HARRAP'S POCKET
FRENCH AND ENGLISH
DICTIONARY

HARRAP'S POCKET FRENCH AND ENGLISH DICTIONARY

FRENCH–ENGLISH, ENGLISH–FRENCH
IN ONE VOLUME

ABRIDGED BY

R. P. JAGO

FROM

HARRAP'S STANDARD FRENCH
AND ENGLISH DICTIONARY

GEORGE G. HARRAP AND COMPANY LTD

LONDON   SYDNEY   TORONTO   BOMBAY

First published 1951
by GEORGE G. HARRAP & CO. LTD.
182 High Holborn, London, W.C.1

MADE IN GREAT BRITAIN AT THE PITMAN PRESS, BATH

PREFACE

HARRAP'S POCKET FRENCH AND ENGLISH DICTIONARY has been based on the two dictionaries edited by the late J. E. Mansion, M.A. The first of these, HARRAP'S STANDARD FRENCH AND ENGLISH DICTIONARY, in two volumes, is the most complete and scholarly work of its kind. The second, HARRAP'S SHORTER FRENCH AND ENGLISH DICTIONARY, provides a work of smaller compass, yet sufficiently comprehensive to cover most of the needs of the advanced student. A third Dictionary, HARRAP'S CONCISE FRENCH AND ENGLISH DICTIONARY, abridged from the SHORTER DICTIONARY, and containing the French-English and English-French parts in one volume, was designed for use in schools and by those whose requirements do not call for the more advanced volumes.

The present volume is adapted more especially to the needs of everyday life and travel.

Difficult points of pronunciation and departures from the normal rules of formation of feminines and plurals are indicated.

REPRESENTATION OF THE PRONUNCIATION

VOWELS

[i] vite, cygne
[i:] rire, lyre, Moïse
[e] été, donner, j'ai
[ɛ] elle, très, peine, mais
[ɛ:] terre, père, paire
[a] chat, là, femme, toit
[a:] rare, tard, noir
[ɑ] pas, âgé, le bois
[ɑ:] sable, âge, tâche
[ɔ] donne, Paul, album
[ɔ:] fort, Laure
[o] dos, impôt, chaud
[o:] fosse, fausse, rôle
[u] tout, goût, août
[u:] cour, Douvres

[y] cru, eu, ciguë
[y:] mur, ils eurent
[ø] feu, ceux, nœud
[ø:] meule, jeûne
[œ] jeune, œuf, cueillir
[œ:] fleur, sœur, œuvre
[ə] le, ce, entremets
[ɛ̃] vin, plein, main, chien, faim
[ɛ̃:] prince, ceindre, plaindre
[ɑ̃] enfant, temps, paon
[ɑ̃:] danse, centre, ample
[ɔ̃] mon, plomb
[ɔ̃:] honte, nombre, comte
[œ̃] lundi, à jeun, parfum
[œ̃:] humble

CONSONANTS

[p] pain, absolu
[b] beau, bleu, abbé
[m] mou, flamme, prisme
[f] feu, bref, phrase
[v] voir, vivre, wagon
[t] table, net, théâtre
[d] donner, sud
[n] né, canne, automne
[s] sou, rébus, cire, action
[z] cousin, zéro, deuxième

[l] lait, aile, table
[ʃ] chose, chercher, schisme
[ʒ] Jean, gilet, manger
[k] camp, képi, quatre, écho
[g] garde, guerre, second
[ɲ] campagne, gniaf
[r] rare, marbre, rhume
[ks] accident, extrême
[gz] exister

SEMI-CONSONANTS

[j] yacht, ration, voyage, cailler
[w] ouate, noir, tramway

[ɥ] muet, huit, lui

DIPHTHONGS

[i:j] fille, famille
[ɛ:j] soleil, veille, paye
[a:j] travail, muraille

[ɑ:j] baille, ferraille
[œ:j] fauteuil, œil

ABBREVIATIONS

A :	*In former use*	*Ind :*	*Industry*
Abs.	*Absolute use*	*indef.*	*Indefinite*
acc.	*Accusative*	*ind.tr.*	*Indirectly transitive*
a., adj.	*Adjective*	*int.*	*Interjection*
adv.	*Adverb*	*interr.*	*Interrogative*
Anat :	*Anatomy*	*inv.*	*Invariable*
Arch :	*Architecture*		
Art :	*Artillery*	*Journ :*	*Journalism*
attrib.	*Attributive*		
Aut :	*Automobilism*	*Lap :*	*Lapidary Arts*
aux.	*Auxiliary*	*Laund :*	*Laundering*
Av :	*Aviation*	*Ling :*	*Linguistics*
		Lit :	*Literary*
Bill :	*Billiards*		
Bot :	*Botany*	*m.*	*Masculine*
		Meas :	*Weights and measures*
Ch :	*Chemistry*	*Med :*	*Medicine*
cogn.	*Cognate*	*Mil :*	*Military*
Coll.	*Collective*	*Miner :*	*Mineralogy*
Com :	*Commerce*	*Mus :*	*Music*
comp.	*Comparative*		
conj.	*Conjunction*	*Nau :*	*Nautical*
Cost :	*Costume*	*neg.*	*Negative*
Cr :	*Cricket*	*neut.*	*Neuter*
Cu :	*Culinary; cuisine*	*nom.*	*Nominative*
		num.a.	*Numeral adjective*
dat.	*Dative*		
Dressm :	*Dressmaking*	*occ.*	*Occasionally*
E :	*Engineering*	*pers.*	*Personal*
Ecc :	*Ecclesiastical*	*Phot :*	*Photography*
El :	*Electricity*	*phr.*	*Phrase*
Ent :	*Entomology*	*pl.*	*Plural*
esp.	*Especially*	*Pol :*	*Politics*
etc.	*Etcetera*	*poss.*	*Possessive*
excl.	*Exclamation;*	*pr.*	*Pronominal*
	exclamative	*pred.*	*Predicative*
		prep.	*Preposition*
f.	*Feminine*	*Pr.n.*	*Proper name*
Fb :	*Football*	*pron.*	*Pronoun*
Fish :	*Fishing*	*Pros :*	*Prosody*
Gram :	*Grammar*	*qch.*	*Quelque chose*
		qn	*Quelqu'un*
Hairdr :	*Hairdressing*		
Harn :	*Harness*	*Rail :*	*Railways*
Her :	*Heraldry*	*rel.*	*Relative*
i.	*Intransitive*	*s., sb.*	*Substantive*
Ich :	*Ichthyology*	*Sch :*	*Schools, etc.*
imp.	*Imperative*	*sg.*	*Singular*
impers.	*Impersonal*	*s.o.*	*Someone*
ind.	*Indicative*	*Sp :*	*Sport*

sth.	Something	tr.	Transitive
sup.	Superlative	Typ :	Typography
Swim :	Swimming		
		usu.	Usually
Ten :	Tennis		
Tex :	Textiles	v.	Verb
Th :	Theatre	Veh :	Vehicles
thg	Thing	Ven :	Venery
Tls :	Tools		
Tp :	Telephony	Z :	Zoology

The symbol = is used to indicate a correspondence between French and English institutions, where the terms thus brought together cannot be considered strictly as translations one of the other. Thus: *Procureur de la République* = public prosecutor.

PART ONE
FRENCH—ENGLISH

A, a, *s.m.* (The letter) A, a.

à, *prep.* I. **1.** (*a*) **Aller à l'école,** to go to school. **Voyage aux Indes,** journey to India. (*b*) **Au voleur!** stop thief! (*c*) **Quinze A,** fifteen all. **2. A jeudi!** see you on Thursday! **3. Être au jardin,** to be in the garden. **Avoir qch. à la main,** to have sth. in one's hand. **4. A deux heures,** at two o'clock. **Au mois de juillet,** in the month of July. **5. Vendre à la douzaine,** to sell by the dozen. **A la française,** French fashion. **Manger à sa faim,** to eat one's fill. **6. Penser à qch.,** to think of sth. **7.** (*a*) **Tasse à thé,** tea-cup. (*b*) **Machine à vapeur,** steam-engine. (*c*) **Homme à barbe noire,** man with a black beard. (*d*) **Le livre est à Jean,** the book is John's. **8.** (*a*) **C'est très gentil à vous,** that's very kind of you. (*b*) **C'est à vous de décider,** it is for you to decide. **C'est à vous,** it is your turn.

II. **1. J'ai à faire,** I have work to do. **2. Un spectacle à ravir,** a delightful sight. **Machine à coudre,** sewing-machine. **3. Je suis prêt à vous écouter,** I am ready to listen to you. **4. Il est à travailler,** he is at work. **5. Laid à faire peur,** frightfully ugly.

abaissement, *s.m.* **1.** A. des prix, lowering of prices. **2.** Falling, abatement. **A. des prix,** dropping of prices. **3.** Abasement.

abaisser, *v.tr.* **1.** To lower. **2.** To reduce. **3.** To humble.
  s'abaisser. **1.** To go down. **2.** S'a. à faire qch., to stoop to doing sth.

abandon, *s.m.* **1.** Surrender. **2.** Forsaking, desertion. **3.** A l'a., neglected. **4.** Lack of restraint.

abandonné, *a.* Forsaken, derelict.

abandonner, *v.tr.* **1.** To forsake, desert, abandon; to leave. **2.** To surrender, give up.
  s'abandonner. (*a*) To neglect oneself. (*b*) To give way (to grief).

abasourdir, *v.tr.* To dumbfound.

abasourdissement, *s.m.* Bewilderment, stupefaction.

abat-jour, *s.m.inv.* (Lamp-)shade

abattage, *s.m.* Felling.

abattement, *s.m.* (*a*) Prostration (*b*) Despondency, low spirits.

abattis, *s.m.pl.* Giblets.

abattoir, *s.m.* Slaughter-house.

abattre, *v.tr.* **1.** (*a*) To knock down; to overthrow. (*b*) To fell. **2.** To slaughter. **3.** To bring down. **4.** To lay (dust). **5.** To dishearten.
  s'abattre. **1.** S'a. sur qch., to pounce upon sth. **2.** To abate.

abattu, *a.* Dejected, low-spirited.

abbaye, *s.f.* Abbey, monastery

abbé, *s.m.* **1.** Abbot. **2.** Priest.

abbesse, *s.f.* Abbess.

abcès [apsɛ], *s.m.* Abscess.

abdication, *s.f.* Abdication.

abdiquer, *v.tr.* To abdicate.

abdomen [-mɛn], *s.m.* Abdomen.

abeille [abɛːj], *s.f.* Bee.

aberration, *s.f.* Aberration.

abhorrer, *v.tr.* To abhor, loathe.

abîme, *s.m.* Abyss, chasm.

abîmer, *v.tr.* To spoil, damage.
  s'abîmer. **1.** To sink. **2.** To spoil.

abject [-ʒɛkt], *a.* Abject; mean.

abjectement, *adv.* Abjectly.

abjuration, *s.f.* Abjuration.

abjurer, *v.tr.* To abjure.

ablution, *s.f.* Ablution, washing.

abnégation, *s.f.* Self-sacrifice.

aboi, *s.m.* Aux abois, at bay.

aboiement, *s.m.* Bark, barking.

abolir, *v.tr.* To abolish, suppress.

abolition, *s.f.* Abolition.

abominable, *a.* Abominable; heinous.

abominablement, *adv.* Abominably.

abomination, *s.f.* Abomination.

abominer, *v.tr.* To abominate.

abondamment, *adv.* Abundantly.

abondance, *s.f.* **1.** Abundance, plenty. **2. Parler d'a.,** to speak extempore.

abondant, *a.* Abundant, plentiful.

abonder, *v.i.* To abound (*en, in*).

abonné, *s.* **1.** Subscriber. **2.** Season-ticket holder.

abonnement, *s.m.* **1.** Subscription. **2. (Carte d')** a., season-ticket.

abonner (s'), *v.pr.* To subscribe.

abord, *s.m.* **1.** Access. **2. Avoir l'a. facile,** to be easy to approach. **3.** *Adv. phr.* **D'a.,** at first. **Dès l'a.,** from the outset.

aborder. **1.** *v.i.* To land. **2.** *v.tr.* (*a*) To accost. (*b*) To approach (a question). (*c*) To board (ship).

aborigène. **1.** *a.* Aboriginal. **2.** *s.pl.* Aborigines.

aboutir, *v.i.* **1. A.** à, dans, en, qch., to end at, in, sth.; to lead to sth. **N'a. à rien,** to come to nothing. **2.** *Abs.* To succeed.

aboutissement, *s.m.* Outcome.

aboyer, *v.i.* To bark.

abrégé, *s.m.* Abridgment, précis.

abréger, *v.tr.* **1.** To shorten; to cut short. **2.** To abbreviate.

abreuver, *v.tr.* **1.** To water (horses). **2.** To flood, irrigate.

abreuvoir, *s.m.* (*a*) Watering-place. (*b*) Drinking-trough.

abréviation, *s.f.* Abbreviation.

abri, *s.m.* Shelter. **A l'a.,** sheltered.

abricot, *s.m.* Apricot.

abricotier, *s.m.* Apricot-tree.

abriter, *v.tr.* To shelter, shield.

abroger, *v.tr.* To abrogate, rescind, repeal (law).

abrupt [-rypt], *a.* **1.** Abrupt, steep. **2.** Abrupt, blunt.

abruptement, *adv.* Abruptly.

abrutir, *v.tr.* To brutalize.
    s'abrutir, to become sottish.

abrutissement, *s.m.* **1.** Degradation. **2.** Sottishness.

absence [aps-], *s.f.* **1.** Absence. **2.** Want (of imagination).

absent [apsã], *a.* (*a*) Absent. (*b*) Missing.

absenter (s') [saps-], *v.pr.* **1.** To absent oneself. **2.** To stay away.

abside [apsid], *s.f.* Apse.

absinthe [apsɛ̃:t], *s.f.* Absinth.

absolu [aps-], *a.* Absolute; positive.

absolument [aps-], *adv.* (*a*) Absolutely. (*b*) Entirely.

absolution [aps-], *s.f.* Absolution.

absorbant [aps-], *a.* **1.** Absorbent. **2.** Absorbing, engrossing.

absorber [aps-], *v.tr.* **1.** To absorb, soak up. **2.** To absorb, engross.

absoudre [aps-], *v.tr.* To absolve.

abstenir (s') [saps-], *v.pr.* To abstain.

abstention [aps-], *s.f.* Abstaining, abstention.

abstinence [aps-], *s.f.* Abstinence.

abstraction [aps-], *s.f.* Abstraction. **Faire a. de qch.,** to leave sth. out of account.

abstraire [aps-], *v.tr.* To abstract.

abstrait [aps-], *a.* **1.** Abstracted. **2.** Abstract (idea); abstruse.

absurde [aps-]. **1.** *a.* Absurd. **2.** *s.m.* Absurdity.

absurdement [aps-], *adv.* Absurdly.

absurdité [aps-], *s.f.* Absurdity.

abus, *s.m.* **1.** (*a*) Abuse, misuse. (*b*) **A. de confiance,** breach of trust. **2.** Error.

abuser. **1.** *v.i.* **A. de qch.** (*a*) To misuse sth. (*b*) To take advantage of sth. **2.** *v.tr.* To deceive.
    s'abuser, to delude oneself; to be mistaken.

abusif, *a.* **1.** Improper. **2.** Excessive.

abusivement, *adv.* Improperly.

acabit, *s.m.* Nature, stamp.

acacia, *s.m.* Acacia.

académicien, *s.m.* Academician.

académie, *s.f.* Academy.

académique, *a.* Academic.

acajou, *s.m.* Mahogany.

acanthe, *s.f.* Acanthus.

acariâtre, *a.* Bad-tempered.

accablant, *a.* **1.** Overwhelming. **2.** Overpowering (heat).

accablé, *a.* Overwhelmed; overcome.

accablement, *s.m.* Dejection.

accabler, *v.tr.* To overpower, overwhelm, crush.

accalmie, *s.f.* Lull.

accaparer, *v.tr.* To monopolize.

accéder, *v.i.* To accede.

accélérateur, *s.m.* Accelerator.

accélération, *s.f.* Acceleration.

accéléré, *a.* Quick; accelerated.

accélérer, *v.tr.* To accelerate.

accent, *s.m.* Accent; stress.

accentuation, *s.f.* Accentuation.

accentuer, *v.tr.* **1.** To stress. **2.** To emphasize.

　　s'accentuer, to become more pronounced, more marked.

acceptabilité, *s.f.* Acceptability.

acceptable, *a.* Acceptable.

acceptation, *s.f.* Acceptance.

accepter, *v.tr.* To accept.

accès, *s.m.* **1.** Access, approach. **2.** Fit.

accessibilité, *s.f.* Accessibility

accessible, *a.* Accessible.

accession, *s.f.* **1.** Accession. **2.** Union. **3.** Adherence.

accessoire. **1.** *a.* Accessory. **2.** *s.m.* Accessory. *pl. Th:* Properties.

accident, *s.m.* **1.** Accident. **Nous sommes arrivés sans a.,** we arrived safely. **2. A. de terrain,** undulation of the ground.

accidenté. **1.** *a.* Uneven, broken. **2.** *s.* Victim of an accident.

accidentel, *a.* Accidental.

accidentellement, *adv.* Accidentally.

acclamation, *s.f.* Acclamation.

acclamer, *v.tr.* To acclaim, cheer.

acclimatation, *s.f.* Acclimatization.

acclimater, *v.tr.* To acclimatize.

accolade, *s.f.* **1.** Embrace. **2.** *Mus:* Bracket.

accommodant, *a.* Good-natured, accommodating.

accommodement, *s.m.* Compromise, arrangement.

accommoder, *v.tr.* **1.** (*a*) To make comfortable. (*b*) To suit. **2.** To dress (food).

　　s'accommoder. **1. S'a. de qch.,** to make the best of sth. **2. S'a. à qch.,** to adapt oneself to sth.

accompagnateur, -trice, *s.* Accompanist.

accompagnement, *s.m.* **1.** Accompanying. **2.** Accompaniment.

accompagner, *v.tr.* To accompany; to escort, attend.

accompli, *a.* Accomplished.

accomplir, *v.tr.* **1.** To accomplish; to fulfil. **2.** To complete.

accomplissement, *s.m.* **1.** Accomplishment; fulfilment. **2.** Completion.

accord, *s.m.* **1.** Agreement. **D'a.,** in agreement. **D'a.!** agreed! **2.** Chord. **3. Être d'a.,** to be in tune.

accorder, *v.tr.* **1.** To reconcile. **2.** To tune. **3.** To grant.

　　s'accorder. **1.** To agree. **2.** To tune (up).

accordeur, *s.m.* Tuner.

accoster, *v.tr.* **1.** To accost; to come up to. **2.** To come on board.

accoucher, *v.i.* To be confined.

accouder (s'), *v.pr.* To lean on one's elbows.

accouplement, *s.m.* (*a*) Coupling. (*b*) Connecting.

accoupler, *v.tr.* To connect.

accourir, *v.i.* To hasten (up).

accoutrement, *s.m.* Dress, garb.

accoutumé, *a.* Accustomed.

accoutumer, *v.tr.* To accustom.

　　s'accoutumer, to get accustomed.

accréditer, *v.tr.* **1.** To accredit. **2.** To credit, believe.

accroc, *s.m.* **1.** Tear, rent. **2.** Hitch, difficulty.

accrocher, *v.tr.* (*a*) To hook. (*b*) To hang (up). (*c*) To tune in.

　　s'accrocher. S'a. à, to fasten on to, cling to.

accroire, *v.tr.* **En faire a. à qn.,** to delude s.o. **S'en faire a.,** to think too much of oneself.

accroissement, *s.m.* Growth; increase.

accroître, *v.tr.* To increase.

　　s'accroître, to grow.

accroupir (s'), *v.pr.* To squat.

accueil [akœ:j], *s.m.* Reception, welcome.

accueillir [akœji:r], *v.tr.* To receive, greet.

acculer, *v.tr.* To drive back; to bring to bay.

accumulateur, *s.m.* Accumulator.

accumulation, *s.f.* Accumulation.

accumuler, *v.tr.* To accumulate.

accusateur, -trice. **1.** *a.* Accusatory. **2.** *s.* Accuser.

accusatif, *a. & s.m.* Accusative.

accusation, *s.f.* Accusation.

accusé. **1.** *a.* Prominent, pronounced. **2.** *s.* Accused.

accuser, *v.tr.* **1.** To accuse. **2.** To acknowledge. **3.** To show up, accentuate.

acerbe, *a.* **1.** Tart, sour. **2.** Harsh.

acerbité, *s.f.* Acerbity.

acéré, *a.* Sharp ; keen.

acétate, *s.m.* Acetate.

acétique, *a.* Acetic.

acétylène, *s.m.* Acetylene.

achalandage, *s.m.* Customers, connection.

acharné, *a.* **1.** Eager. **2.** Inveterate, keen. **3.** Stubborn, desperate.

acharnement, *s.m.* (*a*) Desperate eagerness. (*b*) Relentlessness.

acharner (s'), *v.pr.* **1.** S'a. après qn, to be dead set against s.o. **2.** S'a. sur, to work unceasingly at.

achat, *s.m.* Purchase.

acheminer (s'), *v.pr.* To proceed ; to wend one's way.

acheter, *v.tr.* To buy, purchase. A. qch. à qn, to buy sth. from s.o.

acheteur, -euse, *s.* Purchaser.

achèvement, *s.m.* Completion.

achever, *v.tr.* **1.** To end, finish (off), complete. **2.** To dispatch.

achoppement, *s.m.* Pierre d'a., stumbling-block.

acide. 1. *a.* Acid, sour. **2.** *s.m.* Acid.

acidité, *s.f.* Acidity, sourness.

acier, *s.m.* Steel.

acolyte, *s.m.* Assistant, acolyte.

acompte [akɔ̃:t], *s.m.* Instalment, payment on account.

aconit [-nit], *s.m.* Aconite.

à-coup, *s.m.* Jerk ; sudden stoppage. Par à-coups, by fits and starts.

acoustique, *a.* Acoustic. Tuyau a., speaking-tube.

acquéreur, -euse, *s.* Purchaser.

acquérir, *v.tr.* To acquire, obtain, get, win, gain, secure.

acquiescement, *s.m.* Acquiescence, assent.

acquiescer, *v.ind.tr.* To acquiesce (à, in) ; to agree.

acquis, *a.* Acquired.

acquisition, *s.f.* Acquisition.

acquit, *s.m.* Receipt. " Pour a.," 'paid.'

acquittement, *s.m.* **1.** Discharge, payment. **2.** Acquittal.

acquitter, *v.tr.* **1.** To acquit. **2.** (*a*) To discharge (a debt). (*b*) To receipt (a bill).

　　s'acquitter. 1. S'a. d'un devoir, to discharge a duty. **2.** To acquit oneself.

âcre, *a.* Acrid, bitter, pungent.

âcreté, *s.f.* Acidity, pungency.

acrimonie, *s.f.* Acrimony.

acrimonieusement, *adv.* Acrimoniously.

acrimonieux, *a.* Acrimonious.

acrobate, *s.m.* & *f.* Acrobat.

acrobatique, *a.* Acrobatic.

acte, *s.m.* **1.** Action, deed. **2.** (*a*) Deed, title. (*b*) A. judiciaire, writ. (*c*) Record. **3.** *Th:* Act.

acteur, -trice, *s.* Actor, actress.

actif. 1. *a.* Active, brisk, alert. **2.** *s.m.* Assets ; credit.

action, *s.f.* **1.** Action ; act. **2.** Share. Compagnie par actions, joint-stock company. **3.** Action, lawsuit, trial.

actionnaire, *s.m.* & *f.* Shareholder.

actionner, *v.tr.* **1.** To sue. **2.** To set in motion.

activement, *adv.* Actively.

activer, *v.tr.* To quicken, urge on. s'activer, to bestir oneself.

activité, *s.f.* Activity. En a. n progress, at work.

actrice, *s.f.* Actress.

actuaire, *s.m.* Actuary.

actualité, *s.f.* **1.** Actuality, reality. **2.** Les actualités, current events.

actuel, *a.* Of the present day ; existing, current.

actuellement, *adv.* (Just) now, at the present time.

acuité, *s.f.* Acuteness, sharpness.

adage, *s.m.* Adage, saying.

adaptable, *a.* Adaptable (à, to).

adaptation, *s.f.* Adaptation.

adapter, *v.tr.* To fit ; to adapt.

addenda, *s.m.inv.* Addendum.

addition, *s.f.* **1.** Addition. **2.** Bill, reckoning.

additionnel, *a.* Additional.

additionner, *v.tr.* To add up.

adepte, *s.m.* & *f.* Adept.

adhérence, *s.f.* Adherence.

adhérent, *a.* & *s.* Adherent.

adhérer, *v.i.* **1.** To adhere, stick. **2.** A. à, to join.

adhésif, *a.* & *s.m.* Adhesive.

adhésion, *s.f.* **1.** Adhesion, sticking. **2.** A. à, joining.

adieu, -eux. 1. *adv.* Good-bye. **2.** *s.m.* Farewell. Faire ses adieux à qn, to take leave of s.o.

adipeux, *a.* Adipose, fatty.

adjacent, *a.* Adjacent (à, to) ; bordering (à, on).

adjectif. 1. *a.* Adjectival. **2.** *s.m.* Adjective.

adjoindre, *v.tr.* **1.** To unite (*à*, with). **2.** To add.

adjoint, *s.* Assistant ; deputy.

adjudant, *s.m.* (*a*) Company sergeant-major. (*b*) **A.-major,** adjutant.

adjudicataire, *s.* Highest bidder.

adjudicateur, -trice, *s* Adjudicator, awarder.

adjudication, *s.f.* (*a*) Adjudication, award. (*b*) Knocking-down.

adjuger, *v.tr.* To adjudge, award.

adjurer, *v.tr.* To adjure (*de*, to).

admettre, *v.tr.* To admit. **1.** To let in. **2.** To permit. **3.** To acknowledge.

administrateur, -trice, *s.* Administrator.

administratif, *a.* Administrative.

administration, *s.f.* **1.** Administration. **2.** Government service.

administrer, *v.tr.* To administer ; to govern.

admirable, *a.* Admirable.

admirablement, *adv.* Admirably.

admirateur, -trice, *s.* Admirer

admiratif, *a.* Admiring.

admiration, *s.f.* Admiration.

admirer, *v.tr.* To admire.

admissibilité, *s.f.* Admissibility

admissible, *a.* Admissible.

admission, *s.f.* Admission.

admonestation, *s.f.* Admonition.

admonester, *v.tr.* To admonish

adolescence, *s.f.* Adolescence

adolescent, *s.* Adolescent.

adonner (s'), *v.pr.* **S'a. à qch.** to give oneself up to sth.

adopter, *v.tr.* To adopt

adoptif, *a.* Adopted.

adoption, *s.f.* Adoption.

adorable, *a.* Adorable ; charming.

adorablement, *adv.* Adorably

adorateur, -trice, *s.* Adorer.

adoration, *s.f.* Adoration.

adorer, *v.tr.* To adore, worship.

adossé, *a.* Back to back.

adosser, *v.tr.* To place back to back. **s'adosser,** to set one's back (*à*, *contre*, against).

adoucir, *v.tr.* **1.** To soften ; to sweeten. **2.** To alleviate. **3.** To mollify.

s'adoucir. To grow softer, milder.

adoucissement, *s.* **1.** Softening **2.** Alleviation (of pain).

adresse, *s.f.* **1.** Address, destination. **2.** (*a*) Skill, dexterity. (*b*) Shrewdness

adresser, *v.tr.* To address. **s'adresser. 1.** To apply. "S'a. ici," 'enquire here.' **2. S'a. à,** to address.

adroit, *a.* **1.** Dexterous, skilful. **2.** Shrewd.

adroitement, *adv.* **1.** Skilfully **2.** Adroitly.

adulateur, -trice, *s.* Flatterer

adulation, *s.f.* Adulation.

adulte, *a. & s.m. & f.* Adult.

adultération, *s.f.* Adulteration.

adultère, *s.m.* Adultery.

adultérer, *v.tr.* To adulterate.

advenir, *v.i.* To occur, happen ; to come (about). **Advienne que pourra,** come what may.

adverbe, *s.m.* Adverb.

adverbial, -aux, *a.* Adverbial.

adversaire, *s.m.* Adversary.

adverse, *a.* Adverse, unfavourable.

adversité, *s.f.* **1.** Adversity **2.** Misfortune, trial.

aérage, *s.m.* **aération,** *s.f.* Ventilation

aérer, *v.tr.* To ventilate.

aérien, *a.* Aerial. **Raid a.,** air-raid.

aérodrome, *s.m.* Aerodrome.

aéronaute, *s.m. & f.* Aeronaut.

aéronautique. 1. *a.* Aeronautical. **2.** *s.f.* Aeronautics.

aéroplane, *s.m.* Aeroplane

aéroport, *s.m.* Air-port.

aéroporté, *a.* Airborne.

affabilité, *s.f.* Affability.

affable, *a.* Gracious, affable.

affaiblir, *v.tr.* To weaken. **s'affaiblir,** to become weak.

affaiblissement, *s.m.* **1.** Weakening. **2.** Enfeeblement.

affaire, *s.f.* **1.** (*a*) Business, affair. **Savoir son a.,** to know what one is about. (*b*) Question, matter. **Ce n'est que l'a. d'un instant,** it won't take a minute. (*c*) Thing (required) **Faire l'a.,** to answer the purpose. **Son a. est faite,** he is done for. (*d*) Business, matter. **La belle a.!** pooh, is that all! **S'attirer une (mauvaise) a.,** to get into trouble. **2.** (*a*) Affair, transaction. (*b*) **Avoir a. à, avec, qn,** to have to deal with s.o. **3.** *pl.* (*a*) Things, belongings. (*b*) Business, trade.

affairé, *a.* Busy.

affaissement, *s.m.* **1.** Subsidence. **2.** Depression, despondency.

affaisser (s'), *v.pr.* To subside, collapse.

affamé, *a.* Hungry, starving.

affamer, *v.tr.* To starve.

affectation, *s.f.* Affectation. (*a*) Affectedness. (*b*) Simulation.

affecté, *a.* Affected (person).

affecter, *v.tr.* **1.** To assign. **2.** To simulate. **3.** To have a partiality for. **4.** (*a*) To affect, move. (*b*) To affect (career).

affection, *s.f.* Affection. **1.** Fondness. **2.** *Med :* Complaint.

affectionné, *a.* Affectionate, loving.

affectionner, *v.tr.* To be fond of.

affectueusement, *adv.* Affectionately, lovingly.

affectueux, *a.* Affectionate.

afférent, *a.* Relating (*d*, to).

affermir, *v.tr.* To strengthen.

affermissement, *s.m.* **1.** Strengthening. **2.** Support.

affichage, *s.m.* Placarding. *Sp :* Tableau d'a., telegraph board.

affiche, *s.f.* Placard, poster.

afficher, *v.tr.* **1.** To stick (up), display. **2.** To make a show of.

s'afficher, to show off.

affilé, *a.* Sharp.

affiler, *v.tr.* To sharpen.

affilier, *v.tr.* To affiliate.

affiner, *v.tr.* To improve, refine.

affinité, *s.f.* Affinity.

affirmatif. 1. *a.* Affirmative, positive. Signe a., nod. **2.** *s.f.* L'affirmative, the affirmative.

affirmation, *s.f.* Affirmation.

affirmativement, *adv.* Affirmatively ; positively.

affirmer, *v.tr.* To affirm, assert.

affleurer, *v.tr.* To be level with.

affliction, *s.f.* Affliction.

affligé, *a.* **1.** Afflicted. **2.** Grieved.

affliger, *v.tr.* **1.** To afflict (*de*, with). **2.** To distress.

s'affliger, to grieve (*de*, at).

affluence, *s.f.* **1.** Flow. **2.** Affluence. **3.** Crowd. Heures d'a., rush hours.

affluent, *s.m.* Tributary, affluent.

affluer, *v.i.* **1.** To flow. **2.** To abound. **3.** To flock.

affolé, *a.* Crazy, distracted.

affolement, *s.m.* **1.** Distraction, panic. **2.** Racing of engine).

affoler, *v.tr.* To madden.

s'affoler. 1. To panic. **2.** To become infatuated (*de*, with).

affranchi, *a.* Freed.

affranchir, *v.tr.* **1.** To set free. **2.** To stamp (letter).

s'affranchir, to become free.

affranchissement, *s.m.* **1.** Emancipation. **2.** Stamping (of letter).

affres, *s.f.pl.* Pangs.

affreusement, *adv.* Terribly.

affreux, *a.* Frightful.

affront, *s.m.* Affront, snub.

affronter, *v.tr.* To face, confront.

affût, *s.m.* **1.** Être, se mettre, à l'a. de, to lie in wait for. **2.** Gun-carriage.

afin, *adv.* **1.** A. de, to, in order to. **2.** A. que, so that, in order that.

africain, *a. & s.* African.

Afrique. *Pr.n.f.* Africa.

agaçant, *a.* **1.** Annoying, irritating. **2.** Provocative.

agacement, *s.m.* Irritation.

agacer, *v.tr.* **1.** To set (teeth) on edge ; to grate upon. **2.** To provoke.

agacerie, *s.f.* Provocation.

agate, *s.f.* Agate.

âge, *s.m.* **1.** Age. (*a*) Quel âge avez-vous? how old are you ? (*b*) Le bas âge, infancy. (*c*) Old age. **2.** Generation. **3.** Period. Le moyen âge, the Middle Ages.

âgé, *a.* **1.** Agé de dix ans, aged ten. **2.** Advanced in years.

agence, *s.f.* Agency.

agencement, *s.m.* Arrangement.

agencer, *v.tr.* To arrange ; to adjust.

agenda, *s.m.* Memorandum-book.

agenouillé [-uje], *a.* Kneeling.

agenouiller (s') [-uje], *v.pr.* To kneel (down).

agent, *s.m.* (*a*) Agent. A. d'affaires, man of business. (*b*) A. (de police), policeman. (*c*) A. de change, stock-broker.

agglomération, *s.f.* Agglomeration.

aggravation, *s.f.* Aggravation.

aggraver, *v.tr.* **1.** To aggravate (disease). **2.** To increase.

s'aggraver, to grow worse.

agile, *a.* Agile, nimble.

agilement, *adv.* Nimbly.

agilité, *s.f.* Agility, nimbleness.

agir, *v.i.* To act. **1.** Faire a. qch., to set sth. going. **2.** To act, operate.

s'agir (de), *v.impers.* (*a*) To concern. **De quoi s'agit-il?** what is the question? what is it about? (*b*) **S'a. de faire qch.**, to be a matter of doing sth.

agissant, *a.* Active, bustling.

agitateur, -trice, *s.* Agitator.

agitation, *s.f.* Agitation. **1.** (*a*) Shaking, waving, wagging. (*b*) Discussing. (*c*) **L'a. ouvrière,** labour unrest. **2.** (*a*) Perturbation. (*b*) Restlessness.

agité, *a.* **1.** Rough (sea). **2.** Agitated; troubled (sleep). **3.** Excited.

agiter, *v.tr.* **1.** (*a*) To agitate; to wave; to wag. (*b*) To shake. **2.** To agitate, excite. **3.** To debate.
 s'agiter. (*a*) To be in movement. (*b*) To become excited.

agneau, *s.m.* Lamb.

agonie, *s.f.* Death agony. **Être à l'a.,** to be at one's last gasp.

agonisant. **1.** *a.* Dying. **2.** *s.* Dying person.

agoniser, *v.i.* To be dying.

agrafe, *s.f.* Hook, fastener; clasp

agraire, *a.* Agrarian.

agrandir, *v.tr.* (*a*) To make larger; to enlarge. (*b*) To magnify.
 s'agrandir, to grow larger; to expand.

agrandissement, *s.m.* **1.** (*a*) Enlarging, extending. (*b*) Enlargement. **2.** Increase in power.

agréable, *a.* Agreeable, pleasant, nice. **Pour vous être a.,** to oblige you.

agréablement, *adv.* Pleasantly.

agréer, *v.tr.* To accept. **Agréez mes salutations empressées,** believe me yours sincerely.

agrégé, *a. & s.* Teacher who has qualified for a post in a Lycée.

agrément, *s.m.* **1.** (*a*) Pleasure. **Ouvrages d'a.,** fancy work. (*b*) Charm. **2.** Assent.

agrémenter, *v.tr.* To embellish, ornament, adorn (*de*, with).

agrès, *s.m.pl.* Tackle; rigging.

agresseur, *s.m.* Aggressor.

agressif, *a.* Aggressive.

agression, *s.f.* Aggression.

agressivement, *adv.* Aggressively.

agreste, *a.* Rustic; rural.

agricole, *a.* Agricultural.

agriculteur, *s.m.* Agriculturist.

agriculture, *s.f.* Agriculture.

agripper, *v.tr.* To clutch, grip.
 s'agripper, to cling.

aguerri, *a.* Seasoned, trained.

aguets, *s.m.pl.* **Aux a.,** watchful.

ah, *int.* Ah! oh!

ahuri, *a.* Bewildered. (*a*) Dumbfounded. (*b*) Confused.

ahurir, *v.tr.* To bewilder.

ahurissement, *s.m.* Bewilderment

ai. See AVOIR.

aide[1], *s.f.* (*a*) Help, aid. *Prep.phr.* **A l'a. de,** with the help of. (*b*) Relief, succour.

aide[2], *s.m. & f.* Assistant.

aider, *v.tr.* To help, aid.

aïe [aj], *int.* (Indicating pain) Oh!

aïeul [ajœl], *s.m.* **1.** Grandfather. **2.** (*pl.* aïeux) Ancestor.

aigle. **1.** *s.m. & f.* Eagle. **2.** *s.m.* Lectern.

aiglon, *s.m.* Eaglet.

aigre, *a.* (*a*) Sour, acid (*b*) Sour, crabbed. (*c*) Shrill.

aigrefin[1], *s.m.* Haddock.

aigrefin[2], *s.* Sharper, swindler.

aigrelet, -ette, *a.* Sourish, tart.

aigrement, *adv.* Acrimoniously.

aigrette, *s.f.* **1.** Aigrette. **2.** Egret.

aigreur, *s.f.* Sourness, tartness.

aigrir. **1.** *v.tr.* To embitter. **2.** *v.i.* To turn sour.

aigu, -uë, *a.* **1.** Sharp, pointed. **Angle a.,** acute angle. **2.** Acute; keen. **3.** Shrill. **4.** **Accent a.,** acute accent.

aiguille [egɥi:j], *s.f.* **1.** Needle. **2.** (*a*) **A. de pin,** pine-needle. (*b*) *Rail:* Point. **3.** Spire. **4.** Hand (of clock).

aiguillon [egɥijɔ̃], *s.m.* **1.** (*a*) Goad. (*b*) Incentive. **2.** Sting (of wasp).

aiguillonner [egɥijɔne], *v.tr.* **1.** To goad. **2.** To incite.

aiguiser [eg(ɥ)ize], *v.tr.* (*a*) To whet; to sharpen. (*b*) To point.

ail [a:j], *s.m.* Garlic.

aile, *s.f.* **1.** Wing. **2.** Wing (of aeroplane); sail (of windmill); blade (of propeller).

ailé, *a.* Winged, feathered.

aileron, *s.m.* (*a*) Pinion. (*b*) Fin.

ailleurs [ajœːr], *adv.* **1.** Elsewhere. **2.** *Adv. phr.* **D.a.,** besides, moreover.

aimable, *a.* **1.** Amiable; kind. **Peu a.,** ungracious. **2.** Lovable.

aimablement, *adv.* Amiably, kindly, nicely.

aimant[1], *a.* Loving, affectionate.

aimant[2], *s.m.* Magnet.

aimer, *v.tr.* **1.** (*a*) To like; to be fond of. (*b*) **A. mieux**, to prefer. **2. A. (d'amour)**, to love.

aine, *s.f.* Groin.

aîné, *a.* (*a*) Elder; eldest. *s.* **Il est mon a.**, he is older than I. (*b*) Senior.

aînesse, *s.f.* Primogeniture. **Droit d'a.**, birthright.

ainsi. **1.** *adv.* Thus; so; in a like manner. **S'il en est a.**, if so. **Et a. de suite**, and so on. **Pour a. dire**, so to speak. **2.** *conj.* So, thus. **3.** *Conj.phr.* **A. que**, (just) as; as also.

air, *s.m.* **I.** (*a*) Air, atmosphere. **En plein air**, in the open air. (*b*) **En l'air**, in the air. **Paroles en l'air**, idle talk.
II. air. 1. (*a*) Appearance, look. (*b*) **Avoir l'air**, to look, seem. **2.** Manner, way.
III. air. Tune, air.

airain, *s.m.* Bronze, brass.

aire, *s.f.* **1.** Surface; floor. **A. d'une grange**, threshing-floor. **2.** Area. **3.** Eyrie.

airelle, *s.f.* Bilberry.

aisance, *s.f.* Ease; easy circumstances.

aise. **1.** *s.f.* Ease, comfort. **Être à l'a.**, to be comfortable; to be well-off. **A votre a.!** just as you like! **2.** *a.* **Bien a.**, very glad.

aisé, *a.* **1.** (*a*) Easy, free; comfortable. (*b*) Well-to-do. **2.** Easy (task).

aisément, *adv.* **1.** Comfortably. **2.** Easily.

aisselle, *s.f.* Armpit.

ajonc [aʒɔ̃], *s.m.* Furze, gorse.

ajouré, *a.* Perforated, pierced.

ajournement, *s.m.* Postponement.

ajourner, *v.tr.* To postpone.

ajouter, *v.tr.* To add.

ajustement, *s.m.* Adjustment.

ajuster, *v.tr.* **1.** (*a*) To adjust. (*b*) **A. son fusil**, to take aim with one's gun. **A. qn**, to aim (a gun) at s.o. **2** To put right.

alacrité, *s.f.* Alacrity, eagerness.

alanguissement, *s.m.* Languor.

alarme, *s.f.* Alarm.

alarmer, *v.tr.* **1.** To give the alarm to. **2.** To frighten, alarm.
s'alarmer, to take fright (*de*, at).

albanais, *a. & s.* Albanian.

Albanie. *Pr.n.f.* Albania.

albâtre, *s.m.* Alabaster.

albatros [-trɔs], *s.m.* Albatross.

albinos [-nɔːs], *s. & a. inv.* Albino.

album [-bɔm], *s.m.* **1.** Album, sketch-book. **2.** Trade catalogue.

albumine, *s.f.* Albumin.

alcali, *s.m.* Alkali.

alcalin, *a.* Alkaline.

alchimie, *s.f.* Alchemy.

alcool [-kɔl], *s.m.* Alcohol; spirit(s). **A. à brûler**, methylated spirit.

alcoolique [-kɔl-]. **1.** *a.* Alcoholic, spirituous. **2.** *s.* Drunkard.

alcôve, *s.f.* Alcove, (bed-)recess.

aléa, *s.m.* Risk, hazard, chance.

aléatoire, *a.* Hazardous, risky.

alêne, *s.f.* Awl.

alentour. **1.** *adv.* Around, round about. **2.** *s.m.pl.* Environs.

alerte. **1.** *int.* To arms! **2.** *s.f.* Alarm, warning. **3.** *a.* Alert, brisk.

alezan, *a & s.* Chestnut (horse).

alfa, *s.m.* Alfa(-grass), esparto.

algarade, *s.f.* Storm of abuse.

algèbre, *s.f.* Algebra.

algébrique, *a.* Algebraic.

Alger. *Pr.n.* Algiers.

Algérie. *Pr.n.f.* Algeria.

algérien, *a. & s.* Algerian.

algue [alg], *s.f.* Seaweed.

aliénation, *s.f.* Alienation.

aliéné, *a. & s.* Lunatic.

aliéner, *v.tr.* To alienate.

alignement, *s.m.* Alignment.

aligner, *v.tr.* To align, draw up.
s'aligner, to fall into line.

aliment, *s.m.* Aliment, food.

alimentaire, *a.* Alimentary.

alimenter, *v.tr.* To feed, nourish.

alinéa, *s.m.* Paragraph.

alité, *a.* Confined to (one's) bed.

alizé, *s.m.* Trade-wind.

allaitement, *s.m.* Suckling.

allaiter, *v.tr.* To suckle.

allèchement, *s.m.* Allurement.

allécher, *v.tr.* To allure, entice, tempt.

allée, *s.f.* **1.** **Allées et venues**, coming and going. **2.** (*a*) Walk; path. (*b*) Alley.

allégement, *s.m.* Relief (of pain).

alléger, *v.tr.* To relieve (pain).

allégorique, *a.* Allegorical.

allègre, *a.* Lively, gay, cheerful.

allégresse, *s.f.* Gladness.

alléguer [-ge], *v.tr.* To allege, plead.

Allemagne. *Pr.n.f.* Germany.

allemand, *a. & s.* German.

aller. I. *v.i.* **1.** To go. **2.** (*a*) To be going (well). **Ça ira!** we'll manage! (*b*) To go, work. (*c*) **Comment allez-vous?** how are you? **3. A.** (**à qn**). (*a*) To suit. (*b*) To fit. *F:* **Ça va!** all right! **4.** (*a*) **A. voir qn,** to go and see s.o. (*b*) To be about (to do sth.). **Il va s'en occuper,** he is going to see about it. **5. Y aller.** (*a*) **J'y vais!** on y va! coming! (*b*) **Allons-y!** well, here goes! **Vas-y! allez-y!** go it! **6.** *v.impers.* **Il va de soi, il goes without saying. Il y allait de la vie,** it was a matter of life and death. **7.** *int.* **Allons!** come! **Allons donc!** (i) come along! (ii) nonsense! **s'en aller,** to go away, to depart. II. **aller,** *s.m.* **1.** Going. **Billet d'a. et retour,** return ticket. **2. Pis a.,** last resort; makeshift. **Au pis a.,** if the worst comes to the worst.

alliage, *s.m.* Alloy.

alliance, *s.f.* **1.** Alliance. **2.** Wedding-ring.

allié. **1.** *a.* Allied. **2.** *s.* (*a*) Ally. (*b*) Relation by marriage.

allier, *v.tr.* **1.** To ally, unite. **2.** To alloy, mix.

alligator, *s.m.* Alligator.

allô, allo, *int.* *Tp:* Hullo! hallo!

allocation, *s.f.* **1.** Allocation. **2.** Allowance, grant.

allonger, *v.tr.* **1.** To lengthen. **2.** To stretch out. **3.** To prolong.

allumage, *s.m.* Lighting (of lamp); ignition.

allumer, *v.tr.* **1.** To light. *Abs.* To light up. **2.** To inflame.

allumette, *s.f.* Match.

allure, *s.f.* **1.** (*a*) Walk, bearing. (*b*) Pace. (*c*) Speed. **A toute a.,** at full speed. **2.** (*a*) Demeanour. (*b*) Aspect, look.

allusion, *s.f.* Allusion; hint.

alluvial, -iaux, *a.* Alluvial.

almanach [-na], *s.m.* Almanac.

aloès [aloɛs], *s.m.* Aloe.

aloi, *s.m.* Standard, quality. **De bon a.,** genuine.

alors, *adv.* **1.** Then; at the time. **2.** Therefore, so. **3.** *Conj. phr.* **A. que,** when. **A. même que,** even though. **4.** Then, next.

alouette, *s.f.* Lark.

alourdir, *v.tr.* **1.** To make heavy. **2.** To weigh down (s.o.). **s'alourdir,** to grow heavy; to grow stupid.

alourdissement, *s.m.* Heaviness.

aloyau, -aux, *s.m.* Sirloin.

alpaga, *s.m.* Alpaca.

alpe, *s.f.* Alp, mountain.

alpestre, *a.* Alpine.

alphabet, *s.m.* Alphabet.

alphabétique, *a.* Alphabetical.

alpinisme, *s.m.* Mountaineering.

alpiniste, *s.m. & f.* Mountaineer.

alsacien, *a. & s.* Alsatian.

altération, *s.f.* **1.** Change; deterioration. **2.** Adulteration.

altercation, *s.f.* Altercation.

altéré, *a.* **1.** Broken (voice). **2.** Thirsty.

altérer, *v.tr.* **1.** To change; to impair. **2.** To tamper with. **3.** To make thirsty.

alternatif, *a.* **1.** (*a*) Alternate. (*b*) Alternating (current). **2.** Alternative. **3.** *s.f.* **Alternative,** alternative.

alterner, *v.i.* (*a*) To alternate. (*b*) To take turns.

altesse, *s.f.* Highness.

altier, *a.* Haughty, proud.

altièrement, *adv.* Haughtily.

altitude, *s.f.* Altitude, height.

aluminium [-ɔm], *s.m.* Aluminium.

alun, *s.m.* Alum.

amabilité, *s.f.* **1.** Amiability; kindness. **2.** *pl.* Civilities.

amadou, *s.m.* Touchwood.

amadouer, *v.tr.* To coax.

amaigrir, *v.tr.* To emaciate. **s'amaigrir,** to grow thin.

amaigrissement, *s.m.* Loss of flesh, wasting away.

amalgamation, *s.f.* Amalgamation.

amalgame, *s.m.* Amalgam.

amalgamer, *v.tr.* To amalgamate. **s'amalgamer,** to blend.

amande, *s.f.* Almond.

amandier, *s.m.* Almond-tree.

amant, *s.* Lover.

amarrage, *s.m.* Mooring.

amarre, *s.f.* (Mooring) rope.

amarrer, *v.tr.* To moor.

amas, *s.m.* Heap, pile.

amasser, *v.tr.* **1.** To pile up. **2.** To amass. **3.** To gather together.

amateur, -trice, s. 1. Lover (of sth.). 2. Amateur.

amazone, s.f. 1. (a) Amazon. Le fleuve des Amazones, the Amazon. (b) Horsewoman. 2. Riding-habit.

ambages, s.f.pl. Circumlocution. Parler sans a., to speak to the point.

ambassade, s.f. Embassy.

ambassadeur, s.m. Ambassador.

ambassadrice, s.f. Ambassadress.

ambiance, s.f. Environment.

ambiant, a. Surrounding.

ambigu, -uë, a. Ambiguous.

ambiguïté, s.f. Ambiguity.

ambigument, adv. Ambiguously.

ambitieusement, adv. Ambitiously.

ambitieux, a. Ambitious.

ambition, s.f. Ambition.

ambitionner, v.tr. To be ambitious of; to covet.

ambre, s.m. 1. A. gris, ambergris. 2. A. (jaune), amber.

ambulance, s.f. Ambulance.

ambulant, a. Itinerant, peripatetic. Marchand a., pedlar.

âme, s.f. Soul. (a) Rendre l'âme, to give up the ghost. (b) (Departed) soul, spirit. (c) Heart, feeling.

amélioration, s.f. Amelioration.

améliorer, v.tr. To ameliorate.
s'**améliorer,** to improve.

amen [amɛn], int. Amen.

aménager, v.tr. To fit up.

amende, s.f. 1. Fine. 2. Faire a. honorable, to apologize.

amendement, s.m. Improvement.

amender, v.tr. To amend.
s'**amender,** to improve.

amener, v.tr. To bring. A. à faire qch., to induce to do sth.

aménité, s.f. Amenity, charm.

amer[1] [amɛːr]. 1. a. Bitter. 2. s.m. Bitter(s).

amer[2], s.m. Sea-mark, landmark.

amèrement, adv. Bitterly.

américain, a. & s. American.

Amérique. Pr.n.f. America.

amerrir, v.i. To alight (on sea).

amerrissage, s.m. Alighting (on sea).

amertume, s.f. Bitterness.

améthyste, s.f. Amethyst.

ameublement, s.m. 1. Furnishing. 2. Furniture.

ami. 1. s. Friend. Mon ami, (i) my dear fellow, (ii) my dear. 2. a. Friendly (de, to).

amiable, a. Amicable. Vente à l'a., private sale.

amiante, s.m. Asbestos.

amical, -aux, a. Friendly.

amicalement, adv. In a friendly way.

amidon, s.m. Starch.

amidonner, v.tr. To starch.

amiral, -aux, s.m. 1. Admiral. 2. Flagship.

amirauté, s.f. Admiralty.

amitié, s.f. 1. Friendship, affection. 2. (a) Kindness, favour. (b) pl. Avec mes sincères amitiés, with kind regards.

ammoniaque, s.f. Ammonia.

amnistie, s.f. Amnesty.

amoindrir. 1. v.tr. To reduce; belittle. 2. v.i. & pr. To diminish.

amoindrissement, s.m. Reduction.

amollir, v.tr. 1. To soften. 2. To weaken, enervate.

amollissement, s.m. Softening.

amonceler, v.tr. To pile up, heap up.

amoncellement, s.m. 1. Heaping (up). 2. Heap, pile.

amont, s.m. En a., up-stream.

amorce, s.f. 1. Percussion cap. 2. Bait.

amorcer, v.tr. (a) To bait. (b) To allure.

amorphe, a. Amorphous.

amortir, v.tr. 1. To deaden (pain); to break (fall). 2. To redeem, pay off.

amortissement, s.m. 1. Deadening (of pain); breaking (of fall). 2. Redemption (of debt).

amour, s.m. 1. Love, affection. 2. Mon a., my love, my sweetheart. 3. Cupid.

amoureusement, adv. Lovingly.

amoureux. 1. a. Loving. Être a. de, to be in love with. 2. s. Lover.

amour-propre, s.m. (a) Self-respect; pride. (b) Self-esteem, vanity.

amphibie. 1. a. Amphibious. 2. s.m. Amphibian.

ample, a. 1. Ample. 2. Roomy.

amplement, adv. Amply, fully.

ampleur, s.f. Fullness; volume.

amplifier, v.tr. To amplify.

ampoule, s.f. 1. Bulb (of electric light). 2. Blister.

amputation, s.f. Amputation.

amputer, v.tr. To amputate.

amulette, s.f. Amulet, charm.

amusant, *a.* Amusing, funny.
amusement, *s.m.* Amusement.
amuser, *v.tr.* To amuse, entertain. **s'amuser,** to enjoy oneself.
amygdale [amidal], *s.f.* Tonsil.
an, *s.m.* Year. **Le jour de l'an,** New Year's day.
anachorète, *s.m.* Anchorite.
anachronisme, *s.m.* Anachronism
anagramme, *s.f.* Anagram.
analogie, *s.f.* Analogy.
analogue, *a.* Analogous; similar.
analyse, *s.f.* Analysis.
analyser, *v.tr.* To analyse.
analytique, *a.* Analytical.
ananas [ananɑ(ː)s], *s.m.* Pine-apple.
anarchie, *s.f.* Anarchy.
anarchiste, *a. & s.* Anarchist.
anathème, *s.m.* Anathema.
anatomie, *s.f.* Anatomy.
anatomique, *a.* Anatomical.
ancestral, -aux, *a.* Ancestral.
ancêtre, *s.m. & f.* Ancestor, ancestress.
anchois, *s.m.* Anchovy.
ancien, *a.* **1.** Ancient, old. **2.** Former, old. **3.** Senior.
anciennement, *adv.* Formerly.
ancienneté, *s.f.* **1.** Antiquity. **2.** Seniority; length of service.
ancrage, *s.m.* Anchorage.
ancre, *s.f.* Anchor. **Jeter, mouiller, l'a.,** to anchor.
Andorre. *Pr.n.* Andorra.
André. *Pr.n.m.* Andrew.
âne, *s.m.* **1.** Ass; donkey. **En dos d'âne,** ridged. **2.** Dunce.
anéantir, *v.tr.* To annihilate.
anéantissement, *s.m.* **1.** Annihilation. **2.** Prostration.
anecdote, *s.f.* Anecdote.
anémie, *s.f.* Anaemia.
anémique, *a.* Anaemic, bloodless.
anémone, *s.f.* Anemone.
ânerie, *s.f.* Foolish act or remark.
ânesse, *s.f.* She-ass.
anesthésique, *a. & s.m.* Anaesthetic.
anfractuosité, *s.f.* **1.** Winding. **2.** Cragginess, unevenness.
ange, *s.m.* Angel. **Être aux anges,** to be delighted.
angélique, *a.* Angelic.
angélus [-lyːs], *s.m.* Angelus(-bell).
angine, *s.f.* Quinsy; tonsillitis; angina.
anglais. **1.** *a.* English; British.

Filer à l'anglaise, to take French leave. **2.** *s.* English(wo)man; Briton. **3.** *s.m.* English.
angle, *s.m.* **1.** Angle. **2.** Corner.
Angleterre. *Pr.n.f.* England.
anglo-normand, *a. & s.* **Les îles Anglo-normandes,** the Channel Islands.
angoissant, *a.* Distressing; tense.
angoisse, *s.f.* Anguish; distress
angoisser, *v.tr.* To distress.
anguille [ɑ̃giːj], *s.f.* Eel.
angulaire, *a.* Angular. **Pierre a.,** corner-stone.
anguleux, *a.* Angular; rugged.
anicroche, *s.f.* Difficulty, hitch
ânier, *s.* Donkey-driver.
aniline, *s.f.* Aniline.
animal[1], -aux, *s.m.* Animal.
animal[2], -aux, *a.* **1.** Animal. **2.** Sensual, brutal.
animation, *s.f.* Animation.
animé, *a.* Animated, lively.
animer, *v.tr.* **1.** To animate. **2.** To actuate. **3.** To enliven. **s'animer.** **1.** To come to life. **2.** To become lively.
animosité, *s.f.* Animosity, spite.
anis, *s.m.* **Graine d'a.,** aniseed.
annales, *s.f.pl.* Annals.
annaliste, *s.m.* Annalist.
anneau, *s.m.* **1.** Ring. **2.** (*a*) Link. (*b*) Coil (of serpent).
année, *s.f.* Year, twelvemonth.
annexe, *s.f.* **1.** Annexe, outbuilding. **2.** Enclosure (with letter).
annexer, *v.tr.* To annex.
annexion, *s.f.* Annexation.
annihilation, *s.f.* Annihilation.
annihiler, *v.tr.* To annihilate.
anniversaire. **1.** *a.* Anniversary. **2.** *s.m.* Birthday.
annonce, *s.f.* **1.** (*a*) Announcement. (*b*) *Cards:* Call. (*c*) Indication. **2.** Advertisement.
annoncer, *v.tr.* **1.** To announce. *Cards:* **A. son jeu,** to declare. **2.** To advertise. **3.** (*a*) To foretell. (*b*) To indicate.
annotation, *s.f.* Annotation.
annoter, *v.tr.* To annotate.
annuaire, *s.m.* **1.** Annual. **2.** Calendar. **3.** (Telephone) directory.
annuel, *a.* Annual, yearly.
annuellement, *adv.* Annually, yearly.
annuité, *s.f.* Annuity.

annulaire. 1. *a.* Annular, ring-shaped. **2.** *s.m.* Ring-finger.

annuler, *v.tr.* To annul.

anoblir, *v.tr.* To ennoble.

anoblissement, *s.m.* Ennoblement.

anodin. 1. *a.* Anodyne, soothing. **2.** *s.m.* Palliative ; pain-killer.

anomalie, *s.f.* Anomaly.

ânon, *s.m.* Ass's foal, ass's colt.

ânonner, *v.tr.* To hum and haw.

anonyme. 1. *a.* (*a*) Anonymous. (*b*) Société a., limited company. **2.** *s.m.* Anonymity.

anonymement, *adv.* Anonymously

anormal, -aux, *a.* Abnormal.

anormalement, *adv.* Abnormally.

anse, *s.f.* **1.** Handle (of basket). **2.** Bight, bay.

antagonisme, *s.m.* Antagonism.

antagoniste. 1. *a.* Antagonistic. **2.** *s.* Antagonist.

antarctique, *a.* Antarctic.

antécédent. 1. *a.* Antecedent, previous. **2.** *s.m.* Antecedent.

antédiluvien, *a.* Antediluvian.

antenne, *s.f.* **1.** Aerial (wire). **2.** Antenna, feeler.

antérieur, -e, *a.* **1.** Anterior ; earlier. **2.** Fore-(limb).

antérieurement, *adv.* Previously.

anthologie, *s.f.* Anthology.

anthracite, *s.m.* Anthracite.

anthropoïde, *a. & s.m.* Anthropoid

anthropophage, *a. & s.* Cannibal.

anthropophagie, *s.f.* Cannibalism

anti-aérien, *a.* Anti-aircraft.

antichambre, *s.f.* Waiting-room

anticipatif, *a.* Anticipatory.

anticipation, *s.f.* Anticipation.

anticiper, *v.tr.* To anticipate.

antidérapant, *a.* Non-skid.

antidote, *s.m.* Antidote.

Antilles [ɑ̃tiːj]. *Pr.n.f.pl.* **Les A.,** the West Indies.

antilope, *s.f.* Antelope.

antimoine, *s.m.* Antimony.

antipathie, *s.f.* Antipathy.

antipathique, *a.* Antipathetic.

antipodes, *s.m.pl.* Antipodes.

antiquaire, *s.m.* Antiquary.

antique, *a.* (*a*) Ancient. (*b*) Antique.

antiquité, *s.f.* Antiquity.

antiseptique, *a. & s.m.* Antiseptic.

antithèse, *s.f.* Antithesis.

Antoine. *Pr.n.m.* Anthony.

antre, *s.m.* Cavern : den, lair.

Anvers. *Pr.n.m.* Antwerp.

anxiété [ɑ̃ks-], *s.f.* Anxiety.

anxieusement [ɑ̃ks-], *adv.* Anxiously.

anxieux [ɑ̃ks-], *a.* Anxious, uneasy.

août [u], *s.m.* August.

Apache, *s.m.* Apache ; hooligan.

apaisement, *s.m.* **1.** Pacifying. **2.** Abatement.

apaiser, *v.tr.* **1.** To appease, calm. **2.** To allay ; to quell. **s'apaiser,** to calm down.

apanage, *s.m.* Attribute.

aparté, *s.m.* Aside.

apathie, *s.f.* Apathy ; listlessness.

apathique, *a.* Apathetic ; listless.

apathiquement, *adv.* Apathetically, listlessly.

apercevoir, *v.tr.* To perceive, see. **s'apercevoir de,** to perceive, notice ; to become aware of.

aperçu, *s.m.* **1.** Glimpse. **2.** Outline, sketch, summary.

apéritif, *s.m.* Appetizer.

apiculteur, *s.m.* Bee-keeper.

apiculture, *s.f.* Bee-keeping.

apitoyer, *v.tr.* To move (to pity) ; to incite to pity. **s'apitoyer sur le sort de,** to commiserate with.

aplanir, *v.tr.* **1.** To flatten ; to smooth away. **2.** To level.

aplati, *a.* (*a*) Flattened. (*b*) Deflated.

aplatir, *v.tr.* To flatten. **s'aplatir. 1.** To go flat. **2.** To grovel.

aplomb, *s.m.* **1.** D'a., upright ; plumb. **2.** Assurance, self-possession.

apocryphe, *a.* Apocryphal.

apogée, *s.m* Apogee ; height.

apologie, *s.f.* Defence, vindication. NOTE. Never= EXCUSE, *q.v.*

apoplectique, *a. & s.* Apoplectic

apoplexie, *s.f.* Apoplexy.

apostat, *a. & s.* Apostate ; turncoat.

apostolique, *a.* Apostolic.

apostrophe, *s.f.* Apostrophe.

apothicaire, *s.m.* Apothecary.

apôtre, *s.m.* Apostle.

apparaître, *v.i.* **1.** To appear ; to come into sight. **2.** To become evident.

apparat, *s.m.* State, pomp.

appareil [-rɛːj], *s.m.* (*a*) Apparatus, outfit. (*b*) Device, appliance. (*c*) Instrument. **A. à lampes,** valve set. **A. (photographique),** camera.

appareillage [-rej-], *s.m.* **1.** (*a*) Installation. (*b*) Getting under way. **2.** Outfit; equipment.

appareiller [-rεje], *v.tr.* **1.** To install. **2.** *Abs.* To get under way.

apparemment, *adv.* Apparently.

apparence, *s.f.* **1.** Appearance; look. **2.** Sauver les apparences, to keep up appearances.

apparent, *a.* **1.** (*a*) Visible; apparent. (*b*) Obvious. **2.** Apparent, not real.

apparenté, *a.* Related, akin.

apparier, *v.tr.* To match.

apparition, *s.f.* **1.** Appearance; publication. **2.** Apparition, ghost.

appartement, *s.m.* Flat; suite of rooms.

appartenir, *v.i.* **1.** To belong. **2.** *v. impers.* A. à qn de, to behove s.o. to.

appas, *s.m.pl.* **1.** (Physical) charms. **2.** Lure, attraction.

appât, *s.m.* (*a*) Bait. (*b*) Lure.

appauvrir, *v.tr.* To impoverish.

appauvrissement, *s.m.* Impoverishment.

appel, *s.m.* **1.** Appeal. **2.** Call; summons. **3.** Roll-call.

appeler, *v.tr.* **1.** To call, call to. **2.** (*a*) To call in, send for. A. en justice, to summons. (*b*) Être appelé à qch., to be destined for sth. **3.** To call; to name. **4.** (*a*) To appeal to, call on. (*b*) To call for. **5.** *v.i.* En a. à qn, to appeal to s.o.

s'appeler, to be called, named.

appendice, *s.m.* Appendix.

appendicite, *s.f.* Appendicitis.

appentis, *s.m.* Outhouse.

appesantir, *v.tr.* **1.** To weigh down. **2.** To dull.

appétissant, *a.* Appetizing.

appétit, *s.m.* **1.** Appetite. **2.** Desire.

applaudir. **1.** *v.tr.* To applaud. **2.** *v.ind.tr.* A. à qch., to approve sth.

applaudissement, *s.m.* Applause.

applicable, *a.* Applicable.

application, *s.f.* Application.

appliqué, *a.* Studious, diligent

appliquer, *v.tr.* To apply.

s'appliquer, to apply oneself; to work hard.

appointements, *s.m.pl.* Salary.

apporter, *v.tr.* To bring.

apposer, *v.tr.* To affix, place, put.

appréciable, *a.* Appreciable.

appréciateur, -trice, *a.* Appreciative.

appréciation, *s.f.* **1.** Valuation. **2.** Appreciation. **3.** Rise in value.

apprécier, *v.tr.* **1.** (*a*) To appraise. (*b*) To estimate. **2.** To appreciate.

appréhender, *v.tr.* To apprehend.

appréhensif, *a.* Apprehensive.

appréhension, *s.f.* **1.** Understanding. **2.** Dread.

apprendre, *v.tr.* **1.** (*a*) To learn. (*b*) To hear of. **2.** A. qch. à qn. (*a*) To teach s.o. sth. (*b*) To tell s.o. sth.

apprenti, *s.* (*a*) Apprentice (*b*) Articled clerk. (*c*) Novice.

apprentissage, *s.m.* Apprenticeship.

apprêter, *v.tr.* To prepare; to make ready.

apprivoisé, *a.* Tame.

apprivoisement, *s.m.* Taming.

apprivoiser, *v.tr.* To tame.

approbateur, -trice, *a.* Approving.

approbatif, *a.* Approving.

approbation, *s.f.* Approval, approbation.

approchant, *a.* Approximating, similar (de, to).

approche, *s.f.* **1.** Approach, drawing near. D'une a. difficile, difficult of access. **2.** *pl.* Approaches.

approcher. **1.** *v.tr.* (*a*) To bring, draw, near (de, to). Approchez votre chaise, draw up your chair. (*b*) To approach. **2.** *v.i.* To approach. (*b*) Nous approchons de Paris, we are getting near Paris.

s'approcher, to come near; to approach. S'a. de qch., to draw near (to) sth.

approfondi, *a.* Careful; thorough.

approfondir, *v.tr.* **1.** To deepen. **2.** To go thoroughly into.

appropriation, *s.f.* Appropriation.

approprié, *a.* Appropriate.

approprier, *v.tr.* **1.** S'a. qch., to appropriate sth. **2.** To make appropriate.

approuver, *v.tr.* **1.** (*a*) To approve of, be pleased with. A. de la tête, to nod approval. **2.** To agree to.

approvisionnement, *s.m.* **1.** Provisioning; stocking. **2.** Supply, stock.

approvisionner, *v.tr.* To supply (de, with); to provision.

s'approvisionner, to lay in stores.

approximatif, *a.* Approximate.

approximativement, *adv.* Approximately, roughly.

appui, *s.m.* **1.** Prop, stay. **2.** Support. **A hauteur d'a.,** breast-high.

appuyer, *v.tr.* **1.** To support. **2.** *Abs.* **A. sur,** to press; to stress.
s'appuyer, to lean, rest.

âpre, *a.* **1.** Rough, harsh. **2.** Biting, sharp. **3.** Keen (competition).

âprement, *adv.* **1.** Harshly. **2.** Keenly.

après. **I.** *prep.* **1.** (*a*) After. (*b*) Next to. **2. Courir a.,** to run after. **3.** *Prep. phr.* **D'a.,** according to; after. **4. A. avoir dîné,** after dining.
II. après, *adv.* (*a*) Afterwards, later. **Le jour (d')a.,** the next day. **Et a.?** what then? (*b*) *Conj.phr.* **A. que,** after, when.

après-demain, *adv.* The day after to-morrow.

après-guerre, *s.m.inv.* Post-war period.

après-midi, *s.m.* or *f.inv.* Afternoon.

âpreté, *s.f.* **1.** Roughness; harshness. **2.** Keenness.

à-propos, *s.m.* Aptness.

apte, *a.* **1.** Fitted, qualified. **2.** Apt.

aptitude, *s.f.* Aptitude, fitness.

aquarelle [akwa-], *s.f.* Water-colour.

aquarium [akwarjɔm], *s.m.* Aquarium.

aquatique [akwa-], *a.* Aquatic.

aqueduc [-dyk], *s.m.* Aqueduct.

aquilin, *a.* Aquiline. **Nez a.,** Roman nose.

arabe. **1.** *a. & s.* (*a*) Arab. (*b*) Arabian. **2.** *a. & s.m.* Arabic.

arable, *a.* Arable.

arachide, *s.f.* Pea-nut, earth-nut.

araignée, *s.f.* Spider.

arbitrage, *s.m.* Arbitration.

arbitraire, *a.* Arbitrary.

arbitrairement, *adv.* Arbitrarily.

arbitre[1], *s.m.* (*a*) Arbitrator. (*b*) Umpire. (*c*) Arbiter.

arbitre[2], *s.m.* **Libre a.,** free will.

arbitrer, *v.tr.* **1.** To arbitrate. **2.** To umpire.

arborer, *v.tr.* To hoist (flag).

arbre, *s.m.* **1.** Tree. **2.** Shaft, axle.

arbrisseau, *s.m.* Shrub.

arbuste, *s.m.* Bush; shrub.

arc [ark], *s.m.* **1.** Bow. **2.** Arch. **3.** Arc.

arcade, *s.f.* (*a*) Archway. (*b*) *pl.* Arcade.

arc-bouter, *v.tr.* To buttress.
s'arc-bouter, to brace oneself.

arceau, *s.m.* Arch (of vault).

arc-en-ciel, *s.m.* Rainbow. *pl. arcs-en-ciel* [arkɑ̃sjɛl].

archaïque, [ark-], *a.* Archaic.

archange [ark-], *s.m.* Archangel.

arche[1], *s.f.* Ark.

arche[2], *s.f.* Arch (of bridge).

archéologie [ark-], *s.f.* Archaeology.

archéologue [ark-], *s.m.* Archaeologist.

archer, *s.m.* Archer, bowman.

archet, *s.m.* Bow (of violin).

archevêque, *s.m.* Archbishop.

archipel, *s.m.* Archipelago.

architecte, *s.m.* Architect.

architecture, *s.f.* Architecture.

archives, *s.f.pl.* Archives; records.

archiviste, *s.m. & f.* **1.** Archivist; keeper of records. **2.** Filing clerk.

arctique, *a.* Arctic.

ardemment, *adv.* Ardently.

ardent, *a.* **1.** Burning, scorching. **Charbons ardents,** live coals. **2.** Ardent.

ardeur, *s.f.* **1.** Heat. **2.** Ardour.

ardoise, *s.f.* Slate.

ardu, *a.* **1.** Steep, abrupt. **2.** Arduous, difficult.

are, *s.m.* 100 square metres.

arène, *s.f.* **1.** Sand. **2.** Arena.

aréole, *s.f.* Halo, nimbus.

arête, *s.f.* **1.** (Fish-)bone. **2.** Line; edge; ridge.

argent, *s.m.* **1.** Silver. **2.** Money.

argenterie, *s.f.* (Silver-)plate.

argentin, *a.* Silvery; tinkling.

argile, *s.f.* Clay.

argot, *s.m.* Slang.

arguer [argɥe], *v.tr.* To infer, assert. **2.** *v.i.* To argue.

argument, *s.m.* Argument.

argumenter, *v.i.* To argue.

aride, *a.* Arid, dry, barren.

aridité, *s.f.* Aridity, barrenness.

aristocrate, *s.m. & f.* Aristocrat.

aristocratie, *s.f.* Aristocracy.

aristocratique, *a.* Aristocratic.

arithmétique, *s.f.* Arithmetic.

arlequin, *s.m.* Harlequin.

armateur, *s.m.* (Ship-)owner.

armature, *s.f.* **1.** Framework. **2.** *El:* Armature. **3.** Key-signature.

arme, *s.f.* **1.** Arm, weapon. **Maître d'armes,** fencing-master. **Place**

d'armes, parade-ground. **Passer par les armes,** to be (court-martialled and) shot. **2.** *pl. Her:* Arms.

armée, *s.f.* Army.

armement, *s.m.* **I.** (*a*) Arming. (*b*) *pl.* Armaments. **2.** *Nau:* Fitting out.

armer. I. *v.tr.* **I.** To arm (*de*, with). **2.** To strengthen, reinforce. **3.** To equip (ship). **4.** To cock (fire-arm).
II. **armer,** *v.i.* To arm.

armistice, *s.m.* Armistice.

armoire, *s.f.* **I.** Wardrobe. **2.** Cupboard.

armoiries, *s.f.pl.* (Coat of) arms.

armure, *s.f.* Armour.

armurier, *s.m.* **I.** Gunsmith. **2.** Armourer.

arnica, *s.f.* Arnica.

aromatique, *a.* Aromatic.

arome, *s.m.* Aroma.

arpenter, *v.tr.* To stride along; to pace up and down.

arpenteur, *s.m.* (Land-)surveyor.

arqué, *a.* Arched, curved.

arquer, *v.tr.* To bend. **A. le dos,** to hump the back.

arrache-pied (d'), *adv.phr.* Without interruption.

arracher, *v.tr.* To tear (out); to pull (up). **S'a. les cheveux,** to tear one's hair.

arrangement, *s.m.* Arrangement.

arranger, *v.tr.* To arrange. **I.** To set in order. **2.** To contrive. **3.** To settle.
   s'arranger. I. To manage, contrive. **2.** To come to an agreement.

arrérages, *s.m.pl.* Arrears.

arrestation, *s.f.* Arrest.

arrêt, *s.m.* **I.** Stop, stoppage. **Point d'a.,** stopping place. **"A. fixe,"** 'all cars stop here.' **2.** (*a*) Decree. (*b*) Judgment; sentence. **3.** Arrest.

arrêté. I. *a.* Fixed, decided. **2.** *s.m.* Decision, decree.

arrêter. I. *v.tr.* **I.** To stop; to detain. **2.** To arrest, seize. **3.** To decide. **A. un jour,** to fix a day.
II. **arrêter,** *v.i.* To stop, halt.
   s'arrêter. I. To stop. **2. S'a. à** to dwell on.

arrhes [a:r], *s.f.pl.* Deposit.

arrière. I. *adv.* (**En**) **a.** (*a*) Behind. *Prep.phr.* **En a. de qch.,** behind sth. (*b*) In arrears. (*c*) Backwards.

A.! back! **Faire marche a.,** to reverse. **2.** *a.inv.* Back. *Aut:* **Lanterne a.,** rear light. **3.** *s.m.* (*a*) Back. (*b*) Stern. **4.** *s. Fb:* Back.

arriéré, *a.* **I.** In arrears. **2.** Behind the times. **3.** *s.m.* Arrears.

NOTE. In the following compounds ARRIÈRE is inv., the noun takes the plural.

arrière-boutique, *s.f.* Back-shop.

arrière-cour, *s.f.* Back-yard.

arrière-garde, *s.f.* Rear-guard.

arrière-goût, *s.m.* After-taste.

arrière-main, *s.m. or f.* Back of the hand.

arrière-pensée, *s.f.* (*a*) Mental reservation. (*b*) Ulterior motive.

arrière-plan, *s.m.* Background.

arrière-saison, *s.f.* Late season.

arrière-scène, *s.f.* Back of the stage.

arrimer, *v.tr.* To stow (cargo).

arrimeur, *s.m.* Stevedore.

arrivant, *s.* Person arriving; arrival.

arrivée, *s.f.* Arrival, coming.

arriver, *v.i.* **I.** (*a*) To arrive, come. (*b*) **A. à,** to reach. (*c*) **Il faudra bien en a. là,** it must come to that. **2.** To succeed. **3.** To happen.

arriviste, *s.m. & f.* Thruster.

arrogamment, *adv.* Arrogantly.

arrogance, *s.f.* Arrogance.

arrogant, *a.* Arrogant, overbearing.

arroger (s'), *v.tr.pr.* To arrogate to oneself.

arrondi, *a.* Rounded.

arrondir, *v.tr.* To round (off).
   s'arrondir, to become round; to fill out.

arrondissement, *s.m.* Administrative area; ward.

arrosage, *s.m.* (*a*) Watering. (*b*) Irrigation.

arroser, *v.tr.* (*a*) To water. (*b*) To irrigate a meadow.

arrosoir, *s.m.* Watering-can.

arsenal, -aux, *s.m.* Arsenal.

arsenic [-ik], *s.m.* Arsenic.

art, *s.m.* **I.** Art. **Arts d'agrément,** accomplishments. **2.** Skill. **Ouvrages d'art,** constructive works.

artère, *s.f.* Artery.

artériel, *a.* Arterial.

artichaut, *s.m.* (Globe) artichoke.

article, *s.m.* **I.** (*a*) Article, clause.

(b) Item. (c) Article (in newspaper).
2. Article, commodity; *pl.* goods.
3. *Gram:* Article.
articulation, *s.f.* Articulation.
articuler, *v.tr.* To articulate.
artifice, *s.m.* **1.** Artifice; contrivance. **2.** Feu d'a., fireworks.
artificiel, *a.* Artificial.
artificiellement, *adv.* Artificially.
artificieux, *a.* Crafty, cunning.
artillerie [-tijri], *s.f.* Artillery.
artilleur [-tij-], *s.m.* Gunner.
artisan, *s.m.* Artisan, craftsman.
artiste. **1.** *s.m. & f.* (a) Artist (including musician, etc.). (b) Performer. (c) Artiste. **2.** *a.* Artistic.
artistique, *a.* Artistic.
artistiquement, *adv.* Artistically.
aryen, *a. & s.* Aryan.
as [ɑːs], *s.m.* Ace.
ascendant. **1.** *a.* Ascending, upward. **2.** *s.m.* Ascendancy.
ascenseur, *s.m.* Lift.
ascension, *s.f.* Ascent, ascension; climb.
ascète, *s.m. & f.* Ascetic.
ascétique, *a. & s.* Ascetic.
ascétisme, *s.m.* Asceticism.
asiatique, *a. & s.* Asiatic.
Asie. *Pr.n.f.* Asia.
asile, *s.m.* Shelter, home, refuge.
aspect [aspɛ], *s.m.* **1.** Sight, aspect. **2.** Aspect, appearance.
asperge, *s.f.* Asparagus.
asperger, *v.tr.* To sprinkle with water.
aspérité, *s.f.* Asperity. **1.** Ruggedness, roughness. **2.** Harshness.
asphalte, *s.m.* Asphalt.
asphyxier, *v.tr.* To asphyxiate.
aspirant, *s.* (a) Aspirant; candidate. (b) Midshipman.
aspirateur, *s.m.* **A. de poussières,** vacuum-cleaner.
aspiration, *s.f.* **1.** Aspiration. **2.** (a) Inspiration, inhaling. (b) Suction.
aspirer. **1.** *v.ind.tr.* To aspire. **2.** *v.tr.* (a) To inspire, inhale. (b) To suck up.
aspirine, *s.f.* Aspirin.
assagir, *v.tr.* To make wiser.
assaillant [-ajã], *s.m.* Assailant.
assaillir [-ajiːr], *v.tr.* To assail.
assainir, *v.tr.* To make healthier.
assainissement, *s.m.* Cleansing.
assaisonnement, *s.m.* Seasoning.

assaisonner, *v.tr.* To season.
assassin, *s.* Assassin; murderer.
assassinat, *s.m.* Assassination.
assassiner, *v.tr.* To assassinate.
assaut, *s.m.* **1.** Assault, attack, onslaught. **2.** Match, bout.
assèchement, *s.m.* Drying (up).
assécher, *v.tr.* To dry, drain.
assemblage, *s.m.* Assemblage.
assemblée, *s.f.* Assembly.
assembler, *v.tr.* **1.** To assemble; to collect. **2.** To connect.
  s'assembler, to assemble.
assentiment, *s.m.* Assent, consent.
asseoir, *v.tr.* **1.** To set, seat. **2.** To lay (foundations).
  s'asseoir, to sit down.
assermenté, *a.* Sworn (in).
asservir, *v.tr.* To enslave.
asservissement, *s.m.* (a) Reduction to slavery. (b) Bondage.
assesseur, *s.m.* Assessor.
assez, *adv.* **1.** Enough, sufficient. **J'en ai a.!** I have had enough of it. **2.** Rather, fairly.
assidu, *a.* Assiduous.
assiduité, *s.f.* Assiduity.
assidûment, *adv.* Assiduously.
assiégeant, *s.m.* Besieger.
assiéger, *v.tr.* **1.** To besiege. **2.** To beset, crowd round.
assiette, *s.f.* **1.** N'être pas dans son a., to be out of sorts. **2.** Support, basis. **3.** Plate.
assignation, *s.f.* Writ, summons.
assigner, *v.tr.* **1.** To assign. **2.** To summon, subpoena.
assimilation, *s.f.* Assimilation.
assimiler, *v.tr.* **1.** To assimilate. **2.** To liken, compare (à, to, with)
assis, *a.* Seated.
assise, *s.f.* **1.** Foundation. **2.** *pl.* Assizes.
assistance, *s.f.* **1.** Audience; spectators. **2.** Assistance, help.
assistant, *s.* (a) Bystander, onlooker, spectator. (b) Member of the audience.
assister. **1.** *v.i.* To be present. **2.** *v.tr.* To help, assist.
association, *s.f.* **1.** Association (of ideas). **2.** (a) Society, company; association. (b) Partnership.
associé, *s.* Partner.
associer, *v.tr.* To associate, connect.
  s'associer **1.** To share (à, in).

2. (*a*) To enter into partnership. (*b*) To associate.

assombrir, *v.tr.* (*a*) To darken, obscure. (*b*) To cast a gloom over.
   s'assombrir. (*a*) To cloud over. (*b*) To become gloomy.

assombrissement, *s.m.* **1.** Darkening. **2.** Gloom.

assommant, *a.* **1.** Overwhelming. **2.** Boring, tedious.

assommer, *v.tr.* **1.** To fell (an ox). **2.** To bore.

assommoir, *s.m.* **1.** Club, bludgeon. **2.** Low tavern.

assorti, *a.* **1.** Matched, paired. **2.** Assorted, mixed.

assortiment, *s.m* **1.** Matching. **2.** Assortment.

assortir, *v.tr.* To assort, match

assoupi, *a.* Dozing.

assoupir, *v.tr.* To make drowsy.
   s'assoupir, to doze off.

assoupissement, *s.m.* Drowsiness.

assourdir, *v.tr.* **1.** To deafen. **2.** To deaden (sound).

assourdissant, *a.* Deafening.

assourdissement, *s.m.* (*a*) Deafening. (*b*) Deadening (of sound).

assouvir, *v.tr.* To appease.
   s'assouvir, to satiate oneself.

assouvissement, *s.m.* Satisfying, satisfaction (of hunger).

assujettir, *v.tr.* To subdue.

assujettissement, *s.m.* Subjection.

assumer, *v.tr.* To assume ; to take upon oneself.

assurance, *s.f.* **1.** Assurance. **2.** Insurance.

assuré, *a.* Firm, sure ; assured, confident. **Voix mal assurée**, unsteady voice.

assurément, *adv.* **1.** Firmly. **2.** Assuredly, surely.

assurer, *v.tr.* **1.** (*a*) To make firm ; to secure. (*b*) To ensure. **2.** To assure ; to declare. **3.** To insure.
   s'assurer. 1. To make sure. **2.** To make sure of, to secure. **3.** To get insured.

astérisque, *s.m.* Asterisk.

asthmatique [asm-], *a.* Asthmatic.

asthme [asm], *s.m.* Asthma.

asticot, *s.m.* Maggot.

astiquer, *v.tr.* To polish, furbish.

astral, -aux, *a.* Astral.

astre, *s.m.* Heavenly body ; star.

astreindre, *v.tr.* To compel ; to tie down.

astringent, *a. & s.m.* Astringent.

astrologie, *s.f.* Astrology.

astrologue, *s.m.* Astrologer.

astronome, *s.m.* Astronomer.

astronomie, *s.f.* Astronomy.

astronomique, *a.* Astronomical.

astuce, *s.f.* Astuteness ; wile.

astucieusement, *adv.* Astutely.

astucieux, *a.* Astute, artful.

atelier, *s.m.* (*a*) (Work)shop, workroom. (*b*) Studio.

athée. 1. *a.* Atheistic. **2.** *s.* Atheist.

athéisme, *s.m.* Atheism.

Athènes. *Pr.n.f.* Athens

athlète, *s.m.* Athlete.

athlétique, *a.* Athletic.

athlétisme, *s.m.* Athletics.

atlantique, *a.* **L'océan A.**, *s.m.* **l'A.**, the Atlantic (Ocean).

atlas [atlɑːs], *s.m.* Atlas.

atmosphère, *s.f.* Atmosphere.

atmosphérique, *a.* Atmospheric.

atoll, *s.m.* Atoll ; coral island.

atome, *s.m.* Atom.

atomique, *a.* Atomic.

atout, *s.m.* *Cards:* Trump.

âtre, *s.m.* Fire-place, hearth(-stone).

atroce, *a.* Atrocious ; agonizing.

atrocement, *adv.* **1.** Atrociously, shockingly. **2.** Dreadfully.

atrocité, *s.f.* **1.** Atrociousness **2.** Atrocity.

attabler (s'), *v.pr.* To sit down to table.

attache, *s.f.* **1.** Fastening ; tying up **2.** Tie, fastening ; leash.

attaché. 1. *a.* (*a*) Fastened, tied-up (*b*) Attached, devoted. **2.** *s.m.* **A. militaire**, military attaché.

attachement, *s.m.* Attachment, affection.

attacher, *v.tr.* To attach ; to fasten, bind.
   s'attacher. To attach oneself ; to cling.

attaque, *s.f.* Attack, onslaught.

attaquer, *v.tr.* To attack, assail.
   s'attaquer, to make an attack (*à*, on).

attardé, *a.* Belated ; late.

attarder, *v.tr.* To keep (s.o.) late.
   s'attarder, to linger, loiter.

atteindre, *v.tr.* (*a*) To reach ; to overtake ; to attain. (*b*) To hit.

atteinte, *s.f.* **1.** Reach. **2.** Blow, hit. **Porter a. à,** to injure.

attelage, *s.m.* **1.** Harnessing. **2.** Team. **3.** *Rail:* Coupling.

atteler, *v.tr.* **1.** To harness. **2.** To couple.

attenant, *a.* Contiguous.

attendre, *v.tr.* **1.** To wait for, to await. **Se faire a.,** to be late. **Attendez donc!** wait a bit! **En attendant,** meanwhile. *Conj.phr.* **En attendant que, till. 2.** To expect. **s'attendre à,** to expect.

attendri, *a.* Fond, compassionate.

attendrir, *v.tr.* To soften. **s'attendrir,** to be moved (to pity).

attendrissant, *a.* Moving, touching.

attendrissement, *s.m.* Pity.

attendu. 1. *prep.* Considering; owing to. **2.** *Conj. phr.* **A. que,** considering that.

attentat, *s.m.* Outrage.

attente, *s.f.* **1.** Wait(ing). **Salle d'a.,** waiting-room. **2.** Expectation.

attenter, *v.ind.tr.* To make an attempt (*à,* on).

attentif, *a.* Attentive; careful.

attention, *s.f.* Attention; care. **Faites a.!** take care! **A.!** look out!

attentivement, *adv.* Attentively.

atténuation, *s.f.* **1.** Attenuation, lessening. **2.** Extenuation.

atténuer, *v.tr.* To attenuate, lessen; to mitigate.

atterré, *a.* Crushed (by news).

atterrer, *v.tr.* To overwhelm, astound; to strike with consternation.

atterrir, *v.i.* *Av:* To land.

atterrissage, *s.m.* *Av:* Landing.

attestation, *s.f.* Attestation.

attester, *v.tr.* To testify to.

attiédir, *v.tr.* To warm.

attiédissement, *s.m.* Cooling.

attirail [-ra:j], *s.m.* Gear; outfit.

attirer, *v.tr.* **1.** (*a*) To attract, draw. (*b*) **S'a. un blâme,** to incur a reprimand. **2.** To lure.

attiser, *v.tr.* To poke (fire).

attitré, *a.* Regular, appointed.

attitude, *s.f.* Attitude.

attraction, *s.f.* (*a*) Attraction (of magnet). (*b*) Attractiveness.

attrait, *s.m.* Attraction, lure.

attrape, *s.f.* Trick, catch.

attrape-nigaud, *s.m.* Booby-trap. *pl. attrape-nigauds.*

attraper, *v.tr.* To catch. **1.** (*a*) To (en)trap. (*b*) To trick, cheat. **2.** (*a*) To seize. (*b*) To hit. (*c*) **A. un rhume,** to catch cold.

attrayant, *a.* Attractive.

attribuable, *a.* Attributable.

attribuer, *v.tr.* **1.** To assign. **2.** To attribute; to impute. **3.** To claim.

attribut, *s.m.* Attribute.

attribution, *s.f.* **1.** Attribution **2.** Sphere of duties; functions.

attrister, *v.tr.* To sadden.

attroupement, *s.m.* (Unlawful) assembly.

au = *à le.* See à and LE.

aubaine, *s.f.* Windfall, godsend.

aube[1], *s.f.* Dawn.

aube[2], *s.f.* Paddle, blade (of wheel). **Roue à aubes,** paddle-wheel.

aubépine, *s.f.* Hawthorn.

auberge, *s.f.* Inn.

aubergiste, *s.m. & f.* Innkeeper.

aubier, *s.m.* Sap-wood.

aucun. 1. *pron.* (*a*) Anyone, any. (*b*) No one; not any. **2.** *a.* Any.

aucunement, *adv.* **1.** In any way, at all. **2.** Not at all.

audace, *s.f.* **1.** Boldness, daring. **2.** Impudence.

audacieusement, *adv.* **1.** Boldly. **2.** Impudently.

audacieux, *a.* **1.** Bold, daring. **2.** Impudent.

au-dessous, *adv.* **1.** Below (it); underneath. **2.** *Prep. phr.* **Au-d. de,** below, under; beneath.

au-dessus, *adv.* **1.** Above (it); over. **2.** *Prep.phr.* **A.-d. de,** above; over.

au-devant, *adv.* **1.** Aller a.-d., to go to meet (sth.). **2.** *Prep.phr.* **Aller a.-d. de qn,** to go to meet s.o. **Aller a.-d. des désirs de qn,** to anticipate s.o.'s wishes.

audible, *a.* Audible.

audience, *s.f.* (*a*) Hearing. (*b*) Sitting, court.

audit. See LEDIT.

auditeur, -trice, *s.* Hearer, listener.

auditoire, *s.m.* Audience.

auge, *s.f.* Feeding-trough.

augmentation, *s.f.* Increase.

augmenter, *v.tr. & i.* To increase.

augure, *s.m.* Augury, omen.

augurer, *v.tr.* To augur, forecast.

auguste, *a.* August, majestic.

aujourd'hui, *adv.* To-day; nowadays.

aumône, *s.f.* Alms.

aumônier, *s.m.* Chaplain.

aune[1], *s.m.* Alder.

aune[2], *s.f.* Ell.

auparavant, *adv.* Before(hand), previously.

auprès, *adv.* **1.** Close to. **2.** *Prep. phr.* **A. de.** (*a*) Close to, by; with. (*b*) Compared with.

auquel. See LEQUEL.

auréole, *s.f.* Halo.

Aurigny. *Pr.n.m.* Alderney.

aurore, *s.f.* (*a*) Dawn, day-break. (*b*) **A. boréale,** aurora borealis.

auspices, *s.m. pl.* Auspices.

aussi. **1.** *adv.* (*a*) As. **A. grand que,** as tall as. (*b*) Also, too. (*c*) *Conj. phr.* **A. bien que,** as well as. **2.** *conj.* (*a*) Therefore, so. (*b*) **A. bien,** moreover, besides.

aussitôt, *adv.* (*a*) Immediately, at once. **A. dit, a. fait,** no sooner said than done. (*b*) *Conj.phr.* **A. que,** as soon as.

austère, *a.* Austere.

austèrement, *adv.* Austerely.

austérité, *s.f.* Austerity.

Australie. *Pr.n.f.* Australia.

australien, *a. & s.* Australian.

autant, *adv.* **1.** As much, so much; as many, so many. **2. A. que** (*a*) As much as, as many as. (*b*) As far as, as near as. **3. A. de,** as much, as many, so much, so many. **4.** (*a*) *Conj.phr.* **D'a. que,** more especially as. (*b*) **D'a. plus,** (all) the more.

autel, *s.m.* Altar.

auteur, *s.m.* **1.** Author, perpetrator. **2.** Author, writer. **Droit d'a.,** copyright. **Droits d'a.,** royalties.

authenticité, *s.f.* Authenticity.

authentique, *a.* Authentic.

auto, *s.f.* Motor car.

autobiographie, *s.f.* Autobiography.

autobiographique, *a.* Autobiographical.

autobus [-by:s], *s.m.* Motor bus.

autocar, *s.m.* Motor coach.

autocrate, *s.m.* Autocrat.

autocratie, *s.f.* Autocracy.

autocratique, *a.* Autocratic.

autocratiquement, *adv.* Autocratically.

autographe. **1.** *a.* Autograph(ic). **2.** *s.m.* Autograph.

automate, *s.m.* Automaton.

automatique, *a.* Automatic.

automnal, -aux, *a.* Autumnal.

automne [oton], *s.m. or f.* Autumn.

automobile, *s.f.* (Motor) car.

automobiliste, *s.m. & f.* Motorist.

autopsie, *s.f.* Autopsy; post-mortem (examination).

autorisation, *s.f.* Authorization, authority; permit.

autoriser, *v.tr.* To authorize; to sanction.

autoritaire, *a.* Authoritative, dictatorial.

autorité, *s.f.* Authority.

autour, *adv.* **1.** Round; about. **2.** *Prep.phr.* **A. de,** round, about.

autre, *a. & pron.* **1.** (*a*) Other, further. (*b*) **Nous autres Anglais,** we English. (*c*) **D'un jour à l'a.,** any day. **De temps à a.,** now and then. (*d*) **L'un et l'a.,** both. (*e*) **L'un ou l'a.,** either. **Ni l'un ni l'a.,** neither. (*f*) **Les uns . . ., les autres . . .,** some . . ., some . . . . (*g*) **L'un l'a.,** each other. **2.** (*a*) Other, different. **J'en ai vu bien d'autres,** I've been through worse than that. (*b*) **Nul a., personne** (d')**a.,** nobody else. **A d'autres!** nonsense! (*c*) *indef.pron.m.* **A. chose,** something else. **C'est tout a. chose!** that's quite a different matter!

autrefois, *adv.* Formerly.

autrement, *adv.* Otherwise.

Autriche. *Pr.n.f.* Austria.

autrichien, *a. & s.* Austrian.

autruche, *s.f.* Ostrich.

autrui, *pron.indef.* Others; other people.

auvent, *s.m.* Open shed.

aux = *à les.* See À and LE.

auxiliaire. **1.** *a.* Auxiliary. **2.** *s.* Auxiliary; assistant.

auxquels, -elles. See LEQUEL.

aval, *s.m.* **En a.,** down-stream.

avalanche, *s.f.* Avalanche.

avaler, *v.tr.* To swallow; to devour.

avance, *s.f.* **1.** Advance, lead. **2.** Projection. **3.** (*a*) Advance, loan. (*b*) *pl.* Advances. **4.** *Adv. phr.* (*a*) **Payer d'a.,** to pay in advance. (*b*) **Payable à l'a.,** payable in advance. (*c*) **L'horloge est en a.,** the clock is fast. **Nous sommes en a.,** we are early.

avancé, *a.* Advanced. **A une heure avancée,** at a late hour.

avancement, *s.m.* **1.** (*a*) Advancing, putting forward. (*b*) Promotion. **2.** Advance(ment), progress. **3.** Projection.

avancer. I. *v.tr.* **1.** To advance, put forward. **2.** To make earlier. **3. A. de l'argent,** to advance money. **4.** To promote.

II. **avancer,** *v.i.* **1.** To advance, move forward ; to progress. **2.** (*a*) To be ahead of time. (*b*) To project.

s'avancer. 1. To move forward, to advance. **2.** To progress. **3.** To jut out.

avanie, *s.f.* Insult, affront.

avant. I. **1.** *prep.* Before. **2.** (*a*) *Prep.phr.* **A. de,** before. (*b*) *Conj.phr.* **A. que,** before **3.** *adv.* Before. **4.** *adv.* Forward. **5.** *Adv. phr.* **En a.,** in front ; forward *Prep.phr.* **En a. de,** ahead of.

II. **avant,** *s.m.* **1.** Front. **2.** *Fb :* Forward.

avantage, *s.m.* **1.** Advantage. **Avoir l'a.,** to have the best of it. **2.** *Ten :* (Ad)vantage.

avantager, *v.tr.* To favour.

avantageusement, *adv.* Advantageously, favourably.

avantageux, *a.* Advantageous.

NOTE. In the following compounds AVANT is inv., the noun or adj. takes the plural.

avant-bras, *s.m.* Forearm.

avant-corps, *s.m.* Fore-part.

avant-cour, *s.f.* Fore-court.

avant-coureur, *s.m.* Forerunner, harbinger.

avant-dernier, *a.* Last but one.

avant-garde, *s.f.* Advanced guard.

avant-goût, *s.m.* Foretaste.

avant-hier, *adv* The day before yesterday.

avant-plan, *s.m.* Foreground.

avant-poste, *s.m.* Outpost.

avant-propos, *s.m.* Preface.

avare. 1. *a.* Miserly ; sparing. **2.** *s.* Miser.

avarice, *s.f.* Avarice.

avaricieusement, *adv.* Avariciously.

avaricieux, *a.* Avaricious, stingy.

avarie, *s.f.* Damage, injury.

avarier, *v.tr.* To damage, spoil.

avec. 1. *prep.* With. **2.** *adv.* With (it).

avenant, *a.* **1.** Comely, pleasing. **2. A l'a.,** in keeping ; to match.

avènement, *s.m.* Accession.

avenir, *s.m.* Future. **Dans l'a.,** at some future date. **A l'a.,** in future.

aventure, *s.f.* **1.** Adventure. **2.** Chance, luck. **A l'a.,** at a venture. **3. Dire la bonne a.,** to tell fortunes.

aventurer, *v.tr.* To venture, risk. **s'aventurer,** to venture.

aventureux, *a.* Venturesome.

aventurier, *s.* Adventurer.

avenue, *s.f.* Avenue ; drive.

avéré, *a.* Authenticated ; avowed

averse, *s.f.* Sudden shower.

aversion, *s.f.* Aversion ; dislike. **Prendre en a.,** to take a dislike to.

averti, *a.* Experienced, wide-awake ; well-informed.

avertir, *v.tr.* To warn, notify.

avertissement, *s.m.* Warning ; notice.

aveu, -eux, *s.m.* Confession.

aveuglant, *a.* Blinding ; dazzling.

aveugle, *a.* Blind. *s.* Blind man ; blind woman.

aveuglement, *s.m* Blindness ; infatuation.

aveuglément, *adv.* Blindly.

aveugler, *v.tr.* (*a*) To blind. (*b*) To dazzle.

aviateur, -trice, *s.* Aviator ; airman, air-woman.

aviation, *s.f.* Aviation.

avide, *a.* Greedy ; eager.

avidement, *adv.* Greedily ; eagerly.

avidité, *s.f.* Avidity, greed(iness).

avilir, *v.tr.* To degrade.

avilissant, *a.* Degrading.

avilissement, *s.m.* Degradation.

avion, *s.m.* Aeroplane. **A. de combat,** fighter. **"Par avion,"** 'by air-mail.'

aviron, *s.m.* Oar ; scull. **Engager son a.,** to catch a crab.

avis, *s.m.* **1.** (*a*) Opinion, judgment. **A mon a.,** in my opinion. **J'ai changé d'a.,** I have changed my mind. (*b*) Advice. **2.** Notice, announcement.

avisé, *a.* Prudent ; far-seeing.

aviser, *v.tr.* To advise ; to inform. **s'aviser,** to bethink oneself. **S'a. de,** to take it into one's head to.

aviver, *v.tr.* To quicken ; to brighten.

avocat, *s.* Barrister ; counsel.

avoine, *s.f.* Oats. **Farine d'a.,** oatmeal.

avoir. I. *v.tr.* **1.** (*a*) To have, possess. (*b*) **A. dix ans**, to be ten years old. **2.** To get, obtain. **3.** To ail. **4.** **A. qch. à faire**, to have sth. to do. **5.** *impers.* **Y avoir.** (*a*) **Il y a**, there is, there are. **Il n'y a pas de quoi**, don't mention it. (*b*) **Qu'est-ce qu'il y a?** what is the matter? (*c*) **Il y a deux ans**, two years ago. **6.** **J'ai fini**, I have done.
II. **avoir**, *s.m.* Property.
avoisinant, *a.* Neighbouring.
avoisiner, *v.tr.* To border on.

avortement, *s.m.* Failure.
avorter, *v.i.* To fail.
avoué, *s.m.* Solicitor.
avouer, *v.tr.* **1.** To acknowledge. **2.** To confess.
avril [-ril], *s.m.* April. **Donner un poisson d'a. à**, to make an April-fool of.
axe, *s.m.* Axis.
axiomatique, *a.* Axiomatic.
axiome, *s.m.* Axiom.
azote, *s.m.* Nitrogen.
azur, *s.m.* Azure, blue. **La Côte d'A.**, the Riviera.

B

B, b [be], *s.m.* (The letter) B, b.
babillage [-bij-], *s.m.* **1.** Prattling; twittering. **2.** Prattle.
babillard [-bij-], *s.* Tattler.
babiller [-bije], *v.i.* To prattle.
bâbord, *s.m.* *Nau:* Port (side).
babouin, *s.m.* Baboon.
bac [bak], *s.m.* (*a*) Ferry-boat. (*b*) Ferry.
baccalauréat, *s.m* = Higher school certificate.
bâche, *s.f.* Tarpaulin; tilt.
bachelier, *s.m.* **B. ès lettres**, bachelor of arts.
bacille, *s.m.* Bacillus.
bâcler, *v.tr.* To scamp (work).
bactériologie, *s.f.* Bacteriology
badaud, *s.* Saunterer, stroller.
badigeonner, *v.tr.* To distemper.
badinage, *s.m.* Jesting; banter.
badine, *s.f.* Cane, switch.
badiner. **1.** *v.i.* To jest. **2.** *v.tr.* To tease.
bafouer, *v.tr.* To scoff, jeer, at.
bagage, *s.m.* **1.** Baggage. **2.** *pl.* Luggage.
bagarre, *s.f.* Affray, brawl.
bagatelle, *s.f.* Trifle.
bagne, *s.m.* Convict prison.
bague, *s.f.* (Jewelled) ring.
baguette [-get], *s.f.* Rod, wand.
bah, *int.* **1.** Nonsense! **2.** You don't say so!
bahut, *s.m.* Cupboard, cabinet.
baie[1], *s.f.* Bay, bight.
baie[2], *s.f.* Bay, opening.
baie[3], *s.f.* Berry.
baigner. **1.** *v.tr.* (*a*) To bathe; to dip. (*b*) To wash (coast); to water.

(*c*) To bath. **2.** *v.i.* To soak, steep. **se baigner**, to bathe.
baigneur, -euse, *s.* **1.** Bather **2.** Bath attendant.
baignoire, *s.f.* **1.** Bath. **2.** *Th:* Ground-floor box.
bail [ba:j], **baux**, *s.m.* Lease.
bâillant [bɑjɑ̃], *a.* Yawning.
bâillement [-ɑj-], *s.m.* Yawn.
bâiller [baje], *v.i.* To yawn.
bâillon [bɑjɔ̃], *s.m.* Gag.
bâillonner [-jɔ-], *v.tr.* To gag.
bain, *s.m.* Bath. (*a*) **Salle de bains**, bathroom. (*b*) *pl.* Watering-place; spa. (*c*) Bathing.
baïonnette [bajɔ-], *s.f.* Bayonet.
baiser. I. *v.tr.* **B. qn sur la joue**, to kiss s.o. on the cheek.
II. **baiser**, *s.m.* Kiss.
baissant, *a.* Declining; setting.
baisse, *s.f.* **1.** Subsidence; ebb. **2.** Fall, drop (in prices).
baisser. I. *v.* **1.** *v.tr.* To lower; to let down. **2.** *v.i.* (*a*) To fall; to sink. **se baisser**, to stoop.
II. **baisser**, *s.m.* **B. du rideau**, fall of the curtain.
bal, bals, *s.m.* Ball.
balafre, *s.f.* **1.** Slash, gash. **2.** Scar.
balafrer, *v.tr.* **1.** To gash, slash. **2.** **Visage balafré**, scarred face.
balai, *s.m.* Broom. **Manche a b.**, (i) broomstick, (ii) *Av:* joy-stick.
balance, *s.f.* **1.** Balance; (pair of) scales. **2.** Balancing; balance.
balancement, *s.m.* Swinging.
balancer. I. *v.tr.* **1.** To balance. **2.** To swing, rock.

II. **balancer**, *v.i.* To swing.
se balancer, to swing; to rock.
balançoire, *s.f.* (Child's) swing.
balayage, *s.m.* Sweeping.
balayer, *v.tr.* To sweep; to sweep up.
balayeur, -euse, *s.* **1.** Sweeper. **2.** *s.f.* Balayeuse, carpet-sweeper.
balayures, *s.f.pl.* Sweepings.
balbutiement, *s.m.* Stammering.
balbutier. **1.** *v.i.* To stammer. **2.** *v.tr.* To stammer out.
balcon, *s.m.* **1.** Balcony. **2.** *Th:* Dress-circle.
baleine, *s.f.* **1.** Whale. **2.** Whalebone.
baleinier. **1.** *s.m.* Whaler. **2.** *s.f.* Baleinière, whale-boat.
balise, *s.f.* Beacon; sea-mark.
baliveau, *s.m.* Sapling.
ballade, *s.f.* Ballad.
ballant, *a.* Swinging, dangling.
balle, *s.f.* **1.** Ball. **2.** Bullet. **3.** Bale.
ballet, *s.m.* Ballet.
ballon, *s.m.* **1.** Balloon. **2.** Football.
ballot, *s.m.* Bundle, bale.
ballotter. **1.** *v.tr.* To toss (about). **2.** *v.i.* To toss (on the water).
balnéaire, *a.* **Station b.**, watering-place.
balourd, *s.* Awkward person.
balourdise, *s.f.* **1.** Awkwardness. **2.** Stupid blunder.
baltique. **1.** *a.* Baltic. **2.** *Pr.n.f.* **La B.**, the Baltic (Sea).
balustrade, *s.f.* **1.** Balustrade. **2.** (Hand-)rail; railing.
balustres, *s.m. pl.* Banisters.
bambin, *s.* Little child.
bambou, *s.m.* Bamboo(-cane).
banal, -aux, *a.* Commonplace.
banalité, *s.f.* **1.** Banality, triteness. **2.** Commonplace remark.
banane, *s.f.* Banana.
bananier, *s.m.* Banana-tree.
banc [bɑ̃], *s.m.* **1.** Bench, form; pew; thwart (of boat). **B. des prévenus**, dock. **B. du jury**, jury-box. **2. B. de sable**, sand-bank. **3.** Shoal (of fish).
bancal, -als, *a.* (*a*) Bandy-legged. (*b*) Rickety.
bandage, *s.m.* **1.** Bandage. **2.** Tyre.
bande[1], *s.f.* (*a*) Band, strip. (*b*) *Bill:* Cushion.
bande[2], *s.f.* **1.** Band, party, troop. **2.** Flight, flock; pack.
bandeau, *s.m.* Bandage.

bander[1], *v.tr.* **1.** To bandage, bind (up). **2.** To bend a bow.
bander[2] (**se**), *v.pr.* To combine.
bandit, *s.m.* (*a*) Bandit. (*b*) Ruffian.
bandoulière, *s.f.* **1.** Shoulder-strap. **En b.**, across the back. **2.** Bandolier.
banlieue, *s.f.* Suburbs; outskirts.
banni, *a.* Banished.
bannière, *s.f.* Banner.
bannir, *v.tr.* To banish; to exile.
bannissement, *s.m.* Banishment.
banque, *s.f.* Bank.
banqueroute, *s.f.* Bankruptcy.
banquet, *s.m.* Banquet, feast.
banquette, *s.f.* Bench, seat.
banquier, *s.* Banker.
banquise, *s.f.* Ice-floe, ice-pack.
bans, *s.m. pl.* Banns.
baptême [bat-], *s.m.* Baptism, christening. **Nom de b.**, Christian name.
baptiser [bat-], *v.tr.* To baptize.
baquet, *s.m.* Tub, bucket.
bar, *s.m.* (Public) bar.
baragouin [-gwɛ̃], *s.m.* Gibberish.
baragouiner [-gwi-], *v.tr. & i.* To talk gibberish, to jabber.
baraque, *s.f.* (*a*) Hut, shanty. (*b*) Booth (at fair).
baratte, *s.f.* Churn.
baratter, *v.tr.* To churn.
barbare. **1.** *a.* (*a*) Barbaric. (*b*) Barbarous. **2.** *s.m.* Barbarian.
barbarement, *adv.* **1.** Barbarically. **2.** Barbarously.
barbarie, *s.f.* Barbarity.
barbe, *s.f.* Beard. (*a*) **Rire dans sa b.**, to laugh in one's sleeve. **A la b. de qn**, to s.o.'s face. **Faire la b.**, to shave. (*b*) Awn.
barbelé, *a.* Barbed.
barbiche, *s.f.* Goatee.
barbier, *s.m.* Barber.
barboter, *v.i.* To paddle.
barbouiller [-buje], *v.tr.* To daub; to smear (*de*, with).
se barbouiller, to dirty one's face.
barbu. **1.** *a.* Bearded. **2.** *s.f.* **Barbue**, brill.
barde, *s.m.* Bard, poet.
barème, *s.m.* **1.** Ready-reckoner. **2.** Printed table (of fares).
baril, *s.m.* Barrel, cask, keg.
bariolage, *s.m.* Variegation.
bariolé, *a.* Splashed with colour.
barioler, *v.tr.* To variegate.
baromètre, *s.m.* Barometer.

barométrique, *a.* Barometric.

baron, *s.m.* Baron.

baronne, *s.f.* Baroness.

baronnet, *s.m.* Baronet.

baroque, *a.* Quaint, odd, baroque.

barque, *s.f.* Boat.

barrage, *s.m.* **1.** Barring. **2.** (*a*) Barrier; dam, weir. (*b*) *Mil:* Barrage.

barre, *s.f.* **1.** (*a*) Bar, rod. (*b*) Bar, barrier. (*c*) Bar (of river). **2.** Helm (of ship). **3.** Line, dash, stroke. **4.** Stripe.

barreau, *s.m.* **1.** Small bar; rail. **2.** *Jur:* Bar.

barrer, *v.tr.* **1.** (*a*) To fasten with a bar. (*b*) To bar, obstruct; to dam. "Rue barrée," 'no thoroughfare.' **2.** B. un chèque, to cross a cheque. **3.** To cross out.

barrette, *s.f.* Biretta.

barricade, *s.f.* Barricade.

barricader, *v.tr.* To barricade.

barrière, *s.f.* **1.** Barrier. **2.** Gate (of town); toll-gate, turnpike.

barrique, *s.f.* Large barrel; cask.

baryton, *a. & s.m.* Barytone.

baryum, [-jɔm], *s.m.* Barium.

bas, basse. I. *a.* **1.** Low. **2.** Mean, base, low.

II. **bas,** *adv.* **1.** Low (down). **2.** Mettre bas, to lay down; to overthrow. **3.** Parler tout bas, to speak in a whisper.

III. **bas,** *s.m.* **1.** Lower part. *Adv.phr.* En bas, (down) below; downstairs. *Adv.phr.* A bas, down. A bas les mains! hands off! **2.** Stocking.

IV. **basse,** *s.f.* *Mus:* Bass.

basané, *a.* Sunburnt, tanned.

bascule, *s.f.* Rocker; see-saw.

basculer, *v.tr. & i.* (*a*) To rock, swing. (*b*) To tip (up).

base, *s.f.* **1.** Base. **2.** Basis, foundation.

baser, *v.tr.* To base, found.

bas-fond, *s.m.* **1.** Low ground; swamp. **2.** Shallow, shoal.

basque[1], *a. & s.* Basque.

basque[2], *s.f.* Skirt, tail (of coat).

bass, *s.m.* *Ich:* Bass.

basse, *s.f.* *Mus:* Bass.

basse-cour, *s.f.* Farm-yard, poultry-yard. *pl.* basses-cours.

bassement, *adv.* Basely.

bassesse, *s.f.* **1.** Baseness, lowness. **2.** Low, mean, action.

bassin, *s.m.* **1.** Basin, bowl, pan. **2.** Reservoir. **3.** Dock. **4.** B. houiller, coal-field.

bassinoire, *s.f.* Warming-pan.

basson, *s.m.* Bassoon.

baste, *int.* Pooh! nonsense!

bastingages, *s.m. pl.* Bulwarks.

bât, *s.m.* Pack-saddle.

bataille [-tɑːj], *s.f.* Battle.

batailleur, -euse [-taj-], *a.* Fighting, pugnacious.

bataillon [-tajɔ̃], *s.m.* Battalion.

bâtard, *a. & s.* Bastard.

bateau, *s.m.* Boat. Le train du b., the boat-train.

bateau-citerne, *s.m.* Tanker. *pl.* bateaux-citernes.

bateleur, -euse, *s.* Juggler, tumbler.

batelier, *s.* Boatman; waterman.

bâti, *s.m.* Frame(-work).

batifoler, *v.i.* To frolic, skylark.

bâtiment, *s.m.* **1.** Building, edifice. **2.** Ship, vessel.

bâtir, *v.tr.* To build, erect.

batiste, *s.f.* Cambric.

bâton, *s.m.* **1.** Stick, staff. Mettre des bâtons dans les roues, to put a spoke in (s.o.'s) wheel; to interfere.

bâtonner, *v.tr.* To beat, cudgel.

battant. I. *a.* Beating. Pluie battante, driving rain. Tout b. neuf, brand-new.

II. **battant,** *s.m.* **1.** Clapper, tongue. **2.** Leaf, flap.

battement, *s.m.* Beat(ing); stamp (-ing); clapping; flapping.

batterie, *s.f.* **1.** Battery. **2.** (*a*) Set, collection. (*b*) B. électrique, electric battery.

batteur, -euse, *s.* **1.** Beater. **2.** *s.f.* Batteuse, threshing-machine.

battoir, *s.m.* **1.** Washerwoman's beetle. **2.** (Wooden) bat.

battre, *v.* To beat. **1.** *v.tr.* (*a*) To beat, thrash; to thresh. (*b*) To beat, defeat. (*c*) To fly (a flag). (*d*) To shuffle (cards). **2.** *v.tr. & i.* (*a*) B. la mesure, to beat time. (*b*) Le cœur lui battait, his heart was going pit-a-pat. (*c*) B. des mains, to clap one's hands.

se battre, to fight.

baudet, *s.m.* (Jack)ass.

baudrier, *s.m.* Shoulder-belt.

bauge, *s.f.* Lair.

baume, *s.m.* Balm, balsam.

bavard. 1. *a.* Talkative, garrulous. 2. *s.* Chatterbox.

bavardage, *s.m.* Chatter(ing).

bavarder, *v.i.* 1. To chatter 2. To gossip.

bave, *s.f.* Slaver, dribble.

bavette, *s.f.* Bib.

Bavière. *Pr.n.f.* Bavaria.

bayadère, *s.f.* Nautch-girl.

bazar, *s.m.* Bazaar, emporium.

béant, *a.* Gaping; yawning.

béat, *a.* Sanctimonious, smug.

béatement, *adv.* 1. Blissfully, complacently. 2. Smugly.

béatifier, *v.tr.* To beatify.

béatitude, *s.f.* 1. (*a*) Beatitude. (*b*) Bliss. 2. Smugness, complacency.

beau, bel, *f.* **belle,** *pl.* **beaux, belles.** I. *a.* 1. Beautiful, handsome. **Le b. sexe,** the fair sex. 2. Fine; noble. (*a*) **Un bel esprit,** a wit. (*b*) **Avoir b. jeu,** to have every opportunity. **Le b. côté,** the bright side. (*c*) Smart, spruce. **Le b. monde,** society. (*d*) **B. temps,** fine weather. (*e*) **Au b. milieu,** right in the middle. 3. *Adv.phrs.* **Bel et bien,** entirely, quite. **Tout b.!** steady! gently! **De plus belle,** more than ever. 4. *V.phrs.*(*a*) **L'échapper belle,** to have a narrow escape. (*b*) **Il fait b.** (**temps**), it is fine (weather). (*c*) **Avoir b. faire qch.,** to do sth. in vain.

II. **beau, belle,** *s.* 1. Beauty. 2. *s.m.* Fine. 3. *s.f.* Deciding game.

beaucoup. 1. *s.m.inv.* (*a*) Much. (*b*) (A great) many. **B. de,** much ; (a great) many. (*c*) *Adv.phr.* **De b.,** much, by far. 2. *adv.* Much.

beau-fils, *s.m.* Stepson. *pl. beaux-fils.*

beau-frère, *s.m.* Brother-in-law. *pl. beaux-frères.*

beau-père, *s.m.* 1. Father-in-law. 2. Stepfather. *pl. beaux-pères.*

beaupré, *s.m.* Bowsprit.

beauté, *s.f.* 1. Beauty, loveliness. 2. Beauty; beautiful woman.

beaux-arts, *s.m.pl.* Fine arts.

bébé, *s.m.* Baby.

bec [bɛk], *s.m.* 1. Beak ; bill. **Coup de bec,** peck. **Du bec et des ongles,** tooth and nail. 2. (*a*) Spout. (*b*) **Bec de plume,** pen-nib. (*c*) **Bec de gaz,** gas-burner.

bécasse, *s.f.* Woodcock.

bécassine, *s.f.* Snipe.

bêche, *s.f.* Spade.

bêcher, *v.tr.* To dig.

becqueter, *v.tr.* (Of birds) (*a*) To pick up. (*b*) To peck.

bedeau, *s.m.* Verger.

bédouin, *a. & s.* Bedouin.

bée, *a.f.* Gaping.

beffroi, *s.m.* Belfry.

bégaiement, *s.m.* Stammering.

bégayer, *v.i. & tr.* To stutter, stammer.

bègue [bɛg], *s.* Stammerer.

bégueule [-gœl], *s.f.* Prude

beige, *a.* Beige.

beignet, *s.m.* Fritter.

béjaune, *s.m.* 1. Young bird. 2. Ninny, greenhorn

bel. See BEAU.

bêlement, *s.m.* Bleating, bleat.

bêler, *v.i.* To bleat.

belette, *s.f.* Weasel.

belge, *a. & s.* Belgian.

Belgique. *Pr.n.f.* Belgium.

bélier, *s.m.* Ram.

belladone, *s.f.* Belladonna.

belle. See BEAU.

belle-fille, *s.f.* 1. Step-daughter. 2. Daughter-in-law. *pl. belles-filles.*

belle-mère, *s.f.* 1. Step-mother. 2. Mother-in-law. *pl. belles-mères.*

belle-sœur, *s.f.* Sister-in-law. *pl. belles-sœurs.*

belligérant, *a. & s.m.* Belligerent.

belliqueux, *a.* Warlike.

belvédère, *s.m.* 1. Belvedere ; viewpoint. 2. Summer-house.

bémol, *s.m. Mus.* Flat.

bénédicité, *s.m.* Grace.

bénédictin, *a. & s.* 1. Benedictine. 2. *s.f.* Bénédictine, benedictine.

bénédiction, *s.f.* Blessing.

bénéfice, *s.m.* 1. Profit, gain. 2. Benefit. 3. Benefice.

bénéficier, *v.i.* To profit (*de,* by).

bénévole, *a.* Benevolent ; kindly.

bénévolement, *adv.* Benevolently.

bénignement, *adv.* Benignly, kindly.

bénignité, *s.f.* (*a*) Benignity, kindness. (*b*) Mildness.

bénin, -igne, *a.* (*a*) Benign. (*b*) Mild.

bénir, *v.tr.* 1. (*a*) To bless. (*b*) To thank. 2. To consecrate.

bénit, *a.* Consecrated, blessed. **Eau bénite,** holy water.

bénitier, *s.m.* Holy-water basin.

béquille [-ki:j], *s.f.* Crutch.

bercail [-ka:j], *s.m.* (Sheep)fold.

berceau, *s.m.* **1.** Cradle. **2.** Arbour, bower.

bercer, *v.tr.* **1.** To rock. **2.** To lull; to send to sleep.

   se bercer. 1. To rock, sway. **2.** Se b., de, to cherish.

berceuse, *s.f.* Lullaby.

béret, *s.m.* Beret.

berge, *s.f.* (Steep) bank.

berger, *s.* **1.** Shepherd. **2.** *s.f.* Bergère, easy-chair.

bergerie, *s.f.* Sheepfold.

bergeronnette, *s.f.* Wagtail.

bernacle, *s.f.* Barnacle.

berne, *s.f.* En b., at half-mast.

béryl [-ril], *s.m.* Beryl.

besace, *s.f.* Beggar's wallet.

besicles, *s.f.pl.* Goggles.

bésigue, *s.m. Cards:* Bezique.

besogne, *s.f.* Work; task, job.

besogneux, *a.* Needy, impecunious.

besoin, *s.m.* **1.** Necessity, requirement. (*a*) Au b., if necessary; when required. (*b*) Avoir b. de, to need, want. **2.** Poverty, indigence.

bestial, -aux[1], *a.* Bestial, brutish.

bestiaux[2], *s.m.pl.* Cattle, beasts.

bestiole, *s.f.* Tiny beast.

bétail [-ta:j], *s.m. Coll.* No *pl.* Cattle; live-stock.

bête, *s.f.* **I.** Beast, animal; dumb creature. B. à bon Dieu, lady-bird. **2.** (*a*) Fool, simpleton. (*b*) *a.* Stupid, foolish.

bêtement, *adv.* Stupidly.

bêtise, *s.f.* **1.** Stupidity, silliness. **2.** Nonsense. Faire des bêtises, to play the fool. **3.** Blunder; piece of stupidity.

béton, *s.m.* Concrete.

betterave, *s.f.* Beet(root).

beuglement, *s.m.* **1.** Lowing; bellowing. **2.** Bellow.

beugler, *v.i.* To low; to bellow.

beurre, *s.m.* Butter.

beurrer, *v.tr.* To butter.

bévue, *s.f.* Blunder, mistake.

biais. I. *a.* Oblique, slanting. **2.** *s.m.* Bias (of bowl). En b., askew. Regarder de b., to look sideways at.

bibelot, *s.m.* Curio; trinket.

biberon, *s.m.* Feeding-bottle.

Bible, *s.f.* Bible.

bibliographie, *s.f.* Bibliography.

bibliophile, *s.m.* Bibliophile.

bibliothécaire, *s.m.* Librarian.

bibliothèque, *s.f.* **1.** Library. **2.** Bookcase.

biblique, *a.* Biblical.

biche, *s.f.* Hind, doe.

bicoque, *s.f.* Shanty.

bicorne, *s.m.* Cocked hat.

bicyclette, *s.f.* Bicycle, cycle.

bicycliste, *s.m. & f.* (Bi)cyclist.

bidet, *s.m.* Nag; pony.

bidon, *s.m.* (*a*) Can, drum (for oil). (*b*) *Mil:* Water-bottle.

bielle, *s.f.* Driving-rod.

bien. I. *adv.* **1.** Well. Vous avez b. fait, you did right. Aller b., to be well. Très b.! well done! **2.** (*a*) Right, proper. (*b*) Comfortable. Vous voilà b.! you're in a fine fix! (*c*) Être b. avec, to be on good terms with. **3.** (*a*) Right, really, quite. Je l'avais b. dit! didn't I say so! B. entendu, of course. (*b*) Very. (*c*) Much, many. **4.** *Adv.phr.* Tant b. que mal, somehow (or other). **5.** *Conj.phr.* B. que, though. **6.** *int.* Eh b.! well !

   II. bien, *s.m.* **1.** Good. Grand b. vous fasse! much good may it do you! **2.** Possession, property.

bien-être, *s.m.* No *pl.* (*a*) Well-being; comfort. (*b*) Welfare.

bienfaisance, *s.f.* Beneficence.

bienfaisant, *a.* **1.** Beneficent, charitable. **2.** Beneficial, salutary.

bienfait, *s.m.* Benefit, kindness.

bienfaiteur, -trice, *s.* Benefactor, benefactress.

bienheureux, *a.* **1.** Blissful, happy. **2.** Blessed.

bienséance, *s.f.* Propriety.

bienséant, *a.* Seemly, decorous.

bientôt, *adv.* (Very) soon; before long. A b.! good-bye for the present !

bienveillance [-vɛjɑ̃-], *s.f* Benevolence; kindness.

bienveillant [-vɛjɑ̃], *a.* Kind, benevolent (*envers, pour*, to).

bienvenu, *a. & s.* Welcome.

bienvenue, *s.f.* Welcome. Souhaiter la b. à qn, to welcome s.o.

bière[1], *s.f.* Beer.

bière[2], *s.f.* Coffin.

biffer, *v.tr.* To cross out, cancel.

bifteck [-tɛk], *s.m.* Beefsteak.

bifurcation, *s.f.* Bifurcation, fork. (Gare de) b., junction.

bifurquer, v.tr. & i. To fork.

bigame, a. Bigamous

bigamie, s.f. Bigamy.

bigarrer, v.tr. To variegate, mottle.

bigarrure, s.f. Medley (of colours).

bigorneau, s.m. Winkle.

bigot. 1. a. (Over-)devout. 2. s Zealous church-goer; bigot.

bijou, -oux, s.m. Piece of jewellery; jewel, gem.

bijouterie, s.f. 1. Jeweller's shop. 2. Jewellery; jewels.

bijoutier, s. Jeweller.

bilan, s.m. Balance-sheet.

bilatéral, -aux, a. Bilateral.

bile, s.f. (a) Bile, gall. (b) Bad temper. S'échauffer la b., to worry.

bilieux, a. 1. Bilious. 2. (a) Choleric, irascible, testy. (b) Morose.

bilingue, a. Bilingual.

billard [-jaːr], s.m. 1. Billiards. 2. Billiard-table. 3. Billiard-room.

bille [biːj], s.f. 1. Billiard-ball. 2. Marble.

billet [bije], s.m. 1. Note, short letter. 2. Notice, invitation-card. 3. Ticket. 4. (a) Promissory note, bill. (b) B. de banque, bank-note.

billevesée [bil-, bij-], s.f. Crack-brained notion; nonsense.

billion [biljɔ̃], s.m. One thousand million.

billon [bijɔ̃], s.m. (Monnaie de) b., copper or nickel coinage.

billot [bijo], s.m. Block (of wood).

bimbelot, s.m. 1. Toy. 2. Bauble.

bimbeloterie, s.f. 1. Toy business. 2. Toys, knick-knacks.

bimensuel, a. Fortnightly.

bimoteur, a.m. Twin-engine.

biner, v.tr. To hoe.

binette, s.f. Hoe.

biniou, s.m. Breton (bag-)pipes.

binocle, s.m. Eye-glasses, pince-nez

biographe, s.m. Biographer.

biographie, s.f. Biography.

biographique, a. Biographical.

biologie, s.f. Biology.

biologique, a. Biological.

biologiste, s.m. Biologist.

biparti, f. **-ite,** a. Bipartite.

bipède, s.m. Biped.

biplace, a. & s m. Two-seater.

bique, s.f. She-goat, nanny-goat.

birman, a. & s. Burmese.

Birmanie, Pr.n.f. Burma.

bis[1], a. Pain bis, whole-meal bread.

bis[2] [biːs]. Lt.adv. Twice. 1. No. 10 bis = No. 10A. 2. Repeat. 3. Encore!

biscornu, a. 1. Mis-shapen. 2. Crotchety.

biscuit, s.m. Biscuit; plain cake.

bise, s.f. North wind.

biseau, s.m. Chamfer, bevel.

bismuth, s.m. Bismuth.

bisséqué, a. Bisected.

bissextile, a.f. Année b., leap-year.

bivalve, s.m. Bivalve.

bivouac [-wak], s.m. Bivouac.

bivouaquer [-wake], v.i. To bivouac.

bizarre, a. Peculiar, odd, queer.

bizarrement, adv. Queerly, oddly.

bizarrerie, s.f. 1. Peculiarity, oddness. 2. Whimsicalness.

black-out [-ut], s.m. Black-out.

blafard, a. Pallid, wan; lambent.

blague, s.f. 1. (Tobacco-)pouch. 2. (a) Humbug. Sans b.? really? (b) Joke.

blaguer [-ge]. 1. v.i. To joke. 2. v.tr. To chaff.

blagueur, -euse [-gœ-, -gø-]. 1. s. (a) Humbug. (b) Wag. 2. a. Bantering.

blaireau, s.m. 1. Badger. 2. Shaving-brush.

blâmable, a. Blameworthy.

blâme, s.m. Blame; censure.

blâmer, v.tr. 1. To blame; to find fault with. 2. To reprimand.

blanc, blanche. I. a. 1. White. 2. Light-coloured; pale. s. Un b., a white man. 3. Clean, pure. 4. Blank. Nuit blanche, sleepless night. 5. Armes blanches, side-arms. II. **blanc,** s.m. 1. White. 2. Blank. 3. (a) Saigner à b., to bleed white. (b) Cartouche à b., blank cartridge. 4. Breast (of chicken).

blanc-bec [-bɛk], s.m. Greenhorn. pl. blancs-becs.

blanchaille [-ʃaːj], s.f. Whitebait

blanchâtre, a. Whitish, whity.

blanche, s.f. 1. Bill: White ball. 2. Mus: Minim.

blancheur, s.f. Whiteness.

blanchir. 1. v.tr. (a) To whiten. (b) To bleach. (c) To wash, launder. (d) To whitewash. 2. v.i. To turn white.

blanchissage, s.m. Washing

blanchisserie, *s.f* (*a*) Laundering. (*b*) Laundry.

blanchisseur, -euse, *s.* (*a*) Laundry-man, *f.* laundress. (*b*) *s.f.* Washer-woman.

blasé, *a.* Blasé, indifferent.

blason, *s.m.* (*a*) Coat of arms, armorial bearings. (*b*) Heraldry

blasphème, *s.m.* Blasphemy.

blasphémer, *v.i.* To blaspheme.

blatte, *s.f.* Cockroach.

blé, *s.m.* Corn; wheat.

blême, *a.* **1.** (*a*) Livid. (*b*) Cadaverous. **2.** Pale; wan.

blêmir, *v.i.* To turn pale, livid.

blêmissement, *s.m.* Turning pale.

blessant, *a.* Offensive, cutting.

blessé, *s.* Wounded person.

blesser, *v.tr.* **1.** To wound, hurt. **2.** To offend; to wound the feelings of. **se blesser,** to take offence (*de*, at)

blessure, *s.f.* Wound, hurt, injury.

blet, blette, *a.* Over-ripe, sleepy.

bleu, *pl.* **bleus. 1.**-*a.* Blue. **2.** *s.m.* (*a*) Blue. (*b*) Contusion. **3.** *s.* Recruit. **4.** *s.m.* (*a*) Blue print (*b*) **Petit b.,** express letter.

bleuâtre, *a.* Bluish.

bleuir. 1. *v.tr.* To blue; to make blue. **2.** *v.i.* To become blue.

blindage, *s.m.* Armour-plating.

blindé, *a.* Armoured.

bloc [blɔk], *s.m.* **1.** Block, lump. **2.** Coalition. **Faire b.,** to unite. **3.** Pad (of paper).

blocus [-kyːs], *s.m.* Blockade.

blond. 1. *a.* Fair, flaxen; blond. **Bière blonde,** pale ale. **2.** *s.* Blond(e)

bloquer, *v.tr.* (*a*) To block, obstruct. (*b*) To blockade.

blottir (se), *v.pr.* To cower

blouse, *s.f.* Overall; blouse

bluet, *s.m.* Cornflower.

boa, *s.m.* Boa.

bobine, *s.f.* Bobbin, spool, reel.

bocage, *s.m.* Grove, coppice.

bocal [-kal], **-aux,** *s.m.* (*a*) Bottle (for sweets). (*b*) (Glass) globe.

Boccace. *Pr.n.m.* Boccaccio.

bock, *s.m.* Glass of beer.

bœuf, *pl.* **bœufs** [bœf, bø], *s.m.* **1.** Ox, bullock. **2.** Beef.

bohème, *a. & s.* Bohemian.

bohémien, *a & s* **1.** Bohemian **2.** Gipsy.

boire. I. *v.tr.* **1.** To drink. **B. un**

coup, to have a drink. **B. un affront,** to pocket an insult. **2.** *Abs.* Il boit, he drinks.
    II. **boire,** *s.m.* Drink.

bois, *s.m.* **1.** Wood, forest. **Petit b.,** spinney. **2.** Wood, timber. **3.** Wood-cut. **4.** *pl.* Antlers. **5. B. de lit,** bedstead.

boisé, *a.* Wooded.

boiserie, *s.f.* Woodwork, panelling.

boisseau, *s.m.* Bushel.

boisson, *s.f.* Beverage, drink.

boîte, *s.f.* **1.** Box; canister, tin. **2. B. de nuit,** night-club.

boiter, *v.i.* To limp.

boiteux, *a.* (*a*) Lame. (*b*) Rickety.

boîtier, *s.m.* Case.

bol [bɔl], *s.m.* Bowl, basin.

bolchevisme, *s.m.* Bolshevism.

bolcheviste, *a. & s.* Bolshevist.

bombance, *s.f.* Carousing.

bombardement, *s.m.* Bombardment.

bombarder, *v.tr.* To bombard.

bombe, *s.f.* **1.** Bomb. **2. B. glacée,** ice-pudding.

bombé, *a.* Convex, bulging.

bomber. 1. *v.tr.* (*a*) **B. la poitrine,** to throw out one's chest. (*b*) To bend, arch. **2.** *v.i.* To bulge (out).

bon, bonne. I. *a.* **1.** Good, honest. **2.** Good, nice. **Cela est bon à dire,** it's easier said than done. **3.** Clever, capable. **4.** Right, correct. **5.** Good, kind (*pour, envers,* to). **6.** Good, advantageous. **C'est bon à savoir,** it is worth knowing. **Bon marché,** cheap. **7.** Good, suitable. **8.** Good, favourable. **Souhaiter la bonne année à qn,** to wish s.o. a happy New Year. **9.** Good, sound, safe. **10.** *adv.* **Tenir bon,** to hold one's own. **Sentir bon,** to smell nice. **Il fait bon ici,** it is comfortable here. **11. Pour de bon,** for good (and all). **12.** *int.* Good! agreed!
    II. **bon,** *s.m.* **1.** Order, voucher. **Bon de poste,** postal order. **2.** Bond, bill.

bonbon, *s.m.* Sweet.

bond, *s.m.* **1.** Bound, leap, jump, spring. **2.** (Of ball) Bounce.

bonde, *s.f.* **1.** (*a*) Bung. (*b*) Plug. **2.** Bung-hole, plug-hole.

bondé, *a.* Chock-full, crammed.

bondir, *v.i.* **1.** To leap, bound. **2.** To bounce.

bondissant, *a.* (*a*) Bounding, leaping. (*b*) Skipping, frisking.

bonheur, *s.m.* **1.** Good fortune, good luck, success. **Jouer de b.,** to be in luck. **2.** Happiness.

bonhomie, *s.f.* Good nature.

bonhomme, *s.m.* Simple, good-natured man. **Faux b.,** shifty customer. *pl. bonshommes.*

boniment, *s.m.* Patter.

bonjour, *s.m.* Good day, good morning, good afternoon.

bonne, *s.f.* (*a*) Maid(servant). (*b*) B. d'enfants, nurse. (*c*) Waitress.

bonnement, *adv.* **Tout b.,** simply, plainly.

bonnet, *s.m.* Cap. **B. de police** forage-cap. **Gros b.,** bigwig.

bonneterie, *s.f.* Hosiery.

bonnetier, *s.* Hosier.

bonsoir, *s.m.* Good evening, good night.

bonté, *s.f.* **1.** (*a*) Goodness, kindness. (*b*) *pl.* Kindnesses. **2.** Goodness, excellence.

borax [-aks], *s.m.* Borax.

bord, *s.m.* **1.** (*a*) Side (of ship). **Faux b.,** list. (*b*) Tack, leg. (*c*) Les hommes du b., the ship's company. **2.** Edge; border; brim. **3.** Shore; bank (of river). **B. de la mer,** seaside.

bordée, *s.f. Nau:* **1.** Broadside. **2.** Tack. **3.** Watch.

bordelais, *a.* Of Bordeaux.

border, *v.tr.* (*a*) To border. (*b*) To tuck.

bordure, *s.f.* **1.** Border, rim. **2.** Frame.

borgne, *a.* **1.** (*a*) One-eyed. (*b*) **Rue b.,** blind alley. **2.** Disreputable.

borique, *a.* Boric.

borne, *s.f.* **1.** (*a*) Boundary-stone. (*b*) *pl.* Boundaries, limits. **2.** *El:* Terminal.

borné, *a.* Limited, restricted.

borner, *v.tr.* **1.** To form the boundary of. **2.** To limit, restrict. **se borner,** to restrict oneself.

bosquet, *s.m.* Grove, thicket.

bosse, *s.f.* **1.** Hump. **2.** Bump; swelling. **3.** Dent. **4.** Boss.

bosselage, *s.m.* Embossing.

bosseler, *v.tr.* **1.** To emboss. **2.** To dent.

bosselure, *s.f.* Dent, bruise.

bossoir, *s.m.* Davit.

bossu. **1.** *a.* Hunch-backed; humped (animal). **2.** *s.* Hunchback.

bot [bo], *a.* **Pied bot,** club-foot.

botanique. **1.** *a.* Botanical. **2.** *s.f.* Botany.

botaniste, *s.m. & f.* Botanist.

botte[1], *s.f.* Bunch; truss, bundle.

botte[2], *s.f.* High boot.

bottier, *s.m.* Bootmaker.

bottin, *s.m.* (Postal) directory.

bottine, *s.f.* Boot.

bouc [buk], *s.m.* He-goat.

boucanier, *s.m.* Buccaneer, pirate.

bouche, *s.f.* Mouth. **1. Bonne b.,** tit-bit. **Faire la petite b.,** to be dainty. **2. B. à feu,** piece of artillery. **B. d'eau,** hydrant.

bouchée, *s.f.* **1.** Mouthful. **2.** Vol-au-vent.

boucher[1], *v.tr.* To stop (up). **Se b. le nez,** to hold one's nose.

boucher[2], *s.* Butcher.

boucherie, *s.f.* **1.** Butcher's shop. **2.** Butchery.

bouche-trou, *s.m.* Stop-gap; make-shift. *pl. bouche-trous.*

bouchon, *s.m.* Stopper, plug, bung. **B. de liège,** cork.

boucle, *s.f.* **1.** Buckle, shackle. **2.** Loop; bow. **3.** Ring. **Boucles d'oreilles,** ear-rings. **4.** Curl.

bouclé, *a.* Curly.

boucler, *v.tr.* (*a*) To buckle; to fasten. (*b*) To loop, tie up. **B. la boucle,** to loop the loop. (*c*) To curl.

bouclier, *s.m.* Buckler, shield.

bouddhiste, *a. & s.* Buddhist.

bouder. **1.** *v.i.* To sulk. **2.** *v.tr.* To be sulky with.

bouderie, *s.f.* Sulkiness; sulks.

boudeur, -euse, *a.* Sulky.

boudin, *s.m.* **1.** (Black-)pudding. **2.** (*a*) Corkscrew curl. (*b*) Flange.

boue, *s.f.* **1.** Mud, mire. **2.** Sediment, deposit.

bouée, *s.f.* Buoy. **B. de sauvetage,** life-buoy.

boueur, *s.m.* Scavenger, dustman.

boueux, *a.* Muddy, miry.

bouffée, *s.f.* Puff (of smoke); whiff.

bouffer, *v.tr.* To puff out.

bouffi, *a.* Puffy, swollen; bloated.

bouffissure, *s.f.* Swelling; puffiness.

bouffon, *s.m.* Buffoon.

bouffonnerie, *s.f.* Buffoonery.

bouge, *s.m.* Den, slum, hovel.
bougeoir, *s.m.* Candlestick.
bouger, *v.i.* To budge, stir, move.
bougie, *s.f.* **1.** Candle. **2.** Candle-power. **3.** B. (d'allumage), sparking-plug.
bougon. 1. *s.* Grumbler, grouser. **2.** *a.* Grumpy.
bougonner, *v.i.* To grumble.
bougran, *s.m.* Buckram.
bouillabaisse [buja-], *s.f.* Provença fish-soup ; *bouillabaisse.*
bouillant [bujã], *a.* **1.** Boiling. **2.** Fiery, hot-headed, impetuous.
bouilli [buji], *s.m.* Boiled beef.
bouillie [buji], *s.f.* Pap ; gruel.
bouillir [buji:r], *v.i.* To boil.
bouilloire [bujwa:r], *s.f.* Kettle.
bouillon [bujõ], *s.m.* **1.** Bubble. **2.** B. gras, clear (meat-)soup ; beef-tea.
bouillonnement [bujo-], *s.m.* Bubbling ; boiling ; seething.
bouillonner [bujo-], *v.i.* To bubble.
boulanger, *s.* Baker.
boulangerie, *s.f.* Baker's shop.
boule, *s.f.* **1.** (*a*) Ball, sphere, globe. (*b*) B. de scrutin, ballot-ball. **2.** Jeu de boules, bowling-green. **Partie de boules,** game of bowls.
bouleau, *s.m.* Birch(-tree).
bouledogue, *s.m.* Bull-dog.
boulet, *s.m.* Cannon-ball.
boulette, *s.f.* Pellet.
boulevard, *s.m.* Boulevard.
bouleversant, *a.* Upsetting.
bouleversement, *s.m.* (*a*) Overthrow, upsetting. (*b*) Confusion.
bouleverser, *v.tr.* To upset ; to overthrow ; to throw into confusion.
boulon, *s.m.* Bolt, pin.
bouquet, *s.m.* **1.** (*a*) Bunch of flowers, bouquet. (*b*) Clump (of trees). **2.** Aroma.
bouquetin, *s.m.* Ibex.
bouquin, *s.m.* Old book.
bouquiniste, *s.m.* Second-hand bookseller.
bourbe, *s.f.* Mud ; mire.
bourbeux, *a.* Muddy, miry.
bourbier, *s.m.* Slough, mire.
bourde, *s.f.* **1.** Fib, falsehood. **2.** Blunder, bloomer.
bourdon, *s.m.* **1.** Great bell. **2.** Bumble-bee.
bourdonnement, *s.m.* Humming. buzzing ; booming.

bourdonner. 1. *v.i.* To buzz, hum **2.** *v.tr.* To hum (tune).
bourg, *s.m.* Small market-town.
bourgade, *s.f.* Important village.
bourgeois. I. *s.* **1.** Middle-class man woman. **2.** Governor, boss.
　　II. **bourgeois,** *a.* **1.** Middle-class. **2.** Homely, simple. **3.** Common, unrefined.
bourgeoisie, *s.f.* Middle class.
bourgeon, *s.m.* Bud.
bourgeonner, *v.i.* To bud, shoot.
Bourgogne. 1. *Pr.n.f.* Burgundy. **2.** *s.m.* (Vin de) B., Burgundy (wine).
bourrade, *s.f.* Blow ; thrust.
bourrasque, *s.f.* Squall.
bourreau, *s.m.* Executioner ; hangman.
bourrelet, *s.m.* **1.** Pad, wad, cushion **2.** Rim, flange.
bourrelier, *s.m.* Harness-maker
bourrer, *v.tr.* To stuff, pad.
bourriche, *s.f.* Basket, hamper.
bourrique, *s.f.* (*a*) She-ass ; donkey. (*b*) Dunce, duffer.
bourriquet, *s.m.* Ass's colt.
bourru, *a.* Rough, rude, surly.
bourse, *s.f.* **1.** Purse, bag, pouch. **2.** Scholarship. **3.** Stock exchange B. du Travail, Labour Exchange.
boursier, *s.* Holder of a scholarship
boursouflé, *a.* Swollen ; turgid.
boursoufler, *v.tr.* To puff up.
boursouflure, *s.f.* Puffiness.
bousculade, *s.f.* Scrimmage.
bousculer, *v.tr.* To jostle, hustle.
boussole, *s.f.* Compass.
bout, *s.m.* **1.** Extremity, end. **Au b. du compte,** after all. **Être à b.,** to be exhausted. **Venir à b. de,** to succeed in. **2.** End, tip ; mouthpiece. **A b. portant,** point-blank. **3.** Bit, fragment ; scrap.
boutade, *s.f.* **1.** Whim, caprice. **2.** Sudden outburst. **3.** Sally.
bouteille [butɛ:j], *s.f.* Bottle.
boutique, *s.f.* Shop ; stall.
boutiquier, *s.* Shopkeeper.
bouton, *s.m.* **1.** Bud. **2.** Button ; stud ; *pl.* links. **3.** Knob, handle. **4.** Pimple. **5.** B. d'or, buttercup.
boutonner, *v.tr.* To button (up).
boutonnière, *s.f.* Button-hole.
bouture, *s.f.* Slip, cutting (of plant).
bouvier, *s.m* (*a*) Cowherd. (*b*) Drover.

bouvreuil [-rœ:j], *s.m.* Bullfinch.

bovin, *a.* Bovine.

boxe, *s.f.* Boxing.

boyau, -aux, *s.m.* **1.** Bowel, gut. **2.** Hose-pipe. **3.** Narrow thoroughfare.

bracelet, *s.m.* Bracelet.

braconnage, *s.m.* Poaching.

braconner, *v.tr. & i.* To poach.

braconnier, *s.m.* Poacher.

brai, *s.m.* Pitch, tar.

braillard [-ɑja:r], *s.* Bawler; brawler.

brailler [brɑje], *v.i.* To bawl, shout.

braiment, *s.m.* Braying.

braire, *v.i.* To bray.

braise, *s.f.* (Glowing) embers.

bramer, *v.i.* (Of stag) To bell.

brancard, *s.m.* **1.** Shaft (of carriage). **2.** Stretcher.

brancardier, *s.m.* Stretcher-bearer.

branchage, *s.m. Coll:* Branches.

branche, *s.f.* **1.** Branch; bough. **2.** Leg (of compasses).

brancher, *v.tr.* To connect (up).

branchies, *s.f.pl.* Gills (of fish).

brandir, *v.tr.* To brandish, flourish.

brandissement, *s.m.* Brandishing.

brandon, *s.m.* (Fire-)brand.

branlant, *a.* Shaky; rickety.

branle, *s.m.* **Mettre en b.,** to set going.

branlement, *s.m.* Oscillation.

branler. **1.** *v.tr.* To swing, shake. **2.** *v.i.* To shake; to be loose.

braquer, *v.tr.* (*a*) To point, aim (*sur,* at). (*b*) **B. les yeux sur,** to stare at.

bras, *s.m.* **1.** (*a*) Arm. **Saisir qn à bras-le-corps,** to grapple with s.o. **B. dessus b. dessous,** arm in arm. (*b*) *pl.* Hands, workmen. **2.** Arm (of a chair).

brasier, *s.m.* (*a*) Fire of live coals. (*b*) Source of intense heat.

brassage, *s.m.* **1.** Brewing. **2.** Mixing.

brassard, *s.m.* Armlet, arm-badge.

brasse, *s.f.* **1.** Fathom. **2.** *Swim:* Stroke.

brassée, *s.f.* Armful.

brasser, *v.tr.* **1.** To brew. **2.** To mix, stir (up).

brasserie, *s.f.* **1.** Brewery. **2.** Brewing. **3.** Beer-saloon.

brasseur, -euse, *s.* **1.** Brewer. **2. B. d'affaires,** big-business man.

bravache, *s.m.* Bully.

bravade, *s.f.* Bravado, bluster.

brave, *a.* **1.** Brave, bold. **Un (homme) b.,** a brave man. **2.** Good, worthy. **Un b. homme,** a worthy man.

bravement, *adv.* Bravely, boldly.

braver, *v.tr.* To brave. **1.** To face bravely. **2.** To defy, dare.

bravo. **1.** *int.* Bravo! hear, hear! **2.** *s.m.* Cheer.

bravoure, *s.f.* Bravery, gallantry.

brebis, *s.f.* **1.** Ewe. **2.** Sheep.

brèche, *s.f.* Breach, gap; notch.

bredouille [-du:j], *a.inv.* **Être b.,** to have failed completely.

bredouiller [-duje], *v.i. & tr.* To mumble; to stammer.

bref, *f.* brève. **1.** *a.* Brief, short. **2.** *adv.* Briefly, in short.

breloque, *s.f.* Charm, trinket.

Brésil [-zil]. *Pr.n.m.* Brazil.

brésilien, *a. & s.* Brazilian.

Bretagne. *Pr.n.f.* Brittany.

bretelle, *s.f.* **1.** Strap, sling, suspender. **2.** *pl.* Braces.

breton, *a. & s.* Breton.

breuvage, *s.m.* Beverage, drink.

brève. See BREF.

brevet, *s.m.* **1. B. d'invention,** (letters) patent. **2.** Diploma, certificate.

breveté, *a.* **1.** Patent. **2.** Certificated.

breveter, *v.tr.* To patent.

bréviaire, *s.m.* Breviary.

brévité, *s.f.* Shortness.

bribes, *s.f.pl.* Scraps, fragments.

brick [brik], *s.m.* Brig.

bricole, *s.f.* **1.** Breast-strap. **2.** *pl.* Odd things.

bricoler, *v.i.* To do odd jobs.

bride, *s.f.* (*a*) Bridle. (*b*) Rein(s). **A b. abattue,** at full speed.

brider, *v.tr.* To bridle; to curb.

brièvement, *adv.* Briefly.

brièveté, *s.f.* Brevity.

brigade, *s.f.* Brigade.

brigadier, *s.m.* (*a*) Corporal (of mounted arms). (*b*) Sergeant (of police).

brigand, *s.m.* Brigand; ruffian.

brigandage, *s.m.* Brigandage.

brigue [brig], *s.f.* Intrigue.

brillamment [brij-], *adv.* Brilliantly.

brillant [brijɑ̃]. **1.** *a.* Brilliant. **2.** *s.m.* (*a*) Brilliance, brightness. (*b*) Polish, shine. **3.** *s.m.* Brilliant.

briller [brije], *v.i.* To shine, sparkle.

brin, *s.m.* **1.** Blade (of grass). **2.** Bit, fragment. **3.** Strand (of rope).

brindille [-di:j], *s.f.* Sprig, twig.

brioche, *s.f.* Brioche; bun.

brique, *s.f.* Brick.

briquet, *s.m.* Cigarette-lighter.

brisant. **1.** *a.* Shattering. **2.** *s.m.* (*a*) Reef; shoal. (*b*) Breaker.

brise, *s.f.* Breeze.

brisé, *a.* Broken. **B. de fatigue,** tired out.

brise-lames, *s.m.inv.* Breakwater.

briser, *v.tr.* (*a*) To break, smash. (*b*) To crush. (*c*) To break off. *Abs.* **Brisons là,** let us say no more about it.

    se briser, to break.

brise-vent, *s.m.inv.* Wind-screen.

brisure, *s.f.* Break, crack.

britannique, *a.* British.

broc [bro], *s.m.* Pitcher; jug.

brocanteur, -euse, *s.* Second-hand dealer.

brocart, *s.m.* Brocade.

broche, *s.f.* **1.** Spit. **2.** Peg, pin. **3.** Spindle. **4.** Brooch.

brocher, *v.tr.* **Livre broché,** paper-bound book.

brochet, *s.m.* Pike.

brochette, *s.f.* Skewer.

brochure, *s.f.* Pamphlet.

brodequin, *s.m.* Laced boot.

broder, *v.tr.* To embroider.

broderie, *s.f.* (*a*) Piece of embroidery. (*b*) Embroidery work.

broiement, *s.m.* Crushing.

bromure, *s.m.* Bromide.

broncher, *v.i.* **1.** To stumble. **2.** (*a*) **Sans b.,** without flinching. (*b*) To budge.

bronchial, -aux, *a.* Bronchial.

bronchite, *s.f.* Bronchitis.

bronze, *s.m.* Bronze.

bronzer, *v.tr.* To tan, sunburn.

brosse, *s.f.* **1.** Brush. **2.** *pl.* Brush-wood.

brosser, *v.tr.* To brush.

brosseur, *s.m.* Batman.

brou, *s.m.* Husk (of walnut).

brouette, *s.f.* Wheelbarrow.

brouhaha, *s.m.* Hubbub.

brouillard [bruja:r], *s.m.* Fog.

brouillé [bruje], *a.* Mixed, confused. **Œufs brouillés,** scrambled eggs.

brouiller [bruje], *v.tr.* **1.** To mix up; to jam (a message). **2.** To set at loggerheads.

    se brouiller. **1.** To become confused. **2.** To quarrel; to fall out.

broussaille [-sɑ:j], *s.f.* Brushwood. **Cheveux en b.,** unkempt hair.

brouter, *v.tr.* To browse on.

broutilles [-ti:j], *s.f.pl.* Sprigs, twigs.

broyer, *v.tr.* To pound.

bru, *s.f.* Daughter-in-law.

bruine, *s.f.* Fine rain; drizzle.

bruiner, *v.impers.* To drizzle.

bruissement, *s.m.* Rumbling; brawling (of brook); rustling.

bruit, *s.m.* **1.** (*a*) Noise; din; report (of a gun). (*b*) Noise, fuss. **2.** Rumour.

brûlant, *a.* Burning; on fire.

brûlé, *s.m.* Smell of burning.

brûle-gueule, *s.m.inv.* Short pipe.

brûle-pourpoint (à), *adv.phr.* Point-blank.

brûler. **I.** *v.tr.* **1.** To burn. **2.** To scorch. (*a*) **B. le pavé,** to tear along. (*b*) To bite, nip (buds).

    II. brûler, *v.i.* **1.** To burn; to be on fire. **2.** **B. de curiosité,** to be aflame with curiosity.

brûlure, *s.f.* **1.** Burn, scald. **2.** Frost-nip.

brume, *s.f.* Th ck fog.

brumeux, *a.* Foggy.

brun. **1.** *a.* Brown; dark (complexion). **2.** *s.m.* Brown. **3.** *s.f.* **A la brune,** at dusk.

brunâtre, *a.* Brownish.

brunir. **1.** *v.i.* To become dark. **2.** *v.tr.* To brown, darken.

brusque, *a.* **1.** Abrupt, blunt. **2.** Sudden. *Aut:* **Tournant b.,** sharp turn.

brusquement, *adv.* **1.** Abruptly. **2.** Suddenly.

brusquer, *v.tr.* **1.** To be abrupt with. **2.** To precipitate.

brusquerie, *s.f.* Abruptness.

brut [bryt], *a.* **1.** Brutish. **2.** Raw; crude. **3.** Gross (weight). **4.** *s.f.* **Brute,** brute.

brutal, -aux, *a.* (*a*) Brutal, brutish. (*b*) Coarse, rough.

brutalement, *adv.* (*a*) Brutally. (*b*) Bluntly

brutaliser, *v.tr.* To ill-treat.

brutalité, *s.f.* Brutality.

Bruxelles [brysɛl]. *Pr.n.f.* Brussels.

bruyamment, *adv.* Noisily.

bruyant, *a.* **1.** Noisy. **2.** Loud.

bruyère, *s.f.* **1.** (*a*) Heather. (*b*) Heath(-land). **2.** Briar.

bu. See BOIRE.

buanderie, *s.f.* Wash-house.

bûche, *s.f.* (*a*) (Fire-)log. (*b*) Dolt.

bûcher¹, *s.m.* **1.** Wood-shed. **2.** (*a*) Pile of faggots, stake. (*b*) Funeral-pyre.

bûcher², *v.tr. & i.* To work hard.

bûcheron, *s.m.* (*a*) Woodcutter (*b*) Lumberman.

bucolique, *a.* Bucolic, pastoral.

budget, *s.m.* Budget; estimates.

buée, *s.f.* Steam (on window-panes).

buffet, *s.m.* **1.** Sideboard. **2.** Buffet (at ball); refreshment room.

buffle, *s.m.* Buffalo.

buis, *s.m.* **1.** Box(-tree) **2.** Box (-wood).

buisson, *s.m.* Bush.

bulbe, *s.m. or f. Bot:* Bulb.

bulbeux, *a.* Bulbous (plant)

bulgare, *a. & s.* Bulgarian.

Bulgarie. *Pr.n.f.* Bulgaria

bulle, *s.f.* Bubble.

bulletin, *s.m.* **1.** Bulletin; report. **2.** Ticket, receipt. **B. de vote,** voting paper. **B. de commande,** order form.

bure, *s.f.* Frieze; homespun.

bureau, *s.m.* **1.** Writing-table; desk. **2.** (*a*) Office. **B. de tabac,** tobacconist's shop. (*b*) Board, committee

bureaucrate, *s.m.* Bureaucrat.

bureaucratie, *s.f.* Bureaucracy.

burette, *s.f.* **1.** Cruet. **2.** Oil-can

burlesque, *a.* **1.** Burlesque. **2.** Comical, ludicrous.

bus. See BOIRE.

busard, *s.m.* Buzzard; harrier

buse¹, *s.f.* **1.** Buzzard. **2.** Dolt

buse², *s.f.* Nose-piece, nozzle.

busqué, *a.* Aquiline, hooked (nose).

buste, *s.m.* Bust.

but, *s.m.* **1.** Mark (to aim at); objective. **2.** Goal. **3.** Object, aim. **4.** *Adv.phr.* **De but en blanc,** point-blank.

buté, *a.* Fixed, set.

buter, *v.i.* To strike, knock.
   se buter. Se **b. à.** (*a*) To come up against. (*b*) To be set on.

butin, *s.m.* Booty, spoils, plunder.

butor, *s.m.* **1.** Bittern. **2.** Lout.

butte, *s.f.* **1.** Knoll, mound. **2. Être en b. à,** to be exposed to.

buvard. **1.** *a.* **Papier b.,** blotting-paper. **2.** *s.m.* Blotter.

buvette, *s.f.* Refreshment bar

buveur, -euse, *s.* Drinker.

byzantin, *a. & s.* Byzantine.

C

C, c [se], *s.m.* (The letter) C, c.

ça. See CELA.

çà. 1. *adv.* Hither. **Çà et là,** here and there. **2.** *int.* **Ah çà!** now then!

cabane, *s.f.* Hut, shanty.

cabaret, *s.m.* (*a*) Public-house, tavern. (*b*) Inn, eating-house.

cabestan, *s.m.* Capstan, windlass.

cabillaud [-ijo], *s.m.* Fresh cod.

cabine, *s.f.* (*a*) Cabin; state-room. (*b*) (Telephone) call-box. **C. à signaux,** signal-box.

cabinet, *s.m.* **1.** Closet; small room. **C. de toilette,** dressing room. **C. de travail,** study. **2.** Office. **3.** *Pol:* Cabinet.

câble, *s.m.* Cable.

câbler, *v.tr.* To cable (message).

câblogramme, *s.m.* Cablegram.

cabotage, *s.m.* Coastwise trade.

cabrer. 1. *v.tr. Av:* To elevate (plane). **2.** *v.pr. & i.* To rear.

cabriole, *s.f.* Leap, caper.

cabriolet, *s.m.* Gig.

cacahuète, *s.f.* Pea-nut.

cacao, *s.m.* Cocoa.

cacatoès [-tɔɛːs], *s.m.* Cockatoo

cachalot, *s.m.* Sperm-whale.

cache, *s.f.* Hiding-place; cache.

cache-cache, *s.m.* Hide-and-seek.

cachemire, *s.m.* Cashmere.

cache-nez, *s.m.inv.* Muffler.

cacher, *v.tr.* (*a*) To hide, secrete. (*b*) To hide from view.
   se cacher. 1. To hide **2.** Se **c. à qn,** to hide from s.o.

cachet, *s.m.* **1.** (*a*) Seal. (*b*) Mark, stamp. **2.** Voucher (for lessons)

cacheter, *v.tr.* To seal (up)

cachette, *s.f.* Hiding-place **En c.,** secretly; on the quiet

cachot, *s.m.* Dungeon.

cadavre, *s.m.* Corpse; dead body.

cadeau, *s.m.* Present; gift

cadenas, *s.m.* Padlock.

cadence, *s.f.* Cadence; rhythm.

cadet, -ette, *s.* (*a*) Junior. (*b*) Youngest.

cadran, *s.m.* **1.** Dial. **C. solaire,** sun-dial. **2.** Face (of clock).

cadre, *s.m.* **1.** (*a*) Frame. (*b*) Compass, limits. **2.** Frame(work).

caduc, -uque [kadyk], *a.* **1.** (*a*) Decaying. (*b*) Decrepit. **2.** Deciduous.

cafard. 1. *s.* Sneak. **2.** *s.m.* (*a*) Cockroach. (*b*) Blues, hump.

café, *s.m.* **1.** Coffee. **C. nature,** black coffee. **C. complet,** coffee, milk, roll and butter. **2.** Café.

cafetier. 1. *s.* Owner of a café. **2.** *s.f.* Cafetière, coffee-pot.

cafre, *a. & s.* Kaffir.

cage, *s.f.* **1.** Cage. **2.** Well (of stairs); shaft (of lift).

cagneux, *a.* Knock-kneed.

cagnotte, *s.f.* Pool, kitty.

cagot, -e. 1. *s.* (Canting) hypocrite. **2.** *a.* Sanctimonious.

cagoule, *s.f.* Cowl.

cahier, *s.m.* Exercise book.

cahin-caha, *adv.* **Marcher c.-c.** to limp along.

cahot, *s.m.* Jolt; bump.

cahotement, *s.m.* Jolting, bumping.

cahoter, *v.tr. & i.* To bump along.

cahute, *s.f.* Hut.

caille, *s.f.* Quail.

cailler [kɑje], *v.tr., i., & pr.* To clot, curdle; to congeal.

caillou, -oux [kaju], *s.m.* (*a*) Pebble. (*b*) Boulder.

caillouteux [-ju-], *a.* Flinty, stony; pebbly, shingly.

caïman, *s.m.* Cayman.

Caire (le). *Pr.n.* Cairo.

caisse, *s.f.* **1.** (*a*) (Packing-)case. (*b*) Box, chest. **2.** Body (of vehicle). **3.** (*a*) Cash-box; till. (*b*) Pay-desk. (*c*) Counting-house. (*d*) **Petite c.,** petty cash. (*e*) Fund. (*f*) Bank. **4. Grosse c.,** big drum.

caissier, *s.* Cashier.

caisson, *s.m.* **1.** Caisson. **2.** Locker

cajoler, *v.tr.* To cajole, coax.

cajolerie, *s.f.* Cajolery, coaxing.

calamité, *s.f.* Calamity, disaster.

calamiteux, *a.* Calamitous.

calandre, *s.f.* (*a*) Roller. (*b*) Mangle.

calandrer, *v.tr. Laund:* To mangle.

calcaire, *s.m.* Limestone.

calciner, *v.tr.* To calcine.

calcium [-sjɔm], *s.m.* Calcium.

calcul [-kyl], *s.m.* (*a*) Calculation, reckoning. (*b*) Arithmetic.

calculer, *v.tr.* To calculate.

cale[1], *s.f.* **1.** Hold (of ship). **2.** **C. sèche,** dry dock.

cale[2], *s.f.* Wedge, chock, block.

calèche, *s.f.* Light carriage.

caleçon, *s.m.* (Men's) drawers.

calembour, *s.m.* Pun.

calendrier, *s.m.* Calendar.

calepin, *s.m.* Note-book.

caler, *v.tr.* **1.** To chock (up). **2.** *Aut:* To stall. *v.i.* (Of engine) To stall.

calibre, *s.m.* **1.** Calibre (of fire-arm). **2.** Gauge.

calibrer, *v.tr.* To gauge.

calice[1], *s.m.* Chalice.

calice[2], *s.m.* Calyx.

calicot, *s.m.* Calico.

califourchon (à), *adv.phr.* Astride.

câlin, *a.* Caressing, winning.

câlinerie, *s.f.* **1.** Caressing. **2.** Caress.

calleux, *a.* Horny, callous.

calmant, *a.* Calming; soothing.

calme[1], *s.m.* Calm, calmness.

calme[2], *a.* Calm; cool (manner).

calmement, *adv.* Calmly, coolly.

calmer, *v.tr.* To calm, quiet, allay; to soothe.

se **calmer,** to become calm; to abate.

calomniateur, -trice. 1. *s.* Slanderer. **2.** *a.* Slanderous.

calomnie, *s.f.* Slander, libel.

calomnier, *v.tr.* To slander, libel.

calomnieux, *a.* Slanderous.

calorie, *s.f.* Calorie.

calotte, *s.f.* Skull-cap.

calque, *s.m.* Tracing; traced design.

calquer, *v.tr.* To trace (*sur,* from)

calvitie, *s.f.* Baldness.

camarade, *s.m. & f.* Comrade.

camaraderie, *s.f.* Comradeship; good fellowship.

cambriolage, *s.m.* Housebreaking.

cambrioler, *v.tr.* To burgle.

cambrioleur, -euse, *s.* Housebreaker; burglar.

camée, *s.m.* Cameo.

caméléon, *s.m.* Chameleon.

camélia, *s.m.* Camellia.

camelot, *s.m.* (*a*) Hawker. (*b*) Newsvendor.

camion, *s.m.* Dray, waggon, lorry.

camionnage, *s.m.* Cartage, haulage.

camionneur, *s.m.* Carrier, carman.

camisole, *s.f.* **1.** Dressing-jacket. **2. C. de force,** strait-waistcoat.

camomille [-mi:j], *s.f.* Camomile.

camouflage, *s.m.* Camouflage.

camoufler, *v.tr.* To camouflage.

camp, *s.m.* **1.** Camp. **2.** Party; side.

campagnard. 1. *a.* Country; rustic. **2.** *s.* Countryman; rustic.

campagne, *s.f.* **1.** (*a*) Plain; open country. **En pleine c.,** in the open (country). (*b*) Country(-side). **2.** Campaign.

campanile, *s.m.* Bell-tower.

campanule, *s.f.* Campanula.

campement, *s.m.* Encampment.

camper. 1. *v.i.* To (en)camp. **2.** *v.tr.* To encamp (troops).
  se camper, to plant oneself.

camphre, *s.m.* Camphor.

camus, *a.* Flat-, snub-nosed.

canadien, *a. & s.* Canadian.

canaille [-no:j], *s.f.* Rabble.

canal, -aux, *s.m.* **1.** Channel. **2.** Canal.

canapé, *s.m.* **1.** Sofa, couch. **2.** C. d'anchois, anchovy on toast.

canard, *s.m.* **1.** Duck; drake. **2.** False report.

canarder, *v.tr.* To snipe.

canardeur, *s.m.* Sniper.

canari, *s.m.* Canary.

cancans, *s.m. pl.* Tittle-tattle.

cancer [-se:r], *s.m.* Cancer.

cancéreux, *a.* Cancerous.

candeur, *s.f.* Ingenuousness.

candidat, *s.m.* Candidate, applicant.

candidature, *s.f.* Candidature.

candide, *a.* Ingenuous, artless.

cane, *s.f.* Duck.

caneton, *s.m.* Duckling.

canevas, *s.m.* Canvas.

caniche, *s.m. & f.* Poodle.

canicule, *s.f.* Dog-days.

canif [-nif], *s.m.* Penknife.

canin, *a.* Canine.

caniveau, *s.m.* Gutter.

canne, *s.f.* **1.** Cane, reed. **2.** Walking-stick. **3.** C. à pêche, fishing-rod.

cannelle, *s.f.* Cinnamon.

cannelure, *s.f.* Groove, slot.

cannibale, *s.m.* Cannibal.

cannibalisme, *s.m.* Cannibalism.

canon[1], *s.m.* **1.** Gun, cannon. **2.** Barrel (of rifle).

canon[2], *s.m.* **1.** Canon. **2.** *Mus:* Round, catch.

canonnade, *s.f.* Cannonade.

canonnier, *s.m.* Gunner.

canonnière, *s.f.* Gunboat.

canot, *s.m.* (Open) boat; dinghy.

canotage, *s.m.* Boating, rowing.

canotier, *s.m.* **1.** Oarsman. **2.** Straw-hat.

cantate, *s.f.* Cantata.

cantatrice, *s.f.* (Professional) singer.

cantine, *s.f.* Canteen.

cantinier, *s.* Canteen-keeper.

cantique, *s.m.* (*a*) Canticle. (*b*) Hymn.

canton, *s.m.* Canton, district.

cantonade, *s.f. Th:* Wings. **Parler à la c.,** to speak 'off.'

cantonnement, *s.m.* **1.** Billeting. **2.** Cantonment, billets, quarters.

cantonner, *v.tr.* To billet (troops).

cantonnier, *s.m.* Roadman.

caoutchouc, *s.m.* (India-)rubber.

cap [kap], *s.m.* **1.** Cape, headland. **2.** Head (of ship); course.

capable, *a.* Capable.

capablement, *adv.* Capably, ably.

capacité, *s.f.* Capacity.

cape, *s.f.* (Hooded) cloak. **Rire sous c.,** to laugh up one's sleeve.

capeline, *s.f.* Hooded cape.

capitaine, *s.m.* (*a*) Captain. (*b*) Chief, head, leader.

capital, -aux. 1. *a.* (*a*) Capital. (*b*) Essential, principal. **2.** *s.f.* **Capitale,** capital. **2.** *s.m.* Capital, assets.

capitalisme, *s.m.* Capitalism.

capitaliste, *s.m. & f.* Capitalist.

capitulation, *s.f.* Capitulation.

capituler, *v.i.* To capitulate.

caporal, -aux, *s.m.* **1.** Corporal. **2.** Cut tobacco.

capot, *s.m.* **1.** Hooded great-coat. **2.** Bonnet (of car).

capote, *s.f.* **1.** Great-coat. **2.** Bonnet. **3.** *Veh:* Hood.

capoter, *v.i.* To capsize; to overturn.

câpre, *s.f. Bot:* Caper.

caprice, *s.m.* Caprice, whim.

capricieusement, *adv.* Capriciously, whimsically.

capricieux, *a.* Capricious.

capsule, *s.f.* Capsule.

capter, *v.tr.* **1.** To obtain by insidious means; *Tp:* to tap. **2.** To catch, collect.

captieux, *a.* Fallacious, captious.

captif, *a. & s.* Captive; prisoner.

captivant, *a.* Captivating.

captiver, *v.tr.* To captivate.

captivité, *s.f.* Captivity.
capture, *s.f.* **1.** Capture, seizure. **2.** Capture, prize.
capturer, *v.tr.* To capture.
capuchon, *s.m.* **1.** (*a*) Hood. (*b*) Cowl. **2.** Cap (of fountain-pen).
capucine, *s.f.* Nasturtium.
caque, *s.f.* Keg; herring-barrel.
caquet, *s.m.* Cackle, cackling.
caquetage, *s.m.* **1.** Cackling. **2.** Chatter(ing).
caqueter, *v.i.* **1.** To cackle. **2.** To chatter.
car, *conj.* For, because.
carabine, *s.f.* Carbine.
caractère, *s.m.* **1.** Character; symbol; type. **2.** (*a*) Characteristic. (*b*) Official capacity. **3.** (*a*) Nature, disposition. (*b*) Personality, character.
caractériser, *v.tr.* To characterize.
caractéristique. 1. *a.* Characteristic. **2.** *s.f.* Characteristic.
carafe, *s.f.* Decanter; carafe.
carafon, *s.m.* Small carafe.
carat, *s.m.* Carat.
caravane, *s.f.* Caravan.
caravansérail [-raːj], *s.m.* Caravanserai.
carbonate, *s.m.* Carbonate.
carbone, *s.m.* Carbon.
carbonique, *a.* Carbonic.
carburateur, *s.m.* Carburettor.
carcasse, *s.f.* Carcase; framework.
cardinal, -aux. 1. *a.* Cardinal. **2.** *s.m.* Cardinal.
carême, *s.m.* Lent.
carénage, *s.m.* Stream-lining.
caréner, *v.tr.* To stream-line.
caresse, *s.f.* Caress.
caresser, *v.tr.* **1.** To caress, fondle. **2.** To cherish (hope).
cargaison, *s.f.* Cargo, freight.
cargo, *s.m.* Cargo-boat.
caricature, *s.f.* Caricature.
caricaturer, *v.tr.* To caricature.
caricaturiste, *s.m.* Caricaturist.
carié, *a.* Decayed.
carillon [-ijɔ̃], *s.m.* Chime(s).
carillonner [-ijɔ-], *v.i.* (*a*) To ring a peal. (*b*) To chime.
carlingue [-ɛ̃g], *s.f.* *Av:* Cabin.
carmin, *s.m.* Carmine.
carnage, *s.m.* Carnage, slaughter.
carnassier. 1. *a.* Carnivorous. **2.** *s.m.* Carnivore. **3.** *s.f.* **Carnassière,** game-bag.

carnaval, -als, *s.m.* Carnival.
carnet, *s.m.* Note-book. **C. de chèques,** cheque-book.
carnivore, *a.* Carnivorous.
carotte, *s.f.* Carrot.
carpe, *s.f.* Carp.
carpette, *s.f.* Rug.
carquois, *s.m.* Quiver.
carré. 1. *a.* (*a*) Square. (*b*) Blunt (answer). **2.** *s.m.* (*a*) Square. (*b*) Landing (of staircase). **C. des officiers,** ward-room.
carreau, *s.m.* **1.** (*a*) (Flooring) tile. (*b*) (Window-)pane. **2.** *Cards:* Diamonds.
carrefour, *s.m.* Cross-roads; square, circus.
carrelage, *s.m.* Tiling.
carrelet, *s.m.* Plaice; dab.
carrément, *adv.* Square(ly). **Parler c.,** to speak bluntly.
carrière[1], *s.f.* **1.** Career. **2.** Free play.
carrière[2], *s.f.* Stone-pit, quarry.
carriole, *s.f.* Light covered cart.
carrosse, *s.m.* Coach.
carrure, *s.f.* Breadth across the shoulders.
cartable, *s.m.* School satchel.
carte, *s.f.* **1.** **C. blanche,** a free hand. **2.** Map. **3.** (Piece of) cardboard; card. **C. à jouer,** playing-card. **C. de visite,** visiting-card. **C. postale,** postcard. **4.** Bill of fare.
carter [-tɛːr], *s.m.* Gear-case.
cartilage, *s.m.* Gristle.
carton, *s.m.* **1.** Cardboard. **2.** Cardboard box. **3.** Cartoon.
cartonner, *v.tr.* To bind (book) in boards.
cartouche. 1. *s.m.* Scroll; cartouche. **2.** *s.f.* Cartridge.
cartouchière, *s.f.* Cartridge-pouch.
carvi, *s.m.* Caraway.
cas, *s.m.* **1.** Case, instance. **2.** Case, matter. **3.** **Faire cas de.,** to value. **4.** *Gram:* Case. **5. En ce cas,** in that case. **En tout cas,** in any case, at all events.
casanier, *a.* Stay-at-home.
casaque, *s.f.* **1.** **Tourner c.,** to turn one's coat. **2.** (*a*) Jacket (of jockey). (*b*) (Woman's) jumper.
cascade, *s.f.* Cascade, waterfall.
case, *s.f.* **1.** Hut, cabin. **2.** (*a*) Compartment. (*b*) Square (of chessboard).

caser, *v.tr.* To put away; to file; to find a place for.

se caser, to settle down.

caserne, *s.f.* Barracks.

casier, *s.m.* Set of pigeon-holes.

casino, *s.m.* Casino.

casque, *s.m.* Helmet.

casquette, *s.f.* Peaked cap.

cassant, *a.* **1.** (*a*) Brittle. (*b*) Crisp (biscuit). **2.** Curt, abrupt.

cassation, *s.f.* Annulment. **Cour de c.,** Supreme Court of Appeal.

casse, *s.f.* Breakage, damage.

cassé, *a.* Broken, worn out.

casse-cou, *s.m.inv.* **1.** Death-trap **2.** Dare-devil.

casse-croûte, *s.m.inv.* Snack.

casse-noisette(s), *s.m.inv.* (Pair of) nut-crackers.

casse-noix, *s.m.inv.* (Pair of) nut-crackers.

casser, *v.tr.* **1.** To break, snap. **2.** To cashier. **3.** To quash.

se casser, to break, snap.

casserole, *s.f.* (Sauce)pan, stewpan.

cassette, *s.f.* Casket.

cassis [-sis], *s.m.* Black-currant.

cassonade, *s.f.* Brown sugar.

cassure, *s.f.* Break, fracture.

castagnettes, *s.f.pl.* Castanets.

caste, *s.f.* Caste.

castillan [-tijã], *a. & s.* Castilian.

castor, *s.m.* Beaver.

casuel [-ɥɛl]. **1.** Fortuitous, accidental. **2.** *s.m.* Perquisites.

casuellement [-ɥɛl-], *adv.* Fortuitously, accidentally.

casuiste, *s.m.* Casuist.

casuistique, *s.f.* Casuistry.

cataclysme, *s.m.* Cataclysm.

catacombes, *s.f.pl.* Catacombs.

catalogue [-lɔg], *s.m.* Catalogue.

cataloguer [-ge], *v.tr.* To catalogue.

cataplasme, *s.m.* Poultice

cataracte, *s.f.* Cataract.

catarrhe, *s.m.* Catarrh.

catastrophe, *s.f.* Catastrophe.

catéchiser, *v.tr.* **1.** To catechize. **2.** (*a*) To reason with. (*b*) To lecture.

catéchisme, *s.m.* Catechism.

catégorie, *s.f.* Category.

catégorique, *a.* Categorical. **Refus c.,** flat refusal.

catégoriquement, *adv.* (*a*) Categorically. (*b*) Clearly, explicitly.

cathédrale, *s.f.* Cathedral.

catholique. 1. Orthodox. **2.** *a. & s.* (Roman) Catholic.

Caucase (le). *Pr.n.* The Caucasus.

cauchemar, *s.m.* Nightmare.

cause, *s.f.* **1.** Cause; good reason. *Prep.phr.* **A c. de,** on account of. **2.** *Jur:* Cause, suit. **En connaissance de c.,** with full knowledge of the case.

causer[1], *v.tr.* To cause.

causer[2], *v.i.* To converse, chat.

causerie, *s.f.* (*a*) Talk, chat. (*b*) Chatty lecture.

caustique, *a. & s.m.* Caustic.

cauteleux, *a.* **1.** Cunning. **2.** Wary.

cautériser, *v.tr.* To cauterize.

caution, *s.f.* **1.** Security, guarantee; bail. **Sujet à c.,** unconfirmed (news). **2.** Surety, guaranty.

cautionnement, *s.m.* Guarantee.

cavalcade, *s.f.* **1.** Cavalcade. **2.** Pageant.

cavalerie, *s.f.* Cavalry.

cavalier. 1. *s.* Rider; horseman. **2.** *s.m.* (*a*) *Mil:* Trooper. (*b*) *Chess:* Knight. (*c*) Partner (to lady). **3.** *s.m.* Staple. **4.** *a.* Cavalier, off-hand.

cavalièrement, *adv.* Cavalierly.

cave[1], *a.* Hollow, sunken (cheeks).

cave[2], *s.f.* Cellar, vault.

caveau, *s.m.* Vault.

caver, *v.tr.* To hollow (out).

caverne, *s.f.* (*a*) Cave, cavern. (*b*) Den.

caverneux, *a.* Hollow, sepulchral.

caviar, *s.m.* Caviar(e).

cavité, *s.f.* Cavity, hollow.

ce[1], *dem.pron.neut.* It, that. **1.** (*a*) **C'est faux!** it is untrue! **Est-ce assez?** is that enough? (*b*) **C'est moi, c'est nous, ce sont eux,** it is I, we, they. **Si ce n'est,** except, unless. (*c*) **Ce . . . ici** = CECI. (*d*) **Ce . . . là** = CELA. (*e*) **C'est qu'il fait froid!** it is cold and nò mistake! (*f*) **Est-ce que je peux entrer?** may I come in? **2. Ce disant,** so saying. **3.** (*a*) **Ce qui, ce que,** etc. = what. (*b*) **Ce qui, ce que,** etc. = which. (*c*) **Tout ce qui, que,** everything, all (that). **4. Sur ce,** thereupon.

ce[2] (**cet**), **cette, ces,** *dem. a.* This, that, *pl.* these, those. **1. Ce dernier,** the latter. **2. Ce . . . -ci,** this. **Ce . . . -là,** that. **Prenez cette tasse-ci,** take this cup.

ceci, *dem. pron. neut.* This (thing).

cécité, *s.f.* Blindness.

céder. 1. *v.tr.* (*a*) To give up, yield. (*b*) To transfer. **2.** *v.i.* To yield, give way.

cédille [-di:j], *s.f.* Cedilla.

cèdre, *s.m.* Cedar(-tree, -wood).

ceindre, *v.tr.* **1.** To gird. **C. une épée,** to buckle on a sword. **2.** To encircle.

ceinture, *s.f.* **1.** (*a*) Girdle; belt; sash. **C. de sauvetage,** life-belt. (*b*) Waist. **2.** Girdle.

ceinturon, *s.m.* Sword-belt.

cela, ça, *dem. pron. neut.* (*a*) That (thing). **Qu'est-ce que c'est que c.?** what is that? (*b*) That, it. (*c*) **C'est ça,** that's it, that's right. **Il n'y a que ça,** there's nothing like it. **Et avec c., madame?** and what else, madam?

célébration, *s.f.* Celebration.

célèbre, *a.* Celebrated (*par,* for).

célébrer, *v.tr.* To celebrate.

célébrité, *s.f.* Celebrity.

céleri, *s.m.* Celery.

célérité, *s.f.* Celerity, dispatch.

céleste, *a.* Celestial, heavenly.

célibat, *s.m.* Celibacy.

célibataire, *a.* Unmarried, single. *s.m.* Bachelor. *s.f.* Spinster.

celle. See CELUI.

cellulaire, *a.* **1.** Cellular. **2. Voiture c.,** police-van.

cellule, *s.f.* Cell.

celluloïde, *s.m.* Celluloid.

cellulose, *s.f.* Cellulose.

celtique, *a. & s.m.* Celtic.

celui, celle, *pl.* **ceux, celles,** *dem. pron.* **1.** (*a*) The one; those. (*b*) He, she, those. **2. Celui-ci, ceux-ci,** this (one), these; the latter. **Celui-là, ceux-là,** that (one), those; the former.

cendre, *s.f.* Ash(es), cinders. **Mercredi des Cendres,** Ash-Wednesday.

cendré, *a.* (Ash-)grey; ashy.

cendrée, *s.f.* **Piste en c.,** cinder-track; dirt-track.

cendrier, *s.m.* (*a*) Ash-pan. (*b*) Ash-tray.

Cendrillon [-ijɔ̃]. *Pr.n.f.* Cinderella.

cénotaphe, *s.m.* Cenotaph.

censé, *a.* Supposed.

censeur, *s.m.* **1.** Critic. **2.** (*a*) Censor. (*b*) Auditor.

censure, *s.f.* **1.** (*a*) Censorship. (*b*) Audit. **2.** Censure, blame.

censurer, *v.tr.* **1.** To censure. **2.** To censor.

cent. 1. *num. a.* (A, one) hundred. **Faire les c. pas,** to pace up and down. **2.** *s.m.inv.* A hundred. **Sept pour c.,** seven per cent.

centaine, *s.f.* A hundred (or so).

centaure, *s.m.* Centaur.

centenaire. 1. *a.* Ancient. **2.** *s.m. & f.* Centenarian. **3.** *s.m.* Centenary.

centennal, -aux, *a.* Centennial.

centième, *num. a. & s.* Hundredth.

centigrade, *a.* Centigrade.

centime, *s.m.* Centime.

centimètre, *s.m.* **1.** Centimetre. **2.** Tape-measure.

centipède, *s.m.* Centipede.

central, -aux. 1. *a.* Central. **2.** *s.m.* **C. téléphonique,** telephone exchange.

centralisation, *s.f.* Centralization.

centraliser, *v.tr.* To centralize.

centre, *s.m.* Centre; middle.

centuple, *a. & s.m.* Hundred-fold.

cep [sɛ(p)], *s.m.* Vine-stock.

cèpe, *s.m.* Flap mushroom.

cependant. 1. *adv.* Meanwhile. **2.** *conj.* Yet, still, nevertheless.

cerceau, *s.m.* Hoop.

cercle, *s.m.* **1.** (*a*) Circle. (*b*) Club. **2.** Hoop, ring.

cercler, *v.tr.* To encircle, to ring.

cercueil [-kœ:j], *s.m.* Coffin.

céréales, *s.f.pl.* Cereals.

cérébral, -aux, *a.* Cerebral.

cérémonial, -aux, *a.* Ceremonial.

cérémonie, *s.f.* Ceremony. **Visite de c.,** formal call.

cérémonieux, *a.* Ceremonious.

cerf, *s.m.* Stag.

cerf-volant [sɛrvɔlɑ̃], *s.m.* **1.** Stag-beetle. **2.** (Paper) kite. *pl.* **cerfs-volants.**

cerise. 1. *s.f.* Cherry. **2.** *s.m. & a.inv.* Cerise.

cerisier, *s.m.* Cherry-tree, -wood.

cerne, *s.m.* Ring (round eyes).

cerneau, *s.m.* Green walnut.

cerner, *v.tr.* To encircle, surround. **Avoir les yeux cernés,** to have rings under the eyes.

certain. 1. *a.* (*a*) Certain, sure. (*b*) **Il est c. de réussir,** he is sure he will succeed. (*c*) Fixed, stated. **2.** *indef. a. & pron.* Some, certain.

certainement, *adv.* Certainty.

certes, *adv.* (Oui) c.! yes indeed!

certificat, *s.m.* Certificate, testimonial.

certifier, *v.tr.* To certify, attest.

certitude, *s.f.* Certainty.

céruse, *s.f.* White lead.

cerveau, *s.m.* (*a*) Brain. **Rhume de c.,** cold in the head. (*b*) Intellect, brains. **C. brûlé,** hot-head.

cervelas, *s.m.* Saveloy.

cervelle, *s.f.* **1.** Brain(s) (as matter). **Brûler la c. à qn,** to blow s.o.'s brains out. **2.** Mind, brains. **Se creuser la c.,** to rack one's brains (*pour*, to).

Cervin. *Pr.n.m.* **Le Mont C.,** the Matterhorn.

ces. See CE[2].

cessation, *s.f.* Cessation, ceasing.

cesse, *s.f.* Cease, ceasing.

cesser, *v.tr. & i.* To cease, leave off, stop. **Faire c.,** to put a stop to. **C. de faire,** to cease doing.

cession, *s.f.* Transfer.

cessionnaire, *s.m.* Transferee.

c'est-à-dire, *conj.phr.* That is (to say).

cet. See CE[2].

cétacé, *a. & s.m.* Cetacean.

cette. See CE[2].

ceux. See CELUI.

Ceylan. *Pr.n.m.* Ceylon.

chacal, -als [-kal], *s.m.* Jackal.

chacun, *pron.* **1.** Each; each one. **2.** Everybody, everyone.

chagrin[1], *s.m.* (*a*) Grief, sorrow, affliction. (*b*) Vexation, annoyance.

chagrin[2], *s.m.* Shagreen.

chagrin[3], *a.* **1.** Sad; distressed (*de, at*). **2.** Peevish, fretful.

chagriner, *v.tr.* **1.** To grieve, distress. **2.** To vex, annoy.

se chagriner, to grieve; to fret.

chaîne, *s.f.* **1.** (*a*) Chain. (*b*) Shackles, fetters. **2.** Range (of mountains). **3.** *Tex:* Warp.

chaînon, *s.m.* Link (of chain).

chair, *s.f.* Flesh. **1.** En c. et en os, in the flesh. **Être (bien) en c.,** to be plump. **2.** (*a*) Meat. **C. à canon,** cannon-fodder. (*b*) Pulp (of peach).

chaire, *s.f.* **1.** Pulpit. **2.** (*a*) Chair, desk (of lecturer). (*b*) Professorship.

chaise, *s.f.* Chair, seat.

chaise-longue, *s.f.* Lounge-chair; couch. *pl. chaises-longues.*

chaland[1], *s.m.* Lighter, barge.

chaland[2], *s.* Customer, purchaser.

châle, *s.m.* Shawl.

chalet, *s.m.* (*a*) Chalet. (*b*) Country cottage.

chaleur, *s.f.* (*a*) Heat, warmth. (*b*) Ardour, zeal.

chaleureusement, *adv.* Warmly, cordially.

chaleureux, *a.* Warm; cordial.

chaloupe, *s.f.* Launch; long-boat.

chalumeau, *s.m.* **1.** Straw (for drinking). **2.** Blow-pipe.

chalut, *s.m.* Drag-net; trawl.

chalutier, *s.m.* Trawler; drifter.

chamailler (se) [-aje], *v.pr.* To squabble.

chamarrer, *v.tr.* To bedizen.

chambellan, *s.m.* Chamberlain.

chambranle, *s.m.* Frame (of door).

chambre, *s.f.* **1.** Room, chamber. **C. à deux lits,** double room. **C. d'ami,** spare room. **2.** Chamber, house. **3.** **C. à air,** inner tube. **C. noire,** dark-room.

chambrée, *s.f.* Barrack-room.

chameau, *s.m.* Camel.

chamelier, *s.m.* Camel-driver.

chamelle, *s.f.* She-camel.

chamois, *s.m.* Chamois.

champ[1], *s.m.* **1.** Field. **2.** C. de tir, rifle-range. **3.** Field of action; scope. **Le c. est libre,** the coast is clear.

champ[2], *s.m.* Edge, side.

Champagne. **1.** *s.m.* Champagne. **2.** *s.f.* **Fine c.,** liqueur brandy.

champêtre, *a.* Rustic, rural. **Garde c.,** rural policeman.

champignon, *s.m.* (*a*) **C. comestible,** mushroom. (*b*) **C. vénéneux,** fungus, toadstool.

champion, *s.* Champion.

championnat, *s.m.* Championship.

chance, *s.f.* **1.** Chance. **2.** Luck, fortune. **Avoir de la c.,** to be in luck's way.

chancelant, *a.* Staggering, tottering.

chanceler, *v.i.* To stagger, totter.

chancelier, *s.m.* Chancellor.

chanceux, *a.* **1.** Hazardous. **2.** Lucky.

chancre, *s.m.* Canker.

chancreux, *a.* Cankered.

chandail [-daːj], *s.m.* Sweater.

chandelier, *s.m.* Candlestick.

chandelle, *s.f.* **1.** (Tallow) candle. **Voir trente-six chandelles,** to see stars. **2.** (Of aeroplane) **Monter en c.,** to zoom.

change, *s.m.* **1.** Exchange. **2.** Donner le c. à, to deceive.

changeant, *a.* Changing; changeable.

changement, *s.m.* Change; alteration. C. de marche, reversing gear.

changer. 1. *v.tr.* To change, exchange. **2.** *v.tr.* To change, alter. **3.** *v.i.* To (undergo a) change.

se changer. 1. To change; to alter. **2.** To change one's clothes.

changeur, *s.m.* Money-changer.

chanoine, *s.m.* Canon.

chanson, *s.f.* Song.

chant, *s.m.* **1.** Singing; song. **2.** Melody, air. **3.** Canto.

chantage, *s.m.* Blackmail, extortion.

chanter, *v.tr.* **1.** To sing. Faire c. qn, to blackmail s.o. **2.** To sing; to crow; to chirp.

chanteur, -euse, *s.* Singer, vocalist. Maître c., blackmailer.

chantier, *s.m.* Yard. C. de construction, shipyard.

chantonner, *v.tr. & i.* To hum.

chantre, *s.m.* Chorister. Grand c., precentor.

chanvre, *s.m.* Hemp.

chaos [kao], *s.m.* Chaos, confusion.

chaotique [kaɔ-], *a.* Chaotic.

chapeau, *s.m.* **1.** Hat. Saluer qn d'un coup de c., to raise one's hat to s.o. C. bas, hat in hand. **2.** Cowl (of chimney).

chapelet, *s.m.* (String of) beads. Égrener son c., to tell one's beads.

chapelier, *s.* Hatter.

chapelle, *s.f.* (*a*) Chapel. (*b*) Maître de c., choir-master.

chapellerie, *s.f.* Hat-trade, -shop.

chaperon, *s.m.* **1.** Hood. **2.** Chaperon.

chaperonner, *v.tr.* To chaperon.

chapiteau, *s.m.* Capital (of column).

chapitre, *s.m.* (*a*) Chapter. (*b*) Head(ing); item.

chapon, *s.m.* Capon.

chaque, *a.* Each, every.

char, *s.m.* **1.** Chariot. **2.** C. d'assaut, tank.

charade, *s.f.* Charade.

charançon, *s.m.* Weevil.

charbon, *s.m.* (*a*) C. de bois, charcoal. Être sur des charbons ardents, to be on tenter-hooks. (*b*) Carbon. (*c*) C. de terre, coal.

charbonnier. 1. *s.m. Nau:* Collier. **2.** *s.* Charcoal-burner.

charcuterie, *s.f.* **1.** Pork-butcher's shop. **2.** Pork-butcher's meat.

charcutier, *s.* Pork-butcher.

chardon, *s.m.* Thistle.

chardonneret, *s.m.* Goldfinch.

charge, *s.f.* **1.** Load, burden. Être à c. à, to be a burden to. **2.** Charge, load. **3.** (*a*) Charge, responsibility. Femme de c., housekeeper. (*b*) Office. **4.** Charge, expense. *Prep. phr.* A (la) c. de, on condition of. **5.** *Mil:* Charge. **6.** To instruct. Témoin à c., witness for the prosecution.

chargé, *a.* **1.** Loaded, laden. Temps c., overcast weather. **2.** Lettre chargée, registered letter.

chargement, *s.m.* **1.** Loading. **2.** Cargo, freight, load.

charger, *v.tr.* **1.** To load (*de*, with); to fill (pipe). **2.** To instruct. **3.** To charge. **4.** To register (letter).

se charger de, to undertake.

chariot, *s.m.* **1.** (*a*) Waggon. (*b*) Truck, trolley. **2.** Carriage (of typewriter).

charitable, *a.* Charitable (*envers*, to).

charitablement, *adv.* Charitably.

charité, *s.f.* **1.** Charity. Dame de c., district-visitor. **2.** Act of charity.

charlatan, *s.* Charlatan, quack.

charmant, *a.* Charming, delightful.

charme, *s.m.* **1.** Charm, spell. **2.** Charm, attraction, seductiveness.

charmer, *v.tr.* **1.** To charm, bewitch. **2.** To charm, please.

charnel, *a.* Carnal; sensual.

charnier, *s.m.* Charnel-house.

charnière, *s.f.* Hinge.

charnu, *a.* Fleshy.

charogne, *s.f.* Carrion.

charpente, *s.f.* Frame(work).

charpenterie, *s.f.* Carpentry.

charpentier, *s.m.* Carpenter.

charpie, *s.f.* Lint.

charretée, *s.f.* Cart-load, cartful.

charretier, *s.m.* Carter, carman.

charrette, *s.f.* Cart. C. à bras, hand-cart; barrow.

charrier, *v.tr.* To cart, carry.

charrue, *s.f.* Plough.

charte, *s.f.* Charter.

chas, *s.m.* Eye (of needle).

chasse, *s.f.* **1.** Hunting. Aller à la c., to go hunting or shooting. **2.** C. d'eau, flush.

châsse, *s.f.* Reliquary, shrine.
chasser. 1. *v.tr.* (a) To chase, hunt. (b) To drive away; to dismiss. **C. un clou,** to drive a nail. 2. *v.i.* (a) To hunt; to shoot. (b) To drive.
chasseur, -euse, *s.* 1. (a) Huntsman; hunter. (b) Shooter. 2. *s.m.* Commissionaire; porter; page-boy. 3. *s.m. Av:* Fighter.
châssis, *s.m.* (a) Frame. (b) *Aut:* Chassis. *Av:* Under-carriage.
chaste, *a.* Chaste, pure.
chastement, *adv.* Chastely, purely.
chasteté, *s.f.* Chastity, purity.
chat, *f.* **chatte,** *s.* 1. Cat. **A bon c. bon rat,** tit for tat.
châtaigne, *s.f.* Chestnut.
châtaignier, *s.m.* Chestnut-tree.
châtain, *a.* (Chestnut-)brown.
château, *s.m.* 1. Castle. **Châteaux en Espagne,** castles in the air. 2. (a) Country seat; mansion. (b) Palace.
châtelain, *s.m.* Lord (of manor).
châtelaine, *s.f.* Lady (of manor).
chat-huant, *s.m.* Tawny owl. *pl. chats-huants.*
châtier, *v.tr* To punish, chastise; to chasten.
châtiment, *s.m.* Punishment.
chatoiement, *s.m.* Shimmer; sheen.
chaton, *s.* 1. Kitten. 2. *s.m.* Catkin.
chatouillement [-ujmã], *s.m.* Tickling.
chatouiller [-uje], *v.tr.* To tickle.
chatouilleux [-ujø], *a.* (a) Ticklish. (b) Sensitive, touchy.
chatoyant, *a.* Iridescent, chatoyant.
chatoyer, *v.i.* (a) To shimmer. (b) To glisten, sparkle.
chatte. See CHAT.
chat-tigre, *s.m.* Tiger-cat. *pl. chats-tigres.*
chaud. 1. *a.* Warm; hot. **Pleurer à chaudes larmes,** to weep bitterly. *V.phr.* **Il fait c.,** it is warm (weather). 2. *s.m.* **Avoir c.,** (of pers.) to be warm.
chaudement, *adv.* Warmly.
chaudière, *s.f.* 1. Copper (for washing). 2. Boiler.
chaudron, *s.m.* Cauldron.
chaudronnier, *s.* 1. **C. ambulant,** tinker. 2. Boiler-maker.
chauffage, *s.m.* Warming, heating.
chauffe, *s.f.* 1. Heating. 2. Stoking.
chauffer. 1. *v.tr.* (a) To warm, heat.

(b) **Chauffé au rouge,** red-hot. 2. *v.i.* To get warm, hot.
chauffeur, -euse, *s.* 1. (a) Stoker, fireman. 2. *Aut:* Driver.
chaume, *s.m.* (a) Thatch. (b) Stubble.
chaumière, *s.f.* Thatched cottage.
chaussée, *s.f.* 1. (a) Sea-wall. (b) Causeway. 2. (a) Roadway. (b) Road.
chausse-pied, *s.m.* Shoe-horn. *pl. chausse-pieds*
chausser, *v.tr.* To put on (footwear). **Être bien chaussé,** to be well shod.
chaussette, *s.f.* Sock.
chaussure, *s.f.* Foot-wear.
chauve. 1. *a.* (a) Bald. (b) Bare, denuded. 2. *s.m.* Bald person.
chauve-souris, *s.f. Z:* Bat. *pl. chauves-souris.*
chaux, *s.f.* Lime. **Blanchir à la c.,** to whitewash.
chavirer, *v.i. & tr.* To capsize, upset.
chef [ʃef], *s.m.* 1. Head; chief; principal. **C. de musique,** bandmaster. *Sp:* **C. d'équipe,** captain. **C. de gare,** stationmaster. **C. de train,** guard. 2. Authority. 3. Head(ing).
chef-d'œuvre [ʃɛdœːvr], *s.m.* Masterpiece. *pl. chefs-d'œuvre.*
chef-lieu [ʃefljø], *s.m.* Chief town (of department). *pl. chefs-lieux.*
chemin, *s.m.* 1. (a) Way, road. **C. faisant,** on the way. **Se mettre en c.,** to set out. (b) Road, path, track. **Grand c.,** highway, high road. 2. **C. de fer,** railway.
chemineau, *s.m.* Tramp, vagrant.
cheminée, *s.f.* 1. (a) Fireplace. (b) (Manteau de) **c.,** mantelpiece. 2. (a) Chimney. (b) Funnel (of locomotive).
cheminer, *v.i.* To walk, proceed.
chemise, *s.f.* 1. (a) Shirt. (b) Chemise. 2. Jacket; folder.
chenal, -aux, *s.m.* Channel.
chenapan, *s.m.* Rogue, scoundrel.
chêne, *s.m.* Oak.
chenet, *s.m.* Fire-dog; andiron.
chènevis, *s.m.* Hempseed.
chenille [-niːj], *s.f.* 1. Caterpillar. 2. *Tex:* Chenille.
chenu, *a.* (Of hair) Hoary.
chèque, *s.m.* Cheque.
cher [ʃɛːr], *a.* 1. Dear, beloved. *s.* **Mon c.,** my dear fellow. **Ma chère,** my dear. 2. Dear, expensive.

chercher, *v.tr.* **1.** To look for; to seek. **2. Aller c.,** to (go and) fetch. **Envoyer c.,** to send for. **3. C. à faire qch.,** to endeavour to do sth.

chercheur, -euse, *s.* Seeker, searcher; investigator.

chère, *s.f.* Cheer, fare, living.

chèrement, *adv* Dearly.

chéri. 1. *a.* Cherished, dear. **2.** *s.* Dear one. **Ma chérie,** dearest.

chérir, *v.tr.* To cherish; to love dearly.

cherté, *s.f.* Dearness.

chérubin, *s.m.* Cherub.

chétif, *a.* **1.** Weak, puny, sickly. **2.** Poor, miserable, wretched.

cheval, -aux, *s.m.* **1.** Horse. **A c.,** on horseback. **Être à c. sur,** to sit astride. **2. C. de bois,** vaulting horse. **3.** Horse-power. **Une vingt chevaux,** a twenty horse-power car.

chevaleresque, *a.* Chivalrous.

chevalerie, *s.f.* **1.** Knighthood. **2.** Chivalry.

chevalet, *s.m.* (*a*) Trestle. (*b*) Easel. (*c*) Bridge (of violin).

chevalier, *s.m.* (*a*) Knight. **C. d'industrie,** adventurer, sharper. (*b*) Rider, horseman.

chevalière, *s.f.* Signet-ring.

chevalin, *a.* Equine. **Boucherie chevaline,** horse-butcher's shop.

cheval-vapeur, *s.m.* Horse-power. *pl. chevaux-vapeur.*

chevauchée, *s.f.* **1.** Ride. **2.** Cavalcade.

chevaucher. 1. *v.i.* (*a*) To ride (on horse). (*b*) To overlap. **2.** *v.tr.* To straddle ; to be astride.

chevelu, *a.* **1.** Long-haired. **2.** Hairy.

chevelure, *s.f.* (Head of) hair.

chevet, *s.m.* Bed-head. **Livre de c.,** bedside book.

cheveu, -eux, *s.m.* **1.** (A single) hair. **Couper un c. en quatre,** to split hairs. **2. Les cheveux,** the hair.

cheville [-vi:j], *s.f.* **1.** Peg, pin. **C. en fer,** bolt. **C. ouvrière,** mainspring (of enterprise). **2.** Peg, plug. **3.** Ankle.

chèvre, *s.f.* **1.** Goat; she-goat. **2.** *Veh:* Jack.

chevreau, *s.m.* Kid.

chèvrefeuille [-fœ:j], *s.m.* Honeysuckle.

chevreuil [-rœ:j], *s.m.* Roe-deer.

chevrier, *s.* Goatherd.

chevron, *s.m.* **1.** Rafter. **2.** *Her:* Chevron. **3.** Long-service stripe.

chevroter, *v.i.* To sing, speak, in a quavering voice; to quaver.

chevrotine, *s.f.* Buck-shot.

chez, *prep.* **1. C. qn,** at s.o.'s house. **Je vais c. moi,** I am going home. **C. l'épicier,** at the grocer's. (On letters) **C.,** care of. **2.** With, among. **C.les animaux,** in the animal kingdom.

chic [ʃik]. **1.** *s.m.* (*a*) Skill, knack. (*b*) Smartness, stylishness. **2.** *a. inv. in f., var. in pl.* Smart, stylish.

chicane, *s.f.* Chicanery.

chicanerie, *s.f.* Cavilling.

chicaneur, -euse. 1. *s.* Caviller. **2.** *a.* Captious.

chichement, *adv.* Stingily, meanly.

chicorée, *s.f.* Chicory.

chicot, *s.m.* Stump (of tooth).

chien, *f.* **chienne,** *s.* **1.** Dog. **Entre c. et loup,** in the twilight. **Quel temps de c.!** what beastly weather! **2.** (*a*) Hammer (of gun). (*b*) **C. d'arrêt,** pawl, catch.

chiffon, *s.m.* **1.** (*a*) Rag. (*b*) Piece of lace, of ribbon. **2.** Chiffon.

chiffonner, *v.tr.* To rumple.

chiffonnier, *s.* Rag-and-bone man.

chiffrage, *s.m.* **1.** Reckoning. **2.** Numbering. **3.** Coding.

chiffre, *s.m.* **1.** (*a*) Figure, number. **Marqué en chiffres connus,** marked in plain figures. (*b*) Amount, total. **2.** Cipher, code.

chiffrer, *v.i.* To calculate, reckon.

chiffre-taxe, *s.m.* Postage-due stamp. *pl. chiffres-taxes.*

chimère, *s.f.* Chimera.

chimérique, *a.* **1.** Visionary, fanciful. **2.** Chimerical.

chimie, *s.f.* Chemistry.

chimique, *a.* Chemical. **Un produit c.,** a chemical.

chimiste, *s.m.* Chemist.

chimpanzé, *s.m.* Chimpanzee.

Chine. *Pr.n.f.* China. **Encre de C.,** Indian ink.

chinois, *a. & s.* Chinese.

chinoiserie, *s.f.* Monkey trick.

chipoter, *v.i.* (*a*) To waste time. (*b*) To haggle.

chique, *s.f.* Quid (of tobacco).

chiquenaude, *s.f.* Fillip, flick.

chiromancie [kir-], *s.f.* Palmistry.

chirurgical, -aux, *a.* Surgical.

chirurgie, *s.f.* Surgery.
chirurgien, *s.* Surgeon.
chiure, *s.f.* Fly-speck, -mark.
chlore, *s.m.* Chlorine.
chlorhydrique, *a.* Hydrochloric.
chloroforme, *s.m.* Chloroform.
chlorure, *s.m.* Chloride.
choc, *s.m.* Shock.
chocolat, *s.m.* Chocolate.
chœur [k-], *s.* **1.** Chorus. **2.** Choir.
choisi, *a.* **1.** Selected. **2.** Choice.
choisir, *v.tr.* To choose, select.
choix, *s.m.* Choice, selection. "Au c.," 'all at the same price.'
choléra [kɔl-], *s.m.* Cholera.
chômage, *s.m.* **1.** Abstention from work. **2.** Unemployment.
chômer, *v.i.* **1.** To take a holiday. **2.** To be idle.
chopine, *s.f.* Half-litre mug.
choquant, *a.* Shocking, offensive.
choquer, *v.tr.* **1.** To strike, knock. **2.** To shock.
choral, *pl.* **-als** [kɔr-], *a.* Choral.
choriste [kɔr-], *s.m.* Chorus-singer.
chose, *s.f.* Thing. **Dites des choses aimables de ma part**, remember me kindly.
chou, -oux, *s.m.* **1.** Cabbage. **Faire c. blanc**, to make a duck. **Mon petit c.**, my dear. **2.** **C. à la crème**, cream bun.
choucas, *s.m.* Jackdaw.
choucroute, *s.f.* Sauerkraut.
chou-fleur, *s.m.* Cauliflower. *pl. choux-fleurs.*
choyer, *v.tr.* To pet, coddle.
chrétien, *a. & s.* Christian.
chrétienté, *s.f.* Christendom.
Christ, *s.m.* **Le Christ**, Christ.
christianisme, *s.m.* Christianity.
chromatique, *a.* Chromatic.
chrome, *s.m.* Chromium.
chronique[1], *a.* Chronic.
chronique[2], *s.f.* Chronicle.
chroniqueur, *s.m.* Chronicler.
chronologique, *a.* Chronological.
chronomètre, *s.m.* (*a*) Chronometer. (*b*) Stop-watch.
chrysalide, *s.f.* Chrysalis, pupa.
chrysanthème, *s.m.* Chrysanthemum.
chuchotement, *s.m.* Whispering, whisper.
chuchoter, *v.i. & tr.* To whisper.
chut [ʃyt, ʃt], *int.* Hush! ssh!

chute, *s.f.* **1.** (*a*) Fall. (*b*) (Down)fall. **2.** **C. des reins**, small of the back. **3.** *Ind:* Shoot.
Chypre. *Pr.n.f.* **L'île de C.**, Cyprus.
ci, *dem. pron. inv.* **Comme ci, comme ça**, so so.
ci-après, *adv.* Hereafter; later.
cible, *s.f.* Target.
ciboule, *s.f.* Spring onion.
cicatrice, *s.f.* Scar.
ci-contre, *adv.* (*a*) Opposite. (*b*) Annexed. (*c*) On the other side.
ci-dessous, *adv.* Hereunder; under-mentioned.
ci-dessus, *adv.* Above(-mentioned).
ci-devant, *adv.* Previously.
cidre, *s.m.* Cider.
ciel, *pl.* **cieux**, *s.m.* **1.** Sky, heaven. **A c. ouvert**, out of doors. **2.** Heaven. **(Juste) c.!** (good) heavens!
cierge, *s.m.* Wax candle; taper.
cieux. See CIEL.
cigale, *s.f.* Cicada.
cigare, *s.m.* Cigar.
cigarette, *s.f.* Cigarette.
ci-gisent, ci-gît. Here lie(s).
cigogne, *s.f.* Stork.
ciguë, *s.f.* Hemlock.
ci-inclus, *a.* Enclosed.
ci-joint, *a.* Herewith.
cil [sil], *s.m.* (Eye-)lash.
cime, *s.f.* Summit; top.
ciment, *s.m.* Cement.
cimenter, *v.tr.* To cement.
cimeterre, *s.m.* Scimitar.
cimetière, *s.m.* Cemetery, graveyard.
ciné-actualités, *s.m.* News theatre. *pl. cinés-actualités.*
cinéma, *s.m.* Cinema.
cinglant, *a.* Lashing (rain); cutting, biting.
cingler, *v.tr.* To lash, cut.
cinnamome, *s.m.* Cinnamon.
cinq [sɛ̃k], *num. a. inv. & s.m. inv.* Five. **Le c. mars**, March the fifth.
cinquantaine, *s.f.* (About) fifty.
cinquante, *num. a. inv.* Fifty.
cinquième, *num. a. & s.m.* Fifth.
cintre, *s.m.* **1.** Curve, bend. **2.** Arch (of tunnel). **3.** Coat-hanger.
cintré, *a.* (*a*) Arched. (*b*) Curved.
cirage, *s.m.* Blacking (of boots).
circoncire, *v.tr.* To circumcise.
circoncision, *s.f.* Circumcision.
circonférence, *s.f.* Circumference.
circonflexe, *a.* Circumflex.

circonlocution, *s.f.* Circumlocution.
circonscription, *s.f.* **1.** Circumscription. **2.** Division, district.
circonscrire, *v.tr.* To circumscribe.
circonspect, *a.* Circumspect.
circonspectement, *adv.* Circumspectly.
circonstance, *s.f.* Circumstance, event.
circonstanciel, *a.* Circumstantial.
circonvenir, *v.tr.* To circumvent thwart; outwit.
circuit, *s.m.* Circuit.
circulaire, *a. & s.f.* Circular.
circulation, *s.f.* **1.** Circulation. **2.** Traffic.
circuler, *v.i.* **1.** To circulate. **2.** To move about. **"Circulez!"** 'pass along!'
cire, *s.f.* Wax.
cirer, *v.tr.* To wax. **C. des chaussures,** to black shoes.
cirque, *s.m.* Circus.
cisaille [-zɑːj], *s.f.* Shears.
ciseau, *s.m.* **1.** Chisel. **2.** *pl.* (*a*) Scissors. (*b*) Shears.
ciseler, *v.tr.* To chase (gold); to chisel (wood).
citadelle, *s.f.* Citadel, stronghold.
citadin, *s.* Citizen.
citation, *s.f.* **1.** Quotation. **2.** (*a*) Summons. (*b*) Subpoena.
cité, *s.f.* City. (*a*) (Large) town. (*b*) Housing estate.
citer, *v.tr.* **1.** To quote. **2.** To summon. **3.** To mention (in dispatches).
citerne, *s.f.* Cistern, tank.
citoyen, *s.* Citizen.
citrate, *s.m.* Citrate.
citrique, *a.* Citric.
citron, *s.m.* Lemon.
citronnade, *s.f.* Lemonade.
citronnier, *s.m.* Lemon-tree.
citrouille [-truːj], *s.f.* Pumpkin.
civet, *s.m.* Stew. **C. de lièvre,** jugged hare.
civière, *s.f.* **1.** Hand-barrow. **2.** Stretcher, litter. **3.** Bier.
civil [-vil], *a.* Civil. **En c.,** in plain clothes.
civilement, *adv.* Civilly.
civilisation, *s.f.* Civilization.
civiliser, *v.tr.* To civilize.
civilité, *s.f.* Civility, courtesy.
civique, *a.* Civic.
claie, *s.f.* Hurdle.

clair. **1.** *a.* Clear. (*a*) Unclouded; limpid. (*b*) Obvious, plain. (*c*) Bright; light. **2.** *adv.* Plainly, clearly. **3.** *s.m.* (*a*) Light. (*b*) **Message en c.,** message in plain language.
Claire. *Pr.n.f.* Clara.
clairement, *adv.* Clearly, plainly.
claire-voie, *s.f.* Open-work. *pl.* **claires-voies.**
clairière, *s.f.* Clearing, glade.
clairon, *s.m.* (*a*) Bugle. (*b*) Bugler.
clairsemé, *a.* Scattered, sparse.
clairvoyance, *s.f.* **1.** Perspicacity, clear-sightedness. **2.** Second-sight.
clairvoyant. **1.** *a.* Perspicacious, clear-sighted. **2.** *a. & s.* Clairvoyant.
clameur, *s.f.* Clamour, outcry.
clandestin, *a.* Clandestine, secret.
clapier, *s.m.* Rabbit-hutch.
clapotement, *s.m.* Plash(ing).
clapoter, *v.i.* To chop, plash.
clapotis, *s.m.* Plashing, lapping.
claque, *s.f.* **1.** Smack, slap. **2.** Hired clappers (in Fr. theatres).
claquement, *s.m.* Clapping; slamming; cracking (of whip).
claquemurer, *v.tr.* To immure, mew up.
claquer. **1.** *v.i.* To clap; (of door) to bang; (of teeth) to chatter. **2.** *v.tr. & i.* To slam (the door); to crack (a whip).
clarifier, *v.tr.* To clarify.
clarinette, *s.f.* Clarinet.
clarté, *s.f.* **1.** Clearness clarity. **2.** Light, brightness.
classe, *s.f.* **1.** Class, division. **2.** (*a*) Class, form. (*b*) **Aller en c.,** to go to school.
classement, *s.m.* **1.** Classification. **2.** (*a*) Sorting out. (*b*) Filing.
classer, *v.tr.* **1.** To class(ify). **2.** (*a*) To sort out. (*b*) To file.
classeur, *s.m.* Filing-cabinet, file.
classification, *s.f.* **1.** Classification, classifying. **2.** Sorting out.
classifier, *v.tr.* To classify.
classique, *a.* **1.** For school use. **2.** Classic(al). **3.** *s.m.* Classic.
clause, *s.f.* Clause.
clavicule, *s.f.* Collar-bone.
clavier, *s.m.* Keyboard.
clé, *s.f.,* **clef,** *s.f.* **1.** Key. (*a*) **Fermer à c.,** to lock. (*b*) Key (to a cipher). **2.** *Mus:* Clef. **3.** Wrench. spanner.
clématite, *s.f.* Clematis.

clémence, *s.f.* **1.** Clemency (*pour envers*, to, towards). **2.** Mildness.

clément, *a.* **1.** Clement (*pour, envers*, to, towards). **2.** Mild.

cleptomane, *s.m. & f.* Kleptomaniac.

cleptomanie, *s.f.* Kleptomania.

clerc, *s.m.* Clerk (to lawyer).

clergé, *s.m.* Clergy, priesthood.

clérical, -aux, *a.* Clerical.

clic [klik], *s.m. & int.* Click.

cliché, *s.m.* **1.** *Phot:* Negative. **2.** Stock phrase.

client, *s.* Client, customer.

clientèle, *s.f.* Customers.

clignement, *s.m.* Blinking, winking.

cligner, *v.tr. & i.* **1.** C. les yeux, to blink. **2.** C. de l'œil, to wink.

clignotant, *a.* Blinking; twinkling.

clignotement, *s.m.* Twinkling.

clignoter, *v.i.* (*a*) To blink. (*b*) To twinkle.

climat, *s.m.* Climate.

clin d'œil [klɛ̃dœːj], *s.m.* En un c. d'œil, in the twinkling of an eye.

clinique. (*a*) Nursing-home. (*b*) (Doctor's) surgery.

clinquant, *s.m.* Tinsel.

clique, *s.f.* (Disreputable) set.

cliqueter, *v.i.* To clank; to jingle.

cliquetis, *s.m.* Rattling; chinking; jingling.

cloche, *s.f.* **1.** Bell. **2.** (*a*) Bell-glass, cloche. (*b*) Dish-cover. **3.** Blister.

clocher[1], *s.m.* Belfry; steeple.

clocher[2], *v.i.* To limp, hobble.

clochette, *s.f.* Small bell; hand-bell.

cloison, *s.f.* **1.** Partition, division. **2.** Bulkhead.

cloître, *s.m.* Cloister(s).

clopin-clopant, *adv.* Aller c.-c., to limp along, hobble about.

clopiner, *v.i.* To hobble, limp.

cloporte, *s.m.* Wood-louse.

clos, **1.** *a.* (*a*) Closed; shut up. A la nuit close, after dark. (*b*) Concluded. **2.** *s.m.* Enclosure.

clôture, *s.f.* **1.** Enclosure, fence. **2.** (*a*) Closing. (*b*) Conclusion.

clôturer, *v.tr.* **1.** To enclose. **2.** (*a*) To close down. (*b*) To end.

clou, *s.m.* **1.** (*a*) Nail. (*b*) Star turn. **2.** C. de girofle, clove.

clouer, *v.tr.* **1.** To nail. **2.** Cloué sur place, rooted to the spot.

coagulation, *s.f.* Coagulation.

coaguler (se), *v.pr.* To coagulate, clot; to curdle.

coalition, *s.f.* Coalition, union.

coasser, *v.i.* (Of frog) To croak.

cobalt [-balt], *s.m.* Cobalt.

cobaye, *s.m.* Guinea-pig.

cobra, *s.m.* Cobra.

cocagne, *s.f.* Mât de c., greasy pole.

cocaïne, *s.f.* Cocaine.

cocarde, *s.f.* Cockade, rosette.

coccinelle, *s.f.* Lady-bird.

coche, *s.f.* Notch, nick.

cochenille [-niːj], *s.f.* Cochineal.

cocher, *s.m.* Coachman, driver.

cochon, *s.m.* **1.** Pig, hog. **2.** C. d'Inde, guinea-pig.

coco, *s.m.* **1.** Noix de c., coco-nut. **2.** Liquorice water.

cocon, *s.m.* Cocoon.

cocorico, *s.m.* Cock-a-doodle-doo!

cocotier, *s.m.* Coco-nut palm.

code, *s.m.* **1.** Code. **2.** Statute-book.

codicille, *s.m.* Codicil.

cœur, *s.m.* Heart. **1.** (*a*) En c., heart-shaped. (*b*) Avoir mal au c., to feel sick. Cela soulève le c., it makes one's gorge rise. **2.** Soul, feelings. (*a*) En avoir le c. net, to clear the matter up. (*b*) Apprendre par c., to learn by heart. **3.** Courage, spirit. **4.** (*a*) Travailler de bon c., to work with a will. (*b*) A vous de tout c., yours affectionately. **5.** Middle. midst. **6.** *Cards:* Hearts.

coffre, *s.m.* Chest, bin.

coffre-fort, *s.m.* Safe. *pl. coffres-forts.*

cognac [-nak], *s.m.* Cognac; brandy.

cognée, *s.f.* Axe; hatchet.

cogner, *v.tr.* To knock, thump.

cohérence, *s.f.* Coherence.

cohérent, *a.* Coherent.

cohésion, *s.f.* Cohesion.

cohue, *s.f.* Crowd, mob, throng.

coi, *f.* **coite,** *a.* Quiet.

coiffe, *s.f.* Head-dress, cap.

coiffer, *v.tr.* **1.** (*a*) To cover (the head). (*b*) C. un chapeau, to put on a hat. **2.** C. qn, to dress s.o.'s hair.
se coiffer. 1. To put one's hat on. **2.** To do one's hair.

coiffeur, -euse, *s.* Hairdresser.

coiffure, *s.f.* **1.** Head-dress, head-gear. **2.** Hairdressing.

coin, *s.m.* **1.** (*a*) Corner. (*b*) C. du feu, ingle-nook. Au c. du feu, by the fireside. **2.** Wedge. **3.** Stamp, die.

coincer, v.tr. To wedge, chock (up).
coïncidence, s.f. Coincidence.
coïncident, a. Coincident.
coïncider, v.i. To coincide.
coing, s.m. Quince.
coite. See COI.
col, s.m. 1. Neck (of bottle). 2. Collar. **Faux col,** detachable collar.
3. Pass, col.
coléoptère, s.m. Beetle.
colère. 1. s.f. Anger. 2. a. Angry; irascible.
colérique, a. Choleric, fiery.
colibri, s.m. Humming-bird.
colifichet, s.m. Trinket, bauble.
colimaçon, s.m. Snail. **Escalier en c.,** spiral staircase, winding stairs.
colique, s.f. Colic.
colis, s.m. 1. Parcel package. 2. (Article of) luggage.
collaborateur, -trice, s. Collaborator.
collaboration, s.f. Collaboration.
collaborer, v.i. To collaborate.
collant, a. (a) Sticky. (b) Close-fitting.
collatéral, -aux, a. Collateral.
colle, s.f. Paste; glue; size.
collectif, a. Collective, joint.
collection, s.f. 1. Collecting. 2. Collection.
collectionner, v.tr. To collect.
collectionneur, -euse, s. Collector.
collège, s.m. 1. College. 2. School.
collégien, s. Schoolboy.
collègue, s.m. & f. Colleague.
coller. 1. v.tr. To paste, stick, glue. 2. v.i. To stick, adhere, cling.
collet, s.m. 1. Collar (of coat). 2. Snare, noose.
collier, s.m. 1. Necklace. 2. **C. de chien,** dog-collar.
colline, s.f. Hill.
collision, s.f. Collision.
colloque, s.m. Colloquy.
collusion, s.f. Collusion.
Colomb [kɔlɔ̃]. Pr.n.m. Columbus.
colombe, s.f. Pigeon, dove.
colombier, s.m. Dovecot.
colon, s.m. Colonist, settler.
colonel, s.m. Colonel.
colonial, -aux, a. Colonial.
colonie, s.f. Colony, settlement.
colonisation, s.f. Colonization.
coloniser, v.tr. To colonize.
colonne, s.f. Column.

colophane, s.f. Rosin.
coloration, s.f. 1. Colouring. 2. Colour.
colorer, v.tr. To colour, tint.
colorier, v.tr. To colour.
coloris, s.m. Colour(ing).
colossal, -aux, a. Colossal.
colosse, s.m. Colossus.
colporter, v.tr. (a) To hawk (goods). (b) To spread abroad (news).
colporteur, -euse, s. Pedlar.
combat, s.m. 1. Combat, fight. **Hors de c.,** disabled. 2. Contest.
combattant, s.m. Combatant. **Anciens combattants,** ex-service men.
combattre. 1. v.tr. To combat, to fight (against). 2. v.i. To fight. strive.
combien, adv. 1. (a) How (much)! (b) How many! **C. de gens!** what a lot of people! 2. (a) How much? (b) How many?
combinaison, s.f. 1. (a) Combination; arrangement. (b) Plan, scheme. 2. (Pair of) combinations.
combiner, v.tr. 1. To combine, unite; to arrange. 2. To contrive.
comble[1], s.m. 1. **Ça, c'est le c.!** that beats all! 2. (a) **De fond en c.,** from top to bottom. (b) Highest point; height.
comble[2], a. Packed.
combler, v.tr. 1. To fill. 2. To heap (up). **C. de bienfaits,** to heap kindness on.
combustible, s.m. Fuel.
combustion, s.f. Combustion.
comédie, s.f. Comedy.
comédien, s. Comedian; player.
comestible. 1. a. Edible, eatable. 2. s.m. Article of food.
comète, s.f. Comet.
comique. 1. (a) a. Comic. (b) s.m. Comedian 2. a. Comical, funny.
comiquement, adv. Comically.
comité, s.m. Committee, board.
commandant. 1. a. Commanding. 2. s.m. Commander; major; squadron-leader.
commande, s.f. 1. Order. **Fait sur c.,** made to order. **Payable à la c.,** cash with order. 2. Control.
commandement, s.m. 1. Command, order. 2. Command, authority.
commander. 1. v.tr. (a) To command, order. (b) To be in command

of. (c) To command, dominate.
2. *v.ind.tr.* C. à, to control.

comme[1], *adv.* **1.** (a) As, like.
(b) C'est tout c., it amounts to the
same thing. **2.** *Excl.* How! C. il est
maigre! how thin he is!

comme[2], *conj.* **1.** As; seeing that.
2. (Just) as.

commémoratif, *a.* Commemorative.

commémorer, *v.tr.* To commemorate.

commençant, *s.* Beginner.

commencement, *s.m.* Beginning,
commencement. **Au c.,** at the
outset.

commencer, *v.tr. & i.* To begin,
commence.

comment, *adv.* **1.** How. C. allez-
vous? how are you? C. (dites-
vous)? I beg your pardon? C.
faire? what is to be done? **2.** *Excl.*
What! why! **Mais c. donc!** why,
of course!

commentaire, *s.m.* **1.** Commentary.
2. Comment.

commentateur, -trice, *s.* Commentator, annotator.

commenter, *v.tr & i.* To comment
(up)on.

commérage, *s.m.* Gossip.

commerçant. **1.** *a.* Commercial,
business. **2.** *s.* Merchant, tradesman.

commerce, *s.m.* **1.** Commerce;
trade. **Faire le c. de,** to deal in.
2. Intercourse, dealings.

commercial, -aux, *a.* Commercial;
trading, business.

commère, *s.f.* Gossip.

commettre, *v.tr.* To commit.

commis, *s.m.* **1.** Clerk. **2.** (a) (Shop-)
assistant. (b) C. voyageur, com-
mercial traveller.

commisération, *s.f.* Commiseration, pity.

commissaire, *s.m.* Commissioner;
purser. **C. de police** = police superintendent.

commission, *s.f.* **1.** Commission.
2. Message, errand. **3.** Committee.

commissionnaire, *s.m.* Messenger,
commissionaire.

commode. **1.** *a.* (a) Convenient.
(b) Comfortable (house). (c) Accommodating. **2.** *s.f.* Chest of drawers.

commodément, *adv.* Conveniently,
comfortably.

commodité, *s.f.* Convenience; comfort.

commotion, *s.f.* **1.** Commotion,
disturbance. **2.** Concussion.

commuer, *v.tr.* To commute.

commun. **1.** *a.* (a) Common. (b)
Universal, general. (c) Usual, everyday. (d) Vulgar. **2.** *s.m.* Common run.

communauté, *s.f.* **1.** Community
(of interests). **2.** Society.

commune, *s.f.* Commune.

communément, *adv.* Commonly.

communicant, *a.* Communicating.

communicatif, *a.* Communicative.

communication, *s.f.* Communication. **1.** *Tp:* **Fausse c.,** wrong
number. **2.** Message.

communion, *s.f.* Communion.

communiqué, *s.m.* Official statement.

communiquer, *v.tr. & i.* To communicate.

communisme, *s.m.* Communism.

communiste, *s.m. & f.* Communist.

commutateur, *s.m. El:* Switch.

compact [-pakt], *a.* Compact, dense.

compagne, *s.f.* (Female) companion.

compagnie, *s.f.* **1.** Company. **Fausser c. à qn,** to give s.o. the slip.
Dame de c., (lady) companion.
2. Company; party. **3.** Durand et
C. (usu. Cie), Durand and Co.
4. *Mil:* Company.

compagnon, *s.m.* Companion, comrade.

comparable, *a.* Comparable.

comparaison, *s.f.* Comparison. *Prep.
phr.* En c. de, in comparison with.

comparaître, *v.i. Jur:* To appear.

comparatif, *a. & s.m.* Comparative.

comparativement, *adv.* Comparatively.

comparer, *v.tr.* To compare.

compartiment, *s.m.* Compartment;
partition.

compas, *s.m.* **1.** (Pair of) compasses.
2. C. de mer, mariner's compass.

compassé, *a.* **1.** Stiff, formal.
2. Regular, set.

compassion, *s.f.* Compassion, pity.

compatible, *a.* Compatible.

compatissant, *a.* Compassionate.

compatriote, *s.m. & f.* Compatriot.

compendieux, *a.* Compendious.

compensateur, -trice. **1.** *a.* Com-
pensating. **2.** *s.m.* Compensator.

compensation, s.f. Compensation; set-off.

compenser, v.tr. To compensate; to make up for.

compère, s.m. **1.** Confederate. **2.** Un bon c., a jolly good fellow.

compétemment, adv. Competently.

compétence, s.f. Competence.

compétent, a. Competent.

compilation, s.f. Compilation.

compiler, v.tr. To compile.

complaire, v.ind.tr. **C. à qn,** to please, humour, s.o.
se complaire, to take pleasure (à, in).

complaisamment, adv. **1.** Obligingly. **2.** Complacently.

complaisance, s.f. **1.** Complaisance, obligingness. **2.** Complacency.

complaisant, a. (a) Obliging, complaisant. (b) Complacent.

complément, s.m. Complement.

complet, -ète. 1. a. (a) Complete, entire. (b) Full. **2.** s.m. (a) Suit (of clothes). (b) Adj.phr. **Au c.,** full.

complètement, adv. Completely.

compléter, v.tr. To complete.

complexe. 1. a. Complex; complicated. **2.** s.m. Complex.

complexion, s.f. Constitution, temperament.

complexité, s.f. Complexity.

complication, s.f. Complication.

complice, s. Accomplice.

complicité, s.f. Complicity.

compliment, s.m. **1.** Compliment. **2.** pl. Kind regards, greetings.

complimenter, v.tr. To compliment.

compliqué, a. Complicated, intricate.

compliquer, v.tr. To complicate.

complot, s.m. Plot, conspiracy.

comploter, v.tr. To plot, to scheme.

componction, s.f. Compunction.

comporter, v.tr. **1.** To allow (of). **2.** To call for, require.
se comporter, to behave.

composé. 1. a. (a) Compound. (b) Composed. **2.** s.m. Compound.

composer. 1. v.tr. (a) To compose; to form. (b) Tp: **C. le numéro,** to dial the number. (c) To compose, arrange. **2.** v.i. To compound.
se composer, to consist.

compositeur, -trice, s. Composer.

composition, s.f. **1.** Composition. **2.** Compromise.

compote, s.f. Stewed fruit.

compréhensible, a. Comprehensible.

compréhensif, a. **1.** Comprehensive. **2.** Understanding.

compréhension, s.f. Understanding.

comprendre, v.tr. **1.** To comprise, include. **Y compris,** including. **2.** To understand. **Cela se comprend,** of course.

compression, s.f. Compression.

comprimer, v.tr. To compress.

compromettre, v.tr. & i. To compromise.

comptabilité [kɔ̃t-], s.f. **1.** Bookkeeping. **2.** Counting-house.

comptable [kɔ̃t-], s.m. Accountant, book-keeper.

comptant [kɔ̃t-]. **1.** a. **Argent c.,** ready money. **2.** adv. **Payer c.,** to pay cash.

compte [kɔ̃:t], s.m. Account. (a) Reckoning. **En fin de c.,** all things considered. (b) **Pour mon c.,** for my part. (c) **C. rendu,** report, review. **Se rendre c. de,** to realize.

compter [kɔ̃te]. **1.** v.tr. (a) To count (up), reckon (up). Prep.phr. **A c. de,** (reckoning) from. (b) **C. faire qch.,** to reckon on doing sth. **2.** v.i. (a) **Vous pouvez y c.,** you may depend upon it. (b) To reckon.

compteur [kɔ̃t-], s.m. Meter.

comptoir [kɔ̃t-], s.m. Counter.

compulser, v.tr. To examine, check.

computation, s.f. Computation.

computer, v.tr. To compute.

comte, s.m. Count.

comtesse, s.f. Countess.

concave, a. Concave.

concavité, s.f. Concavity.

concéder, v.tr. **1.** To concede. **2.** To admit.

concentration, s.f. Concentration.

concentrer, v.tr. To concentrate.

conception, s.f. Conception.

concerner, v.tr. To concern, affect.

concert, s.m. Concert.

concerter, v.tr. To concert.

concession, s.f. Concession.

concevable, a. Conceivable.

concevoir, v.tr. To conceive.

concierge, s.m. & f. (House-)porter; caretaker.

conciliant, a. Conciliatory.

conciliation, s.f. Conciliation.

concilier, *v.tr.* To conciliate. reconcile.

concis, *a.* Concise, terse.

concision, *s.f.* Conciseness, brevity.

concitoyen, *s.* Fellow-citizen.

concluant, *a.* Conclusive, decisive.

conclure, *v.tr.* To conclude.

conclusif, *a.* Conclusive.

conclusion, *s.f.* Conclusion.

concombre, *s.m.* Cucumber.

concordance, *s.f.* Concord, agreement.

concorde, *s.f.* Concord, harmony

concorder, *v.i.* To agree, tally.

concourir, *v.i.* **1.** To combine unite. **2.** To compete.

concours, *s.m.* **1.** Concourse. **2.** Co-operation. **3.** Competition. **Hors c.,** not competing.

concret, -ète, *a.* Concrete, solid.

concurremment, *adv.* **1.** Concurrently, jointly. **2.** Competitively.

concurrence, *s.f.* **1.** Concurrence. **2.** Competition, rivalry.

concurrent. 1. *a.* (*a*) Co-operative. (*b*) Competitive. **2.** *s.* Competitor.

condamnation [-dɑn-], *s.f.* Condemnation. **1.** Conviction, sentence. **2.** Reproof.

condamné [-dɑne], *s.* Condemned person.

condamner [-dɑn-], *v.tr.* To condemn. **1.** (*a*) To sentence. **Le médecin l'a condamné,** the doctor has given him up. (*b*) **C. une porte,** to block up a door. **2.** To censure.

condensation, *s.f.* Condensation.

condenser, *v.tr.* To condense.

condescendance, *s.f.* Condescension.

condescendre, *v.i.* To condescend.

condiment, *s.m.* Condiment, seasoning.

condisciple, *s.m.* Fellow-student.

condition, *s.f.* **1.** (*a*) State. (*b*) *pl.* Conditions, circumstances. (*c*) Rank, station. **2.** Condition, stipulation. **A c.,** on approval. **A c. de,** provided that.

conditionnel, *a.* Conditional.

condoléance, *s.f.* Condolence.

conducteur, -trice. 1. *s.* (*a*) Leader, guide. (*b*) Driver. **2.** *a.* Conducting. **3.** *s.m.* Conductor (of heat).

conduire, *v.tr.* **1.** To conduct; to lead. **2.** To drive. **3.** To convey. **4.** To conduct, manage.

   se conduire, to behave.

conduit. *s.m* Passage, conduit, pipe.

conduite, *s.f.* **1.** (*a*) Conducting, leading. (*b*) Driving. **2.** Direction (of affairs). **3.** Conduct, behaviour.

cône, *s.m.* Cone.

confection, *s.f.* **1.** Making; manufacture. **2.** Ready-made clothes.

confectionner, *v.tr.* To make (up); to construct. **Confectionné,** ready-to-wear.

confédération, *s.f.* (Con)federation.

confédéré, *a.* Confederate.

conférence, *s.f.* **1.** Conference. discussion. **2.** Lecture.

conférencier, *s.m.* Lecturer.

conférer, *v.tr. & i.* To confer.

confesse, *s.f.* Confession.

confesser, *v.tr.* **1.** To confess, own. **2.** (Of priest) To confess.

confesseur, *s.m.* Confessor.

confession, *s.f.* Confession.

confiance, *s.f.* **1.** Confidence, trust. **2.** Confidence, sense of security.

confiant, *a.* **1.** Confiding, trustful. **2.** Confident. **3.** Self-confident

confidence, *s.f.* Confidence.

confident, *s.* Confidant, *f.* confidante.

confidentiel, *a.* Confidential.

confidentiellement, *adv.* Confidentially.

confier, *v.tr* **1.** To trust, entrust. **2.** To confide, disclose.

   se confier, to confide (*à*, in).

configuration, *s.f.* Configuration; lie (of the land).

confiner. 1. *v.i.* **C. a,** to border upon. **2.** *v.tr.* To confine, imprison.

confins, *s.m.pl.* Confines.

confire, *v.tr.* To preserve (fruit).

confirmatif, *a.* Confirmative.

confirmation, *s.f.* Confirmation.

confirmer, *v.tr.* To confirm.

confiscation, *s.f.* Confiscation.

confiserie, *s.f.* (*a*) Confectioner's shop. (*b*) Confectionery, preserves.

confiseur, -euse, *s.* Confectioner.

confisquer, *v.tr.* To confiscate.

confiture, *s.f.* Preserve, jam.

conflagration, *s.f.* Conflagration.

conflit, *s.m.* Conflict; clash.

confluent, *s.m.* Confluence.

confondre, *v.tr.* To confound. **1.** (*a*) To mingle. (*b*) To mistake, confuse. **2.** To discomfit.

   se confondre. 1. To intermingle.

2. Se c. en excuses, to apologize profusely.

confondu, *a.* **1.** Disconcerted. **2.** Dumbfounded (*de,* at).

conformation, *s.f.* Conformation.

conforme, *a.* Conformable; consistent (*à,* with).

conformément, *adv.* Conformably (*à,* to); in conformity (*à,* with).

conformer, *v.tr.* (*a*) To form, shape. (*b*) To conform.
  se conformer, to conform.

conformité, *s.f.* Conformity.

confort, *s.m.* Comfort(s).

confortable, *a.* Comfortable, snug.

confortablement, *adv.* Comfortably, snugly.

confraternité, *s.f.* Confraternity.

confrère, *s.m.* Colleague, fellow-member.

confrérie, *s.f.* Confraternity.

confronter, *v.tr.* To confront.

confus, *a.* **1.** Confused; indistinct. **2.** Confused, abashed.

confusément, *adv.* Confusedly.

confusion, *s.f.* Confusion. **1.** (*a*) Disorder. (*b*) Mistake. **2.** Embarrassment.

congé, *s.m.* **1.** Leave. **2.** Dismissal.

congédier, *v.tr.* To dismiss, discharge.

congeler, *v.tr.* To freeze. **Viande congelée,** frozen meat.

congestionné, *a.* Flushed, red (face).

congre, *s.m.* Conger-eel.

congrégation, *s.f.* Congregation.

congrès, *s.m.* Congress.

conifère. 1. *a.* Coniferous. **2.** *s.m.pl.* Conifers.

conique, *a.* Cone-shaped, conical.

conjectural, -aux, *a.* Conjectural.

conjecture, *s.f.* Conjecture, surmise.

conjecturer, *v.tr.* To conjecture.

conjoint, *a.* United, joint.

conjointement, *adv.* (Con)jointly.

conjonction, *s.f.* **1.** Union, connection. **2.** *Gram:* Conjunction.

conjoncture, *s.f.* Conjuncture.

conjugaison, *s.f.* Conjugation.

conjugal, -aux, *a.* Conjugal. **Vie conjugale,** married life.

conjuration, *s.f.* Conspiracy, plot.

conjuré, *s.* Conspirator.

conjurer, *v.tr. & i.* **1.** To plot. **2.** To ward off.

connaissance, *s.f.* **1.** Acquaintance. **2.** Knowledge; understanding. **3.** Consciousness.

connaisseur, -euse, *s.* Expert, connoisseur, judge.

connaître, *v.tr.* To know. **1.** To be acquainted with. **Connu!** that's an old story! **2.** To be versed in.
  se connaître. 1. Se c. à, en, qch., to know all about sth. **2. Il ne se connaît plus de joie,** he is beside himself with joy.

connexion, *s.f.* Connection.

connivence, *s.f.* Connivance.

conque, *s.f.* Conch; marine shell.

conquérant, *a.* Conquering.

conquérir, *v.tr.* (*a*) To conquer. (*b*) To win (over).

conquête, *s.f.* Conquest.

consacré, *a.* **1.** Consecrated; hallowed. **2.** Established.

consacrer, *v.tr.* (*a*) To consecrate; to devote. **2.** To sanctify.

consciemment, *adv.* Consciously.

conscience, *s.f.* **1.** Consciousness. **2.** (*a*) Conscience. (*b*) Conscientiousness.

consciencieusement, *adv.* Conscientiously.

consciencieux, *a.* Conscientious.

conscription, *s.f.* Conscription.

conscrit, *s.m.* Conscript.

consécration, *s.f.* Consecration.

consécutif, *a.* Consecutive.

consécutivement, *adv.* Consecutively.

conseil [-sɛːj], *s.m.* **1.** Counsel; (piece of) advice. **2.** Counsellor, counsel. **3.** Council, committee. **C. de guerre,** court-martial.

conseiller[1] [-sɛj-], *v.tr.* To advise.

conseiller[2], *s.* **1.** Adviser. **2.** Councillor.

consentement, *s.m.* Consent, assent.

consentir, *v.i.* To consent, agree.

conséquemment, *adv.* Consequently.

conséquence, *s.f.* (*a*) Consequence, result. **En c.,** accordingly. (*b*) Inference. (*c*) Importance, consequence.

conséquent. 1. *a.* (*a*) Consistent. (*b*) Following. **2.** *Adv.phr.* **Par c.,** consequently, accordingly.

conservateur, -trice. 1. *s.* Conservator, keeper. **2.** *a.* Preserving.

conservation, *s.f.* (*a*) Preserving. (*b*) Preservation; self-preservation.

conservatoire, *s.m.* School, academy.

conserve, *s.f.* Preserve; preserved food. **Conserves au vinaigre,** pickles.

conserver, *v.tr.* **1.** To preserve. **2.** To keep, retain.

considérable, *a.* Considerable.

considération, *s.f.* Consideration; regard. **Agréez l'assurance de ma haute c.,** I am yours very truly.

considéré, *a.* Esteemed.

considérer, *v.tr.* To consider.

consignation, *s.f.* Consignment.

consigne, *s.f.* **1.** Order(s). **2.** Cloak-room; left-luggage office.

consigner, *v.tr.* To consign.

consistance, *s.f.* (*a*) Consistency. (*b*) Stability.

consistant, *a.* Firm.

consister, *v.i.* To consist (*en*, of).

consolateur, -trice. **1.** *s.* Comforter. **2.** *a.* Consoling, comforting.

consolation, *s.f.* Consolation, solace.

consoler, *v.tr.* To console, comfort.

consolidation, *s.f.* Consolidation, strengthening.

consolider, *v.tr.* To consolidate, strengthen.

se consolider, to grow firm.

consommateur, -trice, *s.* (*a*) Consumer. (*b*) Customer (in café).

consommation, *s.f.* **1.** Consummation. **2.** Consumption. **3.** Drink.

consommé, **1.** *a.* Consummate. **2.** *s.m.* Beef-tea; clear soup.

consommer, *v.tr.* **1.** To consummate. **2.** To consume.

consomption, *s.f.* Consumption.

consonant, *a.* Consonant.

consonne, *s.f.* Consonant.

conspirateur, -trice, *s.* Conspirator.

conspiration, *s.f.* Conspiracy, plot.

conspirer, *v.i.* To conspire.

conspuer, *v.tr.* To boo, hoot.

constamment, *adv.* **1.** Steadfastly. **2.** Continually.

constance, *s.f.* Constancy.

constant, *a.* **1.** (*a*) Steadfast. (*b*) Unshaken. **3.** Constant, uniform.

constatation, *s.f.* Verification.

constater, *v.tr.* **1.** To establish; to find out. **2.** To state.

constellation, *s.f.* Constellation.

consternation, *s.f.* Consternation, dismay.

consterner, *v.tr.* To dismay.

constituant, *a.* Constituent.

constituer, *v.tr.* To constitute. (*a*) To form. (*b*) To set up.

constitution, *s.f.* **1.** Establishing. **2.** Constitution. **3.** Composition.

constitutionnel, *a.* Constitutional.

constructeur, *s.m.* Constructor.

constructif, *a.* Constructive.

construction, *s.f.* Construction.

construire, *v.tr.* To construct; to build; to make.

consul, *s.m.* Consul.

consulaire, *a.* Consular.

consulat, *s.m.* Consulate.

consultatif, *a.* Advisory.

consultation, *s.f.* Consultation.

consulter, *v.tr.* To consult.

consumer, *v.tr.* To consume.

se consumer, to waste away.

contact [-takt], *s.m.* **1.** Contact, touch. **2.** *El:* Connection. **Établir le c.,** to switch on.

contagieux, *a.* Contagious, infectious.

contagion, *s.f.* Contagion.

contamination, *s.f.* Contamination.

contaminer, *v.tr.* To contaminate.

conte, *s.m.* **1.** Story, tale. **2.** Yarn.

contemplation, *s.f.* Contemplation.

contempler, *v.tr.* To contemplate.

contemporain, *a. & s.* Contemporary.

contenance, *s.f.* **1.** Capacity. **2.** Countenance. **Faire bonne c.,** to put a good face on it.

contenir, *v.tr.* **1.** To contain. **2.** To restrain; to control.

se contenir, to keep one's temper.

content, *a.* (*a*) Content. (*b*) Pleased (*de*, with). (*c*) Glad.

contentement, *s.m.* (*a*) Contentment. (*b*) Satisfaction (*de*, at, with).

contenter, *v.tr.* To content, satisfy. **se contenter,** to be satisfied.

contentieux, *a.* Contentious.

contenu. **1.** *a.* Restrained; pent-up. **2.** *s.m.* Contents.

conter, *v.tr.* To tell, relate.

contestable, *a.* Debatable.

contestation, *s.f.* Dispute.

conteste, *s.f.* **Sans c.,** indisputably.

contester, **1.** *v.tr.* To contest, dispute. **2.** *v.i.* To dispute.

conteur, -euse, *s.* **1.** Narrator, teller. **2.** Story-teller.

contexte, *s.m.* Context.

contigu, -uë, *a.* Contiguous, adjoining.

contiguïté, *s.f.* Contiguity.

continence, *s.f.* Continence.

continent[1], *a.* Continent, chaste.

continent[2], *s.m.* 1. Continent. 2. Mainland.

contingent. 1. *a.* Contingent. 2. *s.m.* (*a*) Contingent. (*b*) Quota.

continu, *a.* Continuous, unceasing.

continuation, *s.f.* Continuation.

continuel, *a.* Continual, unceasing.

continuellement, *adv.* Continually.

continuer, *v.tr. & i.* To continue. Continuez! go on !

continuité, *s.f.* Continuity.

contorsion, *s.f.* Contortion.

contour, *s.m.* 1. Outline. 2. Contour.

contourner, *v.tr.* 1. To shape. 2. To pass round. 3. To distort.

contracter[1], *v.tr.* (*a*) To contract. (*b*) To incur.

contracter[2], *v.tr.* To contract. **se contracter,** to contract; to shrink.

contraction, *s.f.* Contraction; shrinking.

contradiction, *s.f.* 1. Contradiction. 2. Inconsistency; discrepancy.

contradictoire, *a.* Contradictory; conflicting.

contraindre, *v.tr.* To constrain. 1. To restrain. 2. To compel.

contraint, *a.* Constrained; forced.

contrainte, *s.f.* Constraint. 1. Restraint. 2. Compulsion.

contraire, *a.* 1. (*a*) Contrary; opposite. Jusqu'à avis c., until further notice. (*b*) *s.m.* Au c., on the contrary. 2. Adverse. *s.m.* Aller au c. de qn, to run counter to s.o.

contrariant, *a.* Provoking; annoying.

contrarié, *a.* 1. Thwarted. 2. Vexed.

contrarier, *v.tr.* 1. To thwart, oppose. 2. To vex, annoy.

contrariété, *s.f.* Vexation, annoyance.

contraste, *s.m.* Contrast; set-off.

contraster, *v.i. & tr.* To contrast.

contrat, *s.m.* Contract, agreement.

contravention, *s.f.* Minor offence; breach.

contre. 1. *prep.* Against. (*a*) Contrary to. (*b*) S'abriter c. la pluie, to shelter from the rain. (*c*) (In exchange) for. (*d*) To. Cinq c. un,

five to one. (*e*) Close to, by. 2. *adv.* Against. 3. *s.m.* Par c., on the other hand.

contre-amiral, *s.m.* Rear-admiral. *pl. contre-amiraux.*

contre-attaque, *s.f.* Counter-attack. *pl. contre-attaques.*

contre-attaquer, *v.tr.* To counter-attack.

contrebande, *s.f.* 1. Contraband, smuggling. 2. Contraband goods.

contrebandier, *s.m.* Smuggler.

contrecarrer, *v.tr.* To cross, thwart.

contre-cœur (à), *adv. phr.* Unwillingly, reluctantly, grudgingly.

contre-coup, *s.m.* (*a*) Rebound. (*b*) After-effects. *pl. contre-coups.*

contredire, *v.tr.* To contradict.

contredit. *Adv.phr.* Sans c., assuredly, unquestionably.

contrée, *s.f.* Region ; country.

contrefaçon, *s.f.* Counterfeit, forgery.

contrefaire, *v.tr.* 1. (*a*) To imitate. (*b*) To feign. 2. To counterfeit.

contrefait, *a.* 1. Feigned. 2. Counterfeit.

contrefort, *s.m.* Spur (of mountain); *pl.* foot-hills.

contremaître, -tresse, *s.* Foreman. forewoman ; overseer.

contremander, *v.tr.* To countermand, cancel, revoke.

contre-partie, *s.f.* Counterpart. *pl. contre-parties.*

contrepoids, *s.m.* Counterpoise.

contre-poison, *s.m.* Antidote. *pl. contre-poisons.*

contrer, *v.i.* Cards : To double.

contre-sens, *s.m.inv.* 1. Misinterpretation. 2. A c.-s., in the wrong way.

contresigner, *v.tr.* To countersign.

contretemps, *s.m.* (*a*) Mishap, hitch. (*b*) Delay, inconvenience.

contre-torpilleur, *s.m.* Destroyer. *pl. contre-torpilleurs.*

contrevenir, *v.ind.tr.* To contravene.

contrevent, *s.m.* Outside shutter.

contribuable, *s.m. & f.* Taxpayer.

contribuer, *v.i.* To contribute.

contribution, *s.f.* 1. Tax or rate. 2. Contribution, share.

contrister, *v.tr.* To sadden, grieve.

contrit, *a.* Contrite, penitent.

contrôle, *s.m.* 1. Roll ; list. 2. Testing. 3. Inspection.

contrôler, *v.tr.* **1.** To inspect; to check. **2.** To hold in check.

contrôleur, -euse, *s.* Inspector examiner; ticket-collector.

controverse, *s.f.* Controversy.

contusion, *s.f.* Contusion, bruise

contusionner, *v.tr.* To bruise.

convaincant, *a.* Convincing.

convaincre, *v.tr* **1.** To convince. **2.** To convict.

convalescence, *s.f.* Convalescence.

convalescent, *a. & s.* Convalescent.

convenable, *a.* **1.** Suitable; proper. **2.** Decent; seemly.

convenablement, *adv.* **1.** Suitably. **2.** Decorously.

convenance, *s.f.* **1.** Suitability, fitness. **2.** Propriety.

convenir, *v.i.* **1.** *(a)* To suit, fit. *(b)* Il convient de, it is advisable to. **2.** *(a)* To agree. **C. de qch.,** to agree about sth. **Il fut convenu,** it was agreed. *(b)* **C. de qch.,** to admit sth.

convention, *s.f.* **1.** Convention. **2.** Covenant.

conventionnel, *a.* Conventional.

convenu, *a.* Agreed.

converger, *v.i.* To converge.

conversation, *s.f.* Conversation, talk.

converser, *v.i.* To converse, talk.

conversion, *s.f.* Conversion.

converti, *s.* Convert.

convertir, *v.tr.* To convert.

    se convertir, to become converted.

convexe, *a.* Convex.

conviction, *s.f.* **1.** Conviction; firm belief. **2.** *Jur:* **Pièce à c.,** exhibit.

convié, *s.* Guest.

convier, *v.tr.* To invite.

convive, *s.m. & f.* *(a)* Guest (at table). *(b)* Table-companion.

convocation, *s.f.* Convocation. summons.

convoi, *s.m.* Convoy.

convoiter, *v.tr.* To covet, desire.

convoitise, *s.f.* Covetousness.

convoquer, *v.tr.* To summon.

convoyer, *v.tr.* To convoy.

convulser, *v.tr.* To convulse.

convulsif, *a.* Convulsive.

convulsion, *s.f.* Convulsion.

convulsionner, *v.tr.* To convulse.

convulsivement, *adv.* Convulsively.

coopératif, *a.* Co-operative.

coopération, *s.f.* Co-operation.

coopérer, *v.i.* To co-operate.

coordonner, *v.tr.* To co-ordinate.

copain, *s.m.* Chum, pal.

copeau, *s.m.* Shaving; chip.

copie, *s.f.* Copy.

copier, *v.tr.* To copy.

copieusement, *adv.* Copiously.

copieux, *a.* Copious.

copiste, *s.m. & f.* Copier. **Faute de c.,** clerical error.

coq [kɔk], *s.m.* *(a)* Cock **Jeune coq,** cockerel. **Coq du village,** cock of the walk. *(b)* Cock, male (of birds). **Coq de bruyère,** grouse.

coq-à-l'âne, *s.m. inv.* Cock-and-bull story.

coque, *s.f.* **1.** *(a)* Shell (of egg). **Un œuf à la c.,** a boiled egg. *(b)* Shell, husk (of nut). **2.** Hull (of ship)

coquelicot, *s.m.* Red poppy.

coqueluche, *s.f* Whooping cough.

coquet, -ette. **1.** *a.* *(a)* Coquettish. *(b)* Smart, dainty. **2.** *s.f.* Flirt.

coqueter, *v.i.* To flirt.

coquetier, *s.m.* Egg-cup.

coquettement, *adv.* Smartly.

coquetterie, *s.f.* Coquetry.

coquillage [-kij-], *s.m.* **1.** Shell-fish. **2.** (Empty) shell (of shell-fish)

coquille [-ki:j], *s.f.* Shell.

coquin, *s.* Rogue, rascal; *f.* hussy.

cor, *s.m.* **1.** Horn. **Cor de chasse,** hunting-horn. **2.** Corn (on the toe).

corail [-rɑ:j], **-aux,** *s.m.* Coral.

corbeau, *s.m.* **1.** Crow; raven. **2.** *Arch:* Corbel, bracket.

corbeille [-bɛ:j], *s.f.* (Open) basket.

corbillard [-bij-], *s.m.* Hearse.

cordage, *s.m.* *(a)* Rope. *(b)* *pl.* Cordage.

corde, *s.f.* **1.** *(a)* Rope, cord, line. **C. à linge,** clothes-line. *(b)* **Usé jusqu'à la c.,** threadbare. **2.** Chord. **3.** Cordes vocales, vocal cords.

cordeau, *s.m.* **1.** Tiré au c., perfectly straight. **2.** Fuse.

cordial, -aux. **1.** *s.m.* Cordial. **2.** *a.* Cordial, hearty.

cordialement, *adv.* Cordially.

cordialité, *s.f.* Cordiality.

cordon, *s.m.* **1.** *(a)* Cord. **C. de la porte,** door-pull. *(b)* Ribbon (of an order). **2.** Cordon (of police).

cordonnier, *s.m.* Shoemaker.

coriace, *a.* Tough.

Corinthe. *Pr.n.f.* Corinth. **Raisins de C.,** currants.

corne, *s.f.* **1.** Horn. **2.** Dog's-ear of a book.

corneille [-nɛ:j], *s.f.* Crow, rook.

cornemuse, *s.f.* Bagpipes.

corner, *v.tr.* (*a*) To trumpet. (*b*) *Abs.* To sound the horn; to hoot.

cornet, *s.m.* **1.** C. à pistons, cornet. **2.** (*a*) C. acoustique, ear-trumpet. (*b*) C. à dés, dice-box.

corniche, *s.f.* **1.** Cornice. **2.** Ledge.

cornichon, *s.m.* Gherkin.

Cornouailles [-nwɑ:j]. *Pr.n.f.* Cornwall.

cornu, *a.* Horned.

cornue, *s.f. Ch:* Retort.

corollaire, *s.m.* Corollary.

corolle, *s.f.* Corolla.

corporation, *s.f.* Corporation.

corporel, *a.* Corporeal; corporal.

corps [kɔ:r], *s.m.* **1.** Body. **Gardes du c.,** the life-guards. **Saisir qn à bras le c.,** to grapple with s.o. **2.** Corpse. **3.** C. célestes, heavenly bodies. **4.** Main part (of sth.). *Nau:* **Perdu c. et biens,** lost with all hands. **5.** Corps.

corps-de-garde, *s.m.inv.* Guardroom.

corps-mort, *s.m.* Moorings.

corpulence, *s.f.* Stoutness.

corpulent, *a.* Stout, fat, corpulent.

corpuscle, *s.m.* Corpuscle.

correct [-ɛkt], *a.* Correct; accurate.

correctement, *adv.* Correctly, accurately.

correction, *s.f.* **1.** Correction **2.** Reproof. **3.** Correctness.

correspondance, *s.f.* **1.** Agreement. **2.** *Rail:* Connection. **3.** (*a*) Intercourse. (*b*) Correspondence.

correspondant. **1.** *a.* Corresponding. **2.** *s.* Correspondent.

correspondre, *v.i.* **1.** To tally, agree (*à*, with). **2.** To correspond.

corridor, *s.m.* Corridor, passage.

corriger, *v.tr.* **1.** To correct. **2.** To chastise.

corroboration, *s.f.* Corroboration.

corroborer, *v.tr.* To corroborate.

corroder, *v.tr.* To corrode.

corrompre, *v.tr.* To corrupt; to deprave.

corrompu, *a.* (*a*) Corrupt, depraved. (*b*) Tainted, putrid.

corrosif, *a. & s.m.* Corrosive.

corrosion, *s.f.* Corrosion.

corrupteur, -trice. **1.** *s.* Corrupter. **2.** *a.* Corrupt (influence).

corruptible, *a.* Corruptible

corruption, *s.f.* Corruption.

corsage, *s.m.* Bodice.

corsaire, *a. & s.m.* Privateer.

corse[1], *a. & s.* Corsican.

Corse[2] **(la).** *Pr.n.* Corsica.

corset, *s.m.* Corset.

cortège, *s.m.* **1.** Train, retinue. **2.** Procession. **C. funèbre,** funeral.

corvée, *s.f.* Irksome task.

cosaque, *s.m.* Cossack.

cosmétique, *a. & s.m.* Cosmetic.

cosmopolite, *a.* Cosmopolitan.

cosse, *s.f.* Pod, husk, hull.

cossu, *a.* Well-to-do (person).

costume, *s.m.* Costume, dress.

costumé, *a.* Fancy-dress (ball).

cote, *s.f.* **1.** Quota. **2.** Quotation.

côte, *s.f.* **1.** Rib. C. à c., side by side. **2.** (*a*) Slope (of hill). (*b*) Hill. **3.** Coast, shore.

côté, *s.m.* **1.** Side. **A mes côtés,** by my side. **D'un côté,** on the one hand. **De tous (les) côtés,** on all sides. **2.** *Adv.phr.* (*a*) **De c.,** on one side; sideways. (*b*) **A c. de,** by the side of; next to.

coteau, *s.m.* Hill.

côtelette, *s.f.* Cutlet; chop.

coterie, *s.f.* Set, clique.

coton, *s.m.* Cotton. **Fil de c.,** sewing cotton.

cotonnier, *s.m.* Cotton plant.

coton-poudre, *s.m.* Gun-cotton.

côtoyer, *v.tr.* To keep close to; to skirt.

cou, *s.m.* Neck. **La peau du cou,** the scruff of the neck.

couchant. **1.** *a.* Soleil c., setting sun. **2.** *s.m.* (*a*) Sunset. (*b*) **Le c.,** the west.

couche, *s.f.* (*a*) Bed, layer. (*b*) Coat (of paint).

coucher. **I.** *v.* **1.** *v.tr.* To put to bed. **2.** *v.i* **C. à l'hôtel,** to sleep at the hotel.

se coucher. (*a*) To go to bed. (*b*) To lie down. (*c*) (Of sun) To set. **II. coucher,** *s.m.* **1.** L'heure du **c.,** bedtime. **2.** Setting (of sun).

couchette, *s.f.* Berth (on train).

coucou, *s.m.* **1.** (*a*) Cuckoo. (*b*) Cuckoo-clock. **2.** Cowslip.

coude, *s.m.* **1.** Elbow. **Coup de c.,** nudge. **2.** Bend, elbow.

cou-de-pied, *s.m.* Instep. *pl. cous-de-pied.*

coudoiement, *s.m.* Elbowing.

coudoyer, *v.tr.* To elbow.

coudre, *v.tr.* To sew, stitch.

coudrier, *s.m.* Hazel(-tree).

coulant, *a.* Running, flowing (liquid). **Nœud c.,** slip-knot; noose.

couler. 1. *v.tr.* (*a*) To pour. (*b*) To sink. **2.** *v.i.* (*a*) To flow, run. (*b*) **C. bas,** to founder.

se couler, to glide, slip.

couleur, *s.f.* **1.** (*a*) Colour, tint. (*b*) Complexion. (*c*) *pl.* Colours, flag. **2.** Paint. **"Attention à la c.!"** 'wet paint.' **3.** *Cards :* Suit.

couleuvre, *s.f.* Snake.

coulisse, *s.f.* **1.** Groove. **2.** *Th :* **Les coulisses,** the wings.

couloir, *s.m.* Corridor.

coup, *s.m.* **1.** (*a*) Knock, blow. **C. de couteau,** stab. (*b*) **C. de feu,** shot. (*c*) **C. de vent,** gust of wind. **2.** Stroke (normal action of sth.). (*a*) **Sur le c. de midi,** on the stroke of twelve. (*b*) **C. d'envoi,** kick-off. (*c*) **C. de bonheur,** stroke of luck. (*d*) Clap, peal. **3.** Influence. **Agir sous le c. de la peur,** to act out of fear. **4.** (*a*) Deed. **C. de tête,** impulsive act. (*b*) **Tout d'un c.,** at one go. **Tout à c.,** suddenly. **C. sur c.,** in rapid succession.

coupable. 1. *a.* Guilty. **2.** *s.m. & f.* Culprit.

coupant. 1. *a.* Cutting, sharp. **2.** *s.m.* Edge.

coupe¹, *s.f.* Cup.

coupe², *s.f.* **1.** (*a*) Cutting. (*b*) Cut (of a coat). **2.** *Cards :* Cut, cutting.

coupé. 1. *a.* Cut up ; broken (sleep). **2.** *s.m.* Brougham ; coupé.

coupe-gorge, *s.m.inv.* Death-trap.

coupe-papier, *s.m.inv.* Paper-knife.

couper, *v.tr.* To cut. **1. Se c. au doigt,** to cut one's finger. **C. la tête à qn,** to cut off s.o.'s head. **2.** *v.i.* **C. au plus court,** to take a short cut. **3.** (*a*) To cut off ; interrupt. (*b*) *Cards :* To trump.

couperosé, *a.* Blotchy (complexion).

couple. 1. *s.m.* Pair, couple. **2.** *s.f.* Two, couple.

coupler, *v.tr.* To couple.

couplet, *s.m.* Verse (of song).

coupole, *s.f.* Cupola.

coupon, *s.m.* **1.** Cutting ; remnant. **2.** Coupon.

coupure, *s.f.* **1.** Cut. **2.** Piece cut out.

cour, *s.f.* **1.** Court. (*a*) **A la c.,** at court. (*b*) **Faire la c.,** to pay court. **2.** Court, yard.

courage, *s.m.* Courage, valour.

courageusement, *adv* Courageously.

courageux, *a.* Courageous, brave.

couramment, *adv.* **1.** Easily ; fluently. **2.** Currently.

courant. 1. *a.* (*a*) Running. (*b*) Flowing. (*c*) **Le cinq c.,** the fifth inst. **2.** *s.m.* (*a*) Current, stream. **C. d'air,** draught. (*b*) Course. **Être au c. de,** to know all about.

courbature, *s.f.* Stiffness, tiredness.

courbe. 1. *a.* Curved. **2.** *s.f.* Curve.

courber. 1. *v.tr.* To bend, curve. **2.** *v.i.* To bend ; to sag.

se courber, to bend, stoop.

coureur, -euse, *s.* **1.** Runner. **2.** (*a*) Wanderer, rover. (*b*) Gadabout. (*c*) **C. de dots,** fortune-hunter.

courge, *s.f.* Gourd ; vegetable marrow.

courir. 1. *v.i.* To run. (*a*) **J'y cours,** I'm going directly. (*b*) To race. (*c*) To be current. **Par le temps qui court,** nowadays. **2.** *v.tr.* **C. un risque,** to run a risk.

courlis, *s.m.* Curlew.

couronne, *s.f.* **1.** Wreath. **2.** Crown ; coronet.

couronnement, *s.m.* Coronation.

couronner, *v.tr.* To crown.

courrier, *s.m.* **1.** Courier ; messenger. **2.** Mail, post. **Par retour du c.,** by return of post.

courroie, *s.f.* Strap.

cours, *s.m.* **1.** Course ; flow. **C. d'eau,** stream. **Au c. de,** during. **2.** Circulation, currency. **3.** **C. du change,** rate of exchange. **4.** Course (of lectures).

course, *s.f.* **1.** Race. **2.** (*a*) Excursion. (*b*) Journey. (*c*) (Business) errand. **3.** Path, course.

court. 1. *a.* Short. **A c.,** hard up. **2.** *adv.* Short. **Tout c.,** simply.

courtepointe, *s.f.* Counterpane.

courtier, *s.m.* Broker.

courtisan, s.m. Courtier.

courtiser, v.tr. To court.

courtois, a. Courteous; polite.

courtoisement, adv. Courteously.

courtoisie, s.f. Courtesy.

couru, a. Popular; sought after.

cousin[1], s. Cousin.

cousin[2], s.m. Gnat, midge.

coussin, s.m. Cushion.

coussinet, s.m. Pad.

coût, s.m. Cost.

couteau, s.m. Knife.

coutelas, s.m. Cutlass.

coutelier, s.m. Cutler.

coutellerie, s.f. Cutlery.

coûter, v.i. To cost. **Coûte que coûte,** at all costs.

coûteux, a. Costly, expensive.

coutil, s.m. Drill, twill.

coutume, s.f. Custom, habit. **Comme de c.,** as usual.

coutumier, a. Customary **Droit c.,** common law.

couture, s.f. **1.** Sewing, needlework. **2.** Seam (in dress).

couturier, s. (a) Dressmaker. (b) s.f. Couturière, seamstress.

couvée, s.f. Brood.

couvent, s.m. (a) Convent, nunnery. (b) Monastery.

couver. 1. v.tr. (a) To sit on (eggs). (b) C. le feu, to brood over the fire. **C. des yeux,** to look fondly at. **2.** v.i. To smoulder.

couvercle, s.m. Lid, cover.

couvert[1], a. **1.** Covered; overcast. **2.** Rester c., to keep one's hat on.

couvert[2], s.m. **1.** Cover(ing), shelter. **2.** Cover, place (at table). **Mettre le c.,** to lay the table.

couverture, s.f. **1.** Covering, cover; blanket. **2.** Roofing.

couvre-feu, s.m.inv. Curfew.

couvre-lit, s.m. Bedspread, counterpane. pl. couvre-lits.

couvre-pied(s), s.m. Coverlet; quilt. pl. couvre-pieds.

couvrir, v.tr. **1.** To cover (de, with). **2.** C. une maison, to roof a house. **se couvrir. 1.** To put on one's hat. **2.** To become overcast.

crabe, s.m. Crab.

crachat, s.m. Spittle, spit.

cracher. 1. v.i. To spit. **2.** v.tr. **C. des injures,** to hurl abuse.

crachin, s.m. Mizzle, fine drizzle.

Cracovie. Pr.n.f. Cracow.

craie, s.f. Chalk.

craindre, v.tr. To fear dread. Il **est à c.,** it is to be feared.

crainte, s.f. Fear, dread; awe.

craintif, a. Timid, timorous.

craintivement, adv. Timidly.

cramoisi, a. & s.m. Crimson.

crampe, s.f. Cramp.

cramponner (se), v.pr. To hold on; to cling.

cran, s.m. **1.** Notch; cog. **2.** Pluck.

crâne. 1. s.m. Skull. **2.** a. (a) Plucky. (b) Jaunty.

crânement, adv. (a) Pluckily. (b) Jauntily.

crapaud, s.m. Toad.

crapuleux, a. Debauched, dissolute.

craquer, v.i. To crack; to crunch; to creak.

crasse. 1. a.f. Gross, crass. **2.** s.f. Dirt.

cratère, s.m. Crater.

cravache, s.f. Riding-whip.

cravate, s.f. (Neck-)tie; scarf.

crayeux, a. Chalky.

crayon, s.m. Pencil. **C. pastel,** crayon.

créance, s.f. Belief, credit.

créancier, s. Creditor.

créateur, -trice. 1. a. Creative. **2.** s. Creator.

création, s.f. Creation, creating.

créature, s.f. Creature.

crécelle, s.f. (Hand-)rattle.

crèche, s.f. **1.** Manger, crib. **2.** Day-nursery, crèche.

crédibilité, s.f. Credibility.

crédit[1], s.m. Credit, repute.

crédit[2], s.m. Credit.

créditeur, -trice, s. Creditor.

credo [kre-], s.m.inv. Creed.

crédule, a. Credulous.

crédulité, s.f. Credulity.

créer, v.tr. To create.

crémaillère [-maj-], s.f. **1. Pendre la c.,** to have a house-warming. **2. Chemin de fer à c.,** rack-railway.

crémation, s.f. Cremation.

crème, s.f. (a) Cream. **a.inv.** Cream (-coloured). (b) Custard.

crémerie, s.f. **1.** Dairy; milk-shop. **2.** Small restaurant.

crémeux, a. Creamy.

créneaux, s.m.pl. Battlements.

crénelé, a. Toothed, notched

créole, a. & s. Creole.

crêpe. 1. *s.f.* Pancake. **2.** *s.m.* Crape.

crépitement, *s.m.* Crackling; sputtering.

crépiter, *v.i.* To crackle; to patter; to sputter.

crépu, *a.* Crisp, fuzzy (hair).

crépusculaire, *a.* Twilight.

crépuscule, *s.m.* Twilight; dusk.

cresson, *s.m.* Cress. **C. de fontaine,** water-cress.

crête, *s.f.* **1.** Comb, crest. **2.** Crest; ridge.

creuser, *v.tr.* **1.** To hollow (out). **2.** To excavate.

creuset, *s.m.* Crucible, melting-pot.

creux. 1. *a.* Hollow. **Voix creuse,** deep voice. **2.** *s.m.* Hollow; trough (of wave).

crevaison, *s.f.* (a) Puncture (in tyre). (b) Bursting (of tyre).

crevasse, *s.f.* Crack (in skin); crevice (in wall); crevasse.

crever. 1. *v.i.* (a) To burst, split. (b) (Of animals) To die. **C. de faim,** to be starving. **2.** *v.tr.* To burst; to puncture (tyre). **C. un œil à qn,** to put out s.o.'s eye.

crevette, *s.f.* Shrimp; prawn.

cri, *s.m.* (a) Cry; chirp. **Cri perçant,** shriek; squeal. (b) Shout, call.

criailler [kriαje], *v.i.* **1.** To cry out bawl. **2.** To whine, complain.

criard, *a.* (a) Squalling, peevish. (b) Shrill. **Couleur criarde,** loud colour.

crible, *s.m.* Sieve, riddle.

criblé, *a.* **C. de dettes,** head over ears in debt.

cribler, *v.tr.* **1.** To sift. **2.** To riddle (de, with).

cric [krik], *s.m.* (Lifting) jack.

cri-cri, *s.m.* *Ent:* Cricket.

criée, *s.f.* Auction.

crier, *v.i.* (a) To cry; to call out, to shout. (b) To squeak; to chirp. (c) To creak.

crime, *s.m.* Crime.

criminel. 1. *a.* (a) Guilty. (b) Criminal. **2.** *s.* Criminal.

crin, *s.m.* Horsehair.

crinière, *s.f.* Mane.

crique, *s.f.* Creek, cove.

crise, *s.f.* **1.** Crisis. **2.** Attack. **Une c. de larmes,** a fit of crying.

crisper, *v.tr.* To contract, clench.

crissement, *s.m.* Grating, grinding.

crisser, *v.tr. & i.* To grate.

cristal, -aux, *s.m.* **1.** Crystal. **2.** C. taillé, cut glass.

cristalliser, *v.tr. & i.* To crystallize.

critique¹. 1. *a.* Critical. **2.** *s.m.* Critic.

critique², *s.f.* Criticism.

critiquer, *v.tr.* To criticize.

croassement, *s.m.* Croak(ing).

croasser, *v.i.* To caw; to croak.

croc [kro], *s.m.* **1.** (a) Hook (b) Pawl, catch. **2.** Fang.

croc-en-jambe, *s.m.* **Faire un c.-en-j. à qn,** to trip s.o. up.

crochet, *s.m.* **1.** Hook. **2.** Poison fang. **3.** Sudden turn (in road).

crochu, *a.* Hooked.

crocodile, *s.m.* Crocodile.

croire. 1. *v.tr.* To believe. **Je (le) crois bien!** I should think so! **N'en croyez rien!** do not believe it! **Croyez-m'en,** be advised by me. **2.** *v.i.* (a) **C. à qch.,** to believe in sth. **C'est à ne pas y c.,** it is beyond all belief. (b) **C. en,** to believe in, have faith in.

croisade, *s.f.* Crusade.

croisé. 1. *a.* Crossed. **Mots croisés,** cross-word. **2.** *s.m.* Crusader.

croisée, *s.f.* Casement-window.

croisement, *s.m.* Crossing.

croiser. 1. *v.tr.* To cross; to fold (the arms); to pass. **Leurs regards se croisèrent,** their eyes met. **2.** *v.i.* To cruise.

croiseur, *s.m.* Cruiser.

croisière, *s.f.* Cruise.

croissance, *s.f.* Growth.

croissant, *s.m.* **1.** Crescent. **2.** Crescent(-roll).

croître, *v.i.* To grow, increase.

croix, *s.f.* Cross. **La C. de guerre,** the Military Cross.

croquant, *a.* Crisp.

croque-mitaine, *s.m.* Bogy(-man), bugaboo. *pl. croque-mitaines.*

croque-mort, *s.m.* (Undertaker's) mute. *pl. croque-morts.*

croquer, *v.tr.* (a) To crunch, munch. **Chocolat à c.,** eating chocolate. (b) To sketch.

croquet, *s.m.* Croquet.

croquis, *s.m.* Sketch.

crosse, *s.f.* **1.** (Hockey-)stick; (golf-) club. **2.** (a) Crook. (b) Butt (of rifle).

crotale, *s.m.* Rattlesnake.

crotte, *s.f.* **1.** Dung. **2.** Mud. dirt.

crotter, *v.tr.* To dirty, soil.

crouler, *v.i.* To collapse.

croupe, *s.f.* **1.** Monter en c., to ride pillion. **2.** Ridge (of hill).

croupier, *s.m.* Croupier.

croupir, *v.i.* **1.** To wallow. **2.** (Of water) To stagnate.

croustillant [-tijã], *a.* Crisp.

croûte, *s.f.* **1.** Crust; rind. **2.** Scab. **3.** Daub.

croyance, *s.f.* Belief (*à*, in).

croyant. **1.** *a.* Believing. **2.** *s.* Believer.

cru¹, *a.* Raw; crude.

cru², *s.m.* Vin du cru, local wine.

cruauté, *s.f.* Cruelty (*envers*, to).

cruche, *s.f.* Pitcher, jug.

crucifier, *v.tr.* To crucify.

crucifix, *s.m.* Crucifix.

crucifixion, *s.f.* Crucifixion.

crudité, *s.f.* Crudity.

crue, *s.f.* Rising (of river); flood.

cruel, *a.* Cruel (*envers*, to).

cruellement, *adv.* Cruelly.

crûment, *adv.* Crudely, roughly.

crustacés, *s.m.pl.* Shell-fish.

crypte, *s.f.* Crypt.

cube. **1.** *s.m.* Cube. **2.** *a.* Cubic

cubique, *a.* Cubic(al), cube.

cueillette [kœjɛt], *s.f.* Gathering, picking.

cueillir [kœjiːr], *v.tr.* To pick gather.

cuiller, cuillère [kɥijɛːr], *s.f.* Spoon

cuillerée [kɥij-], *s.f.* Spoonful.

cuir, *s.m.* **1.** Hide. **2.** (*a*) Leather. (*b*) C. à rasoir, strop.

cuirasse, *s.f.* **1.** Cuirass. **2.** Armour (of warship).

cuirassé. **1.** *a.* Armoured. **2.** *s.m.* Battleship.

cuire. **1.** *v.tr.* To cook. **2.** *v.i.* (*a*) To cook. (*b*) To burn, smart. Il vous en cuira. you shall smart for it.

cuisant, *a.* Smarting, burning.

cuisine, *s.f.* **1.** Kitchen. **2.** (*a*) Cookery. **Faire la c.,** to do the cooking.

cuisinier, *s.* Cook.

cuisse, *s.f.* Thigh; leg (of poultry).

cuistre, *s.m.* Cad.

cuivre, *s.m.* Copper. **C. jaune,** brass.

cuivré, *a.* **1.** Copper-coloured. **2.** Sons cuivrés, brassy tones.

cul [ky], *s.m.* Bottom.

culasse, *s.f.* Breech (of gun).

culbute, *s.f.* (*a*) Somersault. (*b*) Tumble.

cul-de-jatte, *s.m.* Legless cripple. *pl. culs-de-jatte.*

culinaire, *a.* Culinary.

culminant, *a.* **Point c.,** highest point; height, climax.

culotte, *s.f.* Breeches.

culpabilité, *s.f.* Culpability, guilt.

culte, *s.m.* **1.** Worship. **2.** Cult.

cultivateur, *s.m.* Cultivator; farmer.

cultivé, *a.* **1.** Cultivated. **2.** Cultured.

cultiver, *v.tr.* To cultivate; to till.

culture, *s.f.* **1.** (*a*) Cultivation. (*b*) *pl.* Land under cultivation. **2.** Culture.

cupide, *a.* Covetous, grasping.

cupidité, *s.f.* Cupidity, greed.

Cupidon. *Pr.n.m.* Cupid.

curable, *a.* Curable.

curateur, -trice, *s.* Trustee. administrator; guardian.

curatif, *a. & s.m.* Curative.

cure, *s.f.* **1.** Care. **2.** (Course of) treatment; cure.

curé, *s.m.* Parish priest.

cure-dents, *s.m.inv.* Tooth-pick.

curée, *s.f.* Spoils.

curieusement, *adv.* **1.** Inquisitively. **2.** Curiously, quaintly.

curieux, *a.* Curious. (*a*) Interested. (*b*) Inquisitive (*de.* about). (*c*) Odd.

curiosité, *s.f.* Curiosity. **1.** (*a*) Interest. (*b*) Inquisitiveness. (*c*) Oddness. **2.** Curio.

cuve, *s.f.* Vat, tun.

cuvette, *s.f.* Wash-basin.

cyanure, *s.m.* Cyanide.

cycle, *s.m.* Cycle.

cyclisme, *s.m.* Cycling.

cycliste, *s.m. & f.* Cyclist.

cyclone, *s.m.* Cyclone.

cygne, *s.m.* Swan.

cylindre, *s.m.* Cylinder.

cylindrique, *a.* Cylindrical.

cymbale, *s.f.* Cymbal.

cynique. **1.** *a.* Shameless; brazen. **2.** *s.m.* Shameless person.

cyniquement, *adv.* Shamelessly.

cynisme, *s.m.* Shamelessness.

cyprès, *s.m.* Cypress.

cytise, *s.m.* Laburnum.

D

D, d [de], *s.m.* (The letter) D, d.

dactylo(graphe), *s.m. & f.* Typist.

dada, *s.m.* Hobby.

dague, *s.f.* Dagger; dirk.

dahlia, *s.m.* Dahlia.

daigner, *v.tr.* To deign, condescend.

daim, *s.m.* (Fallow-)deer; buck.

dais [dɛ], *s.m.* Canopy.

dalle, *s.f.* (*a*) Flag(stone). (*b*) Slab.

daltonisme, *s.m.* Colour-blindness.

Damas. **1.** *Pr.n.m.* Damascus. **2.** *s.m.* Damask.

dame¹, *s.f.* **1.** (*a*) Lady. (*b*) Married woman. **Dames de charité,** district-visitors. **2.** (*a*) Jeu de dames (game of) draughts. (*b*) King (at draughts); queen (at cards and chess).

dame², *int.* D. oui! rather!

damier, *s.m.* Draught-board.

damné [dɑne], *a. & s.* Damned.

damner [dɑne], *v.tr.* To damn.

dandiner (se), *v.pr.* To have a rolling gait.

Danemark [-mark]. *Pr.n.m.* Denmark.

danger, *s.m.* Danger, peril. **Pas de d.!** never fear!

dangereusement, *adv.* Dangerously.

dangereux, *a.* Dangerous (*pour*, to).

danois. **1.** *a.* Danish. **2.** *s.* Dane. **3.** *s.m.* Danish.

dans, *prep.* **1.** (*a*) In. (*b*) Within. (*c*) Into. (*d*) Out of. **Boire d. un verre,** to drink out of a glass. **2.** In, within, during. **3.** **D. la nécessité de,** under the necessity of. **D. cette occasion,** on that occasion.

dansant, *a.* Dancing.

danse, *s.f.* Dance, dancing. **D. de Saint-Guy,** St. Vitus's dance.

danser, *v.i.* To dance.

danseur, -euse, *s.* **1.** Dancer. **2.** Partner (at dance).

dard, *s.m* Sting (of insect); forked tongue.

darder, *v.tr.* To shoot forth.

dare-dare, *adv.* In hot haste.

date, *s.f.* Date.

dater. **1.** *v.tr.* To date (letter). **2.** *v.i.* **A d. de ce jour,** from to-day.

datte, *s.f. Bot:* Date.

dattier, *s.m.* Date-palm.

dauphin, *s.m.* **1.** Dolphin. **2.** Dauphin.

davantage, *adv.* More.

de. **I.** *prep.* **1.** (*a*) From. (*b*) **Il partit de nuit,** he left by night. (*c*) **Accompagné de,** accompanied by. (*d*) **D'une voix douce,** in a gentle voice. (*e*) **Sauter de joie,** to leap for joy. (*f*) **Agé de seize ans,** sixteen years old. **2.** Of. (*a*) **Le livre de Pierre,** Peter's book. (*b*) **Un pont de fer,** an iron bridge. (*c*) **Le journal d'hier,** yesterday's paper. (*d*) **Quelque chose de bon,** something good. **3.** **Manquer de courage,** to lack courage.

II. **de,** serving as a link word. **1.** **Indigne de vivre,** unfit to live. **2.** **Un drôle de garçon,** a funny chap.

III. **de,** partitive particle. **Sans faire de fautes,** without making any mistakes. **Vous êtes des lâches,** you are cowards.

dé¹, *s.m. Gaming:* Die. **Coup de dé,** cast of the die.

dé², *s.m.* Thimble.

débâcle, *s.f.* **1.** Break(ing) up. **2.** Downfall, collapse.

déballer, *v.tr.* To unpack.

débandade, *s.f.* Rout; stampede.

débander, *v.tr.* To disband.

débarbouiller (se) [-buje], *v.pr.* To wash one's face.

débarcadère, *s.m.* Landing-stage, wharf.

débardeur, *s.m.* Docker, stevedore.

débarquement, *s.m.* Unloading; landing, disembarkment.

débarquer. **1.** *v.tr.* To unload; to disembark, land. **2.** *v.i.* To land, disembark; to alight.

débarras, *s.m.* Riddance. **Chambre de d.,** lumber-room.

débarrasser, *v.tr.* To relieve. **se débarrasser,** to get rid (*de*, of).

débat, *s.m.* **1.** Debate. **2.** Dispute.

débattre, *v.tr.* To debate, discuss. **se débattre,** to struggle.

débauche, *s.f.* Debauch(ery).

débauché, *a.* Debauched, profligate.

débilité, *s.f.* Debility, weakness.

débit¹, *s.m.* (*a*) (Retail) sale. (*b*) (Retail) shop. **D. de tabac,** tobacconist's. **D. de boissons,** public house.

débit², *s.m.* Debit.

débitant, s. Retail dealer ; retailer.
débiter[1], v.tr. **1.** To retail. **2.** D.
des histoires, to spin yarns.
débiter[2], v.tr. To debit.
débiteur, -trice, s. Debtor.
déblayer, v.tr. **1.** To clear away.
2. To clear.
déboire, s.m. Disappointment.
débonnaire, a. Good-natured.
débordant, a. **1.** Overflowing (de
with). **2.** Projecting, protruding.
déborder, v.tr. & i. To overflow.
débouché, s.m. **1.** Outlet. **2.** Opening ; chance of success.
déboucher[1], v.tr. **1.** To clear. **2.** To
uncork.
déboucher[2], v.i. To emerge, issue.
déboucler, v.tr. To unbuckle (belt).
débours, s.m.pl. Disbursement ; out-
of-pocket expenses.
debout, adv. **1.** (a) Upright, on end ;
standing. Se tenir d., to stand.
"Places d. seulement," 'standing
room only.' (b) Être d., to be up.
Allons, d.! come, get up! **2.** Vent
d., head-wind.
déboutonner, v.tr. To unbutton.
débraillé [-raje], a. Untidy.
débris, s.m.pl. Remains, debris.
débrouiller [-bruje], v.tr To unravel ; to straighten out.
se débrouiller, to extricate oneself (from difficulties) ; to manage.
début, s.m. **1.** First appearance.
2. Beginning, start, outset.
débutant, s. Beginner, tyro.
débuter, v.i. **1.** To make one's first
appearance. **2.** To begin.
deçà, adv. On this side.
décacheter, v.tr. To unseal, open.
décade, s.f. Decade.
décadence, s.f. Decadence, decline.
décadent, a. Decadent ; in decay.
décamper, v.i. To decamp.
décanter, v.tr. To decant.
décapiter,v.tr. To decapitate, behead.
décédé, a. & s. Deceased, defunct.
décéder, v.i. To die.
déceler, v.tr. To disclose ; to
divulge, betray.
décembre, s.m. December.
décemment, adv. Decently.
décence, s.f. (a) Decency. (b) Propriety.
décent, a. (a) Decent ; modest.
(b) Proper, seemly.

décentraliser, v.tr. To decentralize.
déception, s.f. Disappointment.
décerner, v.tr. To award, bestow
décès, s.m. Decease, death.
décevant, a. **1.** Deceptive ; delusive.
2. Disappointing.
décevoir, v.tr. **1.** To deceive, delude.
2. To disappoint.
déchaînement, s.m. (a) Breaking
loose. (b) Outburst.
déchaîner, v.tr. To let loose.
se déchaîner, to break out.
décharge, s.f. **1.** (a) Unloading.
(b) Discharge. **2.** (a) Relief. (b)
Témoin à d., witness for the defence.
(c) Release. **3.** Outlet.
déchargement, s.m. Unloading.
décharger, v.tr. **1.** (a) To unload.
(b) To unburden. (c) To discharge.
2. (a) To lighten. (b) To acquit.
décharné, a. Emaciated ; gaunt ;
bony.
déchausser, v.tr. To take off (s.o.'s)
shoes.
se déchausser, to take off one's
shoes.
déchéance, s.f. **1.** Downfall. **2.**
Lapse ; forfeiture.
déchet, s.m. Waste, refuse.
déchiffrer, v.tr. To decipher.
déchiqueté, a Jagged (edge).
déchiqueter, v.tr. To cut into
shreds.
déchirant, a. Heart-rending.
déchirement, s.m. Tearing, rending.
déchirer, v.tr. To tear (up, open).
déchu, a. Fallen ; lapsed (policy).
décidé, a. **1.** Settled. **2.** Resolute ;
determined. **3.** Decided.
décidément, adv. **1.** Resolutely.
2. Decidedly, positively.
décider, v.tr. **1.** To decide, settle.
2. To persuade, induce.
se décider, to make up one's
mind.
décimal, -aux, a. Decimal
décimale, s.f. Decimal.
décimer, v.tr. To decimate.
décisif, a. **1.** Decisive ; conclusive.
2. Peremptory.
décision, s.f. Decision
décisivement, adv. Decisively.
déclamation, s.f. **1.** Oratory. **2.** (a)
Declamation. (b) Ranting.
déclamer, v.tr. **1.** To declaim.
2. To rant, spout.

déclaration, *s.f.* Declaration ; proclamation. **D. sous serment,** affidavit.

déclarer, *v.tr.* **1.** To declare, make known. **2.** To declare, announce. **se déclarer 1.** To declare. **2.** To break out.

déclic [-klik], *s.m.* Pawl, catch.

déclin, *s.m.* Decline, close.

déclinaison, *s.f.* Declension.

décliner. I. *v.i.* To wane. II. **décliner,** *v.tr.* To decline.

déclivité, *s.f.* Declivity, slope.

décocher, *v.tr.* To let fly.

décoiffer (se), *v.pr.* To remove one's head-dress.

décolérer, *v.i.* To calm down.

décoller, *v.tr.* (Of aeroplane) To take off.

décolleté, *a.* Low-necked.

décoloration, *s.f.* Discolouration.

décombres, *s.m.pl.* Rubbish, debris.

décommander, *v.tr.* To countermand.

décomposé, *a.* **Visage d.,** drawn distorted, face.

décomposer, *v.tr.* To decompose.

décomposition, *s.f.* **1.** Decomposition. **2.** Distortion (of features).

déconcertant, *a.* Disconcerting.

déconcerté, *a.* Abashed ; taken aback.

déconcerter, *v.tr.* **1.** To upset. **2.** To disconcert.

déconfit, *a.* Crest-fallen, discomfited.

déconfiture, *s.f.* Collapse, failure.

décontenancé, *a.* Abashed ; put out.

décontenancer, *v.tr.* To put out of countenance.

déconvenue, *s.f.* Disappointment ; mortification.

décor, *s.m.* **1.** Decoration. **2.** *Th :* *pl.* Scenery.

décorateur, *s.m.* (House-)decorator.

décoration, *s.f.* Decoration.

décorer, *v.tr.* To decorate.

décorum [-rom], *s.m.* Decorum.

découcher, *v.i.* To sleep out.

découper, *v.tr.* **1.** To cut up ; to carve. **Couteau à d.,** carving-knife. **2.** To cut out. **Scie à d.,** fret-saw. **se découper,** to stand out, show up (*sur,* against).

découplé, *a.* **Bien d.,** well set up.

découpure, *s.f.* **1.** Fretwork. **2.** Indentation (in coastline).

découragé, *a.* Discouraged, despondent, downhearted.

découragement, *s.m.* Discouragement.

décourager, *v.tr.* **1.** To discourage, dishearten. **2.** To discountenance. **se décourager** to become disheartened.

décousu, *a.* Disconnected, disjointed.

découvert. 1. *a.* (a) Uncovered. (b) Open. **2. A d.,** uncovered, unprotected.

découverte, *s.f.* Discovery.

découvrir, *v.tr.* **1.** (a) To uncover. (b) To disclose. **2.** To perceive. **3.** To discover ; to detect. **se découvrir,** to take off one's hat.

décrépit, *a.* Decrepit, senile.

décrépitude, *s.f.* Decrepitude.

décret, *s.m.* Decree ; fiat, order.

décréter, *v.tr.* To decree.

décrier, *v.tr.* To disparage, decry.

décrire, *v.tr.* To describe.

décrocher, *v.tr.* To unhook ; to take down.

décroissance, *s.f.* Decrease.

décroître, *v.i.* To decrease, diminish.

décrotter, *v.tr.* To clean (boots).

décrotteur, *s.m.* Shoeblack.

décrottoir, *s.m.* Door-scraper.

décuple, *a. & s.m.* Tenfold.

décupler, *v.tr. & i.* To increase tenfold.

dédaigner, *v.tr.* To scorn, disdain.

dédaigneusement, *adv.* Disdainfully.

dédaigneux, *a.* Disdainful.

dédain, *s.m.* Disdain, scorn.

dédale, *s.m.* Labyrinth, maze.

dedans. 1. *adv.* Inside ; within ; in (it). **Donner d.,** to fall into the trap. **En d.,** inside ; within. **2.** *s.m.* Inside interior. **Au d.,** inside, within.

dédicace, *s.f.* Dedication.

dédier, *v.tr.* To dedicate.

dédire (se), *v.pr.* **Se d. de,** to retract.

dédit, *s.m.* **1.** Retraction, withdrawal. **2.** Breaking (of promise).

dédommagement, *s.m.* Compensation, damages.

dédommager, *v.tr.* To indemnify, compensate.

déduction, *s.f.* Deduction. (a) Inference. (b) Allowance.

déduire, *v.tr.* **1.** To deduce, infer. **2.** To deduct.

déesse, s.f. Goddess.

défaillance [-faj-], s.f. (a) Failing. (b) Fainting fit; swoon.

défaillir [-faj-], v.i. (a) To become feeble. (b) To faint, swoon.

défaire, v.tr. 1. To undo; to untie. 2. To defeat.
  se défaire. 1. To come undone. 2. To get rid.

défait, a. (a) Discomposed. (b) Dishevelled.

défaite, s.f. Defeat.

défaut, s.m. 1. Default, absence, lack. A d. de., for lack of, failing. 2. (a) Fault, short-coming. (b) Defect, flaw. Prendre en d., to catch napping.

défaveur, s.f. Disfavour, discredit.

défavorable, a. Unfavourable.

défection, s.f. Defection from a cause.

défectueux, a. Defective, faulty.

défectuosité, s.f. Defect, flaw.

défendable, a. Defensible.

défendeur, -eresse, s. Defendant.

défendre, v.tr. 1. (a) To defend; to uphold. (b) To protect. 2. To forbid.
  se défendre. 1. To defend oneself. 2. Se d. de, to refrain from.

défense, s.f. 1. Defence. Sans d., defenceless. 2. pl. (a) Defences. (b) Tusks. 3. Prohibition. "D. d'entrer, de fumer," 'no admittance,' 'no smoking.'

défenseur, s.m. (a) Protector. (b) Supporter, upholder.

défensif, a. & s.f. Defensive.

déférence, s.f. Deference, respect.

déférer, v.i. To defer (to s.o.).

déferler, v.i. (Of waves) To break.

défi, s.m. (a) Challenge. (b) Defiance.

défiance, s.f. 1. Mistrust, distrust. 2. D. de soi-même, diffidence.

défiant, a. Mistrustful, distrustful.

déficit [-sit], s.m. Deficit; shortage.

défier, v.tr. (a) To challenge. (b) To defy. (c) To brave.
  se défier de, to distrust.

défigurer, v.tr. To disfigure.

défilé, s.m. 1. Defile, gorge. 2. March past; parade.

défiler, v.i. (a) To march past. (b) To walk in procession.

défini, a. Definite.

définir, v.tr. To define.
  se définir, to become distinct.

définitif, a. Definitive; final. Adv.phr. En définitive, finally.

définition, s.f. Definition.

définitivement, adv. Definitively.

déflation, s.f. Deflation.

défoncé, a. 1. Stove in; battered. 2. Chemin d., broken, bumpy, road.

défoncer, v.tr. 1. To stave in; to smash in. 2. To break up.

déformation, s.f. (a) Deformation. (b) Distortion.

déformer, v.tr. To deform; to put out of shape; to distort.

défraîchi, a. (Shop-)soiled.

défrayer, v.tr. D. qn., to defray s.o.'s expenses.

défricher, v.tr. To bring into cultivation; to break (new ground).

défroque, s.f. Cast-off clothing.

défunt, a. & s. Defunct, deceased.

dégagé, a. (a) Free, untrammelled. (b) Free and easy.

dégagement, s.m. Release.

dégager, v.tr. 1. (a) To disengage. (b) To clear. 2. To emit, give off.
  se dégager. 1. To get free. 2. To escape.

dégainer, v.tr. To unsheathe, draw.

dégarni, a. Empty; stripped.

dégarnir, v.tr. To dismantle; to strip.

dégâts, s.m.pl. Damage.

dégel, s.m. Thaw.

dégeler, v.tr. & i. To thaw.

dégénération, s.f. Degeneration, degeneracy.

dégénéré, a. & s. Degenerate.

dégénérer, v.i. To degenerate.

dégingandé, a. Ungainly.

dégivrer, v.tr. To de-ice.

dégonflement, s.m. Deflation.

dégonfler, v.tr. To deflate.
  se dégonfler, to collapse, to go flat.

dégorger. 1. v.tr. To disgorge. 2. v.i. To overflow.

dégourdir, v.tr. To remove stiffness from.
  se dégourdir, to lose one's stiff feeling.

dégoût, s.m. Disgust, distaste.

dégoûtant, a. Disgusting, nasty.

dégoûté, a. 1. Disgusted (de, with); sick (of). 2. Squeamish.

dégoûter, v.tr. To disgust.
  se dégoûter, to take a dislike.

dégoutter, v.i. To drip, trickle.

dégradant, a. Degrading, lowering.

dégradation, s.f. Degradation.

dégrader, *v.tr.* To degrade.
  se dégrader, to lower oneself.
dégrafer, *v.tr.* To unfasten, undo.
degré, *s.m.* Step; degree.
dégringolade, *s.f.* **1.** Tumble. **2.** Collapse.
dégringoler, *v.tr. & i.* To tumble down.
dégriser, *v.tr.* To sober.
déguenillé [-gnije], *a.* Ragged, tattered.
déguerpir [-gɛr-], *v.i.* To decamp.
déguisement [-gi-], *s.m.* Disguise.
déguiser [-gi-], *v.tr.* To disguise.
déguster, *v.tr.* To taste; to sip.
dehors. **1.** *adv.* (a) Out, outside. "Ne pas se pencher d.!" 'do not lean out of the window!' (b) **En d.,** (on the) outside; outwards. **2.** *s.m.* (a) Outside, exterior. (b) *pl.* (Outward) appearance.
déité, *s.f.* Deity.
déjà, *adv.* **1.** Already. **2.** Before, previously.
déjeuner. **I.** *v.i.* (a) To breakfast. (b) To lunch; to take lunch.
  II. déjeuner, *s.m.* (a) (**Premier**) d., breakfast. **Petit d.,** coffee with rolls, etc. (b) (**Second**) d., lunch.
déjouer, *v.tr.* To thwart; to foil; to frustrate.
delà. **1.** *prep.* Beyond. **2.** *adv.* **Au d.,** beyond.
délabré, *a.* Tumble-down; impaired.
délabrement, *s.m.* Disrepair, decay.
délabrer, *v.tr.* To dilapidate; to ruin.
  se délabrer, to fall into decay; to become impaired.
délacer, *v.tr.* To unlace.
délai, *s.m.* **1.** Delay. **2.** Respite, time allowed. **A court d.,** at short notice.
délaisser, *v.tr.* To forsake, desert.
délassement, *s.m.* Rest, relaxation.
délasser, *v.tr.* To rest, refresh.
  se délasser, to take relaxation.
délateur, *s.m.* Informer, spy.
délayer, *v.tr.* To add water to.
délectable, *a.* Delightful, pleasant.
délégation, *s.f.* Delegation.
délégué, *a. & s.* (a) Delegate. (b) Deputy.
déléguer, *v.tr.* To delegate.
délétère, *a.* Deleterious; pernicious.
délibération, *s.f.* **1.** Deliberation, discussion. **2.** Reflection.

délibéré, *a.* Deliberate.
délibérément, *adv.* Deliberately.
délibérer. **1.** *v.i.* (a) To deliberate. (b) To reflect. **2.** *v.tr.* To discuss.
délicat, *a.* Delicate. **1.** Dainty. **2.** Fine, refined. **3.** Sensitive; frail. **4.** Difficult.
délicatement, *adv.* Delicately.
délicatesse, *s.f.* Delicacy. **1.** Fineness. **2.** Refinement. **3.** Fragility. **4.** Difficulty, awkwardness.
délices, *s.f.pl.* Delight(s), pleasure(s).
délicieusement, *adv.* Deliciously; delightfully.
délicieux, *a.* Delicious; delightful.
délié, *a.* Slender, fine; glib.
délier, *v.tr.* To untie, undo.
délimiter, *v.tr.* To delimit; to define (powers).
délinquant, *s.* Offender, delinquent.
délire, *s.m.* Delirium.
délirer, *v.i.* To be delirious; to rave.
délit, *s.m.* Misdemeanour, offence.
délivrance, *s.f.* **1.** Deliverance, rescue. **2.** Delivery; issue.
délivrer, *v.tr.* **1.** To deliver; to rescue. **2.** To deliver, hand over.
déloger. **1.** *v.i.* To go off. **2.** *v.tr.* To eject; to dislodge.
déloyal, -aux, *a.* Disloyal, false; unfair; foul (play).
déloyauté, *s.f.* Disloyalty, perfidy.
delta, *s.m.* Delta.
déluge, *s.m.* Deluge, flood.
déluré, *a.* Sharp, knowing, smart.
démagogue, *s.m.* Demagogue.
demain, *adv. & s.m.* To-morrow.
demande, *s.f.* **1.** (a) Request, application. (b) Demand. **2.** Question.
demander, *v.tr.* **1.** To ask (for). **On vous demande,** somebody wants to see you. **D. qch. à qn.,** to ask s.o. for sth. **2.** To desire, require. **3.** To ask, enquire.
démangeaison, *s.f.* Itching; longing.
démanger, *v.i.* To itch.
démarcation, *s.f.* Demarcation. **Ligne de d.,** dividing line.
démarche, *s.f.* **1.** Gait, walk. **2.** Step; proceeding.
démarrer. **1.** *v.tr.* To unmoor. **2.** *v.i.* (Of vehicle) To start; to drive off.
démasquer, *v.tr.* To unmask; to expose.

démêler, *v.tr.* To disentangle; to comb out.

se démêler, to extricate oneself.

démembrer, *v.tr.* To dismember.

déménagement, *s.m.* Removal.

déménager, *v.tr. & i.* To move house, to remove.

démence, *s.f.* Insanity, madness.

démener (se), *v.pr.* **1.** To struggle. **2.** To bestir oneself.

dementi, *s.m.* Denial, contradiction.

démentir, *v.tr.* **1.** To contradict; to deny. **2.** To belie.

se démentir, to contradict oneself.

démesuré, *a.* Inordinate; unbounded.

démesurément, *adv.* Inordinately; enormously.

démettre (se), *v.pr.* To retire.

demeure, *s.f.* (Place of) residence, dwelling place; abode.

demeurer, *v.i.* **1.** To remain; to stay. **2.** To live, reside.

demi. 1. *a.* Half. **2.** *s.m.* (*a*) Half. (*b*) A d. mort, half-dead. **3.** *s.f.* Demie, half-hour.

NOTE. In all the following compounds DEMI is *inv.*; the second component takes the plural.

demi-cercle, *s.m.* Semicircle.

demi-circulaire, *a.* Semicircular.

demi-dieu, *s.m.* Demigod.

demi-frère, *s.m.* Stepbrother.

demi-heure, *s.f.* Une d.-h., half an hour.

demi-monde, *s.m.* Outskirts of society.

demi-mot (à), *adv.phr.* Entendre à d.-m., to take a hint.

demi-place, *s.f.* Half-fare; half-price.

demi-sœur, *s.f.* Stepsister.

demi-solde, *s.f.* *Mil:* Half-pay.

démission, *s.f.* Resignation.

demi-voix (à), *adv.phr.* In an undertone; under one's breath.

démobilisation, *s.f.* Demobilization.

démobiliser, *v.tr.* To demobilize.

démocrate, *s.m. & f.* Democrat.

démocratie, *s.f.* Democracy.

démocratique, *a.* Democratic.

démodé, *a.* Old-fashioned; obsolete.

demoiselle, *s.f.* **1.** (*a*) Spinster. (*b*) D. d'honneur, bridesmaid. **2.** Young lady. **3.** Dragon-fly.

démolir, *v.tr.* To demolish pull down.

démolition, *s.f.* Demolition.

démon, *s.m.* Demon, devil, fiend.

démoniaque, *a.* Demoniac(al).

démonstratif, *a.* Demonstrative.

démonstration, *s.f.* Demonstration.

démonté, *a.* **1.** Dismounted. **2.** Stormy (sea). **3.** Abashed.

démonter, *v.tr.* **1.** To unhorse. Se laisser d., to get upset. **2.** To dismantle; to remove (tyre).

démontrable, *a.* Demonstrable.

démontrer, *v.tr.* To demonstrate.

démoralisation, *s.f.* Demoralization.

démoraliser, *v.tr.* To demoralize.

démuni, *a.* Unprovided (*de*, with).

démunir (se), *v.pr.* Se d. de qch., to part with sth.

dénaturé, *a.* Unnatural; hard-hearted; perverted.

dénaturer, *v.tr.* To misrepresent, distort.

dénégation, *s.f.* Denial.

dénicher, *v.tr.* (*a*) To find. (*b*) To dislodge.

dénier, *v.tr.* To deny.

dénigrement, *s.m.* Disparagement.

dénigrer, *v.tr.* To disparage.

dénombrement, *s.m.* Enumeration.

dénombrer, *v.tr.* To enumerate.

dénominateur, *s.m.* Denominator.

dénomination, *s.f.* Denomination, name.

dénommer, *v.tr.* To denominate.

dénoncer, *v.tr.* **1.** To declare. **2.** (*a*) To denounce. (*b*) To expose.

dénonciateur, -trice. 1. *s.* Informer. **2.** *a.* Tell-tale (look).

dénonciation, *s.f.* Denunciation.

dénoter, *v.tr.* To denote, betoken.

dénouer, *v.tr.* To unknot; to undo.

denrée, *s.f.* Commodity; food-stuff.

dense, *a.* Dense, crowded; close.

densité, *s.f.* Denseness, density.

dent, *s.f.* **1.** Tooth. Coup de d., bite. Rire à belles dents, to laugh heartily. Être sur les dents, to be worn out. **2.** Tooth (of saw); cog; prong.

dental, -aux, *a.* Dental.

denté, *a.* Cogged, toothed.

dentelé, *a.* Notched, indented

dentelle, *s.f.* Lace.

dentellière, *s.f.* Lace-maker.

dentelure, *s.f.* Indentation.

dentifrice, *s.m.* Dentifrice.

dentiste, *s.m.* Dentist.
dénudé, *a.* Bare, denuded.
dénuder, *v.tr.* To denude.
dénué, *a.* Devoid.
dénuement, *s.m.* Destitution.
dénuer, *v.tr.* To divest, strip.
départ, *s.m.* Departure, starting.
département, *s.m.* Department.
départir, *v.tr.* To divide.
dépasser, *v.tr.* **1.** (*a*) To pass beyond. (*b*) To overtake. **2.** To exceed.
dépaysé, *a.* Out of one's element.
dépècement, *s.m.* Cutting up.
dépecer, *v.tr.* To cut up; to carve.
dépêche, *s.f.* (*a*) Despatch. (*b*) Telegram.
dépêcher, *v.tr.* To dispatch.
 se dépêcher, to make haste. Dépêchez-vous! hurry up!
dépeindre, *v.tr.* To depict.
dépenaillé [-naj-], *a.* Ragged.
dépendance, *s.f.* **1.** Dependence. **2.** (*a*) Dependency. (*b*) *pl.* Outbuildings.
dépendant, *a.* Dependent (*de*, on).
dépendre, *v.i.* To depend (*de*, on).
dépens, *s.m.pl.* Cost, expenses.
dépense, *s.f.* Expenditure, outlay.
dépenser, *v.tr.* To spend.
dépérir, *v.i.* To waste away.
dépérissement, *s.m.* Wasting away.
dépeupler, *v.tr.* To depopulate.
dépiécer, *v.tr.* To cut to pieces
dépit, *s.m.* Spite; chagrin.
dépiter, *v.tr.* To vex.
déplacé, *a.* Out of place.
déplacement, *s.m.* **1.** Displacement. **2.** Travelling.
déplacer, *v.tr.* **1.** To displace. **2.** To oust.
déplaire, *v.ind.tr.* To displease.
 se déplaire, to be dissatisfied.
déplaisant, *a.* Unpleasant.
déplaisir, *s.m.* Displeasure, chagrin.
déplier, *v.tr.* To unfold, spread out.
 se déplier, to open out.
déploiement, *s.m.* **1.** Spreading out, unfolding. **2.** Display.
déplorable, *a.* Deplorable.
déplorer, *v.tr.* To deplore, lament.
déployer, *v.tr.* **1.** To unfold. **2.** To display.
dépopulation, *s.f.* Depopulation.
déportation, *s.f.* Deportation.
déporter, *v.tr.* To deport.
déposer, *v.tr.* **1.** (*a*) To deposit. **2.**

(*a*) To register (trade-mark). (*b*) To lodge (a complaint). **3.** To depose.
déposition, *s.f.* Deposition.
dépôt, *s.m.* **1.** (*a*) Depositing. (*b*) Deposit. **2.** Depository, depot. **3.** Deposit, sediment.
dépouille [-puːj], *s.f.* **1.** Skin, hide. **D. mortelle,** mortal remains. **2.** *pl.* Spoils, booty.
dépouiller [-puje], *v.tr.* To deprive, strip; to despoil.
dépourvu, *a.* Destitute, devoid. Être pris au d., to be caught napping.
dépravation, *s.f.* Depravation.
dépraver, *v.tr.* To deprave.
dépréciateur, -trice, *a.* Disparaging.
dépréciation, *s.f.* **1.** Depreciation. **2.** Disparagement.
déprécier, *v.tr.* **1.** To depreciate. **2.** To disparage.
déprédation, *s.f.* Depredation.
dépression, *s.f* **1.** Hollow, dip. **2.** Depression; dejection.
déprimé, *a.* Depressed.
déprimer, *v.tr.* To depress.
depuis, *prep.* **1.** (*a*) Since, for. **D. quand êtes-vous ici?** how long have you been here? (*b*) *adv.* Since (then); afterwards. (*c*) **D. que,** since. **2.** From.
députation, *s.f.* Deputation.
député, *s.m.* Deputy.
députer, *v.tr.* To depute.
déraciner, *v.tr.* **1.** To uproot. **2.** To eradicate.
dérailler [-raje], *v.i.* To run off the rails.
déraisonnable, *a.* Unreasonable.
déraisonner, *v.i.* To talk nonsense.
dérangement, *s.m.* Derangement.
déranger, *v.tr.* (*a*) To disarrange. (*b*) To disturb. (*c*) To upset.
 se déranger, to move, stir. **Ne vous dérangez pas,** don't trouble.
déraper, *v.tr. & i. Aut:* To skid.
derechef [-ʃef], *adv.* Yet again.
déréglé, *a.* **1.** Out of order. **2.** Lawless; wild (life); immoderate.
dérèglement, *s.m.* Profligacy.
dérégler, *v.tr.* To upset, disarrange.
dérider, *v.tr.* To smoothe.
dérision, *s.f.* Derision, mockery.
dérisoire, *a.* Ridiculous, laughable.
dérivation, *s.f.* Derivation.
dérive, *s.f.* Leeway, drift.
dériver¹, *v.i.* To be derived.

dériver², *v.i.* To drift.

dernier, *a. & s.* **1.** Last, latest. (*a*) Dans ces derniers temps, latterly. (*b*) Le mois d., last month. **2.** (*a*) Utmost, highest. (*b*) Lowest; worst.

dernièrement, *adv.* Lately, latterly.

dérobé, *a.* Hidden, concealed. A la dérobée, stealthily, secretly.

dérober, *v.tr.* **1.** (*a*) To steal. (*b*) D. qn au danger, to save s.o. from danger. **2.** To hide.

se **dérober**, to escape, steal away, slip away (*à*, from).

déroger, *v.i.* To derogate (*à*, from).

dérouler, *v.tr.* To unroll; to unwind.

se **dérouler**, to unfold.

déroute, *s.f.* Rout.

dérouter, *v.tr.* **1.** To lead astray; to put off. **2.** To confuse, baffle.

derrière. 1. *prep.* Behind. **2.** *adv.* (*a*) Behind, at the back. Pattes de d., hind legs. (*b*) Aft. **3.** *s.m.* (*a*) Back. (*b*) Hind part.

derviche, *s.m.* Dervish.

des = de les.

dès, *prep.* Since, from; as early as. Dès le matin, first thing in the morning. *Conj.phr.* Dès que, as soon as. *Adv.phr.* Dès lors, ever since (then).

désabuser, *v.tr.* To disabuse, undeceive (*de*, with regard to).

désaccord, *s.m.* **1.** (*a*) Disagreement. (*b*) Clash. Discord.

désaccoutumer, *v.tr.* To disaccustom.

désaffection, *s.f.* Disaffection.

désagréable, *a.* Disagreeable, unpleasant.

désagréablement, *adv.* Disagreeably, unpleasantly.

désagrégation, *s.f.* Disintegration.

désagréger, *v.tr.* To disintegrate.

se **désagréger**, to break up.

désagrément, *s.m.* Source of annoyance; unpleasant occurrence.

désaltérer (se), *v.pr.* To quench (one's thirst).

désappointement, *s.m.* Disappointment.

désappointer, *v.tr.* To disappoint.

désapprobateur, -trice *a.* Disapproving, censorious.

désapprobation, *s.f.* Disapproval.

désapprouver, *v.tr.* To disapprove of, object to.

désarmé, *a.* **1.** Disarmed. **2.** Unarmed, defenceless.

désarmement, *s.m.* Disarmament.

désarmer, *v.tr. & i.* To disarm.

désarroi, *s.m.* Disarray, disorder.

désassocier, *v.tr.* To dissociate.

désastre, *s.m.* Disaster, calamity.

désastreusement, *adv.* Disastrously.

désastreux, *a.* Disastrous.

désavantage, *s.m.* Disadvantage, drawback.

désavantageusement, *adv.* Disadvantageously.

désavantageux, *a.* Disadvantageous.

désaveu, *s.m.* Disavowal; disclaimer.

désavouer, *v.tr.* To disavow.

descendance, *s.f.* **1.** Descent, lineage. **2.** *Coll:* Descendants.

descendant. 1. *a.* Descending. Train d., down train. **2.** *s.* Descendant.

descendre. I. *v.i.* **1.** (*a*) To descend; to come, go, down. (*b*) To come, go, downstairs. **2.** (*a*) To alight. "Tout le monde descend!" 'all change!' (*b*) D. à un hôtel, to put up at a hotel. **II. descendre**, *v.tr.* **1.** To go down. **2.** (*a*) To take, bring, down. (*b*) To lower. (*c*) To shoot down.

descente, *s.f.* **1.** Descent. **2.** Letting down, lowering. **3.** D. de bain, bath-mat. D. de lit, (bed-side) rug.

descriptif [des-], *a.* Descriptive.

description [des-], *s.f.* Description.

désenchantement, *s.m.* (*a*) Disenchantment. (*b*) Disillusion.

désenchanter, *v.tr.* (*a*) To disenchant. (*b*) To disillusion.

déséquilibré, *a.* Unbalanced.

déséquilibrer, *v.tr.* To unbalance.

désert¹, *a.* Desert; lonely.

désert², *s.m.* Desert, wilderness.

déserter, *v.tr.* To desert.

déserteur, *s.m.* Deserter.

désertion, *s.f.* Desertion.

désespérant, *a.* Heart-breaking.

désespéré, *a.* Desperate.

désespérément, *adv.* **1.** Despairingly, hopelessly. **2.** Desperately.

désespérer. 1. *v.i.* To despair. **2.** *v.tr.* To drive to despair.

se **désespérer**, to be in despair.

désespoir, *s.m.* Despair.

déshabiller [-bije], *v.tr.* To undress.

se **déshabiller**, to undress.

déshériter, *v.tr.* To disinherit.

déshonneur, *s.m.* Dishonour.
déshonorer, *v.tr.* To dishonour.
désignation, *s.f.* Designation.
désigner, *v.tr.* **1.** To designate, show. **2.** To appoint.
désillusion, *s.f.* Disillusion.
désillusionner, *v.tr.* To disillusion.
désinfectant, *a. & s.m.* Disinfectant.
désinfecter, *v.tr.* To disinfect.
désinfection, *s.f.* Disinfection.
désintéressé, *a.* (*a*) Disinterested. (*b*) Unselfish.
désintéressement, *s.m.* Disinterestedness.
désintéresser, *v.tr.* To buy out.
 se désintéresser, to take no further interest (*de*, in).
désinvolte, *a.* (*a*) Easy, free. (*b*) Airy.
désinvolture, *s.f.* Free and easy manner.
désir, *s.m.* Desire (*de*, for); wish
désirable, *a.* Desirable.
désirer, *v.tr.* To desire, want. Cela laisse à d., it is not satisfactory. Madame désire? what can I show you, madam?
désireux, *a.* Desirous.
désister (se), *v.pr.* To desist.
désobéir, *v.ind.tr.* D. à, to disobey.
désobéissance, *s.f.* Disobedience.
désobéissant, *a.* Disobedient.
désobligeant, *a.* (*a*) Disobliging. (*b*) Disagreeable, ungracious.
désobliger, *v.tr.* **1.** To disoblige. **2.** To offend.
désœuvré, *a.* Unoccupied, idle.
désœuvrement, *s.m.* Idleness.
désolant, *a.* Distressing, sad.
désolation, *s.f.* Desolation.
désolé, *a.* **1.** Desolate. **2.** Grieved.
désoler, *v.tr.* **1.** To devastate (country). **2.** To distress.
 se désoler, to grieve.
désordonné, *a.* **1.** Disordered. **2.** Disorderly, dissolute.
désordre, *s.m.* **1.** Disorder, confusion. **2.** Disorderliness. **3.** *pl.* Disturbances, riots.
désorganisation, *s.f.* Disorganization.
désorganiser, *v.tr.* To disorganize.
désorienté, *a.* At a loss.
désormais, *adv.* Henceforth.
despote, *s.m.* Despot.
despotique, *a.* Despotic.
despotiquement, *adv.* Despotically.

despotisme, *s.m.* Despotism.
dessaisir, *v.tr.* To dispossess.
dessécher, *v.tr.* **1.** To dry up. **2.** To desiccate.
dessein, *s.m.* **1.** Design, plan. **2.** Intention, purpose. A d., on purpose.
desserrer, *v.tr.* To loosen.
dessert, *s.m.* Dessert.
desservir[1], *v.tr.* (Of railway) To serve.
desservir[2], *v.tr.* To clear (the table).
dessiccation, *s.f.* Desiccation.
dessin, *s.m.* **1.** (*a*) Drawing, sketching. (*b*) Drawing, sketch. **2.** Design.
dessinateur, -trice, *s.* **1.** Designer. **2.** Draughtsman, -woman.
dessiner, *v.tr.* **1.** To draw, sketch. **2.** To design.
 se dessiner, to stand out, take form.
dessous. **1.** *adv.* Under(neath), below. Vêtements de d., underclothing. En d., underneath; down (-wards). **2.** *s.m.* Lower part. Avoir le d., to get the worst of it.
dessus. **1.** *adv.* Above, over; (up)on. En d., on top; above. **2.** *s.m.* (*a*) Top, upper part. Avoir le d., to have the upper hand.
destin, *s.m.* Fate, destiny.
destinataire, *s.m. & f.* Addressee; consignee.
destination, *s.f.* Destination. Trains à d. de Paris, trains for Paris.
destinée, *s.f.* Destiny.
destiner, *v.tr.* To destine.
destitué, *a.* Deprived.
destituer, *v.tr.* To dismiss, discharge.
destitution, *s.f.* Dismissal.
destructeur, -trice. **1.** *a.* Destroying; destructive. **2.** *s.* Destroyer.
destructif, *a.* Destructive.
destruction, *s.f.* Destruction.
désuétude, *s.f.* Disuse, desuetude.
désuni, *a.* Disunited, at variance.
désunir, *v.tr.* To disunite, divide.
détaché, *a.* **1.** (*a*) Loose. (*b*) Isolated. **2.** Detached, unconcerned.
détachement, *s.m.* **1.** Detaching. **2.** Indifference (*de*, to). **3.** Detachment (of troops).
détacher, *v.tr.* To detach. (*a*) To unfasten. (*b*) To separate; to cut off.
 se détacher. **1.** To come undone. **2.** To break off.

détail [-ta:j], *s.m.* **1.** (*a*) Dividing up. (*b*) Retail. **2.** Detail.

détailler [-taje], *v.tr.* **1.** (*a*) To divide up. (*b*) To retail. **2.** To detail.

détaler, *v.i.* To decamp.

détendre, *v.tr.* To slacken, relax.

détendu, *a.* Slack.

détenir, *v.tr.* **1.** To keep. **2.** (*a*) To detain. (*b*) To withhold, keep back.

détente, *s.f.* **1.** Relaxation. **2.** Trigger

détention, *s.f.* Detention.

détenu, *s.* Prisoner.

détérioration, *s.f.* Deterioration.

détériorer, *v.tr.* To make worse.
  se détériorer, to deteriorate ; to spoil.

détermination, *s.f.* Determination

déterminé, *a.* Determined.

déterminer, *v.tr.* **1.** To settle. **2.** To cause ; to bring about. **3.** To resolve (*de,* to).

déterrer, *v.tr.* To unearth.

détestable, *a.* Detestable, hateful.

détestation, *s.f.* Detestation.

détester, *v.tr.* To detest, hate

détonateur, *s.m.* Detonator.

détonation, *s.f.* Detonation ; report.

détoner, *v.i.* To detonate, explode.

détour, *s.m.* Turning ; roundabout way. **Sans d.,** plainly.

détourné, *a.* Indirect, circuitous.

détournement, *s.m.* **1.** Diversion. **2.** Misappropriation

détourner, *v.tr.* **1.** (*a*) To divert ; to turn aside. (*b*) To turn away, avert. **2.** To misappropriate.

détracteur, -trice, *s.* Detractor.

détraquer, *v.tr.* To put out of order.

détrempe, *s.f.* Distemper.

détremper, *v.tr.* To moisten, soak.

détresse, *s.f.* Distress.

détriment, *s.m.* Detriment, loss

détroit, *s.m.* Strait, straits.

détromper, *v.tr.* To undeceive

détrôner, *v.tr.* To dethrone.

détruire, *v.tr.* **1.** To demolish. **2.** To destroy, ruin

dette, *s.f.* Debt.

deuil [dœ:j], *s.m.* **1.** (*a*) Mourning, sorrow. **2.** Mourning.

deux, *num.a.inv.* & *s.m.* Two. **Charles D.,** Charles the Second.

deuxième, *num. a.* & *s* Second.

deuxièmement, *adv.* Secondly.

deux-points, *s.m.* Colon.

dévaliser, *v.tr.* To rob.

devancer, *v.tr.* **1.** To precede. **2.** To outstrip. **3.** To forestall.

devancier, *s.* Predecessor.

devant. 1. *prep.* Before, in front of. **2.** *adv.* Before, in front. **3.** *s.m.* Front (part). **Prendre les devants,** to go on ahead.

devanture, *s.f.* (*a*) Front(age). (*b*) D. **de magasin,** shop-front.

dévastateur, -trice, *a.* Devastating.

dévastation, *s.f.* Devastation.

déveine, *s.f.* (Run of) ill-luck.

développement, *s.m.* Development, growth.

développer, *v.tr.* To develop.

devenir, *v.pred.* (*a*) To become. **Qu'est-il devenu?** what has become of him ? (*b*) To grow into.

dévergondé, *a.* & *s.* Profligate.

déverser, *v.tr.* To pour.

dévêtir, *v.tr.* (*a*) To undress. (*b*) To take off (garment).
  se dévêtir. 1. To undress **2.** To divest oneself.

déviation, *s.f.* Deviation.

dévider, *v.tr.* To unwind.

dévier, *v.i.* To deviate. **Faire d.,** to deflect.

devin, devineresse, *s.* Soothsayer

deviner, *v.tr.* To guess.

devinette, *s.f.* Riddle, conundrum

dévisager, *v.tr.* To stare at.

devise, *s.f.* (*a*) Device (*b*) Motto. (*c*) Slogan.

deviser, *v.i.* To chat, gossip.

dévoiler, *v.tr.* **1.** To unveil **2.** To reveal, disclose.

devoir. I. *v.tr.* **1.** Should, ought. **Il aurait dû m'avertir,** he should have warned me. **2.** Must, have to. **3.** Am to. **Je dois partir demain,** I am to start to-morrow. **4.** Must. **Vous devez avoir faim,** you must be hungry. **5.** To owe.
  II. **devoir,** *s.m.* **1.** (*a*) Duty. **Se mettre en d. de,** to prepare (to). (*b*) *Sch :* Exercise. **2.** *pl.* Respects.

dévorant, *a.* Consuming ; devouring.

dévorer, *v.tr.* To devour ; to consume.

dévot. 1. *a.* Devout, religious. **2.** *s.* Devout person.

dévotement, *adv.* Devoutly.

dévotion, *s.f.* Devotion ; piety.

dévoué, *a.* Devoted, staunch.

dévouement, *s.m.* Self-sacrifice; devotion to duty.

dévouer, *v.tr.* To devote.

dextérité, *s.f.* Dexterity, skill (*à* in).

diable, *s.m.* **1.** Devil. **Pauvre d.!** poor beggar! **2. D.** (*à ressort*) Jack-in-the-box.

diablement, *adv.* Awfully.

diablotin, *s.m.* Little devil; imp.

diabolique, *a.* Diabolical, fiendish.

diacre, *s.m.* Deacon.

diadème, *s.m.* Diadem.

diagnostic, *s.m.* Diagnosis.

diagnostiquer, *v.tr.* To diagnose.

diagonal, -aux. **1.** *a.* Diagonal. **2.** *s.f.* Diagonale, diagonal (line).

diagonalement, *adv.* Diagonally.

diagramme, *s.m.* Diagram.

dialecte, *s.m.* Dialect.

dialogue, *s.m.* Dialogue.

diamant, *s.m.* Diamond.

diamétral, -aux, *a.* Diametrical.

diamètre, *s.m.* Diameter.

diane, *s.f.* Reveille.

diapason, *s.m.* **1.** Diapason, pitch. **2.** Tuning-fork.

diaphane, *a.* Diaphanous.

diaphragme, *s.m.* Diaphragm.

diaprer, *v.tr.* To variegate.

diarrhée, *s.f.* Diarrhoea.

dictateur, *s.m.* Dictator.

dictatorial, -aux, *a.* Dictatorial.

dictature, *s.f.* Dictatorship.

dictée, *s.f.* Dictation.

dicter, *v.tr.* To dictate.

diction, *s.f.* Diction; elocution.

dictionnaire, *s.m.* Dictionary.

dicton, *s.m.* Common saying.

dièse, *s.m.* *Mus:* Sharp.

diète, *s.f.* Diet, regimen.

dieu, -ieux, *s.m.* God. **1. Grands dieux!** heavens! **2.** (*a*) **S'il plaît à D.,** God willing; D.V. (*b*) **D. merci!** thank heaven! **3.** *int.* **Mon D.!** dear me!

diffamateur, -trice, *s.* Slanderer.

diffamation, *s.f.* Slander, libel.

diffamatoire, *a.* Defamatory, slanderous, libellous.

diffamer, *v.tr.* To slander, libel.

différemment, *adv.* Differently.

différence, *s.f.* Difference.

différencier, *v.tr.* To differentiate.

différend, *s.m.* Difference, dispute.

différent, *a.* Different.

différer. **1.** *v.tr.* To defer; to put off. **2.** *v.i.* To differ.

difficile, *a.* Difficult.

difficilement, *adv.* With difficulty.

difficulté, *s.f.* Difficulty.

difforme, *a.* Deformed, misshapen.

difformité, *s.f.* Deformity.

diffus, *a.* Diffused; diffuse.

diffuser, *v.tr.* **1. Lumière diffusée,** flood-lighting. **2.** To broadcast.

diffusion, *s.f.* **1.** Diffusion; spread. **2.** Broadcasting. **3.** Verbosity

digérer, *v.tr.* To digest.

digestible, *a.* Digestible.

digestif, *a.* Digestive.

digestion, *s.f.* Digestion.

digital, -aux, *a.* **Empreinte digitale,** finger-print.

digne, *a.* **1.** Deserving, worthy. **2.** Dignified.

dignement, *adv.* **1.** Suitably. **2.** With dignity; worthily.

dignitaire, *s.m.* Dignitary.

dignité, *s.f.* Dignity.

digression, *s.f.* Digression.

digue, *s.f.* (*a*) Dike, dam. (*b*) Breakwater; sea-wall.

dilapidation, *s.f.* Squandering.

dilapider, *v.tr.* To squander.

dilatation, *s.f.* Dilation; distension

dilater, *v.tr.* To dilate, expand.

dilemme, *s.m.* Dilemma.

diligemment, *adv.* Diligently.

diligence, *s.f.* **1.** (*a*) Diligence. (*b*) Haste, dispatch. **2.** (Stage-)coach.

diligent, *a.* Diligent, industrious.

diluer, *v.tr.* To dilute (*de.* with).

dilution, *s.f.* Dilution.

dimanche, *s.m.* Sunday.

dimension, *s.f.* Dimension, size.

diminuer, *v.tr. & i.* To lessen: to diminish; to abate.

diminutif, *a. & s.m.* Diminutive.

diminution, *s.f.* Diminution, lessening; abatement.

dinde, *s.f.* Turkey(-hen).

dindon, *s.m.* Turkey-cock.

dindonneau, -x, *s.m.* Young turkey.

dîner. **I.** *v.i.* To dine. **II. dîner,** *s.m.* Dinner.

dîneur, -euse, *s.* Diner

diocèse, *s.m.* Diocese.

diphtongue, *s.f.* Diphthong.

diplomate, *s.m.* Diplomatist.

diplomatie, *s.f.* Diplomacy.

diplomatique, *a.* Diplomatic.

diplôme, *s.m.* Diploma.

dire. I. *v.tr.* 1. To say, tell. (*a*) **Qu'en dira-t-on?** what will people say? **Je vous l'avais bien dit!** didn't I tell you so? **Comme on dit,** as the saying goes. **Dites toujours!** go on! say it! **A vrai d.,** to tell the truth. **Vous l'avez dit,** quite so. **Il n'y a pas à d.,** there is no denying it. **Dites donc,** I say! (*b*) **Il ne se le fit pas d. deux fois,** he didn't wait to be told twice. (*c*) **Faire d. qch. à qn,** to make s.o. tell sth. 2. **D. à qn de faire qch.,** to tell s.o. to do sth. 3. (*a*) To express. (*b*) To suit; to appeal to. 4. (*a*) **Vouloir d.,** to mean. (*b*) **Qu'est-ce à d.?** what does this mean?

II. **dire,** *s.m.* Statement, assertion.

direct [-ɛkt], *a.* Direct. straight. **Train d.,** through train.

directement, *adv.* Directly, straight.

directeur, -trice. 1. *s.* Director, directress; head; principal. 2. *a.* Directing, controlling.

direction, *s.f.* 1. (*a*) Guidance. (*b*) Board of directors. 2. Direction, course. **Train d. de,** train for. 3. *pl.* Directions.

directorat, *s.m.* Directorate.

dirigeant, *a.* Directing, guiding.

diriger, *v.tr.* 1. To direct, control. 2. (*a*) To direct; to guide. (*b*) To level, point (*sur*, at).

se diriger, to make one's way.

discernable, *a.* Discernible, visible.

discernement, *s.m.* 1. Perception: discrimination. 2. Discernment.

discerner, *v.tr.* To discern, distinguish.

disciple, *s.m.* Disciple, follower.

disciplinaire, *a.* Disciplinary.

discipline, *s.f.* Discipline.

discipliner, *v.tr.* To discipline.

discontinuer, *v.tr.* To discontinue.

discordant, *a.* Discordant.

discorde, *s.f.* Discord, dissension.

discourir, *v.i.* To discourse.

discours, *s.m.* 1. Talk. 2. Discourse 3. Speech, address.

discourtois, *a.* Discourteous.

discrédit, *s.m.* Discredit; disrepute.

discréditer, *v.tr.* To disparage; to discredit.

discret, -ète, *a.* (*a*) Discreet. (*b*) Quiet. unobtrusive.

discrètement, *adv.* 1. Discretely. 2. Unobtrusively.

discrétion, *s.f.* 1. Discretion. 2. **A d.,** unconditionally; unlimited.

disculpation, *s.f.* Exculpation.

disculper, *v.tr.* To exculpate, exonerate.

discursif, *a.* Discursive.

discussion, *s.f.* Discussion, debate.

discutable, *a.* Debatable, arguable.

discuter, *v.tr.* (*a*) To discuss, debate. (*b*) To question, dispute.

disette, *s.f.* Scarcity, dearth.

diseur, -euse, *s.* **Diseuse de bonne aventure,** fortune-teller.

disgrâce, *s.f.* Disfavour, disgrace.

disgracié, *a.* Out of favour.

disgracieux, *a.* 1. Uncouth. 2. Ungracious.

disjoindre, *v.tr.* To disjoin, sever.

dislocation, *s.f.* Dislocation.

disloquer, *v.tr.* To dislocate.

disparaître, *v.i.* To disappear.

disparate. 1. *a.* (*a*) Dissimilar. (*b*) Ill-matched. 2. *s.f.* Incongruity.

disparition, *s.f.* Disappearance.

disparu, *a.* 1. Missing. 2. Extinct.

dispendieux, *a.* Expensive, costly.

dispensaire, *s.m.* Dispensary.

dispensation, *s.f.* 1. Dispensation. 2. *Pharm:* Dispensing.

dispenser, *v.tr.* 1. To exempt. 2. To dispense.

disperser, *v.tr.* To disperse, scatter.

dispersion, *s.f.* Dispersion.

disponibilité, *s.f.* Availability.

disponible, *a.* Available.

dispos, *a.m.* Fit, well, in good form.

disposer. 1. *v.tr.* To dispose. 2. *v.ind.tr.* **Les moyens dont je dispose,** the means at my disposal.

se disposer, to make ready.

dispositif, *s.m.* Apparatus, device.

disposition, *s.f.* Disposition. 1. Arrangement; lie (of the land). 2. (*a*) State (of mind) (*b*) Tendency. (*c*) *pl.* Natural aptitude. 3. *pl.* Arrangements. 4. Disposal.

disproportionné, *a.* Disproportionate.

dispute, *s.f.* Altercation, quarrel.

disputer, *v.tr.* 1. To dispute. 2. *v.i.* To quarrel, wrangle.

se disputer, to quarrel.

disque, *s.m.* (*a*) Disk. disc. (*b*) (Gramophone) record.

disquisition, s.f. Disquisition.
dissection, s.f. Dissection.
dissemblable, a. Dissimilar.
dissemblance, s.f. Dissimilarity.
dissémination, s.f. Dissemination.
disséminer, v.tr. To disseminate.
dissension, s.f. Dissension discord
dissentiment, s.m. Dissent.
disséquer, v.tr. To dissect.
dissertation, s.f. Dissertation.
dissidence, s.f. Dissidence; dissent.
dissident. 1. a. Dissident, dissentient. **2.** s. Dissenter.
dissimilaire, a. Dissimilar, unlike.
dissimulation, s.f. **1.** Dissimulation;
deceit. **2.** Concealment.
dissimulé, a. Dissimulating, secretive.
dissimuler, v.tr. To dissemble, dissimulate conceal. *Abs.* To dissemble.
   se dissimuler, to hide.
dissipation, s.f. Dissipation.
dissipé, a. Dissipated; gay.
dissiper, v.tr. (*a*) To dissipate; to
dispel. (*b*) To dissipate, waste.
   se dissiper. 1. To vanish. **2.** To
amuse oneself.
dissolu, a. Dissolute, profligate.
dissolution, s.f. **1.** Dissolution.
2. (*a*) Dissolving. (*b*) Solution.
dissolvant, a. & s.m. (Dis)solvent.
dissonance, s.f. **1.** Dissonance. **2.**
Mus: Discord.
dissonant, a. Dissonant, discordant.
dissoudre, v.tr. **1.** To dissolve.
2. To disintegrate.
   se dissoudre. 1. To dissolve.
2. To break up.
dissuader, v.tr. To dissuade.
distance, s.f. Distance.
distancer, v.tr. To outdistance.
distant, a. Distant.
distendre, v.tr. To distend.
distension, s.f. Distension.
distillation, s.f. Distilling.
distiller, v.tr. To distil.
distillerie, s.f. Distillery.
distinct [-tĕ:kt], a. Distinct.
distinctement, adv. Distinctly.
distinctif, a. Distinctive.
distinction, s.f. Distinction. **1.** Sans
d., indiscriminately. **2.** Honour.
distinguable, a. Distinguishable.
distingué, a. Distinguished.
distinguer, v.tr. **1.** To distinguish.
2. To discern.

   se distinguer. 1. To distinguish
oneself. **2.** To stand out.
distique, s.m. Couplet.
distraction, s.f. **1.** Absence of mind.
2. Diversion, amusement.
distraire, v.tr. **1.** To distract.
2. To divert, amuse.
   se distraire, to amuse oneself.
distrait, a. Absent-minded.
distraitement, adv. Absent-mindedly.
distribuer, v.tr. To distribute.
distributeur, -trice, s. Distributor.
distribution, s.f. Distribution. **D.**
de prix, speech-day. **D. d'eau,**
water supply.
dit, a. (*a*) Settled fixed. (*b*) (So-)
called.
divaguer, v.i. (*a*) To digress. (*b*)
To ramble (in delirium).
divan, s.m. Divan; couch.
divergence, s.f. Divergence.
divergent, a. Divergent.
diverger, v.i. To diverge.
divers, a. pl. (*a*) Diverse, varied.
Faits d., news items. (*b*) *Indef. adj.*
Various, sundry.
diversement, adv. Diversely.
diversifier, v.tr. To diversify, vary
diversion, s.f. Diversion, change.
diversité, s.f. Diversity.
divertir, v.tr. To entertain, amuse.
divertissant, a. Diverting, amusing.
divertissement, s.m. Diversion.
dividende, s.m. Dividend.
divin, a. Divine.
divinité, s.f. Divinity.
diviser, v.tr. To divide.
divisible, a. Divisible.
division, s.f. Division.
divorce, s.m. Divorce.
divulguer, v.tr. To divulge.
dix, num.a.inv. & s.m. **1.** Ten. **2.** Le
dix mai, the tenth of May.
dix-huit. 1. Eighteen. **2.** Le dix-huit
mai, the eighteenth of May.
dix-huitième, a. Eighteenth.
dixième, num. a & s.m. Tenth.
dix-neuf. 1. Nineteen. **2.** Le dix-
neuf mai, the nineteenth of May
dix-neuvième, Nineteenth.
dix-sept. 1. Seventeen. **2.** Le dix-
sept mai, the seventeenth of May.
dix-septième, Seventeenth
dizaine, s.f. (About) ten.
docile, a. Docile.

docilement, *adv.* Submissively
docilité, *s.f.* Docility.
docte, *a.* Learned.
docteur, *s.m.* Doctor.
doctrine, *s.f.* Doctrine, tenet.
document, *s.m.* Document.
documentaire, *a* Documentary.
dodu, *a.* Plump.
dogmatique. I. *a.* Dogmatic.
dogme, *s.m.* Dogma, tenet.
dogue, *s.m.* Mastiff.
doigt, *s.m.* Finger. (*a*) **Donner sur les doigts à qn**, to rap s.o. over the knuckles. (*b*) **Être à deux doigts de**, to be within an ace of. (*c*) **D. de pied**, toe.
doigtier, *s.m.* Finger-stall.
doléances, *s.f.pl.* Complaints.
dolent, *a.* Whining, doleful.
domaine, *s.m.* I. Domain; estate, property. **2.** Field, scope.
dôme, *s.m.* Dome, cupola.
domestique. I. *a.* Domestic. **2.** *s.m. & f.* (Domestic) servant.
domicile, *s.m.* Residence. **A d.**, at one's private house.
domicilié, *a.* Resident, domiciled.
dominant, *a.* Dominating, dominant.
domination, *s.f.* Domination, sway.
dominer. I. *v.i.* To rule. **2.** *v.tr.* To dominate. (*a*) To rule. (*b*) To tower above.
dominical, -aux, *a.* **L'oraison dominicale**, the Lord's prayer.
domino, *s.m.* Domino.
dommage, *s.m.* I. (*a*) Damage, injury. (*b*) **Quel d.!** what a pity! **2.** *pl.* (*a*) Damage. (*b*) *Jur:* **Dommages-intérêts**, damages.
dompter [dɔ̃te], *v.tr.* To tame; to subdue; to master.
dompteur, -euse [dɔ̃t-], *s.* Tamer.
don, *s.m.* Gift.
donation, *s.f.* Donation, gift.
donc [dɔ̃k]. I. *conj.* Therefore, consequently. **2.** *adv.* [dɔ̃] **Mais taisez-vous d.!** do hold your tongue! **Pensez d.!** just think!
donjon, *s.m.* Keep (of castle)
données, *s.f.pl.* Data.
donner, *v.tr.* To give. I. **Je vous le donne en vingt**, I give you twenty guesses. **S'en d.**, to have a good time. **D. les cartes**, to deal (the cards). **2.** (*a*) To provide, furnish; to yield. **Cela donne à penser**, this

gives food for reflection. (*b*) **D. faim à qn**, to make s.o. hungry. **3.** To attribute. **D. raison à qn**, to agree with s.o. **4.** (*a*) To look out (*sur*, on). (*b*) **D. de la tête contre**, to knock one's head against. **D. dans le piège**, to fall into the trap.
dont, *rel.pron.* (*a*) From, by, with, whom or which. (*b*) Of whom, which. (*c*) Whose.
doré, *a* Gilded, gilt.
dorénavant, *adv.* Henceforth.
dorer, *v.tr.* To gild.
dorloter, *v.tr.* To fondle; to pamper.
dormant, *a.* Sleeping.
dormeur, -euse, *s.* Sleeper.
dormir, *v.i.* I. To sleep; to be asleep. **D. sur les deux oreilles**, to sleep soundly. **2.** To be dormant
dortoir, *s.m.* Dormitory.
dorure, *s.f.* I. Gilding. **2.** Gilt.
dos, *s.m.* Back.
dose, *s.f.* Dose.
dossier, *s.m.* I. Back (of seat). **2.** (*a*) Documents, file. (*b*) Record
dot [dɔt], *s.f.* Dowry.
doter, *v.tr.* (*a*) To dower. (*b*) To endow.
douairière, *a. & s.f.* Dowager
douane, *s.f.* Customs.
douanier. I. *a.* Customs. **2.** *s.m.* Custom-house officer.
double. I. *a.* Double, twofold. **2.** *adv.* Double. **3.** *s.m.* (*a*) Double. (*b*) Duplicate.
doublement, *adv.* Doubly.
doubler. I. *v.tr.* (*a*) To double; to understudy. *Aut:* **Défense de d.**, overtaking forbidden. (*b*) To line (coat). **2.** *v.i.* To double.
doublure, *s.f.* I. Lining. **2.** *Th:* Understudy.
douce. See DOUX.
doucement, *adv.* Gently, softly.
doucereux, *a.* I. Sweetish, sickly. **2.** Mealy-mouthed, smooth-tongued.
douceur, *s.f.* I. (*a*) Sweetness. (*b*) *pl.* Sweet things. **2.** Softness. **3.** Pleasantness. **4.** Gentleness.
douche, *s.f.* Shower-bath
doué, *a.* Gifted.
douer, *v.tr.* To endow (*de*, with).
douillet, -ette [duj-], *a.* Soft, downy.
douleur, *s.f.* Suffering. I. Pain, ache. **2.** Sorrow, grief woe.

douloureusement, *adv.* **1.** Painfully. **2.** Sorrowfully.

douloureux, *a.* Painful. **1.** Aching; sore. **2.** Sad, distressing.

doute, *s.m.* Doubt, misgiving.

douter, *v.i.* To doubt. **D. de,** to mistrust.
se douter de, to suspect.

douteusement, *adv.* Doubtfully.

douteux, *a.* Doubtful, uncertain.

Douvres. *Pr.n.f.* Dover.

doux, *f.* **douce,** *a.* (*a*) Sweet; smooth, soft. **Eau douce,** fresh water. (*b*) Pleasant. (*c*) Gentle.

douzaine, *s.f.* Dozen.

douze, *num.a.inv. & s.m.inv.* Twelve. **Le d. mai,** the twelfth of May.

douzième, *num. a & s.m.* Twelfth.

doyen, *s.* **1.** Dean. **2.** Senior.

dragée, *s.f.* Sugar(ed) almond.

dragon, *s.m* **1.** Dragon. **2.** Dragoon.

drague, *s.f.* Dredger.

draguer, *v.tr.* To dredge.

dragueur, *a. & s.m.* Dredger. **D. de mines,** mine-sweeper.

dramatique, *a.* Dramatic.

dramatiquement, *adv.* Dramatically.

dramatiser, *v.tr.* To dramatize.

dramaturge, *s.m. & f.* Dramatist.

drame, *s.m.* (*a*) Drama (*b*) Play.

drap, *s.m.* **1.** Cloth. **2. D. de lit,** sheet. **Dans de beaux draps,** in a sorry plight.

drapeau, *s.m.* Flag; colour.

draper, *v.tr.* To drape.

draperie, *s.f.* Drapery.

drapier, *s.* Draper, clothier.

dresser, *v.tr.* **1.** To erect. **2.** To draw up. **3.** To adjust. **4.** To train.
se dresser. (*a*) To stand up. (*b*) To sit up; to become all attention.

dressoir, *s.m.* Sideboard, dresser.

drogue, *s.f.* Drug.

droit[1]**,** *a.* **1.** Straight, upright. **2.** (*a*) Direct, straight. **Allez tout d.,** keep straight on. **3.** Straightforward. **4.** (*a*) Right. (*b*) *s.f.* **Droite,** right hand.

droit[2]**,** *s.m.* **1.** Right. **A bon d.,** with good reason. **Faire d. à,** to accede to. **2.** Charge, due. **3.** Law.

droiture, *s.f.* Uprightness, rectitude.

drôle[1]**,** *s.m.* Rascal, knave, scamp.

drôle[2]**,** *a.* Funny, droll, odd.

drôlement, *adv.* Funnily, drolly.

dromadaire, *s.m.* Dromedary.

dru. **1.** *a.* Thick, close-set. **2.** *adv.* **Tomber dru,** to fall thick and fast.

druide, -esse, *s* Druid, druidess.

du = *de le.*

dû, due. **1.** *a.* Due. (*a*) Owing. (*b*) Proper. **2.** *s.m.* Due.

duc, *s.m.* Duke.

ducal, -aux, *a.* Ducal.

duché, *s.m.* Duchy, dukedom.

duchesse, *s.f.* Duchess.

ductile, *a.* Ductile.

duègne, *s.f.* Duenna.

duel, *s.m.* Duel, encounter.

duelliste, *s.m* Duellist.

dûment, *adv.* Duly ; in due form.

dune, *s.f.* Dune, sand-hill ; down.

Dunkerque. *Pr.n.f.* Dunkirk

duo, *s.m.* Duet.

dupe, *s.f.* Dupe.

duper, *v.tr.* To dupe, to gull.

duperie, *s.f.* **1.** Dupery, deception. **2.** Take-in.

duplicité, *s.f.* Duplicity, deceit.

dur, *a.* **1.** Hard; tough. **2. Avoir l'oreille dure,** to be hard of hearing. **3.** Hard, harsh.

durabilité, *s.f.* Durability.

durable, *a.* Durable, lasting.

durant, *prep.* During.

durcir. **1.** *v.tr.* To harden. **2.** *v.i. & pr.* To grow hard.

durcissement, *s.m.* Hardening.

durée, *s.f.* **1.** Lasting quality ; wear. **2.** Duration.

durement, *adv* **1.** Hard ; hardly. **2.** Harshly, severely.

durer, *v.i.* To last endure.

dureté, *s.f.* **1.** Hardness ; toughness. **2.** Difficulty. **3.** Harshness.

durillon [-rij5], *s.m.* Corn (on foot).

duvet, *s.m.* Down (on chin).

dynamique. **1.** *a* Dynamic. **2.** *s.f.* Dynamics.

dynamite, *s.f.* Dynamite.

dynamo, *s.f.* Dynamo.

dynastie, *s.f.* Dynasty.

dysenterie, *s.f.* Dysentery.

dyspepsie, *s.f.* Dyspepsia.

E

E, e [e], *s.m.* (The letter) E, e.

eau, *s.f.* Water. **1.** Ville d'eau, watering-place. **2.** (*a*) Cours d'eau, watercourse, stream. (*b*) Eau courante dans les chambres, hot and cold water in the rooms.

eau-de-vie, *s.f.* Spirits ; brandy.

eau-forte, *s.f.* **1.** Nitric acid. **2.** Etching. *pl. eaux-fortes.*

ébahir, *v.tr.* To astound, flabbergast.

ébahissement, *s.m.* Amazement.

ébats, *s.m.pl.* Gambols, revels.

ébauche, *s.f.* Rough sketch.

ébaucher, *v.tr.* To sketch out.

ébène, *s.f.* Ebony.

ébéniste, *s.m.* Cabinet-maker.

éblouir, *v.tr.* To dazzle.

éblouissement, *s.m.* **1.** Dazzling. **2.** Dizziness, vertigo.

éborgner, *v.tr.* To put (s.o.'s) eye out.

éboulement, *s.m.* **1.** Caving in. **2.** Land-slide, landslip.

ébouler (s'), *v.pr.* To crumble.

éboulis, *s.m.* Mass of debris.

ébouriffer, *v.tr.* To dishevel, ruffle.

ébranlement, *s.m.* **1.** Shaking ; shock. **2.** Perturbation, commotion.

ébranler, *v.tr.* To shake ; to set in motion.
  s'ébranler. 1. To shake, totter. **2.** (Of train) To start.

ébrécher, *v.tr.* To notch.

ébrouer (s'), *v.pr.* **1.** (Of horse) To snort. **2.** (Of bird) To take a bath.

ébruiter, *v.tr.* To noise abroad.

ébullition, *s.f.* Ebullition, boiling.

écaille [eka:j], *s.f.* **1.** Scale (of fish). **2.** Shell (of oyster).

écale, *s.f.* Shell (of nut).

écaler, *v.tr.* To shell (nuts).

écarlate, *s.f.* & *a.* Scarlet.

écarquiller [-kije], *v.tr.* To open (the eyes) wide.

écart[1], *s.m.* **1.** Deviation. Faire un é., to step aside ; to shy. **2.** Se tenir à l'é., to stand aside.

écart[2], *s.m.* *Cards :* Discard.

écarté, *a.* **1.** Lonely. **2.** Apart.

écartement, *s.m.* **1.** (*a*) Separation. (*b*) Setting aside. **2.** Space, gap.

écarter[1], *v.tr.* **1.** To separate, part. **2.** To move aside. **3.** To divert.
  s'écarter, to move aside.

écarter[2], *v.tr.* *Cards :* To discard.

ecclésiastique. 1. *a.* Ecclesiastical. **2.** *s.m.* Ecclesiastic, clergyman.

écervelé, *a.* Hare-brained.

échafaud, *s.m.* Scaffold.

échalas, *s.m.* Vine-prop ; hop-pole.

échalote, *s.f.* Shallot.

échancrer, *v.tr.* To notch.

échancrure, *s.f.* Notch ; indentation.

échange, *s.m.* Exchange.

échanger, *v.tr.* To exchange.

échantillon [-tijɔ̃], *s.m.* Sample.

échappée, *s.f.* Space, interval ; vista.

échapper, *v.i.* To escape. (*a*) É. à toute définition, to baffle definition. (*b*) **Laisser é. une larme,** to let fall a tear.
  s'échapper, to escape ; to break free.

écharpe, *s.f.* (*a*) Sash. (*b*) Armsling.

échasse, *s.f.* Stilt.

échauder, *v.tr.* To scald.

échauffant, *a.* Heating.

échauffement, *s.m.* **1.** Heating. **2.** Over-excitement.

échauffer, *v.tr.* (*a*) To overheat. (*b*) To warm.
  s'échauffer. (*a*) **Ne vous échauffez pas,** don't get excited. (*b*) To warm (up).

échéance, *s.f.* Date (of payment).

échec [-ɛk], *s.m.* **1.** (*a*) Check. É. et mat, checkmate. (*b*) Check, failure. **2.** *pl.* Chess.

échelle, *s.f.* **1.** Ladder. **2.** Scale.

échelon, *s.m.* Rung.

échelonner, *v.tr.* To space out ; to stagger (holidays).

écheveau, *s.m.* Hank, skein.

échevelé, *a.* Dishevelled.

échine, *s.f.* Spine, backbone.

échiquier, *s.m.* Chess-board.

écho [eko], *s.m.* Echo.

échoir, *v.i.* **1.** To fall (to s.o.). Le cas échéant, in case of need. **2.** To fall due.

échoppe, *s.f.* Booth ; street stall.

échouer, *v.i.* (*a*) To run aground. (*b*) To fail.

éclabousser, *v.tr.* To splash. (be)-spatter.

éclaboussure, *s.f.* Splash, spatter.

éclair, *s.m.* **1.** Flash of lightning; *pl.* lightning. **2.** Flash. **3.** Éclair.

éclairage, *s.m.* Lighting; illumination.

éclaircie, *s.f.* **1.** Break, opening, rift (in clouds). **2.** Clearing.

éclaircir, *v.tr.* **1.** To clear (up). **2.** To solve, explain.
 s'éclaircir. (*a*) To clear (up). (*b*) To enlighten oneself.

éclaircissement, *s.m.* (*a*) Enlightenment. (*b*) Clearing up.

éclairé, *a.* Enlightened; well-informed.

éclairer. **1.** *v.tr.* (*a*) To light, illuminate. (*b*) To enlighten. **2.** *v.impers.* Il éclaire, it is lightening.

éclaireur, *s.m.* Scout.

éclat, *s.m.* **1.** Splinter. **Voler en éclats,** to fly into pieces. **2.** Burst. **Rire aux éclats,** to laugh heartily. **3.** Brilliancy.

éclatant, *a.* **1.** Bursting. **2.** Loud. **3.** Dazzling; vivid; brilliant.

éclatement, *s.m.* Bursting; shivering.

éclater. **1.** *v.tr.* To burst. **2.** *v.i.* To burst, explode; to fly (into pieces). **É. de rire,** to burst out laughing. **3.** *v.i.* To sparkle.

éclipse, *s.f.* Eclipse.

éclipser, *v.tr.* To eclipse.
 s'éclipser, to disappear, vanish.

éclisse, *s.f.* Splint.

éclore, *v.i.* **1.** (Of eggs) To hatch (out). **2.** (Of flowers) To open.

écluse, *s.f.* (Canal) lock.

éclusier, *s.* Lock-keeper.

écœurant, *a.* Disgusting; sickening.

écœurement, *s.m.* Disgust.

écœurer, *v.tr.* To disgust.

école, *s.f.* School. **Faire l'é. buissonnière,** to play truant.

écolier, *s.* Scholar.

éconduire, *v.tr.* To show out.

économe. **1.** *s.m. & f.* Bursar, steward. **2.** *a.* Economical, thrifty.

économie, *s.f.* **1.** Economy. **2.** *pl.* Savings.

économique, *a.* Economical.

économiser, *v.tr.* To economize, save.

écorce, *s.f.* Bark; rind, peel.

écorcher, *v.tr.* **1.** To skin. **2.** To graze.

écorchure, *s.f.* Scratch, graze.

écossais. **1.** *a.* Scottish. **2.** *s.* Scot.

Écosse. *Pr.n.f.* Scotland.

écosser, *v.tr.* To shell (peas).

écot, *s.m.* **1.** Share, quota. **2.** Score, reckoning.

écoulement, *s.m.* Flow, discharge.

écouler. **1.** *v.pr.* (*a*) To flow out. (*b*) To pass, elapse. **2.** *v.tr.* To sell.

écourter, *v.tr.* To shorten.

écoute, *s.f.* **1.** Se tenir aux écoutes, to keep one's ears open. **2.** Listening in.

écouter, *v.tr.* **1.** (*a*) To listen to. (*b*) To listen in. **2.** To pay attention to.

écran, *s.m.* Screen.

écrasement, *s.m.* Crushing.

écraser, *v.tr.* To crush; to squash. **Se faire é.,** to get run over.
 s'écraser, to crumple up; to crash.

écrevisse, *s.f.* Crayfish.

écrier (s'), *v.pr.* (*a*) To cry (out). (*b*) To exclaim.

écrin, *s.m.* (Jewel-)case.

écrire, *v.tr.* To write. **Machine à é.,** typewriter. **É. à la machine,** to type.

écrit. **1.** *a.* Written. **2.** *s.m.* Writing.

écriteau, *s.m.* Placard, bill, notice.

écriture, *s.f.* **1.** Writing. **2.** (*a*) *pl.* Papers. (*b*) **L'É. sainte,** Holy Scripture.

écrivain, *s.m.* Author, writer.

écrou, *s.m.* (Screw-)nut.

écroulement, *s.m.* Collapse.

écrouler (s'), *v.pr.* To collapse.

écu, *s.m.* **1.** (*a*) *A:* Shield. (*b*) Coat of arms. **2.** *A:* Crown (= 3 francs).

écueil [ekœ:j], *s.m.* Reef.

écuelle, *s.f.* Bowl, basin.

écume, *s.f.* **1.** (*a*) Froth; foam. (*b*) Scum. **2. É. de mer,** meerschaum.

écumer. **1.** *v.tr.* To skim. **2.** *v.i.* To foam, froth.

écureuil [-rœ:j], *m.* Squirrel.

écurie, *s.f.* Stable.

écusson, *s.m.* Escutcheon.

écuyer. **1.** *s.m.* Equerry. **2.** *s.* Rider.

édifiant, *a.* Edifying.

édification, *s.f.* Edification.

édifice, *s.m.* Building, edifice.

édifier, *v.tr.* **1.** To erect. **2.** To edify.

Édimbourg. *Pr.n.* Edinburgh.

édit, *s.m.* Edict.

éditer, *v.tr.* To edit.

éditeur, -trice, *s.* **1.** Editor (of text). **2.** Publisher.

édition, *s.f.* **1.** Edition. **2.** Publishing.

Édouard. *Pr.n.m.* Edward.

édredon, *s.m.* Eider-down.

éducation, *s.f.* (*a*) Education. (*b*) Training. (*c*) Upbringing, breeding.

effacement, *s.m.* **1.** Obliteration. **2.** Retirement; self-effacement.

effacer, *v.tr.* To efface, obliterate.

s'effacer, to stand aside.

effarement, *s.m.* Fright, alarm.

effarer, *v.tr.* To frighten, scare.

s'effarer, to be frightened (*de,* at, by); to take fright (*de,* at).

effaroucher, *v.tr.* To startle.

s'effaroucher, to be startled (*de,* at, by); to take fright (*de,* at).

effectif, *a.* Effective.

effectivement, *adv.* **1.** Effectively. **2.** Actually. **3.** (In answer) That is so.

effectuer, *v.tr.* To effect, carry out.

efféminé, *a.* Effeminate, unmanly.

effervescence, *s.f.* Effervescence.

effervescent, *a.* Effervescent.

effet, *s.m.* **1.** Effect, result. **A cet e.,** to this end. **2.** (*a*) Action, operation. (*b*) **En e.,** as a matter of fact; indeed. **3.** Impression. **4.** *pl.* Possessions.

efficace, *a.* Efficacious, effectual.

efficacité, *s.f.* Efficacy; efficiency.

effigie, *s.f.* Effigy.

effilé, *a.* Slender; tapering.

effleurer, *v.tr.* To touch lightly.

effluve, *s.m.* Effluvium, emanation.

effondrement, *s.m.* Breaking down; subsidence; collapse.

effondrer, *v.tr.* To break (sth.) down.

s'effondrer, to fall in; to break down.

efforcer (s'), *v.pr.* To strive.

effort, *s.m.* **1.** Effort, exertion. **2.** Strain, stress.

effrayamment, *adv.* Frightfully.

effrayant, *a.* Frightful, terrifying, dreadful, appalling.

effrayer, *v.tr.* To frighten, scare.

s'effrayer, to take fright.

effréné, *a.* Unbridled; frantic.

effriter, *v.tr.* To crumble.

s'effriter, to crumble.

effroi, *s.m.* Fright, terror, fear.

effronté, *a.* Shameless; impudent.

effrontément, *adv.* Shamelessly.

effronterie, *s.f.* Effrontery.

effroyable, *a.* Frightful, dreadful.

effroyablement, *adv.* Frightfully.

effusion, *s.f.* Effusion, outpouring. **E. de sang,** bloodshed.

égal, -aux, *a.* **1.** (*a*) Equal. (*b*) Level. even. **2.** (All) the same.

également, *adv.* **1.** Equally, alike. **2.** Also, likewise.

égaler, *v.tr.* To equal, be equal to.

égaliser, *v.tr.* **1.** To equalize. **2.** To level.

égalité, *s.f.* **1.** Equality; *Ten:* deuce. **2.** Evenness, regularity.

égard, *s.m.* Consideration, respect. (*a*) **Avoir é. à,** to pay regard to. **A l'é. de,** with respect to. (*b*) *pl.* Attentions.

égaré, *a.* **1.** Stray, lost; out-of-the-way. **2.** Distraught.

égarement, *s.m.* **1.** (*a*) Mislaying. (*b*) Bewilderment. **2.** Wildness. **3.** Frenzy.

égarer, *v.tr.* To mislead.

s'égarer, to lose one's way.

égayer, *v.tr.* To enliven.

églantier, *s.m.* Sweet briar.

église, *s.f.* Church.

égoïsme, *s.m.* Selfishness.

égoïste. **1.** *s.m. & f.* Selfish person. **2.** *a.* Selfish.

égorger, *v.tr.* To slaughter

égout, *s.m.* Sewer; drain.

égouttement, *s.m.* Drip(ping).

égratigner, *v.tr.* To scratch.

égratignure, *s.f.* Scratch.

Égypte. *Pr.n.f.* Egypt.

égyptien, *a. & s.* Egyptian.

eh, *int.* Hey! **Eh bien!** well!

éjection, *s.f.* Ejection.

élaborer, *v.tr.* To elaborate.

élan[1], *s.m.* **1.** (*a*) Spring, dash. (*b*) Impetus. **2.** Burst, outburst.

élan[2], *s.m.* Elk, moose.

élancé, *a.* Tall and slim; slender

élancer, *v.i.* To throb.

s'élancer. **1.** To spring; to rush (*sur,* at). **2.** To shoot up.

élargir, *v.tr.* **1.** (*a*) To widen. (*b*) To enlarge. **2.** To release.

s'élargir. (*a*) To widen out. (*b*) To grow, extend.

élargissement, *s.m.* Enlarging; release.

élasticité, *s.f.* Elasticity.

élastique, *a. & s.m.* Elastic.

électeur, -trice, *s.* Elector, voter.

élection, *s.f.* **1.** Election. **2.** Choice.

électoral, -aux, *a.* Electoral.

électricien, *s.m.* Electrician.
électricité, *s.f.* Electricity.
électrique, *a.* Electric.
électriser, *v.tr.* To electrify.
électrocution, *s.f.* Electrocution
élégamment, *adv.* Elegantly.
élégance, *s.f.* Elegance; stylishness.
élégant, *a.* Elegant, stylish.
élégie, *s.f.* Elegy.
élément, *s.m.* **1.** Element. **2.** *pl.* Rudiments.
élémentaire, *a.* Elementary.
éléphant, *s.m.* Elephant.
élevage, *s.m.* Breeding, raising.
élévation, *s.f.* **1.** Elevation, lifting. **2.** Rise. **3.** Height. **4.** High ground.
élève, *s.m. & f.* Pupil; student.
élevé, *a.* **1.** High; noble, lofty. **2.** Bred.
élever, *v.tr.* **1.** To elevate; to raise. **2.** To bring up, rear; to breed.
 s'élever. **1.** To rise (up); to amount. **2.** To raise oneself.
éleveur, -euse, *s.* Breeder.
elfe, *s.m* Elf, brownie.
éligibilité, *s.f.* Eligibility.
éligible, *a.* Eligible.
élimination, *s.f.* Elimination.
éliminer, *v.tr.* To eliminate.
élire, *v.tr.* To elect, choose.
élite, *s.f.* Élite; flower, pick.
elle, *pers.pron.f.* **1.** She; it. **2.** Her, it.
elle-même, *pers.pron.f.* Herself, itself.
elles, *pers.pron.f.pl.* **1.** They. **2.** Them.
elles-mêmes, *pers.pron.f.pl.* Themselves.
élocution, *s.f.* Elocution.
éloge, *s.m.* **1.** Eulogy. **2.** Praise.
éloigné, *a.* Far; distant; remote.
éloignement, *s.m.* **1.** Removal; postponement. **2.** (*a*) Absence. (*b*) Distance, remoteness. (*c*) Aversion.
éloigner, *v.tr.* (*a*) To remove. (*b*) To postpone, put off.
 s'éloigner, to move off.
éloquemment, *adv.* Eloquently.
éloquence, *s.f.* Eloquence.
éloquent, *a.* Eloquent.
élu. **1.** *a.* Chosen; successful. **2.** *s.pl.* Elect.
élucidation, *s.f.* Elucidation
élucider, *v.tr.* To elucidate.
éluder, *v.tr.* To elude, evade.
émaciation, *s.f.* Emaciation.
émacié, *a* Emaciated; wasted

émail [ema:j], *pl.* **émaux,** *s.m.* Enamel.
émailler [emaje], *v.tr.* **1.** To enamel. **2.** (Of flowers) To dot (the fields).
émanation, *s.f.* Emanation.
émancipation, *s.f.* Emancipation
émanciper, *v.tr.* To emancipate
émaner, *v.i.* To emanate, issue.
émaux. See ÉMAIL.
emballage, *s.m.* **1.** Packing, wrapping. **2.** Spurt.
emballer, *v.tr.* **1.** To pack; to wrap up. **2.** *Abs.* To spurt.
 s'emballer. (*a*) (Of horse) To bolt. (*b*) (Of engine) To race. (*c*) To be carried away (by excitement).
embarcadère, *s.m.* Landing-stage; wharf, quay.
embarcation, *s.f.* (Ship's) boat.
embardée, *s.f.* Yaw, lurch.
embargo, *s.m.* Embargo.
embarquement, *s.m.* Embarkation.
embarquer. **1.** *v.tr.* To embark; to ship; to hoist in (boat). **2.** *v.i. & pr.* To embark.
embarras, *s.m.* **1.** Encumbrance. **2.** Difficulty trouble. **3.** Embarrassment.
embarrassant, *a.* **1.** Cumbersome. **2.** Embarrassing, awkward.
embarrassé, *a.* **1.** Encumbered. **2.** Embarrassed.
embarrasser, *v.tr.* To embarrass. **1.** To (en)cumber. **2.** To trouble, inconvenience.
embaucher, *v.tr.* To engage; to hire.
embaumer, *v.tr.* **1.** To embalm. **2.** To perfume, scent.
embellir. **1.** *v.tr.* To embellish. **2.** *v.i.* To improve in looks.
embellissement, *s.m.* **1.** Embellishment. **2.** Improvement (in looks).
embêtant, *a.* **1.** Annoying. **2.** Tiresome.
embêter, *v.tr* **1.** To annoy, vex. **2.** To bore.
emblée (d'), *adv.phr.* Straight off.
emblématique, *a.* Emblematic(al).
emblème, *s.m.* **1.** (*a*) Emblem, device. (*b*) Badge, crest. **2.** Symbol, sign.
emboîter, *v.tr* To fit together. E. le pas, to fall into step.
embonpoint, *s.m.* Stoutness.
embouchure, *s.f.* **1.** Mouthpiece. **2.** Opening, mouth.

embourber (s'), *v.pr* To stick in the mud.

embranchement, *s.m.* **1.** Branching (off). **2.** Branch; branch-line.

embrasé, *a.* Blazing; fiery.

embrasement, *s.m.* Conflagration.

embraser, *v.tr.* To set ablaze.
 s'embraser, to catch fire.

embrassement, *s.m.* Embrace.

embrasser, *v.tr.* **1.** (*a*) To embrace. (*b*) To adopt (career). **2.** To include.

embrasure, *s.f* Embrasure; window-recess.

embrouillement [ãbrujmã], *s.m.* **1.** Entanglement. **2.** Confusion.

embrouiller [ãbruje], *v.tr.* **1.** To tangle. **2.** To confuse, muddle.
 s'embrouiller, to get muddled.

embrumé, *a.* Misty; clouded.

embrun, *s.m.* Spray, spindrift.

embryon, *s.m.* Embryo.

embûche, *s.f.* Ambush, snare.

embuscade, *s.f.* Ambush.

embusquer (s'), *v.pr* To lie in ambush.

émeraude, *s.f. & a.inv.* Emerald.

émerger, *v.i.* **1.** To emerge. **2.** To come into view.

émeri, *s.m.* Emery.

émerveillé [-vɛje], *a.* Amazed, wonder-struck.

émerveiller [-vɛje], *v.tr.* To amaze; to fill with admiration.
 s'émerveiller, to marvel (*de*, at).

émétique, *s.m.* Emetic.

émetteur, -trice. **1.** *s.m.* Transmitter. **2.** *a.* Poste é., broadcasting station.

émettre, *v.tr.* **1.** (*a*) To emit; to give off. (*b*) To broadcast. **2.** To issue.

émeu, *s.m.* Emu. *pl.* émeus.

émeute, *s.f.* Riot. Chef d'é., ring-leader.

émietter, *v.tr.* To crumble.

émigrant, *s.* Emigrant.

émigration, *s.f.* Emigration.

émigré, *s.* (*a*) Emigrant. (*b*) Émigré.

émigrer, *v.i.* **1.** To migrate. **2.** To emigrate.

éminemment, *adv.* Eminently.

éminence, *s.f.* Eminence.

éminent, *a.* Eminent; distinguished.

émissaire, *s.m.* Emissary. *a.* Bouc é., scapegoat.

émission, *s.f.* **1.** (*a*) Emission. (*b*) Broadcasting. **2.** Issue.

emmagasiner, *v.tr.* To store.

emmailloter [ãmaj-], *v.tr.* To swaddle; to bind (up).

emmêler, *v.tr.* (*a*) To tangle. (*b*) To mix up; to muddle.

emmener, *v.tr.* To take away.

emmitoufler, *v.tr.* To muffle.

émoi, *s.m.* Emotion, agitation.

émoluments, *s.m.pl.* Emoluments.

émotion, *s.f.* Emotion; excitement.

émoudre, *v.tr.* To grind, sharpen.

émoussé, *a.* Blunt.

émousser, *v.tr.* (*a*) To blunt; to take the edge off. (*b*) To dull, deaden.

émouvant, *a.* Moving. (*a*) Touching. (*b*) Stirring, thrilling.

émouvoir, *v.tr.* To move. (*a*) To stir up. (*b*) To affect, touch.
 s'émouvoir. **1.** To get excited. **2.** To be touched.

empailler [ãpaje], *v.tr.* To stuff

empaqueter, *v.tr.* To pack up.

emparer (s'), *v.pr.* S'e. de qch., to take possession of sth.

empêchement, *s.m.* Hindrance.

empêcher, *v.tr.* To prevent, hinder, impede.
 s'empêcher, to refrain.

empereur, *s.m.* Emperor.

empeser, *v.tr.* To starch.

empester, *v.tr.* To make stink.

empêtrement, *s.m.* Entanglement.

empêtrer, *v.tr.* To entangle; to trammel.

emphase, *s.f.* Bombast.

emphatique, *a.* Bombastic.

empiétement, *s.m.* Encroachment.

empiéter, *v.i.* To encroach.

empiler, *v.tr.* To stack, to pile (up).

empire, *s.m.* **1.** (*a*) Dominion; sway. (*b*) Control. **2.** Empire.

empirer, **1.** *v.tr.* To make worse. **2.** *v.i.* To grow worse.

emplacement, *s.m.* (*a*) Site (*b*) Location. (*c*) Place, spot.

emplâtre, *s.m.* Pharm: Plaster.

emplette, *s.f.* Purchase. Aller faire ses emplettes, to go shopping.

emplir, *v.tr.* To fill (up).

emploi, *s.m.* **1.** Use. E. du temps, time-table. **2.** Employment, post.

employé, *s.* Employee, assistant.

employer, *v.tr.* **1.** To employ, use. **2.** To employ (s.o.).

empocher, *v.tr.* To pocket.

empoigner, *v.tr.* 1. To grasp, seize. 2. To arrest. 3. To thrill, grip.

empois, *s.m.* Starch.

empoisonner, *v.tr.* To poison. **s'empoisonner**, to take poison.

empoisonneur, -euse, *s.* Poisoner.

emporté, *a.* Quick-tempered.

emportement, *s.m.* Transport (of anger).

emporter, *v.tr.* 1. To take away. 2. (*a*) To carry away. (*b*) To take (by assault). 3. **L'e. sur**, to get the better of.
s'emporter, to lose one's temper.

empourpré, *a.* Crimson.

empourprer, *v.tr.* To tinge with crimson.
s'empourprer, to turn crimson.

empreindre, *v.tr.* To impress, stamp.

empreinte, *s.f.* Impress, print.

empressé. 1. *a.* Eager, zealous. 2. *s.* Busybody.

empressement, *s.m.* Eagerness, readiness, alacrity.

empresser (s'), *v.pr.* 1. To hurry, hasten. 2. **S'e. auprès de**, to dance attendance on.

emprisonnement, *s.m.* Imprisonment.

emprisonner, *v.tr.* To imprison.

emprunt, *s.m.* Borrowing; loan. **Nom d'e.**, assumed name.

emprunté, *a.* (*a*) Assumed (name); (*b*) Borrowed.

emprunter, *v.tr.* To borrow.

emprunteur, -euse, *s.* Borrower.

ému, *a.* Affected; moved.

émulation, *s.f.* Emulation, rivalry.

émule, *s.m. & f.* Emulator, rival.

en[1], *prep.* 1. In, (in)to. **En tramway**, by tram. **En tête**, at the head. **Aller en France**, to go to France. 2. In. **En cinq jours**, (with)in five days. 3. (*a*) **En réparation**, under repair. **En faction**, on guard. (*b*) **Montre en or**, gold watch. (*c*) **De mal en pis**, from bad to worse. 4. **En philosophe**, philosophically. 5. While. **En attendant**, in the meantime.

en[2]. I. *adv.* 1. From there; thence. 2. On that account.
II. **en**, *pron.inv.* 1. Of him, her, it, them. 2. Some, any. 3. **Prenez-en dix**, take ten.

enamourer (s'), *v.pr.* To fall in love.

encadrement, *s.m.* 1. Framing. 2. Framework; frame; setting.

encadrer, *v.tr.* To frame.

encaisser, *v.tr.* To encash, collect.

encan, *s.m.* (Public) auction.

enceinte, *s.f.* Enclosure.

encens, *s.m.* Incense.

encercler, *v.tr.* To encircle.

enchaînement, *s.m.* 1. Chaining (up). 2. Chain, series; sequence.

enchaîner, *v.tr.* 1. To chain up. 2. To link (up), connect.

enchanté, *a.* 1. Enchanted. 2. Delighted (*de*, with).

enchantement, *s.m.* 1. Enchantment. 2. Charm. 3. Delight.

enchanter, *v.tr.* 1. To enchant. 2. To charm, delight.

enchanteur, -eresse. 1. *s.* Enchanter, enchantress. 2. *a.* Bewitching.

enchère, *s.f.* Bid(ding). **Mettre aux enchères**, to put up for auction.

enchérir, *v.i.* (*a*) To go up in price. (*b*) **E. sur**, to outbid.

enchérisseur, -euse, *s.* Bidder.

enchevêtré, *a.* Tangled.

enchevêtrement, *s.m.* Tangle.

enchevêtrer, *v.tr.* To mix up, confuse.

enclin, *a.* Inclined, disposed.

enclos, *s.m.* Enclosure; paddock.

enclume, *s.f.* Anvil.

encoignure, *s.f.* Corner, angle.

encolure, *s.f.* 1. **Gagner par une e.**, to win by a neck. 2. Size in collars.

encombrant, *a.* Cumbersome.

encombre, *s.m.* Hindrance.

encombrement, *s.m.* (*a*) Litter; congestion (of traffic). (*b*) Overcrowding.

encombrer, *v.tr.* To encumber.

encontre (à l'), *adv.phr.* **A l'e. de**, against; in opposition to.

encore, *adv.* 1. (*a*) Still. **Hier e.**, only yesterday. (*b*) Yet. (*c*) More, again. **E. une tasse de café**, another cup of coffee. 2. (*a*) **E. si**, if even. (*b*) *Conj.phr.* **E. (bien) que**, (al-) though; even though.

encourageant, *a.* Encouraging.

encouragement, *s.m.* Encouragement.

encourager, *v.tr.* To encourage.

encourir, *v.tr.* To incur.

encre, *s.f.* Ink. **E. sympathique,** invisible ink.

encrier, *s.m.* Inkpot; inkstand.

encyclopédie, *s.f.* Encyclopedia.

endetter (s'), *v.pr.* To get into debt.

endiablé, *a.* (a) Reckless, devil-may-care. (b) Wild, frenzied (music).

endiguer, *v.tr.* To dam up.

endimanché, *a.* Dressed in (one's) Sunday best.

endolori, *a.* Painful, sore; tender.

endommager, *v.tr.* To damage.

endormi, *a.* **1.** (a) Asleep. (b) Sleepy. (c) Dormant. **2.** Numb.

endormir, *v.tr.* **1.** To put to sleep. **2.** To allay.
s'**endormir,** to fall asleep.

endosser, *v.tr.* **1.** To put on; to take on. **2.** To endorse.

endroit, *s.m.* **1.** Place, spot. **2.** Side, aspect.

enduire, *v.tr.* To smear, coat.

enduit, *s.m.* Coat, coating.

endurable, *a.* Endurable.

endurance, *s.f.* Endurance.

endurant, *a.* Patient; long-suffering.

endurci, *a.* **1.** Hardened. **2.** Callous.

endurcir, *v.tr.* **1.** To harden. To inure.

endurcissement, *s.m.* **1.** Hardening. **2.** Hardness; obduracy.

endurer, *v.tr.* To endure, bear.

énergie, *s.f.* Energy; force, vigour.

énergique, *a.* (a) Energetic. (b) Strong, drastic.

énergiquement, *adv.* Energetically.

énervement, *s.m.* State of nerves.

énerver, *v.tr.* **1.** To enervate. **2.** É. qn, to get on s.o.'s nerves.

enfance, *s.f.* **1.** Childhood. **Première e.,** infancy. **2.** Seconde e., dotage.

enfant, *s.m. & f.* Child; boy; girl. **E. trouvé,** foundling.

enfantement, *s.m.* Childbirth.

enfanter, *v.tr.* To give birth to.

enfantillage [-tij-], *s.m.* Childishness.

enfantin, *a.* **1.** Infantile. **2.** Childish.

enfer, *s.m.* Hell. **Les enfers,** the underworld; Hades.

enfermer, *v.tr.* **1.** To shut up. **Sentir l'enfermé,** to smell stuffy. **2.** To shut in; to enclose.

enfiévré, *a.* Fevered.

enfiler, *v.tr.* **1.** To thread; to file; to string. **2.** To go along. **3.** To slip on (clothes).

enfin, *adv.* (a) Finally, lastly. (b) In fact, in short. (c) At last.

enflammé, *a.* **1.** Burning. blazing; fiery. **2.** Glowing.

enflammer, *v.tr.* To inflame.
s'**enflammer,** to take fire.

enflé, *a.* Swollen.

enfler, *v.tr., i. & pr.* To swell.

enflure, *s.f.* Swelling.

enfoncé, *a.* **1.** Smashed (in). **2.** Sunken.

enfoncement, *s.m.* **1.** Driving (in); breaking open. **2.** Depression; recess.

enfoncer, *v.tr.* (a) To drive (in); to thrust on, in. (b) To break (open).
s'**enfoncer,** to penetrate.

enfouir, *v.tr.* To hide in the ground.

enfourcher, *v.tr.* To bestride.

enfourchure, *s.f.* Fork, crotch.

enfreindre, *v.tr.* To infringe, transgress.

enfuir (s'), *v.pr.* To flee, fly; to run away.

enfumer, *v.tr.* To fill with smoke.

engageant, *a.* Engaging, prepossessing, winning; inviting.

engagement, *s.m.* **1.** Pawning. **2.** Engagement.

engager, *v.tr.* **1.** To pawn; to pledge. **2.** To engage. **3.** (a) To catch, entangle. (b) To fit, insert. **4.** To begin; to open. **5.** To urge.
s'**engager.** **1.** To undertake. **2.** (a) To take service. (b) To enlist. **3.** (a) (Of rope) To foul. (b) **S'e. dans,** to enter. (c) To begin.

engelure, *s.f.* Chilblain.

engendrer, *v.tr.* To engender.

engin, *s.m.* Engine, machine; device.

engloutir, *v.tr.* **1.** To swallow. **2.** To engulf; to swallow up.

engloutissement, *s.m.* Swallowing up; engulfment.

engorger, *v.tr.* To choke (up).

engouement, *s.m.* Infatuation.

engouffrer, *v.tr.* To engulf.

engourdi, *a.* **1.** Numb. **2.** Dull.

engourdir, *v.tr.* To (be)numb.

engourdissement, *s.m.* **1.** Numbness. **2.** Dullness, sluggishness.

engrais, *s.m.* Manure.

engraisser. **1.** *v.tr.* To fatten. **2.** *v.i.* To grow stout.

enhardir, *v.tr.* To embolden.
s'**enhardir,** to pluck up courage.

énigmatique, *a.* Enigmatic(al).

énigme, *s.f.* Enigma, riddle.

enivrant, *a.* Intoxicating, heady.

enivrement, *s.m.* Intoxication.

enivrer, *v.tr.* To intoxicate.

enjambée, *s.f.* Stride.

enjamber, *v.tr.* (*a*) To bestride. (*b*) To step over; to span.

enjeu, -eux, *s.m.* *Gaming:* Stake.

enjoindre, *v.tr.* To enjoin.

enjôler, *v.tr.* To coax, wheedle.

enjôleur, -euse. 1. *s.* Coaxer. **2.** *a.* Coaxing.

enjoliver, *v.tr.* To embellish

enjoué, *a.* Playful, sprightly.

enjouement, *s.m.* Sprightliness.

enlacer, *v.tr.* (*a*) To entwine (*b*) To clasp in one's arms.

enlaidir. 1. *v.tr.* To make ugly; to disfigure. **2.** *v.i.* To grow ugly.

enlèvement, *s.m.* **1.** Removal. **2.** Carrying off. **3.** Storming.

enlever, *v.tr.* **1.** (*a*) To remove; to carry away. (*b*) E. qch. à qn, to take sth. from s.o. **2.** To carry off; to kidnap. **3.** To storm. **4.** To raise.

enliser (s'), *v.pr.* To get bogged.

ennemi. 1. *s.* Enemy. **2.** *a.* Hostile.

ennui, *s.m.* **1.** Worry. anxiety. **2.** Boredom.

ennuyant, *a.* Annoying, vexing.

ennuyer, *v.tr.* **1.** (*a*) To annoy, worry. (*b*) To importune. **2.** To weary.

s'ennuyer, to be bored; to weary.

ennuyeux, *a.* **1.** (*a*) Boring, tedious. (*b*) Importunate. **2.** Annoying.

énoncer, *v.tr.* **1.** To state (opinion). **2.** To articulate (word).

énonciation, *s.f.* **1.** Stating, expressing. **2.** Enunciation; articulation.

enorgueillir (s') [-gœj-], *v.pr.* To pride oneself (*de*, on).

énorme, *a.* Enormous, huge.

énormément, *adv.* Enormously.

énormité, *s.f.* (*a*) Enormity. (*b*) Vastness.

enquérir (s'), *v.pr.* To inquire, make inquiries (*de*, after).

enquête, *s.f.* Inquiry, investigation.

enraciné, *a.* Deep-rooted.

enraciner, *v.tr.* To establish.

s'enraciner, to take root.

enragé, *a.* (*a*) Mad. (*b*) Keen.

enrager. 1. *v.tr.* To enrage. **2.** *v.t.* To fume.

enregistrement, *s.m.* Registration.

enregistrer, *v.tr.* To register, record.

enrhumer (s'), *v.pr.* To catch cold.

enrichir, *v.tr.* To enrich.

s'enrichir, to grow rich.

enrôlement, *s.m.* Enrolment.

enrôler, *v.tr.* To enrol.

enroué, *a.* Hoarse, husky.

enrouement, *s.m.* Hoarseness.

enrouler, *v.tr.* To roll up; to wrap up.

ensanglanté, *a.* Covered with blood.

enseigne, *s.f.* (*a*) Sign, index. (*b*) Sign(-board). (*c*) Ensign.

enseignement, *s.m.* **1.** Teaching. **2.** Education, instruction.

enseigner, *v.tr.* **1.** To show; to point out. **2.** To teach.

ensemble. 1. *adv.* Together. **Le tout e.,** the general effect. **2.** *s.m.* (*a*) Whole. **Vue d'e.,** general view. (*b*) Unity.

enserrer, *v.tr.* (*a*) To enclose. (*b*) To squeeze.

ensevelir, *v.tr.* To bury.

ensevelissement, *s.m.* Burial.

ensoleillé [-lèje], *a.* Sunny.

ensorcelé, *a.* Bewitched.

ensorceler, *v.tr.* To bewitch.

ensuite, *adv.* After(wards), then.

ensuivre (s'), *v.pr.* To follow, result.

entacher, *v.tr.* To sully, besmirch.

entaille [ɑ̃tɑːj], *s.f.* (*a*) Notch, nick; groove. (*b*) Gash, slash.

entailler [ɑ̃tɑje], *v.tr.* (*a*) To notch. nick. (*b*) To gash, cut, slash.

entamer, *v.tr.* **1.** To cut into. **2.** To begin; to broach.

entassement, *s.m.* Accumulation.

entasser, *v.tr.* (*a*) To accumulate; to heap (up). (*b*) To pack together.

s'entasser. 1. To accumulate. **2.** To crowd together.

entendement, *s.m.* Understanding.

entendre, *v.tr.* **1.** To intend, mean. **2.** (*a*) To hear. **E. dire qch. à qn,** to hear s.o. say sth. (*b*) To listen to. **3.** To understand. **C'est entendu,** agreed. **Bien entendu!** of course!

s'entendre. 1. To agree. **2.** To be skilled (*à*, in).

entendu, *a.* (*a*) Business-like, sensible. (*b*) Knowing, shrewd.

entente, *s.f.* **1.** (*a*) Understanding. (*b*) **A double e.,** with a double meaning. **2.** Agreement. **E. cordiale,** friendly understanding.

enterrement, *s.m.* Burial, interment.

enterrer, *v.tr.* To bury, inter.

en-tête, *s.m.* (a) Heading. (b) Headline. *pl.* en-têtes.

entêté, *a.* Obstinate, headstrong.

entêtement, *s.m.* Obstinacy.

entêter (s'), *v.pr.* To be obstinate.

enthousiasme, *s.m.* Enthusiasm.

enthousiasmer, *v.tr.* To fire with enthusiasm.

enthousiaste. 1. *s.m. & f.* Enthusiast. **2.** *a.* Enthusiastic.

entier, *a.* **1.** Entire, whole. **2.** Complete, full. **3.** *Adv.phr.* En e., entirely, in full.

entièrement, *adv.* Entirely, wholly.

entonner, *v.tr.* **1.** To intone. **2.** To strike up (a song).

entonnoir, *s.m.* **1.** Funnel. **2.** Shellhole, crater.

entorse, *s.f.* Sprain, wrench, twist.

entour, *s.m.* A l'e., around, round about. A l'e. de, round.

entourage, *s.m.* **1.** Surroundings. **2.** Set; circle; environment.

entourer, *v.tr.* To surround (de, with).

entr'acte, *s.m.* **1.** Interval. **2.** Entr'acte, interlude. *pl.* entr'actes.

entr'aider (s'), *v.pr.* To help one another.

entrailles [ɑ̃trɑːj], *s.f.pl.* **1.** Entrails. **2.** Être sans e., to be ruthless.

entr'aimer (s'), *v.pr.* To love one another.

entrain, *s.m.* Liveliness, briskness.

entraînement, *s.m.* **1.** (a) Carrying away. (b) Enthusiasm. **2.** Allurement. **3.** Training.

entraîner, *v.tr.* **1.** To carry along; to carry away. **2.** To entail, involve. **3.** To train.

entrave, *s.f.* **1.** Shackle. **2.** Impediment.

entraver, *v.tr.* **1.** To shackle; to hobble. **2.** To hinder, impede.

entre, *prep.* **1.** Between. **E.** deux âges, middle-aged. **2.** (a) Among(st). (b) E. les mains de, into the hands of. (c) L'un d'e. eux, one of them.

entrebâillé [-bɑje], *a.* Ajar.

entre-choquer (s'), *v.pr.* (a) To collide. (b) To knock against one another.

entrecôte, *s.f.* Rib of beef.

entrecoupé, *a.* Interrupted, broken.

entrecouper, *v.tr.* **1.** To intersect. **2.** To interrupt.

entrée, *s.f.* **1.** Entry, entering. **2.** Admission. "E. interdite," 'no admittance.' **3.** Way in; entrance. **4.** Entrée.

entrefaite, *s.f.* Sur ces entrefaites, meanwhile.

entrelacement, *s.m.* Interlacing.

entrelacer, *v.tr.* To interlace.

entremêler, *v.tr.* To (inter-)mix. s'entremêler, to mingle.

entremise, *s.f.* Intervention.

entrepôt, *s.m.* Warehouse, store.

entreprenant, *a.* Enterprising.

entreprendre, *v.tr.* To undertake.

entrepreneur, -euse, *s.* Contractor.

entreprise, *s.f.* Undertaking; venture.

entrer, *v.i.* **1.** To enter; to go in; to come in. **2.** To enter into, take part in.

entre-regarder (s'), *v.pr.* To look at one another.

entresol, *s.m.* Entresol; mezzanine.

entretenir, *v.tr.* **1.** To maintain. **2.** To talk to (de, about). s'entretenir, to talk, converse.

entretien, *s.m.* **1.** Maintenance. **2.** Support. **3.** Conversation; interview.

entrevoir, *v.tr.* To catch a glimpse of. Laisser e., to drop a hint of.

entrevue, *s.f.* Interview.

entr'ouvert, *a.* Half-open. **2.** Gaping, yawning.

entr'ouvrir, *v.tr.* To half-open.

énumération, *s.f.* Enumeration.

énumérer, *v.tr.* To enumerate.

envahir, *v.tr.* To invade.

envahissement, *s.m.* Invasion.

envahisseur, *s.m.* Invader.

enveloppe, *s.f.* **1.** Envelope, cover (-ing); wrapper. **2.** Exterior.

enveloppement, *s.m.* Envelopment.

envelopper, *v.tr.* To envelop. (a) To wrap up. (b) To cover.

envenimer, *v.tr.* **1.** To envenom. **2.** To aggravate; to embitter.

envers[1], *s.m.* Wrong side, reverse. A l'e., inside out; wrong way up.

envers[2], *prep.* Towards.

envie, *s.f.* **1.** Desire, longing. Avoir e. de, to want. **2.** Envy.

envier, *v.tr.* To envy. **1.** To covet. **2.** To begrudge.

envieusement, *adv.* Enviously.

envieux, *a.* Envious.

environ. **1.** *adv.* About. **2.** *s.m.pl.* Surroundings, environs.

environner, *v.tr.* To surround.

envisager, *v.tr.* To face, envisage. (*a*) To look in the face. (*b*) To consider.

envoi, *s.m.* **1.** Sending, consignment. **2.** Consignment, parcel.

envol, *s.m.* (*a*) Flight. (*b*) *Av:* Take-off.

envoler (s'), *v.pr.* (*a*) To fly away; to take flight. (*b*) *Av:* To take off.

envoyé, *s.m.* Envoy; messenger.

envoyer, *v.tr.* To send. **E. promener qn,** to send s.o. to the right-about.

épagneul, *s.* Spaniel.

épais, -aisse, *a.* Thick.

épaisseur, *s.f.* **1.** Thickness; depth. **2.** Density, thickness.

épaissir, *v.tr., i. & pr.* To thicken.

épanchement, *s.m.* Outpouring, effusion.

épancher, *v.tr.* To pour out; to shed. **s'épancher,** to unbosom oneself.

épandre, *v.tr.* To spread. **s'épandre,** to spread.

épanoui, *a.* In full bloom; full-blown. **Visage é.,** beaming face.

épanouir (s'), *v.pr.* **1.** To open out, bloom. **2.** (Of face) To light up.

épanouissement, *s.m.* **1.** (*a*) Opening out. (*b*) Beaming. **2.** Bloom.

épargne, *s.f.* Saving, thrift.

épargner, *v.tr.* **1.** To save (up). **2.** To save. **3.** To spare.

éparpiller [-pije], *v.tr.* To scatter

épars, *a.* Scattered.

épatant, *a.* Wonderful; fine.

épater, *v.tr.* To astound.

épaule, *s.f.* Shoulder.

épaulette, *s.f.* (*a*) Shoulder-strap. (*b*) Epaulette.

épave, *s.f.* (*a*) Waif. (*b*) Wreck; derelict. (*c*) *pl.* Wreckage.

épée, *s.f.* Sword.

épeler, *v.tr.* To spell (out).

éperdu, *a.* Distracted, bewildered.

éperdument, *adv.* Distractedly.

éperon, *s.m.* **1.** Spur. **2.** Ram.

éperonner, *v.tr.* (*a*) To spur. (*b*) To ram.

épervier, *s.m.* Sparrow-hawk.

épeuré, *a.* Frightened, scared.

éphémère, *a.* Ephemeral.

épi, *s.m.* Ear (of grain); spike.

épice, *s.f.* Spice. **Pain d'é.,** gingerbread.

épicé, *a.* Highly spiced.

épicer, *v.tr.* To spice.

épicerie, *s.f.* **1.** Spices. **2.** (*a*) Groceries. (*b*) Grocer's shop.

épicier, *s.* Grocer.

épidémie, *s.f.* Epidemic; outbreak.

épiderme, *s.m.* Epidermis.

épier, *v.tr.* **1.** To watch; to spy upon. **2.** To be on the look-out for.

épigramme, *s.f.* Epigram.

épilepsie, *s.f.* Epilepsy.

épileptique, *a. & s.* Epileptic.

épilogue, *s.m.* Epilogue.

épinard, *s.m.* Spinach.

épine, *s.f.* **1.** Thorn-bush. **2.** Thorn, prickle. **3.** É. dorsale, spine, back-bone.

épineux, *a.* Thorny prickly.

épingle, *s.f.* Pin. **Coups d'é.,** pin-pricks.

épingler, *v.tr.* To pin.

épique, *a.* Epic.

épiscopal, -aux, *a.* Episcopal.

épisode, *s.m.* Episode.

épitaphe, *s.f.* Epitaph.

épithète, *s.f.* Epithet.

épitomé, *s.m.* Epitome, abridgment.

épître, *s.f.* Epistle.

éploré, *a.* Tearful, weeping.

éplucher, *v.tr.* To peel (potatoes)

épluchures, *s.f.pl.* Peelings.

éponge, *s.f.* Sponge.

éponger, *v.tr.* S'é. le front, to mop one's brow.

épopée, *s.f.* Epic (poem).

époque, *s.f.* **1.** Epoch, era, age. **2.** A l'é. de, at the time of.

épouse. See ÉPOUX.

épouser, *v.tr.* **1.** To marry, wed. **2.** To espouse.

épousseter, *v.tr.* To dust.

épouvantable, *a.* Dreadful, frightful.

épouvantail [-ta:j], *s.m.* **1.** Scarecrow. **2.** Bugbear.

épouvante, *s.f.* Terror, fright.

épouvanter, *v.tr.* To terrify. **s'épouvanter,** to take fright.

époux, -ouse, *s.* Husband, *f.* wife; spouse.

éprendre (s'), *v.pr.* To become enamoured.

épreuve, *s.f.* **1.** (*a*) Proof, test. A l'é. de, proof against. (*b*) *Sp:* Event. **2.** Trial, ordeal. **3.** (*a*) *Typ:* Proof. (*b*) *Phot:* Print.

épris, *a.* In love (*de*, with).

éprouvé, *a.* Well-tried.

éprouver, *v.tr.* 1. To test. try 2. To feel, experience.

éprouvette, *s.f.* Test-tube

épuisant, *a.* Exhausting.

épuisé, *a.* Exhausted.

épuisement, *s.m.* Exhaustion.

épuiser, *v.tr.* To exhaust.
s'épuiser, to become exhausted.

équanimité [ekwa-]. *s.f.* Equanimity.

équateur [ekwa-]. 1. *s.m.* Equator. Sous l'é., at the equator. 2. *Pr.n.m.* Ecuador.

équatorial, -aux [ekwa-], *a.* Equatorial.

équerre, *s.f.* *Tls:* Square.

équestre, *a.* Equestrian.

équilibre, *s.m.* Equilibrium.

équilibré, *a.* In equilibrium ; balanced.

équilibrer, *v.tr.* To balance.

équinoxe, *s.m.* Equinox.

équinoxial, -aux, *a.* Equinoctial.

équipage, *s.m.* 1. Crew. 2. Equipage. 3. Apparel, attire.

équipe, *s.f.* 1. Gang (of workmen). Travailler par équipes, to work in shifts. Chef d'é., foreman. 2. *Sp:* Team ; side.

équipement, *s.m.* Equipment.

équiper, *v.tr.* To equip ; to fit out.

équitable, *a.* Equitable, fair.

équitablement, *adv.* Equitably.

équité, *s.f.* Equity, fairness.

équivalent, *a. & s.m.* Equivalent.

équivaloir, *v.i.* To be equivalent ; to be equal in value.

équivoque. 1. *a.* (*a*) Equivocal, ambiguous. (*b*) Questionable, dubious. 2. *s.f.* Ambiguity.

équivoquer, *v.i.* To equivocate

érable, *s.m.* Maple.

érafler, *v.tr.* To scratch, graze.

éraflure, *s.f.* Slight scratch ; graze.

éraillé [-oje], *a.* Frayed.

ère, *s.f.* Era ; epoch.

érection, *s.f.* Erection ; setting up.

éreinter, *v.tr.* To exhaust.

ergot, *s.m.* Spur (of cock).

ériger, *v.tr.* 1. To erect, set up. 2. To establish, set up.

ermitage, *s.m.* Hermitage.

ermite, *s.m.* Hermit.

éroder, *v.tr.* To erode, abrade.

érosion, *s.f.* Erosion ; wearing away.

errant, *a.* 1. Rambling, roving. 2. Erring, misguided.

erre, *s.f.* (Head)way (of ship).

errer, *v.i.* 1. To roam, wander. 2. To err ; to be mistaken.

erreur, *s.f.* Error.

erroné, *a.* Erroneous, mistaken.

érudit. 1. *a.* Erudite. 2. *s.* Scholar.

érudition, *s.f.* Erudition, learning.

éruption, *s.f.* Eruption.

ès [es] = en les. **Docteur ès lettres,** doctor of literature.

escabeau, *s.m.* (Wooden) stool.

escadre, *s.f.* *Navy:* Squadron

escadrille [-ri:j], *s.f.* Flotilla.

escadron, *s.m.* *Mil:* Squadron.

escalade, *s.f.* Scaling, climbing.

escalader, *v.tr.* To scale, climb.

escale, *s.f.* 1. Place of call. 2. Call.

escalier, *s.m.* Staircase ; stairs. E. roulant, escalator.

escalope, *s.f.* Cutlet.

escamotage, *s.m.* 1. Conjuring. 2. Sneaking, filching.

escamoter, *v.tr.* 1. To make vanish. 2. To sneak, filch.

escamoteur, *s.m.* Conjurer.

escapade, *s.f.* Escapade ; prank.

escarbille [-bi:j], *s.f.* Cinder.

escarboucle, *s.f.* *Lap:* Carbuncle.

escargot, *s.m.* Snail.

escarmouche, *s.f.* Skirmish.

escarpé, *a.* Steep, precipitous.

escarpement, *s.m.* 1. Steepness. 2. Abrupt descent.

escarpin, *s.m.* (Dancing-)shoe

esclavage, *s.m.* Slavery.

esclave, *s.m. & f.* Slave.

escompte [eskɔ̃:t], *s.m.* Discount.

escompter [-kɔ̃te], *v.tr.* 1. To dis count. 2. To reckon upon.

escorte, *s.f.* Escort ; convoy.

escorter, *v.tr.* To escort ; to convoy.

escouade, *s.f.* Squad, gang.

escrime, *s.f.* Fencing.

escroc, *s.m.* Swindler, sharper.

escroquerie, *s.f.* Swindle.

espace, *s.m.* Space.

espacé, *a.* At wide intervals.

espacer, *v.tr.* To space (out).

espadrille [-ri:j], *s.f.* (*a*) Canvas shoe. (*b*) Bathing sandal.

Espagne. *Pr.n.f.* Spain.

espagnol. 1. *a.* Spanish. 2. *s.* Spaniard. 3. *s.m.* Spanish.

espèce, *s.f.* **1.** (*a*) Kind, sort. (*b*) *pl.* Specie, cash, coin. **2.** Species.

espérance, *s.f.* Hope.

espérer, *v.tr.* To hope.

espiègle, *a. & s.* Mischievous.

espion, *s.* Spy.

espionnage, *s.m.* Espionage, spying.

espionner, *v.tr.* To spy (up)on. *Abs.* To spy.

espoir, *s.m.* Hope.

esprit, *s.m.* **1.** (*a*) Spirit. (*b*) Ghost, phantom. (*c*) Sprite. **2.** (*a*) Mind. (*b*) Wit. **3.** Spirit, feeling.

Esquimau, -aux, *s. & a.* Eskimo.

esquisse, *s.f.* Sketch; outline.

esquisser, *v.tr.* To sketch, outline.

esquiver, *v.tr.* To avoid, evade. **s'esquiver,** to slip away.

essai, *s.m.* **1.** Trial, test(ing). **A l'e.,** on approval. **2.** (*a*) Attempt(ing), try. **Coup d'e.,** first attempt. (*b*) *Lit:* Essay.

essaim, *s.m.* Swarm (of bees).

essaimer, *v.i.* (Of bees) To swarm.

essayer, *v.tr.* **1.** (*a*) To test, try. (*b*) To try on. (*c*) To assay. **2. E. de faire qch.,** to try to do sth.

essence, *s.f.* **1.** (*a*) Petrol. (*b*) Essence, extract. **2.** Spirit; gist.

essentiel, *a. & s.m.* Essential.

essentiellement, *adv.* Essentially.

essieu, -eux, *s.m.* Axle.

essor, *s.m.* Flight, soaring.

essoufflé, *a.* Out of breath.

essoufflement, *s.m.* Breathlessness.

essouffler, *v.tr.* To blow, wind. **s'essouffler,** to get out of breath.

essuie-main(s), *s.m.inv.* Towel.

essuyer [esɥije], *v.tr.* **1.** To wipe; to wipe up. **2.** To suffer endure.

est¹ [ɛst], *s.m.* East.

est² [ɛ]. See ÊTRE.

estaminet, *s.m.* **1.** Public house. **2.** Bar; tap-room.

estampe, *s.f.* Print, engraving.

esthétique, *a.* Aesthetic.

estimable, *a.* Estimable.

estimation, *s.f.* (*a*) Valuing, appraising. (*b*) Estimate, valuation.

estime, *s.f.* Esteem, regard.

estimer, *v.tr.* **1.** To estimate. **2.** (*a*) To consider. (*b*) To esteem.

estomac, *s.m.* Stomach.

estrade, *s.f.* Dais; platform, stage.

estropié, *a.* Crippled, maimed.

estropier, *v.tr.* To cripple. maim

estuaire, *s.m.* Estuary.

esturgeon, *s.m.* Sturgeon

et [e], *conj.* And **Et . . . et . . .** both . . and . .

étable, *s.f.* Cow-shed; cattle-shed.

établi, *s.m.* (Work-)bench.

établir, *v.tr.* **1.** (*a*) To establish; to fix. (*b*) To prove. **2.** To draw up. **3.** To institute. **4.** To set up. **s'établir,** to establish oneself, to take up one's abode.

établissement, *s.m.* Establishment.

étage, *s.m.* **1.** Story, floor. **2.** (*a*) Tier, step. (*b*) Degree, rank.

étai, *s.m.* Stay, prop.

étain, *s.m.* **1.** Tin. **2.** Pewter.

étalage, *s.m.* Display, show.

étaler, *v.tr.* To display.

étalon¹, *s.m.* Stallion.

étalon², *s.m.* Standard (of weights).

étameur, *s.m.* (*a*) Tinsmith. (*b*) É. ambulant, tinker.

étamine, *s.f.* Stamen.

étampe, *s.f.* Stamp, die.

étanche, *a.* Watertight.

étancher, *v.tr* (*a*) To stanch. (*b*) To quench.

étang, *s.m.* Pond, pool.

étape, *s.f.* Stage (of journey); halting-place.

état, *s.m.* **1.** State, condition. **2.** (*a*) Statement, return. (*b*) **Faire é. de,** to take into account. (*c*) É. civil, civil status. **3.** Profession trade. **4.** State; government.

état-major, *s.m.* (*a*) (General) staff. **Carte d'é.-m.,** ordnance map (*b*) Headquarters. *pl. états-majors.*

États-Unis (les), *Pr.n.m.pl.* The United States (of America).

étau, -aux, *s.m.* *Tls:* Vice.

étayer, *v.tr.* To stay, prop (up).

été¹, *s.m* Summer.

été². See ÊTRE.

éteindre, *v.tr.* To extinguish. **s'éteindre.** (*a*) To die out. (*b*) To fade; to die away.

éteint, *a.* (*a*) Extinguished. **Le feu est é.,** the fire is out. (*b*) Extinct. (*c*) Dull; faint.

étendard, *s.m.* Colours, standard.

étendre, *v.tr.* **1.** To spread, stretch. **2.** To extend. **s'étendre. 1.** To lie at full length.

2. (*a*) To extend, stretch. (*b*) To spread.

étendu. I. *a.* (*a*) Extensive. (*b*) Outstretched. **2.** *s.f.* Étendue, extent; stretch.

éternel, *a.* Eternal.

éternellement, *adv.* Eternally

éternité, *s.f.* Eternity.

éternuement, *s.m.* **I.** Sneezing. **2.** Sneeze.

éternuer, *v.i.* To sneeze.

éthéré, *a.* Ethereal, airy.

éthique. I. *a.* Ethical. **2.** *s.f.* Ethics.

ethnologie, *s.f.* Ethnology.

Étienne. *Pr.n.m.* Stephen.

étinceler, *v.i.* **I.** To throw out sparks. **2.** To sparkle.

étincelle, *s.f.* Spark.

étincellement, *s.m.* Sparkling.

étiqueter, *v.tr.* To label; to ticket.

étiquette, *s.f.* **I.** Label, ticket. **2.** Etiquette.

étirer, *v.tr.* To stretch; to draw out. **s'étirer,** to stretch oneself.

étoffe, *s.f.* Stuff, material; fabric.

étoile, *s.f.* Star. **I. Coucher à la belle é.,** to sleep in the open. **2.** Asterisk, star. **3.** *Th:* Star.

étoilé, *a.* Starry, starlit.

étonnamment, *adv.* Astonishingly.

étonnant, *a.* Astonishing, surprising.

étonnement, *s.m.* Astonishment, surprise, wonder, amazement.

étonner, *v.tr.* To astonish, surprise. **s'étonner,** to be astonished, surprised, to wonder (*de,* at).

étouffant, *a.* Suffocating; sultry.

étouffer. I. *v.tr.* (*a*) To suffocate, smother. (*b*) To stifle; to suppress. **2.** *v.i. & pr.* To suffocate, choke.

étourderie, *s.f.* **I.** Thoughtlessness. **2.** Thoughtless action.

étourdi, *a.* Thoughtless; foolish.

étourdiment, *adv.* Thoughtlessly.

étourdir, *v.tr.* **I.** To stun, daze. **2.** To deaden.

étourdissant, *a.* Stunning.

étourdissement, *s.m.* Giddiness.

étourneau, *s.m.* Starling.

étrange, *a.* Strange, peculiar, queer.

étrangement, *adv.* Strangely.

étranger. I. (*a*) *a.* Foreign. (*b*) *s.* Foreigner, alien. (*c*) *s.m.* **A l'é.,** abroad. **2.** (*a*) *a.* Strange. (*b*) *s.* Stranger. **3.** *a.* Extraneous.

étrangeté, *s.f.* Strangeness, oddness.

étranglé, *a.* Constricted; choking.

étranglement, *s.m.* (*a*) Strangling. (*b*) Constriction.

étrangler. (*a*) *v.tr.* To strangle. (*b*) *v.i.* **É. de colère,** to choke with rage.

étrave, *s.f.* Stem (of ship).

être. I. *v.i. & pred.* **I.** To be; to exist. **2.** (*a*) **Nous étions trois,** there were three of us. **Nous sommes le dix,** to-day is the tenth. (*b*) **Il est midi,** it is twelve o'clock. (*c*) **Où en sommes-nous?** how far have we got? (*d*) **C'en est trop!** this is past bearing. (*e*) **Il n'en est rien!** nothing of the kind! **3.** (*a*) **Ê à,** to belong to. (*b*) **C'est à vous de jouer,** it is your turn to play. **4.** **Il est arrivé,** he has arrived.

II. être, *s.m.* Being.

étrécir, *v.tr.* To narrow. **s'étrécir. I.** To contract. **2.** To shrink.

étreindre, *v.tr.* To embrace; to clasp.

étreinte, *s.f.* (*a*) Embrace. (*b*) Grasp, grip.

étrenne, *s.f.* New-Year's gift.

étrier, *s.m.* Stirrup.

étroit, *a.* **I.** Narrow; confined. **2.** Tight; tight(-fitting).

étroitement, *adv.* **I.** Narrowly. **2.** Tightly, closely.

étude, *s.f.* **I.** (*a*) Study (*b*) Research. **2.** Office (of notary).

étudiant, *s.* Student.

étudier, *v.tr.* To study.

étui, *s.m.* Case, box.

étymologie, *s.f.* Etymology.

eu [y], **eûmes** [ym]. SEE AVOIR.

eunuque, *s.m.* Eunuch.

euphémisme, *s.m.* Euphemism.

eurent [y:r]. SEE AVOIR.

Europe. *Pr.n.f.* Europe.

européen, *a. & s.* European.

euss-e, -es, etc. [ys]. SEE AVOIR.

Eustache. *Pr.n.m.* Eustace.

eux, *pers.pron.mpl.* (*a*) They. (*b*) Them.

eux-mêmes, *pers.pron.m.pl.* Themselves.

évacuation, *s.f.* Evacuation.

évacuer, *v.tr.* To evacuate.

évader (s'), *v.pr.* To escape.

évaluation, *s.f.* Valuation, appraisement; estimate.

évaluer, *v.tr.* To value. appraise ; to estimate.

évangile, *s.m.* Gospel.

évanouir (s'), *v.pr.* **1.** To vanish, disappear. **2.** To faint, swoon.

évanouissement, *s.m.* Swoon.

évaporation, *s.f.* Evaporation.

évaporer (s'), *v.pr.* To evaporate.

évasif, *a* Evasive.

évasion, *s.f* **1.** Escape. **2.** Quibble. evasion.

évasivement, *adv.* Evasively.

évêché, *s.m.* **1.** Bishopric, diocese, see. **2.** Bishop's palace.

éveil [evɛ:j], *s.m.* **1.** (a) Awakening. (b) **En é.,** on the alert. **2.** Warning.

éveillé, *a.* **1.** Awake. **2.** Wide-awake.

éveiller [evɛje], *v.tr.* To wake up. **s'éveiller,** to wake (up).

événement, *s.m.* Event.

éventail [-ta:j], *s.m.* Fan.

éventer, *v.tr.* **1.** To air. **2.** To fan.

éventrer, *v.tr.* To rip open.

éventualité, *s.f.* Possibility. eventuality.

éventuel. 1. *a.* Possible. **2.** *s.m.* Eventuality, contingency.

éventuellement, *adv.* Possibly contingently ; on occasion.

évêque, *s.m.* Bishop.

évertuer (s'), *v.pr.* To do one's utmost ; to exert oneself.

éviction, *s.f.* Eviction.

évidemment, *adv.* **1.** Evidently, obviously. **2.** Certainly ; of course.

évidence, *s.f.* (a) Obviousness clearness. (b) Conspicuousness.

évident, *a.* Evident, obvious

évier, *s.m.* (Scullery) sink.

évincer, *v.tr.* **1.** To evict **2.** To oust, supplant.

évitable, *a.* Avoidable.

éviter, *v.tr.* To avoid, shun.

évocation, *s.f.* Evocation.

évoluer, *v.i.* **1.** To perform evolutions. **2.** To evolve, develop.

évolution, *s.f.* Evolution.

évoquer, *v.tr.* (a) To evoke. call forth. (b) To call to mind.

exact [-zakt], *a.* Exact. (a) Accurate, correct. (b) Strict. (c) Punctual.

exactement, *adv.* Exactly

exaction, *s.f.* Exaction.

exactitude, *s.f.* (a) Exactness, accuracy, exactitude. (b) Punctuality.

exagération, *s.f.* Exaggeration.

exagérer, *v.tr.* To exaggerate.

exaltation, *s.f.* **1.** Exalting, glorifying. **2.** Exaltation ; excitement.

exalté. 1. *a.* (a) Impassioned. (b) Hotheaded. (c) Uplifted. **2.** *s.* Fanatic.

exalter, *v.tr.* **1.** To exalt. **2.** To excite, inflame. **s'exalter,** to grow enthusiastic.

examen, *s.m.* Examination.

examinateur, -trice, *s.* Examiner.

examiner, *v.tr.* To examine.

exaspération, *s.f.* Exasperation

exaspérer, *v.t.* To exasperate.

exaucer, *v.tr.* To fulfil (wish).

excavation, *s.f.* Excavation.

excaver, *v.tr.* To excavate.

excédent, *s.m.* Excess, surplus.

excéder, *v.tr.* **1.** To exceed go beyond. **2.** To tire out.

excellemment, *adv.* Excellently.

excellence, *s.f.* **1.** Excellence. **Par e.,** pre-eminently. **2.** Excellency.

excellent, *a.* Excellent.

exceller, *v.i.* To excel.

excentricité, *s.f.* Eccentricity.

excentrique, *a.* Eccentric odd.

excepté, *prep.* Except, but, save.

excepter, *v.tr.* To except, exclude.

exception, *s.f.* Exception.

exceptionnel, *a.* Exceptional.

exceptionnellement, *adv.* Exceptionally.

excès, *s.m.* (a) Excess. (b) *pl.* Excesses.

excessif, *a.* Excessive ; undue.

excessivement, *adv.* Excessively

excitabilité, *s.f.* Excitability.

excitable, *a.* Excitable.

excitant, *a.* Exciting, stimulating.

excitation, *s.f.* **1.** Excitation ; incitement. **2.** Excitement.

exciter, *v.tr.* To excite.

exclamation, *s.f.* Exclamation.

exclamer (s'), *v.pr.* (a) To exclaim. (b) To protest loudly.

exclure, *v.tr.* To exclude, leave out.

exclusif, *a.* Exclusive, sole.

exclusion, *s.f.* Exclusion.

exclusivement, *adv.* Exclusively.

excommunication, *v.tr.* Excommunication.

excommunier, *v.tr* To excommunicate.

excrétion, *s.f.* Excretion.

excroissance, *s.f.* Excrescence.

excursion, *s.f.* Excursion; tour.
excusable, *a.* Excusable.
excusablement, *adv.* Excusably.
excuse, *s.f.* 1. Excuse. 2. *pl.* Apology.
excuser, *v.tr.* To excuse.
   s'excuser, to excuse oneself; to apologize.
exécrable, *a.* Execrable.
exécrablement, *adv.* Execrably.
exécration, *s.f.* Execration.
exécrer, *v.tr.* To execrate, loathe.
exécutant, *s.* Performer.
exécuter, *v.tr.* 1. To execute; to carry out. 2. To execute; to put to death.
   s'exécuter, to comply.
exécuteur, -trice, *s.* Executor, executrix.
exécutif, *a.* Executive.
exécution, *s.f.* 1. Execution, performance. 2. E. capitale, execution.
exemplaire[1], *a.* Exemplary.
exemplaire[2], *s.m.* (a) Specimen (of work). (b) Copy (of book).
exemple, *s.m.* 1. Example. 2. Lesson, warning. 3. Par e., for instance *int.* Par e.! the idea!
exempt [egzã], *a.* Exempt, free.
exempter [-zõte], *v.tr.* To exempt, excuse.
exemption, *s.f.* Exemption; immunity; freedom.
exercé, *a.* Practised (à, in).
exercer, *v.tr.* To exercise. 1. To train. 2. To make use of. 3. To practise.
   s'exercer. S'e. à, to practise.
exercice, *s.m.* Exercise. 1. (a) Prendre de l'e., to take exercise. (b) Drill. 2. Practice; use.
exhalaison, *s.f.* Exhalation.
exhaler, *v.tr.* To exhale, emit.
exhaussement, *s.m.* Raising.
exhiber, *v.tr.* To exhibit, show.
exhibition, *s.f.* Show; exhibition
exhorter, *v.tr.* To exhort, urge.
exhumer, *v.tr.* To exhume.
exigeant, *a.* Exacting: hard to please.
exigence, *s.f.* (a) Unreasonable demand. (b) Exigency, requirement(s).
exiger, *v.tr.* 1. To exact; to insist upon. 2. To require, call for.
exigible, *a.* Exigible.
exigu, -uë, *a.* Tiny; scanty.
exiguïté, *s.f.* Scantiness.

exil, *s.m.* Exile, banishment.
exilé, *s.* Exile.
exiler, *v.tr.* To exile, banish.
existant, *a.* Existing, existent.
existence, *s.f.* Existence.
exister, *v.i.* To exist, be; to live
exode, *s.m.* Exodus.
exonération, *s.f.* Exoneration.
exonérer, *v.tr.* To exonerate.
exorbitant, *a.* Exorbitant.
exorciser, *v.tr.* To exorcize.
exotique, *a.* Exotic.
expansif, *a.* Expansive.
expansion, *s.f.* Expansion.
expatriation, *s.f.* Expatriation
expatrier, *v.tr.* To expatriate.
expectant, *a.* Expectant.
expédient. 1. *a.* Expedient. 2. *s.m.* Expedient, device, shift.
expédier, *v.tr.* 1. To dispatch. 2. To expedite. 3. To forward.
expéditeur, -trice, *s.* Sender.
expéditif, *a.* Expeditious.
expédition, *s.f.* 1. Expedition. 2. (a) Forwarding. (b) Consignment.
expérience, *s.f.* 1. Experience. 2. Experiment, test.
expérimental, -aux, *a.* Experimental.
expérimenté, *a.* Experienced.
expérimenter, *v.tr.* To test, try. *Abs.* To make an experiment
expert, *a. & s.m.* Expert.
expertement, *adv.* Expertly.
expiation, *s.f.* Expiation.
expiatoire, *a.* Expiatory.
expier, *v.tr.* To expiate, atone for.
expiration, *s.f.* Expiration.
expirer, *v.tr. & i.* To expire.
explétif, *a. & s.m.* Expletive.
explicable, *a.* Explicable.
explicatif, *a.* Explanatory.
explication, *s.f.* Explanation.
explicite, *a.* Explicit, clear, plain.
explicitement, *adv.* Explicitly.
expliquer, *v.tr.* (a) To explain. (b) To account for.
   s'expliquer, to explain oneself; to have it out (with s.o.).
exploit, *s.m.* Exploit; feat.
exploitation, *s.f.* Exploitation.
exploiter, *v.tr.* To exploit.
explorateur, -trice, *s.* Explorer.
exploration, *s.f.* Exploration.
explorer, *v.tr.* To explore.
explosif, *a. & s.m.* Explosive.

explosion, *s.f.* Explosion.
exportateur, -trice, *s.* Exporter.
exportation, *s.f.* Exportation.
exporter, *v.tr.* To export.
exposé. 1. *a.* (*a*) In an exposed position. (*b*) Liable. **2.** *s.m.* Statement.
exposer, *v.tr.* **1.** To exhibit. show. **2.** To expose.
exposition, *s.f* **1.** (*a*) Exhibition. (*b*) Exposure.
exprès¹, -esse, *a.* Express, explicit.
exprès², *adv.* Intentionally.
express, *a. & s.m.* Express (train).
expressément, *adv.* Expressly.
expressif, *a.* Expressive.
expression, *s.f.* Expression.
exprimable, *a.* Expressible.
exprimer, *v.tr.* To express.
exproprier, *v.tr.* To expropriate.
expulser, *v.tr.* To expel; to eject.
expulsion, *s.f* Expulsion; eviction.
expurger, *v.tr.* To expurgate.
exquis, *a.* Exquisite.
exsangue [-sã:g] *a.* Bloodless.
exsuder, *v.tr. & i.* To exude.
extase, *s.f* Ecstasy; trance.
extasier (s'), *v.pr* To go into ecstasies.
extatique, *a.* Ecstatic.
extension, *s.f.* Extension.
exténuation, *s.f.* Extenuation.
exténuer, *v.tr.* To extenuate.
extérieur, -e. 1. *a.* (*a*) Exterior, external (*b*) Foreign **2.** *s.m.* Exterior.
extérieurement, *adv.* **1.** Externally, outwardly. **2.** On the surface.
extermination, *s.f.* Extermination.
exterminer, *v.tr.* To exterminate.

externat, *s.m.* Day-school.
externe. 1. *a.* External, outer. **2.** *s.* Day-pupil.
extincteur, *s.m.* Fire-extinguisher.
extinction, *s.f.* **1.** Extinction. **2.** (*a*) Dying out. (*b*) Loss (of voice).
extirper, *v.tr.* To extirpate.
extorquer, *v.tr.* To extort.
extorsion, *s.f.* Extortion.
extra. 1. *s.m.* Extra. **2.** *a.inv.* Extra-special.
extraction, *s.f.* Extraction. **1.** Extracting. **2.** Descent, lineage.
extrader, *v.tr.* To extradite.
extradition, *s.f.* Extradition.
extra-fin, *a.* Superfine.
extraire, *v.tr.* To extract
extrait, *s.m.* Extract.
extraordinaire, *a.* Extraordinary.
extraordinairement, *adv.* Extraordinarily.
extravagamment, *adv.* Extravagantly.
extravagance, *s.f* Extravagance; absurdity.
extravagant, *a.* Extravagant.
extrême. 1. *a.* Extreme. (*a*) Farthest. (*b*) Intense, excessive. **2.** *s.m.* Extreme limit.
extrêmement, *adv.* Extremely.
extrême-Orient (l'), *s.m.* The Far East.
extrémiste, *s.m. & f.* Extremist.
extrémité, *s.f.* (*a*) Extremity, end; tip. (*b*) Extremity, extreme.
exubérance, *s.f.* Exuberance.
exubérant, *a.* Exuberant.
exultation, *s.f.* Exultation.
exulter, *v.i.* To exult, rejoice

F

F, f [ɛf], *s.f.* (The letter) F, f.
fable, *s.f.* (*a*) Fable. (*b*) Story, tale.
fabricant, *s.* Maker, manufacturer.
fabrication, *s.f.* Manufacture, making.
fabrique, *s.f.* **1. Marque de f.,** trademark. **2.** Factory, works.
fabriquer, *v.tr.* To manufacture.
fabuleux, *a.* Fabulous.
façade, *s.f.* Façade, front(age).
face, *s.f.* **1.** Face. **2.** (*a*) **Faire f. à,** to cope with. (*b*) **De f.,** full-face. **3.** *Prep.phr.* **En f. de,** opposite.

facétie, *s.f.* Joke, jest.
facétieusement, *adv.* Facetiously.
facétieux, *a.* Facetious, waggish.
facette, *s.f.* Facet.
fâché, *a.* **1.** Sorry. **2.** Angry.
fâcher, *v.tr.* **1.** To grieve. **2.** To anger.
se fâcher, to get angry.
fâcheux, *a.* Troublesome, tiresome.
facile, *a.* **1.** Easy **2.** Facile, ready, quick.
facilement, *adv.* Easily, readily.
facilité, *s.f.* **1.** Easiness. **Avec f.,**

with ease. **2.** Aptitude, talent, facility.

faciliter, *v.tr.* To facilitate.

façon, *s.f.* **1.** (a) Making. (b) Make; cut (of a coat). **2.** (a) Manner, way. **De la bonne f.,** properly. (b) **Sans façon(s),** unceremoniously. (c) **De cette f.,** thus. **En aucune f.!** by no means! **3.** *Conj.phr.* **De f. à,** so as to.

faconde, *s.f.* Fluency of speech.

façonner, *v.tr.* To work, shape.

facteur, -trice, *s.* **1.** (a) Carrier. (b) Porter. (c) Postman. **2.** Agent. **3.** *s.m.* Factor.

factice, *a.* Factitious; artificial.

factieux, *a.* Factious.

faction, *s.f* **1.** Sentry-duty, guard. **2.** Faction.

factionnaire, *s.m.* Sentry, sentinel.

facture, *s.f.* Invoice.

facultatif, *a.* Optional.

faculté, *s.f.* (a) Option, right. (b) Faculty. (c) *pl.* Resources.

fade, *a.* Insipid, flavourless.

fadeur, *s.f.* Insipidity

fagot, *s.m.* Faggot.

faible. **1.** *a.* (a) Feeble, weak. (b) Light; faint. **2.** *s.m* Weakness, failing.

faiblement, *adv.* Feebly, weakly.

faiblesse, *s.f.* **1.** (a) Feebleness, weakness. (b) Smallness (of sum). **2.** Failing.

faiblir, *v.i.* To grow weak.

faïence, *s.f.* Crockery; earthenware.

failli [faji], *s.* Bankrupt.

faillibilité [faji-], *s.f* Fallibility

faillible [faji-], *a.* Fallible.

faillir [fajiːr], *v.i.* **1.** To fail. **2.** J'ai failli manquer le train, I nearly missed the train.

faillite [fajit], *s.f.* Failure, insolvency. **Faire f.,** to go bankrupt.

faim, *s.f.* Hunger. **Manger à sa f.,** to eat one's fill.

faîne, *s.f.* Beech-nut.

fainéant. **1.** *a.* Idle, lazy, slothful. **2.** *s.* Idler, sluggard.

faire, *v.tr.* I. To make. **1.** Tout fait, ready-made. **2.** (a) Se f. des amis, to make friends (b) F. des provisions, to lay in provisions.

II. **faire,** *v.tr.* To do. **1.** (a) Que f.? what is to be done? **Faites vite!** look sharp! **Bonne à tout f.,** general servant. **C'est bien fait!**

it serves you right! (b) To say. **2.** (a) **Toute réflexion faite,** all things considered. (b) **F. de l'auto,** to go in for motoring. **3.** To matter. **Cela ne fait rien,** never mind.

III. **faire.** **1.** To form. **2. A qui de f.?** whose deal is it? **3. N'avoir que f. de,** to have no occasion for. **4.** To play (the fool).

IV. **faire.** **1.** (a) **N'en faites rien,** do no such thing. (b) **C'(en) est fait de lui,** it's all up with him. **2. Rien n'y fit,** nothing availed. **Qu'y f.?** how can it be helped?

V. **faire,** *impers.* **Quel temps fait-il?** what is the weather like?

VI. **faire.** **Je ne fais que d'arriver,** I have only just arrived.

VII. **faire.** **1. Faites-le entrer,** show him in. **2.** (a) **F. f.,** to have made. (b) **Un bruit se fit entendre,** a noise was heard. **3. F. f. qch. à qn,** to get s.o. to do sth.

se faire. **1.** (a) To develop. (b) To become. **La nuit se fait,** night is falling. (c) To adapt oneself. **2.** *Impers.* **Il se fait tard,** it is growing late.

faisan, *s.* Pheasant.

faisceau, *s.m.* Bundle; cluster.

fait, *s.m.* (a) Act, deed. (b) Fact. **Être au f. de la question,** to know how things stand. **En f., de f.,** as a matter of fact. **En f. de,** as regards. (c) Occurrence.

fait-divers, *s.m.* News item. **Faits-divers,** news in brief.

faîte, *s.m.* Top, summit.

falaise, *s.f.* Cliff.

fallacieux, *a.* Fallacious, misleading.

falloir, *v. impers.* **1.** To be wanting, necessary. **S'en f.,** to be lacking, wanting. **Tant s'en faut,** far from it. **Comme il faut,** proper(ly). **2.** (a) To be necessary. **Il nous faut le voir,** we must see him. (b) **Il viendra s'il le faut,** he will come if necessary.

falsification, *s.f.* Falsification; forgery; adulteration.

falsifier, *v.tr.* To falsify; to adulterate.

fameusement, *adv.* Famously.

fameux, *a.* Famous.

familial, -aux, *a.* Family.

familiariser (se), *v.pr.* To familiarize oneself.

familiarité, *s.f.* Familiarity.
familier, *a.* 1. Domestic. 2. Familiar.
familièrement, *adv.* Familiarly.
famille, [-mi:j], *s.f.* Family; household. **En f.,** at home; without ceremony.
famine, *s.f.* Famine, starvation.
fanal, -aux, *s.m.* Lantern, light. **F. de tête,** head-light.
fanatique. 1. *a.* Fanatic(al). 2. *s.* Fanatic.
fanatisme, *s.m.* Fanaticism.
faner (se), *v.pr.* To wither, fade.
fanfare, *s.f.* 1. (*a*) Flourish (of trumpets). (*b*) Fanfare. 2. Brass band.
fanfaronnade, *s.f.* Piece of brag.
fange, *s.f.* Mud, mire, filth.
fangeux, *a.* Miry, muddy.
fantaisie, *s.f.* 1. (*a*) Imagination. (*b*) Fantasia. 2. Fancy, whim.
fantasque, *a.* Odd, whimsical.
fantassin, *s.m.* Foot-soldier, infantryman.
fantastique, *a.* Fantastic; fanciful.
fantoche, *s.m.* Marionette, puppet.
fantôme, *s.m.* Phantom, ghost.
faon [fã], *s.m.* Fawn.
farce, *s.f.* (*a*) Farce. (*b*) Prank.
farceur, -euse, *s.* Wag, joker.
farcir, *v.tr.* To stuff (poultry).
fard, *s.m.* Paint, rouge, make-up.
fardeau, *s.m.* Burden, load.
farder (se), *v.pr.* To make up.
farine, *s.f.* Flour; meal.
farouche, *a.* 1. Fierce, savage. 2. (*a*) Shy, timid. (*b*) Unsociable.
fascicule, *s.m.* Instalment; part.
fascination, *s.f.* Fascination.
fasciner, *v.tr.* To fascinate
fascisme, *s.m.* Fascism.
fasciste, *s.m. & f.* Fascist.
faste, *s.m.* Ostentation, display.
fastidieusement, *adv.* Fastidiously.
fastidieux, *a.* Dull, tedious.
fastueux, *a.* Sumptuous.
fat [fat]. 1. *a.m.* Conceited, foppish. 2. *s.m.* Conceited ass; fop.
fatal, -als, *a.* 1. Fatal; mortal. 2. Fated, inevitable.
fatalement, *adv.* 1. Fatally, mortally. 2. Inevitably.
fatalisme, *s.m.* Fatalism.
fataliste, *s.* Fatalist.
fatalité, *s.f.* 1. Fate, fatality 2. Mischance, calamity.

fatigant, *a.* 1. Tiring, fatiguing. 2. Tiresome, tedious.
fatigue, *s.f.* Fatigue, weariness.
fatiguer, *v.tr.* To fatigue, tire. **se fatiguer,** to tire; to get tired.
fatuité, *s.f.* Self-conceit
faubourg, *s.m.* Suburb.
faucher, *v.tr.* To mow, cut.
faucheur, -euse, *s.* 1. Mower. 2. *s.f.* Faucheuse, mowing-machine.
faucille [-si:j], *s.f.* Sickle.
faucon [-kɔ̃], *s.m.* Falcon, hawk.
faufiler (se), *v.pr.* To slip (in).
faune[1], *s.m.* Faun.
faune[2], *s.f.* Fauna, animal life.
faussaire, *s.m. & f.* Forger.
fausse. See FAUX[1].
faussement, *adv.* Falsely.
fausser, *v.tr.* To make false. **F. parole,** to break one's word.
fausseté, *s.f.* 1. Falseness, falsity. 2. Falsehood, untruth.
faute, *s.f.* 1. Lack, want. **Faire f.,** to be lacking. **Sans f.,** without fail. **F. de,** for want of. 2. (*a*) Fault, mistake. (*b*) Transgression.
fauteuil [-tœ:j], *s.m.* Arm-chair. **F. d'orchestre,** orchestra stall
fautif, *a.* In fault.
fauve. 1. *a.* Tawny. 2. *s.m.* Les (grands) fauves, wild beasts.
fauvette, *s.f.* Warbler.
faux[1], **fausse.** I. *a.* False. 1. Untrue. 2. Not genuine. (*a*) Counterfeit. (*b*) Treacherous, shifty. 3. Wrong, mistaken. **Faire un f. pas,** to blunder. *adv.* **Chanter f.,** to sing out of tune. *Adv.phr.* **A f.,** wrongly. II. **faux,** *s.f.* Forgery.
faux[2], *s.f.* Scythe.
faux-monnayeur, *s.m.* Coiner.
faveur, *s.f.* Favour. **Billet de f.,** complimentary ticket.
favorable, *a.* Favourable.
favorablement, *adv.* Favourably.
favori, -ite. 1. *a. & s.* Favourite. 2. *s.m.pl.* (Side-)whiskers.
favoriser, *v.tr.* To favour.
favoritisme, *s.m.* Favouritism.
fébrile, *a.* Feverish.
fécond, *a.* Prolific, fruitful, fertile.
fécondité, *s.f.* 1. Fruitfulness. 2. Fertility.
fédération, *s.f.* Federation
fée, *s.f.* Fairy.
féerie, *s.f.* Fairyland.

féerique, *a.* Fairy-like, enchanting.

feindre, *v.tr.* To feign, sham ; to pretend.

feinte, *s.f.* Feint, pretence

fêlé, *a.* Cracked.

félicitations, *s.f.pl.* Congratulations.

félicité, *s.f.* Felicity, bliss.

féliciter, *v.tr.* To congratulate.

félin, *a.* Feline.

fêlure, *s.f.* Crack ; split.

femelle, *s.f. & a.* Female.

féminin, *a.* Feminine.

femme [fam], *s.f.* **1.** Woman. **2.** Wife. **3.** F. de chambre, housemaid ; stewardess.

fenaison, *s.f.* Hay-harvest.

fendre, *v.tr.* To split.

fenêtre, *s.f.* Window.

fente, *s.f.* (a) Crack, crevice. (b) Slot.

féodal, -aux, *a.* Feudal.

fer, *s.m.* **1.** Iron. **2.** Sword. **3.** *pl.* Irons, fetters. **4.** Fer à cheval, horseshoe.

fer-blanc, *s.m.* Tin.

férié, *a.* Jour f., (general) holiday.

férir, *v.tr.* Sans coup f., without striking a blow.

ferme[1]. **1.** *a.* Firm, steady. **2.** *adv.* Firmly ; hard. Tenir f., to stand fast.

ferme[2], *s.f.* Farm.

fermé, *a.* **1.** Closed. **2.** Inscrutable.

fermement, *adv.* Firmly, steadily.

ferment, *s.m.* Ferment.

fermentation, *s.f.* Fermentation.

fermenter, *v.i.* To ferment.

fermer. 1. *v.tr.* (a) To close shut. (b) F. la marche, to bring up the rear. **2.** *v.i.* To close, shut. se fermer, to close, shut.

fermeté, *s.f.* Firmness.

fermeture, *s.f.* **1.** Closing, shutting. F. éclair, zip fastener.

fermier, *s.* Farmer.

féroce, *a.* Ferocious, savage.

férocement, *adv.* Ferociously.

férocité, *s.f.* Ferocity.

ferraille [fɛrɑːj], *s.f.* Old iron.

ferré, *a.* Iron-shod.

ferrer, *v.tr.* To shoe (a horse).

fertile, *a.* Fertile, fruitful.

fertilisation, *s.f.* Fertilization.

fertiliser, *v.tr.* To fertilize.

fertilité, *s.f.* Fertility ; fruitfulness.

fervemment, *adv.* Fervently.

fervent, *a.* Fervent, ardent.

ferveur, *s.f.* Fervour ; ardour.

festin, *s.m.* Feast, banquet.

feston, *s.m.* Festoon.

fête, *s.f.* **1.** Feast, festival. Jour de f., holiday. Souhaiter la f. à, to wish many happy returns. **2.** Fête, entertainment. **3.** Festivity.

fêter, *v.tr.* To celebrate.

fétiche, *s.m.* Fetish.

fétide, *a.* Fetid, stinking.

feu[1], **feux,** *s.m.* **1.** (a) Fire ; light (for pipe). Visage en feu, flushed face. (b) Heat, ardour. **2.** Faire du feu, to light a fire. **3.** Armes à feu, firearms. Faire feu, to fire. Tué au feu, killed in action. **4.** Light. Feux de circulation, traffic lights.

feu[2], *a.* Late, deceased.

feuillage [fœjaːʒ], *s.m.* Foliage.

feuille [fœːj], *s.f.* **1.** Leaf. **2.** Sheet (of paper).

feuilleter [fœjte], *v.tr.* To turn over the pages of (book).

feutre, *s.m.* **1.** Felt. **2.** Felt hat.

fève, *s.f.* Bean.

février, *s.m.* February.

fi, *int.* Fie ! for shame ! Faire fi de, to turn up one's nose at.

fiacre, *s.m.* Cab.

fiançailles [-sɑːj], *s.f.pl.* Betrothal

fiancé, *s.* Fiancé.

fiancer (se), *v.pr.* To become engaged.

fibre, *s.f.* Fibre.

fibreux, *a.* Fibrous, stringy.

ficeler, *v.tr.* To tie up.

ficelle, *s.f.* String, twine.

fiche, *s.f.* (a) Slip (of paper). (b) Card, ticket. (c) Index card.

fichier, *s.m.* Card-index.

fictif, *a.* Fictitious, imaginary.

fiction, *s.f.* Fiction ; invention.

fidèle, *a.* Faithful, loyal, staunch.

fidèlement, *adv.* Faithfully.

fidélité, *s.f.* Fidelity ; allegiance.

fiel, *s.m.* Gall.

fier[1] [fjɛːr], *a.* **1.** Proud. **2.** Haughty.

fier[2] **(se),** *v.pr.* To trust. Fiez-vous à moi, leave it to me.

fièrement, *adv.* **1.** Proudly **2.** Haughtily.

fierté, *s.f.* Pride.

fièvre, *s.f.* Fever.

fiévreusement, *adv.* Feverishly.

fiévreux, *a.* Feverish.

figer, *v.tr.* To coagulate. se figer, to coagulate. sourire figé, set smile.

figue, s.f. Fig.

figuier, s.m. Fig-tree.

figuratif, a. Figurative.

figurativement, adv. Figuratively.

figure, s.f. **1.** Figure, form. **2.** (a) Face, countenance. **Les figures,** the court-cards. (b) Appearance.

figuré, a. Figurative.

figurer. 1. v.tr. To represent. **2.** v.i. To appear, figure.
   se figurer, to imagine.

fil [fil], s.m. **1.** (a) Thread. (b) Wire. **2.** Grain (of wood). **3.** Fil de l'eau, current. **4.** Edge.

filament, s.m. Filament.

filant, a. Étoile filante, shooting star.

filasse, s.f. **1.** Tow. **2.** Oakum.

file, s.f. File; line.

filer. I. v.tr. **1.** To spin. **2.** To shadow.
   II. **filer,** v.i. To slip by.

filet[1], s.m. **1.** Small thread; thin streak. **2.** Fillet, undercut.

filet[2], s.m. Net. **F. à bagages,** luggage rack.

filial, -als, -aux. I. a. Filial. **2.** s.f. Filiale, branch.

filigrane, s.m. Water-mark.

fille [fiːj], s.f. **1.** Daughter. **2.** Girl. **Jeune f.,** girl. **Nom de jeune f.,** maiden name. **Vieille f.,** old maid.

filleul [fijœl], s. God-child.

film [film], s.m. Film.

filon, s.m. Vein, seam, lode.

filou, s.m. Pickpocket, thief.

fils [fis], s.m. Son. **M. Duval f.,** Mr Duval junior.

filtre, s.m. Filter, percolator.

filtrer. 1. v.tr. To filter, strain. **2.** v.i. & pr. To filter, percolate.

fin[1], s.f. **1.** End, close. **2.** End, aim.

fin[2], a. (a) Fine, choice. s.f. **Une fine,** a liqueur brandy. (b) Subtle, shrewd. **Avoir l'oreille fine,** to be quick of hearing. (c) Fine, small.

final, -als, a. Final.

finalement, adv. Finally.

finalité, s.f. Finality.

finance, s.f. Finance.

financer, v.tr. To finance.

financier. 1. a. Financial. **2.** s.m. Financier.

finement, adv. **1.** Delicately **2.** Shrewdly.

finesse, s.f. **1.** Good quality; delicacy.

2. (a) Shrewdness. (b) Cunning. **3.** Fineness (of dust).

fini, a. **1.** Finished, ended. **2.** (a) Accomplished. (b) s.m. Finish. **3.** Finite.

finir. 1. v.tr. To finish, end. **2.** v.i. To end, finish. **En f. avec qch.,** to have done with sth.

finlandais. 1. a. Finnish. **2.** s. Finn.

Finlande. Pr.n.f. Finland.

finnois. 1. a. & s.m. Finnish. **2.** s. Finn.

firmament, s.m. Firmament.

fiscal, -aux, a. Fiscal.

fission, s.f. Splitting.

fissure, s.f. Fissure, cleft.

fixe, a. **1.** Fixed, firm. **2.** Fixed, settled. **Arrêt f.,** all cars stop here.

fixement, adv. Fixedly.

fixer, v.tr. **1.** To fix; to make firm, fast; to stare at. **2.** To fix, determine.

fixité, s.f. Fixity.

flacon, s.m. Bottle; flask.

flagorner, v.tr. To toady to.

flagorneur, -euse, a. Toady.

flagrant, a. Flagrant, glaring.

flair, s.m. (a) Scent. (b) Flair.

flairer, v.tr. (a) To scent. (b) To smell.

flamand, a. Flemish.

flamant, s.m. Flamingo.

flambant, a. Blazing, flaming. adv. **F. neuf,** brand-new.

flambeau, s.m. Torch.

flamber. 1. v.i. To flame. blaze. **2.** v.tr. To singe.

flamboyant, a. **1.** Flaming; fiery. **2.** Flamboyant

flamboyer, v.i. To blaze.

flamme, s.f. **1.** Flame. **2.** Pennant, streamer.

flanc, s.m. Flank, side.

flanelle, s.f. Flannel. **F. de coton,** flannelette.

flâner, v.i. To lounge; to stroll.

flânerie, s.f Dawdling, idling.

flâneur, -euse, s. (a) Idler. dawdler; stroller. (b) Loafer.

flanquer, v.tr. To throw.

flaque, s.f. **1.** Puddle, pool. **2. F. de neige,** patch of snow.

flasque, a. Flaccid; flabby.

flatter, v.tr. **1.** To stroke, caress. **2.** To delight. **3.** To flatter.
   se flatter, to flatter oneself.

flatterie, *s.f.* Flattery.

flatteur, -euse. 1. *a.* (*a*) Pleasing. (*b*) Flattering. 2. *s.* Flatterer.

fléau, -aux, *s.m.* 1. Flail. 2. Scourge.

flèche, *s.f.* 1. Arrow. 2. Spire.

fléchir. 1. *v.tr.* (*a*) To bend. (*b*) To move to pity. 2. *v.i.* To give way.

fléchissement, *s.m.* Bending.

flegmatique, *a.* Phlegmatic.

flegme, *s.m.* Phlegm.

Flessingue. *Pr.n.* Flushing.

flétan, *s.m.* Halibut.

flétrir, *v.tr.* To blight.

fleur, *s.f.* 1. Flower; blossom, bloom. 2. A f. d'eau, at water-level. Yeux à f. de tête, prominent eyes.

fleuri, *a.* 1. In bloom. 2. Florid.

fleurir, *v.i.* (*a*) To flower, bloom. (*b*) To flourish. prosper.

fleuriste, *s.m. & f.* Florist.

fleuve, *s.m.* (Large) river.

flexibilité, *s.f.* Flexibility.

flexible, *a.* Flexible, pliable.

flibustier, *s.m.* Buccaneer.

flirter, *v.i.* To flirt.

flocon, *s.m.* Flake.

floconneux, *a.* Fleecy, fluffy.

floral, -aux, *a.* Floral.

flore, *s.f.* Flora.

florissant, *a.* Flourishing.

flot, *s.m.* 1. (*a*) Wave. (*b*) Flots de larmes, floods of tears. 2. A f., afloat.

flottaison, *s.f.* Floating.

flottant, *a.* Floating; flowing.

flotte, *s.f.* Fleet.

flotter, *v.i.* (*a*) To float. (*b*) To wave. (*c*) To waver.

flottille [-ti:j], *s.f.* Flotilla.

flou, *a.* Woolly (outline); hazy.

fluctuation, *s.f.* Fluctuation.

fluctuer, *v.i.* To fluctuate.

fluet, -ette, *a.* Thin, slender.

fluide, *a. & s.m.* Fluid.

flûte, *s.f.* 1. Flute. 2. Long thin roll (of bread).

flûté, *a.* **Voix flûtée,** piping voice.

flux [fly], *s.m.* Flow; flood.

fluxion, *s.f.* Inflammation.

foi, *s.f.* Faith. 1. **Ma foi, oui!** indeed, yes! 2. Belief, trust. 3. (Religious) faith.

foie, *s.m.* Liver.

foin, *s.m.* Hay.

foire, *s.f.* Fair.

fois, *s.f.* Time, occasion. **Une f.,**

once. **Deux f.,** twice. **A la f.,** at one and the same time.

foison, *s.f.* **A f.,** plentifully.

foisonner, *v.i.* To abound (*de,* in).

fol, *a.* See FOU.

folâtre, *a.* Playful, frolicsome.

folâtrer, *v.i.* To sport, romp, frolic.

folie, *s.f.* 1. Madness. 2. Folly; piece of folly.

folle. See FOU.

follement, *adv.* Madly. 1. Foolishly, unwisely. 2. Extravagantly.

fomenter, *v.tr.* To foment.

foncé, *a.* Dark (colour).

foncer, *v.i.* To rush, swoop (down).

foncier, *a.* Innate.

foncièrement, *adv.* At bottom.

fonction, *s.f.* Function; office. **Faire f. de,** to act as.

fonctionnaire, *s.m.* Civil servant.

fonctionnement, *s.m.* Functioning, working.

fonctionner, *v.i.* 1. To function. 2. To act, work.

fond, *s.m.* 1. Bottom. *Adv.phr.* **A f.,** thoroughly. 2. Foundation. **Article de f.,** leading article. **Au f.,** at bottom. 3. Back, far end.

fondamental, -aux, *a.* Fundamental; basic; primary.

fondateur, -trice, *s.* Founder.

fondation, *s.f.* Foundation.

fondé, *a.* Founded, justified.

fondement, *s.m.* Foundation; base.

fonder, *v.tr.* To found.

fondre. 1. *v.tr.* (*a*) To smelt. (*b*) To melt. (*c*) To dissolve. 2. *v.i.* (*a*) To melt. (*b*) To melt, dissolve. 3. *v.i.* To swoop down.

fondrière, *s.f.* (*a*) Bog, quagmire. (*b*) Muddy hole.

fonds, *s.m.* 1. (*a*) F. de commerce, business. (*b*) Stock(-in-trade). 2. (*a*) Funds. (*b*) Means, resources.

fontaine, *s.f.* 1. Spring, source. well. 2. Fountain.

fonte[1], *s.f.* 1. (*a*) Melting. (*b*) Smelting. (*c*) Casting. 2. Cast iron.

fonte[2], *s.f.* Holster.

fonts, *s.m.pl.* Font.

forain, *a.* **Spectacle f.,** travelling show.

forban, *s.m.* Corsair, pirate.

forçat, *s.m.* Convict.

force, *s.f.* 1. Strength, force. (*a*) **Être à bout de forces,** to be exhausted. (*b*) Force, violence. **F. lui**

fut, he was compelled. **De gré ou de f.,** willy-nilly. **2.** Force, power. **3.** *a.inv.* Many. **4. A f. de,** by dint of.

forcé, *a.* Forced; strained.

forcément, *adv.* Perforce.

forcené, *à.* Frantic, frenzied.

forcer, *v.tr.* To force. **1.** To compel. **2.** To do violence to; to break open.

forer, *v.tr.* To drill, bore.

foret, *s.m.* *Tls:* Drill.

forêt, *s.f.* Forest.

forfait[1]**,** *s.m.* Heinous crime.

forfait[2]**,** *s.m.* Contract. **Acheter à f.,** to buy outright.

forge, *s.f.* **1.** Smithy. **2.** *pl.* Iron-works.

forger, *v.tr.* To forge.

forgeron, *s.m.* (Black)smith.

formaliste, *a.* Formal, stiff.

formalité, *s.f.* Formality; ceremony.

formation, *s.f.* Formation.

forme, *s.f.* **1.** Form, shape. **2.** Form; method of procedure. **Pour la f.,** for form's sake. **3.** Last; mould. **Chapeau haut de f.,** top hat.

formel, *a.* Formal, strict; explicit; categorical.

formellement, *adv.* Formally.

former, *v.tr.* To form.

formidable, *a.* Formidable; tremendous.

formule, *s.f.* **1.** Formula **2.** (Printed) form.

formuler, *v.tr.* To formulate.

fort. I. *a.* **1.** *(a)* Strong. **Forte mer,** heavy sea. **D'une voix forte,** in a loud voice. **C'est plus f. que moi!** I can't help it! *(b)* **Se faire f.,** to undertake *(de,* to). **2.** Large; stout. II. **fort,** *adv.* **1.** Strongly. **2.** Very; much. III. **fort,** *s.m.* **1.** Strong part. **Le f. de l'hiver,** the depth of winter. **2.** Fort.

fortement, *adv.* Strongly; stoutly.

forteresse, *s.f.* Fortress, stronghold.

fortifiant, **1.** *a.* Fortifying, invigorating. **2.** *s.m.* Tonic.

fortification, *s.f.* Fortification.

fortifier, *v.tr.* To strengthen; to fortify.

fortuit, *a.* Fortuitous; chance.

fortuitement, *adv.* Accidentally.

fortune, *s.f.* **1.** Fortune, chance, luck. **2.** Fortune, riches.

fortuné, *a.* **1.** Fortunate. **2.** Rich.

fosse, *s.f.* **1.** Pit, hole. **2.** Grave.

fossé, *s.m.* Ditch, trench.

fossette, *s.f.* Dimple.

fossile, *a. & s.m.* Fossil.

fossoyeur, *s.m.* Grave-digger.

fou, fol, folle. **1.** *a.* *(a)* Mad, insane. *(b)* Foolish. *(c)* Prodigious. **Succès fou,** tremendous success. **2.** *s.* *(a)* Lunatic. *(b)* Fool. **3.** *s.m.* *Chess:* Bishop.

foudre, *s.f.* Thunderbolt, lightning.

foudroiement, *s.m.* Blasting.

foudroyant, *a.* Crushing.

foudroyer, *v.tr.* To strike down; to blast.

fouet, *s.m.* Whip, lash.

fouetter, *v.tr.* To whip, flog; to beat.

fougère, *s.f.* Fern; bracken.

fougue, *s.f.* Fire, ardour, spirit.

fougueux, *a.* Fiery, ardent, spirited.

fouille [fuːj], *s.f.* Excavation.

fouiller [fuje]. **1.** *v.tr.* *(a)* To dig, excavate. *(b)* To search. **2.** *v.i.* To rummage.

fouine, *s.f.* (Stone-)marten. **A figure de f.,** weasel-faced.

foule, *s.f.* Crowd; throng.

fouler, *v.tr.* **1.** To crush; to trample. **2.** To sprain.

foulure, *s.f.* Sprain, wrench.

four, *s.m.* **1.** *(a)* Oven. *(b)* **Petits fours,** fancy biscuits. **2.** Kiln, furnace.

fourberie, *s.f.* Deceit, cheating.

fourche, *s.f.* (Pitch)fork.

fourcher, *v.i.* To fork, branch.

fourchette, *s.f.* (Table) fork.

fourchu, *a.* Forked.

fourgon, *s.m.* Van, waggon.

fourmi, *s.f.* Ant. **Avoir des fourmis,** to have pins and needles.

fourmilière, *s.f.* Ant-hill.

fourmillement [-mij-], *s.m.* **1.** Swarming. **2.** Tingling; pins and needles.

fourmiller [-mije], *v.i.* To swarm.

fournaise, *s.f.* (Fiery) furnace.

fourneau, *s.m.* *(a)* Furnace; bowl (of pipe). *(b)* Stove, range.

fournir, *v.tr.* To supply, furnish.

fournisseur, -euse, *s.* Purveyor, caterer.

fourniture, *s.f.* **1.** Supplying, providing. **2.** *pl.* Supplies.

fourrager, *v.i.* To forage.

fourré, *s.m.* Thicket.

fourreau, *s.m.* Sheath, cover, case.
fourrer, *v.tr.* To stuff, cram.
fourreur, *s.m.* Furrier.
fourrure, *s.f.* Fur, skin.
fourvoyer, *v.tr.* To mislead.
foyer, *s.m.* **1.** Fire(-place), hearth, grate. **2.** Centre. **3.** (*a*) Hearth, home. (*b*) F. du public, foyer. F. des acteurs, green-room. **4.** Focus.
frac [frak], *s.m.* Dress-coat.
fracas, *s.m.* Din; crash.
fraction, *s.f.* Fraction.
fracture, *s.f.* **1.** Breaking open. **2.** Fracture.
fracturer, *v.tr.* **1.** To break open. **2.** To fracture.
fragile, *a.* **1.** Fragile; brittle. **2.** Frail.
fragilité, *s.f.* **1.** Fragility; brittleness. **2.** Frailty.
fragment, *s.m.* Fragment.
frai, *s.m.* Spawn.
fraîche. See FRAIS[1].
fraîchement, *adv.* **1.** Coolly. **2.** Freshly, recently.
fraîcheur, *s.f.* **1.** Coolness, chilliness. **2.** Freshness.
frais[1]**, fraîche,** *a.* Fresh. (*a*) Cool. (*b*) New, recent.
frais[2]**,** *s.m.pl.* Expenses, cost.
fraise, *s.f.* Strawberry.
fraisier, *s.m.* Strawberry-plant.
framboise, *s.f.* Raspberry.
framboisier, *s.m.* Raspberry-cane.
franc[1]**,** *s.m.* Franc.
franc[2]**, franche,** *a.* **1.** Free. **2.** (*a*) Frank; open. (*b*) Real, downright.
français. 1. *a. & s.m.* French. **2.** *s.* Frenchman, Frenchwoman.
France. *Pr.n.f.* France.
franche. See FRANC[2].
franchement, *adv.* Frankly, candidly, openly.
franchir, *v.tr.* (*a*) To jump (over); to get over. (*b*) To cross.
franchise, *s.f.* **1.** Freedom. **2.** Exemption. En f., post-free. **3.** Frankness.
franc-maçon, *s.m.* Freemason. *pl. francs-maçons.*
franc-maçonnerie, *s.f.* Freemasonry.
franco, *adv.* Free, carriage-free.
François. *Pr.n.m.* Francis, Frank.
Françoise. *Pr.n.f.* Frances.
franc-parler, *s.m.* Plain speaking.

frange, *s.f.* Fringe.
frappant, *a.* Striking (likeness).
frapper, *v.tr.* **1.** (*a*) To strike, hit. On frappe, there's a knock. F. du pied, to stamp. (*b*) To strike (coin). **2.** To ice.
fraternel, *a.* Fraternal.
fraternellement, *adv.* Fraternally.
fraternisation, *s.f.* Fraternizing.
fraterniser, *v.i.* To fraternize.
fraternité, *s.f.* Fraternity, brotherhood.
fraude, *s.f.* **1.** Fraud, deception; smuggling. **2.** Fraudulence, deceit.
frauder. 1. *v.tr.* To defraud, cheat. **2.** *v.i.* To cheat.
fraudeur, -euse, *s.* Defrauder.
frauduleusement, *adv.* Fraudulently.
frauduleux, *a.* Fraudulent.
frayer, *v.tr.* Se f. un passage, to clear a way (for oneself).
frayeur, *s.f.* Fright; fear, dread.
fredonner, *v.tr.* To hum.
frégate, *s.f.* Frigate. Capitaine de f., commander.
frein, *s.m.* **1.** Bit. Mettre un f. à, to curb. **2.** Brake.
freiner, *v.tr.* To put on the brakes.
frêle, *a.* Frail, weak.
frelon, *s.m.* Hornet.
frémir, *v.i.* **1.** To quiver. **2.** To tremble, shake.
frémissement, *s.m.* **1.** Quivering. **2.** (*a*) Shuddering. (*b*) Shudder.
frêne, *s.m.* Ash(-tree).
frénésie, *s.f.* Frenzy, madness.
frénétique, *a.* Frantic, frenzied.
frénétiquement, *adv.* Frantically.
fréquemment, *adv.* Frequently.
fréquence, *s.f.* Frequency.
fréquent, *a.* Frequent.
fréquenter, *v.tr.* (*a*) To frequent. (*b*) To associate with.
frère, *s.m.* Brother.
fresque, *s.f.* Fresco.
fret, *s.m.* Freight.
frétillant [-tijã], *a.* **1.** (Of fish) Wriggling. **2.** Full of life; lively.
frétiller [-tije], *v.i.* To wriggle; to quiver.
friable, *a.* Friable, crumbly.
friand, *a.* (*a*) Fond of delicacies. (*b*) Morceau f., dainty morsel.
friandise, *s.f.* **1.** Love of good food. **2.** Dainty, tit-bit.

friche, *s.f.* Waste land; fallow land.

fricot, *s.m.* Made-up dish; stew.

fricoter, *v.tr. & i.* To stew.

friction, *s.f.* Friction.

frileusement, *adv.* Cosily, snugly.

frileux, *a.* Sensitive to cold; chilly.

frimas, *s.m.* (Hoar-)frost; rime.

friperie, *s.f.* Rubbish, frippery.

fripier, *s.* Wardrobe dealer.

fripon. 1. *s.* Rogue, rascal, knave. **2.** *a.* Roguish, knavish.

frire, *v.tr. & i.* To fry.

frise[1], *s.f. Arch :* Frieze.

frise[2], *s.f. Tex :* Frieze.

frisé, *a.* Curly; crisp (hair).

friser, *v.tr.* **1.** To curl, wave. **2.** To touch, skim.

frisson, *s.m.* (*a*) Shiver. (*b*) Shudder. (*c*) Thrill.

frissonnement, *s.m.* Shivering.

frissonner, *v.i.* (*a*) To shiver. (*b*) To be thrilled. (*c*) To quiver.

frit, *a.* Fried.

frivole, *a.* Frivolous, shallow.

frivolité, *s.f.* Frivolity.

froid. I. *a.* **1.** Cold. **Il fait f.,** it is cold. **J'ai f.,** I am cold. **2. Battre f. à,** to cold-shoulder.
II. **froid,** *s.m.* Cold.

froidement, *adv.* Coldly, frigidly.

froideur, *s.f.* Coldness.

froissement, *s.m.* **1.** Crumpling; rustle. **2.** Giving offence.

froisser, *v.tr.* **1.** To crumple. **2.** To give offence to.
se froisser, to take offence.

frôlement, *s.m.* Slight rubbing.

frôler, *v.tr.* To touch lightly.

fromage, *s.m.* Cheese.

froment, *s.m.* Wheat.

froncement, *s.m.* **F. des sourcils,** frown; scowl.

froncer, *v.tr.* **F. les sourcils,** to knit one's brows; to frown.

fronde, *s.f.* (*a*) Sling. (*b*) (Toy) catapult.

front, *s.m.* **1.** Forehead, brow. **2.** Face, front. **Faire f. à,** to face. **3. De f.,** abreast.

frontal, -aux, *a.* Frontal, front.

frontière, *s.f.* Frontier; border.

frontispice, *s.m.* Frontispiece.

frottement, *s.m.* Friction.

frotter, *v.tr.* To rub.

froufrou, *s.m.* Rustle, swish.

fructifier, *v.i.* To bear fruit.

fructueusement, *adv.* Fruitfully.

fructueux, *a.* Fruitful.

frugal, -aux, *a.* Frugal.

frugalement, *adv.* Frugally.

frugalité, *s.f.* Frugality.

fruit, *s.m.* Fruit.

fruitier. 1. *a.* **Arbre f.,** fruit-tree. **2.** *s.* Fruiterer; greengrocer.

fruste, *a.* Worn; rough.

frustrer, *v.tr.* To frustrate.

fugitif, *a. & s.* **1.** Fugitive; runaway. **2. Désir f.,** passing desire.

fuir. 1. *v.i.* (*a*) To flee, run away. (*b*) To recede. (*c*) To leak. **2.** *v.tr.* To shun.

fuite, *s.f.* **1.** Flight, running away. **2.** Leak; leakage.

fulminer, *v.i.* To fulminate.

fumée, *s.f.* (*a*) Smoke. (*b*) Steam.

fumer. 1. *v.i.* (*a*) To smoke. (*b*) To steam; to fume. **2.** *v.tr.* To smoke.

fumet, *s.m.* Smell; bouquet.

fumeur, -euse, *s.* Smoker.

fumeux, *a.* Smoky, smoking.

fumier, *s.m.* **1.** Manure, dung. **2.** Dunghill; manure heap.

fumoir, *s.m.* Smoking-room.

funèbre, *a.* **1.** Funeral. **Marche f.,** dead-march. **2.** Funereal, gloomy.

funérailles [-rɑ:j], *s.f.pl.* Funeral.

funeste, *a.* Deadly, fatal.

funiculaire, *s.m.* Funicular railway.

furet, *s.m.* Ferret.

fureter, *v.i.* To ferret, pry about.

fureur, *s.f.* **1.** Fury, rage. **2.** Passion.

furibond, *a.* Furious; full of fury.

furie, *s.f.* Fury.

furieusement, *adv.* Furiously.

furieux, *a.* Furious; in a passion.

furoncle, *s.m.* Boil.

furtif, *a.* Furtive, stealthy.

furtivement, *adv.* Furtively.

fuseau, *s.m.* Spindle.

fusée, *s.f.* (*a*) Rocket. **F. éclairante,** flare. (*b*) Fuse.

fuselé, *a.* Stream-lined.

fusible, *s.m. El.E :* Fuse.

fusil, *s.m.* Gun; rifle.

fusillade [-zij-], *s.f.* Fusillade.

fusiller [-zije], *v.tr.* To shoot.

fusion, *s.f.* Fusion.

fût[2], *s.m.* **1.** (*a*) Shaft (of column). (*b*) Bole. **2.** Cask, barrel.

futaie, *s.f.* Wood, forest.

futile, *a.* Futile, trifling.

futilement, *adv.* Futilely.
futilité, *s.f.* Futility.
futur, *a.* Future.

fuyant, *a.* **1.** Fleeting. **2.** Receding (forehead). **3.** Shifty.
fuyard, *s.* Runaway.

G

G, g [ʒe], *s.m.* (The letter) G, g.
gâcher, *v.tr.* To spoil; to bungle.
gâchis, *s.m.* Muddle, mess.
gaffe, *s.f.* **1.** Boat-hook. **2.** Blunder.
gage, *s.m.* **1.** Pledge, security. **Mettre en g.,** to pawn. **2.** Token, sign. **3.** Forfeit. **4.** *pl.* Wages, pay.
gager, *v.tr.* To wager, bet.
gageure, *s.f.* Wager, bet.
gagnant. 1. *a.* Winning. **2.** *s.* Winner.
gagne-pain, *s.m.inv.* Bread-winner.
gagner, *v.tr.* **1.** (*a*) To earn. (*b*) To gain. **2.** To win, gain. **3.** To reach. **4.** To overtake.
gai, *a.* Gay; merry; cheerful.
gaiement, *adv.* Gaily, brightly.
gaieté, gaîté, *s.f.* Gaiety, mirth. **De g. de cœur,** wantonly.
gaillard [gaj-]. **1.** *a.* (*a*) Vigorous. (*b*) Merry. **2.** *s.m.* (Merry) fellow. **3.** *s.m.* **G. d'avant,** forecastle. **G. d'arrière,** quarter-deck.
gaîment, *adv.* = GAIEMENT.
gain, *s.m.* (*a*) Gain. (*b*) Earnings.
gaine, *s.f.* Sheath, casing.
galamment, *adv.* Gallantly.
galant. 1. *a.* (*a*) Gay, elegant. (*b*) Gallant. **2.** *s.m.* Lover.
galanterie, *s.f.* Politeness.
galère, *s.f.* Galley.
galerie, *s.f.* **1.** (*a*) Gallery. (*b*) Arcade. **2.** Balcony; gallery.
galet, *s.m.* (*a*) Pebble. **Gros g.,** boulder. (*b*) *pl.* Shingle.
galetas, *s.m.* Garret, attic.
galette, *s.f.* Girdle-cake.
galeux, *a.* Mangy. **Brebis galeuse,** black sheep.
galimatias, *s.m.* Farrago; jumble of words.
Galles. *Pr.n.f.* **Le pays de G.,** Wales.
gallois. 1. *a.* Welsh. **2.** *s.* Welshman, -woman.
galoche, *s.f.* (*a*) Clog. (*b*) Overshoe.
galon, *s.m.* **1.** Braid. **2.** *pl.* Stripes; gold braid.
galop, *s.m.* Gallop.
galoper, *v.i. & tr.* To gallop.
galopin, *s.* Urchin; young scamp.

galvaniser, *v.tr.* To galvanize.
gambade, *s.f.* Leap, gambol.
gambader, *v.i.* To leap; to gambol.
gamelle, *s.f.* Mess-tin, -kettle.
gamin, *s.* (*a*) Street-arab, urchin. (*b*) Youngster.
gamme, *s.f.* **1.** Scale gamut. **2.** Range, series.
gammée, *a.f.* **Croix g.,** swastika.
Gand. *Pr.n.m.* Ghent.
gant, *s.m.* Glove.
ganter, *v.tr.* To glove. **G. du sept,** to take sevens in gloves.
gantier, *s.* Glover.
garage, *s.m.* **1.** Shunting. **Voie de g.,** siding. **2.** Storage. **3.** Garage.
garagiste, *s.m.* Garage keeper.
garant, *s.* (*a*) Guarantor, surety. (*b*) Authority, guarantee.
garantie, *s.f.* Guarantee.
garantir, *v.tr.* **1.** To warrant, guarantee. **2.** To shelter, protect.
garçon, *s.m.* **1.** (*a*) Boy, lad. (*b*) Son. **2.** Young man. **G. d'honneur,** best man. **3.** Bachelor. **4.** Servant; waiter; steward.
garde[1]**,** *s.m.* **1.** (*a*) Keeper (*b*) Watchman.
garde[2]**,** *s.f.* **1.** (*a*) Guardianship, care, custody. **Avoir en g.,** to have charge of. (*b*) Protection. (*c*) Keeping. **2.** (*a*) Watch(ing). (*b*) Care, guard. **Être sur ses gardes,** to be on one's guard. *Mil:* **"G. à vous!"** 'attention!' **3.** (*a*) **Prendre g. à,** to beware of. (*b*) **Prendre g. à, de, faire qch.,** to be careful to do sth. (*c*) **Prenez g. de tomber,** mind you don't fall. **4.** Guard. (*a*) **Être de g.,** to be on guard. (*b*) **La g.,** the Guards. **5.** Hilt.
garde-à-vous, *s.m. Mil:* Attention.
garde-barrière, *s.m. & f.* Gate-keeper (at level-crossing). *pl. gardes-barrière(s).*
garde-boue, *s.m.inv.* Mudguard.
garde-chasse, *s.m.* Gamekeeper. *pl. gardes-chasse(s).*
garde-côte, *s.m.* Coast-guard(sman). *pl. gardes-côte(s).*

garde-feu, *s.m.inv.* (a) Fender. (b) Fire-guard.

garde-fou, *s.m.* **1.** Parapet. **2.** Railing (of bridge). *pl.* garde-fous.

garde-malade. 1. *s.m.* Male nurse. **2.** *s.f.* (Sick-)nurse. *pl.* gardes-malades.

garde-manger, *s.m.inv.* Larder.

garder, *v.tr.* To keep. **1.** To guard, protect. **2.** (a) To retain. (b) To preserve. **3.** To remain in (a place). **4.** To observe, respect.
   se garder. 1. To protect oneself. Garde-toi! look out for yourself! **2. Se g. de,** to beware of.

garde-robe, *s.f.* (a) Wardrobe. (b) Clothes. *pl.* garde-robes.

gardien, *s.* Guardian, keeper; caretaker.

gare[1], *int.* Look out !

gare[2], *s.f.* (Railway) station.

garenne, *s.f.* (Rabbit-)warren.

garer, *v.tr.* To shunt.

gargouille [-gu:j], *s.f.* (a) (Water-)spout. (b) Gargoyle.

garnement, *s.m.* Scamp, rogue.

garni, *a.* Furnished.

garnir, *v.tr.* **1.** To furnish, provide (de, with). **2.** To trim.

garnison, *s.f.* Garrison.

garniture, *s.f.* **1.** Fittings. **2.** Trimming(s).

garrotter, *v.tr.* To pinion.

gars [gɑ], *s.m.* Young fellow ; lad.

Gascogne. *Pr.n.f.* Gascony. **Le Golfe de G.,** the Bay of Biscay.

gascon, *a. & s.* Gascon.

gaspiller [-pije], *v.tr.* To squander ; to waste.

gastronomie, *s.f.* Gastronomy.

gâté, *a.* Spoilt.

gâteau, *s.m.* Cake ; (open) tart.

gâter, *v.tr.* To spoil.
   se gâter, to spoil, deteriorate.

gauche, *a.* **1.** Awkward, clumsy. **2.** Left. **3.** *Adv.phr.* A g., to the left.

gauchement, *adv.* Awkwardly.

gaucherie, *s.f.* Awkwardness.

gaufre, *s.f.* Waffle.

gaufrette, *s.f.* Wafer biscuit.

gaule, *s.f.* (Long thin) pole, stick.

gaulois. 1. *a.* Gallic. **2.** *s.* Gaul.

Gautier. *Pr.n.m.* Walter.

gaver, *v.tr.* To cram.

gaz [gɑ:z], *s.m.* Gas.

gaze, *s.f.* Gauze.

gazelle, *s.f.* Gazelle.

gazette, *s.f.* Gazette ; news-sheet.

gazeux, *a.* **1.** Gaseous. **2.** Aerated ; fizzy.

gazon, *s.m.* (a) Turf, sward. (b) Lawn, green.

gazouillement [-ʒuj-], *s.m.* Twittering ; babbling.

gazouiller [-zuje], *v.i.* To twitter ; to babble ; to prattle.

geai, *s.m.* Jay.

géant. 1. *s.* Giant, *f.* giantess. **2.** *a.* Gigantic.

geindre, *v.i.* To whine, whimper.

gel [ʒɛl], *s.m.* Frost, freezing.

gélatine, *s.f.* Gelatine

gélatineux, *a.* Gelatinous.

gelé, *a.* **1.** Frozen. **2.** Frost-bitten.

gelée, *s.f.* **1.** Frost. **2.** Jelly.

geler. 1. *v.tr.* To freeze. **2.** *v.i.* (a) To freeze. (b) *Impers.* Il gèle à pierre fendre, it is freezing hard.
   se geler, to freeze, solidify.

gelure, *s.f.* Frost-bite.

gémir, *v.i.* To groan, moan, wail.

gémissement, *s.m.* Groan, moan.

gemme. (a) *s.f.* Gem ; precious stone. (b) *a.* Sel g., rock-salt.

gênant, *a.* **1.** Cumbersome ; in the way. **2.** Embarrassing, awkward.

gencive, *s.f.* Gum.

gendarme, *s.m.* Gendarme.

gendarmerie, *s.f.* **1.** Body of gendarmes. **2.** Headquarters (of gendarmes)

gendre, *s.m.* Son-in-law.

gêne, *s.f.* **1.** Discomfort **Sans g.,** free and easy. **2.** Want.

gêné, *a.* Embarrassed ; ill at ease.

généalogie, *s.f.* Genealogy ; pedigree.

généalogique, *a.* Genealogical. **Arbre g.,** family-tree ; pedigree.

gêner, *v.tr.* **1.** To constrict. **2.** To hinder. **3.** To inconvenience.
   se gêner, to put oneself out.

général, -aux. **1.** *a.* General. **Répétition générale,** *s.f.* **générale,** dress-rehearsal. **2.** *s.m.* General. **3.** *s.f.* **Générale,** alarm call.

généralement, *adv.* Generally.

généraliser, *v.tr.* To generalize.

généralité, *s.* Generality.

générateur, -trice. 1. *a.* Generating. **2.** Generator.

génération, *s.f.* Generation.

générer, *v.tr.* To generate.

généreusement, *adv.* Generously.

généreux, *a.* Liberal, generous.

générique, *a.* Generic.

générosité, *s.f.* Generosity; munificence.

Gênes. *Pr.n.f.* Genoa.

genèse, *s.f.* Genesis, origin.

genêt, *s.m.* Broom.

gêneur, -euse, *s.* Spoil-sport.

Genève. *Pr.n.f.* Geneva.

genévrier, *s.m.* Juniper(-tree).

génie, *s.m.* 1. (*a*) Genius. (*b*) Genie, jinnee. 2. (*a*) Engineering. (*b*) **Le g.,** the engineers.

genièvre, *s.m.* 1. Juniper-berry; juniper-tree. 2. Gin.

génisse, *s.f.* Heifer.

génois, *a. & s.* Genoese.

genou, -oux, *s.m* Knee. **A genoux!** kneel down!

genre, *s.m.* 1. Genus, kind. **Le g. humain,** mankind. 2. Kind, manner. 3. (Artistic) style. 4. Gender.

gens, *s.m.pl.* 1. People, folk. 2. **Le droit des g.,** the law of nations.

gentil, -ille [ʒɑ̃ti, -i:j], *a.* (*a*) Pleasing, nice. (*b*) **Sois g.,** be a good boy.

gentilhomme [-tij-], *s.m.* Gentleman. *pl. gentilshommes* [ʒɑ̃tizɔm]

gentillesse [-tij-], *s.f.* 1. (*a*) Graciousness. (*b*) **Auriez-vous la g. de,** would you be so kind as to. 2. *pl.* Gracious words.

gentiment, *adv.* Nicely; prettily.

géographie, *s.f.* Geography.

géographique, *a* Geographic(al). **Carte g.,** map.

geôlier [ʒolje], *s.m.* Gaoler.

géologie, *s.f.* Geology.

géologique, *a.* Geological.

géologue, *s.m.* Geologist.

géométrie, *s.f.* Geometry.

géométrique, *a.* Geometric(al).

géranium [-ɔm], *s.m.* Geranium.

gérant, *s.* Manager, director.

gerbe, *s.f.* Sheaf; shower (of sparks); spray (of water).

gerçure, *s.f.* Crack, cleft; chap.

gérer, *v.tr.* To manage.

germain, *a.* **Frère g.,** own brother. **Cousin g.,** first cousin.

germe, *s.m.* Germ.

germer, *v.i.* To germinate; to shoot.

germination, *s.f.* Germination.

gésier, *s.m.* Gizzard.

gésir, *v.i.* To lie. **Ci-gît,** here lies.

geste, *s.m.* Gesture, movement; wave (of the hand).

gesticulation, *s.f.* Gesticulation.

gesticuler, *v.i.* To gesticulate.

gestion, *s.f.* Management.

geyser [-zɛ:r], *s.m.* Geyser.

gibecière [ʒibs-], *s.f.* 1. Game-bag. 2. Satchel.

gibet, *s.m.* Gibbet, gallows.

gibier, *s.m.* Game.

giboulée, *s.f.* Sudden shower.

gicler, *v.i.* To squirt out.

gicleur, *s.m.* (Spray) nozzle; jet.

gifle, *s.f.* Slap in the face; box on the ear.

gifler, *v.tr.* To slap, smack. (s.o.'s) face; to box (s.o.'s) ears.

gigantesque, *a.* Gigantic; huge.

gigot, *s.m.* Leg of mutton

gigue, *s.f.* Jig.

gilet, *s.m.* Waistcoat, vest.

gingembre, *s.m.* Ginger.

girafe, *s.f.* Giraffe.

giration, *s.f.* Gyration.

giratoire, *a.* Gyratory

girofle, *s.m.* Clove.

giroflée, *s.f.* **G. des jardins.** stock. **G. des murailles,** wallflower.

giron, *s.m* Lap.

girouette, *s.f.* Weathercock; vane.

gisement, *s.m.* Layer; deposit.

gîte, *s.m.* Resting-place.

givre, *s.m.* Hoar-frost, rime.

glabre, *a.* Glabrous, smooth.

glace, *s.f.* 1. Ice. 2. (*a*) (Plate-)glass. (*b*) (Looking-)glass, mirror. (*c*) Window. 3. Ice(-cream)

glacé, *a.* 1. (*a*) Frozen. (*b*) Iced. 2. Glazed.

glacer, *v.tr.* To freeze.

glacial, -als, *a.* Icy; frosty; frigid.

glacier, *s.m.* Glacier.

glaçon, *s.m* (*a*) Block of ice. (*b*) Icicle.

gladiateur, *s.m.* Gladiator.

glaïeul, *s.m.* Gladiolus.

glaire, *s.f.* White of egg

glaise, *s.f.* Clay.

gland, *s.m.* 1. Acorn. 2. Tassel.

glande, *s.f.* Gland.

glaner, *v.tr.* To glean.

glaneur, -euse, *s.* Gleaner.

glapir, *v.i.* To yelp; (of fox) to bark.

glapissement, *s.m.* Yapping, yelping; barking (of fox).

glas, *s.m.* Knell

glauque, *a.* Glaucous ; sea-green.
glissade, *s.f.* **1.** Slip. **2.** Slide.
glissant, *a.* **1.** Slippery. **2.** Sliding.
glissement, *s.m.* **1.** Sliding ; slip.
  2. Landslip, land-slide.
glisser. I. *v.i.* **1.** To slip. **2.** To slide.
  3. To glide.
  II. **glisser,** *v.tr.* To slip.
  se glisser, to creep, steal.
global, -aux, *a.* Total, inclusive.
globe, *s.m.* **1.** Globe, sphere. **2.** G.
  de l'œil, eyeball.
globulaire, *a.* Globular.
globule, *s.m.* Globule.
gloire, *s.f.* **1.** Glory. **2.** Pride.
glorieusement, *adv.* **1.** Gloriously.
  2. Proudly.
glorieux, *a.* **1.** Glorious. **2.** Proud.
  3. *s.m.* Boaster.
glorifier, *v.tr.* To praise, glorify.
  to boast.
  se glorifier, to boast.
glossaire, *s.m.* Glossary, dictionary.
glouglou, *s.m.* Gurgle, bubbling.
gloussement, *s.m.* Clucking ; gob-
  bling ; chuckling.
glousser, *v.i.* To cluck ; to gobble ;
  to chuckle.
glouton. **1.** *a.* Greedy, gluttonous.
  2. *s.* Glutton.
gloutonnement, *adv.* Gluttonously.
gloutonnerie, *s.f.* Gluttony.
glu, *s.f.* Bird-lime.
gluant, *a.* Sticky, gummy.
glutineux, *a.* Glutinous.
glycérine, *s.f.* Glycerine.
gnome [gno:m], *s.m.* Gnome.
gobelet, *s.m.* Goblet, cup.
gober, *v.tr* To swallow, gulp down.
  G. des mouches, to stand gaping.
godille [-di:j], *s.f.* Scull.
goéland, *s.m.* (Sea-)gull.
goélette, *s.f.* Schooner.
goémon, *s.m.* Seaweed.
goguenard, *a.* Mocking, bantering
golfe, *s.m.* Gulf, bay.
gomme, *s.f.* **1.** Gum. G. arabique,
  gum-arabic. **2.** G. à effacer, (india-)
  rubber.
gommeux, *a.* Gummy, sticky.
gommier, *s.m.* Gum-tree.
gond, *s.m.* Hinge-pin.
gondole, *s.f.* Gondola.
gonflement, *s.m.* Inflating, inflation.
gonfler. **1.** *v.tr.* (a) To inflate ; to
  pump up ; to puff out. (b) To swell.
  2. *v.i* & *pr.* To swell.

gorge, *s.f.* **1.** (a) Throat, neck. (b)
  Bosom, bust. **2.** Throat, gullet.
  3. Gorge, pass.
gorgée, *s.f.* Mouthful, draught
gorger, *v.tr.* To stuff, gorge.
gorille [-ri:j], *s.m.* Gorilla.
gosier, *s.m.* Throat ; gullet.
gosse, *s.m.* & *f.* Youngster, kid.
gothique, *a.* Gothic.
goudron, *s.m.* Tar.
gouffre, *s.m.* Gulf, pit, abyss.
goujat, *s.m.* Boor, churl, cad.
goule, *s.f.* Ghoul.
goulet, *s.m.* Narrow part, neck.
goulot, *s.m.* Neck (of bottle).
goulûment, *adv.* Greedily.
goupille [-pi:j], *s.f.* (Linch)pin.
goupillon [-pijɔ̃], *s.m.* Sprinkler (for
  holy water).
gourde, *s.f.* **1.** Gourd. **2.** Water-
  bottle.
gourdin, *s.m.* Club, bludgeon
gourmand. **1.** *a.* Greedy. **2.** *s.*
  Gourmand, glutton.
gourmandise, *s.f.* **1.** Greediness.
  2. *pl.* Sweetmeats, dainties.
gourmet, *s.m.* Gourmet, epicure.
gousse, *s.f.* Pod, shell, husk.
gousset, *s.m.* (a) Gusset. (b) Waistcoat pocket.
goût, *s.m.* **1.** (Sense of) taste. **2.**
  Flavour, taste. **3.** Les gens de g.,
  people of taste.
goûter. I. *v.tr.* **1.** To taste. **2.** To
  enjoy. **3.** G. à qch., to take a little
  of sth.
  II. **goûter,** *s.m.* (Afternoon) snack.
goutte, *s.f.* **1.** Drop. **2.** Spot, splash.
  3. Small quantity. **4.** *Adv.phr.*
  Ne . . . goutte, not at all. **5.** Gout.
gouttelette, *s.f.* Droplet, globule.
goutteux, *a.* Gouty.
gouttière, *s.f.* **1.** Gutter. **2.** Rain-
  pipe.
gouvernail [-na:j], *s.m.* Rudder, helm.
gouvernante, *s.f.* Housekeeper.
gouverne, *s.f.* Guidance, direction.
gouvernement, *s.m.* Government.
gouverner, *v.tr.* **1.** To steer. **2.** To
  govern, rule.
gouverneur, *s.m.* Governor.
goyave, *s.f.* Guava.
grabat, *s.m.* Mean bed ; pallet.
grâce, *s.f.* **1.** Grace, charm. De
  bonne g., willingly. **2.** Favour.
  De g.! for pity's sake ! **3.** (a)

Pardon. **4.** Thanks. (*a*) *pl.* **Action de grâces,** thanksgiving. (*b*) *Prep. phr.* **G. à,** thanks to

gracieusement, *adv.* Graciously.

gracieux, *a.* **1.** Graceful. **2.** Gracious.

grade, *s.m.* **1.** Rank ; dignity, grade. **2.** (University) degree.

gradin, *s.m.* Step, tier.

graduation, *s.f.* **1.** Graduation. **2.** Scale.

gradué, *a.* (*a*) Graduated. (*b* Graded, progressive.

graduel, *a.* Gradual.

graduellement, *adv.* Gradually.

grain[1], *s.m.* **1.** (*a*) Grain. (*b*) Corn. **2.** Berry, bean (of coffee). **G. de raisin,** grape. **G. de beauté,** mole. **3.** Particle. **4.** Bead. **5.** Grain, texture.

grain[2], *s.m.* Squall ; gust of wind.

graine, *s.f.* Seed. **Monter en g.,** to run to seed.

graissage, *s.m.* Greasing, lubrication.

graisse, *s.f.* Grease, fat. **G. de rôti,** dripping.

graisser, *v.tr.* To grease, lubricate.

graisseux, *a.* (*a*) Greasy, oily. (*b*) Fatty.

grammaire, *s.f.* Grammar.

grammatical, -aux, *a.* Grammatical.

grammaticalement, *adv.* Grammatically.

gramme, *s.m.* Gram(me).

gramophone, *s.m.* Gramophone.

grand, *a.* **1.** (*a*) Tall ; large, big. (*b*) Chief, main. **G. ressort,** mainspring. (*c*) Grown up. (*d*) *adv.* Wide. **2.** Large, many. **En grande partie,** to a great extent. **3.** Il fait g. jour, it is broad daylight. **Il est g. temps,** it is high time. **4.** *s.m.* Les grands, the great ones.

grand'chose, *indef. pron. m.* Much.

Grande-Bretagne. *Pr.n.f.* Great Britain.

grandeur, *s.f.* **1.** (*a*) Size ; height. (*b*) Extent ; scale. **2.** Greatness.

grandiose, *a.* Grand, imposing.

grandir, *v.i.* To grow up ; to increase.

grand'mère, *s.f.* Grandmother. *pl. grand'mères.*

grand'messe, *s.f.* High mass. *pl. grand'messes.*

grand-oncle, *s.m.* Great-uncle *pl. grands-oncles.*

grand-père, *s.m.* Grandfather. *pl. grands-pères.*

grand'route, *s.f* Highway, high road. *pl. grand'routes.*

grand'rue, *s.f* High street main street. *pl. grand'rues.*

grands-parents, *s.m.pl.* Grandparents.

grange, *s.f.* Barn.

granit, *s.m.* Granite.

granulaire, *a.* Granular.

granuler, *v.tr.* To granulate.

granuleux, *a.* Granular.

graphique. **1.** *a.* Graphic. **2.** *s.m.* Diagram.

graphiquement, *adv.* Graphically.

graphite, *s.m.* Graphite, plumbago.

grappe, *s.f.* Cluster, bunch.

grappin, *s.m.* Grapnel, hook.

gras, grasse, *a.* **1.** (*a*) Fat ; fatty. (*b*) Rich. **Faire g.,** to eat meat. (*c*) *s.m.* Fat (of meat). **2.** Fat, stout. **3.** Greasy ; oily.

grasseyer, *v.i.* To roll one's r's.

gratification, *s.f.* Gratuity ; bonus.

gratifier, *v.tr.* **G. qn de qch.,** to bestow sth. upon s.o.

gratis [-tis], *adv.* Gratis.

gratitude, *s.f.* Gratitude.

gratte-ciel, *s.m.inv.* Sky-scraper.

grattement, *s.m.* Scratching.

gratter, *v.tr.* **1.** To scrape, scratch. **2.** To erase.

grattoir, *s.m.* Scraper.

gratuit, *a.* Gratuitous.

gratuitement, *adv.* Gratuitously.

grave, *a.* **1.** (*a*) Grave ; solemn ; sober. (*b*) Important. **2.** Deep (voice).

gravement, *adv.* **1.** Gravely **2.** Seriously.

graver, *v.tr.* To cut, engrave.

graveur, *s.m.* Engraver ; carver.

gravier, *s.m.* Gravel, grit.

gravir, *v.tr.* To climb ; to ascend.

gravité, *s.f.* Gravity.

graviter, *v.i.* To gravitate.

gravure, *s.f.* **1.** Engraving. **G. sur bois,** woodcut. **G. à l'eau-forte,** etching. **2.** Picture.

gré, *s.m.* **1.** Liking, taste. **2.** Will, pleasure. **De mon plein gré,** of my own accord. **Bon gré mal gré,** willynilly. **3.** Savoir gré, to be grateful.

grec, grecque. 1. *a. & s.m.* Greek. **2.** *s.* Greek.

Grèce. *Pr.n.f.* Greece.

grecque. See GREC.

gredin, s. Rogue, scoundrel.

gréement, s.m. Rigging.

greffe, s.f. **1.** Graft, slip. **2.** Grafting.

greffier, s.m. **1.** Clerk (of the court). **2.** Registrar.

grégaire, a. Gregarious.

grêle[1], a. Slender, thin; high-pitched.

grêle[2], s.f. Hail.

grêler, v.impers. **Il grêle,** it hails.

grêlon, s.m. Hail-stone.

grelot, s..m. Bell.

grelotter, v.i. To tremble, shiver.

grenade, s.f. **1.** Pomegranate **2.** Grenade, bomb.

grenat, s.m. Garnet.

grenier, s.m. **1.** Granary. **2.** Garret.

grenouille [-nu:j], s.f. Frog.

grès, s.m. Sandstone.

grésil, s.m. Frozen pellets of snow.

grésillement [-zij-], s.m. Crackling; chirping.

grésiller [-zije], v.i. (a) To crackle; to sizzle. (b) To chirp.

grève, s.f. **1.** Strand; beach **2.** Strike (of workmen).

gréviste, s.m. & f. Striker.

grief [griɛf], s.m. Grievance.

grièvement, adv. Severely, grievously.

griffe, s.f. Claw; talon.

griffonner, v.tr. To scrawl, scribble.

grignoter, v.tr. To nibble.

gril [gri], s.m. Grid(iron), grill.

grillade [grijad], s.f. Grill, grilled steak.

grillage [grija:ʒ], s.m. Grating.

grille [gri:j], s.f. (a) Bars. (c) Railings. (d) Fire-grate.

griller [grije], v.tr. **1.** To grill; to toast. **2.** To scorch.

grillon [grijɔ̃], s.m. Cricket.

grimace, s.f. Grimace, wry face.

grimacer, v.i. To grimace.

grimper, v.i. & tr. To climb (up).

grimpeur, -euse, a. Climbing.

grincement, s.m. Grinding; gnashing.

grincer, v.i. To grate; to grind; to creak.

grincheux, a. Grumpy, crabbed.

grippe, s.f. **1.** Dislike. **2.** Influenza.

gris, a. **1.** (a) Grey. (b) Grey-haired. **2.** Intoxicated.

grisâtre, a. Greyish.

griser, v.tr. To intoxicate.
  se griser, to get tipsy.

griserie, s.f. **1.** Tipsiness. **2.** Intoxication, exhilaration.

grisou, s.m. Fire-damp.

grive, s.f. Thrush.

grognard. 1. a. Grumbling. **2.** s. Grumbler, grouser.

grognement, s.m. **1.** (a) Grunt. (b) Growl. **2.** Grumbling.

grogner, v.i. **1.** (a) To grunt. (b) To growl. **2.** To grumble.

groin, s.m. Snout (of pig).

grommeler, v.i. To grumble.

grondement, s.m. **1.** Growl(ing). **2.** Rumbling.

gronder. 1. v.i. (a) To growl. (b) To rumble. **2.** v.tr. To scold.

gronderie, s.f. Scolding; rating.

grondeur, -euse, a Grumbling, scolding.

gros, grosse. 1. a. (a) Big, stout. **G. mot,** coarse expression. **G. temps,** heavy weather. **Avoir le cœur g.,** to be sad at heart. (b) adv. **Gagner g.,** to earn a great deal. **2.** s.m. (a) Bulk, chief part. (b) **En g.,** wholesale. **3.** s.f. **Grosse,** gross; twelve dozen.

groseille [-zɛ:j], s.f. **1.** Currant. **2. G. à maquereau,** gooseberry.

groseillier [-zɛje], s.m. **1.** Currant-bush. **2. G. à maquereau,** gooseberry-bush.

grosse. See GROS.

grosseur, s.f. Size, bulk, volume.

grossier, a. (a) Coarse, rough. (b) **Faute grossière,** glaring blunder. (c) Rude (envers, to).

grossièrement, adv. **1.** Coarsely. **2.** Rudely.

grossièreté, s.f. (a) Coarseness. (b) Rudeness.

grossir. 1. v.tr. To enlarge, swell. **2.** v.i. To increase, swell.

grossissant, a. **1.** Growing, swelling. **2.** Magnifying.

grossissement, s.m. Increase in size.

grotesque, a. Ludicrous, absurd.

grotte, s.f. Grotto.

grouiller [gruje], v.i. To crawl, swarm (de, with).

groupe, s.m. Group; cluster.

groupement, s.m. Grouping.

grouper, v.tr. To group.
  se grouper, to gather.

gruau, s.m. **1. G. d'avoine,** groats. **2.** Gruel.

grue, *s.f.* Crane.

gué, *s.m.* Ford.

guenille [-ni:j], *s.f.* **En guenilles,** in rags (and tatters).

guenon, *s.f.* She-monkey.

guêpe, *s.f.* Wasp.

guêpier, *s.m.* Wasps' nest.

guère, *adv.* Hardly ; not much, not many.

guéridon, *s.m.* Pedestal table.

guérilla [-rija], *s.f.* Band of guerrillas.

guérir. 1. *v.tr.* To cure, heal. **2.** *v.i.* (a) To recover. (b) To heal.

guérison, *s.f.* **1.** Recovery. **2.** (a) Cure. (b) Healing.

guérite, *s.f.* Sentry-box.

guerre, *s.f.* **1.** War, warfare. **2.** Strife, feud. *Adv.phr.* **De g.** lasse, for the sake of peace.

guerrier. 1. *a.* Warlike. **2.** *s.m.* Warrior.

guet, *s.m.* Watch(ing) ; look-out.

guet-apens, *s.m.* Ambush, snare. *pl.* **guets-apens.**

guêtre, *s.f.* Gaiter.

guetter, *v.tr.* To be on the look-out for.

gueule, *s.f.* **1.** Mouth ; jaws. **2.** Mouth ; muzzle (of gun).

gueux, *s.* Beggar ; tramp.

gui, *s.m.* Mistletoe.

guichet, *s.m.* **1.** (a) Wicket. (b) Grating (in door). **2.** Booking-office.

guide¹, *s.m.* **1.** Guide ; conductor. **2.** Guide(-book).

guide², *s.f.* Rein.

guider, *v.tr.* To guide, direct, lead.

guidon, *s.m.* Handle-bar.

guigne, *s.f.* Bad luck.

guignol, *s.m.* (a) Punch. (b) Punch and Judy show.

Guillaume [gij-]. *Pr.n.m.* William.

guillemets [gijmɛ], *s.m.pl.* Inverted commas, quotation marks.

guillotine [gij-], *s.f.* Guillotine.

guillotiner [gij-], *v.tr.* To guillotine.

guimauve, *s.f.* Marsh-mallow.

guimpe, *s.f.* (Nun's) wimple.

guindé, *a.* Stiff, stilted.

guirlande, *s.f.* Garland, wreath.

guise, *s.f.* Manner, way, fashion. **En g. de,** by way of.

guitare, *s.f.* Guitar.

guttural, -aux, *a.* Guttural.

Guyane (la). *Pr.n.f.* Guiana.

gymnase, *s.m.* Gymnasium.

gymnaste, *s.m.* Gymnast.

gymnastique. 1. *a.* Gymnastic. **2.** *s.f.* Gymnastics.

gyro, *a.* **Sens g.,** roundabout.

H

Words beginning with an 'aspirate' h are shown by an asterisk.

H, h [aʃ], *s.m. & f.* (The letter) H, h.

*ha, *int.* **1.** Ah ! **2.** Ha, ha ! ha, ha !

habile, *a.* Clever, able ; artful.

habilement, *adv.* Cleverly, ably.

habileté, *s.f.* (a) Ability, skill. (b) Cleverness, smartness.

habillé, *a.* Dressed.

habillement [abij-], *s.m.* **1.** Clothing. **2.** Clothes, dress ; apparel.

habiller [abije], *v.tr.* (a) To dress. (b) To clothe.

s'habiller, to dress.

habit, *s.m.* **1.** Dress, costume ; *pl.* clothes. **2.** (a) Coat. (b) **En h.,** in evening-dress.

habitable, *a.* Habitable.

habitant, *s.* (a) Inhabitant ; resident. (b) Occupier. (c) Inmate.

habitation, *s.f.* **1.** Habitation. **2.** Dwelling(-place), residence.

habiter. 1. *v.tr.* (a) To inhabit, to live in. (b) To occupy. **2.** *v.i.* To live, reside.

habitude, *s.f.* (a) Habit, custom. **D'h.,** usually. (b) Knack.

habitué, *s.* Frequenter.

habituel, *a.* Usual ; habitual.

habituellement, *adv.* Habitually.

habituer, *v.tr.* To accustom.

s'habituer, to get accustomed.

*hache, *s.f.* Axe.

*haché, *a.* Staccato, jerky.

*hacher, *v.tr.* To chop (up) ; to mince.

*hachette, *s.f.* Hatchet.

*hachis, *s.m.* Mince.

*hagard, *a.* Haggard, wild.

*haie, *s.f.* (a) Hedge. (b) Line, row.

*haillon [ajɔ̃], *s.m.* Rag.

*haine, *s.f.* Hatred ; detestation.

*haineux, *a.* Full of hatred.

*haïr, v.tr. To hate, detest.
*haïssable, a. Hateful. detestable.
*halage, s.m. Towing.
*hâle, s.m. Tan; sunburn.
*hâlé, a. Tanned; weather-beaten.
haleine, s.f. Breath.
*haler, v.tr. To tow; to haul.
*hâler, v.tr. To tan.
  se hâler, to get sunburnt.
*haletant, a. Panting, breathless.
*halètement, s.m. Panting.
*haleter, v.i. To pant; to gasp.
*halle, s.f. (Covered) market.
*hallier, s.m. Thicket, copse, brake.
hallucination, s.f. Hallucination.
*halte, s.f. 1. Stop, halt. 2. Stopping-place, resting-place.
*hamac [amak], s.m. Hammock.
*hameau, s.m. Hamlet.
hameçon, s.m. (Fish-)hook.
*hampe, s.f. Staff, pole; shaft.
*hanche, s.f. 1. Hip. 2. Haunch.
*hangar, s.m. 1. Shed; lean-to.
  H. à bateaux, boat-house. 2. Hangar.
*hanneton, s.m. Cockchafer.
*hanter, v.tr. To frequent, haunt.
*hantise, s.f. Obsession.
*happer, v.tr. To snap up.
*harangue, s.f. Harangue; speech.
*haranguer, v.tr. To harangue.
*harasser, v.tr. (a) To tire (out), exhaust. (b) To harass, worry.
*harcelant, a. Harassing, tormenting.
*harceler, v.tr. To harass, torment.
*hardes, s.f.pl. (Worn) clothes.
*hardi, a. Bold, audacious. (a) Daring. (b) Rash. (c) Impudent.
*hardiesse, s.f. Boldness, hardihood. (a) Daring. (b) Impudence.
*hardiment, adv. Boldly.
*harem [arɛm], s.m. Harem.
*hareng, s.m. Herring.
*hargneux, a. Snarling; peevish.
*haricot, s.m. H. (blanc), haricot bean. Haricots verts, French beans.
  H. d'Espagne, scarlet runner.
harmonie, s.f. Harmony; agreement.
harmonieux, a. Harmonious.
harmoniser, v.tr. To harmonize.
*harnachement, s.m. Harness, trappings.
*harnacher, v.tr. To harness.
*harnais, s.m. Harness.
*harpe, s.f. Harp.
*harpie, s.f. Harpy.

*harpon, s.m. Harpoon.
*harponner, v.tr. To harpoon.
*hasard, s.m. (a) Chance, luck, accident. Au h., at random (b) Risk, danger.
*hasarder, v.tr. To risk, venture.
  se hasarder, to venture.
*hasardeux, a. 1. Hazardous, perilous. 2. Daring, foolhardy.
*hâte, s.f. Haste, hurry A la h., in haste.
*hâter, v.tr. To hasten; to expedite.
  se hâter, to hasten, hurry.
*hâtif, a. (a) Forward, early; premature. (b) Hasty, hurried.
*hâtivement, adv. (a) Prematurely. (b) Hastily.
*hausse, s.f. Rise, rising.
*haussement, s.m. Raising; lifting.
*hausser. 1. v.tr. To raise, lift. H. les épaules, to shrug. 2. v.i. To rise.
*haut. I. a. 1. High. (a) Tall; lofty. (b) Exalted. (c) Raised. A haute voix, aloud. 2. Upper, higher.
  II. haut, adv. High (up), above, up. Parler h., to speak loudly.
  III. haut, s.m. 1. Height. 2. Top. 3. Regarder de h. en bas, to look down on. En h., above; upstairs.
*hautain, a. Haughty.
*hautbois, s.m. Oboe.
*hautement, adv. 1. Highly. 2. (a) Loudly. (b) Openly. 3. Loftily.
*hauteur, s.f. 1. Height, elevation. A la h. de, abreast of, level with. 2. Haughtiness. 3. Eminence.
*haut-fond, s.m. Shoal, shallow. pl. hauts-fonds.
*haut-le-corps, s.m.inv Sudden start.
*haut-parleur, s.m. Loud-speaker. pl. haut-parleurs.
*hâve, a. Haggard, gaunt; sunken.
*havre, s.m. Harbour, port.
*havresac [-sak], s.m. Knapsack.
*Haye (la). Pr.n.f. The Hague.
*hé, int. 1. Hullo! I say! 2. Hey! 3. Hé! hé! well, well!
hebdomadaire, a. & s.m. Weekly.
héberger, v.tr To harbour; to lodge, shelter.
hébété, a. Dazed, bewildered.
hébétement, s.m. Stupefaction.
hébéter, v.tr. To dull; to daze.
hébraïque, a. Hebraic, Hebrew.
hébreu, -eux, a. & s.m. Hebrew.

hécatombe, *s.f.* Hecatomb.
*****hein,** *int.* Eh? what?
hélas [elɑːs], *int.* Alas!
*****héler,** *v.tr.* To hail, call.
hélice, *s.f.* Propeller, screw.
héliographe, *s.m.* Heliograph.
*****hem** [ɛm], *int.* (A)hem! hm!
hémisphère, *s.m.* Hemisphere.
hémisphérique, *a.* Hemispheric(al).
hémorragie, *s.f.* Haemorrhage.
*****henné,** *s.m.* Henna.
*****hennir,** *v.i.* To whinny; to neigh.
*****hennissement,** *s.m.* (a) Whinnying, neighing (b) Whinny, neigh.
Henri. *Pr.n.m.* Henry.
héraldique, *a.* Heraldic.
*****héraut,** *s.m.* Herald.
herbacé, *a.* Herbaceous.
herbage, *s.m.* Grass-land; pasture.
herbe, *s.f.* **1.** Herb, plant. **Omelette aux fines herbes,** savoury omelet. **Mauvaise h.,** weed **2.** Grass. **3.** En h., in embryo.
herbeux, *a.* Grassy.
herbivore. 1. *a.* Herbivorous, grass-eating. **2.** *s.m.* Herbivore.
herboriste, *s.m. & f.* Herbalist.
Hercule. *Pr.n.m.* Hercules.
herculéen, *a.* Herculean.
héréditaire, *a.* Hereditary.
hérédité, *s.f.* Heredity.
hérésie, *s.f.* Heresy.
hérétique. 1. *a.* Heretical. **2.** *s.* Heretic.
*****hérissé,** *a* **1.** Bristling (de, with). **2.** Bristly.
*****hérisser,** *v.tr.* To bristle (up).
se hérisser, to stand on end.
*****hérisson,** *s.m.* Hedgehog.
héritage, *s.m.* Inheritance, heritage.
hériter. 1. *v.i.* **H de.** to inherit. **2.** *v.tr.* To inherit.
héritier, *s.* Heir, *f.* heiress.
hermétiquement, *adv.* Hermetically.
hermine, *s.f.* Stoat; ermine.
héroïne, *s.f.* Heroine.
héroïque, *a.* Heroic.
héroïquement, *adv.* Heroically.
héroïsme, *s.m.* Heroism.
*****héron,** *s.m.* Heron.
*****héros,** *s.m.* Hero.
*****herse,** *s.f.* **1.** Harrow. **2.** Portcullis.
hésitant, *a.* Hesitating.
hésitation, *s.f.* Hesitation.
hésiter, *v.i.* **1.** To hesitate, waver. **2.** To falter.
hétérogène, *a.* Heterogeneous.

*****hêtre,** *s.m.* Beech.
*****heu,** *int.* (a) Ah! (b) H'm!
heure, *s.f.* Hour. **1.** (a) **La dernière h.,** stop-press news. **Heures supplémentaires,** overtime. (b) **Quelle h. est-il?** what is the time? **Cinq heures,** five o'clock. (c) **H. d'éclairage,** lighting-up time. **Être à l'h.,** to be punctual. (d) **Pour l'h.,** for the present. **2.** *Adv.phrs.* **De bonne h.,** early. **Tout à l'heure,** (i) just now; (ii) directly. **3.** *int.* **A la bonne h.!** well done!
heureusement, *adv.* Happily. (a) Successfully. (b) Luckily.
heureux, *a.* **1.** Happy. **2.** (a) Successful. (b) Lucky. **3.** Favourable, fortunate. **4.** Felicitous, apt.
*****heurt,** *s.m.* Shock, knock.
*****heurter,** *v.tr. & i.* **1.** To knock (against); to run into. **2.** To shock, offend.
hexagone. 1. *a.* Hexagonal. **2.** *s.m.* Hexagon.
hiberner, *v.i.* To hibernate.
*****hibou, -oux,** *s.m.* Owl.
*****hideur,** *s.f.* Hideousness.
*****hideusement,** *adv.* Hideously.
*****hideux,** *a.* Hideous.
hier [ieːr], *adv.* Yesterday. **H. soir,** last night.
*****hiérarchie,** *s.f.* Hierarchy.
hiéroglyphe, *s.m.* (a) Hieroglyph. (b) *pl.* Hieroglyphics.
hilarant, *a* Mirth-provoking **Gaz h.,** laughing gas.
hilare, *a.* Hilarious, mirthful.
hilarité, *s.f.* Hilarity, mirth.
hindou, *a. & s.* Hindu.
hippique, *a.* Relating to horses; equine. **Concours h.,** horse-show.
hippopotame, *s.m.* Hippopotamus.
hirondelle, *s.f.* **1.** Swallow. **2.** Small river steamboat.
hirsute, *a.* Hirsute, hairy.
*****hisser,** *v.tr.* To hoist (up), pull up.
histoire, *s.f.* **1.** (a) History. (b) **H. naturelle,** natural history. **2.** Story, tale. **3.** Fib, story. **4.** **Faire des histoires,** to make a fuss.
historien, *s.* Historian.
historique, *a.* Historic(al).
historiquement, *adv.* Historically.
hiver [iveːr], *s.m.* Winter.
hivernal, -aux, *a.* Winter.
hiverner, *v.i.* To winter.

*ho, *int.* **1.** Hi! **2.** Oh!

*hochement, *s.m.* Shaking; tossing.

*hocher, *v.tr. & i.* H. (de) la tête, (i) to shake one's head; (ii) to nod; (iii) to toss the head.

*holà, *int.* **1.** Hallo! **2.** Stop!

*hollandais. **1.** *a. & s.* Dutch. **2.** *s.* Dutchman, -woman.

*Hollande. *Pr.n.f.* Holland.

holocauste, *s.m.* Holocaust.

*homard, *s.m.* Lobster.

homélie, *s.f.* Homily.

homéopathique, *a.* Homoeopathic.

homicide[1]. **1.** *s.m. & f.* Homicide. **2.** *a.* Homicidal.

homicide[2], *s.m.* Homicide. H. involontaire, manslaughter.

hommage, *s.m.* **1.** Homage. **2.** *pl.* Respects. **3.** Tribute.

homme, *s.m.* Man; mankind.

homogène, *a.* Homogeneous.

homonyme. **1.** *a.* Homonymous. **2.** *s.m.* (*a*) Homonym. (*b*) Namesake.

homuncule, *s.m.* Manikin, dwarf.

*Hongrie. *Pr.n.f.* Hungary.

*hongrois, *a. & s.* Hungarian.

honnête, *a.* **1.** Honest, honourable. **2.** Courteous, well-bred. **3.** Reasonable, fair.

honnêtement, *s.m.* **1.** Honestly. **2.** Civilly. **3.** Reasonably. **4.** Fairly.

honnêteté, *s.f.* **1.** Honesty, uprightness. **2.** Courtesy. **3.** Fairness.

honneur, *s.m.* **1.** Honour. Piquer qn d'h., to put s.o. on his mettle. **2.** Faire h. au dîner, to do justice to the dinner. J'ai l'h. de vous faire savoir, I beg to inform you. Jouer pour l'h., to play for love. **3.** *pl.* Faire les honneurs, to do the honours. **4.** *pl. Cards :* Honours.

honorabilité, *s.f.* Respectability.

honorable, *a.* (*a*) Honourable. (*b*) Respectable.

honorablement, *adv.* Honourably.

honoraire. **1.** *a.* Honorary. **2.** *s.m.pl.* Fee(s); honorarium.

honorer, *v.tr.* **1.** (*a*) To honour; to respect. Votre honorée du, your favour of the. (*b*) To honour to. **2.** To do credit to (s.o.).

*honte, *s.f.* (*a*) Shame. Faire h. à, to put to shame. (*b*) Fausse h., bashfulness.

*honteusement, *adv.* Shamefully; disgracefully.

*honteux, *a.* **1.** Ashamed. **2.** Shameful, disgraceful.

hôpital, -aux, *s.m.* Hospital, infirmary.

*hoquet, *s.m.* Hiccup.

horaire. **1.** *a.* Signal h., time-signal. **2.** *s.m.* Time-table.

*horde, *s.f.* Horde.

*horion, *s.m.* Blow, punch, knock.

horizon, *s.m.* Horizon, sky-line.

horizontal, -aux, *a.* Horizontal.

horizontalement, *adv.* Horizontally.

horloge, *s.f.* Clock.

horloger, *s.m.* Watchmaker.

horlogerie, *s.f.* **1.** Clock-making. Mouvement d'h., clockwork. **2.** Watchmaker's shop.

*hormis, *prep.* Except, but, save.

horreur, *s.f.* Horror.

horrible, *a.* Horrible.

horriblement, *adv.* Horribly.

horripilant, *a.* Hair-raising.

*hors, *prep.* **1.** (*a*) Out of, outside. (*b*) Except. **2.** *Prep.phr.* H. de, out of, outside (of). Être h. de soi, to be beside oneself.

*hors-la-loi, *s.m.inv.* Outlaw.

horticole, *a.* Horticultural.

horticulture, *s.f.* Horticulture, gardening.

hospice, *s.m.* **1.** Hospice. **2.** Almshouse, home, asylum.

hospitalier, *a.* Hospitable.

hospitalité, *s.f.* Hospitality.

hostie, *s.f.* (Eucharistic) host.

hostile, *a.* Hostile; unfriendly.

hostilité, *s.f.* **1.** Hostility (*contre*, to); enmity. **2.** *pl.* Hostilities.

hôte, hôtesse, *s.* **1.** Host, *f.* hostess; landlord, landlady. **2.** Guest.

hôtel, *s.m.* **1.** Mansion, town-house. **2.** Public building. H. de ville, town-hall. **3.** (*a*) Hotel. (*b*) H. meublé, hotel (providing bed and breakfast).

hôtelier, *s.* Innkeeper.

hôtellerie, *s.f.* Hostelry, inn.

*hotte, *s.f.* Basket.

*houblon, *s.m.* Hop(s).

*houe, *s.f.* Hoe.

*houer, *v.tr.* To hoe.

*houille [u:j], *s.f.* **1.** Coal. **2.** H. blanche, water-power.

*houillère [uj-]. *s.f.* Coal-mine.

*houilleur [ujœ:r], *s.m.* Collier.

*houle, *s.f.* Swell, surge (of sea).

*houlette, *s.f.* (Shepherd's) crook.

*houleux, a. Swelling, surging.

*houppe, s.f. (a) Tuft; pompon; powder-puff. (b) Tassel.

*hourra, int. & s.m. Hurrah!

*houspiller [-pije], v.tr. To hustle; to jostle; to handle roughly.

*housse, s.f. (Furniture) cover.

*houssine, s.f. Switch.

*houx, s.m. Holly.

*hublot, s.m. Scuttle, port-hole.

*huche, s.f. Bin.

*huées, s.f.pl. Booing, hooting.

*huer. I. v.i. (a) To shout; halloo. (b) To hoot. 2. v.tr. To boo.

*Hugues. Pr.n.m. Hugh.

huile, s.f. Oil.

huiler, v.tr. To oil; to lubricate.

huileux, a. Oily, greasy.

huissier, s.m. I. Usher. 2. Bailiff.

*huit, num.a. & s.m.inv. Eight. H. jours, a week. D'aujourd'hui en h., to-day week.

*huitaine, s.f. Week.

*huitième. I. num.a. & s. Eighth. 2. s.m. Eighth.

huître, s.f. Oyster.

*huit-reflets [ҷitrəflɛ], s.m.inv Top hat.

humain, a. I. Human. 2. Humane.

humainement, adv. I. Humanly. 2. Humanely.

humanitaire, a. & s. Humanitarian.

humanité, s.f. Humanity.

humble, a. Humble, lowly.

humblement, adv. Humbly.

humecter, v.tr. To damp, moisten.

*humer, v.tr. To suck in, up.

humeur, s.f. (a) Humour, mood. (b) Temper. Avec h., testily.

humide, a. Damp, moist. Temps h. et froid, raw weather.

humidité, s.f. Humidity, damp(ness), moisture. "Craint l'h.," 'to be kept dry.'

humiliant, a. Humiliating.

humiliation, s.f. Humiliation.

humilier, v.tr. To humiliate.

humilité, s.f. Humility.

humoriste, s.m. & f. Humorist.

humoristique, a. Humorous.

humour, s.m. Humour.

*hurlement, s.m. Howl(ing).

*hurler. I. v.i. To howl; to roar. 2. v.tr. To bawl out.

*hussard, s.m. Hussar.

*hutte, s.f. Hut, shed, shanty.

hybride, a. & s.m. Hybrid.

hydrate, s.m. Hydrate.

hydraulique, a. Hydraulic.

hydravion, s.m. Seaplane.

hydrogène, s.m. Hydrogen

hydrophile, a. Absorbent.

hydrophobie, s.f. Hydrophobia

hydropisie, s.f. Dropsy.

hyène, s.f. Hyena.

hygiène, s.f. Hygiene.

hygiénique, a. Hygienic; sanitary.

hymne. I. s.m. Patriotic song. 2. s.f. Hymn.

hypnotiser, v.tr. To hypnotize.

hypnotisme, s.m. Hypnotism.

hypocrisie, s.f. Hypocrisy; cant.

hypocrite. I. a. Hypocritical. 2. s.m. & f. Hypocrite.

hypocritement, adv. Hypocritically.

hypothécaire, s.m. & f. Mortgagee.

hypothèque, s.f. Mortgage.

hypothéquer, v.tr. To mortgage.

hypothèse, s.f. Hypothesis.

hypothétique, a. Hypothetical.

hystérie, s.f. Hysteria.

hystérique, a. Hysterical.

I

I, i [i], s.m. I. (The letter) I, i. 2. i grec, (the letter) Y, y

ibex [-ɛks], s.m. Ibex.

ibis [-is], s.m. Ibis.

iceberg [-bɛrk], s.m. Iceberg.

ici, adv. I. Here. Ici-bas, here below, on earth. Passez par ici, step this way. Tp: Ici Dupont, Dupont speaking. 2. Now. Jusqu'ici, up to now; hitherto. D'ici peu, before long.

idéal, -aux, a. & s.m. Ideal.

idéalement, adv. Ideally.

idéalisme, s.m. Idealism.

idéaliste. I. a. Idealistic. 2. s.m. & f. Idealist.

idée, s.f. I. Idea. (a) Notion. I. fixe, obsession. (b) View, opinion. (c) Whim, fancy. 2. Mind.

identification, s.f. Identification

identifier, v.tr. To identify.

identique, a. Identical (à, with).

identiquement, adv. Identically

identité, *s.f.* Identity.

idiomatique, *a.* Idiomatic.

idiome, *s.m.* Language.

idiosyncrasie, *s.f.* Idiosyncrasy.

idiot. 1. *a.* Idiotic. 2. *s.* Idiot.

idiotie, *s.f.* Idiocy.

idiotisme, *s.m.* Idiom.

idolâtre, *a.* Idolatrous.

idolâtrie, *s.f.* Idolatry.

idole, *s.f.* Idol, image.

idylle, *s.f.* Idyl ; romance.

idyllique, *a.* Idyllic.

if, *s.m.* Yew(-tree).

ignare, *s.m. & f.* Ignoramus.

ignoble, *a.* Ignoble ; base.

ignominie, *s.f.* Ignominy, shame.

ignominieusement, *adv.* Ignominiously.

ignominieux, *a.* Ignominious.

ignorance, *s.f.* Ignorance.

ignorant. 1. *a.* Ignorant, uninstructed. 2. *s.* Ignoramus, dunce.

ignoré, *a.* Unknown.

ignorer, *v.tr* Not to know ; to be ignorant of.

il, ils. 1. *pers. pron. nom. m.* He, it ; they. 2. *inv.* It, there. (*a*) Il était une fois, there was once. (*b*) Il faut partir, we must start. Il y a, there is ; there are.

île, *s.f.* 1. Island. 2. Island site.

illégal, -aux, *a.* Illegal, unlawful.

illégalement, *adv.* Illegally.

illégalité, *s.f* Illegality.

illégitime, *a.* Illegitimate ; unlawful.

illégitimité *s.f* Illegitimacy : unlawfulness.

illettré, *a.* Illiterate, uneducated.

illicite, *a.* Illicit, unlawful.

illicitement, *adv* Illicitly.

illimité, *a.* Unlimited, boundless.

illisible, *a.* Illegible, unreadable.

illisiblement, *adv.* Illegibly.

illogique, *a.* Illogical ; inconsequent.

illogiquement, *adv.* Illogically.

illumination, *s.f* Illumination.

illuminer, *v.tr.* 1. To light up. 2. To enlighten.

illusion, *s.f* 1. Illusion 2. Delusion.

illusoire, *a.* Illusory.

illustrateur, *s.m* Illustrator

illustration, *s.f.* Illustration.

illustre, *a.* Illustrious, renowned.

illustrer, *v.tr.* 1. To render illustrious. 2. To illustrate.

s'illustrer, to become famous.

îlot, *s.m.* Islet, small island.

image, *s.f.* 1. Image 2. (*a*) Likeness. (*b*) Picture.

imaginable, *a.* Imaginable.

imaginaire, *a.* Imaginary ; fancied.

imaginatif, *a.* Imaginative.

imagination, *s.f.* Imagination

imaginer, *v.tr.* To imagine.

imbécile. 1. *a* (*a*) Imbecile. (*b*) Silly, idiotic. 2. *s.m. & f.* Idiot ; fool.

imbécillité, *s.f.* (*a*) Imbecility. (*b*) Silliness, stupidity.

imberbe, *a.* Beardless ; callow.

imbiber, *v.tr.* To soak.

s'imbiber, to absorb.

imbu, *a.* Imbued, soaked.

imbuvable, *a.* Undrinkable.

imitateur, -trice, *s.* Imitator.

imitatif, *a.* Imitative.

imitation, *s.f.* Imitation.

imiter, *v.tr.* To imitate.

immaculé, *a.* Immaculate.

immangeable, *a.* Uneatable.

immanquable, *a.* Inevitable.

immatériel, *a* Immaterial, unsubstantial.

immaturité, *s.f.* Immaturity.

immédiat, *a.* Immediate.

immédiatement, *adv.* Immediately.

immémorial, -aux, *a.* Immemorial.

immense, *a.* 1. Immeasurable, boundless. 2. Immense, vast, huge.

immensément, *adv.* Immensely.

immensité, *s.f.* Immensity.

immerger, *v.tr.* To immerse, dip.

immérité, *a.* Undeserved.

immersion, *s.f.* Immersion.

immesurable, *a.* Immeasurable.

immeuble, *s.m.* (*a*) Real estate. (*b*) House ; premises.

immigrant, *a. & s.* Immigrant.

immigration, *s.f.* Immigration.

immigré, *s.* Immigrant, settler.

immigrer, *v.i.* To immigrate.

imminence, *s.f.* Imminence.

imminent, *a.* Imminent.

immiscer (s'), *v.pr.* To interfere.

immobile, *a.* 1. Motionless, still. 2. Immovable ; firm.

immobilité, *s.f.* Immobility

immodéré, *a.* Immoderate.

immodérément. *adv* Immoderately.

immodeste, *a.* Immodest.

immodestie, *s.f.* Immodesty.

immonde, *a.* Filthy ; vile.

immondices, *s.f.pl.* Dirt, refuse.
immoral, -aux, *a.* Immoral.
immoralité, *s.f.* Immorality.
immortalité, *s.f.* Immortality.
immortel. 1. *a.* Immortal. **2.** *s.f.* Immortelle, everlasting (flower).
immuable, *a.* Immutable, unalterable ; fixed, unchanging.
immuablement, *adv.* Immutably.
immunité, *s.f.* Immunity.
immutabilité, *s.f.* Immutability.
impair, *a.* Odd, uneven.
impalpable, *a.* Impalpable.
impardonnable, *a.* Unpardonable.
imparfait, *a.* **1.** Unfinished, uncompleted. **2.** Imperfect, defective.
imparfaitement, *adv.* Imperfectly.
impartial, -aux, *a.* Impartial, unbiassed, fair-minded, unprejudiced.
impartialement, *adv.* Impartially.
impartialité, *s.f.* Impartiality.
impasse, *s.f.* **1.** Blind alley. **2.** Deadlock.
impassibilité, *s.f.* Impassibility.
impassible, *a.* Impassive.
impassiblement, *adv.* Impassively.
impatiemment, *adv.* Impatiently.
impatience, *s.f.* (*a*) Impatience. (*b*) Eagerness.
impatient, *a.* (*a*) Impatient. (*b*) Eager.
impatienter, *v.tr.* To put out of patience.
    s'impatienter, to lose patience.
impayable, *a.* Priceless.
impeccabilité, *s.f.* Impeccability.
impeccable, *a.* Impeccable.
impécunieux, *a.* Impecunious.
impénétrabilité, *s.f.* **1.** Impenetrability. **2.** Inscrutability.
impénétrable, *a.* **1.** Impenetrable ; impervious. **2.** Inscrutable.
impénitence, *s.f.* Impenitence.
impénitent, *a.* Impenitent, unrepentant.
impératif, *a.* Imperative.
impérativement, *adv.* Imperatively.
impératrice, *s.f.* Empress.
imperceptible, *a.* Imperceptible.
imperceptiblement, *adv.* Imperceptibly.
imperfection, *s.f.* Imperfection.
impérial, -aux. 1. *a.* Imperial. **2.** *s.f.* Impériale, top(-deck) (of tram).
impérieux, *a.* **1.** Imperious, haughty. **2.** Imperative, pressing.

impérissable, *a.* Imperishable.
imperméable. 1. *a.* Impervious ; waterproof. **2.** *s.m.* Waterproof.
impersonnel, *a.* Impersonal.
impertinemment, *adv.* Impertinently, rudely.
impertinence, *s.f.* Impertinence
impertinent, *a.* Impertinent.
imperturbabilité, *s.f.* Imperturbability.
imperturbable, *a.* Imperturbable.
imperturbablement, *adv.* Imperturbably.
impétueusement, *adv.* Impetuously.
impétueux, *a.* Impetuous.
impétuosité, *s.f.* Impetuosity.
impie, *a.* Impious ; blasphemous.
impiété, *s.f.* Impiety, godlessness.
impitoyable, *a.* (*a*) Pitiless ; ruthless. (*b*) Relentless.
impitoyablement, *adv.* (*a*) Pitilessly. (*b*) Relentlessly.
implacabilité, *s.f.* Implacability.
implacable, *a.* Implacable, relentless.
implacablement, *adv.* Implacably.
implanter, *v.tr.* To implant.
    s'implanter, to take root.
implicite, *a.* Implicit.
implicitement, *adv.* Implicitly.
impliquer, *v.tr.* To implicate.
implorer, *v.tr.* To implore.
impoli, *a.* Impolite, rude.
impoliment, *adv.* Impolitely.
impolitesse, *s.f.* Impoliteness.
impolitique, *a.* Impolitic.
impopulaire, *a.* Unpopular.
impopularité, *s.f.* Unpopularity.
importance, *s.f.* Importance ; consequence, moment ; extent.
important, *a.* (*a*) Important ; considerable. (*b*) Consequential.
importateur, -trice, *s.* Importer.
importation, *s.f.* Importation.
importer[1], *v.tr.* To import.
importer[2], *v.i.* To be of importance ; to matter. **N'importe,** no matter, never mind.
importun. 1. *a.* Importunate ; tiresome ; unwelcome. **2.** *s.* Nuisance.
importuner, *v.tr.* To importune.
importunité, *s.f.* Importunity.
imposant, *a.* Imposing ; stately.
imposer. 1. *v.tr.* **1.** To impose ; to set ; to lay down. **2.** To tax.

II. **imposer**, *v.i.* **1.** To inspire respect. **2.** En i. à, to impose on.
s'imposer. 1. To assert oneself. **2.** S'i. à, to thrust oneself upon.

imposition, *s.f.* (*a*) Imposing, laying down. (*b*) Taxation.

impossibilité, *s.f.* Impossibility.

impossible, *a.* Impossible.

imposteur, *s.m.* Impostor.

imposture, *s.f.* Imposture.

impôt, *s.m.* Tax, duty.

impotence, *s.f.* Helplessness

impotent, *a.* Helpless.

impraticable, *a.* Impracticable.

imprécation, *s.f.* Imprecation, curse.

imprécis, *a.* Vague, indefinite.

imprégnation, *s.f.* Impregnation.

imprégner, *v.tr.* To impregnate.

imprenable, *a.* Impregnable.

impression, *s.f.* **1.** Impressing; printing. **Faute d'i.**, misprint. **2.** Impression.

impressionnable, *a.* Impressionable.

impressionnant, *a.* Impressive.

impressionner, *v.tr.* To impress.

imprévoyable, *a.* Unforeseeable.

imprévoyance, *s.f.* (*a*) Want of foresight. (*b*) Improvidence.

imprévoyant, *a.* (*a*) Wanting in foresight. (*b*) Improvident.

imprévu, *a.* Unforseen, unexpected.

imprimé, *s.m* Printed paper or book.

imprimer, *v.tr.* **1.** To impart; to inspire. **2.** To print; to impress.

imprimerie, *s.f.* **1.** Printing. **2.** Printing-office; press.

imprimeur, *s.m.* Printer.

improbabilité, *s.f.* Improbability.

improbable, *a.* Improbable.

improbité, *s.f.* Dishonesty.

improductif, *a.* Unproductive.

impromptu. 1. *adv.* Impromptu. **2.** *a.inv.* Impromptu; extempore.

impropre, *a.* (*a*) Incorrect, wrong. (*b*) Unfit (*à*, for).

improprement, *adv.* Improperly.

impropriété, *s.f.* Impropriety.

improviser, *v.tr.* To improvise.

improviste (à l'), *adv.phr* Unexpectedly; unawares.

imprudemment, *adv.* Imprudently.

imprudence, *s.f.* Imprudence.

imprudent, *a.* Imprudent, rash.

impudemment, *adv.* Shamelessly, impudently.

impudence, *s.f.* Impudence. (*a*) Effrontery. (*b*) Shamelessness.

impudent, *a.* **1.** Shamelessly immodest. **2.** Impudent, insolent.

impuissance, *s.f.* Impotence, powerlessness, helplessness.

impuissant, *a.* Impotent, helpless.

impulsif, *a.* Impulsive.

impulsion, *s.f.* **1.** Impulse; impetus. **2. Sous l'i. du moment**, on the spur of the moment.

impunément, *adv.* With impunity.

impuni, *a.* Unpunished.

impunité, *s.f.* Impunity.

impur, *a.* Impure.

impureté, *s.f.* Impurity.

imputation, *s.f.* Imputation, charge.

imputer, *v.tr.* To impute, attribute.

inabordable, *a.* Unapproachable inaccessible.

inacceptable, *a.* Unacceptable.

inaccessibilité, *s.f.* Inaccessibility.

inaccessible, *a.* Inaccessible, unapproachable.

inaccompagné, *a.* Unaccompanied.

inaccoutumé, *a.* Unaccustomed; unwonted.

inachevé, *a.* Unfinished.

inactif, *a.* Inactive; idle.

inaction, *s.f.* Inaction, idleness.

inactivité, *s.f.* Inactivity.

inadmissibilité, *s.f.* Inadmissibility.

inadmissible, *a.* Inadmissible.

inadvertamment, *adv.* Inadvertently.

inadvertance, *s.f.* **1.** Inadvertency. **2.** Oversight.

inaltérable, *a.* (*a*) Unalterable. (*b*) Unfailing, unvarying.

inamovible, *a.* Irremovable.

inanimé, *a.* **1.** Inanimate, lifeless. **2.** Senseless, unconscious.

inanité, *s.f.* Inanity, futility.

inapaisable, *a.* Inappeasable.

inapaisé, *a.* Unappeased.

inaperçu, *a.* (*a*) Unseen (*b*) Unnoticed.

inapplicable, *a.* Inapplicable.

inappréciable, *a.* **1.** Inappreciable. **2.** Inestimable, invaluable.

inapprécié, *a.* Unappreciated.

inapte, *a.* Inapt; unfit (*à*, for).

inaptitude, *s.f.* Inaptitude.

inarticulé, *a.* Inarticulate.

inassouvi, *a.* Unappeased.

inattaquable, *a.* Unassailable.

inattendu, *a.* Unexpected.
inattentif, *a.* Inattentive.
inaudible, *a.* Inaudible.
inaugural, -aux, *a.* Inaugural.
inauguration, *s.f.* Inauguration.
inaugurer, *v.tr.* To inaugurate.
inautorisé, *a.* Unauthorized.
incalculable, *a.* Incalculable.
incandescence, *s.f.* Incandescence.
incandescent, *a.* Incandescent.
incantation, *s.f.* Incantation.
incapable, *a.* **1.** Incapable, unfit.
2. Unable.
incapacité, *s.f.* Incapacity, unfitness.
incarcération, *s.f.* Incarceration.
incarcérer, *v.tr.* To incarcerate
incarnat, *a.* Rosy, pink.
incarnation, *s.f.* Incarnation.
incarné, *a.* Incarnate.
incartade, *s.f.* Outburst; tirade.
incendiaire, *a.* Incendiary.
incendie, *s.m.* Fire; conflagration.
1. volontaire, arson.
incendier, *v.tr.* To set on fire.
incertain, *a.* (*a*) Uncertain, doubtful. (*b*) Unreliable.
incertitude, *s.f.* (*a*) Uncertainty,
incertitude, doubt. (*b*) Indecision.
incessamment, *adv.* **1.** Unceasingly,
incessantly. **2.** Immediately.
incessant, *a.* Unceasing, ceaseless.
incidemment, *adv.* Incidentally.
incident, *s.m.* Incident.
incinérer, *v.tr.* (*a*) To burn to ashes.
(*b*) To cremate.
incisif, *a.* Incisive, sharp, cutting
incision, *s.f.* Incision.
incisivement, *adv.* Incisively.
incitation, *s.f.* Incitement (*d*, to).
inciter, *v.tr* To ncite; to urge
(on).
incivil [-vil], *a.* Uncivil, rude.
incivilement, *adv.* Uncivilly.
incivilisé, *a.* Uncivilized.
incivilité, *s.f.* Incivility, rudeness.
inclémence, *s.f.* Inclemency.
inclément, *a.* Inclement; severe
inclinaison, *s.f.* Incline; slant.
inclination, *s.f.* Inclination. **1.**
Bending. **2.** (*a*) Propensity. (*b*) Attachment.
incliné, *a.* Inclined.
incliner. 1. *v.tr.* To incline. (*a*) To
slope. (*b*) To tip up. (*c*) To bend,
bow. (*d*) To predispose. **2.** *v.i.* (*a*)
To lean, slope. (*b*) To feel inclined.

s'incliner. 1. To slant, slope.
2. To bow.
inclus, *a.* (*a*) Enclosed (*b*) Included.
inclusif, *a.* Inclusive.
inclusion, *s.f.* Inclusion.
inclusivement, *adv.* Inclusively.
incohérence, *s.f.* Incoherence.
incohérent, *a.* Incoherent.
incolore, *a.* Colourless.
incomber, *v.i.* To be incumbent
(*d*, on).
incombustible, *a.* Incombustible ;
fireproof.
incommensurable, *a.* **1.** Incom-
mensurate. **2.** Immeasurable, huge.
incommode, *a.* Inconvenient.
incommodément, *adv.* Inconveniently.
incommoder, *v.tr.* To inconvenience, incommode.
incomparable, *a.* Incomparable.
incomparablement, *adv.* Incom-
parably.
incompatibilité, *s.f.* Incompati-
bility.
incompatible, *a.* Incompatible.
incompétence, *s.f.* Incompetence.
incompétent, *a.* Incompetent.
incomplet, -ète, *a.* Incomplete.
incomplètement, *adv.* Incompletely.
incompréhensible, *a.* Incomprehensible.
incompris, *a.* Misunderstood.
inconcevable, *a.* Inconceivable.
inconditionnel, *a.* Unconditional.
inconduite, *s.f.* Misconduct.
incongru, *a.* **1.** Incongruous, foolish.
2. Improper.
incongruité, *s.f.* (*a*) Incongruity,
absurdity. (*b*) Impropriety.
inconnu. 1. *a.* & *s.m.* Unknown.
2. *s.* Unknown person.
inconsciemment, *adv.* Unconsciously.
inconscience, *s.f.* Unconsciousness.
inconscient, *a.* Unconscious.
inconséquemment, *adv.* Inconse-
quently.
inconséquence, *s.f.* Inconsequence.
inconséquent, *a.* Inconsequent.
inconsistance, *s.f.* Inconsistency.
inconsistant, *a.* Inconsistent.
inconsolable, *a.* Unconsolable.
inconstance, *s.f.* Inconstancy.
inconstant, *a.* **1.** Inconstant **2.**
Changeable.

incontestable, *a.* Incontestable.

incontinent[1], *a.* Incontinent.

incontinent[2], *adv.* At once, forthwith.

inconvenance, *s.f.* (*a*) Unsuitableness. (*b*) Impropriety.

inconvenant, *a.* Improper, unseemly.

inconvénient, *s.m.* Drawback.

incorporer, *v.tr.* To incorporate.

incorrect [-rɛkt], *a.* Incorrect.

incorrectement, *adv.* Incorrectly.

incorrigible, *a.* Incorrigible.

incorruptible, *a.* Incorruptible.

incrédibilité, *s.f.* Incredibility.

incrédule, *a.* Incredulous.

incrédulité, *s.f.* Incredulity.

incrimination, *s.f.* Incriminating.

incriminer, *v.tr.* To incriminate.

incroyable, *a.* Incredible, unbelievable.

incroyablement, *adv.* Incredibly.

incruster, *v.tr.* To encrust.

incubation, *s.f.* Incubation.

incube, *s.m.* Incubus, nightmare.

inculpation, *s.f.* Indictment.

inculper, *v.tr.* To indict, charge.

inculquer, *v.tr.* To inculcate.

inculte, *a.* Uncultivated; waste.

incurable, *a. & s.* Incurable.

incursion, *s.f.* Inroad, incursion.

Inde. *Pr.n.f.* (*a*) India. (*b*) **Les Indes,** the Indies.

indécemment, *adv.* Indecently.

indécence, *s.f.* Indecency.

indécent, *a.* Indecent, improper.

indécis, *a.* **1.** Unsettled; doubtful; vague. **2.** Undecided.

indécisif, *a.* Indecisive.

indéfendable, *a.* Indefensible.

indéfini, *a.* Indefinite.

indéfiniment, *adv.* Indefinitely.

indéfinissable, *a.* Indefinable; nondescript.

indélébile, *a.* Indelible.

indélicat, *a.* Indelicate; coarse.

indélicatesse, *s.f.* Indelicacy.

indemne, *a.* (*a*) Without loss (*b*) Undamaged. (*c*) Uninjured.

indemnisation, *s.f.* Indemnification.

indemniser, *v.tr.* To indemnify.

indemnité, *s.f.* Indemnity.

indéniable, *a.* Undeniable.

indépendamment, *adv.* Independently.

indépendance, *s.f.* Independence.

indépendant, *a.* **1.** Independent. **2.** Self-contained (flat).

indescriptible, *a.* Indescribable.

indésirable, *a. & s.* Undesirable.

indestructible, *a.* Indestructible.

indéterminé, *a.* Undetermined, indefinite.

index [-ɛks], *s.m.inv.* **1.** (*a*) Forefinger. (*b*) Pointer. **2.** Index.

indicateur, -trice. 1. *a.* Poteau i., sign-post. Lampe indicatrice, telltale lamp. **2.** *s.m* (*a*) Time-table. (*b*) Indicator.

indicatif, *a.* Indicative.

indication, *s.f.* Indication.

indice, *s.m.* **1.** Indication, sign; mark, token. **2.** Index.

indicible, *a.* Inexpressible, unutterable; unspeakable.

indiciblement, *adv.* Inexpressibly.

indien. 1. *a. & s.* Indian. **2.** *s.f.* **Indienne,** chintz.

indifféremment, *adv.* Indifferently.

indifférence, *s.f.* Indifference.

indifférent, *a.* Indifferent; unconcerned.

indigence, *s.f.* Poverty, want.

indigène, *a. & s.* Native.

indigent, *a.* Poor, needy, indigent.

indigeste, *a.* Indigestible.

indigestion, *s.f.* Indigestion.

indignation, *s.f.* Indignation.

indigne, *a.* Unworthy.

indigné, *a.* Indignant (*de*, at).

indignement, *adv.* Unworthily.

indigner, *v.tr.* To make indignant. **s'indigner,** to become indignant.

indignité, *s.f.* **1.** Unworthiness. **2.** Indignity.

indiquer, *v.tr.* To indicate. (*a*) To point to. (*b*) To show. (*c*) To betoken. (*d*) To name.

indirect [-rɛkt], *a.* (*a*) Indirect. (*b*) Circumstantial.

indirectement, *adv.* Indirectly.

indiscipliné, *a.* Undisciplined.

indiscret, -ète, *a.* Indiscreet.

indiscrètement, *adv.* Indiscreetly.

indiscrétion, *s.f.* Indiscretion.

indiscutable, *a.* Indisputable.

indiscutablement, *adv.* Indisputably, unquestionably.

indispensable, *a.* Indispensable.

indisposé, *a.* Indisposed, unwell.

indisposer, *v.tr.* To upset.

indisposition, *s.f.* Indisposition.

indistinct [-ɛ̃(:kt)], *a.* Indistinct.
indistinctement, *adv.* Indistinctly.
indistinguible [-gi-], *a.* Indistinguishable.
individu, *s.m.* Individual.
individualité, *s.f.* Individuality.
individuel, *a.* Individual.
individuellement, *adv.* Individually.
indivisible, *a.* Indivisible.
indolemment, *adv.* Indolently.
indolence, *s.f.* Indolence, sloth.
indolent, *a.* Indolent, slothful.
indomptable [-dɔ̃t-], *a.* Unconquerable ; untamable.
indompté [-dɔ̃te], *a.* Unconquered.
indu, *a.* **1.** Not due. **2.** Undue.
indubitable, *a.* Beyond doubt, indubitable, unquestionable.
indubitablement, *adv.* Indubitably.
induction, *s.f.* Induction.
indulgence, *s.f.* Indulgence.
indulgent, *a.* Indulgent, lenient.
indûment, *adv.* Unduly.
industrie, *s.f.* **1.** (*a*) Activity ; industry. (*b*) Ingenuity. **2.** Industry,
trade.
industriel. 1. *a.* Industrial. **2.** *s.m.*
Manufacturer.
industrieusement, *adv.* Busily, in-
dustriously.
industrieux, *a.* Busy, industrious.
inébranlable, *a.* (*a*) Immovable,
firm. (*b*) Resolute.
inédit, *a.* Unpublished.
ineffable, *a.* Ineffable, unutterable.
ineffaçable, *a.* Ineffaceable.
inefficace, *a.* Ineffectual.
inégal, -aux, *a.* **1.** Unequal. **2.** (*a*)
Uneven, rough. (*b*) Irregular.
inégalé, *a.* Unequalled.
inégalement, *adv.* Unequally, unevenly.
inégalité, *s.f.* **1.** Inequality disparity. **2.** Unevenness.
inélégant, *a.* Inelegant.
inéligible, *a.* Ineligible.
inepte, *a.* Inept, foolish.
ineptement, *adv.* Ineptly, foolishly
ineptie, *s.f.* Ineptitude.
inépuisable, *a.* Inexhaustible.
inéquitable, *a.* Inequitable, unfair.
inéquitablement, *adv.* Inequitably.
inerte, *a.* Inert ; sluggish ; dull.
inertie, *s.f.* Inertia.
inespéré, *a.* Unhoped-for.
inestimable, *a.* Inestimable.

inévitable, *a.* **1.** Unavoidable. **2.**
Inevitable.
inévitablement, *adv.* Inevitably.
inexact [-zakt], *a.* **1.** Inexact, inaccurate. **2.** Unpunctual.
inexactitude, *s.f.* **1.** Inaccuracy, inexactitude. **2.** Unpunctuality.
inexcusable, *a.* Inexcusable.
inexistant, *a.* Non-existent.
inexorable, *a.* Inexorable. unrelenting.
inexorablement, *adv.* Inexorably.
inexpérience, *s.f.* Inexperience.
inexpérimenté, *a.* Inexperienced.
inexplicable, *a.* Inexplicable.
inexploré, *a.* Unexplored.
inexprimable, *a.* Inexpressible.
inexpugnable, *a.* Impregnable.
inextinguible, *a.* Inextinguishable.
inextricable, *a.* Inextricable.
infaillibilité [ɛ̃faji-], *s.f.* Infallibility.
infaillible [ɛ̃fajibl], *a.* Infallible.
infailliblement [-faji-], *adv.* Infallibly.
infâme, *a.* Infamous ; unspeakable.
infamie, *s.f.* **1.** Infamy dishonour.
2. Vile, foul, deed.
infanterie, *s.f.* Infantry
infantile, *a.* Infantile.
infatigable, *a.* Indefatigable.
infatigablement, *adv.* Indefatigably.
infatuation, *s.f.* Infatuation.
infatuer, *v.tr.* To infatuate.
infect [ɛ̃fɛkt], *a.* Foul ; noisome.
infecter, *v.tr.* **1.** To infect (*de.* with).
2. To pollute, taint.
infectieux, *a.* Infectious.
infection, *s.f.* Infection.
inférer, *v.tr.* To infer.
inférieur, -e, *a.* **1.** Inferior ; lower.
2. I. à, inferior to ; below **3.** *s.*
Inferior.
infernal, -aux, *a.* Infernal.
infertile, *a.* Unfruitful, barren.
infester, *v.tr.* To infest, overrun.
infidèle. 1. *a.* Unfaithful ; false.
2. *s.* Infidel.
infidélité, *s.f.* Infidelity ; unfaith-
fulness.
infime, *a.* Tiny, minute.
infini, *a. & s.m.* Infinite *Adv.phr.*
A l'i., to infinity
infiniment, *adv* Infinitely ; extremely.
infinité, *s.f.* Infinity.
infinitésimal, -aux, *a.* Infinitesimal.
infinitif, *a. & s.m.* Infinitive.

infirme. 1. *a.* (*a*) Infirm. (*b*) Disabled. (*c*) Feeble. **2.** *s.* Cripple.
infirmerie, *s.f.* Infirmary.
infirmier. 1. *s.m.* Hospital attendant. **2.** *s.f.* **Infirmière,** (sick-)nurse.
infirmité, *s.f.* Infirmity.
inflammable, *a.* Inflammable
inflammation, *s.f.* Inflammation.
inflexibilité, *s.f.* Inflexibility.
inflexible, *a.* Inflexible.
inflexiblement, *adv.* Inflexibly.
inflexion, *s.f.* Inflexion, inflection.
infliger, *v.tr.* To inflict.
influence, *s.f.* Influence.
influencer, *v.tr.* To influence.
influent, *a.* Influential.
informateur, -trice, *s.* Informant.
informatif, *a.* Informative.
information, *s.f.* (*a*) Inquiry. (*b*) Information.
informe, *a.* Shapeless.
informer, *v.tr. & i.* To inform.
s'informer, to make inquiries.
infortune, *s.f.* Misfortune.
infortuné, *a.* Unfortunate, unlucky
infraction, *s.f.* Infraction; infringement; breach.
infranchissable, *a.* Impassable.
infréquent, *a.* Infrequent, rare.
infructueusement, *adv.* Fruitlessly.
infructueux, *a.* (*a*) Unfruitful. (*b*) Fruitless, unavailing.
infuser, *v.tr.* To infuse
infusion, *s.f.* Infusion.
ingambe, *a.* Nimble, alert.
ingénier (s'), *v.pr.* To exercise one's wits.
ingénieur, *s.m.* Engineer.
ingénieusement, *adv.* Ingeniously.
ingénieux, *a.* Ingenious, clever.
ingéniosité, *s.f.* Ingenuity.
ingénu, *a.* Ingenuous, artless.
ingénuité, *s.f.* Ingenuousness.
ingénument, *adv.* Ingenuously.
ingérer (s'), *v.pr.* To meddle (*dans,* with).
inglorieux, *a* Inglorious.
ingouvernable, *a.* Ungovernable.
ingrat, *a.* **1.** Ungrateful. **2.** Thankless. **3.** Unpleasing.
ingratitude, *s.f.* **1.** Ingratitude. **2.** Thanklessness.
ingrédient, *s.m.* Ingredient.
inhabile, *a.* Inapt; unskilled.
inhabilement, *adv.* Awkwardly.
inhabitable, *a.* Uninhabitable.

inhabité, *a.* Uninhabited.
inhaler, *v.tr.* To inhale.
inhérent, *a.* Inherent (*à,* in).
inhospitalier, *a* Inhospitable.
inhumain, *a.* Inhuman; unfeeling.
inhumanité, *s.f.* Inhumanity.
inimaginable, *a.* Unimaginable.
inimitable, *a.* Inimitable.
inimitié, *s.f.* Enmity, hostility.
inintelligent, *a.* Unintelligent.
inintelligible, *a.* Unintelligible.
ininterrompu, *a.* Uninterrupted; unbroken.
inique, *a.* Iniquitous.
iniquement, *adv.* Iniquitously.
iniquité, *s.f.* Iniquity.
initial, -aux. 1. *a.* Initial; starting. **2.** *s.f.* Initiale, initial.
initiateur, -trice. 1. *s.* Initiator. **2.** *a.* Initiatory.
initiation, *s.f.* Initiation (*à,* into)
initiative, *s.f.* Initiative.
initié, *s.* Initiate; one in the know.
initier, *v.tr.* To initiate (*à,* in).
injecté, *a.* Inflamed; bloodshot.
injecter, *v.tr.* To inject.
injection, *s.f.* Injection.
injonction, *s.f.* Injunction, behest.
injudicieusement, *adv.* Injudiciously.
injudicieux, *a.* Injudicious.
injure, *s.f.* **1.** Wrong, injury **2.** Insult; *pl.* abuse.
injurier, *v.tr.* To abuse.
injurieux, *a.* Insulting, abusive
injuste, *a.* Unjust, unfair.
injustement, *adv.* Unjustly.
injustice, *s.f.* Injustice, unfairness
injustifiable, *a.* Unjustifiable.
injustifié, *a.* Unjustified.
inlassable, *a.* Untiring; tireless.
inlassablement, *adv.* Untiringly.
inné, *a.* Innate, inborn.
innocemment, *adv.* Innocently.
innocence, *s.f.* Innocence.
innocent, *a. & s.* Innocent.
innombrable, *a.* Innumerable.
innovation, *s.f.* Innovation.
inoccupé, *a.* Unoccupied.
inoculation, *s.f.* Inoculation.
inoculer, *v.tr.* To inoculate.
inodore, *a.* Odourless; scentless
inoffensif, *a.* Inoffensive.
inondation, *s.f.* Inundation; flood
inonder, *v.tr.* To inundate, flood.

inopiné, *a.* Sudden, unexpected.

inopportun, *a.* Inopportune.

inopportunément, *adv.* **1.** Inopportunely. **2.** Unseasonably.

inorganique, *a.* Inorganic.

inoubliable, *a.* Unforgettable.

inouï, *a.* Unheard of.

inqualifiable, *a.* Beyond words.

inquiet, -ète, *a.* (*a*) Restless, fidgety. (*b*) Anxious, uneasy.

inquiétant, *a.* Disquieting.

inquiéter, *v.tr.* To disquiet.

  s'inquiéter, to get uneasy.

inquiétude, *s.f.* Disquiet. (*a*) Restlessness. (*b*) Anxiety, uneasiness.

inquisiteur, *a.m.* Inquisitorial.

inquisition, *s.f.* Inquisition.

insaisissable, *a.* Elusive.

insanité, *s.f.* Insanity.

insatiable, *a.* Insatiable.

inscription, *s.f.* **1.** (*a*) Writing down. (*b*) Registration. **2.** Inscription.

inscrire, *v.tr.* (*a*) To inscribe, write down. (*b*) To register.

  s'inscrire, to put down one's name.

inscrutable, *a.* Inscrutable.

inscrutablement, *adv.* Inscrutably.

insecte, *s.m.* Insect.

insécurité, *s.f.* Insecurity.

insensé, *a.* (*a*) Mad, insane. (*b*) Senseless, foolish.

insensibilité, *s.f.* (*a*) Insensibility. (*b*) Callousness.

insensible, *a.* **1.** (*a*) Insensitive. (*b*) Callous. **2.** Imperceptible.

insensiblement, *adv.* Imperceptibly, insensibly.

inséparable, *a.* Inseparable.

insérer, *v.tr.* To insert.

insertion, *s.f.* Insertion.

insidieusement, *adv.* Insidiously.

insidieux, *a.* Insidious.

insigne[1], *a.* **1.** Distinguished ; remarkable. **2.** Arrant.

insigne[2], *s.m.* Badge.

insignifiance, *s.f.* Insignificance.

insignifiant, *a.* Insignificant.

insinuant, *a.* Insinuating.

insinuation, *s.f.* Insinuation.

insinuer, *v.tr.* To insinuate.

  s'insinuer, to creep (in).

insipide, *a.* Insipid.

insipidité, *s.f.* Insipidity.

insistance, *s.f.* Insistence.

insister, *v.i.* To insist.

insociable, *a.* Unsociable.

insolation, *s.f.* Sunstroke.

insolemment, *adv.* Insolently.

insolence, *s.f.* Insolence, impertinence.

insolent, *a.* Insolent, impertinent.

insolite, *a.* Unusual, unwonted.

insoluble, *a.* Insoluble.

insolvable, *a.* Insolvent.

insomnie, *s.f.* Insomnia, sleeplessness.

insondable, *a.* Unfathomable.

insouciamment, *adv.* Unconcernedly, heedlessly.

insouciance, *s.f.* (*a*) Unconcern. (*b*) Thoughtlessness, casualness.

insouciant, *a.* (*a*) Careless. (*b*) Heedless, thoughtless, casual.

insoupçonné, *a.* Unsuspected.

insoutenable, *a.* Untenable.

inspecter, *v.tr.* To inspect.

inspecteur, -trice, *s.* Inspector ; overseer ; shop-walker ; surveyor.

inspection, *s.f.* Inspection ; survey.

inspirateur, -trice, *a.* Inspiring.

inspiration, *s.f.* Inspiration.

inspirer, *v.tr.* To inspire.

instabilité, *s.f.* Instability.

instable, *a.* Unstable.

installation, *s.f.* **1.** Installation. **2.** (*a*) Fittings. (*b*) Plant.

installer, *v.tr.* (*a*) To install. (*b*) To set up ; to fit up, equip.

instamment, *adv.* Insistently, earnestly.

instance, *s.f.* (*a*) Instancy, solicitation. (*b*) *pl.* Requests, entreaties.

instant[1], *a.* Pressing, urgent.

instant[2], *s.m.* Moment, instant.

instantané. **1.** *a.* Instantaneous. **2.** *s.m.* Snapshot.

instantanément, *adv.* Instantaneously.

instar de (à l'), *prep.phr.* After the fashion, manner, of ; like.

instaurer, *v.tr.* To found, to set up.

instigateur, -trice, *s.* Instigator.

instigation, *s.f.* Instigation.

instiller, *v.tr.* To instil.

instinct [ɛ̃stɛ̃], *s.m.* Instinct.

instinctif, *a.* Instinctive.

instinctivement, *adv.* Instinctively.

instituer, *v.tr.* To institute.

institut, *s.m.* Institute, institution.

instituteur, -trice. (*a*) *s.* (School-) teacher. (*b*) *s.f.* **Institutrice,** governess.

institution, *s.f.* **1.** Institution. **2.** Establishment; academy.

instructeur, *s.m.* Instructor, teacher. **Sergent i.,** drill-sergeant.

instructif, *a.* Instructive.

instruction, *s.f.* **1.** Instruction. **2.** Education. **3. Juge d'i.,** examining magistrate.

instruire, *v.tr.* **1.** To inform **2.** To teach, instruct.

instruit, *a.* Educated; well-read.

instrument, *s.m.* Instrument.

insu, *s.m.* **A l'i. de** without the knowledge of.

insubordination, *s.f.* Insubordination.

insubordonné, *a.* Insubordinate.

insuccès, *s.m.* Unsuccess; failure.

insuffisamment, *adv.* Insufficiently.

insuffisance, *s.f.* Insufficiency.

insuffisant, *a.* Insufficient.

insulaire. 1. *a.* Insular. **2.** *s.* Islander.

insultant, *a* Insulting, offensive.

insulte, *s.f.* Insult.

insulter, *v.tr.* To insult, affront.

insupportable, *a.* Unbearable.

insurgé, *s.* Insurgent, rebel.

insurger (s'), *v.pr.* To revolt.

insurmontable, *a* Insurmountable.

insurrection, *s.f.* Insurrection.

intact [ɛ̃takt], *a.* Intact; untouched.

intangible, *a.* Intangible.

intégral, -aux, *a.* Integral, whole.

intégralement, *adv.* Wholly, fully.

intégrité, *s.f.* Integrity.

intellect [-lɛkt], *s.m.* Intellect.

intellectuel, *a.* Intellectual.

intellectuellement, *adv.* Intellectually.

intelligemment, *adv.* Intelligently.

intelligence, *s.f.* **1.** Understanding. **2.** Intelligence. **3. En bonne i.,** on good terms.

intelligent, *a.* Intelligent.

intelligible, *a.* Intelligible.

intelligiblement, *adv.* Intelligibly.

intempérance, *s.f.* Intemperance.

intempérant, *a.* Intemperate.

intempérie, *s.f.* Inclemency.

intempestif, *a.* Untimely; inopportune.

intenable, *a.* Untenable.

intendant, *s.m.* (*a*) Steward, bailiff. (*b*) Manager.

intense, *a.* Intense; severe; deep.

intensif, *a.* Intensive.

intensifier, *v.tr.* To intensify.

intensité, *s.f.* Intensity; force.

intention, *s.f.* Intention. (*a*) Purpose, design. (*b*) Will, wish. **A l'i. de,** for (the sake of).

intentionné, *a.* Disposed.

intentionnel, *a.* Intentional.

intentionnellement, *adv.* Intentionally.

intercéder, *v.i.* To intercede.

intercepter, *v.tr.* To intercept.

interception, *s.f.* Interception.

interdiction, *s.f* Interdiction; prohibition.

interdire, *v.tr.* To forbid.

interdit, *a.* Disconcerted.

intéressant, *a.* Interesting.

intéressé, *a.* **1.** Interested. **2.** Selfish, self-seeking.

intéresser, *v.tr.* (*a*) To interest. (*b*) To give an interest. (*c*) To concern. **s'intéresser,** to become interested; to take an interest.

intérêt, *s.m.* Interest. **1.** Share. **2.** Advantage. **Ligne d'i. local,** branch-line. **3. Porter i. à,** to take an interest in. **4. I. composé,** compound interest.

intérieur,-e. 1. *a.* (*a*) Interior; inner. (*b*) Inward. **2.** *s.m.* (*a*) Interior, inside. (*b*) Home, house.

intérieurement, *adv* Inwardly internally.

interjection, *s.f.* Interjection.

interloquer, *v.tr* To disconcert.

intermède, *s.m.* **1.** Medium, intermediary. **2.** Interlude.

intermédiaire. 1. *a.* Intermediate. **2.** *s.m.* Agent; intermediary.

interminable, *a.* Interminable.

interminablement, *adv.* Endlessly.

intermittent, *a.* Intermittent.

internat, *s.m.* Boarding-school.

international, -aux. *a* International.

interne. 1. *a.* Internal. **2.** *s.* (*a*) Boarder. (*b*) Resident medical student.

internement, *s.m.* Internment.

interner, *v.tr.* To intern.

interpeller, *v.tr.* To call upon.

interpoler, *v.tr.* To interpolate.

interposer, *v.tr.* To interpose. **s'interposer,** to intervene.

interprétation, *s.f.* Interpretation.

interprète, *s.m. & f.* Interpreter.

interpréter, *v.tr.* To interpret.

interrogateur, -trice. I. *a.* Interrogatory. **2.** *s* Questioner.
interrogatif, *a.* Interrogative.
interrogation, *s.f.* Interrogation.
interroger, *v.tr.* To interrogate.
interrompre, *v.tr.* (*a*) To interrupt. (*b*) To stop, suspend.
  s'interrompre, to break off.
interruption, *s.f* Interruption.
intersection, *s.f.* Intersection.
interstice, *s.m.* Interstice; chink.
intervalle, *s.m.* Interval; space.
intervenir, *v.i.* **I.** To intervene. **2.** To happen, occur.
intervention, *s.f.* Intervention.
intestin, *s.m.* Intestine, bowel.
intimation, *s.f.* Notification.
intime, *a.* Intimate.
intimement, *adv.* Intimately.
intimidant, *a.* Intimidating.
intimidation, *s.f.* Intimidation.
intimider, *v.tr.* To intimidate.
intimité, *s.f.* Intimacy. (*a*) Closeness. (*b*) Privacy.
intolérable, *a.* Intolerable.
intolérablement, *adv.* Intolerably.
intoléramment, *adv.* Intolerantly.
intolérance, *s.f.* Intolerance
intolérant, *a.* Intolerant.
intoxiquer, *v.tr.* To poison.
intraitable, *a.* (*a*) Intractable, unmanageable. (*b*) Obstinate.
intransigeant, *a.* Uncompromising.
intrépide, *a.* Intrepid, dauntless.
intrépidement, *adv.* Intrepidly
intrépidité, *s.f.* Intrepidity.
intrigant. I. *a.* Intriguing, scheming. **2.** *s.* Intriguer, schemer.
intrigue, *s.f.* **I.** (*a*) Intrigue (*b*) (Love-)affair. **2.** Plot.
intriguer. I. *v.tr.* To puzzle. **2.** *v.i* To scheme. plot, intrigue.
intrinsèque, *a.* Intrinsic.
introduction, *s.f.* Introduction.
introduire, *v.tr.* To introduce; to bring in; to admit.
  s'introduire, to get in, enter.
introuvable, *a* Not to be found.
intrus, *s.* Intruder.
intrusion, *s.f* Intrusion.
intuitif, *a.* Intuitive.
intuition, *s.f.* Intuition.
inusable, *a.* Hard-wearing.
inusité, *a.* Not in common use.
inutile, *a.* (*a*) Useless, unavailing; vain. (*b*) Needless, unnecessary.

inutilement, *adv.* (*a*) Uselessly. (*b*) Needlessly.
invaincu, *a.* Unconquered.
invalide. I. *a.* Invalid. **2.** ». (*a*) Invalid. (*b*) *s.m* Disabled soldier; pensioner.
invariable, *a.* Invariable.
invariablement, *adv.* Invariably.
invasion, *s.f.* Invasion.
invective, *s.f.* Invective.
invendable, *a.* Unsaleable.
inventaire, *s.m.* Inventory
inventer, *v.tr.* To invent.
inventeur, *s.m.* Inventor.
inventif, *a.* Inventive.
invention, *s.f.* **I.** Invention, inventing. **2.** Invention; device.
inverse. I. *a.* Inverse, opposite. **2.** *s.m.* Opposite, reverse.
inversement, *adv.* Inversely.
inversion, *s.f.* Inversion.
invertébré, *a.* Invertebrate.
investigateur, -trice. I. *a.* Investigating. **2.** *s.* Investigator.
investigation, *s.f.* Investigation.
investir, *v.tr.* To invest
invétéré, *a.* Inveterate.
invincible, *a.* Invincible.
inviolable, *a.* Inviolable; sacred
invisibilité, *s.f.* Invisibility.
invisible, *a.* Invisible.
invitation, *s.f.* Invitation.
inviter, *v.tr.* **I.** To invite. **2.** To request.
invocation, *s.f.* Invocation.
involontaire, *a.* Involuntary, unintentional.
invoquer, *v.tr.* To invoke.
invraisemblable, *a* Unlikely, improbable.
invraisemblance, *s.f* Unlikeliness, improbability.
invulnérable, *a.* Invulnerable.
iode, *s.m.* Iodine.
iodure, *s.m.* Iodide.
iota, *s.m.* Pas un i., not a jot.
irascible, *a.* Irascible.
iris [iris], *s.m.* **I.** Iris (of eye). **2.** Iris, flag.
irisé, *a.* Iridescent.
irlandais. I. *a. & s.m.* Irish. **2.** *s.* Irishman; Irishwoman.
Irlande. *Pr.n.f.* Ireland.
ironie, *s.f.* Irony.
ironique, *a.* Ironical.
ironiquement, *adv.* Ironically.

irradier, *v.i.* To (ir)radiate.
irrationnel, *a.* Irrational.
irréalisable, *a.* Unrealizable.
irréconciliable, *a.* Irreconcilable.
irrécouvrable, *a.* Irrecoverable.
irréel, *a.* Unreal.
irréfléchi, *a.* **1.** Unconsidered, thoughtless. **2.** Hasty, rash.
irréflexion, *s.f.* Thoughtlessness.
irréfutable, *a.* Irrefutable.
irrégularité, *s.f.* Irregularity.
irrégulier, *a.* Irregular.
irrégulièrement, *adv.* Irregularly.
irrémédiable, *a.* Irremediable.
irremplaçable, *a.* Irreplaceable.
irréparable, *a.* Irreparable.
irréprochable, *a.* Irreproachable.
irrésistible, *a.* Irresistible.
irrésistiblement, *adv.* Irresistibly
irrésolu, *a.* Irresolute, wavering.
irrésolument, *adv.* Irresolutely.
irrespectueusement, *adv.* Disrespectfully.
irrespectueux, *a.* Disrespectful.
irresponsabilité, *s.f.* Irresponsibility.
irresponsable, *a.* Irresponsible.
irrévérence, *s.f.* Irreverence.
irrévérencieux, *a.* Irreverent.
irrévocable, *a.* Irrevocable.
irrévocablement, *adv.* Irrevocably.
irrigation, *s.f.* Irrigation.

irriguer, *v.tr.* To irrigate.
irritabilité, *s.f.* Irritability.
irritable, *a.* Irritable.
irritant, *a.* Irritating.
irritation, *s.f.* Irritation.
irriter, *v.tr.* To irritate.
s'irriter, to grow angry.
irruption, *s.f.* Irruption. **Faire i.** dans, to burst into.
islandais, *a.* Icelandic.
Islande. *Pr.n.f.* Iceland.
isolant, *a.* (*a*) Isolating. (*b*) Insulating.
isolateur, *s.m.* Insulator.
isolé, *a.* **1.** Isolated. **2.** Insulated.
isolement, *s.m.* **1.** Isolation, loneliness. **2.** Insulation.
isoler, *v.tr.* **1.** To isolate **2.** To insulate.
issu, *a.* Descended ; born.
issue, *s.f.* **1.** Issue, end. **2.** Outlet
isthme, *s.m.* Isthmus.
Italie. *Pr.n.f.* Italy.
italien, *a. & s.* Italian.
italique, *a. & s.m.* Italic ; italics.
itinéraire, *s.m.* Itinerary ; route.
itinérant, *a.* Itinerant.
ivoire, *s.m.* Ivory.
ivre, *a.* Drunk ; intoxicated.
ivresse, *s.f.* Intoxication
ivrogne, *s.m.* Drunkard.

J

J, j [ʒi], *s.m.* (The letter) J, j.
jabot, *s.m.* **1.** Crop (of bird). **2.** Shirt-frill, ruffle.
jacasser, *v.i.* To chatter, jabber.
jacinthe, *s.f.* Hyacinth. **J. des bois,** blue-bell.
Jacques. *Pr.n.m.* James.
jactance, *s.f.* Boastfulness, brag.
jade, *s.m.* Jade(-stone).
jadis [ʒadis], *adv.* Formerly, once.
jaguar [-gwaːr], *s.m.* Jaguar.
jaillir [ʒajiːr], *v.i.* To spring (up) ; to gush (forth) ; (of sparks) to fly.
jaillissement [ʒaji-], *s.m.* Gush(ing).
jais, *s.m. Miner :* Jet.
jalonner, *v.tr.* To stake out.
jalousement, *adv.* Jealously.
jalousie, *s.f* **1.** Jealousy **2.** Venetian blind.
jaloux, *a.* Jealous.
jamaïque (la). *Pr.n.f.* Jamaica.

jamais, *adv.* **1.** Ever. **A tout j.,** for ever and ever. **2.** (With neg.) Never. **J. de la vie!** never ! **3.** *s.m.* **Au grand j.!** never, never !
jambe, *s.f.* Leg. **Prendre ses jambes à son cou,** to take to one's heels.
jambon, *s.m.* Ham.
jante, *s.f.* Rim (of wheel)
janvier, *s.m.* January.
Japon (le). *Pr.n.m.* Japan.
japonais, *a. & s.* Japanese
japper, *v.i.* To yelp, yap.
jaquette, *s.f.* (*a*) Tail-coat, morning coat. (*b*) (Woman's) jacket.
jardin, *s.m.* Garden.
jardinage, *s.m.* Gardening.
jardiner, *v.i.* To garden.
jardinier, *s.* Gardener.
jarretelle, *s.f.* (Stocking) suspender.
jarretière, *s.f.* Garter.
jars, *s.m.* Gander.

jaser, *v.i.* To chatter; to gossip.
jaseur, -euse. 1. *a.* Talkative. **2.** *s.* Chatterbox; gossip.
jasmin, *s.m.* Jasmine.
jatte, *s.f.* Bowl; basin.
jauge, *s.f.* Gauge.
jauger, *v.tr.* To gauge.
jaunâtre, *a.* Yellowish.
jaune. 1. *a.* Yellow. **Chaussures jaunes,** brown shoes. *adv.* **Rire j.,** to give a sickly smile. **2.** *s.m.* (*a*) Yellow. (*b*) **J. d'œuf,** yolk (of egg).
jaunir, *v.tr. & i.* **1.** To colour yellow. **2.** To turn yellow.
jaunisse, *s.f.* Jaundice.
je, *pers.pron.nom.* I.
Jean [ʒɑ̃]. *Pr.n.m.* John.
Jeanne [ʒɑn]. *Pr.n.f.* Jane.
jésuite, *s.m.* Jesuit.
Jésus. *Pr.n.m.* Jesus.
jet, *s.m.* **1.** Throw, cast. **2.** Jet, gush. **3.** Spout.
jetée, *s.f.* Jetty, pier.
jeter, *v.tr.* To throw, fling, cast.
  se jeter, to jump; to fling oneself.
jeton, *s.m. Cards:* Counter.
jeu, jeux, *s.m.* **1.** Play; sport. **Jeu de mots,** pun. **Jeu d'esprit,** witticism. **2.** (*a*) Game. **Jouer franc jeu,** to play fair. (*b*) **Jeu de boules,** bowling-green. **3.** Set. **Jeu de cartes,** pack of cards. **4.** Gaming, play. **Jouer gros jeu,** to play high. **Faites vos jeux!** put down your stakes!
jeudi, *s.m.* Thursday.
jeun (à), *adj.phr.* Fasting.
jeune, *a.* (*a*) Young; youthful. (*b*) Younger; junior.
jeûne, *s.m.* (*a*) Fast. (*b*) Fasting.
jeûner, *v.i.* To fast.
jeunesse, *s.f.* (*a*) Youth. (*b*) Youthfulness.
joaillerie [ʒwajri], *s.f.* Jewellery.
joaillier [ʒwaje], *s.* Jeweller.
joie, *s.f.* **1.** Joy; delight; gladness. **Feu de j.,** bonfire. *Adv.phr.* **A cœur j.,** to one's heart's content. **2.** Mirth, merriment.
joindre, *v.tr.* **1.** To join; to clasp. (*a*) To bring together. (*b*) To add. **2.** To adjoin.
  se joindre, to join, unite.
joint. 1. *a.* Joined, united. **2.** *s.m.* Joint, join.

jointure, *s.f.* Joint, join.
joli, *a.* Pretty; nice.
joliment, *adv.* Prettily, nicely.
jonc [ʒɔ̃], *s.m.* (*a*) Rush. (*b*) **Canne de j.,** Malacca cane.
joncher, *v.tr.* To strew.
jonction, *s.f.* Junction, joining.
jongler, *v.i.* To juggle.
jonglerie, *s.f.* Juggling.
jongleur, *s.m.* Juggler.
jonque, *s.f.* (Chinese) junk.
joue, *s.f.* Cheek. **Coucher qn en j.,** to aim (a gun) at s.o.
jouer, *v.* To play. **I.** *v.i.* **1. J. aux cartes,** to play cards. **J. du piano,** to play the piano. **2.** To gamble. **3.** To work, to act. **II. jouer,** *v.tr.* **1.** To stake. **2.** (*a*) To play. (*b*) To act; to perform. **3.** To trick.
  se jouer. 1. Faire qch. en se jouant, to do sth. with great ease. **2.** To make game (of s.o.).
jouet, *s.m.* Toy, plaything.
joueur, -euse, *s.* **1.** (*a*) Player. **Être bon j.,** to be a good loser. (*b*) Performer. **2.** Gambler.
joufflu, *a.* Chubby.
joug, *s.m.* Yoke.
jouir, *v.i.* **J. (de),** to enjoy.
jouissance, *s.f.* Enjoyment. (*a*) Pleasure. (*b*) Possession, tenure.
joujou, -oux, *s.m.* Toy, plaything.
jour [ʒuːr], *s.m.* Day. **1.** (Day)light. (*a*) **Le petit j.,** the morning twilight. **Il fait grand j.,** it is broad daylight. (*b*) **Mettre au j.,** to bring to light. (*c*) Light. **2.** Aperture, opening. **A j.,** open-work. **3.** **Plat du j.,** special dish for the day. **De nos jours,** nowadays. **Mettre à j.,** to bring up to date.
journal, -aux, *s.m.* **1.** Journal, diary. **J. de bord,** log-book. **2.** Newspaper, journal.
journalier, *a.* Daily; everyday.
journalisme, *s.m.* Journalism.
journaliste, *s.m. & f.* Journalist.
journée, *s.f.* **1.** Day(time). **Dans la j.,** in the course of the day. **2.** (*a*) **Femme de j.,** charwoman. (*b*) Day's wages. (*c*) **Gagner la j.,** to win the day.
journellement, *adv.* Daily.
jovial, -aux, *a.* Jovial, jolly, merry.
jovialement, *adv.* Jovially.

jovialité, *s.f.* Joviality, jollity
joyau, -aux, *s.m.* Jewel.
joyeusement, *adv.* Joyous.y joy-fully.
joyeux, *a.* Merry, joyous.
jubilant, *a.* Jubilant.
jubilation, *s.f.* Jubilation
jubilé, *s.m.* Jubilee.
jubiler, *v.i.* To exult.
jucher, *v.i.* To roost ; to perch.
   se jucher. **1.** To roost. **2.** To perch oneself.
juchoir, *s.m.* Perch ; hen-roost.
judiciaire, *a.* Judicial.
judiciairement, *adv.* Judicially.
judicieusement, *adv.* Judiciously.
judicieux, *a.* Judicious, discerning.
juge, *s.m.* Judge. **J. de paix,** police-court magistrate.
jugé, *s.m.* Au j., by guess-work.
jugement, *s.m.* Judgment. **1.** (*a*) Trial. (*b*) Decision ; sentence. **2.** Opinion. **3.** Discernment.
juger, *v.tr* **1.** (*a*) To judge ; to try ; to pass sentence on. (*b*) To pass judgment on **2.** (*a*) To think. (*b*) To judge.
jugulaire. **1.** *a. & s.f.* Jugular (vein). **2.** *s.f.* Chin-strap.
juif [ʒɥif]. **1.** *a.* Jewish ; Jew. **2.** *s.* Jew, *f.* Jewess. **Petit i.,** funny-bone.
juillet [ʒɥijɛ], *s.m.* July
juin [ʒɥɛ̃], *s.m.* June.
jumeau, -elle. **1.** *a. & s.* Twin. **Trois jumeaux,** triplets.

II jumelles, *s.f.pl.* Binoculars. **J. de théâtre,** opera-glasses.
jument, *s.f.* Mare
jupe, *s.f.* Skirt.
jupon, *s.m.* Petticoat, underskirt.
juré, *s.m.* Juryman.
jurement, *s.m.* Swearing ; oath.
jurer, *v.tr.* **1.** To swear. **2.** *Abs.* (*a*) To curse. (*b*) (Of colours) To clash.
juridiction, *s.f.* Jurisdiction.
juridique, *a.* Judicial ; legal.
juron, *s.m.* Oath
jury, *s.m.* Jury.
jus, *s.m.* **1.** Juice. **2.** Gravy
jusant, *s.m.* Ebb(-tide).
jusque, *prep.* **1.** As far as ; up to. **2.** Till, until **3.** *Conj.phr* **Jusqu'à ce que,** till, until.
juste, *a.* **1.** Just right, fair. **2.** Right, exact. **Trop j.,** tight **3.** *adv.* (*a*) Rightly. (*b*) Exactly, precisely. (*c*) Barely. **Comme de j.,** as is only fair.
justement, *adv.* **1.** Justly. iightly. **2.** Precisely exactly, just.
justesse, *s.f.* Exactness, accuracy.
justice, *s.f* **1.** Justice **En toute j.,** by rights. **2.** Law.
justifiable, *a.* Justifiable.
justification, *s.f* Justification
justifier, *v.tr.* To justify, vindicate.
   se justifier, to clear oneself.
juteux, *a.* Juicy
juvénile, *a.* Juvenile ; youthful.
juxtaposer, *v.tr.* To place side by side.

K

K, k [kɑ], *s.m.* (The letter) K, k.
kaki, *s.m. & a.inv.* Khaki.
kangourou, *s.m.* Kangaroo.
képi, *s.m.* Kepi ; peaked cap.
kilogramme, *s.m.* Kilogramme (= 2.2 lbs).
kilomètre, *s.m.* Kilometre (= ·624 mile).

kilométrique, *a.* **Borne k.,** kilo-metre stone.
kiosque, *s.m.* **1.** (*a*) Kiosk. **K. à musique,** bandstand. (*b*) Newspaper-stall. **2.** Conning-tower.
klaxon, *s.m.* Klaxon, hooter.
klaxonner, *v.i.* To sound the hooter.
krach [krak], *s.m.* Crash ; failure.

L

L, l [ɛl], *s.f.* (The letter) L, l.
la, *def.art. & pron.f.* See LE[1], [2].
là, *adv.* **1.** There. (*a*) **Passer par là,** go that way. (*b*) **Que dites-vous là?**

what is that you are saying? **Ce, cette,** *etc.*, . . . **-là,** see CE[1] **1,** CE[2] **2.** **2.** Then. **D'ici là,** between now and then. **3.** *int.* **Oh là là!** oh dear me !

là-bas, *adv.* (Over) yonder.
labeur, *s.m.* Labour, toil, hard work.
laboratoire, *s.m.* Laboratory.
laborieusement, *adv.* Laboriously.
laborieux, *a.* 1. Toilsome, arduous. 2. Laborious, hard-working.
labour, *s.m.* Tilling; ploughing.
labourer, *v.tr.* To till; to plough.
laboureur, *s.m.* Ploughman.
labyrintne, *s.m.* Labyrinth, maze.
lac [lak], *s.m.* Lake.
lacer, *v.tr.* To lace (up).
lacération, *s.f.* Laceration.
lacérer, *v.tr.* To lacerate.
lacet, *s.m.* 1. Lace (of shoe). 2. Hair-pin bend. 3. Noose, snare.
lâche, *a.* 1. Loose, slack; lax. 2. Cowardly; *s.m.* coward.
lâchement, *adv.* 1. Indolently, slackly. 2. In a cowardly manner.
lâcher, *v.tr.* To release. (*a*) To slacken. (*b*) To let go. **L** pied, to give ground. (*c*) To set free.
lâcheté, *s.f.* 1. Cowardice. 2. Dastardliness.
laconique, *a.* Laconic.
laconiquement, *adv.* Laconically.
là-contre, *adv.* To the contrary.
lacs [lɑ], *s.m.* Noose snare.
lacune, *s.f.* Lacuna, gap.
là-dedans, *adv.* In there; within.
là-dehors, *adv.* Without, outside.
là-dessous, *adv.* Under that.
là-dessus, *adv.* On that.
ladite, *see* LEDIT.
ladre, *a.* Niggardly stingy.
ladrerie, *s.f.* Meanness, stinginess.
lagune, *s.f.* Lagoon.
là-haut, *adv.* Up there.
laid, *a.* (*a*) Ugly; unsightly; plain. (*b*) Unseemly, mean, shabby.
laideur, *s.f.* 1. Ugliness; plainness. 2. Unseemliness, meanness.
laine, *s.f.* Wool.
laineux, *a.* Fleecy; woolly.
laïque, *a.* Laic; secular.
laisse, *s.f.* Leash, lead.
laisser, *v.tr.* 1. To let, allow. **Laissez-le** faire! leave it to him! 2. (*a*) To leave. **L.** là, to leave in the lurch. (*b*) Laissez donc! please do not trouble. (*c*) Ne pas l. de faire qch., not to fail to do sth.
laisser-aller, *s.m.inv.* Slovenliness.
laisser-faire, *s.m.* Non-interference.
laissez-passer, *s.m.inv.* Pass, permit.

lait, *s.m.* Milk. **Frère de l.,** foster-brother. **Cochon de l.,** sucking-pig.
laiterie, *s.f.* Dairy.
laiteux, *a.* Milk-like, milky.
laitier, *s.* (*a*) Milkman; milkmaid. (*b*) Dairymaid; dairyman.
laiton, *s.m.* Brass.
laitue, *s.f.* Lettuce. **L.** pommée, cabbage lettuce.
lambeau, *s.m.* Scrap, bit, shred.
lambris, *s.m.* Wainscoting; dado.
lame, *s.f.* 1. (*a*) Thin plate; slat. (*b*) Blade. 2. Wave. **L.** de fond, ground-swell.
lamentable, *a.* Lamentable, deplorable; woeful.
lamentablement, *adv.* Lamentably; woefully.
lamentation, *s.f.* Lamentation.
lamenter (se), *v.pr.* To lament; to wail; to bewail.
lampadaire, *s.m.* Standard lamp.
lampe, *s.f.* 1. Lamp. 2. (*a*) **L.** de poche, electric torch. (*b*) (Wireless) valve.
lampée, *s.f.* Draught, gulp.
lamper, *v.tr.* To swig, toss off.
lampion, *s.m.* Fairy-light.
lance, *s.f.* (*a*) Spear. (*b*) Lance.
lance-bombes, *s.m.inv.* 1. Trench mortar. 2. Bomb rack.
lancer, *v.tr.* 1. To throw, fling **L.** un avion, to catapult a plane. 2. (*a*) To start, set going. (*b*) To launch. **se lancer,** to rush; to launch out.
lancette, *s.f.* Lancet.
lancier, *s.m.* Lancer.
lancinant, *a.* Shooting (pain).
lande, *s.f.* Sandy moor; heath.
langage, *s.m.* Language; speech.
langes, *s.m.pl.* Swaddling-clothes.
langoureusement, *adv.* Languidly.
langoureux, *a.* Languid.
langouste, *s.f.* Spiny lobster; crayfish.
langue, *s.f.* 1. Tongue. **Tirer la l.,** to put out one's tongue. 2. Language, speech.
languette, *s.f.* Tongue (of shoe).
langueur, *s.f.* Languor; listlessness.
languir, *v.i.* To languish, pine.
languissant, *a.* 1. Languid. 2. Languishing.
lanière, *s.f.* Thin strap; thong.
lanterne, *s.f.* Lantern. **L.** vénitienne, Chinese lantern.

laper, *v.tr.* To lap (up).

lapereau, *s.m.* Young rabbit.

lapider, *v.tr.* To throw stones at.

lapin, *s.* Rabbit.

laps [laps], *s.m.* Space (of time).

laquais, *s.m.* Lackey footman.

laque, *s.f.* Lacquer.

laquelle, *pron.f.* See LEQUEL.

laquer, *v.tr.* To lacquer, to japan.

larcin, *s.m.* Larceny ; petty theft.

lard, *s.m.* Bacon.

large. 1. *a.* (*a*) Broad, wide. (*b*) Large, big, ample. **2.** *s.m.* (*a*) Open sea. **Au l. de Cherbourg,** off Cherbourg. (*b*) Breadth.

largement, *adv.* (*a*) Broadly, widely. (*b*) Amply.

largeur, *s.f.* Breadth, width.

larme, *s.f.* Tear.

larmoyant, *a.* Weeping, tearful.

larmoyer, *v.i* **1.** (Of the eyes) To water. **2.** To snivel.

larve, *s.f.* Larva ; grub.

las, lasse, *a.* Tired, weary.

lascif, *a.* Lascivious, lewd.

lascivement, *adv.* Lasciviously.

lasser, *v.tr.* To tire, weary.

     se lasser, to grow weary ; to tire.

lassitude, *s.f.* Lassitude. weariness.

lasso, *s.m.* Lasso.

latent, *a.* Latent ; hidden.

latéral, -aux, *a.* Lateral.

latin, *a. & s.m.* Latin. **Le Quartier l.,** the students' quarter (of Paris).

latitude, *s.f.* Latitude.

latte, *s.f.* Lath, batten, slat.

laudatif, *a* Laudatory.

laurier, *s.m.* Laurel.

lavabo, *s.m.* Wash-hand basin.

lavande, *s.f* Lavender.

lavandière, *s.f* Washerwoman.

lave, *s.f.* Lava.

laver, *v.tr.* To wash. **Se l. les mains,** to wash one's hands. **L. la vaisselle,** to wash up.

     se laver, to wash (oneself).

lavoir, *s.m.* Wash-house.

laxatif, *a. & s.m.* Laxative, aperient.

le[1], la, les, *def.art.* The. **1.** (*a*) **Il est arrivé le lundi,** he arrived on Monday. (*b*) **La France,** France. (*c*) **Le colonel Chabot,** Colonel Chabot. (*d*) **Le Havre,** Havre. (*e*) **A la Noël,** at Christmas. (*f*) **Elle ferma les yeux,** she closed her eyes. **2. Je préfère le café au thé,** I prefer coffee to tea.

3. Cent francs la livre, a hundred francs a pound

le[2], la, les, *pers.pron.* **1.** Him, her, it, them. **2.** *Neut. pron.* **Le.** (*a*) **Êtes-vous mère?—Je le suis,** are you a mother ?—I am. (*b*) So. **Il me l'a dit,** he told me so. (*c*) **Vous le devriez,** you ought to.

lécher, *v.tr.* To lick.

leçon, *s.f.* Lesson.

lecteur, -trice, *s.* Reader.

lecture, *s.f.* Reading.

ledit, ladite, *pl.* **lesdits, lesdites,** *a.* The aforesaid.

légal, -aux, *a.* Legal ; statutory.

légalement, *adv.* Legally lawfully.

légaliser, *v tr.* To legalize.

légalité, *s.f.* Legality, lawfulness.

légataire, *s.m. & f* Legatee.

légation, *s.f.* Legation.

légendaire, *a.* Legendary.

légende, *s.f.* **1.** Legend. **2.** (*a*) Inscription. (*b*) List of references.

léger, *a.* **1.** (*a*) Light. **Avoir la main légère,** to be quick with one's hands. (*b*) Slight ; gentle ; faint. **2.** *Adv. phr.* **A la légère,** lightly.

légèrement, *adv.* **1.** (*a*) Lightly. (*b*) Slightly. **2.** W.thout consideration.

légèreté, *s.f.* **1.** (*a*) Lightness. (*b*) Slightness. **2.** Levity ; flightiness.

légion, *s.f.* Legion.

légionnaire, *s.m.* Soldier of the Foreign Legion.

législateur, -trice, *s.* Legislator, law-giver.

législatif, *a.* (*a*) Legislative. (*b*) **Election législative,** parliamentary election.

législation, *s.f.* Legislation.

légitime, *a.* **1.** Legitimate, lawful. **2.** Justifiable. **L défense,** self-defence.

légitimement, *adv.* Legitimately.

legs [lɛ], *s.m.* Legacy, bequest.

léguer, *v tr.* To bequeath.

légume, *s.m.* Vegetable **Légumes verts,** greens.

Léman. *Pr.n.m.* **Le lac L.,** the Lake of Geneva.

lendemain, *s.m.* Next day. **Le l. matin,** the next morning.

lent, *a.* Slow.

lentement, *adv.* Slowly.

lenteur, *s.f.* Slowness.

lentille [-ti:j], *s.f.* **1.** Lentil. **2.** Lens.

léonin, *a.* Leonine, lion-like.

léopard, *s.m.* Leopard.

lèpre, *s.f.* Leprosy.

lépreux. 1. *a.* Leprous. **2.** *s.* Leper.

lequel, laquelle, lesquels, lesquelles. 1. *rel.pron.* Who, whom; which. **2.** *interr.pron.* Which (one)?

lesdit(e)s. See LEDIT.

lèse-majesté, *s.f.* High treason.

lesquels, -elles. See LEQUEL.

lessive, *s.f.* **1.** Lye. **2. Faire la l.,** to do the washing.

lest [lɛst], *s.m.* Ballast.

leste, *a.* Light; nimble, agile.

lestement, *adv.* Lightly, nimbly.

léthargie, *s.f.* Lethargy, apathy.

léthargique, *a.* Lethargic.

lettre, *s.f.* Letter. **1. En toutes lettres,** in full. **2. Au pied de la l.,** literally. **3.** (*a*) Epistle. (*b*) **L. de change,** bill of exchange. **4.** *pl.* Literature.

lettré, *a.* Lettered, well-read.

leur¹. 1. *poss.a.* Their. **2. Le leur, la leur, les leurs.** (*a*) *poss.pron.* Theirs. (*b*) *s.m.* Their own.

leur², *pers.pron.* See LUI¹.

leurre, *s.m.* Bait, lure.

leurrer, *v.tr.* To lure.

levain, *s.m.* Leaven.

levant. 1. *a.m.* Rising. **2.** *s.m.* (*a*) East. (*b*) Levant.

levé, *a.* (*a*) Raised. **A main levée,** free-hand. (*b*) Up; out of bed.

levée, *s.f.* **1.** (*a*) Raising, lifting. (*b*) Gathering; collection (of letters). **2.** (*a*) Embankment, sea-wall. (*b*) *Cards :* Trick.

lever. I. *v.tr.* **1.** (*a*) To raise, to lift (up). **2.** To gather (crops).

se lever, (*a*) To stand up. (*b*) To get up; to rise.

II. lever, *s.m.* **1.** (*a*) Rising; getting up. (*b*) Levee. **2. L. de rideau,** curtain-raiser.

levier, *s.m.* **1.** Lever. **2.** Crow-bar.

levraut, *s.m.* Leveret; young hare.

lèvre, *s.f.* Lip. **Du bout des lèvres,** in a forced manner. **Pincer les lèvres,** to purse one's lips.

lévrier, *s.m.* Greyhound.

levure, *s.f.* Yeast.

lexique, *s.m.* Lexicon.

lézard, *s.m.* Lizard.

lézardé, *a.* Cracked, full of cracks.

liaison, *s.f.* (*a*) Joining, binding. (*b*) Liaison.

liane, *s.f.* Liana.

liasse, *s.f.* Bundle (of letters); file.

Liban. *Pr.n.m.* Lebanon.

libellule, *s.f.* Dragon-fly.

libéral, -aux, *a.* & *s.* Liberal.

libéralement, *adv.* Liberally.

libéralité, *s.f.* Liberality.

libérateur, -trice, *s.* Liberator.

libération, *s.f.* Liberation, freeing, releasing.

libérer, *v.tr.* To liberate, release.

liberté, *s.f.* **1.** Liberty, freedom. **Jour de l.,** day off. **2. Prendre des libertés,** to take liberties.

libertin, *s.* Libertine, rake.

libraire, *s.m.* & *f.* Bookseller.

librairie, *s.f.* Bookshop.

libre, *a.* **1.** Free. **2.** Clear; vacant. *Tp :* **"Pas libre,"** 'line engaged.' (Taxi sign) **"Libre,"** 'for hire.'

libre-échange, *s.m.* Free trade.

librement, *adv.* Freely.

licence, *s.f.* Licence. **1.** Leave, permission. **2.** Abuse of liberty.

licencié, *s.* Licentiate, **L. ès lettres,** (approx. =) master of arts.

licencieux, *a.* Licentious.

lichen [likɛn], *s.m.* Lichen. **L. d'Islande,** Iceland moss.

licite, *a.* Lawful, permissible.

licou, *pl.* **-ous,** *s.m.* Halter.

lie, *s.f.* Lees, dregs.

lié, *a.* Bound, tied.

liège, *s.m.* Cork.

lien, *s.m.* Tie, bond.

lier, *v.tr.* **1.** To bind, tie. **2. L. conversation,** to enter into conversation.

se lier, to form a friendship.

lierre, *s.m.* Ivy.

lieu, -eux, *s.m.* **1.** Place. (*a*) Locality, spot. **De bon l.,** from a good source. (*b*) *pl.* Premises. **2.** (*a*) **Avoir l.,** to take place. (*b*) Grounds, cause. (*c*) **Au l. de,** instead of. **3. Lieux communs,** commonplaces.

lieue, *s.f.* League (= 4 kilometres).

lieutenant, *s.m.* (*a*) Lieutenant. (*b*) **Premier l.,** second mate.

lièvre, *s.m.* Hare.

lignage, *s.m.* Lineage, descent.

ligne, *s.f.* Line. **1.** (*a*) Cord. (*b*) **Grandes lignes,** broad outline. (*c*) **Hors l.,** out of the common. **2.** (Railway) line.

lignée, s.f. Issue; descendants.

ligoter, v.tr. To bind hand and foot.

ligue, s.f. League, confederacy.

lilas, s.m. Lilac.

limace, s.f. Slug.

limaçon, s.m. Snail.

limande, s.f. Dab.

lime, s.f. File.

limer, v.tr. To file; to file down.

limier, s.m. Bloodhound.

limitation, s.f. Limitation.

limite, s.f. **1.** Boundary; limit. **2. Cas l.,** border-line case. **Vitesse l.,** maximum speed.

limité, a. Limited, restricted.

limiter, v.tr. **1.** To bound. **2.** To limit; to restrict.

limitrophe, a. Adjacent; abutting.

limon[1], s.m. Mud, silt.

limon[2], s.m. Veh: Shaft.

limon[3], s.m. Sour lime.

limonade, s.f. **1.** Lemonade. **2.** pl. Mineral waters.

limoneux, a. Muddy.

limpide, a. Limpid, clear.

limpidité, s.f. Limpidity, clarity.

lin, s.m. Flax. **Graine de lin,** linseed.

linceul, s.m. Winding-sheet, shroud.

linéament, s.m. Lineament, feature.

linge, s.m. **1.** (Made-up) linen. **2. Essuyer avec un l.,** to wipe with a cloth.

lingère, s.f. Wardrobe keeper.

lingerie, s.f. Underclothing, linen.

lingot, s.m. Ingot. **Or, argent, en lingots,** bullion.

linguiste [-gɥist], s.m. & f. Linguist.

liniment, s.m. Liniment.

linoléum [-ɔm], s.m. Linoleum.

linotte, s.f. Linnet.

linteau, s.m. Lintel.

lion, s. Lion, f. lioness.

lionceau, s.m. Lion's cub.

lippu, a. Thick-lipped.

liquéfier, v.tr. To liquefy.

liqueur, s.f. (a) Liquor, drink. (b) Liqueur.

liquidation, s.f. **1.** Liquidation. **2.** Selling off; clearance sale.

liquide. 1. a. Liquid. **2.** s.m (a) Liquid. (b) Liquor.

liquider, v.tr. **1.** To liquidate. **2.** To realize; to sell off.

lire, v.tr. To read. "Dans l'attente de vous l.," "hoping to hear from you.'

lis, s.m. Lily.

Lisbonne. Pr.n.f. Lisbon.

liseron, s.m. Bindweed, convolvulus.

lisibilité, s.f. Legibility.

lisible, a. Legible.

lisiblement, adv. Legibly.

lisière, s.f. **1.** Selvedge. **2.** Edge, border.

lisse, a. Smooth, polished; sleek.

lisser, v.tr. To smooth; to preen.

liste, s.f. List, roll, register.

lit, s.m. **1.** Bed. (a) **Lit à colonnes,** four-poster. **Lit d'ami,** spare bed. **Garder le lit,** to be laid up. (b) Bedstead. **2.** (a) Bed layer. (b) Bed, bottom.

litanie, s.f. Litany.

literie, s.f. Bedding.

litige, s.m. Litigation; suit.

litigieux, a. Litigious.

litre, s.m. Litre (about 1¾ pint).

littéraire, a. Literary.

littéral, -aux, a. Literal.

littéralement, adv. Literally.

littérateur, s.m Man of letters.

littérature, s.f. Literature.

littoral, -aux, s.m. Coastline; littoral; seaboard.

liturgie, s.f. Liturgy.

livide, a. Livid; ghastly.

Livourne. Pr.n. Leghorn.

livraison, s.f. **1.** Delivery. **2.** Part, instalment.

livre[1], s.f. **1.** Pound. **2. L. sterling,** pound sterling.

livre[2], s.m. Book. (a) **Jouer à l. ouvert,** to play at sight. (b) **Tenue des livres,** book-keeping.

livrée, s.f. Livery.

livrer, v.tr. **1.** (a) To deliver; to give up. **Livré à soi-même,** left to oneself. (b) **L. bataille,** to join battle. **2.** To deliver (goods). **se livrer,** to give oneself up.

livret, s.m. **1.** Small book. **2.** Libretto.

lobe, s.m. Lobe (of ear).

local, -aux. 1. a. Local. **2.** s.m. Premises, building.

localement, adv. Locally.

localité, s.f. Locality, place, spot.

locataire, s.m. & f. **1.** Tenant, occupier. **2.** Lodger.

location, s.f. (a) Hiring. (b) Renting; letting. **Agent de l.,** house-agent. (c) **Bureau de l.,** box-office.

locomotive, s.f. Locomotive, engine.

locution, s.f. Expression, phrase.

loge, *s.f.* **1.** Hut; lodge. **2.** *Th*: Box.

logement, *s.m.* **1.** Lodging, housing. **2.** Accommodation; lodgings. **Le l. et la nourriture,** board and lodging.

loger. 1. *v.i.* To lodge. **L. en garni,** to be in lodgings. **2.** *v.tr.* (*a*) To lodge, house. (*b*) To place, put.

logique. 1. *a.* Logical. **2.** *s.f.* Logic.

logiquement, *adv.* Logically.

logis, *s.m.* Home, house.

loi, *s.f.* (*a*) Law. **Faire la loi,** to lay down the law. **Hors la loi,** outlawed. (*b*) Act (of Parliament); law. **Projet de loi,** bill.

loin, *adv.* **1.** (*a*) Far. (*b*) *s.m.* **De l.,** from afar. **Au l.,** in the distance. **2.** Distant. **De l. en l.,** at long intervals.

lointain. 1. *a.* Distant, remote. **2.** *s.m.* **Dans le l.,** in the distance.

loisible, *a.* Permissible, optional.

loisir, *s.m.* Leisure.

Londres. *Pr.n.* London.

long, longue. 1. *a.* Long. *Adv.phr.* **A la longue,** in the long run. **2.** *s.m.* Length. (*a*) **De l. en large,** up and down. **Le l. de,** along; alongside. (*b*) **Regard qui en dit l.,** look which speaks volumes.

longe, *s.f.* Loin (of veal).

longer, *v.tr.* To keep to the side of; to skirt.

longitude, *s.f.* Longitude.

longtemps, *adv.* Long; a long time.

longuement, *adv.* **1.** For a long time. **2.** Slowly, deliberately.

longueur, *s.f.* Length.

longue-vue, *s.f.* Telescope, spyglass. *pl. longues-vues.*

lopin, *s.m.* Plot (of ground).

loquace [-kwas], *a.* Loquacious.

loquacité [-kwas-], *s.f.* Loquacity.

loque, *s.f.* Rag.

loquet, *s.m.* Latch.

lorgner, *v.tr.* To stare at.

lorgnette, *s.f.* Opera-glass.

lorgnon, *s.m.* (*a*) Pince-nez, eyeglasses. (*b*) (Handled) lorgnette.

lors, *adv.* (*a*) **Depuis l.,** ever since then. **L. de,** at the time of; when.

lorsque, *conj.* When.

losange, *s.m.* Lozenge.

lot [lo], *s.m.* **1.** (*a*) Share; lot. (*b*) Prize. **2.** Lot, parcel.

loterie, *s.f.* (*a*) Lottery. (*b*) Raffle.

lotion, *s.f.* Lotion.

lotir, *v.tr.* **1.** To divide into lots. **2. Bien loti,** well provided for.

louable, *a.* Laudable, praiseworthy; conmendable (*de,* for).

louablement, *adv.* Laudably.

louage, *s.m.* Hiring, hire.

louange [lwã:ʒ], *s.f.* Praise.

louche, *a.* **1.** Squint-eyed. **2.** (*a*) Ambiguous. (*b*) Shady, suspicious.

loucher, *v.i.* To squint.

louer¹, *v.tr.* To hire; to rent.

louer², *v.tr.* To praise, commend. **se louer,** to be pleased (*de,* with).

loueur, -euse, *s.* Hirer out.

loup, *s.m.* Wolf. **A pas de l.,** stealthily. **Un froid de l.,** bitterly cold.

loupe, *s.f.* **1.** Wen; excrescence (on tree). **2.** Lens, magnifying-glass.

loup-garou, *s.m.* (*a*) Werewolf. (*b*) Bugaboo. *pl. loups-garous.*

lourd, *a.* (*a*) Heavy; ungainly; ponderous. (*b*) Clumsy; dull. (*c*) Weighty. (*d*) Close, sultry.

lourdaud, *s.* (*a*) Lout. (*b*) Dullard.

lourdement, *adv.* Heavily, awkwardly, clumsily.

lourdeur, *s.f.* Heaviness; clumsiness; dullness; sultriness.

loutre, *s.f.* Otter.

louve, *s.f.* She-wolf.

louveteau, *s.m.* Wolf-cub.

louvoyer, *v.i. Nau:* To tack.

loyal, -aux, *a.* **1.** Honest, fair. **2.** Loyal, faithful.

loyalement, *adv.* **1.** Honestly, fairly. **2.** Loyally.

loyauté, *s.f.* **1.** Honesty, uprightness. **2.** Loyalty, fidelity.

loyer, *s.m.* Rent.

lubie, *s.f.* Whim, fad.

lubrifiant, *s.m.* Lubricant.

lubrification, *s.f.* Lubrication.

lubrifier, *v.tr.* To lubricate.

lucarne, *s.f.* (*a*) Dormer-window. (*b*) Skylight.

lucide, *a.* Lucid, clear.

lucidement, *adv.* Lucidly, clearly.

lucidité, *s.f.* Lucidity, clearness.

luciole, *s.f.* Fire-fly.

lucratif, *a.* Lucrative, profitable.

lucre, *s.m.* Lucre, profit.

lueur [lɥ-], *s.f.* **1.** Gleam, glimmer. **2. L. momentanée,** flash.

lugubre, *a.* Lugubrious, dismal.

lugubrement, *adv.* Lugubriously.

lui[1], *pl.* **leur,** *pers. pron. m. & f.* (To) him, her, it, them.

lui[2], *pl.* **eux,** *pers. pron. m.* (*a*) He, it, they. (*b*) Him, it, them. (*c*) Him(self), it(self), them(selves).

lui-même, *pers.pron.m.* Himself, itself.

luire, *v.i.* To shine.

luisant, *a.* Shining; gleaming.

lumière, *s.f.* Light.

luminaire, *s.m.* Luminary, star.

lumineux, *a.* Luminous.

lunaire, *a.* Lunar.

lunatique, *a.* Capricious.

lune, *s.f.* **1.** Moon. **L. de miel,** honeymoon. **2. Pierre de l.,** moonstone.

lunette, *s.f.* **1. L. d'approche,** telescope; field-glass. **2.** *pl.* Spectacles. **3.** Wish-bone.

lustre, *s.m.* **1.** Lustre, polish, gloss. **2.** Chandelier.

luth, *s.m.* Lute.

lutin, *s.m.* Sprite; imp.

lutrin, *s.m.* Lectern.

lutte, *s.f.* **1.** Wrestling. **2.** (*a*) Contest, struggle. (*b*) Strife.

lutter, *v.i.* **1.** To wrestle. **2.** To struggle, contend. **L. de vitesse avec,** to race.

lutteur, -euse, *s.* Wrestler.

luxe, *s.m.* Luxury. **Train de l.,** firstclass and Pullman train.

luxueusement, *adv.* Luxuriously.

luxueux, *a.* Luxurious; rich.

luxure, *s.f.* Lust.

luxurieux, *a.* Lustful.

lycée, *s.m.* (In Fr.) Secondary school.

lycéen, *s.* Pupil at a *lycée.*

lynx [lɛ̃:ks], *s.m.* Lynx.

Lyon. *Pr.n.* Lyons.

lyonnais, *a. & s.* (Native) of Lyons.

lyrique, *a.* Lyric(al).

M

M, m [ɛm], *s.f.* (The letter) M, m.

ma, *poss.a.f.* See MON.

macareux, *s.m.* Puffin.

macaron, *s.m.* Macaroon.

macaroni, *s.m.* Macaroni.

macédoine, *s.f.* (*a*) **M. de fruits,** fruit salad. (*b*) Medley.

macérer, *v.tr.* To macerate; to steep.

mâcher, *v.tr.* To chew, masticate.

machin, *s.m.* Gadget; thing(amy).

machinal, -aux, *a.* Mechanical.

machinalement, *adv.* Mechanically.

machination, *s.f.* Machination, plot.

machine, *s.f.* **1.** Machine. (*a*) **Ecriture à la m.,** typewriting. *pl.* Machinery. (*b*) Bicycle. (*c*) Gadget. **2.** Engine. (*a*) **M. à vapeur,** steamengine. (*b*) Locomotive.

machiner, *v.tr.* To scheme, plot.

mâchoire, *s.f.* Jaw.

mâchonner, *v.tr.* **1.** To chew; to munch. **2.** To mumble.

maçon, *s.m.* Mason; bricklayer.

maçonnerie, *s.f.* Masonry.

macule, *s.f.* Stain, spot, blemish.

maculer, *v.tr.* To stain, spot.

madame, *pl.* **mesdames,** *s.f.* **1.** (*a*) Mrs. (*b*) (*pl.* **ces dames**) The mistress. **Ces dames n'y sont pas,** the ladies are not at home. **2.** Madam.

madeleine, *s.f.* Sponge-cake.

mademoiselle, *pl.* **mesdemoiselles,** *s.f.* **1.** Miss. **2.** (*pl.* **ces demoiselles**) The lady. **Que prendront ces demoiselles?** what can I offer you, ladies?

Madère. 1. *Pr.n.f.* Madeira. **2.** *s.m.* Madeira (wine).

madone, *s.f.* Madonna.

madrier, *s.m.* Plank.

magasin, *s.m.* **1.** (*a*) (Large) shop; stores. **Demoiselle de m.,** shopassistant. (*b*) Store, warehouse. **2.** Magazine (of rifle).

magicien, *s.* Magician, wizard, sorcerer; *f.* sorceress.

magie, *s.f.* Magic, wizardry.

magique, *a.* Magic(al).

magiquement, *adv.* Magically.

magistral, -aux, *a.* Magisterial; masterly.

magistrat, *s.m.* Magistrate; judge.

magnanime, *a.* Magnanimous.

magnanimement, *adv.* Magnanimously.

magnésie, *s.f.* **1.** Magnesia. **2. Sulfate de m.,** Epsom salts.

magnésium [-zjɔm] *s.m.* Magnesium.

magnétique, *a.* Magnetic.

magnétiser, *v.tr.* To magnetize.

magnétisme, *s.m.* Magnetism.

magnéto, *s.f.* Magneto.

magnificence, *s.f.* Magnificence, splendour.

magnifier [-gni-], *v.tr.* To magnify.

magnifique, *a.* Magnificent, grand; gorgeous.

magnifiquement, *adv.* Magnificently, grandly.

mahométan, *a. & s.* Mahometan.

mai, *s.m.* May.

maigre. **1.** *a.* Thin; lean. **M. repas**, frugal meal. **Jour m.**, fast-day. **2.** *s.m.* Lean.

maigreur, *s.f.* **1.** Thinness, leanness. **2.** Poorness, meagreness.

maigrir, *v.i.* To grow thin, lean.

mail [maːj], *s.m.* Avenue, promenade.

maille [maːj], *s.f.* **1.** (*a*) Stitch. (*b*) Link (of chain). **2.** Mesh.

maillet [maje], *s.m.* Mallet.

maillon [majɔ̃], *s.m.* Link.

maillot[1] [majo], *s.m.* Swaddling-clothes.

maillot[2], *s.m.* (*a*) Tights. (*b*) **M. de bain**, bathing-costume.

main, *s.f.* **1.** Hand. (*a*) **En venir aux mains**, to come to blows. **Haut les mains!** hands up! **A bas les mains!** hands off! (*b*) **En un tour de m.**, in a twinkling. **Se faire la m.**, to get one's hand in. (*c*) **Gagner haut la m.**, to win hands down. (*d*) *Adv.phr.* **De longue m.**, for a long time (past). **2.** Hand(writing). **3.** *Cards:* Hand. **4. M. courante**, hand-rail.

main-d'œuvre, *s.f.* Labour.

maintenant, *adv.* Now.

maintenir, *v.tr.* To maintain. **1.** (*a*) To keep, hold, in position. (*b*) To support. (*c*) To uphold. **se maintenir. 1.** To last well. **2.** To hold on.

maintien, *s.m.* **1.** Maintenance, keeping. **2.** Bearing, carriage.

maire, *s.m.* Mayor.

mairie, *s.f.* Town-hall.

mais. 1. *a.* **M. oui!** why, certainly! **M. non!** not at all! **2.** *conj.* But.

maïs [mais], *s.m.* Maize. **Farine de m.**, cornflour.

maison, *s.f.* **1.** House. (*a*) **M. de commerce**, business house. (*b*) Home. **A la m.**, at home. **2.** Family.

maître, -esse, *s.* **1.** (*a*) Master, *f.*

mistress. (*b*) **M. d'école**, schoolmaster. (*c*) Works owner. (*d*) **M. d'équipage**, boatswain. **M. d'hôtel**, butler; head waiter; chief steward. **2.** *Attrib.* Chief, principal.

maîtrise, *s.f.* Mastery.

maîtriser, *v.tr.* To master.

majesté, *s.f.* **1.** Majesty. **2.** (*a*) Stateliness. (*b*) Grandeur.

majestueusement, *adv.* Majestically.

majestueux, *a.* Majestic.

majeur, -e, *a.* (*a*) Major, greater. **Le lac M.**, Lake Maggiore. (*b*) **Force majeure**, absolute necessity. (*c*) Of age.

major, *s.m.* Medical officer; M.O.

majoration, *s.f.* Increase.

majorer, *v.tr.* To raise the price of.

majorité, *s.f.* Majority.

majuscule, *a. & s.f.* Capital (letter).

mal[1], *pl.* **maux**, *s.m.* **1.** Evil. (*a*) Hurt, harm. **Prendre en mal**, to take amiss. (*c*) Wrong(doing); evil. **2.** (*a*) Ailment; pain. **Mal de tête**, headache. **Mal de mer**, seasickness. **Faire (du) mal à**, to hurt. (*b*) **Se donner du mal**, to take pains.

mal[1], *adv.* **1.** (*a*) Badly, ill. (*b*) **Aller mal**, to be ill. (*c*) **Pas mal**, a fair amount. **2.** (*a*) Not right. (*b*) Uncomfortable; badly off. (*c*) **Se trouver mal**, to faint.

malade. 1. *a.* Ill, sick. **2.** *s.* Patient; invalid.

maladie, *s.f.* Illness, sickness.

maladif, *a.* Sickly.

maladresse, *s.f.* **1.** Clumsiness, awkwardness. **2.** Blunder.

maladroit. 1. *a.* (*a*) Clumsy, awkward. (*b*) Blundering.

maladroitement, *adv.* Clumsily.

malaise, *s.m.* **1.** Uneasiness, discomfort. **2.** Indisposition.

malaisé, *a.* Difficult.

malaria, *s.f.* Malaria.

malavisé, *a.* Ill-advised.

malchance, *s.f.* Bad luck.

malchanceux, *a.* Unlucky.

mâle, *a. & s.m.* **1.** Male; cock (bird). **2.** Manly; virile.

malédiction, *s.f.* Curse.

malencontreux, *a.* **1.** Untoward. **2.** Unlucky.

malentendu, *s.m.* Misunderstanding.

malfaisance, *s.f.* Maleficence.

malfaisant, *a.* Maleficent; evil-minded; harmful; evil.

malfaiteur, -trice, *s.* Malefactor.

malgré, *prep.* In spite of.

malhabile, *a.* Unskilful; clumsy.

malheur, *s.m.* **1.** Misfortune; untoward accident. **2.** Bad luck. **Jouer de m.,** to be unlucky.

malheureusement, *adv.* Unfortunately, unluckily.

malheureux, *a.* (*a*) Unfortunate, unhappy. **Le m.!** (the) poor man! **M.!** wretch! (*b*) Unlucky.

malhonnête, *a.* (*a*) Dishonest. (*b*) Rude.

malhonnêteté, *s.f.* (*a*) Dishonesty. (*b*) Rudeness.

malice, *s.f.* (*a*) Malice. (*b*) Mischievousness.

malicieusement, *adv.* (*a*) Mischievously. (*b*) Archly, slyly.

malicieux, *a.* (*a*) Mischievous. (*b*) Waggish, sly, arch.

maligne. See MALIN.

malignité, *s.f.* Malignity.

malin, -igne, *a.* **1.** Malignant. **2.** Shrewd, cunning.

malingre, *a.* Sickly, puny.

malle, *s.f.* Trunk, box. **Faire sa m.,** to pack.

mallette, *s.f.* (*a*) **M. de camping,** tea-basket. (*b*) Attaché case.

malmener, *v.tr.* To ill-treat.

malodorant, *a.* Evil-smelling.

malpeigné, *a.* Unkempt, tousled

malpropre, *a.* Dirty; untidy.

malpropreté, *s.f.* Dirtiness.

malsain, *a.* **1.** Unhealthy. **2.** Unwholesome.

malséant, *a.* Unseemly; unbecoming.

Malte. *Pr.n.f.* Malta.

maltraiter, *v.tr.* To ill-treat.

malveillance [-vej-], *s.f.* Malevolence, ill-will.

malveillant [-vejã], *a.* (*a*) Malevolent; malicious. (*b*) Spiteful.

maman, *s.f.* Mamma.

mamelle, *s.f* Breast; udder.

mammifère, *s.m.* Mammal.

manche¹, *s.f.* **1.** (*a*) Sleeve. (*b*) **M. d'incendie,** fire-hose. **2.** *Cards:* Game. **3.** Strait, channel. **La M.,** the (English) Channel.

manche², *s.m.* Handle. **M. à balai,** (i) broomstick; (ii) joy-stick.

manchette, *s.f.* Cuff.

manchon, *s.m.* (*a*) **M. d'embrayage,** clutch. (*b*) Gas-mantle.

manchot. 1. *a. & s.* One-armed (person). **2.** *s.m.* Penguin.

mandarine, *s.f.* Tangerine.

mandat, *s.m.* **1.** Mandate. **2.** Warrant.

mandataire, *s.m. & f.* **1.** Proxy. **2.** Attorney.

mandat-poste, *s.m* Money order. *pl. mandats-poste.*

mander, *v.tr.* **1.** To report. **2.** To instruct. **3.** To summon.

manège, *s.m.* **1.** (*a*) Riding-school. (*b*) Roundabout. **2.** Trick.

mangeable, *a.* Edible, eatable.

mangeoire, *s.f.* Manger.

manger. I. *v.tr.* **1.** To eat. **Salle à m.,** dining-room. **Donner à m. à,** to feed. **2.** To squander.
II. manger, *s.m.* Food.

maniable, *a.* Manageable; handy.

maniaque, *s.* **1.** Maniac. **2.** Faddist.

manie, *s.f.* Mania.

manier, *v.tr.* **1.** To feel; to handle. **2.** To wield.

manière, *s.f.* **1.** Manner, way. **De (telle) m. que,** so that. **2.** *pl.* Manners.

maniéré, *a.* Affected; genteel.

maniérisme, *s.m.* Mannerism.

manifestant, *s.* Demonstrator.

manifestation, *s.f.* (*a*) Manifestation. (*b*) Demonstration.

manifeste¹, *a.* Manifest, evident.

manifeste², *s.m.* Manifesto.

manifestement, *adv.* Manifestly.

manifester, *v.tr.* **1.** To manifest; to evince. **2.** *Abs.* To demonstrate. **se manifester,** to appear.

manigance, *s.f.* (*a*) Intrigue. (*b*) *pl.* Underhand practices.

manigancer, *v.tr.* To scheme.

manipulation, *s.f.* Manipulation.

manipuler, *v.tr.* To manipulate.

manivelle, *s.f.* Crank.

mannequin, *s.m.* **1.** (*a*) Lay figure. (*b*) Dummy. **2.** Mannequin.

manœuvre. 1. *s.f.* (*a*) Working, driving. (*b*) Drill; manœuvre. (*c*) Shunting. (*d*) Scheme, manœuvre. **2.** *s.m.* Labourer.

manœuvrer. 1. *v.tr.* (*a*) To work, operate. (*b*) To shunt. **2.** *v.i.* To manœuvre.

manoir, *s.m.* Manor-house.

manquant, *a.* Missing; lacking.

manque, *s.m.* Lack, want.

manqué, *a.* Missed ; unsuccessful.

manquement, *s.m.* Failure.

manquer. I. *v.i.* 1. (*a*) **M. de,** to lack be short of. (*b*) **Il a manqué (de) tomber,** he nearly fell. (*c*) *Impers.* **Il s'en manque de beaucoup,** far from it. 2. To fail. (*a*) To be wanting. (*b*) To give way. (*c*) To be missing. (*d*) **M. à sa parole,** to break one's word. *Abs.* To fail ; to miscarry.

II. **manquer,** *v.tr.* To miss.

mansarde, *s.f.* Attic, garret.

manteau, *s.m.* Cloak, mantle.

manucure, *s.m. & f.* Manicurist.

manuel. 1. *a.* Manual. 2. *s.m.* Manual, handbook.

manufacture, *s.f.* Factory ; works.

manufacturer, *v.tr.* To manufacture.

manufacturier. 1. *a.* Manufacturing. 2. *s.m.* Manufacturer.

manuscrit, *a. & s.m.* Manuscript.

mappemonde, *s.f.* Map of the world in two hemispheres.

maquereau, *s.m.* Mackerel.

maquillage [-kij-], *s.m.* Make-up.

maquiller [-kije], *v.tr.* To make up.

maquis, *s.m* Scrub bush ; underground forces.

maraîcher, *s.* Market-gardener.

marais, *s.m.* Marsh ; bog, fen.

marâtre, *s.f.* Cruel stepmother or mother.

maraude, *s.f.* Marauding.

marauder, *v.i.* To maraud.

maraudeur, -euse, *s.* Marauder.

marbre, *s.m.* Marble.

marbré, *a.* Marbled ; mottled.

marc [ma:r], *s.m.* Coffee-grounds.

marchand. 1. *s.* Dealer, merchant ; tradesman. **M. des quatre saisons,** costermonger. 2. *a.* **Navire m.,** merchant ship.

marchander, *v.tr.* To haggle.

marchandise, *s.f.* Merchandise.

marche, *s.f.* 1. Step, stair. 2. (*a*) Walking. **Ralentir sa m.,** to slacken one's pace. **Se mettre en m.,** to start off. (*b*) March. 3. **M. arrière,** reverse. 4. (*a*) Running, working. (*b*) Course.

marché, *s.m.* 1. (*a*) Deal, bargain. **Pardessus le m.,** into the bargain. (*b*) **Bon m.,** cheapness. 2. Market.

marchepied, *s.m.* Footboard ; running-board.

marcher, *v.i.* 1. To tread. 2. (*a*) To walk, go. (*b*) To march. 3. (*a*) To move, go. (*b*) To work, run, go.

marcheur, -euse, *s.* Walker.

mardi, *s.m.* Tuesday. **M. gras,** Shrove Tuesday.

mare, *s.f.* Pool ; pond.

marécage, *s.m.* Bog, swamp.

marécageux, *a.* Boggy, swampy.

maréchal, -aux, *s.m.* (*a*) (Field-) marshal. (*b*) **M. des logis,** (cavalry) sergeant.

marée, *s.f.* 1. Tide. 2. Fresh fish. **Train de m.,** boat-train.

margarine, *s.f.* Margarine.

marge, *s.f.* (*a*) Border. (*b*) Margin.

marginal, -aux, *a.* Marginal.

Marguerite. 1. *Pr.n.f.* Margaret. 2. *s.f.* Daisy.

marguillier [-gije], *s.m.* Churchwarden.

mari, *s.m.* Husband.

mariable, *a.* Marriageable.

mariage, *s.m.* Marriage ; wedding.

Marie. *Pr.n.f.* Mary, Maria.

marié, *a. & s.* Married (person).

marier, *v.tr.* To marry.
  se marier, to marry. **Se m. avec qn,** to marry s.o.

marin. 1. *a.* Marine. 2. *s.m.* Sailor.

marine, *s.f.* **La m. marchande,** the mercantile marine. **La m. de guerre,** the Navy.

marital, -aux, *a.* Marital.

maritime, *a.* Maritime **Gare m.,** harbour station.

marmelade, *s.f.* Compote (of fruit). **M. de pommes,** stewed apples.

marmite, *s.f.* (*a*) (Cooking-)pot ; pan. (*b*) Dixy, camp-kettle.

marmotter, *v.tr.* To mumble, mutter.

Maroc (le) [-rɔk]. *Pr.n.m.* Morocco.

marocain, *a. & s.* Moroccan.

maroquin, *s.m.* Morocco(-leather).

marotte, *s.f.* Fad, hobby.

marquant, *a.* Prominent outstanding.

marque, *s.f.* Mark ; token.

marqué, *a.* Marked.

marquer. 1. *v.tr.* To mark. (*a*) To put a mark on. (*b*) To record, note. (*c*) To indicate 2. *v.i.* To stand out.

marqueur, -euse, *s.* Marker.

marquis, *s.m.* Marquis, marquess.

marquise, *s.f.* **1.** Marchioness. **2.**
(*a*) Awning. (*b*) Marquee.

marraine, *s.f.* Godmother.

marron, *s.m.* **1.** (*a*) Chestnut. (*b*)
M. d'Inde, horse-chestnut. **2.** Maroon.
3. *a.* Chestnut.

marronnier, *s.m.* Chestnut-tree.
M. d'Inde, horse-chestnut tree.

Mars [mars]. **1.** *Pr.n.m.* **Champ de
M.,** parade-ground. **2.** *s.m.* March.

Marseille [-sɛːj]. *Pr.n.* Marseilles.

marsouin, *s.m.* Porpoise.

marteau, *s.m.* (*a*) Hammer. (*b*)
Knocker.

marteler, *v.tr.* To hammer.

martial, -aux, *a.* Martial.

martin-pêcheur, *s.m.* Kingfisher.
pl. **martins-pêcheurs.**

martre, *s.f.* Marten.

martyr, *s.* Martyr.

martyre, *s.m.* Martyrdom.

martyriser, *v.tr.* To martyrize.

mascarade, *s.f.* Masquerade.

mascaret, *s.m.* Bore, tidal wave.

mascotte, *s.f.* Mascot, charm.

masculin, *a.* **1.** Male. **2.** Masculine.

masque, *s.m.* Mask.

masquer, *v.tr.* To mask; to hide,
screen.

massacre, *s.m.* Massacre.

massacrer, *v.tr.* To massacre.

massage, *s.m.* Massage.

masse, *s.f.* Mass. **En m.,** in a body.

massepain, *s.m.* Marzipan.

masser[1], *v.tr.* To mass.
se masser, to form a crowd.

masser[2], *v.tr.* To massage.

masseur, -euse, *s.* Masseur, *f.* masseuse.

massif. 1. *a.* (*a*) Massive. (*b*) Solid.
2. *s.m.* (*a*) Clump (of shrubs). (*b*)
Mountain mass.

massue, *s.f.* Club, bludgeon.

mastic [-tik], *s.m.* Putty.

mastiquer, *v.tr.* To masticate, chew.

masure, *s.f.* Tumbledown cottage.

mat[1] [mat], *a.* Mat, unpolished, dull.
Son mat, dull sound; thud.

mat[2] [mat], *s.m.* (Check)mate.

mât [mɑ], *s.m.* Mast, pole.

matelas, *s.m.* Mattress.

matelasser, *v.tr.* To pad, cushion.

matelot, *s.m.* Sailor, seaman.

mater, *v.tr.* To (check)mate.

matérialiser, *v.tr.* To materialize.

matérialiste, *s.* Materialist.

matériaux, *s.m.pl.* Materials.

matériel. 1. *a.* (*a*) Material. (*b*)
Materialistic. **2.** *s.m.* Plant, imple-
ments. **M. roulant,** rolling-stock.

matériellement, *adv.* Materially;
physically

maternel, *a.* Maternal.

maternellement, *adv.* Maternally.

maternité, *s.f* Maternity.

mathématicien, *s.* Mathematician.

mathématique. 1. *a.* Mathematical.
2. *s.f. pl.* Mathematics.

matière, *s.f.* **1.** Material. **2.** Matter,
substance. **3.** Subject. **Table des
matières,** table of contents.

matin. 1. *s.m.* Morning. **De grand
m.,** early in the morning. **2.** *adv.*
Se lever très m., to get up very early.

mâtin, *s.m.* Mastiff.

matinal, -aux, *a.* (*a*) Morning.
(*b*) Early.

matinée, *s.f.* **1.** Morning. **2.**
Matinée; afternoon performance.

matois, *a.* Sly, cunning, crafty.

matou, *s.m.* Tom-cat.

matraque, *s.f.* Bludgeon.

matrice, *s.f.* Matrix; die.

matrimonial, -aux, *a.* Matrimonial.

matrone, *s.f.* Matron.

mâture, *s.f.* Masts.

maturité, *s.f.* Maturity, ripeness.

matutinal, -aux, *a.* Matutinal.

maudire, *v.tr.* To curse.

maudissement, *s.m.* Cursing.

maudit, *a.* (Ac)cursed.

maugréer, *v.i.* To curse, fume.

Maure, *s.m.* Moor.

mauresque. 1. *a.* Moorish. **2.** *s.f.*
Moorish woman.

Maurice. *Pr.n.m.* **L'île M.,** Mauritius.

mausolée, *s.m* Mausoleum.

maussade, *a.* (*a*) Surly, sullen.
(*b*) Dull, cheerless.

mauvais, *a.* (*a*) Evil; bad, wicked.
(*b*) Ill-natured. (*c*) Nasty, unpleasant. **M. pas,** dangerous situation. *Adv.* **Il fait m.,** the weather is
bad. (*d*) Wrong.

mauve, *a. & s.m.* Mauve, purple.

maxime, *s.f.* Maxim.

maximum [-mɔm], *a. & s.m.* Maximum.

mazagran, *s.m.* Glass of black coffee.

mazout, *s.m.* Oil fuel.

me, *pers.pron.* (*a*) Me. (*b*) (To) me.
(*c*) Myself.

méandre, *s.m.* Meander, winding.

mécanicien, *s.m.* (a) Mechanic. (b) Engine-driver; engineer.

mécanique. 1. *a.* Mechanical. **2.** *s.f.* Mechanics

mécaniquement, *adv.* Mechanically.

mécanisme, *s.m.* Mechanism.

méchamment, *adv.* **1.** Naughtily, wickedly. **2.** Spitefully.

méchanceté, *s.f.* (a) Wickedness. (b) Unkindness, spitefulness.

méchant, *a.* **1.** (a) Miserable, wretched. (b) Unpleasant. **2.** (a) Wicked, evil; naughty. (b) Spiteful.

mèche, *s.f.* **1.** (a) Wick. (b) Fuse. **2.** Lock (of hair). **3.** Bit, drill.

mécompte [-kɔ̃:t], *s.m.* Miscalculation, error.

méconnaissable, *a.* Unrecognizable.

méconnaître, *v.tr.* To misappreciate; to disregard.

méconnu, *a.* Unappreciated; misunderstood.

mécontent. 1. *a.* Discontented, displeased. **2.** *s.* Malcontent.

mécontentement, *s.m.* Dissatisfaction (de with); disaffection.

mécontenter, *v.tr.* To displease.

Mecque (la). *Pr.n.f.* Mecca.

mécréant. 1. *a.* Misbelieving. **2.** *s.* Misbeliever.

médaille [-da:j], *s.f.* Medal.

médaillon [-dajɔ̃], *s.m* **1.** Medallion **2.** Locket.

médecin, *s.m.* Doctor, physician

médecine, *s.f.* Medicine.

médiateur, -trice, *s.* Mediator.

médiation, *s.f.* Mediation.

médical, -aux, *a.* Medical.

médicinal, -aux, *a.* Medicinal.

médiéval, -aux, *a.* Mediaeval.

médiocre, *a.* Mediocre.

médiocrité, *s.f.* Mediocrity.

médire, *v.i.* M. de, to speak ill of; to slander.

médisance, *s.f.* Slander, backbiting.

médisant. 1. *a.* Backbiting. **2.** *s.* Slanderer, backbiter.

méditatif, *a.* Meditative.

méditation, *s.f.* Meditation.

méditer. 1. *v.i.* To meditate, to muse. **2.** *v.tr* To contemplate.

Méditerranée (la). *Pr.n.f.* The Mediterranean.

mediterranéen, *a.* Mediterranean.

médium [-djɔm], *s.m.* Medium.

méduse, *s.f.* Jelly-fish.

méfait, *s.m.* Misdeed, ill deed.

méfiance, *s.f.* Distrust, mistrust.

méfiant, *a.* Distrustful.

méfier (se), *v.pr.* Se m. de, to distrust.

mégarde (par), *adv.phr.* Inadvertently; through carelessness.

mégère, *s.f.* Shrew, termagant.

meilleur [-jœ:r], *a.* **1.** Better. **2.** Le m., the better; the best. *s.* The best.

mélancolie, *s.f.* Melancholy.

mélancolique, *a.* Melancholy.

mélancoliquement, *adv* Mournfully, gloomily.

mélange, *s.m.* Mixture; blend.

mélanger, *v.tr.* To mix; to blend.

mélasse, *s.f.* Molasses; treacle. M. raffinée, golden syrup.

mêlé, *a.* Tangled; involved.

mêlée, *s.f.* Scrimmage.

mêler, *v.tr.* To mix, mingle, blend. M. les cartes, to shuffle the cards. se mêler, to mix, mingle, blend. Se m. de, to take a hand in.

mélodie, *s.f.* Melody, tune.

mélodieusement, *adv.* Melodiously.

mélodieux, *a.* Melodious, tuneful.

mélodramatique, *a.* Melodramatic.

mélodrame, *s.m.* Melodrama.

melon, *s.m.* **1.** Melon **2.** (Chapeau) m., bowler (hat).

membrane, *s.f.* Membrane.

membraneux, *a.* Membranous

membre, *s.m.* Member; limb.

même. 1. *a.* (a) Same. En m. temps, at the same time; at once. (b) Very. C'est cela m., that's the very thing. **2.** *adv.* Even. **3.** De m., n the same way; likewise. Tout de m., all the same. Être à m. de, to be in a position to.

mémoire[1], *s.f.* (a) Memory. (b) Recollection, remembrance.

mémoire[2], *s.m.* **1.** (a) Memorial (b) Memoir. **2.** Account; bill.

mémorable, *a.* Memorable.

mémorandum [-dɔm], *s.m.* **1.** Memorandum, note. **2.** Note-book.

mémorial, -aux, *s.m.* Memorial.

menaçant, *a.* Menacing, threatening

menace, *s.f.* Threat, menace

menacer, *v.tr.* To threaten, menace.

ménage, *s.m.* **1.** (a) Housekeeping. (b) Femme de m., charwoman. **2.** Household, family.

ménagement, *s.m.* Caution, care.

ménager[1], *v.tr.* **1.** To save; to be sparing of. **M. qn**, to deal tactfully with s.o. **2.** To contrive, arrange.

ménager[2]. **1.** *a.* Thrifty, sparing **2.** *s.f.* **Ménagère.** housekeeper, housewife.

ménagerie, *s.f.* Menagerie.

mendiant. 1. *a.* Mendicant. begging **2.** *s.* Beggar.

mendicité, *s.f.* Mendicity, begging.

mendier, *v.i. & tr.* To beg.

menée, *s.f.* Intrigue. *pl.* Schemings.

mener, *v.tr.* **1.** To lead; to take. **2.** To drive; to ride; to steer. **3.** To manage, conduct.

meneur, -euse, *s.* (*a*) Leader. (*b*) Ringleader.

menottes, *s.f. pl.* Handcuffs.

mensonge, *s.m.* Lie, falsehood.

mensonger, *a.* Lying; deceitful.

mensuel, *a.* Monthly.

mental, -aux, *a.* Mental.

mentalement, *adv.* Mentally.

mentalité, *s.f.* Mentality.

menteur, -euse. 1. *a.* (*a*) Lying. (*b*) False, deceptive. **2.** *s.* Liar.

menthe, *s.f.* Mint. **M poivrée**, peppermint.

mention, *s.f.* (*a*) Mention. (*b*) Reference.

mentionner, *v.tr.* To mention.

mentir, *v.i.* To lie; to tell lies.

menton, *s.m.* Chin.

menu. 1. *a.* Small. (*a*) Fine; slender; tiny. **Menue monnaie**, small change. (*b*) Trifling; petty. **2.** *adv.* Small. fine. **3.** *s.m.* (*a*) **Par le m.**, in detail. (*b*) Bill of fare, menu

menuet, *s.m.* Minuet.

menuiserie, *s.f.* Joinery, woodwork. carpentry.

menuisier, *s.m.* Joiner; carpenter.

méprendre (se), *v.pr.* To be mistaken, to make a mistake.

mépris, *s.m.* Contempt, scorn.

méprisable, *a.* Contemptible.

méprisant, *a.* Contemptuous.

méprise, *s.f.* Mistake misapprehension.

mépriser, *v.tr.* To despise, scorn.

mer, *s.f.* Sea. (*a*) **Un homme à la mer!** man overboard! (*b*) **Basse mer**, low water.

mercantile, *a.* Mercantile.

mercenaire, *a. & s.m.* Mercenary.

mercerie, *s.f.* Haberdashery.

merci. 1. *s.f.* Mercy. **2.** *adv.* (*a*) Thank you. (*b*) No, thank you.

mercier, *s.* Haberdasher.

mercredi, *s.m.* Wednesday.

mercure, *s.m.* Mercury quicksilver.

mère, *s.f.* Mother.

méridien, *s.m.* Meridian.

méridional, -aux. 1. *a* South(ern). **2.** *s.* Southerner.

mérinos [-nɔs], *s.m.* Merino.

mérite, *s.m.* Merit. (*a*) Desert, worth. (*b*) Excellence, talent.

mériter, *v.tr.* **1.** To deserve, merit. **2.** To earn.

méritoire, *a.* Meritorious, deserving.

merlan, *s.m.* Whiting.

merle, *s.m.* Blackbird.

merluche, *s.f.* Hake.

merveille [-vɛːj], *s.f.* Marvel, wonder **A m.**, excellently.

merveilleusement [-vɛj-], *adv.* Marvellously, wonderfully.

merveilleux [-vɛjø], *a.* Marvellous, wonderful.

mes. See MON.

mésalliance, *s.f.* Misalliance.

mésaventure, *s.f.* Misadventure.

mesdames, -demoiselles. See MADAME, MADEMOISELLE.

mésintelligence, *s.f* Disagreement.

mesmérique *a.* Mesmeric.

mesquin, *a.* (*a*) Mean, shabby; paltry, petty. (*b*) Mean, stingy.

mesquinement, *adv.* Meanly, shabbily; pettily.

mesquinerie, *s.f.* Meanness. (*a*) Pettiness. (*b*) Niggardliness.

message, *s.m.* Message.

messager, *s.* **1.** Messenger. **2.** Carrier.

messagerie, *s.f.* Carrying trade.

messe, *s.f.* *Ecc:* Mass.

messieurs. See MONSIEUR.

mesurage, *s.m.* Measurement.

mesure, *s.f.* Measure. **1.** (*a*) Measurement(s). *Adv.phr.* **A m.**, in proportion. **A m. que**, (in proportion) as. (*b*) **Prendre des mesures**, to take action. **2.** **Garder la m.**, to keep within bounds. **Être en m. de**, to be in a position to. **3.** *Mus:* (*a*) Bar. (*b*) Time.

mesuré, *a.* Measured; temperate.

mesurer, *v.tr.* **1.** To measure. **2.** To calculate; to weigh.

métal, -aux, *s.m.* Metal.

métallique, *a.* Metallic.

métallurgie, *s.f.* Metallurgy.

métamorphose, *s.f.* Metamorphosis, transformation.

métamorphoser, *v.tr.* To metamorphose, transform.

   se métamorphoser, to change completely

métaphore, *s.f.* Metaphor.

métaphorique, *a.* Metaphorical.

métaphoriquement, *adv.* Metaphorically.

météore, *s.m.* Meteor.

météorique, *a.* Meteoric.

météorologique, *a.* Meteorological. Bulletin m., weather report.

méthode, *s.f.* Method, system.

méthodique, *a.* Methodical.

méthodiquement, *adv.* Methodically.

méticuleusement, *adv.* Meticulously.

méticuleux, *a.* Meticulous.

métier, *s.m.* **1.** Trade, profession, craft. M. manuel, handicraft. **2.** M. à tisser, loom.

métis, -isse. **1.** *a.* Half-bred; mongrel. **2.** *s.* Half-breed; mongrel.

mètre¹, *s.m.* *Pros:* Metre.

mètre², *s.m.* **1.** *Meas:* Metre (= 3 28 ft.). **2.** (Metre) rule.

métrique¹, *a.* Metrical.

métrique², *a.* Metric.

Métro (le), *s.m.* The Underground (railway) (in Paris).

métropole, *s.f.* Metropolis.

métropolitain, *a.* Metropolitan.

mets [me], *s.m.* Food; viand; dish.

mettre, *v.tr.* **1.** (*a*) To put, lay, place. (*b*) To put on. **2.** To set (going). **3.** To admit, grant; to consider.

   se mettre. **1.** (*a*) To go, get. (*b*) To begin, to set about. (*c*) Se m. à faire qch., to begin to do sth. **2.** Être bien mis, to be well dressed. **3.** Se m en route, to start on one's way.

meuble. **1.** *a.* Movable. **2.** *s.m.* Piece of furniture.

meublé. **1.** *a.* Furnished. **2.** *s.m.* Furnished apartment(s).

meubler, *v.tr.* To furnish.

meugler, *v.i.* To low, moo.

meule, *s.f.* **1.** Millstone; grindstone. **2.** Stack, rick.

meunier, *s.* Miller.

meurtre, *s.m.* Murder.

meurtri, *a.* Bruised.

meurtrier. **1.** *a.* Murderous; deadly. **2.** *s.* Murderer, *f.* murderess. **3.** *s.f.* Meurtrière, loop-hole.

meurtrir, *v.tr.* To bruise.

meurtrissure, *s.f.* Bruise.

meute, *s.f.* Pack (of hounds).

mexicain, *a. & s.* Mexican.

Mexique (le). *Pr.n.m.* Mexico.

mi, *adv.* Half, mid, semi-.

miaou, *s.m.* Miaow, mew.

mi-août [miu], *s.f.inv.* Mid-August.

miasme, *s.m.* Miasma.

miauler, *v.i.* To mew; to caterwaul.

mica, *s.m.* Mica.

mi-carême, *s.f.* Mid-Lent.

miche, *s.f.* Round loaf.

micheline, *s.f.* Rail-car.

mi-chemin (à), *adv.phr.* Half-way.

mi-clos, *adj.* Half-closed.

mi-corps (à), *adv.phr.* To the waist.

microbe, *s.m.* Microbe, germ.

microphone, *s.m.* Microphone.

microphoniste, *s.m. & f.* Announcer.

microscope, *s.m.* Microscope.

microscopique, *a.* Microscopic(al).

midi, *s.m.* **1.** Midday, noon, twelve o'clock. M. et demi, half-past twelve. **2.** South. Chambre au m., room facing south.

mie, *s.f.* Crumb (of loaf)

miel, *s.m.* Honey.

mielleusement, *adv.* With honeyed words.

mielleux, *a.* Honeyed; soft-spoken.

mien, mienne. (*a*) *poss.pron.* Le mien, la mienne, les miens, les miennes, mine. (*b*) *s.m. pl.* My own people.

miette, *s.f.* Crumb; morsel.

mieux, *adv.* **1.** Better. (*a*) Pour m. dire, to be more exact. *Adv.phr.* A qui m. m., to vie with one another. (*b*) More comfortable. (*c*) *s.neut.* Faute de m., for want of something better. **2** Le mieux, (the) best. (*a*) Le m. du monde, on the best of terms. (*b*) *s.neut.* Faire de son m., to do one's best.

mièvre, *a.* (*a*) Fragile, delicate. (*b*) Finical, affected.

mignard, *a.* Affected, mincing.

mignardise, *s.f.* Affectation.

mignon. **1.** *a.* Dainty, tiny. **2.** *s.* Pet, darling, favourite.

migraine, *s.f.* Sick headache.

migration, *s.f.* Migration.

mijoter, *v.i.* To simmer.

milice, *s.f.* Militia.

milieu, -eux, *s.m.* **1.** Middle, midst. **Au beau m.,** right in the middle. **2.** Surroundings, environment. **3.** Middle course; mean.

militaire. 1. *a* Military. **2.** *s.m.* Soldier.

militer, *v.i.* To militate.

mille[1], *num.a.inv & s.m.inv.* Thousand.

mille[2], *s.m.* Mile.

millénium [-jɔm], *s.m.* Millennium.

millésime, *s.m.* Date (on coin).

millet [mijɛ], *s.m.* Millet.

milliard, *s.m.* One thousand million(s).

milliardaire, *a. & s.m.* Multimillionaire.

millième, *num.a. & s.m.* Thousandth.

millier, *s.m.* (About a) thousand.

million, *s.m.* Million.

millionnaire, *a. & s.* Millionaire.

mime, *s.m.* Mimic.

mimer, *v.tr.* To mimic, to ape.

mimique. 1. *a.* Mimic. **2.** *s.f.* Mimicry.

minable, *a.* Seedy-looking; shabby.

minauder, *v.i.* To simper, smirk.

minauderie, *s.f.* Simpering.

mince, *a.* Thin; slender, slim.

minceur, *s.f.* Thinness; slimness.

mine[1], *s.f.* **1.** Mine. **2. M. de plomb,** graphite, black-lead.

mine[2], *s.f.* Appearance look. (*a*) **Avoir bonne m.,** to look well. (*b*) **Faire bonne m.,** to be pleasant.

miner, *v.tr.* To mine, undermine.

minerai, *s.m.* Ore.

minéral, -aux. 1. *a.* Mineral **Source minérale,** spa. **2.** *s.m.* Mineral.

mineur[1], **-euse,** *s.m.* Miner.

mineur[2], **-eure. 1.** *a.* (*a*) Minor. lesser. (*b*) Under age. **2.** *s.* Minor.

miniature, *s.f.* Miniature.

minime, *a.* Small; trivial; trifling.

minimum [-mɔm], *a. & s.m* Minimum.

ministère, *s.m.* **1.** Agency. **2.** Ministry.

ministériel, *a.* Ministerial.

ministre, *s.m.* Minister.

minorité, *s.f.* Minority.

minuit, *s.m.* Midnight. **M. et demi,** half-past twelve at night.

minuscule, *a.* (*a*) Small, minute, tiny. (*b*) **Lettre m.,** *s. f* m., small letter.

minute, *s.f.* Minute.

minutie, *s.f.* Minute detail; trifle.

minutieusement, *adv.* Thoroughly, minutely.

minutieux, *a.* Scrupulously careful; minute, detailed.

mioche, *s.m & f.* Small child; urchin.

miracle, *s.m.* Miracle.

miraculeusement, *adv.* Miraculously.

miraculeux, *a.* Miraculous.

mirage, *s.m.* Mirage.

mire, *s.f.* Aiming. **Point de m.,** aim; cynosure.

mirer, *v.tr.* To aim at. **se mirer,** to look at oneself.

mirifique, *a.* Wonderful.

miroir, *s.m.* Mirror, looking-glass.

miroitant, *a.* Flashing.

miroitement, *s.m.* Flashing.

miroiter, *v.i.* To flash; to sparkle.

misanthrope. 1. *s.m.* Misanthrope. **2.** *a.* Misanthropic(al).

misanthropie, *s.f.* Misanthropy.

mise, *s.f.* **1.** (*a*) Placing; putting. (*b*) Setting. **M. en marche,** starting. **2.** Dress, attire. **3.** (*a*) Stake. (*b*) Bid.

misérable. 1. *a.* (*a*) Miserable; wretched. (*b*) Despicable. **2.** *s.* (*a*) Poor wretch. (*b*) Scoundrel.

misérablement, *adv.* Miserably.

misère, *s.f.* **1.** (*a*) Misery. (*b*) Trouble, ill. **2.** Destitution. **3.** Trifle.

miséricorde, *s.f.* Mercy.

miséricordieux, *a. & s* Merciful.

mission, *s.f.* Mission.

missionnaire, *s.m.* Missionary.

missive, *s.f.* Missive; letter.

mite, *s.f.* **1.** Mite. **2.** Clothes-moth.

mité, *a.* Moth-eaten.

mitigation, *s.f.* Mitigation.

mitiger, *v.tr.* To mitigate.

mitrailler [-rɑje], *v.tr* To rake with machine-gun fire.

mitraillette [-rɑj-], *s.f.* Sub machine-gun.

mitrailleuse [-rɑj-], *s.f.* Machinegun.

mi-vitesse (à), *adv.phr.* At halfspeed.

mi-voix (à), *adv.phr* In an undertone.

mixte, *a.* Mixed.

mobile. 1. *a.* (*a*) Mobile, movable. (*b*) Unstable, fickle. (*c*) Moving; changing. **2.** *s.m.* Driving power; motive.

mobilier, *s.m.* Furniture.

mobilisation, *s.f.* Mobilization.

mobiliser, *v.tr.* To mobilize.

mobilité, *s.f.* Mobility.

mocassin, *s.m.* Moccasin.

mode[1], *s.f.* **1.** Fancy, fashion. **A la m. de**, after the style of. **2.** *pl.* (*a*) Fashions. (*b*) Millinery.

mode[2], *s.m.* Method, mode. "**M. d'emploi**," 'directions for use.'

modèle. 1. *s.m.* Model; pattern. **2.** *s.m.* (Artist's) model. **3.** *a.* Model.

modeler, *v.tr.* To model; to mould.

modération, *s.f.* Moderation.

modéré, *a.* Moderate; temperate.

modérément, *adv.* Moderately.

modérer, *v.tr.* To moderate.
  se modérer, to control oneself.

moderne, *a.* Modern.

modeste, *a.* Modest; unassuming.

modestement, *adv.* Modestly.

modestie, *s.f.* Modesty.

modicité, *s.f.* Moderateness.

modification, *s.f.* Modification.

modifier, *v.tr.* To modify; to alter, change.

modique, *a.* Moderate, reasonable.

modiste, *s.f.* Milliner.

modulation, *s.f.* Modulation.

moduler, *v.tr.* To modulate.

moelle [mwal], *s.f.* **1.** Marrow. **2.** Pith.

moelleusement [mwal-], *adv.* Softly, luxuriously.

moelleux [mwalø], *a.* **1.** Pithy. **2.** (*a*) Soft, velvety; mellow. (*b*) *s.m.* Softness.

mœurs [mœrs], *s.f.pl.* Manners; customs; habits.

moi. 1. *pers.pron.* (*a*) I. **Moi, je veux bien**, for my part, I am willing. (*b*) Me. **A moi, help! Ce livre est à moi**, this book is mine. (*c*) **Laissez-moi tranquille**, leave me alone. **Donnez-le-moi**, give it (to) me. **2.** *s.m.* Ego, self.

moignon, *s.m.* Stump (of limb).

moi-même, *pers.pron.* Myself.

moindre, *a.* **1.** Less(er). **2. Le, la, moindre**, the least.

moine, *s.m.* Monk, friar.

moineau, *s.m.* Sparrow.

moins. 1. *adv.* (*a*) Less. *Prep.phr.* **A m. de**, unless. **A m. que**, unless. (*b*) **Le moins**, least. **Pas le m. du monde**, not in the least. *Adv.phr.* **Du m.**, at least, at all events. **Au m.**, at least. **2.** *prep.* Minus, less. **Une heure m. cinq**, five minutes to one.

moiré, *a.* Watered, moiré.

mois, *s.m.* Month.

moisi. 1. *a.* Mouldy; musty. **2.** *s.m.* Mould, mildew.

moisir, *v.i. & pr.* To go mouldy.

moisissure, *s.f.* **1.** Mildew; mould. **2.** Mouldiness, mustiness.

moisson, *s.f.* **1.** (*a*) Harvest(ing). (*b*) Harvest-time. **2.** Crop.

moissonner, *v.tr.* To reap; to harvest.

moissonneur, -euse, *s.* **1.** Harvester, reaper. **2.** *s.f.* **Moissonneuse**, reaping-machine.

moite, *a.* Moist; clammy

moiteur, *s.f.* Moistness.

moitié. 1. *s.f.* Half. *Adv.phr.* **A m.**, half. **2.** *adv.* **M. l'un, m. l'autre**, half and half.

mol. See MOU.

môle, *s.m.* Mole; breakwater.

molécule, *s.f.* Molecule.

molestation, *s.f.* Molestation.

molester, *v.tr.* To molest.

molle. See MOU.

mollement, *adv.* (*a*) Softly. (*b*) Slackly, feebly.

mollesse, *s.f.* (*a*) Softness; flabbiness. (*b*) Slackness, lifelessness.

mollet, *s.m.* Calf (of leg).

moment, *s.m.* Moment. **Au bon m.**, in the nick of time. *Conj.phr.* **Du m. que**, seeing that

momentané, *a.* Momentary.

momentanément, *adv.* Momentarily.

momie, *s.f.* Mummy.

mon, ma, mes, *poss.a.* My.

monarchie, *s.f.* Monarchy.

monarchique, *a.* Monarchic(al).

monarque, *s.m.* Monarch.

monastère, *s.m.* Monastery.

monceau, *s.m.* Heap, pile.

mondain, *a.* Mundane, worldly. *s.* Worldling.

monde, *s.m.* **1.** World. (*a*) **Pour rien au m.**, not for the world. (*b*) Society. **2.** People. (*a*) **Avoir du m.**, to have

company **Tout le m.**, everybody.
(b) Servants

monégasque, a. & s. (Native) of Monaco.

monétaire, a. Monetary.

moniteur, -trice, s. Monitor.

monnaie, s.f. **1.** Money. **Pièce de m.,** coin **La Monnaie,** the Mint. **2.** Change.

monnayer, v.tr To coin, mint.

monogramme, s.m. Monogram.

monographie, s.f. Monograph

monologue, s.m. Monologue.

monologuer, v.i. To soliloquize.

monomane, s. Monomaniac.

monomanie, s.f. Monomania.

monoplace, a. & s.m. Single-seater.

monopole, s.m. Monopoly.

monopoliser, v.tr To monopolize

monosyllabe, s.m. Monosyllable.

monotone, a. Monotonous.

monotonie, s.f. Monotony.

monseigneur, s.m. **1.** (a) His Highness; his Grace. (b) Your Highness; your Grace. **2. Pince m.,** jemmy.

monsieur [məsjø], pl. **messieurs,** s.m. **1.** (a) Mr; Messrs. **M. de duc,** the Duke. (b) Master. (c) **M. n'y est pas,** Mr X is not at home. **2.** Sir. **Bonsoir, messieurs,** good evening, gentlemen. **3.** Gentleman.

monstre. 1. s.m. Monster. **2.** a. Huge; colossal; monster.

monstrueux, a. Monstrous.

mont, s.m. Mount, mountain.

montagnard, s. Mountaineer.

montagne, s.f Mountain. **Montagnes russes,** switchback.

montagneux, a. Mountainous

montant. 1. a. Rising, ascending. **Train m.,** up train **2.** s.m. Total amount.

monté, a. Mounted; worked up; excited.

montée, s.f. **1.** Rise; climb. **2.** Ascent.

monter. I. v.i. **1.** (a) To climb (up), mount, ascend; to go upstairs. (b) To climb on, into (sth.). **2.** (a) To rise, to go up. (b) To ascend; to climb.
II. **monter,** v.tr. **1.** To mount. **2.** (a) To raise, take up. (b) **Se m. la tête,** to get excited. **3.** To set, mount; to erect; to equip.
se monter, to amount.

montre, s.f. **1.** Display. **2.** Watch

montrer, v.tr. To show.
se montrer, to prove.

montueux, a. Hilly.

monture, s.f. **1.** Mount. **2.** Setting; mount(ing).

monument, s.m. **1.** Monument. **2.** Historic building.

monumental, -aux, a. Monumental.

moquer (se), v.pr. **Se m. de,** to make fun of. **Vous vous moquez,** you're joking.

moquerie, s.f Mockery; derision.

moqueur, -euse. 1. a. Mocking. **2.** s. Mocker, scoffer.

moral, -aux. 1. a. (a) Moral. (b) Mental, intellectual. **2.** s.m. (State of) mind; morale.

morale, s.f. **1.** (a) Morals. (b) Ethics **2.** Moral.

moralement, adv. Morally.

moraliser, v.i. To moralize.

moraliste, s.m. & f. Moralist.

moralité, s.f. (a) Morality. (b) Morals; honesty.

morbide, a. Morbid.

morbidement, adv. Morbidly.

morbidité, s.f. Morbidity.

morceau, s.m. **1.** Morsel, piece. **2.** Piece; bit, scrap.

morceler, v.tr To parcel out.

mordant. 1. a. Mordant, biting. **2.** s.m. (a) Bite (b) Mordancy, pungency.

mordre, v.tr. & ind.tr. To bite. (a) **M. à, dans,** to take a bite out of. (b) To catch, engage.

morfondre (se), v.pr. To be bored.

morgue, s.f **1.** Pride, arrogance. **2.** Mortuary, morgue.

moribond, a. Moribund.

morigéner, v.tr. To lecture.

morne, a. Dejected; gloomy; dull.

morose, a. Morose, moody.

morphine, s.f. Morphia.

mors, s.m. **1.** Jaw (of vice). **2.** Harn: Bit.

morse¹, s.m. Walrus.

Morse². Pr.n.m. Morse.

morsure, s.f. Bite.

mort¹. 1. See MOURIR **2.** a. Dead. **3.** s Dead person; deceased. **4.** s.m. Cards: Dummy.

mort², s.f. Death.

mortalité, s.f. Mortality.

mortel, a. & s. Mortal.

mortellement, *adv.* Mortally.

mortier, *s.m.* Mortar.

mortifiant, *a.* Mortifying.

mortification, *s.f.* Mortification.

mortifier, *v.tr.* To mortify.

mortuaire, *a.* Mortuary. **Drap m.,** pall.

morue, *s.f.* Cod.

mosaïque, *s.f.* Mosaic.

Moscou. *Pr.n.* Moscow.

mosquée, *s.f* Mosque.

mot, *s.m.* Word. **Au bas mot,** at the lowest estimate. **Écrire un mot à qn,** to drop s.o. a line. **Bon mot,** witty remark.

moteur, -trice. 1. *a.* Motive, driving. **2.** *s.m.* Motor, engine.

motif, *s.m.* (*a*) Motive. incentive; reason. (*b*) Motif.

motion, *s.f.* Motion, proposal.

motiver, *v.tr.* **1.** To state the reason for. **2.** To justify, warrant.

motocyclette, *s.f.* Motor (bi)cycle.

motocycliste, *s.* Motor cyclist.

motte, *s.f.* **1.** Mound. **2.** Clod, lump; sod, turf.

mou, mol, *f.* **molle. 1.** *a.* Soft; slack; weak, flabby. **2.** *s.m.* Slack.

mouchard, *s.m.* Sneak, informer.

mouche, *s.f.* **1.** Fly. **Prendre la m.,** to take offence. **Quelle m. vous pique?** what is the matter with you? **2.** (*a*) Spot, speck. (*b*) Bull's-eye. **3.** River steamer.

moucher (se), *v.pr.* To wipe, blow, one's nose.

moucheron, *s.m.* Midge.

moucheter, *v.tr.* To spot, speckle.

moucheture, *s.f.* Spot, speck, fleck.

mouchoir, *s.m.* Handkerchief.

moudre, *v.tr.* To grind.

moue, *s.f* Pout.

mouette, *s.f.* Sea-gull.

mouillage [-ja:ʒ], *s.m.* **1.** (*a*) Anchoring. (*b*) Laying (of mine). **2.** Anchorage.

mouillé [muje], *a.* **1.** Moist, damp, wet. **Poule mouillée,** milksop. **2.** At anchor.

mouiller [muje], *v.tr.* **1.** To wet, moisten. **2.** (*a*) To anchor. (*b*) To lay (mine).

moule[1], *s.m.* Mould; matrix.

moule[2], *s.f.* Mussel.

mouler, *v.tr* To cast; to mould.

moulin, *s.m.* Mill. **M. à vent,** windmill.

moulu, *a.* Ground, powdered.

moulure, *s.f.* Moulding.

mourant. 1. *a.* Dying. **2.** *s.* Dying person.

mourir, *v.i.* To die. **Il est mort hier,** he died yesterday.

mousquetaire, *s.m.* Musketeer.

mousse[1], *s.f.* **1.** Moss. **2.** Froth, foam; lather.

mousse[2], *s.m.* Ship's boy.

mousseline, *s.f.* Muslin.

mousser, *v.i.* To froth; to lather.

mousseux, *a.* **1.** Mossy. **2.** (*a*) Frothy. (*b*) Sparkling (wine).

moustache, *s.f.* (*a*) Moustache. (*b*) Whiskers (of cat).

moustiquaire, *s.f.* Mosquito-net.

moustique, *s.m.* (*a*) Mosquito. (*b*) Gnat.

moutard, *s.m.* (*a*) Urchin. (*b*) Brat.

moutarde, *s.f* Mustard.

mouton, *s.m.* **1.** Sheep. **2.** Mutton. **3.** *pl.* White horses (on sea).

moutonné, *a.* Fleecy (sky).

mouvant, *a.* (*a*) Mobile. (*b*) **Sable m.,** quicksand.

mouvement, *s.m.* Movement. **1.** Motion. **Se mettre en m.,** to start off. **2.** (*a*) Change, modification. **Être dans le m.,** to be in the swim. (*b*) Agitation. (*c*) Impulse. **3.** Traffic. **Mouvements des trains,** train arrivals and departures. **4.** Action. **M. d'horlogerie,** clock-work.

mouvementé, *a.* **1.** Animated, lively. **2.** Terrain m., undulating ground.

mouvoir, *v.tr.* **1.** To move. **2.** To drive; to propel.

se mouvoir, to move, stir.

moyen[1]. **1.** *a.* (*a*) Middle. (*b*) Average, mean. (*c*) Medium. **2.** *s.f.* Moyenne, average.

moyen[2], *s.m.* Means. **Au m. de,** by means of. **Y a-t-il m. de le faire?** is it possible to do it?

moyennant, *prep.* On condition. **M. finances,** for a consideration.

moyeu, -eux, *s.m.* Hub.

muable, *a.* Changeable mutable.

mue, *s.f.* **1.** Moulting; shedding of antlers or skin. **2.** Breaking of voice.

muer, *v.i.* (*a*) To moult; to shed the skin or antlers. (*b*) (Of voice) To break.

muet, -ette. 1. *a.* Dumb, mute. (*a*) Speechless. (*b*) **Rester m.,** to remain silent. **2.** *s.* Dumb person.

mufle, *s.m.* Muzzle ; snout.

mugir, *v.i.* (*a*) To low ; to bellow. (*b*) To roar ; to boom.

mugissement, *s.m.* (*a*) Lowing ; bellowing. (*b*) Roaring. booming.

muguet [-gɛ], *s.m.* Lily of the valley.

mulâtre, *a. & s.* Mulatto.

mule¹, *s.f.* (She-)mule.

mule², *s.f.* Bedroom slipper.

mulet, *s.m.* (He-)mule.

muletier, *s.m.* Muleteer.

mulot, *s.m.* Field-mouse.

multicolore, *a.* Multi-coloured.

multiple. **1.** *a.* Multiple, manifold. **2.** *s.m.* Multiple.

multiplication, *s.f.* Multiplication.

multiplicité, *s.f.* Multiplicity.

multiplié, *a.* Multiple ; manifold.

multiplier, *v.tr. & i.* To multiply. **se multiplier.** (*a*) To multiply. (*b*) To be here, there, and everywhere.

multitude, *s.f.* Multitude ; crowd.

municipal, -aux, *a.* Municipal.

municipalité, *s.f.* Municipality.

munificence, *s.f.* Munificence.

munificent, *a.* Munificent.

munir, *v.tr.* To furnish, equip.

munitions, *s.f.pl.* Stores, supplies.

mur, *s.m.* Wall. **Mettre au pied du mur,** to drive into a corner.

mûr, *a.* Ripe ; mellow ; mature.

muraille [-ra:j], *s.f.* Wall.

mûre, *s.f.* **1.** Mulberry. **2. M. (de ronce),** blackberry.

mûrement, *adv.* With mature consideration.

murer, *v.tr.* To wall in ; to wall up.

mûrier, *s.m.* Mulberry(-tree).

mûrir, *v.tr. & i.* To ripen, mature.

murmure, *s.m.* Murmur, murmuring.

murmurer, *v.tr. & i.* (*a*) To murmur. (*b*) To grumble.

musc [mysk], *s.m.* Musk.

muscade, *s.f.* Nutmeg.

muscle, *s.m.* Muscle.

musclé, *a.* Muscular ; brawny.

musculeux, *a.* Muscular, brawny.

muse, *s.f.* Muse.

museau, *s.m.* Muzzle, snout.

musée, *s.m.* (*a*) Museum. (*b*) **M. de peinture,** picture-gallery.

museler, *v.tr.* To muzzle.

muselière, *s.f.* Muzzle.

musette, *s.f.* Haversack.

musical, -aux, *a.* Musical.

musicalement, *adv.* Musically.

musicien, *a. & s.* **1.** Musician. **2.** Bandsman.

musique, *s.f.* **1.** Music. **2.** Band.

musulman, *a. & s.* Moslem.

mutable, *a.* Changeable, mutable.

mutation, *s.f.* Change, alteration.

mutilation, *s.f.* (*a*) Mutilation, maiming. (*b*) Defacement.

mutilé, *a. & s.* **Mutilés de guerre,** disabled ex-service men.

mutiler, *v.tr.* (*a*) To mutilate, maim. (*b*) To deface.

mutin. **1.** *a.* (*a*) Insubordinate ; unruly. (*b*) Roguish. **2.** *s.m.* Mutineer.

mutiner (se), *v.pr.* To rise in revolt ; to mutiny, to rebel.

mutisme, *s.m.* Dumbness, muteness.

mutuel, *a.* Mutual.

mutuellement, *adv.* Mutually.

myope, *a. & s.* Short-sighted (person).

myopie, *s.f.* Short-sightedness.

myosotis [-tis], *s.m.* Forget-me-not.

myriade, *s.f.* Myriad.

myrrhe, *s.f.* Myrrh.

myrte, *s.m.* Myrtle.

myrtille [-ti:j], *s.f.* Bilberry.

mystère, *s.m.* Mystery.

mystérieusement, *adv.* Mysteriously.

mystérieux, *a.* Mysterious.

mystification, *s.f.* (*a*) Mystification. (*b*) Hoax.

mystifier, *v.tr.* (*a*) To mystify. (*b*) To hoax.

mystique, *a. & s.* Mystic.

mythe, *s.m.* Myth, legend.

mythique, *a.* Mythical.

mythologie, *s.f.* Mythology.

mythologique, *a.* Mythological.

N

N, n [ɛn], *s.f.* (The letter) N, n.

nacelle, *s.f.* **1.** Skiff, wherry. **2.** Cockpit (of aeroplane).

nacre, *s.f.* Mother of pearl.

nacré, *a.* Nacreous, pearly.

nage, *s.f.* **1.** Rowing, sculling. **2.** Swimming. **En n.,** bathed in perspiration.

nageoire, *s.f.* Fin.

nager, *v.i.* **1.** To row; to scull. **2.** To swim.

nageur, -euse, *s.* (a) Swimmer. (b) Oarsman; rower.

naguère [-gɛ:r], *adv.* Not long since.

naïf, *a.* **1.** Artless, ingenuous, naive. **2.** Simple-minded.

nain, *a. & s.* Dwarf.

naissance, *s.f.* Birth.

naître, *v.i.* (a) To be born. (b) To spring up, come up. (c) To originate, rise.

naïvement, *adv.* Artlessly, ingenuously; naively.

naïveté, *s.f.* (a) Artlessness, simplicity. (b) Guilelessness.

naphte, *s.m.* Naphtha.

nappe, *s.f.* **1.** (a) Table-cloth. (b) Cloth, cover. **2.** Sheet (of ice).

narcisse, *s.m.* Narcissus.

narcotique, *a. & s.m.* Narcotic.

narguer, *v.tr.* To flout.

narine, *s.f.* Nostril.

narquois, *a.* Quizzing, bantering.

narrateur, -trice, *s.* Narrator.

narratif, *a.* Narrative.

narration, *s.f.* **1.** Narrating, narration. **2.** Narrative.

narrer, *v.tr.* To narrate, relate.

nasal, -als, -aux, *a.* Nasal.

nasalement, *adv.* Nasally.

naseau, *s.m.* Nostril.

nasillard [-zij-], *a.* Ton n., twang; snuffle.

nasiller [-zije], *v.i.* To snuffle.

natal, -als, -aux, *a.* Native.

natalité, *s.f.* Birth-rate.

natation, *s.f.* Swimming.

natif. **1.** *a.* (a) Native. (b) Natural, inborn. **2.** *s.m.* Native.

nation, *s.f.* Nation.

national, -aux. **1.** *a.* National. **2.** *s.m.pl.* Nationals.

nationalité, *s.f.* Nationality.

natte, *s.f.* **1.** Mat, matting. **2.** Plait, braid.

naturalisation, *s.f.* Naturalization.

naturaliser, *v.tr.* To naturalize.

naturaliste, *s.* Naturalist.

nature, *s.f.* Nature. **1.** N. morte, still-life. **2.** (a) Kind, character. (b) Character, disposition. **3.** *a.inv.* Pommes n., plain boiled potatoes. Café n., plain black coffee.

naturel. **1.** *a.* Natural. (a) De grandeur naturelle, life-size. (b) Natural, unaffected. **2.** *s.m.* Native. **3.** *s.m.* Nature

naturellement, *adv.* Naturally.

naufrage, *s.m.* (Ship)wreck.

naufragé. **1.** *a.* (Ship)wrecked. **2.** *s.* Castaway.

nauséabond, *a.* Nauseous.

nausée, *s.f.* (a) Nausea. (b) Avoir des nausées, to feel squeamish.

nautique, *a.* Nautical.

naval, -als, *a.* Naval, nautical.

navarin, *s.m.* Haricot mutton.

navet, *s.m.* Turnip.

navette, *s.f.* Shuttle.

navigabilité, *s.f.* **1.** Navigability. **2.** Seaworthiness; airworthiness.

navigable, *a.* **1.** Navigable. **2.** Seaworthy; airworthy.

navigateur, *s.m.* Navigator.

navigation, *s.f.* Navigation. Compagnie de n., shipping company.

naviguer, *v.i.* To sail, navigate. **2.** *v.tr.* To navigate.

navire, *s.m.* Ship, vessel.

navrant, *a.* Heart-rending.

navré, *a.* Heart-broken; woe-begone; dreadfully sorry

navrer, *v.tr.* To grieve deeply.

nazi, *s.* Nazi.

nazisme, *s.m.* Naziism.

ne, *neg.adv.* Not. **1.** N'importe, it doesn't matter. **2.** Je n'ai que faire de, I don't need. **3.** (a) Je crains qu'il (ne) prenne froid, I am afraid he may catch cold. (b) A moins qu'on (ne) vous appelle, unless they call you.

néanmoins, *adv.* Nevertheless; for all that; yet; still.

néant, *s.m.* Nothingness, nought.

nébuleux. **1.** *a.* (a) Nebulous. (b) Cloudy, hazy.

nécessaire. **1.** *a.* Necessary, needful. **2.** *s.m.* (a) Necessaries, the needful. (b) Outfit. N. de toilette, dressing-case.

nécessairement, *adv.* Necessarily.

nécessité, *s.f.* Necessity; want.

nécessiter, *v.tr.* To necessitate.

nécessiteux, *a.* Needy, in want.

nectar, *s.m.* Nectar

nef [nef], *s.f.* Nave.

néfaste, *a.* Luckless, ill-omened.

nèfle, *s.f.* Medlar.

négatif. 1. *a. &* s.*m.* Negative.
2. *s.f.* Négative, negative.

négation, *s.f.* Negation, denial.

négativement, *adv.* Negatively.

négligé. 1. *a.* (*a*) Neglected. (*b*) Careless. **2.** *s.m.* Dishabille.

négligeable, *a.* Negligible.

négligemment, *adv.* **1.** Negligently, carelessly. **2.** Casually.

négligence, *s.f.* Negligence.

négligent, *a.* **1.** Negligent, careless ; neglectful. **2.** Indifferent.

négliger, *v.tr.* To neglect.
   se négliger, to neglect one's person.

négoce, *s.m.* Trade, business.

négociabilité, *s.f.* Negotiability.

négociable, *a.* Negotiable.

négociant, *s.* Merchant ; trader.

négociation, *s.f.* **1.** Negotiation. **2.** Transaction.

négocier, *v.tr.* To negotiate.

nègre, négresse, *s.* Negro, *f.* negress.

neige, *s.f.* Snow. **N. fondue,** sleet ; slush.

neiger, *v.impers.* To snow.

neigeux, *a.* Snowy ; snow-covered.

nénuphar, *s.m.* Water-lily.

néolithique, *a.* Neolithic.

néon, *s.m.* Neon.

néo-Zélandais, *s.* New Zealander.

népotisme, *s.m.* Nepotism.

nerf, *s.m.* **1.** Nerve. **Attaque de nerfs,** (fit of) hysterics. **2.** Sinew.

nerveusement, *adv.* **1.** Energetically. **2.** Impatiently, irritably.

nerveux, *a.* **1.** Nervous. **2.** Sinewy, wiry ; vigorous. **3.** Highly-strung.

nervosité, *s.f.* Irritability.

n'est-ce pas, *adv.phr.* Is it not so ?

net, nette [net], *a.* **1.** Clean, spotless. **2.** (*a*) Clear ; distinct. (*b*) **Poids net,** net weight. **3.** *adv.* Plainly, outright. **S'arrêter net,** to stop dead.

nettement, *adv.* **1.** (*a*) Cleanly. (*b*) Clearly. **2.** Plainly.

netteté, *s.f.* **1.** Cleanness ; cleanliness. **2.** Clearness ; distinctness.

nettoyage, *s.m.* Cleaning.

nettoyer, *v.tr.* To clean ; to scour.

neuf[1], *num. a. inv. &* s.*m. inv.* Nine.

neuf[2] [nœf]. **1.** *a.* New. **2.** *s.m.* Il y a du n., I have news for you. *Adv.phr.* **A** n., anew.

neutraliser, *v.tr.* To neutralize.

neutralité, *s.f.* Neutrality.

neutre. 1. *a.* Neuter. **2.** *a. &* s.*m.* Neutral.

neuvième. 1. *num. a. &* s. Ninth. **2.** *s.m.* Ninth (part).

neveu, -eux, *s.m.* Nephew.

névralgie, *s.f.* Neuralgia.

névrite, *s.f.* Neuritis.

névrosé, *a. &* s. Neurotic.

nez, *s.m.* Nose. (*a*) Sense of smell ; scent. (*b*) **Nez à nez,** face to face. **Rire au nez de qn,** to laugh in s.o.'s face.

ni, *conj.* Nor, or. (*a*) **Ni moi** (non plus), neither do I. (*b*) **Il ne mange ni ne boit,** he neither eats nor drinks. (*c*) **Ni . . . ni,** neither . . . nor.

niais. 1. *a.* Simple foolish. **2.** *s.* Fool, simpleton.

niaisement, *adv.* Foolishly.

niaiserie, *s.f.* **1.** Silliness. **2.** Nonsense.

niche[1], *s.f.* **1.** Niche, nook, recess. **2. N. à chien,** dog-kennel.

niche[2], *s.f.* Trick, prank.

nicher. 1. *v.i.* To build a nest ; to nest. **2.** *v.tr.* To put, lodge.

niçois, *a. &* s. (Native) of Nice.

nid, *s.m.* **1.** Nest. **2. Nid de pie,** crow's-nest.

nièce, *s.f.* Niece.

nier, *v.tr.* To deny.

nigaud. (*a*) *s.* Simpleton, booby. (*b*) *a.* Simple.

Nil (le) [lənil]. *Pr.n.m.* The Nile.

nimbe, *s.m.* Nimbus, halo.

nippes, *s.f.pl.* Garments.

nippon, -one, *a.* Japanese.

nitrate, *s.m.* Nitrate.

nitre, *s.m.* Nitre, saltpetre.

niveau, *s.m.* Level. **N. de vie,** standard of living. **Être au n. de,** to be on a par with.

niveler, *v.tr.* To level, to even up.

nivellement, *s.m.* Levelling.

noble, *a. &* s. Noble.

noblement, *adv.* Nobly.

noblesse, *s.f.* Nobility.

noce, *s.f.* **1.** (*a*) Wedding. (*b*) Wedding-party. (*c*) **Épouser qn en secondes noces,** to marry for the second time. **2. Faire la n.,** to go on the spree.

noceur, -euse, *s.* Fast liver.

nocif, *a.* Injurious, noxious.

nocturne. 1. *a.* Nocturnal. **2.** *s.m.* Nocturne.

Noé. *Pr.n.m.* Noah.

Noël, *s.m.* **1.** Christmas. **La nuit de N.,** Christmas Eve. **2.** Carol.

nœud, *s.m.* (*a*) Knot. (*b*) Crux. (*c*) *Cost:* Bow.

noir. 1. *a.* Black. (*a*) Dark, swarthy. (*b*) Dark; gloomy. **Il fait n.,** it is dark. **Bête noire,** pet aversion. **2.** *s.* Black (man, woman). **3.** *s.m.* **Broyer du n.,** to be in the dumps.

noirâtre, *a.* Blackish, darkish.

noiraud, *a.* Swarthy.

noirceur, *s.f.* Blackness.

noircir. 1. *v.i.* To become black; to darken. **2.** *v.tr.* To blacken.

noircissement, *s,m,* Blackening.

noise, *s.f.* **Chercher n. à,** to try to pick a quarrel with.

noisetier, *s.m.* Hazel(-tree).

noisette. 1. *s.f.* Hazel-nut. **2.** *a.inv.* Hazel.

noix, *s.f.* **1.** Walnut. **2.** Nut.

nom, *s.m.* **1.** Name. **Nom de famille,** surname. **Nom et prénoms,** full name. **2.** Noun.

nomade. 1. *a.* Nomadic. **2.** *s.* Nomad.

nombre, *s.m.* Number. **N. de** a good many.

nombrer, *v.tr.* To number, reckon.

nombreux, *a.* Numerous.

nombril, *s.m.* Navel.

nominal, -aux, *a.* Nominal. **Valeur nominale,** face-value.

nominalement, *adv.* Nominally.

nominateur, *s.m.* Nominator.

nominatif, *a. & s.m.* Nominative.

nomination, *s.f.* **1.** Nomination. **2.** Appointment.

nommer, *v.tr.* **1.** To name. **2.** To mention by name. **3.** To appoint. **se nommer,** to be called, named.

non, *adv.* No; not. **Je pense que non,** I think not. **Faire signe que non,** to shake one's head.

nonagénaire, *a. & s.* Nonagenarian.

nonchalamment, *adv.* Nonchalantly.

nonchalance, *s.f.* Nonchalance.

nonchalant, *a.* Nonchalant.

non-lieu, *s.m.* No ground for action.

nonne, *s.f.* Nun.

nonobstant [-ops-]. **1.** *prep.* Notwithstanding. **2.** *adv.* Nevertheless.

non-sens [-sã:s], *s.m.inv.* Meaningless sentence or action.

non-valeur, *s.f.* Inefficient employee. *pl. non-valeurs.*

nord, *s.m.* **1.** North. **La mer du N.,** the North Sea. **L'Amérique du N.,** North America. **2.** *a.inv* North, northern.

nord-est, *s.m.* North-east.

nord-ouest, *s.m.* North-west.

normal, -aux. 1. *a.* (*a*) Normal. **École normale,** training college. (*b*) Standard. **2.** *s.f.* **Normale,** normal.

normalement, *adv.* Normally.

normand, *a. & s.* Norman. **Les îles Normandes,** the Channel Islands.

Normandie. *Pr.n.f.* Normandy.

norme, *s.f.* Norm, standard.

Norvège. *Pr.n.f.* Norway.

norvégien. 1. *a. & s.* Norwegian. **2.** *s.m.* Norwegian.

nos. See NOTRE.

nostalgie, *s.f.* Home-sickness.

notabilité, *s.f.* Notability.

notable, *a. & s.m.* Notable.

notablement, *adv.* Notably.

notaire, *s.m.* Notary.

notamment, *adv.* (*a*) More particularly; especially. (*b*) Among others.

note, *s.f.* **1.** Note; memorandum, minute. **2.** Mark. **3.** Bill account.

noter, *v.tr.* **1.** To note; to take notice of. **2.** To put down, jot down.

notice, *s.f.* Notice, account.

notification, *s.f.* Notification.

notifier, *v.tr.* To notify; to intimate.

notion, *s.f.* Notion, idea.

notoire, *a.* Well-known; notorious.

notoirement, *adv.* Notoriously.

notoriété, *s.f.* Notoriety; repute.

notre, *pl.* **nos,** *poss.a.* Our.

nôtre. 1. *poss.pron.* Ours; our own. **2.** *s.m.* Our own.

nouer, *v.tr.* **1.** To tie, knot. **2. N. conversation,** to enter into conversation.

noueux, *a.* Knotty; gnarled.

nouilles [nu:j], *s.f.pl.* Noodle(s).

nourri, *a.* **1.** Nourished, fed. **2.** Rich; full.

nourrice, *s.f.* (Wet-)nurse.

nourricier, *s.* (Père) n., foster-father.

nourrir, *v.tr.* To nourish. **1. To nurture. 2.** To feed. **3.** To harbour; to cherish.

nourrissant, *a.* Nourishing.

nourrisson, *s.* **1.** Infant. **2.** Foster-child.

nourriture, *s.f.* **1.** Food, nourishment. **2.** Board, keep.

nous, *pers.pron.* **1.** (*a*) We. (*b*) Us; to us. (*c*) Ourselves. (*d*) Each other. **2. N. autres Anglais,** we English. **A n.,** ours.

nous-mêmes, *pers.pron.pl.* Ourselves.

nouveau, -el, -elle, -eaux, *a.* **1.** New. *s.m.* **J'ai appris du n.,** I have some news. **2.** (*a*) New, recent, fresh. (*b*) Newly, recently. **N. riche,** upstart. **3.** Another, further. **4. De n.,** again, afresh. **A n.,** anew, afresh.

nouveau-né, *a.* & *s.* New-born (child). *pl. nouveau-né(e)s.*

nouveauté, *s.f.* **1.** Newness, novelty. **2.** Change, innovation. **3.** *pl.* Fancy goods. **Marchand de nouveautés,** linen-draper.

nouvel, -elle[1]. See NOUVEAU.

nouvelle[2], *s.f.* **1.** (*a*) (Piece of) news. (*b*) *pl.* **Envoyez-moi de vos nouvelles,** let me hear from you. **2.** Novelette; short story.

nouvellement, *adv.* Newly, lately.

Nouvelle-Zélande. *Pr.n.f.* New Zealand.

novembre, *s.m.* November.

novice, *s.m.* & *f.* Novice; tyro.

noyade, *s.f.* Drowning (fatality).

noyau, -aux, *s.m.* **1.** Stone (of fruit); kernel. **2.** Nucleus.

noyé, *a.* Drowned.

noyer[1], *s.m.* Walnut(-tree).

noyer[2], *v.tr.* To drown. **Yeux noyés de larmes,** eyes filled with tears.
    se noyer. (*a*) To drown oneself. (*b*) To be drowned.

nu. 1. *a.* (*a*) Naked; bare; nude. **Aller les pieds nus, aller nu-pieds,** to go bare-footed. (*b*) Uncovered, plain. **2. Mettre à nu,** to lay bare, expose.

nuage, *s.m.* (*a*) Cloud. (*b*) Mist (before the eyes).

nuageux, *a.* Cloudy; overcast.

nuance, *s.f.* Shade; hue.

nudiste, *s.m.* & *f.* Nudist.

nudité, *s.f.* Nudity, nakedness.

nuée, *s.f.* (*a*) Cloud. (*b*) Swarm.

nues, *s.f.pl.* Skies. **Tomber des n.,** to be thunderstruck.

nuire, *v.ind.tr.* To be hurtful; to do harm.

nuisible, *a.* Hurtful, harmful.

nuit, *s.f.* Night. (*a*) **Cette n.,** (i) to-night; (ii) last night. (*b*) **De n.,** by night. (*c*) Darkness. **Il se fait n.,** it is growing dark. **A la n. tombante,** at nightfall. **A (la) n. close,** after dark.

nuitamment, *adv.* By night.

nul, nulle. 1. (*a*) *ind.f. a.* No; not one. (*b*) *ind.f.pron.* No one; no-body. **2.** *a.* Null and void. **Partie nulle,** drawn game.

nullement, *adv.* Not at all.

nullifier, *v.tr.* To nullify.

nullité, *s.f.* **1.** Nullity, invalidity. **2.** Incompetence; incapacity.

numéral, -aux, *a.* & *s.m.* Numeral.

numérique, *a.* Numerical.

numériquement, *adv.* Numerically.

numéro, *s.m.* Number.

numéroter, *v.tr.* To number.

nuptial, -aux, *a.* Nuptial, bridal.

nuque, *s.f.* Nape of the neck.

nutritif, *a.* Nutritious, nourishing.

nutrition, *s.f.* Nutrition.

nymphe, *s.f.* Nymph.

O

O, o [o], *s.m.* (The letter) O, o.

ô, *int.* O! oh!

oasis, *s.f.* Oasis.

obéir, *v.ind.tr.* To obey. **O. à,** to obey. *v.tr.* **Se faire o.,** to enforce obedience.

obéissance, *s.f.* Obedience.

obéissant, *a.* Obedient, dutiful.

obélisque, *s.m.* Obelisk.

obèse, *a.* Obese, fat, corpulent.

obésité, *s.f.* Obesity, corpulence.

objecter, *v.tr.* To object.

objectif. 1. *a.* Objective. **2.** *s.m.*

Aim, object(ive), end. **3.** *s.m.* Lens.

objection, *s.f.* Objection.

objet, *s.m.* **1.** Object, thing. **2.** Object, aim, purpose.

obligation, *s.f.* **1.** Obligation; duty. **2.** Bond, debenture. **3.** Obligation, favour.

obligatoire, *a.* Obligatory; compulsory, binding.

obligé, *a.* (*a*) Obliged, compelled. (*b*) Grateful.

obligeamment, *adv.* Obligingly.

obligeance, *s.f.* Obligingness.
obligeant, *a.* Obliging ; kind.
obliger, *v.tr.* **1.** To oblige, compel.
2. O. qn, o oblige s.o.
  s'obliger, to bind oneself ; to
undertake.
oblique, *a.* Oblique.
obliquement, *adv.* Obliquely.
oblitération, *s.f.* Obliteration.
oblitérer, *v.tr.* To obliterate.
oblong, -ongue, *a.* Oblong.
obscène [ɔp-], *a.* Obscene ; lewd.
obscénité [ɔp-], *s.f.* Obscenity.
obscur [ɔp-], *a.* **1.** Dark. **2.** Obscure ;
dim.
obscurcir [ɔp-], *v.tr.* To obscure ;
to dim.
  s'obscurcir, to grow dark ; to
become dim.
obscurcissement [ɔp-], *s.m.* Darkening ; growing dimness.
obscurément [ɔp-], *adv.* Obscurely
dimly.
obscurité [ɔp-], *s.f.* Obscurity.
obséder [ɔp-] *v.tr.* (*a*) To beset.
(*b*) To obsess.
obsèques [ɔp-], *s.f.pl.* Obsequies.
obséquieusement [ɔp-], *adv.* Obsequiously.
obséquieux [ɔp-], *a.* Obsequious.
observance [ɔp-], *s.f.* Observance.
observateur, -trice [ɔp-]. **1.** *s.*
Observer. **2.** *a.* Observant, observ-
ing.
observation [ɔp-], *s.f.* **1.** Observance. **2.** Observation ; remark.
observatoire [ɔp-], *s.m.* Observatory.
observer [ɔp-], *v.tr.* To observe.
(*a*) To keep (to), to comply with
(*b*) To watch. (*c*) To notice.
obsession [ɔp-], *s.f.* Obsession.
obstacle [ɔp-], *s.m.* Obstacle.
obstination [ɔp-], *s.f.* Obstinacy,
stubbornness.
obstiné [ɔp-], *a.* Stubborn, obstinate.
obstinément [ɔp-], *adv.* Obstinately,
stubbornly.
obstiner (s') [ɔp-], *v.pr.* To persist
(*d*, in).
obstructif [ɔp-], *a.* Obstructive.
obstruction [ɔp-], *s.f.* Obstruction.
obstruer [ɔp-], *v.tr.* To obstruct.
obtenir [ɔp-], *v.tr.* To obtain, get ;
to gain, procure.
obturer [ɔp-], *v.tr.* To stop (tooth).
obtus [ɔp-], *a.* **1.** Blunt. **2.** Obtuse.

obus [ɔby(:)s], *s.m.* Shell.
obvier, *v.ind.tr.* O. à, to obviate.
occasion, *s.f.* **1.** (*a*) Opportunity,
occasion, chance. (*b*) Bargain. D'o.,
second-hand. **2.** Occasion. Pour l'o.,
for the nonce. **3.** Reason, occasion.
occasionnel, *a.* Occasional.
occasionnellement, *adv.* Occasionally.
occasionner, *v.tr.* To cause.
occident, *s.m.* West.
occidental, -aux, *a.* West(ern).
occulte, *a.* Occult ; hidden.
occupant, *s.* Occupant.
occupation, *s.f.* Occupation.
occupé, *a.* Busy ; engaged ; taken.
occuper, *v.tr.* To occupy.
  s'occuper. 1. To keep oneself
busy. **2.** Je m'en occuperai, I shall
see to it.
occurrence, *s.f.* Occurrence event.
océan, *s.m.* Ocean.
océanique, -e, *a.* Oceanic.
ocre, *s.f.* Ochre.
octave, *s.f.* Octave.
octobre, *s.m.* October.
octogénaire, *a. & s.* Octogenarian.
octogonal, -aux, *a.* Octagonal.
octogone, *s.m.* Octagon.
octroi, *s.m.* (*a*) Town dues. (*b*) Toll-
house.
octroyer, *v.tr.* To grant.
oculaire. 1. *a.* Ocular. Témoin o.,
eyewitness. **2.** *s.m.* Eyepiece.
oculiste, *s.m.* Oculist.
ode, *s.f.* Ode.
odeur, *s.f.* **1.** Odour, smell. **2.** Scent.
odieusement, *adv.* Odiously, hate-
fully.
odieux, *a.* Odious ; hateful.
odorant, *a.* Odorous.
odorat, *s.m.* (Sense of) smell.
œil [œ:j], *pl.* **yeux,** *s.m.* **1.** Eye.
Ouvrir de grands yeux, to open
one's eyes wide. Cela saute aux
yeux, it is obvious. **2.** Sight, look,
eye. Chercher des yeux, to look
about for. A vue d'œil visibly.
Coup d'œil, glance.
œillade [œjad], *s.f.* Glance, ogle.
œillet [œjɛ], *s.m.* **1.** Eyelet. **2.** Pink,
O. de poète, sweet-william.
œuf [œf], *pl.* **œufs** [ø], *s.m.* (*a*) Egg.
Œuf mollet, soft-boiled egg. Œuf
sur le plat, fried egg. (*b*) *pl.* Roe.
œuvre, *s.f.* **1.** (*a*) Work, working.

(b) Œ. de bienfaisance, charitable institution. 2. Work, production.

offensant, a. Offensive, insulting.

offense, s.f. 1. Offence. 2. Sin, trespass.

offenser, v.tr. 1. To offend. 2. (a) To injure. (b) To shock.
s'offenser, to take offence (de, at).

offensif. 1. a. Offensive. 2. s.f. L'offensive, the offensive.

offensivement, adv. Offensively.

offertoire, s.m. Offertory.

office. 1. s.m. (a) Office, functions. (b) Service. (c) Divine Service. (d) Bureau, office. 2. s.f. Servants' hall.

officiel, a. Official; formal.

officiellement, adv. Officially.

officier¹, v.i. To officiate.

officier², s.m. Officer.

officieusement, adv. 1. Officiously. 2. Unofficially.

officieux. 1. a. (a) Officious. (b) Unofficial. 2. s. Busybody.

offrande, s.f. Offering.

offre, s.f. Offer, proposal; tender.

offrir, v.tr. To offer.
s'offrir. 1. To offer oneself. 2. To present itself.

offusquer, v.tr. To offend, shock.
s'offusquer, to take offence (de, at).

ogre, ogresse, s. Ogre; ogress.

oh, int. Oh! O!

ohé, int. Hi! ahoy!

oie, s.f. Goose.

oignon [ɔɲɔ̃], s.m. 1. (a) Onion. (b) Bulb. 2. Bunion.

oindre, v.tr. To anoint.

oiseau, s.m. Bird.

oiseau-mouche, s.m. Humming-bird. pl. oiseaux-mouches.

oiseux, a. Idle.

oisif. 1. a. Idle. 2. s. Idler.

oisillon [-zijɔ̃], s.m. Fledgling.

oisivement, adv. Idly.

oisiveté, s.f. Idleness.

oison, s.m. Gosling.

olive, s.f. Olive.

olivier, s.m. Olive-tree.

olympique, a. Olympic.

ombrage, s.m. 1. Shade. 2. Umbrage.

ombragé, a. Shaded, shady.

ombrager, v.tr. (a) To shade. (b) To overshadow.

ombrageux, a. 1. Shy, skittish (horse). 2. Easily offended; touchy.

ombre, s.f. 1. Shadow 2. Shade. 3. Darkness. 4. Ghost.

ombrelle, s.f. Parasol, sunshade.

omelette, s.f. Omelette

omettre, v.tr. To omit; to leave out.

omission, s.f. Omission.

omnibus [-byːs]. 1. s.m. Omnibus. 2. a.inv. Train o., slow train.

omnipotent, a. Omnipotent.

omnivore, a. Omnivorous.

omoplate, s.f. Shoulder-blade.

on, indef.pron. One, people, they, we, etc. On dit, it is said. On frappe, there is a knock at the door.

oncle, s.m. Uncle.

onction, s.f. Unction.

onctueusement, adv. Unctuously.

onctueux, a. Unctuous.

onde, s.f. Wave.

ondée, s.f. Heavy shower.

on-dit, s.m.inv. Rumour, hearsay.

ondoyant, a. Undulating, wavy.

ondulation, s.f. 1. Undulation. 2. Hairdr: Wave.

ondulé, a. Undulating; wavy; corrugated.

onduler. 1. v.i. To undulate, ripple. 2. v.tr. Se faire o., to have one's hair waved.

onduleux, a. Wavy, sinuous.

onéreux, a. Onerous.

ongle, s.m. (Finger-)nail; claw. Coup d'o., scratch.

onguent [ɔ̃gã], s.m Ointment, salve.

ont. See AVOIR.

onze, num. a. inv. & s.m. inv. Eleven. Le o. avril, the eleventh of April.

onzième. 1. num. a. & s. Eleventh. 2. s.m. Eleventh (part)

opale, s.f. Opal.

opaque, a. Opaque.

opéra, s.m. Opera.

opérateur, -trice, s. Operator.

opératif, a. Operative.

opération, s.f. 1. Operation; working; process. 2. Transaction.

opérer, v.tr. To operate. 1. To bring about. 2. (a) To carry out, perform. (b) Se faire o., to undergo an operation. 3. Abs. To work, act.
s'opérer, to take place.

opérette, s.f. Operetta; musical comedy.

opiat, s.m. Opiate narcotic.

opiner, v.i. To be of opinion.

opiniâtre, a. Obstinate.

opiniâtrement, *adv.* Obstinately; doggedly.

opiniâtreté, *s.f.* Obstinacy.

opinion, *s.f.* Opinion; view.

opium [-jɔm], *s.m.* Opium.

opossum [-sɔm], *s.m.* Opossum.

opportun, *a.* (*a*) Opportune, timely. (*b*) Expedient.

opportunément, *adv.* Opportunely.

opportunité, *s.f.* (*a*) Opportuneness. (*b*) Expediency.

opposé. 1. *a.* Opposed, opposing; opposite. **2.** *s.m.* Contrary.

opposer, *v.tr.* **1.** To oppose. O. une vigoureuse résistance, to offer a vigorous resistance. **2.** To compare; to contrast (*à*, with).

    s'opposer à to oppose.

opposition, *s.f.* **1.** Opposition. **2.** Contrast.

oppresser, *v.tr.* To oppress; to weigh down.

oppresseur, *s.m.* Oppressor.

oppressif, *a.* Oppressive.

oppression, *s.f.* Oppression.

opprimé, *a.* Oppressed down-trodden.

opprimer, *v.tr.* To oppress, crush.

opprobre, *s.m.* Opprobrium.

opter, *v.i.* O. pour, to decide in favour of.

opticien, *s.m.* Optician.

optimisme, *s.m.* Optimism.

optimiste. 1. *a.* Optimistic; sanguine. **2.** *s.* Optimist.

option, *s.f.* Option, choice.

optique. 1. *a.* Optical. **2.** *s.f.* Optics.

opulence, *s.f.* Opulence, affluence.

opulent, *a.* Opulent, rich; affluent.

or¹, *s.m.* Gold.

or², *conj.* Now. **Or donc,** well then.

oracle, *s.m.* Oracle.

orage, *s.m.* Storm.

orageusement, *adv.* Stormily.

orageux, *a.* Stormy.

oraison, *s.f.* **1.** O funèbre, funeral oration. **2.** Prayer.

oral, -aux, *a.* Oral; verbal.

oralement, *adv.* Orally, by word of mouth.

orange, *s.f.* **1.** Orange. **2.** *s.m.* Orange (colour).

oranger, *s.m.* Orange-tree.

orateur, *s.m.* Orator, speaker.

oratoire, *a.* Oratorical.

oratorio, *s.m.* Oratorio.

orbe, *s.m.* Orb; globe; sphere.

orbite, *s.f.* Orbit.

orchestral, -aux [-kɛs-], *a.* Orchestral.

orchestre [-kɛs-], *s.m.* Orchestra.

orchidée [-ki-], *s.f.* Orchid.

ordinaire. 1. *a.* Ordinary, usual, common. **Vin o.,** table wine. **2.** *s.m.* Wont, custom. **D'o.,** usually.

ordinairement, *adv.* Ordinarily.

ordonnance, *s.f.* **1.** Order. **2.** Officier d'o., aide-de-camp. **3.** (*a*) Orderly. (*b*) Batman. **4.** Prescription.

ordonné, *a.* Orderly.

ordonner, *v.tr.* **1.** To arrange. **2.** To order, command; to prescribe.

ordre, *s.m.* Order. **1.** Homme d'o., orderly man. **2.** O. public, law and order. **3.** (*a*) Order; class. **De premier o.,** first-rate. (*b*) Decoration; order. **4.** (*a*) Command; warrant. (*b*) Billet à o., promissory note.

ordure, *s.f.* **1.** Dirt filth. **2.** *pl.* Refuse.

orée, *s.f.* Edge, verge.

oreille [ɔrɛːj], *s.f.* Ear. **1.** Baisser l'o., to be crestfallen. **2.** Souffler à l'o. de, to whisper to. **Faire la sourde o.,** to turn a deaf ear.

oreiller [ɔrɛje], *s.m.* Pillow.

orfèvre, *s.m.* Goldsmith.

orfraie, *s.f.* Osprey.

organe, *s.m.* **1.** Organ. **2.** Agent, means, medium.

organique, *a.* Organic.

organiquement, *adv.* Organically.

organisateur, -trice, *s.* Organizer.

organisation, *s.f.* Organization.

organiser, *v.tr.* To organize.

organisme, *s.m.* Organism; system.

organiste, *s.m. & f.* Organist.

orge. 1. *s.f.* Barley. **2.** *s.m.* O. perlé, pearl-barley.

orgie, *s.f.* Orgy.

orgue [ɔrg], *s.m.* **1.** Organ. **2.** O. de Barbarie, barrel-organ.

orgueil [-gœːj], *s.m.* Pride.

orgueilleusement [-gœj-]. *adv.* Proudly.

orgueilleux [-gœj-], *a.* Proud.

orient, *s.m.* Orient, East.

oriental, -aux, *a.* Eastern, oriental.

orienter, *v.tr.* **1.** To direct, guide. **2.** To take the bearings of.

    s'orienter, to take one's bearings

orifice, *s.m.* Aperture, opening.

originaire, *a.* Originating; native.

originairement, *adv.* Originally.

original, -aux, *a.* 1. Original. 2. (*a*) Novel, fresh. (*b*) Odd.

originalité, *s.f.* (*a*) Originality. (*b*) Eccentricity, oddity.

origine, *s.f.* Origin. 1. Beginning. 2. Source, derivation.

originel, *a.* Primordial, original.

originellement, *adv.* Originally.

oripeau, *s.m.* Tinsel.

orme, *s.m.* Elm.

ormeau, *s.m.* (Young) elm.

orné, *a.* Ornate.

ornement, *s.m.* Ornament. adornment, embellishment.

ornemental, -aux, *a.* Ornamental.

ornementation, *s.f.* Ornamentation.

ornementer, *v.tr.* To ornament.

orner, *v.tr.* To ornament. adorn.

ornière, *s.f.* Rut.

ornithologie, *s.f.* Ornithology.

orphelin, *s.* Orphan.

orphelinat, *s.m.* Orphanage.

orteil [-tɛːj], *s.m.* Toe.

orthodoxe, *a.* Orthodox.

orthodoxie, *s.f.* Orthodoxy.

orthographe, *s.f.* Orthography, spelling.

orthographier, *v.tr.* To spell.

ortie, *s.f.* Nettle. **O. brûlante,** stinging nettle.

os [ɔs; *pl.* o], *s.m.* Bone. **Trempé jusqu'aux os,** wet through.

oscillant, *a.* Oscillating; rocking.

oscillation, *s.f.* Oscillation. (*a*) Swing. (*b*) Rocking. (*c*) Vibration.

osciller, *v.i.* To oscillate. 1. To swing; to rock. 2. To waver.

osé, *a.* Bold, daring.

oseille [ozɛːj], *s.f.* Sorrel.

oser, *v.tr.* To dare, venture.

osier, *s.m.* Osier, water-willow. **Panier d'o.,** wicker-basket.

ossature, *s.f.* Frame.

osselet, *s.m.* Knuckle-bone.

ossements, *s.m.pl.* Bones, remains.

osseux, *a.* Bony.

ossuaire, *s.m.* Ossuary.

ostensible, *a.* Patent to all.

ostensiblement, *adv.* Openly.

ostentation, *s.f.* Ostentation, show.

ostraciser, *v.tr.* To ostracize.

ostracisme, *s.m.* Ostracism.

otage, *s.m.* Hostage.

otarie, *s.f.* Sea-lion.

ôter, *v.tr.* To remove, take away; to take off.

ou, *conj.* Or. **Ou . . ou . .,** either . . . or . . . .

où, *adv.* 1. Where? **D'où?** whence? **D'où vient?** how does it happen? **Jusqu'où?** how far? 2. (*a*) Where. **N'importe où,** anywhere. **Partout où il va,** wherever he goes. (*b*) When. (*c*) In which, at which. 3. **Où que vous soyez,** wherever you may be.

ouate, *s.f.* (*a*) Wadding. (*b*) Cotton-wool.

ouaté, *a.* 1. Padded; quilted. 2. Fleecy; soft (footstep).

ouater, *v.tr.* To pad; to quilt.

oubli, *s.m.* 1. (*a*) Forgetfulness. (*b*) Oblivion. 2. Oversight.

oublier, *v.tr.* (*a*) To forget. (*b*) To overlook, neglect.
　s'oublier, to forget oneself.

oublieux, *a.* Forgetful.

Ouessant, *Pr.n.m.* Ushant.

ouest [wɛst]. 1. *s.m.* West. 2. *a.inv.* Western, west.

ouf [uf], *int.* Ah! ha!

oui, *adv.* Yes. **Je crois que oui,** I think so. **Faire signe que oui,** to nod assent. **Oui-dà!** yes, rather!

ouï-dire, *s.m.inv.* Hearsay.

ouïe, *s.f.* 1. (Sense of) hearing. 2. *pl.* Gills (of fish).

ouïr, *v.tr.* To hear.

ouragan, *s.m.* Hurricane.

Oural (l'), *Pr.n.* The Ural.

ourdir, *v.tr.* To hatch (plot).

ourler, *v.tr.* To hem.

ourlet, *s.m.* Hem.

ours [urs], *s.* Bear.

oursin, *s.m.* Sea-urchin.

ourson, *s.m.* Bear's cub.

outarde, *s.f.* Bustard.

outil [uti], *s.m.* Tool, implement.

outillage [-jaːʒ], *s.m.* Gear, plant.

outiller [-je], *v.tr.* To equip, supply.

outrage, *s.m.* Outrage.

outrageant, *a.* Insulting, outrageous.

outrager, *v.tr.* 1. To insult. 2. To outrage.

outrageusement, *adv.* Outrageously.

outrageux, *a.* Insulting, outrageous.

outrance, *s.f.* A o., to the bitter end. **Guerre à o.,** war to the knife.

outre[1], *s.f.* Leather bottle.

outre². **1.** *prep.* (a) Beyond. (b) In addition to. **2.** *adv.* (a) **Passer o.**, to proceed further. (b) **En o.**, besides.

outré, *a.* Beside oneself.

outrecuidance, *s.f* Presumptuousness.

outrecuidant, *a.* Presumptuous.

outremer, *s.m.* Ultramarine.

outre-mer, *adv.phr.* Overseas.

outrepasser, *v.tr.* To go beyond; to exceed.

outrer, *v.tr* **1.** To carry to excess; to overdo **2.** To provoke beyond measure.

ouvert, *a.* Open.

ouvertement, *adv.* Openly, frankly.

ouverture, *s.f.* **1.** (a) Opening. (b) Overture. (c) **Heures d'o.**, business hours; visiting hours.

ouvrable, *a.* **Jour o.**, working day.

ouvrage, *s.m.* **1.** (a) Work. (b) Workmanship. **2.** Piece of work; product. **Boîte à o.**, work-box.

ouvre-boîtes, *s.m.inv.* Tin-opener.

ouvreuse, *s.f.* Usherette.

ouvrier. **1.** *s.* (a) Worker; workman. (b) **Première ouvrière**, forewoman. **2.** *a.* Working; workman's.

ouvrir. **1.** *v.tr.* To open. (a) To turn on. (b) To open up (c) To begin. **2.** *v.i.* To open.
 s'ouvrir, to open; to unbosom oneself.

ovale, *a. & s.m.* Oval.

ovation, *s.f.* Ovation.

ovoïde, *a.* Ovoid, egg-shaped.

oxalique, *a.* Oxalic.

oxhydrique, *a.* **Lumière o.**, limelight.

oxyde, *s.m.* Oxide.

oxygène, *s.m.* Oxygen.

oxygéné, *a.* **Eau oxygénée**, peroxide of hydrogen.

ozone, *s.m.* Ozone.

P

P, p [pe], *s.m.* (The letter) P, p.

pacificateur, -trice. 1. *a.* Pacifying. **2.** *s.* Peacemaker.

pacification, *s.f.* Pacification.

pacifier, *v.tr.* To pacify; to appease.

pacifique, *a.* (a) Pacific, peaceable. (b) Peaceful, quiet.

pacifiquement, *adv.* Peaceably.

pacifiste, *s.m. & f.* Pacifist.

pacte, *s.m.* Compact, pact.

pactiser, *v.i.* To come to terms.

pagaie, *s.f.* Paddle.

paganisme, *s.m.* Paganism.

pagayer, *v.tr. & i.* To paddle.

page¹, *s.f.* Page. **A la p.**, up-to-date.

page², *s.m.* Page(-boy).

pagne, *s.m.* Loin-cloth.

pagode, *s.f.* Pagoda.

païen, *a. & s.* Pagan, heathen.

paillasse [-jas]. **1.** *s.f.* Straw mattress. **2.** *s.m.* Clown, buffoon.

paillasson [-jas-], *s.m.* (Door-)mat.

paille [pɑːj], *s.f.* Straw. (a) **Feu de p.**, flash in the pan. **Sur la p.**, in great want. (b) *a.inv.* Straw-coloured.

pailleté [paj-], *a.* Spangled.

paillette [-jɛt], *s.f.* Spangle.

pain, *s.m.* **1.** Bread. **2.** Loaf. (a) **Petit p.**, (French) roll. (b) **P. de savon**, cake of soap. **3. P. à cacheter**, (sealing) wafer.

pair. 1. *a.* (a) Equal. **De p.**, on a par. (b) Even (number). **2.** *s.m.* Equal; peer. **3.** *s.m.* Equality; par. **Au p.**, with board and lodging but no salary.

paire, *s.f.* Pair; brace.

pairesse, *s.f.* Peeress.

pairie, *s.f.* Peerage.

paisible, *a.* Peaceful, quiet.

paisiblement, *adv.* Peacefully, quietly.

paître. 1. *v.tr.* (a) To graze. (b) To feed upon. **2.** *v.i.* To graze.

paix, *s.f.* Peace.

palace, *s.m.* Sumptuous hotel or cinema.

palais¹, *s.m.* **1.** Palace. **2. P. de Justice**, law-courts.

palais², *s.m.* Palate.

pale, *s.f.* Blade (of oar).

pâle, *a.* Pale.

palefrenier, *s.m.* Groom, ostler.

palet, *s.m.* Quoit.

paletot, *s.m.* Overcoat, greatcoat.

palette, *s.f.* **1.** (Table-tennis) bat. **2.** Paddle. **3.** Palette.

palétuvier, *s.m.* Mangrove.

pâleur, *s.f.* Pallor, paleness.

palier, *s.m.* (*a*) Landing (of stairs). (*b*) Stage degree.

pâlir, *v.i.* To become pale; to fade.

palissade, *s.f.* (*a*) Palisade. (*b*) Stockade. (*c*) (Street) hoarding.

palliatif, *a. & s.m.* Palliative.

pallier, *v.tr.* To palliate.

palme, *s.f.* Palm(-branch). **Remporter la p.,** to bear the palm.

palmé, *a.* Web-footed.

palmier, *s.m.* Palm-tree.

palombe. *s.f* Ring-dove, woodpigeon.

palourde, *s.f.* Clam.

palpable, *a.* Palpable.

palper, *v.tr.* To feel; to finger.

palpitant, *a* Palpitating, throbbing. quivering; thrilling.

palpitation, *s.f.* Palpitation.

palpiter, *v.i.* To palpitate. (*a*) To quiver. (*b*) To throb. (*c*) To thrill.

pâmer, *v.i. & pr.* To swoon. **Se p.** **de joie,** to be overjoyed.

pâmoison, *s.f* Swoon; fainting fit.

pamplemousse, *s.m.* Grape-fruit.

pan¹, *s.m.* **1.** Skirt, flap; tail. **2. Pan de mur,** bare wall.

pan², *int.* Bang!

panacée, *s.f.* Panacea.

panache, *s.m.* (*a*) Plume. **P. de fumée,** wreath of smoke. (*b*) **Il a du p.,** he has an air about him.

panais, *s.m.* Parsnip.

panama, *s.m.* Panama hat.

pancarte, *s.f.* **1.** Placard bill. **2.** Jacket (for documents).

pandit, *s.m.* Pundit.

panégyrique, *s.m.* Panegyric.

panier, *s.m.* **1.** Basket. **2.** Ponycarriage.

panique. **1.** *a.* Panic. **2.** *s.f.* Panic, scare; stampede.

panne, *s.f.* Breakdown; hold-up.

panneau, *s.m.* Panel.

panoplie, *s.f.* Panoply.

panorama, *s.m.* Panorama.

panoramique, *a* Panoramic.

pansement, *s.m.* Dressing (of a wound).

panser, *v.tr* To dress (wound).

pantalon, *s.m.* (*a*) Trousers. (*b*) Knickers.

pantelant, *a.* Panting.

panteler, *v.i.* To pant.

panthère, *s.f.* Panther.

pantin, *s.m.* Nonentity; puppet.

pantomime, *s.f.* Pantomime.

pantoufle, *s.f.* Slipper.

paon [på], *s.m.* Peacock.

paonne [pan], *s.f* Peahen.

papa, *s.m.* Papa, dad(dy).

papal, -aux, *a.* Papal.

papauté, *s.f.* Papacy.

pape, *s.m.* Pope.

paperasse, *s.f.* Old archives.

paperasserie, *s.f.* Red tape.

papeterie, *s.f.* Stationer's shop.

papetier, *s* Stationer.

papier, *s.m* Paper. **1. P. à lettres,** note-paper **2.** Document. paper.

papillon [-pij-], *s.m.* **1.** Butterfly. **P. de nuit,** moth **2.** Inset (in book).

papillote [-pij-], *s.f.* **1.** Curl-paper. **2.** Twist of paper; frill.

papilloter [-pij-], *v.i.* To blink.

pâque. **1.** *s.f.* Passover. **2.** *s.m.* Pâques, Easter.

paquebot, *s.m.* Liner.

pâquerette, *s.f.* Daisy.

Pâques. See PÂQUE.

paquet, *s.m.* **1.** Parcel. packet. **2. P. de mer,** heavy sea.

par, *prep.* **1.** (*a*) By; through. **Par tout le pays,** all over the country. **Par ici,** this way. (*b*) **Par le froid qu'il fait,** in this cold weather. **2.** (*a*) Faire qch. par soi-même, to do sth. unaided. (*b*) **Par trop aimable,** far too kind. **3. Par pitié!** for pity's sake! **4. Trois fois par jour,** three times a day.

parabole, *s.f.* Parable.

parachute, *s.m.* Parachute.

parachutiste, *s.m. & f.* Parachutist.

parade, *s.f.* Parade. **Faire p. de,** to show off.

parader, *v.i.* To parade, make a display.

paradis, *s.m.* Paradise.

paradoxal, -aux, *a.* Paradoxical.

paradoxe, *s.m.* Paradox.

paraffine, *s.f.* Paraffin.

parages, *s.m.pl.* Localities; regions.

paragraphe, *s.m.* Paragraph.

paraître, *v.i.* To appear. **1.** (*a*) To come in sight. (*b*) To be published. "**Vient de p.,**" 'just published.' **2.** To be visible, apparent. **3.** To seem, to look. **A ce qu'il paraît,** as it would appear.

parallèle. **1.** *a. & s.f.* Parallel.

2. *s.m.* (*a*) Parallel, comparison. (*b*) Parallel (of latitude).

paralyser, *v.tr.* To paralyse.

paralysie, *s.f.* Paralysis.

paralytique, *a. & s.* Paralytic.

parangon, *s.m.* Paragon; pattern.

parapet, *s.m.* Parapet.

paraphrase, *s.f.* Paraphrase.

paraphraser, *v.tr.* To paraphrase.

parapluie, *s.m.* Umbrella.

parasite. 1. *s.m.* Parasite. **2.** *a.* Parasitic.

parasitique, *a.* Parasitical.

paratonnerre, *s.m.* Lightning-conductor.

paravent, *s.m.* Draught-screen.

parbleu, *int.* Why, of course!

parc [park], *s.m.* **1.** Park. **2. P. pour autos,** car-park, parking-place.

parcage, *s.m.* Parking. "**P. interdit,**" 'no parking.'

parcelle, *s.f.* Small fragment; particle; plot, patch.

parceller, *v.tr.* To portion out.

parce que, *conj.phr.* Because.

parchemin, *s.m.* Parchment.

par-ci par-là, *adv.* Here and there.

parcimonie, *s.f.* Parsimony.

parcimonieux, *a.* Parsimonious.

parcourir, *v.tr.* **1.** To travel through, go over, traverse. **2.** To glance through.

parcours, *s.m.* **1.** (*a*) Distance covered (*b*) Route; course. **2.** Run, trip.

par-dessous, *prep. & adv* Under, beneath, underneath.

par-dessus, *prep. & adv.* Over.

pardessus, *s.m.* Overcoat.

pardon, *s.m.* Pardon; forgiveness.

pardonner, *v.tr.* To pardon, forgive.

paré, *a.* Adorned, bedecked.

pare-boue, *s.m.inv.* Mudguard (of motor-car, bicycle).

pare-brise, *s.m.inv.* Wind-screen.

pare-choc(s), *s.m.inv.* Bumper.

parégorique, *a. & s.m.* Paregoric.

pareil, -eille [-rɛːj]. **1.** *a.* (*a*) Like, alike; similar. (*b*) Same, identical. (*c*) Such; like that. **2.** *s.* (*a*) Like. (*b*) Equal, match. **3.** *s.f.* **La pareille,** the like.

pareillement [-rej-], *adv.* **1.** In like manner. **2.** Also; likewise.

parement, *s.m.* **1.** Adorning. **2.** Ornament, adornment.

parent, *s.* **1.** *s.m.pl.* Parents. **2.** Relation.

parenté, *s.f.* **1.** Kinship, relationship. **2.** *Coll.* Kindred.

parenthèse, *s.f.* Parenthesis.

parer[1], *v.tr.* **1.** To prepare; to trim. **2.** To adorn, embellish. **se parer,** to adorn oneself.

parer[2]. **1.** *v.tr.* To avoid ward off. **2.** *v.ind.tr.* P. à, to provide, guard, against.

paresse, *s.f.* (*a*) Laziness, idleness. (*b*) Sluggishness.

paresseusement, *adv.* Idly, lazily.

paresseux. 1. *a.* (*a*) Lazy, idle. (*b*) Sluggish. **2.** *s.* Lazy person.

parfaire, *v.tr.* To finish off, perfect.

parfait, *a.* Perfect. (*a*) Faultless. C'est p.! excellent! (*b*) Thorough.

parfaitement, *adv.* **1.** (*a*) Perfectly. (*b*) Thoroughly. **2.** Quite so; certainly.

parfois, *adv.* Sometimes, at times.

parfum, *s.m.* Perfume; scent.

parfumer, *v.tr.* To scent.

parfumerie, *s.f.* Perfumery.

pari, *s.m.* **1.** Bet, wager. **2.** Betting.

paria, *s.m.* Pariah.

parier, *v.tr.* To bet, to wager.

Paris. *Pr.n.m.* Paris. **Articles de P.,** fancy goods.

parisien, *a. & s.* Parisian.

parjure[1], *s.m.* Perjury.

parjure[2]. **1.** *a.* Perjured. **2.** *s.* Perjurer.

parlant, *a.* Speaking; talking.

parlé. 1. *a.* Spoken. **2.** *s.m.* Patter; spoken part (in opera).

parlement, *s.m.* Parliament.

parlementaire[1], *a.* Parliamentary.

parlementaire[2]. *a.* **Drapeau p.,** white flag.

parlementer, *v.i.* To parley.

parler. I. *v.i.* To speak, talk. **Entendre p. de,** to hear of. **Faire p. de soi,** to get talked about. **II. parler,** *s.m.* Speech, language.

parleur, -euse, *s.* Talker, speaker.

parmi, *prep.* Among(st), amid(st).

parodie, *s.f.* Parody; skit.

parodier, *v.tr.* To parody.

paroi, *s.f.* (*a*) Partition-wall. (*b*) Wall (of rock).

paroisse, *s.f.* Parish.

paroissial, -aux, *a.* Parochial; parish.

paroissien, *s.* Parishioner.

parole, *s.f.* **1.** Word; remark. **2.** Promise, word. **3.** Speech, speaking. (*a*) Delivery. (*b*) **Prendre la p.,** to begin to speak.

paroxysme, *s.m.* Paroxysm.

parquer, *v.tr.* To park.

parrain, *s.m.* Godfather; sponsor.

parsemer, *v.tr.* To strew, sprinkle.

part, *s.f.* **1.** Share, portion. (*a*) **Mettre qn de part à demi,** to go half-shares with s.o. (*b*) **Pour ma p.,** as for me. (*c*) **Prendre en bonne p.,** to take in good part. **2.** Share, participation. **Faire p. à,** to inform. **Billet de faire p.,** intimation. **3.** **Nulle p.,** nowhere. **Autre p.,** somewhere else. **De p. en p.,** through and through. **D'une p.,** on the one hand. **Dites-lui de ma p.,** tell him from me. **4.** **A p.,** apart, separately.

partage, *s.m.* **1.** Division. **2.** Share, portion.

partager, *v.tr.* **1.** To divide; to share out. **2.** To share.
se partager, to divide.

partance, *s.f.* Departure. **En p. pour,** bound for.

partant[1], *adv.* Consequently, therefore.

partant[2], *a.* Departing.

partenaire, *s.* Partner.

parterre, *s.m.* **1.** Flower-bed. **2.** *Th:* Pit.

parti, *s.m.* **1.** Party. **Prendre p. pour,** to side with. **2.** **Un bon p.,** a good match. **3.** Decision, choice. **Prendre (un) p.,** to make up one's mind. **P. pris,** bias. **4.** Advantage.

partial, -aux, *a.* Partial; biased.

partialité, *s.f.* Partiality; bias.

participant, *s.* Participant.

participation, *s.f.* Participation.

participe, *s.m.* Participle.

participer, *v.i.* **1.** To participate (*à,* in). **2.** To partake.

particulariser, *v.tr.* To particularize.

particularité, *s.f.* **1.** Detail, particular. **2.** Peculiarity.

particule, *s.f.* Particle, atom.

particulier. 1. *a.* (*a*) Particular, special. (*b*) Peculiar, characteristic. (*c*) Unusual. (*d*) Private. **2.** *s.* Private person. **3.** *s.m.* **En p.,** particularly; privately.

particulièrement, *adv.* (*a*) Particularly, (e)specially. (*b*) Peculiarly.

partie, *s.f.* **1.** Part. **En grande p.,** to a great extent. **2.** (*a*) Party. (*b*) Game, match.

partiel, *a.* Partial, incomplete.

partiellement, *adv.* Partially.

partir, *v.i.* (*a*) To depart, leave; to go away. **Nous voilà partis!** now we're off! (*b*) To part, to give way; to go off. **P. de rire,** to burst out laughing. (*c*) To emanate, spring (from). (*d*) **A p. d'aujourd'hui,** from to-day.

partisan, *s.* Partisan.

partition, *s.f. Mus:* Score.

partout. *adv* Everywhere; on all sides.

parure, *s.f.* (*a*) Dress, finery. (*b*) Ornament.

parvenir, *v.i.* **1.** To arrive. **2.** (*a*) To attain, reach; to succeed. (*b*) *Abs.* To succeed in life.

parvenu, *s.* Parvenu, upstart.

pas[1], *s.m.* **1.** Step, pace, stride. (*a*) **Allonger le pas,** to step out. **Faux pas,** slip. **Avoir le pas sur,** to have precedence of. (*b*) **Au pas,** at a walking pace. **2.** Footprint. **3.** Pass; strait. **Le Pas de Calais,** the Straits of Dover. **Mauvais pas,** tight corner.

pas[2], *neg.adv.* Not. **Non pas!** not at all!

passable, *a.* Passable, tolerable.

passablement, *adv.* Passably.

passage, *s.m.* Passage. **1.** Crossing; going past. **Droit de p.,** right of way. **"P. interdit,"** 'no thoroughfare.' **2.** (*a*) Way, way through. (*b*) Arcade. (*c*) **P. à niveau,** level crossing.

passager. 1. *a.* Fleeting transitory. **2.** *s.* Passenger.

passant, *s.* Passer-by.

passe, *s.f.* **1.** Permit; pass. **2.** **En mauvaise p.,** in a tight corner.

passé. 1. *a.* (*a*) Past; gone by. (*b*) Faded. **2.** *s.m.* Past. **Oublions le p.,** let bygones be bygones.

passe-lacet, *s.m.* Bodkin. *pl. passe-lacets.*

passe-montagne, *s.m.* Balaclava helmet. *pl. passe-montagnes.*

passe-partout, *s.m.inv.* Master-key.

passe-passe, *s.m.* Conjuring.

passeport, *s.m.* Passport.

passer. I. *v.i.* **1.** To pass; to go past; to proceed. **En passant,** by the way

P. son chemin, to go one's way.
2. To undergo, pass through. **3.** To pass away. (a) To disappear, to cease. (b) To elapse, to go by. **4.** To die. **5.** *Pred.* (a) To become. (b) To pass for.
II. **passer,** *v.tr.* **1.** To pass, cross. **2.** (a) To carry across. (b) To pass; to hand. **3.** To pass, spend. **4.** To pass, go beyond. **5.** To pass over. **6.** P. une loi, to pass a law.
se passer. 1. To happen; to take place. **2.** Se p. de, to do without.
passereau, *s.m.* Sparrow.
passerelle, *s.f.* **1.** Foot-bridge. **2.** *Nau:* Bridge.
passe-temps, *s.m.inv.* Pastime.
passeur, *s.m.* Ferryman.
passible, *a.* Liable (*de,* to, for).
passif. 1. *a.* Passive. **2.** *s.m.* Liabilities.
passion, *s.f.* Passion.
passionné, *a.* Passionate; ardent.
passionnel, *a.* Crime p., crime due to jealousy.
passionnément, *adv.* Passionately.
passionner, *v.tr.* To impassion.
passivement, *adv.* Passively.
pastel, *s.m.* Pastel.
pastèque, *s.f.* Water-melon.
pasteur, *s.m.* Pastor.
pastille [-ti:j], *s.f.* Lozenge, jujube.
pastoral, -aux, *a.* Pastoral.
pat [pat], *s.m.inv. Chess:* Stalemate.
pataud, *a.* Clumsy.
patauger, *v.i.* (a) To flounder (in the mud). (b) To paddle (in sea).
pâte, *s.f.* Paste; dough.
pâté, *s.m.* **1.** (Meat) pie. **2.** Blot, blob.
patent, *a.* (a) Patent. (b) Obvious, evident.
patente, *s.f.* Licence.
patère, *s.f.* Hat-peg, coat-peg.
paternel, *a.* Paternal.
paternellement, *adv.* Paternally.
paternité, *s.f.* Paternity.
pâteux, *a.* (a) Pasty, clammy. (b) Thick (voice); muddy (ink).
pathétique. 1. *a.* Pathetic touching. **2.** *s.m.* Pathos.
pathétiquement, *adv.* Pathetically.
pathologie, *s.f.* Pathology.
patiemment, *adv.* Patiently.
patience, *s.f.* Patience.
patient. 1. *a.* Patient. **2.** *s.* Condemned man.

patienter, *v.i.* To exercise patience.
patin, *s.m.* (a) Skate. (b) Runner (of sledge); skid (of aeroplane).
patinage, *s.m.* Skating.
patiner, *v.i.* To skate.
patineur, -euse, *s.* Skater.
pâtir, *v.i.* To suffer (for others).
pâtisserie, *s.f.* **1.** (a) Pastry. (b) *pl.* Cakes. **2.** Tea-rooms.
pâtissier, *s.* Pastry-cook.
patois, *s.m.* Patois.
pâtre, *s.m.* Herdsman; shepherd.
patriarcal, -aux, *a.* Patriarchal.
patriarche, *s.m.* Patriarch.
patrie, *s.f.* Fatherland.
patrimoine, *s.m.* Patrimony.
patriote, *s.* Patriot.
patriotique, *a.* Patriotic.
patriotiquement, *adv.* Patriotically.
patriotisme, *s.m.* Patriotism.
patron, *s.* **1.** Patron. **2.** (a) Employer; proprietor (b) Skipper. **3.** *s.m.* Pattern.
patronage, *s.m.* Patronage.
patronner, *v.tr.* To patronize.
patrouille [-ru:j], *s.f.* Patrol.
patrouiller [-ruje], *v.i.* To patrol.
patte, *s.f.* **1.** Paw; foot (of bird); leg (of insect). **2.** Fluke (of anchor). **3.** Tab, strap.
patte-d'oie, *s.f.* **1.** Road junction. **2.** Crow's-foot. *pl. pattes-d'oie.*
pâturage, *s.m.* Pasture.
pâture, *s.f.* Food, feed, fodder.
pâturer, *v.i.* To graze, to feed.
paume, *s.f.* Palm (of hand).
paupière, *s.f.* Eyelid.
pause, *s.f.* Pause.
pauvre. 1. *a.* Poor. **2.** *s.* Poor person; pauper.
pauvrement, *adv.* Poorly.
pauvreté, *s.f.* Poverty.
pavage, *s.m.* **1.** Paving. **2.** Pavement.
pavaner (se), *v.pr.* To strut (about).
pavé, *s.m.* **1.** Paving-stone. **2.** (a) Pavement. (b) Paved road.
paver, *v.tr.* To pave.
pavillon [-vijɔ̃], *s.m.* **1.** Pavilion. **2.** Flag, colours.
pavoiser, *v.tr.* To deck with flags.
pavot, *s.m.* Poppy.
paye, *s.f.* Pay; wages.
payement, *s.m.* Payment.
payer, *v.tr.* To pay. (a) P. d'audace, to take the risk. P. d'effronterie, to put a bold face on it. (b) To pay,

settle. (*c*) To pay for. **P. qch à qn**, to pay s.o. for sth.

pays[1] [pe(j)i], *s.m.* Country. (*a*) Land. (*b*) Region. district. (*c*) Native land; home. **Avoir le mal du p.**, to be homesick.

pays[2], *s.* Nous sommes p., we are from the same parts.

paysage, *s.m.* Landscape; scenery.

paysan, *s. & a.* Peasant.

péage, *s.m.* Toll.

peau, *s.f.* **1.** Skin. **2.** Pelt, fur; hide. **3.** Peel, skin.

Peau-Rouge, *s.m.* Red Indian, red-skin. *pl. Peaux-Rouges.*

pêche[1], *s.f.* Peach.

pêche[2], *s.f.* **1.** Fishing. **2.** Catch (of fish). **3.** Fishery.

péché, *s.m.* Sin; transgression.

pécher, *v.i.* To sin.

pêcher[1], *s.m.* Peach-tree.

pêcher[2], *v.tr.* **1.** To fish for. **2. P. une truite**, to catch a trout.

pécheur, pécheresse, *s.* Sinner.

pêcheur, -euse, *s.* Fisherman, -woman.

pécuniaire, *a.* Pecuniary.

pédale, *s.f.* Pedal; treadle.

pédaler, *v.i.* To pedal.

pédant, *s.* Pedant.

pédestre, *a.* Pedestrian.

pédicure, *s.m. & f.* Chiropodist.

peigne, *s.m.* Comb.

peigner, *v.tr.* To comb (out).

se peigner, to comb one's hair.

peignoir, *s.m.* Dressing-gown.

peindre, *v.tr.* **1.** To paint. **Papier peint**, wall-paper. **2.** To depict.

peine, *s.f.* **1.** Punishment, penalty. **2.** Sorrow, affliction. **3.** Pains, trouble. **4.** Difficulty **5. A p.**, hardly, scarcely.

peiner. **1.** *v.tr.* To pain, vex, distress. **2.** *v.i.* To toil, labour.

peintre, *s.m.* Painter.

peinture, *s.f.* **1.** Painting. **2.** Paint, colour. "Attention à la p.!" 'wet paint.'

pelage, *s.m.* Coat, wool, fur.

pelé, *a.* Bald; bare.

pêle-mêle. **1.** *adv.* Pell-mell. **2.** *s.m.inv.* Jumble, medley, confusion.

peler. **1.** *v.tr.* To peel, skin **2.** *v.i. & pr.* To peel.

pèlerin, *s.* Pilgrim.

pèlerinage, *s.m.* Pilgrimage.

pélican, *s.m.* Pelican.

pelle, *s.f.* **1.** Shovel, scoop. **2.** Blade (of oar)

pelletée, *s.f.* Shovelful, spadeful.

pelleterie, *s.f.* Fur; peltry.

pelletier, *s.* Furrier.

pellicule, *s.f Phot :* Film.

pellucide, *a.* Pellucid, limpid.

pelote, *s.f.* Ball (of wool). **P. à épingles**, pincushion.

peloton, *s.m.* **1.** Ball (of wool). **2.** Squad, party.

pelouse, *s.f.* Lawn; grass-plot.

peluche, *s.f.* Plush.

pelure, *s.f.* Peel, skin; paring; rind.

pénal, -als, -aux, *a.* Penal.

pénalité, *s.f.* Penalty.

penaud, *a.* Crestfallen chapfallen.

penchant. **1.** *a.* Sloping, leaning. **2.** *s.m.* (*a*) Slope, declivity. (*b*) Leaning, tendency.

pencher, *v.tr & i.* To incline, bend, lean.

se pencher, to bend, lean.

pendaison, *s.f.* (Death by) hanging.

pendant. **I.** *a.* **1.** Hanging, pendent. **2.** Pending; in suspense. **II. pendant**, *s.m.* **1.** Pendant. **2.** Match, fellow. **III. pendant**, *prep.* During. *Conj. phr.* **P. que**, while, whilst.

pendeloque, *s.f.* Pendant; drop.

pendre. **1.** *v.tr.* To hang (up). **2.** *v.i.* To hang (down).

pendu, *a.* Hanged, hung; hanging.

pendule. **1.** *s.m.* Pendulum **2.** *s.f.* Clock.

pêne, *s.m.* Bolt (of lock); latch.

pénétrable, *a.* Penetrable.

pénétrant, *a.* Penetrating; sharp.

pénétration, *s.f.* Penetration

pénétrer, *v.* **1.** *v.i.* To penetrate. **I.** *v.i.* To enter. **2.** *v.tr.* To penetrate; to fathom.

se pénétrer, to become imbued.

pénible, *a.* **1.** Laborious. toilsome. **2.** Painful, distressing.

péniblement, *adv.* Painfully.

péniche, *s.f.* Coal-barge; lighter.

pénicilline, *s.f.* Penicillin.

péninsulaire, *a.* Peninsular.

péninsule, *s.f.* Peninsula.

pénitence, *s.f* **1.** Penitence, repentance. **2.** Penance.

pénitencier, *s.m.* Penitentiary.

pénitent, *a. & s.* Penitent.

penne, *s.f.* Feather.

pennon, s.m. Pennon.
pénombre, s.f. Half-light.
pensée[1], s.f. Pansy.
pensée[2], s.f. Thought.
penser, v. To think. **1.** v.ind.tr. P. à, to think of. **Vous n'y pensez pas!** you don't mean it! **2.** v.i. **Pensez donc!** just fancy! **3.** v.tr. (a) **Je** le **pensais bien,** I thought as much. (b) To expect.
penseur, -euse, s. Thinker.
pensif, a. Thoughtful, pensive.
pension, s.f. **1.** Pension, allowance. **2.** (a) **Être en p. chez,** to board with. (b) **P de famille,** residential hotel. **3.** Boarding-school.
pensionnaire, s.m. & f. **1.** Pensioner. **2.** Boarder.
pensionnat, s.m. Boarding-school.
pensionner, v.tr. To pension.
pensivement, adv. Pensively.
pente, s.f. Slope, gradient.
Pentecôte, s.f. Whitsun(tide).
pénurie, s.f. (a) Scarcity, shortage; lack. (b) Poverty.
pépier, v.i. To cheep, chirp.
pépin, s.m. Pip; stone.
pépinière, s.f. Seed-bed; nursery.
pépiniériste, s.m. Nurseryman.
perçant, a. Piercing; shrill.
percé, a. Pierced; holed.
percée, s.f. Glade; vista.
perce-neige, s.f.inv. Snowdrop.
perce-oreille, s.m Earwig. pl. **perce-oreilles.**
percepteur, -trice, s. (a) Tax-collector. (b) Bus or tram conductor.
perceptible, a. Perceptible.
perceptiblement, adv. Perceptibly.
perceptif, a. Perceptive.
perception, s.f. **1.** Perception. **2.** Collection; receipt.
percer. 1. v.tr. (a) To pierce, to go through. (b) To perforate; to make an opening in. (c) To bore. **2.** v.i. To pierce; to come through.
percevoir, v.tr. **1.** To perceive, discern. **2.** To collect.
perche[1], s.f. (Thin) pole.
perche[2], s.f. Ich: Perch.
percher, v.i. To perch, roost. **se percher,** to alight, perch.
perchoir, s.m. Perch, roost.
perclus, a. Stiff-jointed; crippled.
percolateur, s.m. Percolator.
percussion, s.f. Percussion, impact.

perdant. 1. a Losing. **2.** s. Loser.
perdition, s.f Perdition.
perdre, v.tr **1.** To ruin, destroy. **2.** To lose; to waste. **se perdre,** to be lost.
perdreau, s.m. Young partridge.
perdrix, s.f. Partridge.
perdu, a. **1.** Ruined. **2.** Lost. **Heures perdues,** spare time. **3.** A **corps p.,** recklessly.
père, s.m. Father. **M Dupont p., Mr Dupont senior.**
pérégrination, s.f. Peregrination.
péremptoire, a. Peremptory.
péremptoirement, adv Peremptorily.
perfection, s.f. Perfection.
perfectionnement, s.m. **1.** Perfecting; improving. **2.** Improvement.
perfectionner, v.tr. **1.** To perfect. **2.** To improve.
perfide, a. Treacherous; perfidious.
perfidie, s.f. Treachery, perfidy.
perforation, s.f. Perforation.
perforer, v.tr. To perforate.
péricliter, v.i. To be in jeopardy.
péril [-ril], s.m. Peril, danger; risk.
périlleusement [-rij-], adv. Perilously.
périlleux [-rij-], a. Perilous.
périmé, a. Out-of-date; no longer available; lapsed.
périmètre, s.m. Perimeter.
période, s.f Period.
périodique, a. & s.m. Periodical.
périodiquement, adv. Periodically.
péripétie, s.f. Change (of fortune).
périr, v.i. To perish.
périscope, s.m. Periscope.
périssable, a. Perishable.
périssoire, s.f. (Single-seater) canoe.
perle, s.f. **1.** Pearl. **2.** Bead.
perler, v.i. To form in beads.
permanence, s.f. Permanence.
permanent. 1. a. Permanent. **Spectacle p.,** continuous performance. **2.** s.f. Hairdr: Permanente, perm.
permettre, v.tr To permit, allow. **Permettez!** excuse me! **Vous permettez?** may I?
permis. 1. a. Allowed, permissible. **2.** s.m. Permit; licence. **P. de conduire,** driving-licence. **P. de circulation,** car-licence.
permission, s.f (a) Permission, leave. (b) Leave of absence.

6

pernicieux, *a.* Pernicious, injurious.
pérorer, *v.i.* To hold forth.
Pérou (le). *Pr.n.m.* Peru.
perpendiculaire, *a. & s.* Perpendicular.
perpétration, *s.f.* Perpetration.
perpétrer, *v.tr.* To perpetrate.
perpétuation, *s.f.* Perpetuation.
perpétuel, *a.* Perpetual; (imprisonment) for life.
perpétuellement, *adv.* Perpetually.
perpétuer, *v.tr.* To perpetuate.
  se perpétuer, to endure.
perpétuité, *s.f.* Perpetuity.
perplexe, *a.* **1.** Perplexed, puzzled. **2.** Perplexing.
perplexité, *s.f.* Perplexity.
perquisition, *s.f.* Thorough inquiry.
perquisitionner, *v.i.* To make a search.
perron, *s.m.* (Flight of) steps.
perroquet, *s.m.* Parrot.
perruche, *s.f.* Parakeet.
perruque, *s.f.* Wig.
persécuter, *v.tr.* To persecute.
persécuteur, -trice, *s.* Persecutor.
persécution, *s.f.* Persecution.
persévérance, *s.f.* Perseverance.
persévérant, *a.* Persevering.
persévérer, *v.i.* To persevere.
persil, *s.m.* Parsley.
persistance, *s.f.* Persistence.
persistant, *a.* Persistent.
persister, *v.i.* To persist.
personnage, *s.m.* (*a*) Personage. (*b*) Character (in play).
personnalité, *s.f.* Personality.
personne. **1.** *s.f.* Person. (*a*) Les grandes personnes, the grown-ups. (*b*) En p., in person; personally. **2.** *pron.indef.m.inv.* (*a*) Anyone. (*b*) No one; nobody.
personnel. **1.** *a.* Personal. **2.** *s.m.* Personnel, staff; hands.
personnellement, *adv.* Personally, in person.
personnification, *s.f.* (*a*) Personification. (*b*) Impersonation.
personnifier, *v.tr.* (*a*) To personify. (*b*) To impersonate.
perspectif. **1.** *a.* Perspective. **2.** *s.f.* Perspective, outlook, view, prospect.
perspicace, *a.* Perspicacious.
perspicacité, *s.f.* Perspicacity.
persuader, *v.tr.* To persuade; convince.

persuasif, *a.* Persuasive.
persuasion, *s.f.* **1.** Persuasion. **2.** Conviction, belief.
perte, *s.f.* **1.** Ruin, destruction. **2.** Loss. En pure p., to no purpose. **3.** Loss, leakage.
pertinemment, *adv.* Pertinently.
pertinent, *a.* Pertinent; relevant.
perturbateur, -trice. **1.** *a.* Disturbing, upsetting. **2.** *s.* Disturber.
perturbation, *s.f* Perturbation.
pervers, *a.* Perverse, depraved.
perversement, *adv.* Perversely.
perversion, *s.f.* Perversion.
perversité, *s.f.* Perversity.
pervertir, *v.tr.* To pervert.
pesamment, *adv.* Heavily.
pesant, *a.* Heavy, weighty.
pesanteur, *s.f.* **1.** Weight. **2.** (*a*) Heaviness. (*b*) Dullness.
pesée, *s.f.* Weighing.
peser. **1.** *v.tr.* To weigh. **2.** *v.i.* To weigh; to be heavy.
pessimisme, *s.m.* Pessimism.
pessimiste. **1.** *a.* Pessimistic. **2.** *s.* Pessimist.
peste, *s.f.* Plague, pestilence.
pestilentiel, *a.* Pestilential.
pétale, *s.m.* Petal.
pétard, *s.m.* Cracker.
pétillant [-tijã], *a.* Crackling; sparkling.
pétillement [-tij-], *s.m.* Crackling; sparkling; bubbling.
pétiller [-tije], *v.i.* To crackle; to sparkle, bubble.
petit, *a.* Small, little. **1.** En p., in miniature. **2.** Insignificant, petty. **3.** Mean, paltry. **4.** *s.* Little one. **5.** *s.m.pl.* Young (of animals).
petite-fille, *s.f.* Grand-daughter. *pl. petites-filles.*
petitesse, *s.f* (*a*) Smallness. (*b*) Meanness, pettiness.
petit-fils, *s.m* Grandson *pl. petits-fils.*
pétition, *s.f.* Petition.
pétitionnaire, *s.m. & f.* Petitioner.
pétitionner, *v.i.* To petition.
petit-lait, *s.m.* Whey.
petits-enfants, *s.m.pl.* Grand-children.
pétrel, *s.m.* Petrel.
pétrification, *s.f.* Petrifaction.
pétrifier, *v.tr.* To petrify.
pétrir, *v.tr.* To knead; to mould.

pétrole, *s.m.* Petroleum ; paraffin oil.
pétulance, *s f.* Liveliness.
pétulant, *a.* Lively, irrepressible.
peu. 1. *adv.* (*a*) Little. **Quelque peu,** somewhat. **Peu de chose,** little ; not much. (*b*) Few. (*c*) Not very. **2.** *s.m.* (*a*) Little, bit. **Écoutez un peu,** just listen. (*b*) **Sous peu,** before long. **Depuis peu,** lately.
peuplade, *s.f.* Small tribe.
peuple, *s.m.* People.
peuplement, *s.m.* Peopling.
peupler, *v.tr.* To people, populate.
peuplier, *s.m.* Poplar.
peur, *s.f.* Fear, fright, dread.
peureusement, *adv.* Timorously.
peureux, *a.* Timorous ; timid.
peut-être, *adv.* Perhaps, possibly.
pharaon, *s.m.* **1.** Pharaoh. **2.** Faro.
phare, *s.m.* **1.** Lighthouse. **2.** Head-light.
pharisien, *s.m.* Pharisee.
pharmacie, *s.f.* (*a*) Pharmacy ; chemist's shop. (*b*) Dispensary.
pharmacien, *s.* Chemist.
phase, *s.f.* Phase.
phénique, *a.* Carbolic.
phénix [-niks], *s.m.* Phoenix.
phénol, *s.m.* Carbolic acid.
phénoménal, -aux, *a.* Phenomenal.
philanthrope, *s.m.* Philanthropist.
philatélie, *s.f.* Philately.
philatélique, *a.* Philatelic.
philatéliste, *s.m. & f.* Philatelist.
Philippe. *Pr.n.m.* Philip.
philistin, *a. & s.* Philistine.
philologue, *s.m.* Philologist.
philosophe. 1. *s.m. & f.* Philosopher, sage. **2.** *a.* Philosophical.
phonétique, *a.* Phonetic.
phonétiquement, *adv.* Phonetically.
phoque, *s.m.* Seal.
phosphate, *s.m.* Phosphate.
phosphore, *s.m.* Phosphorus.
phosphorescent, *a.* Phosphorescent.
photographe, *s.m.* Photographer.
photographie, *s.f.* **1.** Photography. **2.** Photograph.
photographier, *v.tr.* To photograph.
photographique, *a.* Photographic.
phrase, *s.f.* Sentence ; phrase.
phraséologie, *s.f.* Phraseology.
phrénologiste, *s.m.* Phrenologist.
phtisie, *s.f.* Consumption.
phtisique, *a. & s.* Consumptive.
physiologie, *s.f.* Physiology.

physiologique, *a.* Physiological.
physiologiste, *s.m.* Physiologist.
physionomie, *s.f.* Physiognomy ; face, countenance ; appearance.
physique. 1. *a.* Physical ; bodily. **2.** *s.f.* Physics. **3.** *s.m.* Physique.
physiquement, *adv.* Physically.
piaffer, *v.i.* (*a*) To paw the ground. (*b*) To prance.
pianiste, *s.m. & f.* Pianist.
piano, *s.m.* Piano **P. à queue,** grand piano.
piauler, *v.i.* To cheep ; to whimper.
pic[1] [pik], *s.m.* **1.** Pick, pickaxe. **2.** (Mountain-)peak. *Adv.phr.* **A pic,** perpendicular(ly) ; sheer ; precipitous.
pic[2], *s.m.* Woodpecker.
picorer. 1. *v.i.* (Of bird) To pick, peck, for food.
picotement, *s.m.* Pricking, tingling.
picoter, *v.tr.* **1.** (*a*) (Of bird) To peck. (*b*) To sting, make smart. **2.** *v.i.* To smart, tingle.
pie. 1. *s.f.* Magpie. **2.** *a.* Piebald.
pièce, *s.f.* **1.** Piece. (*a*) **P. de gibier,** head of game. **P. d'eau,** sheet of water. (*b*) **P. de théâtre,** play. **2.** (*a*) Piece ; part. (*b*) Room. (*c*) Patch. **3.** Fragment, bit.
pied, *s.m.* **1.** (*a*) Foot. **Mettre p. à terre,** to alight ; to step ashore. **Coup de p.,** kick. **Aller à p.,** to walk. (*b*) Footing. **Le p. me manqua,** I lost my footing. **Tenir p.,** to stand fast. **2.** (*a*) Foot ; base. (*b*) Leg (of chair) ; stem, foot (of glass). (*c*) **P. de céleri,** head of celery. (*d*) Stand, rest.
pied-à-terre [-tate:r], *s.m.inv.* (Small) occasional lodging, shooting-box.
piédestal, -aux, *s.m.* Pedestal.
piège, *s.m.* Trap, snare.
pierre[1], *s.f.* Stone. **Faire d'une p. deux coups,** to kill two birds with one stone.
Pierre[2]. *Pr.n.m.* Peter.
pierreries, *s.f.pl.* Precious stones.
pierreux, *a.* Stony.
piété, *s.f.* Piety.
piétinement, *s.m.* Trampling.
piétiner. 1. *v.tr.* To trample on. **2.** *v.i.* **P. de rage,** to dance with rage.
piéton, *s.m.* Pedestrian.
piètre, *a.* Wretched, poor ; paltry.
pieu, -eux, *s.m.* Stake ; post.

pieusement, *adv.* Piously.

pieuvre, *s.f* Octopus.

pieux, *a.* Pious.

pigeon, *s.* Pigeon.

pignon, *s.m.* Gable, gable-end.

pile[1], *s.f.* **1.** Pile; heap. **2.** Pier (of bridge). **3.** Battery. **P. de rechange,** refill (for torch).

pile[2], *s.f.* **P. ou face,** heads or tails.

piler, *v.tr.* To pound; to crush.

pilier, *s.m.* Pillar, column, post.

pillage [-ja:ʒ], *s.m.* Pillage, looting.

pillard [pija:r] **1.** *a.* Thieving. **2.** *s.* Pillager, looter

piller [pije], *v.tr.* To pillage, sack.

pilon, *s.m.* **1.** Pestle. **2.** Drumstick (of fowl).

pilorier, *v.tr.* To pillory.

pilotage, *s.m.* Pilotage, piloting.

pilote, *s.m.* Pilot.

piloter, *v.tr.* To pilot.

pilule, *s.f.* Pill.

piment, *s.m.* Red pepper.

pimpant, *a.* Smart, spruce.

pin, *s.m.* Pine(-tree), fir(-tree).

pinacle, *s.m.* Pinnacle.

pince, *s.f.* **1.** Grip, hold. **2.** (*a*) Pincers, pliers; forceps. **P. à sucre,** sugar-tongs. (*b*) Clip. (*c*) Crow-bar. **3.** Claw

pincé, *a.* Affected, prim.

pinceau, *s.m.* (Artist's) paint-brush.

pincée, *s.f.* Pinch (of snuff).

pince-nez, *s.m.inv.* Eye-glasses.

pincer, *v.tr.* **1.** To pinch, nip. **2.** To grip, hold fast.

pincettes, *s.f.pl.* (Fire-)tongs.

pingouin, *s.m.* Auk.

pinson, *s.m.* Chaffinch.

pintade, *s.f.* Guinea-fowl.

pioche, *s.f.* Pickaxe, pick.

piolet, *s.m.* Ice-axe.

pion, *s.m.* **1.** Usher; junior master. **2.** (*a*) Pawn. (*b*) Draughtsman.

pionnier, *s.m.* Pioneer.

pipe, *s.f.* Pipe.

piquant. **1.** *a.* Pungent; piquant. **2.** *s.m.* Prickle; quill; spike.

pique[1]. **1.** *s.f.* Pike. **2.** *s.m.* *Cards:* Spade(s).

pique[2], *s.f* Pique, ill-feeling.

piqué, *a.* **1.** Quilted; padded. **2.** **Descente piquée,** nose-dive.

pique-nique, *s.m* Picnic. *pl. pique-niques*

piquer, *v.tr.* **1.** (*a*) To prick, sting.

(*b*) To nettle, pique; to arouse. **2.** To stick, insert. **3.** **P une tête,** to take a header.

se piquer. 1. To take offence. **2.** **Se p. de,** to pride oneself on.

piquet, *s.m.* **1.** Peg. stake. post. **2.** Picket.

piqûre, *s.f.* **1.** (*a*) Prick, sting. (*b*) Hypodermic injection. **2.** Puncture.

pirate, *s.m.* Pirate.

piraterie, *s.f.* Piracy.

pire, *a.* **1.** Worse. **2.** **Le p.,** the worst.

pis[1], *s.m.* Udder.

pis[2], *adv.* **1.** Worse. **2.** **Le pis,** (the) worst. **3.** **Pis aller,** *s.m. inv.* Last resource; makeshift.

piscine, *s.f* Swimming-bath.

pissenlit, *s.m.* Dandelion.

pistache, *s.f.* Pistachio(-nut).

piste, *s.f.* **1.** (*a*) Race-track. (*b*) **P. d'envol,** runway. **P. d'atterrissage,** landing strip. **2.** Track, trail; scent.

pistolet, *s.m.* Pistol.

piston, *s.m.* Piston.

piteusement, *adv.* Piteously.

piteux, *a.* Piteous, woeful.

pitié, *s.f.* Pity, compassion. **Faire p.,** to arouse pity.

pitoyable, *a.* (*a*) Pitiable. (*b*) Paltry.

pittoresque, *a.* (*a*) Picturesque, quaint. (*b*) Pictorial.

pivoine, *s.f.* Peony.

pivot, *s.m.* Pivot, pin, axis; swivel.

pivoter, *v.i.* To pivot; to turn; to swivel, revolve.

placard, *s.m.* **1.** Wall-cupboard. **2.** Poster, bill, placard.

placarder, *v.tr.* To post up.

place, *s.f.* Place. **1.** (*a*) Position. (*b*) Stead. **A votre p.,** if I were you. (*c*) **P. aux dames!** ladies first! **2.** (*a*) Seat. (*b*) Situation, office. **3.** Locality, spot; square. **Sur p.,** on the spot.

placement, *s.m.* **1.** (*a*) Bureau de p., employment bureau. (*b*) Sale, disposal. **2.** Investment.

placer, *v.tr.* To place. **1.** (*a*) To put, set. (*b*) To find a situation for. (*c*) To invest. **2.** To sell, dispose of. **se placer. 1.** To take one's place. **2.** To obtain a situation.

placide, *a.* Placid; calm.

placidité, *s.f.* Placidity.

plafond, *s.m.* Ceiling.

plage, *s.f.* (*a*) Beach. shore. (*b*) Seaside resort.

plagiat, *s.m.* Plagiarism.

plaid, *s.m.* Travelling-rug.

plaider, *v.tr.* To plead.

plaideur, -euse, *s.* Litigant.

plaie, *s.f.* Wound, sore.

plaignant, *s.* Plaintiff.

plaindre, *v.tr.* To pity.
    se plaindre, to complain.

plaine, *s.f.* Plain ; flat open country.

plain-pied, *s.m.* **1.** Rooms on one floor. **2.** *Adv.phr.* De p.-p., on a level.

plainte, *s.f.* **1.** Moan, groan. **2.** Complaint.

plaintif, *a.* Plaintive, doleful.

plaintivement, *adv.* Plaintively.

plaire, *v.ind.tr.* P. à qn, to please s.o. *Impers.* S'il vous plaît, (if you) please. Plaît-il? I beg your pardon ?
    se plaire, to be pleased.

plaisamment. *adv.* Drolly, amusingly.

plaisance, *s.f.* Pleasure.

plaisant. 1. *a.* (*a*) Funny, amusing. (*b*) Ridiculous. **2.** *s.m.* Wag, joker.

plaisanter. 1. *v.i.* To joke, jest. **2.** *v.tr.* To chaff, banter.

plaisanterie, *s.f.* Joke, jest ; joking.

plaisir, *s.m.* Pleasure. **1.** Delight. A p., ad lib. **2.** Amusement, enjoyment. Train de p., excursion train.

plan¹. 1. *a.* Even, level, flat. **2.** *s.m.* (*a*) Plane. (*b*) **Premier p.,** foreground ; down-stage.

plan², *s.m.* Plan. (*a*) Drawing ; draft. (*b*) Scheme, project, design.

planche, *s.f.* **1.** (*a*) Board, plank. (*b*) Shelf. **2.** Plate, engraving.

plancher, *s.m.* Floor.

planer, *v.i.* (*a*) To soar ; to hover. (*b*) *Av :* To glide.

planète, *s.f.* Planet.

plantation, *s.f.* Plantation.

plante¹, *s.f.* Sole (of the foot).

plante², *s.f.* Plant.

planter, *v.tr.* **1.** To plant, set. **2.** To fix. P. là, to leave in the lurch.
    se planter. to (take one's) stand.

planteur, *s.m.* Planter.

planton, *s.m.* Orderly.

plantureux, *a.* Copious ; lavish.

plaque, *s.f.* **1.** Plate ; sheet ; slab. **2.** Plaque. **3.** Badge. **P. matricule,** number plate.

plastique. 1. *a.* Plastic. **2.** *s.m.pl.* Plastics.

plastron, *s.m.* **1.** Breast-plate. **2.** P. de chemise, shirt-front.

plat. 1. *a.* (*a*) Flat, level. **Calme p.,** dead calm. (*b*) Dull, tame. (*c*) Tomber à p., to fall flat. **2.** *s.m.* (*a*) Flat (part) ; blade. (*b*) Dish. (*c*) *Cu :* Course.

platane, *s.m.* Plane-tree.

plat-bord, *s.m.* Gunwale. *pl. plats-bords.*

plateau, *s.m.* **1.** (*a*) Tray. (*b*) Pan, scale. **2.** Plateau. **3.** Disc, plate.

plate-bande, *s.f.* (*a*) Grass border. (*b*) Flower-bed. *pl. plates-bandes.*

plate-forme, *s.f.* Platform ; foot-plate. *pl. plates-formes.*

platine, *s.m.* Platinum.

platitude, *s.f.* **1.** Flatness, dullness. **2.** Platitude.

platonique, *a.* Platonic.

plâtras, *s.m.* Debris ; rubbish.

plâtre, *s.m.* Plaster. **P. de moulage,** plaster of Paris.

plâtrer, *v.tr.* To plaster.

plausible, *a.* Plausible.

plébéien, *a. & s.* Plebeian.

plein. 1. *a.* Full. (*a*) Filled. (*b*) Complete, entire. (*c*) Solid. (*d*) **En p.** visage, full in the face. **En p. air,** in the open. **2.** *s.m.* (*a*) **Faire le p.** d'essence, to fill up with petrol. (*b*) **La saison bat son p.,** the season is in full swing. (*c*) **En p. dans le** centre, right in the middle.

pleinement, *adv.* Fully, entirely.

plénipotentiaire, *a. & s.m.* Plenipotentiary.

pleurer. 1. *v.tr.* To weep, mourn, for. **2.** *v.i.* (*a*) To weep, to cry. (*b*) (Of the eyes) To water, to run.

pleurnicher, *v.i.* To whimper.

pleuvoir, *v.i.* To rain.

pli, *s.m.* **1.** (*a*) Fold ; pleat ; tuck. (*b*) Wrinkle. **Pli de terrain,** fold of the ground. (*c*) Crease. **2.** Cover, envelope.

pliable, *a.* Pliable, flexible.

pliant. 1. *a.* (*a*) Pliant. (*b*) Folding. **2.** *s.m.* Folding chair ; camp-stool.

plie, *s.f.* Plaice.

plier. 1. *v.tr.* (*a*) To fold, fold up. (*b*) To bend. **2.** *v.i.* (*a*) To bend. (*b*) To submit, yield.

plissement, *s.m.* **1.** Corrugation. **2.** Crumpling ; crinkling.

plisser. 1. *v.tr.* (*a*) To pleat. (*b*) To crease, crumple ; to pucker. **2.** *v.i.* & *pr.* To crease.

plomb, *s.m.* **1.** Lead. **2.** *Ven :* Shot. **3.** Fil à p., plumb-line. A p., vertical(ly). **4.** P. de sûreté, fuse, cut-out.

plombé, *a.* Leaden ; livid.

plomberie, *s.f.* Plumbing.

plombier, *s.m.* Plumber.

plongée, *s.f.* Plunge, dive.

plongeoir, *s.m.* Diving-board.

plongeon, *s.m.* Plunge, dive.

plonger. 1. *v.i.* To plunge. (*a*) To dive. (*b*) To submerge. **2.** *v.tr.* To plunge, immerse.

se plonger, to mmerse oneself.

plongeur, -euse. 1. *a.* Diving. **2.** *s.m.* Diver.

ployer. 1. *v.tr.* To bend. **2.** *v.i.* To bow (under burden).

pluie, *s.f.* Rain.

plumage, *s.m.* Plumage, feathers.

plume, *s.f.* **1.** Feather. **2.** Pen ; nib. Dessin à la p., pen-and-ink drawing

plumeau, *s.m.* Feather-duster.

plumer, *v.tr.* To pluck ; to fleece.

plumet, *s.m.* Plume (of helmet).

plupart (la) *s.f* The most : the greater part.

pluriel, *a.* & *s.m.* Plural.

plus. 1. *adv.* (*a*) More. Deux fois p. grand, twice as large. P. de, more than. P. loin, farther on. P. tôt, sooner. (*b*) (Le) p., most. (*c*) Ne . . . p., no more, no longer. P. de doute, there is no more doubt about it. (*d*) Non p., (not) either. Ni moi non p., neither do I. (*e*) Plus, also. (*f*) De p., more. De p. en p., more and more. En p., in addition. **2.** *s.m.* (*a*) More. (*b*) Most. Tout au p., at (the very) most.

plusieurs, *a.* & *pron.pl.* Several.

plutôt, *adv.* (*a*) Rather, sooner. (*b*) Rather ; on the whole.

pluvieux, *a.* Rainy ; wet.

pneumatique. 1. *a.* Pneumatic. **2.** *s.m.* (*a*) Pneumatic tyre. (*b*) Express letter.

pneumonie, *s.f.* Pneumonia.

poche, *s.f.* **1.** Pocket. **2.** Bag, pouch. P. d'air, air-pocket.

pocher, *v.tr.* To poach (eggs). Œil poché, black eye.

pochette, *s.f.* (*a*) Hand-bag. (*b*) Pocket-case.

poêle[1] [pwɑːl], *s.f.* Frying-pan.

poêle[2], *s.m.* Stove.

poeme, *s.m.* Poem.

poésie, *s.f.* **1.** Poetry. **2.** Poem.

poete, *s.m.* Poet.

poétesse, *s.f.* Woman poet.

poétique, *a.* Poetical.

poétiquement, *adv.* Poetically.

poids [pwɑ], *s.m.* Weight. **1.** (*a*) Vendre au p., to sell by weight. (*b*) Importance. **2.** Load, burden.

poignant, *a.* Poignant.

poignard, *s.m.* Dagger.

poignarder, *v.tr.* To stab.

poigne, *s.f.* Grip, grasp.

poignᴇe, *s.f.* **1.** (*a*) Handful. (*b*) P. de main, handshake. **2.** Handle.

poignet, *s.m.* **1.** Wrist. **2.** (*a*) Wristband. (*b*) Cuff.

poil [pwal], *s.m.* Hair ; fur.

poilu. 1. *a.* Hairy shaggy. **2.** *s.m.* French soldier.

poinçon, *s.m.* **1.** Bradawl. **2.** (*a*) Punch. (*b*) P. de contrôle, hall-mark.

poinçonner, *v.tr.* To punch, clip.

poindre, *v.i.* To dawn.

poing, *s.m.* Fist. Dormir à poings fermés, to sleep soundly.

point[1], *s.m.* **1.** Hole (in strap). **2.** Stitch. **3.** Point. (*a*) Le p. du jour, daybreak. A p., nommé, in the nick of time. (*b*) P. d'appui, fulcrum ; purchase. Au p., in focus. **4.** (*a*) Point, dot ; full stop. Deux points, colon. P. et virgule, semicolon. P. d'exclamation, note of exclamation. (*b*) Point ; score. (*c*) Mark. (*d*) Speck, spot. **5.** (*a*) Point, degree. A ce p., so much so. (*b*) En bon p., in good condition. (*c*) A p., in the right condition ; to a turn. **6.** Point, particular.

point[2], *adv.* Not.

pointe, *s.f.* **1.** (*a*) Point ; head (of arrow) ; toe (of shoe). Coup de p., thrust. Sur la p. des pieds, on tiptoe. (*b*) P. du jour, daybreak. **2.** Foreland, headland ; spit.

pointer[1], *v.tr.* **1.** To check, tick off. **2.** To point, level.

pointer[2]. **1.** *v.tr.* To thrust. **2.** *v.i.* To appear ; to sprout.

pointillé [-tije], *a.* Dotted ; stippled.

pointilleux [-tijø], *a.* **1.** Captious. **2.** Particular ; fastidious.

pointu, *a.* Sharp-pointed.

pointure, *s.f.* Size (in shoes, etc.).

poire, *s.f.* 1. Pear. 2. Bulb (of horn).

poireau, *s.m.* Leek.

poirier, *s.m.* Pear-tree.

pois, *s.m.* 1. Pea. **P. de senteur,** sweet pea. 2. **Petits pois,** green peas.

poison, *s.m.* Poison.

poisson, *s.m.* Fish. **P. rouge,** gold-fish.

poitrail [-rɑ:j], *s.m.* Breast (of horse).

poitrinaire, *a. & s.* Consumptive.

poitrine, *s.f.* Breast, chest; bosom.

poivre, *s.m.* Pepper.

poivré, *a.* Peppery; pungent.

poivrer, *v.tr.* To pepper.

poivrière, *s.f.* Pepper-castor.

poix, *s.f.* Pitch; cobbler's wax.

polaire, *a.* Polar. **L'étoile p.,** the pole-star.

pôle, *s.m.* Pole.

poli. 1. *a.* (*a*) Polished. (*b*) Polite. 2. *s.m.* Polish.

police[1], *s.f.* 1. **Faire la p.,** to keep order. **Tribunal de simple p.,** police-court. 2. Police.

police[2], *s.f.* (Insurance) policy.

policier, *a.* Police. **Roman p.,** detective novel.

poliment, *adv.* Politely, civilly.

polir, *v.tr.* To polish.

polisson, *s.* Naughty child.

politesse, *s.f.* Politeness; civility.

politicien, *s.* Politician.

politique. 1. *a.* (*a*) Political. (*b*) Politic, prudent. 2. *s.f.* (*a*) Policy. (*b*) Politics.

politiquement, *adv.* Politically.

polluer, *v.tr.* To pollute, defile.

pollution, *s.f.* Pollution, defilement.

Pologne. *Pr.n.f.* Poland.

polonais. 1. (*a*) *a. & s.m.* Polish. (*b*) *s.* Pole. 2. *s.f.* Polonaise, polonaise.

poltron. 1. *a.* Timid. 2. *s.* Poltroon.

polycopier, *v.tr.* To manifold.

polygame. 1. *a.* Polygamous. 2. *s.* Polygamist.

polyglotte, *a. & s.* Polyglot.

polytechnique, *a.* Polytechnic.

pommade, *s.f.* Pomade, pomatum.

pomme, *s.f.* 1. (*a*) Apple. **P. sauvage,** crab-apple. (*b*) **P. de terre,** potato. **Bifteck aux pommes,** steak and chips. (*c*) **P. de pin,** pine-cone. 2. Knob.

pommelé, *a.* Dappled, mottled.

pommeraie, *s.f.* Apple-orchard.

pommette, *s.f.* Cheek-bone.

pommier, *s.m.* Apple-tree.

pompe[1], *s.f.* Pon.p, ceremony, display. **Entrepreneur de pompes funèbres,** undertaker.

pompe[2], *s.f.* Pump. **P. à incendie,** fire-engine.

pomper, *v.tr.* To pump

pompeusement, *adv.* Pompously

pompeux, *a.* Pompous.

pompier, *s.m.* Fireman.

pompon, *s.m.* Pompon; tuft.

ponce, *s.f.* (Pierre) p., pumice-stone.

ponctualité, *s.f.* Punctuality.

ponctuation, *s.f.* Punctuation.

ponctuel, *a.* Punctual.

ponctuellement, *adv.* Punctually.

ponctuer, *v.tr.* To punctuate.

pondre, *v.tr.* To lay (eggs).

poney [pɔnɛ], *s.m.* Pony.

pont, *s.m.* 1. Bridge. **P. tournant,** swing-bridge. 2. Deck.

pontife, *s.m.* Pontiff

pont-levis, *s.m.* Drawbridge. *pl. ponts-levis.*

ponton, *s.m.* Pontoon.

populace, *s.f.* Populace, rabble.

populaire, *a.* Popular.

populairement, *adv.* Popularly.

popularité, *s.f.* Popularity.

population, *s.f.* Population.

populeux, *a.* Populous.

porc, *s.m.* 1. Pig. 2. Pork.

porcelaine, *s.f.* Porcelain, china.

porc-épic, *s.m.* Porcupine. *pl. porcs-épics.*

porche, *s.m.* Porch.

porcherie, *s.f.* Piggery; pigsty.

pore, *s.m.* Pore.

poreux, *a.* Porous.

port[1], *s.m.* Harbour, haven, port.

port[2], *s.m.* 1. Carrying. 2. Cost of transport; postage. **En p. dû,** carriage forward. 3. Bearing, carriage.

portable, *a.* Portable.

portage, *s.m.* (*a*) Porterage, conveyance, transport. (*b*) Portage.

portail, -ails [-ta:j], *s.m.* Portal.

portant, *a.* **Être bien p.,** to be in good health.

portatif, *a.* Portable. **Armes portatives,** small-arms.

porte, *s.f.* 1. Gate(way), entrance. **P. cochère,** carriage entrance. 2. Door. 3. Eye (of hook and eye).

porté, *a.* Inclined, disposed.
porte-affiches, *s.m.inv.* Notice-board.
porte-aiguilles, *s.m.inv.* Needle-case.
porte-avions, *s.m.inv.* Aircraft carrier.
porte-bagages, *s.m.inv.* (*a*) Luggage-rack. (*b*) Luggage-carrier.
porte-billets, *s.m.inv.* (Bank-)note case.
porte-cigares, *s.m.inv.* Cigar-case.
porte-cigarette, *s.m.* Cigarette-holder. *pl. porte-cigarettes.*
porte-cigarettes, *s.m.inv.* Cigarette-case.
porte-clefs, *s.m.inv.* Turnkey.
porte-crayon, *s.m.inv.* Pencil-case.
portée, *s.f* **1.** (*a*) Litter, brood (*b*) *Mus:* Stave. **2.** (*a*) Reach; range; scope. (*b*) Bearing, full significance.
portefaix, *s.m.* Porter.
porte-fenêtre, *s.f.* French window. *pl. portes-fenêtres.*
portefeuille [-fœːj], *s.m.* **1.** Portfolio **2.** Pocket-book.
portemanteau, *s.m.* Coat(-and-hat)-rack, -stand.
porte-mine, *s.m.inv.* Pencil-case.
porte-monnaie, *s.m.inv.* Purse.
porte-parole, *s.m.inv.* Spokesman.
porte-plume, *s.m.inv.* Penholder; pen. **P.-p. réservoir**, fountain-pen.
porter. **1.** *v.tr.* To carry. (*a*) To bear, support. (*b*) To wear. (*c*) To carry, convey, take. (*d*) To induce, incline. (*e*) To produce. (*f*) **P. témoignage**, to bear witness. **2.** *v.i* (*a*) To rest, bear. (*b*) To hit, reach
  se porter, (of health), to be.
porte-serviette(s), *s.m.inv.* Towel-rail.
porteur, -euse, s. Porter, carrier, bearer.
porte-voix, *s.m.inv.* Speaking-trumpet; megaphone.
portier, *s.* Porter, door-keeper.
portière, *s.f.* Door (of carriage).
portion, *s.f.* Portion, share, part.
portique, *s.m.* Portico, porch.
Porto. **1.** *Pr.n.* Oporto. **2.** *s.m.* (Vin de) P., port (wine).
portrait, *s.m.* Portrait, likeness.
portugais, *a. & s.* Portuguese.

pose, *s.f.* **1.** (*a*) Pose, posture. (*b*) Posing, affectation. **2.** *Phot:* Exposure.
posé, *a.* Staid, grave; steady.
poser. **1.** *v.i.* (*a*) To rest, lie. (*b*) To pose; to sit. (*c*) To pose; to put on side. **2.** *v.tr.* To place, put; to lay down.
  se poser, to settle, alight.
poseur, -euse, *a. & s.* Affected (person).
positif, *a.* (*a*) Positive, actual. **C'est p.**, that's so. (*b*) Matter-of-fact.
position, *s.f.* Position. **1.** (*a*) Situation, site. (*b*) Posture; stance. (*c*) Condition, circumstances. **2.** Post, situation.
positivement, *adv.* Positively.
possédé, *a.* Possessed; infatuated.
posséder, *v.tr.* To be in possession of. (*a*) To possess own. (*b*) To curb, control.
  se posséder, to contain oneself.
possesseur, *s.m.* Possessor, owner.
possessif, *a.* Possessive.
possession, *s.f.* **1.** Possession. **2.** Property; *pl.* possessions.
possibilité, *s.f.* Possibility.
possible. **1.** *a.* Possible. **2.** *s.m.* **Dans la mesure du p.**, as far as possible.
postal, -aux, *a.* Postal.
poste[1], *s.f.* (*a*) Post. (*b*) Post office. **Bureau de p.**, post office.
poste[2], *s.m.* **1.** (*a*) Post, station. (*b*) **P. d'incendie**, fire-station. **P. de police**, police station. (*c*) **"Ici p. de Toulouse,"** 'Toulouse calling.' (*d*) **P. de T.S.F.**, wireless set. **2.** Post, place, appointment.
poster, *v.tr.* To post; to station.
postérieur, -e, *a.* Posterior. (*a*) Subsequent. (*b*) Hinder, hind.
postérieurement, *adv.* Subsequently.
postérité, *s.f.* Posterity.
posthume, *a.* Posthumous.
postiche, *a.* False; imitation.
post-scriptum [-tɔm], *s.m.inv.* Post-script.
postulant, *s.* Candidate, applicant.
posture, *s.f.* Posture, attitude.
pot, *s.m.* Pot, jug, can, jar.
potable, *a.* Drinkable. **Eau p.**, drinking water.
potage, *s.m.* Soup.
potager, *a.* **Herbe potagère**, pot-herb. **Jardin p.**, kitchen-garden.

potasse, *s.f.* Potash.

pot-au-feu, *s.m.inv.* **1.** Stock-pot. **2.** Boiled beef with vegetables.

pot-de-vin, *s.m.* **1.** Douceur. **2.** Bribe. *pl.* pots-de-vin.

poteau, *s.m.* Post, pole, stake.

potelé, *a.* Plump and dimpled.

potence, *s.f.* Gallows, gibbet.

potentat, *s.m.* Potentate.

potentiel, *a.* Potential.

potentiellement, *adv.* Potentially.

poterie, *s.f.* Pottery.

potiche, *s.f.* (Large) vase.

potion, *s.f.* Potion, draught.

potiron, *s.m.* Pumpkin.

pou, *pl.* **poux,** *s.m.* Louse.

pouah, *int.* Faugh! ugh!

poubelle, *s.f.* Dustbin.

pouce, *s.m.* Thumb. **Manger sur le p.,** to take a snack.

pouding, *s.m.* Pudding.

poudre, *s.f.* Powder; dust.

poudrer, *v.tr.* To powder; to dust on.

poudreux, *a.* Dusty.

poudrier, *s.m.* Compact.

pouf [puf]. **I.** *int.* (a) Plop! (b) Phew! **2.** *s.m.* Puff; advertisement.

pouffer, *v.i. & pr.* (Se) p. (de rire), to burst out laughing.

poulailler [-laje], *s.m.* (a) Hen-house (b) *Th:* Gallery.

poulain, *s.m.* Colt, foal.

poularde, *s.f.* (Table-)fowl.

poule, *s.f.* **1.** Hen; fowl. **Lait de p.,** egg-flip. **Chair de p.,** goose-flesh. **2.** (a) (At games) Pool. (b) Sweepstake.

poulet, *s.m.* Chicken.

pouliche, *s.f.* Filly.

poulie, *s.f.* Pulley.

poulpe, *s.m.* Octopus.

pouls [pu], *s.m.* Pulse.

poumon, *s.m.* Lung.

poupe, *s.f.* Stern, poop.

poupée, *s.f.* Doll.

pour. I. *prep.* For. **1.** (a) Instead of. (b) Because of, for the sake of. (c) With regard to. **P. moi,** for my part. (d) **Dix p. cent,** ten per cent. **2.** (a) (In order) to. (b) Because of. **3.** (a) **P. que,** in order that. (b) **P. peu que,** if only, if ever.

II. pour, *s.m.* **Le p. et le contre,** the pros and cons.

pourboire, *s.m.* Tip, gratuity.

pourceau, *s.m.* Hog, pig, swine

pourcentage, *s.m.* Percentage.

pourchasser, *v.tr.* To pursue.

pourlécher (se), *v.pr.* **Se p. les lèvres,** to lick one's lips.

pourparlers, *s.m.pl.* (a) Parley. (b) Negotiations.

pourpre. I. *s.f.* (a) Purple (dye). (b) Imperial dignity. **2.** *a. & s.m.* Crimson.

pourquoi, *adv. & conj.* Why? **P. faire?** what for? **P. cela?** why so?

pourri, *a.* Rotten; putrid.

pourrir. I. *v.i.* To rot, decay. **2.** *v.tr.* To rot. **se pourrir,** to go bad.

pourriture, *s.f.* **1.** Rot, decay. **2.** Rottenness.

poursuite, *s.f.* **1.** Pursuit; chase. **2.** *pl.* Prosecution.

poursuivre, *v.tr.* **1.** To pursue; to chase. **2.** To proceed against **3.** To pursue, follow up *Abs* **Poursuivez,** go on; continue.

pourtant, *adv.* Nevertheless, however.

pourtour, *s.m.* Circumference.

pourvoir, *v.* To provide. **1.** *v.ind.tr.* **P. aux frais,** to defray the cost. **2.** *v.tr.* (a) To supply (de. with). (b) To equip. fit.

pourvoyeur, -euse, Purveyor; caterer

pourvu que, *conj.phr.* Provided (that); so long as.

pousse, *s.f.* Young shoot, sprout.

poussée, *s.f.* **1.** Thrust. **2.** Pushing, pressure. **3.** Push, shove.

pousser. I. *v.tr.* (a) To push, shove, thrust. (b) To drive, impel (c) To push on. (d) To put forth, shoot out. (e) To utter. **2.** *v.i.* (a) To push. (b) To grow.

poussière, *s.f.* **1.** Dust. **2. P. d'eau,** spray; spindrift.

poussiéreux, *a.* Dusty.

poussif, *a.* Wheezy, short-winded.

poussin, *s.m.* (a) Chick. (b) Spring chicken.

poutre, *s.f.* **1.** Beam. **2.** Girder.

pouvoir. I. *v.tr.* **1.** To be able; 'can.' **On n'y peut rien,** t can't be helped. **N'en plus p.,** to be exhausted. *v.pr.* **Si cela se peut,** if possible. **2.** 'May'; to be allowed. **3.** To be possible.

II. pouvoir, *s.m.* Power. **1.** Force, means. **2.** Influence. **Être au p. de qn,** to be in s.o.'s power.

3. (a) Authority; competency; power. (b) **Au p.**, in power. **4.** Power of attorney; procuration.

prairie, s.f. Meadow.

praticabilité, s.f Practicability.

praticable, a Practicable.

praticien, s.m. Practitioner.

pratique¹, a Practical useful.

pratique², s.f. **1.** Practice; application (of theory). **2.** Practice, experience. **3.** Custom, business. **4.** Customer

pratiquement, adv. Practically.

pratiquer, v.tr **1.** To practise; to employ **2. P une ouverture.,** to make an opening **3.** To frequent.

pré, s.m. Meadow.

préalable, a. (a) Previous. (b) Preliminary.

préambule, s.m. Preamble.

précaire, a. Precarious.

précairement, adv. Precariously.

précaution, s.f. **1.** Precaution **2.** Caution; wariness; care.

précédemment, adv. Previously.

précédence, s.f. Precedence.

précédent. 1. a. Preceding, previous, former. **2.** s.m. Precedent.

précéder, v.tr To precede.

précepte, s.m. Precept.

précepteur, -trice, s. Tutor; (private) teacher; f. governess.

prêcher, v.tr. To preach.

précieusement, adv. Preciously. **1.** Very carefully. **2.** Affectedly.

précieux, a. (a) Precious. (b) Valuable. (c) Affected.

précipice, s.m. Precipice.

précipitamment, adv. Precipitately.

précipitation, s.f. Precipitancy.

précipité, a. Precipitate; hasty.

précipiter, v.tr. To precipitate.
    se précipiter, to dash. to rush.

précis. 1. a. Precise, exact. definite **2.** s.m Abstract, summary

précisément, adv. Precisely, exactly.

préciser, v.tr. (a) To specify; to state precisely. (b) Abs. To be precise.

précision, s.f. **1.** Precision, exactness, accuracy. **2.** pl. Full particulars.

précoce, a. Precocious; forward

précocité, s.f. Precocity.

préconiser, v.tr. To recommend.

précurseur. 1. s.m. Precursor. **2.** a.m. Precursory.

prédécesseur, s.m. Predecessor.

prédicateur, s.m. Preacher.

prédiction, s.f. Prediction.

prédilection, s.f. Predilection.

prédire, v.tr. To predict.

prédisposer, v.tr. To predispose.

prédisposition, s.f. Predisposition.

prédominance, s.f. Predominance.

prédominant, a. Predominant.

prédominer, v.i. To predominate.

prééminence, s.f. Pre-eminence.

prééminent, a. Pre-eminent.

préfabriqué, a. Prefabricated.

préface, s.f. Preface, foreword.

préfecture, s.f Prefecture

préférable, a. Preferable; better.

préférablement, adv. Preferably.

préféré, a. & s. Favourite.

préférence, s.f. Preference.

préférer, v.tr. To prefer.

préfet, s.m. Prefect.

préfixe, s.m. Prefix.

préhensile, a. Prehensile.

préhistorique, a. Prehistoric.

préjudice, s.m. Prejudice, detriment.

préjudiciable, a. Prejudicial detrimental.

préjudicier, v.i. To be detrimental.

préjugé, s.m. Prejudice.

préjuger, v.tr. To prejudge.

prélasser (se), v.pr. To loll.

prélat, s.m. Prelate.

prélever, v.tr. To deduct in advance.

préliminaire. 1. a. Preliminary. **2.** s.m.pl. Preliminaries.

prélude, s.m. Prelude.

préluder, v.i. To prelude.

prématuré, a. Premature, untimely.

prématurément, adv. Prematurely.

préméditation, s.f. Premeditation.

préméditer, v.tr To premeditate.

prémices, s.f.pl. First-fruits.

premier, a. First. **1.** (a) **Du p. coup,** at the first attempt. **Le p. venu,** anyone. **Première vitesse,** bottom gear. (b) **Matières premières,** raw materials. **2. Au p.,** on the first floor. **3. P. ministre,** Prime Minister. **Monter en première,** to travel first (class).

première, s.f. Th: First-night.

premièrement, adv. First, firstly.

premier-né, a. & s. First-born.

prémonition, s.f. Premonition.

prémunir (se), v.pr. To provide oneself (de, with).

prendre, I. *v.tr.* To take. **1.** To take (up), to take hold of. (*a*) **P.** qch. **sur la table,** to take sth. from the table. (*b*) **P. des pensionnaires** to take in boarders. (*c*) **P.** qch à qn, to take sth. from s.o. (*d*) **A tout p.,** everything considered. **2.** To take, capture. **Qu'est-ce qui lui prend?** what's up with him now? **Bien lui en prit,** it was lucky for him. **3.** (*a*) **P. des voyageurs,** to take up passengers. (*b*) To take; to engage. (*c*) **P.** pour exemple, to take as an example. (*d*) To take, mistake (*e*) **P. un bain,** to take a bath. (*f*) **P. de l'âge,** to be getting on in years. **4. P. le train,** to take the train. **P. le large,** to take to the open sea.

II. **prendre,** *v.i.* **1.** (*a*) To set. (*b*) To freeze (*c*) To jam. **2.** To catch.

se prendre. 1. (*a*) To catch, to be caught (*b*) **Se p. d'amitié,** to take a liking. **2. S'en p. à,** to blame **3. Il sait comment s'y p.,** he knows how to set about it.

preneur, -euse, *s.* Taker.
prénom, *s.m.* Christian name.
préoccupation, *s.f.* Preoccupation.
préoccuper, *v.tr.* To preoccupy.
préparatifs, *s.m.pl.* Preparations.
préparation, *s.f.* Preparation.
préparatoire, *a.* Preparatory.
préparer, *v.tr.* To prepare; to get ready.

se préparer. 1. To prepare. **2.** To make ready.

prépondérance, *s.f.* Preponderance.
prépondérant, *a.* Preponderant.
préposé, *s.* Official in charge.
préposition, *s.f.* Preposition.
prérogative, *s.f.* Prerogative.
près. 1. *adv.* Near. **2.** *Adv.phr.* **A peu p.,** nearly, about. **Au plus p.,** to the nearest point. **De p.,** near; from close to. **3.** *Prep.phr.* **P. de,** near, close to. **P. de partir,** about to start.

présage, *s.m.* Presage, foreboding.
présager, *v.tr.* To presage.
prescription, *s.f.* Directions.
prescrire, *v.tr.* To prescribe.
préséance, *s.f.* Precedence: priority.
présence, *s.f.* Presence.
présent[1], *a.* Present. **A p.,** just now.
présent[2], *s.m.* Present, gift.

présentation, *s.f.* **1.** Presentation. **2.** Introduction.
présentement, *adv.* At present.
présenter, *v.tr.* **1.** To present; to offer. **2.** To present, introduce.

se présenter. 1. To offer; to arise. **2.** To present oneself.

préservation, *s.f.* Preservation.
préserver, *v.tr.* To preserve.
présidence, *s.f.* (*a*) Presidency. (*b*) Chairmanship.
président, *s.* **1.** President. **2.** Chairman.
présidentiel, *a.* Presidential.
présider, *v.tr. & i.* (*a*) To preside over. (*b*) To preside.
présomption, *s.f.* Presumption.
présomptueux, *a.* Presumptuous.
presque, *adv.* Almost, nearly. **2.** Scarcely, hardly. **P amais,** hardly ever.
presqu'île, *s.f.* Peninsula.
pressant, *a.* Pressing, urgent.
presse, *s.f.* **1.** Press, pressing-machine. **2.** Press, newspapers. **3.** Press, crowd. **4.** Haste, urgency.
pressé, *a.* **1.** Pressed, crowded. **2.** Pressed; in a hurry.
pressentiment, *s.m.* Presentiment.
pressentir, *v.tr.* To have a presentiment of.
presse-papiers, *s.m.inv.* Paperweight.
presser, *v.tr.* To press. **1.** To squeeze. **2.** To hurry, push on. **P. le pas,** to hasten one's steps. *Abs.* **L'affaire presse,** the matter is urgent.

se presser. 1. To press, crowd. **2.** To hurry.

pression, *s.f.* Pressure.
preste, *a.* Quick, nimble; alert.
prestement, *adv.* Quickly, nimbly.
prestesse, *s.f.* Quickness, alertness.
prestidigitateur, *s.m.* Conjurer.
prestidigitation, *s.f.* Conjuring.
prestige, *s.m.* **1.** Glamour. **2.** Prestige; high reputation.
prestigieux, *a.* Marvellous.
présumer, *v.tr.* To presume.
prêt[1], *a.* Ready, prepared.
prêt[2], *s.m.* Loan; advance.
prétendant, *s.* **1.** Applicant; claimant. **2.** *s.m.* Suitor.
prétendre, *v.tr.* **1.** To claim; to require. **2.** To maintain, assert; to mean. **3.** To aspire.

prétendu. **I.** *a.* Alleged would-be.
2. *s* Intended.
prétentieusement *adv.* Pretentiously.
prétentieux, *a.* Pretentious showy.
prétention, *s.f* Pretension, claim.
prêter, *v.tr.* **I.** To lend. **P.** attention, to pay attention. **2.** To attribute. **3.** *v.ind.tr.* To give rise.
  se prêter. **I.** To lend oneself.
2. To indulge (*à,* in).
prêteur, -euse, *s.* Lender. **P.** sur gages, pawnbroker.
prétexte, *s.m.* Pretext, excuse.
prétexter, *v.tr.* To pretext.
prêtre, *s.m.* Priest.
preuve, *s.f* Proof, evidence.
prévaloir, *v.i* To prevail.
prévarication, *s.f* Breach of trust.
prévariquer, *v.i* To betray one's trust
prévenance, *s.f* Attention ; kindness.
prévenant, *a.* **I.** Kind attentive.
2. Pleasing, prepossessing.
prévenir, *v.tr* **I.** (*a*) To anticipate.
(*b*) To prevent. **2.** To predispose.
3. To inform, forewarn
préventif, *a.* Preventive.
prévention, *s.f.* Prejudice, bias.
prévenu, **I.** *a.* Prejudiced biased.
2. *s* Accused.
prévision, *s.f.* Forecast ; anticipation.
prévoir, *v.tr.* **I.** To foresee, forecast.
2. To provide for.
prévôt, *s.m.* Provost.
prévoyance, *s.f* Foresight, precaution. **Société de p.,** provident society.
prévoyant, *a.* Provident ; far-sighted.
prier, *v.tr.* **I.** To pray. **2.** To ask beg. **Je vous en prie!** oh do !
prière, *s.f.* **I.** Prayer. **2.** Request.
prieur, -e, *s* Prior ; *f.* prioress.
prieuré, *s.m.* Priory.
primaire, *a.* Primary.
prime, *s.f* **I.** Premium. **2.** Bounty, bonus.
primer, *v.tr.* To excel, surpass.
prime-sautier, *a.* Impulsive.
primeur, *s.f.* Early product (fruit vegetables, etc.).
primevère, *s.f.* Primrose.
primitif, *a.* Primitive ; primary.
primitivement, *adv.* Primitively.
prince, *s.m.* Prince.
princesse, *s.f.* Princess.
princier, *a.* Princely.

principal, -aux. **I.** *a.* Principal, chief. **2.** *s.m* (*a*) Principal ; headmaster. (*b*) Principal thing. (*c*) *Com:* Principal.
principauté, *s.f.* Principality.
principe, *s.m.* Principle.
printemps [-tã], *s.m.* Spring.
priorité, *s.f.* Priority. **Route de p.,** major road.
pris, *a.* (*a*) Engaged, occupied. (*b*) **P. de colère,** in a passion.
prise, *s.f.* **I.** Hold, grasp. (*a*) **Lâcher p.,** to let go. (*b*) **Aux prises,** in conflict. **2.** Congealing setting.
3. (*a*) Taking ; capture. (*b*) *Nau:* Prize. **4.** **P. de tabac,** pinch of snuff.
priser, *v.tr.* (*a*) To appraise. (*b*) To prize.
prismatique, *a.* Prismatic.
prisme, *s.m* Prism.
prison, *s.f.* Prison.
prisonnier, *s.* Prisoner.
privation, *s.f.* **I.** Deprivation. **2.** Privation, hardship.
privé, *a.* Private.
priver, *v.tr.* To deprive.
  se priver, to deny oneself.
privilège, *s.m.* Privilege.
privilégié, *a.* Privileged.
privilégier, *v.tr.* To privilege.
prix, *s.m.* **I.** (*a*) Value, worth, cost.
(*b*) Price. **C'est hors de p.,** the price is prohibitive. **N'avoir pas de p.,** to be priceless. (*c*) Charge. **2.** Reward, prize.
probabilité, *s.f.* Probability.
probable, *a* Probable, likely.
probablement, *adv.* Probably.
probe, *a.* Honest, upright.
probité, *s.f.* Probity, integrity.
problématique, *a.* Problematical
problème, *s.m.* Problem.
procédé, *s.m.* **I.** Proceeding, dealing, conduct. **2.** Process ; method.
procéder, *v.i.* To proceed.
procédure, *s.f.* **I.** Procedure. **2.** Proceedings.
procès, *s.m.* Lawsuit ; trial.
procession, *s.f.* Procession.
procès-verbal, *s.m.* **I.** Report ; minute. **2.** Policeman's report. *pl. procès-verbaux.*
prochain. **I.** *a.* (*a*) Nearest. (*b*) Next. (*c*) Near at hand. **2.** *s.m.* Neighbour, fellow-creature.
prochainement, *adv.* Shortly, soon

proche. 1. *adv.* Near. 2. *a* Near, neighbouring.

proclamation, *s.f.* Proclamation.

proclamer, *v.tr.* To proclaim.

procuration. *s.f.* Proxy. power of attorney.

procurer, *v.tr.* To procure (*à*, for). Se p. de l'argent, to raise money.

procureur, *s.m.* P. de la République = public prosecutor.

prodige, *s.m.* Prodigy, marvel.

prodigieusement, *adv.* Prodigiously.

prodigieux, *a.* Prodigious.

prodigue, *a.* Prodigal; lavish.

prodiguer, *v.tr.* 1. To be lavish of. 2. To waste. squander.

producteur, -trice, *s.* Producer.

productif, *a.* Productive.

production, *s.f.* 1. Production. 2. Yield; output.

produire, *v.tr.* To produce. se produire, to occur, happen.

produit, *s.m.* Product; proceeds.

proéminence, *s.f.* Prominence.

proéminent, *a.* Prominent.

profanation, *s.f.* Profanation, desecration.

profane. 1. *a.* Profane. 2. *s.* Uninitiated person; layman.

profaner, *v.tr.* To profane; to desecrate; to violate.

proférer, *v.tr.* To utter.

professer, *v.tr* To teach; to exercise, carry on.

professeur, *s.m.* Professor; teacher.

profession, *s.f.* 1. Profession, declaration. 2. Occupation, profession.

professionnel, *a.* Professional.

profil [-fil] *s m.* Profile, side-face.

profit, *s.m.* Profit, benefit.

profitable, *a.* Profitable.

profitablement, *adv.* Profitably.

profiter, *v.i.* 1. (*a*) P. de, to profit by; to turn to account. (*b*) To make a profit.

profiteur, *s.m.* Profiteer.

profond, *a.* (*a*) Deep (*b*) Profound.

profondément, *adv.* Profoundly, deeply.

profondeur, *s.f.* Depth.

profus, *a.* Profuse.

profusément, *adv.* Profusely

profusion, *s.f* Profusion.

progéniture, *s.f.* Progeny, offspring.

programme, *s.m.* Programme.

progrès, *s.m.* Progress

progresser, *v.i.* To progress.

progressif, *a.* Progressive

progressivement. *adv.* Progressively.

prohiber, *v.tr.* To prohibit, forbid

prohibitif, *a* Prohibitive.

prohibition, *s.f* Prohibition.

proie, *s.f* Prey

projecteur, *s.m* Searchlight.

projectile, *s.m.* Projectile; missile.

projection, *s.f* Projection.

projet, *s.m.* Project, plan.

projeter, *v.tr* To project. 1. To throw 2. To plan, contemplate se projeter, to stand out

prolifique, *a.* Prolific.

prolixe, *a.* Prolix, verbose, wordy.

prolixité, *s.f.* Prolixity, verbosity.

prologue, *s.m.* Prologue.

prolongation, *s.f.* Prolongation.

prolongé. *a* Prolonged; long-drawn.

prolongement, *s.m.* Extension

prolonger, *v.tr* To prolong; to extend. se prolonger, to be prolonged; to continue, extend.

promenade, *s.f.* 1. (*a*) Walking. (*b*) Stroll, outing. P. à cheval, ride. P. en bateau. row. sail. 2. Promenade, walk.

promener, *v.tr.* 1. To take, lead, about. 2. P. sa main sur, to pass one's hand over. se promener, to walk; to go for a walk, for a drive, etc.

promeneur, -euse *s.* Walker, pedestrian.

promesse, *s.f.* Promise, assurance.

promettre, *v.tr.* To promise.

promontoire, *s.m* Promontory.

promotion, *s.f.* Promotion.

prompt [prɔ̃] *a.* Prompt, ready.

promptement [prɔ̃t-] *adv.* Promptly.

promptitude [prɔ̃t-] *s.f* Promptitude; quickness.

promu, *a.* Promoted, raised.

promulguer, *v.tr* To promulgate.

pronom, *s.m.* Pronoun.

prononcé, *a.* Pronounced, decided.

prononcer, *v.tr.* To pronounce. (*a*) To utter. (*b*) To deliver. *Abs.* To declare. se prononcer, to express one's opinion; to make a decision.

prononciation, *s.f.* Pronunciation

pronostic [-tik], *s.m.* Forecast.
pronostiquer, *v.tr.* To forecast.
propagande, *s.f.* Propaganda.
propagation, *s.f.* Propagation.
propager, *v.tr.* To propagate.
  se propager, to spread.
propension, *s.f.* Propensity.
prophète, prophétesse, *s.* Prophet
  seer; *f.* prophetess.
prophétie, *s.f* Prophecy.
prophétique, *a.* Prophetic.
prophétiser, *v.tr.* (*a*) To prophesy
  (*b*) To foretell.
propice, *a.* Propitious; favourable.
propitiation, *s.f.* Propitiation.
propitiatoire, *a.* Propitiatory.
proportion, *s.f.* **1.** Proportion. ratio.
  2. *pl.* Size.
proportionné, *a.* **1.** Proportioned.
  2. Proportionate.
proportionnel, *a.* Proportional.
proportionnellement, *adv.* Proportionately.
propos, *s.m.* **1.** Purpose. **2.** Subject.
  A ce p., in this connection. A
  p., to the point; in the nick of
  time; by the way. **3.** Utterance
  remark; *pl.* talk.
proposer, *v.tr.* To propose.
  se proposer. 1. To come forward. **2.** To have (sth.) in view.
proposition, *s.f.* Proposal.
propre, *a.* (*a*) Proper. (*b*) Peculiar.
  (*c*) Own. (*d*) Appropriate. P. à
  tout, fit for anything. (*e*) Clean.
proprement, *adv.* **1.** Properly **2.**
  Cleanly, neatly.
propreté, *s.f* Cleanliness; neatness.
propriétaire, *s.m. & f.* **1.** Proprietor;
  owner. **2.** Landlord, landlady.
propriété, *s.f.* **1.** (*a*) Ownership
  (*b*) Property. estate. **2.** Property.
  characteristic. **3.** Propriety.
propulsion, *s.f.* Propulsion.
proroger, *v.tr.* **1.** To prorogue.
  2. To extend (time-limit).
prosaïque, *a.* Prosaic.
prosaïquement, *adv.* Prosaically.
prosateur, -trice, *s.* Prose-writer.
proscrire, *v.tr.* To proscribe,
  outlaw.
proscrit. 1. *a.* Proscribed. **2.** *s.*
  Outlaw.
prose, *s.f.* Prose.
prospecter, *v.tr.* To prospect.
prospecteur, *s.m.* Prospector.

prospectus [-ty:s], *s.m.* **1.** Prospectus. **2.** Handbill.
prospère, *a.* **1.** Favourable. **2.** Prosperous, thriving, flourishing.
prospérer, *v.i.* To prosper, thrive.
prospérité, *s.f.* Prosperity.
prosterné, *a.* Prostrate.
prosterner (se), *v.pr.* (*a*) To prostrate oneself; to bow down. (*b*) To
  grovel.
prostituée, *s.f.* Prostitute.
prostration, *s.f.* Prostration.
protecteur, -trice. 1. *s.* (*a*) Protector. (*b*) Patron. **2.** *a* (*a*) Protecting. (*b*) Patronizing.
protection, *s.f.* **1.** Protection. **2.**
  Patronage, nfluence.
protectorat, *s.m.* Protectorate.
protégé, *s.* (*a*) Protégé. *f.* protégée.
  (*b*) Dependant.
protéger, *v.tr.* To protect. **1.** To
  shelter, guard. **2.** To patronize.
protestant, *a. & s.* Protestant.
protestation, *s.f.* **1.** Protestation,
  asseveration. **2.** Protest.
protester. 1. *v.tr.* To protest, asseverate. **2.** *v.i.* To protest.
protubérance, *s.f.* Protuberance;
  knob.
protubérant, *a.* Protuberant.
proue, *s.f.* Prow.
prouesse, *s.f.* Prowess.
prouver, *v.tr.* To prove.
provenance, *s.f* Source, origin.
  En p. de, coming from.
provençal, -aux, *a. & s.* Provencal.
provenir, *v.i.* To proceed, come; to
  originate.
proverbe, *s.m.* Proverb.
proverbial, -aux, *a.* Proverbial.
providence, *s.f.* Providence.
providentiel, *a.* Providential.
province, *s.f.* Province.
provincial, -aux, *a. & s.* Provincial.
provision, *s.f.* **1.** Provision, store,
  supply. **2.** Funds, reserve.
provisoire, *a.* Provisional.
provisoirement, *adv.* Provisionally.
provocant, *a.* Provocative.
provocation, *s.f.* Provocation.
provoquer, *v.tr.* **1.** To provoke.
  2. To instigate. **3.** To cause.
proximité, *s.f.* Proximity.
prude. 1. *a.* Prudish. **2.** *s.f.* Prude.
prudemment, *adv.* Prudently; carefully.

prudence, s.f. Prudence, carefulness.
prudent, a. Prudent, discreet.
prune, s.f. Plum. **P. de Damas,** damson.
pruneau, s.m Prune, dried plum.
prunelle, s.f. **1.** Sloe. **2.** Pupil (of the eye).
prunellier, s.m. Blackthorn.
prunier, s.m. Plum-tree.
psalmodier, v.i. To intone, to chant.
psaume, s.m. Psalm.
pseudonyme. 1. a. Pseudonymous. **2.** s.m. Pseudonym.
psychique, a. Psychic(al).
psychologie [-kɔl-], s.f. Psychology.
psychologique [-kɔl-], a. Psychological.
psychologue [-kɔl-], s.m. Psychologist.
puant, a. Stinking, noisome.
puanteur, s.f. Stench; foul smell.
public, -ique [-lik]. **1.** a. Public. **2.** s.m. Public, people.
publication, s.f. Publication.
publicité, s.f. Publicity, advertising.
publier, v.tr. To publish.
publiquement, adv. Publicly.
puce, s.f. Flea.
pudeur, s.f. Modesty; shame.
pudibond, a. Easily shocked.
pudique, a. Modest; chaste.
pudiquement, adv. Modestly.
puer, v.i. To stink, smell.
puéril [-ril], a. Puerile, childish
puérilement, adv. Childishly.
pugilat, s.m. Pugilism, boxing.
pugiliste, s.m. Pugilist, boxer.
puis, adv. (a) Then, afterwards next. (b) Besides.
puiser, v.tr. To draw; to derive.
puisque, conj. Since, as.
puissamment, adv. Powerfully.
puissance, s.f. Power; force.
puissant, a. Powerful, mighty.

puits [pɥi], s.m. **1.** Well hole. **2.** Shaft, pit.
pulluler, v.i. To swarm.
pulpe, s.f. Pulp.
pulper, v.tr. To pulp.
pulpeux, a. Pulpy.
pulsation, s.f. Pulsation. **1.** Throbbing. **2.** Throb; (heart-)beat.
pulvérisation, s.f. (a) Pulverization. (b) Spraying.
pulvériser, v.tr. (a) To pulverize. (b) To spray.
punaise, s.f. **1.** Bug. **2.** Drawing-pin.
punir, v.tr. To punish; to avenge.
punition, s.f. Punishment.
pupille[1] [-pil], s.m. & f. Ward.
pupille[2], s.f. Pupil (of the eye).
pupitre, s.m. Desk. **P. à musique,** music-stand.
pur, a. Pure. **1. Pur hasard.** mere chance. **2. Ciel pur,** clear sky.
purée, s.f. (a) **P. de pommes de terre,** mashed potatoes. (b) Thick soup.
pureté, s.f. Purity; pureness.
purgatif, a. & s.m. Purgative.
purgatoire, s.m. Purgatory.
purge, s.f. **1.** Purge. **2.** Paying off, redemption.
purger, v.tr. (a) To purge, cleanse. (b) To redeem, pay off.
purification, s.f. Purification.
purifier, v.tr. To purify, cleanse.
puritain, s. Puritan.
pur-sang, s.m.inv. Thoroughbred.
pusillanime, a. Pusillanimous.
putatif, a. Supposed, presumed.
putois, s.m. Polecat.
putréfaction, s.f. Putrefaction.
putréfier, v.tr. To putrefy.
putride, a. Putrid, tainted.
pygmée, s.m. & f. Pygmy.
pyjama, s.m. Pyjamas.
pyramide, s.f. Pyramid.
python, s.m. Python.

Q

Q, q [ky], s.m. (The letter) Q, q.
quadrille [-ri:j], s.m. Quadrille.
quadrillé [-rije], a. Squared, cross-ruled; chequered.
quadrimoteur, -trice [kwad-], a. Av: Four-engined.
quadrupède [kwad-]. **1.** a. Four-footed. **2.** s.m. Quadruped.

quadruple [kwad-], a. & s.m. Quadruple, fourfold.
quai, s.m. (a) Quay, wharf, pier. (b) Embankment. (c) Platform. **Le train est à q.,** the train is in
qualificatif, a. Qualifying.
qualification, s.f. **1.** Qualifying. **2.** Designation, name, title.

qualifié, *a.* Qualified.

qualifier, *v.tr.* To style, term.
se qualifier. **1.** To style oneself
2. To qualify.

qualité, *s.f* **1.** Quality. **2.** Quality
property. **3.** Capacity, occupation
Avoir q. to be qualified. **4.** Title
rank.

quand. When **1.** *conj.* Even if, even
though Q. même, all the same. **2.**
adv. Depuis q. how long.

quant, *adv.* Q. à, as for.

quantième, *s.m.* Day of the month

quantité, *s.f* Quantity

quarantaine, *s.f.* **1.** (About) forty.
2. Quarantine.

quarante, *num.a.inv.* & *s.m.inv.*
Forty.

quart, *s.m.* **1.** Quarter, fourth part.
Deux heures et q., a quarter past
two. **2.** Watch. Être de q., to be
on watch.

quartier, *s.m.* **1.** Quartei. **2.** Part,
portion. **3.** (*a*) District. (*b*) Q.
général, headquarters.

quartz [kwarts], *s.m.* Quartz.

quasi, *adv.* Quasi, almost.

quatorze, *num.a.inv.* & *s.m.inv*
Fourteen.

quatre, *num.a.inv.* & *s.m.inv.* Four.

Quatre-Cantons. *Pr.n.* Le lac des
Q.-C., the Lake of Lucerne.

quatre-vingt-dix, *num.a.* & *s.m*
Ninety.

quatre-vingts, *num.a.* & *s.m* Eighty.

quatrième. 1. *num.a.* & *s.* Fourth.
2. *s.m.* Fourth (part).

quatuor [kwatyɔːr], *s.m.* Quartet.

que¹, *rel.pron.* That; whom; which;
what.

que², *interr.pron.neut.* **1.** What? **2.** (*a*)
Why? (*b*) Qu'il est beau! how
handsome he is! Que de gens!
what a lot of people!

que³, *conj.* That; lest. **1.** (*a*) Qu'elle
entre! let her come in! (*b*) Whether.
2. Aussi grand que moi, as tall as I.
3. (*a*) Ne . . . que, only. Il ne fait
que de sortir, he has only just gone
out. (*b*) Ne . . . pas que, not only.

quel, quelle, *a.* & *pron.* What,
which. **1.** Q. que soit le résultat,
whatever the result may be. **2.** Quels
sont ces messieurs? who are these
gentlemen? **3.** Quel homme! what
a man!

quelconque, *a.* **1.** Any (whatever).
2. Some sort of.

quelque 1. *a.* (*a*) Some, any. (*b*)
Some, a few (*c*) Q. . . . qui, que,
whatever. **2.** *adv.* (*a*) Some about.
(*b*) Q . . . que, however.

quelque chose, *indef. pron. m. ınv.*
Something, anything.

quelquefois, *adv.* Sometimes; now
and then.

quelque part, *adv.* Somewhere.

quelqu'un *indef. pron.* **1.** *m.* & *f.*
One (or other). Quelques-un(e)s
d'entre nous, a few of us. **2.** *m.*
Someone; anyone.

quenouille [-nuːj], *s.f.* Distaff.

querelle, *s.f.* Quarrel dispute.

quereller, *v.tr.* To quarrel with
se quereller, to quarrel, wrangle

querelleur, -euse, *a* Quarrelsome.

quérir, quérir, *v.tr.* To fetch.

qu'est-ce que, *interr.pron.* What?
Qu'est-ce que c'est que ça? what's
that?

qu'est-ce qui, *interr. pron.* What?

question, *s.f.* (*a*) Question, query
(*b*) Question, matter.

questionner, *v.tr.* To question.

quête, *s.f.* **1.** Quest, search. **2.** Faire
la q., to take up the collection.

quêter, *v.tr* To collect (alms)

queue, *s.f.* **1.** Tail **2.** Handle (of
pan); pin (of brooch); pigtail
3. Queue. Faire (la) q., to queue up.
4. *Bill:* Cue.

qui¹, *rel.pron.* **1.** Who, that, which
2. Whom; which. **3.** (*a*) Qui que,
whoever, whomever? (*b*) Qui que
ce soit, anyone (whatever).

qui², *interr.pron.m.sg.* **1.** Who?
whom? **2.** What?

quiconque, *indef.pron.m.sg.* **1.** Whoever; anyone who. **2.** Anybody.

qui est-ce que, *interr.pron.* Whom?

qui est-ce qui, *interr.pron.* Who?

quiétude, *s.f.* Quietude.

quille¹ [kiːj], *s.f.* Ninepin. skittle.

quille², *s.f.* Keel.

quincaillerie [-kaj-], *s.f.* Hardware
ironmongery.

quincaillier [-kaje], *s.m.* Ironmonger.

quinine, *s.f.* Quinine

quinte, *s.f.* Q. de tox x. fit of coughing.

quintuple, *a.* & *s.m.* Fivefold.

quinzaine, *s.f.* **1.** (About) fifteen
2. Fortnight.

quinze, *num.a.inv. & s.m.inv.* **1.** Fifteen. **2. Q. jours,** a fortnight.

quiproquo, *s.m.* Mistake; misunderstanding.

quittance, *s.f.* Receipt, discharge.

quitte, *a.* Free, quit.

quitter, *v.tr.* To leave, quit; to take off.

qui-vive, *s.m.inv.* Who goes there? Sur le q.-v., on the alert.

quoi¹, *rel.pron.* **1.** What. **2. De q.,** enough. Il n'y a pas de q., don't mention it. **3. Sans q.,** otherwise.

4. Q. qui, q. que, whatever. **Q. qu'il en soit,** be that as it may. **Q. que ce soit,** anything (whatever).

quoi², *interr.pron.* What? **A q. bon?** what's the use?

quoique, *conj.* (Al)though.

quolibet, *s.m.* Gibe.

quote-part, *s.f.* Share, quota portion. *pl. quotes-parts.*

quotidien. 1. *a.* Daily, everyday. **2.** *s.m.* Daily (paper).

quotidiennement, *adv.* Daily.

R

R, r [εːr], *s.f.* (The letter) R, r.

rabais, *s.m.* Discount; reduction.

rabaisser, *v.tr.* **1.** To lower. **2.** (a) To depreciate. (b) To humble.

rabat-joie, *s.m. & f.inv.* Kill-joy.

rabattre, *v.tr.* **1.** To lower. **2.** To reduce; take down. **3.** To beat back.

rabbin, *s.m.* Rabbi.

rabot, *s.m.* Tls: Plane.

raboter, *v.tr.* To plane.

rabougri, *a.* Stunted.

rabrouer, *v.tr.* To scold, snub.

racommodage, *s.m.* **1.** Mending, repairing. **2.** Mend, repair.

raccommoder, *v.tr.* **1.** To mend, repair. **2.** To reconcile.

raccorder, *v.tr.* To join, connect.

raccourci. 1. *a.* Shortened; short. **2.** *s.m.* (a) Abridgement. (b) Short cut.

raccourcir. 1. *v.tr.* (a) To shorten. (b) To abridge; to cut short. **2.** *v.i. & pr.* To grow shorter; to shrink.

raccourcissement, *s.m.* **1.** Shortening. **2.** Shrinking.

raccrocher, *v.tr.* To hang up again.

race, *s.f.* Race. **1.** Strain. **2.** Breed.

rachat, *s.m.* Repurchase; redemption.

racheter, *v.tr.* (a) To buy back. (b) To redeem.

racine, *s.f.* Root.

racler, *v.tr.* To scrape.

raconter, *v.tr.* To tell, relate.

raconteur, -euse, *s.* Narrator.

radar, *s.m.* Radar.

rade, *s.f.* Roadstead roads.

radeau, *s.m.* Raft.

radiateur, *s.m.* Radiator.

radiation, *s.f.* Radiation.

radical, -aux, *a. & s.m.* Radical.

radicalement, *adv.* Radically.

radieux, *a.* Radiant; beaming.

radio. 1. *s.m.* Wireless message; radio. **2.** *s.f.* Wireless.

radioactif, *a.* Radio-active.

radiodiffuser, *v.tr.* To broadcast.

radiodiffusion, *s.f.* Broadcasting.

radioémission, *s.f.* **1.** Broadcasting. **2.** Broadcast.

radiogramme, *s.m.* Radiogram.

radis, *s.m.* Radish.

radium [-jɔm], *s.m.* Radium.

radotage, *s.m.* Drivel; dotage.

radoter, *v.i.* To drivel.

radoteur, -euse, *s.* Dotard.

radoucir, *v.tr.* To calm, soften. **se radoucir. 1.** To grow softer. **2.** To grow milder.

radoucissement, *s.m.* (a) Softening. (b) Getting milder.

rafale, *s.f.* Squall; blast.

raffermir, *v.tr.* **1.** To make firm(er). **2.** To confirm, strengthen. **se raffermir,** to harden.

raffermissement, *s.m.* **1.** Making firmer. **2.** Strengthening.

raffinage, *s.m.* Refining.

raffiné, *a.* Refined.

raffinement, *s.m.* **1.** Refining. **2.** Refinement.

raffiner, *v.tr.* To refine. **se raffiner,** to become refined.

raffinerie, *s.f.* Refinery.

raffoler, *v.i.* To be very fond.

rafraîchir, *v.tr.* **1.** To refresh; to air. **2.** To freshen up. **se rafraîchir,** to refresh oneself.

rafraîchissant, *a.* Refreshing.

rafraîchissement, *s.m.* **1.** Freshening up. **2.** *pl.* Refreshments.

rage, *s.f.* **1.** Madness; rabies. **2.** Rage, fury.

rageur, -euse, *a.* Passionate.

rageusement, *adv.* Angrily.

ragoût, *s.m.* Stew, ragout.

raid [red], *s.m.* **1.** Raid. **2.** Long-distance run or flight.

raide. 1. *a.* (*a*) Stiff; tight. (*b*) Stiff; unbending. (*c*) Steep; abrupt. **2.** *adv.* **Tomber r. mort,** to fall stone-dead.

raideur, *s.f.* **1.** Stiffness. **2.** Steepness.

raidillon [-dijɔ̃], *s.m.* Abrupt path.

raidir, *v.tr.* To stiffen; to tighten. **se raidir,** to stiffen, to grow stiff.

raie¹, *s.f.* **1.** Line, stroke. **2.** Stripe. **3.** Parting (of the hair).

raie², *s.f.* Ray, skate.

raifort, *s.m.* Horse-radish.

rail [rɑ:j], *s.m.* Rail.

railler [rɑje], *v.tr.* To jeer at. **se railler,** to make game.

raillerie [rɑjri], *s.f.* Raillery.

railleur, -euse [rɑjœ:r, -ø:z]. **1.** *a.* Bantering, scoffing. **2.** *s.* Banterer, scoffer.

rainure, *s.f.* Groove, furrow.

raisin, *s.m.* **Le r., du r.,** grapes. **Grappe de r.,** bunch of grapes. **R. sec,** raisin. **R. de Smyrne,** sultana.

raison, *s.f.* **1.** Reason, motive. **R. d'être,** reason, justification. **2.** Reason. **Parler r.,** to talk sense. **Rendre r. de qch.,** to explain sth. **3.** **Avoir r.** to be right. **Comme de r.,** as one might expect. **4.** Satisfaction. **Avoir r. de,** to get the better of. **5.** **R. sociale,** name, style. **6. A r. de,** at the rate of.

raisonnable, *a.* Reasonable.

raisonnablement, *adv.* Reasonably.

raisonné, *a.* Reasoned. **Catalogue r.,** descriptive catalogue.

raisonnement, *s.m.* Reasoning.

raisonner. 1. *v.i.* To reason; to argue. **2.** *v.tr.* To reason with.

raisonneur, -euse. **1.** *a.* Argumentative. **2.** *s.* Reasoner, arguer.

rajeunir. 1. *v.tr.* To rejuvenate. **2.** *v.i.* To grow young again.

rajeunissement, *s.m.* Rejuvenation.

rajustement, *s.m.* Readjustment.

rajuster, *v.tr.* To readjust.

râle, *s.m.* Rattle (in the throat); death-rattle.

ralentir, *v.tr. & i.* To slacken, slow down.

ralentissement, *s.m.* Slackening; slowing down.

râler, *v.i.* To rattle (in one's throat).

ralliement, *s.m.* Rally; assembly.

rallier, *v.tr.* **1.** (*a*) To rally, assemble. (*b*) To rejoin (ship). **2.** To win over.

rallonger, *v.tr.* To lengthen.

rallumer, *v.tr.* To relight.

ramage, *s.m.* Song, warbling.

ramasser, *v.tr.* **1.** To gather together. **2.** To collect, gather. **3.** To pick up. **se ramasser. 1.** To collect, gather. **2.** To pick oneself up.

rame, *s.f.* Oar, scull.

rameau, *s.m.* **1.** (*a*) (Small) branch; bough. (*b*) **Le dimanche des Rameaux,** Palm Sunday. **2.** Branch, subdivision.

ramener, *v.tr.* To bring back.

ramer, *v.i.* To row.

ramier, *s.m.* Ring-dove.

ramification, *s.f.* Ramification.

ramifier (se), *v.pr.* To branch out.

ramollir, *v.tr.* To soften.

ramoner, *v.tr.* To sweep (chimney).

ramoneur, *s.m.* Chimney-sweep.

rampant, *a.* (*a*) Creeping; crawling. (*b*) Grovelling, cringing.

rampe, *s.f.* **1.** Slope, rise, incline. **2.** Banisters. **3.** Footlights.

ramper, *v.i.* To creep, crawl.

rancart, *s.m.* **Mettre au r.,** to discard.

rance, *a.* Rancid, rank.

rancidité, *s.f.* Rancidity, rancidness.

rancœur, *s.f.* Rancour; bitterness.

rançon, *s.f.* Ransom.

rançonner, *v.tr.* To ransom.

rancune, *s.f.* Rancour, spite.

rancunier, *a.* Vindictive, spiteful.

randonnée, *s.f.* Outing, run, trip.

rang, *s.m.* **1.** (*a*) Row, line. (*b*) **Sortir du r.,** to rise from the ranks. **2.** (*a*) Rank; station. **Par r. de,** according to. (*b*) Status.

rangé, *a.* **1.** Orderly. **2.** Steady.

rangée, *s.f.* Row, line; tier.

ranger, *v.tr.* **1.** To arrange; to draw up. **2.** To put away. **3.** To arrange, tidy. **se ranger. 1.** To draw up, line up. **2.** To get out of the way. **3.** To settle down.

ranimer, *v.tr.* To revive; to put fresh life into.

se ranimer, to revive.

Raoul [-ul]. *Pr.n.m.* Ralph.

rapace, *a.* Rapacious.

rapacité, *s.f.* Rapacity.

rapatriement, *s.m.* Repatriation.

rapatrier, *v.tr.* To repatriate.

râpe, *s.f.* Rasp; grater.

râpé, *a.* Threadbare.

râper, *v.tr.* To rasp; to grate.

rapetisser. 1. *v.tr.* To make smaller. **2.** *v.i. & pr.* To shorten; to shrink.

rapide. 1. *a.* (*a*) Rapid, fast. (*b*) Steep. **2.** *s.m.* (*a*) Rapid. (*b*) Express.

rapidement, *adv.* (*a*) Rapidly. (*b*) Steeply.

rapidité, *s.f.* Rapidity, swiftness.

rapiécer, *v.tr.* To piece, patch.

rapière, *s.f.* Rapier.

rappel, *s.m.* Recall.

rappeler, *v.tr.* **1.** (*a*) To recall; to call back. (*b*) R. à l'ordre, to call to order. **2.** To call back to mind.

se rappeler, to recall, remember.

rapport, *s.m.* I. **1.** Return, yield. Maison de r., block of flats. **2.** Report; account.
  II. **rapport. 1.** Relation, connection. En r., in keeping. Par r. à, in comparison with. **2.** Proportion. **3.** Relations, intercourse.

rapporter, *v.tr.* **1.** To bring back. **2.** To bring in, yield. **3.** To report. **4.** To revoke.

se rapporter. 1. To agree. **2.** To refer. **3.** S'en r. à, to rely on.

rapporteur, *s.m.* Reporter, recorder.

rapproché, *a.* Near.

rapprochement, *s.m.* **1.** Bringing together. **2.** Coming together.

rapprocher, *v.tr.* (*a*) To bring closer. (*b*) To bring together.

se rapprocher, to draw near (*de*, to).

rapsodie, *s.f.* Rhapsody.

rapt [rapt], *s.m.* Abduction.

raquette, *s.f.* **1.** *Games:* Racket. **2.** Snow-shoe.

rare, *a.* **1.** Rare, uncommon. **2.** Sparse, scanty.

rarement, *adv.* Rarely, seldom.

rareté, *s.f.* **1.** Scarceness. **2.** Rarity.

ras. 1. *a.* (*a*) Close-cropped. A poil ras, short-haired. (*b*) Rase campagne, open country. **Faire table** rase, to make a clean sweep. **2.** *s.m.* Au ras de, flush with.

raser, *v.tr.* **1.** To shave. **2.** To raze. **3.** To graze, skim (over).

se raser, to shave

rasoir, *s.m.* Razor.

rassasier, *v.tr* **1.** To satisfy. **2.** To sate, satiate.

se rassasier, to eat one's fill.

rassemblement, *s.m.* **1.** Assembling, gathering. **2.** Assemblage, crowd.

rassembler, *v.tr.* To assemble; to gather together.

se rassembler, to assemble.

rasseoir, *v.tr.* To settle, compose.

se rasseoir, to resume one's seat.

rasséréner(se), *v.pr.* To brighten up.

rassis, *a.* (*a*) Staid, sedate. (*b*) Pain r., stale bread.

rassurer, *v.tr.* To reassure, cheer.

se rassurer, to feel reassured.

rat, *s.m.* Rat.

rataplan, *s.m.* Rat-tat, rub-a-dub.

ratatiné, *a.* Wizened.

ratatiner (se), *v.pr.* To shrivel (up).

rate, *s.f.* Spleen.

raté. 1. *s.* Failure. **2.** *s.m.* Misfire.

râteau, *s.m.* Rake.

râtelier, *s.m.* **1.** Rack. **2.** Row of teeth.

rater. 1. *v.i.* (*a*) To miss fire. (*b*) To fail; to miscarry. **2.** *v.tr.* To miss.

ratière, *s.f.* Rat-trap.

ratification, *s.f.* Ratification.

ratifier, *v.tr.* To ratify; to approve.

ration, *s.f.* Ration(s), allowance.

rationnel, *a.* Rational.

rationnellement, *adv.* Rationally.

rationnement, *s.m.* Rationing.

rationner, *v.tr.* To ration.

ratisser, *v.tr.* To rake.

rattacher, *v.tr.* **1.** To refasten. **2.** (*a*) To bind. (*b*) To connect.

se rattacher, to be connected.

rattraper, *v.tr.* **1.** To recapture. **2.** To catch up.

se rattraper, to recoup oneself.

raturer, *v.tr.* To erase, scratch out.

rauque, *a.* Hoarse, raucous, harsh.

ravage, *s.m.* Havoc, ravages.

ravager, *v.tr.* To ravage.

ravauder, *v.tr.* To mend, patch.

ravi, *a.* **1.** Entranced. **2.** Delighted.

ravin, *s.m.* Ravine, gully.

raviner, *v.tr.* To hollow out.

ravir, *v.tr.* To ravish.

raviser (se), *v.pr.* To change one's mind.

ravissant, *a* Delightful.

ravissement, *s.m.* Rapture.

raviver, *v.tr* 1. To revive. 2. To brighten up.

rayer, *v.tr.* 1. *a)* To scratch; to score *(b)* To rule line. *(c)* To stripe. 2. To strike out.

rayon[1], *s.m.* 1. Ray; beam. 2. Radius. 3. Spoke.

rayon[2], *s.m.* 1. R. de miel, honeycomb. 2. *(a)* Shelf. *(b)* Department (in shop).

rayonnant, *a* Radiant, beaming.

rayonne, *s.f.* Rayon; artificial silk.

rayonnement, *s.m.* *(a)* Radiation *(b)* Radiance.

rayonner, *v.i.* *(a)* To radiate *(b)* To beam, shine.

rayure, *s.f.* 1. *(a)* Stripe, streak. *(b)* Scratch. *(c)* Groove. 2. Erasure.

raz [rɑ], *s.m.* Strong current; race.

réaction, *s.f.* Reaction. **Avion à r.,** jet plane.

réactionnaire, *a. & s* Reactionary.

réagir, *v.i.* To react.

réalisation, *s.f.* Realization; carrying into effect carrying out.

réaliser, *v.tr.* 1. To effect. 2. To realize (assets).

se réaliser, to come true

réalisme, *s.m* Realism.

réaliste. 1. *a.* Realistic. 2. *s.* Realist.

réalité, *s.f.* Reality.

réapparition, *s.f.* Reappearance.

réarmement, *s.m.* Rearmament.

réarmer, *v.tr* To rearm.

rébarbatif, *a.* Grim, forbidding.

rebâtir, *v.tr.* To rebuild.

rebattre, *v.tr.* 1. To beat again. 2. To say over and over again.

rebattu, *a.* *(a)* **Sentier r.,** beaten track. *(b)* Hackneyed.

rebelle. 1. *a.* Rebellious; stubborn, obstinate. 2. *s.m. & f.* Rebel.

rebeller (se), *v.pr.* To rebel.

rébellion, *s.f* Rebellion, rising.

rebond, *s.m* Rebound, bounce.

rebondi, *a.* Chubby; plump.

rebondir, *v.i.* To rebound; bounce.

rebondissement, *s.m.* Rebound.

rebord, *s.m* Edge border.

rebours, *s.m.* **A r.,** against the grain, the wrong way.

rebrousser, *v.tr.* **R. chemin,** to turn back.

rebuffade, *s.f* Rebuff; snub.

rebut, *s.m.* Papier de r., waste paper. **Mettre au r.,** to throw away.

rebuter, *v.tr.* 1. To rebuff. 2. To discourage.

récalcitrant, *a.* Recalcitrant.

récapitulation, *s.f.* Recapitulation

récapituler, *v.tr.* To recapitulate.

recéler, *v.tr.* To conceal.

receleur, -euse, *s.* Receiver, fence.

récemment, *adv.* Recently, lately.

recensement, *s.m.* *(a)* Census. *(b)* Counting (of votes).

récent, *a.* Recent, late.

récépissé, *s.m.* Receipt.

réceptacle, *s.m.* Receptacle.

récepteur, -trice. 1. *a.* Receiving. 2. *s.m.* Receiver.

réception, *s.f.* 1. *(a)* Receipt. *(b)* Acceptance. 2. *(a)* Welcome. *(b)* Reception; at home. 3. (Hotel) receiving desk.

recette, *s.f.* 1. Receipts, returns. 2. Recipe.

receveur, -euse, *s.* 1. Receiver. 2. *(a)* R. des postes, postmaster. *(b)* Conductor (of bus).

recevoir, *v.tr.* 1. *(a)* To receive. *(b)* Être reçu, to pass; to qualify as. 2. To accept, admit.

rechange, *s.m.* Replacement. **Pièces de r.,** spare parts.

réchapper, *v.i.* To escape.

rechargement, *s.m.* Reloading.

recharger, *v.tr* To reload.

réchauffer, *v.tr.* To warm up (again). **se réchauffer,** to warm oneself.

rêche, *a.* Harsh, rough.

recherche, *s.f.* *(a)* Quest, search. *(b)* Research. *(c)* Searching.

recherché, *a.* 1. Choice, select. 2. Studied, strained.

rechercher, *v.tr.* *(a)* To search for, inquire into. *(b)* To seek (after).

rechigner, *v.i.* To jib.

rechute, *s.f.* Relapse, set-back.

récidive, *s.f.* Relapse (into crime).

récif, *s.m.* Reef.

récipient, *s.m.* Container, vessel.

réciprocité, *s.f* Reciprocity.

réciproque, *a.* Reciprocal, mutual.

réciproquement, *adv* Reciprocally.

récit, *s.m.* Narrative; account.

récitateur, -trice, *s.* Reciter.

récitation, *s.f.* Recitation, reciting.

réciter, *v.tr.* To recite.

réclamation, *s.f.* (*a*) Complaint; protest. (*b*) Claim, demand.

réclame, *s.f.* (*a*) Advertising; publicity. (*b*) Advertisement.

réclamer. 1. *v.i.* To complain. **2.** *v.tr.* (*a*) To claim. (*b*) To beg for (*c*) To call for.

reclus, *s.* Recluse.

recoin, *s.m.* Nook, recess.

récolte, *s.f.* Harvest.

récolter, *v.tr.* To harvest.

recommandable, *a.* Advisable.

recommandation, *s.f.* **1.** Recommendation. **2.** Advice, injunction.

recommander, *v.tr.* **1.** To recommend. **2.** To advise. **3.** To register (letter).

recommencer. 1. *v.tr.* To recommence; to begin again. **2.** *v.i.* To start afresh.

récompense, *s.f.* Recompense, reward.

récompenser, *v.tr.* To reward, recompense.

réconciliable, *a.* Reconcilable.

réconciliation, *s.f.* Reconciliation.

réconcilier, *v.tr.* To reconcile. **se réconcilier,** to make it up.

reconduire, *v.tr.* To see home; to take back.

réconfortant, *a.* Comforting.

reconnaissable, *a.* Recognizable.

reconnaissance, *s.f.* **1.** Recognition. **2.** Acknowledgment. **3.** Reconnoitring. **4.** Gratitude.

reconnaissant, *a.* (*a*) Grateful. (*b*) Thankful.

reconnaître, *v.tr.* **1.** To recognize; to know again. **2.** To recognize, acknowledge. **3.** To reconnoitre.

reconquérir, *v.tr.* To regain.

reconstituer, *v.tr.* To reconstitute.

reconstitution, *s.f.* Reconstitution.

reconstruction, *s.f.* Reconstruction.

reconstruire, *v.tr.* To reconstruct, rebuild.

recourber, *v.tr.* To bend back.

recourir, *v.i.* To have recourse.

recours, *s.m.* Recourse, resource.

recouvrement, *s.m.* Recovery.

recouvrer, *v.tr.* To recover.

recouvrir, *v.tr.* **1.** To re-cover. **2.** To cover (over).

récréation, *s.f.* Recreation.

récréer, *v.tr.* To entertain.

récrier (se), *v.pr.* To cry out.

récrimination, *s.f.* Recrimination.

récriminer, *v.i.* To recriminate.

recroquevillé, *a.* Shrivelled.

recrudescence, *s.f.* Recrudescence.

recrue, *s.f.* Recruit.

recrutement, *s.m.* Recruiting.

recruter, *v.tr.* To recruit.

rectangle. 1. *a.* Right-angled. **2.** *s.m.* Rectangle.

rectangulaire, *a.* Rectangular.

rectification, *s.f.* Rectification.

rectifier, *v.tr.* To rectify.

rectitude, *s.f.* Rectitude.

reçu. (*a*) *a.* Received, recognized. (*b*) *s.m.* Receipt.

recueil [-kœːj], *s.m.* Collection.

recueillement [-kœj-], *s.m.* Self-communion, meditation contemplation.

recueilli [-kœji], *a.* Collected, meditative.

recueillir [-kœj-], *v.tr.* **1.** To collect, gather. **2.** To take in; to shelter. **se recueillir,** to collect one's thoughts.

recul, *s.m.* **1.** Retirement; backing. **2.** Recoil.

reculé, *a.* Distant, remote.

reculement, *s.m.* **1.** Backing. **2.** Moving back; postponement.

reculer. 1. *v.i.* To move back; to recoil. **Ne r. devant rien,** to shrink from nothing. **2.** *v.tr.* (*a*) To move back. (*b*) To postpone. **se reculer,** to draw back.

reculons (à), *adv.phr.* Backwards.

récupérer, *v.tr.* To recover.

récurrence, *s.f.* Recurrence.

récurrent, *a.* Recurrent.

rédacteur, -trice, *s.* **1.** Writer. **2.** R. en chef, editor.

rédaction, *s.f.* **1.** (*a*) Drafting. (*b*) Editing. **2.** Editorial staff.

reddition, *s.f.* Surrender (of town).

rédemption, *s.f.* Redemption.

redevable, *a.* Indebted.

redevance, *s.f.* Dues.

rédiger, *v.tr.* **1.** To draw up, draft; to write. **2.** To edit.

redingote, *s.f.* Frock-coat.

redire, *v.tr.* **1.** To tell, say, again; to repeat. **2.** Trouver à r., to take exception.

redondance, *s.f.* Redundancy.

redondant, *a.* Redundant.

redoublement, *s.m.* Redoubling.

redoubler, *v.tr. & v.i.* To redouble.

redoutable, *a.* Redoubtable.

redouter, *v.tr.* To dread, fear.

redressement, *s.m.* Rectification, righting.

redresser, *v.tr* 1. (*a*) To straighten (out). (*b*) To redress; to rectify.

se **redresser,** to draw oneself up

réduction, *s.f* Reduction.

réduire, *v.tr.* To reduce.

réduit, *s.m.* Retreat; nook.

réel, *a.* Real, actual.

réélire, *v.tr.* To re-elect.

réellement, *adv.* Really, actually.

refaire, *v.tr.* To remake; to do again.

se **refaire,** to recuperate.

réfectoire, *s.m.* Refectory.

référence, *s.f.* Reference.

référer, *v.tr.* To refer, ascribe.

se **référer,** to refer.

refermer, *v.tr.* To shut again.

réfléchi, *a.* Reflective, thoughtful.

réfléchir. 1. *v.tr.* To reflect. 2. *v.i.* To reflect. Donner à r., to give food for thought.

réflecteur, *s.m.* Reflector

reflet, *s.m.* Reflection.

refléter, *v.tr.* To reflect.

réflexe, *a* Reflex.

réflexion, *s.f.* Reflection.

refluer, *v.i* To flow back; to ebb.

reflux [fly] *s.m.* Ebb

réformateur, –trice, *s.* Reformer.

réformation, *s.f.* Reformation.

réforme, *s.f.* 1. Reformation, reform. 2. Discharge.

reformer, *v.tr.* To re-form.

réformer, *v.tr.* 1. To reform, amend. 2. To discharge; to retire.

se **réformer,** to reform.

refouler, *v.tr.* To force back

réfractaire, *a.* Refractory.

réfraction, *s.f.* Refraction.

refrain, *s.m.* Refrain; chorus.

refréner, *v.tr.* To curb, bridle.

réfrigérant, *s.m.* Refrigerator.

réfrigération, *s.f.* Refrigeration.

refroidir. 1. *v.tr.* To cool, chill. 2. *v.i. & pr.* To grow cold.

refroidissement, *s.m.* 1. Cooling (down). 2. Chill.

refuge, *s.m.* Refuge; shelter.

réfugié, *s.* Refugee.

réfugier (se), *v.pr.* To take refuge.

refus, *s.m.* Refusal.

refuser, *v.tr.* 1. To refuse. 2. To reject.

se **refuser,** to refuse; to object.

réfutation, *s.f.* Refutation.

réfuter, *v.tr.* To refute.

regagner, *v.tr.* To regain.

regain, *s.m.* Renewal.

régal, -als, *s.m.* Feast; treat.

régaler, *v.tr.* To entertain, feast.

se **régaler,** to feast.

regard, *s.m.* Look, glance, gaze. Chercher du r., to look round for. En r. de, facing. Au r. de, compared with.

regarder, *v.tr.* 1. (*a*) To regard, consider. (*b*) *v.ind.tr.* R. à, to pay attention to. (*c*) To concern. 2. To look at. *abs.* R. à, to look in at. R. par, to look out of. 3. To look on to; to face.

régate, *s.f.* Regatta.

régence, *s.f.* Regency.

régénération, *s.f.* Regeneration.

régent, *s.* Regent.

régie, *s.f.* 1. Administration. 2. Excise.

regimber, *v.i.* To kick; to jib.

régime, *s.m.* 1. Regime. 2. Diet. 3. Object. 4. Bunch.

régiment, *s.m.* Regiment.

régimentaire, *a.* Regimental.

région, *s.f.* Region, territory, area.

régional, -aux, *a.* Regional, local.

régir, *v.tr.* To govern, rule.

régisseur, *s.m.* Steward; stage-manager.

registre, *s.m.* Register.

réglable, *a.* Adjustable.

réglage, *s.m.* (*a*) Regulating, adjusting. (*b*) Tuning.

règle, *s.f.* 1. Rule. ruler. 2. Rule. En r., in order. Bataille en r., stand-up fight.

réglé, *a.* Regular; steady.

règlement, *s.m.* 1. Settlement, adjustment. 2. Regulation(s).

réglementaire, *a.* Regular.

réglementation, *s.f.* Regulation.

réglementer, *v.tr.* To regulate.

régler, *v.tr.* 1. To rule. 2. To regulate. 3. (*a*) To settle. (*b*) To set in order.

réglisse, *s.f.* Liquorice.

règne, *s.m.* 1. Reign. 2. Kingdom.

régner, *v.i.* To reign, rule; to prevail.

regorger, *v.i.* To abound; to be crowded.

régression, *s.f.* Regression.

regret, *s.m.* Regret. **A r.,** reluctantly.

regrettable, *a.* Regrettable.

regretter, *v.tr.* To regret.

régulariser, *v.tr* To regularize.

régularité, *s.f.* (*a*) Regularity. (*b*) Steadiness. (*c*) Equability.

régulateur, -trice. 1. *a.* Regulating. **2.** *s.m.* Regulator.

régulier, *a.* (*a*) Regular. (*b*) Steady. (*c*) Equable.

régulièrement, *adv.* (*a*) Regularly (*b*) Steadily, evenly.

rehausser, *v.tr* **1.** To raise. **2.** To heighten, enhance.

réimprimer, *v.tr.* To reprint.

Reims [rɛ̃:s] *Pr.n.m.* Rheims.

rein, *s.m* **1.** Kidney **2.** *pl.* Loins, back.

reine, *s.f.* Queen.

reine-Claude, *s.f.* Greengage. *pl. reines-Claude.*

réintégration, *s.f.* Reinstatement.

réintégrer, *v.tr.* **1.** To reinstate. **2.** To return to.

réitération, *s.f.* Reiteration.

réitérer, *v.tr.* To reiterate.

rejet, *s.m.* Rejection.

rejeter, *v.tr.* **1.** To throw back. **2.** To transfer. **3.** To reject.

rejeton, *s.m.* **1.** Shoot, sucker. **2.** Scion, descendant, offspring.

rejoindre, *v.tr.* To rejoin.

rejouer, *v.tr.* To replay.

réjoui, *a.* Jolly, joyous, cheerful.

réjouir, *v.tr.* To delight, gladden. **se réjouir. 1.** To rejoice; to be glad. **2.** To make merry.

réjouissance, *s.f.* Rejoicing.

relâchant, *a.* Relaxing.

relâche. 1. *s.m.* Relaxation; respite. **2.** *s.f.* (*a*) Call. (*b*) Port of call.

relâché, *a.* Relaxed; slack.

relâchement, *s.m.* Relaxation.

relâcher. 1. *v.tr.* (*a*) To loosen. (*b*) To relax; to abate. **2.** *v.tr.* To release. **se relâcher,** to slacken.

relais, *s.m.* Relay; shift.

relancer, *v.tr.* **1.** To throw back. **2. R. le moteur,** to restart the engine.

relaps [-laps], *s.* Backslider.

relater, *v.tr.* To relate, state.

relatif, *a.* Relative.

relation, *s.f.* Relation. **1. R. étroite,** close connection. **2.** Account, narrative.

relativement, *adv.* Relatively.

relayer, *v.tr.* To relay.

reléguer, *v.tr.* To relegate.

relent, *s.m.* Musty smell or taste.

relève, *s.f.* Relief; changing.

relevé. 1. *a.* Exalted. **2.** *s.m.* Summary.

relèvement, *s.m.* **1.** (*a*) Raising up. (*b*) Picking up. (*c*) Re-establishment. **2.** Rise

relever. 1. *v.tr.* **1.** (*a*) To raise, lift. (*b*) To pick up. **2.** To call attention to. **3.** To bring into relief; to heighten. **4.** To relieve.
II. relever, *v.i.* **1.** To have just recovered. **2.** To be dependent (*de, on*).
se relever. 1. To rise to one's feet. **2.** To recover.

relief [-jɛf], *s.m.* Relief.

relier, *v.tr.* (*a*) To connect, join. (*b*) To bind (book).

relieur, *s.m.* (Book)binder.

religieusement, *adv.* Religiously.

religieux. 1. *a* Religious. **2.** *s.* Monk; *f.* nun.

religion, *s.f.* Religion.

reliquaire, *s.m.* Reliquary, shrine.

relique, *s.f.* Relic.

relire, *v.tr.* To read again.

reliure, *s.f.* Binding.

reluire, *v.i.* To shine; to glitter.

reluisant, *a.* Shining, glittering.

remanier, *v.tr.* To alter, adapt.

remarier (se), *v.pr.* To remarry.

remarquable, *a.* Remarkable.

remarquablement, *adv.* Remarkably.

remarque, *s.f.* Remark.

remarquer, *v.tr.* (*a*) To remark, notice, observe. **Faire r.,** to point out. (*b*) **Se faire r.,** to attract attention.

rembarquer, *v.tr. & i.* To re-embark.

remblai, *s.m.* Embankment, bank.

rembourrer, *v.tr.* To stuff, pad.

remboursement, *s.m.* Reimbursement, repayment, refunding.

rembourser, *v.tr.* To repay.

rembrunir, *v.tr.* To cast a gloom over.

se rembrunir, to cloud over.

remède, *s.m.* Remedy, cure.

remédiable, *a.* Remediable.

remédier, *v.ind.tr.* R. à, to remedy

remerciement, *s.m.* Thanks.

remercier, *v.tr.* 1. To thank (*de* for). 2. To dismiss.

remettre, *v.tr.* 1. To put back. (*a*) To put on again. **R. un os,** to set a bone (*b*) To calm, compose. (Se) r., to recall. 2. To hand (over) 3. To remit. ;. To postpone.

se remettre. 1. To start again. 2. To recover. **Remettez-vous!** calm yourself! 3. S'en r. à, to leave it to (s.o.).

réminiscence, *s.f* Reminiscence.

remise, *s.f.* 1. (*a*) Delivery. (*b*) Remission. 2. (*a*) Remittance. (*b*) Allowance. 3. Coach-house.

remiser, *v.tr.* To put up (vehicle).

rémission, *s.f.* Remission.

remmener, *v.tr.* To lead away.

remonter. 1. *v.i.* (*a*) To go up (again) (*b*) To go back. 2. *v.tr.* (*a*) To re-ascend. (*b*) To take, carry up : to pull up. (*c*) To wind (up).

remontrance, *s.f.* Remonstrance.

remords [-mɔːr], *s.m.* Remorse. Pris de r., conscience-stricken.

remorque, *s.f.* 1. Towing. 2. Towline. 3. Trailer.

remorquer, *v.tr.* To tow ; to haul.

remorqueur, *s.m.* Tug-boat ; tug.

remous, *s.m.* Eddy ; wash (of ship).

rempart, *s.m.* Rampart.

remplaçant, *s* Substitute ; locum tenens.

remplacement, *s.m.* Replacing, substitution.

remplacer, *v.tr.* 1. To take, fill, the place of. 2. (*a*) To replace. (*b*) To supersede.

remplir, *v.tr.* 1. To fill up ; to refill. 2. To fulfil. **R. un rôle,** to fill a part.

se remplir, to fill.

remporter, *v.tr.* 1. To take back or away. 2. To carry off ; to win.

remuant, *a.* Restless, bustling.

remue-ménage, *s.m.inv* Stir, bustle, confusion.

remuer. 1. *v.tr.* To move ; to shift ; to stir. 2. *v.i.* To move, stir.

se remuer, to move, stir.

rémunérateur, -trice, *a.* Remunerative.

rémunération *s.f.* Remuneration payment.

rémunérer, *v.tr.* To remunerate

renâcler, *v.i.* To snort.

renaissance, *s.f* (*a*) Rebirth. (*b*) Revival.

renaître, *v.i.* To spring up again ; to reappear ; to revive.

renard, *s.m.* (*a*) Fox (*b*) Blackleg.

renarde, *s.f* Vixen, she-fox.

renardeau, *s.m* Fox-cub.

renchérir, *v.i.* (*a*) To get dearer. (*b*) To improve (*sur*, upon).

renchérissement, *s.m.* Rise in price.

rencontre, *s.f* (*a*) Meeting, encounter Aller à la r. de, to go to meet. Connaissance de r., chance acquaintance. (*b*) Collision.

rencontrer, *v.tr* To meet, to fall in with.

se rencontrer. 1. (*a*) To meet. (*b*) To collide. 2. To agree.

rendement, *s.m.* (*a*) Produce, yield ; return, profit (*b*) Output.

rendez-vous, *s.m.inv* Rendezvous. 1. Appointment. 2. Resort, haunt.

rendormir (se), *v.pr* To go to sleep again.

rendre, *v.tr.* 1. (*a*) To give back, return. (*b*) To render, give. (*c*) To yield ; to produce. 2. To convey, deliver. 3. To give up, surrender. 4. *Pred.* **Il se rend ridicule,** he is making himself ridiculous.

se rendre. 1. To make one's way ; to go. 2. To surrender ; to yield.

rendu, *a.* Exhausted.

rêne, *s.f.* Rein.

renégat, *s.* Renegade, turncoat.

renfermé, *s.m.* **Sentir le r.,** to smell stuffy.

renfermer, *v.tr.* 1. To shut up. 2. To contain, comprise.

renflement, *s.m.* Swelling.

renfler, *v.tr. & i.* To swell (out).

renfoncement, *s.m.* Hollow.

renforcer, *v.tr.* (*a*) To reinforce. (*b*) To strengthen.

renfort, *s.m.* Reinforcement(s).

renfrogné, *a.* Frowning ; glum.

renfrogner (se), *v.pr.* To frown.

rengorger (se), *v.pr.* To swagger.

reniement, *s.m.* Repudiation.

renier, *v.tr.* To repudiate.

reniflement, *s.m.* **1.** Sniffing, snuffling. **2.** Sniff.

renifler, *v.i.* To sniff.

renne, *s.m.* Reindeer.

renom, *s.m.* Renown, fame.

renommé, *a.* Renowned, famed.

renommée, *s.f.* Renown, fame.

renoncement, *s.m.* Renunciation.

renoncer. **1.** *v.ind.tr.* (*a*) R. à, to renounce, give up. (*b*) To revoke. **2.** *v.tr.* To renounce.

renonciation, *s.f.* Renunciation.

renouer, *v.tr.* To renew, resume.

renouveler, *v.tr.* To renew.
  se renouveler. **1.** To be renewed. **2.** To recur.

renouvellement, *s.m.* Renewal.

rénovateur, -trice. **1.** *a.* Renovating. **2.** *s.* Renovator.

rénovation, *s.f.* Renovation.

renseignement, *s.m.* (Piece of) information. **Prendre des renseignements,** to make inquiries.

renseigner, *v.tr.* To inform.
  se renseigner, to make inquiries (*sur,* about).

rente, *s.f.* **1.** Annuity. **2.** *pl.* (Unearned) income.

rentier, *s.* (*a*) Stockholder fundholder. (*b*) Annuitant.

rentrée, *s.f.* **1.** (*a*) Return. (*b*) Reopening. **2.** Getting in (of crops).

rentrer. **I.** *v.i.* **1.** (*a*) To go in again. R. dans ses droits, to recover one's rights. (*b*) To return home. (*c*) To call in (one's money). **2.** To enter, go in.
  II. rentrer, *v.tr.* To take in, bring in.

renverse, *s.f.* A la r., backwards.

renversé, *a.* **1.** Inverted, reversed. **2.** Upset.

renversement, *s.m.* **1.** Reversal, inversion. **2.** Overthrow.

renverser, *v.tr.* (*a*) To reverse, invert. R. les rôles, to turn the tables. (*b*) To turn upside down. (*c*) To knock over; to overturn, upset. (*d*) To overthrow.
  se renverser, to fall over; to upset; to fall back.

renvoi, *s.m.* **1.** Return. **2.** Dismissal. **3.** Postponement. **4.** Reference.

renvoyer, *v.tr.* **1.** To send back; to return. **2.** (*a*) To send away. (*b*) To

dismiss. **3.** To put off, postpone. **4.** To refer.

réorganisation, *s.f.* Reorganization.

réorganiser, *v.tr* To reorganize.

réouverture, *s.f.* Reopening.

répandre, *v.tr.* **1.** To pour out; to spill, shed. **2.** To spread; to give off. **3.** To scatter.
  se répandre. (*a*) To spill; to run over. (*b*) To spread.

répandu, *a.* Wide-spread, prevalent.

reparaître, *v.i.* To reappear

réparateur, -trice. **1.** *a.* Repairing, restoring. **2.** *s.* Repairer.

réparation, *s.f.* Reparation. **1.** Repairing. **2.** Atonement, amends.

réparer, *v.tr.* **1.** To repair, mend. **2.** To make amends; to put right.

reparler, *v.i.* To speak again.

repartie, *s.f.* Retort, rejoinder.

repartir, *v.i.* **1.** To set out again. **2.** To retort, reply.

répartir, *v.tr.* To distribute, share out.

répartition, *s.f.* **1.** Distribution; sharing out. **2.** Apportionment.

repas, *s.m.* Meal, repast.

repasser. **1.** *v.i.* To repass. **2.** *v.tr* (*a*) To cross again. (*b*) To sharpen grind. (*c*) To iron.

repêcher, *v.tr.* To fish out (again).

repentant, *a.* Repentant.

repentir (se). **I.** *v.pr.* Se r. de, to repent.
  II. repentir, *s.m.* Repentance.

répercussion, *s.f.* Repercussion; reverberation.

répercuter, *v.tr.* To reverberate.

repère, *s.m.* Point de r., landmark.

repérer, *v.tr.* To locate; to spot.

répertoire, *s.m.* **1.** List. **2.** Repertory. **3.** Repertoire.

répéter, *v.tr.* (*a*) To repeat. (*b*) To rehearse.
  se répéter. **1.** To repeat oneself. **2.** To recur.

répétiteur, -trice, *s.* (*a*) Assistant-master, -mistress. (*b*) Private tutor.

répétition, *s.f.* **1.** (*a*) Repetition. Fusil à r., repeating rifle. (*b*) Reproduction, replica. **2.** Rehearsal.

repeupler, *v.tr.* To repeople.

répit, *s.m.* Respite; breathing-space.

replacer, *v.tr.* To replace.

replanter, *v.tr.* To replant.

replet, -ète, *a.* Stoutish.

réplétion, *s.f.* Repletion.

repli, *s.m.* **1.** Fold, crease. **2.** Coil.

replier, *v.tr.* To fold up (again).
　se replier. (*a*) To fold up, turn back. (*b*) To wind, turn.

réplique, *s.f.* **1.** Retort, rejoinder. **2.** *Th:* Cue. **3.** Replica.

répliquer, *v.i.* To retort, rejoin.

répondre. 1. *v.tr.* To answer. **2.** *v.ind.tr.* **R. à,** to answer; to comply with. **3.** *v.i.* **R. de,** to answer for.

réponse, *s.f.* Answer; response.

repos, *s.m.* **1.** (*a*) Rest, repose. (*b*) Pause. **2.** Peace, tranquillity.

reposer. I. *v.tr.* To rest.
　II. reposer, *v.i.* To lie, rest.
　se reposer, to rest, repose.

repoussant, *a.* Repulsive, repellent.

repousser, *v.tr.* (*a*) To push back, repulse; to reject. (*b*) To repel.

repoussoir, *s.m.* Set-off, foil.

répréhensible, *a.* Reprehensible.

répréhension, *s.f.* Reprehension.

reprendre. 1. *v.tr.* (*a*) To take again, retake. (*b*) To take back. (*c*) To resume; to regain. *Abs.* To reply. (*d*) To reprove. **2.** *v.i.* To recommence; to return.
　se reprendre. 1. To recover oneself. **2.** To correct oneself.

représailles [-za:j], *s.f.pl.* Reprisals.

représentant, *s.* Representative.

représentatif, *a.* Representative.

représentation, *s.f.* **1.** Representation. **2.** Performance. **3.** Remonstrance, protest.

représenter, *v.tr.* **1.** To represent. **2.** (*a*) To perform. (*b*) To act, personate.

répressif, *a.* Repressive.

répression, *s.f.* Repression.

réprimande, *s.f.* Reprimand.

réprimander, *v.tr.* To reprimand.

réprimer, *v.tr.* To repress.

repris, *s.* **R. de justice,** old offender

reprise, *s.f.* **1.** Retaking **2.** (*a*) Resumption, renewal. (*b*) **A plusieurs reprises,** on several occasions. **3.** Darn.

repriser, *v.tr.* To mend, darn.

réprobateur, -trice, *a.* Reproachful; reproving.

réprobation, *s.f.* Reprobation.

reproche, *s.m.* Reproach.

reprocher, *v.tr.* **1.** To reproach. **2.** To grudge.

reproductif, *a.* Reproductive.

reproduction, *s.f.* **1.** Reproduction. **2.** Copy.

reproduire, *v.tr.* To reproduce.
　se reproduire. 1. To recur; to happen again. **2.** To breed, multiply.

réprouvé, *s.* Reprobate.

reptile, *s.m.* Reptile.

repu, *a.* Satiated; full.

républicain, *a. & s.* Republican.

république, *s.f.* (*a*) Republic. (*b*) Commonwealth.

répudiation, *s.f.* **1.** Repudiation. **2.** Renunciation.

répudier, *v.tr.* **1.** To repudiate. **2.** To renounce.

répugnance, *s.f.* **1** Repugnance. **2.** Reluctance

répugnant, *a.* Repugnant.

répugner, *v.i.* **1.** To feel repugnance; to feel reluctant. **2. Il me répugne de,** I am reluctant to.

répulsion, *s.f.* Repulsion.

réputation, *s.f.* Reputation, repute.

réputé, *a.* Well-known; of repute.

réputer, *v.tr.* To repute, consider.

requérir, *v.tr.* **1.** To ask for; to solicit. **2.** To require.

requête, *s.f.* Request, petition.

requin, *s.m.* Shark. **Peau de r.,** shagreen.

requis, *a.* Required; requisite.

réquisition, *s.f.* Requisition.

réquisitionner, *v.tr.* To requisition.

rescinder, *v.tr.* To rescind, annul.

rescision, *s.f.* Annulment.

rescousse, *s.f.* Rescue.

réseau, *s.m.* Network; system.

réséda, *s.m.* Mignonette.

réservation, *s.f.* Reservation.

réserve, *s.f.* **1.** (*a*) Reservation (*b*) Reserve. **2.** Reserve, caution.

réservé, *a.* Reserved.

réserver, *v.tr.* To reserve.
　se réserver, to hold back, wait.

réserviste, *s.m.* Reservist.

réservoir, *s.m.* **1.** Reservoir. **2.** Tank.

résidence, *s.f.* Residence.

résider, *v.i.* **1.** To reside, dwell, live. **2.** To lie; to consist.

résidu, *s.m.* Residue.

résignation, *s.f.* Resignation.

résigné, *a.* Resigned; meek.

résigner, *v.tr.* To resign.

résilience, *s.f.* Resilience.

résine, *s.f.* Resin.

résineux, *a.* Resinous.
résistance, *s.f.* Resistance. **1.** Opposition. **2.** (*a*) Strength. (*b*) Endurance.
résistant, *a.* Resistant; strong.
résister, *v.ind.tr.* To resist.
résolu, *a.* Resolute; determined.
résolument, *adv.* Resolutely.
résolution, *s.f.* **1.** Termination. **2.** Resolution.
résonance, *s.f.* Resonance.
résonner, *v.i.* To resound.
résoudre, *v.tr.* **1.** To terminate. **2.** To solve. **3.** To resolve (*de*, on).
   se résoudre, to make up one's mind.
respect [-spɛ], *s.m.* Respect, regard.
respectabilité, *s.f.* Respectability.
respectable, *a.* Respectable.
respectablement, *adv.* Respectably.
respecter, *v.tr.* To respect.
respectif, *a.* Respective.
respectivement, *adv.* Respectively.
respectueusement, *adv* Respectfully.
respectueux, *a.* Respectful; dutiful.
respirateur, *s.m.* Respirator.
respiration, *s.f.* Respiration, breathing.
respirer, *v.i. & tr.* To breathe.
resplendir, *v.i.* To shine.
resplendissant, *a.* Resplendent.
responsabilité, *s.f.* Responsibility; liability.
responsable, *a.* Responsible, answerable.
ressac [-sak], *s.m.* **1.** Undertow. **2.** Surf.
ressaisir, *v.tr.* To recapture.
   se ressaisir, to recover oneself.
ressemblance, *s.f.* Resemblance, likeness.
ressemblant, *a.* Like, alike.
ressembler, *v.ind. tr.* R. à, to resemble, to be like.
   se ressembler, to be (a)like.
ressentiment, *s.m.* Resentment.
ressentir, *v.tr.* (*a*) To feel. (*b*) To resent. (*c*) To feel, experience.
   se ressentir de, to feel the effects of.
resserré, *a.* Confined, cramped.
resserrement, *s.m.* **1.** Tightening. **2.** Tightness; oppression.
resserrer, *v.tr.* **1.** To contract, close up. **2.** To tighten.
   se resserrer, to contract, shrink.

ressort, *s.m.* **1.** (*a*) Elasticity. (*b*) Spring. **2.** Resort.
ressortir, *v.i.* **1.** (*a*) To come, go, out again. (*b*) *v.tr.* To bring out again. **2.** (*a*) To stand out. (*b*) To result, follow.
ressource, *s.f.* Resource. **1.** Resourcefulness. **2.** Expedient, shift. **3.** *pl.* Resources, means.
ressusciter, *v.tr. & i.* To resuscitate; revive.
restant, *a.* (*a*) Remaining, left. (*b*) Poste restante, *poste restante*.
restaurant. 1. *a.* Restorative. **2.** *s.m.* Restaurant.
restaurateur, *s.m.* Restaurant keeper.
restauration, *s.f.* Restoration.
restaurer, *v.tr.* (*a*) To restore. (*b*) To refresh.
   se restaurer, to take refreshment.
reste, *s.m.* **1.** Rest, remainder. Et le r., and so on. De r., over and above. Au r., du r., besides. **2.** *pl.* Remains.
rester, *v.i.* To remain. **1.** To be left. **2.** (*a*) To stay (behind). (*b*) *Pred.* R. tranquille, to keep still. **3.** To stay, dwell.
restituer, *v.tr* To restore.
restitution, *s.f.* Restoration.
restreindre, *v.tr.* To restrict.
   se restreindre, to retrench.
restreint, *a* Restricted, limited.
restrictif, *a.* Restrictive.
restriction, *s.f.* Restriction, limitation. R. mentale, mental reservation.
résultant, *a.* Resultant; resulting.
résultat, *s.m.* Result, outcome.
résulter, *v.i.* To result, follow.
résumé, *s.m.* Summary, résumé.
résumer, *v.tr.* To sum up.
résurrection, *s.f.* Resurrection.
rétablir, *v.tr.* To re-establish.
   se rétablir. 1. (*a*) To recover. (*b*) To be restored. **2.** To re-establish oneself.
rétablissement, *s.m.* **1.** Re-establishment; reinstatement. **2.** Recovery.
retard, *s.m.* Delay, slowness. En r., late.
retardataire, *s.* (*a*) Late-comer. (*b*) Laggard.
retarder. 1. *v.tr.* To delay. **2.** *v.i* To be late, slow.
retenir, *v.tr.* **1.** (*a*) To hold (back); to detain. (*b*) To secure. **2.** (*a*) To

retain. (b) To engage; to reserve. **3.** To restrain.

    se retenir, to hold oneself in; to refrain.

retentir, v.i. To resound, echo.

retentissant, a. Resounding.

retentissement, s.m. Sound echo; stir.

retenu, a. Prudent, circumspect.

retenue, s.f. Reserve, discretion.

réticence, s.f. Reticence, reserve.

rétif, a. Restive, stubborn.

retiré, a. Retired, remote.

retirer, v.tr. To pull out; to withdraw; to take off.

    se retirer, to retire withdraw.

retomber, v.i. **1.** To fall (down) again. **2.** To fall (back). **3.** To hang down.

retors, a. Crafty, wily, intriguing.

retour, s.m. **1.** (a) Twisting, winding. (b) Turn, vicissitude. (c) Recurrence. **2.** Return. Être de r., to be back.

retourner. **1.** v.tr. (a) To turn inside out. (b) To turn over. (c) To turn round. **2.** v.tr. To return. **3.** v.i. To return; to go back.

    se retourner, to turn (round); to turn over.

retracer, v.tr. To retrace.

rétracter, v.tr. To retract.

retrait, s.m. **1.** Withdrawal. **2.** Recess. En r., set back.

retraite, s.f. **1.** Retreat, retirement. **2.** Tattoo. **3.** Retirement. R. de vieillesse, old-age pension. **4.** (a) Retreat. (b) Refuge; lair.

retranchement, s.m. **1.** Cutting off. **2.** Entrenchment.

retrancher, v.tr. **1.** To cut off. **2.** To entrench.

rétréci, a. Narrow, contracted.

rétrécir, v.i. & pr. To contract; to grow narrow.

rétrécissement, s.m. (a) Contracting. (b) Shrinking.

rétribuer, v.tr. To remunerate, pay.

rétribution, s.f. Remuneration.

rétrograde, a. Retrograde.

rétrograder, v.i. To go back.

rétrospectif, a. Retrospective.

retrousser, v.tr. To turn up.

retrouver, v.tr. To find (again).

réunion, s.f. **1.** Reunion. **2.** Assembly, meeting.

réunir, v.tr. To join together.

    se réunir, to meet.

réussi, a. Successful.

réussir. **1.** v.i. To succeed. **2.** v.tr. To make a success of.

réussite, s.f. **1.** Success. **2.** Cards: Patience.

revanche, s.f. **1.** Revenge. **Jouer la r.,** to play the return game. **2.** Requital. En r., on the other hand.

rêve, s.m. Dream.

revêche, a. **1.** Harsh. **2.** Crabbed.

réveil [-vɛːj], s.m. **1.** (a) Waking, awakening. (b) Reveille. **2.** Alarm (-clock).

réveille-matin [-vɛj-], s.m.inv. Alarm (-clock).

réveiller [-veje] v.tr. **1.** To wake up. **2.** To awaken.

    se réveiller, to wake (up).

révélateur, -trice. **1.** a. Revealing, tell-tale. **2.** s.m. Developer.

révélation, s.f. Revelation.

révéler, v.tr. (a) To reveal, disclose. (b) To show; to betray.

    se révéler, to be revealed.

revenant. **1.** a. Pleasing, prepossessing. **2.** s.m. Ghost.

revendication, s.f. Claim, demand.

revendiquer, v.tr. To claim.

revendre, v.tr. To resell.

revenir, v.i. **1.** To return; to come back; to go back (on a promise). **2. Son visage ne me revient pas,** I don't like his looks. **3. Je n'en reviens pas!** I can't get over it! R. à soi, to recover consciousness. **4.** En r. à qch., to revert to sth. **5.** (a) To cost. (b) **Cela revient au même,** it comes to the same thing.

revenu, s.m. Income; revenue.

rêver, v.i. & tr. To dream.

réverbération, s.f. Reverberation.

réverbère, s.m. Street-lamp.

révéremment, adv. Reverently.

révérence, s.f. **1.** Reverence. **2.** Bow; curtsey.

révérend, a. Reverend.

révérer, v.tr. To revere.

rêverie, s.f. Reverie; dreaming.

revers, s.m. (a) Reverse; wrong side; other side. (b) Facing, lapel.

réversible, a. Reversible.

réversion, s.f. Reversion.

revêtement, s.m. Facing, coating.

revêtir, *v.tr.* **1.** To reclothe. **2.** To clothe, dress ; to invest. **3.** To put on.
  se revêtir de, to put on ; to assume.

rêveur, -euse, *a.* Dreamy.

revient, *s.m.* **Prix de r.,** cost price.

revirement, *s.m.* Sudden change.

reviser, *v.tr.* To revise.

reviseur, *s.m.* Reviser.

revision, *s.f.* Revision.

revivre, *v.i.* To live again ; to revive.

révocable, *a.* Revocable.

révocation, *s.f.* **1.** Revocation, rescinding. **2.** Removal, dismissal.

revoir, *v.tr.* **1.** To see again. *s.m.inv.* **Au r.,** good-bye. **2.** To revise.

révoltant, *a.* Revolting.

révolte, *s.f.* Revolt, rebellion.

révolter, *v.tr.* To shock, disgust.
  se révolter, to revolt, rebel.

révolution, *s.f.* Revolution.

révolutionnaire. (*a*) *a. & s.* Revolutionary. (*b*) *s.* Revolutionist.

revolver [-vɛːr], *s.m.* Revolver.

révoquer, *v.tr.* **1.** To revoke ; to countermand. **2.** To dismiss.

revue, *s.f.* **1.** Review. **2.** Revue.

rez-de-chaussée, *s.m.inv.* (*a*) Ground level. (*b*) Ground-floor.

rhabiller [-bije], *v.tr.* To reclothe.
  se rhabiller, to dress again.

rhétorique, *s.f.* Rhetoric.

Rhin (le). *Pr.n.m.* The Rhine.

rhinocéros [-rɔs], *s.m.* Rhinoceros.

rhubarbe, *s.f.* Rhubarb.

rhum [rɔm], *s.m.* Rum.

rhumatismal, -aux, *a.* Rheumatic.

rhumatisme, *s.m.* Rheumatism.

rhume, *s.m.* Cold.

riant, *a.* **1.** Smiling. **2.** Cheerful.

ricanement, *s.m.* Sneering laugh.

ricaner, *v.i.* To laugh unpleasantly.

riche, *a.* **1.** Rich, wealthy, well-off. **2.** Valuable ; handsome.

richement, *adv.* Richly.

richesse, *s.f.* **1.** Wealth ; riches. **2.** Richness.

ricin, *s.m* **Huile de r.,** castor oil.

ricocher, *v.i.* (*a*) To glance off. (*b*) To ricochet.

ricochet, *s.m.* (*a*) Rebound. (*b*) Ricochet.

rictus [-tyːs], *s.m.* Grin.

ride, *s.f.* **1.** Wrinkle. **2.** Ripple.

ridé, *a.* **1.** Wrinkled. **2.** Ribbed corrugated, fluted.

rideau, *s.m.* Screen ; curtain.

rider, *v.tr.* **1.** (*a*) To wrinkle, line. (*b*) To corrugate. **2.** To ripple.

ridicule. 1. *a.* Ridiculous, ludicrous. **2.** *s.m.* (*a*) Absurdity. (*b*) Ridicule.

ridiculement, *adv.* Ridiculously.

ridiculiser, *v.tr.* To ridicule.

rien. I. *pron. indef. m.* **1.** Anything. **2.** Nothing, not anything. (*a*) **Cela ne fait r.,** that doesn't matter. **Il n'en est r.!** nothing of the kind ! (*b*) **En moins de r.,** in less than no time. (*c*) **R. que,** nothing but, only, merely. **II. rien,** *s.m.* **1.** Trifle. **2.** Just a little.

rieur, -euse. 1. *a.* Laughing ; fond of laughter. **2.** *s.* Laughter.

rigide, *a.* Rigid ; tense ; fixed.

rigidement, *adv.* Rigidly ; tensely.

rigidité, *s.f.* Rigidity ; tenseness.

rigole, *s.f.* Drain, gutter, channel.

rigoureusement, *adv.* Rigorously. (*a*) Severely. (*b*) Strictly.

rigoureux, *a.* Rigorous. **1.** Severe, harsh. **2.** Strict.

rigueur, *s.f.* **1.** Rigour, harshness, severity. **2.** Strictness. **De r.,** compulsory. **A la r.,** if need be.

rime, *s.f.* Rhyme.

rimer, *v.i.* To rhyme.

rincer, *v.tr.* To rinse.

riposte, *s.f.* Riposte ; retort.

riposter, *v.i.* To retort.

rire. I. *v.i.* **1.** To laugh. **R. de,** to laugh at. **2.** To jest, joke. **Pour r.,** for fun. **3.** To smile (**d,** on).
  se rire de, to laugh at.
II. rire, *s.m.* (*a*) Laughter, laughing. (*b*) Laugh.

ris¹, *s.m.* Reef (in sail).

ris², *s.m.* **Ris de v.,** sweetbread.

risée, *s.f.* (*a*) Mockery. (*b*) Laughing-stock, butt.

risible, *a.* Ludicrous, laughable.

risque, *s.m.* Risk.

risqué, *a.* Risky.

risquer, *v.tr.* To risk, venture.
  se risquer, to take a risk.

rite, *s.m.* Rite.

rituel, *a. & s.m.* Ritual.

rivage, *s.m.* Bank ; shore ; strand.

rival, -aux, *a. & s.* Rival.

rivaliser, *v.i.* **R. avec,** (i) to rival ; (ii) to vie with.

rivalité, *s.f.* Rivalry, emulation.

rive, *s.f.* Bank ; shore.

river, *v.tr.* (*a*) To rivet. (*b*) **To clinch.**

riverain, *a.* Waterside.

rivet, *s.m.* Rivet.

riveter, *v.tr.* To rivet.

rivière, *s.f.* River, stream.

rixe, *s.f.* Brawl, scuffle, affray.

riz [ri], *s.m.* Rice.

rizière, *s.f.* Rice-plantation.

robe, *s.f.* **1.** (*a*) Dress, gown, frock. (*b*) R. de chambre, dressing-gown. (*c*) Robe, gown. **2.** Coat (of horse).

robinet, *s.m.* (Stop-)cock ; tap.

robre, *s.m. Cards :* Rubber.

robuste, *a.* Robust ; strong.

robustement, *adv.* Robustly, stoutly.

robustesse, *s.f.* Robustness.

roc [rɔk], *s.m.* Rock.

rocailleux [-kaj-], *a.* Rocky, stony.

roche, *s.f.* Rock, boulder.

rocher, *s.m.* Rock ; crag.

rocheux, *a.* Rocky, stony.

rôder, *v.i.* To prowl ; to loiter.

rôdeur, -euse. 1. *a.* Prowling. **2.** *s.* Prowler.

rogner, *v.tr.* To clip, trim, pare.

rognon, *s.m.* Kidney.

rogue, *a.* Arrogant. haughty.

roi, *s.m.* King.

roitelet, *s.m.* Wren.

rôle, *s.m.* **1.** Roll ; list ; register. A tour de r., by turns. **2.** Part, rôle.

romain. I. *a. & s.* Roman. **2.** *s.f.* Romaine, cos lettuce.

roman, *s.m.* (*a*) Novel. (*b*) Romance.

romance, *s.f.* (Sentimental) song.

romancier, *s.* Novelist.

romanesque, *a.* Romantic.

romantique, *a.* Romantic.

romarin, *s.m.* Rosemary.

rompre. I. *v.tr.* To break. (*a*) To break in two. (*b*) To burst. **Se r. la tête,** to cudgel one's brains. (*c*) R. le silence, to break the silence. (*d*) To break in. **2.** *v.i.* To break. se rompre, to break ; to snap.

rompu, *a.* (*a*) Broken. R. de fatigue, worn out. (*b*) Broken in.

romsteck [-tɛk], *s.m.* Rump-steak.

ronce, *s.f.* **1.** Bramble ; blackberry-bush. **2.** Thorns.

rond. I. 1. *a.* Round ; plump ; full. **2.** *s.m.* Round, ring, circle. **II. ronde,** *s.f.* **1.** Round(s) ; beat. **2.** A la r., around.

rondelle, *s.f.* (*a*) Ring. (*b*) Washer.

rondement, *adv.* Roundly, briskly, smartly.

rondeur, *s.f.* **1.** Roundness, rotundity. **2.** Outspokenness.

rond-point, *s.m.* Circus (where roads meet). *pl. ronds-points.*

ronflant, *a.* **1.** Snoring. **2.** Rumbling, booming, humming.

ronflement, *s.m.* **1.** (*a*) Snoring. (*b*) Snore. **2.** Rumbling, booming.

ronfler, *v.i.* **1.** To snore. **2.** To roar ; to boom.

rongeant, *a.* Gnawing.

ronger, *v.tr.* **1.** To gnaw. **2.** To corrode ; to eat away.

rongeur, -euse. 1. *a.* Rodent, gnawing. **2.** *s.m.* Rodent.

ronronnement, *s.m.* (*a*) Purring. (*b*) Humming.

ronronner, *v.i.* (*a*) To purr. (*b*) To hum.

roquet, *s.m.* (*a*) Pug-dog. (*b*) Cur.

rosace, *s.f.* Rose(-window).

rosaire, *s.m.* Rosary.

rosâtre, *a.* Pinkish.

rosbif [-bif], *s.m.* Roast beef.

rose. 1. *s.f.* Rose. (*a*) R. mousseuse, moss rose. (*b*) R. trémière, hollyhock. **2.** (*a*) *a.* Pink. (*b*) *s.m.* Rose ; pink. **3.** *s.f.* R. des vents, compass-card.

rosé, *a.* Roseate, rosy.

roseau, *s.m.* Reed.

rosée, *s.f.* Dew.

roséole, *s.f.* German measles.

rosette, *s.f.* Bow ; rosette.

rosier, *s.m.* Rose-tree, rose-bush.

rossée, *s.f.* Beating, thrashing.

rosser, *v.tr.* To give a beating.

rossignol, *s.m.* Nightingale.

rotatif, *a.* Rotary.

rotation, *s.f.* Rotation.

rôti, *s.m.* Roast.

rôtie, *s.f.* Round of toast.

rôtir. I. *v.tr.* To roast ; to toast. **2.** *v.i.* To roast.

rotonde, *s.f.* Rotunda.

rotondité, *s.f.* Rotundity.

rotule, *s.f.* Knee-cap.

rouage, *s.m.* Wheels ; works.

rouan, *a.* Roan.

roucoulement, *s.m.* Cooing.

roucouler, *v.i.* To coo.

roue, *s.f.* Wheel.

roué. 1. *s.m.* Rake, profligate. **2.** *a. & s.* Cunning, artful (person).

rouer, *v.tr.* R. de coups, to thrash soundly.

rouet, *s.m.* Spinning-wheel.

rouge. 1. *a.* Red. **Fer r.,** red-hot iron. **2.** *s.m.* (*a*) Red. (*b*) Rouge. **Bâton de r.,** lipstick.

rougeâtre, *a.* Reddish.

rouge-gorge, *s.m.* Robin. *pl. rouges-gorges.*

rougeole, *s.f.* Measles.

rougeur, *s.f.* **1.** Redness. **2.** Blush, flush.

rougir. 1. *v.tr.* (*a*) To redden. (*b*) To flush. **2.** *v.i.* (*a*) To redden, to turn red. (*b*) To blush; to flush. **R. de,** to be ashamed of.

rouille [ru:j], *s.f.* Rust.

rouillé [ruje], *a.* Rusted, rusty.

rouiller [ruje], *v.tr.* To rust. **se rouiller,** to rust (up).

roulant, *a.* Rolling; sliding.

rouleau, *s.m.* **1.** Roller. **2.** Roll; coil.

roulement, *s.m.* **1.** Rolling. **2.** Rumbling; roll.

rouler. 1. *v.tr.* (*a*) To roll (along). (*b*) To roll (the lawn). **2.** *v.i.* (*a*) To roll. *Av:* **R. sur le sol,** to taxi. **R. par le monde,** to knock about the world. (*b*) To roll, rumble. (*c*) To run. **se rouler.** (*a*) To roll. (*b*) To roll up.

roulette, *s.f.* **1.** Caster; roller. **2.** Roulette.

roulier, *s.m.* Carter; carrier.

roulis, *s.m.* Rolling.

roulotte, *s.f.* Caravan.

roumain, *a. & s.* Rumanian.

Roumanie. *Pr.n.f.* Rumania.

roupie, *s.f.* Rupee.

roussâtre, *a.* Reddish.

rousse. See ROUX.

rousseur, *s.f.* Redness. **Tache de r.,** freckle.

roussi, *a.* Browned; scorched.

roussir. 1. *v.tr.* (*a*) To redden. (*b*) To scorch. **2.** *v.i.* (*a*) To turn brown. (*b*) To scorch.

route, *s.f.* **1.** Road(way), path. **R. nationale,** main road, highway. **2.** Route, way. **Se mettre en r.,** to set out.

routine, *s.f.* Routine.

routinier, *a.* Routine.

rouvrir, *v.tr. & i.* To reopen. **se rouvrir,** to reopen.

roux, rousse. 1. (*a*) *a.* (Russet-)red; red. (*b*) *s.* Red-haired person. **2.** *s.m.* Russet.

royal, -aux, *a.* Royal, regal, kingly.

royalement, *adv.* Royally, regally.

royaliste, *a. & s.* Royalist.

royaume, *s.m.* Kingdom, realm.

royauté, *s.f.* Royalty; kingship.

ruade, *s.f.* Lashing out, fling out.

ruban, *s.m.* **1.** (*a*) Ribbon, band. (*b*) **Mètre à r.,** measuring-tape. **2.** Metal strip.

rubicond, *a.* Rubicund, florid.

rubis, *s.m.* Ruby.

rubrique, *s.f.* (*a*) Rubric. (*b*) Heading.

ruche, *s.f.* (Bee-)hive.

rucher, *s.m.* Apiary.

rude, *a.* **1.** (*a*) Unpolished. (*b*) Rough; harsh; rugged. **2.** (*a*) Hard, arduous. (*b*) Gruff, brusque. **3.** Hearty.

rudement, *adv.* Roughly.

rudesse, *s.f.* **1.** Uncouthness. **2.** Roughness. **3.** (*a*) Severity. (*b*) Bluntness.

rudiment, *s.m.* Rudiment.

rudimentaire, *a.* Rudimentary.

rudoyer, *v.tr.* To treat roughly

rue[1], *s.f.* Street, thoroughfare.

rue[2], *s.f.* Rue.

ruée, *s.f.* Rush.

ruelle, *s.f.* Lane, by-street, alley.

ruer, *v.i.* To kick, to lash out. **se ruer,** to hurl oneself.

rugir, *v.i.* To roar; to howl.

rugissement, *s.m.* **1.** Roaring; howling. **2.** Roar.

rugueux, *a.* Rugged, rough.

ruine, *s.f.* Ruin.

ruiner, *v.tr.* To ruin, destroy.

ruineux, *a.* Ruinous.

ruisseau, *s.m.* Brook; stream.

ruisseler, *v.i.* **1.** To stream (down), run (down). **2.** To run.

ruissellement, *s.m.* Streaming.

rumeur, *s.f.* **1.** (*a*) Murmur. (*b*) Din, clamour. **2.** Rumour, report.

rumination, *s.f.* Rumination.

ruminer, *v.tr. & i.* To ruminate.

rupture, *s.f.* Breaking; rupture.

rural, -aux, *a.* Rural.

ruse, *s.f.* Ruse, trick, dodge.

rusé, *a. & s.* Artful, crafty, sly.

russe, *a. & s.* Russian.

Russie. *Pr.n.f.* Russia.

rustique, *a.* Rustic.

rustre. 1. *a.* Boorish. **2.** *s.m.* Boor, churl, lout.

rythme, *s.m.* Rhythm.

rythmique, *a.* Rhythmic.

S

S, s [ɛs], *s.f.* (The letter) S, s.

sa, *a.poss.f.* See SON[1].

sabbat, *s.m.* (Jewish) Sabbath.

sable[1], *s.m.* Sand.

sable[2], *s.m.* Sable, black.

sablière, *s.f.* Sand-pit, gravel-pit.

sablonneux, *a.* Sandy.

sabord, *s.m.* Port(-hole).

saborder, *v.tr.* To scuttle.

sabot, *s.m.* **1.** Wooden shoe. **2.** Hoof. **3.** Drag, skid.

sabotage, *s.m.* Sabotage.

saboter, *v.tr.* To botch; to sabotage

sabre, *s.m.* Sabre; sword.

sabrer, *v.tr.* To sabre.

sac[1] [sak], *s.m.* Sack, bag. **Sac de nuit**, travelling-bag.

sac[2], *s.m.* Sacking, pillage.

saccade, *s.f* Jerk, start, jolt.

saccadé, *a.* Jerky, abrupt.

saccager, *v.tr.* To sack, pillage.

saccharine [-kar-], *s.f.* Saccharine.

sacerdoce, *s.m.* Priesthood.

sacerdotal, -aux, *a.* Priestly.

sachet, *s.m.* Sachet.

sacoche, *s.f.* Satchel, wallet.

sacre, *s.m.* Coronation.

sacré, *a.* **1.** Sacred. **2.** Confounded.

sacrement, *s.m.* Sacrament.

sacrer, **1.** *v.tr.* To anoint; to consecrate. **2.** *v.i.* To swear.

sacrifice, *s.m.* Sacrifice.

sacrifier, *v.tr.* To sacrifice.

sacrilège[1], *s.m.* Sacrilege.

sacrilège[2], *a.* Sacrilegious.

sacristain, *s.m.* Sacristan; sexton.

sacristie, *s.f.* Sacristy, vestry.

sacro-saint, *a.* Sacrosanct.

sadiste, *s.m. & f.* Sadist.

safran, *s.m.* Saffron.

sagace, *a.* Sagacious, shrewd.

sagacité, *s.f.* Sagacity, shrewdness.

sagaie, *s.f.* Assegai.

sage, *a.* **1.** Wise. **2.** Judicious. **3.** Well-behaved; good.

sage-femme, *s.f.* Midwife. *pl. sages-femmes.*

sagement, *adv.* Wisely, prudently.

sagesse, *s.f.* **1.** (*a*) Wisdom. (*b*) Prudence. **2.** Good behaviour.

sagou, *s.m.* Sago.

saignant, *a.* **1.** Bleeding. **2.** Raw, underdone.

saigner, *v.i. & tr.* To bleed.

saillant [sajã]. **1.** *a.* (*a*) Projecting. (*b*) Salient. **2.** *s.m.* Salient.

saillie [saji], *s.f.* **1.** Sally; flash of wit. **2.** Projection.

saillir [saji:r], *v.i.* To jut out.

sain, *a.* Healthy, hale; sane

saindoux, *s.m.* Lard.

sainement, *adv.* **1.** Healthily, wholesomely. **2.** Sanely.

saint. 1. *a.* (*a*) Holy. (*b*) Saintly. (*c*) Hallowed. **2.** *s.* Saint.

Saint-Esprit (le). *Pr.n.m.* The Holy Ghost.

sainteté, *s.f.* Holiness saintliness; sanctity.

saisie, *s.f.* (*a*) Seizure. (*b*) Distraint.

saisir, *v.tr.* To seize. (*a*) To grasp; to take hold of. (*b*) To perceive.
se saisir de, to lay hands on.

saisissant, *a.* Striking; thrilling.

saisissement, *s.m.* Seizure. (*a*) Surprise, thrill. (*b*) Shock.

saison, *s.f.* Season. **De s.**, in season.

salade, *s.f.* Salad.

salaire, *s.m.* Wage(s); pay; reward.

sale, *a.* Dirty. (*a*) Unclean; soiled. (*b*) Offensive, nasty.

salé, *a.* Salt; salted.

saler, *v.tr.* To salt.

saleté, *s.f.* **1.** (*a*) Dirtiness. (*b*) Dirt, filth. **2.** Nastiness.

salière, *s.f.* Salt-cellar.

salin, *a.* Saline, briny; salty.

salir, *v.tr.* To dirty, soil.

salive, *s.f.* Saliva, spittle.

salle, *s.f.* **1.** Hall; (large) room. **2.** *Th:* House.

Salomon. *Pr.n.m.* Solomon.

salon, *s.m.* (*a*) Drawing-room. (*b*) Saloon; cabin. (*c*) **S. de thé**, tea-room(s).

salpêtre, *s.m.* Saltpetre, nitre.

saltimbanque, *s.m.* Mountebank.

salubre, *a.* Salubrious; wholesome.

salubrité, *s.f.* Salubrity.

saluer, *v.tr.* (*a*) To salute; to bow to. (*b*) To greet, to hail.

salut, *s.m.* **1.** (*a*) Safety. (*b*) Salvation. **2.** (*a*) Bow, greeting. (*b*) Salute.

salutaire, *a.* Salutary, wholesome.

salutation, *s.f.* Salutation, greeting.

salve, *s.f.* Salvo.

samedi, *s.m.* Saturday.

sanctifier, *v.tr.* To sanctify.

sanction, *s.f.* Sanction. **1.** Approbation. **S. royale,** royal assent. **2.** Penalty.

sanctionner, *v.tr.* To sanction. **1.** To approve. **2.** To penalize.

sanctuaire, *s.m.* Sanctuary

sandale, *s.f.* Sandal.

sandwich [-witʃ], *s.m.* Sandwich.

sang, *s.m.* **1.** Blood. **2.** (*a*) Blood, race. (*b*) Blood, kinship.

sang-froid, *s.m.* Coolness, composure.

sanglant, *a.* Bloody; blood-stained.

sangle, *s.f.* Strap, band, webbing.

sangler, *v.tr.* **1.** To strap. **2.** To thrash, lash.

sanglier, *s.m.* Wild boar.

sanglot, *s.m.* Sob.

sangloter, *v.i.* To sob.

sangsue, *s.f.* Leech.

sanguin [-gɛ̃], *a.* Full-blooded.

sanguinaire [-gin-], *a.* Sanguinary.

sanitaire, *a.* Sanitary.

sans, *prep.* **1.** Without. **2.** But for. **S. cela, s. quoi,** otherwise, else.

sans-façon. **1.** *s.m.* Homeliness. **2.** *a.inv.* Homely; without ceremony.

sans-fil, **1.** *s.inv.* **1.** *s.f.* Wireless. **2.** *s.m.* Wireless message.

sans-gêne. **1.** *s.m.* Off-handedness. **2.** *a.inv.* Unceremonious.

sans-travail, *s.m.pl.* Unemployed.

santé, *s.f.* Health; well-being. **A votre s.!** good health!

saper, *v.tr.* To sap, undermine.

sapeur, *s.m.* Sapper.

sapeur-pompier, *s.m.* Fireman. **Les sapeurs-pompiers,** the fire-brigade.

sapin, *s.m.* (*a*) Fir(-tree). (*b*) **Bois de s.,** deal.

sarbacane, *s.f.* Blow-pipe.

sarcasme, *s.m.* Taunt; gibe.

sarcastique, *a.* Sarcastic.

sarcler, *v.tr.* To weed; to hoe.

sarcloir, *s.m.* Dutch hoe.

sarcophage, *s.m.* Sarcophagus.

Sardaigne, *Pr.n.f.* Sardinia.

sarde, *a. & s.* Sardinian.

sardine, *s.f.* Sardine.

sardonique, *a.* Sardonic.

sarment, *s.m.* Vine-shoot.

sarrasin, *s.m.* Buckwheat.

sarrau, *pl.* **-s, -x,** *s.m.* Smock.

sas[1] [sɑ], *s.m.* Sieve, screen, riddle.

sas[2], *s.m.* Lock.

Satan, *Pr.n.m.* Satan.

satané, *a.* Devilish, confounded.

satanique, *a.* Satanic; fiendish.

satellite, *s.m.* Satellite.

satiété, *s.f.* Satiety; surfeit.

satin, *s.m.* Satin.

satire, *s.f.* Satire.

satirique, *a.* Satirical.

satiriquement, *adv.* Satirically.

satisfaction, *s.f.* **1.** Satisfaction. **2.** Reparation, amends.

satisfaire, *v.* To satisfy. **1.** *v.tr.* (*a*) To content. (*b*) To make amends to. **2.** *v.ind.tr.* **S. à.,** to satisfy; to answer; to fulfil.

satisfaisant, *a.* Satisfying, satisfactory.

satisfait, *a.* Satisfied, contented.

saturation, *s.f.* Saturation.

saturer, *v.tr.* To saturate.

saturnin, *a.* Saturnine.

satyre, *s.m.* Satyr.

sauce, *s.f.* Sauce.

saucière, *s.f.* Sauce-boat.

saucisse, *s.f.* Sausage.

saucisson, *s.m.* (Large) sausage.

sauf[1] [sof], *a.* Safe, unhurt.

sauf[2], *prep.* Save, but, except.

sauf-conduit, *s.m.* Safe-conduct; pass. *pl. sauf-conduits.*

sauge, *s.f.* Sage.

saugrenu, *a.* Absurd, preposterous.

saule, *s.m.* Willow.

saumâtre, *a.* Brackish, briny.

saumon, *s.m.* **1.** Salmon. **2.** Ingot.

saumure, *s.f.* Brine; pickle.

saupoudrer, *v.tr.* To sprinkle, powder.

saupoudroir, *s.m.* Dredger, castor.

saur [sɔːr], *a.m.* **Hareng s.,** red herring.

saut, *s.m.* Leap, jump, vault. **Au s. du lit,** on getting out of bed. **S. périlleux,** somersault.

saute, *s.f.* Jump. **S. de vent,** shift, change of wind.

saute-mouton, *s.m.* Leap-frog.

sauter. **1.** *v.i.* (*a*) To jump, leap, skip. **S. au cou de,** to hug. (*b*) To explode; to blow up; to fly off. (*c*) (Of wind) To shift. **2.** *v.tr.* To jump (over).

sauterelle, *s.f.* Grasshopper; locust.

sautiller [-tije], *v.i.* To hop; to skip.

sauvage. **1.** *a.* (*a*) Savage; wild,

untamed. (*b*) Unsociable; shy. **2.** *s.*
(*a*) Savage. (*b*) Unsociable person.

sauvagement, *adv.* Savagely.

sauvagerie, *s.f.* **1.** (State of) sav-
agery. **2.** Unsociability.

sauvegarde, *s.f.* Safeguard.

sauvegarder, *v.tr.* To safeguard.

sauve-qui-peut, *s.m.inv.* Stampede.

sauver, *v.tr.* To save, rescue.
se sauver. **1.** To escape. **2.** To
run away.

sauvetage, *s.m.* (*a*) Life-saving;
rescue. **Canot de s.,** lifeboat. **Échelle
de s.,** fire-escape. (*b*) Salvage.

sauveur, *s.m.* Preserver, deliverer.

savamment, *adv.* (*a*) Learnedly
(*b*) Knowingly, wittingly.

savant. **1.** *a.* (*a*) Learned, scholarly.
(*b*) Skilful. **2.** *s.* Scientist; scholar.

saveur, *s.f.* Savour, taste.

Savoie. *Pr.n.f.* Savoy.

savoir. **I.** *v.tr.* To know. **1.** To be
aware of. **Sans le s.,** unconsciously.
Pas que je sache, not that I am aware
of. **2.** (*a*) **C'est à s.,** that remains to
be seen. (*b*) **Faire s. qch. à qn,** to
inform s.o. of sth. (*c*) (**A**) **s.,** namely.
3. To know how, to be able.
II. savoir, *s.m.* Knowledge.
learning.

savoir-faire, *s.m.* Ability; tact.

savoir-vivre, *s.m.* Good breeding.

savon, *s.m.* Soap. **Eau de s.,** soap-
suds.

savonner, *v.tr.* To soap; to lather.

savonnette, *s.f.* Cake of toilet-soap.

savonneux, *a.* Soapy.

savourer, *v.tr.* To relish, enjoy.

savoureux, *a.* Savoury, tasty.

sbire, *s.m.* Myrmidon (of the law).

scabreux, *a.* **1.** Difficult, risky.
2. Indelicate; improper.

scandale, *s.m.* Scandal.

scandaleusement, *adv.* Scandalously, disgracefully.

scandaleux, *a.* Scandalous.

scandaliser, *v.tr.* To scandalize.

scandinave, *a. & s.* Scandinavian.

scaphandrier, *s.m.* Diver.

scarabée, *s.m.* **1.** Beetle. **2.** Scarab.

scarlatine, *s.f.* Scarlet fever.

sceau, *s.m.* Seal.

scélérat, *s.* Scoundrel.

scélératesse, *s.f.* Villainy.

scellé. **1.** *a.* Sealed; under seal.
2. *s.m.* Seal.

sceller, *v.tr.* (*a*) To seal; to seal up.
(*b*) To ratify, confirm.

scène, *s.f.* **1.** Stage. **Entrer en s.,** to
come on. **Metteur en s.,** producer.
2. Scene.

scénique, *a.* Scenic; theatrical.

scepticisme, *s.m.* Scepticism.

sceptique. **1.** *a.* Sceptical. **2.** *s.*
Sceptic.

sceptre, *s.m.* Sceptre.

schampooing, *s.m.* Shampoo.

schisme, *s.m.* Schism.

sciatique. **1.** *a.* Sciatic. **2.** *s.f.*
Sciatica.

scie, *s.f.* Saw.

sciemment, *adv.* Knowingly.

science, *s.f.* **1.** Knowledge, learning;
skill. **2.** Science.

scientifique, *a.* Scientific.

scientifiquement, *adv.* Scientific-
ally.

scier, *v.tr.* **1.** To saw. **2.** To saw off.

scierie, *s.f.* Saw-mill.

scinder, *v.tr.* To divide, split up.

scintillant, *a.* Scintillating; twinkling; sparkling.

scintillation, *s.f.* Scintillation.

scintiller, *v.i.* To scintillate; to
twinkle.

scission, *s.f.* Scission, split.

sciure, *s.f.* **S. de bois,** sawdust.

scolaire, *a.* School.

sconse, *s.m.* Skunk (fur).

scorpion, *s.m.* Scorpion.

scrupule, *s.m.* Scruple.

scrupuleusement, *adv.* Scrupulously.

scrupuleux, *a.* Scrupulous.

scruter, *v.tr.* To scrutinize; to scan.

scrutin, *s.m.* Poll. **Dépouiller le s.,**
to count the votes.

sculpter [skylte], *v.tr.* To carve.

sculpteur [skylt-], *s.m.* Sculptor.

sculpture [skylt-], *s.f.* Sculpture.
S. sur bois, wood-carving.

se, *pers.pron.* (*a*) Oneself; himself,
herself, itself, themselves. (*b*) Each
other, one another.

séance, *s.f.* **1.** Sitting; session.
2. Performance; seance.

séant. **1.** *s.m.* **Sur son s.,** sitting (up).
2. *a.* Becoming; fitting.

seau, *s.m.* Pail, bucket. **S. à charbon,**
coal-scuttle.

sec [sɛk], **sèche,** *a.* **1.** (*a*) Dry. (*b*)
Dried. (*c*) **Perte sèche,** dead loss.

2. (*a*) Spare ; lean. (*b*) Sharp, curt.
(*c*) Barren ; dry. **3.** *Adv.phr.* **A sec,**
dry.

sécession, *s.f.* Secession.

sèche. See SEC.

sèchement, *adv.* Curtly, tartly.

sécher, *v.tr.* **1.** To dry (up). **2.** *v.i.*
To dry.

sécheresse, *s.f.* **1.** (*a*) Dryness.
(*b*) Drought. **2.** Curtness.

second. 1. *a.* Second. **2.** *s.m.* (*a*)
Second floor. (*b*) Principal assistant ;
second (in command). **3.** *s.f.*
Seconde. (*a*) Second (class). (*b*)
Second (of time).

secondaire, *a.* Secondary.

seconder, *v.tr.* **1.** To second, back
up. **2.** To forward, promote.

secouer, *v.tr.* **1.** (*a*) To shake. (*b*) To
shake up, rouse. **2.** To shake off.
se secouer. (*a*) To shake oneself.
(*b*) To bestir oneself.

secourable, *a.* Helpful.

secourir, *v.tr.* To succour, help.

secours, *s.m.* Help, succour, aid.
Sortie de s., emergency exit.

secousse, *s.f.* Shake ; jolt, jerk.

secret[1], **-ète,** *a.* Secret ; hidden.

secret[2], *s.m.* **1.** Secret. **2.** Secrecy
privacy.

secrétaire, *s.m. & f.* Secretary.

secrètement, *adv.* Secretly.

secte, *s.f.* Sect.

secteur, *s.m.* Sector.

section, *s.f.* **1.** Section **2.** Stage (on
bus route).

séculaire, *a.* Century-old.

séculier. 1. *a.* (*a*) Secular. (*b*) Laic.
2. *s.* Layman.

sécurité, *s.f.* **1.** Security. **2.** Safety

sédatif, *a. & s.m.* Sedative.

sédentaire, *a.* Sedentary.

sédiment, *s.m.* Sediment, deposit.

séditieux, *a.* Seditious.

sédition, *s.f.* Sedition ; mutiny.

séducteur, -trice. 1. *s.* (*a*) Tempter.
(*b*) *s.m.* Seducer. **2.** *a.* Tempting.

séduction, *s.f.* Seduction.

séduire, *v.tr.* **1.** To seduce. **2.** To
fascinate, captivate.

séduisant, *a.* **1.** Seductive. **2.** Fascinating, attractive.

segment, *s.m.* Segment.

ségrégation, *s.f.* Segregation

seiche, *s.f.* Cuttle-fish.

seigle, *s.m.* Rye.

seigneur, *s.m.* Lord.

sein, *s.m.* Breast, bosom.

seize, *num.a.inv. & s.m.inv.* Sixteen.

séjour, *s.m.* **1.** Stay, sojourn. **2.**
Abode ; residence.

séjourner, *v.i.* To stay, sojourn.

sel, *s.m.* Salt.

sélection, *s.f.* Selection, choice.

selle, *s.f.* Saddle.

seller, *v.tr.* To saddle.

sellier, *s.m.* Saddler, harness-maker.

selon, *prep.* According to. **C'est s.,**
it all depends.

Seltz [sɛls], *s.m.* **Eau de S.,** soda-
water.

semaine, *s.f.* (*a*) Week. (*b*) Working
week. (*c*) Week's pay.

sémaphore, *s.m.* Semaphore.

semblable. 1. *a.* (*a*) Alike ; similar ;
like. (*b*) Such. **2.** *s.* Like. (*b*) **Nos
semblables,** our fellow-men.

semblablement, *adv.* Similarly.

semblant, *s.m.* Semblance, appearance. **Faire s. de,** to pretend to.

sembler, *v.i.* (*a*) To seem, appear.
(*b*) *Impers.* **A ce qu'il me semble,** as
it strikes me.

semelle, *s.f.* Sole (of shoe).

semence, *s.f.* **1.** Seed. **2.** (*a*) **S. de
perles,** seed pearls. (*b*) (Tin)tacks.

semer, *v.tr.* **1.** To sow. **2.** To spread,
scatter.

semestre, *s.m.* Half-year.

semestriel, *a.* Half-yearly.

semeur, -euse, *s.* Sower.

semi-circulaire, *a.* Semicircular.

sémillant [-mijã], *a.* Sprightly.

séminaire, *s.m.* Seminary.

semis, *s.m.* **1.** Sowing. **2.** Seedlings.

sémitique, *a.* Semitic.

semonce, *s.f.* Reprimand scolding.

semoule, *s.f.* Semolina.

sénat, *s.m.* Senate.

sénateur, *s.m.* Senator.

séné, *s.m.* Senna.

sénile, *a.* Senile.

sénilité, *s.f.* Senility.

sens [sã:s], *s.m.* **1.** Sense ; judgment ;
meaning. **2.** Direction, way. **Rue à
s. unique,** one-way street. **"S. interdit,"** 'no entry.' **S. dessus dessous,**
topsy-turvy.

sensation, *s.f.* Sensation.

sensationnel, *a.* Sensational.

sensé, *a.* Sensible, judicious

sensibilité, *s.f.* Sensibility.

sensible, *a.* **1.** (*a*) Sensitive, susceptible. (*b*) Sympathetic. (*c*) Sensitive, tender. **2.** Sensible; perceptible.

sensiblement, *adv.* Appreciably
perceptibly.

sensualité, *s.f.* Sensuality.

sensuel, *a.* Sensual.

sente, *s.f.* Footpath; track.

sentence, *s.f.* Sentence, judgment.

sentencieux, *a.* Sententious.

senteur, *s.f.* Scent, perfume.

sentier, *s.m.* (Foot)path.

sentiment, *s.m.* **1.** Feeling. (*a*) Sensation. (*b*) Sense, consciousness.
2. Opinion.

sentimental, -aux, *a.* Sentimental.

sentimentalité, *s.f.* Sentimentality.

sentinelle, *s.f.* Sentry; sentinel.

sentir. **1.** *v.tr.* (*a*) To feel. (*b*) To
be conscious. (*c*) To smell. **2.** *v.i.*
(*a*) To taste of, smell of. (*b*) To smell.
se sentir, to feel.

seoir [swa:r], *v.i.* To suit, become.

sépale, *s.m.* Sepal.

séparable, *a.* Separable.

séparation, *s.f* Separation.

séparé, *a.* **1.** Separate, different.
2. Separated, apart.

séparément, *adv.* Separately

séparer, *v.tr.* To separate.
se séparer. **1.** To separate part.
2. To divide. **3.** To break up.

sépia, *s.f.* Sepia.

sept [se(t)], *num.a.inv.* & *s.m.inv.*
Seven.

septembre, *s.m.* September.

septentrional, -aux, *a.* Northern.

septième [setjɛm]. **1.** *num.a.* & *s.*
Seventh. **2.** *s.m.* Seventh (part).

septique, *a.* Septic.

septuagénaire, *a.* & *s.* Septuagen-
arian.

sépulcral, -aux, *a.* Sepulchral.

sépulcre, *s.m.* Sepulchre.

séquence, *s.f.* Sequence.

séquestrer, *v.tr.* To sequestrate.

séraphique, *a.* Seraphic, angelic.

serbe, *a.* & *s.* Serb, Serbian.

Sercq. *Pr.n.* Sark

serein[1], *a.* Serene, calm.

serein[2], *s.m.* Evening dew.

sérénade, *s.f.* Serenade.

sérénité, *s.f.* Serenity, calmness.

serf [sɛrf], **serve,** *s.* Serf.

serge, *s.m.* Serge.

sergent, *s.m.* Sergeant. **S. de ville,**
policeman.

série, *s.f.* Series; succession. **Fabrication en s.,** mass production.

sérieusement, *adv.* Seriously.

sérieux. **1.** *a.* Serious, (*a*) Grave.
(*b*) Serious-minded. (*c*) Earnest.
(*d*) Important. **2.** *s.m.* Seriousness.
gravity.

serin, *s.m.* Canary.

seringue, *s.f.* Syringe, squirt.

seringuer, *v.tr.* (*a*) To syr.nge.
(*b*) To squirt.

serment, *s.m.* (Solemn) oath. **Prêter
s.,** to take an oath.

sermon, *s.m.* Sermon.

sermonner, *v.tr.* To lecture.

serpe, *s.f.* Bill-hook.

serpent, *s.m.* Serpent, snake.

serpenter, *v.i.* To wind, meander.

serpentin. **1.** *a.* Serpentine. **2.** *s.m.*
(Paper) streamer.

serpolet, *s.m.* Wild thyme.

serre, *s.f.* **1.** Greenhouse. **S. chaude,**
hothouse. **2.** (*a*) Grip. (*b*) Claw
talon.

serré, *a.* Tight; compact.

serrement, *s.m.* Squeezing, pressure. **S. de cœur,** pang.

serrer, *v.tr.* **1.** To put away, stow
away. **2.** To press, squeeze, clasp.
3. To tighten; to clench. **4.** To
close, close up.
se serrer. **1.** To keep close together; to crowd. **2.** To tighten.

serrure, *s.f.* Lock. **Trou de la s.,**
key-hole.

serrurier, *s.m.* Locksmith.

servant. **1.** *a.* Serving. **2.** *s.f.* **Servante,** (maid-)servant.

serve, *s.f.* See SERF.

serviable, *a.* Obliging.

service, *s.m.* **1.** (*a*) Service. **Escalier
de s.,** backstairs. (*b*) Department
2. (*a*) Duty. **Officier de s.,** orderly
officer. (*b*) Attendance. **3.** (*a*)
Course (of a meal). (*b*) **Premier s.,**
first lunch *or* dinner. **4.** Set.

serviette, *s.f.* **1.** (*a*) (Table-)napkin
(*b*) Towel. **2.** Portfolio.

servile, *a.* Servile.

servilité, *s.f.* Servility.

servir, *v.* To serve. **1.** *v.i.* (*a*) To be
useful. (*b*) **S. de,** to serve as. **2.**
v.tr. (*a*) To serve, wait on. **Madame
est servie,** dinner is served, madam

(b) To serve up, dish up. (c) To help **se servir de,** to use.

serviteur, s.m. Servant.

servitude, s.f. Servitude.

ses. See SON[1].

session, s.f. Session, sitting.

seuil [sœːj], s.m. Threshold ; doorstep.

seul, a. **1.** (a) Only, single. **Pas un s.,** not a single one. (b) Mere, bare. **2. Un homme s.,** a man by himself. **Dames seules,** ladies only. **Je l'ai fait tout s.,** I did it (by) myself. **3. S. un homme,** only a man.

seulement, adv. **1.** (a) Only (b) Solely, merely. **2.** Even.

sève, s.f. Sap.

sévère, a. Severe. **1.** Stern. **2.** Strict.

sévèrement, adv. **1.** Severely. **2.** Strictly.

sévérité, s.f. Severity ; sternness.

sévir, v.i. To rage.

sevrer, v.tr. To wean.

sexagénaire, a. & s. Sexagenarian

sexe, s.m. Sex.

sexuel, a. Sexual.

seyant, a. Becoming.

si[1], conj. **1.** If. **2.** Whether. **3.** What if ; suppose.

si[2], adv. **1.** So ; so much. (a) Such. (b) As. (c) **Si bien que,** with the result that. **2.** Yes. **Si fait,** yes indeed.

siamois, a. & s. Siamese.

Sibérie. Pr.n.f. Siberia.

sibérien, a. & s. Siberian.

sibilant, a. Sibilant, hissing.

Sicile. Pr.n.f. Sicily.

sicilien, a. & s. Sicilian.

sidecar, s.m. Side-car.

siècle, s.m. **1.** Century. **2.** Age.

siège, s.m. **1.** Seat, centre. **2.** Siege. **3.** Seat, chair.

sien, sienne. 1. poss.a. His, hers, its, one's. **2.** poss.pron. **Le sien, la sienne, les siens, les siennes,** (a) His, hers, its, one's. (b) s.m. **Y mettre du s.,** to contribute to sth. (c) s.pl. His own, her own, one's own.

sieste, s.f. Siesta, nap.

sifflant, a. Hissing ; whistling.

sifflement, s.m. Whistling, whistle.

siffler. 1. v.i. To whistle ; to hiss ; to whizz. **2.** v.tr. (a) To whistle. (b) To whistle for. (c) To hiss.

sifflet, s.m. Whistle.

siffleur, -euse, s. Whistler.

siffloter, v.i. To whistle to oneself.

signal, -aux, s.m. Signal.

signalement, s.m. Description.

signaler, v.tr. **1.** (a) To make conspicuous. (b) To report. **2.** To signal. **3.** To give a description of. **se signaler,** to distinguish oneself.

signaleur, s.m. Signaller ; signalman.

signataire, s.m. & f. Signatory, subscriber.

signature, s.f. **1.** Signing. **2.** Signature.

signe, s.m. Sign. **1.** Indication ; mark. **2.** Symbol. **3.** Gesture.

signer, v.tr. To sign. **se signer,** to cross oneself.

significatif, a. Significant.

signification, s.f. Meaning, signification, sense, import.

significativement, adv. Significantly.

signifier, v.tr. To mean, signify.

silence, s.m. Silence.

silencieusement, adv. Silently.

silencieux, a. Silent. (a) Taciturn. (b) Noiseless. (c) Still, peaceful.

silex [-leks], s.m. Flint.

silhouette, s.f. Silhouette.

sillage [sijaːʒ], s.m. (a) Wake, wash. (b) Slip-stream.

sillon [sijɔ̃], s.m. (a) Furrow (b) Line, wrinkle.

sillonner [sijɔ-], v.tr. (a) To furrow. (b) To streak.

similaire, a. Similar ; like.

similairement, adv. Similarly.

similarité, s.f. Similarity, likeness.

similitude, s.f. Similitude ; resemblance, likeness ; similarity.

simple, a. **1.** Simple. **2.** (a) Ordinary, common. **S. soldat,** private. (b) Plain. (c) Easy. **3.** (a) Simpleminded. (b) Half-witted.

simplement, adv. Simply.

simplicité, s.f. **1.** Simplicity ; plainness. **2.** Artlessness, simpleness.

simplification, s.f. Simplification.

simplifier, v.tr. To simplify.

simulacre, s.m. Semblance.

simulation, s.f. Simulation, feint.

simulé, a. Feigned ; sham.

simuler, v.tr. To simulate, feign.

simultané, a. Simultaneous.

simultanément, adv. Simultaneously.

sincère, *a.* Sincere. **1.** Frank, candid. **2.** Genuine.

sincèrement, *adv.* Sincerely.

sincérité, *s.f.* (*a*) Sincerity, frankness, candour. (*b*) Genuineness.

sinécure, *s.f.* Sinecure.

singe, *s.m.* Monkey, ape.

singer, *v.tr.* To ape, mimic.

singularité, *s.f.* Singularity. **1.** Peculiarity. **2.** Oddness.

singulier, *a.* Singular. **1.** Remarkable. **2.** Odd.

singulièrement, *adv.* Singularly.

sinistre. 1. *a.* Sinister, ominous. **2.** *s.m.* Disaster, catastrophe.

sinon, *conj.* Otherwise, else, if not.

sinueux, *a.* Sinuous ; winding.

sinuosité, *s.f.* (*a*) Sinuosity, winding. (*b*) Bend (of river).

siphon, *s.m.* Siphon.

sirène, *s.f.* **1.** Siren ; charmer. **2.** Siren, hooter.

sirop, *s.m.* Syrup.

situation, *s.f.* Situation.

situer, *v.tr.* To place, situate.

six, *num.a.inv.* & *s.m.* Six.

sixième [siz-]. **1.** *num.a.* & *s.* Sixth. **2.** *s.m.* Sixth (part).

ski, *s.m.* **1.** Ski. **2.** Skiing.

slave. 1. *a.* Slav, Slavonic. **2.** *s.* Slav.

smoking [-kiŋ], *s.m.* Dinner-jacket

sobre, *a.* Temperate, abstemious.

sobrement, *adv.* Soberly.

sobriété, *s.f.* Sobriety.

sobriquet, *s.m.* Nickname.

soc [sɔk], *s.m.* Ploughshare.

sociabilité, *s.f.* Sociability.

sociable, *a.* Sociable.

social, -aux, *a.* Social.

socialisme, *s.m.* Socialism.

socialiste. 1. *a.* Socialistic ; socialist. **2.** *s.* Socialist.

société, *s.f.* Society. **1.** (*a*) Community. (*b*) Company. **2.** Association.

socle, *s.m.* Base, pedestal, plinth.

socque, *s.m.* Clog, patten.

sœur, *s.f.* Sister ; nun.

sofa, *s.m.* Sofa, settee.

soi, *pers.pron.* Oneself ; himself herself, itself, etc.

soi-disant. 1. *a.inv.* (*a*) Self-styled. (*b*) So-called. **2.** *adv.* Supposedly.

soie, *s.f.* **1.** Bristle. **2.** Silk. **Papier de s.,** tissue paper.

soierie, *s.f.* Silk goods ; silks.

soif [swaf], *s.f.* Thirst.

soigné, *a.* Carefully done. **Repas s.,** Carefully cooked meal.

soigner, *v.tr.* To look after, take care of, attend to.

soigneusement, *adv.* Carefully.

soigneux, *a.* Careful ; painstaking

soi-même, *pers.pron.* Oneself.

soin, *s.m.* Care. (*a*) "**Aux (bons) soins de,**" 'care of.' (*b*) Attention, trouble. **Avoir s.,** to take care.

soir, *s.m.* (*a*) Evening. **Du s.,** p.m. (*b*) Afternoon.

soirée, *s.f.* **1.** (Duration of) evening. **2.** (*a*) (Evening) party. (*b*) Représentation de s., evening performance.

soit [swat]. **1. S.!** all right ! **2.** *conj.* **S. . . . s. . . . ; s. . . . ou . . .,** either . . . or . . . ; whether . . . or . . . .

soixantaine [swasã-], *s.f.* About sixty. **Avoir passé la s.,** to be in the sixties.

soixante [swasã:t], *num.a.inv.* & *s.m.inv.* Sixty.

soixante-dix, *num.a.inv.* & *s.m.inv.* Seventy.

sol [sɔl], *s.m.* Ground, earth ; soil.

solaire, *a.* Solar.

soldat, *s.m.* Soldier.

solde¹, *s.f.* Pay.

solde², *s.m.* **1.** Balance. "**Pour s.,**" 'in settlement.' **2. Vente de soldes,** clearance sale.

sole, *s.f. Ich* : Sole.

soleil [-lɛ:j], *s.m.* **1.** Sun. **2.** Sunshine. **Coup de s.,** touch of sunstroke. **3.** Sunflower. **4.** Catherine-wheel.

solennel, *a.* Solemn.

solennellement, *adv.* Solemnly.

solennité, *s.f.* Solemnity.

solidaire, *a.* Jointly responsible.

solidarité, *s.f.* **1.** Joint responsibility. **2. Grève de s.,** sympathetic strike.

solide. 1. *a.* (*a*) Solid. (*b*) Sound, solvent. **2.** *s.m.* Solid.

solidement, *adv.* Solidly, firmly.

solidifier, *v.tr.* To solidify.

solidité, *s.f.* Solidity ; strength.

soliloque, *s.m.* Soliloquy.

soliste, *s.m.* & *f.* Soloist.

solitaire. 1. *a.* Solitary, lonely. **2.** *s.m.* (*a*) Recluse. (*b*) Solitaire.

solitude, *s.f.* **1.** Solitude, loneliness. **2.** Lonely spot ; solitude.

solive, *s.f.* Joist, beam.

sollicitation, *s.f.* Solicitation.

solliciter, *v.tr.* To solicit.

solliciteur, -euse, *s.* Petitioner; applicant.

sollicitude, *s.f.* (*a*) Solicitude; care. (*b*) Anxiety, concern.

solo, *s.m.* Solo.

solubilité, *s.f.* Solubility

soluble, *a.* Soluble.

solution, *s.f.* Solution.

solvabilité, *s.f.* Solvency.

solvable, *a.* Solvent.

sombre, *a.* Dark, sombre, gloomy.

sombrement, *adv.* Sombrely.

sombrer, *v.i.* To founder; to sink.

sommaire, *a. & s.m.* Summary.

sommairement, *adv.* Summarily.

somme[1], *s.f.* **Bête de s.,** beast of burden.

somme[2], *s.f.* Sum, amount. **S. toute,** upon the whole. **En s.,** in short.

somme[3], *s.m.* Nap; short sleep.

sommeil [-mɛːj], *s.m.* **1.** Sleep, slumber. **2.** Avoir s., to be sleepy.

sommeiller [-meje], *v.i.* To doze, nod; to sleep lightly; to slumber.

sommelier, *s.m.* Wine-waiter.

sommer, *v.tr.* To summon.

sommet, *s.m.* Top, summit; apex.

sommier, *s.m.* **S. élastique,** spring-mattress.

somnambule, *s.* Somnambulist.

somnolence, *s.f.* Somnolence, sleepiness, drowsiness.

somnolent, *a.* Somnolent, drowsy.

somnoler, *v.i.* To drowse, doze.

somptueusement, *adv.* Sumptuously.

somptueux, *a.* Sumptuous.

son[1], **sa, ses,** *poss.a.* His, her, its, one's.

son[2], *s.m.* Sound.

son[3], *s.m.* Bran.

sonate, *s.f.* Sonata.

sondage, *s.m.* (*a*) Sounding; boring. (*b*) Probing.

sonde, *s.f.* **1.** Sounding-line; plummet. **Jeter la s.,** to heave the lead **2.** Probe.

sonder, *v.tr.* **1.** To sound; to fathom. **2.** To probe; to examine.

songe, *s.m.* Dream.

songer, *v.i.* **1.** (*a*) To dream. (*b*) To muse; to day-dream. **2.** (*a*) **S. à,** to think of. (*b*) To imagine.

songerie, *s.f.* (Day-)dreaming.

songeur, -euse, *a.* Dreamy.

sonnant, *a.* **1.** Striking. **A dix heures sonnantes,** on the stroke of ten. **2.** **Espèces sonnantes,** hard cash.

sonné, *a.* Past.

sonner. **1.** *v.i.* To sound; to strike; to ring. **2.** *v.tr.* To sound; to ring.

sonnerie, *s.f.* **1.** Ringing. **2.** S. électrique, electric bell. **3.** (Trumpet-, bugle-) call.

sonnet, *s.m.* Sonnet.

sonnette, *s.f.* **1.** (*a*) Small bell. (*b*) Handbell. (*c*) House-bell. **2.** **Serpent à sonnettes,** rattlesnake.

sonneur, *s.m.* Bell-ringer.

sonore, *a.* Sonorous.

sophiste, *s.m.* Sophist.

sophistique. **1.** *a.* Sophistic(al). **2.** *s.f.* Sophistry.

soporifique, *a. & s.m.* Soporific. **Potion s.,** sleeping-draught.

soprano, *s.m. & f.* Soprano.

sorbet, *s.m.* Sorbet; water-ice.

sorcellerie, *s.f.* Witchcraft, sorcery.

sorcier, *s.* Sorcerer, *f.* sorceress; wizard, *f.* witch. **Vieille sorcière.** old hag.

sordide, *a.* Sordid; squalid.

sort, *s.m.* **1.** Lot; destiny, fate. **2.** Chance, fortune. **Tirer au s.,** to draw lots. **3.** Spell, charm.

sortant, *a.* Coming out.

sorte, *s.f.* **1.** Manner, way. **En s. que,** so that. **2.** Sort, kind.

sortie, *s.f.* **1.** Going out, coming out departure, exit. **2.** Trip, excursion. **3.** Outburst. **4.** Exit; way out.

sortilège, *s.m.* Spell, charm.

sortir. **I.** *v.i.* **1.** (*a*) To go *or* come out. (*b*) **S. en courant,** to run out. (*c*) To have just come out. **2.** To go out, go from home. **3.** To get out, extricate oneself. **4.** To spring, descend (from). **5.** To stand out, project.

II. sortir, *v.tr* To take out, bring out.

III. sortir, *s.m.* **Au s. du théâtre,** on coming out of the theatre.

sot, sotte. **I.** *a.* Silly, stupid, foolish. **2.** *s.* Fool, dolt.

sottement, *adv.* Stupidly, foolishly.

sottise, *s.f.* **1.** Stupidity, folly. **2.** Foolish act *or* word.

soubresaut, *s.m.* Sudden start.

souche, *s.f.* **1.** Stump (of tree). **2.** Counterfoil.

souci[1], *s.m.* Marigold.

souci[2], *s.m.* Care. **1.** Solicitude. **2.** Anxiety, worry.

soucier (se), *v.pr.* To concern oneself; to care; to mind.

soucieux, *a.* (*a*) Anxious, concerned. (*b*) Full of care; worried.

soucoupe, *s.f.* Saucer.

soudain. 1. *a.* Sudden, unexpected. **2.** *adv.* Suddenly; all of a sudden.

soudainement, *adv.* Suddenly.

soudaineté, *s.f.* Suddenness.

soude, *s.f.* Soda.

souder, *v.tr.* To weld.

se souder, (of bone) to knit.

souffle, *s.m.* Breath. **1.** Puff, blast. **2.** Respiration, breathing.

souffler. 1. *v.i.* (*a*) To blow. (*b*) To pant. **2.** *v.tr.* (*a*) To blow; to blow out (a candle). (*b*) To breathe. utter. (*c*) To prompt.

soufflet, *s.m.* **1.** (Pair of) bellows. **2.** (*a*) Box on the ear, slap. (*b*) Affront.

souffleter, *v.tr.* To slap.

souffleur, -euse, *s.* Prompter.

souffrance, *s.f.* Suffering, pain.

souffrant, *a.* (*a*) Suffering; in pain. (*b*) Unwell, ailing.

souffrir, *v.* To suffer. **1.** *v.tr.* (*a*) To endure. (*b*) To permit. **2.** *v.i.* To feel pain.

soufre, *s.m.* Sulphur.

souhait, *s.m.* Wish, desire. **A s.**, to one's liking.

souhaitable, *a.* Desirable.

souhaiter, *v.tr.* To wish, desire.

souiller [-je], *v.tr.* **1.** To soil, dirty. **2.** To pollute. **3.** To tarnish, sully.

souillure [-jyːr], *s.f.* **1.** Spot; stain. **2.** Blot, blemish.

soûl [su], *a.* Drunk, tipsy.

soulagement, *s.m.* Relief; solace.

soulager, *v.tr.* To ease; to relieve.

se soulager, to relieve one's feelings.

soulèvement, *s.m.* (*a*) Rising, heaving. (*b*) Revolt, rising.

soulever, *v.tr.* **1.** To raise; to lift (up). **2.** To rouse, stir up.

se soulever, to rise.

soulier, *s.m.* Shoe.

souligner, *v.tr.* (*a*) To underline. (*b*) To emphasize.

soumettre, *v.tr.* **1.** To subdue. **2.** To submit, refer.

se soumettre, to submit, yield.

soumis, *a.* Submissive.

soumission, *s.f.* (*a*) Submission. (*b*) Obedience.

soupape, *s.f.* Valve.

soupçon, *s.m.* **1.** Suspicion. **2.** Small quantity, dash.

soupçonner, *v.tr.* To suspect.

soupçonneusement, *adv.* Suspiciously.

soupçonneux, *a.* Suspicious.

soupe, *s.f.* Soup.

soupente, *s.f.* Loft, garret.

souper. 1. *v.i.* To have supper. **II. souper**, *s.m.* Supper.

soupeser, *v.tr.* To feel, try, the weight of.

soupière, *s.f.* Soup-tureen.

soupir, *s.m.* Sigh.

soupirant, *s.m.* Suitor.

soupirer, *v.i.* (*a*) To sigh. (*b*) **S. après**, to long for.

souple, *a.* Supple, pliant; flexible; versatile.

souplement, *adv.* Supply, lithely.

souplesse, *s.f.* Suppleness, flexibility, pliability; versatility.

source, *s.f.* Source. **1.** Spring(-head). **Eau de s.**, spring water. **2.** Origin; authority.

sourcil [-si], *s.m.* Eyebrow.

sourciller [-sije], *v.i.* **1.** To knit one's brows. **2.** To flinch.

sourd, *a.* **1.** (*a*) Deaf. (*b*) *s.* Deaf person. **2.** Dull; muffled.

sourdement, *adv.* Dully.

souriant, *a.* Smiling.

souricière, *s.f.* Mouse-trap.

sourire. I. *v.i.* **1.** To smile. **2.** **S. à**, to please. **II. sourire**, *s.m.* Smile.

souris, *s.f.* Mouse.

sournois, *a.* Artful, sly, crafty.

sournoisement, *adv.* Slyly.

sous, *prep.* Under(neath), beneath, below. **S. les tropiques**, in the tropics.

NOTE. Compound nouns and adjectives of which the first element is *sous* vary in the plural.

sous-bois, *s.m.* Underwood.

souscripteur, *s.m.* Subscriber.

souscription, *s.f.* Subscription.

souscrire, *v.tr.* To subscribe.

sous-entendre, *v.tr.* To imply.

sous-main, *s.m.* Blotting-pad.

sous-maître, -maîtresse, s. Assistant master; assistant mistress.

sous-marin. I. a. Submarine; submerged. 2. s.m. Submarine.

sous-mentionné, a. Undermentioned.

sous-officier, s.m. Non-commissioned officer.

ous-produit, s.m. By-product.

soussigné, a. & s. Undersigned.

sous-sol, s.m. Basement.

sous-titre, s.m. Sub-title.

soustraction, s.f. (a) Removal, abstraction. (b) Subtraction.

soustraire, v.tr. I. To abstract. 2. To screen, shield. 3. To subtract.
   se soustraire à, to avoid.

sous-vêtement, s.m. Under-garment.

soutane, s.f. Cassock.

soute, s.f. Store-room; bunker.

soutenable, a. Tenable.

soutenir, v.tr. To sustain, support.
   I. (a) To hold up. (b) To keep, maintain. (c) To back (up). (d) To uphold; to affirm. 2. To withstand.
   se soutenir. I. To hold up, keep up. 2. To last, continue.

soutenu, a. Sustained.

souterrain. I. a. Underground, subterranean. 2. s.m. Subway.

soutien, s.m. Support prop.

soutirer, v.tr. To draw off; to tap.

souvenir, s.m. I. Remembrance, recollection. 2. Memento. 3. Keepsake, souvenir.

souvenir (se). v.pr. **Se s. de,** to remember.

souvent, adv. Often.

souverain. I. a. Sovereign; supreme. 2. s. Sovereign.

souveraineté, s.f. Sovereignty.

soviet [-vjet], s.m. Soviet.

soviétique, a. Soviet.

soyeux, a. Silky.

spacieux, a. Spacious, roomy.

spasme, s.m. Spasm.

spatule, s.f. Spatula.

spécial, -aux, a. Special.

spécialement, adv. Especially.

spécialiser, v.tr. To specialize.

spécialiste, s.m. & f. Specialist.

spécialité, s.f. Speciality.

spécieusement, adv. Speciously.

spécieux, a. Specious; plausible.

spécifier, v.tr. To specify

spécifique, a. & s.m. Specific.

spécifiquement, adv. Specifically.

spécimen [-men], s.m. Specimen.

spectacle, s.m. I. Spectacle. sight. 2. Play. 3. Show, display.

spectateur, -trice, s. Spectator, onlooker, bystander.

spectral, -aux, a. Spectral.

spectre, s.m. Spectre, ghost.

spéculateur, -trice, s. Speculator.

spéculatif, a. Speculative.

spéculation, s.f. Speculation.

spéculer, v.i. To speculate.

sphère, s.f. Sphere.

sphérique, a. Spherical.

sphinx [sfɛ̃ks], s.m. Sphinx.

spinal, -aux, a. Spinal.

spiral, -aux. I. a. Spiral. 2. s.f. Spirale, spiral.

spirite. I. a. Spiritualistic. 2. s. Spiritualist.

spiritisme, s.m. Spiritualism.

spirituel, a. I. Spiritual. 2. Witty.

spirituellement, adv I. Spiritually. 2. Wittily

spiritueux. I. a. Spirituous 2. s.m.pl. Spirits.

splendeur, s.f. Splendour (a) Brilliance. (b) Magnificence.

splendide, a. Splendid.

splendidement, adv. Splendidly.

spoliateur, -trice, s. Despoiler.

spoliation, s.f. Spoliation.

spolier, v.tr. To despoil, rob.

spongieux, a. Spongy.

spontané, a. Spontaneous.

spontanéité, s.f Spontaneity.

spontanément, adv Spontaneously.

sporadique, a. Sporadic.

sporadiquement, adv. Sporadically.

spore, s.f. Spore.

sport, s.m. Sports; games.

sportif, a. Sporting; (of) sport.

square [skwa:r], s.m. (Public) square.

squelette, s.m. Skeleton.

stabilisation, s.f. Stabilization.

stabiliser, v.tr. To stabilize.

stabilité, s.f. Stability, firmness

stable, a. Stable; firm, steady.

stade, s.m. Stadium, sports-ground.

stagnant [stagnã], a. Stagnant.

stagnation [stagn-], s.f. Stagnation.

stalactite, s.f. Stalactite.

stalle, s.f. Stall (in cathedral); (numbered) seat (in theatre).

stance, s.f. Stanza.

stand [stă:d], *s.m.* **1.** Stand (on race-course). **2.** Shooting-gallery.

station, *s.f.* **I.** (*a*) (Action of) standing. (*b*) Position. **2.** Break of journey ; (short) halt. **3.** (*a*) Station ; stage ; taxi-rank. (*b*) Resort. **S. balnéaire,** watering-place.

stationnaire, *a.* Stationary.

stationnement, *s.m.* Stopping, standing. "S. interdit," 'no parking.'

stationner, *v.i.* **I.** To stop ; to take up one's position. **2.** To stand ; to park.

statique. I. *a.* Static. **2.** *s.f.* Statics.

statistique. I. *a.* Statistical. **2.** *s.f.* Statistics.

statue, *s.f.* Statue.

statuer, *v.tr.* To decree, enact.

stature, *s.f.* Stature, height.

statut, *s.m.* Statute, ordinance.

statutaire, *a.* Statutory.

stellaire, *a.* Stellar.

sténodactylographe, *s.m. & f.* Shorthand-typist.

sténographe, *s.m. & f.* Shorthand writer.

sténographie, *s.f.* Shorthand.

sténographier, *v.tr.* To take down in shorthand.

stéréoscope, *s.m.* Stereoscope.

stéréoscopique, *a.* Stereoscopic.

stéréotyper, *v.tr.* To stereotype.

stérile, *a.* Sterile ; barren.

stérilisation, *s.f.* Sterilization.

stériliser, *v.tr.* To sterilize.

stéthoscope, *s.m.* Stethoscope.

stigmate, *s.m.* Stigma.

stigmatiser, *v.tr.* To stigmatize.

stimulant. I. *a.* Stimulating. **2.** *s.m.* (*a*) Stimulant. (*b*) Stimulus.

stimulation, *s.f.* Stimulation.

stimuler, *v.tr.* To stimulate.

stipulation, *s.f.* Stipulation.

stipuler, *v.tr.* To stipulate.

stock, *s.m.* Stock (of goods).

stoïcien. I. *a.* Stoical. **2.** *s.* Stoic.

stoïcisme, *s.m.* Stoicism.

stoïque. I. *a.* Stoical. **2.** *s.* Stoic.

stoïquement, *adv.* Stoically.

stop [stɔp], *int.* Stop !

stopper, *v.i. & tr.* To stop.

store, *s.m.* (Window-)blind.

strabisme, *s.m.* Squinting.

strapontin, *s.m.* Folding seat.

strass, *s.m.* Paste (jewellery).

stratagème, *s.m.* Stratagem.

stratégie, *s.f.* Strategy.

stratégique, *a.* Strategic(al).

stratégiquement, *adv.* Strategically.

stratégiste, *s.m.* Strategist.

strict [-rikt], *a.* Strict ; severe.

strictement, *adv.* Strictly.

strident, *a.* Strident, harsh.

strié, *a.* **I.** Scored, scratched. **2.** Streaked.

strier, *v.tr.* **I.** To score, scratch. **2.** To streak.

strophe, *s.f.* Stanza, verse.

structural, -aux, *a.* Structural.

structure, *s.f.* Structure.

studieusement, *adv.* Studiously.

studieux, *a.* Studious.

stupéfaction, *s.f.* Stupefaction.

stupéfait, *a.* Stupefied, amazed.

stupéfiant. I. *a.* Amazing. **2.** *s.m.* Narcotic ; drug.

stupéfier, *v.tr.* (*a*) To bemuse. (*b*) To astound, amaze.

stupeur, *s.f.* Stupor.

stupide, *a.* Stupid.

stupidement, *adv.* Stupidly.

stupidité, *s.f.* Stupidity.

style, *s.m.* Style.

stylet, *s.m.* Stiletto, stylet.

stylographe, *s.m.* Fountain-pen.

su, *s.m.* Knowledge.

suaire, *s.m.* Winding-sheet ; shroud.

suave, *a.* (*a*) Sweet. (*b*) Suave.

suavement, *adv.* (*a*) Sweetly, pleasantly. (*b*) Suavely.

suavité, *s.f.* (*a*) Sweetness. (*b*) Suavity.

subalterne. I. *a.* Subordinate. **2.** *s.m.* Underling, subaltern.

subir, *v.tr.* To undergo ; to suffer.

subit, *a.* Sudden, unexpected.

subitement, *adv.* Suddenly.

subjugation, *s.f.* Subjugation.

subjuguer, *v.tr.* To subjugate.

sublime, *a.* Sublime ; lofty, exalted.

sublimité, *s.f.* Sublimity.

submerger, *v.tr.* **I.** To submerge. **2.** To overwhelm.

submersion, *s.f.* Submersion.

subordonné, *a.* Subordinate.

subordonner, *v.tr.* To subordinate.

subreptice, *a.* Surreptitious.

subrepticement, *adv.* Surreptitiously.

subséquent [syp-], *a.* Subsequent.

subside [syp-], *s.m.* Subsidy.

subsidence [syp-], *s.f.* Subsidence.

subsidiaire [syp-], *a.* Subsidiary.

subsistance [syp-], *s.f.* Subsistence, sustenance.

subsistant [syp-], *a.* Subsisting.

subsister [syp-], *v.i.* To subsist.

substance, *s.f.* Substance.

substantiel, *a.* Substantial.

substantiellement, *adv.* Substantially.

substantif, *a. & s.m* Substantive.

substituer, *v.tr.* To substitute.

substitut, *s.m.* Assistant; deputy.

substitution, *s.f.* Substitution.

subterfuge [syp-], *s.m.* Subterfuge.

subtil [syptil], *a.* **1.** Subtle. **2.** (*a*) Acute. (*b*) Delicate, fine.

subtilement [syp-], *adv.* Subtly.

subtilité [syp-], *s.f.* Subtlety.

suburbain, *a.* Suburban.

subvenir, *v.ind.tr.* S. à, to provide for.

subvention, *s.f.* Subsidy.

subventionner, *v.tr.* To subsidize.

subversif, *a.* Subversive.

subvertir, *v.tr.* To subvert.

suc [syk], *s.m.* Juice; sap.

succéder, *v.ind.tr.* S. à, to succeed, follow; to inherit.

succès, *s.m.* **1.** Result. **2.** Success.

successeur, *s.m.* Successor.

successif, *a.* Successive.

succession, *s.f.* Succession.

successivement, *adv.* Successively.

succinct [-sɛ̃, -sɛ̃kt], *a.* Succinct.

succinctement [-sɛ̃tmã], *adv.* Succinctly, briefly.

succion, *s.f.* Suction; sucking.

succomber, *v.i.* To succumb.

succulence, *s.f.* Succulence.

succulent, *a.* Succulent, juicy.

succursale, *s.f.* Branch.

sucer, *v.tr.* To suck.

sucre, *s.m.* Sugar.

sucré, *a.* Sugared; sweet.

sucrer, *v.tr.* To sugar; to sweeten.

sucreries, *s.f. pl.* Sweetmeats, sweets.

sucrier, *s.m.* Sugar-basin.

sud [syd], *s.m. & a.inv.* South.

sud-est. 1. *s.m.* South-east. **2.** *a.inv.* South-easterly; south-eastern.

sud-ouest. 1. *s.m.* South-west. **2.** *a.inv.* South-westerly; south-western.

Suède. *Pr.n.f.* Sweden.

suédois. 1. *a.* Swedish. **2.** *s.* Swede. **3.** *s.m. Ling:* Swedish.

suer, *v.i.* To sweat. **1.** To perspire. **2.** To exude.

sueur, *s.f.* Sweat, perspiration.

suffire, *v.i.* (*a*) To suffice; to be sufficient. (*b*) S. à, to be equal to

suffisamment, *adv.* Sufficiently.

suffisance, *s.f.* **1.** Sufficiency, adequacy. **2.** Self-conceit.

suffisant, *a.* **1.** Sufficient, adequate. **2.** Self-satisfied, conceited.

suffixe, *s.m.* Suffix.

suffocant, *a.* Suffocating, stifling.

suffocation, *s.f.* Suffocation.

suffoquer. **1.** *v.tr.* To suffocate, stifle. **2.** *v.i.* To choke (*de*, with).

suffrage, *s.m.* Suffrage, vote.

suggérer, *v.tr.* To suggest.

suggestif, *a.* Suggestive.

suggestion, *s.f.* Suggestion.

suicide, *s.m.* Suicide.

suicidé, *s.* Suicide.

suicider (se), *v.pr.* To commit suicide.

suie, *s.f.* Soot.

suif [sɥif], *s.m.* Tallow.

suinter, *v.i.* To ooze.

Suisse[1]. *Pr.n.f.* Switzerland.

suisse[2]. **1.** *a.* Swiss. **2.** *s.m.* (*a*) Swiss. (*b*) Church officer; hall porter. (*c*) Petit s., small cream cheese.

Suissesse, *s.f.* Swiss (woman).

suite, *s.f.* **1.** (*a*) Continuation; effect. A la s. de, following. De s., in succession. Tout de s., at once, immediately. Dans la s., subsequently. (*b*) Sequel. (*c*) Coherence. **2.** Suite. **3.** Series. **4.** Consequence. Par s. de, in consequence of.

suivant[1], *prep.* According to.

suivant[2]. **1.** *a.* Next, following. **2.** *s.m.* Follower, attendant.

suivi, *a.* Connected; close.

suivre, *v.tr.* **1.** (*a*) To follow. "Prière de faire s.," 'please forward.' "A s.," 'to be continued.' (*b*) To attend. (*c*) To pursue. (*d*) To pay heed to. **2.** (*a*) To come after. (*b*) To result from. **3.** (*a*) To go along. (*b*) To obey.

sujet[1], **-ette**, *a. & s.* Subject.

sujet[2], *s.m.* **1.** Subject. **2.** Individual.

sujétion, *s.f.* Subjection.

sulfate, *s.m.* Sulphate.

sulfure, *s.m.* Sulphide.

sulfureux, *a.* Sulphureous.

sulfurique, *a.* Sulphuric.

sultan, *s.m.* Sultan.

sultane, *s.f.* Sultana, sultaness.

superbe, *a.* Superb; stately.
superbement, *adv.* Superbly.
supercherie, *s.f.* Deceit; swindle.
superficie, *s.f.* Area.
superficiel, *a.* Superficial.
superficiellement, *adv.* Superficially.
superfin, *a.* Superfine.
superflu. 1. *a.* Superfluous. **2.** *s.m.* Superfluity.
superfluité, *s.f.* Superfluity.
supérieur, -eure. **1.** *a.* (*a*) Upper. (*b*) Superior. (*c*) Higher. **2.** *s.* Superior.
supériorité, *s.f.* Superiority.
superlatif, *a.* Superlative.
superstitieux, *a.* Superstitious.
superstition, *s.f.* Superstition.
supplanter, *v.tr.* To supplant; to supersede.
suppléant. **1.** *s.* Substitute; deputy. **2.** *a.* Acting, temporary.
suppléer. 1. *v.tr.* (*a*) To supply, make up. (*b*) To take the place of **2.** *v.i.* S. à, to make up for.
supplément, *s.m.* (*a*) Supplement. (*b*) Extra payment; excess fare.
supplémentaire, *a.* Supplementary. Heures supplémentaires, overtime.
suppliant. 1. *a.* Supplicating, pleading. **2.** *s.* Supplicant.
supplication, *s.f.* Supplication.
supplice, *s.m.* (*a*) Torture. (*b*) Torment, anguish.
supplier, *v.tr.* To beseech, implore.
supplique, *s.f.* Petition.
support, *s.m.* **1.** Support, prop, stay **2.** Rest; stand.
supportable, *a.* Bearable, tolerable.
supporter, *v.tr.* **1.** To support. **2.** (*a*) To endure. (*b*) To tolerate.
supposé, *a.* Supposed, alleged; assumed.
supposer, *v.tr.* **1.** To suppose. assume, imagine. **2.** To imply.
supposition, *s.f.* Supposition.
suppression, *s.f.* Suppression.
supprimer, *v.tr.* To suppress.
supputation, *s.f.* Computation.
supputer, *v.tr.* To compute.
suprématie, *s.f.* Supremacy.
suprême, *a.* Supreme.
suprêmement, *adv.* Supreme.y.
sur¹, *prep.* **1.** (*a*) On, upon. (*b*) Towards. (*c*) Over, above. (*d*) About, concerning. **2.** (*a*) About, towards.

(*b*) Sur quoi, whereupon. **3.** Out of. **4. Huit pieds sur six,** eight foot by six.
sur², *a.* Sour; tart.
sûr, *a.* Sure. **1.** (*a*) Safe, secure. (*b*) Trustworthy. **2.** Certain. A coup sûr, for certain.
surabondance, *s.f.* Superabundance.
surabondant, *a.* Superabundant.
suranné, *a.* Antiquated.
surcharge, *s.f.* **1.** Overloading. **2.** (*a*) Overload. (*b*) Excess weight. **3.** Additional charge.
surcharger, *v.tr.* (*a*) To overload. (*b*) To overcharge.
surchauffer, *v.tr.* To overheat.
surcroît, *s.m.* Addition, increase.
surdité, *s.f.* Deafness.
sureau, *s.m.* Elder(-tree).
sûrement, *adv.* **1.** Surely, certainly. **2.** Securely, safely.
sûreté, *s.f.* **1.** Safety, security. **La S.,** the Criminal Investigation Department. **2.** Sureness.
surexciter, *v.tr.* To excite
surface, *s.f.* Surface.
surfaire, *v.tr.* To overcharge.
surgir, *v.i.* To rise; to loom (up).
surhomme, *s.m.* Superman.
surhumain, *a.* Superhuman.
surintendant, *s.m.* Superintendent.
sur-le-champ, *adv.* At once.
surlendemain, *s.m.* Next day but one.
surmené, *a.* Jaded; fagged.
surmener, *v.tr.* To overwork.
surmonter, *v.tr.* To surmount.
surnager, *v.i.* (*a*) To float on the surface. (*b*) To remain afloat.
surnaturel, *a.* Supernatural.
surnom, *s.m.* Nickname.
surnuméraire, *a. & s.m.* Supernumerary.
surpasser, *v.tr.* **1.** To surpass. **2.** To go beyond; to outdo.
surpeuplé, *a.* Over-populated.
surplis, *s.m.* Surplice.
surplomber, *v.i. & tr.* To overhang.
surplus, *s.m.* Surplus, excess.
surprenant, *a.* Surprising, astonishing.
surprendre, *v.tr.* **1.** To surprise. **2.** To astonish.
surpris, *a.* Surprised.
surprise, *s.f.* Surprise.
sursaut, *s.m.* Start, jump.
sursauter, *v.i.* To start; to jump.

sursis, *s.m.* Respite; reprieve.
surtout, *adv.* Particularly especially, principally, above all.
surveillance [-vɛj-], *s.f.* Supervision, surveillance.
surveillant [-vɛj-], *s.* Supervisor, superintendent, overseer.
surveiller [-vɛj-], *v.tr.* To supervise oversee, superintend.
survenir, *v.i.* To supervene, happen; to arise.
survivance, *s.f.* Survival.
survivant. 1. *a.* Surviving. **2.** *s.* Survivor.
survivre, *v.ind.tr.* To survive.
survoler, *v.tr.* To fly over.
sus [sy(s)]. **En sus,** in addition.
susceptibilité, *s.f.* **1.** Susceptibility. **2.** Touchiness.
susceptible, *a.* Susceptible (*a*) Sensitive. (*b*) Touchy.
susciter, *v.tr.* (*a*) To raise up (*b*) To create; to give rise to.
suscription, *s.f.* Superscription, address.
susdit, *a. & s.* Aforesaid.
susmentionné, *a. & s.* Abovementioned, aforesaid.
susnommé, *a. & s.* Above-named.
suspect [-pɛ(kt)]. **1.** *a.* Suspicious, doubtful, suspect. **2.** *s.m.* Suspect.
suspecter, *v.tr.* To suspect.
suspendre, *v.tr.* To suspend.
suspendu, *a.* Suspended; hanging.
suspens (en), *adv.phr.* In suspense.
suspension, *s.f.* Suspension.
suspicion, *s.f.* Suspicion.
susurrer, *v.i.* To murmur, whisper.
svelte, *a.* Slender, slim.
sveltesse, *s.f.* Slenderness, slimness.
sybarite, *a. & s.* Sybarite.

sycomore, *s.m.* Sycamore.
sycophante. 1. *s.m.* Sycophant. **2.** *a.* Sycophantic.
syllabe, *s.f.* Syllable.
syllabique, *a.* Syllabic.
sylphe, *s.m.,* **sylphide,** *s.f.* Sylph.
sylvestre, *a.* Woodland; sylvan.
sylviculture, *s.f.* Forestry.
symbole, *s.m.* Symbol.
symbolique, *a.* Symbolic(al).
symboliquement, *adv.* Symbolically.
symboliser, *v.tr.* To symbolize.
symbolisme, *s.m.* Symbolism.
symétrie, *s.f.* Symmetry.
symétrique, *a.* Symmetrical.
symétriquement, *adv.* Symmetrically.
sympathie, *s.f.* Sympathy; nstinctive attraction; liking.
sympathique, *a.* **1.** Sympathetic. **2.** Likable, attractive, congenial.
sympathiquement, *adv.* Sympathetically.
sympathiser, *v.i.* To sympathize.
symphonie, *s.f.* Symphony.
symptôme, *s.m.* Symptom.
synchroniser [-krɔn-], *v.tr.* To synchronize.
syncope, *s.f.* **1.** Syncope; swoon. **2.** Syncopation.
syndicaliste, *s.m.* Trade-unionist.
syndicat, *s.m.* Syndicate. **S. ouvrier,** trade-union.
synonyme. 1. *a.* Synonymous (*de,* with). **2.** *s.m.* Synonym.
synthétique, *a.* Synthetic.
Syrie. *Pr.n.f.* Syria.
systématique, *a.* Systematic.
systématiquement, *adv.* Systematically.
système, *s.m.* System.

T

T, t [te], *s.m.* (The letter) T, t.
ta, *poss.a.f.* See TON[1].
tabac [taba], *s.m.* Tobacco.
tabatière, *s.f.* Snuff-box.
table, *s.f.* **1.** Table. **2.** (*a*) Slab; tablet. (*b*) List, catalogue.
tableau, *s.m.* **1.** Board. **T. de distribution,** switchboard. **2.** (*a*) Picture, painting. (*b*) Tableau. **3.** List, table.
tablette, *s.f.* **1.** (*a*) Shelf. (*b*) Flat slab. **2.** Cake, slab; tablet, lozenge.

tablier, *s.m.* **1.** Apron. **T. d'enfant,** pinafore. **2.** Dash-board.
tabou, *s.m. & a.* Taboo.
tabouret, *s.m.* Stool; footstool.
tache, *s.f.* Stain, spot; blot.
tâche, *s.f.* Task.
tacher, *v.tr.* To stain, spot; to sully.
tâcher, *v.i.* To try, endeavour.
tacheté, *a.* Spotted; speckled.
tacite, *a.* Tacit; implied.
tacitement, *adv.* Tacitly.

taciturne, *a.* Taciturn.

taciturnité, *s.f.* Taciturnity.

tact [takt], *s.m.* Tact.

tacticien, *s.m.* Tactician.

tactique. 1. *a.* Tactical. **2.** *s.f.* Tactics.

taffetas, *s.m.* T. gommé, sticking-plaster.

taie, *s.f.* T. d'oreiller, pillow-case.

taillade [tajad], *s.f.* Cut, slash.

taillader [tajade], *v.tr.* To slash.

taille [ta:j, tɑ:j], *s.f.* **1.** Cutting. **2.** Cut (of garment). **3.** Edge. **4.** (*a*) Stature, height. (*b*) Figure, waist.

taille-crayons, *s.m.inv.* Pencil-sharpener.

tailler [taje], *v.tr.* To cut; to hew; to trim.

tailleur, -euse [taj-], *s.* **1.** (*a*) Cutter; hewer. (*b*) Tailor, tailoress. **2.** *s.m.* Tailor-made costume.

taillis [taji], *s.m.* Copse; brushwood.

taire, *v.tr.* To say nothing about.
se taire, to be silent.

talc [talk], *s.m.* Talc; French chalk.

talent, *s.m.* Talent, faculty, gift.

talisman, *s.m.* Talisman.

talon, *s.m.* **1.** Heel. **2.** (*a*) *Cards:* Talon. (*b*) Fag-end, remnant. (*c*) Counterfoil.

talonner, *v.tr.* (*a*) To follow closely. (*b*) To spur on, urge.

talus, *s.m.* **1.** Slope. **2.** Bank; ramp.

tamarin, *s.m.* Tamarind.

tambour, *s.m.* **1.** Drum. **T.** de basque, tambourine. **2.** Drummer. **3.** Revolving door.

tambour-major, *s.m.* Drum-major. *pl.* tambours-majors.

tamis, *s.m.* Sieve, sifter; strainer.

Tamise (la). *Pr.n.* The Thames.

tamiser, *v.tr.* To sift; to strain.

tampon, *s.m.* **1.** Plug. **2.** (*a*) (Inking-)pad. (*b*) Rubber stamp. **3.** Buffer.

tancer, *v.tr.* To rate, scold.

tandem [-dɛm], *s.m.* Tandem.

tandis que, *conj.phr.* (*a*) Whereas. (*b*) While, whilst.

tangage, *s.m.* Pitching (of ship).

tangente, *s.f.* Tangent.

tangible, *a.* Tangible.

tango, *s.m.* Tango.

tanguer, *v.i.* (Of ship) To pitch.

tanière, *s.f.* Den, lair.

tanner, *v.tr.* To tan.

tanneur, *s.m.* Tanner.

tant, *adv.* **1.** (*a*) So much. **Pour t. faire,** if it comes to that. **T. s'en faut,** far from it. **T. soit peu,** ever so little. **Si t. est que,** if indeed. (*b*) So many; as many. (*c*) So; to such a degree. **En t. que,** in so far as. (*d*) However. (*e*) **T. mieux,** so much the better. **T. pis!** so much the worse. **2.** (*a*) As much, as well (as). (*b*) As long, as far (as).

tante, *s.f.* Aunt.

tantôt, *adv.* **1.** Soon, presently. **2.** Just now. **3. T. triste, t. gai,** now sad, now gay.

taon [tɔ̃], *s.m.* Gad-fly, horse-fly.

tapage, *s.m.* Din, uproar; row.

tapageur, -euse. 1. *a.* Noisy; uproarious. **2.** *s.* Roisterer, rowdy.

tape, *s.f.* Tap, rap, pat, slap.

tapioca, *s.m.* Tapioca.

tapir (se), *v.pr.* To squat, cower.

tapis, *s.m.* **1.** Cloth, cover. **2.** Carpet.

tapisser, *v.tr.* To paper (room).

tapisserie, *s.f.* Tapestry, hangings.

tapissier, *s.* Upholsterer.

tapoter, *v.tr.* To pat; to strum.

taquin. 1. *a.* Teasing. **2.** *s.* Tease.

taquiner, *v.tr.* To tease; to worry.

tard, *adv.* Late.

tarder, *v.i.* **1.** To delay. **2.** *Impers.* Il lui tarde, he is longing (*de*, to).

tardif, *a.* Tardy, belated; backward.

tardivement, *adv.* Tardily.

tare, *s.f.* Defect, blemish.

tarif [-rif], *s.m.* (*a*) Tariff, price-list. (*b*) Scale of charges.

tarir. 1. *v.tr.* (*a*) To dry up. (*b*) To exhaust. **2.** *v.i.* To dry up, run dry.

tartare, *a. & s.* Tartar.

tarte, *s.f.* (Open) tart; flan.

tartelette, *s.f.* Tartlet.

tartine, *s.f.* Slice of bread and butter.

tartrique, *a.* Tartaric.

tas [tɑ], *s.m.* Heap, pile; lot.

tasse, *s.f.* Cup.

tasser, *v.tr.* To compress, squeeze, together; to pack.
se tasser. **1.** To settle; to sink. **2.** To crowd together.

tâter, *v.tr.* To feel, touch; to finger.

tâtonnement, *s.m.* Groping.

tâtonner, *v.i.* To grope.

tâtons (à), *adv.phr.* Gropingly.

tatouer, *v.tr.* To tattoo.

taudis, *s.m.* Miserable room; hovel.

taupe, *s.f.* Mole.

taupinière, *s.f.* Mole-hill.

taureau, *s.m.* Bull.

taux, *s.m.* Rate ; established price ; scale.

taverne, *s.f.* Tavern ; public house.

taxation, *s.f.* Taxation.

taxe, *s.f.* **1.** Charge ; rate. **2.** Tax.

taxer, *v.tr.* **1.** To tax. **2.** To accuse

taxi, *s.m.* Taxi(-cab).

taxiphone, *s.m.* Public call-box.

tchécoslovaque, *a. & s.* Czecho-slovak.

Tchécoslovaquie. *Pr.n.f.* Czecho-slovakia.

tchèque, *a. & s.* Czech.

te, *pers. pron. sg.* **1.** (*a*) You. (*b*) (To) you. (*c*) Yourself. **2.** Thee, thyself.

technique [tɛk-]. **1.** *a.* Technical. **2.** *s.f.* Technique.

techniquement [tɛk-], *adv.* Tech-nically.

teindre, *v.tr.* **1.** To dye. **2.** To stain, tinge.

teint, *s.m.* **1.** Dye, colour. **Bon t.,** fast dye. **2.** Complexion, colour.

teinte, *s.f.* Tint, shade, hue.

teinter, *v.tr.* To tint.

teinture, *s.f.* **1.** Dyeing. **2.** (*a*) Dye (*b*) Colour, tinge. **3.** Tincture.

teinturier, *s.* Dyer.

tel, telle, *a.* **1.** Such. **Un tel,** such a. **2.** (*a*) Like ; as. (*b*) **Tel que,** such as, like. (*c*) **Tel quel,** just as it is. **3.** *pron.* Such a one. **Tel qui,** he who. *s.* **Un tel, une telle,** so-and-so.

télégramme, *s.m.* Telegram.

télégraphe, *s.m.* Telegraph.

télégraphie, *s.f.* Telegraphy.

télégraphier, *v.tr. & i.* To wire.

télégraphique, *a.* Telegraphic.

télégraphiste, *s.* Telegraphist. **Fac-teur t.,** telegraph-messenger.

télépathie, *s.f.* Telepathy.

télépathique, *a.* Telepathic.

téléphone, *s.m.* Telephone.

téléphoner, *v.tr. & i.* To telephone.

téléphonie, *s.f.* Telephony.

téléphonique, *a.* Telephonic. **Cabine t.,** telephone box.

téléphoniste, *s.m. & f.* Telephonist ; telephone operator.

télescope, *s.m.* Reflecting telescope.

télescopique, *a.* Telescopic.

télévision, *s.f.* Television.

tellement, *adv.* **1.** In such a manner ; so. **2.** To such a degree ; so.

téméraire, *a.* Rash, reckless.

témérairement, *adv.* Rashly.

témérité, *s.f.* Temerity, rashness.

témoignage, *s.m.* **1.** Testimony, evidence. **2. En t. de,** as a token of.

témoigner. **1.** *v.i.* To testify ; to bear witness. **2.** *v.tr. or ind.tr.* **T. (de),** To testify to.

témoin, *s.m.* Witness ; second.

tempe, *s.f. Anat :* Temple.

tempérament, *s.m.* (*a*) Constitution, temperament. (*b*) Temper.

tempérance, *s.f.* Temperance.

tempérant, *a.* Temperate.

température, *s.f.* Temperature.

tempéré, *a.* Temperate, moderate.

tempérer, *v.tr.* To temper.

tempête, *s.f.* Storm ; tempest.

tempétueux, *a.* Tempestuous.

temple, *s.m.* Temple.

temporaire, *a.* Temporary.

temporairement, *adv.* Temporarily.

temporel, *a.* Temporal.

temporiser, *v.i.* To temporize.

temps [tã], *s.m.* **1.** Time. (*a*) While, period. **Entre t.,** meanwhile. (*b*) Term. (*c*) Age, times. **Au t. jadis,** in times past. (*d*) Hour. **Il n'est plus t.,** it is too late. **2.** Weather. **Par tous les temps,** in all weathers. **3.** Tense. **4.** Beat ; time.

tenable, *a.* Tenable, defensible.

tenace, *a.* Tenacious ; retentive.

ténacité, *s.f.* Tenacity.

tenaille [-nɑːj], *s.f.* Pincers ; tongs.

tenant, *a.* **Séance tenante,** forthwith.

tendance, *s.f.* Tendency, trend.

tendon, *s.m.* Tendon, sinew.

tendre[1], *a.* Tender. (*a*) Soft ; early (age). (*b*) Fond, affectionate.

tendre[2]. **1.** *v.tr.* (*a*) To stretch. (*b*) To lay (carpet). (*c*) To stretch out, hold out. **2.** *v.i.* To tend, lead. **se tendre,** to become taut.

tendresse, *s.f.* Tenderness ; love.

tendu, *a.* Tense, taut, tight

ténèbres, *s.f.pl.* Darkness, gloom.

ténébreux, *a.* Gloomy, dark.

teneur, *s.f.* Tenor, purport.

tenir. **1.** *v.tr.* **1.** To hold. (*a*) **Tiens! tenez!** here ! (*b*) To contain. (*c*) **T. de,** to have, derive, from. (*d*) To keep, stock. **2.** To keep (a shop) ; to have charge of. **3.** To hold ; to maintain ; to keep (to). **4.** To hold back, restrain. **5.** To occupy.

II. **tenir,** *v.i.* **1.** (*a*) To hold ; to adhere. (*b*) To remain. **2.** (*a*) **T. (bon),** to hold out, to stand fast. (*b*) To last. **3. T. pour,** to be in favour of. **4. T. à.** (*a*) To value, prize. (*b*) To be bent on. (*c*) To depend on, result from. **5. T. de,** to take after.

se tenir. 1. (*a*) To keep, be, remain. (*b*) **Se t. à,** to hold on to. **2.** To contain oneself. **3. S'en t. à,** to confine oneself to.

tennis [-nis], *s.m.* **1.** (Lawn) tennis. **2.** Tennis court.

tenor, *s.m.* Tenor.

tension, *s.f.* Tension.

tentacule, *s.m.* Tentacle, feeler.

tentant, *a.* Tempting, alluring.

tentateur, -trice, *s.* Tempter, temptress.

tentatif. 1. *a.* Tentative. **2.** *s.f.* Tentative, attempt, endeavour.

tentation, *s.f.* Temptation.

tente, *s.f.* (*a*) Tent. (*b*) Awning.

tenter, *v.tr.* **1.** To tempt. **2.** To attempt, try.

tenture, *s.f.* Hangings, tapestry.

tenu. *a.* (*a*) **Bien t.,** well-kept. (*b*) **Être t. de, à,** to be obliged to.

ténu, *a.* Tenuous, thin ; slender.

tenue, *s.f.* **1.** (*a*) Session. (*b*) Keeping, managing. **2.** Bearing, behaviour. **3.** Dress. **En grande t.,** in full dress.

térébenthine, *s.f.* Turpentine.

terme[1], *s.m.* **1.** Term, end, limit. **2.** (Appointed) time. **3.** (*a*) Quarter ; term. (*b*) Quarter's rent.

terme[2], *s.m.* **1.** Term, expression. **2.** *pl.* Wording ; terms. **3.** *pl.* Terms, footing.

terminaison, *s.f.* Termination.

terminer, *v.tr.* **1.** To terminate. **2.** To end, finish ; to conclude.

se terminer, to come to an end.

terminus [-ny:s], *s.m.* Terminus.

terne, *a.* Dull, lustreless, leaden.

ternir, *v.tr.* To tarnish, dull, dim.

terrain, *s.m.* Ground. (*a*) (Piece of ground, plot of land. (*b*) (Football) field ; (golf) course.

terrasse, *s.f.* (*a*) Terrace ; bank. (*b*) Pavement (in front of a café).

terrasser, *v.tr.* **1.** To embank. **2.** To lay low ; to throw.

terre, *s.f.* **1.** Earth. (*a*) World. (*b*) Ground, land. **2.** Soil, land. **3.** Estate, property. **4.** Clay. **T. cuite,** terra-cotta.

Terre-Neuve. 1. *Pr.n.f.* Newfoundland. **2.** *s.m.inv.* Newfoundland dog.

terrestre, *a.* Terrestrial ; earthly.

terreur, *s.f.* Terror ; dread.

terreux, *a.* (*a*) Earthy. (*b*) Grubby, dirty. (*c*) Dull ; sickly.

terrible, *a.* Terrible, dreadful.

terriblement, *adv.* Terribly.

terrier[1], *s.m.* Burrow, hole ; earth.

terrier[2], *a.m. & s.m.* Terrier.

terrifiant, *a.* Terrifying.

terrifier, *v.tr.* To terrify.

terrine, *s.f.* (Earthenware) pot.

territoire, *s.m.* Territory.

territorial, -aux, *a.* Territorial.

terroriser, *v.tr.* To terrorize.

terroriste, *s.m.* Terrorist.

tertre, *s.m.* Hillock, mound, knoll.

tes, *a.poss.* See TON[1].

testament[1], *s.m.* Will, testament.

testament[2], *s.m.* Testament.

testateur, -trice, *s.* Testator, testatrix.

têtard, *s.m.* Tadpole.

tête, *s.f.* Head. **1.** (*a*) **Tenir t. à,** to stand up to. (*b*) Face, appearance. **2.** Headpiece, brains. **Mauvaise tête,** unruly boy, workman. **En faire à sa t.,** to have one's way. **3.** (*a*) Leader. (*b*) Summit, top. (*c*) Front.

tête-à-tête, *s.m.inv.* Tête-à-tête.

têtu, *a.* Stubborn, obstinate.

teuton. 1. *a.* Teuton(ic). **2.** *s.* Teuton.

texte, *s.m.* (*a*) Text. **Gravure hors t.,** plate. (*b*) Letterpress.

textile, *a. & s.m.* Textile.

texture, *s.f.* Texture.

thé, *s.m.* **1.** Tea. **2.** Tea-party.

théâtral, -aux, *a.* Theatrical.

théâtralement, *adv.* Theatrically.

théâtre, *s.m.* **1.** Theatre. **2.** Stage. **3.** (*a*) **Pièce de t.,** play. **Coup de t.,** dramatic turn. (*b*) Plays, dramatic works ; drama.

théière, *s.f.* Teapot.

thème, *s.m.* Theme, subject.

théologie, *s.f.* Theology.

théologien, *s.m.* Theologian ; divine.

théologique, *a.* Theological.

théorème, *s.m.* Theorem.

théorie, *s.f.* Theory.

théorique, *a.* Theoretic(al).

théoriquement, *adv.* Theoretically.

théoriser, *v.tr. & i.* To theorize.

thermal, -aux, *a.* Thermal.

thermomètre, *s.m.* Thermometer.

thèse, *s.f.* Proposition, argument. Pièce à t., problem play.

thon, *s.m.* Tunny(-fish).

thorax [-aks], *s.m.* Thorax, chest.

thym, *s.m.* Thyme.

tiare, *s.f.* Tiara.

tic [tik], *s.m.* (a) Tic; twitching. (b) Habit; trick.

ticket, *s.m.* Numbered slip, check.

tiède, *a.* Tepid; lukewarm.

tièdement, *adv.* Lukewarmly.

tiédeur, *s.f.* Tepidity.

tien, tienne[1]. **1.** *poss.a.* Yours; thine. **2.** Le tien, la tienne, les tiens, les tiennes. (a) *poss.pron.* Yours; thine. (b) *s.m.* (i) Your own; yours. (ii) *pl.* Your own.

tiens, *int.* **1.** Hullo! **2.** T., t., indeed? well, well!

tiers, *f.* tierce, *s.* (a) Third. (b) Third person, third party.

tige, *s.f.* **1.** (a) Stem, stalk. (b) Trunk. **2.** (a) Shaft; shank. (b) Rod.

tigre, tigresse, *s.* Tiger. tigress.

tigré, *a.* Striped.

tilleul [tijœl], *s.m.* Lime-tree.

timbale, *s.f.* **1.** Kettle-drum. **2.** Metal drinking-cup. **3.** Pie-dish.

timbre, *s.m.* **1.** (a) Bell; gong. (b) Timbre. **2.** Stamp; postmark.

timbré, *a.* **1.** Sonorous. **2.** Stamped.

timbre-poste, *s.m.* Postage stamp. *pl. timbres-poste.*

timbre-quittance, *s.m.* Receipt stamp. *pl. timbres-quittance.*

timbrer, *v.tr.* To stamp.

timide, *a.* Timid. (a) Timorous. (b) Shy; diffident.

timidement, *adv.* Timidly.

timidité, *s.f.* Timidity.

timonerie, *s.f.* Signalling.

timonier, *s.m. Nau:* Signalman.

tintement, *s.m.* **1.** Ringing. **2.** Tinkling; jingling.

tinter. **1.** *v.tr.* To ring. **2.** *v.i.* To ring; to tinkle; to clink.

tir, *s.m.* **1.** Shooting; gunnery. **2.** Fire, firing. **3.** Rifle-range.

tirade, *s.f.* Tirade.

tirage, *s.m.* **1.** Pulling, hauling. **2.** Draught. **3.** Drawing.

tirailler [-raje], *v.tr.* To pull about.

tirailleur [-raj-], *s.m.* Skirmisher.

tire, *s.f.* Voleur à la t., pickpocket.

tiré, *a.* Drawn, worn-out.

tire-bouchon, *s.m.* Corkscrew. *pl. tire-bouchons.*

tire-bouton, *s.m.* Button-hook. *pl. tire-boutons.*

tirelire, *s.f.* Money-box.

tirer. **I.** *v.tr.* **1.** To pull out; stretch. **2.** To pull, tug, draw. **3.** To pull off, draw off. **4.** To take out, extract. **5.** To draw. **6.** To shoot, fire. **II. tirer,** *v.i.* **1.** To pull. **2.** To incline (to); to verge (on).

tiret, *s.m.* (a) Hyphen. (b) Dash.

tireur, -euse, *s.* **1.** Drawer. **2.** (a) Shooter; marksman. (b) Fencer.

tiroir, *s.m.* Drawer.

tisane, *s.f.* Infusion (of herbs).

tison, *s.m.* (Fire-)brand.

tisonner, *v.tr.* To poke, stir (the fire).

tisonnier, *s.m.* Poker.

tissage, *s.m.* Weaving.

tisser, *v.tr.* To weave.

tisserand, *s.* Weaver.

tissu, *s.m.* (a) Texture. (b) Fabric, tissue.

titan, *s.m.* Titan.

titanesque, titanique, *a.* Titanic.

titre, *s.m.* **1.** Title. **2.** (a) Diploma, certificate. (b) Title-deed. (c) Bond, certificate; *pl.* securities. **3.** Title right.

titré, *a.* **1.** Titled. **2.** Certificated.

tituber, *v.i.* To reel; to stagger.

titulaire. **1.** *a.* Titular. **2.** *s.* Holder; bearer (of passport).

toast [tɔst], *s.m.* Toast; health.

toaster [tɔs-], *v.tr.* To toast.

toboggan, *s.m.* Toboggan.

tocsin, *s.m.* Tocsin; alarm-bell.

toi, *pers. pron.* (a) You. (b) Thou, thee.

toile, *s.f.* (a) Linen. (b) Cloth. (c) Canvas.

toilette, *s.f.* **1.** Wash-stand. **2.** Lavatory.

toi-même, *pers.pron.* Thyself; yourself.

toiser, *v.tr.* To measure.

toison, *s.f.* Fleece.

toit, *s.m.* Roof; house-top.

toiture, *s.f.* Roofing, roof.

tôle, *s.f.* Sheet-metal.

tolérable, *a.* Bearable, tolerable.

tolérablement, *adv.* Tolerably.

tolérance, *s.f.* Tolerance.

tolérant, *a.* Tolerant.

tolérer, *v.tr.* To tolerate.

tomate, *s.f.* Tomato.

tombal, *a.* Pierre tombale, tomb-stone.

tombant, *a.* Falling.

tombe, *s.f.* Tomb, grave.

tombeau, *s.m.* Tomb; monument.

tombée, *s.f.* Fall.

tomber, *v.i.* 1. To fall. Laisser t., to drop. 2. To abate, subside. 3. T. sur, to come across. 4. To fail. 5. To fall, hang down.

tombereau, *s.m.* Cart.

tome, *s.m.* (Heavy) volume; tome.

ton¹, ta, tes, *poss.a.* (a) Your. (b) Thy.

ton², *s.m.* 1. (a) Tone. (b) Manners. Le bon ton, good form. 2. (a) Pitch. (b) Key. 3. Tone, tint.

tondeur, -euse. 1. *s.* Shearer. 2. *s.f.* Tondeuse. (a) Clippers. (b) Mower.

tondre, *v.tr.* To shear; to clip; to mow.

tonique, *a. & s.m.* Tonic.

tonnage, *s.m.* Tonnage.

tonne, *s.f.* 1. Tun. 2. Ton.

tonneau, *s.m.* Cask, barrel.

tonnelet, *s.m.* Small cask; keg.

tonnelle, *s.f.* Arbour, bower.

tonner, *v.i.* To thunder.

tonnerre, *s.m.* Thunder.

tonsure, *s.f.* Tonsure.

tonte, *s.f.* (a) Sheep-shearing. (b) Clip.

topaze, *s.f.* Topaz.

topinambour, *s.m.* Jerusalem arti-choke.

topographie, *s.f.* Topography.

topographique, *a.* Topographical.

toque, *s.f.* (a) Cap. (b) Toque.

toqué, *a.* Crazy.

torche, *s.f.* Torch.

torchon, *s.m.* Dish-cloth; duster.

tordre, *v.tr.* To twist; to wring. se tordre, to writhe, twist.

toréador, *s.m.* Bull-fighter.

tornade, *s.f.* Tornado.

torpédo, *s.m. or f.* Open touring-car.

torpeur, *s.f.* Torpor.

torpille [-pi:j], *s.f.* Torpedo.

torpiller [-pije], *v.tr.* To torpedo.

torpilleur [-pij-], *s.m.* Torpedo-boat.

torrent, *s.m.* Torrent.

torrentiel, *a.* Torrential.

torride, *a.* Torrid.

tors, *a.* Twisted.

tort, *s.m.* Wrong. 1. Error, fault. A t., wrongly. 2. Injury, harm.

torticolis, *s.m.* Stiff neck.

tortiller [-tije], *v.tr.* To twist. se tortiller. 1. To wriggle, twist. 2. To squirm.

tortue, *s.f.* Tortoise; turtle.

tortueusement, *adv.* Tortuously.

tortueux, *a.* Tortuous; winding.

torture, *s.f.* Torture.

torturer, *v.tr.* To torture.

tôt, *adv.* (a) Soon. Tôt ou tard, sooner or later. (b) Early.

total, -aux. 1. *a.* Total, complete, whole. 2. *s.m.* Whole, total.

totalement, *adv.* Totally, entirely.

totalitaire, *a.* Totalitarian.

totalité, *s.f.* Totality, whole.

toton, *s.m.* Teetotum.

touage, *s.m.* Towing; warping.

touchant. 1. *a.* Touching, moving. 2. *prep.* Touching, concerning.

touche, *s.f.* 1. Touch, touching. 2. Key (of typewriter).

toucher. I. *v.* To touch. 1. *v.tr.* (a) To hit; to be paid; to draw. (b) To move, affect. (c) To concern, affect. 2. (a) *v.tr.* To touch on; to allude to. (b) *v.ind.tr.* To meddle, interfere. 3. *v.i.* T. à, to be in touch with; to border on. se toucher, to touch, adjoin. II. **toucher,** *s.m.* Touch.

touer, *v.tr.* To tow.

touffe, *s.f.* Tuft; wisp; clump.

touffu, *a.* Bushy; thick.

toujours, *adv.* 1. Always, ever. 2. Still. 3. Nevertheless, all the same.

toupet, *s.m.* 1. (a) Tuft of hair. (b) Forelock. 2. Cheek, impudence.

toupie, *s.f.* Top; peg-top.

tour¹ [tu:r], *s.f.* 1. Tower. 2. Castle, rook.

tour², *s.m.* 1. Lathe. 2. (a) Circum-ference, circuit. Sp: Lap. (b) T. de cou, necklet. (c) Turn; shape; course. 3. (a) Round, turn. (b) Stroll. (c) Trip, tour. 4. T. à t., by turns. 5. Trick, feat.

tourbe, *s.f.* Peat, turf.

tourbeux, *a.* Peaty, boggy.

tourbillon [-bijɔ̃], *s.m.* 1. Whirl-wind; swirl. 2. (a) Whirlpool. (b) Eddy.

tourbillonner [-bij-], *v.i.* To whirl (round); to eddy, swirl.

tourelle, *s.f.* Turret.

tourisme, *s.m.* Touring.

touriste, *s.m. & f.* Tourist.

tourment, *s.m.* (*a*) Torment, torture. (*b*) Anguish, pain.

tourmente, *s.f.* Storm, tempest.

tourmenté, *a.* (*a*) Tormented. (*b*) Agitated; turbulent.

tourmenter, *v.tr.* **1.** To torment. **2.** To worry.
    se tourmenter, to fret, worry.

tournant. 1. *a.* Turning; revolving. **2.** *s.m.* Turning, bend.

tournedos, *s.m.* Fillet steak.

tournée, *s.f.* Round; tour.

tourner, *v.* To turn. **1.** *v.tr.* (*a*) To revolve, turn round. (*b*) To change, convert. (*c*) To turn over. (*d*) To get round; to evade. **2.** *v.i.* (*a*) To revolve; to go round. (*b*) **Tournez à gauche,** turn to the left. (*c*) To turn out, result.
    se tourner, to turn (round).

tournesol [-sɔl], *s.m.* Sunflower.

tournevis [-vis], *s.m.* Screw-driver.

tourniquet, *s.m.* Turnstile.

tournoi, *s.m.* Tournament.

tournoiement, *s.m.* Whirling.

tournoyer, *v.i.* To whirl; to eddy.

tournure, *s.f.* **1.** Turn, course. **2.** Shape, form, figure.

tourte, *s.f.* Raised pie.

tourterelle, *s.f.* Turtle-dove.

tous. See TOUT.

Toussaint (la). *Pr.n.f.* All Saints' day; All-Hallows.

tousser, *v.i.* To cough.

tout, toute, *pl.* **tous, toutes. I.** *a.* **1.** Any, every, all. **2. A toute vitesse,** at full speed. **3.** The whole; all. **4. Tous (les) deux,** both.
    II. tout, *pron.* **1.** All, everything. **C'est à dire,** I needn't say more. **2.** *pl.* **Tous à la fois,** all together.
    III. tout, *s.m.* **Le t.,** the whole. **Pas du t.,** not at all.
    IV. tout, *adv.* **1.** Quite, entirely. **T. fait,** ready-made. **T. à fait,** quite. **2. T. en parlant,** while speaking. **3. Être t. oreilles,** to be all ears.

toutefois, *adv.* Yet, however.

tout-puissant, *f.* **toute-puissante,** *a.* Almighty, omnipotent. *pl.* **tout(es)-puissant(e)s.**

toux, *s.f.* Cough.

toxicomane, *s.m. & f.* Drug addict.

tracas, *s.m.* Worry, trouble, bother.

tracasser, *v.tr.* To worry, bother.
    se tracasser, to worry.

tracasserie, *s.f.* Worry, fuss.

trace, *s.f.* Trace.

tracé, *s.m.* Outline, sketch.

tracer, *v.tr.* To trace.

tract [trakt], *s.m.* Tract.

tracteur, *s.m.* Tractor.

traction, *s.f.* Traction. **T. avant,** (car with) front-wheel drive.

tradition, *s.f.* Tradition.

traditionnel, *a.* Traditional.

traducteur, -trice, *s.* Translator.

traduction, *s.f.* **1.** Translating. **2.** Translation.

traduire, *v.tr.* (*a*) To translate. (*b*) To interpret, explain.

trafic [-fik], *s.m.* Traffic.

trafiquer, *v.i.* To traffic, trade.

tragédie, *s.f.* Tragedy.

tragédien, *s.* Tragedian.

tragique, *a.* Tragic.

tragiquement, *adv.* Tragically.

trahir, *v.tr.* To betray; to reveal.

trahison, *s.f.* Treachery; treason.

train, *s.m.* **1.** (*a*) Train, string, line. (*b*) (Railway-)train. (*c*) Suite. **2.** Movement. (*a*) Pace. (*b*) **Mettre en t.,** to set going. **3. Être en t.,** to be in good form.

traînant, *a.* **1.** Dragging, trailing. **2.** Languid, listless; drawling.

traînard, *s.m.* Straggler.

traîneau, *s.m.* Sledge.

traînée, *s.f.* Trail; train.

traîner. 1. *v.tr.* To drag, pull, draw, along; to spin out. **2.** *v.i.* (*a*) To lag behind. (*b*) To linger. (*c*) To lie about.
    se traîner, to crawl (along).

traire, *v.tr.* To milk.

trait, *s.m.* **1.** Pulling. **Tout d'un t.,** at one stretch. **2.** (*a*) Throwing. (*b*) Shaft; dart. **3.** Draught, gulp. **4.** (*a*) Stroke, line; dash. (*b*) **T. d'union,** hyphen. **5.** (*a*) Feature. (*b*) Trait. **6.** Act, deed.

traitable, *a.* Tractable, manageable.

traite, *s.f.* **1.** Stretch; stage. **2.** Transport; trading. **3.** Milking.

traité, *s.m.* **1.** Treatise. **2.** Treaty.

traitement, *s.m.* **1.** Treatment. **2.** Salary; pay.

traiter, *v.tr.* **1.** To treat. **2.** (*a*) To negotiate. (*b*) To discuss, deal with. **3.** *v.i.* (*a*) To treat (*de*, for). (*b*) To deal (*de*, with).

traître, traîtresse. 1. *a.* Treacherous. **2.** *s.* Traitor, traitress.

traîtreusement, *adv.* Treacherously.

traîtrise, *s.f.* Treachery.

trajet, *s.m.* Journey; passage.

trame, *s.f.* Woof, weft.

tramway [tramwɛ], *s.m.* Tram(car).

tranchant. 1. *a.* (*a*) Cutting, sharp (*b*) Trenchant. **2.** *s.m.* Edge.

tranche, *s.f.* **1.** (*a*) Slice; rasher. (*b*) Block, portion. **2.** Slab. **3.** Edge.

tranchée, *s.f.* **1.** Trench; cutting. **2.** *pl.* Colic.

trancher, *v.tr.* (*a*) To slice; to cut. (*b*) To cut short. (*c*) To decide.

tranquille [-kil], *a.* Tranquil. (*a*) Still. (*b*) Quiet. (*c*) Undisturbed.

tranquillement [-kil-], *adv.* Tranquilly, calmly, quietly.

tranquilliser [-kil-], *v.tr.* To tranquillize; to soothe.
   se tranquilliser, to ca.m down.

tranquillité [-kil-], *s.f.* **1.** Tranquillity, quiet. **2.** Peace.

transaction, *s.f.* (*a*) Transaction; *pl.* dealings. (*b*) Compromise.

transatlantique. 1. *a.* Transatlantic **2.** *s.m.* (Atlantic) liner.

transborder, *v.tr.* To trans-ship.

transcendant, *a.* Transcendent.

transcripteur, *s.m.* Transcriber.

transcription, *s.f.* **1.** Transcription. **2.** Transcript, copy.

transcrire, *v.tr.* To transcribe.

transe, *s.f.* **1.** Fright. **2.** Trance.

transférable, *a.* Transferable.

transférer, *v.tr.* To transfer.

transfert, *s.m.* Transfer.

transfigurer, *v.tr.* To transfigure.

transformation, *s.f.* Transformation.

transformer, *v.tr.* To transform.
   se transformer, to change, turn.

transgresser, *v.tr.* To transgress.

transgression, *s.f.* Transgression.

transi, *a.* Perished with cold.

transiger, *v.i.* To compromise.

transitif, *a.* Transitive.

transition, *s.f.* Transition.

transitoire, *a.* Transitory, transient.

transmettre, *v.tr.* To transmit; to pass on, convey.

transmissible, *a.* Transferable.

transmission, *s.f.* **1.** Transmission. **2.** Transfer; conveyance.

transmuer, *v.tr.* To transmute.

transmutation, *s.f.* Transmutation.

transparaître, *v.i.* To show through.

transparence, *s.f.* Transparency.

transparent, *a.* Transparent.

transpercer, *v.tr.* To transfix.

transpiration, *s.f.* **1.** Perspiring. **2.** Sweat, perspiration.

transpirer, *v.i.* **1.** To perspire. **2.** To transpire; to leak out.

transplanter, *v.tr.* To transplan..

transport, *s.m.* Transport.

transportation, *s.f.* Conveyance.

transporter, *v.tr.* To transport.

transposer, *v.tr.* To transpose.

transposition, *s.f.* Transposition.

transversal, -aux, *a.* Transverse.

trapèze, *s.m.* Trapeze.

trappe, *s.f.* **1.** Trap. **2.** Trap-door.

trappeur, *s.m.* Trapper.

trapu, *a.* Thick-set, squat, stocky.

traquenard, *s.m.* Trap, deadfall.

traquer, *v.tr.* To hunt down.

traqueur, *s.m.* Tracker.

travail [-va:j], **aux**, *s.m.* Work. **1.** (*a*) Labour. (*b*) Working, operation. (*c*) Employment. **2.** Piece of work.

travaillé [-vaje], *a.* (*a*) Worked, wrought. (*b*) Laboured.

travailler [-vaje]. **1.** *v.tr.* To work. **2.** *v.i.* To work, labour.

travailleur, -euse [-vaj-]. **1.** *a.* Industrious hard-working. **2.** *s.* Worker.

travailliste [-vaj-], *a.* Labour.

travée, *s.f.* Span.

travers, *s.m.* **1.** En t. de, across. A t., au t. de, through **2.** De t.. askew, awry.

traverse, *s.f.* **1.** (Chemin de) t.. cross-road. **2.** *Rail:* Sleeper.

traversée, *s.f.* Passage, crossing.

traverser, *v.tr.* **1.** To cross; to go through. **2.** To cross, thwart.

traversin, *s.m.* Bolster.

travestir, *v.tr.* **1.** To disguise. Bal travesti, fancy-dress ball. **2.** To travesty.

travestissement, *s.m.* **1.** (*a*) Disguising. (*b*) Disguise. **2.** Travesty.

trébucher, *v.i.* To stumble, totter.

trèfle, *s.m.* **1.** Trefoil. clover. **2.** *Cards:* Clubs.

treillis [trɛji], *s.m.* Trellis; lattice.

treize, *num.a.inv. & s.m.inv.* Thirteen.

treizième, *num.a. & s.* Thirteenth.

tréma, *s.m.* Diaeresis.

tremblant, *a.* Trembling; unsteady.

tremble, *s.m.* Aspen.

tremblement, *s.m.* **1.** Trembling. **2.** Tremor. **T. de terre,** earthquake.

trembler, *v.i.* To tremble, shake; to quake; to flicker; to quaver.

trembleur, *s.m.* Buzzer.

trembloter, *v.i.* To quiver; to flicker.

trémousser, *v.i.* To flutter.

trempe, *s.f.* (*a*) Temper (of steel). (*b*) Quality; stamp.

trempé, *a.* (*a*) Wet, soaked. (*b*) Tempered; hardened.

tremper. **1.** *v.tr.* (*a*) To soak, steep. (*b*) To temper. **2.** *v.i.* To soak.

tremplin, *s.m.* Spring-board.

trentaine, *s.f.* (About) thirty.

trente, *num.a.inv. & s.m.inv.* Thirty.

trentième, *num.a. & s.* Thirtieth.

trépas, *s.m.* Death, decease.

trépassé, *a. & s.* Dead, deceased.

trépidation, *s.f.* Trepidation.

trépied, *s.m.* (*a*) Tripod. (*b*) Trivet.

trépigner, *v.i.* **T de colère,** to dance with rage.

très, *adv.* Very, most; (very) much.

trésor, *s.m.* **1.** Treasure. **2.** Treasury.

trésorerie, *s.f.* Treasury.

trésorier, *s.* Treasurer; paymaster.

tressaillement [-saj-], *s.m.* Start (of surprise); quiver; thrill.

tressaillir [-saj-], *v.i.* To start; to give a start; to wince. **Faire t.,** to startle.

tresse, *s.f.* Plait, tress.

tresser, *v.tr.* To plait; to weave.

tréteau, *s.m.* Trestle, support.

treuil [trœːj], *s.m.* Winch, windlass.

trêve, *s.f.* (*a*) Truce. (*b*) Respite.

triangle, *s.m.* Triangle.

triangulaire, *a.* Triangular.

tribord, *s.m.* Starboard.

tribu, *s.f.* Tribe.

tribulation, *s.f.* Tribulation; trial.

tribunal, -aux, *s.m.* Tribunal.

tribune, *s.f.* **1.** Tribune, platform. **2.** (*a*) Gallery. (*b*) Grand stand.

tribut, *s.m.* Tribute.

tributaire, *a. & s.m.* Tributary.

tricher, *v.i. & tr.* To cheat.

tricherie, *s.f.* Cheating.

tricheur, -euse, *s.* Cheat; trickster.

tricolore, *a.* Tricolour(ed).

tricorne, *s.m.* Three-cornered hat.

tricot, *s.m.* **1.** Knitting. **2.** Vest.

tricoter, *v.tr.* To knit.

tricycle, *s.m.* Tricycle.

trident, *s.m.* Trident.

triennal, -aux, *a.* Triennial.

trier, *v.tr.* (*a*) To sort. (*b*) To pick.

trieur, -euse, *s.* Sorter.

trigonométrie, *s.f.* Trigonometry.

trimestre, *s.m.* **1.** Quarter; three months; term. **2.** Quarter's pay.

trimestriel, *a.* Quarterly.

tringle, *s.f.* Rod.

trinité, *s.f.* **1.** Trinity. **2.** (**Ile de) la T.,** Trinidad.

trinquer, *v.i.* To clink glasses.

triomphal, -aux, *a.* Triumphal.

triomphalement, *adv.* Triumphantly.

triomphant, *a.* Triumphant.

triomphe, *s.m.* Triumph. **Arc de t.,** triumphal arch.

triompher, *v.i.* To triumph. **T. de,** to overcome.

tripes, *s.f.pl.* Tripe.

triple, *a. & s.m.* Treble, triple.

triplement, *adv.* Trebly.

tripot, *s.m.* Gambling-den.

tripotage, *s.m.* **1.** Odd jobs. **2.** Jobbery.

tripoter, *v.i.* To do odd jobs.

triste, *a.* Sad. **1.** (*a*) Sorrowful, melancholy. (*b*) Dreary. **2.** Unfortunate.

tristement, *adv.* **1.** Sadly, mournfully. **2.** Gloomily.

tristesse, *s.f.* (*a*) Sadness; melancholy. (*b*) Dullness, dreariness.

triton, *s.m.* Newt.

trivial, -als, *a.* Vulgar, low, coarse.

trivialement, *adv.* Vulgarly.

trivialité, *s.f.* Vulgarity, coarseness.

troc [trɔk], *s.m.* Exchange; barter.

troène, *s.m.* Privet.

trognon, *s.m.* Core; stump.

trois, *num.a.inv. & s.m.* Three.

troisième, *num.a. & s.* Third.

trombe, *s.f.* **1.** Waterspout. **2.** Whirlwind.

trombone, *s.m.* Trombone.

trompe, *s.f.* **1.** (*a*) Trump, horn. (*b*) Hooter. **2.** Proboscis; trunk.

tromper, *v.tr.* To deceive. **1.** (*a*) To cheat. (*b*) To betray. **2.** (*a*) To disappoint. (b) To outwit. (c) To while away.

se tromper, to be mistaken.

tromperie, s.f. (a) Deceit. fraud. (b) Illusion.

trompette. 1. s.f. Trumpet. **2.** s.m. Trumpeter.

trompeur, -euse. 1. a. (a) Deceitful. (b) Deceptive. **2.** s. Deceiver.

trompeusement, adv. (a) Deceitfully. (b) Deceptively.

tronc [trɔ̃], s.m. **1.** Trunk; stem. **2.** Collecting-box.

tronçon, s.m. (Broken) piece, stump.

trône, s.m. Throne.

tronquer, v.tr. To curtail, cut down.

trop. 1. adv. Too. (a) **T. fatigué,** overtired. (b) Too much. **T. travailler,** to over-work. **2.** s.m. Too much, too many. **Être de t.,** to be in the way.

trophée, s.m. Trophy.

tropical, -aux, a. Tropical.

tropique, s.m. Tropic.

trop-plein, s.m. Overflow.

troquer, v.tr. To exchange, barter.

trot, s.m. Trot.

trotter, v.i. To trot; to scamper.

trottiner, v.i. To toddle.

trottinette, s.f. Scooter.

trottoir, s.m. Footway, pavement.

trou, s.m. Hole.

troublant, a. Disturbing. **1.** Disquieting. **2.** Perturbing.

trouble¹, a. **1.** Turbid, cloudy; dim; murky. **2.** Confused.

trouble², s.m. (a) Confusion, disorder. (b) Agitation, perturbation.

troubler, v.tr. **1.** To make thick, muddy. **2.** To disturb. **3.** To perturb. (a) To confuse. (b) To agitate, excite.

se troubler. 1. To cloud over. **2.** To falter; to get confused.

trouée, s.f. Gap, opening, breach.

trouer, v.tr. To make a hole in.

troupe, s.f. **1.** (a) Troop, band. (b) Troupe. (c) Herd. **2.** pl. Troops, forces.

troupeau, s.m. Herd, drove; flock.

trousse, s.f. **1.** Bundle, package. **2.** Case, kit (of instruments).

trousseau, s.m. **1.** Bunch (of keys). **2.** (a) Outfit. (b) Trousseau.

trousser, v.tr. To truss.

trouvaille [-va:j], s.f. Find, windfall.

trouver, v.tr. **1.** To find. **2.** To discover, hit upon. **3.** To think, deem.

se trouver. 1. (a) To be. (b) To feel. **2.** To happen; to turn out.

truc [tryk], s.m. **1.** (a) Knack. (b) Trick, dodge. **2.** Contraption, gadget.

truculence, s.f. Truculence.

truculent, a. Truculent.

truelle, s.f. **1.** Trowel. **2. T. à poisson,** fish-slice.

truffe, s.f. Truffle.

truie, s.f. Sow.

truite, s.f. Trout.

truquer, v.tr. To fake.

tu, pers.pron. (a) You. (b) Thou.

tube, s.m. Tube, pipe.

tubercule, s.m. Tuber.

tuberculose, s.f. Tuberculosis.

tubulaire, a. Tubular.

tuer, v.tr. To kill. **Se faire t.,** to get killed. **Tué à l'ennemi,** killed in action.

se tuer. (a) To kill oneself. (b) To get killed.

tuerie, s.f. Slaughter, carnage.

tue-tête (à), adv.phr. At the top of one's voice.

tueur, s.m. Killer, slayer.

tuile, s.f. (Roofing) tile.

tulipe, s.f. Tulip.

tumeur, s.f. Tumour.

tumulte, s.m. Tumult, uproar.

tumultueusement, adv. Tumultuously; boisterously.

tumultueux, a. Tumultuous, noisy.

tunique, s.f. Tunic.

tunnel, s.m. Tunnel.

turban, s.m. Turban.

turbidité, s.f. Turbidity.

turbine, s.f. Turbine.

turbot, s.m. Turbot.

turbulence, s.f. Turbulence.

turbulent, a. Turbulent.

turc, f. turque [tyrk]. **1.** a. Turkish. **2.** s. (a) Turk. (b) s.m. Turkish.

turlututu, int. Fiddlesticks!

turque, a. & s.f. See TURC.

Turquie. Pr.n.f. Turkey.

turquoise, s.f. Turquoise.

tutelle, s.f. Guardianship.

tuteur, -trice, s. Guardian.

tutoyer, v.tr. To address as **tu** and **toi**; to be on familiar terms with.

tuyau, -aux, s.m. **1.** (a) Pipe, tube. **T. d'incéndie,** fire-hose. (b) Stem (of pipe). **2.** Tip; wrinkle.

tympan, s.m. Drum (of ear).

type, *s.m.* Type.
typhoïde, *a.* Typhoid.
typhon, *s.m.* Typhoon.
typique, *a.* Typical.
typographie, *s.f.* Typography.

tyran, *s.m.* Tyrant.
tyrannie, *s.f.* Tyranny.
tyrannique, *a.* Tyrannical.
tyranniquement, *adv.* Tyrannically.
tyranniser, *v.tr.* To tyrannize over.

U

U, u [y], *s.m.* (The letter) U, u.
ulcère, *s.m.* Ulcer.
ultérieur, -eure, *a.* 1. Ulterior.
2. Subsequent; later.
ultérieurement, *adv.* Subsequently.
ultimatum [-tɔm], *s.m.* Ultimatum.
ultime, *a.* Ultimate, final, last.
ululer, *v.i.* (Of owl) To hoot.
un, une. 1. *num.a. & s.* One. **Une
heure,** one o'clock. 2. *Indef.pron.*
One. **Les uns disent,** some say.
3. *Indef.art.* A, an.
unanime, *a.* Unanimous.
unanimement, *adv.* Unanimously.
uni, *a.* 1. United. 2. Smooth, level,
even.
unième, *num.a.* First.
uniforme, *a. & s.m.* Uniform.
uniformément, *adv.* Uniformly.
uniformité, *s.f.* Uniformity.
union, *s.f.* 1. Union. 2. Unity.
unique, *a.* Unique.
uniquement, *adv.* Solely, uniquely.
unir, *v.tr.* 1. To unite, join. 2. To
smooth, level.
  s'unir, to unite, join.
unisson, *s.m.* Unison.
unité, *s.f.* 1. Unit. 2. Unity.
univers, *s.m.* Universe.
universel, *a.* Universal. **Légataire
u.,** residuary legatee.
universellement, *adv.* Universally.
université, *s.f.* University.
uranium [-njɔm], *s.m.* Uranium.
urbain, *a.* Urban; town.

urbanisme, *s.m.* Town-p.anning.
urbanité, *s.f.* Urbanity.
urgemment, *adv.* Urgently.
urgence, *s.f.* Urgency.
urgent, *a.* Urgent, pressing.
urinoir, *s.m.* (Public) urinal.
urne, *s.f.* Urn; ballot-box.
us [y:s], *s.m.pl.* Usages.
usage, *s.m.* 1. (a) Use, employment.
(b) Wear, service. 2. (a) Usage;
custom. (b) Experience; breeding.
usé, *a.* Worn.
user. 1. *v.ind.tr.* **U. de,** to use. 2. *v.tr.*
(a) To use (up). (b) To wear (out).
  s'user, to wear (away).
usine, *s.f.* Works, factory.
usinier, *s.m.* Mill-owner.
usité, *a.* Used; in use; current.
ustensile, *s.m.* Utensil, implement.
usuel, *a.* Usual, habitual.
usuellement, *adv.* Usually.
usure[1], *s.f.* Usury.
usure[2], *s.f.* Wear (and tear).
usurier, *s.* Usurer.
usurpateur, -trice. 1. *s.* Usurper.
2. *a.* Usurping.
usurpation, *s.f.* Usurpation.
usurper, *v.tr.* To usurp.
utile, *a.* Useful, serviceable.
utilement, *adv.* Usefully; profitably.
utiliser, *v.tr.* To utilize.
utilité, *s.f.* Utility; service.
utopie, *s.f.* Utopia.
utopique, *a.* Utopian.
utopiste, *s.* Utopian.

V

V, v [ve], *s.m.* (The letter) V, v.
vacance, *s.f.* 1. Vacancy. 2. *pl.*
Vacation, holidays.
vacant, *a.* Vacant, unoccupied.
vacarme, *s.m.* Uproar, din.
vacations, *s.f.pl.* 1. Fees. 2. Vacation.
vaccination, *s.f.* Vaccination.
vacciner, *v.tr.* To vaccinate.

vache, *s.f.* Cow.
vacher, *s.* Cowherd.
vacillant [-sillā, -sijā], *a.* 1. Unsteady; flickering. 2. Wavering.
vacillation [-silla-, -sija-], *s.f.* 1.
Unsteadiness. 2. Wavering.
vaciller [-sille, -sije], *v.i.* 1.(a) To be
unsteady. (b) To flicker. 2. To waver.

vacuité, *s.f.* Vacuity, emptiness.

vacuum [-yɔm], *s.m.* Vacuum.

va-et-vient, *s.m.inv.* Coming and going.

vagabond. 1. *a.* Vagabond; roving. **2.** *s.* Vagabond; vagrant.

vagabondage, *s.m.* Vagrancy.

vagissement, *s.m.* Cry, wail(ing).

vague¹, *s.f.* Wave. **V. de fond,** tidal wave.

vague². 1. *a.* Vague, indefinite; dim. **2.** *s.m.* Vagueness.

vague³. 1. *a.* **Regard v.,** vacant stare. **2.** *s.m.* Empty space.

vaguement, *adv.* Vaguely; dimly.

vaillamment [vaj-], *adv.* Valiantly.

vaillance [vaj-], *s.f.* Valour, bravery.

vaillant [vajɑ̃], *a.* Valiant, brave.

vain, *a.* **1.** Vain. (*a*) Sham, unreal, empty. (*b*) Ineffectual. **2.** Conceited.

vaincre, *v.tr.* To vanquish, defeat. **2.** To overcome, conquer.

vainement, *adv.* Vainly.

vainqueur. 1. *s.m.* Victor, conqueror. **2.** *a.m.* Conquering.

vaisseau, *s.m.* Vessel.

vaisselle, *s.f.* Table-service; plates and dishes. **Laver la v.,** to wash up. **Eau de v.,** dish-water.

val, *s.m.* Valley, vale.

valable, *a.* Valid; available.

valet, *s.m.* **1.** Knave, jack. **2. V. de chambre,** valet. **V. de pied,** footman.

valeur, *s.f.* **1.** Value, worth. **2.** (*a*) Asset. (*b*) *pl.* Bills. securities. **3.** Valour.

valeureux, *a.* Valorous, brave.

valide, *a.* **1.** Valid. **2.** Able-bodied.

validité, *s.f.* Validity.

valise, *s.f.* (*a*) Valise. (*b*) Suit-case.

vallée, *s.f.* Valley.

vallon, *s.m.* Small valley; glen.

valoir, *v.tr. & i.* (*a*) To be worth. **A v.,** on account. (*b*) To be equivalent to. (*c*) **Il vaut mieux,** (it is) better. **Autant vaut,** (we may) as well. (*d*) **Faire v.,** to make the most of. **2.** To deserve, merit. **3.** To bring in, yield.

valse, *s.f.* Waltz.

valser, *v.i.* To waltz.

valve, *s.f.* Valve.

vandalisme, *s.m.* Vandalism.

vanille [-ni:j], *s.f.* Vanilla.

vanité, *s.f.* Vanity. **1.** Futility. **2.** Conceit, vainglory.

vaniteux, *a.* Vain, conceited.

vanne, *s.f.* Sluice(-gate), water-gate.

vanneau, *s.m.* Lapwing, peewit.

vanner, *v.tr.* To winnow.

vantard. 1. *a.* Boastful, bragging. **2.** *s.* Braggart, boaster.

vantardise, *s.f.* **1.** Bragging boastfulness. **2.** Boast.

vanter, *v.tr.* To praise up. **se vanter,** to boast. brag; to pride oneself.

vanterie, *s.f.* **1.** Boasting. **2.** Boast.

va-nu-pieds, *s.m. & f.inv.* Tatterdemalion; barefoot tramp.

vapeur¹, *s.f.* Vapour; haze; steam.

vapeur², *s.m.* Steamer, steamship.

vaporeux, *a.* Vaporous.

vaporisateur, *s.m.* (*a*) Atomizer, sprayer. (*b*) Scent-spray.

vaporiser, *v.tr.* To atomize, spray.

vareuse, *s.f.* (*a*) (Sailor's) jersey. (*b*) Pilot-coat.

variable, *a.* (*a*) Variable. (*b*) Changeable.

variation, *s.f.* Variation.

varié, *a.* Varied.

varier, *v.tr. & i.* To vary.

variété, *s.f.* Variety; diversity.

Varsovie. *Pr.n.f.* Warsaw.

vase¹, *s.m.* Vase, vessel, receptacle.

vase², *s.f.* Mud, silt, slime, ooze

vaseline, *s.f.* Vaseline.

vaseux, *a.* Muddy, slimy.

vasistas [-tɑ:s], *s.m.* Fanlight.

vasque, *s.f.* Basin (of fountain).

vaste, *a.* Vast, immense, spacious.

vastement, *adv.* Vastly, spaciously.

vaurien, *s.* Waster, rotter. bad lot

vautour, *s.m.* Vulture.

vautrer (se), *v.pr.* To wallow.

veau, *s.m.* **1.** Calf. **2.** Veal. **3.** Calf (-leather).

vedette, *s.f.* **1.** Motor-launch. **2.** (*a*) **Mots en v.,** words displayed in bold type. (*b*) *Th:* Star.

végétal, -aux. 1. *a* Plant; vegetable. **2.** *s.m.* Plant.

végétarien, *a. & s.* Vegetarian.

végétarisme, *s.m.* Vegetarianism.

végétation, *s.f.* Vegetation.

végéter, *v.i.* To vegetate.

véhémence, *s.f.* Vehemence.

véhément, *a.* Vehement, violent.

véhémentement, *adv.* Vehemently.

véhicule, *s.m.* Vehicle.

veille [vɛ:j], *s.f.* **1.** (*a*) Sitting up (at

night). (b) Vigil. (c) Look-out. (d) Wakefulness. **2.** Eve; preceding day.

veillée [vɛje], *s.f.* **1.** Watching, vigil. **2.** Evening (spent in company).

veiller [vɛje]. **1.** *v.i.* (a) To sit up, keep awake. (b) To watch. (c) **V.** sur, to look after. (d) **V. à,** to see to. **2.** *v.tr.* To watch over.

veilleur, -euse [vɛj-]. **1.** *s.* Watcher. **2.** *s.f.* Veilleuse, night-light.

veine, *s.f.* **1.** Vein. **2.** (a) Vein; lode. (b) Vein, mood. (c) Luck.

vélin, *s.m.* Vellum.

velléité, *s.f.* Slight desire.

vélo, *s.m.* Bike, push-bike.

vélocité, *s.f.* Speed, velocity.

velours, *s.m.* Velvet.

velouté. 1. *a.* Velvety; downy. **2.** *s.m.* Softness; bloom (of fruit).

velu, *a.* Hairy.

vélum [velɔm], *s.m.* Awning.

venaison, *s.f.* Venison.

vénal, -als, -aux, *a.* Venal.

venant. 1. *a.* Thriving. **2.** *s.m.* **A tout v.,** to all comers.

vendable, *a.* Saleable, marketable.

vendange, *s.f.* Vintage.

vendanger, *v.tr & i* To gather (the grapes).

vendangeur, -euse, *s.* Vintager.

vendetta, *s.f.* Vendetta.

vendeur, -euse, *s.* Seller; salesman, saleswoman; vendor.

vendre, *v.tr.* **1.** To sell. **A v.,** for sale. **2.** To betray.

vendredi, *s.m.* Friday **Le v. saint,** Good Friday.

vénéneux, *a.* Poisonous (plant).

vénérable, *a.* Venerable.

vénération, *s.f.* Veneration.

vénérer, *v.tr.* To venerate. reverence, revere.

vengeance, *s.f.* **1.** Revenge. **2.** Vengeance, retribution.

venger, *v.tr.* To avenge. 　**se venger,** to be revenged.

vengeur, -eresse. 1. *s.* Avenger. **2.** *a.* Avenging, vengeful.

véniel, -elle, *a.* Venial (sin).

venimeux, *a.* Venomous; poisonous.

venin, *s.m.* Venom.

venir, *v.i.* To come. **1.** (a) **Faire v.,** to send for, fetch. (b) **V. de faire,** to have just done. **Il vient de sortir,** he has just gone out. **2. D'où vient(-il) que?** how is it that? **3.** (a)

To occur; to come. (b) **V. à faire,** to happen to do. **4.** (a) To attain, reach. (b) **V. à bien,** to succeed. (c) **En v. aux mains,** to come to blows.

Venise. *Pr.n.f.* Venice.

vénitien, *a. & s.* Venetian.

vent, *s.m.* **1.** (a) Wind. **Coup de v.,** gust of wind; gale. **Côté du v.,** weather-side. (b) **Aire de v.,** point of the compass. (c) Air. **2. Avoir v. de,** to get wind of.

vente, *s.f.* Sale **Salle des ventes,** auction-room.

ventilateur, *s.m.* Ventilator.

ventilation, *s.f.* Ventilation.

ventiler, *v.tr.* To ventilate, air.

ventre, *s.m.* Stomach. **V. à terre,** at full speed.

ventriloque, *s.m. & f.* Ventriloquist.

ventriloquie, *s.f.* Ventriloquism.

ventru, *a.* Corpulent, portly.

venu, *s.* Comer.

venue, *s.f.* Coming, arrival.

vêpres, *s.f.pl.* Vespers; evensong.

ver, *s.m.* **1.** Worm. **2.** (a) Grub, maggot. (b) **Ver luisant,** glow-worm. (c) **Ver à soie,** silk-worm.

véracité, *s.f.* Veracity.

véranda, *s.f.* Veranda.

verbal, -aux, *a.* Verbal.

verbalement, *adv.* Verbally.

verbe, *s.m.* Verb.

verbeux, *a.* Verbose, long-winded.

verbosité, *s.f.* Verbosity, wordiness.

verdâtre, *a.* Greenish.

verdeur, *s.f.* Greenness.

verdict [-dikt], *s.m.* Verdict.

verdir, *v.i.* To become, turn, green.

verdoyant, *a.* Verdant, green.

verdure, *s.f.* **1.** (a) Greenness. (b) Verdure. **2.** Green-stuff, greens.

verge, *s.f.* Rod, wand, switch.

verger, *s.m.* Orchard.

verglas, *s.m.* Glazed frost.

vergogne, *s.f.* **Sans v.,** shameless.

vergue, *s.f. Nau:* Yard.

véridique, *a.* Veracious.

véridiquement, *adv.* Veraciously.

vérification, *s.f.* Verification.

vérifier, *v.tr.* **1.** To verify; to check; to audit. **2.** To verify, confirm.

véritable, *a.* **1.** True. **2.** Genuine.

vérité, *s.f.* **1.** Truth. **En v.,** really, actually. **2.** Fact, truth.

vermeil, -eille [-mɛːj]. **1.** *a.* Vermilion; rosy. **2.** *s.m.* Silver-gilt.

vermicelle, *s.m.* Vermicelli.

vermillon [-mijɔ̃], *s.m.* Vermilion.

vermine, *s.f.* Vermin.

vermoulu, *a.* Worm-eaten.

vermout(h) [-mut], *s.m.* Vermouth.

verni, *a.* Varnished. **Cuir v.,** patent leather.

vernir, *v.tr.* To varnish ; to polish.

vernis, *s.m.* Varnish, polish.

vérole, *s.f.* **Petite v.,** smallpox.

verre, *s.m.* **1.** Glass. **Papier de v.,** sand-paper. **2. V. grossissant,** magnifying glass. **3.** (*a*) **V. à boire,** (drinking-)glass. (*b*) Glass(ful). **4. V. soluble,** water-glass.

verrerie, *s.f.* Glassware.

verrou, *s.m.* Bolt, bar.

verrouiller [-ruje], *v.tr.* To bolt.

verrue, *s.f.* Wart.

vers[1]**,** *s.m.* Verse, line (of poetry).

vers[2]**,** *prep.* **1.** Toward(s), to. **2.** Toward(s) ; about.

versant, *s.m.* Slope, side ; bank.

versatile, *a.* Changeable, inconstant.

versatilité, *s.f.* Inconstancy.

verse, *s.f.* **A v.,** in torrents.

versé, *a.* Versed, experienced.

verser, *v.tr.* (*a*) To overturn. (*b*) To pour (out). (*c*) To shed. (*d*) To pay (in).

version, *s.f.* Version ; account.

verso, *s.m.* **"Voir au v.,"** 'see overleaf.

vert. 1. *a.* (*a*) Green. (*b*) Unripe. (*c*) Sharp ; severe. **2.** *s.m.* Green.

vert-de-gris, *s.m.* Verdigris.

vertébral, -aux, *a.* Vertebral.

vertical, -aux, *a.* Vertical ; upright.

verticalement, *adv.* Vertically.

vertige, *s.m.* Dizziness, giddiness.

vertigineux, *a.* Dizzy, giddy.

vertu, *s.f.* **1.** Virtue. **2.** Quality, property. **En v. de,** by virtue of.

vertueux, *a.* Virtuous.

verve, *s.f.* Animation, zest.

vessie, *s.f* Bladder.

veste, *s.f.* (Short) jacket.

vestiaire, *s.m.* Cloakroom.

vestibule, *s.m.* (Entrance-)hall.

vestige, *s.m.* Mark ; trace.

veston, *s.m.* (Man's) jacket. **Complet v.,** lounge suit.

vêtement, *s.m.* Garment. *pl.* Clothes, clothing.

vétéran, *s.m.* Veteran.

vétérinaire. 1. *a.* Veterinary. **2.** *s.m.* Veterinary surgeon.

vétille [-ti:j], *s.f.* Bagatelle, trifle.

vêtir, *v.tr.* To clothe ; to dress.
 se vêtir, to dress.

veto [veto], *s.m.* Veto.

vétusté, *s.f.* Decay, decrepitude.

veuf [vœf]. **1.** *a.* Widowed. **2.** *s.* Widower.

veuve, *s.f.* Widow.

vexation, *s.f.* Harassing.

vexatoire, *a.* Vexatious.

vexer, *v.tr.* To vex. **1.** To plague, harass. **2.** To annoy, provoke.

viabilité, *s.f.* Condition (of road).

viable, *a.* (Road) fit for traffic.

viaduc [-dyk], *s.m.* Viaduct.

viager, *a.* For life.

viande, *s.f.* Meat ; flesh.

vibrant, *a.* **1.** Vibrating, vibrant. **2.** (*a*) Resonant. (*b*) Stirring.

vibrateur, *s.m.* Buzzer.

vibration, *s.f.* Vibration.

vibratoire, *a.* Vibratory.

vibrer, *v.i.* To vibrate.

vicaire, *s.m.* Curate.

vice, *s.m.* **1.** Vice. **2.** Fault, defect.

vice-amiral, *s.m.* Vice-admiral. *pl. vice-amiraux.*

vice-roi, *s.m.* Viceroy. *pl. vice-rois.*

vicié, *a.* Vitiated, corrupt.

vicier, *v.tr.* To vitiate, corrupt.

vicieux, *a.* Vicious.

vicinal, -aux, *a.* **Chemin v.,** by-road.

vicissitude, *s.f.* Vicissitude.

vicomte, *s.m.* Viscount.

vicomtesse, *s.f.* Viscountess.

victime, *s.f.* Victim.

victoire, *s.f.* Victory.

victorieusement, *adv.* Victoriously.

victorieux, *a.* Victorious (*de,* over).

victuailles [-tɥaːj], *s.f.pl.* Victuals.

vidangeur, *s.m.* Scavenger.

vide. 1. *a.* Empty ; blank ; void. **2.** *s.m.* (*a*) Empty space ; void. (*b*) Vacuum. (*c*) Emptiness.

vider, *v.tr.* **1.** To empty ; to clear out. **2.** To clean (fish) ; to draw (fowl).
 se vider, to empty.

vie, *s.f.* Life. **1. Être en vie,** to be alive. **Il y va de la vie,** it's a case of life and death. **2.** Lifetime. **3.** Existence, mode of life. **Changer de vie,** to mend one's ways. **4.** Living, livelihood.

vieil. See VIEUX.

vieillard [-ejaːr], *s.m.* Old man.

vieille [vjɛːj]. **1.** See VIEUX. **2.** *s.f.* Old woman.

vieillesse [-ɛjes], *s.f.* (Old) age.

vieillir [-ɛjiːr]. **1.** *v.i.* (*a*) To grow old. (*b*) To age. **2.** *v.tr.* To age.

vierge. 1. *s.f.* Virgin, maiden. **2.** *a.* Virgin. **Page v.,** blank page.

vieux, vieil, *f.* **vieille** [vjø, vjɛ(ː)j], *a.* **1.** Old. (*a*) **Se faire v.,** to be getting on. **Mes v.,** my old people. (*b*) Of long standing. **2.** Old, ancient; worn. **V. papiers,** waste paper. *Adj.phr.inv.* **V. jeu,** old-fashioned.

vif. 1. *a.* (*a*) Alive, living. **De vive force,** by main force. **De vive voix,** by word of mouth. **Eau vive,** running water. (*b*) Lively, animated; fast. (*c*) Sharp. (*d*) Keen, quick. (*e*) Bright. **2.** *s.m.* Living flesh; quick.

vif-argent, *s.m.* Quicksilver.

vigie, *s.f.* Look-out.

vigilance, *s.f.* Vigilance.

vigilant, *a.* Vigilant, watchful.

vigile, *s.f.* Vigil.

vigne, *s.f.* **1.** (*a*) Vine. (*b*) Vineyard. **2. V. vierge,** Virginia creeper.

vigneron, *s.* Vine-grower.

vignette, *s.f.* Vignette.

vignoble, *s.m.* Vineyard.

vigoureusement, *adv.* Vigorously.

vigoureux, *a.* Vigorous, sturdy.

vigueur, *s.f.* **1.** Vigour, strength. **2. Entrer en v.,** to come into force.

vil, *a.* **1.** Cheap, low-priced. **2.** Low(ly); base. **3.** Vile, base.

vilain. 1. *s.* (*a*) Scurvy fellow. (*b*) Naughty child. **2.** *a.* (*a*) Nasty, unpleasant. (*b*) Ugly; wretched. (*c*) Mean.

vilement, *adv.* Vilely, basely.

vilenie, *s.f.* **1.** Meanness, stinginess. **2.** Mean action; foul deed.

vilipender, *v.tr.* To vilify, abuse.

villa [vil-], *s.f.* Villa.

village [vil-], *s.m.* Village.

villageois [vil-]. **1.** *s.* Villager. **2.** *a.* Rustic, country.

ville [vil], *s.f.* Town. **En v.,** out; not at home. **Toilette de v.,** out-door dress.

villégiature [vil-], *s.f.* (*a*) Stay in the country. (*b*) **En v.,** on holiday.

villégiaturiste [vil-], *s.m. & f.* Holiday-maker.

vin, *s.m.* Wine.

vinaigre, *s.m.* Vinegar.

vinaigrier, *s.m.* Vinegar-cruet.

vindicatif, *a.* Vindictive, spiteful.

vindicativement, *adv.* Vindictively.

vingt [vɛ̃], *num.a.inv. & s.m.inv.* Twenty.

vingtaine [vɛ̃tɛn], *s.f.* (About) twenty.

vingtième [vɛ̃tjɛm]. **1.** *num. a. & s.* Twentieth. **2.** *s.m.* Twentieth (part).

viol, *s.m.* ·Rape.

violacé, *a.* Purplish-blue.

violation, *s.f.* Violation, breach.

violâtre, *a.* Purplish.

violemment, *adv.* Violently.

violence, *s.f.* Violence force.

violent, *a.* Violent.

violer, *v.tr.* To violate.

violet, -ette[1], *a.* Violet; purple.

violette[2], *s.f.* Violet.

violon, *s.m.* **1.** (*a*) Violin. (*b*) Violin (player). **2. Violons de mer,** fiddles (for the tables).

violoncelle, *s.m.* Violoncello.

violoniste, *s.m. & f.* Violinist.

vipère, *s.f.* Viper, adder.

virage, *s.m.* **1.** Turning; tacking. **2.** (Sharp) turn, corner, bend.

virago, *s.f.* Virago, termagant.

virer. 1. *v.i.* To turn. (*a*) To take a corner. (*b*) To slew round. (*c*) **V. de bord,** to tack. **2.** *v.tr.* To turn over.

virginal, -aux, *a.* Maidenly.

virginité, *s.f.* Virginity.

virgule, *s.f.* (*a*) Comma. (*b*) = (Decimal) point.

viril [-ril], *a.* Virile; manly.

virilité, *s.f.* Virility manliness.

virole, *s.f.* Ferrule.

virtuel, *a.* Virtual.

virtuellement, *adv.* Virtually.

virtuose, *s.m. & f.* Virtuoso.

virulence, *s.f.* Virulence.

virulent, *a.* Virulent.

vis [vis], *s.f.* Screw.

visa, *s.m.* Visa.

visage, *s.m.* Face, countenance.

vis-à-vis. 1. *Adv.phr.* Opposite. **2.** *Prep.phr.* **Vis-à-vis de.** (*a*) Opposite, facing. (*b*) With regard to. **3.** *s.m.* Person opposite; partner.

visée, *s.f.* **1.** Aim. **Ligne de v.,** line of sight. **2.** *pl.* Aims, designs.

viser. 1. *v.i.* To aim. **2.** *v.tr.* (*a*) To aim, take aim, at; to address (the ball). (*b*) To have in view. (*c*) To allude to.

viseur, *s.m.* View-finder.

visibilité, *s.f.* Visibility.

visible, *a.* **1.** (*a*) Visible, perceptible. (*b*) Evident. **2.** (*a*) At home. (*b*) Disengaged.

visiblement, *adv.* **1.** Visibly, perceptibly. **2.** Obviously, evidently.

visière, *s.f.* (*a*) Peak (of cap). (*b*) Eye-shade.

vision, *s.f.* Vision.

visionnaire, *a. & s.* Visionary.

visite, *s.f.* Visit. **1.** (*a*) (Social) call. (*b*) Caller, visitor. **2.** Attendance. **3.** Inspection; survey. **V. de la douane,** customs examination.

visiter, *v.tr.* **1.** To visit; to attend. **2.** To examine, inspect.

visiteur, -euse, *s.* Caller. visitor.

vison, *s.m.* Mink.

visqueux, *a.* Viscous, sticky.

visser, *v.tr.* To screw, screw down.

visuel, *a.* Visual. **Champ v.,** field of vision.

vital, -aux, *a.* Vital.

vitalité, *s.f.* Vitality.

vitamine, *s.f.* Vitamin.

vite. 1. *a.* Swift, speedy. **2.** *adv.* Quickly. **Faites v.!** make haste! **Au plus v.,** as quickly as possible.

vitesse, *s.f.* Speed, rapidity; velocity; rate. **Indicateur de v.,** speedometer. **Boîte de vitesses,** gear-box.

vitrage, *s.m.* Glass partition *or* door.

vitrail [-ra:j] **-aux,** *s.m.* Leaded glass window; stained glass window.

vitre, *s.f.* Pane; window-pane.

vitré, *a.* Glazed.

vitrer, *v.tr.* To glaze.

vitreux, *a.* Vitreous; glassy.

vitrier, *s.m.* Glazier.

vitrine, *s.f.* **1.** Shop-window **2.** Glass case, glass cabinet.

vitupération, *s.f.* Vituperation.

vivace, *a.* (*a*) Long-lived. (*b*) Hardy; perennial.

vivacité, *s.f.* **1.** Hastiness. **2.** (*a*) Acuteness; intensity. (*b*) Vividness. **3.** Vivacity; liveliness.

vivant. 1. *a.* (*a*) Alive, living. **Langue vivante,** modern language. (*b*) Lively, animated. (*c*) Vivid, live. **2.** *s.m.* **De son v.,** during his lifetime.

vivement, *adv.* **1.** Briskly; sharply. **2.** Keenly, deeply.

vivifiant, *a.* Invigorating, bracing.

vivifier, *v.tr.* To invigorate.

vivre. I. *v.i.* To live. **1. Vive le roi!** long live the King! **Qui vive?** who

goes there? **2. Savoir v.,** to know how to behave. **3. Avoir de quoi v.,** to have enough to live on.

II. vivres, *s.m.pl.* Provisions.

vocabulaire, *s.m.* Vocabulary.

vocal, -aux, *a.* Vocal.

vocalement, *adv.* Vocally.

vocation, *s.f.* Vocation.

vociférer, *v.i.* To vociferate.

vœu, -x, *s.m.* **1.** Vow. **2.** Wish.

vogue, *s.f.* Fashion, vogue.

voici, *prep.* **1.** Here is, are. **2.** Ago.

voie, *s.f.* **1.** (*a*) Way, road, track. **Par v. de terre,** by land; overland. (*b*) **V. ferrée,** railway track. **V. de garage,** siding. (*c*) **V. d'eau,** leak. **2.** Way. **En bonne v.,** going well. **Voies de fait,** acts of violence.

voilà, *prep.* There is, are. **En v. assez!** that will do! **En v. une idée!** what an idea! **V. tout,** that's all.

voile. I. *s.f.* Sail.

II. voile, *s.m.* (*a*) Veil. (*b*) Voile.

voilé, *a.* (*a*) Veiled, dim; muffled. (*b*) Fogged.

voiler, *v.tr.* (*a*) To veil. (*b*) To veil, obscure; to muffle.

se voiler, to cloud over.

voilier, *s.m.* Sailing-ship.

voir, *v.tr.* To see. **1.** To set eyes upon; to sight. **A le v.,** to judge by his looks. **Faites v.!** let me see it! **2.** (*a*) **V. venir,** to see coming. (*b*) **faire qch. à qn,** to see s.o. do sth. **3.** To visit. **4.** (*a*) To understand. (*b*) To perceive. **Cela se voit,** that is obvious. **5.** *int.* **Voyons!** (i) let us see; (ii) come! come! **6. Être bien vu,** to be highly esteemed (*de.* by).

voire, *adv.* Nay. **V. même,** and even.

voisin. 1. *a.* Neighbouring, adjoining. **2.** *s.* Neighbour.

voisinage, *s.m.* **1.** Proximity, vicinity. **2.** Neighbourhood.

voiture, *s.f.* (*a*) Carriage, motor car. **Aller en v.,** to drive. (*b*) Cart, van. **V. d'enfant,** perambulator. (*c*) (Railway) coach, carriage. **"En v.!"** 'take your seats!'

voiturier, *s.m.* Carter, carrier.

voix, *s.f.* **1.** Voice. **2. D'une commune v.,** by common consent. **Mettre aux v.,** to put to the vote.

vol¹, *s.m.* **1.** (*a*) Flying, flight. **Au vol,** on the wing. **Vue à vol d'oiseau,**

bird's-eye view. (b) **Vol piqué**, dive.
2. Flock, flight.

vol², *s.m.* Theft; stealing, robbery. **Vol à l'étalage,** shop-lifting.

volage, *a.* Fickle, inconstant.

volaille [-la:j], *s.f.* Poultry, fowls.

volant. I. *a.* **1.** Flying; fluttering. **2.** Loose; movable.
II. **volant,** *s.m.* **1.** Fly-wheel. **2.** Steering-wheel. **3.** Flounce.

volatil, *a.* Volatile.

volatiliser, *v.tr.* To volatilize.

vol-au-vent, *s.m.inv.* Puff-pie; vol-au-vent.

volcan, *s.m.* Volcano.

volcanique, *a.* Volcanic.

volée, *s.f.* **1.** Flight (of bird). **Prendre sa v.,** to take wing. **2.** Flock, flight. **3.** (*a*) Volley; shower. (*b*) **Sonner à toute v.,** to set all the bells a-ringing.

voler¹, *v.i.* To fly.

voler², *v.tr.* **1.** To steal. **2.** To rob.

volet, *s.m.* Shutter.

voleter, *v.i.* To flutter.

voleur, -euse, *s.* Thief, robber, burglar. **Au v.!** stop thief!

volière, *s.f.* Aviary.

volition, *s.f.* Volition.

volontaire, *a.* **1.** Voluntary. **2.** *s.m.* Volunteer. **3.** Self-willed **Menton v.,** firm chin.

volontairement, *adv.* **1.** Voluntarily, willingly. **2.** Obstinately, wilfully.

volonté, *s.f.* **1.** Will. **A v.,** at pleasure, ad lib. **2. Bonne v.,** willingness.

volontiers [-tje], *adv.* (*a*) Willingly gladly. (*b*) Readily.

volte-face, *s.f.inv.* Face-about.

voltiger, *v.i.* To fly about; to flit; to flutter.

volubilis [-lis], *s.m.* Convolvulus

volubilité, *s.f* Volubility.

volume, *s.m.* **1.** Volume tome. **2.** Volume; bulk, mass.

volumineux, *a.* Voluminous.

volupté, *s.f.* Pleasure; delight.

voluptueusement, *adv.* Voluptuously.

voluptueux, *a.* Voluptuous.

volute, *s.f.* Volute; scroll; wreath (of smoke).

vomir, *v.tr.* To vomit.

vomissement, *s.m.* Vomiting.

vorace, *a.* Voracious.

voracement, *adv.* Voraciously.

voracité, *s.f.* Voracity, voraciousness.

vos. See VOTRE.

votant, *s.* Voter.

votation, *s.f.* Voting.

vote, *s.m.* (*a*) Vote. (*b*) Voting, ballot(ing), poll. **Droit de v.,** franchise.

voter, *v.i. & tr.* To vote

votif, *a.* Votive.

votre, *pl.* **vos,** *poss.a.* Your.

vôtre, *poss.pron.* Yours; your own. **A la v.!** here's to you!

vouer, *v.tr.* To vow, dedicate.

vouloir. I. *v.tr* **1.** To will; to be determined on. **2.** (*a*) To want, to wish (for). **Faites comme vous voudrez,** do as you please. **Je ne le veux pas!** I will not have it! **Que voulez-vous!** well, well! (*b*) **En v. à qn,** to bear s.o. a grudge. **Ne m'en veuillez pas,** don't be vexed with me. **3.** (*a*) To will, require, demand. (*b*) To want, wish. **Que voulez-vous que je fasse?** what would you have me do? (*c*) To try to. (*d*) To mean, intend. (*e*) **V. bien,** to consent, be willing. **Veuillez vous asseoir,** kindly sit down. **4.** To be convinced. to insist. **5.** To require, need.
II. **vouloir,** *s.m.* Will.

voulu, *a.* **1.** Required, requisite. **2.** Deliberate, intentional.

vous, *pers.pron. sg. & pl.* **1.** (*a*) You. (*b*) You, to you. (*c*) Yourself. (*d*) **Vous vous connaissez,** you know one another. **2. C'est à vous de jouer,** it is your turn to play.

vous-même(s), *pers.pron* Yourself; yourselves.

voûte, *s.f.* Vault, arch.

voûté, *a.* (*a*) Vaulted arched. (*b*) Stooping, bent.

voûter, *v.tr.* To arch, vault. **se voûter,** to become bowed.

voyage, *s.m.* Journey, voyage. **V. d'agrément,** pleasure trip. **Il est en v.,** he is travelling. **Compagnon de v.,** fellow-traveller.

voyager, *v.i.* To travel; to make a journey.

voyageur, -euse. **1.** *s.* Traveller; passenger. **2.** *a.* (*a*) Travelling. (*b*) **Pigeon v.,** carrier-pigeon.

voyant, *a.* Gaudy, loud; showy.

voyelle, *s.f* Vowel.

vrai. 1. *a.* (*a*) True, truthful. (*b*) True, real, genuine. (*c*) Downright, regular. **2.** *adv.* Truly, really, indeed. A **v. dire**, truth to say. **3.** *s.m.* Truth.

vraiment, *adv.* Really, truly. **V.?** indeed? is that so?

vraisemblable, *a.* Probable, likely.

vraisemblablement, *adv.* Probably, very likely.

vraisemblance, *s.f.* Probability, likelihood.

vrille [vri:j], *s.f.* **1.** Tendril. **2.** Gimlet. **3.** *Av:* Spin.

vrombir, *v.i.* To buzz: to hum.

vrombissement, *s.m.* Buzzing; humming.

vu. 1. *s.m.* **Au vu de tous,** openly. **2.** *prep.* Considering, seeing.

vue, *s.f.* **1.** Sight. **A perte de vue,** as far as the eye can reach. **2.** View.

vulgaire. 1. *a.* Vulgar. (*a*) Common. (*b*) Low, coarse. **2.** *s.m.* **Le v.,** the common people.

vulgariser, *v.tr.* To popularize. **se vulgariser,** to grow vulgar.

vulgarité, *s.f.* Vulgarity.

vulnérabilité, *s.f.* Vulnerability.

vulnérable, *a.* Vulnerable.

W

W, w [dublǝve], *s.m.* (The letter) W, w.

wagon [vagɔ̃], *s.m.* Carriage, coach; waggon, truck.

wagon-lit, *s.m.* Sleeping-car. *pl. wagons-lits.*

wagon-restaurant, *s.m.* Restaurant-car; dining-car. *pl. wagons-restaurants.*

water-closet [-tɛrklozɛt], *s.m.* Water-closet. *pl. water-closets.*

whist, *s.m.* Whist.

X

X, x [iks], *s.m.* (The letter) X, x. **Rayons X,** X rays.

Xérès [kerɛs], *s.m.* **Vin de X,** sherry.

Y

Y, y¹ [igrɛk], *s.m.* (The letter) Y, y.

y². 1. *adv.* There; here; thither. **Madame y est-elle?** is Mrs X at home? **2.** *pron.inv.* (*a*) By it; at it; to it; to him; to her, etc. **3. Ça y est!** it's done! that's it!

yacht [jak], *s.m.* Yacht.

yeuse, *s.f.* Ilex, holm-oak.

yeux. *s.f.* See ŒIL.

yole, *s.f.* Gig, yawl.

yougoslave, *a. & s.* Jugo-Slav.

Yougoslavie (la). *Pr.n.f.* Jugoslavia.

youyou, *s.m.* Dinghy. *pl. youyous.*

Z

Z, z [zɛd], *s.m.* (The letter) Z, z.

zagaie, *s.f.* Assegai.

zèbre, *s.m.* Zebra.

zébré, *a.* Striped (*de*, with).

zélateur, -trice, *s.* Zealot.

zèle, *s.m.* Zeal, ardour.

zélé, *a. & s* Zealous.

zénith, *s.m.* Zenith.

zéphire, zéphyr(e), *s.m.* Zephyr.

zéro, *s.m.* **1.** Cipher, nought. *Ten:* **Trois à zéro,** three love. **2.** Starting point, zero. **"Zéro,"** 'off' (on electric stove).

zeste, *s.m.* **Z. confit,** candied peel.

zézaiement, zézayement, *s.m.* Lisping, lisp.

zézayer, *v.i. & tr.* To lisp.

zibeline, *s.f.* Sable.

zigzag [-zag], *s.m.* Zigzag. **Éclair en z.,** forked lightning.

zigzaguer, *v.i.* To zigzag.

zinc [zɛ̃:g], *s.m.* Zinc.

zodiaque, *s.m.* Zodiac.

zone, *s.f.* Zone.

zoologie [zɔɔlɔʒi], *s.f.* Zoology.

zoologique [-zɔɔ-], *a.* Zoological.

zoologiste [-zɔɔ-], *s.m.* Zoologist.

zouave, *s.m.* Zouave.

zoulou, *a. & s.* Zulu. *pl. zoulous.*

Zoulouland. *Pr.n.* Zululand.

A]   **A**   **[above-named**

A, a¹, s. (La lettre) A, a m. **AI,** de première qualité.

a², *indef. art.* **1.** Un, une. **2. To have a taste for,** avoir le goût de. **3. Fivepence a pound,** cinq pence la livre. **Three times a week,** trois fois par semaine. **4. Two at a time,** deux à la fois. **5.** (*a*) **He is an Englishman,** il est Anglais. (*b*) **In a cab,** en fiacre.

aback, *adv.* **Taken a.,** déconcerté interdit.

abandon, *v.tr.* Abandonner; délaisser; renoncer à.

abandonment, *s.* Abandon *m.*

abase, *v.tr.* Abaisser.

abasement, *s.* Abaissement *m.*

abash, *v.tr.* Décontenancer.

abate. 1. *v.tr.* Diminuer; relâcher. **2.** *v.i.* Diminuer; s'apaiser.

abatement, *s.* **1.** Diminution *f*; apaisement *m.* **2.** Rabais *m.*

abbess, *s.* Abbesse *f.*

abbey, *s.* Abbaye *f.*

abbot, *s.* Abbé *m.*

abbreviate, *v.tr.* Abréger.

abbreviation, *s.* Abréviation *f.*

abdicate, *v.tr. & i.* Abdiquer.

abdication, *s.* Abdication *f.*

abduct, *v.tr.* Enlever.

abduction, *s.* Enlèvement *m.*

abed, *adv.* Au lit; couché.

aberration, *s.* Aberration *f.*

abet, *v.tr.* Encourager.

abeyance, *s.* Suspension *f.* **In a.,** en suspens.

abhor, *v.tr.* Abhorrer.

abhorrence, *s.* Horreur *f.*

abhorrent, *a.* Répugnant.

abide. 1. *v.i.* **To a. by,** rester fidèle à. **2.** *v.tr.* Sentir.

ability, *s.* **1.** Capacité *f*, pouvoir *m.* **2.** Habileté *f.*

abject, *a.* **1.** Abject. **2.** Bas, vil.

abjection, *s.* Abjection *f*, misère *f.*

abjectly, *adv.* Abjectement.

abjure, *v.tr.* Abjurer; renier.

ablaze, *adv.* En feu, en flammes.

able, *a.* **1.** (*a*) Capable, habile. (*b*) **To be a.,** (i) savoir, être capable de; (ii) pouvoir, être à même de. **2. Bien fait.**

able-bodied, *a.* Fort, robuste

ably, *adv.* Habilement.

abnegation, *s.* Abnégation *f.*

abnormal, *a.* Anormal, -aux.

abnormally, *adv.* Anormalement.

aboard. 1. *adv* A bord **2.** *prep.* A bord de.

abode, *s.* **1.** Demeure *f*, résidence *f.* **2. Place of a.,** domicile *m.*

abolish, *v.tr.* Abolir, supprimer

abolition, *s.* Abolition *f.*

abominable, *a* Abominable.

abominably, *adv.* Abominablement.

abominate, *v.tr* Abominer.

abomination, *s.* Abomination *f.*

aboriginal, *a.* Indigène, aborigène.

aborigines, *s.pl.* Aborigènes *m*

abortive, *a.* Avorté, manqué.

abound, *v.i.* Abonder (*in with.* en).

abounding, *a.* Abondant.

about, *adv. & prep.* **1.** (*a*) Autour (de). (*b*) De côté et d'autre. (*c*) **Turn (and turn) a.,** à tour de rôle **2. To turn sth. a.,** retourner qch. **3.** Environ, presque. **That's a. right,** c'est à peu près cela. **A. three o'clock,** vers trois heures **4.** Au sujet de. **What is it all a.?** de quoi s'agit-il? **To speak a.,** parler de. **5.** (*a*) **A. to,** sur le point de. (*b*) **While you are a.** it, pendant que vous y êtes

above, *adv. & prep.* **1.** Au-dessus (de). (*a*) **From a.,** d'en haut. (*b*) **Par-dessus**; à l'amont de. (*c*) Supérieur à. **A. all,** surtout. **2. As a.,** comme ci-dessus. **3.** Plus de.

above-board, *a.* Franc, *f.* franche.

above-mentioned *a.* Sus-mentionné.

above-named, *a.* Sus-nommé.

abreast, *adv.* (*a*) De front. (*b*) To walk a., marcher côte à côte. A. of the times, de son temps

abridge, *v.tr.* Abréger.

abridg(e)ment, ‹. **1.** Diminution *f.* **2.** Abrégé *m*

abroad, *adv.* **1.** A l'étranger. **2.** To get a., se répandre.

abrupt, *a.* **1.** Brusque; brusqué. **2.** Abrupt, escarpé.

abruptly, *adv.* **1.** Brusquement. **2.** Abruptement.

abruptness, *s.* **1.** Brusquerie *f.* **2.** Raideur *f.*

abscess, *s.* Abcès *m.*

abscond, *v.i.* S'enfuir.

absence, *s.* **1.** Absence *f.* **2.** In the a. of, faute de. **3.** A. of mind, distraction *f.*

absent¹, *a.* Absent.

absent², *v.pr* To a. oneself, s'absenter.

absentee, *s.* Absent *m.*

absent-minded, *a.* Distrait.

absent-mindedly, *adv.* Distraitement.

absent-mindedness, *s.* Distraction *f.*

absolute, *a.* (*a*) Absolu. (*b*) Véritable.

absolutely, *adv.* Absolument.

absolution, *s.* Absolution *f.*

absolve, *v.tr.* Absoudre.

absorb, *v.tr.* Absorber.

absorbent, *a.* & *s.* Absorbant (*m*).

absorbing, *a.* Absorbant.

abstain, *v.i.* S'abstenir.

abstemious, *a.* Sobre, tempérant.

abstemiously, *adv.* Frugalement.

abstemiousness, *s.* Sobriété *f.*

abstention, *s.* Abstention *f.*

abstinence, *s.* Abstinence *f.*

abstract¹, *a.* & *s.* Abstrait (*m*).

abstract², *s.* Résumé *m*, abrégé *m.*

abstract³, *v.tr.* Soustraire (*from.* à).

abstracted, *a.* Distrait; rêveur.

abstractedly, *adv* Distraitement.

abstraction, *s.* Soustraction *f.*

abstruse, *a.* Abstrus.

absurd, *a.* Absurde.

absurdity, *s.* Absurdité *f.*

absurdly, *adv.* Absurdement.

abundance, *s.* Abondance *f.*

abundant, *a.* Abondant; copieux.

abundantly, *adv.* Abondamment; copieusement.

abuse¹, *s.* **1.** Abus *m.* **2.** Insultes *fpl* injures *fpl.*

abuse², *v.tr* **1.** Abuser de. **2.** Injurier.

abusive, *a.* Injurieux.

abut, *v.i.* & *tr.* Se toucher; confiner à.

abutting, *a.* Aboutissant (*on*, à).

abyss, *s.* Abîme *m*, gouffre *m.*

acacia, *s.* Acacia *m.*

academic, *a.* Académique.

academical, *a.* Universitaire.

academy, *s.* Académie *f.*

acanthus, *s.* Acanthe *f.*

accede, *v.i.* To a. to, accueillir.

accelerate. 1. *v.tr.* Accélérer; activer. **2.** *v.i.* S'accélérer.

acceleration, *s* Accélération *f.*

accelerator, *s.* Accélérateur *m.*

accent¹, *s.* Accent *m.* In broken accents, d'une voix brisée.

accent², *v.tr.* Accentuer; appuyer sur.

accentuate, *v.tr.* Accentuer.

accentuated, *a.* Accentué.

accentuation, *s.* Accentuation *f.*

accept, *v.tr.* & *ind.tr.* Accepter; agréer; admettre.

acceptable, *a.* Acceptable, agréable.

acceptance, *s.* Acceptation *f*; consentement *m* à recevoir.

acceptation, *s.* Acception *f.*

access, *s.* Accès *m*; abord *m.* **Easy of a.,** abordable.

accessible, *a.* **1.** Accessible, approchable. **2.** Accueillant.

accession, *s.* **1.** (*a*) Augmentation *f.* (*b*) Adhésion *f.* **2.** Accession *f.* **A. to the throne,** avènement *m* au trône.

accessory. 1. *a.* Accessoire. **2.** *s.* Accessoire *m.* **3.** *s.* Complice *m.*

accident, *s.* Accident *m.* **By a.,** accidentellement.

accidental, *a.* (*a*) Accidentel, fortuit. (*b*) Accessoire.

accidentally, *adv.* Accidentellement.

acclaim, *v.tr* Acclamer.

acclamation, *s.* Acclamation *f.*

acclimatization, *s.* Acclimatation *f.*

acclimatize, *v.tr.* Acclimater.

acclivity, *s.* Montée *f*, côte *f.*

accommodate, *v.tr.* **1.** (*a*) Accommoder (*b*) Ajuster. adapter. **2.** Loger, recevoir.

accommodating, *a.* Complaisant.

accommodation, *s.* **1.** Accommodement *m.* **2.** (*a*) Commodité *f.* (*b*) Logement *m.* (*c*) Avance *f*, prêt *m.*

accompaniment, *s.* Accompagnement *m*; accessoires *mpl.*

acc_ompanist, s. Accompagnateur, -trice.

accompany, v.tr. Accompagner.

acc_omplice, s. Complice mf.

accomplish, v.tr. Accomplir.

accomplishcd, a. (a) Accompli. (b) Qui possède de nombreux talents.

acc_omplishment, s. **1.** Accomplissement m. **2.** pl. Arts m d'agrément.

accord¹, s. **1.** Accord m. **2.** Of one's own a., de son plein gré.

accord², **1.** v.i. S'accorder. **2.** v.tr. Accorder, concéder.

accordance, s. Accord m.

according, adv. **1.** Conj.phr. A. as, selon que. **2.** Prep.phr. (a) A. to, selon. A. to age, par rang d'âge. (b) A. to, d'après.

accordingly, adv. En conséquence.

accost, v.tr. Accoster, aborder.

account¹, s. **1.** (a) Compte m, note f. A sum on a., un acompte. (b) Exposé m. (c) To turn to a., tirer parti de. (d) To call to a., demander une explication à. **2.** (a) To be of a., être en grande estime. To take into a., tenir compte de. (b) On a. of, à cause de. On no a., dans aucun cas. **3.** Récit m. By all accounts, au dire de tout le monde.

account², v.tr. & ind.tr. To a. for (sth.), rendre raison de ; expliquer.

accountable, a. Responsable (for, de ; to, envers).

accountancy, s. Comptabilité f.

accountant, s. Comptable m.

accoutrement, s. Équipement m.

accredit, v.tr. Accréditer.

accrue, v.i. **1.** Provenir, dériver. **2.** S'accumuler.

accumulate, **1.** v.tr. Accumuler. **2.** v.i. S'accumuler.

accumulation, s. Accumulation f.

accumulator, s. Accumulateur m.

accuracy, s. Exactitude f.

accurate, a. Exact, juste, précis.

accurately, adv. Exactement, avec précision.

accursed, a. Maudit.

accusation, s. Accusation f.

accuse, v.tr. Accuser.

accused, s. Prévenu(e).

accuser, s. Accusateur, -trice.

accustom, v.tr. Accoutumer, habituer.

accustomed, a. **1.** Accoutumé, habitué. **2.** Habituel.

ace, s. As m.

acerbity, s. Acerbité f ; âpreté f.

acetic, a. Acétique.

acetylene, s. Acétylène m.

ache¹, s. Mal m, douleur f.

ache², v.i. My head aches, j'ai mal à la tête.

achieve, v.tr. **1.** Accomplir ; réaliser. **2.** Atteindre.

achievement, s. **1.** Accomplissement m, réalisation f. **2.** Exploit m (haut) fait.

aching, a. Douloureux, endolori.

acid. **1.** a. (a) Acide. (b) Aigre. **2.** s. Acide m.

acidity, s. Ac dité f

acknowledge, v.tr. **1.** Reconnaître ; avouer. **2.** Accuser réception de.

acknowledg(e)ment, s. (a) Reconnaissance f ; reçu m. A. of receipt, accusé m. de réception. (b) Aveu m.

acme, s. Sommet m, apogée m.

aconite, s. Aconit m.

acorn, s. Gland m.

acoustic, a. Acoustique.

acoustics, s.pl. Acoustique f.

acquaint, v.tr. **1.** Informer (with, de). **2.** To be acquainted with s.o., connaître qn.

acquaintance, s. Connaissance f. He improves upon a., il gagne à être connu.

acquaintanceship, s. Relations fpl.

acquiesce, v.i. Acquiescer (in, à).

acquiescence, s. **1.** Acquiescement m (in, à). **2.** Soumission f (in à).

acquiescent, a. Consentant.

acquire, v.tr. Acquérir. To a. a habit, prendre une habitude.

acquirement, s. **1.** Acquisition f. **2.** pl. Connaissances fpl

acquisition, s. Acquisition f.

acquisitive, a. Apre au gain.

acquit, v.tr. Acquitter.

acquittal, s. Acquittement m.

acrid, a. Acre.

acridity, s. Acreté f.

acridly, adv. Avec âcreté.

acrimonious, a. Acrimonieux.

acrimoniously, adv. Avec acrimonie.

acrimony, s. Acrimonie f.

acrobat, s. Acrobate mf.

acrobatic, a. Acrobatique.

across, adv. & prep. En travers (de). **1.** (a) To walk a., traverser. To go a., franchir. (b) To come a., rencontrer.

8

2. (*a*) The distance a., la distance en largeur. (*b*) De l'autre côté de.

act[1], *s.* **1.** Acte *m.* Act of Parliament, loi *f.* **2.** Action *f.* In the act, sur le fait.

act[2]. **1.** *v.tr.* Jouer (une pièce); remplir (un rôle); faire (l'imbécile). **2.** *v.i.* Agir. (*a*) To act for the best, faire pour le mieux. (*b*) Marcher. To act as, faire fonction de. (*c*) Jouer.

acting[1], *a.* Remplissant les fonctions de.

acting[2], *s.* **1.** Action *f.* **2.** Jeu *m.*

action, *s.* **1.** Action *f.* To take a., agir. To put out of a., détraquer. **2.** Action, acte *m.* fait *m.* **3.** Action, combat *m.* Killed in a., tué à l'ennemi.

active, *a.* **1.** Actif; agile, alerte. **2.** On a. service, en campagne.

activity, *s.* Activité *f.*

actor, *s.* Acteur *m.*

actress, *s.* Actrice *f.*

actual, *a.* **1.** Réel, véritable. **2.** Actuel, présent.

actually, *adv.* **1.** (*a*) Réellement. He a. . . . il alla jusqu'à . . . . **2.** Actuellement, à présent.

actuate, *v.tr.* Pousser.

acumen, *s.* Pénétration *f,* finesse *f.*

acute, *a.* **1.** Aigu, -uë. **2.** Fin, pénétrant.

acutely, *adv.* Vivement; intensément.

acuteness, *s.* **1.** Acuité *f.* **2.** Finesse *f*; pénétration *f.*

adapt, *v.tr.* Adapter, ajuster.

adaptability, *s* Faculté *f* d'adaptation.

adaptable, *a.* Adaptable.

adaptation, *s.* Adaptation *f.*

add, *v.tr.* **1.** Ajouter; joindre. **2.** Additionner.

adder, *s.* Vipère *f.*

addict[1], *s.* Personne adonnée à (qch.). Drug a. toxicomane *mf.*

addict[2], *v.tr.* To be addicted, s'adonner, se livrer.

addiction, *s.* Penchant *m.*

addition, *s.* Addition *f.* In a., en outre, de plus.

additional, *a.* Additionnel, supplémentaire.

additionally, *adv.* En outre (*to,* de).

addle, *v.tr.* Pourrir, gâter.

address[1], *s.* **1.** Habileté *f.* **2.** Adresse *f.* **3.** Discours *m.*

address[2], *v.tr.* **1.** Adresser. **2.** Abor-

der, accoster; adresser la parole à. **3.** *Golf:* Viser.

addressee, *s.* Destinataire *mf.*

adduce, *v.tr.* Alléguer; citer.

adept. **1.** *a.* Expert habile. **2.** *s.* Adepte *mf.*

adequacy, *s.* Suffisance *f.*

adequate, *a.* Suffisant.

adequately, *adv.* Suffisamment.

adhere, *v.i.* Adhérer.

adherence, *s.* **1.** Adhérence *f,* adhésion *f.* **2.** Attachement *m.*

adherent. **1.** *a* Adhérent. **2.** *s.* Adhérent, -e.

adhesion, *s.* Adhésion.

adhesive, *a.* Adhésif, collant.

adieu, *int.* Adieu!

adjacent, *a.* Adjacent; attenant.

adjective, *s.* Adjectif *m.*

adjoin, *v.tr* Avoisiner; toucher à.

adjoining, *a.* (*a*) Contigu, -uë; avoisinant. (*b*) Voisin.

adjourn. **1.** *v.tr.* Ajourner, renvoyer. **2.** *v.i.* S'ajourner.

adjournment, *s.* (*a*) Ajournement *m.* (*b*) Renvoi *m.*

adjudge, *v.tr.* Prononcer sur, juger.

adjudicate, *v.tr.* & *i.* Juger, décider.

adjudication, *s.* Jugement *m,* arrêt *m.*

adjudicator, *s.* Arbitre *m*; juge *m.*

adjunct, *s.* Accessoire *m.*

adjure, *v.tr.* Adjurer, conjurer.

adjust, *v.tr.* (*a*) Arranger; ajuster. To a. oneself, s'adapter. (*b*) Régler.

adjustable, *a.* Ajustable.

adjustment, *s.* **1.** Ajustement *m.* **2.** Réglage *m.*

adjutant, *s.* Adjudant major.

administer, *v.tr.* Administrer; dispenser (la justice).

administration, *s.* Administration *f.*

administrative, *a.* Administratif.

administrator, *s.* Administrateur *m.*

admirable, *a.* Admirable.

admirably, *adv.* Admirablement.

admiral, *s.* Amiral *m,* pl. -aux.

admiralty, *s.* The A., l'Amirauté *f*; le Ministère de la Marine.

admiration, *s.* Admiration *f.*

admire, *v.tr.* Admirer.

admirer, *s.* Admirateur, -trice.

admiring, *a.* Admiratif.

admiringly, *adv.* Avec admiration.

admissible, *a.* Admissible.

admission, *s.* **1.** Admission *f*; entrée *f.* **2.** Confession *f*; aveu *m.*

admit. 1. *v.tr.* (*a*) Admettre ; livrer passage à. 'A. bearer,' "laissez passer." (*b*) Admettre ; reconnaître. **2.** *v.ind.tr.* To a. of, permettre admettre.

admittance, *s.* Entrée *f* (*to.* dans) ; accès *m.*

admittedly, *adv.* De l'aveu général.

admixture, *s.* Mélange *m.*

admonish, *v.tr* (*a*) Admonester. (*b*) Exhorter.

admonition, *s.* Remontrance *f.*

ado, *s.* **1.** Agitation *f.* Without more ado, sans plus de façons. **2.** Difficulté *f,* peine *f.*

adolescence, *s* Adolescence *f.*

adolescent, *a. & s.* Adolescent, -e.

adopt, *v.tr.* Adopter.

adopted, *a.* Adoptif.

adoption, *s* Adoption *f.*

adorable, *a.* Adorable.

adorably, *adv.* Adorablement.

adoration, *s.* Adoration *f.*

adore, *v.tr.* Adorer.

adorer, *s.* Adorateur, -trice.

adorn, *v.tr.* Orner, parer (*with,* de).

adornment, *s.* Ornement *m,* parure *f.*

adrift, *adv.* A la dérive.

adroit, *a.* Adroit ; habile.

adroitly, *adv.* Adroitement.

adroitness, *s.* Adresse *f,* dextérité *f.*

adult, *a. & s.* Adulte (*mf*).

adulterate, *v.tr.* Adultérer.

adulteration, *s.* Adultération *f.*

adulterer, *s.* Adultère *mf.*

adultery, *s.* Adultère *m.*

advance[1], *s.* **1.** (*a*) Marche *f* en avant. To make an a., avancer. A. guard, avant-garde *f* (*b*) To pay in a., payer d'avance. **2.** Avancement *m,* progrès *m.* **3.** (*a*) Avance *f.* (*b*) Augmentation *f ;* hausse *f.*

advance[2]. I. *v.tr.* **1.** Avancer. **2.** Augmenter, hausser.
II. **advance,** *v.i.* **1.** S'avancer. **2.** Hausser.

advanced, *a.* Avancé.

advancement, *s.* Avancement *m.*

advantage, *s.* Avantage *m.* To take a. of, profiter de ; exploiter. To turn to a., tirer parti de. To show off to a., faire valoir.

advantageous, *a.* Avantageux (*to,* pour) ; profitable.

advantageously, *adv.* Avantageusement.

advent, *s.* **1.** Avent *m.* **2.** Venue *f.*

adventure[1], *s.* Aventure *f.*

adventure[2], *v.tr.* Aventurer.

adventurer, *s* Aventurier *m.*

adventuress, *s.* Aventurière *f.*

adventurous, *a.* Aventureux.

adverb, *s* Adverbe *m.*

adversary, *s.* Adversaire *m.*

adverse, *a.* Adverse. (*a*) Contraire. (*b*) Ennemi (*to.* de). (*c*) Défavorable.

adversely, *adv.* (*a*) To act a. to, agir au contraire de. (*b*) To influence a., exercer une influence défavorable sur.

adversity, *s.* Adversité *f.*

advertise, *v.tr. & i.* Faire de la réclame (pour).

advertisement, *s.* **1.** Publicité *f.* **2.** (*a*) Annonce *f.* (*b*) Affiche *f.*

advertiser, *s.* Auteur *m* de l'annonce.

advertising, *s.* Publicité *f,* réclame *f.*

advice, *s.* **1.** Conseil *m.* **2.** Avis *m.*

advisability, *s.* Opportunité *f.*

advisable, *a.* Convenable.

advise, *v.tr.* (*a*) Conseiller (*b*) Recommander.

advisedly, *adv.* A dessein.

adviser, *s.* Conseiller *m.*

advisory, *a.* Consultatif.

advocacy, *s.* Appui *m.*

advocate[1], *s.* **1.** Avocat *m.* **2.** Défenseur *m.*

advocate[2], *v.tr.* Préconiser.

aerate, *v.tr.* **1.** Aérer. **2.** Gazéifier.

aerated, *a.* (*a*) Aéré. (*b*) Gazeux.

aeration, *s.* Aération *f.*

aerial. 1. *a.* Aérien. **2.** *s.* Antenne *f.*

aerodrome, *s.* Aérodrome *m.*

aeronaut, *s.* Aéronaute *m.*

aeronautic(al), *a.* Aéronautique.

aeroplane, *s.* Aéroplane *m ;* avion *m.*

aesthetic(al), *a.* Esthétique.

affability, *s.* Affabilité *f.*

affable, *a.* Affable (*to,* envers).

affably, *adv.* Avec affabilité.

affair, *s.* Affaire *f.*

affect[1], *v.tr.* (*a*) Affecter. (*b*) Simuler.

affect[2], *v.tr.* **1.** Atteindre, attaquer ; influer sur ; altérer. **2.** Affecter, affliger. **3.** Toucher, concerner.

affectation, *s.* Affectation.

affected[1], *a.* (*a*) Affecté. maniéré. (*b*) Simulé.

affected[2], *a.* (*a*) Atteint. (*b*) Ému.

affectedly, *adv.* Avec affectation.

affecting, *a* Touchant, attendrissant.

affection, *s.* Affection *f*

affectionate, *a.* Affectueux.

affectionately, *adv.* Affectueusement.

affidavit, *s.* Déclaration *f* sous serment.

affinity, *s.* Affinité *f.*

affirm, *v.tr.* Affirmer, soutenir.

affirmation, *s.* Affirmation *f,* assertion *f.*

affirmative. 1. *a.* Affirmatif. **2.** *s.* The answer is in the a., la réponse est oui.

affix, *v.tr.* Attacher.

afflict, *v.tr.* Affliger; désoler.

afflicting, *a.* Affligeant.

affliction, *s.* **1.** Affliction *f.* **2.** Calamité *f,* revers *m.*

affluence, *s.* Abondance *f,* richesse *f.*

affluent, *a.* Opulent, riche.

afflux, *s.* Concours *m.*

afford, *v.tr.* **1.** *(a)* Avoir les moyens; être en mesure. *(b)* I can a. to wait, je peux attendre. **2.** Fournir, offrir.

affray, *s.* Bagarre *f,* échauffourée *f.*

affront¹, *s.* Affront *m,* offense *f.*

affront², *v.tr.* Insulter.

afire, *adv. & pred.a.* En feu.

aflame, *adv. & pred. a.* En flammes.

afloat, *adv. & pred. a.* **1.** A flot. **2.** To be a., courir, circuler.

afoot, *adv.* **1.** A pied. **2.** To be a., être sur pied. **3.** There's something a., il se prépare quelque chose.

aforesaid, *a.* Susmentionné, susdit.

afraid, *pred. a.* Pris de peur. To be a., avoir peur; craindre.

afresh, *adv.* De nouveau, à nouveau.

Africa. *Pr.n.* L'Afrique *f.*

African, *a. & s.* Africain, -e.

aft, *adv.* Sur, à, vers, l'arrière.

after. I. *adv.* Après; plus tard. The week a., la semaine d'après.

II. after, *prep.* **1.** Après. The police are a. you, la police est à vos trousses. What is he a.? qu'est-ce qu'il a en tête? **2.** A. all, au bout du compte; enfin. The day a., le lendemain (de). The day a. to-morrow, après-demain. It is a. five, il est cinq heures passées. **3.** D'après suivant.

III. after, *conj.* Après que.

after-effect(s), *s.(pl.)* Suites *fpl,* contre-coup *m.*

afternoon, *s.* Après-midi *m or f.* Good a.! bonjour!

after-taste, *s.* Arrière-goût *m.*

afterthought, *s.* Réflexion *f* après coup.

afterwards, *adv.* Après, plus tard ensuite.

again, *adv.* **1.** *(a)* De nouveau, encore. Don't do it a.! ne recommencez pas! A and a., à plusieurs reprises. Now and a., de temps en temps. *(b)* To send back a., renvoyer. **2.** *(a)* De plus, d'ailleurs. *(b)* (Then) a. d'autre part.

against, *prep.* **1.** *(a)* Contre. A. one's will, à contre-cœur. A. the rules, contraire aux règlements. *(b)* A l'encontre de. Over a., en face de. **3.** To show up a., se détacher sur.

agate, *s.* Agate *f.*

age¹, *s.* **1.** Age *m.* *(a)* What age are you? quel âge avez-vous? To be under age, être mineur. To come of age, atteindre sa majorité *(b)* (Old) age, vieillesse *f.* **2.** Age, époque *f.* The Middle Ages, le moyen âge.

age², *v.i. & tr.* Vieillir.

aged, *a.* **1.** Agé, vieux. **2.** Agé de.

agency, *s.* **1.** *(a)* Action *f.* *(b)* Entremise *f.* **2.** Agence *f.*

agent, *s.* *(a)* Agent *m.* *(b)* Régisseur *m.*

agglomeration, *s.* Agglomération *f.*

aggrandizement. *s.* Agrandissement *m.*

aggravate, *v.tr.* **1.** Aggraver. **2.** Agacer, exaspérer.

aggravating, *a.* Exaspérant.

aggravation, *s.* *(a)* Aggravation *f.* *(b)* Agacement *m,* exaspération *f.*

aggregate. 1. *a.* Collectif. **2.** *s.* *(a)* Ensemble *m.* *(b)* In the a., en somme.

aggression, *s.* Agression *f.*

aggressive, *a.* Agressif.

aggressively, *adv.* Agressivement.

aggressor, *s.* Agresseur *m.*

aggrieve, *v.tr.* Chagriner, blesser.

aghast, *pred. a.* Consterné (at, de).

agile, *a.* Agile, leste.

agility, *s.* Agilité *f.*

agitate, *v.tr.* **1.** Agiter. **2.** *Abs.* Faire de l'agitation.

agitated, *a.* Agité; troublé.

agitation, *s.* Agitation *f.*

agitator, *s.* Agitateur *m.*

aglow, *adv. & pred. a.* **1.** Embrasé. **2.** Rayonnant.

ago. 1. *a.* Il y a. **2.** *adv.* Long ago, il y a longtemps.

agog, *adv. & pred. a.* (*a*) Impatient. (*b*) En émoi.

agonized, *a.* 1. (Cri) d'angoisse. 2. Angoissé.

agonizing, *a.* Atroce.

agony, *s.* Angoisse *f.*

agree, *v.i. & tr.* 1. Consentir ; faire droit ; admettre ; convenir. 2. (*a*) Être d'accord ; tomber d'accord. (*b*) S'accorder. 3. Convenir (*with*, à).

agreeable, *a.* 1. Agréable ; aimable (*to*, envers). 2. I am a., je veux bien.

agreeably, *adv.* 1. Agréablement. 2. Conformément (*to, with.* à).

agreed, *a.* Convenu.

agreement, *s.* 1. Convention *f*, contrat *m.* 2. Accord *m.* To come to an a., tomber d'accord 3. Conformité *f.*

agricultural, *a.* Agricole.

agriculture, *s.* Agriculture *f.*

agriculturist, *s.* Agriculteur *m.*

aground, *adv.* Échoué ; au sec. To run a., échouer.

ague, *s.* Fièvre intermittente.

ah, *int.* Ah ! ha !

ahead, *adv.* 1. Devant. To draw a. of, dépasser. To go a., avancer. 2. En avant. To look a., penser à l'avenir.

ahem, *int.* Hum !

aid[1], *s.* Aide *f*, assistance *f*, appui *m.* In aid of, au profit de.

aid[2], *v.tr.* Aider, assister.

aide-de-camp, *s.* Officier *m* d'ordonnance.

ail, *v.tr.* What ails you? qu'est-ce que vous avez ?

ailing, *a.* Souffrant, malade.

ailment, *s.* Mal *m* ; maladie (légère).

aim[1], *s.* To miss one's aim, manquer son but. To take aim at, viser. 2. But, objet *m.*

aim[2]. 1. *v.tr.* (*a*) To aim a blow, allonger un coup. (*b*) Diriger. 2. *v.ind.tr.* To aim at. coucher en joue ; viser.

aimless, *a.* Sans but, sans objet.

aimlessly, *adv.* Sans but.

air[1], *s.* I. Air *m.* (*a*) By air, par la voie des airs. There is something in the air, il se prépare quelque chose. (*b*) *Attrib.* Air raid, raid aérien.
 II. **air.** *Mus :* Air.
 III. **air.** Air, mine *f.* To put on airs, se donner des airs.

air[2], *v.tr.* 1. Aérer. 2. Faire parade de.

air-borne, *a.* Aéroporté.

aircraft, *s.* Avions *mpl.*

air-force, *s.* Armée *f* de l'air.

airily, *adv.* Légèrement.

airing, *s.* 1. Ventilation *f.* 2. Promenade *f* ; tour *m.*

air-line, *s.* Service *m* de transports aériens.

air-liner, *s.* Grand avion de transport.

air-mail, *s.* Poste aérienne. By a.-m., par avion.

airman, *s.* Aviateur *m.*

air-pocket, *s.* *Av.* Trou *m* d'air.

air-port, *s.* Aéroport *m.*

airship, *s.* Dirigeable *m.*

air-tight, *a.* Étanche à l'air.

airy, *a.* 1. Ouvert à l'air. 2. Léger. 3. Insouciant.

aisle, *s.* Nef latérale.

ajar, *adv. & pred. a.* Entrebâillé.

akin, *adv. & pred.a.* 1. Apparenté. 2. To be a., ressembler.

alabaster, *s.* Albâtre *m.*

alacrity, *s.* Empressement *m.*

alarm[1], *s.* 1. Alarme *f*, alerte *f.* 2. Avertisseur *m.*

alarm[2], *v.tr.* (*a*) Alarmer. (*b*) Alerter.

alarm(-clock), *s.* Réveille-matin *m inv.*

alarming, *a.* Alarmant.

alarum. Réveille-matin *m inv.*

alas, *int.* Hélas !

albatross, *s.* Albatros *m.*

albino, *s.* Albinos *mf.*

album, *s.* Album *m.*

albumin, *s.* Albumine *f.*

alcohol, *s.* Alcool *m.*

alcoholic, *a.* Alcoolique.

alcove, *s.* 1. Alcôve *f.* 2. Niche *f.*

alder, *s.* Aune *m.*

Alderney. *Pr.n.* Aurigny *m.*

ale, *s.* Ale *f.* Pale ale, bière blanche.

alert. 1. *a.* (*a*) Alerte, vigilant. (*b*) Actif, vif. 2. *s.* Alerte *f.* To be on the a., être sur le qui-vive.

alertly, *adv.* D'une manière alerte.

alertness, *s.* 1. Vigilance *f.* 2. Vivacité *f*, prestesse *f.*

alfresco, *a. & adv.* En plein air.

algebra, *s.* Algèbre *f.*

algebraic, *a.* Algébrique.

Algeria. *Pr.n.* L'Algérie *f.*

Algerian, *a. & s.* Algérien, -ienne.

Algiers. *Pr.n.* Alger *m.*

alias. **1.** *adv.* Autrement dit. **2.** *s.* Nom *m* d'emprunt.

alibi, *s.* Alibi *m.*

alien, *a. & s.* Étranger, -ère.

alienate, *v.tr.* Aliéner; éloigner, s'aliéner.

alienation, *s.* Aliénation *f.*

alight[1], *v.i.* **1.** Descendre. **2.** S'abattre, se poser.

alight[2], *pred. a.* Allumé; en feu.

align. **1.** *v.tr.* Aligner. **2.** *v.i.* S'aligner; se mettre en ligne.

alignment, *s.* Alignement *m.*

alike. **1.** *pred. a.* Semblable, pareil. **You are all a.!** vous vous ressemblez tous ! **2.** *adv.* Pareillement ; de même.

aliment, *s.* Aliment *m.*

alimony, *s.* Pension *f* alimentaire.

alive, *a.* **1.** (*a*) Vivant, en vie. **Dead or a.,** mort ou vif. (*b*) **To keep a.,** entretenir. **2. To be a. to,** se rendre compte de. **3. Look a.!** dépêchez-vous ! **4. To be a. with,** fourmiller de.

alkali, *s.* Alcali *m.*

alkaline, *a.* Alcalin.

alkaloid, *a. & s.* Alcaloïde (*m*).

all. **I.** *a., pron., & adv.* **1.** Tout, tous. (*a*) **All the way,** tout le long du chemin. **For all his wealth,** malgré sa fortune. **With all speed,** au plus vite. **At all hours,** à toute heure. (*b*) **All of us,** nous tous. (*c*) **Take it all,** prenez le tout. *Ten:* **Fifteen all,** quinze à. (*d*) **For all he may say,** quoi qu'il en dise. **All's well,** tout va bien. **2.** (*a*) **Once for all,** une fois pour toutes. **For all I know,** autant que je sache. (*b*) **Most of all,** surtout ; le plus. (*c*) **At all,** aucunement. **Not at all,** pas du tout. (*d*) **All but,** presque. **I all but fell,** j'ai failli tomber. (*e*) **All in all,** à tout prendre. **3.** *adv.* **Tout. She is all ears,** elle est tout oreilles. **All the better,** tant mieux. **All at once,** tout à coup ; tous à la fois.

II. all, *s.* **To lose one's all,** perdre tout son avoir.

allay, *v.tr.* Apaiser, calmer.

allaying, *s.* Apaisement *m.*

allegation, *s.* Allégation *f.*

allege, *v.tr.* Alléguer, prétendre.

alleged, *a.* Prétendu.

allegiance, *s.* Fidélité *f*, obéissance *f.*

alleviate, *v.tr.* Alléger, soulager.

alleviation, *s.* Allègement *m.*

alley, *s.* Allée *f*; ruelle *f*, passage *m.*

All Fools' Day, *s.* Le premier avril.

alliance, *s.* Alliance *f.* **To enter into an a.,** s'allier.

allied, *a.* Allié.

alligator, *s.* Alligator *m.*

allocate, *v.tr.* Allouer, assigner.

allocation, *s.* **1.** Allocation *f.* **2.** Part assignée.

allot, *v.tr.* **1.** Attribuer, assigner. **2.** Répartir, distribuer.

allotment, *s.* **1.** (*a*) Attribution *f.* (*b*) Partage *m.* **2.** (*a*) Portion *f.* (*b*) *pl.* Jardins ouvriers.

allow, *v.tr.* **1.** Admettre. **2.** Permettre, souffrir. **To a. s.o. to do sth.,** permettre à qn de faire qch. **3.** (*a*) Accorder (qch.) à (qn). (*b*) *ind.tr.* **To a. for,** tenir compte de.

allowable, *a.* Admissible.

allowance, *s.* **1.** (*a*) Pension *f.* (*b*) **Travelling a.,** frais *mpl* de voyage. (*c*) Ration *f.* **2.** Remise *f.* **3. To make a. for,** tenir compte de.

alloy, *s.* Alliage *m.*

allude, *v.ind.tr.* Faire allusion.

allure, *v.tr.* Attirer, séduire.

allurement, *s.* Attrait *m*; appât *m.*

alluring, *a.* Attrayant, séduisant.

allusion, *s.* Allusion *f.*

ally[1], *s.* Allié, -e.

ally[2]. **1.** *v.tr.* Allier. **2.** *v.i.* S'allier.

almanac, *s.* Almanach *m.*

almighty, *a. & s.* Tout-puissant.

almond, *s.* **1.** Amande *f.* **Burnt a.,** praline *f.* **2.** A.(-tree), amandier *m.*

almoner, *s.* Aumônier *m.*

almost, *adv.* Presque ; à peu près. **He a. fell,** il faillit tomber.

alms, *s.sg. or pl.* Aumône *f.*

aloe, *s.* **1.** Aloès *m.* **2.** *pl.* **Bitter aloes,** amer *m* d'aloès.

aloft, *adv.* En haut.

alone, *pred.a.* **1.** Seul ; rien que. **2. To leave a.,** laisser tranquille ; laisser faire.

along. **1.** *prep.* Le long de. **2.** *adv.* **To move a.,** avancer. **Come a.!** arrivez donc !

alongside, *adv. & prep.* Le long de. **To come a.,** accoster.

aloof, *adv. & pred.a* A l'écart, éloigné.

aloofness, *s.* Attitude distante.

aloud, *adv.* A haute voix ; (tout) haut.

alp, s. Alpe f.

alpaca, s. Alpaga m.

alpenstock, s. Alpenstock m; bâton ferré.

alphabet, s. Alphabet m.

alphabetical, a. Alphabétique.

alphabetically, adv. Alphabétiquement.

alpine, a. Alpestre.

already, adv. Déjà.

also, adv. Aussi; également.

altar, s. Autel m.

alter. 1. v.tr. Changer (de). **2.** v.i. Changer.

alteration, s. Changement m.

altercation, s. Altercation f.

alternate¹, a. Alternatif, alterné.

alternate², v.i. Alterner; se succéder.

alternately, adv. Alternativement; tour à tour.

alternating, a. Alternant, alterné.

alternation, s. Alternance f.

alternative. 1. a. Alternatif. **2.** s. Alternative f; choix m.

alternatively, adv. **1.** Alternativement; tour à tour. **2.** Avec l'alternative de.

although, conj. Quoique, bien que.

altitude, s. **1.** Altitude f, élévation f. **2.** Hauteur f.

altogether, adv. (a) Entièrement, tout à fait. (b) Somme toute. (c) En tout.

alum, s. Alun m.

aluminium, s. Aluminium m.

always, adv. Toujours.

a.m. Avant midi; du matin.

amalgam, s. Amalgame m.

amalgamate. 1. v.tr. Amalgamer. **2.** v.i. Fusionner.

amalgamation, s. Fusion f.

amass, v.tr. Amasser, accumuler.

amateur, s. Amateur m.

amateurish, a. D'amateur.

amaze, v.tr. Confondre, stupéfier.

amazed, a. Confondu, stupéfait.

amazement, s. Stupéfaction f; stupeur f.

amazing, a. Stupéfiant.

amazingly, adv. Étonnamment.

ambassador, s. Ambassadeur m.

amber, s. Ambre m. **A.** light, feu jaune.

ambergris, s. Ambre gris.

ambiguity, s. **1.** Ambiguïté f. **2.** Équivoque f.

ambiguous, a. **1.** Ambigu. -uë; équivoque. **2.** Incertain.

ambiguously, adv. Avec ambiguïté.

ambit, s. **1.** Circuit m tour m. **2.** Étendue f, portée f.

ambition, s. Ambition f.

ambitious, a. Ambitieux.

ambitiously, adv. Ambitieusement.

ambulance, s. Ambulance f.

ambuscade, s. Embuscade f.

ambush¹, s. Embuscade f. **In a.,** embusqué.

ambush², v.tr. Attirer dans un piège.

ameliorate, v.tr. Améliorer.

amelioration, s. Amélioration f.

amen, int. Amen; ainsi soit-il.

amenable, a. Soumis; docile. **A. to** reason, raisonnable.

amend. 1. v.tr. Amender; corriger. **2.** v.i. S'amender, se corriger.

amendment, s. (a) Modification f; rectification f. (b) Amendement m.

amends, s.pl. Réparation f.

amenity, s. **1.** Aménité f. **2.** pl. Commodités f.

America. Pr.n. L'Amérique f. North A., l'Amérique du Nord.

American, a. & s. Américain, -aine.

amethyst, s. Améthyste f.

amiability, s. Amabilité f.

amiable, a. Aimable (to, envers).

amiably, adv. Aimablement.

amicable, a. Amical.

amicably, adv. Amicalement.

amid(st), prep. Au milieu de; parmi.

amiss, adv. & pred.a. **1.** Mal. **To** take a., prendre en mauvaise part. **2.** Mal à propos.

ammonia, s. Ammoniaque f.

ammunition, s. Munitions fpl.

amnesty, s. Amnistie f.

among(st), prep. Parmi, entre; au milieu de.

amorous, a. Amoureux.

amount¹, s. **1.** Somme f, montant m, total m. **2.** Quantité f.

amount², v.i. **1.** S'élever, (se) monter. **2.** Équivaloir, revenir.

amphibious, a. Amphibie.

amphitheatre, s. Amphithéâtre m.

ample, a. Ample.

amplify, v.tr. Amplifier.

amplitude, s. Amplitude f.

amply, adv. Amplement.

amputate, v.tr. Amputer.

amputation, s. Amputation f.

amulet, *s.* Amulette *f.*

amuse, *v.tr.* Amuser, divertir.

amusement, *s.* Amusement *m*; divertissement *m.*

amusing, *a.* Amusant, divertissant.

Amy. *Pr.n.* Aimée *f.*

an. See A².

anaemia, *s.* Anémie *f.*

anaemic, *a.* Anémique.

anaesthetic, *a. & s.* Anesthésique (*m*).

anagram, *s.* Anagramme *f.*

analogous, *a.* Analogue.

analogy, *s.* Analogie *f.*

analyse, *v.tr.* Analyser.

analysis, *s.* Analyse *f.*

analyst, *s.* Analyste *m.*

analytic(al), *a.* Analytique.

anarchist, *s.* Anarchiste *mf.*

anarchy, *s.* Anarchie *f.*

anathema, *s.* Anathème *m.*

anathematize, *v.tr.* (*a*) Anathématiser. (*b*) Maudire.

anatomical, *a.* Anatomique.

anatomy, *s.* Anatomie *f.*

ancestor, *s.* Ancêtre *m.*

ancestral, *a.* Héréditaire ; de famille.

ancestry, *s.* **1.** Lignage *m*; ascendance *f.* **2.** *Coll.* Ancêtres *mpl*; aïeux *mpl.*

anchor¹, *s.* Ancre *f.*

anchor². **1.** *v.tr.* Ancrer. **2.** *v.i.* Jeter l'ancre ; mouiller.

anchorage, *s.* Mouillage *m.*

anchored, *a.* Ancré, mouillé.

anchorite, *s.* Anachorète *m.*

anchovy, *s.* Anchois *m.*

ancient, *a.* Ancien ; antique.

and, *conj.* Et. **1.** (*a*) **To walk two and two,** marcher deux à deux. (*b*) **Better and better,** de mieux en mieux. **2. Wait and see,** attendez voir. **Try and help me,** tâchez de m'aider.

Andrew. *Pr.n.* André *m.*

anecdote, *s.* Anecdote *f.*

anemone, *s.* Anémone *f.*

anew, *adv.* De nouveau.

angel, *s.* Ange *m.*

angelic, *a.* Angélique.

anger¹, *s.* Colère *f*; emportement *m.*

anger², *v.tr.* Irriter, mettre en colère.

angered, *a.* Irrité, furieux.

angle, *s.* (*a*) Angle *m.* (*b*) Coin *m.*

angler, *s.* Pêcheur *m* à la ligne.

angling, *s.* Pêche *f* à la ligne.

angrily, *adv.* En colère, avec colère.

angry, *a.* Fâché, irrité, courroucé (**with,** contre). **To get a.,** se fâcher. **To make a.,** fâcher ; mettre en colère.

anguish, *s.* Angoisse *f*; douleur *f.*

angular, *a.* Anguleux.

animal, *s.* Animal *m.*

animate¹, *a.* Animé ; doué de vie.

animate², *v.tr.* (*a*) Animer. (*b*) Encourager, stimuler.

animated, *a.* Animé.

animation, *s.* Animation *f*; feu *m.*

animosity, *s.* Animosité *f.*

aniseed, *s.* (Graine *f* d')anis *m.*

ankle, *s.* Cheville *f.*

annals, *s.pl.* Annales *f.*

annex, *v.tr.* Annexer.

annexation, *s.* Annexion *f.*

annexe, *s.* Annexe *f.*

annihilate, *v.tr.* Anéantir ; annihiler.

annihilation, *s.* Anéantissement *m*; annihilation *f.*

anniversary, *s.* Anniversaire *m.*

annotate, *v.tr.* Annoter.

announce, *v.tr.* Annoncer.

announcement, *s.* Annonce *f.*

announcer, *s.* Microphoniste *mf.*

annoy, *v.tr.* **1.** Contrarier. **2.** Gêner, ennuyer.

annoyance, *s.* **1.** Contrariété *f*, chagrin *m.* **2.** Désagrément *m*, ennui *m.*

annoyed, *a.* Contrarié, ennuyé.

annoying, *a.* Contrariant, ennuyeux.

annual. **1.** *a.* Annuel. **2.** *s.* (*a*) Plante annuelle. (*b*) Annuaire *m.*

annually, *adv.* Annuellement ; tous les ans.

annuitant, *s.* **1.** Pensionnaire *mf.* **2.** Rentier, -ière.

annuity, *s.* Rente (annuelle).

annul, *v.tr.* Annuler ; abroger.

anoint, *v.tr.* Oindre.

anomalous, *a.* Anomal, -aux.

anomaly, *s.* Anomalie *f.*

anonymity, *s.* Anonyme *m*, anonymat *m.*

anonymous, *a.* Anonyme.

anonymously, *adv.* Anonymement.

another, *a. & pron.* **1.** Encore (un). **Without a. word,** sans un mot de plus. **2.** (*a*) Un(e) autre. (*b*) Nouveau, -elle. **3.** (*a*) **Taking one (thing) with a.,** l'un dans l'autre. (*b*) **One a.,** l'un l'autre, les uns les autres.

answer¹, *s.* **1.** Réponse *f*; réplique *f.* **2.** Solution *f.*

answer[2], *v.tr. & i.* **1.** Répondre (à). (*a*) To a. the door, aller ouvrir. (*b*) To a. a prayer, exaucer une prière. **2.** Réussir. To a. the purpose, remplir le but. **3.** To a. for, répondre de.

answerable, *a.* Responsable.

ant, *s.* Fourmi *f.*

antagonism, *s.* Antagonisme *m.*

antagonistic, *a.* Opposé, contraire.

antarctic, *a.* Antarctique.

antecedent. **1.** *a.* Antécédent ; antérieur, -e. **2.** *s.* Antécédent *m.*

antelope, *s.* Antilope *f.*

anterior, *a.* Antérieur, -e.

anthem, *s.* **1.** Motet *m.* **2.** National a., hymne national.

ant-hill. Fourmilière *f.*

anthology, *s.* Anthologie *f.*

Anthony. *Pr.n.* Antoine *m.*

anthracite, *s.* Anthracite *m.*

anthropology, *s.* Anthropologie *f.*

anti-aircraft, *a.* Anti-aérien ; contre-avion(s).

anticipate, *v.tr.* **1.** (*a*) Anticiper sur. (*b*) Escompter. **2.** Prévenir, devancer. **3.** Prévoir, se promettre.

anticipation, *s.* Anticipation *f.*

antics, *s.pl.* Gambades *f*, cabrioles *f.*

antidote, *s.* Antidote *m.* contre-poison *m.*

antipathetic, *a.* Antipathique.

antipathy, *s.* Antipathie *f* (*to*, pour).

antipodes, *s.pl.* Antipodes *m.*

antiquarian. **1.** *a.* Archéologique **2.** *s.* Archéologue *m.*

antiquary, *s.* Archéologue *m.*

antiquated, *a.* Vieilli ; démodé.

antique. **1.** *a.* Antique ; suranné. **2.** *s.* Objet *m* antique. A. dealer, antiquaire *m.*

antiquity, *s.* **1.** Ancienneté *f.* **2.** *pl.* Antiquités.

antiseptic, *a. & s.* Antiseptique (*m*).

antithesis, *s.* **1.** Antithèse *f* (*to*, *of*, de). **2.** Opposé *m*, contraire *m* (de).

antler, *s.* Andouiller *m.*

antonym, *s.* Antonyme *m.*

Antwerp. *Pr.n.* Anvers *m.*

anvil, *s.* Enclume *f.*

anxiety, *s.* (*a*) Inquiétude *f* ; anxiété *f.* (*b*) Sollicitude *f.*

anxious, *a.* **1.** (*a*) Inquiet, -ète ; soucieux. (*b*) Inquiétant. **2.** Désireux.

anxiously, *adv.* **1.** (*a*) Avec inquiétude. (*b*) Anxieusement. **2.** Avec impatience.

any. **I.** *a. & pron.* **1.** (*a*) Du, de la, des ; en. (*b*) Aucun. **2.** Not any, ne . . . aucun, nul. I can't find any, je n'en trouve pas **3.** (*a*) N'importe (le)quel ; quelconque. Any but he, tout autre que lui. Any day, d'un jour à l'autre. (*b*) Tout.

II. any, *adv.* I cannot go any further, je ne peux aller plus loin.

anybody, anyone, *s. & pron.* **1.** Quelqu'un ; personne. **2.** Not a., ne . . . personne. **3.** N'importe qui ; tout le monde ; le premier venu ; quiconque. A. but he, tout autre que lui.

anyhow. **1.** *adv.* Tant bien que mal. **2.** *conj.* En tout cas, de toute façon.

anything, *pron. & s.* **1.** Quelque chose ; rien. If a. should happen, s'il arrivait quelque malheur. **2.** Not a., ne . . . rien. Hardly a., presque rien. **3.** N'importe quoi ; tout. A. but, rien moins que.

anyway, *conj.* En tout cas.

anywhere, *adv.* **1.** N'importe où ; quelque part. A. else, partout ailleurs. **2.** Not . . . a., nulle part.

apart, *adv.* A part. **1.** De côté. **2.** Séparé. To come a., se défaire.

apartment, *s.* (*a*) Salle *f*, chambre *f* ; pièce *f.* (*b*) *pl.* Logement *m* ; appartement *m.* To let furnished apartments, louer en meublé.

apathetic, *a.* Apathique, indifférent.

apathetically, *adv.* Apathiquement.

apathy, *s.* Apathie *f*, nonchalance *f.*

ape[1], *s.* Singe.

ape[2], *v.tr.* Singer ; imiter ; mimer.

aperient, *a. & s.* Laxatif (*m*).

aperture, *s.* Ouverture *f*, orifice *m.*

apex, *s.* Sommet *m* ; point culminant.

apiary, *s.* Rucher *m.*

apiece, *adv.* Chacun ; (la) pièce.

apocryphal, *a.* Apocryphe.

apologetic, *a.* D'excuse.

apologetically, *adv.* En s'excusant.

apologize, *v.i.* S'excuser.

apology, *s.* Excuses *fpl.*

apostate, *a. & s.* Apostat (*m*).

apostle, *s.* Apôtre *m.*

apostrophe, *s.* Apostrophe *f.*

apostrophize, *v.tr.* Apostropher.

appal, *v.tr.* Consterner ; épouvanter.

appalling, *a.* Épouvantable, effroyable.

apparatus, *s.* Appareil *m.*

apparel, *s.* Vêtement(s) *m.*

apparent, *a.* Apparent, évident.

apparently, *adv.* **1.** Évidemment. **2.** Apparemment.

apparition, *s.* **1.** Apparition *f.* **2.** Fantôme *m,* revenant *m.*

appeal[1], *s.* **1.** Appel *m.* **2.** Prière *f.*

appeal[2], *v.i.* **1.** En appeler. **2.** Faire appel. **3.** S'adresser ; sourire.

appealing, *a.* Suppliant.

appealingly, *adv.* D'un ton, d'un regard, suppliant.

appear, *v.i.* **1.** Paraître, apparaître ; se montrer. **2.** Se présenter ; comparaître. **To appear for,** représenter. **3.** Paraître. **So it appears,** il paraît que oui.

appearance, *s.* **1.** Apparition *f* ; entrée *f.* **2.** Apparence *f,* air *m,* mine *f.*

appease, *v.tr.* Apaiser.

appeasement, *s.* Apaisement *m.*

append, *v.tr.* Attacher, joindre.

appendage, *s.* Accessoire *m.*

appendicitis, *s.* Appendicite *f.*

appendix, *s.* Appendice *m.*

appertain, *v.i.* **1.** Appartenir. **2.** Se rapporter.

appetite, *s.* Appétit *m.*

appetizer, *s.* Apéritif *m.*

appetizing, *a.* Appétissant.

applaud, *v.tr.* Applaudir.

applause, *s.* Applaudissements *mpl.*

apple, *s.* **1.** Pomme *f.* **2. A. of the eye,** prunelle *f* de l'œil.

apple-pie, *s.* Tourte *f* aux pommes.

apple-sauce, *s.* Compote *f* de pommes.

apple-tart, *s.* Tourte *f* aux pommes.

apple-tree, *s.* Pommier *m.*

appliance, *s.* (*a*) Appareil *m,* dispositif *m.* (*b*) *pl.* Accessoires *m.*

applicable, *a.* **1.** Applicable. **2.** Approprié.

applicant, *s.* Candidat *m* ; solliciteur, -euse.

application, *s.* **1.** Application *f.* **2.** Assiduité *f,* application *f.* **3.** Demande *f,* sollicitation *f.*

apply, *v.tr. & i.* **1.** (*a*) Appliquer. (*b*) S'appliquer. **2.** S'adresser, recourir. **To a. for,** solliciter.

appoint, *v.tr.* **1.** Nommer. **2.** Fixer, arrêter.

appointed, *a.* **1.** Désigné ; fixé. **2.** Équipé. monté.

appointment, *s.* **1.** Rendez-vous *m.*

2. (*a*) Nomination *f.* (*b*) Place *f,* charge *f,* emploi *m.* **3.** *pl.* Équipement *m.*

apportion, *v.tr.* Répartir.

apportionment, *s.* Partage *m.*

apposite, *a.* Juste ; approprié.

appositely, *adv.* A propos.

appraise, *v.tr.* Priser, évaluer.

appraisement, *s.* Évaluation *f.*

appreciable, *a.* Appréciable ; sensible.

appreciably, *adv.* Sensiblement.

appreciate. 1. *v.tr.* Apprécier ; faire cas de. **2.** *v.i.* Augmenter de valeur ; monter.

appreciation, *s.* **1.** Appréciation *f* ; estimation *f.* **2.** Accroissement *m,* hausse *f,* de valeur.

appreciative, *a.* **1.** Élogieux. **2. To be a. of,** apprécier.

apprehend, *v.tr.* **1.** Arrêter. **2.** Comprendre. **3.** Appréhender, redouter.

apprehension, *s.* **1.** Arrestation *f.* **2.** Compréhension *f.* **3.** Appréhension *f.*

apprehensive, *a.* Timide, craintif. **To be a. of,** redouter.

apprentice, *s.* Apprenti -ie.

apprise, *v.tr.* Prévenir.

approach[1], *s.* Approche *f.* **1. To make approaches,** faire des avances. **2.** Voie *f* d'accès.

approach[2]. **1.** *v.i.* Approcher, s'approcher. **2.** *v.tr.* S'approcher de ; aborder, approcher. **To be easy to a.,** avoir l'abord facile.

approbation, *s.* Approbation *f.*

appropriate[1], *a.* **1.** Approprié. **2.** Propre, convenable.

appropriate[2], *v.tr.* **1.** S'approprier. **2.** Approprier, affecter.

appropriately, *adv.* Convenablement ; à propos.

appropriateness, *s.* Convenance *f,* justesse *f,* à-propos *m.*

appropriation, *s.* **1.** Appropriation *f.* **2.** Affectation *f.*

approval, *s.* **1.** Approbation *f,* agrément *m.* **2.** Ratification *f.* **3. On a.,** à condition.

approve. 1. *v.tr.* Approuver ; ratifier. **2.** *v.ind.tr.* **To a. of,** approuver.

approving, *a.* Approbateur, -trice.

approximate, *a.* Approximatif.

approximately, *adv.* Approximativement.

appurtenance, s. Accessoire m.

apricot, s. Abricot m.

April, s. Avril m.

apron, s. Tablier m.

apse, s. Abside f, apside f.

apt, a. **1.** Juste, fin. **2.** (a) Enclin, porté. (b) Sujet. **3.** Intelligent.

aptitude, s. Aptitude f.

aptly, adv. **1.** Avec justesse. **2.** Adroitement.

aptness, s. Justesse f, à-propos m.

aquarium, s. Aquarium m.

aquatic, a. Aquatique.

aqueduct, s. Aqueduc m.

aquiline, a. Aquilin.

Arab, a. & s. Arabe (mf).

Arabia. Pr.n. L'Arabie f.

Arabian, a. Arabe, d'Arabie. **The A. Nights,** les Mille et une Nuits.

Arabic. **1.** a. (Gomme) arabique; (langue) arabe. **2.** s. L'arabe m.

arable, a. Arable, labourable.

arbiter, s. Arbitre m.

arbitrarily, adv. Arbitrairement.

arbitrary, a. Arbitraire.

arbitrate. **1.** v.tr. Arbitrer, juger. **2.** v.i. Arbitrer.

arbitration, s. Arbitrage m.

arbitrator, s. Arbitre m.

arbour, s. Tonnelle f.

arc, s. Arc m.

arcade, s. Arcade f.

arch[1], s. **1.** Voûte f, arc m; cintre m. **2.** Arche f; pont m (de chemin de fer).

arch[2]. **1.** v.tr. Arquer; cambrer. **2.** v.i. Se voûter.

arch[3], a. Espiègle; malicieux.

archaeologist, s. Archéologue m.

archaeology, s. Archéologie f.

archaic, a. Archaïque.

archangel, s. Archange m.

archbishop, s. Archevêque m.

archdeacon, s. Archidiacre m.

arched, a. (a) En voûte; voûté. (b) Arqué, cambré.

archery, s. Tir m à l'arc.

archipelago, s. Archipel m.

architect, s. Architecte m.

architecture, s. Architecture f.

archives, s.pl. Archives f.

archly, adv. D'un air espiègle.

archway, s. Passage voûté; portail m.

arctic, a. Arctique.

ardent, a. Ardent.

ardently, adv. Ardemment.

ardour, s. Ardeur f.

arduous, a. Ardu.

arduously, adv. Péniblement.

area, s. **1.** Cour f d'entrée en sous-sol. **2.** Aire f, superficie f. **3.** Étendue f; région f.

arena, s. Arène f.

Argentina. Pr.n. L'Argentine f.

arguable, a. Discutable, soutenable.

argue. **1.** v.tr. (a) Prouver, indiquer, démontrer. (b) Discuter, débattre. **2.** v.i. (a) Argumenter. (b) Discuter, disputer.

argument, s. **1.** Argument m. **For the sake of a.,** à titre d'exemple. **2.** Discussion f, dispute f.

argumentative, a. Raisonneur, -euse.

arid, a. Aride.

aright, adv. Bien, juste.

arise, v.i. (a) S'élever, survenir, se présenter. (b) Provenir, résulter.

aristocracy, s. Aristocratie f.

aristocrat, s. Aristocrate mf.

aristocratic, a. Aristocratique.

arithmetic, s. Arithmétique f, calcul m.

arithmetical, a. Arithmétique.

ark, s. Arche f.

arm[1], s. Bras m. **Arm-in-arm,** bras dessus bras dessous. **She took my arm,** elle me prit le bras. **To put one's arm round s.o.,** prendre qn par la taille. **At arm's length,** à distance.

arm[2], s. **1.** Arme f. **2.** pl. Armoiries f, armes.

arm[3]. **1.** v.tr. Armer. **2.** v.i. S'armer; prendre les armes.

armament, s. **1.** Armement m. **2.** Forces fpl; armée f, flotte navale.

arm-chair, s. Fauteuil m.

armed, a. Armé (with, de).

armful, s. Brassée f.

armistice, s. Armistice m.

armlet, s. Brassard m.

armour, s. Armure f.

armourer, s. Armurier m.

armour-plated, a. Cuirassé; blindé.

armoury, s. Magasin m d'armes.

armpit, s. Aisselle f.

army, s. **1.** Armée f. **To join the a.,** se faire soldat. **2.** Foule f.

arnica, s. Arnica f.

aroma, s. Arome m; bouquet m.

aromatic, a. Aromatique.

around. **1.** adv. Autour, à l'entour. **2.** prep. Autour de.

arouse, *v.tr.* **1.** (*a*) Réveiller, éveiller. (*b*) Stimuler. **2.** Exciter, susciter.

arraign, *v.tr.* (*a*) Accuser. (*b*) Attaquer, s'en prendre à.

arraignment, *s.* **1.** Mise *f* en accusation. **2.** Censure *f*.

arrange, *v.tr.* Arranger. **1.** Disposer, ranger. **2.** To a. to, s'arranger pour. **3.** Ajuster.

arrangement, *s.* **1.** Arrangement *m*, disposition *f*. **2.** Accommodement *m*.

arrant, *a.* Insigne, achevé.

array¹, *s.* Étalage *m*.

array², *v.tr.* Ranger; disposer.

arrear(s), *s.* Arriéré *m*.

arrest¹, *s.* Arrestation *f*.

arrest², *v.tr.* Arrêter.

arrival, *s.* **1.** Arrivée *f*. On a., à l'arrivée. **2.** A new a., un nouveau venu.

arrive, *v.i.* Arriver.

arrogance, *s.* Arrogance *f*.

arrogant, *a.* Arrogant.

arrogantly, *adv.* Avec arrogance.

arrogate, *v.tr.* S'arroger.

arrow, *s.* Flèche *f*.

arrow-head, *s.* Tête *f*, fer *m*, pointe *f*, de flèche.

arsenal, *s.* Arsenal *m*, -aux.

arsenic, *s.* Arsenic *m*.

arson, *s.* Incendie *m* volontaire.

art, *s.* **1.** Art *m*. The (fine) arts, les beaux-arts. **2.** Adresse *f*, habileté *f*, artifice *m*.

arterial, *a.* A. road, grande voie de communication.

artery, *s.* Artère *f*.

artful, *a.* (*a*) Adroit. (*b*) Rusé.

artfully, *adv.* **1.** Adroitement. **2.** Artificieusement.

artfulness, *s.* **1.** Art *m*, adresse *f*; ingéniosité *f*. **2.** Astuce *f*.

artichoke, *s.* **1.** Artichaut *m*. **2.** Jerusalem a., topinambour *m*.

article, *s.* **1.** Article *m*. **2.** (*a*) Objet *m*. (*b*) A. of clothing, pièce *f* d'habillement.

articulate¹, *a.* Net, distinct.

articulate², *v.tr. & i.* Articuler.

artifice, *s.* **1.** Artifice *m*, ruse *f*. **2.** Art *m*, habileté *f*, adresse *f*.

artificial, *a.* **1.** Artificiel. **2.** Factice, simulé.

artificially, *adv.* Artificiellement.

artillery, *s.* Artillerie *f*.

artisan, *s.* Artisan *m*, ouvrier *m*.

artist, *s.* (*a*) Artiste *mf*. (*b*) Artiste peintre *mf*.

artiste, *s.* Artiste *mf*.

artistic, *a.* Artistique.

artistically, *adv.* Artistement.

artless, *a.* **1.** Naturel; sans artifice. **2.** Naïf.

artlessly, *adv.* **1.** Naturellement, simplement. **2.** Naïvement.

artlessness, *s.* **1.** Naturel *m*, simplicité *f*. **2.** Naïveté *f*.

as. **I.** *adv.* **1.** Aussi, si. **2.** As to., quant à; au sujet de.

II. as, *conj. & rel. adv.* **1.** (*a*) Que. **As . . . as,** aussi . que. (*b*) Comme. **2.** (*a*) **Leave it as it is,** laissez-le tel qu'il est. **As it is,** les choses étant ainsi. (*b*) **To treat as,** traiter en. **3.** **As he grew older,** en vieillissant. **4.** Comme, puisque. **5.** **Be so good as to,** soyez assez bon pour.

III. as, *rel. pron.* Tel que, comme.

asbestos, *s.* Amiante *m*.

ascend. **1.** *v.i.* Monter, s'élever. **2.** *v.tr.* (*a*) **To a. the throne,** monter sur le trône. (*b*) Gravir.

ascendancy, *s.* Ascendant *m*.

ascent, *s.* **1.** Ascension *f*. **2.** Montée *f*.

ascertain, *v.tr.* S'informer. s'assurer. de; constater.

ascertainment, *s.* Vérification *f*.

ascetic. **1.** *a.* Ascétique. **2.** *s.* Ascète *mf*.

ascribable, *a.* Attribuable.

ascribe, *v.tr.* Attribuer, imputer.

ash¹, *s.* Frêne *m*.

ash², *s.* Cendre *f*.

ashamed, *a.* Honteux, confus. To be a., avoir honte.

ash-bin, *s.* Cendrier *m*.

ashen, *a.* Pâle comme la mort.

ashore, *adv.* À terre.

ash-pan, *s.* Cendrier *m*.

ash-tray, *s.* Cendrier *m*.

Ash Wednesday, *s* Le mercredi des Cendres.

Asia. *Pr.n.* L'Asie *f*.

Asiatic, *a. & s.* Asiatique (*mf*); d'Asie.

aside. **1.** *adv.* De côté; à l'écart; à part. **To stand a.,** se ranger. **2.** *s.* Aparté *m*.

asinine, *a.* Stupide, sot.

ask, *v.tr. & i.* Demander. **1.** To ask s.o. a question, faire une question à qn. **2. To ask s.o. to do sth.,** demander à qn de faire qch. **3. To ask about,** se renseigner sur. **4.** (a) **To ask for s.o.,** demander à voir qn. (b) **To ask for sth.,** demander qch. **5.** Inviter.

askance, adv. De travers.

askew, adv. De biais, de côté.

aslant, adv. Obliquement, de biais.

asleep, adv. & pred.a. Endormi. **To be a.,** dormir. **To fall a.,** s'endormir.

asparagus, s. Asperges fpl.

aspect, s. **I.** Exposition f. vue f. **2.** Aspect m, air m.

aspen, s. Tremble m.

asperity, s. Apreté f; sévérité f.

aspersion, s. Calomnie f.

asphalt, s. Asphalte m.

asphyxia, s. Asphyxie f.

asphyxiate, v.tr. Asphyxier.

aspirant, s. Aspirant, -ante.

aspirate, v.tr. Aspirer.

aspiration, s. Aspiration f.

aspire, v.i. Aspirer.

aspirin, s. Aspirine f. **An a.,** un comprimé d'aspirine.

aspiring, a. Ambitieux.

ass, s. **I.** Ane f ânesse. **2.** Sot, f. sotte; âne.

assail, v.tr. Assaillir, attaquer.

assailant, s Assaillant m.

assassin, s. Assassin m.

assassinate, v.tr. Assassiner.

assassination, s. Assassinat m.

assault[1], s. **I.** (a) Assaut m. (b) Attaque. **2. A. and battery,** voies fpl de fait.

assault[2], v.tr. Attaquer.

assay[1], s. Essai m.

assay[2], v.tr. Essayer, titrer.

assemblage, s. **I.** Assemblage m **2.** (a) Réunion f. (b) Collection f.

assemble. I. v.tr. Assembler **2.** v.i. S'assembler; se rassembler.

assembly, s. **I.** Assemblée f. **2.** Assemblement m, réunion f.

assent[1], s. Assentiment m.

assent[2], v.i Accéder, acquiescer.

assert, v.tr. **I.** (a) Revendiquer, faire valoir. (b) **To a. oneself,** s'imposer. **2.** Affirmer

assertion, s. Affirmation f.

assertive, a. Péremptoire.

assertiveness, s. Assurance f.

assess, v.tr. **I.** Estimer évaluer. **2.** Taxer.

assessment, s. (a) Évaluation f. (b) Imposition f. (c) Cotisation f.

assessor, s. Assesseur m.

asset, s. **I.** Possession f; avoir m. **II. assets,** s.pl. Actif m.

assiduity, s. Assiduité f, diligence f.

assiduous, a. Assidu.

assiduously, adv. Assidûment.

assign, v.tr. **I.** Assigner. **2.** Céder, transférer.

assignation, s. Rendez-vous m.

assignment, s. **I.** Cession f. transfert m. **2.** Tâche assignée.

assimilate, v.tr Assimiler.

assist. I. v.tr. (a) Aider. (b) Secourir, assister. **2.** v.i. Prendre part; assister.

assistance, s. Aide f, secours m, assistance f. **To be of a. to,** aider; être utile à.

assistant. I. a. Auxiliaire; adjoint. **2.** s. Aide mf; commis m; demoiselle f de magasin.

assizes, s.pl. Assises fpl.

associate[1], s. (a) Associé m, adjoint m. (b) Compagnon m, camarade mf.

associate[2]. **I.** v.tr. Associer (à qch.). **2.** v.i. S'associer. (b) **To a. with,** fréquenter.

association, s. **I.** (a) Association f. (b) Fréquentation f. **2.** Association, société f.

assort, v.tr (a) Assortir. (b) Classer, ranger.

assortment, s. Assortiment m.

assuage, v.tr. Apaiser; satisfaire.

assume, v.tr. **I.** Prendre; affecter. **2.** Prendre sur soi, assumer. **3.** S'attribuer, s'approprier. **4.** Simuler. **5.** Présumer, supposer.

assumed, a. Supposé. feint. **A. name,** pseudonyme m.

assuming, a. Présomptueux.

assumption, s. Supposition f.

assurance, s. (a) Assurance f. (b) Promesse (formelle). (c) Affirmation f.

assure, v.tr. Assurer.

assuredly, adv. Assurément.

asterisk, s. Astérisque m.

astern, adv. (a) A l'arrière. (b) En arrière.

asthma, s. Asthme m.

asthmatic, a. Asthmatique.

astir, adv. & pred. a. **I.** En mouvement. **2.** Debout, levé. **3.** Agité.

astonish, *v.tr.* Étonner, surprendre.

astonishing, *a.* Étonnant, surprenant.

astonishingly, *adv.* Étonnamment.

astonishment, *s.* Étonnement *m*, surprise *f*.

astound, *v.tr.* Confondre ; stupéfier.

astounding, *a.* Abasourdissant.

astray, *adv. & pred. a.* Égaré. **To go a.,** s'égarer. **To lead a.,** dévoyer.

astride, *adv., pred.a., & prep.* A califourchon ; à cheval sur.

astringent, *a.* Astringent.

astrologer, *s.* Astrologue *m*.

astrology, *s.* Astrologie *f*.

astronomer, *s.* Astronome *m*.

astronomical, *a.* Astronomique.

astronomy, *s.* Astronomie *f*.

astute, *a.* Fin, avisé.

astutely, *adv.* Astucieusement.

astuteness, *s.* **1.** Finesse *f*, sagacité *f*. **2.** Astuce *f*.

asylum, *s.* Asile *m*, refuge *m*.

at, *prep.* **A. 1.** (a) At sea, en mer. (b) At the tailor's, chez le tailleur. **2.** Two at a time, deux à la fois. At night, la nuit. **3.** At my request, sur ma demande. **4.** (a) To look at, regarder. Surprised at, étonné de. (b) To be at work, être au travail. While we are at it, pendant que nous y sommes.

atheism, *s.* Athéisme *m*.

atheist, *s.* Athée *mf*.

Athens. *Pr.n.* Athènes *f*.

athlete, *s.* Athlète *m*.

athletic, *a.* Athlétique.

athletics, *s.pl.* Sports *m* (athlétiques).

athwart. **1.** *adv.* En travers. **2.** *prep.* En travers de.

Atlantic, *a. & s.* Atlantique *m*.

atlas, *s.* Atlas *m*.

atmosphere, *s.* Atmosphère *f*.

atmospheric(al). **1.** *a.* Atmosphérique. **2.** *s.pl.* **Atmospherics**, parasites *m*.

atom, *s.* Atome *m*.

atomic, *a.* Atomique.

atone, *v.ind.tr.* To a. for, expier.

atonement, *s.* Expiation *f* réparation *f*.

atrocious, *a.* **1.** Atroce. **2.** Exécrable.

atrociously, *adv.* **1.** Atrocement. **2.** Exécrablement.

atrocity, *s.* Atrocité *f*.

attach. **1.** *v.tr.* Attacher, lier. **2.** *v.i* S'attacher.

attaché, *s.* Attaché *m*. **A. case,** *s.* Mallette *f* (pour documents)

attached, *a.* Attaché.

attachment, *s.* **1.** Accessoire *m*. **2.** Attachement *m*.

attack[1], *s.* Attaque *f*. **To make an a. upon,** attaquer.

attack[2], *v.tr.* Attaquer ; s'attaquer à.

attacker, *s.* Attaquant *m*.

attain. **1.** *v.tr.* Atteindre, arriver à. **2.** *v.ind.tr.* To a. to, atteindre à.

attainable, *a.* Accessible.

attainment, *s.* **1.** Réalisation *f*. **2.** Connaissance *f* ; savoir *m*.

attempt[1], *s.* **1.** Tentative *f*, essai *m*. First a., coup *m* d'essai. At the first a., du premier coup. **2.** Attentat *m* (on, contre).

attempt[2], *v.tr.* **1.** (a) Essayer, tenter. (b) Attempted murder, tentative *f* d'assassinat. **2.** To a. s.o.'s life, attenter à la vie de qn.

attend. **1.** *v.ind.tr.* To a. to. (a) Faire attention à. (b) Écouter. (c) S'occuper de. **2.** *v.tr.* Soigner. **3.** *v.tr. & ind.tr.* To a. on, servir. **4.** *v.tr.* To a. school, aller à l'école. To a. a meeting, assister à une réunion.

attendance, *s.* **1.** (a) Soins *mpl*. (b) In a. on, de service auprès de. **2.** Présence *f*.

attendant. **1.** *a.* Présent. **2.** *s.* (a) Serviteur *m*, domestique *mf* ; gardien, -ienne ; ouvreuse *f*. (b) *pl.* Suivants *m*, gens *m*.

attention, *s.* **1.** (a) Attention *f*. Pay a.! faites attention ! To attract a., se faire remarquer. (b) Soins *mpl*. **2.** A.! garde à vous !

attentive, *a.* **1.** Attentif. **2.** Empressé (to, auprès de).

attentively, *adv* Attentivement.

attenuate, *v.tr.* Atténuer.

attest. (a) *v.tr.* Attester. (b) *v.ind.tr.* To a. to, témoigner de.

attic, *s.* Mansarde *f*.

attire, *s.* Vêtement *m* ; costume *m*.

attitude, *s.* Attitude *f*, pose *f*.

attorney[1], *s.* Mandataire *m*.

attorney[2]. *s.* Power of a., procuration *f*.

attract, *v.tr.* Attirer.

attraction, *s.* **1.** Attraction *f*. **2.** *pl.* Attractions, attraits *mpl*. **3.** The chief a., le clou.

attractive, *a.* Attrayant, séduisant.

attractively, *adv.* D'une manière attrayante.

attributable, *a.* Attribuable.

attribute[1], *s.* Attribut *m*, qualité *f.*

attribute[2], *v.tr.* Attribuer, imputer.

attribution, *s.* Attribution *f.*

auburn, *a.* Châtain roux.

auction[1], *s.* Vente *f* aux enchères *fpl.*

auction[2], *v.tr.* Vendre aux enchères.

auctioneer, *s.* Commissaire-priseur *m.*

audacious, *a.* Audacieux ; hardi.

audacity, *s.* Audace *f.*

audible, *a.* Audible ; intelligible.

audibly, *adv.* Distinctement.

audience, *s.* **1.** Audience *f.* **2.** Assistance *f*, auditoire *m.*

audit[1], *s.* Vérification *f* (de comptes).

audit[2], *v.tr.* Vérifier (des comptes).

auditor, *s.* Expert *m* comptable.

aught, *s.* Quelque chose *m.* **For a. I know,** autant que je sache.

augment. **1.** *v.tr.* Augmenter, accroître (by, de). **2.** *v.i.* Augmenter.

augmentation, *s.* Augmentation *f.*

augury, *s.* Augure *m* ; présage *m.*

august[1], *a.* Auguste ; majestueux.

August[2], *s.* Août *m.*

aunt, *s.* Tante *f.*

aureole, *s.* Auréole *f.*

auricular, *a.* Auriculaire.

auspices, *s.pl.* Auspices *m.*

auspicious, *a.* **1.** (*a*) Propice. (*b*) De bon augure. **2.** Heureux.

auspiciously, *adv.* Favorablement.

austere, *a.* Austère.

austerely, *adv.* Austèrement.

austerity, *s.* Austérité *f.*

Australia. *Pr.n.* L'Australie *f.*

Australian, *a. & s.* Australien.

Austria. *Pr.n.* L'Autriche *f.*

Austrian, *a. & s.* Autrichien, -enne.

authentic, *a.* Authentique.

authenticate, *v.tr.* **1.** Certifier. **2.** Vérifier.

authenticity, *s.* Authenticité *f.*

author, *s.* Auteur *m.*

authoritative, *a.* **1.** Péremptoire. **2.** Revêtu d'autorité.

authoritatively, *adv.* **1.** Péremptoirement. **2.** Avec autorité.

authority, *s.* **1.** Autorité *f.* **2.** Autorisation *f.* **3.** (*a*) A. on, autorité en. (*b*) On good a., de bonne source.

authorization, *s.* Autorisation *f.*

authorize, *v.tr.* Autoriser.

authorized, *a.* Autorisé.

autobiographical, *a.* Autobiographique.

autobiography, *s.* Autobiographie *f.*

autocracy, *s.* Autocratie *f.*

autocrat, *s.* Autocrate *m.*

autocratic, *a.* Autocratique.

autograph, *s.* Autographe *m.*

automatic, *a. & s.* Automatique. **A. machine,** distributeur *m* automatique.

automatically, *adv.* Automatiquement.

automaton, *s.* Automate *m.*

autonomy, *s.* Autonomie *f.*

autopsy, *s.* Autopsie *f.*

autumn, *s.* Automne *m.*

autumnal, *a.* Automnal ; d'automne.

auxiliary, *a. & s.* Auxiliaire *mf.*

avail[1], *s.* Avantage *m*, utilité *f.* **Without a.,** inutile(ment).

avail[2], *v.tr. & i.* **1.** Servir ; être efficace. **2. To a. oneself of,** se servir de.

availability, *s.* **1.** Disponibilité *f.* **2.** Validité *f.*

available, *a.* **1.** (*a*) Disponible. (*b*) Accessible. **2.** Valable, bon.

avalanche, *s.* Avalanche *f.*

avarice, *s.* Avarice *f.*

avaricious, *a.* Avare, avaricieux.

avenge, *v.tr.* Venger.

avenger, *s.* Vengeur, -eresse.

avenging, *a.* Vengeur, *f.* -eresse.

avenue, *s.* (*a*) Avenue *f.* (*b*) Chemin *m* d'accès.

aver, *v.tr.* Avérer, déclarer, affirmer.

average[1], *s.* Moyenne *f.* **On an a.,** en moyenne.

average[2], *a.* Moyen.

averse, *a.* Opposé.

aversion, *s.* **1.** Aversion *f*, répugnance *f.* **2. Pet a.,** bête noire.

avert, *v.tr.* Détourner.

aviary, *s.* Volière *f.*

aviation, *s.* Aviation *f.*

aviator, *s.* Aviateur, -trice.

avid, *a.* Avide.

avidity, *s.* Avidité *f.*

avocation, *s.* (*a*) Occupation *f.* (*b*) Vocation *f*, profession *f.*

avoid, *v.tr.* Éviter.

avoidable, *a.* Évitable.

avow, *v.tr.* **1.** Reconnaître. **2.** Déclarer. **3.** Avouer, admettre.

avowal, *s.* Aveu *m.*

avowed, *a.* Avéré.

avowedly, *adv.* Franchement.

await, *v.tr.* Attendre.

awake[1]. **I.** *v.i.* S'éveiller, se réveiller. **2.** *v.tr.* Éveiller réveiller.

awake[2], *pred.a.* **I.** Éveillé. **I was a.,** je ne dormais pas. **Wide a.,** bien éveillé. **2. To be a to,** avoir conscience de

awaken, *v.tr. & i.* = AWAKE[1].

award[1], *s.* **I.** Arbitrage *m*; adjudication *f*. **2.** Récompense *f*.

award[2], *v.tr.* Adjuger, décerner.

aware, *a* Avisé, informé, instruit. **To be a. of,** savoir. **Not that I am a. of,** pas que je sache.

away, *adv.* Loin; au loin. **I.** (*a*) **To go a.,** partir, s'en aller. (*b*) **To run a.,** s'enfuir. **To take s.o. a.,** emmener qn. **To carry a.,** emporter. **2.** Sing **a.!** continuez à chanter! **3.** (*a*) **Far a.,** dans le lointain; au loin. **Five paces a.,** à cinq pas de là. (*b*) Éloigné. (*c*) **When he is a.,** lorsqu'il n'est pas là.

awe, *s.* Crainte *f*, terreur *f*; respect *m*.

awe-inspiring, *a.* Terrifiant, imposant.

awesome, *a.* Terrifiant.

awe-struck, *a.* **I.** Frappé d'une terreur mystérieuse. **2.** Intimidé.

awful, *a.* **I.** Terrible; redoutable. **2.** (*a*) Terrifiant. (*b*) Imposant.

awfully, *adv.* Terriblement; effroyablement.

awhile, *adv.* Pendant quelque temps; un moment.

awkward, *a.* **I.** Gauche, maladroit. **2.** Embarrassé, gêné. **3.** Fâcheux gênant. **4.** Incommode.

awkwardly, *adv.* **I.** Gauchement. **2.** D'une manière embarrassée **3.** D'une façon gênante.

awkwardness, *s.* **I.** Gaucherie *f*. **2.** Embarras *m*. **3.** Inconvénient *m*.

awl, *s.* Alène *f*.

awning, *s.* Tente *f*, vélum *m*.

awry, *adv. & pred.a.* De travers.

axe, *s.* Hache *f*; cognée *f*.

axiom, *s.* Axiome *m*.

axiomatic, *a.* (*a*) Axiomatique. (*b*) Évident.

axis, *s.* Axe *m*.

axle, *s.* **I.** Essieu *m*. **2.** Arbre *m*, axe *m*.

azure, *s.* Azur *m*.

B

B, b. (La lettre) B, b *m*.

babble[1], *s.* **I.** Babil *m*, babillage *m*. **2.** Bavardage *m*.

babble[2], *v.i.* (*a*) Babiller. (*b*) Bavarder, jaser. (*c*) Murmurer.

babbling, *a.* Babillard.

babel, *s.* Vacarme *m*.

baboon, *s.* Babouin *m*.

baby, *s.* **I.** Bébé *m*. **2.** *Attrib.* (*a*) D'enfant. (*b*) De petites dimensions. **B. car,** voiturette *f*.

babyhood, *s.* Première enfance.

babyish, *a.* De bébé; puéril.

bachelor, *s.* **I.** Célibataire *m*, garçon *m*. **2.** Bachelier, -ière. **B. of Arts,** *approx.* = licencié ès lettres.

bacillus, *s.* Bacille *m*.

back[1]. **I.** *s.* **I.** (*a*) Dos *m*. **To fall on one's back,** tomber à la renverse. **To put s.o.'s b. up,** mettre qn en colère. (*b*) Les reins *m*. **2.** (*a*) Dossier *m* (d'une chaise). (*b*) Revers *m*. (*c*) Derrière *m*; arrière *m*.

II. back, *a.* Arrière, de derrière.

III. back, *adv.* (*a*) En arrière.

Stand b.! rangez-vous! (*b*) **To call b.,** rappeler. **To come b.,** revenir. (*c*) **As soon as I get b.,** dès mon retour.

back[2], **I.** *v.tr.* **I.** Soutenir, appuyer; parier sur (un cheval). **2.** Refouler. **II. back,** *v.i.* Aller en arrière.

back out, *v.i.* Retirer sa promesse.

back up, *v.tr.* Soutenir.

backbite, *v.tr.* Médire de.

backbiting, *s.* Médisance *f*.

backbone, *s.* Épine dorsale, échine *f*.

backer, *s.* **I.** Parieur, -euse. **2.** Partisan *m*.

back-fire[1], *s.* Contre-allumage *m*.

back-fire[2], *v.i.* Pétarder.

background, *s.* Fond *m*, arrière-plan *m*. **To keep in the b.,** s'effacer.

backing, *s.* Renfort *m*, support *m*.

back-number, *s.* Vieux numéro.

back-pay, *s.* Arriéré *m* de solde.

backslide, *v.i.* Retomber dans l'erreur.

backslider, *s.* Relaps, *f*. relapse.

backstairs, *s.* Escalier *m* de service.

backward. 1. *a.* (*a*) En arrière. (*b*) En retard ; arriéré. **2.** *adv.* = BACK-WARDS.

backwardness, *s.* Retard *m.*

backwards, *adv.* En arrière ; (marcher) à reculons ; (tomber) à la renverse. **B. and forwards,** de long en large.

backwash, *s.* Remous *m.*

bacon, *s.* Lard *m.*

bacteria, *s.pl.* Bactéries *f.*

bad. I. *a.* Mauvais. **1.** (*a*) **To go bad,** se gâter. (*b*) **In a bad way,** en mauvais état. **From bad to worse,** de mal en pis. **2.** (*a*) Méchant. **A bad lot,** un vilain personnage. (*b*) **A bad cold,** un gros rhume. **That's too bad!** c'est trop fort ! (*c*) Grave (accident). (*d*) **She has a bad finger,** elle a mal au doigt. **My bad leg,** ma jambe malade.
II. **bad,** *s.* (*a*) Mauvaise fortune. (*b*) **To go to the bad,** mal tourner. (*c*) **To the bad,** en perte de.

badge, *s.* **1.** Insigne *m* ; plaque *f* ; brassard *m.* **2.** Symbole *m.*

badger¹, *s.* Blaireau *m.*

badger², *v.tr.* Harceler.

bad-looking, *a.* **Not b.-l.,** pas mal.

badly, *adv.* **1.** Mal. **2.** Grièvement (blessé). **3. To want b.,** avoir grand besoin de.

badness, *s.* **1.** Mauvaise qualité ; mauvais état. **2.** Méchanceté *f.*

bad-tempered, *a.* Acariâtre.

baffle, *v.tr.* (*a*) Confondre, déconcerter. (*b*) Déjouer ; frustrer.

bag¹, *s.* **1.** Sac *m.* **2.** Poche *f.*

bag², *v.i.* Bouffer.

bagatelle, *s.* **1.** Bagatelle *f.* **2.** Billard anglais.

bagful, *s.* Sac plein ; plein sac.

baggage, *s.* Bagage *m.*

baggy, *a.* (Vêtement) trop ample.

bagpipes, *s.pl.* Cornemuse *f.*

Bahamas(the). *Pr.n.* Les Lucayes *f.*

bail¹, *s.* Caution *f,* garant *m.*

bail², *v.tr.* **To b. out,** vider.

bailiff, *s.* Huissier *m.*

bait¹, *s.* Amorce *f* ; appât *m.*

bait², *v.tr.* **1.** Harceler. **2.** Amorcer.

baize, *s.* Serge *f,* reps *m.*

bake. 1. *v.tr.* Cuire. faire cuire. **2.** *v.i.* Cuire.

bakehouse, *s.* Boulangerie *f.*

bakelite, *s.* Bakélite.

baker, *s.* Boulanger, -ère. **Baker's shop,** boulangerie *f.*

baking, *s.* Cuisson *f.*

baking-powder, *s.* Poudre *f* à lever.

Balaclava. *Pr.n.* **B. helmet,** passe-montagne *m.*

balance¹, *s.* **1.** Balance *f.* **2.** Équilibre *m.* **To keep one's b.,** se tenir en équilibre. **3.** (*a*) **B. in hand,** solde créditeur. (*b*) **On b.,** à tout prendre.

balance². **1.** *v.tr.* (*a*) Balancer, peser. (*b*) Équilibrer ; faire contrepoids à. **2.** *v.i.* (*a*) Se faire contrepoids ; se balancer. (*b*) Osciller, balancer.

balanced, *a.* Équilibré ; compensé.

balance-sheet, *s.* Bilan *m.*

balancing¹, *a.* Compensateur, -trice.

balancing², *s.* **1.** Balancement *m.* **2.** (*a*) Mise *f* en équilibre. (*b*) Règlement *m,* solde *m.* **3.** Ajustement *m.*

balcony, *s.* Balcon *m.*

bald, *a.* **1.** Chauve. **2.** Plat ; sec.

bald-headed, *a.* Chauve.

baldly, *adv.* Nûment, platement.

baldness, *s.* **1.** (*a*) Calvitie *f.* (*b*) Nudité *f.* **2.** Platitude *f.*

bale¹, *s.* Balle *f,* ballot *m.*

bale², *v.i.* **To b. out,** se lancer en parachute.

Balearic, *a.* **The B. Islands,** les Baléares.

baleful, *a.* Sinistre, funeste.

balk¹, *s.* **1.** Obstacle *m.* **2.** Poutre *f.*

balk². **1.** *v.tr.* (*a*) Frustrer. (*b*) Entraver. **2.** *v.i.* Refuser. **To b. at,** reculer devant.

ball¹, *s.* **1.** Boule *f* ; balle *f* (de tennis) ; ballon *m* (de football) ; bille *f* (de billard) ; pelote *f* (de laine). **2.** Globe *m* (de l'œil).

ball², *s.* Bal *m, pl.* bals.

ballad, *s.* **1.** Romance *f.* **2.** Ballade *f.*

ballast, *s.* Lest *m.*

ball-bearings, *s.pl.* Roulement *m* à billes.

ball-cartridge, *s.* Cartouche *f* à balle.

ballet, *s.* Ballet *m.*

ballet-dancer, *s.* Danseur, -euse, d'opéra ; ballerine *f.*

balloon, *s.* Ballon *m,* aérostat *m.*

ballot¹, *s.* Scrutin *m,* vote *m.*

ballot². *v.i.* (*a*) Voter au scrutin. (*b*) Tirer au sort.

ballot-box, *s.* Urne *f* de scrutin.

balloting, *s.* **1.** Élection *f* au scrutin. **2.** Tirage *m* au sort.

ball-room, s. Salle f de bal.
balm, s. Baume m.
balmy, a. Embaumé, parfumé.
balsam, s. Baume m.
Baltic, a. & s. Baltique f.
baluster, s. Balustre m.
balustrade, s. Balustrade f.
bamboo, s. Bambou m.
ban[1], s. (a) Ban m, proscription f. (b) Interdit m.
ban[2], v.tr. Interdire.
banal, a. Banal, -aux.
banality, s. Banalité f.
banana, s. Banane f. **B.(-tree),** bananier m.
band[1], s. (a) Lien m; cercle m; ruban m. **Elastic b.,** élastique m. (b) Bande f.
band[2], s. **1.** (a) Bande f, troupe f. (b) Compagnie f. **2.** (a) Orchestre m. (b) Musique f. **Brass b.,** fanfare f.
band[3], v.i. To b. (together), se bander.
bandage[1], s. Bandage m; bandeau m.
bandage[2], v.tr. Bander.
bandbox, s. Carton m à chapeau(x).
bandit, s. Bandit m, brigand m.
bandmaster, s. Chef m de musique.
bandolier, s. Bandoulière f.
bandsman, s. Musicien m.
bandstand, s. Kiosque m à musique.
bandy[1], v.tr. (Se) renvoyer (des paroles); échanger (des plaisanteries).
bandy[2], a. Bancal, -als.
bandy-legged, a. Bancal, -als.
bane, s. Fléau m, peste f.
baneful, a. Funeste; pernicieux.
banefully, adv. Pernicieusement.
bang[1], s. Coup (violent); détonation f.
bang[2]. **1.** v.i. (a) Frapper avec bruit. (b) Claquer. **2.** v.tr. (a) Frapper (violemment). (b) (Faire) claquer.
bang[3], int. Pan! v'lan! boum!
bang[4], s. Coiffure f à la chien.
banging, s. (a) Coups violents; claquement m. (b) Détonations fpl.
bangle, s. Bracelet m.
banish, v.tr. Bannir, exiler.
banishment, s. Bannissement m, proscription f, exil m.
banisters, s.pl. Balustres m; rampe f.
banjo, s. Banjo m.
bank[1], s. **1.** (a) Talus m; remblai m. (b) Banc m (de sable). **2.** Berge f, rive f.

bank[2]. **1.** v.tr. (a) To b. up, remblayer. (b) Couvrir (un feu). **2.** v.i. S'entasser. **3.** v.i. Pencher l'avion.
bank[3], s. Banque f. **B. account,** compte en banque.
bank, v.tr. & i. Mettre en banque.
bank-book, s. Livret m de banque.
banker, s. Banquier m.
bank-holiday, s. Fête légale.
banking, s. Opérations fpl de banque.
bank-note, s. Billet m de banque.
bankrupt, a. & s. Failli, -e; banqueroutier, -ère. **To go b.,** faire faillite.
bankruptcy, s. Faillite f; banqueroute f.
banner, s. Bannière f, étendard m.
banns, s.pl. Bans m.
banquet, s. Banquet m.
banter[1], s. Badinage m.
banter[2], v.tr. & i. Badiner.
bantering, a. Railleur, -euse.
baptism, s. Baptême m.
baptize, v.tr. Baptiser.
bar[1], s. **1.** (a) Barre f. (b) pl. Barreaux m. **2.** Empêchement m, obstacle m. **3.** Called to the bar, reçu avocat. **4.** Bar m; buvette f. **5.** (a) Barre, ligne f. (b) Mesure f.
bar[2], v.tr. **1.** Barrer. **2.** Défendre, prohiber.
barb[1], s. Barbillon m.
barb[2], v.tr. Garnir de barbillons.
Barbados. Pr.n. La Barbade.
barbarian, a. & s. Barbare (mf).
barbaric, a. Barbare.
barbarism, s. Barbarie f.
barbarity, s. Barbarie f, cruauté f.
barbarous, a. **1.** Barbare. **2.** Cruel, barbare, inhumain.
barbarously, adv. Cruellement.
barbed, a. **B. wire,** fil de fer barbelé.
barber, s. Barbier m, coiffeur m.
bard, s. Barde m.
bare[1], a. **1.** Nu; dénudé. **To lay b.,** mettre à nu, exposer. **Cards:** Ace b., as sec. **2.** Faible. **A b. living,** juste de quoi vivre.
bare[2], v.tr. Mettre à nu.
barefaced, a. Éhonté, cynique.
barefoot, adv. Nu-pieds; pieds nus.
barefooted, a. Aux pieds nus; les pieds nus.
bare-headed, a. & adv. Nu-tête, tête nue.
barely, adv. A peine, tout juste.
bareness, s. Nudité f, dénuement m.

bargain[1], s. **1.** (a) Marché m, affaire f. (b) Occasion f. **Into the b.,** par-dessus le marché. **2. B. sale,** vente de soldes.

bargain[2], v.i. (a) Négocier. (b) Marchander.

barge, s. Chaland m, péniche f.

baritone, s. Baryton m.

bark[1], s. Écorce f. **Peruvian b.,** quinquina m.

bark[2], s. Aboiement m, aboi m.

bark[3], v.i. Aboyer.

bark[1], s. Barque f.

barking, s. Aboiement m.

barley, s. Orge f.

barley-sugar, s. Sucre m d'orge.

barmaid, s. Demoiselle f de comp-toir.

barman, s. Garçon m de comptoir.

barn, s. Grange f.

barnacle, s. Bernache f.

barn-door, s. Porte f de grange.

barometer, s. Baromètre m.

baron, s. Baron m.

baroness, s. Baronne f.

baronet, s. Baronnet m.

barrack, s. Caserne f; quartier m.

barrack room, s. Chambrée f.

barrage, s. Tir m de barrage.

barred, a. Barré; muni de barreaux.

barrel, s. **1.** Tonneau m, barrique f, fût m. **2.** Cylindre m; canon m (de fusil).

barrel-organ, s. Orgue m de Bar-barie.

barren, a. Stérile, improductif.

barrenness, s. Stérilité f.

barricade[1], s. Barricade f.

barricade[2], v.tr. Barricader.

barrier, s. Barrière f.

barrister, s. Avocat m.

barrow, s. **1.** Charrette f à bras; civière f. **2.** Baladeuse f; voiture f à bras.

barter[1], s. Échange m; troc m.

barter[2], v.tr. Échanger, troquer.

Bartholomew, Pr.n. Barthélemy m.

basalt, s. Basalte m.

base[1], s. Base f.

base[2], v.tr. Baser, fonder.

base[3], a. Bas, vil.

baseless, a. Sans base, sans fonde-ment.

basely, adv. Bassement, vilement.

basement, s. Sous-sol m.

baseness, s. Bassesse f.

bash, v.tr. Cogner; défoncer.

bashful, a. (a) Timide. (b) Modeste, pudique.

bashfully, adv. (a) Timidement. (b) Pudiquement.

bashfulness, s. Timidité f; fausse honte.

basic, a. Fondamental.

basin, s. (a) Bassin m; écuelle f, bol m. (b) Cuvette f.

basis, s. Base f; fondement m.

bask, v.i. Se chauffer; prendre le soleil.

basket, s. Corbeille f; panier m.

basketful, s. Plein panier.

basket-work, s. Vannerie f.

bass, a. & s. Basse f. **B. voice,** voix de basse.

bassoon, s. Basson m.

bastard. I. a. & s. Bâtard, -e. **2.** a. Faux, f. fausse.

bastion, s. Bastion m.

bat[1], s. Chauve-souris f, pl. chauves-souris.

bat[2], s. Batte f.

bat[3], v.i. Être au guichet.

batch, s. Lot m.

bate, v.tr. **With bated breath,** en baissant la voix.

bath[1], s. **1.** Bain m. **Turkish baths,** hammam m. **2.** Baignoire f.

bath[2]. **1.** v.tr. Baigner. **2.** v.i. Prendre un bain.

bathe[1], s. Bain m; baignade f.

bathe[2]. **1.** v.tr. (a) Baigner. (b) Laver. **2.** v.i. Se baigner.

bather, s. Baigneur, -euse.

bathing, s. Bains mpl.

bathing-costume, s. Costume m de bain(s).

bathing-drawers, s.pl. Caleçon m de bain.

bath-mat, s. Descente f de bain.

bath-room, s. Salle f de bain(s).

bath-tub, s. Baignoire f.

batman, s. Ordonnance m or f.

baton, s. Bâton m.

batsman, s. Batteur m.

battalion, s. Bataillon m.

batter[1], s. Pâte f lisse.

batter[2], v.tr. Battre.

battered, a. Délabré; bossué.

battering-ram, s. Bélier m.

battery, s. **1.** Batterie f. **2.** El: Pile f.

battle, s. Bataille f, combat m.

battle-axe, s. Hache f d'armes.

battle-field, s. Champ m de bataille.

battlements, s.pl. (a) Créneaux m. (b) Parapet m, rempart m.

battleship, s. Cuirassé m.

baulk[1,2], = BALK[1,2].

bawl, v.tr. & i. Brailler; crier à tue-tête.

bay[1], s. Bay(-tree), laurier m.

bay[2], s. Baie f.

bay[3], s. Enfoncement m; baie f.

bay[4], s. Aboi m, aboiement m. At bay, aux abois.

bay[5], v.i. Aboyer.

bay[6], a. & s. Bai (m).

baying, s. Aboiement m.

bayonet[1], s. Baïonnette f.

bayonet[2], v.tr. Percer d'un coup de baïonnette.

bay-window, s. Fenêtre f en saillie.

bazaar, s. 1. Bazar m. 2. Vente f de charité.

be, v.i. Être. 1. (a) He is an Englishman, il est Anglais. (b) Three and two are five, trois et deux font cinq. 2. (a) To be in danger, se trouver en danger. Here I am, me voici. (b) How are you? comment allez-vous? (c) How much is that? combien cela coûte-t-il? (d) To-morrow is Friday, c'est demain vendredi. 3. (a) To be cold, avoir froid. (b) To be twenty, avoir vingt ans. 4. (a) That may be, cela se peut. (b) Impers. There is, there are, il y a. 5. I have been into every room, j'ai visité toutes les pièces. Has anyone been? est-il venu quelqu'un? 6. Impers. (a) It is fine, il fait beau. (b) It is said, on dit. As it were, pour ainsi dire. 7. (a) I am doing sth., je fais qch. (b) He is allowed, on lui permet. He is to be pitied, il est à plaindre. What is to be done? que faire? (c) I am to see him to-morrow, je dois le voir demain. 8. To be for s.o., tenir pour qn. 9. He is back.—Is he? il est de retour.—Vraiment?

beach, s. Plage f, grève f, rivage m.

beacon, s. Balise f.

bead, s. 1. To tell one's beads, dire son chapelet. 2. Perle f. (String of) beads, collier m.

beading, s. Garniture f de perles.

beadle, s. Bedeau m.

beak, s. Bec m.

beaker, s. Gobelet m; coupe f.

beam[1], s. 1. Poutre f; solive f. 2. Rayon m.

beam[2], v.i. Rayonner.

beaming, a. Rayonnant; radieux.

bean, s. Fève f. **French beans,** haricots verts.

bear[1], s. 1. Ours m. **She-b.,** ourse f. Bear's cub, ourson m. 2. Baissier m.

bear[2], v.tr. & i. (a) Porter. To b. oneself well, se bien comporter. (b) Supporter, soutenir. To b. with, être indulgent pour. (c) To b. to the right, appuyer à droite. (d) Donner naissance à. **bear out,** v.tr. Confirmer. **bear up,** v.i. To b. up against, faire face à.

bearable, a. Supportable.

beard, s. Barbe f.

bearded, a. Barbu.

beardless, a. Imberbe; sans barbe.

bearer, s. 1. (a) Porteur, -euse. (b) Titulaire mf (d'un passeport).

bearing, s. 1. Port m, maintien m. 2. (a) Beyond (all) b., insupportable. (b) To take one's bearings, s'orienter. (c) Portée f. **B. on,** rapport m avec.

bearish, a. Bourru.

beast, s. Bête f.

beastly, a. (a) Bestial, -aux. (b) Sale, dégoûtant.

beat[1], s. 1. (a) Battement m; batterie f. (b) Mesure f, temps m. 2. Ronde f.

beat[2], v.tr. & i. Battre. 1. To b. a retreat, se retirer. 2. (a) That beats everything! ça c'est le comble! (b) To b. the record, battre le record. **beat back,** v.tr. Repousser, refouler. **beat down,** v.tr. Abattre. **beat in,** v.tr. Enfoncer, défoncer. **beat off,** v.tr. Repousser.

beaten, a. Battu.

beating, s. 1. Battement m. 2. (a) Coups mpl; rossée f. (b) Défaite f.

beau, s. Prétendant m; galant m.

beautiful, a. Beau, belle.

beautify, v.tr. Embellir, enjoliver.

beauty, s. Beauté f.

beaver, s. Castor m.

becalmed, a. Encalminé.

because. 1. conj. Parce que. 2. Prep. phr. B. of, à cause de.

beckon, v.tr. & i. Faire signe; appeler de la main.

become. 1. v.i. Devenir; se faire.

(a) To b. old, vieillir. **To b. accustomed,** s'accoutumer. (b) **What has b. of X?** qu'est devenu X? **2.** v.tr Convenir à, aller (bien) à.

becoming, a. **1.** Convenable bienséant. **2.** Seyant.

becomingly, adv. Convenablement.

bed, s. **1.** Lit m. **To go to bed,** se coucher. **To take to one's bed,** s'aliter. **To get out of bed,** se lever. **2.** Banc m (d'huîtres).

bed-clothes, s.pl. Couvertures f (de lit).

bed-cover, s. Dessus m de lit.

bedding, s. Literie f.

bedfellow, s. Camarade mf de lit.

bedizen, v.tr. Attifer, chamarrer.

bedlam, s. Charivari m, tohu-bohu m.

bed-post, s. Colonne f de lit.

bed-ridden, a. Cloué au lit.

bedroom, s. Chambre f à coucher.

bedside, s. Chevet m; bord m du lit.

bedstead, s. Bois m de lit, lit m.

bedtime, s. Heure f du coucher.

bee, s. Abeille f.

beech, s. Hêtre m.

beech-nut, s. Faîne f.

beef, s. Bœuf m. **Roast b.,** rosbif m.

beef-steak, s. Bifteck m, tournedos m.

beef-tea, s. Bouillon m.

beehive, s. Ruche f.

bee-keeper, s. Apiculteur m.

bee-line, s. **To make a b.-l.** for, aller droit vers.

beer, s. Bière f.

beeswax, s. Cire f d'abeilles.

beet, s. Betterave f.

beetle, s. Coléoptère m; scarabée m.

beetroot, s. Betterave f.

befitting, a. Convenable, seyant.

before. 1. adv. (a) En avant; devant. (b) Auparavant, avant; précédent. **The day b.,** la veille. **I have seen him b.,** je l'ai déjà vu. **2.** prep. (a) Devant. **B. my eyes,** sous mes yeux. (b) Avant. **3.** conj. Avant que; avant de.

beforehand, adv. Préalablement; d'avance.

befriend, v.tr. Secourir.

beg, v.tr. & i. **1.** Mendier. **2.** Solliciter; supplier. **I beg (of) you** je vous en prie!

beget, v.tr. **1.** Engendrer. **2.** Causer.

beggar[1], s. **1.** Mendiant, -e, pauvre, -esse. **2. Poor b.!** pauvre diable! **Lucky b.!** veinard!

beggar[2], v.tr. Réduire à la mendicité.

beggarly, a. Chétif, misérable.

beggary, s. Mendicité f, misère f.

begging, s. Mendicité f.

begin, v.tr. & i. Commencer; se mettre à. **To b. with,** tout d'abord. **To b. again,** recommencer.

beginner, s. Commençant, -e, débutant, -e.

beginning, s. Commencement m; début m; origine f.

begrudge, v.tr. Donner à contrecœur; envier à.

beguile, v.tr. **1.** Enjôler séduire. **2.** Distraire, amuser.

behalf, s. **1.** On b. of, au nom de; de la part de. **2. In b. of,** en faveur de.

behave, v.i. Se conduire, se comporter. **To know how to b.,** savoir vivre. **B. yourself!** sois sage!

behaviour, s. Tenue f, maintien m; conduite f.

behead, v.tr. Décapiter.

behest, s. Ordre m.

behind. 1. adv. Derrière; par derrière. (a) **To remain b.,** rester en arrière. (b) En retard. **2.** prep. (a) Derrière. (b) En arrière de, en retard sur.

behindhand, adv. & pred. a. En arrière; en retard; attardé.

behold, v.tr. Voir; apercevoir.

being[1], a. **For the time b.,** pour le moment.

being[2], s. **1.** Existence. **2.** Être.

belabour, v.tr. Rouer de coups.

belated, a. **1.** Attardé. **2.** Tardif.

belch. 1. v.i. Éructer. **2.** v.tr. Vomir (des flammes).

beleaguer, v.tr. Assiéger.

belfry, s. Beffroi m, clocher m.

Belgian, a. & s. Belge (mf).

Belgium. Pr.n. La Belgique.

belief, s. **1.** Croyance f. **2. B. in.,** confiance f en.

believe. 1. v.tr. Croire; ajouter foi à. **To make s.o. b.,** faire accroire à qn. **2.** v.i. Croire. **3. To make b.** faire semblant.

believer, s. **1.** Croyant, -e. **2. A b.** in, un partisan de.

belittle, v.tr. Rabaisser, déprécier.

bell, s. Cloche f; clochette f; sonnette f; timbre m; grelot m. **Electric b.,** sonnerie f (électrique). **To ring the b.,** sonner.

belladonna, *s.* Belladone *f.*

belle, *s.* Beauté *f.*

belligerent, *a. & s.* Belligérant (*m*).

bellow[1], *s.* (*a*) Beuglement *m*, mugissement *m.* (*b*) Hurlement *m.*

bellow[2], *v.i.* Beugler, mugir ; hurler.

bellows, *s.pl* Soufflet *m.*

bell-pull, *s.* Cordon *m* de sonnette.

bell-push, *s.* Bouton *m.*

bell-ringer, *s.* Sonneur *m.*

bell-tower, *s.* Clocher *m.*

belly, *s.* Ventre *m.*

belong, *v.i.* **1.** Appartenir. **2.** Faire partie (*to*, de).

belongings, *s.pl.* Affaires *f*, effets *m.*

beloved, *a. & s.* Bien-aimé(e).

below. 1. *adv.* (*a*) En bas, (au-)dessous. **Here b.,** ici-bas. (*b*) Ci-dessous. **2.** *prep.* (*a*) Au-dessous de. (*b*) Sous.

belt, *s.* **1.** Ceinture *f* ; ceinturon *m* ; baudrier *m.* **2.** Courroie *f.*

bemoan, *v.tr* Pleurer, déplorer.

bemuse, *v.tr.* Stupéfier.

bench, *s.* **1.** Banc *m* ; banquette *f.* **2.** Établi *m.*

bend[1], *s.* Courbure *f* ; courbe *f* ; coude *m* ; virage *m* ; méandre *m.*

bend[2], *v.tr. & i.* **1.** Courber ; plier ; fléchir ; baisser. **2.** *v.tr.* Tendre. **bend down,** *v.i.* Se courber ; se baisser. **bend forward,** *v.i.* Se pencher en avant.

beneath. 1. *adv.* Dessous, au-dessous. **2.** *prep.* Au-dessous de ; sous. **It is b.** him, il est indigne de lui.

benedictine. 1. *a. & s.* Bénédictin, -e. **2.** *s.* Bénédictine *f.*

benediction, *s.* Bénédiction *f.*

benefaction, *s.* Bienfait *m.*

benefactor, *s.* Bienfaiteur, -trice.

benefice, *s.* Bénéfice *m.*

beneficence, *s.* Bienfaisance *f.*

beneficent, *a.* Bienfaisant.

beneficial, *a.* Profitable, avantageux.

beneficially, *adv.* Avantageusement.

beneficiary, *s.* Bénéficiaire *m.*

benefit[1], *s.* **1.** Avantage *m*, profit *m* ; bénéfice *m.* **2.** Indemnité *f.*

benefit[2]. **1.** *v.tr.* Faire du bien, être avantageux, profiter, à. **2.** *v.i.* To b. by, profiter de.

benevolence, *s.* Bienveillance *f*, bonté *f.*

benevolent, *a.* Bienveillant.

benevolently, *adv.* Avec bienveillance.

benign, *a.* Bénin, *f.* bénigne.

benignant, *a.* Bénin, *f.* bénigne.

bent[1], *s.* Penchant *m*, inclination *f.*

bent[2], *a.* **1.** (*a*) Courbé, plié. **B.** back, dos voûté. (*b*) Faussé. **2.** Résolu, décidé (*on*, à).

benumb, *v.tr.* Engourdir, transir.

bequeath, *v.tr.* Léguer.

bequest, *s.* Legs *m.*

bereave, *v.tr.* Priver.

bereavement, *s.* Perte *f* ; deuil *m.*

beret, *s.* Béret *m.*

berry, *s.* Baie *f.*

berth, *s.* **1.** (*a*) To give a wide b., éviter. (*b*) Poste *m* de mouillage. **2.** Couchette *f.* **3.** Place *f*, emploi *m.*

beryl, *s.* Béryl *m.*

beseech, *v.tr.* Supplier, adjurer, conjurer (*to*, de).

beseeching, *a.* Suppliant.

beset, *v.tr.* Entouré (*with*, de).

beside, *prep.* **1.** A côté, auprès, de. **2.** (*a*) **B. the point,** en dehors du sujet. (*b*) **B. oneself,** hors de soi.

besides. 1. *adv.* (*a*) En outre, en plus. (*b*) D'ailleurs. **2.** *prep.* En plus de.

besiege, *v.tr.* Assiéger.

bespatter, *v.tr.* Éclabousser.

bespeak, *v.tr.* Commander ; retenir.

bespoke, *a.* (Fait) sur mesure.

best[1]. **1.** *a. & s.* (*a*) (Le) meilleur, (la) meilleure ; le mieux. **B. man,** garçon d'honneur. **In one's b.,** endimanché. **The b. of it,** le plus beau de l'affaire. **To do one's b.,** faire son mieux. **To get the b. of it,** avoir le dessus. (*b*) *Adv.phr.* **At b.,** pour dire le mieux. **To the b. of my belief,** à ce que je crois. **2.** *adv.* (Le) mieux. **As b. I could,** de mon mieux.

best[2], *v.tr* L'emporter sur.

bestial, *a.* Bestial, -aux.

bestow, *v.tr.* Accorder, donner.

best-seller, *s.* Livre *m* à succès.

bet[1], *s.* Pari *m*, gageure *f.*

bet[2], *v.tr.* Parier.

betide, *v.tr.* Woe b. him, malheur à lui.

betimes, *adv.* De bonne heure.

betoken, *v.tr.* **1.** Dénoter. **2.** Présager, annoncer.

betray, *v.tr.* Trahir.

betrayal, *s.* Trahison *f.*

betrothal, *s.* Fiançailles *fpl.*

betrothed, *a. & s.* Fiancé(e).

better[1]. **1.** *a. & s.* Meilleur. **I had hoped for b. things,** j'avais espéré mieux.

2. Mieux. That's b., voilà qui est mieux. **So much the b.,** tant mieux. **To get b.,** s'améliorer; guérir. **To be b.,** aller mieux. **To get the b. of,** l'emporter sur. **3.** *adv.* (*a*) Mieux. **To think b. of it,** se raviser. (*b*) B. known, plus connu.

better², *v.tr.* (*a*) Améliorer. (*b*) Surpasser.

betting, *s.* Les paris *m*.

between, *prep.* Entre. (*a*) **B. now and Monday,** d'ici (à) lundi. **B. twenty and thirty,** de vingt à trente. (*b*) **B. ourselves,** entre nous.

bevel, *s.* Biseau *m*, biais *m*.

bevelled, *a.* En biseau.

beverage, *s.* Breuvage *m*, boisson *f*.

bevy, *s.* Bande *f*, troupe *f*.

bewail, *v.tr.* Pleurer.

beware, *v.ind.tr.* Se méfier. **B.!** prenez garde !

bewilder, *v.tr.* Désorienter, égarer; ahurir.

bewildered, *a.* Désorienté; ahuri.

bewildering, *a.* Déroutant.

bewilderment, *s.* Désorientation *f*; ahurissement *m*.

bewitch, *v.tr.* Ensorceler.

bewitching, *a.* Ensorcelant; ravissant.

beyond. 1. *adv.* Au delà, par delà, plus loin. **2.** *prep.* Au delà de, par delà. **It is b. me,** cela me dépasse. **B. doubt,** hors de doute.

bias, *s.* **1.** Déviation *f*. **2.** Prévention *f*; parti pris.

biased, *a.* Partial, -aux.

bib, *s.* Bavette *f*.

Bible, *s.* Bible *f*.

biblical, *a.* Biblique.

bibliography, *s.* Bibliographie *f*.

bicarbonate, *s.* Bicarbonate *m*.

bicker, *v.i.* Se chamailler.

bicycle, *s.* Bicyclette *f*.

bid¹, *s.* (*a*) Enchère *f*, offre *f*. (*b*) *Cards:* Appel *m*.

bid², *v.tr. & i.* **1.** Commander, ordonner (à). **2. To bid fair,** promettre. **3.** (*a*) **To bid for,** mettre une enchère sur. (*b*) *Cards:* Appeler.

bidding, *s.* Commandement *m* ordre *m*.

bier, *s.* Civière *f*.

big. 1. *a.* (*a*) Grand ; gros. (*b*) Lourd (de conséquences). **2.** *adv.* **To talk big,** faire l'important.

bigamist, *s.* Bigame *mf*

bigamy, *s.* Bigamie *f*.

bigot, *s.* Fanatique *mf*.

bigoted, *a.* Fanatique.

bigotry, *s.* Fanatisme *m*.

bigwig, *s.* Gros bonnet.

bile, *s.* Bile *f*.

bilge, *s.* Eau *f* de cale.

bilingual, *a.* Bilingue.

bilious, *a.* Bilieux.

biliousness, *s.* Attaque *f* de bile.

bill¹, *s.* Bec *m*.

bill², *s.* **1.** Note *f*, mémoire *m*; addition *f*. **2. B. of exchange,** lettre *f* de change. **3.** Affiche *f*, placard *m*. **4. B. of fare,** carte *f* du jour. **5.** Projet *m* de loi.

billet¹, *s.* **1.** Logement *m*. **2.** Place *f*, emploi *m*.

billet², *v.tr.* Loger.

billiard-ball, *s.* Bille *f* de billard.

billiard-room, *s.* Salle *f* de billard.

billiards, *s.pl.* (Jeu *m* de) billard *m*

billiard-table, *s.* Billard *m*.

billion, *s.* Trillion *m*.

billow, *s.* Grande vague; lame *f*.

billy-goat, *s.* Bouc *m*.

bin, *s.* Coffre *m*, huche *f*.

bind, *v.tr.* Attacher, lier. **1. Bound hand and foot,** pieds et poings liés. **2.** Bander (une blessure). **3.** Relier. **Bound in paper,** broché. **4.** Lier engager.

binding¹, *a.* Obligatoire (*upon*, pour).

binding², *s.* Reliure *f*.

biographer, *s.* Biographe *m*.

biographical, *a.* Biographique.

biography, *s.* Biographie *f*.

biology, *s.* Biologie *f*.

biped, *a. & s.* Bipède (*m*).

birch, *s.* **1.** Bouleau *m*. **2.** Verge *f*.

bird, *s.* Oiseau *m*.

bird-cage, *s.* Cage *f* d'oiseau.

bird-catcher, *s.* Oiseleur *m*.

bird-lime, *s.* Glu *f*.

bird's-eye, *s.* **B.-e. view,** vue à vol d'oiseau.

biretta, *s.* Barrette *f*.

birth, *s.* Naissance *f*. **By b.,** de naissance.

birth-certificate, *s.* Acte *m* de naissance.

birthday, *s.* Anniversaire *m* de naissance.

birth-place, *s.* Lieu *m* de naissance.

birth-rate, *s.* Natalité *f*

Biscay. *Pr.n.* **The Bay of B.,** le golfe de Gascogne.

biscuit, *s.* Biscuit *m.* **Fancy biscuits,** petits fours.

bisect, *v.tr.* Couper, diviser.

bishop, *s.* **1.** Évêque *m.* **2.** *Chess:* Fou *m.*

bishopric, *s.* Évêché *m.*

bismuth, *s.* Bismuth *m.*

bit[1], *s.* **1.** Mors *m.* **2.** Mèche *f.*

bit[2], *s.* **1.** (*a*) Morceau *m.* (*b*) Bout *m*, brin *m.* **2.** **A bit** (of), un peu (de). **A good bit,** sensiblement. **Not a bit** (of it)! n'en croyez rien !

bitch, *s.* Chienne *f.*

bite[1], *s.* **1.** (*a*) Coup *m* de dent. (*b*) *Fish:* Touche *f.* **2.** (*a*) Morsure *f.* (*b*) Piqûre *f.*

bite[2], *v.tr.* Mordre ; piquer.

biting, *a.* Mordant ; cuisant ; cinglant.

bitter, *a.* **1.** Amer ; (vent) piquant ; implacable. **B. experience,** expérience cruelle. **2.** *s.pl.* Amer(s) *m.*

bitter-end, *s.* **To the b.-e.,** à outrance ; jusqu'au bout.

bitterly, *adv.* **1.** Amèrement, avec amertume. **2.** Cruellement.

bitterness, *s.* (*a*) Amertume *f.* (*b*) Rigueur *f.* ; aigreur *f.*

bivalve, *a. & s.* Bivalve (*m*).

bivouac[1], *s.* Bivouac *m.*

bivouac[2], *v.i.* Bivouaquer.

bizarre, *a.* Bizarre.

black[1]. **I.** *a.* Noir. **B. and blue,** tout bleu. **B. eye,** œil poché. **II. black,** *s.* Noir *m.* **In b. and white,** par écrit.

black[2], *v.tr.* **1.** Noircir. **To b. boots,** cirer des chaussures. **2. To b. out,** obscurcir ; blackouter.

black-beetle, *s.* Blatte *f*, cafard *m.*

blackberry, *s.* Mûre *f* (de ronce).

blackbird, *s.* Merle *m.*

blackboard, *s.* Tableau noir.

blacken. **1.** *v.tr.* Noircir ; obscurcir. **2.** *v.i.* Devenir noir.

blackguard, *s.* Vaurien *m.*

blackguardly, *a.* Ignoble, canaille

blacking, *s.* Cirage *m.*

blacking-brush, *s.* Brosse *f* à cirer.

blackish, *a.* Noirâtre.

black-lead, *s.* Mine *f* de plomb.

blackleg, *s.* Renard *m* ; jaune *m.*

blackmail[1], *s.* Chantage *m.*

blackmail[2], *v.tr.* Faire chanter.

blackmailer, *s.* Maître-chanteur *m.*

blackness, *s.* Noirceur *f* ; obscurité *f.*

black-out, *s.* Blackout *m.*

blacksmith, *s.* Forgeron *m.*

blackthorn, *s.* **1.** Épine noire. **2.** Gourdin *m.*

bladder, *s.* Vessie *f.*

blade, *s.* **1.** Brin *m* (d'herbe). **2.** (*a*) Lame *f* (de couteau). (*b*) Sabre *m*, épée *f.* **3.** Pelle *f*, pale *f* (d'aviron).

blame[1], *s.* **1.** Reproches *mpl* ; condamnation *f.* **2.** Faute *f*, blâme *m.*

blame[2], *v.tr.* Blâmer, condamner. **He is to b.** il y a de sa faute.

blameless, *a.* Innocent, irréprochable.

blameworthy, *a.* Blâmable.

blanch. **1.** *v.tr.* Blanchir. **2.** *v.i.* Blêmir, pâlir.

blancmange, *s.* Blanc-manger *m.*

bland, *a.* Doux, *f.* douce ; affable ; débonnaire.

blandishment, *s.* Flatterie *f* ; cajoleries *fpl.*

blandly, *adv.* Avec affabilité.

blank. **I.** *a.* **1.** Blanc, *f.* blanche ; en blanc. **2. B. look,** regard sans expression. **II. blank,** *s.* **1.** Blanc *m.* vide *m.* **2.** Billet blanc.

blanket, *s.* Couverture *f.*

blankly, *adv.* D'un air confondu ; sans expression.

blaspheme, *v.i. & tr.* Blasphémer.

blasphemous, *a.* Blasphématoire.

blasphemy, *s.* Blasphème *m.*

blast[1], *s.* **1.** Coup *m* de vent ; rafale *f.* **2.** Son *m.* **3. In full b.,** en pleine activité. **4.** Souffle *m.*

blast[2], *v.tr.* (*a*) Faire sauter. (*b*) Ruiner ; détruire. (*c*) Foudroyer.

blasting, *s.* Anéantissement *m* ; foudroiement *m.*

blatant, *a.* **1.** Criard. **2.** Criant.

blaze[1], *s.* **1.** Flamme(s) *f*, flambée *f.* **2.** Flamboiement *m* ; éclat *m.*

blaze[2], *v.i.* (*a*) Flamber ; flamboyer.

blazer, *s.* Blazer *m.*

blazing, *a.* (*a*) En feu ; enflammé ; embrasé. (*b*) Flambant.

blazon, *v.tr.* Publier, proclamer.

bleach, *v.tr. & i.* Blanchir.

bleaching, *s.* Blanchiment *m.*

bleak, *a.* **1.** (Terrain) exposé au vent. **2.** Morne. **3.** Froid.

bleat, *v.i.* Bêler.

bleating, s. Bêlement m.

bleed, v.tr. & i. Saigner.

bleeding[1], a. Saignant.

bleeding[2], s. Saignement m.

blemish[1], s. 1. Défaut m; imperfection f. 2. Tache f, tare f.

blemish[2], v.tr. Tacher, souiller.

blench, v.i. Sourciller, broncher.

blend[1], s. Mélange m.

blend[2]. 1. v.tr. Mélanger. 2. v.i. Se mêler, se confondre; s'allier.

blending, s. Mélange m; alliance f.

bless, v.tr. Bénir. **To be blessed with,** jouir de. **Well, I'm blest!** par exemple!

blessed, a. (a) Saint. (b) Bienheureux.

blessing, s. Bénédiction f; avantage m.

blight[1], s. Fléau m.

blight[2], v.tr. Flétrir.

blind[1], a. 1. Aveugle. **B. in one eye,** borgne. **To turn a b. eye to,** refuser de voir. 2. **B. alley,** cul-de-sac m, impasse f.

blind[2], v.tr. Aveugler.

blind[3], s. 1. Store m. **Venetian b.,** jalousie f. 2. Masque m, feinte f.

blindfold, a. & adv. 1. Les yeux bandés. 2. Aveuglément.

blindly, adv. Aveuglément; en aveugle.

blindness, s. 1. Cécité f. 2. Aveuglement m.

blink, v.i. Cligner les yeux; clignoter.

blinking, s. Clignotement m.

bliss, s. Béatitude f, félicité f.

blissful, a. (Bien)heureux.

blister[1], s. Ampoule f, bulle f.

blister[2], v.tr. Faire venir les ampoules à.

blithe, a. Joyeux.

blithely, adv. Joyeusement.

blizzard, s. Tempête f de neige.

bloated, a. Boursouflé, bouffi.

bloater, s. Hareng bouffi.

blob, s. Tache f; pâté m.

block[1], s. 1. (a) Bloc m. (b) Billot m. 2. Pâté m, îlot m (de maisons). 3. Encombrement m.

block[2], v.tr. Bloquer, obstruer. **block up,** v.tr. (a) Boucher, bloquer. (b) Obstruer.

blockade[1], s. Blocus m.

blockade[2], v.tr. Bloquer.

blockhead, s. Lourdaud m.

blond, a. & s. Blond, -e.

blood, s. Sang m. (a) **His b. was up,** il était monté. **In cold b.,** de sang-froid. **Bad b.,** inimitié f. (b) **B. horse,** (cheval) pur-sang m.

blood-curdling, a. A vous tourner les sangs.

bloodhound, s. Limier m.

bloodless, a. 1. Exsangue, anémié. 2. Sans effusion de sang.

blood-poisoning, s. Empoisonnement m du sang.

blood-relation, s. Parent(e) par le sang.

bloodshed, s. 1. Effusion f de sang. 2. Carnage m.

bloodshot, a. Injecté de sang.

blood-stain, s. Tache f de sang.

blood-stained, a. Taché de sang.

blood-sucker, s. Sangsue f, vampire m.

bloodthirsty, a. Sanguinaire; altéré de sang.

blood-vessel, s. Vaisseau sanguin.

bloody, a. Sanglant; sanguinaire.

bloom[1], s. 1. Fleur f. **In full b.,** épanoui; en pleine fleur. 2. Velouté m.

bloom[2], v.i. Fleurir; être en fleur.

blooming, a. Fleurissant; en fleur.

blossom[1], s. Fleur f.

blossom[2], v.i. Fleurir. **blossom out,** v.i. S'épanouir.

blot[1], s. Tache f; pâté m.

blot[2], v.tr. 1. Tacher, souiller. 2. Sécher l'encre. **blot out,** v.tr. 1. Effacer. 2. Exterminer.

blotch, s. Tache f, éclaboussure f.

blotchy, a. 1. Couperosé. 2. Tacheté.

blotter, s. Buvard m; bloc buvard.

blotting-pad, s. (Bloc) buvard m; sous-main m.

blotting-paper, s. Papier buvard.

blouse, s. Blouse f.

blow[1]. I. v.i. Souffler.
II. **blow,** v.tr. 1. Souffler. 2. **To b. the horn,** sonner du cor. 3. **To b. a fuse,** faire sauter les plombs. **blow about.** 1. v.i. Voler çà et là. 2. v.tr. Faire voler çà et là. **blow away,** v.tr. Emporter. **blow down,** v.tr. Abattre, renverser. **blow in.** 1. v.tr. Enfoncer. 2. v.i. Entrer. **blow off,** v.tr. (a) Emporter; souffler. (b) Purger (de la vapeur). **blow out,** v.tr. (a) Souffler, éteindre. (b) Gonfler. **blow over,**

v.tr. Renverser. **blow up. 1.** *v.i.*
Éclater, sauter. **2.** *v.tr.* (*a*) Faire
sauter. (*b*) Gonfler. (*c*) Semoncer.

blow², *s.* **1.** Coup *m.* **To come to
blows,** en venir aux mains. **2.** Coup
(du sort).

blow-fly, *s.* Mouche *f* à viande.

blow-pipe, *s.* **1.** Chalumeau *m.*
2. Sarbacane *f.*

blubber¹, *s.* Graisse *f* de baleine.

blubber², *v.i.* Pleurnicher.

bludgeon¹, *s.* Gourdin *m.*

bludgeon², *v.tr.* Asséner des coups
de gourdin à.

blue. I. *a.* Bleu, azuré. **B. spectacles,**
lunettes bleutées.

II. blue, *s.* **1.** Bleu *m,* azur *m.*
Out of the b., soudainement. **2.**
Indigo *m*; bleu (d'empois). **3.** *s.pl.*
To have the blues, avoir le cafard.

Bluebeard. *Pr.n.* Barbe-bleue *m.*

blue-bell, *s.* Jacinthe *f* des bois.

blue-black, *a.* Noir tirant sur le bleu.

bluebottle, *s.* Mouche *f* à viande.

blue jacket, *s.* Matelot.

blue-stocking, *s.* Bas-bleu *m.*

bluff¹. I. *a.* Brusque.

II. bluff, *s.* Cap *m* à pic; à-pic *m.*

bluff², *s.* Bluff *m.*

bluff³, *v.tr.* Faire du bluff.

bluish, *a.* Bleuâtre; bleuté.

blunder¹, *s.* Bévue *f,* erreur *f.*

blunder², *v.i. & tr.* **1.** Faire une
bévue, une maladresse. **2.** Se
heurter (contre qn).

blunderer, *s.* Maladroit, -e.

blundering, *a.* Brouillon, maladroit.

blunt¹, *a.* **1.** Émoussé; contondant.
2. Brusque.

blunt², *v.tr.* Émousser.

bluntly, *adv.* Brusquement, carrément.

bluntness, *s.* **1.** Manque *m* de tranchant. **2.** Brusquerie *f,* franchise *f.*

blur¹, *s.* **1.** Tache *f.* **2.** Brouillard *m.*

blur², *v.tr.* Brouiller.

blurt, *v.tr.* To b. out, laisser échapper.

blush¹, *s.* Rougeur *f.*

blush², *v.i.* Rougir.

blushing, *a.* Rougissant; timide.

bluster¹, *s.* (*a*) Fureur *f,* fracas *m.*
(*b*) Rodomontades *fpl.*

bluster², *v.i.* (*a*) Souffler en rafales.
(*b*) Faire le rodomont.

blustering, *a.* (*a*) Violent. (*b*)
Bravache.

boa, *s.* Boa *m.*

boar, *s.* Verrat *m.* **Wild b.,** sanglier *m.*

board¹, *s.* **1.** Planche *f.* **2.** (*a*) Table
f. (*b*) Nourriture *f,* pension *f.* **B.
and lodging,** pension et chambre(s).
With b. and lodging, nourri et logé.
(*c*) Table de jeu. **3.** (*a*) Commission
f. (*b*) **B. of directors,** (conseil *m*
d') administration *f.* **4.** Bord *m.* **On
b. (ship),** à bord d'un navire.

board². **1.** (*a*) *v.i.* Être en pension.
(*b*) *v.tr.* Nourrir. **3.** *v.tr.* Aller à
bord.

boarder, *s.* Pensionnaire *mf.*

boarding-house, *s.* Pension *f* de
famille.

boarding-school, *s.* Pensionnat *m,*
internat *m.*

boast¹, *s.* Vanterie *f.*

boast². 1. *v.i.* Se vanter. **2.** *v.tr.*
Être fier de posséder.

boaster, *s.* Vantard *m,* fanfaron *m.*

boastful, *a.* Vantard.

boastfully, *adv.* Avec vanterie.

boastfulness, *s.* Vantardise *f.*

boasting, *s.* Vantardise *f.*

boat, *s.* Bateau *m*; canot *m*; barque
f; navire *m.*

boat-builder, *s.* Constructeur *m* de
canots.

boat-hook, *s.* Gaffe *f.*

boat-house, *s.* Hangar *m* à bateaux.

boating, *s.* Canotage *m.*

boatman, *s.* Batelier *m.*

boat-race, *s.* Course *f* de bateaux.

boatswain, *s.* Maître *m* d'équipage.

boat-train, *s.* Train *m* du bateau.

bob¹, *s.* Coiffure *f* à la Ninon.

bob², *v.tr.* **To bob one's hair,** se faire
couper les cheveux à la nuque.

bobbin, *s.* Bobine *f.*

bode, *v.tr. & i.* Présager.

bodice, *s.* Corsage *m.*

bodiless, *a.* Sans corps.

bodily, *a.* Corporel, physique.

bodkin, *s.* (*a*) Passe-lacet *m.* (*b*)
Poinçon *m.*

body, *s.* Corps *m.* **1.** (*a*) (Dead) b.,
cadavre *m.* (*b*) Consistance *f.* **2. To
come in a b.,** venir en masse. **3.** Bâti
m, corps, caisse *f.*

body-guard, *s.* Garde *f* du corps.

bog¹, *s.* Fondrière *f*; marécage *m.*

bog², *v.tr.* Embourber, enliser.

bogey, *s.* **1.** Épouvantail *m.* **2.** *Golf:*
La normale du parcours.

bogey-man, s. Croque-mitaine m.

boggle, v.i. Rechigner.

boggy, a. Marécageux.

bogus, a. Faux, f. fausse; feint.

bogy, s. Épouvantail m.

Bohemian, a. De bohème.

boil[1], s. Furoncle m.

boil[2]. **1.** v.i. Bouillir. **2.** v.tr. Faire bouillir; faire cuire à l'eau. **Boiled egg,** œuf à la coque.

boiler, s. Chaudière f.

boiling, a. Bouillant. adv. **B. hot,** tout bouillant.

boisterous, a. Bruyant, turbulent; violent.

boisterously, adv. Bruyamment.

bold, a. **1.** Hardi; audacieux; assuré, confiant. **2.** Impudent effronté.

boldly, adv. **1.** Hardiment. **2.** Effrontément.

boldness, s. **1.** Hardiesse f; audace f. **2.** Effronterie f.

bole, s. Fût m, tronc m.

Bolshevik, a. & s. Bolcheviste (mf).

Bolshevism, s. Bolchevisme m.

bolster, s. Traversin m.

bolt[1], s. **1.** Verrou m. **2.** Boulon m; cheville f.

bolt[2]. **1.** v.i. (a) Décamper, déguerpir. (b) S'emballer, s'emporter. **2.** v.tr. Gober. **3.** v.tr. Verrouiller.

bomb[1], s. Bombe.

bomb[2], v.tr. Lancer des bombes sur.

bombard, v.tr. Bombarder.

bombardment, s. Bombardement m.

bombast, s. Grandiloquence f.

bombastic, a. Emphatique.

bomber, s. Avion m de bombardement.

bombing, s. Bombardement m.

bona fide, a. & adv. De bonne foi. **B. f. offer,** offre sérieuse.

bond, s. **1.** Lien m; attache f. **2.** (a) Contrat m; obligation f. (b) Bon m. (c) Caution f.

bondage, s. Esclavage m, servitude f.

bone, s. **1.** Os m. **2.** pl. (Of the dead) Ossements m.

bone-dry, a. Sec à l'absolu.

bonfire, s. Feu m de joie.

bonnet, s. **1.** Capote f; béguin m. **2.** Capot m.

bonus, s. Surpaye f; prime f.

bony, a. **1.** Osseux. **2.** Décharné.

boo[1]. **1.** int. Hou! **2.** s. Huée f.

boo[2], v.tr. & i. Huer, conspuer.

booby, s. Nigaud, -e, benêt m.

booing, s. Huées fpl.

book[1], s. **1.** (a) Livre m. (b) Livret m. **2.** Registre m; carnet m.

book[2], v.tr. **1.** Inscrire, enregistrer. **2.** Retenir, réserver. **3.** Abs. Prendre son billet.

bookbinder, s. Relieur m.

bookbinding, s. Reliure f.

bookcase, s. Bibliothèque f.

booking, s. Enregistrement m; location f; réservation f.

booking-office, s. Guichet m.

book-keeper, s. Comptable m.

book-keeping, s. Comptabilité f.

booklover, s. Bibliophile m.

book-maker, s. Bookmaker m.

book-mark, s. Signet m.

book-post, s. Service postal des imprimés.

bookseller, s. Libraire mf. **Second-hand b.,** bouquiniste m.

book-shelf, s. Rayon m.

bookshop, s. Librairie f.

bookstall, s. Bibliothèque f.

book-worm, s. Bouquineur m.

boom[1], s. Barrage m.

boom[2], s. Grondement m; mugissement m.

boom[3], v.i. Retentir, gronder, mugir.

boom[4], s. **1.** Hausse f rapide. **2.** Vague f de prospérité.

boom[5], v.i. Être en hausse.

boon, s. Bienfait m, avantage m.

boor, s. Rustre m, rustaud m.

boorish, a. Rustre, grossier.

boorishness, s. Grossièreté f.

boost, v.tr. Faire de la réclame pour.

boot, s. Chaussure f, bottine f.

boot-black, s. Décrotteur m.

booth, s. Baraque f, tente f.

bootlace, s. Lacet m.

boot-maker, s. Bottier m, cordonnier m.

boots, s. Garçon m d'étage.

booty, s. Butin m.

boracic, a. Borique. **B. ointment,** pommade à l'acide borique. **B. powder,** poudre boriquée.

borax, s. Borax m.

border[1], s. **1.** Bord m; lisière f; marge f; frontière f. **2.** Bordure.

border[2]. **1.** v.tr. Border. **2.** v.i. **To b. on,** toucher, confiner, à; être voisin de.

bordering, *a.* (*a*) Contigu, -uë, aboutissant (*on*, à). (*b*) B. **on,** qui frise.

border-land, *s.* (*a*) Pays *m* frontière, limitrophe; marche *f.* (*b*) Les confins *m* de l'au-delà.

border-line, *s.* **1.** Ligne *f* de séparation; frontière *f.* **2.** B.-l. **case,** cas limite.

bore¹, *s.* Calibre *m.*

bore², *v.tr. & i.* Creuser. To b. **through,** percer, perforer.

bore³, *s.* (*a*) Raseur, -euse. (*b*) Ennui *m*, scie *f.*

bore⁴, *v.tr.* Raser, assommer.

bore⁵, *s.* Mascaret *m*; raz *m* de marée.

boredom, *s.* Ennui *m.*

boric, *a.* Borique.

boring, *a.* Assommant, rasant.

born, *p.p.* To be b., naître.

borough, *s.* Ville *f.*

borrow, *v.tr.* Emprunter (*from*, à).

borrower, *s.* Emprunteur, -euse.

bosh, *s. & int.* Bêtises *fpl.*

bosom, *s.* **1.** Giron *m*, sein *m.* **2.** Poitrine *f.*

boss¹, *s.* Protubérance *f.*

boss², *s.* (*a*) Patron *m*; chef *m.* (*b*) Contremaître *m.*

botanical, *a.* Botanique.

botanist, *s.* Botaniste *mf.*

botany, *s.* Botanique *f.*

both. 1. *a. & pron.* Tous (les) deux, toutes (les) deux; l'un(e) et l'autre. To hold in b. **hands,** tenir à deux mains. B. **alike,** l'un comme l'autre. **2.** *adv.* B. . . . **and** . . . ., et . . . et . . . .

bother¹, *s.* Ennui *m*; tracas *m.*

bother². 1. *v.tr.* Gêner, ennuyer, tourmenter. **2.** *v.i.* S'inquiéter (*about*, de).

bothered, *a.* Inquiet, -ète; embarrassé.

bottle¹, *s.* **1.** Bouteille *f*; flacon *m*; bocal *m.* **2. Feeding b.,** biberon *m.*

bottle², *v.tr.* Mettre en bouteilles. **bottle up,** *v.tr.* **1.** Embouteiller. **2.** Étouffer.

bottle-neck, *s.* Étranglement *m*, embouteillage *m.*

bottom, *s.* **1.** (*a*) Bas *m.* (*b*) Fond *m* To be at the b. **of,** être la cause de. **2.** Bas-fond *m.* **3.** Derrière *m*, postérieur *m.*

bottomless, *a.* Sans fond.

bough, *s.* Branche *f*, rameau *m.*

boulder, *s.* Gros galet.

bounce¹, *s.* Vantardise *f.*

bounce², *v.i.* Rebondir.

bound¹, *s.* Limite *f*, borne *f.* To put out of bounds, consigner.

bound², *v.tr.* Borner, limiter.

bound³, *s.* Bond *m*, saut *m.*

bound⁴, *v.i.* Bondir, sauter.

bound⁵, *a.* En partance (*for*, pour).

bound⁶, *a.* **1.** Lié. **2.** Obligé, tenu. I'll be b., j'en suis sur.

boundary, *s.* Limite *f*, bornes *fpl.*

boundless, *a.* Sans bornes; illimité.

bounteous, *a.* Libéral, -aux; généreux.

bountiful, *a.* Bienfaisant.

bounty, *s.* **1.** Générosité *f.* **2.** (*a*) Don *m*, gratification *f.* (*b*) Indemnité *f*; prime *f.*

bouquet, *s.* Bouquet *m.*

bout, *s.* **1.** Tour *m*, reprise *f.* **2.** Accès *m.*

bow¹, *s.* **1.** Arc *m.* **2.** Archet *m* (de violon). **3.** Nœud *m.*

bow², *s.* Salut *m.*

bow³. 1. *v.i.* S'incliner. To bow to, saluer. To bow down, se prosterner. **2.** *v.tr.* (*a*) Incliner, baisser; fléchir. (*b*) Courber, voûter. **bow down,** *v.i.* Se baisser.

bow⁴, *s.* Avant *m*, étrave *f.*

bowels, *s.pl.* Intestins *m*, entrailles *f.*

bower, *s.* Berceau *m* de verdure.

bowl¹, *s.* **1.** Bol *m*, jatte *f.* **2.** Fourneau *m* (de pipe).

bowl², *s.* Boule *f.*

bowl³, *v.tr.* (*a*) Rouler. (*b*) Servir (la balle). **bowl along,** *v.i.* Rouler rapidement. **bowl over,** *v.tr.* Renverser.

bowler¹, *s.* Serveur *m.*

bowler², *s.* Chapeau *m* melon.

bowling-green, *s.* Jeu *m* de boules.

bowsprit, *s.* Beaupré *m.*

bowstring, *s.* Corde *f* d'arc.

bow-window, *s.* Fenêtre *f* en saillie

box¹, *s.* Buis *m.*

box². 1. *s.* (*a*) Boîte *f*; coffret *m*; caisse *f*; carton *m.* (*b*) (*For alms*) Tronc *m.* **2.** Loge *f.*

box³, *s.* Box on the ear, gifle *f.*

box⁴. 1. *v.tr.* To box s.o.'s ears, gifler qn. **2.** *v.i.* Boxer; faire de la boxe.

boxed, *a.* B. in, encaissé ; sans issue.

boxer, *s.* Boxeur *m*, pugiliste *m*.

boxing, *s.* La boxe, le pugilat.

boxing-day, *s.* Le lendemain de Noël.

boxing-gloves, *s.pl.* Gants de boxe.

boxing-match, *s.* Match *m* de boxe.

box-office, *s.* Bureau *m* de location.

box-room, *s.* Chambre *f* de débarras.

boxwood, *s.* Buis *m*.

boy, *s.* (*a*) Garçon *m.* (*b*) Élève *m.*

boycott[1], *s.* Mise *f* en interdit.

boycott[2], *v.tr* Boycotter.

boyhood, *s.* Enfance *f.* première jeunesse (d'un garçon).

brace, *s.* **1.** Attache *f*; croisillon *m.* **2.** *pl.* Bretelles *f.* **3.** *inv.* Couple *f.* **4.** B. (and bit), vilebrequin *m.*

bracelet, *s.* Bracelet *m.*

bracing, *a.* Fortifiant, tonifiant.

bracken, *s.* Fougère *f.*

bracket[1], *s.* (*a*) Support *m*; console *f*; corbeau *m.* (*b*) Parenthèse *f.*

bracket[2], *v.tr.* **1.** Mettre entre crochets. **2.** Réunir par une accolade.

brackish, *a.* Saumâtre.

bradawl, *s.* Poinçon *m.*

brag[1], *s.* Vantardise *f.*

brag[2], *v.i.* Se vanter ; fanfaronner.

braggart, *s.* Fanfaron *m*, vantard *m.*

bragging[1], *a.* Vantard.

bragging[2], *s.* Vantardise *f.*

braid[1], *s.* Galon *m*, ganse *f.*

braid[2], *v.tr.* **1.** Tresser, natter. **2.** Galonner, soutacher.

brain[1], *s.* **1.** Cerveau *m.* **2.** *pl.* Cervelle *f.* To rack one's brains, se creuser la cervelle, le cerveau.

brain[2], *v.tr.* Casser la tête à ; assommer.

brainless, *a.* Stupide.

brain-wave, *s.* Inspiration *f*, bonne idée.

brain-work, *s.* Travail *m* de tête.

brainy, *a.* Intelligent.

braise, *v.tr.* Braiser. Braised beef, bœuf en daube.

brake[1], *s.* Frein *m.*

brake[2], *v.tr.* Appliquer le frein sur. *Abs.* Serrer le frein ; freiner.

bramble, *s.* Ronce *f.*

bran, *s.* Son *m.*

branch[1], *s.* **1.** Branche *f*, rameau *m.* **2.** (*a*) Branche, bras *m.* (*b*) Succursale *f*, filiale *f.*

branch[2], *v.i.* **1.** To b. (out), se ramifier. **2.** (Se) bifurquer.

branch-line, *s.* Embranchement *m*; ligne *f* d'intérêt local.

brand[1], *s.* **1.** Brandon *m*, tison *m.* **2.** (*a*) Fer chaud. (*b*) Marque (faite avec un fer chaud). **3.** (*a*) Marque. (*b*) Sorte *f*, qualité *f.*

brand[2], *v.tr.* Marquer (au fer chaud).

brandish, *v.tr.* Brandir.

brand-new, *a.* Tout flambant neuf.

brandy, *s.* Eau-de-vie *f*, cognac *m.* Liqueur b., fine champagne.

brass, *s.* Cuivre *m* jaune ; laiton *m.*

brassy[1], *s.* *Golf:* Brassie *m.*

brassy[2], *a.* (Son) cuivré, cl:ironnant.

brat, *s.* Marmot *m*, mioche *mf.*

bravado, *s.* Bravade *f.*

brave[1]. **I.** *a.* Courageux, brave. **2.** *s.* Brave *m.*

brave[2], *v.tr.* Braver, défier.

bravely, *adv.* Courageusement.

bravery, *s.* Bravoure *f*, vaillance *f.*

bravo, *int.* Bravo !

brawl[1], *s.* Rixe *f*, bagarre *f.*

brawl[2], *v.i.* Brailler.

brawler, *s.* Braillard, -e.

brawling[1], *a.* **1.** Braillard. **2.** Murmurant.

brawling[2], *s.* **1.** Braillement *m.* **2.** Murmure *m.*

brawn, *s.* **1.** Muscles *mpl.* **2.** Fromage *m* de cochon.

brawny, *a.* Musclé.

bray, *v.i.* Braire.

brazen[1], *a.* **1.** D'airain. **2.** Effronté.

brazen[2], *v.tr.* To b. it out, payer d'effronterie.

Brazil. *Pr.n.* Le Brésil.

Brazilian, *a. & s.* Brésilien, -ienne.

Brazil-nut, *s.* Noix *f* du Brésil.

breach[1], *s.* **1.** Infraction *f.* B. of faith, violation *f* de foi. B. of trust, abus *m* de confiance. **2.** Brèche *f.*

breach[2], *v.tr.* Ouvrir une brèche dans.

bread, *s.* Pain *m.* A loaf of b., un pain, une miche. B. and butter, pain beurré. B. and milk, panade *f* au lait.

bread-crumb, *s.* **1.** Miette *f* (de pain). *Cu:* Bread-crumbs, chapelure *f*; (*when cooked*) gratin *m.*

bread-fruit, *s.* Fruit *m* à pain. B.-f. tree, arbre *m* à pain ; jaquier *m.*

bread-knife, *s.* Couteau *m*, scie *f*, à pain.

bread-poultice, s. Cataplasme m à la mie de pain.

bread-sauce, s. Sauce f à la mie de pain.

breadth, s. Largeur f.

break[1], s. **1.** Rupture f. (a) Brisure f, fracture f ; brèche f. **B. in the voice,** altération f de la voix. **B. in a journey,** arrêt m. **Without a b.,** sans interruption. (b) Rupture, brouille f. **2.** (a) Repos m, répit m. (b) Intervalle m. **3.** B. of day, point m du jour. **4.** Bill : Série f, suite f.

break[2]. I. v.tr. **1.** (a) Casser, briser, rompre. (b) To b. one's journey, interrompre son voyage. **2.** To b. bounds, violer la consigne. **3.** Briser, crever (le cœur à qn). **4.** To b. a fall, amortir une chute. **5.** Ruiner. **To b. the bank,** faire sauter la banque. **6.** To b. one's word, manquer de parole.

II. **break,** v.i. **1.** (Se) casser, se rompre, se briser ; (of wave) déferler. **2.** To b. with s.o., rompre avec qn. **3.** Poindre. **break away.** 1. v.tr. Détacher. **2.** v.i. Se détacher ; s'échapper. **break down.** I. v.tr. Abattre, démolir ; vaincre. **2.** v.i. (a) Échouer. (b) Rester en panne. **break in.** I. v.tr. Enfoncer ; défoncer. **2.** v.i. (a) To b. in upon, interrompre. Abs. Intervenir. (b) S'introduire par effraction. **break loose,** v.i. **1.** S'évader, s'échapper. **2.** Se déchaîner. **break off.** 1. v.tr. (a) Casser, rompre. (b) Interrompre, abandonner. **2.** v.i. (a) Se détacher. (b) Discontinuer. **break open,** v.tr. Enfoncer, forcer. **break out,** v.i. **1.** Éclater. **2.** S'échapper, s'évader. **break through,** v.tr. Percer ; enfoncer. Abs. Se frayer un passage. **break up.** 1. v.tr. Mettre en morceaux ; démolir ; disperser. **2.** v.i. (a) Se démembrer ; se disperser. (b) Se séparer. (c) Entrer en vacances. (d) Se gâter.

breakable. I. a. Cassant, fragile. **2.** s.pl. Objets m fragiles.

breakage, s. Casse f.

break-down, s. **1.** Arrêt complet. **2.** Panne f.

breaker, s. Brisant m ; vague déferlante.

breakfast[1], s. (Petit) déjeuner. **To have b.,** déjeuner.

breakfast[2], v.i. Déjeuner (le matin).

breakwater, s. Brise-lames m inv.

breast[1], s. **1.** Sein m. **2.** Poitrine f ; poitrail m (de cheval) ; blanc m (de volaille).

breast[2], v.tr. Affronter, faire front à.

breast-plate, s. Plastron m ; cuirasse f.

breast-pocket, s. Poche f de poitrine.

breath, s. Haleine f, souffle m, respiration f. **To draw b.,** respirer. **To gasp for b.,** haleter. **To waste one's b.,** perdre ses paroles. **Out of b.,** essoufflé. **Below one's b.,** à mi-voix.

breathe. I. v.i. Respirer, souffler. II. **breathe,** v.tr. **1.** Respirer. **To b. in, b. out, the air,** aspirer, exhaler, l'air. **2.** To b. one's last, rendre le dernier soupir.

breathing, s. Respiration f ; souffle m.

breathing-space, s. Le temps de souffler ; répit m.

breathless, a. **1.** Hors d'haleine ; essoufflé. **B. suspense,** attente fiévreuse.

breathlessly, adv. **1.** En haletant. **2.** En retenant son haleine.

breech, s. **1.** (Pair of) breeches, culotte f. **2.** Culasse f.

breed[1], s. Race f ; lignée f.

breed[2]. I. v.tr. **1.** Produire, engendrer ; faire naître. **2.** Élever. II. **breed,** v.i. Multiplier ; se reproduire.

breeder, s. Éleveur m.

breeding, s. **1.** (a) Reproduction f. (b) Élevage m. **2.** (a) Éducation. (b) (Good) b., bonnes manières ; savoir-vivre m.

breeze, s. Brise f.

breezy, a. **1.** Venteux. **2.** Désinvolte.

Breton, a. & s. Breton.

breviary, s. Bréviaire m.

brevity, s. Brièveté f.

brew. I. v.tr. (a) Brasser. (b) Abs. Brasser ; faire de la bière. **2.** v.i. (a) S'infuser. (b) Couver ; se préparer.

brewer, s. Brasseur m.

brewery, s. Brasserie f.

briar, s. (a) Églantier m. (b) pl. Ronces f.

bribe[1], s. Payement m illicite ; pot-de-vin m.

bribe[2], *v.tr.* Corrompre, soudoyer.
bribery, *s.* Corruption *f*.
brick, *s.* (*a*) Brique *f*. (*b*) **Box of bricks**, boîte de constructions.
bricklayer, *s.* Maçon *m*.
bridal, *a.* Nuptial, -aux.
bride, *s.* Épousée *f*; (nouvelle) mariée.
bridegroom, *s.* (Nouveau) marié.
bridesmaid, *s.* Demoiselle *f* d'honneur.
bridge[1], *s.* **1.** Pont *m*. **2.** Passerelle *f* (de commandement). **3.** Dos *m*, arête *f* (du nez).
bridge[2], *v.tr.* Jeter un pont sur. **To b. a gap**, combler une lacune.
bridge[3], *s. Cards :* Bridge *m*.
bridle[1], *s.* (*a*) Bride *f*. (*b*) Frein *m*.
bridle[2]. **1.** *v.tr.* Maîtriser, brider. **2.** *v.i.* Se rengorger; se rebiffer.
brief[1], *a.* Bref; court. **In b.**, en raccourci. **To be b.**, bref.
brief[2], *s.* Dossier *m*. **To hold a b.**, être chargé d'une cause.
briefly, *adv.* Brièvement; en peu de mots.
brier, *s.* Pipe *f* en bruyère.
brig, *s.* Brick *m*.
brigade, *s.* Brigade *f*.
brigadier, *s.* Général *m* de brigade.
brigand, *s.* Brigand *m*, bandit *m*.
brigandage, *s.* Brigandage *m*.
bright, *a.* **1.** (*a*) Lumineux. (*b*) Vif, éclatant. **2.** (*a*) Vif, animé. (*b*) Éveillé. **A b. idea**, une idée lumineuse.
brighten. **1.** *v.tr.* Faire briller; égayer. **2.** *v.i.* S'éclaircir. **His eyes brightened**, ses yeux s'allumèrent.
brightly, *adv.* Brillamment; avec éclat.
brightness, *s.* Éclat *m*; clarté *f*; vivacité *f*.
brilliance, *s.* Éclat *m*, brillant *m*.
brilliant[1], *a.* Brillant, éclatant.
brilliant[2], *s.* Brillant *m*.
brilliantly, *adv.* Brillamment.
brim[1], *s.* Bord *m*.
brim[2], *v.i.* **To b. over**, déborder.
brimful, *a.* Débordant.
brine, *s.* Eau salée; saumure *f*.
bring, *v.tr.* (*a*) Amener (qn); apporter (qch.). (*b*) **To b. luck**, porter bonheur (à). (*c*) **To b. into question**, mettre en question. (*d*) **To b. to pass**, amener, faire arriver. (*e*) **To b. oneself to**, se résoudre à.

bring about, *v.tr.* (*a*) Amener, causer. (*b*) Effectuer, accomplir.
bring along, *v.tr.* Amener (qn); apporter (qch.). **bring away**, *v.tr.* Emmener (qn); emporter (qch.).
bring back, *v.tr.* Rapporter (qch.); ramener (qn). **bring down**, *v.tr.* **1.** Abattre; faire tomber. **To b. d. the house**, faire crouler la salle. **2.** (*a*) Faire descendre. (*b*) Descendre.
bring forth, *v.tr.* Produire. **bring forward**, *v.tr.* Avancer. **bring in**, *v.tr.* **1.** Introduire. **2.** Rapporter. **3.** Rendre (un verdict); déclarer (coupable). **bring off**, *v.tr.* Réussir, conduire à bien. **bring on**, *v.tr.* **1.** Produire, occasionner. **2.** Introduire. **bring out**, *v.tr.* **1.** Sortir. **2.** Faire ressortir. **3.** Publier. **bring over**, *v.tr.* **1.** Transporter, amener. **2.** Gagner. **bring round**, *v.tr.* **1.** (*a*) Rappeler à la vie. (*b*) Remettre de bonne humeur. **2.** (R)amener. **bring to**, *v.tr.* Faire reprendre connaissance à. **bring together**, *v.tr.* Réunir; mettre en contact. **bring up**, *v.tr.* **1.** Monter. **2.** Élever. **3.** Citer en justice. **4.** Mettre sur le tapis.
bringing up, *s.* Éducation *f*.
brink, *s.* Bord *m*.
briny, *a.* Saumâtre, salé.
brisk, *a.* Vif, actif, alerte.
briskly, *adv.* Vivement; avec entrain.
briskness, *s.* (*a*) Vivacité *f*, animation *f*, entrain *m*. (*b*) Activité *f*.
bristle[1], *s.* Soie *f*; poil *m* raide.
bristle[2], *v.i.* (*a*) Se hérisser. (*b*) **To b. with**, être hérissé de.
bristling, *a.* Hérissé (*with*, de).
bristly, *a.* Couvert de poils raides; hérissé.
Britain. *Pr.n.* **Great B.**, la Grande-Bretagne.
British, *a.* Britannique; anglais. *s.pl.* **The B.**, les Anglais *m*.
Briton, *s.* Anglais, -aise.
Brittany. *Pr.n.* La Bretagne.
brittle, *a.* Fragile, cassant.
brittleness, *s.* Fragilité *f*.
broach, *v.tr.* Entamer.
broad. **1.** *a.* Large. **In b. daylight**, en plein jour. **2.** *s.* **The b. of the back**, le milieu du dos.
broad-brimmed, *a.* A larges bords.
broadcast[1]. **1.** *adv.* **Scattered b.**,

répandu à profusion. 2. *a.* (Omni-)
diffusé. **B. announcement,** radioémission *f.*
broadcast². I. *v.tr.* **1.** Faire savoir
partout. **2.** Radiodiffuser.
    II. broadcast, *s.* Radio-émission *f.*
broaden. 1. *v.tr.* Élargir. **2.** *v.i.*
S'élargir.
broadly, *adv.* Largement. **B. speak-**
ing, généralement parlant.
broad-minded, *a.* **To be b.-m.,**
avoir l'esprit large.
broad-mindedness, *s.* Largeur *f*
d'esprit.
broad-shouldered, *a.* Trapu.
broadside, *s.* Bordée *f.*
broadsword, *s.* Sabre *m* ; latte *f.*
brocade, *s.* Brocart *m.*
brogue¹, *s.* Soulier *m* de golf.
brogue², *s.* (*a*) Accent *m* de terroir.
(*b*) Accent irlandais.
broil¹, *s.* Querelle *f* ; bagarre *f.*
broil², *v.tr. & i.* Griller.
broiling, *a.* Ardent, brûlant.
broken, *a.* (*a*) Cassé, brisé, rompu.
(*b*) Interrompu. (*c*) **In a b. voice,**
d'une voix entrecoupée. (*d*) **B. down,**
Cassé ; en panne.
broken-hearted, *a.* Au cœur brisé.
broker, *s.* Courtier *m.*
bronchial, *a.* Bronchial, -aux.
bronchitis, *s.* Bronchite *f.*
bronze. 1. *s.* Bronze *m.* **2.** *Attrib.*
De, en, bronze.
brooch, *s.* Broche *f.*
brood¹, *s.* Couvée *f.*
brood², *v.i.* Broyer du noir. **To b.**
over the fire, couver le feu.
brook, *s.* Ruisseau *m.*
broom, *s.* **1.** Genêt *m.* **2.** Balai *m.*
broomstick, *s.* Manche *m* à balai.
broth, *s.* Bouillon *m*, potage *m.*
brother, *s.* Frère *m.*
brotherhood, *s.* Fraternité *f.*
brother-in-law, *s.* Beau-frère *m.*
pl. beaux-frères.
brotherly, *a.* De frère ; fraternel.
brow, *s.* **1.** Sourcil *m.* **2.** Front *m.*
browbeat, *v.tr.* Intimider, rudoyer.
brown. 1. *a.* (*a*) Brun. **B. shoes,**
chaussures jaunes. **B. bread,** pain
bis. (*b*) Bruni. **2.** *s.* Brun *m.*
brownie, *s.* Farfadet *m.*
brownish, *a.* Brunâtre.
browse, *v.tr. & i.* Brouter.
bruise¹, *s.* Meurtrissure *f.*

bruise², *v.tr.* Meurtrir.
brunette, *a. & s.* Brune *f.*
brunt, *s.* Choc *m.* **To bear the b.,**
payer de sa personne.
brush¹, *s.* **1.** Broussailles *fpl.* **2.** (*a*)
Brosse *f.* (*b*) (**Paint-)b.,** pinceau *m.*
(*c*) Queue *f.* **3.** Coup *m* de brosse.
4. Échauffourée *f.*
brush². 1. *v.tr.* (*a*) Brosser. **To b.**
one's hair, se brosser les cheveux.
(*b*) Effleurer, frôler. **2.** *v.i.* **To b.**
against, frôler en passant. **brush**
aside, *v.tr.* Écarter. **brush down.**
v.tr. Donner un coup de brosse à.
brushwood, *s.* Broussailles *fpl.*
brusque, *a.* Brusque ; rude, bourru.
brusquely, *adv.* Avec brusquerie.
brusqueness, *s.* Brusquerie *f.*
Brussels. *Pr.n.* Bruxelles *f.*
brutal, *a.* Brutal, -aux.
brutality, *s.* Brutalité *f* (*to,* envers).
brutalize, *v.tr.* Abrutir.
brutally, *adv.* Brutalement.
brute. 1. *s.* Brute *f.* **2.** *a.* **By b. force**
de vive force.
brutishness, *s.* **1.** Bestialité *f.* **2.**
Abrutissement *m.*
bubble¹, *s.* Bulle *f.*
bubble², *v.i.* Bouillonner ; pétiller.
bubble over, *v.i.* Déborder.
buccaneer, *s.* Boucanier *m* ; pirate *m.*
buck, *s.* (*a*) Daim *m* ; chevreuil *m.*
(*b*) Mâle *m.*
bucket, *s.* Seau *m.*
bucketful, *s.* Plein seau.
buck-jump¹, *s.* Saut *m* de mouton.
buck-jump², *v.i.* Faire le saut de
mouton.
buckle¹, *s.* Boucle *f.*
buckle². 1. *v.tr.* Boucler. **2.** *v.i.* Se
déformer, gauchir.
buckram, *s.* Bougran *m.*
buck-shot, *s.* Chevrotine *f.*
bucolic, *a.* Bucolique.
bud¹, *s.* **1.** Bourgeon *m.* **2.** Bouton *m.*
bud², *v.i.* Boutonner.
Buddha, *s.* (Le) Bouddha.
Buddhist. 1. *s.* Bouddhiste *mf.* **2.** *a.*
Bouddhique.
budge, *v.i.* Bouger.
budget, *s.* **1.** Tas *m* ; collection *f.*
2. Budget *m.*
buff, *s.* Jaune clair *inv.*
buffalo, *s.* Buffle *m.*
buffer, *s.* Tampon *m.*
buffet¹, *s.* Coup *m* (de poing).

buffet², *v.tr. & i.* (*a*) Bourrer de coups. (*b*) Secouer.

buffet³, *s.* Buffet *m.*

buffeting, *s.* Succession *f* de coups, de chocs.

buffoon, *s.* Bouffon *m*, paillasse *m.*

buffoonery, *s.* Bouffonneries *fpl.*

bug, *s.* Punaise *f.*

bugbear, *s.* Cauchemar *m.*

bugle, *s.* Clairon *m.*

bugler, *s.* Clairon *m.*

build¹, *s.* Carrure *f*, taille *f.*

build², *v.tr.* **1.** Bâtir; construire. **2.** Fonder. **build up**, *v.tr.* Affermir.

builder, *s.* Entrepreneur *m* (en bâtiments).

building, *s.* **1.** Construction *f.* B. land, terrain *m* à bâtir. **2.** Bâtiment *m*; maison *f.* **Public b.**, édifice public.

bulb, *s.* **1.** Bulbe *m*, oignon *m.* **2.** Ampoule *f*; lampe *f.*

bulbous, *a.* Bulbeux.

Bulgaria. *Pr.n.* La Bulgarie.

Bulgarian, *a. & s.* Bulgare (*mf*).

bulge¹, *s.* Bombement *m*, ventre *m.*

bulge², *v.tr. & i.* Bomber; faire saillie.

bulging, *a.* Bombé.

bulk, *s.* **1.** Grandeur *f*, grosseur *f*, volume *m.* **2.** Masse *f*, plupart *f.*

bulkhead, *s.* Cloison *f.*

bulky, *a.* **1.** Volumineux. **2.** Gros *f.* grosse.

bull, *s.* **1.** (*a*) Taureau *m.* (*b*) Mâle *m.* **2.** Haussier *m.* **3.** Noir *m*, mouche *f.*

bull-dog, *s.* Bouledogue *m.*

bullet, *s.* Balle *f.*

bulletin, *s.* Bulletin *m.*

bull-fight, *s.* Course *f* de taureaux.

bull-fighter, *s.* Toréador *m.*

bullfinch, *s.* Bouvreuil *m.*

bullock, *s.* Bœuf *m.*

bull-ring, *s.* Arène (pour les courses de taureaux).

bull's-eye, *s.* Noir *m*, mouche *f.*

bully¹, *s.* Tyran *m.*

bully², *v.tr.* Intimider, malmener.

bullying¹, *a.* Brutal, -aux.

bullying², *s.* Intimidation *f* brutalité *f.*

bulrush, *s.* Massette *f*

bulwarks, *s. pl.* Bastingage *m.*

bumble-bee, *s.* Bourdon *m.*

bump¹, *s.* **1.** Choc (sourd); heurt *m*; cahot *m.* **2.** Bosse *f.*

bump². **1.** *v.tr* Cogner, frapper. **2.** *v.i.* Se cogner, se heurter.

bumper, *s.* **1.** Rasade *f.* **B. crop**, récolte magnifique. **2.** Pare-choc *m inv.*

bumpkin, *s.* Rustre *m*, lourdaud *m.*

bumptious, *a.* Présomptueux, suffisant.

bumptiously. *adv.* D'un air suffisant.

bumptiousness, *s.* Suffisance *f.*

bumpy, *a.* Cahoteux.

bun, *s.* Petit pain au lait.

bunch, *s.* Bouquet *m*; grappe *f*; trousseau *m* (de clefs).

bundle¹, *s.* Paquet *m*; liasse *f*; fagot *m.*

bundle², *v.tr.* To b. (up), empaqueter; mettre en liasse.

bungalow, *s.* Maison *f* sans étage.

bungle, *v.tr.* Bousiller, gâcher.

bungler, *s.* (*a*) Bousilleur, -euse; gâcheur, -euse. (*b*) Maladroit, -e.

bungling¹, *a.* Maladroit.

bungling², *s.* Maladresse *f.*

bunion, *s.* Oignon *m.*

bunk, *s.* Couchette *f.*

bunker, *s.* **1.** Soute *f.* **2.** *Golf*: Banquette *f.*

bunting, *s.* *Coll*: Drapeaux *m*, pavillons *m.*

buoy¹, *s.* Bouée *f*; balise flottante.

buoy², *v.tr.* To b. up, soutenir.

buoyancy, *s.* **1.** Flottabilité *f.* **2.** Entrain *m*; élasticité *f.*

buoyant, *a.* **1.** Flottable; léger. **2.** Plein d'entrain.

burden¹, *s.* **1.** Fardeau *m*, charge *f.* Beast of b., bête de somme. **2.** (*a*) Refrain *m.* (*b*) Substance *f*, fond *m.*

burden², *v.tr.* Charger (*with*, de).

burdensome, *a.* Onéreux.

bureau, *s.* Bureau *m.*

bureaucrat, *s.* Bureaucrate *m.*

burglar, *s.* Cambrioleur *m.*

burglary, *s.* Cambriolage *m.*

burgle, *v.tr.* Cambrioler.

Burgundy. **1.** *Pr.n.* La Bourgogne. **2.** *s.* (Vin *m* de) bourgogne *m.*

burial, *s.* Enterrement *m.*

burial-service, *s* Office *m* des morts.

burlesque, *a. & s.* Burlesque (*m*).

burly, *a* Solidement bâti.

Burma. *Pr.n.* La Birmanie.

Burmese, *a. & s.* Birman, -e.

burn¹, *s.* Brûlure *f.*

burn². **1.** *v.tr.* Brûler. **To b. one's**

9

fingers, se brûler les doigts. **To be burnt to death,** être carbonisé. **2.** *v.i.* Brûler. **burn away. 1.** *v.tr.* Brûler, consumer. **2.** *v.i.* Se consumer. **burn down,** *v.tr.* Brûler, incendier. **burn out. 1.** *v.tr.* Griller (une lampe). **2.** *v.i.* Se consumer. **burn up. 1.** *v.tr.* Brûler; consumer. **2.** *v.i.* Flamber.

burner, *s.* Bec *m* (de gaz).

burning, *a.* Brûlant, ardent.

burnish, *v.tr.* Brunir; polir.

burnt, *a.* Brûlé, carbonisé.

burr, *s.* Teigne *f.*

burrow[1], *s.* Terrier *m.*

burrow[2], *v.i.* Fouiller.

bursar, *s.* Économe *m.*

burst. 1. *v.i.* (a) Éclater, faire explosion; crever. (b) **To b. into tears,** se mettre à pleurer. **2.** *v.tr.* Faire éclater; crever; rompre. **burst asunder. 1.** *v.tr.* Rompre. **2.** *v.i.* Se rompre. **burst in. 1.** *v.tr.* Enfoncer. **2.** *v.i.* Faire irruption. **burst open. 1.** *v.tr.* Enfoncer. **2.** *v.i.* S'ouvrir tout d'un coup. **burst out,** *v.i.* S'écrier, s'exclamer. **To b. out laughing,** éclater de rire.

bury, *v.tr.* Enterrer; ensevelir.

burying, *s.* Enterrement *m.*

bus, *s.* Omnibus *m.*

bush, *s.* **1.** (a) Buisson *m.* (b) Fourré *m,* taillis *m.* **2.** Brousse *f.*

bushel, *s.* Boisseau *m.*

bushy, *a.* Touffu.

busily, *adv.* Activement; avec empressement.

business, *s.* **1.** Affaire *f,* besogne *f,* occupation *f.* **It is my b. to,** c'est à moi de. **It's none of your b.,** cela ne vous regarde pas. **2.** (a) Les affaires *f.* **To mean b.,** avoir des intentions sérieuses. *Attrib:* B. hours, heures d'ouverture. **B. house,** maison de commerce. **B. man,** homme d'affaires. (b) Fonds *m* de commerce.

business-like, *a.* **1.** Pratique. **2.** Sérieux.

bust, *s.* Buste *m,* gorge *f,* poitrine *f.*

bustle[1], *s.* Remue-ménage *m.*

bustle[2]. **1. To b.** (about), se remuer. **2.** *v.tr.* Faire dépêcher.

bustling, *a.* Affairé; empressé.

busy[1], *a.* Affairé, occupé.

busy[2], *v.tr. & pr.* **To b. oneself,** s'occuper (*with,* à)

busybody, *s.* Officieux, -euse.

but. 1. *conj.* Mais. **But yet,** néanmoins. **2.** *adv.* Ne . . que; seulement. **But yesterday,** pas plus tard qu'hier. **Had I but known!** si j'avais su! **3.** *conj. or prep.* (a) Excepté. **Anything but,** rien moins que. (b) **But for,** sans. **But for that,** à part cela.

butcher[1], *s.* Boucher *m.*

butcher[2], *v.tr.* Égorger, massacrer.

butchery, *s.* Tuerie *f,* boucherie *f.*

butler, *s.* Maître *m* d'hôtel.

butt[1], *s.* **1.** Gros bout, talon *m.* **2.** Crosse *f* (de fusil).

butt[2], *s.* But *m;* plastron *m.*

butt[3], *s.* Coup *m* de tête, de corne.

butt[4], *v.i. & tr.* Donner un coup de corne à. **To b.** (into), donner du front, buter, contre.

butt-end, *s.* Extrémité inférieure; gros bout.

butter[1], *s.* Beurre *m.*

butter[2], *v.tr.* Beurrer.

butter-bean, *s.* Haricot *m* beurre.

buttercup, *s.* Bouton *m* d'or.

butter-dish, *s.* Beurrier *m.*

butterfly, *s.* Papillon *m.*

butter-scotch, *s.* Caramel *m* au beurre.

button[1], *s.* Bouton *m.*

button[2], *v.tr.* **To b. up,** boutonner.

button-hole, *s.* Boutonnière *f.*

button-hook, *s.* Tire-bouton *m.*

buttress[1], *s.* Contrefort *m.*

buttress[2], *v.tr.* Arc-bouter, étayer.

buxom, *a.* Aux formes rebondies.

buy, *v.tr.* Acheter (*from,* à). **buy back,** *v.tr.* Racheter. **buy up,** *v.tr.* Rafler, accaparer.

buyer, *s.* Acheteur, -euse; acquéreur *m.*

buzz[1], *s.* Bourdonnement *m.*

buzz[2], *v.i.* Bourdonner.

buzzard, *s.* Buse *f,* busard *m.*

buzzer, *s.* Vibreur *m,* vibrateur *m.*

buzzing, *s.* Bourdonnement *m.*

by. 1. *prep.* **1.** (Au)près de, à côté de. **By the sea,** au bord de la mer. **By oneself,** seul; à l'écart. **2.** Par. **3.** (a) Par, de. **Made by hand,** fait à la main. **By force,** de force. **Three feet by two,** trois pieds sur deux. **By tram,** en tramway. (b) **By doing that,** en faisant cela. **4.** By

rights, à la rigueur. **By the pound,**
à la livre. **5. By turn(s),** tour à tour.
One by one, un à un. **6. By day,** de
jour, le jour. **7. By Monday,** d'ici
lundi. **By now,** déjà. **8. By far,** de
beaucoup.
   II. **by,** *adv.* **1.** Près. **Close by,**
tout près. **2.** De côté. **3.** *Adv.phr.*
By and by, tout à l'heure, bientôt.
By the by, à propos.
   III. **by,** *a.* Secondaire.
by-election, *s.* Élection *f* de remplacement.
bygone, *a.* Passé, d'autrefois.

by-law, *s.* Arrêté municipal.
by-pass[1], *s.* Route *f* de contourne-
ment.
by-pass[2], *v.tr.* Contourner.
by-path, *s.* Sentier détourné.
by-play, *s.* Jeu *m* accessoire; aparté
mimé.
by-product, *s.* Sous-produit *m.*
by-road, *s.* Chemin détourné.
bystander, *s.* Assistant *m*; spectateur, -trice.
by-way, *s.* Chemin détourné.
by-word, *s.* **1.** Proverbe *m*, dicton *m.*
2. Risée *f.*

C

C, c. (La lettre) C, c *m.*
cab, *s.* Voiture *f* de place. (*a*) Fiacre
m. (*b*) Taxi *m.*
cabbage, *s.* Chou *m*, *pl.* choux.
cabbage-lettuce, *s.* Laitue pommée.
cab-driver, *s.* Cocher *m* de fiacre.
cabin, *s.* **1.** Cabane *f*, case *f.* **2.** (*a*)
Cabine *f.* (*b*) Carlingue *f.*
cabinet, *s.* **1.** (*a*) Meuble *m* à tiroirs.
(*b*) Glass c., vitrine *f.* **2.** Cabinet *m*,
ministère *m.* **C. minister,** ministre *m*
d'État.
cabinet-maker, *s.* Ébéniste *m.*
cable[1], *s.* **1.** Câble *m.* **2.** Câblogramme *m.*
cable[2], *v.tr. & i.* Câbler.
cablegram, *s.* Câblogramme *m.*
cabman, *s.* Cocher *m* de fiacre.
cachou, *s.* Cachou *m.*
cackle[1], *s.* Caquet *m.*
cackle[2], *v.i.* Caqueter.
cactus, *s.* Cactus *m.*
cad, *s.* Goujat *m*, pleutre *m*, cuistre *m.*
cadaverous, *a.* Cadavéreux.
caddie, *s.* Caddie *m.*
caddy, *s.* Boîte *f* à thé.
cadence, *s.* Cadence *f.*
café, *s.* Café.
cage[1], *s.* Cage *f.*
cage[2], *v.tr.* Encager; mettre en
cage.
Cairo. *Pr.n.* Le Caire.
cajole, *v.tr.* Cajoler; enjôler.
cake[1], *s.* **1.** Gâteau *m.* **2.** Pain *m* (de
savon); tablette *f* (de chocolat).
cake[2], *v.i.* Former une croûte.
Caked with mud, plaqué de boue.
calamitous, *a.* Calamiteux.

calamity, *s.* **1.** Calamité *f.* malheur
m. **2.** Désastre *m.*
calcium, *s.* Calcium *m.*
calculate, *v.tr. & i.* Calculer; estimer. *Abs.* Compter.
calculated, *a.* Délibéré, calculé.
calculating, *a.* Calculateur, -trice.
calculation, *s.* Calcul *m.*
calendar, *s.* Calendrier *m*
calf[1], *s.* Veau *m.*
calf[2], *s.* Mollet *m.*
calf's-foot, *s.* Pied *m* de veau.
calibre, *s.* Calibre *m.*
calico, *s.* Calicot *m.*
call[1], *s.* **1.** Appel *m*; cri *m.* **2. Within
c.,** à portée de voix. **3.** Visite *f.*
Port of c., port d'escale. **4.** Demande *f.*
call[2]. I. *v.tr.* **1.** (*a*) Appeler; crier.
London calling! ici Londres! (*b*)
To c. to s.o., crier à qn. **2.** (*a*) Convoquer. (*b*) Réveiller. **3.** Traiter de.
To c. names, injurier.
   II. **call,** *v.i.* (*a*) **Has anyone called?**
est-il venu quelqu'un? (*b*) S'arrêter;
faire escale. **call back.** **1.** *v.tr.*
Rappeler. **2.** *v.i.* Repasser. **call for,**
v.ind.tr. (*a*) **To c. for help,** crier
au secours. (*b*) Venir prendre.
(*c*) Demander. **call forth,** *v.tr.*
Produire, faire naître. **call in,** *v.tr.*
1. Faire entrer. **2.** Faire appel à.
call on, *v.i.* **1.** Faire visite chez.
2. Invoquer. **call out,** *v.i.* Appeler;
appeler au secours. **call up,** *v.tr.*
1. Évoquer. **2.** Appeler au téléphone.
3. Appeler sous les armes. **call
upon,** *v.i.* (*a*) Invoquer. (*b*) **To c. u.
s.o. for sth.,** demander qch. à qn.

call-box, s. Cabine f (téléphonique). Public c.-b. taxiphone m.

call-boy, s. Avertisseur m.

caller, s. Visiteur, -euse.

calling, s. 1. Convocation f. 2. Vocation f, état m.

callous, a. Insensible, endurci.

callously, adv. Sans pitié, sans cœur.

calm[1], s. Calme m; tranquillité f.

calm[2], a. Calme, tranquille.

calm[3]. 1. v.tr. Calmer, apaiser. To c. down, pacifier. 2. v.i. To c. down se calmer.

calmly, adv. Avec calme; tranquillement.

calmness, s. Tranquillité f, calme m.

calumniate, v.tr. Calomnier.

calumniator, s. Calomniateur, -trice.

calumny, s. Calomnie f.

cambered, a. Arqué, courbé.

cambric, s. Batiste f.

camel, s. Chameau m. She-c., chamelle f.

camel-driver, s. Chamelier m.

cameo, s. Camée m.

camera, s. Appareil m photographique.

camouflage[1], s. Camouflage m.

camouflage[2], v.tr. Camoufler.

camp[1], s. Camp m; campement m.

camp[2], v.t. Camper.

campaign, s. Campagne f.

camp-bed, s. Lit m de sangle.

camp-chair, s. Chaise pliante.

camphor, s. Camphre m.

camphorated, a. Camphré.

can[1], s. Bidon m.

can[2], modal aux. v. 1. Pouvoir. 1 cannot allow that, je ne saurais permettre cela That cannot be, cela ne se peut pas. What can it be? qu'est-ce que cela peut bien être? 2. Savoir. I can swim, je sais nager. 3. You can but try vous pouvez toujours essayer.

Canada, Pr.n. Le Canada.

Canadian, a. & s. Canadien, -enne.

canal, s. Canal m, -aux

canary, s. Serin m.

cancel, v.tr Annuler; biffer.

cancellation, s. Annulation f.

cancer, s. Cancer m.

candid, a. Franc, f. franche; sincère.

candidate, s. Candidat, -e.

candidly, adv. Franchement, sincèrement.

candied, a Candi ; confit.

candle, s. 1. Wax c., bougie f. Tallow c., chandelle f. 2. Roman c., chandelle romaine.

candle-grease, s Suif m.

candle-power, s. Bougie f.

candlestick, s. Bougeoir m.

candour, s. Franchise f sincérité f

cane[1], s. Canne f.

cane[2], v.tr Battre à coups de canne.

canine, a. Canin ; de chien.

caning, s. Correction f.

canister, s. Boîte f (en fer blanc).

canker[1], s. Chancre m.

canker[2], v.tr (a) Ronger (b) Corrompre.

cannibal, s. & a. Cannibale (mf); anthropophage (mf).

cannibalism, s. Cannibalisme m. anthropophagie f.

cannon[1], s. 1. Canon m. 2. Bill: Carambolage m.

cannon[2], v.i. 1. Caramboler. 2. To c. into, heurter.

cannonade, s. Canonnade f.

cannon-ball, s. Boulet m.

canoe, s. 1. Périssoire f. 2. Pirogue f.

canon[1], s. Règle f, critère m.

canon[2], s. Chanoine m.

canopy, s. Dais m; auvent m, marquise f.

cant, s. (a) Jargon m. (b) Langage m hypocrite.

cantankerous, a. Revêche, acariâtre.

cantata, s Cantate f.

canteen, s. 1. Cantine f 2. Bidon m.

canter[1], s. Petit galop. To win in a c., arriver bon premier.

canter[2], v.i Aller au petit galop.

canting, a. Hypocrite.

canto, s Chant m.

canvas, s. 1. Toile f a voiles. Under c., sous la tente. 2. Toile.

canvass, v.tr Solliciter (des suffrages).

canyon, s. Cañon m ; gorge f.

caoutchouc, s. Caoutchouc m.

cap[1], s. 1. Bonnet m; casquette f; toque f. Skull cap, calotte f. 2. Chapeau m (de protection); capuchon m. 3. Amorce f.

cap[2], v.tr. 1. Coiffer. 2. Coiffer, couronner (with de). 3. To cap it all, pour comble.

capability, s. Capacité.

capable, a. 1. Capable. 2. Susceptible.

capably, *adv.* Avec compétence.

capacious, *a.* Vaste, spacieux.

capacity, *s.* **1.** (*a*) Contenance *f.* (*b*) Rendement *m.* **Seating c.,** nombre *m* de places. **House filled to c.,** salle comble. **2.** Capacité; aptitude *f.*

cape¹, *s.* Pèlerine *f*, cape *f.*

cape², *s.* Cap *m*, promontoire *m.*

caper¹, *s.* Câpre *f.*

caper², *s.* Entrechat *m*, gambade *f.*

caper³, *v.i.* Faire des entrechats; gambader.

capital¹, *s.* Chapiteau *m.*

capital², I. *a.* **1.** Capital, -aux. **C. letter,** majuscule *f.* **2.** *s.* Capitale. **3. C. punishment,** peine capitale. **4. C.!** fameux!

II. **capital,** *s.* Capital *m*, capitaux *mpl*, fonds *mpl.* **To make c. out of,** profiter de.

capitalism, *s.* Capitalisme *m.*

capitalist, *s.* Capitaliste *mf.*

capitally, *adv.* Admirablement.

capitulate, *v.i.* Capituler.

capitulation, *s.* Capitulation *f.*

capon, *s.* Chapon *m*, poulet *m.*

caprice, *s.* Caprice *m.*

capricious, *a.* Capricieux.

capriciously, *adv.* Capricieusement.

capriciousness, *s.* Humeur capricieuse, inégale.

capsicum, *s.* Piment *m.*

capsize, **1.** *v.i.* Chavirer. **2.** *v.tr.* Faire chavirer.

capstan, *s.* Cabestan *m.*

capsule, *s.* Capsule *f.*

captain, *s.* **1.** (*a*) Chef *m*, capitaine *m.* (*b*) Chef d'équipe. **2.** Capitaine. **Group c.,** colonel *m.*

captaincy, *s.* Grade *m* de capitaine. **To obtain one's c.,** passer capitaine.

captious, *a.* **1.** Captieux. **2.** Pointilleux, vétilleux.

captiously, *adv.* Pointilleusement.

captivate, *v.tr.* Charmer, captiver.

captivating, *a.* Séduisant; captivant.

captivation, *s.* Séduction *f.*

captive, **1.** *a.* Captif. **2.** *s.* Captif, -ive, prisonnier, -ière.

captivity, *s.* Captivité *f.*

captor, *s.* Celui qui s'est emparé de qn.

capture¹, *s.* Capture *f*, prise *f.*

capture², *v.tr.* Capturer; prendre.

car, *s.* Automobile *f.*

carafe, *s.* Carafe *f.*

caramel, *s.* **1.** Caramel *m.* **2.** Bonbon *m* au caramel.

carat, *s.* Carat *m.*

caravan, *s.* **1.** Caravane *f.* **2.** Roulotte *f.*

caraway, *s.* Carvi *m.*

carbine, *s.* Carabine *f.*

carbolic, *a.* Phénique. **C. acid,** phénol *m.*

carbon, *s.* **1.** Carbone *m.* **2.** Papier *m* carbone.

carbonate, *s.* Carbonate *m.*

carbon-copy, *s.* Copie *f*, double *m*, au carbone.

carbonic, *a.* Carbonique. **C. acid gas,** anhydride *m* carbonique.

carbon-paper, *s.* Papier *m* carbone.

carbuncle, *s.* **1.** Escarboucle *f.* **2.** Anthrax *m*; bourgeon *m.*

carburettor, *s.* Carburateur *m.*

carcase, *s.* Cadavre *m*; corps *m.*

card, *s.* Carte *f*; billet *m.* **It is on the cards,** il est bien possible. **He's a c.,** c'est un original

cardboard, *s.* Carton *m.*

card-case, *s.* Porte-cartes *m inv.*

cardigan, *s.* Gilet *m* de tricot.

cardinal, I. *a.* Cardinal, -aux. II. **cardinal,** *s.* Cardinal *m.*

card-index, *s.* Fichier *m*; classeur *m.*

card-sharper, *s.* Tricheur *m*; bonneteur *m.*

card-table, *s.* Table *f* de jeu.

care¹, *s.* **1.** Souci *m*, inquiétude *f.* **2.** Soin(s) *m(pl)*, attention *f*, ménagement *m.* **Take c.!** faites attention! prenez garde! **3.** Soin(s), charge *f*, tenue *f.* **C. of,** aux bons soins de. **Want of c.,** incurie *f*, négligence *f.*

care², *v.i.* **1.** Se soucier, s'inquiéter, se préoccuper. **I don't c.!** ça m'est égal! **2.** To c. for, soigner. **3.** To c. for, aimer.

career¹, *s.* **1.** Course *f.* **2.** Carrière *f.*

career², *v.i.* **To c. along,** être en pleine course.

care-free, *a.* Libre de soucis; insouciant.

careful, *a.* **1.** Soigneux; attentif (*of*, à). **Be c.!** prenez garde! faites attention! **2.** Prudent, circonspect.

carefully, *adv.* **1.** Soigneusement; attentivement. **2.** Prudemment.

carefulness, *s.* **1.** Soin *m*, attention *f.* **2.** Prudence *f.*

careless, *a.* **1.** (*a*) Insouciant; nonchalant. (*b*) **C. mistake,** faute d'inattention. **2.** Négligent.

carelessly, *adv.* Avec insouciance; négligemment.

carelessness, *s.* **1.** (*a*) Insouciance *f*. (*b*) Inattention *f*. **2.** Négligence *f*.

caress[1], *s.* Caresse *f*.

caress[2], *v.tr.* Caresser.

caressing, *a.* Caressant.

care-taker, *s.* Concierge *mf*; gardien *m*.

care-worn, *a.* Rongé par le chagrin.

cargo, *s.* Cargaison *f*.

cargo-boat, *s.* Cargo *m*.

caricature[1], *s.* Caricature *f*.

caricature[2], *v.tr.* Caricaturer.

caricaturist, *s.* Caricaturiste *m*.

carman, *s.* Camionneur *m*, charretier *m*.

carmine. **1.** *s.* Carmin *m*. **2.** *a.* Carminé; carmin *inv*.

carnage, *s.* Carnage *m*.

carnal, *a.* **1.** Charnel. **2.** Mondain.

carnation[1], *a.* Incarnat.

carnation[2], *s.* Œillet *m*.

carnival, *s.* Carnaval *m*, *pl.* -als.

carnivora, *s.pl.* Carnassiers *m*.

carnivorous, *a.* Carnassier.

carol, *s.* Chant *m*. **Christmas c.,** noël *m*.

carouse, *v.i.* Faire la fête.

carp[1], *s.* Carpe *f*.

carp[2], *v.i.* Trouver à redire.

carpenter, *s.* Charpentier *m*; menuisier *m*.

carpentry, *s.* Charpenterie *f*.

carpet[1], *s.* Tapis *m*.

carpet[2], *v.tr.* Recouvrir d'un tapis.

carpeted, *a.* Couvert d'un tapis; tapissé (*with*, de).

carpet-sweeper, *s.* Balai *m* mécanique.

carriage, *s.* **1.** Port *m*, transport *m*. **2.** Port, maintien *m*. **3.** Voiture *f*; wagon *m*.

carriage-window, *s.* Glace *f* (de voiture).

carrier, *s.* **1.** (*a*) Porteur, -euse. (*b*) Camionneur *m*, roulier *m*. **2.** **Aircraft c.,** porte-avions *m inv*.

carrier-pigeon, pigeon voyageur.

carrion, *s.* Charogne *f*.

carrot, *s.* Carotte *f*.

carry, *v.tr.* **1.** Porter; transporter. **2.** **To c. into effect,** mettre à exécu-

tion. **3.** Emporter d'assaut. **To c. all before one,** vaincre toutes les résistances. **To c. one's point,** imposer sa manière de voir. **4.** Adopter; faire adopter. **5.** Supporter. **6.** *Abs.* Porter. **carry along,** *v.tr.* Emporter, entraîner. **carry away,** *v.tr.* **1.** Emporter; emmener, enlever. **2.** Entraîner. **carry off,** *v.tr.* **1.** Emporter; emmener, enlever. **2.** Remporter. **carry on,** *v.tr.* Poursuivre; continuer; exercer; entretenir; soutenir. **carry out,** *v.tr.* Mettre à exécution, effectuer. **carry through,** *v.tr.* Mener à bonne fin.

carrying, *s.* **1.** Port *m*, transport *m*. **2.** Adoption *f*, vote *m*.

cart[1], *s.* Charrette *f*.

cart[2], *v.tr.* Charrier, charroyer.

carter, *s.* Charretier *m*, roulier *m*.

cartful, *s.* Charretée *f*.

cart-horse, *s.* Cheval *m* de trait.

cart-load, *s.* Charretée *f*, voiturée *f*.

carton, *s.* Carton *m*.

cartoon, *s.* Carton *m*; dessin *m* humoristique.

cartridge, *s.* Cartouche *f*.

cart-shed, *s.* Remise *f*.

cart-wheel, *s.* Roue *f* de charrette.

carve, *v.tr.* **1.** Sculpter, graver. **2.** Découper.

carving, *s.* **1.** Sculpture *f*. **2.** Découpage *m* de la viande.

carving-fork, *s.* Fourchette *f* à découper.

carving-knife, *s.* Couteau *m* à découper.

cascade, *s.* Chute *f* d'eau; cascade *f*.

case[1], *s.* **1.** Cas *m*. **If that is the c.,** s'il en est ainsi. **In any c.,** en tout cas. **Just in c.,** à tout hasard. **In most cases,** en général. **2.** Malade *mf*; blessé, -e. **3.** Cause *f*, affaire *f*.

case[2], *s.* **1.** Caisse *f*; colis *m*. **2.** Étui *m*; écrin *m*.

case-hardened, *a.* Endurci.

casement-window, *s.* Croisée *f*.

cash[1], *s.* Espèces *fpl*; argent comptant. **Hard c.,** espèces sonnantes. **C. with order,** payable à la commande.

cash[2], *v.tr.* Toucher.

cash-book, *s.* Livre *m* de caisse.

cash-box, *s.* Caisse *f*.

cash-desk, *s.* Caisse *f*.

cashier[1], *s.* Caissier, -ière. **Cashier's desk**, caisse *f.*

cashier[2], *v.tr.* Casser (un officier).

cashmere, *s.* Cachemire *m.*

cash-register, *s.* Caisse enregistreuse.

casino, *s.* Casino *m.*

cask, *s.* Barrique *f*, tonneau *m.*

casket, *s.* Coffret *m*, cassette *f.*

cassock, *s.* Soutane *f.*

cast[1], *s.* **1.** (*a*) Jet *m*; coup *m* (de dés); lancer *m* (du filet). (*b*) Bas *m* de ligne. **2.** Moulage *m.* **3.** Addition *f.* **4.** Distribution *f.*

cast[2], *v.tr.* **1.** Jeter, lancer. **2.** Additionner. **cast aside**, *v.tr.* Se défaire de. **cast away**, *v.tr.* (*a*) Jeter au loin; rejeter. (*b*) **To be c. a.**, faire naufrage. **cast down**, *v.tr.* (*a*) Baisser. (*b*) **To be c. d.**, être abattu. **cast off**, *v.tr.* Rejeter. **cast up**, *v.tr.* **1.** Reprocher. **2.** Rejeter.

castanets, *s.pl.* Castagnettes *f.*

castaway, *s.* Naufragé, -e.

caste, *s.* Caste *f.*

castigate, *v.tr.* Châtier, corriger.

castigation, *s.* Châtiment *m.*

castle[1], *s.* **1.** Château (fort). **2.** *Chess :* Tour *f.*

castle[2], *v.tr. Chess :* Roquer.

castor, *s.* **1.** Saupoudroir *m.* **2.** Roulette *f.*

castor oil, *s.* Huile *f* de ricin.

casual, *a.* (*a*) Fortuit, accidentel. (*b*) Insouciant.

casually, *adv.* (*a*) En passant. (*b*) Négligemment.

casualty, *s.* **1.** Accident *m.* **C. ward**, salle des accidentés. **2.** Mort, -e ; blessé, -e.

cat, *s.* **1.** (*a*) Chat, *f.* chatte. **Tom cat**, matou *m.* (*b*) **An old cat**, une vieille chipie. **2. The great cats**, les grands félins.

cataclysm, *s.* Cataclysme *m.*

catacombs, *s.pl.* Catacombes *f.*

catalogue[1], *s.* Catalogue *m*, liste *f.*

catalogue[2], *v.tr.* Cataloguer.

catapult[1], *s.* **1.** Fronde *f.* **2.** Catapulte *f* (de lancement).

catapult[2], *v.tr.* Lancer (un avion).

cataract, *s.* Cataracte *f.*

catarrh, *s.* Catarrhe *m.*

catastrophe, *s.* Catastrophe *f.*

catastrophic, *a.* Désastreux.

cat-burglar, *s.* Monte-en-l'air *m.*

catch[1], *s.* **1.** Prise *f.* **2.** Loquet *m.*

catch[2]. I. *v.tr.* **1.** Attraper, prendre. **2.** (*a*) Saisir ; rencontrer. (*b*) Accrocher. **3.** Attraper ; contracter. II. **catch**, *v.i.* **1.** S'accrocher. **2.** Prendre. **3.** Attacher. **catch up**, *v.tr.* Rattraper.

catching, *a.* Contagieux, infectieux.

catchword, *s.* Scie *f*, rengaine *f.*

catchy, *a.* Entraînant.

catechism, *s.* Catéchisme *m.*

catechize, *v.tr.* **1.** Catéchiser. **2.** Interroger.

categorical, *a.* Catégorique.

categorically, *adv.* Catégoriquement.

category, *s.* Catégorie *f.*

cater, *v.i.* **To c. for**, approvisionner ; pourvoir à.

caterer, *s.* Approvisionneur ; pourvoyeur.

catering, *s.* Approvisionnement *m.*

caterpillar, *s.* Chenille *f.*

caterwaul, *v.i.* Miauler.

caterwauling, *s.* Miaulements *mpl.*

catgut, *s.* Corde *f* de boyau.

cathedral, *a.* Cathédrale *f.*

Catherine. *Pr.n.* Catherine *f.* **C. wheel**, soleil *m.*

catholic. **1.** *a.* (*a*) Universel. (*b*) Tolérant. **2.** *a. & s.* Catholique (*mf*).

catholicism, *s.* Catholicisme *m.*

catkin, *s.* Chaton *m.*

cat's-paw, *s.* **1.** Risette *f.* **2.** Instrument *m.*

cattle, *s.* Bétail *m* ; bestiaux *mpl.*

cattle-shed, *s.* Étable *f.*

cattle-truck, *s.* Fourgon *m* à bestiaux.

cauldron, *s.* Chaudron *m.*

cauliflower, *s.* Chou-fleur *m*, *pl.* choux-fleurs.

cause[1], *s.* **1.** Cause *f.* **2.** Raison *f*, motif *m*, sujet *m.*

cause[2], *v.tr.* Causer, occasionner.

causeway, *s.* (*a*) Chaussée *f.* (*b*) Levée *f*, digue *f.*

caustic, *a. & s.* Caustique (*m*).

caustically, *adv.* D'un ton mordant.

cauterize, *v.tr.* Cautériser.

caution[1], *s.* **1.** Précaution *f*, prudence *f.* **2.** (*a*) Avis *m*, avertissement *m.* (*b*) Réprimande *f.*

caution[2], *v.tr.* Avertir.

cautious, *a.* Circonspect, prudent.

cautiously, *adv.* Avec circonspection ; prudemment.

cautiousness, *s.* Prudence *f.*

cavalcade, *s.* Cavalcade *f.*

cavalier. **1.** *s.* Cavalier *m.* **2.** *a.* Cavalier, désinvolte.

cavalierly, *adv.* Cavalièrement.

cavalry, *s.* Cavalerie *f.*

cave[1], *s.* Caverne *f*, antre *m.*

cave[2], *v.i* To c. in, s'effondrer.

cavern, *s.* Caverne *f.*

cavernous, *a.* Caverneux.

caviare, *s.* Caviar *m.*

cavil, *v.i.* Chicaner (*at*, sur).

cavilling, *a.* Chicaneur, -euse.

cavity, *s.* Cavité *f* ; creux *m.*

caw, *v.i.* Croasser.

cawing, *s.* Croassement *m.*

cease, *v.tr. & i.* Cesser.

ceasing, *s.* Cessation *f.* **Without c.**, sans arrêt.

ceaseless, *a.* Incessant ; sans arrêt.

ceaselessly, *adv.* Sans cesse.

cedar, *s.* Cèdre *m.*

cede, *v.tr.* Céder.

cedilla, *s.* Cédille *f.*

ceiling, *s.* Plafond *m.*

celebrate, *v.tr.* Célébrer.

celebrated, *a.* Célèbre (*for*, par).

celebration, *s.* Célébration *f.*

celebrity, *s.* Célébrité *f.*

celerity, *s.* Célérité *f.*

celery, *s.* Céleri *m.*

celestial, *a.* Céleste.

celibacy, *s.* Célibat *m.*

celibate. **1.** *a.* Célibataire ; de célibataire. **2.** *s.* Célibataire *mf.*

cell, *s.* **1.** Cellule *f.* **2.** Élément *m.* **Dry c.**, pile sèche.

cellar, *s.* Cave *f.*

'cello, *s.* Violoncelle *m.*

cellular, *a.* Cellulaire.

celluloid, *s.* Celluloïd *m.*

cellulose, *s.* Cellulose *f.*

Celtic, *a.* Celtique ; celte.

cement[1], *s.* Ciment *m.*

cement[2], *v.tr.* Cimenter.

cemetery, *s.* Cimetière *m.*

cenotaph, *s.* Cénotaphe *m.*

censer, *s.* Encensoir *m.*

censor[1], *s.* Censeur *m.*

censor[2], *v.tr.* **To be censored**, passer par le contrôle.

censorious, *a.* Sévère.

censorship, *s.* Censure *f.*

censure[1], *s.* Censure *f*, blâme *m.*

censure[2], *v.tr.* Censurer.

census, *s.* Recensement *m.*

cent, *s.* **Per c.**, pour cent.

centenarian, *a. & s.* Centenaire (*mf*).

centenary, *a. & s.* Centenaire (*m*).

centigrade, *a.* Centigrade.

central, *a.* Central, -aux.

centralize, *v.tr.* Centraliser.

centrally, *adv.* Centralement.

centre, *s.* **1.** Centre *m* ; milieu *m.* **In the c.**, au centre. **2.** *Attrib.* Central, -aux.

century, *s.* **1.** Siècle *m.* **2.** *Cr :* Centaine *f.*

cereal, *a. & s.* Céréale (*f*).

cerebral, *a.* Cérébral, -aux.

ceremonial. **1.** *a.* De cérémonie. **2.** *s.* Cérémonial *m.*

ceremonious, *a.* Cérémonieux.

ceremoniously, *adv.* Cérémonieusement.

ceremony, *s.* Cérémonie *f.* **To stand on c.**, faire des façons.

certain, *a.* Certain. (*a*) **To know sth. for c.**, être bien sûr de qch. (*b*) **To make c. of**, (i) s'assurer de ; (ii) s'assurer.

certainly, *adv.* (*a*) Certainement ; certes. (*b*) Assurément ; parfaitement.

certainty, *s.* (*a*) Certitude *f* ; chose certaine. **Of a c.**, à coup sûr. (*b*) Conviction *f.*

certificate, *s.* **1.** Certificat *m* ; titre *m* (d'actions). **2.** Diplôme *m.* **3.** Acte *m.* **4.** **Savings c.**, bon *m* d'épargne.

certificated, *a.* Diplômé, titré.

certify, *v.tr.* (*a*) Certifier, déclarer. **To c. a death**, constater un décès. (*b*) Authentiquer.

certitude, *s.* Certitude *f.*

cessation, *s.* Cessation *f*, arrêt *m.*

cession, *s.* Cession *f* ; abandon *m.*

Ceylon. *Pr.n.* Ceylan *m.*

chafe. **1.** *v.tr.* (*a*) Frictionner. (*b*) Écorcher. **2.** *v.i.* (*a*) S'érailler. (*b*) **To c. at**, s'énerver de.

chaff[1], *s.* Raillerie *f* ; persiflage *m.*

chaff[2], *v.tr.* Railler.

chaffinch, *s.* Pinson *m.*

chafing, *s.* **1.** Friction *f.* **2.** (*a*) Écorchement *m.* (*b*) Usure *f.*

chagrin[1], *s.* Chagrin *m*, dépit *m.*

chagrin[2], *v.tr.* Chagriner, dépiter.

chain[1], *s.* Chaîne *f.*

chain², *v.tr.* **I.** Attacher par une chaîne. **2. To c. down,** retenir par une chaîne. **Chained up,** à la chaîne.

chair, *s.* (*a*) Chaise *f*, siège *m*. **To take a c.,** s'asseoir. (*b*) **To be in the c.,** présider. **To take the c.** prendre la présidence.

chair-back, *s.* Dossier *m* de chaise.

chairman, *s.* Président, -ente.

chalice, *s.* Calice *m*.

chalk, *s.* Craie *f*. **French c.,** stéatite *f*.

chalky, *a.* **I.** Crayeux. **2.** Pâle.

challenge¹, *s.* (*a*) Défi *m*; provocation *f*. (*b*) Interpellation *f*.

challenge², *v.tr.* **I.** (*a*) Défier; provoquer. (*b*) Interpeller. **2.** Disputer, relever.

challenger, *s.* Provocateur, -trice.

challenging, *a.* Provocateur, -trice.

chamber, *s.* Chambre *f*.

chamberlain, *s.* Chambellan *m*.

chambermaid. *s.* Femme *f* de chambre.

chamber-music, *s.* Musique *f* de chambre.

chamois, *s.* Chamois *m*.

chamois-leather, *s.* (Peau *f* de) chamois *m*.

champagne, *s.* Vin *m* de Champagne; champagne *m*.

champion¹, *s.* Champion *m*.

champion², *v.tr.* Soutenir, défendre.

championship, *s.* **I.** Championnat *m*. **2.** Défense *f*.

chance¹, *s.* **I.** Chance *f*, hasard *m*, sort *m*. **By c.,** par hasard. **The chances are,** il y a fort à parier. **On the off c.,** à tout hasard. **2.** Occasion *f*. **To take one's c.,** risquer les chances. **3. To take a c.,** encourir un risque. **4.** *Attrib* Fortuit, accidentel.

chance². **I.** *v.i.* **To c. to do sth.,** faire qch. par hasard. **2.** *v.tr.* **To c. it,** risquer le coup.

chancel, *s.* **I.** Sanctuaire *m*. **2.** Chœur *m*.

chancellor, *s.* Chancelier *m*.

change¹, *s.* **I.** Changement *m*; revirement *m*. **For a c.,** comme distraction *f*; pour changer. **2. C. of clothes,** vêtements *mpl* de rechange. **3.** Change *m*. **4.** Monnaie *f*.

change². **I.** *v.tr.* Changer. (*a*) Modifier. (*b*) **To c. one's clothes,** changer de vêtements. (*c*) **All c.!** tout le monde descend! (*d*) Échanger. **2.** *v.i.* (Se) changer; se modifier.

changeable, *a.* Changeant; variable, inconstant.

changing, *a.* Changeant.

changing-room, *s.* Vestiaire *m*.

channel, *s.* **I.** (*a*) Passe *f*, chenal *m*. (*b*) **The (English) C.,** la Manche. **The C. Islands,** les îles Anglo-normandes. **2.** Canal, conduit *m*. **3.** Voie *f*.

chant¹, *s.* Chant *m*.

chant², *v.tr.* Psalmodier.

chaos, *s.* Chaos *m*.

chaotic, *a.* Chaotique, désorganisé.

chaotically, *adv.* Sans ordre.

chap¹, *s.* Gerçure *f*, crevasse *f*.

chap², *v.tr.* Gercer, crevasser.

chap³, *s.* Type *m*, individu *m*.

chapel, *s.* (*a*) Chapelle *f*. (*b*) Temple *m*.

chaperon¹, *s.* Chaperon *m*.

chaperon², *v.tr.* Chaperonner.

chaplain, *s.* Aumônier *m*.

chaplet, *s.* Chapelet *m*.

chapter, *s.* Chapitre *m*.

char, *v.tr.* Carboniser.

char-à-banc, *s.* Autocar *m*.

character, *s.* **I.** Caractère *m*. **2.** Lettre *f*. **3. A public c.,** une personnalité. **A bad c.,** un mauvais sujet.

characteristic. **I.** *a.* Caractéristique. **2.** *s.* Particularité *f*.

charcoal, *s.* Charbon *m* (de bois).

charge¹, *s.* **I.** Charge *f*. **2.** Frais *mpl*, prix *m*. **No c. for admission,** entrée gratuite. **3.** (*a*) Commission *f*, devoir *m*. (*b*) Emploi *m*; fonction *f*. **4.** Garde *f*, soin *m*. **To give in c.,** faire arrêter. **5.** Accusation *f*. **6.** Charge, attaque *f*.

charge², *v.tr. & i.* Charger.

chargeable, *a.* **I.** A la charge (*to*, de). **2.** Imputable.

charitable, *a.* **I.** Charitable. **2.** De bienfaisance, de charité.

charitably, *adv.* Charitablement.

charity, *s.* **I.** Charité *f*. **2.** (*a*) Acte *m* de charité. (*b*) Charité, aumônes *fpl*.

charm¹, *s.* **I.** Charme *m*; sortilège *m*. **2.** (*a*) Amulette *f*. (*b*) Breloque *f*. **3.** Charme, agrément *m*.

charm², *v.tr.* Charmer, enchanter.

charmer, *s.* Charmeur, -euse.

charming, *a.* Charmant, ravissant.

chart, *s.* **I.** Carte *f* (marine). **2.** Diagramme *m*.

charter[1], *s.* **1.** Charte *f.* **2.** Affrètement *m.*

charter[2], *v.tr.* Affréter, fréter.

charwoman, *s.* Femme *f* de journée.

chary, *a.* Circonspect.

chase[1], *s.* Chasse *f*, poursuite *f.*

chase[2], *v.tr.* Poursuivre.

chasm, *s.* Gouffre béant.

chassis, *s.* Châssis *m.*

chaste, *a.* Chaste, pudique.

chasten, *v.tr.* Châtier, éprouver.

chastened, *a.* Assagi ; radouci.

chastise, *v.tr.* Châtier ; corriger.

chastisement, *s.* Châtiment *m.*

chastity, *s.* Chasteté *f.*

chat[1], *s.* Causerie *f*, causette *f.*

chat[2], *v.i.* Causer, bavarder.

chatter[1], *s.* Caquet(age) *m*, jacasserie *f* ; bavardage *m.*

chatter[2], *v.i.* **1.** Bavarder, caqueter. **2.** Claquer.

chattering, *s.* **1.** Bavardage *m.* **2.** Claquement *m.*

chauffeur, *s.* Chauffeur, -euse ; conducteur, -trice.

cheap. 1. *a.* (*a*) (A) bon marché. **Cheaper**, (à) meilleur marché. (*b*) De peu de valeur. **2.** *adv.* (A) bon marché.

cheaply, *adv.* (A) bon marché.

cheapness, *s.* Bon marché.

cheat[1], *s.* (*a*) Trompeur, -euse, escroc *m.* (*b*) Tricheur, -euse.

cheat[2], *v.tr.* **1.** Tromper. **To c. out of**, frustrer de. **2.** Tricher.

cheating, *s.* **1.** Tromperie *f.* **2.** Tricherie *f.*

check[1], *s.* **1.** Échec *m.* **2.** Arrêt *m*, pause *f.* **3.** Frein *m.* **4.** Contrôle *m.*

check[2], *v.tr.* (*a*) Faire échec à ; arrêter. (*b*) Refouler. (*c*) Réprimander. (*d*) Vérifier. **To c. (off)**, pointer. **To c. (up)**, contrôler.

check[3], *s.* Carreau *m* ; à carreaux.

checking, *s.* **1.** Répression *f.* **2.** Contrôle *m* ; vérification *f.*

checkmate[1], *s.* Échec et mat *m.*

checkmate[2], *v.tr.* **1.** Faire échec et mat à. **2.** Déjouer.

cheek, *s.* **1.** Joue *f.* **2.** Effronterie *f.*

cheek-bone, *s.* Pommette *f*

cheeky, *a.* Effronté.

cheer[1], *s.* Hourra *m* ; *pl.* acclamations *f.*

cheer[2]. **1.** *v.tr.* (*a*) Égayer. (*b*) Applaudir. **2.** *v.i.* (*a*) **To c. up**, reprendre sa gaieté. (*b*) Pousser des hourras ; applaudir.

cheerful, *a.* Gai ; de bonne humeur ; riant ; réconfortant.

cheerfully, *adv.* **1.** Allégrement. **2.** De bon cœur.

cheerfulness, *s.* Gaieté *f* ; contentement *m.*

cheerily, *adv.* Gaiement.

cheering[1], *a.* Encourageant.

cheering[2], *s.* Applaudissements *mpl.*

cheerless, *a.* Morne, triste.

cheery, *a.* Joyeux, gai.

cheese, *s.* Fromage *m.*

chef, *s.* Chef *m* de cuisine.

chemical. 1. *a.* Chimique. **2.** *s.pl.* Produits *m* chimiques.

chemise, *s.* Chemise *f* (de femme).

chemist, *s.* **1.** Pharmacien. **Chemist's shop**, pharmacie *f.* **2.** Chimiste *m.*

chemistry, *s.* Chimie *f.*

cheque, *s.* Chèque *m.*

cheque-book, *s.* Carnet *m* de chèques.

chequered, *a.* Accidenté.

cherish, *v.tr.* **1.** Chérir. **2.** Caresser.

cherry. 1. *s.* Cerise *f.* **2.** *a.* Cerise *inv.*

cherry-orchard, *s.* Cerisaie *f.*

cherry-stone, *s.* Noyau *m* de cerise.

cherry-tree, *s.* Cerisier *m.*

cherub, *s.* Chérubin *m.*

chess, *s.* Jeu *m* d'échecs. **To play c.**, jouer aux échecs.

chess-board, *s.* Échiquier *m.*

chess-men, *s.pl.* Pièces *f* (du jeu d'échecs).

chest, *s.* **1.** Coffre *m.* **2.** Poitrine *f.*

chestnut. 1. *s.* (*a*) Châtaigne *f* ; marron *m.* (*b*) C.(-tree), châtaignier *m* ; marronnier *m.* **2.** *Attrib.* : Châtain ; (cheval) alezan.

chew, *v.tr.* Mâcher, mastiquer.

chicanery, *s.* Chicanerie *f.*

chick, *s.* Poussin *m.*

chicken, *s.* Poulet *m.* **Spring c.**, poussin *m.*

chicory, *s.* Chicorée *f.*

chide, *v.tr. & i.* Gronder.

chief. I. *s.* Chef *m.* **II. chief**, *a.* Principal, -aux ; premier ; (en) chef.

chiefly, *adv.* **1.** Surtout, avant tout. **2.** Principalement.

chieftain, *s.* Chef *m.*

chiffon, *s.* Chiffon *m*, gaze *f.*

chilblain, *s.* Engelure *f.*

child, s. Enfant mf. **From a c.,** dès son enfance.
child-birth, s. Enfantement m.
childhood, s. Enfance f.
childish, a. Enfantin, d'enfant.
childishly, adv. Comme un enfant; puérilement.
childishness, s. Enfantillage m, puérilité f.
childless, a. Sans enfant(s).
childlike, a. Enfantin; naïf.
child's-play, s. Jeu m d'enfant.
chill¹, s. **1.** (a) Froid m. (b) Frisson m. **2. To take the c. off,** tiédir.
chill², a. Froid, glacé.
chill³, v.tr. Refroidir, glacer; faire frissonner.
chilliness, s. Froid m, froideur f.
chilly, a. **1.** (a) Frileux. (b) **To feel c.,** avoir froid. **2.** Froid.
chime¹, s. Carillon m.
chime². **1.** v.i. Carillonner. **To c. in with,** s'harmoniser avec. **2.** v.tr. Carillonner.
chimera, s. Chimère f.
chimerical, a. Chimérique.
chimney, s. Cheminée f. **Lamp c.,** verre m de lampe.
chimney-corner, s. Coin m du feu.
chimney-piece, s. Cheminée f.
chimney-pot, s. Pot m de cheminée.
chimney-sweep, s. Ramoneur m.
chimpanzee, s. Chimpanzé m.
chin, s. Menton m.
China. **1.** Pr.n. La Chine. **2.** s. Porcelaine f; faïence fine.
Chinese. **1.** a. & s. Chinois, -e. **2.** s. Le chinois.
chink¹, s. Fente f, crevasse f; entre-bâillement m.
chink². **1.** v.tr. Faire sonner; faire tinter. **2.** v.i. Sonner.
chintz, s. Perse f, indienne f.
chip¹, s. **1.** Éclat m, copeau m. **2.** Brisure f. **3.** **Chips,** pommes de terre frites.
chip², v.tr. **1.** Tailler par éclats. **2.** (a) Ébrécher; écorner.
chiropodist, s. Pédicure mf.
chiropody, s. Chirurgie f pédicure.
chirp, v.i. Pépier, gazouiller.
chisel¹, s. Ciseau m.
chisel², v.tr. Ciseler.
chivalrous, a. Chevaleresque.
chivalry, s. Conduite f chevaleresque
chlorate, s. Chlorate m.

chloride, s. Chlorure m.
chloroform, s. Chloroforme m.
chock, s. Cale f; tin m, coin m.
chocolate. **1.** s. Chocolat m. **2.** a. Chocolat inv.
choice¹, s. **1.** Choix m. (a) **For c.,** de préférence. (b) Alternative f. **2.** Assortiment m.
choice², a. Choisi; de choix.
choir, s. Chœur m.
choir-boy, s. Enfant m de chœur.
choir-master, s. Maître m de chapelle.
choke. **1.** v.tr. Étouffer, suffoquer; obstruer. **2.** v.i. Étouffer, suffoquer.
choking, s. **1.** Étouffement m. **2.** Engorgement m.
choleric, a. Colérique, irascible.
choose, v.tr. **1.** Choisir; faire choix de. **2. When I c.,** quand je voudrai.
choosing, s. Choix m.
chop¹, s. Côtelette f.
chop², v.tr. Couper, fendre. **chop down,** v.tr. Abattre. **chop off,** v.tr. Trancher. **chop up,** v.tr. Couper en morceaux.
chopper, s. Couperet m, hachoir m.
choppy, a. **C. sea,** mer hachée.
choral, a. **1.** Choral (no m. pl.). **2.** Chanté en chœur.
chord¹, s. Corde f.
chord², s. Accord m.
chortle, v.i. Glousser de joie.
chorus, s. **1.** Chœur m. **2.** Refrain m.
chosen, a. Choisi. **s. The c.,** les élus.
Christ. Pr.n. Le Christ.
christen, v.tr. Baptiser.
christening, s. Baptême m.
Christian, a. & s. Chrétien, -ienne.
Christianity, s. Christianisme m.
Christmas, s. Noël m.
Christmas-box, s. = Étrennes fpl.
Christmas-card, s. Carte f de Noël.
Christmas-day, s. Le jour de Noël.
Christmas-eve, s. La veille de Noël.
Christmas-tree, s. Arbre m de Noël.
chrome, s. (a) **C. leather,** cuir chromé. (b) **C. yellow,** jaune de chrome.
chromium, s. Chrome m.
chronic, a. (a) Chronique. (b) Constant, continuel.
chronicle, s. Chronique f.
chronological, a. Chronologique.
chronometer, s. Chronomètre m.
chrysalis, s. Chrysalide f.

chrysanthemum, *s.* Chrysanthème *m.*

chubby, *a.* Boulot, -otte ; joufflu.

chubby-cheeked, *a.* Joufflu.

chuckle[1], *s.* Rire étouffé.

chuckle[2], *v.i.* Rire sous cape.

chum, *s.* Camarade *mf.*

chump, *s.* (*a*) Tronçon *m.* (*b*) C.-chop, côtelette *f* de gigot.

chunk, *s.* Gros morceau.

church, *s.* **1.** Église *f.* **2. C. service,** office *m.* **To go to c.,** aller à l'office.

churchwarden, *s.* Marguillier *m.*

churchyard, *s.* Cimetière *m.*

churlish, *a.* (*a*) Mal élevé ; grossier. (*b*) Hargneux.

churlishness, *s.* (*a*) Grossièreté *f.* (*b*) Tempérament hargneux.

churn[1], *s.* Baratte *f.*

churn[2], *v.tr.* Baratter ; battre.

cicerone, *s.* Cicerone *m.*

cider, *s.* Cidre *m.*

cigar, *s.* Cigare *m.*

cigar-case, *s.* Étui *m* à cigares.

cigarette, *s.* Cigarette *f.*

cigarette-case, *s.* Étui *m* à cigarettes.

cigarette-holder, *s.* Porte-cigarette *m,* *pl.* porte-cigarettes.

cinder, *s.* **1.** Cendre *f.* **2.** *pl.* Escarbilles *fpl.*

Cinderella. *Pr.n.* Cendrillon *f.*

cinder-track, *s.* Piste *f* (en) cendrée.

cine-camera, *s.* Camera *f.*

cinema, *s.* Cinéma *m.*

cinnamon, *s.* Cannelle *f.*

cipher, *s.* **1.** Zéro *m.* **2.** (*a*) Chiffre *m.* (*b*) Message chiffré.

circle, *s.* **1.** Cercle *m.* **2. Upper c.,** seconde galerie. **3.** Milieu *m.* coterie *f.*

circuit, *s.* **1.** Pourtour *m.* **2.** (*a*) Révolution *f.* (*b*) Tournée *f.* **3.** Détour *m.* **4.** Circuit. **Short c.,** court-circuit *m.*

circuitous, *a.* Détourné.

circular, *a. & s.* Circulaire (*f*).

circulate. **1.** *v.i.* Circuler. **2.** *v.tr.* Faire circuler.

circulation, *s.* Circulation *f* ; tirage *m.*

circumcise, *v.tr.* Circoncire.

circumcised, *a.* Circoncis.

circumcision, *s.* Circoncision *f.*

circumference, *s.* Circonférence *f.*

circumflex, *a. & s.* **C.** (accent), accent *m* circonflexe.

circumlocution, *s.* Circonlocution *f.* ambages *fpl.*

circumscribe, *v.tr.* Limiter.

circumscribed, *a.* Restreint, limité.

circumspect, *a.* Circonspect.

circumspection, *s.* Circonspection *f*

circumspectly, *adv.* Prudemment ; avec circonspection *f.*

circumstance, *s.* **1.** Circonstance, détail *m,* fait *m.* **2.** *pl.* (*a*) Circonstances *f.* **That depends on circumstances,** c'est selon. (*b*) Moyens.

circumstantial, *a.* **1.** Circonstanciel. **C. evidence,** preuves indirectes. **2.** Circonstancié, détaillé.

circumvent, *v.tr.* Circonvenir.

circus, *s.* (*a*) Cirque *m.* (*b*) Rond-point *m.*

cistern, *s.* (*a*) Réservoir *m* à eau. (*b*) Citerne *f.*

citadel, *s.* Citadelle *f.*

cite, *v.tr.* Citer.

citizen, *s.* Citoyen, -enne.

citrate, *s.* Citrate *m.*

citric, *a.* Citrique.

city, *s.* (*a*) Grande ville. (*b*) Cité *f.*

civet, *s.* Civette *f.*

civic, *a.* Civique.

civil, *a.* **1.** Civil. **2. C. defence,** défense passive. **3.** Poli, courtois.

civilian, *s. & a.* Civil (*m*).

civility, *s.* Civilité *f* ; politesse *f*

civilization, *s.* Civilisation *f.*

civilize, *v.tr.* Civiliser.

civilly, *adv.* Civilement, poliment.

claim[1], *s.* **1.** Demande *f* ; réclamation *f.* **2.** Droit *m,* titre *m.* **3.** Créance *f.* **4.** Concession (minière).

claim[2], *v.tr.* (*a*) Réclamer ; demander. (*b*) Prétendre, affirmer.

claimant, *s.* Prétendant, -ante.

clamber, *v.i.* Grimper **To c. over.** escalader.

clamminess, *s.* Moiteur froide.

clammy, *a.* **1.** (Froid et) moite. **2.** Gluant, collant.

clamorous, *a.* Bruyant, braillard.

clamour[1], *s.* Clameur *f* ; cris *mpl.*

clamour[2], *v.i.* Pousser des clameurs. **To c. for,** réclamer à grands cris.

clamp[1], *s.* Crampon *m.*

clamp[2], *v.tr.* Agrafer.

clan, *s.* **1.** Clan *m.* **2.** (*a*) Tribu *f.* (*b*) Coterie *f.*

clandestine, *a.* Clandestin.

clang[1], *s.* Son *m* métallique.

clang[2], *v.i.* Retentir, résonner.

clank[1], *s.* Cliquetis *m.*

clank². **1.** *v.i.* Résonner. **2.** *v.tr.* Faire sonner.

clap¹, *s.* (*a*) Battement *m.* **To give a c.,** applaudir. (*b*) Coup *m* ; tape *f.*

clap². **1.** *v.tr.* (*a*) Applaudir. **To c. one's hands,** battre des mains. **To c. on the back,** donner une tape dans le dos. (*b*) Battre (des ailes). **2.** *v.i.* Applaudir.

clapper, *s.* Battant *m.*

clapping, *s.* Battement *m* des mains ; applaudissements *mpl.*

claret, *s.* Vin *m* de Bordeaux rouge.

clarinet, *s.* Clarinette *f.*

clarion, *s.* Clairon *m.*

clarity, *s.* Clarté *f.*

clash¹, *s.* **1.** Fracas *m* ; résonnement *m* ; cliquetis *m.* **2.** Conflit *m* ; échauffourée *f.*

clash², *v.i.* (*a*) Résonner. (*b*) Jurer ; faire disparate ; se heurter.

clasp¹, *s.* **1.** Agrafe *f* ; fermeture *f* ; fermoir *m.* **2.** Étreinte *f.*

clasp², *v.tr.* **1.** Agrafer. **2.** Serrer, étreindre. **3.** Joindre.

class¹, *s.* **1.** Classe *f.* **2. The upper c.,** les gens du monde. **The lower classes,** le prolétariat. **The middle c.,** la bourgeoisie. **3.** Sorte *f,* genre *m.*

class², *v.tr.* Classer.

classic, *a.* & *s.* Classique (*m*).

classical, *a.* Classique.

classification, *s.* Classification *f.*

classify, *v.tr.* Classer.

class-room, *s.* (Salle *f* de) classe *f.*

clatter, *s.* Bruit *m,* vacarme *m.*

clause, *s.* Clause *f,* article *m.*

claw¹, *s.* Griffe *f* ; serre *f* ; pince *f.*

claw². **1.** *v.tr.* Griffer, égratigner. **2.** *v.i.* **To c. at,** s'accrocher à.

clay, *s.* Argile *f.*

clean¹. **I.** *a.* Propre, net. **C. break,** cassure nette. **C. hands,** (i) mains propres ; (ii) mains nettes.
II. clean, *adv.* **1.** Tout à fait. **I c. forgot,** j'ai absolument oublié. **2. C. through,** de part en part.

clean², *s.* Nettoyage *m.*

clean³, *v.tr.* Nettoyer. **clean up,** *v.tr.* **1.** Nettoyer. **2.** *Abs.* Faire le nettoyage.

clean-handed, *a.* Aux mains nettes.

cleaning, *s.* Nettoyage *m.*

cleanliness, *s.* Propreté *f* ; netteté *f.*

cleanly¹, *a.* Propre (par habitude).

cleanly², *adv.* Proprement, nettement.

cleanness, *s.* **1.** Propreté *f.* **2.** Netteté *f.*

cleanse, *v.tr.* **1.** Curer. **2.** Purifier.

clean-shaven, *a.* Sans barbe ni moustache ; glabre.

cleansing¹, *a.* Assainissant, purifiant.

cleansing², *s.* **1.** Curage *m.* **2.** Purification *f.*

clear¹. **I.** *a.* **1.** Clair, limpide ; net, *f.* nette. **2.** Certain, évident. **3.** Lucide. **4. To be c. about,** être convaincu de. **5. C. majority,** majorité absolue. **6.** Libre, dégagé. **'All c.!'** "fin d'alerte."
II. clear, *a.* or *adv.* **To keep c. of,** éviter.

clear². **I.** *v.tr.* **1.** Éclaircir. **2.** Innocenter. **To c. oneself,** se disculper. **3.** Dégager ; désencombrer. **C. the way!** faites place ! **To c. the table,** enlever le couvert. **4. To c. the letter-box,** lever les lettres. **5. To c. a barrier,** franchir une barrière. **6.** Affranchir ; solder.
II. clear, *v.i.* **To c. (up),** s'éclaircir. **To c. (away),** se dissiper.

clear away, *v.tr.* Enlever, ôter.

clear off, *v.tr.* S'acquitter de.

clear out, *v.tr.* Nettoyer. **clear up**, *v.tr.* Éclaircir, élucider.

clearance, *s.* **C. sale,** vente *f* de soldes.

clear-cut, *a.* Net, *f.* nette.

clear-headed, *a.* Perspicace.

clearing, *s.* **1.** Désinculpation *f.* **2.** Dégagement *m.* **3.** Éclaircie *f.*

clearly, *adv.* Clairement, nettement. **To see c.,** voir clair.

clearness, *s.* **1.** Clarté *f.* **2.** Netteté *f.*

clear-sighted, *a.* Clairvoyant.

cleave, *v.tr.* Fendre.

cleaver, *s.* Fendoir *m.*

clef, *s.* Clef *f.*

cleft, *s.* Fente *f,* fissure *f.* crevasse *f.*

clematis, *s.* Clématite *f.*

clemency, *s.* **1.** Clémence *f* (*to,* envers). **2.** Douceur *f.*

clement, *a.* **1.** Clément, indulgent (*to,* envers). **2.** Doux, *f.* douce.

clench, *v.tr.* Serrer.

clergy, *s.* **1.** Clergé *m.* **2.** Membres *m* du clergé.

clergyman, *s.* Ecclésiastique *m.*

cleric, *s.* Ecclésiastique *m.*

clerical, *a.* **1.** Clérical, -aux. **2. C. error,** faute de copiste.

clerk, *s.* Employé, -ée, de bureau; commis *m.*

clerkship, *s.* Emploi *m*, place *f*, de commis. ,

clever, *a.* **1.** Habile, adroit. **2.** (*a*) Intelligent. (*b*) Ingénieux.

cleverly, *adv.* Habilement, adroitement.

cleverness, *s.* **1.** Habileté *f*, adresse *f*. **2.** Intelligence *f*.

click¹, *s.* Bruit sec ; clic *m* ; cliquetis *m*.

click², *v.tr.* & *i.* Cliqueter ; claquer.

client, *s.* Client, -ente.

clientele, *s.* Clientèle *f*.

cliff, *s.* Falaise *f*.

climate, *s.* Climat *m.*

climax, *s.* Comble *m.*

climb¹, *s.* **1.** Ascension *f.* **2.** Montée *f.*

climb², *v.tr.* & *i.* **1.** Monter, gravir ; grimper à. **To c.** over, franchir. **2.** S'élever. **3.** Prendre de l'altitude. **climb down,** *v.i.* Descendre.

climber, *s.* Ascensionniste *mf.*

climbing¹, *a.* Grimpant.

climbing², *s.* Escalade *f* ; montée *f.*

clinch, *v.tr.* (*a*) River. (*b*) Conclure.

cling, *v.i.* (*a*) S'attacher, s'accrocher. **To c. close to,** se serrer contre. (*b*) Adhérer.

clinic, *s.* Clinique *f.*

clinical, *a.* Clinique. **C. thermo-meter,** thermomètre médical.

clink¹, *s.* Tintement *m*, choc *m.*

clink². **I.** *v.i.* Tinter. **2.** *v.tr.* Faire tinter. **To c. glasses,** trinquer.

clip¹, *s.* Pince *f*, attache *f.*

clip², *v.tr.* Pincer, serrer.

clip³, *v.tr.* **1.** Tondre ; tailler. **2.** Poinçonner.

clique, *s.* Coterie *f.*

cloak¹, *s.* Manteau *m.*

cloak², *v.tr.* (*a*) Couvrir d'un manteau. (*b*) Masquer.

cloak-room, *s.* **1.** Vestiaire *m.* **2.** Consigne *f.*

clock, *s.* Horloge *f* ; pendule *f.*

clockwork, *s.* Mouvement *m* d'hor-logerie. **Like c.,** comme sur des roulettes.

clod, *s.* Motte *f* (de terre).

clog¹, *s.* **1.** Entrave *f.* **2.** Galoche *f.*

clog², *v.tr.* (*a*) Boucher, obstruer. (*b*) Entraver.

cloister, *s.* Cloître *m.*

close¹. **I.** *a.* **1.** (*a*) Bien fermé ; clos. (*b*) Renfermé. **C. weather,** temps lourd. (*c*) Exclusif. (*d*) **C. season,** chasse fermée. **2.** **C. connection,** rapport étroit. **C. friend,** ami(e) intime. **C. resemblance,** ressem-blance exacte. **3.** Réservé. **4.** Avare, regardant.
  II. close, *adv.* **1.** Étroitement. **2.** Près, de près. **3.** (*a*) Serré, serrés. **3. C. at hand, c. by,** tout près.

close², *s.* (*a*) Clos *m*, enclos *m.* (*b*) Enceinte *f.*

close³, *s.* Fin *f*, conclusion *f.*

close⁴. **I.** *v.tr.* **1.** Fermer. **2.** Con-clure, terminer. **3.** Serrer.
  II. close, *v.i.* **1.** (Se) fermer ; refermer. **2.** Finir ; se terminer.

close down. **I.** *v.tr.* Fermer. **2.** *v.i.* (*a*) Fermer. (*b*) Terminer l'émission.

close up. **1.** *v.tr.* Boucher ; barrer. **2.** *v.i.* (*a*) S'obturer. (*b*) Se serrer.

closed, *a.* Fermé ; obturé. **With c. eyes,** les yeux clos.

close-fitting, *a.* Collant.

closely, *adv.* Étroitement.

closeness, *s.* **1.** Rapprochement *m*, proximité *f.* **2.** (*a*) Manque *m* d'air. (*b*) Lourdeur *f.* **3.** Réserve *f.*

closet, *s.* **1.** Cabinet *m.* **2.** Armoire *f*, placard *m.*

closing¹, *a.* Dernier ; final, -als.

closing², *s.* **1.** Fermeture *f.* **2.** Clôture *f.*

clot¹, *s.* Caillot *m.*

clot², *v.i.* Se cailler ; se figer.

cloth, *s.* **1.** (*a*) Drap *m.* (*b*) Toile *f.* **2.** Linge *m* ; torchon *m.*

clothe, *v.tr.* Vêtir, habiller (*in*, de).

clothes, *s.pl.* Vêtements *m*, habits *m.*

clothes-basket, *s.* Panier *m* au linge sale.

clothes-horse, *s.* Séchoir *m.*

clothes-line, *s.* Étendoir *m.*

clothes-peg, *s.* Pince *f* ; fichoir *m.*

clothes-prop, *s.* Perche *f* d'étendoir.

clothier, *s.* (*a*) Drapier *m.* (*b*) Mar-chand *m* de confections.

clothing, *s.* Habillement *m* ; vête-ments *mpl.*

cloud¹, *s.* **1.** Nuage *m.* **Under a c.,** l'objet de soupçons. **2.** Nuée *f.*

cloud². **1.** *v.tr.* Couvrir, voiler. **2.** *v.i.* Se couvrir (de nuages) ; s'assombrir.

clouded, *a.* (Ciel) couvert.

cloudiness, *s.* **1.** Aspect nuageux. **2.** Turbidité *f.*

cloudy, *a.* **1.** (Temps) couvert; nuageux. **2.** Trouble.

clove, *s.* Clou *m* de girofle.

clover, *s.* Trèfle *m.*

clown, *s.* **1.** Rustre *m*, manant *m.* **2.** (*a*) Bouffon *m.* (*b*) Clown *m.*

cloy, *v.tr.* Rassasier; écœurer.

cloying, *a.* Rassasiant, affadissant.

club[1], *s.* **1.** (*a*) Massue *f*, gourdin *m.* (*b*) *Golf:* Club *m.* **2.** *Cards:* Trèfle *m.* **3.** (*a*) Cercle *m.* (*b*) Association *f.*

club[2]. **1.** *v.tr.* Frapper avec une massue. **2.** *v.i.* To c. together, se cotiser.

clucking, *s.* Gloussement *m.*

clue, *s.* Indication *f*, indice *m*; définition *f.*

clump, *s.* Groupe *m*, bouquet *m.*

clumsily, *adv.* Maladroitement.

clumsiness, *s.* Maladresse *f.*

clumsy, *a.* **1.** Maladroit, gauche. **2.** Lourd, informe.

cluster[1], *s.* Groupe *m*; grappe *f.*

cluster[2], *v.i.* Se grouper.

clutch[1], *s.* Embrayage *m.* To let in the c., embrayer.

clutch[2], *v.tr. & ind.tr.* Saisir, empoigner. To c. at, se raccrocher à.

clutch[3], *s.* Couvée *f* (d'œufs).

clutter[1], *s.* Encombrement *m.*

clutter[2], *v.tr.* To c. up, encombrer (*with*, de).

coach[1], *s.* **1.** Voiture *f*, wagon *m.* **2.** (*a*) Répétiteur *m.* (*b*) Entraîneur *m.*

coach[2], *v.tr.* Entraîner.

coachman, *s.* Cocher *m.*

coagulate. **1.** *v.tr.* Coaguler, figer. **2.** *v.i.* Se coaguler, se figer.

coagulation, *s.* Coagulation *f.*

coal[1], *s.* Charbon *m* (de terre); houille *f.*

coal[2], *v.tr.* Faire le charbon.

coal-cellar, *s.* Cave *f* au charbon.

coalesce, *v.i.* S'unir; se fondre.

coalescence, *s.* Coalescence *f.*

coal-field, *s.* Bassin houiller.

coaling, *s.* Charbonnage *m.*

coalition, *s.* Coalition *f.*

coalman, *s.* Charbonnier *m.*

coal-merchant, *s.* Marchand *m* de charbon.

coal-mine, *s.* Mine *f* de houille.

coal-scuttle, *s.* Seau *m* à charbon.

coal-shovel, *s.* Pelle *f* à charbon.

coal-tar, *s.* Goudron *m* de houille.

coarse, *a.* Grossier; vulgaire.

coarsely, *adv.* Grossièrement.

coarseness, *s.* Grossièreté *f*, brutalité *f.*

coast[1], *s.* Côte *f*, rivage *m.*

coast[2], *v.i. & tr.* Suivre la côte.

coast-guard, *s.* Garde-côte *m*, *pl.* gardes-côte.

coastline, *s.* Littoral *m.*

coat[1], *s.* **1.** (*a*) Habit *m.* (*b*) C. and skirt, costume *m* tailleur. (*c*) C. of arms, armoiries *fpl.* **2.** Robe *f* (d'un chien). **3.** Couche *f* (de peinture).

coat[2], *v.tr.* Enduire (*with*, de).

coated, *a.* Enduit (*with*, de); chargé.

coat-hanger, *s.* Cintre *m*; portevêtements *m inv.*

coat-hook, *s.* Patère *f.*

coax, *v.tr.* Cajoler, enjôler.

coaxing[1], *a.* Câlin.

coaxing[2], *s.* Cajolerie *f.*

cobble[1], *s.* Galet *m*, caillou *m.*

cobble[2], *v.tr.* Paver de galets.

cobbler, *s.* Savetier *m.*

cobra, *s.* Cobra *m.*

cobweb, *s.* Toile *f* d'araignée.

cocaine, *s.* Cocaïne *f.*

cochineal, *s.* Cochenille *f.*

cock[1], *s.* **1.** Coq *m.* **2.** (*a*) Robinet *m.* (*b*) At full c., au cran d'armé.

cock[2], *v.tr.* **1.** Dresser (les oreilles). **2.** Cocked hat, chapeau à cornes. **3.** Armer (un fusil).

cockade, *s.* Cocarde *f.*

cockatoo, *s.* Cacatoès *m.*

cockchafer, *s.* Hanneton *m.*

cock-crow, *s.* Chant *m* du coq.

cockerel, *s.* Jeune coq *m.*

cock-fight, *s.* Combat *m* de coqs.

cockle, *s.* Bucarde *f*, clovisse *f.*

cockpit, *s.* **1.** Poste *m* des blessés. **2.** Carlingue *f.*

cockroach, *s.* Blatte *f.*

cock-sure, *a.* Sûr de soi.

cocktail, *s.* Cocktail *m.*

cocoa, *s.* Cacao *m.*

coco-nut, *s.* **1.** Noix *f* de coco. **2.** C.-nut palm, cocotier *m.*

cocoon, *s.* Cocon *m.*

cod, *s.* Morue *f*; cabillaud *m.*

coddle, *v.tr.* Gâter, choyer.

code, *s.* **1.** Code *m.* **2.** (*a*) C. word, mot convenu. (*b*) Chiffre *m.*

codicil, *s.* Codicille *m.*

codify, *v.tr.* Codifier.

cod-liver-oil, *s.* Huile *f* de foie de morue.

coefficient, *s.* Coefficient *m.*

coerce, *v.tr.* Forcer, contraindre.

coercion, *s.* Coercition *f*, contrainte *f.*

coffee, *s.* Café *m.* **Black c.,** café noir ; café nature. **White c.,** café au lait ; café crème.

coffee-bean, *s.* Grain *m* de café

coffee-cup, *s.* Tasse *f* à café.

coffee-grounds, *s.pl.* Marc *m* de café.

coffee-pot, *s.* Cafetière *f.*

coffer, *s.* Coffre *m.*

coffin, *s.* Cercueil *m*

cog, *s.* Dent *f.*

cogency, *s.* Force *f*, puissance *f.*

cogent, *a.* Puissant ; valable.

cogitate, *v.i.* Méditer, réfléchir.

cogitation, *s* Réflexion *f*, délibération *f*

cognizance, *s.* Connaissance *f.*

cognizant, *a.* Instruit.

cognomen, *s.* Surnom *m.*

cog-wheel, *s.* Roue dentée.

cohere, *v.i.* Se tenir ensemble ; adhérer.

coherent, *a.* Cohérent.

coherently, *adv.* Avec cohérence.

cohesion, *s.* Cohésion *f* ; adhérence *f.*

cohesive, *a.* Cohésif.

coil¹, *s.* **1.** Rouleau *m.* **2.** Pli *m*, repli *m* ; anneau *m.* **3.** Enroulement *m*, bobine *f.*

coil². **1.** *v.tr.* (En)rouler. **2.** *v.i.* Serpenter.

coiling, *s.* Enroulement *m* ; bobinage *m.*

coin¹, *s.* Pièce *f* de monnaie.

coin², *v.tr.* **1.** Frapper. **2.** Inventer.

coinage, *s.* (*a*) Système *m* monétaire. (*b*) Monnaie(s) *f.*

coincide, *v.i.* **1.** Coïncider. **2.** S'accorder, être d'accord.

coincidence, *s.* Coïncidence *f.*

coiner, *s.* Faux monnayeur.

coke, *s.* Coke *m.*

colander, *s.* Passoire *f.*

cold¹, *a.* Froid. (*a*) **It is c.,** il fait froid. **To grow c.,** se refroidir. **C. storage,** conservation par le froid. (*b*) **To be c., to feel c.,** avoir froid.

cold², *s.* **1.** Froid *m.* **2.** Rhume *m.* **To have a c.,** être enrhumé. **C. in the head,** rhume de cerveau.

cold-blooded, *a.* **1.** A sang froid. **2.** Froid, insensible ; délibéré.

coldly, *adv.* Froidement.

coldness, *s.* Froideur *f.*

collaborate, *v.i.* Collaborer.

collaboration, *s.* Collaboration *f.*

collaborator, *s.* Collaborateur, -trice.

collapse¹, *s.* **1.** Écroulement *m*, effondrement *m.* **2.** Affaissement subit.

collapse², *v.i.* S'affaisser ; s'écrouler, s'effondrer.

collapsible, *a.* Pliant.

collar¹, *s.* **1.** (*a*) Col *m* ; collet *m* (de manteau). **Lace c.,** collerette *f.* (*b*) Faux col. **Size in collars,** encolure *f.* **2.** Collier *m.*

collar², *v.tr.* Colleter ; saisir au collet.

collar-bone, *s.* Clavicule *f.*

collate, *v.tr.* Collationner.

collateral, *a.* Collatéral, -aux.

collation, *s.* Collation *f.*

colleague, *s.* Collègue *mf* ; confrère *m.*

collect. **1.** *v.tr.* (*a*) Rassembler ; assembler. (*b*) Collectionner. (*c*) Percevoir, lever. (*d*) **To c. oneself,** se reprendre. **To c. one's thoughts,** se recueillir. **2.** *v.i.* S'assembler, se rassembler ; s'amasser.

collected, *a.* (*a*) Recueilli. (*b*) De sang-froid.

collecting-box, *s.* tronc *m.*

collection, *s.* **1.** Rassemblement *m* ; perception *f* (des impôts) ; levée *f* (des lettres). **2.** Quête *f.* **3.** Amas *m.* **4.** Collection *f* ; recueil *m.*

collector, *s.* (*a*) Collecteur, -trice. (*b*) Percepteur *m.* (*c*) Collectionneur, -euse.

college, *s.* Collège *m.*

collide, *v.i.* Se rencontrer, se heurter.

collier, *s.* **1.** Houilleur *m* ; mineur *m.* **2.** (Navire *m*) charbonnier *m.*

colliery, *s.* Houillère *f.*

collision, *s.* Collision *f*, rencontre *f.*

colloquial, *a.* Familier ; de (la) conversation.

colloquialism, *s.* Expression familière.

colloquially, *adv.* Familièrement.

colloquy, *s.* Colloque *m*, entretien *m.*

collusion, *s.* Collusion *f.*

colon, *s.* Deux-points *m.*

colonel, *s.* Colonel *m.*

colonial, *a. & s.* Colonial *m*, -aux.

colonist, *s.* Colon *m.*

colonization, *s.* Colonisation *f.*

colonize, *v.tr.* Coloniser.

colony, *s.* Colonie *f.*

colossal, *a.* Colossal, -aux.

colossus, *s.* Colosse *m.*

colour[1], *s.* **1.** Couleur *f.* **2.** Matière colorante ; pigment *m.* **3.** Teint *m,* couleurs. **To change c.,** changer de visage. **4.** *pl.* Pavillon *m* ; drapeau *m.* **5. To give c. to,** rendre vraisemblable.

colour[2]. **1.** *v.tr.* (*a*) Colorer ; colorier. (*b*) Donner de l'éclat à. **2.** *v.i.* Rougir.

colour-blind, *a.* Daltonien.

colour-blindness, *s.* Daltonisme *m.*

coloured, *a.* Coloré ; colorié ; de couleur.

colouring, *s.* (*a*) Coloris *m.* (*b*) Teint *m.*

colourless, *a.* Sans couleur.

colt, *s.* Poulain *m,* pouliche *f.*

column, *s.* Colonne *f.*

coma, *s.* Coma *m.*

comatose, *a.* Comateux.

comb[1], *s.* **1.** Peigne *m* **2.** Crête *f.*

comb[2], *v.tr.* Peigner. **comb out,** *v.tr.* **1.** Démêler. **2.** Éliminer les non-valeurs de.

combat[1], *s.* Combat *m.*

combat[2], *v.i. & tr.* Combattre.

combatant. *a. & s.* Combattant, -ante.

combative, *a.* Combatif.

combination, *s.* Combinaison *f.*

combine. 1. *v.tr.* Combiner ; allier (*with,* à). **2.** *v.i.* (*a*) S'unir, s'associer. (*b*) Se combiner.

combined, *a.* Combiné, d'ensemble.

combustible, *a. & s* Combustible (*m*).

combustion, *s.* Combustion *f.*

come, *v.i.* **1.** Venir, arriver. (*a*) Here he comes! le voilà qui arrive! Coming! voilà! on y va! **To c. for,** venir chercher. **C. now!** allons! voyons! (*b*) **To c. to oneself,** reprendre connaissance. **2. C. what may,** advienne que pourra. **3.** (*a*) How much does it c. to? combien cela fait-il? It comes to this, cela revient à ceci. (*b*) It must c. to that, il faudra bien en arriver là. **4.** (*a*) **To c. expensive,** coûter cher. (*b*) You c. first, vous venez en premier. **come about,** *v.i* Arriver, se passer, se produire. **come across,** *v.i.* Tomber sur. **come after,** *v.i.* (*a*) Suivre. (*b*) Succéder à. **come again,** *v.i.*

Revenir. **come against,** *v.i.* Heurter, frapper. **come along,** *v.i.* **1.** Arriver, venir. **2.** Survenir. **come apart,** *v.i.* Se séparer, se défaire. **come away,** *v.i.* **1.** Partir, s'en aller. **2.** Se détacher. **come back,** *v.i.* Revenir. **come before,** *v.i.* **1.** Précéder. **2.** Primer. **come between,** *v.i.* S'interposer entre. **come by,** *v.i.* **1.** Passer. **2.** Obtenir. **come down,** *v.i.* **1.** Descendre. **2.** (*a*) Baisser. (*b*) Tomber. **come forward,** *v.i.* **1.** S'avancer. **2.** Se présenter. **come in,** *v.i.* **1.** Entrer. **2.** (*a*) **To c. in useful,** servir. (*b*) **To c. in first,** arriver premier. **come into,** *v.i.* **1.** Se présenter à. **2.** Entrer en possession de. **come off,** *v.i.* (*a*) Se détacher. (*b*) Avoir lieu ; réussir. (*c*) **To c. off badly,** s'en mal tirer. **come on,** *v.i.* (*a*) S'avancer. **Come on!** allons! (*b*) Faire des progrès. (*c*) Survenir. **come out,** *v.i.* **1.** (*a*) Sortir ; se mettre en grève. (*b*) Paraître ; éclore. (*c*) S'effacer. (*d*) Se résoudre. **come round,** *v.i.* (*a*) Reprendre connaissance. (*b*) Se ranger. **come through,** *v.i.* **1.** Passer par ; surmonter. **2.** Pénétrer. **come to,** *v.i.* Revenir à soi. **come together,** *v.i.* S'assembler, se réunir. **come under,** *v.i.* **1.** Subir. **2.** Être compris sous. **come up,** *v.i.* (*a*) Monter. (*b*) **To c. up to,** s'approcher de. (*c*) Pousser. (*d*) Répondre (*to,* à). (*e*) Se heurter (*against.* contre). **come upon,** *v.i.* Rencontrer par hasard.

comedian, *s.* Comédien -ienne.

comedy, *s.* Comédie *f.*

comely, *a.* Avenant.

comer, *s.* **First c.,** premier venu. **All comers,** tout le monde.

comet, *s.* Comète *f.*

comfort[1], *s.* **1.** Consolation *f* ; soulagement *m.* **2.** Bien-être *m.* **3.** Confort *m* ; aisance *f.*

comfort[2], *v.tr* Consoler, soulager.

comfortable, *a.* **1.** Confortable ; commode, aisé ; agréable. **2.** Tranquille.

comfortably, *adv.* Confortablement, commodément.

comforter, *s.* Consolateur, -trice.

comforting, *a.* Réconfortant.

comfortless, *a.* Incommode ; triste.

comic, *a.* Comique. **C. opera**, opéra bouffe.

comical, *a.* Comique, risible.

coming[1], *a.* Prochain, qui approche ; d'avenir.

coming[2], *s.* Venue *f* ; arrivée *f.*

comma, *s.* (*a*) Virgule *f.* (*b*) **Inverted commas**, guillemets *m.*

command[1], *s.* **1.** Ordre *m*, commandement *m.* **Word of c.**, commandement. **2.** Commandement ; gouvernement *m.* **3.** (*a*) Maîtrise *f.* (*b*) **At c.**, à sa disposition.

command[2], *v.tr.* **1.** Ordonner, commander (à). **2.** Avoir à sa disposition. **3.** **To c. attention**, forcer l'attention. **4.** Dominer.

commandant, *s.* Commandant *m.*

commandeer, *v.tr.* Réquisitionner.

commander, *s.* (*a*) Commandant *m.* **C.-in-chief**, généralissime *m.* (*b*) Capitaine *m* de frégate.

commanding, *a.* **1.** Commandant. **2.** De commandement. **3.** Imposant.

commandment, *s.* Commandement *m.*

commemorate, *v.tr.* Commémorer.

commence, *v.tr. & i.* Commencer.

commencement, *s.* Commencement *m*, début *m.*

commend, *v.tr.* **1.** Recommander, confier. **2.** Louer.

commendable, *a.* Louable.

commendation, *s.* Éloge *m*, louange *f.*

commensurate, *a.* Proportionné.

comment[1], *s.* Commentaire *m* ; observation *f.*

comment[2], *v.i.* Faire des observations.

commentary, *s.* Commentaire *m.*

commentator, *s.* Commentateur, -trice.

commerce, *s.* Commerce *m.*

commercial, *a.* Commercial, -aux.

commiserate, *v.tr. & i.* Compatir (*with*, à).

commiseration, *s.* Commisération *f*, compassion *f.*

commissary, *s.* Commissaire *m.*

commission[1], *s.* Commission *f.* **1.** Brevet *m.* **2.** Ordre *m*, mandat *m.* **3.** **To put into c.**, armer. **4.** Commission ; pourcentage *m.* **5.** Perpétration *f.*

commission[2], *v.tr.* **1.** (*a*) Commissionner. (*b*) Commander. **2.** Armer.

commissionaire, *s.* Commissionnaire *m.*

commissioned, *a.* Muni de pouvoirs ; commissionné.

commissioner, *s.* Commissaire *m.*

commit, *v.tr.* **1.** Commettre, confier. **2.** **To c. to prison**, envoyer en prison. **To c. for trial**, renvoyer aux assises. **3.** **To c. oneself**, se compromettre. **4.** Commettre (un crime).

commitment, *s.* Engagement *m.*

committee, *s.* Comité *m*, commission *f*, conseil *m.*

commodious, *a.* Spacieux.

commodity, *s.* Marchandise *f*, denrée *f*, article *m.*

commodore, *s.* Chef *m* de division ; commodore *m.*

common[1], *a.* **1.** Commun. **2.** (*a*) Ordinaire. **In c. use**, d'usage courant. (*b*) De peu de valeur. **The c. people**, les gens du peuple. **3.** Vulgaire.

common[2], *s.* **1.** Terrain communal. **2.** **In c.**, en commun.

commonly, *adv.* Ordinairement.

commonplace. **1.** *s.* Lieu commun. **2.** *a.* Banal, -aux.

commons, *s.pl.* **1.** Peuple. **2.** **Short c.**, maigre chère.

commonwealth, *s.* **1.** État *m* ; république *f.* **2.** Commonwealth *m.*

commotion, *s.* **1.** Confusion *f*, commotion *f.* **2.** Troubles *mpl.*

communal, *a.* Communal, -aux.

commune, *v.i.* Converser.

communicable, *a.* Communicable.

communicant, *s.* **1.** Informateur, -trice. **2.** Communiant, -e.

communicate, *v.tr. & i.* Communiquer.

communication, *s.* **1.** Communication *f.* **2.** **To get into c.**, communiquer.

communicative, *a.* Communicatif.

communion, *s.* **1.** Relations *fpl*, rapports *mpl.* **2.** Communion.

communism, *s.* Communisme *m.*

communist, *s.* Communiste *mf.*

community, *s.* **1.** Communauté *f.* **2.** Société *f.*

commute, *v.tr.* **1.** Interchanger. **2.** Échanger ; racheter.

compact[1], *s.* Convention *f*, pacte *m.*

compact[2], *a.* Compact ; serré, tassé.

compact[3], *s.* Poudrier *m.*

compactness, *s.* Compacité *f*; concision *f*.

companion, *s.* **1.** (*a*) Compagnon, *f.* compagne. (*b*) (**Lady's**)**c.**, dame *f* de compagnie. **2. Lady's c.,** nécessaire *m* à ouvrage.

companionable, *a.* D'une société agréable.

companionship, *s.* (*a*) Compagnie *f.* (*b*) Camaraderie *f*.

company, *s.* **1.** Compagnie *f.* **To part c.,** se séparer (*with*, de). **2.** (*a*) Assemblée *f*, compagnie; (*b*) Monde *m.* **3.** Compagnie; société. **Limited c.,** société à responsabilité limitée. **4.** (*a*) *Th*: Troupe *f.* (*b*) **The ship's c.,** l'équipage *m*.

comparable, *a.* Comparable.

comparative, *a.* **1.** Comparatif. **2.** Relatif.

comparatively, *adv.* **1.** Comparativement. **2.** Relativement.

compare. **1.** *v.tr.* Comparer. **Compared with,** auprès de. **2.** *v.i.* Être comparable (*with*, à). **To c. favourably with,** ne le céder en rien à.

comparing, *s.* Comparaison *f*.

comparison, *s.* Comparaison *f.* **In c. with,** auprès de.

compartment, *s.* **1.** Compartiment *m.* **2.** Case *f*.

compass¹, *s.* **1.** (**A pair of**) **compasses,** un compas. **2.** Pourtour *m.* **3.** Étendue *f*, registre *m.* **4.** Boussole *f*; compas.

compass², *v.tr.* Atteindre.

compassion, *s.* Compassion *f*.

compassionate, *a.* Compatissant.

compatibility, *s.* Compatibilité *f*.

compatible, *a.* Compatible.

compatriot, *s.* Compatriote *mf*.

compel, *v.tr.* Contraindre, obliger.

compendious, *a.* Abrégé, succinct.

compendium, *s.* Abrégé *m*.

compensate. **1.** *v.tr.* (*a*) Dédommager. (*b*) Rémunérer. **2.** *v.i.* **To c. for,** remplacer; compenser.

compensation, *s.* Compensation *f*; dédommagement *m*; indemnité *f*.

compete, *v.i.* **1.** Faire concurrence (*with*, à). **2.** Concourir.

competence, *s.* **1.** Suffisance *f* de moyens d'existence. **2.** Compétence *f.* **3.** Attributions *fpl*.

competent, *a.* **1.** Capable. **2.** Compétent.

competently, *adv.* Avec compétence.

competition, *s.* **1.** Rivalité *f*, concurrence *f.* **2.** Concours *m*.

competitor, *s.* Concurrent, -e.

compilation, *s.* Compilation *f*.

compile, *v.tr.* Compiler.

compiler, *s.* Compilateur, -trice.

complacency, *s.* **1.** Satisfaction *f.* **2.** Suffisance *f*.

complacent, *a.* Content de soi-même; suffisant.

complacently, *adv.* Avec satisfaction; avec suffisance.

complain, *v.i.* Se plaindre.

complainant, *s.* Plaignant, -e.

complaint, *s.* **1.** Grief *m*; plainte *f.* **2.** Maladie *f*, mal *m*.

complaisance, *s.* Complaisance *f*.

complaisant, *a.* Complaisant.

complement, *s.* **1.** Plein *m.* **2.** Complément *m*.

complementary, *a.* Complémentaire.

complete¹, *a.* **1.** Complet, ète; entier. **2.** Achevé.

complete², *v.tr.* Compléter, achever.

completely, *adv.* Complètement, totalement.

completion, *s.* Achèvement *m*.

complex, *a. & s.* Complexe (*m*)

complexion, *s.* **1.** Teint *m.* **2.** Aspect *m*.

complexity, *s.* Complexité *f*.

compliance, *s.* Acquiescement *m*; conformité *f*.

compliant, *a.* Obligeant.

complicated, *a.* Compliqué.

complication, *s.* Complication *f*.

complicity, *s.* Complicité *f*.

compliment¹, *s.* Compliment *m*.

compliment², *v.tr.* Complimenter, féliciter (*on*, de).

complimentary, *a.* Flatteur, -euse.

comply, *v.i.* Se conformer (*with*, à); accéder (*with*, à).

component. **1.** *a.* Constituant. **2.** *s.* Composant *m*.

comportment, *s.* Conduite *f*.

compose, *v.tr.* **1.** Composer. **2.** Arranger. **3.** Calmer.

composed, *a.* Calme, tranquille.

composedly, *adv.* Tranquillement.

composer, *s.* Compositeur, -trice.

composition, *s.* **1.** Composition *f.* **2.** Mélange *m*, composé *m.* **3.** Accommodement *m*.

composure, s Calme m.
compound¹. I. a. (a) Composé. (b) Complexe.
II. **compound,** s. Composé m.
compound². I. v.tr. (a) Composer. (b) Accommoder, arranger. 2. v.i. S'arranger.
comprehend, v.tr. Comprendre.
comprehensible, a. Compréhensible, intelligible.
comprehension, s. Compréhension f.
comprehensive, a. Compréhensif.
compress, v.tr. Comprimer.
compression, s. Compression f.
comprise, v.tr. Comprendre.
compromise¹, s. Compromis m.
compromise². I. v.tr. (a) Compromettre. (b) Arranger. 2. v.i. Transiger.
compromising, a. Compromettant.
compulsion, s. Contrainte f.
compulsorily, adv. Obligatoirement.
compulsory, a. Obligatoire.
compunction, s. Componction f; remords m; scrupule m.
computation, s. Calcul m.
compute, v.tr. Computer calculer.
comrade, s. Camarade m.
comradeship, s. Camaraderie f.
concave, a. Concave.
concavity, s. Cavité f.
conceal, v.tr. Cacher ; dissimuler.
concealed, a Caché, dissimulé. **C.** turning, virage masqué.
concealment, s. **1.** Dissimulation f. **2.** Action f de cacher. **Place of c.,** cachette f, retraite f.
concede, v.tr. Concéder.
conceit, s. Vanité f, suffisance f.
conceited, a. Suffisant.
conceitedly, adv. Avec suffisance.
conceivable, a Concevable.
conceive, v.tr. **1.** Concevoir. **2.** v.i. **To c. of,** (s')imaginer.
concentrate. **1.** v.tr Concentrer. **2.** v.i Se concentrer.
concentration, s. Concentration f.
conception, s. Conception f ; idée f.
concern¹, s. **1.** (a) Rapport m. (b) Intérêt m. **2.** Souci m. **3.** (a) Entreprise f. (b) Appareil m, machin m.
concern². v.tr. **1.** Concerner, regarder, intéresser. **2.** (a) **The persons concerned,** les intéressés. (b) **To be concerned about,** s'inquiéter de.

concerning, prep. Concernant, touchant, en ce qui concerne.
concert¹, s. **1.** Concert m, accord m. **2.** Concert ; séance musicale.
concert². **1.** v.tr. Concerter. **2.** v.i Se concerter.
concession, s. Concession f.
conciliate, v.tr. Concilier réconcilier.
conciliation, s. Conciliation f.
conciliatory, a. Conciliant.
concise, a. Concis.
concisely, adv. Avec concision.
conciseness, s. Concision f.
conclude, v.tr. & i. **1.** Conclure ; arranger. **2.** Terminer.
concluding, a. Final, -als.
conclusion, s. **1.** Conclusion f. **2.** Fin f. **In c.,** pour conclure. **3. To come to the c.,** conclure. **To try conclusions,** se mesurer.
conclusive, a. Concluant, décisif.
conclusively, adv. D'une manière concluante.
concoct, v.tr. **1.** Confectionner. **2.** Imaginer.
concoction, s. (a) Confectionnement m. (b) Boisson f, potion f.
concord, s. Concorde f, harmonie f.
concordance, s. Concordance f.
concordant, a Concordant.
concourse, s. Foule f, rassemblement m, concours m.
concrete. **1.** a. Concret, -ète. **2.** s. Béton m.
concur, v.i. **1.** Concourir, coïncider. **2.** Être d'accord ; s'accorder.
concurrence, s **1.** (a) Concours m ; coopération f. (b) Simultanéité f. **2.** (a) Accord m. (b) Assentiment m.
concurrent, a. Concourant.
concurrently, adv. Concurremment.
concussion, s. **1.** Ébranlement m. **2.** Commotion (cérébrale).
condemn, v.tr. Condamner.
condemnation, s. (a) Condamnation f. (b) Censure f, blâme m.
condensation, s. Condensation f.
condense. **1.** v.tr. Condenser ; concentrer. **2.** v.i. Se condenser.
condescend, v.i. **1.** Condescendre. **2.** Se montrer condescendant.
condescending. a. Condescendant (to, envers).
condescension, s. Condescendance f.
condign, a. Mérité, exemplaire.

condiment, s. Condiment m.

condition, s. Condition f. **1.** On c., à (la) condition. **2.** (a) État m, situation f. In c., en forme. (b) État civil.

conditional, a. Conditionnel.

conditionally, adv. Conditionnellement ; sous condition.

condole, v.i. To c. with, exprimer ses condoléances à.

condolence, s. Condoléance f.

condone, v.tr. Pardonner.

conduce, v.i. Contribuer, tendre.

conducive, a. Favorable.

conduct¹, s. Conduite f.

conduct², v.tr. **1.** Conduire ; mener ; accompagner. **2.** (a) Mener, gérer. (b) Diriger. **3.** To c. oneself, se comporter, se conduire. **4.** Être conducteur de.

conductor, s. **1.** (a) Conducteur, -trice ; accompagnateur m. (b) Receveur, -euse. (c) Chef m d'orchestre. **2.** Conducteur.

cone, s. Cône m.

confection, s. Confection f.

confectioner, s. Confiseur m.

confectionery, s. Confiserie f.

confederacy, s. Confédération f.

confederate. 1. a. Confédéré. **2.** s. (a) Confédéré m. (b) Complice mf.

confederation, s. Confédération f.

confer. 1. v.tr. Conférer ; accorder. **2.** v.i. Conférer.

conference, s. Conférence f, entretien m, consultation f.

confess, v.tr. **1.** (a) Confesser, avouer. (b) Abs. Faire des aveux. (c) v.ind.tr. To c. to, avouer. **2.** (a) Se confesser. (b) Confesser.

confessed, a. Confessé, avoué.

confession, s. **1.** Confession f, aveu m. **2.** Confesse f.

confessor, s. Confesseur m.

confidant, f. **confidante,** s. Confident, -ente.

confide. 1. v.tr. Confier. **2.** v.i. To c. in, se confier à.

confidence, s. **1.** (a) Confiance f. (b) Assurance f. **2.** Confidence f.

confidence-trick, s. Vol m à l'américaine.

confident. 1. a. (a) Assuré, sûr ; confiant. (b) Effronté. **2.** s. Confident, -ente.

confidential, a. **1.** Confidentiel. **2.** C. clerk, homme m de confiance.

confidentially, adv. Confidentiellement.

confidently, adv. **1.** Avec confiance. **2.** Avec assurance.

confiding, a. Confiant ; sans soupçons.

confidingly, adv. Avec confiance.

configuration, s. Configuration f.

confine, v.tr. (a) (R)enfermer. Confined to bed, alité. (b) To c. oneself, se borner. (c) Confined space, espace restreint.

confinement, s. **1.** Emprisonnement m, réclusion f. In solitary c., au secret. **2.** Couches fpl.

confines, s.pl. Confins m.

confirm, v.tr. (R)affermir ; confirmer.

confirmation, s. Confirmation f.

confirmed, a. Invétéré.

confiscate, v.tr. Confisquer.

confiscation, s. Confiscation f.

conflagration, s. (a) Conflagration f, embrasement m. (b) Incendie m.

conflict¹, s. Conflit m, lutte f.

conflict², v.i. Être en conflit, en contradiction.

conflicting, a. Opposé (with, à) ; incompatible.

confluence, s. Confluent m.

conform, v.i. Se conformer.

conformable, a. **1.** Conforme. **2.** Accommodant.

conformation, s. Conformation f.

conformity, s. Conformité f.

confound, v.tr. **1.** Confondre. **2.** C. it! zut !

confounded, a. Maudit, sacré.

confront, v.tr. **1.** Affronter, faire face à. **2.** Confronter.

confuse, v.tr. **1.** Mêler, brouiller. **2.** Confondre. **3.** (a) Embrouiller. (b) Troubler.

confused, a. (a) Embrouillé. (b) Bouleversé. (c) Confus.

confusedly, adv. Confusément.

confusing, a. Embrouillant.

confusion, s. **1.** Confusion f. **2.** Désordre m, remue-ménage m.

confutation, s. Réfutation f.

confute, v.tr. **1.** Convaincre d'erreur. **2.** Réfuter.

congeal. 1. v.tr. Congeler. **2.** v.i. (a) Se congeler. (b) Se figer.

congenial, a. Sympathique ; aimable ; agréable.

conger, s. C.(-eel), congre m.

congest. **1.** v.tr. Encombrer, embouteiller. **2.** v.i. S'embouteiller.

congested, a. Encombré. **C. area,** région surpeuplée.

congestion, s. **1.** Congestion f. **2.** Encombrement m.

conglomeration, s. Conglomération f.

congratulate, v.tr. Féliciter (on, de).

congratulation, s. Félicitation f.

congregate, v.i. S'assembler.

congregation, s. **1.** Rassemblement m. **2.** Assistance f; paroissiens mpl.

congress, s. Congrès m.

conical, a. Conique.

coniferous, a. Conifère.

conjectural, a. Conjectural, -aux.

conjecture¹, s. Conjecture f.

conjecture², v.tr. Conjecturer.

conjoin, v.i. S'unir; s'associer.

conjoined, a. Conjoint.

conjoint, a. Conjoint, associé.

conjugal, a. Conjugal, -aux.

conjugate, v.tr. Conjuguer.

conjugation, s. Conjugaison f.

conjunction, s. Conjonction f. In c., de concert.

conjuncture, s. Conjoncture f, circonstance f, occasion f.

conjure, (a) v.tr. Conjurer. **To c. up,** évoquer. (b) v.i. Faire des tours de passe-passe.

conjuring, s. **1.** **C. up,** évocation f. **2.** Prestidigitation f.

conjuror, s. Prestidigitateur m.

connect. **1.** v.tr. (a) (Re)lier; (ré-)unir; joindre. (b) Allier. **2.** v.i. Se lier, se relier, se joindre; faire correspondance (avec un train).

connected, a. **1.** Suivi. **2.** Apparenté.

connection, s. **1.** Rapport m, liaison f; connexion f, suite f. **In this c.,** à ce propos. **2.** (a) Parenté f. (b) Parent, -e. **3.** Correspondance f. **4.** Contact m.

conning-tower, s. Blockhaus m; kiosque m (de sous-marin).

connivance, s. Connivence f.

connive, v.i. **To c. at,** fermer les yeux sur.

connoisseur, s. Connaisseur, -euse.

connubial, a. Conjugal, -aux.

conquer, v.tr. **1.** Conquérir. **2.** Vaincre.

conquering, a. Conquérant.

conqueror, s. Conquérant m.

conquest, s. Conquête f.

conscience, s. Conscience f.

conscience-stricken, a. Pris de remords.

conscientious, a. **1.** Consciencieux. **2.** **C. objector,** objecteur m de conscience.

conscientiously, adv. Consciencieusement.

conscientiousness, s. Conscience f; droiture f.

conscious, a. **1.** (a) **To be c. of,** avoir conscience de. **To become c. of,** s'apercevoir de. (b) Conscient. **2.** **To become c.,** reprendre connaissance.

consciously, adv. Consciemment.

consciousness, s. **1.** (a) Conscience f. (b) Sentiment m intime. **2.** Connaissance f. **To regain c.,** revenir à soi.

conscript¹, a. & s. Conscrit (m).

conscript², v.tr. Enrôler, engager.

conscription, s. Conscription f.

consecrate, v.tr. Consacrer.

consecrated, a. Consacré; bénit.

consecration, s. Consécration f.

consecutive, a. Consécutif.

consecutively, adv. Consécutivement.

consensus, s. Consensus m, unanimité f.

consent¹, s. Consentement m, assentiment m.

consent², v.i. Consentir.

consequence, s. **1.** Conséquence f; suites fpl. **In c.,** par conséquent. **In c. of,** par suite de. **2.** Importance f.

consequent, a. **1.** Résultant. **2.** Conséquent, logique.

consequential, a. **1.** Conséquent. **2.** Suffisant; plein d'importance.

consequently, adv. & conj. Par conséquent; conséquemment.

conservative, a. & s. Conservateur, -trice.

conservator, s. Conservateur, -trice.

conservatory, s. Serre f.

conserve, v.tr. Conserver, préserver.

consider, v.tr. **1.** (a) Considérer; réfléchir à. **All things considered,** tout bien considéré. (b) Prendre en considération; étudier. **2.** Regarder à. **3.** Trouver; estimer.

considerable, a. Considérable.

considerably, adv. Considérablement.

considerate, *a.* Prévenant, plein d'égards.

considerately, *adv.* Avec égards, avec prévenance.

consideration, *s.* **1.** Considération *f.* (*a*) After due c., après mûre réflexion. (*b*) On no c., à aucun prix. **2.** Rémunération *f.* **3.** Out of c. for, par égard pour. **4.** Importance *f.*

considering, *prep.* Eu égard à ; vu.

consign, *v.tr.* Consigner, expédier.

consignee, *s.* Consignataire *m.*

consignment, *s.* Envoi *m.*

consignor, *s.* Consignateur *m.*

consist, *v.i.* Consister (*of*, en) ; se composer.

consistence, *s.* Consistance *f.*

consistency, *s.* Uniformité *f.*

consistent, *a.* **1.** Conséquent. **2.** Compatible.

consistently, *adv.* **1.** Conséquemment. **2.** Conformément (*with*, à).

consolation, *s.* Consolation *f.*

console, *v.tr.* Consoler.

consolidate, *v.tr.* Consolider.

consolidation, *s.* Consolidation *f.*

consoling, *a.* Consolant.

consonance, *s.* Consonance *f* ; accord *m.*

consonant, *s.* Consonne *f.*

consort[1], *s.* Époux, -ouse.

consort[2], *v.i.* To c. with, fréquenter.

conspicuous, *a.* **1.** Visible ; manifeste. **2.** Frappant, marquant. To make oneself c., se faire remarquer.

conspicuously, *adv.* Manifestement.

conspiracy, *s.* Conspiration *f.*

conspirator, *s.* Conspirateur, -trice.

conspire, *v.i.* Conspirer.

constable, *s.* Gardien *m* de la paix. Chief c. = commissaire *m* de police.

constabulary, *s.* Police.

constancy, *s.* Constance *f.*

constant, *a.* (*a*) Constant. (*b*) Incessant, continuel. (*c*) Loyal, -aux.

constantly, *adv.* Constamment, continuellement.

constellation, *s.* Constellation *f.*

consternation, *s.* Consternation *f.*

constituency, *s.* Circonscription électorale.

constituent, *s.* **1.** *a.* Constituant. **2.** *s.* Élément constitutif. **3.** *s.pl.* Électeurs *m.*

constitute, *v.tr.* Constituer.

constitution, *s.* Constitution *f.*

constitutional, *a.* Constitutionnel.

constitutionally, *adv.* **1.** Constitutionnellement. **2.** Par tempérament.

constrain, *v.tr.* **1.** Contraindre, forcer. **2.** Retenir de force.

constrained, *a.* Forcé ; gêné.

constraint, *s.* Contrainte *f.*

constrict, *v.tr.* Resserrer, étrangler.

constriction, *s.* Resserrement *m.*

construct, *v.tr.* Construire ; bâtir.

construction, *s.* **1.** Construction *f.* **2.** Interprétation *f.*

constructive, *a.* Constructif.

constructor, *s.* Constructeur *m.*

construe, *v.tr.* Interpréter.

consul, *s.* Consul *m.*

consular, *a.* Consulaire.

consulate, *s.* Consulat *m.*

consult, *v.tr. & i.* **1.** Consulter. **2.** To c. together, délibérer.

consultation, *s.* Consultation *f.*

consulting-hours, *s.pl.* Heures *f* de consultation.

consume, *v.tr.* (*a*) Consumer. (*b*) Consommer.

consumer, *s.* Consommateur, -trice.

consummate[1], *a.* Consommé.

consummate[2], *v.tr.* Consommer.

consummation, *s.* **1.** Consommation *f.* **2.** Fin *f* ; but *m.*

consumption, *s.* **1.** Consommation *f.* **2.** Phtisie *f* ; consomption *f.*

consumptive, *a. & s.* Poitrinaire (*mf*), phtisique (*mf*).

contact, *s.* Contact *m.*

contagion, *s.* Contagion *f.*

contagious, *a.* Contagieux.

contain, *v.tr.* Contenir.

container, *s.* (*a*) Récipient *m* ; réservoir *m.* (*b*) Boîte *f.*

contaminate, *v.tr.* Contaminer.

contamination, *s.* Contamination *f.*

contemplate, *v.tr.* **1.** (*a*) Contempler. (*b*) *v.i.* Méditer. **2.** (*a*) Envisager. (*b*) Projeter.

contemplation, *s.* **1.** (*a*) Contemplation *f.* (*b*) Méditation *f.* **2.** To have in c., projeter.

contemplative, *a.* Contemplatif.

contemporaneous, *a.* Contemporain (*with*, de).

contemporaneously, *adv.* En même temps.

contemporary, *a.* Contemporain (*with*, de). C. events, événements actuels.

contempt, *s.* Mépris *m*; dédain *m*.

contemptible, *a.* Méprisable; indigne.

contemptibly, *adv.* D'une manière méprisable.

contemptuous, *a.* 1. Dédaigneux. 2. Méprisant; de mépris.

contemptuously, *adv.* Avec mépris.

contend. 1. *v.i.* Combattre, lutter. To c. with s.o. for sth., contester qch. à qn. 2. *v.tr.* Prétendre.

content[1], *s.* (*a*) Contenance *f*. (*b*) *pl.* Contenu *m*; table *f* des matières.

content[2], *s.* Contentement *m*, satisfaction *f*.

content[3], *a.* Satisfait (*with*, de).

content , *v.tr.* Contenter, satisfaire.

contented, *a.* Satisfait. content (*with*, de).

contentedly, *adv.* Sans se plaindre; content.

contention, *s.* 1. Dispute *f*, débat *m*. 2. Prétention *f*.

contentious, *a.* Disputeur, -euse.

contentment, *s.* Contentement *m*.

contest[1], *s.* (*a*) Combat *m*, lutte *f*. (*b*) Concours *m*.

contest[2], *v.tr.* (*a*) Contester, débattre. (*b*) Disputer.

context, *s.* Contexte *m*.

contiguity, *s.* Contiguïté *f*. In c., contigu, -uë (*with*, à).

contiguous, *a.* Contigu, -uë; attenant.

continent, *s.* Continent *m*.

continental, *a.* Continental, -aux.

contingency, *s.* Éventualité *f*; cas imprévu *m*.

contingent. 1. *a.* (*a*) Éventuel, fortuit. (*b*) C. on, sous réserve de. To be c. upon, dépendre de. 2. *s.* Contingent *m*.

continual, *a.* Continuel.

continually, *adv.* Continuellement; sans cesse.

continuance, *s.* Continuation *f*.

continuation, *s.* 1. Continuation *f*. 2. Prolongement *m*; suite *f*.

continue. 1. *v.tr.* (*a*) Continuer. 'To be continued,' "à suivre." (*b*) Perpétuer. 2. *v.i* (*a*) (Se) continuer. (*b*) To c. in office, garder sa charge.

continuity, *s.* Continuité *f*.

continuous, *a.* Continu.

continuously, *adv.* Continûment; sans interruption.

contort, *v.tr.* Tordre, contourner.

contorted, *a.* Contorsionné, contourné.

contortion, *s.* Contorsion *f*.

contour, *s.* Contour *m*; profil *m*.

contraband, *s.* Contrebande *f*.

contract[1], *s.* 1. Pacte *m*; contrat *m*. 2 Entreprise *f*; adjudication *f*. 3. *Cards:* Contrat.

contract[2]. I. 1. *v.tr.* Contracter; crisper. 2. *v.i.* Se contracter, se resserrer, se rétrécir. II. **contract,** *v.tr.* (*a*) Contracter; prendre. (*b*) S'engager par traité.

contraction, *s.* Contraction *f*.

contractor, *s.* Entrepreneur *m*.

contradict, *v.tr.* Contredire.

contradiction, *s.* Contradiction *f*.

contradictory, *a.* Contradictoire.

contralto, *s.* Contralte *m*.

contrariness, *s.* Esprit *m* contrariant.

contrary. 1. *a.* (*a*) Contraire; opposé. (*b*) Indocile. 2. *s.* Contraire *m*. 3. *adv.* Contrairement.

contrast[1], *s.* Contraste *m*.

contrast[2], *v.tr. & i.* Contraster.

contravene, *v.tr.* Transgresser, enfreindre.

contribute, *v.tr. & i.* Contribuer; aider.

contribution, *s.* Contribution *f*.

contributor, *s.* Collaborateur, -trice.

contrite, *a.* Contrit, pénitent.

contrition, *s.* Contrition *f*. .

contrivance, *s.* 1. Invention *f*. 2. Appareil *m*, dispositif *m*.

contrive, *v.tr.* (*a*) Inventer, combiner. (*b*) Pratiquer, ménager.

control[1], *s.* (*a*) Autorité *f*. (*b*) Maîtrise *f*. (*c*) Gouverne *f*, manœuvre *f*. (*d*) Contrôle *m*.

control[2], *v.tr.* 1. Diriger; régler. To c. the traffic, réglementer la circulation. 2. Maîtriser, gouverner.

controller, *s.* 1. Contrôleur, -euse. 2. Contrôleur *m*; commande *f*.

controversial, *a.* Controversable.

controversy, *s.* Controverse *f*.

controvert, *v.tr.* Controverser.

contumacious, *a.* Récalcitrant.

contumacy, *s.* Entêtement *m*.

contumely, *s.* 1. Insolence *f*; souverain mépris. 2. Honte *f*.

contusion, *s.* Contusion *f*.

conundrum, *s.* Énigme *f*.

convalescence, *s.* Convalescence *f*.

convalescent, *a. & s.* Convalescent.

convene. **1.** *v.tr.* Convoquer, réunir. **2.** *v.i.* S'assembler, se réunir.

convenience, *s.* **1.** Commodité *f*, convenance *f*. **2.** *pl.* Commodités. agréments *m*.

convenient, *a.* Commode. **It c.** to you, si cela ne vous dérange pas.

conveniently, *adv.* Commodément ; sans inconvénient.

convent, *s.* Couvent *m*.

convention, *s.* **1.** Convention *f*. **2.** *pl.* Convenances *fpl*, bienséances *fpl*.

conventional, *a* Conventionnel ; de convention.

converge, *v.i.* Converger.

converging, *a.* Convergent, concourant.

conversant, *a.* Familier.

conversation, *s.* Conversation *f*, entretien *m*.

converse, *v.i.* Causer.

conversely, *adv.* Réciproquement.

conversion, *s.* Conversion *f*.

convert¹, *s.* Converti, -ie.

convert², *v.tr.* Convertir.

convex, *a.* Convexe.

convey, *v.tr.* **1.** Transporter, porter. **2.** Transmettre ; communiquer.

conveyance, *s.* **1.** Transport *m* ; transmission *f*. **2.** Véhicule *m*.

convict¹, *s.* Forçat *m*.

convict², *v.tr* Convaincre ; condamner.

conviction, *s.* **1.** Condamnation *f*. **2.** Persuasion *f*. **3.** Conviction *f*.

convince, *v.tr.* Convaincre.

convincing, *a.* Convaincant.

convivial, *a.* Joyeux, jovial, -aux.

convoke, *v.tr.* Convoquer.

convolution, *s.* Circonvolution *f*.

convolvulus, *s.* Volubilis *m*.

convoy¹, *s.* Convoi *m*.

convoy², *v.tr.* Convoyer, escorter.

convulse, *v.tr.* **1.** Bouleverser ; ébranler. **2.** Faire tordre.

convulsion, *s.* **1.** Bouleversement *m*. **2.** *pl.* Convulsions *f*.

convulsive, *a.* Convulsif.

coo, *v.i.* Roucouler.

cooing, *s.* Roucoulement *m*.

cook¹, *s.* Cuisinier, -ière.

cook², **1.** *v.tr.* (Faire) cuire. *Abs.* Faire la cuisine. **2.** *v.i.* Cuire.

cookery, *s.* Cuisine *f*.

cooking, *s.* **1.** Cuisson *f*. **2.**

Cuisine *f*. **C.** utensils articles de cuisine.

cool¹. **1.** *a.* (*a*) Frais, *f.* fraîche. **It is c.,** il fait frais. (*b*) **To keep c.,** garder son sang-froid. **2.** *s.* Fraîcheur *f*.

cool². **1.** *v.tr.* Rafraîchir, refroidir. **2.** *v.i.* Se refraîchir, (se) refroidir.

cool down, *v.i.* S'apaiser, se calmer.

cooling¹, *a.* Rafraîchissant.

cooling², *s.* Rafraîchissement *m*.

coolly, *adv.* **1.** Fraîchement. **2.** De sang-froid. **3.** Sans gêne.

coolness, *s.* **1.** Fraîcheur *f*. **2.** (*a*) Sang-froid *m*. (*b*) Aplomb *m*. **3.** Froideur.

co-operate, *v.t.* Coopérer.

co-operation, *s.* Coopération *f*.

co-operative, *a.* Coopératif.

co-ordination, *s.* Coordination *f*.

cope¹, *s.* Chape *f*.

cope², *v.i.* **To c. with,** tenir tête à.

copious, *a.* Copieux, abondant.

copiously, *adv.* Copieusement.

copper, *s.* **1.** Cuivre *m*. **2.** Chaudière *f*. **3.** *Attrib.* En cuivre.

coppice, *s.* Taillis *m*, hallier *m*.

copse, *s.* Taillis *m*.

copy¹, *s.* **1.** Copie *f*. **2.** Modèle *m*. **3.** Exemplaire *m* ; numéro *m*.

copy², *v.tr.* Copier.

copying, *s.* Transcription *f* ; imitation *f*.

copyright, *s.* Droit *m* d'auteur ; propriété *f* littéraire.

coquetry, *s.* Coquetterie *f*.

coquette¹, *s.* Coquette *f*.

coquette², *v.i.* Faire la coquette.

coquettish, *a.* Coquet, -ette.

coral, *s.* Corail *m*, -aux.

cord, *s.* Corde *f* ; cordon *m* ; ficelle *f*.

cordial. **1.** *a.* Cordial, -aux. **2.** *s.* Cordial *m*.

cordiality, *s.* Cordialité *f*.

cordially, *adv.* Cordialement.

core, *s.* Cœur *m* ; trognon *m*.

cork¹, *s.* **1.** Liège *m*. **2.** Bouchon *m*.

cork², *v.tr.* Boucher.

corkscrew, *s.* Tire-bouchon *m*, *pl.* tire-bouchons.

cormorant, *s.* Cormoran *m*.

corn¹, *s.* Blé *m*.

corn², *s.* Cor *m*.

corned, *a.* **C. beef,** bœuf de conserve.

corner, *s.* **1.** Coin *m*, angle *m*. **2.** Coin ; encoignure *f*. **3.** Tournant *m* ; virage *m*.

corner-cupboard, s. Encoignure f.

cornet, s. Cornet m à pistons.

corn-field, s. Champ m de blé.

cornflour, s. Farine f de maïs.

cornflower, s. Bluet m.

cornice, s. Corniche f.

corollary, s. Corollaire m.

coronation, s. Couronnement m.

coronet, s. (a) Couronne. (b) Diadème m.

corporal[1], a. Corporel.

corporal[2], s. Caporal m, -aux.

corporation, s. Conseil municipal.

corps, s. Corps m.

corpse, s. Cadavre m.

corpulence, s. Corpulence f.

corpulent, a. Corpulent.

correct[1], v.tr. **1.** Corriger. **2.** Rectifier. **3.** Reprendre.

correct[2], a. **1.** Correct, exact ; juste. **2.** Bienséant.

correction, s. Correction f.

correctly, adv. Correctement.

correctness, s. Correction f, convenance f ; exactitude f, justesse f.

correspond, v.i. Correspondre.

correspondence, s. Correspondance f.

correspondent, s. Correspondant m.

corresponding, a. Correspondant.

correspondingly, adv. Également.

corridor, s. Couloir m, corridor m. **C. carriage,** wagon m à couloir.

corroborate, v.tr. Corroborer.

corroboration, s. Corroboration f.

corrode, **1.** v.tr. Corroder ; ronger. **2.** v.i. Se corroder.

corrosion, s. Corrosion f.

corrosive, a. & s. Corrosif (m).

corrugated, a. Gaufré ; ondulé.

corrupt[1], a. Corrompu.

corrupt[2], v.tr. Corrompre.

corruption, s. Corruption f.

corset, s. Corset m.

Corsica. Pr.n. La Corse.

Corsican, a. & s. Corse (mf).

cosily, adv. Confortablement.

cosiness, s. Confortable m.

cosmetic, a. & s. Cosmétique (m).

cosmopolitan, a. Cosmopolite.

cost[1], s. **1.** Coût m, frais mpl. **At all costs,** à tout prix. **2.** pl. Frais d'instance.

cost[2], v.i. Coûter ; revenir à. **C. what it may,** coûte que coûte.

coster(monger), s. Marchand ambulant ; marchand des quatre saisons.

costliness, s. **1.** Somptuosité f. **2.** Haut prix ; prix élevé.

costly, a. **1.** (a) Précieux. (b) Riche, somptueux. **2.** Coûteux.

costume, s. Costume m.

cosy, a. Chaud, confortable.

cot, s. Lit m d'enfant.

coterie, s. Coterie f.

cottage, s. **1.** Chaumière f. **2.** Villa f.

cottager, s. Paysan, -anne.

cotton, s. **1.** Coton m. **2.** Fil m d'Écosse. **3.** Attrib. (a) De, en, coton. (b) Cotonnier.

cotton-mill, s. Filature f de coton.

cotton-plantation, s. Cotonnerie f.

cotton-wool, s. Ouate f.

couch[1], s. Canapé m, divan m.

couch[2], **1.** v.tr. Coucher. **2.** v.i. (a) Se coucher. (b) Se tapir.

cough[1], s. Toux f.

cough[2], v.i. Tousser.

coughing, s. Toux f.

cough-lozenge, s. Pastille pectorale.

council, s. Conseil m.

council-chamber, s. Salle f du conseil.

councillor, s. Conseiller m.

counsel, s. **1.** Délibération f ; consultation f. **2.** Conseil m, avis m. **3.** Avocat m ; conseil.

counsel[2], v.tr. Conseiller.

counsellor, s. Conseiller m.

count[1], s. (a) Compte m ; calcul m. **To keep c. of,** compter. (b) Total m.

count[2]. **1.** v.tr. Compter ; calculer. **2.** v.i. Compter. **3.** Avoir de l'importance.

count[3], s. Comte m.

countenance[1], s. **1.** Visage m, figure f, mine f. **2. To give c. to,** appuyer.

countenance[2], v.tr. **1.** Autoriser, approuver. **2.** Encourager, appuyer.

counter[1], s. **1.** Fiche f ; jeton m. **2.** (a) Guichets mpl ; caisse f. (b) Comptoir m.

counter[2]. **1.** a. Contraire, opposé. **2.** adv. En sens inverse ; à contre-sens.

counteract, v.tr. Neutraliser.

counter-attack[1], s. Contre-attaque f.

counter-attack[2], v.tr. & i. Contre-attaquer.

counter-attraction, s. Attraction opposée.

counterbalance, v.tr. Contre-balancer ; compenser.

countercharge, s. Contre-accusation f.

counterfeit[1]. **1.** *a.* Contrefait ; faux. C. coin, fausse monnaie. **2.** *s.* Contrefaçon *f.*

counterfeit[2], *v.tr.* **1.** Contrefaire. **2.** Simuler, feindre.

counterfoil, *s.* Souche *f*, talon *m.*

countermand, *v.tr.* Contremander ; révoquer.

counterpane, *s.* Courtepointe *f.*

counterpart, *s.* Contre-partie *f* ; double *m.*

counterpoise, *s.* Contrepoids *m.*

countersign, *v.tr.* Contresigner.

countess, *s.* Comtesse *f.*

counting-house, *s.* Comptabilité *f.*

countless, *a.* Innombrable.

country, *s.* **1.** (*a*) Pays *m* ; contrée *f*, région *f.* Open c., rase campagne. (*b*) Patrie *f.* **2.** Campagne *f.*

countryman, *s.* **1.** Compatriote *m.* **2.** Paysan *m.*

countrywoman, *s.* **1.** Compatriote *f.* **2.** Paysanne *f.*

county, *s.* Comté *m.* C. town, chef-lieu (*pl.* chefs-lieux) *m* de comté.

couple[1], *s.* **1.** Couple *f.* **2.** Couple *m.* The young c., les jeunes époux.

couple[2], *v.tr.* (*a*) Coupler ; associer. (*b*) Atteler, accrocher.

couplet, *s.* Distique *m.*

coupon, *s.* Coupon *m.*

courage, *s.* Courage *m.*

courageous, *a.* Courageux.

courageously, *adv.* Courageusement.

courier, *s.* Courrier *m*, messager *m.*

course, *s.* **1.** (*a*) Cours *m* ; marche *f.* In c. of time, à la longue. In the ordinary c., normalement. In due c., en temps voulu, en temps utile. (*b*) Of c., bien entendu. (*c*) As a matter of c., comme de juste. **2.** Traitement *m*, régime *m.* **3.** Route *f*, direction *f.* **4.** Service *m*, plat *m.* **5.** (*a*) Champ *m*, terrain *m.* (*b*) Piste *f.*

court[1], *s.* **1.** Ruelle *f.* **2.** Cour *f.* **3.** The Law Courts, le palais de justice. Police c., tribunal de simple police. **4.** Tennis *m.*

court[2], *v.tr.* **1.** Courtiser ; faire la cour à. **2.** Aller au-devant de.

courteous, *a.* Courtois, poli.

courteously, *adv.* Courtoisement.

courteousness, *s.* Courtoisie *f.*

courtesy, *s.* Courtoisie *f.*

courtier, *s.* Courtisan *m.*

courtly, *a.* **1.** Courtois. **2.** Élégant.

court-martial[1], *s.* Conseil *m* de guerre.

court-martial[2], *v.tr.* Faire passer en conseil de guerre.

courtship, *s.* Cour *f.*

courtyard, *s.* Cour *f.*

cousin, *s.* Cousin, -ine. First c., cousin(e) germain(e).

cove, *s.* Anse *f* ; petite baie.

covenant[1], *s.* **1.** Convention *f*, contrat *m.* **2.** Pacte *m*, traité *m.*

covenant[2]. **1.** *v.tr* Stipuler. **2.** *v.i.* Convenir.

cover[1], *s.* **1.** Couverture *f* ; tapis *m.* Outer c., enveloppe *f* (de pneu). **2.** Couvercle *m.* **3.** Enveloppe *f.* **4.** (*a*) Abri *m.* (*b*) Couvert *m*, fourré *m.*

cover[2], *v.tr.* **1.** Couvrir (with, de). **2.** Comprendre, englober. **cover up**, *v.tr.* Recouvrir ; dissimuler.

covering, *s.* **1.** Recouvrement *m.* **2.** Couverture *f*, enveloppe *f.*

covert, *a.* Caché, voilé.

covet, *v.tr.* Convoiter.

covetous, *a.* Avide.

covetously, *adv.* Avidement.

covetousness, *s.* Convoitise *f.*

cow[1], *s.* Vache *f.*

cow[2], *v.tr.* Intimider, dompter.

coward, *s. & a.* Lâche (*mf*).

cowardice, *s.* Lâcheté *f.*

cowardly, *a.* Lâche.

cower, *v.i.* Se blottir, se tapir.

cowherd, *s.* Vacher *m* ; bouvier *m.*

cow-house, *s.* Étable *f.*

cowl, *s.* Capuchon *m.*

cowslip, *s.* Coucou *m.*

coxcomb, *s.* Petit-maître *m*, *pl.* petits-maîtres.

coxswain, *s.* **1.** Patron *m* (d'une chaloupe). **2.** Barreur *m.*

coy, *a.* Timide, farouche.

coyness, *s.* Timidité *f*, réserve *f.*

crab[1], *s.* Crabe *m*, cancre *m.* To catch a c., engager un aviron.

crab[2], *s.* Pomme *f* sauvage.

crabbed, *a.* Maussade, grincheux.

crack[1]. **I.** *s.* **1.** Claquement *m* ; détonation *f.* **2.** (*a*) Fente *f* ; fissure *f* ; fêlure *f.* (*b*) Entrebâillement *m.* **II.** **crack**, *a.* D'élite. C. player as *m.*

crack[2], *int.* Clac ! crac ! pan !

crack[3]. **I.** *v.tr.* **1.** Faire claquer. **2.** (*a*) Fêler. (*b*) Casser. **3.** To c. a joke, lâcher une plaisanterie.

II. **crack**, *v.i.* **1.** Craquer; claquer. **2.** Se fêler.

cracked, *a.* Fêlé fendu. C. voice voix cassée.

cracker, *s.* Pétard *m.*

crackle, *v.i.* Craqueter; pétiller.

cradle, *s.* Berceau *m.*

cradle-song, *s.* Berceuse *f.*

craft, *s.* **1.** Ruse *f*; fourberie *f.* **2.** Métier *m*; profession *f.* **3.** *Coll:* Embarcations *f.*

craftily, *adv.* Astucieusement.

craftiness, *s* Ruse *f*, astuce *f.*

craftsman, *s.* **1.** Artisan *m.* **2.** Artiste *m* dans son métier.

crafty, *a.* Astucieux, rusé.

crag, *s.* Rocher escarpé.

cram. 1. *v.tr.* (*a*) Fourrer; bonder. (*b*) Bourrer. **2.** *v.i.* S'entasser.

cramming, *s.* Entassement *m.*

cramp[1], *s.* Crampe *f.*

cramp[2], *v.tr.* **1.** Donner des crampes à. **2.** Gêner.

cramped, *a.* A l'étroit; gêné.

crane[1], *s.* Grue *f.*

crane[2], *v.tr. & i.* Tendre, allonger.

cranium, *s.* Crâne *m.*

crank[1], *s.* Manivelle *f.*

crank[2], *v.tr.* To c. up a car, lancer une auto à la main.

crank[3], *s.* Excentrique *mf.*

crankiness, *s.* Humeur *f* difficile.

cranky, *a.* D'humeur difficile.

crape, *s.* Crêpe noir.

crash[1], *s.* **1.** Fracas *m.* **2.** Débâcle *f.* **3.** *int.* Patatras !

crash[2], *v.i.* (*a*) Retentir; éclater avec fracas. (*b*) Tomber avec fracas. (*c*) S'écraser sur le sol.

crass, *a.* Crasse; grossier.

crate, *s.* Caisse *f* à claire-voie.

crater, *s.* **1.** Cratère *m.* **2.** Entonnoir *m.*

crave, *v.tr. & i.* Implorer.

craven, *a. & s.* Poltron (*m*).

cravenness, *s.* Lâcheté *f.*

craving, *s.* Désir ardent.

crawfish, *s.* Écrevisse *f*; langouste *f.*

crawl[1], *s.* Rampement *m.*

crawl[2], *v.i.* **1.** Ramper. **2.** (*a*) Se traîner. (*b*) Avancer lentement.

crawling, *a.* **1.** Rampant. **2.** Grouillant (*with*, de).

crayfish, *s.* **1.** Écrevisse *f.* **2.** Langouste *f.*

crayon, *s.* Pastel *m.*

craze, *s.* Manie *f.*

crazily, *adv.* Follement.

craziness, *s.* Folie *f*, démence *f.*

crazy, *a.* Fou, *f.* folle; toqué; affolé.

creak[1], *s.* Grincement *m*; craquement *m.*

creak[2], *v.i.* Crier, grincer; craquer.

cream[1], *s.* Crème *f.*

cream[2], *v.tr.* Écrémer.

creamy, *a.* Crémeux.

crease[1], *s.* (Faux) pli *m.*

crease[2], *v.tr.* (*a*) Plisser. (*b*) Chiffonner, froisser.

create, *v.tr.* Créer; produire.

creation, *s.* Création *f.*

creative, *a.* Créateur, -trice.

creator, *s.* Créateur, -trice.

creature, *s.* **1.** Créature *f*, être *m.* **2.** Animal *m*, bête *f.* **3.** *Attrib:* C. comforts, l'aisance matérielle.

credence, *s.* Créance *f*, foi *f.*

credentials, *s.pl.* **1.** Certificat *m.* **2.** Papiers *m* d'identité.

credible, *a.* Croyable; digne de foi.

credit[1], *s.* **1.** Croyance *f*, foi *f.* **2.** Crédit *m*, influence *f.* **3.** Mérite *m.* It does him c., cela lui fait honneur. **4.** (*a*) Crédit. (*b*) Avoir *m.*

credit[2], *v.tr.* **1.** Ajouter foi à; croire. **2.** Attribuer. **3.** Créditer (*with*, de).

creditable, *a.* Estimable, honorable.

creditably, *adv.* Honorablement.

creditor, *s.* Créancier, -ière.

credulity, *s.* Crédulité *f.*

credulous, *a.* Crédule.

creed, *s.* **1.** Credo *m.* **2.** Croyance *f.* **3.** Profession *f* de foi.

creek, *s.* Crique *f*, anse *f.*

creel, *s.* Panier *m* de pêche.

creep, *v.i.* Ramper; se traîner, se glisser.

creeper, *s.* Plante grimpante.

cremate, *v.tr.* Incinérer.

cremation, *s.* Incinération *f.*

creosote, *s.* Créosote *f.*

crêpe, *s,* Crêpe *m.*

crescent, *s.* (*a*) Croissant *m.* (*b*) Rue *f* en arc de cercle.

cress, *s.* Cresson *m.*

crest, *s.* **1.** Crête *f.* **2.** Armoiries *fpl.*

crestfallen, *a.* Abattu.

crevasse, *s.* Crevasse *f.*

crevice, *s.* Fente *f*; lézarde *f*; fissure *f.*

crew, *s.* **1.** Équipage *m*; équipe *f.* **2.** Bande *f*, troupe *f.*

crib, *s.* **1.** Mangeoire *f*, râtelier *m*. **2.** Lit *m* d'enfant.

cricket¹, *s.* Grillon *m*, cricri *m*.

cricket², *s.* Cricket *m*.

cricketer, *s.* Joueur *m* de cricket.

crime, *s.* (*a*) Crime *m*. (*b*) Délit *m*.

criminal. 1. *a.* Criminel. **The C.** Investigation Department, la Sûreté. **2.** *s.* Criminel, -elle.

criminally, *adv.* Criminellement.

crimson, *a. & s.* Cramoisi (*m*).

cringe, *v.i.* S'humilier, ramper.

cringing, *a.* **1.** Craintif. **2.** Servile.

crinkle. 1. *v.tr.* Froisser, chiffonner. Crinkled paper, papier gaufré. **2.** *v.i.* Se froisser.

cripple¹, *s.* Estropié, -ée; boiteux, -euse; infirme *mf*.

cripple², *v.tr.* (*a*) Estropier. (*b*) Disloquer; paralyser.

crisis, *s.* Crise *f*.

crisp, *a.* (*a*) Croquant, croustillant. (*b*) Tranchant. (*c*) Vif.

crispness, *s.* **1.** Qualité croustillante. **2.** Netteté *f*. **3.** Froid vif.

criterion, *s.* Critérium *m*.

critic, *s.* (*a*) Critique *m*. (*b*) Censeur *m*.

critical, *a.* Critique.

critically, *adv.* **1.** En critique. **2.** Dangereusement.

criticism, *s.* Critique *f*.

criticize, *v.tr.* **1.** Critiquer, faire la critique de. **2.** Censurer, blâmer.

croak¹, *s.* Coassement *m*; croassement *m*.

croak², *v.i.* **1.** Coasser; croasser. **2.** Grogner.

croaking, *s.* Coassement *m*; croassement *m*.

crockery, *s.* Faïence *f*, poterie *f*.

crocodile, *s.* Crocodile *m*.

crocus, *s.* Crocus *m*.

crone, *s.* Vieille (femme).

crony, *s.* Compère *m*, commère *f*.

crook, *s.* **1.** Houlette *f*. **2.** Angle *m*; coude *m*. **3.** Escroc *m*.

crooked, *a.* (*a*) Courbé; crochu; tortueux. (*b*) Malhonnête.

croon, *v.tr.* Chantonner; fredonner.

crooner, *s.* Fredonneur, -euse.

crop¹, *s.* **1.** Récolte *f*, moisson *f*. **2.** Coupe *f*. Eton c., cheveux *mpl* à la garçonne.

crop², *v.tr.* (*a*) Tondre, couper. (*b*) Brouter.

croquet, *s.* Croquet *m*.

cross¹, *s.* **1.** Croix *f*. **The Red C.,** la Croix rouge. **2.** Contrariété *f*, ennui *m*.

cross². 1. *v.tr.* (*a*) Croiser. (*b*) **To c. oneself,** se signer. (*c*) Barrer (un chèque). (*d*) Traverser; passer (sur). **2.** *v.i.* (*a*) Se croiser. (*b*) Faire la traversée. **cross out,** *v.tr.* Biffer, rayer. **cross over,** *v.i.* Passer de l'autre côté.

cross³, *a.* **1.** (*a*) Transversal, -aux. (*b*) (Entre-)croisé. (*c*) Contraire, opposé. **2.** Maussade; fâché.

cross-bow, *s.* Arbalète *f*.

cross-breed, *s.* Métis, -isse.

cross-examination, *s.* Interrogatoire *m* contradictoire.

cross-examine, *v.tr.* Interroger contradictoirement.

crossing, *s.* **1.** (*a*) Traversée *f*; passage *m*. (*b*) **Pedestrian c.,** passage pour piétons. **2.** Croisement *m*. **Level c.,** passage à niveau.

cross-legged, *a.* Les jambes croisées.

crossly, *adv.* Avec humeur.

cross-purposes, *s.pl.* **We are at c.-p.,** il y a malentendu *m*.

cross-road, *s.* **1.** Chemin *m* de traverse. **2.** Cross-roads, carrefour *m*.

crosswise, *adv.* En travers.

cross-word, *s.* Mots croisés.

crotch, *s.* Fourche *f*, enfourchure *f*.

crotchety, *a.* Capricieux; à l'humeur difficile.

crouch, *v.i.* Se tapir, s'accroupir.

croupier, *s.* Croupier *m*.

crow¹, *s.* Corneille *f*. **As the c. flies,** à vol d'oiseau.

crow², *v.i.* Chanter.

crow-bar, *s.* Pince *f* (à levier).

crowd¹, *s.* **1.** Foule *f*. **2.** Grande quantité, tas *m*.

crowd². 1. *v.tr.* (*a*) Serrer, (en)tasser. (*b*) Remplir, bonder. **2.** *v.i.* Se presser en foule.

crowing, *s.* Chant *m*.

crown¹, *s.* **1.** Couronne *f*. **C. prince,** prince héritier. **2.** Couronne. **Half a c.,** une demi-couronne. **3.** Sommet *m*.

crown², *v.tr.* Couronner.

crowning¹, *a.* Final, -als; suprême.

crowning², *s.* Couronnement *m*.

crow's-nest, *s.* Nid *m* de pie.

crucial, *a.* Décisif, critique.

crucible, *s.* Creuset *m*.

crucifix, *s.* Crucifix *m*, christ *m*.
crucifixion, *s.* Crucifixion *f*.
crucify, *v.tr.* Crucifier.
crude, *a.* (*a*) Brut. (*b*) Cru. (*c*) Grossier.
crudely, *adv.* Crûment, grossièrement.
crudity, *s.* Crudité *f*.
cruel, *a.* Cruel.
cruelly, *adv.* Cruellement.
cruelty, *s.* Cruauté *f* (*to,* envers).
cruet, *s.* Burette *f*.
cruise, *s.* Croisière *f*. **Pleasure c.,** voyage *m* d'agrément.
cruiser, *s.* Croiseur *m*.
crumb, *s.* 1. Miette *f*. 2. Mie *f*.
crumble. 1. *v.tr.* Émietter; effriter. 2. *v.i.* S'émietter; s'écrouler.
crumple, *v.tr.* Friper, froisser.
crunch[1], *s.* Bruit *m* de broiement.
crunch[2], *v.tr.* Croquer, broyer.
crusade, *s.* Croisade *f*.
crusader, *s.* Croisé *m*.
crush[1], *s.* Presse *f*, foule *f*.
crush[2], *v.tr.* (*a*) Écraser; fourrer. (*b*) Accabler. (*c*) Froisser. (*d*) Broyer.
crushing, *a.* Écrasant.
crust, *s.* Croûte *f*.
crustacean, *s.* Crustacé *m*.
crusted, *a.* Couvert d'une croûte.
crusty, *a.* 1. (Pain) qui a une forte croûte. 2. Bourru.
crutch, *s.* Béquille *f*.
crux, *s.* Nœud *m*.
cry[1], *s.* 1. Cri *m*; plainte *f*. 2. **To have a good cry,** donner libre cours à ses larmes.
cry[2], *v.tr. & i.* 1. Crier. 2. S'écrier. 3. Pleurer. **cry out.** 1. *v.tr.* Crier. 2. *v.i.* (*a*) Pousser des cris; s'écrier. (*b*) Se récrier.
crying[1], *a.* 1. Criant. 2. Qui pleure.
crying[2], *s.* Pleurs *mpl*, larmes *fpl*.
crypt, *s.* Crypte *f*.
cryptic, *a.* Secret, occulte.
crystal, *s.* Cristal *m*, -aux.
crystallize. 1. *v.tr.* **Crystallized fruits,** fruits candis. 2. *v.i.* (Se) cristalliser.
cub, *s.* Petit *m*.
cube, *s.* Cube *m*.
cubic, *a.* Cube. **C. capacity,** volume *m*.
cubical, *a.* Cubique.
cuckoo, *s.* Coucou *m*.

cuckoo-clock, *s.* Coucou *m*.
cucumber, *s.* Concombre *m*.
cud, *s.* **To chew the cud,** ruminer.
cuddle[1], *s.* Étreinte *f*, embrassade *f*.
cuddle[2]. 1. *v.tr.* Serrer doucement dans ses bras. 2. *v.i.* **To c. up to,** se pelotonner contre.
cudgel[1], *s.* Gourdin *m*, trique *f*.
cudgel[2], *v.tr.* Bâtonner.
cue[1], *s.* (*a*) Réplique *f*. (*b*) Avis *m*, mot *m*, indication *f*.
cue[2], *s.* Queue *f*.
cuff[1], *s.* 1. Poignet *m*; manchette *f*. 2. Parement *m*.
cuff[2], *s.* Taloche *f*, calotte *f*.
cuff[3], *v.tr.* Talocher, calotter.
cuirass, *s.* Cuirasse *f*.
culinary, *a.* Culinaire.
culminate, *v.i.* Se terminer.
culmination, *s.* Point culminant.
culpability, *s.* Culpabilité *f*.
culpable, *a.* Coupable.
culpably, *adv.* Coupablement.
culprit, *s.* Coupable *mf*.
cult, *s.* Culte *m*.
cultivate, *v.tr.* Cultiver.
cultivated, *a.* Cultivé.
cultivation, *s.* Culture *f*.
cultivator, *s.* Cultivateur *m*.
culture, *s.* Culture *f*.
cultured, *a.* Cultivé, lettré.
cumber, *v.tr.* Encombrer (*with,* de).
cumbersome, *a.* Encombrant, gênant, incommode.
cunning[1], *s.* Ruse *f*, finesse *f*.
cunning[2], *a.* Rusé; astucieux.
cunningly, *adv.* Avec ruse; astucieusement.
cup, *s.* 1. Tasse *f*. 2. Timbale *f*.
cupboard, *s.* Armoire *f*; placard *m*.
cupful, *s.* Pleine tasse.
Cupid. *Pr.n.* Cupidon *m*.
cupidity, *s.* Cupidité *f*.
cupola, *s.* Coupole *f*.
cur, *s.* 1. Roquet *m*. 2. Cuistre *m*.
curable, *a.* Guérissable; curable.
curacy, *s.* Vicariat *m*, vicairie *f*.
curate, *s.* Vicaire *m*.
curative, *a. & s.* Curatif (*m*).
curator, *s.* Conservateur *m*.
curb[1], *s.* 1. Frein *m*. 2. Bordure *f* (de trottoir).
curb[2], *v.tr.* Réprimer, refréner.
curdle. 1. *v.tr.* Cailler; figer (le sang). 2. *v.i.* Se cailler; se figer.
cure[1], *s.* 1. Guérison *f*. 2. Remède *m*.

cure², *v.tr.* Guérir.
curing, *s.* Guérison *f.*
curio, *s.* Curiosité *f*; bibelot *m.*
curiosity, *s.* Curiosité *f.*
curious, *a.* Curieux.
curiously, *adv.* Singulièrement.
curl¹, *s.* Boucle *f.*
curl², *v.tr. & i.* Boucler, friser. **curl up.** **1.** *v.tr.* To c. up one's lip, retrousser la lèvre. **2.** *v.i.* Se mettre en boule.
curl-paper, *s.* Papillote *f.*
curly, *a.* Bouclé, frisé.
currant, *s.* **1.** Groseille *f.* **Black c.**, cassis *m.* **2.** Raisin *m* de Corinthe.
currant-bush, *s.* Groseillier *m.*
currency, *s.* **1.** Circulation *f*, cours *m.* **2.** Échéance *f.* **3.** Monnaie *f.*
current¹, *a.* Courant; en cours. **C. events**, actualités *f.*
current², *s.* Courant *m.*
currently, *adv.* Couramment.
curry, *s.* Cari *m.*
curse¹, *s.* **1.** (*a*) Malédiction *f.* (*b*) Imprécation *f*; juron *m.* **2.** Fléau *m.*
curse². **1.** *v.tr.* Maudire. **2.** *v.i.* Blasphémer; sacrer, jurer.
cursed, *a.* Maudit.
cursing, *s.* **1.** Malédictions *fpl.* **2.** Jurons *mpl.*
cursorily, *adv.* Rapidement; à la hâte.
cursory, *a.* Rapide, superficiel.
curt, *a.* Brusque; sec, *f.* sèche.
curtail, *v.tr.* **1.** Raccourcir; écourter. **2.** Diminuer; restreindre.
curtailment, *s.* Raccourcissement *m*; restriction *f*, diminution *f.*
curtain, *s.* Rideau *m.*
curtly, *adv.* Sèchement.
curtness, *s.* Brusquerie *f.*
curtsey¹, *s.* Révérence *f.*
curtsey², *v.i.* Faire une révérence.
curve¹, *s.* Courbe *f.*
curve². **1.** *v.tr.* Courber. **2.** *v.i.* Se courber; décrire une courbe.
curved, *a.* Courbé, courbe.
cushion, *s.* **1.** Coussin *m.* **2.** *Bill*: Bande *f.*
custard, *s.* Crème *f* (au lait).
custodian, *s.* Gardien, -ienne.
custody, *s.* **1.** Garde *f.* **In safe c.**, en lieu sûr. **2.** To take into c., arrêter.
custom, *s.* **1.** Coutume *f*, usage *m*,

habitude *f.* **2.** *pl. Adm*: Douane *f.* **Customs officer**, douanier *m.* **3.** (*a*) Clientèle *f.* (*b*) Patronage *m.*
customary, *a.* Accoutumé, habituel.
customer, *s.* Client, -ente.
custom-house, *s.* Douane *f.*
cut¹, *s.* **1.** Coupe *f.* **2.** Taillade *f.* **3.** Coupure *f*; entaille *f.* **4.** **Short cut**, raccourci *m.*
cut², *v.tr. & i.* **1.** Couper; tailler. **To cut one's finger**, se couper au doigt. **2.** (*a*) **To cut to ribbons**, déchiqueter. (*b*) **To cut short**, couper court à. **cut away**, *v.tr.* Retrancher. **cut down**, *v.tr.* **1.** (*a*) Abattre. (*b*) Sabrer. **2.** Rogner; restreindre. **cut off**, *v.tr.* Couper, détacher. **cut out**, *v.tr.* **1.** (*a*) Couper; exciser. **2.** Découper; tailler. **3.** Retrancher. **cut up**, *v.tr.* Couper; découper.
cut³, *a.* **1.** Taillé. **2.** **Cut prices**, prix réduits.
cute, *a.* Malin, -igne; rusé.
cutlery, *s.* Coutellerie *f.*
cutlet, *s.* Côtelette *f*; escalope *f.*
cutter, *s.* Canot *m*; cotre *m.*
cutting¹, *a.* **1.** Tranchant *m.* **2.** Cinglant. **3.** Mordant.
cutting², *s.* **1.** Taille *f.* **2.** Coupon *m*, bout *m*; coupure *f.* **3.** Tranchée *f.*
cuttle-fish, *s.* Seiche *f.*
cyanide, *s.* Cyanure *m.*
cycle¹, *s.* **1.** Cycle *m.* **2.** Bicyclette *f.*
cycle², *v.i.* Faire de la bicyclette; aller à bicyclette.
cycling, *s.* Cyclisme *m.*
cyclist, *s.* Cycliste *mf.*
cyclone, *s.* Cyclone *m.*
cygnet, *s.* Jeune cygne *m.*
cylinder, *s.* Cylindre *m.*
cylindrical, *a.* Cylindrique.
cymbal, *s.* Cymbale *f.*
cynic, *s.* Censeur *m* caustique; railleur *m*; sceptique *m.*
cynical, *a.* Sarcastique; sceptique.
cynically, *adv.* D'un ton sceptique.
cynicism, *s.* Scepticisme railleur.
cynosure, *s.* Point *m* de mire.
cypress, *s.* Cyprès *m.*
Cyprus. *Pr.n.* L'île *f* de Chypre *f.*
Czechoslovak, *s.* Tchécoslovaque *mf.*
Czechoslovakia. *Pr.n.* La Tchécoslovaquie.

D

D, d, s. (La lettre) D, d, m.

dab¹, s. **1.** Tape f. **2.** Tache f.

dab², v.tr. **1.** Lancer une tape à (qn). **2.** Tapoter.

dab³, s. Ich: Limande f, carrelet m.

dabble. 1. v.tr. Humecter, mouiller. **2.** v.i. Barboter.

dad, daddy, s. Papa m.

daddy-long-legs, s. Tipule f.

dado, s. Lambris m.

daffodil, s. Narcisse m des bois.

daft, a. **1.** Écervelé. **2.** Toqué.

dagger, s. **1.** Poignard m, dague f. At daggers drawn, à couteaux tirés. **2.** Typ: Croix f.

dahlia, s. Dahlia m.

daily. 1. a. Journalier, quotidien. **2.** adv. Journellement, quotidiennement. **3.** s. Quotidien m.

daintily, adv. Délicatement; d'une manière raffinée.

daintiness, s. Délicatesse f, raffinement m.

dainty¹, s. Friandise f.

dainty², a. **1.** Friand, délicat. **2.** Délicat, exquis.

dairy, s. Laiterie f.

dairymaid, s. Fille f de laiterie.

dairyman, s. Laitier m; crémier m.

dais, s. Estrade f; dais m.

daisy, s. Pâquerette f; marguerite f.

dale, s. Vallée f, vallon m.

dally, v.i. **1.** Badiner. **2.** Tarder.

dam¹, s. Barrage m.

dam², v.tr. Contenir, endiguer.

damage¹, s. **1.** Dommage m, dégâts mpl; avarie f. **2.** Préjudice m, tort m. **3.** pl. Dommages-intérêts m.

damage², v.tr. **1.** Endommager; avarier; abîmer. **2.** Nuire à.

damaged, a. Avarié, endommagé.

damaging, a. Préjudiciable, nuisible.

damask, a. & s. Damas m

dame, s. Dame f.

damn, v.tr. **1.** (a) Condamner. (b) Perdre. **2.** Damner. **3.** int. Sacristi !

damnation, s. Damnation f.

damned, a. **1.** Damné. **2.** (a) Sacré, satané. (b) adv. Diablement.

damning¹, a. Portant condamnation.

damning², s. **1.** Condamnation f. **2.** Damnation f.

damp¹, s. Humidité f.

damp², v.tr. **1.** Mouiller; humecter. **2.** Refroidir.

damp³, a. Humide.

dampness, s. Humidité f; moiteur f.

damsel, s. Demoiselle f.

damson, s. Prune f de Damas.

dance¹, s. **1.** Danse f. **2.** Bal m, pl. bals; soirée dansante.

dance². 1. v.i. (a) Danser. To d. with, faire danser. (b) To d. with rage, trépigner de colère. **2.** v.tr. Danser.

dance-hall, s. Bal public; dancing m

dancer, s. Danseur, -euse.

dancing¹, a. Dansant.

dancing², s. Danse f.

dancing-master, s. Maître m de danse.

dandelion, s. Pissenlit m.

dandy, s. Dandy m, gommeux m.

Dane, s. Danois, -oise.

danger, s. Danger m, péril m.

dangerous, a. Dangereux, périlleux.

dangerously, adv. Dangereusement.

dangle. 1. v.i. Pendiller. pendre. **2.** v.tr. Faire pendiller.

Danish. 1. a. Danois. **2.** s. Ling: Le danois.

dank, a. Humide.

dapper, a. Tiré à quatre épingles.

dappled, a. Pommelé.

dare. 1. Modal aux. Oser. I d. say, sans doute. **2.** v.tr. (a) Oser. (b) Braver. (c) Défier.

dare-devil, s. Casse-cou m inv.

daring¹, a. Audacieux.

daring², s. Audace f.

daringly, adv. Audacieusement.

dark¹, a. **1.** Sombre; obscur, noir. It is d., il fait nuit. **2.** Foncé. **3.** Brun; basané. **4.** To keep sth. d., tenir qch. secret.

dark², s. **1.** Ténèbres fpl, obscurité f. **2.** In the d., dans l'ignorance.

darken. 1. v.tr. Obscurcir; assombrir. **2.** v.i. S'obscurcir.

darkly, adv. Obscurément.

darkness, s. **1.** Obscurité f, ténèbres fpl. **2.** Teinte foncée.

dark-room, s. Cabinet noir.

darling, s. & a. Favori, -ite. My d.! mon chéri ! ma chérie !

darn¹, s. Reprise f.

darn², *v.'r.* Repriser.

darning, *s.* Reprise *f.*

darning-needle. *s.* Aiguille *f* à repriser.

dart¹, *s.* (*a*) Dard *m* trait *m.* (*b*) Fléchette *f.*

dart². **1.** *v.tr.* Darder. **2.** *v.i.* Se précipiter, s'élancer, foncer.

dash¹, *s.* **1.** Coup *m*, heurt *m*, choc *m.* **2.** Soupçon *m*, goutte *f.* **3.** Trait *m* ; tiret *m.* **4.** Élan *m* ; ruée *f* **5.** Élan, fougue *f.*

dash². **1.** *v.tr.* (*a*) Lancer ; jeter. (*b*) Déconcerter. **2.** *v.i.* (*a*) Se heurter, le mort, la morte. (*b*) Se précipiter, s'élancer (*at*, sur). **dash along**, *v.i.* Avancer à fond de train. **dash away**. **1.** *v.tr.* Écarter violemment. **2.** *v.i.* S'éloigner en coup de vent.

dash-board, *s.* Tablier *m.*

dashing, *a.* Impétueux ; plein d'élan.

dastard, *s.* Lâche *m.*

dastardly, *a.* **1.** Lâche. **2.** Infâme.

data, *s.pl.* Données *f.*

date¹, *s.* Datte *f.*

date², *s.* Date *f.* **Up to d.**, à la page. **To bring up to d.**, remettre au point.

date³, *v.tr. & i.* Dater.

date-palm, *s.* Dattier *m.*

dative, *a. & s.* Datif (*m*).

daub¹, *s.* Barbouillage *m.*

daub², *v.tr.* Barbouiller (*with*, de).

daughter, *s.* Fille *f.*

daughter-in-law, *s.* Belle-fille *f*, *pl.* belles-filles ; bru *f.*

daunt, *v.tr.* Intimider, décourager.

dauntless, *a.* Intrépide.

dauntlessly, *adv.* Intrépidement.

davit, *s.* Bossoir *m*, davier *m.*

dawdle, *v.i.* Flâner.

dawdler, *s.* Flâneur, -euse.

dawdling, *s.* Flânerie *f.*

dawn¹, *s.* Aube *f.* aurore *f.* **At d.**, au point du jour.

dawn², *v.i.* Poindre ; naître ; se faire jour (*on*, à).

day, *s.* **1.** Jour *m* ; journée *f.* **It's a fine day**, il fait beau aujourd'hui. **All day (long)**, toute la journée. **By the day**, à la journée. **Twice a day**, deux fois par jour. **This day week**, (d')aujourd'hui en huit. **The day before**, la veille (de). **The day after**, le lendemain (de). **Day after day**, tous les jours. **2.** (*a*) **Day of the month**, quantième *m* du mois.

Day off, jour de congé. (*b*) Fête *f.* **3. The good old days**, le bon vieux temps. **In our days**, de nos jours. **To this day**, encore aujourd'hui.

day-boy, *s.* Externe *m.*

day-break, <. Point *m* du jour ; aube *f.*

day-dream, *s.* Rêverie *f.*

daylight, *s.* Jour *m* ; lumière *f* du jour.

day-time, *s.* Le jour, la journée.

daze¹, *s.* **In a d.**, hébété, stupéfait.

daze², *v.tr.* (*a*) Stupéfier. (*b*) Étourdir.

dazed, *a.* (*a*) Stupéfié ; hébété. (*b*) Tout étourdi.

dazzle, *v.tr.* Éblouir, aveugler.

dazzling, *a.* Éblouissant.

deacon, *s.* Diacre *m.*

dead. **I.** *a.* **1.** Mort. **The d. man, woman**, le mort, la morte. **D. letters**, lettres tombées au rebut. **2. To come to a d. stop**, s'arrêter net. **D. calm**, calme plat. **D. silence**, silence de mort. **D. on time**, à la minute. **D. loss**, perte sèche.

II. dead, *s.* **1.** *pl.* **The d.**, les morts *m* ; les trépassés *m.* **2. At d. of night**, au milieu de la nuit.

III. dead, *adv.* (*a*) Absolument. **D. slow**, au grand ralenti. (*b*) **To stop d.**, s'arrêter net.

dead-and-alive, *a.* Mort, sans animation.

dead-beat, *a.* Épuisé, éreinté, fourbu.

deaden, *v.tr* Amortir ; étouffer ; émousser.

dead-end, *s.* Cul-de-sac *m.*

dead-lock, *s.* Impasse *f.*

deadly. **1.** *a.* Mortel. **2.** *adv.* Mortellement.

dead-march, *s.* Marche *f* funèbre.

dead-weight, *s.* Poids mort.

deaf, *a.* Sourd. **D. and dumb**, sourd-muet, *f.* sourde-muette **To turn a d. ear**, faire la sourde oreille.

deafen, *v.tr.* Assourdir ; rendre sourd.

deafening, *a.* Assourdissant.

deafness, *s.* Surdité *f.*

deal¹, *s. & adv.* **A good d.**, beaucoup.

deal², *s.* **1.** Donne *f.* **Whose d. is it?** à qui de donner ? **2.** Marché *m.*

deal³. **I.** *v.tr.* **1. To d. out**, distribuer. **2.** Donner, porter. **3.** Donner (les cartes).

II. deal, *v.i.* **1. To d. with**, avoir affaire à ; traiter de. **2. To d. with**,

10

traiter, négocier, avec. **3.** Faire la donne ; donner.

deal¹, s. Bois m de pin, de sapin.

dealer, s. **1.** *Cards:* Donneur m. **2.** (a) Négociant m. (b) Marchand, -ande (*in*, de).

dealing, s. **1.** Distribution f. **2.** pl. Relations f. **3.** Conduite f.

dean, s. Doyen m.

dear. I. a. (a) Cher. D. Madam, Madame, Mademoiselle. **D.** Sir, Cher Monsieur. (b) Cher, coûteux.
II. **dear,** s. Cher, f. chère.
III. **dear,** adv. Cher.
IV. **dear,** int. D. me! mon Dieu ! Oh d.! oh là là !

dearly, adv. **1.** Cher, chèrement. **2.** Tendrement.

dearth, s. Disette f, pénurie f.

death, s. **1.** Mort f. **2.** Décès m. *Journ:* Deaths, Nécrologie f. **3.** At death's door, à l'article de la mort.

death-bed, s. Lit m de mort.

death-blow, s. Coup mortel, fatal.

deathly, adv. Mortellement.

death-rate, s. Mortalité f.

death's-head, s. Tête f de mort.

death-trap, s. Casse-cou m inv.

death-warrant, s. Ordre m d'exécution.

debar, v.tr. Exclure ; défendre à

debase, v.tr. Avilir, dégrader.

debasement, s. Avilissement m.

debasing, a. Avilissant.

debatable, a. Contestable, discutable.

debate¹, s. Débat m, discussion f.

debate². **1.** v.tr. Débattre, discuter. **2.** v.i. Discuter, disputer.

debauch¹, s. Débauche f.

debauch², v.tr. Débaucher.

debauched, a. Débauché, corrompu.

debauchery, s. Débauche f.

debility, s. Débilité f.

debit¹, s. Débit m, doit m.

debit², v.tr. Débiter.

debris, s. Débris mpl.

debt, s. Dette f ; créance f. Bad debts, mauvaises créances. In d., endetté.

debtor, s. Débiteur, -trice.

début, s. Début m.

decadence, s. Décadence f.

decadent, a. Décadent.

decamp, v.i. Décamper, filer.

decant, v.tr. Décanter.

decanter, s. Carafe f.

decapitate, v.tr. Décapiter.

decapitation, s. Décapitation f.

decay¹, s. **1.** Décadence f ; délabrement m. To fall into d., tomber en ruine. **2.** Pourriture f.

decay², v.i. (a) Tomber en décadence. (b) Dépérir. (c) Pourrir.

decayed, a. **1.** Déchu. **2.** Pourri. D. tooth, dent gâtée.

decease, s. Décès m.

deceased. **1.** a. Décédé. **2.** Défunt, défunte.

deceit, s. Tromperie f, duperie f.

deceitful, a. Trompeur, -euse ; fourbe ; faux, f. fausse.

deceitfully, adv. **1.** Frauduleusement. **2.** Faussement.

deceive, v.tr. Tromper, abuser.

deceiver, s. Trompeur, -euse ; fourbe m.

deceiving, a. Trompeur -euse ; décevant.

December, s. Décembre m.

decency, s. Décence f, bienséance f.

decent, a. (a) Bienséant, convenable. (b) Décent, honnête, modeste.

decently, adv. Décemment, convenablement.

deception, s. Tromperie f, duperie f.

deceptive, a. Trompeur. -euse ; décevant.

decide. **1.** v.tr. (a) Décider (de). (b) Se décider. **2.** v.i Se décider (on, à) ; fixer.

decided, a. **1.** Arrêté ; décidé ; catégorique. **2.** Incontestable.

decidedly, adv. **1.** Résolument. **2.** Décidément.

deciding, a. Décisif.

decimal. **1.** a. Décimal, -aux. **2.** s. Décimale f.

decimate, v.tr. Décimer.

decipher, v.tr. Déchiffrer.

decision, s. Décision f.

decisive, a. **1.** Décisif. **2.** Tranchant ; net, nette.

decisively, adv. Décisivement.

deck¹, s. Pont m.

deck², v.tr. Parer, orner (*with*, de). To d. oneself out, s'endimancher.

deck-chair, s. Transatlantique m.

declaim, v.i. & tr. Déclamer.

declaration, s. (a) Déclaration f. (b) *Cards:* Annonce f.

declare. **1.** v.tr. Déclarer. Well, I d.! par exemple ! **2.** v.i. Se déclarer

declared, a. Ouvert, avoué.
decline[1], s. Déclin m; baisse f.
decline[2]. I. v.tr. Refuser; décliner.
Abs: S'excuser.
 II. **decline,** v.i. Décliner; baisser.
decompose. I. v.tr. Décomposer.
 2. v.i. Se décomposer.
decomposition, s. Décomposition f.
decorate, v.tr. Décorer (*with,* de).
decoration, s. **1** Décoration f.
 2. Décor m.
decorative, a Décoratif.
decorator, s. Décorateur m.
decorous, a. Bienséant, convenable.
decorum, s. Décorum m.
decoy[1], s. Appât m, leurre m.
decoy[2], v.tr. Leurrer.
decrease[1], s. Diminution f.
decrease[2], v.tr. & i. Diminuer.
decreasing, a. Décroissant.
decree[1], s. **1.** Décret m, édit m,
 arrêté m. **2.** Jugement m.
decree[2], v.tr. Décréter, ordonner.
decrepit, a. Décrépit; caduc, -uque.
decrepitude, s. Décrépitude f.
decry, v.tr. Décrier, dénigrer.
dedicate, v.tr. Dédier.
dedication, s. Dédicace f.
deduce, v.tr. Déduire.
deduct, v.tr. Déduire, retrancher.
deduction, s. Déduction f.
deed, s. **1.** (a) Action f. (b) Foul d.,
 forfait m. (c) Fait. **2.** Acte.
deem, v.tr. Juger, estimer, croire.
deep. I. a. **1.** Profond. **D.** in study,
 plongé dans l'étude. **2.** Foncé.
 sombre. **3.** Rusé.
 II. **deep,** adv. Profondément.
 III. **deep,** s. Océan m.
deepen. **1.** v.tr. (a) Approfondir,
 creuser. (b) Rendre plus intense.
 2. v.i. Devenir plus profond;
 s'approfondir.
deep-laid, a. Habilement ourdi.
deeply, adv. Profondément. **To go
 d. into,** pénétrer fort avant dans.
deepness, s. **1.** Profondeur f;
 gravité f. **2.** Astuce f.
deep-rooted, a. Profondément enraciné.
deer, s. Cerf. **Fallow d.,** daim m.
deerskin, s. Peau f de daim.
deface, v.tr. Défigurer; mutiler.
defacement, s. Défiguration f, mutilation f.
defame, v.tr. Diffamer.

default[1], s. **1.** Défaut m. **2.** *Prep.phr.*
 In d. of, à défaut de.
default[2], v.i. Faire défaut.
defaulter, s. **1.** Délinquant. -ante.
 2. Retardataire m.
defeat[1], s. **1.** Défaite f. **2.** Renversement m; insuccès m.
defeat[2], v.tr. **1.** Battre, défaire.
 2. Renverser, faire échouer.
defect, s. Défaut m.
defective, a. Défectueux.
defence, s. Défense f. **Witness for
 the d.,** témoin m à décharge.
defenceless, a. Sans défense.
defend, v.tr. **1.** Défendre, protéger.
 2. Défendre, justifier.
defendant, a. & s. Défendeur, -eresse.
defender, s. Défenseur m.
defensive. **1.** a. Défensif **2.** s.
 Défensive f.
defer[1], v.tr. Différer ajourner
defer[2], v.i. Déférer.
deference, s. Déférence f.
deferential, a. De déférence.
deferment, s. Ajournement m.
deferred, a. Différé.
defiance, s. Défi m. **To set at d.,** défier.
defiant, a. (a) Provocant; de défi.
 (b) Intraitable.
defiantly, adv. D'un air de défi.
deficiency, s. **1.** Manque m, insuffisance f. **2.** Défaut m; imperfection f.
deficient, a. Défectueux, insuffisant.
 To be d. in, manquer de.
deficit, s. Déficit m.
defile[1], s. Défilé m.
defile[2], v.i. Défiler.
defile[3], v.tr. Souiller, salir; polluer.
defilement, s. Souillure f.
define, v.tr. **1.** Définir. **2.** Déterminer; délimiter.
definite, a. Défini; bien déterminé.
 D. answer, réponse catégorique
definitely, adv. Décidément.
definition, s. Définition f.
deflate, v.tr. Dégonfler.
deflation, s. Dégonflement m.
deflect, v.tr. Détourner.
deform, v.tr. Déformer.
deformation, s. Déformation f.
deformed, a. Contrefait, difforme.
deformity, s. Difformité f.
defraud, v.tr. **1.** Frauder. **2.** Frustrer.
defray, v.tr. Payer; couvrir. **To d.
 s.o.'s expenses,** défrayer qn.
deft, a. Adroit, habile.

deftly, *adv.* Adroitement, prestement.
deftness, *s* Adresse *f*, habileté *f*.
defunct, *a* Défunt; décédé.
defy, *v.tr.* Défier; mettre au défi.
degeneracy, *s* Dégénération *f*.
degenerate[1] *a.* & *s.* Dégénéré -ée
degenerate[2], *v.i.* Dégénérer.
degeneration, *s* Dégénération *f*.
degradation, *s.* Dégradation *f*.
degrade, *v.tr.* Dégrader.
degrading, *a* Avilissant, dégradant.
degree, *s.* **1.** Degré *m.* By degrees, petit à petit. **2.** Grade *m.* To take one's d. prendre ses grades.
de-ice, *v.tr.* Dégivrer.
de-icing, *s.* Dégivrage *m.*
deign, *v.tr.* Daigner.
deity, *s.* Déité *f*, divinité *f*.
deject, *v.tr.* Abattre, décourager.
dejected, *a.* Triste, abattu.
dejection, *s.* Découragement *m.*
delay[1], *s.* **1.** Délai *m,* retard *m.* Without further d., sans plus tarder. **2.** Retardement *m.*
delay[2]. **1.** *v.tr.* (*a*) Différer, retarder. (*b*) Retenir, arrêter. **2.** *v.i.* (*a*) Tarder. (*b*) S'attarder.
delegate[1], *s.* Délégué *m.*
delegate[2], *v.tr.* Déléguer.
delegation, *s.* Délégation *f.*
delete, *v.tr.* Effacer, rayer.
deleterious, *a.* Délétère.
deletion, *s.* Rature *f*, suppression *f.*
deliberate[1], *a.* **1.** Délibéré. **2.** (*a*) Réfléchi, avisé. (*b*) Sans hâte.
deliberate[2], *v.tr.* & *i.* Délibérer.
deliberately, *adv.* **1.** A dessein; exprès. **2.** Délibérément.
deliberation, *s.* **1.** (*a*) Délibération *f.* (*b*) *pl* Débats *m.* **2.** With d., après réflexion.
delicacy, *s.* Délicatesse *f.*
delicate, *a* Délicat.
delicately, *adv.* Avec délicatesse.
delicious, *a.* Délicieux, exquis.
deliciously, *adv.* Délicieusement.
delight[1], *s* **1.** Délices *fpl.* délice *m.* **2.** Joie *f*
delight[2]. **1.** *v.tr.* Enchanter, ravir. **2.** *v.i.* Se délecter.
delighted, *a.* Enchanté, ravi.
delightful, *a.* Délicieux, ravissant.
delightfully *adv* Délicieusement; à ravir.
delineate, *v.tr.* Tracer, décrire.
delineation, *s.* Description *f.*

delinquency, *s.* **1.** Culpabilité *f.* **2.** Délit *m,* faute *f.*
delinquent, *a.* & *s.* Coupable (*mf*).
delirious, *a.* En délire; délirant.
delirium, *s.* Délire *m.*
deliver, *v.tr.* **1.** Délivrer. **2.** Livrer. To d. up, restituer. **3.** To d. a message, faire une commission. **4.** Porter donner· lancer; livrer. **5.** Prononcer.
deliverance, *s.* Délivrance *f.*
deliverer, *s.* Libérateur -trice; sauveur *m.*
delivery, *s.* **1.** Livraison *f.* **2.** Débit *m,* diction *f.*
dell, *s.* Vallon *m,* combe *f.*
delta, *s* Delta *m*
delude, *v.tr.* **1.** Abuser, tromper. **2.** Duper; en faire accroire à.
deluge[1], *s.* Déluge *m.*
deluge[2], *v.tr.* Inonder (*with*, de).
delusion, *s.* Illusion *f*, erreur *f.* To be under a d., se faire illusion.
delusive, *a.* Illusoire.
demand[1], *s* Demande *f.* réc.amation *f* revendication *f*
demand[2], *v.tr* Réclamer; exiger.
demean, *v.pr.* To d. oneself, s'abaisser, se dégrader.
demeanour, *s.* Tenue *f* maintien *m.*
demented, *a.* Dément.
demise, *s.* Décès *m,* mort *f.*
demobilization, *s.* Démobilisation *f.*
demobilize, *v.tr.* Démobiliser.
democracy, *s.* Démocratie *f.*
democrat, *s.* Démocrate *mf.*
democratic, *a.* Démocratique.
demolish, *v.tr.* Démolir.
demolition, *s.* Démolition *f.*
demon, *s.* Démon *m,* diable *m.*
demoniacal, *a.* Démoniaque.
demonstrate. **1.** *v.tr.* (*a*) Démontrer. (*b*) Décrire. expliquer **2.** *v.i* Manifester
demonstration, *s.* **1.** Démonstration *f.* **2.** Manifestation *f.*
demonstrative, *a.* Démonstratif.
demonstrator, *s.* **1.** Démonstrateur *m.* **2.** Manifestant *m.*
demoralization, *s.* Démoralisation *f.*
demoralize, *v.tr.* **1.** Dépraver, corrompre. **2.** Démoraliser.
demur[1], *s* Hésitation *f.*
demur[2], *v.i.* Soulever des objections.
demure, *a.* **1.** Posé; réservé. **2.** D'une modestie affectée.

demurely, *adv.* **1.** D'un air posé. **2.** Avec une modestie affectée.

demureness, *s.* **1.** Gravité *f* de maintien. **2.** Modestie affectée.

den, *s.* Tanière *f*, repaire *m*.

denial, *s.* **1.** Refus *m*. **2.** Démenti *m*.

denizen, *s.* Habitant, -ante.

Denmark. *Pr.n.* Le Danemark.

denomination, *s.* **1.** Dénomination *f*. **2.** Culte *m*. **3.** Catégorie *f*.

denote, *v.tr.* **1.** Dénoter. **2.** Signifier.

denounce, *v.tr.* **1.** (*a*) Dénoncer. (*b*) Démasquer. **2.** S'élever contre.

dense, *a.* **1.** Épais, -aisse ; compact. **2.** Stupide.

density, *s.* **1.** Épaisseur *f* ; densité *f*. **2.** Stupidité *f*.

dent[1], *s.* Marque *f* de coup ; bosselure *f* ; renfoncement *m*.

dent[2], *v.tr.* Bosseler, bossuer.

dental, *a.* Dentaire. **D. surgeon,** chirurgien dentiste.

dentifrice, *s.* Dentifrice *m*.

dentist, *s.* Dentiste *m*.

dentistry, *s.* Art *m* dentaire.

denude, *v.tr.* Dénuder.

denunciation, *s.* **1.** Dénonciation *f*. **2.** Condamnation *f*.

deny, *v.tr.* **1.** Nier ; démentir. **2.** Refuser. **3. To d. oneself,** se priver.

depart, *v.i.* **1.** S'en aller, partir. **2.** Sortir (d'une règle).

departed, *a.* **1.** Passé. **2.** Mort.

department, *s.* (*a*) Département *m* ; service *m* (*b*) Rayon *m*.

departmental, *a.* Départemental, -aux.

departure, *s.* **1.** Départ *m*. **To take one's d.,** s'en aller. **2. A new d.,** une nouvelle tendance.

depend, *v.i.* **1.** Dépendre (on, de). **That depends,** c'est selon. **2.** Compter. **D. upon it,** comptez là-dessus.

dependable, *a.* Digne de confiance.

dependant, *s.* Protégé, -ée.

dependence, *s.* **1.** Dépendance *f* (on, de). **2.** Confiance *f*.

dependent. 1. *a.* (*a*) Dépendant (on, de). (*b*) A la charge (on, de). **2.** *s.* Protégé, -ée.

depict, *v.tr.* Peindre, dépeindre.

deplete, *v.tr.* Épuiser.

depletion, *s.* Épuisement *m*.

deplorable, *a.* Déplorable, lamentable.

deplorably, *adv.* Lamentablement.

deplore, *v.i.* Déplorer.

depopulate, *v.tr.* Dépeupler.

depopulation, *s.* Dépopulation *f*.

deport, *v.tr.* Expulser.

deportation, *s.* Expulsion *f*.

deportment, *s.* (*a*) Tenue *f*, maintien *m*. (*b*) Conduite *f*.

depose, *v.tr.* Déposer.

deposit[1], *s.* **1.** Dépot *m*. **2. To pay a d.,** verser une provision.

deposit[2], *v.tr.* Déposer.

deposition, *s.* Déposition *f*.

depositor, *s.* Déposant, -ante.

depository, *s.* Dépôt *m*, entrepôt *m*.

depot, *s.* Dépôt *m* ; entrepôt *m*.

depravation, *s.* Dépravation *f*.

deprave, *v.tr.* Dépraver.

depravity, *s.* Dépravation *f*.

deprecate, *v.tr.* Désapprouver.

deprecating, *a.* Désapprobateur, -trice.

deprecation, *s.* Désapprobation *f*.

depreciate. 1. *v.tr* Déprécier. **2.** *v.i.* Se déprécier.

depreciation, *s.* Dépréciation *f*.

depredation, *s.* Déprédation *f*.

depredator, *s.* Déprédateur, -trice.

depress, *v.tr.* **1.** Abaisser ; baisser. **2.** Décourager.

depressed, *a.* Triste, abattu.

depressing, *a.* Attristant.

depression, *s.* **1.** Abaissement *m*. **2.** Dépression *f*. **3.** Affaissement *m*. **4.** Découragement *m*.

deprivation, *s.* Privation *f*, perte *f*.

deprive, *v.tr.* Priver.

depth, *s.* **1.** Profondeur *f*. **2.** Hauteur *f* ; épaisseur *f*. **3.** Intensité *f* (de coloris). **4.** Fond *m* ; milieu *m*.

deputation, *s.* Députation *f*.

depute, *v.tr.* Députer, déléguer.

deputize, *v.i.* **To d. for,** remplacer.

deputy, *s.* **1.** Délégué *m*. **2.** Député *m*.

derange, *v.tr.* Déranger.

derangement, *s.* Dérangement *m*.

derelict. 1. *a.* Abandonné. **2.** *s.* Navire abandonné ; épave *f*.

dereliction, *s.* **1.** Abandon *m*. **2. D. of duty,** manquement *m* au devoir.

deride, *v.tr.* Tourner en dérision ; railler, se moquer de.

derision, *s.* Dérision *f*. **Object of d.,** objet de risée *f*.

derisive, *a.* Moqueur, -euse.

derivation, *s.* Dérivation *f*.

derivative, *a. & s.* Dérivé (*m*).

derive, *v.tr. & i.* **1.** (*a*) Tirer; trouver (*from*, à). (*b*) Venir. **2.** To be derived, dériver, (pro-)venir.

derogatory *a.* Dérogeant, qui déroge.

dervish, *s.* Derviche *m*.

descend. **1.** *v.i.* (*a*) Descendre. (*b*) S'abattre, tomber. (*c*) S'abaisser. **2.** *v.tr.* Descendre.

descendant, *s.* Descendant, -ante.

descent, *s.* **1.** Descente *f*. **2.** Descendance *f*.

describe, *v.tr.* (*a*) Décrire. (*b*) Qualifier (*as*, de).

description, *s.* **1.** (*a*) Description *f*. (*b*) Signalement *m*. **2.** Sorte *f*, espèce *f*.

descriptive, *a.* Descriptif.

descry, *v.tr.* Apercevoir, aviser.

desecrate, *v.tr.* Profaner.

desecration, *s.* Profanation *f*.

desecrator, *s.* Profanateur, -trice.

desert[1], *s.* Mérite *m*.

desert[2], *a. & s.* Désert (*m*).

desert[3], *v.tr.* (*a*) Déserter. (*b*) Abandonner, délaisser.

deserted, *a.* Abandonné; désert.

deserter, *s.* Déserteur *m*.

desertion, *s.* Abandon *m*, délaissement *m*.

deserve, *v.tr.* Mériter.

deservedly, *adv.* A juste titre.

deserving, *a.* Méritant; méritoire.

desiccate, *v.tr.* Dessécher.

design[1], *s.* **1.** Dessein *m*, intention *f*. **2.** Dessin *m*, modèle *m*.

design[2], *v.tr.* **1.** Destiner (*for*, à). **2.** Projeter, se proposer. **3.** (*a*) Préparer. (*b*) Créer.

designate, *v.tr.* **1.** Désigner, nommer. **2.** Indiquer.

designation, *s.* Désignation *f*.

designedly, *adv.* A dessein.

designer, *s.* Dessinateur, -trice.

designing, *a.* Artificieux, intrigant.

desirability, *s.* Avantage *m*; attrait *m*.

desirable, *a.* Désirable; à désirer; souhaitable; avantageux.

desire[1], *s.* **1.** Désir *m*, souhait *m*. **2.** Demande *f*.

desire[2], *v.tr.* **1.** Désirer; avoir envie de. **2.** (*a*) Demander (*of*, à). (*b*) Prier.

desirous, *a.* Désireux.

desist, *v.i.* **1.** Cesser. **2.** Renoncer (*from*, à).

desk, *s.* **1.** Pupitre *m*; bureau *m*. **2.** Pay at the d.! payez à la caisse!

desolate, *a.* **1.** Désert. **2.** Affligé.

desolation, *s.* Désolation *f*.

despair[1], *s.* Désespoir *m*. In d., au désespoir. To drive to d., désespérer.

despair[2], *v.i.* (*a*) Désespérer. (*b*) *Abs.* Perdre espoir.

despairing, *a.* Désespéré.

despairingly, *adv.* En désespéré.

despatch, *s. & v.* = DISPATCH[1], [2].

desperado, *s.* Homme *m* capable de tout.

desperate, *a.* **1.** Désespéré. **2.** Acharné.

desperately, *adv.* Désespérément avec acharnement.

desperation, *s.* Désespoir *m*.

despicable, *a.* Méprisable.

despicably, *adv.* Bassement.

despise, *v.tr.* (*a*) Mépriser. (*b*) Dédaigner.

despite, *prep.* En dépit de.

despoil, *v.tr.* Dépouiller, spolier.

despoiler, *s.* Spoliateur, -trice.

despond, *v.i.* Perdre courage.

despondency, *s.* Abattement *m*.

despondent, *a.* Découragé, abattu.

despot, *s.* Despote *m*; tyran *m*.

despotic, *a.* **1.** Despotique. **2.** Arbitraire, despote.

despotically, *adv.* Despotiquement, arbitrairement.

despotism, *s.* Despotisme *m*.

dessert, *s.* Dessert *m*.

dessert-spoon, *s.* Cuiller *f* à dessert.

destination, *s.* Destination *f*.

destine, *v.tr.* Destiner (*for*, à).

destiny, *s.* Destin *m*, destinée *f*.

destitute, *a.* **1.** Dépourvu, dénué. **2.** Indigent; sans ressources.

destitution, *s.* Dénuement *m*, indigence *f*.

destroy, *v.tr.* Détruire; anéantir.

destroyer, *s.* **1.** Destructeur. -trice. **2.** Contre-torpilleur *m*.

destroying, *a.* Destructeur -trice.

destructible, *a.* Destructible.

destruction, *s.* Destruction *f*.

destructive, *a.* Destructeur, -trice; destructif.

destructiveness, *s.* **1.** Pouvoir destructeur. **2.** Penchant *m* à détruire.

destructor, *s.* Destructeur, -trice.

desultory, *a.* Décousu; sans suite.

detach, *v.tr.* Détacher, séparer.

detached, *a.* Détaché.

detachment, *s.* **1.** Séparation *f.* **2.** Détachement *m.*

detail¹, *s.* Détail *m*, particularité *f.*

detail², *v.tr.* Détailler.

detain, *v.tr.* **1.** Détenir. **2.** Retenir ; empêcher de partir.

detect, *v.tr.* **1.** Découvrir. **2.** Apercevoir.

detection, *s.* Découverte *f.*

detective, *s.* Agent *m* de la sûreté. D. novel, roman policier.

detention, *s.* **1.** Détention *f.* **2.** Retard *m* (inévitable) ; arrêt *m.*

deter, *v.tr.* Détourner, décourager.

deteriorate, *v.i.* (Se) détériorer.

deterioration, *s.* Détérioration *f.*

determination, *s.* **1.** Détermination *f.* **2.** Expiration *f.*

determine, *v.tr. & i.* **1.** (*a*) Déterminer, fixer. (*b*) Constater. **2.** Décider. **3.** Résoudre.

determined, *a.* Déterminé, résolu.

deterrent, *s.* To act as a d., exercer un effet préventif.

detest, *v.tr.* Détester.

detestable, *a.* Détestable.

detestation, *s.* Détestation *f.* To hold in d., détester.

detonate, *v.tr.* Faire détoner.

detonation, *s.* Détonation *f.*

detonator, *s.* Détonateur *m.*

detour, *s.* Détour *m.*

detract, *v.i.* To d. from, amoindrir ; nuire à.

detractor, *s.* Détracteur, -trice

detriment, *s.* Détriment *m.*

detrimental, *a.* Nuisible.

detrimentally, *adv.* Nuisiblement.

deuce¹, *s.* **1.** Deux *m.* **2.** *Ten :* A deux ; égalité *f.*

deuce², *s.* Diantre *m*, diable *m.*

devastate, *v.tr.* Dévaster, ravager.

devastating, *a.* Dévastateur, -trice.

devastation, *s.* Dévastation *f.*

develop. I. *v.tr.* **1.** Développer **2.** Engendrer. **3.** Révéler.
II. **develop,** *v.i.* **1.** Se développer. **2.** Se manifester.

developer, *s.* Révélateur *m.*

developing, *s.* Développement *m.*

development, *s.* Développement *m.*

deviate, *v.i.* Dévier, s'écarter.

deviation, *s.* Déviation *f* ; écart *m.*

device, *s.* **1.** (*a*) Expédient *m.* (*b*)

Stratagème *m.* **2.** Dispositif *m*, appareil *m.* **3.** Emblème *m*, devise *f.*

devil, *s.* **1.** Diable *m.* **2.** Démon *m.*

devilish, *a.* (*a*) Diabolique. (*b*) Maudit, satané.

devilry, *s.* **1.** Méchanceté *f.* **2.** To be full of d., avoir le diable au corps.

devious, *a.* Détourné, tortueux.

devise, *v.tr.* Combiner ; inventer.

devoid, *a.* Dénué, dépourvu.

devolve, *v.i.* Incomber (*on*, à).

devote, *v.tr.* Vouer, consacrer.

devoted, *a.* Dévoué, attaché.

devotedly, *adv.* Avec dévouement.

devotion, *s.* **1.** Dévotion *f.* **2.** Dévouement *m.*

devour, *v.tr.* Dévorer.

devourer, *s.* Dévorateur, -trice.

devouring, *a.* Dévorateur, -trice.

devout, *a.* **1.** Dévot, pieux. **2.** Fervent, sincère.

devoutly, *adv.* **1.** Dévotement. **2.** Sincèrement.

dew, *s.* Rosée *f.*

dewdrop, *s.* Goutte *f* de rosée.

dexterity, *s.* Dextérité *f* ; habileté *f.*

dexterous, *a.* Adroit, habile.

dexterously, *adv.* Avec dextérité ; habilement.

diabolical, *a.* Diabolique.

diabolically, *adv.* Diaboliquement.

diadem, *s.* Diadème *m.*

diagnose, *v.tr.* Diagnostiquer.

diagnosis, *s.* Diagnostic *m.*

diagonal. **I.** *a.* Diagonal -aux. **2.** *s.* Diagonale *f.*

diagonally, *adv.* Diagonalement.

diagram, *s.* Diagramme *m*, tracé *m.*

dial¹, *s.* Cadran *m.*

dial², *v.tr.* To d. a number, composer un numéro.

dialect, *s.* Dialecte *m* ; patois *m.*

dialling, *s.* D. tone, signal *m* de numérotage.

dialogue, *s.* Dialogue *m.*

diameter, *s.* Diamètre *m.*

diametrical, *a.* Diamétral, -aux.

diametrically. *adv.* Diamétralement.

diamond, *s.* **1.** Diamant *m* **2.** *Cards :* Carreau *m.*

diamond-shaped, *a.* En losange

Diana. *Pr.n.* Diane *f.*

diaphanous, *a.* Diaphane.

diaphragm, *s.* Diaphragme *m.*

diarrhoea, *s.* Diarrhée *f.*

diary, s. Journal m.

diatribe, s. Diatribe f.

dice, s.pl. See DIE[1] I.

dice-box, s. Cornet m à dés.

dictate. 1. v.tr. Dicter. 2. v.i. Faire la loi.

dictation, s. Dictée f.

dictator, s. Dictateur m.

dictatorial, a. Impérieux.

dictionary, s. Dictionnaire m.

die[1], s I. Dé m.
II. **die.** 1. Coin m. 2. Matrice f.

die[2], v.i. 1. Mourir ; crever. **To be dying,** être à l'agonie. **Never say die!** tenez bon! 2. **To die of laughing,** mourir de rire. **To be dying,** mourir d'envie (de faire qch.). **die away,** v.i. S'affaiblir ; s'éteindre. **die down,** v.i. Baisser ; s'apaiser ; se calmer. **die out,** v.i. S'éteindre ; disparaître.

diet[1], s. 1. Nourriture f. 2. Régime m.

diet[2], v.tr. Mettre au régime.

differ, v.i. 1. Différer ; être différent. 2. Ne pas s'accorder.

difference, s. 1. Différence f, écart m. **It makes no d.,** cela ne fait rien. 2. **To split the d.,** partager le différend. 3. Dispute f.

different, a. 1. Différent. 2. Divers.

differentiate, v.tr Différencier.

differently, adv. 1. Différemment. 2. Diversement.

difficult, a. Difficile.

difficulty, s. 1. Difficulté f. 2. Obstacle m. 3. Embarras m.

diffidence, s. Manque m d'assurance ; modestie excessive.

diffident, a Qui manque d'assurance.

diffidently, adv. Timidement ; en hésitant.

diffuse[1], a. Diffus.

diffuse[2], v.tr. Répandre ; diffuser.

diffusely, adv. Avec prolixité.

dig, v.tr. 1. (a) Bêcher. (b) Creuser. 2. Enfoncer. **dig up,** v.tr. Déraciner ; mettre à jour ; piocher.

digest[1], s Sommaire m, abrégé m.

digest[2], v.tr. 1. (a) Mettre en ordre. (b) Résumer. 2. Digérer.

digestible, a. Digestible.

digestion, s. Digestion f.

digestive, a. Digestif.

digging, s. 1. Bêchage m. 2. pl. (a) Placer m. (b) Logement m, garni m.

digit, s. 1. (a) Doigt m. (b) Doigt de pied. 2. Chiffre m.

dignified, a. Plein de dignité.

dignify, v.tr. Donner de la dignité à.

dignitary, s. Dignitaire m

dignity, s. Dignité f.

digress, v.i. Faire une digression.

digression, s. Digression f, écart m.

dike, s. Digue f, levée f.

dilapidated, a. Délabré.

dilapidation, s. Délabrement m.

dilate, v.i. (a) Se dilater. (b) S'étendre.

dilation, s. Dilatation f.

dilatory, a. Lent ; tardif.

dilemma, s. Embarras m.

diligence, s. Assiduité f, diligence f.

diligent, a. Assidu, diligent.

diligently, adv. Avec assiduité ; diligemment.

dilute, v.tr. Diluer.

dilution, s. Dilution f.

dim[1], a. Faible ; pâle.

dim[2], v.tr. (a) Obscurcir ; ternir. (b) **To dim the head-lights,** baisser les phares.

dimension, s. Dimension f.

diminish. 1. v.tr. Diminuer ; amoindrir. 2. v.i. Diminuer.

diminished, a. Diminué, amoindri.

diminution, s. Diminution f.

diminutive, a. Tout petit ; minuscule.

dimly, adv. Faiblement, sans éclat.

dimness, s. 1. Faiblesse f ; obscurité f. 2. Imprécision f.

dimple, s. Fossette f.

dimpled, a. A fossettes.

din, s. Tapage m, vacarme m.

dine, v.i. Dîner. **To d. out,** dîner en ville.

diner, s. Dîneur, -euse.

dinghy, s Canot m, youyou m. Collapsible d., berthon m.

dinginess, s. Manque m de fraîcheur.

dingy, a. Défraîchi ; terne.

dining, s. Dîner m.

dining-car, s. Wagon-restaurant m, pl. wagons-restaurants.

dining-room, s. Salle f à manger.

dinner, s. Dîner m. **Public d.,** banquet m.

dinner-dance, s. Dîner suivi de bal.

dinner-jacket, s. Smoking m.

dinner-service, s. Service m de table.

dinner-time, s. L'heure f du dîner.

dint, s. By d. of, à force de.

dip[1], s. **1.** Plongement m. **2.** Plongée f. **3.** Baignade f.

dip[2]. I. v.tr. **1.** Plonger, tremper. **2.** Immerger. **3.** Baisser subitement. II. dip, v.i. **1.** Plonger. **2.** Incliner ; pencher.

diphtheria, s. Diphtérie f.

diploma, s. Diplôme m.

diplomacy, s. Diplomatie f.

diplomat, s. Diplomate m.

diplomatic, a. **1.** Diplomatique. **2.** Adroit, prudent.

diplomatically, adv. **1.** Diplomatiquement. **2.** Avec tact.

diplomatist, s. Diplomate m.

dipping, s. Plongée f, immersion f.

dire, a. Affreux ; lugubre ; noir. D. necessity, nécessité implacable.

direct[1], v.tr. **1.** Adresser. **2.** Gouverner ; gérer. **3.** (a) Attirer. (b) Diriger. **4.** Indiquer le chemin à. **5.** Ordonner à. As directed, selon les instructions.

direct[2]. **1.** a. (a) Direct ; immédiat. (b) Franc, f. franche. (c) Formel ; catégorique. **2.** adv. Directement ; tout droit.

direction, s. **1.** Direction f, administration f. **2.** Adresse f. **3.** Direction, sens m. **4.** pl Instructions f.

directly. **1.** adv. (a) Directement ; tout droit. (b) Absolument. (c) Tout de suite. **2.** conj. Aussitôt que, dès que.

directness, s. Franchise f.

director, s. Administrateur m, directeur m.

directory, s. Annuaire m (des téléphones). Post-office d. = Bottin.

dirge, s. Chant m funèbre.

dirt, s. Saleté f. **1.** Boue f, crotte f, ordure f. **2.** Malpropreté f.

dirtiness, s. Saleté f, malpropreté f.

dirt-track, s. Piste f en cendrée.

dirty[1], a. **1.** Sale, malpropre, crasseux ; crotté. **2.** D. weather, mauvais temps ; gros temps. **3.** D. trick, vilain tour.

dirty[2], v.tr. Salir, crotter, encrasser.

disability, s. (a) Incapacité f. (b) Physical d., infirmité f.

disable, v.tr. Mettre hors de combat ; estropier.

disablement, s. **1.** Mise f hors de combat. **2.** Invalidité f ; incapacité f.

disabuse, v.tr. Désabuser.

disadvantage, s. Désavantage m, inconvénient m. At a d., au dépourvu.

disadvantageous, a. Désavantageux, défavorable.

disaffected, a. Désaffectionné.

disaffection, s. Désaffection f.

disagree, v.i. **1.** (a) Être en désaccord. (b) Donner tort (with, à). **2.** Se brouiller. **3.** Ne pas convenir à.

disagreeable, a. Désagréable.

disagreeably, adv. Désagréablement ; fâcheusement.

disagreement, s. **1.** Différence f. **2.** Désaccord m. **3.** Différend m, querelle f.

disappear, v.i. Disparaître.

disappearance, s. Disparition f.

disappoint, v.tr. (a) Désappointer. (b) Décevoir, chagriner. (c) Décevoir ; tromper.

disappointing, a. Décevant.

disappointment, s. Déception f, désappointement m ; mécompte m.

disapprobation, s. Désapprobation f.

disapproval, s. Désapprobation f.

disapprove, v.i. To d. of. désapprouver.

disarm, v.tr. & i. Désarmer.

disarmament, s. Désarmement m.

disarrange, v.tr. Déranger.

disarrangement, s. Dérangement m.

disaster, s. Désastre m ; sinistre m.

disastrous, a. Désastreux ; funeste.

disastrously, adv. Désastreusement.

disbelief, s. Incrédulité f.

disbelieve. **1.** v.tr. Ne pas croire. **2.** v.i. Ne pas croire (in, à).

disbeliever, s. Incrédule mf.

disburden, v.tr. Décharger.

disburse, v.tr. Débourser.

disbursement, s. **1.** Déboursement m. **2.** pl. Débours mpl.

disc, s. Disque m, rondelle f.

discard, v.tr. Se défaire de.

discern, v.tr. Distinguer, discerner.

discernible, a. Perceptible.

discerning, a. Judicieux ; pénétrant.

discernment, s. Discernement m.

discharge[1], s. **1.** Déchargement m. **2.** Décharge f. **3.** Renvoi m. **4.** (a) Mise f en liberté. (b) Acquittement m. **5.** Accomplissement m. **6.** (a) Payement m. (b) Quittance f.

discharge[2], v.tr. **1.** Décharger **2.**

Congédier. **3.** Libérer. **4.** Lancer.
5. (*a*) S'acquitter de. (*b*) Acquitter.
disciple, *s.* Disciple *m.*
disciplinarian, *s.* Disciplinaire *m.*
discipline, *s.* Discipline *f.*
disclaim, *v.tr.* Désavouer.
disclose, *v.tr.* Découvrir; divulguer.
disclosure, *s.* Mise *f* à découvert;
révélation *f*; divulgation *f.*
discolour, *v.tr.* Décolorer.
discolouration, *s.* Décoloration *f.*
discomfiture, *s.* **1.** Déconfiture *f.*
2. Déconvenue *f.*
discomfort, *s.* (*a*) Manque *m* de
confort. (*b*) Malaise *m*, gêne *f.*
discompose, *v.tr.* Troubler.
discomposure, *s.* Trouble *m.*
disconcert, *v.tr.* Déconcerter.
disconcerting, *a.* Déconcertant.
disconnect, *v.tr.* Désunir, disjoindre; décrocher.
disconnected, *a.* **1.** Détaché **2.**
Décousu.
disconsolate, *a.* Inconsolable; désolé.
discontent, *s.* Mécontentement *m.*
discontented, *a.* Mécontent (*with*,
de); peu satisfait.
discontinuance, *s.* Discontinuation *f.*
discontinue. 1. *v.tr.* Discontinuer;
cesser. **2.** *v.i.* Cesser.
discord, *s.* **1.** Discorde *f*, désunion *f.*
2. Dissonance *f*; accord dissonant.
discordant, *a.* **1.** (*a*) Discordant.
(*b*) Dissonant. **2.** Opposé.
discount¹, *s.* **1.** Remise *f*, rabais *m.*
2. Escompte *m.*
discount², *v.tr.* **1.** Escompter. **2.** (*a*)
Ne pas tenir compte de. (*b*) Rabattre.
discountenance, *v.tr.* Décourager.
discourage, *v.tr.* Décourager.
discouragement, *s.* Découragement *m.*
discouraging, *a.* Décourageant.
discourse¹, *s.* Discours *m.*
discourse², *v.i.* (*a*) Discourir. (*b*)
Causer.
discourteous, *a.* Discourtois.
discourtesy, *s.* Impolitesse *f.*
discover, *v.tr.* Découvrir, trouver.
discoverer, *s.* Découvreur, -euse.
discovery, *s.* Découverte *f.*
discredit¹, *s.* **1.** Doute *m.* **2.** Discrédit *m*; déconsidération *f.*
discredit², *v.tr.* **1.** Ne pas croire;
mettre en doute. **2.** Discréditer.

discreditable, *a.* Peu digne.
discreet, *a.* **1.** Avisé, sage. **2.** Discret, -ète.
discreetly, *adv.* **1.** Avec réserve.
2. Discrètement.
discrepancy, *s.* Désaccord *m*; divergence *f.*
discretion, *s.* **1.** Discrétion *f.* **2.**
Sagesse *f*, jugement *m.*
discriminate. 1. *v.tr.* Distinguer.
2. *v.i.* (*a*) Distinguer. (*b*) Faire des
distinctions.
discriminating, *a.* Plein de discernement.
discrimination, *s.* **1.** Discernement
m. **2.** Jugement *m.* **3.** Distinction *f.*
discursive, *a.* Décousu, sans suite.
discuss, *v.tr.* Discuter, débattre;
délibérer.
discussion, *s.* Discussion *f.*
disdain¹, *s.* Dédain *m.*
disdain², *v.tr.* Dédaigner.
disdainful, *a.* Dédaigneux.
disdainfully, *adv.* Dédaigneusement.
disease, *s.* Maladie *f*; mal *m.*
diseased, *a.* **1.** Malade. **2.** Morbide.
disembark, *v.tr. & i.* Débarquer.
disembarkation, *s.* Débarquement *m.*
disembarrass, *v.tr.* Débarrasser.
disenchanted, *a.* Désenchanté.
disengage. 1. *v.tr.* Dégager. **2.** *v.i.*
Se dégager.
disengaged, *a.* Libre, inoccupé.
disentangle, *v.tr.* Démêler.
disfavour, *s.* Défaveur *f.*
disfigure, *v.tr.* Défigurer; enlaidir.
disfigurement, *s.* Défiguration *f.*
disgorge, *v.tr.* Dégorger, rendre.
disgrace¹, *s.* **1.** Disgrâce *f.* **2.** Honte
f, déshonneur *m.*
disgrace², *v.tr.* **1.** Disgracier. **2.**
Déshonorer.
disgraceful, *a.* Honteux, déshonorant, scandaleux.
disgracefully, *adv.* Honteusement.
disguise¹, *s.* **1.** Déguisement *m.* In
d., déguisé. **2.** Feinte *f*; fausse
apparence.
disguise², *v.tr* Déguiser; travestir;
dissimuler.
disgust¹, *s.* **1.** Dégoût. **2.** Profond
mécontentement.
disgust², *v.tr.* Dégoûter; écœurer.
disgusting, *a.* Dégoûtant.
dish, *s.* **1.** Plat *m.* **Vegetable d.,**
légumier *m.* **2.** Plat; mets *m.*

dish-cloth, s. Torchon m.
dish-cover, s. I. Couvercle m. 2. Cloche f.
dishearten, v.tr. Décourager.
disheartening, a. Décourageant.
dishevel, v.tr. Ébouriffer.
dishevelled, a. I. Échevelé. 2. Aux vêtements chiffonnés.
dishonest, a. Malhonnête.
dishonestly, adv. Malhonnêtement.
dishonesty, s. Improbité f.
dishonour¹, s. Déshonneur m.
dishonour², v.tr. Déshonorer.
dishonourable, a. I. Sans honneur. 2. Déshonorant, honteux.
dishonourably, adv. D'une façon peu honorable.
dish-water, s. Eau f de vaisselle.
disillusion, v.tr. Désillusionner.
disillusionment, s. Désillusionnement m.
disinclination, s. Répugnance f, aversion f.
disinclined, a. Peu disposé.
disinfect, v.tr. Désinfecter.
disinfectant, a. & s. Désinfectant (m).
disingenuous, a. Sans franchise
disinherit, v.tr. Déshériter.
disintegrate. I. v.tr. Désagréger ; effriter. 2. v.i. Se désagréger.
disintegration, s. Désagrégation f.
disinter, v.tr. Déterrer, exhumer.
disinterested, a. Désintéressé.
disinterestedness, s. Désintéressement m.
disjointed, a. Disjoint, sans suite.
dislike¹, s. Aversion f, répugnance f.
dislike², v.tr. Ne pas aimer ; détester. **To take a d. to,** prendre en grippe.
dislocate, v.tr. (a) Désorganiser. (b) Luxer, déboîter.
dislocation, s. (a) Désorganisation f. (b) Luxation f, déboîtement m.
dislodge, v.tr. Déloger.
disloyal, a. Infidèle ; déloyal, -aux.
disloyalty, s. Infidélité f, déloyauté f.
dismal, a. Sombre, triste ; lugubre.
dismally, adv. Lugubrement, tristement.
dismantle, v.tr. Dégarnir.
dismay¹, s. Consternation f.
dismay², v.tr. Consterner.
dismiss, v.tr. I. Congédier ; donner congé à ; destituer. 2. (a) Congédier

(aimablement). (b) Dissoudre. 3. Bannir, chasser. 4. (a) Écarter. (b) Acquitter.
dismissal, s. Congédiemen m, renvoi m; destitution f.
dismount. I. v.i. Mettre pied à terre. 2. v.tr. Démonter.
disobedience, s. Désobéissance f.
disobedient, a. Désobéissant.
disobey, v.tr. Désobéir à.
disobliging, a. Désobligeant.
disorder¹, s. I. Désordre m, confusion f. 2. Désordre, tumulte m.
disorder², v.tr. Déranger.
disordered, a. I. Désordonné ; en désordre. 2. Dérangé.
disorderliness, s. Désordre m.
disorderly, a. I. Désordonné ; en désordre. 2. Turbulent.
disorganize, v.tr. Désorganiser.
disown, v.tr. Désavouer ; renier.
disparage, v.tr. Déprécier, dénigrer.
disparagement, s. Dénigrement m.
disparaging, a. I. Dépréciateur. -trice. 2. Peu flatteur, -euse.
disparagingly, adv. En termes peu flatteurs.
disparity, s. Inégalité f.
dispassionate, a. I. Sans passion ; calme. 2. Impartial, -aux.
dispassionately, adv. I. Avec calme. 2. Sans parti pris.
dispatch¹, s. I. Expédition f ; envoi m. 2. Mise f à mort. 3. Promptitude f, diligence f. 4. Dépêche f.
dispatch², v.tr. I. Expédier ; envoyer. 2. Tuer.
dispatch-box, s Valise diplomatique.
dispel, v.tr. Chasser, dissiper.
dispensary, s. I. Dispensaire m policlinique f. 2. Pharmacie f.
dispensation, s. Décret m, arrêt m.
dispense. I. v.tr. (a) Dispenser, distribuer. (b) Administrer 2. v.i. **To d. with,** se passer de.
dispensing, s. I. Dispensation f distribution f. 2. Préparation f.
dispersal, s. Dispersion f.
disperse. I. v.tr. Disperser ; dissiper. 2. v.i. Se disperser.
dispersion, s. Dispersion f.
dispirit, v.tr. Décourager, abattre.
displace, v.tr. I. Déplacer. 2. (a Destituer. (b) Remplacer.
displacement, s. Déplacement m.

display[1], *s.* **1.** Manifestation *f.* **2.** Étalage *m*; parade *f*, apparat *m*.

display[2], *v.tr* **1.** Exhiber, exposer. **2.** Montrer, manifester. **3.** Étaler, afficher. **4.** Découvrir, révéler.

displease, *v.tr* Déplaire à, contrarier, mécontenter.

displeasing, *a.* Déplaisant, désagréable.

displeasure, *s.* Déplaisir *m*, mécontentement *m*.

disposal, *s.* **1.** Disposition *f*. **2.** For d., à vendre.

dispose, *v.tr & t.* **1.** Disposer, arranger. **2.** To d. of, se défaire de ; régler. **3.** To d. of, écouler ; céder.

disposed, *a.* Intentionné, disposé.

disposition, *s.* **1.** Disposition *f*. **2.** Caractère *m*. **3.** Penchant *m*, tendance *f.*

dispossess, *v.tr.* Déposséder.

disproportionate, *a.* Disproportionné ; hors de proportion.

disprove, *v.tr.* Réfuter ; démontrer la fausseté de.

dispute[1], *s.* **1.** Contestation *f*, débat *m*. Beyond d., incontestable. **2.** Querelle *f*, dispute *f*.

dispute[2]. **1.** *v.i* Se disputer. **2.** *v.tr.* Contester.

disqualification, *s.* **1.** Incapacité *f* **2.** Cause *f* d'incapacité (*for*, à).

disqualify, *v.tr.* **1.** Rendre incapable. **2.** Disqualifier.

disquiet, *v.tr.* Inquiéter ; troubler.

disquieting, *a.* Inquiétant.

disquietude, *s.* Inquiétude *f*.

disregard, *v.tr.* Ne tenir aucun compte de.

disreputable, *a.* **1.** Déshonorant ; honteux. **2.** De mauvaise réputation. **3.** Minable.

disrepute, *s.* To bring into d., discréditer.

disrespect, *s.* Manque *m* d'égards, de respect (*for*, envers).

disrespectful, *a.* Irrespectueux.

disrespectfully, *adv.* Avec irrévérence.

dissatisfaction, *s.* Mécontentement *m* (*with*, *at*, de).

dissatisfied, *a.* Mécontent (*with*, de).

dissatisfy, *v.tr.* Mécontenter.

dissect, *v.tr.* Disséquer.

dissection, *s.* Dissection *f.*

dissemble, *v.tr.* Dissimuler.

dissembling, *s.* Dissimulation *f.*

dissension, *s.* Dissension *f.*

dissent[1], *s.* Dissentiment *m*.

dissent[2], *v.i.* **1.** Différer. **2.** Être dissident.

dissenter, *s.* Dissident, -ente.

dissentient, *a. & s.* Dissident, -ente.

dissenting, *a.* Dissident.

dissertation, *s.* Dissertation *f.*

dissimilar, *a.* Dissemblable.

dissimulate, *v.tr. & i.* Dissimuler.

dissimulation, *s.* Dissimulation *f.*

dissipate. **1.** *v.tr.* Dissiper. **2.** *v.i.* Se dissiper.

dissipated, *a.* Dissipé.

dissipation, *s.* Dissipation *f.*

dissociate, *v.tr.* Désassocier.

dissolute, *a.* Dissolu, débauché.

dissolution, *s.* Dissolution *f.*

dissolve. **1.** *v.tr.* Dissoudre. **2.** *v.i.* Se dissoudre ; fondre.

dissuade, *v.tr.* Dissuader.

dissuasion, *s.* Dissuasion *f.*

distaff, *s.* Quenouille *f*

distance, *s.* **1.** (*a*) Distance *f*, éloignement *m*. Seen from a d., vu de loin. (*b*) Lointain *m*. **2.** Distance, intervalle *m*.

distant, *a.* **1.** (*a*) Éloigné ; lointain. D. likeness, faible ressemblance. (*b*) Éloigné, reculé. **2.** Réservé, distant.

distantly, *adv.* **1.** De loin. D. related, d'une parenté éloignée. **2.** Avec réserve.

distaste, *s.* Dégoût *m* (*for*, de) ; aversion *f*, répugnance *f*.

distasteful, *a.* Désagréable. To be d., répugner.

distemper, *s.* Détrempe *f*.

distend. **1.** *v.tr.* Dilater, gonfler. **2.** *v.i.* (*a*) Se dilater. (*b*) Se distendre.

distension, *s.* Dilatation *f*, distension *f*, gonflement *m*.

distil, *v.tr.* Distiller.

distillery, *s.* Distillerie *f.*

distinct, *a.* **1.** Distinct, différent. **2.** Distinct, net, *f.* nette. **3.** Marqué.

distinction, *s.* Distinction *f.*

distinctive, *a.* Distinctif.

distinctly, *adv.* **1.** Distinctement, clairement. **2.** Décidément.

distinctness, *s.* Clarté *f*, netteté *f.*

distinguish. **1.** *v.tr.* (*a*) Distinguer, discerner. (*b*) Distinguer, différencier. (*c*) To d. oneself, se signaler. **2.** *v.i.* Faire une distinction.

distinguishable, *a.* **1.** Que l'on peut distinguer. **2.** Perceptible.

distinguished, *a.* Distingué.

distort, *v.tr.* (*a*) Tordre ; décomposer. (*b*) Fausser, dénaturer.

distorted, *a.* Tordu, contourné ; convulsé.

distortion, *s.* Déformation *f.*

distract, *v.tr.* **1.** Distraire. **2.** Affoler.

distracted, *a.* Affolé, éperdu.

distraction, *s.* **1.** Distraction *f.* **2.** Confusion *f.* **3.** Affolement *m.*

distress[1], *s.* **1.** Détresse *f.* **2.** Misère *f* ; gêne *f.*

distress[2], *v.tr.* **1.** Affliger, angoisser. **2.** Épuiser, excéder.

distressed, *a.* Affligé, désolé.

distressing, *a.* Affligeant.

distribute, *v.tr.* Distribuer, répartir.

distribution, *s.* Distribution *f* ; répartition *f.*

distributor, *s.* Distributeur, -trice.

district, *s.* **1.** Région *f*, contrée *f.* **2.** (*a*) District. (*b*) Quartier *m.*

distrust[1], *s.* Méfiance *f*, défiance *f.*

distrust[2], *v.tr.* Se méfier de.

distrustful, *a.* Défiant, méfiant.

disturb, *v.tr.* **1.** Déranger ; troubler ; agiter. **2.** Inquiéter, troubler.

disturbance, *s.* **1.** Trouble *m* ; dérangement *m.* **2.** Bruit *m*, tapage *m.*

disturbing, *a.* Perturbateur, -trice.

disunite, *v.tr.* Désunir.

disuse, *s.* Désuétude *f.*

disused, *a.* Hors d'usage.

ditch, *s.* Fossé *m.*

ditto, *a. & s.* Idem ; de même.

divan, *s.* Divan *m.*

dive[1], *s.* (*a*) Plongeon *m.* (*b*) Plongée *f.* (*c*) Vol piqué ; piqué *m.*

dive[2], *v.i.* (*a*) Plonger ; piquer une tête. (*b*) Piquer.

diver, *s.* (*a*) Plongeur *m.* (*b*) Scaphandrier *m.*

diverge, *v.i.* Diverger, s'écarter.

divergence, *s.* Divergence *f.*

divergent, *a.* Divergent.

diverging, *a.* Divergent.

diverse, *a.* **1.** Divers, différent. **2.** Divers, varié.

diversify, *v.tr.* Diversifier.

diversion, *s.* **1.** Détournement *m.* **2.** (*a*) Diversion *f.* (*b*) Divertissement *m.*

diversity, *s.* Diversité *f.*

divert, *v.tr.* **1.** Détourner ; distraire. **2.** Divertir, amuser.

diverting, *a.* Divertissant, amusant.

divest, *v.tr.* Dépouiller, priver.

divide. **1.** *v.tr.* (*a*) Diviser. (*b*) Partager, répartir. (*c*) Séparer. (*d*) Désunir. **2.** *v.i.* Se diviser, se partager.

dividend, *s.* Dividende *m.*

divination, *s.* Divination *f.*

divine[1]. **1.** *a.* Divin. **2.** *s.* Théologien *m.*

divine[2], *v.tr.* Deviner.

divinely, *adv.* Divinement.

diving-board, *s.* Plongeoir *m*, tremplin *m.*

diving-dress, *s.* Scaphandre *m.*

divinity, *s.* Divinité *f*

divisible, *a.* Divisible.

division, *s.* **1.** Division *f*, partage *m* ; scission *f.* **2.** Répartition *f.* **3.** Division, désunion *f.* **4.** Cloison *f.*

divorce[1], *s.* Divorce *m.*

divorce[2], *v.tr.* (*a*) Divorcer. (*b*) To d. s.o., divorcer d'avec qn.

divot, *s.* Motte *f* (de gazon).

divulge, *v.tr.* Divulguer.

dizziness, *s.* Étourdissement *m*, vertige *m.*

dizzy, *a.* **1.** Pris d'étourdissement ; pris de vertige. To make d., étourdir. **2.** Vertigineux.

do. I. *v.tr.* **1.** Faire. To do right, bien faire. It isn't done, cela ne se fait pas. What is to be done? que faire ? What can I do for you? en quoi puis-je vous servir ? Do what we would, malgré tous nos efforts. Well done! à la bonne heure ! **2.** Cuire, faire cuire. Done to a turn, cuit à point. **3.** To have done, avoir fini. Have done! finissez donc ! **4.** How do you do? comment allez-vous ? **5.** That will do, (i) c'est bien ; (ii) en voilà assez !

II. **do**, *verb substitute.* **1.** He writes better than I do, il écrit mieux que moi. **2.** Did you see him?— I did, l'avez-vous vu ?—Oui (, je l'ai vu). I like coffee ; do you? j'aime le café ; et vous ? You like him, don't you? vous l'aimez, n'est-ce pas ? Don't! ne faites pas cela ! **3.** You like Paris? so do I, vous aimez Paris ? moi aussi.

III. **do**, *v.aux.* **1.** He did go, il y est bien allé. Do sit down, asseyez-vous donc ! **2.** We do not know, nous ne le savons pas. **Don't do it!** n'en faites rien !

IV. **do**. **1.** To do well by, bien agir envers. **2.** I'm done for, j'ai mon compte ; je suis perdu. **3.** To have to do with, avoir affaire à ; avoir rapport à. **4.** Do without, passer de. **do again,** *v.tr.* **1.** Refaire. **2.** I wont do it again, je ne le ferai plus. **do away,** *v.i.* To do away with, abolir ; détruire. **do out,** *v.tr.* Faire, nettoyer. **do up,** *v.tr.* **1.** (*a*) Réparer ; décorer. (*b*) Blanchir (le linge). **2.** Faire, envelopper ; boutonner, agrafer. **3.** To be done up, être éreinté.

docile, *a.* Docile.

docilely, *adv.* Docilement.

docility, *s.* Docilité *f.*

dock[1], *v.tr.* Diminuer, rogner.

dock[2], *s.* (*a*) Bassin *m.* The docks, les docks *m.* (*b*) Dry d., cale sèche.

dock[3]. **1.** *v.tr.* Faire entrer au bassin. **2.** *v.i.* Entrer au bassin.

dock[4], *s.* Banc *m* des prévenus

docket, *s.* Étiquette *f*, fiche *f.*

dockyard, *s.* Chantier *m* de construction de navires.

doctor[1], *s.* **1.** Docteur *m.* **2.** Médecin *m.* Woman d., docteur femme

doctor[2], *v.tr.* Soigner.

doctrine, *s.* Doctrine *f*

document, *s.* Document *m.*

documentary, *a.* Documentaire.

dodge[1], *s.* Ruse *f*, artifice *m.*

dodge[2]. **1.** *v.i.* (*a*) Se jeter de côté. (*b*) Biaiser. **2.** *v.tr.* Esquiver ; éviter

doe, *s.* **1.** Daine *f.* **2.** Lapine *f.*

doeskin, *s.* Peau *f* de daim

doff, *v.tr.* Enlever, ôter.

dog[1], *s.* **1.** Chien *m.* Dog racing, courses de lévriers. **2.** Lucky dog! (le) veinard !

dog[2], *v.tr.* Suivre à la piste ; filer. Dogged by, poursuivi par.

dog-biscuit, *s.* Biscuit *m* de chien.

dog-collar, *s.* Collier *m* de chien.

dog-days, *s.pl.* Canicule *f.*

dog-fight, *s.* **1.** Combat *m* de chiens. **2.** Mêlée générale.

dogged, *a.* Obstiné, résolu, tenace.

doggedly, *adv.* Avec ténacité ; opiniâtrement.

doggedness, *s.* Persévérance *f.*

dogma, *s.* Dogme *m.*

dogmatic, *a.* **1.** Dogmatique. **2.** Autoritaire, tranchant.

dogmatically, *adv.* D'un ton autoritaire, tranchant.

dogmatize, *v.i.* Dogmatiser.

dog's-ear, *v.tr.* Corner.

dog-show, *s.* Exposition canine.

dog-tired, *a.* Éreinté.

doing, *s.* **1.** (*a*) That requires some d., ce n'est pas facile. (*b*) This is so-and-so's d., cela est du fait d'un tel. **2.** *pl.* Ce qu'on fait. (*a*) Agissements *mpl.* (*b*) Événements *mpl,* grande activité.

dole[1], *s.* (*a*) Aumône *f.* (*b*) Unemployment d., secours *m* de chômage. To go on the d., s'inscrire au chômage.

dole[2], *v.tr.* To d. out, distribuer parcimonieusement.

doleful, *a.* Lugubre ; douloureux.

dolefully, *adv.* Tristement, douloureusement.

doll, *s.* Poupée *f.*

dolmen, *s.* Dolmen *m.*

dolorous, *a.* **1.** Douloureux **2.** Triste, plaintif.

dolphin, *s.* Dauphin *m.*

dolt, *s.* Sot *m*, benêt *m* ; lourdaud *m.*

domain, *s.* Domaine *m.*

dome, *s.* Dôme *m.*

domestic, *a.* **1.** Domestique. D. servant, domestique *mf.* **2.** D. animal, animal domestique.

domicile, *s.* Domicile *m.*

dominant, *a.* Dominant.

dominate, *v.tr. & i.* Dominer.

dominating, *a.* Dominant.

domination, *s.* Domination *f.*

domineer, *v.i.* **1.** Se montrer autoritaire. **2.** To d. over, tyranniser.

domineering, *a.* Autoritaire.

dominion, *s.* **1.** Domination *f* **2.** Possession *f* ; dominion *m.*

domino, *s.* **1.** Domino *m.* **2.** To play dominoes, jouer aux dominos.

don[1], *s.m.* Professeur (d'université).

don[2], *v.tr.* Revêtir ; mettre.

donate, *v.tr.* Faire un don de.

donation, *s.* Donation *f*, don *m.*

donkey, *s.* **1.** Ane, *f.* ânesse ; baudet *m.* **2.** Imbécile *mf*, âne *m.*

donkey-cart, *s.* Charrette *f* à âne.

donor, *s.* **1.** Donateur, -trice. **2.** D. of blood, donneur, -euse, de sang.

doom[1], *s.* **1.** Destin *m* (funeste) ;

sort (malheureux). **2.** Perte *f*, ruine *f*.

doom², *v.tr.* **Doomed**, perdu. **Doomed to failure**, condamné à l'insuccès.

door, *s.* **1.** Porte *f*. **To turn out of doors**, mettre à la porte. **2.** Portière *f* (de voiture).

door-keeper, *s.* Portier *m*; concierge *mf*.

door-mat, *s.* Paillasson *m*.

door-step, *s.* Seuil *m*.

doorway, *s.* **In the d.**, sous la porte.

dormant, *a.* Assoupi, endormi.

dormitory, *s.* Dortoir *m*.

dormouse, *s.* Loir *m*.

dose, *s.* Dose *f*.

dot¹, *s.* Point *m*.

dot², *v.tr.* **1.** Mettre un point sur. **2.** Pointiller. **Dotted line**, ligne en pointillé.

dotage, *s.* Radotage *m*.

dotard, *s.* Radoteur *m*.

dote, *v.i.* **1.** Radoter. **2. To d. (up)on**, aimer à la folie.

double¹. **I.** *a.* **1.** Double. **With a d. meaning**, à deux sens. **D. bedroom**, chambre à deux personnes. **2. Bent d.**, courbé en deux. **3.** Deux fois plus. **4. D. time**, pas redoublé.
II. double, *adv.* **1. D. as long**, deux fois plus long. **2. To see d.**, voir double.
III. double, *s.* **1.** Double *m*; deux fois autant. **2.** Double; sosie *m*. **3. Men's doubles**, double messieurs.

double². **I.** *v.tr.* **1.** Doubler. **2.** *Cards:* Contrer.
II. double, *v.i.* **1.** Doubler, se doubler. **2.** Faire un brusque crochet. **double up**, **1.** *v.i.* (*a*) Se plier (en deux); se replier. **To d. up with laughter**, se tordre de rire. **2.** *v.tr.* Faire plier en deux.

double-barrelled, *a.* A deux coups.

double-dealing, *s.* Duplicité *f*.

double-edged, *a.* A deux tranchants.

double-width, *a.* Grande largeur.

doubly, *adv.* Doublement.

doubt¹, *s.* Doute *m*. **Beyond a d.**, sans le moindre doute. **No d.**, sans doute.

doubt². **1.** *v.tr.* Douter **2.** *v.i.* Hésiter; douter.

doubtful, *a.* **1.** Douteux. **2.** (*a*) Indécis, incertain. (*b*) **To be d. of**, douter de. **3.** Suspect; louche.

doubtfully, *adv.* **1.** D'un air de doute. **2.** En hésitant.

doubtfulness, *s.* **1.** Ambiguïté *t*. **2.** Irrésolution *f*.

doubtless, *adv.* Sans doute.

dough, *s.* Pâte *f*.

dove, *s.* Colombe *f*.

Dover. *Pr.n.* Douvres *m*. **The Straits of D.**, le Pas de Calais.

dovetail, *v.i.* Se rejoindre, se raccorder.

dowager, *s.* Douairière *f*.

dowdiness, *s.* Manque *m* d'élégance.

dowdy, *a.* Sans élégance.

down¹, *s.* Duvet *m*.

down², *s.* Duvet *m*.

down³. **I.** *adv.* **1.** Vers le bas. **To go d.**, aller en bas; descendre. **To fall d.**, tomber par terre. **Cash d.**, argent comptant. **D. with the traitors!** à bas les traîtres! **2.** Baissé. **D. there**, là-bas. **Face d.**, face en dessous. **Your tyres are d.**, vos pneus sont à plat. *Cards:* **To be two d.**, avoir deux de chute. **3. To be d. on**, en vouloir à. **D. in the mouth**, abattu
II. down, *prep* En bas de; le long de.
III. down, *a.* **D. train**, train descendant.

down-at-heel, *a.* Râpé.

downcast, *a.* **1.** Abattu. **2.** Baisse

downfall, *s.* Chute *f*.

down-hearted, *a.* Découragé; abattu.

downpour, *s.* Forte pluie.

downright. **1.** *adv.* (*a*) Tout à fait; complètement. (*b*) Nettement, catégoriquement. **2.** *a.* (*a*) Direct. (*b*) Absolu, véritable.

downstairs, *adv.* En bas. **To come go, d.**, descendre.

down-stream, *adv.* En aval.

downtrodden, *a.* Foulé aux pieds; opprimé, tyrannisé.

downward, *a.* Descendant, de haut en bas.

downwards, *adv.* De haut en bas; en descendant; en bas.

dowry, *s.* Dot *f*.

doze¹, *s.* Petit somme.

doze², *v.i.* Sommeiller; être assoupi.

dozen, *s.* Douzaine *f*.

drab, *a.* (*a*) Gris. (*b*) Terne.

draft[1], *s.* I. **1.** Traite *f*; lettre *f* de change. **2.** Tracé *m*; ébauche *f*. **3.** Brouillon *m*.
II. **draft**, *s* = DRAUGHT I.

draft[2], *v.tr* Rédiger; faire le brouillon de.

drag. 1. *v.tr.* (*a*) Traîner, tirer. (*b*) Draguer. **2.** *v.i.* Traîner. **drag along**, *v.tr.* Traîner, entraîner. **drag away**, *v.tr.* Entraîner, emmener, de force. **drag on**, *v.i.* Traîner en longueur; s'éterniser.

dragon, *s.* Dragon *m*.

dragon-fly ‹ Libellule *f*; demoiselle *f*.

dragoon, ‹ Dragon *m*.

drain[1], *s.* **1.** Tranchée *f*, rigole *f*. **2.** Égout *m*. **3.** Tuyau *m* d'écoulement.

drain[2]. **1.** *v.tr.* (*a*) Assécher (*b*) Épuiser. **2.** *v.i.* S'écouler.

drainage, *s* Système *m* d'écoulement des eaux.

drake, *s.* Canard *m* mâle.

drama, *s.* Drame *m*.

dramatic, *a.* Dramatique. **The d. works of**, le théâtre de.

dramatically, *adv.* Dramatiquement.

dramatist, *s.* Auteur *m* dramatique; dramaturge *m*.

dramatize, *v.tr.* Dramatiser.

draper, *s.* Marchand *m* d'étoffes de nouveautés.

drapery, *s.* Draperie *f*.

drastic, *a.* Énergique, rigoureux.

drastically, *adv* Énergiquement, rigoureusement.

draught, *s.* I. **1.** Traction *f*. **2.** Coup *m* de filet; pêche *f*. **3.** Trait *m*, gorgée *f*. **At a d.**, d'un seul trait. **4.** Potion *f*. **5.** Tirant *m* d'eau. **6.** *pl.* = (Jeu *m* de) dames *fpl*. **7.** Courant *m* d'air.
II. **draught**, *s.* = DRAFT[1] I.

draught-board, *s.* = Damier *m*.

draught-screen, *s.* Paravent *m*.

draughtsman, *s.* **1.** Dessinateur *m*. **2.** Pion *m*.

draughty, *a.* **1.** Plein de courants d'air. **2.** Exposé à tous les vents.

draw[1], *s.* **1.** Tirage *m* au sort. **2.** Attraction *f*; clou *m*. **3.** Partie nulle.

draw[2]. I. *v.tr.* **1.** Tirer; traîner. **2.** Attirer. **3.** (*a*) Tirer, retirer. (*b*) Arracher. (*c*) Puiser; tirer.

(*d*) Toucher. **4.** Vider. **5.** (*a*) Tracer; tirer (*b*) Dessiner. **6.** Tirer, jauger.
II. **draw**, *v.i.* **1.** (*a*) To d. near to, s'approcher de. (*b*) To d. to an end, tirer toucher, à sa fin. **2.** To let the tea d., laisser infuser le thé. **draw along**, *v.tr.* Traîner, entraîner. **draw aside**, *v.tr.* (*a*) Détourner, écarter. (*b*) Prendre à l'écart. **2.** *v.i.* S'écarter; se ranger. **draw away**, *v.tr.* (*a*) Entraîner. (*b*) Détourner. **draw back. 1.** *v.tr.* Tirer en arrière; retirer. **2.** *v.i.* (Se) reculer. **draw down**, *v.tr.* Faire descendre; baisser. **draw off**, *v.tr.* (*a*) Retirer, ôter. (*b*) Détourner. (*c*) Soutirer. **draw out, 1.** *v.tr.* Retirer; arracher. **2.** Prolonger. **draw up. 1.** *v.tr.* (*a*) Relever. To d. oneself up, se (re)dresser. (*b*) Approcher. (*c*) Ranger. (*d*) Dresser, rédiger. **2.** *v.i.* S'approcher (*to, de*).

drawback, *s.* Inconvénient *m*.

drawer, *s.* **1.** Tireur, -euse. **2.** Tiroir *m*. Chest of drawers, commode *f*. **3.** *pl.* Caleçon *m*; pantalon *m*.

drawing, *s.* **1.** Tirage *m*. **2.** Dessin *m*.

drawing-board, *s.* Planche *f* à dessin.

drawing-paper, *s.* Papier *m* à dessin.

drawing-pin, *s.* Punaise *f*.

drawing-room, *s.* Salon *m*.

drawl[1], *s.* Voix traînante.

drawl[2], *v.i.* Parler d'une voix traînante.

drawn, *a.* **1.** Tiré. **2.** D. match, partie égale, nulle.

dread[1], *s.* Crainte *f*, épouvante *f*.

dread[2], *v.tr.* Redouter, craindre.

dreadful, *a.* **1.** Terrible, redoutable. **2.** Atroce, épouvantable.

dreadfully, *adv.* Terriblement, affreusement.

dream[1], *s.* Rêve *m*, songe *m*.

dream[2], *v.tr. & i.* **1.** Rêver. **2.** Rêvasser. **3.** Little did I d., je ne songeais guère.

dreamer, *s.* Rêveur, -euse.

dreaming, *s.* Rêves *mpl*, songes *mpl*.

dreamy, *a.* Rêveur, -euse.

dreariness, *s.* Tristesse *f*.

dreary, *a.* Triste, morne.

dredge, *v.tr. & i.* Draguer.

dredger[1], *s.* Drague *f*.

dredger[2], *s.* Saupoudroir *m*.

dregs, *s.pl.* Lie *f*.

drench, *v.tr.* Tremper, mouiller.
drenching, *a.* D. rain, pluie battante.
Dresden. *P.n.* Dresde *f.* D. china, porcelaine *f* de Saxe.
dress[1], *s.* 1. Habillement *m.* In full d., en grande tenue. 2. Robe *f*, costume *m*, toilette *f.*
dress[2], *v.tr.* 1. (*a*) Habiller, vêtir. (*b*) *v.pr.* & *i.* S'habiller; faire sa toilette. 2. Orner, parer (*with*, de). 3. Aligner. *v.i.* S'aligner. 4. Panser. 5. (*a*) To d. s.o.'s hair, coiffer qn. (*b*) Apprêter **dress up**, *v.tr* Habiller, parer.
dress-circle, *s.* (Premier) balcon.
dress-coat, *s.* Frac *m.*
dresser[1], *s.* Buffet *m*; dressoir *m.*
dresser[2], *s.* Habilleur, -euse.
dressing, *s.* 1. Habillement *m*, toilette *f.* 2. Pansement *m.*
dressing-case, *s.* Nécessaire *m*, sac *m* (de voyage).
dressing-gown, *s.* Robe *f* de chambre; peignoir *m.*
dressing-room, *s.* 1. Cabinet *m* de toilette. 2. Loge *f* (d'acteur).
dressing-table, *s.* (Table *f* de) toilette *f*; coiffeuse *f.*
dressmaker, *s.* (*a*) Couturière *f.* (*b*) Couturier *m.*
dressmaking, *s.* 1. Couture *f* 2. Confections *fpl* pour dames.
dress-suit, *s.* Habit *m.*
dried, *a.* Séché, desséché. D. fruits, fruits secs.
drift[1], *s.* 1. (*a*) Mouvement *m.* (*b*) Direction *f*, sens *m.* 2. Dérive *f.* 3. But *m*, tendance *f.*
drift[2], *v.i.* (*a*) Flotter; dériver. (*b*) To let things d., laisser aller les choses.
drifter, *s.* Chalutier *m.*
driftwood, *s.* Bois flottant, bois flotté.
drill[1], *s.* 1. Foret *m*, mèche *f.* 2. Exercice *m.*
drill[2]. 1. *v.tr.* Forer; perforer. 2. *v.tr.* Faire faire l'exercice à. 3. *v.i.* Faire l'exercice.
drill[3], *s.* Coutil *m.*
drill-sergeant, *s.* Sergent instructeur.
drink[1], *s.* 1. (*a*) Boire *m.* (*b*) To give s.o. a d., donner à boire à qn. (*c*) Consommation *f.* To have a d., boire un coup. 2. Boisson *f*, breuvage *m.* Strong d., spiritueux *mpl.* 3. Boisson; ivrognerie *f.*

drink[2], *v.tr.* Boire. **drink up**, *v.tr.* Achever de boire; vider.
drinkable, *a.* (*a*) Buvable. (*b*) Potable.
drinker, *s.* Buveur, -euse.
drinking, *s.* Ivrognerie *f.*
drinking-fountain, *s.* Fontaine publique.
drinking-trough, *s.* Abreuvoir *m.*
drinking-water, *s.* Eau *f* potable.
drip, *v.i.* Dégoutter; tomber goutte à goutte.
dripping[1], *a.* Ruisselant.
dripping[2], *s.* 1. Dégouttement *m.* 2. Graisse *f* de rôti.
drive[1], *s.* 1. Promenade *f* en voiture; course *f.* 2. Battue *f.* 3. Énergie *f.*
drive[2]. I. *v.tr.* 1. Chasser, pousser. 2. Faire marcher; conduire. 3. Pousser; contraindre. 4. Enfoncer. 5. To d. a bargain conclure un marché.
II. **drive**, *v.i.* 1. Chasser, être charrié. To let d., décocher un coup. 2. Se rendre en voiture. **drive along**, *v.tr.* Chasser, pousser. **drive away**, *v.tr.* Chasser. **drive back**, *v.tr.* Repousser, refouler. **drive in**, *v.tr.* Enfoncer; visser. **drive off**, *v.tr.* Chasser. **drive out**, *v.tr* Chasser.
driver, *s.* Mécanicien *m*; conducteur, -trice, chauffeur, -euse; cocher *m.*
driving, *a.* 1. D. force, force motrice. 2. D. rain, pluie battante.
driving-wheel, *s.* Roue motrice.
drizzle[1], *s.* Bruine *f*, crachin *m.*
drizzle[2], *v.i.* Bruiner, crachiner.
droll, *a.* Drôle, bouffon, plaisant.
drone, *s* 1. (*a*) Abeille *f* mâle; faux bourdon. (*b*) Fainéant *m.* 2. Bourdonnement *m.*
droop, *v.i.* Pencher, languir.
drop[1], *s* 1. (*a*) Goutte *f.* (*b*) Pendant *m*, pendeloque *f.* 2. Chute *f*
drop[2]. I. *v.i.* 1. Tomber goutte à goutte, dégoutter. 2. Tomber; se laisser tomber. 3. Baisser.
II. **drop**, *v.tr.* 1. Laisser tomber; lâcher. 2. Perdre. 3. Omettre, supprimer. 4. Baisser. 5. Abandonner; laisser. **drop in**, *v.i.* Entrer en passant. **drop off**, *v.i.* Tomber, se détacher. **drop out**, *v.tr.* Omettre, supprimer.
dross, *s.* Rebut *m.*

drought, *s.* Sécheresse *f*; disette *f* d'eau.

drove, *s.* (*a*) Troupeau *m* en marche. (*b*) Multitude *f*, foule *f*.

drown, *v.tr.* **1.** Noyer. **To be drowned,** se noyer. **2.** Inonder. **3.** Étouffer, couvrir.

drowned, *a.* Noyé.

drowse, *v.i.* Somnoler, s'assoupir.

drowsiness, *s.* Somnolence *f*.

drowsy, *a.* Assoupi, somnolent. **To be d.,** avoir sommeil.

drubbing, *s.* Raclée *f*.

drudge, *s.* Femme *f*, homme *m*. de peine.

drudgery, *s.* Travail pénible.

drug[1], *s.* **1.** Drogue *f*. **2.** Narcotique *m*, stupéfiant *m*. **3.** **A d. in the market,** invendable.

drug[2], *v.tr.* **1.** Donner un narcotique à. **2.** Mettre un narcotique à.

druggist, *s.* Pharmacien *m*.

drum[1], *s.* **1.** Tambour *m*, caisse *f*. Big d., grosse caisse. **2.** Tympan *m* **3.** Tonneau *m*; tonnelet *m*.

drum[2]. **1.** *v.i.* Tambouriner; battre du tambour. **2.** *v.tr.* Enfoncer.

drum-major, *s.* Tambour-major *m*

drummer, *s.* Tambour *m*.

drummer-boy, *s.m.* Petit tambour.

drumming, *s.* Tambourinage *m*: bruit *m* de tambour.

drumstick, *s.* **1.** Baguette de tambour. **2.** Pilon *m*.

drunk, *pred.a.* (*a*) Ivre, gris. **To get d.,** s'enivrer. (*b*) Enivré, grisé.

drunkard, *s.* Ivrogne, *f.* ivrognesse.

drunken, *a.* Ivrogne.

drunkenness, *s* **1.** Ivresse *f*. **2.** Ivrognerie *f*.

dry[1], *a.* **1.** Sec, *f.* sèche; à sec. Dry land, terre ferme. **2.** Aride.

dry[2]. **1.** *v.tr.* Sécher; faire sécher. **2.** *v.i.* Sécher, se dessécher. **dry up,** *v.i.* Se dessécher, tarir.

dryad, *s.* Dryade *f*.

dry-cleaning, *s.* Nettoyage *m* à sec.

dry-foot, *a. & adv.* A pied sec.

drying, *s.* Assèchement *m*. dessèchement *m*; essuyage *m*.

dryly, *adv.* Sèchement.

dryness, *s.* **1.** Sécheresse *f*; aridité *f*. **2.** Sévérité *f*; aridité.

dry-shod, *a. & adv.* A pied sec.

dual, *a.* Double.

dubious, *a* **1.** (*a*) Douteux; incer-

tain. (*b*) Équivoque, louche. **2.** Hésitant.

dubiously, *adv.* D'un air de doute.

dubiousness, *s.* **1.** Incertitude *f*. **2.** Caractère douteux, équivoque *f*.

ducal, *a.* Ducal, -aux; de duc.

duchess, *s.* Duchesse *f*.

duck[1], *s.* **1.** (*a*) Cane *f*. (*b*) Canard *m*. Wild d., canard sauvage. **2.** **D.,** duck's egg, zéro *m*.

duck[2]. **1.** *v.i.* Se baisser (subitement). **2.** *v.tr.* (*a*) Plonger dans l'eau (*b*) Baisser subitement.

ducking, *s.* Plongeon *m* (involontaire); bain forcé.

duckling, *s.* Caneton *m*.

ductile, *a.* Ductile.

dudgeon, *s.* Ressentiment *m*.

due[1]. **1.** *a.* (*a*) Exigible; échu. **To fall d.,** échoir. (*b*) Dû, *f.* due; juste. (*c*) **What is it due to?** à quoi cela tient-il? (*d*) **The train is due at two o'clock,** le train arrive à deux heures. **2.** *adv.* **Due north,** droit vers le nord.

due[2], *s.* **1.** Dû *m* **2.** *pl.* Droits *mpl.*

duel, *s.* Duel *m*.

duelling, *s.* Le duel.

duellist, *s.* Duelliste *m*

duenna, *s.* Duègne *f*.

duet, *s.* Duo *m*.

duke, *s.* Duc *m*.

dukedom, *s.* Duché *m*.

dull, *a.* **1.** Lent, lourd. **2.** Sourd, mat. **3.** Terne, morne. **4.** Ennuyeux. **5.** Terne, mat. **6.** Lourd, sombre. **7.** Émoussé.

dullness, *s.* **1.** Pesanteur *f* de l'esprit. **2.** Matité *f*. **3.** Ennui *m*. **4.** Stagnation *f*. **5.** Émoussement *m*. **6.** Manque d'éclat; faiblesse *f*.

dull-witted, *a.* A l'esprit lourd.

dully, *adv.* **1.** Lourdement; ennuyeusement. **2.** Sourdement.

duly, *adv.* **1.** Dûment; convenablement. **2.** En temps voulu.

dumb, *a.* Muet,*f.* muette. **D. animals,** les bêtes. **To strike d.,** abasourdir.

dumbfound, *v.tr.* Abasourdir.

dumbly, *adv.* Sans rien dire; en silence.

dumbness, *s.* Mutisme *m*.

dummy, *s.* **1.** Homme *m* de paille. **2.** (*a*) Mannequin *m*. (*b*) Faux paquet. **3.** *Cards:* Mort *m*. **4.** *Attrib:* Postiche; faux, *f.* fausse.

dump, s. 1. Tas *m*, amas *m*. 2. Dépôt *m*.

dun¹, *a.* Brun foncé.

dun², s. Créancier importun.

dun³, *v.tr.* Importuner.

dunce, s. Ignorant, -ante ; âne *m*

dune, s. Dune *f*.

dungeon, s. Cachot *m*.

dunghill, s. Fumier *m*.

dupe¹, s. Dupe *f*.

dupe², *v.tr.* Duper, tromper.

duplicate¹. 1. *a.* Double. **D. parts,** pièces de rechange. 2. s. Double *m*. In d., en double exemplaire.

duplicate², *v.tr.* Faire le double de.

duplicating-machine, s. Duplicateur *m*.

duplication, s. Duplication *f*.

duplicity, s. Duplicité *f*.

durability, s. Durabilité *f*.

durable, *a.* Durable ; résistant.

duration, s. Durée *f* ; étendue *f*.

during, *prep.* Pendant, durant ; au cours de.

dusk, s. (*a*) Obscurité. (*b*) Crépuscule *m*.

dusky, *a.* 1. Sombre, obscur. 2. (*a*) Bistré. (*b*) Noirâtre.

dust¹, s. Poussière *f*.

dust², *v.tr.* 1. Saupoudrer (*with*, de). 2. Épousseter.

dustbin, s. Poubelle *f*.

dust-cart, s. Tombereau *m* aux ordures.

dust-coat, s. Cache-poussière *m inv*.

duster, s. Chiffon *m* (à épousseter). **Feather d.,** plumeau *m*.

dustman, s. Boueur *m*.

dust-pan, s. Ramasse-poussière *m inv*.

dusty, *a.* Poussiéreux, poudreux ; recouvert de poussière.

Dutch. 1. *a.* Hollandais ; de Hollande. 2. s. (*a*) **The D.,** les Hollandais. (*b*) Le hollandais.

Dutchman, s. Hollandais *m*.

dutiable, *a.* Soumis aux droits de douane ; taxable.

dutiful, *a.* Respectueux, soumis.

dutifully, *adv.* Avec soumission.

duty, s. 1. Obéissance *f*, respect *m*. 2. Devoir *m* (*to,* envers). 3. Fonction(s) *f(pl)*. **To do d. for,** remplacer. 4. Service *m*. **On d.,** de service. 5. Droit *m*.

dwarf¹, s. & *a.* Nain, -e

dwarf², *v.tr.* Rapetisser.

dwell, *v.i.* 1. Habiter ; demeurer, résider. 2. Rester. 3. **To d. on,** s'appesantir sur.

dwelling, s. 1. (*a*) Séjour *m*. (*b*) Insistance *f*. 2. Demeure *f*.

dwelling-house, s. Maison *f* d'habitation.

dwelling-place, s. Demeure *f*, résidence *f*.

dwindle, *v.i.* Diminuer.

dwindling, s. Diminution *f*.

dye¹, s. (*a*) Teinture *f*. (*b*) Teinte *f*.

dye², *v.tr.* Teindre.

dyeing, s. Teinture *f*.

dyer, s. Teinturier *m*.

dye-works, s. Teinturerie *f*.

dying, *a.* Mourant, agonisant.

dyke, s. Digue *f*, levée *f*.

dynamic, *a.* Dynamique.

dynamite¹, s. Dynamite *f*.

dynamite², *v.tr.* Dynamiter.

dynamo, s. Dynamo *f*.

dynasty, s. Dynastie *f*.

dysentery, s. Dysenterie *f*.

dyspepsia, s. Dyspepsie *f*.

dyspeptic, *a.* & s. Dyspepsique (*mf*).

E

E, e, s. (La lettre) E, e *m*.

each. 1. *a.* Chaque. 2. *pron.* (*a*) Chacun, -une. (*b*) **E. other,** l'un l'autre, les uns les autres.

eager, *a.* Ardent, passionné ; impatient. **E. for gain,** âpre au gain.

eagerly, *adv.* Ardemment, passionnément ; avidement.

eagerness, s. Ardeur *f* ; impatience *f* ; vif désir.

eagle, s. Aigle *mf*.

eaglet, s. Aiglon *m*.

ear¹, s. Oreille *f*. **To keep one's ears open,** se tenir aux écoutes.

ear², s. Épi *m*.

ear-ache, s. **To have ear-a.,** avoir mal *m* à l'oreille.

earl, s. Comte *m*.

earldom, s. Comté *m*.

early. 1. *a.* 1. (*a*) Matinal. **To be an e. riser,** se lever matin. (*b*) **E. youth,** première jeunesse. 2. Précoce,

hâtif. **E. death,** mort prématurée.
3. Prochain. **At an e. date** prochainement

II **early,** adv. (a De bonne
heure ; tôt. **Earlier,** de meilleure
heure ; plus tôt. **E. in the afternoon,**
au commencement de l'après-midi.
As e. as, dès ; aussitôt que. (b) **To
die e.,** mourir prématurément.

ear-mark, v.tr Assigner. affecter.

earn, v.tr. Gagner.

earnest[1]. **1.** a. (a) Sérieux. **E.
worker,** ouvrier consciencieux. (b)
Pressant ; fervent. **2.** s. **In e,**
sérieusement.

earnest[2], s. Gage m, garantie f.

earnestly, adv. Sérieusement ; instamment.

earnestness, s. Gravité f, sérieux m.

earnings, s.pl. **1.** Salaire m, gages
mpl. **2.** Profits mpl, bénéfices mpl.

ear-ring, s. Boucle d'oreille

ear-shot, s. **Within ear-s.** à portée
de voix.

earth, s. **1.** Terre f. (a) Le monde.
(b) Le sol. **2.** Terrier m tanière f
To run to e., dénicher

earthen, a. De terre.

earthenware, s. Poterie f : faïence f.

earthly, a. Terrestre.

earthquake, s. Tremblement m de
terre.

earthworks, s.pl. Travaux mpl en
terre.

earthworm, s. Ver m de terre.

earthy, a. Terreux.

ear-trumpet, s. Cornet m acoustique.

earwig, s. Perce-oreille m, pl. perce-oreilles.

ease[1], adv. **1.** Tranquillité f ; repos m
bien-être m, aise f. **2.** (a) Loisir m
(b) Oisiveté f. **3.** (a) Aisance f.
(b) Simplicité f ; facilité f **With e.,**
facilement ; aisément.

ease[2], v.tr. **1.** (a) Adoucir. calmer ;
soulager. (b) Calmer. **2.** Débarrasser **3.** Détendre. relâcher.

easel, s. Chevalet m.

easily, adv. **1.** Tranquillement, à son
aise paisiblement. **2** Facilement,
sans difficulté

easiness, s. **1.** Bien-être m. **2.** Aisance f **3.** Facilité f.

east. **1.** s. (a) Est m, orient m, levant
m. (b) **The Far, Middle, Near, E.,**

l'extrême, moyen, proche, Orient. **2.**
adv. A 'est à l'orient. **3.** adj.
D'est.

Easter, s. Pâques m.

easterly 1. a. D'est. **2.** adv Vers
l'est

eastern, a Est ; oriental, -aux.

eastward, a (a) A l'est (b) Du côté
de l'est.

eastwards, adv. A l'est ; vers l'est.

easy. **1** a. **1.** (a) A l'aise (b) Tranquille ; sans inquiétude **2.** Aisé,
libre **3.** (a) Facile. aisé. **Within e.
reach,** à distance commode. (b)
Facile, accommodant. (c) **By e.
stages,** à petites étapes **An e. first,**
bon premier
II. easy, adv. En douceur ; à
son aise. **To go e. with,** ménager

easy-chair, s Fauteuil m : bergère f.

easy-going, a. (a) Insouciant. (b)
D'humeur facile.

eat, v.tr. Manger **eat away,** v.tr.
Ronger, éroder **eat up,** v.tr.
Achever de manger, dévorer.

eatable. 1. a. Bon à manger. **2.** s.pl.
Provisions f de bouche.

eating, s Manger m

eating-house, s. Restaurant m.

eavesdrop, v.i. Écouter aux portes.

eavesdropper, s Écouteur. -euse.
aux portes

ebb[1], s. **1.** Reflux m, jusant m. **2.**
Déclin m. **At a low ebb,** très bas.

ebb[2], v.i. **1.** Baisser **To ebb and
flow,** monter et baisser **2.** Décliner.

ebb-tide, s Marée descendante ;
jusant m ; reflux m

ebony, s Ébène f ; bois m d'ébène.

eccentric, a. & s Excentrique (mf).

eccentricity, s Excentricité f

ecclesiastic, a & s Ecclésiastique (m)

echo[1], s Écho m

echo[2]. **1.** v.tr Répéter **2.** v.i (a)
Faire écho. (b) Retentir.

eclipse[1], s Éclipse f.

eclipse[2], v.tr Éclipser.

economical. a (a) Économe (b)
Économique.

economically, adv Économiquement

economics, s.pl. L'économie f politique

economist, s Économiste m.

economize, v.tr Économiser, ménager. Abs Faire des économies

economy, s. Économie f.

ecstasy, s 1. Transport m; ravissement m. 2. Extase f.

ecstatic, a. Extatique.

eddy¹, s. Remous m; tourbillon m.

eddy², v.i. Faire des remous; tourbillonner, tournoyer

edge, s. 1. Fil m, tranchant m. **To take the e. off,** émousser. 2. Arête f, angle m. 3. Bord m, rebord m. **With gilt edges,** doré sur tranches. **On e.,** énervé. 4. Lisière f, bordure f; bord; rive f

edged, a. Tranchant, acéré.

edgeways, adv. **To get a word in e.,** glisser un mot.

edible, 1. a. Comestible; bon à manger. 2. s.pl. Comestibles m.

edict, s. Édit m.

edification, s. Édification f.

edifice, s. Édifice m.

edify, v.tr. Édifier.

edit, v.tr (a) Annoter, éditer. (b) Rédiger, diriger.

edition, s. Édition f.

editor, s. 1. Annotateur m, éditeur m. 2. Rédacteur m en chef

editorial, 1. a. Éditorial, -aux. 2. s. Article m de fond, de tête.

educate, v.tr. Instruire.

education, s. 1. Éducation f. 2. Enseignement m, instruction f.

educational, a. D'éducation.

Edward. Pr.n. Édouard m.

eel, s. Anguille f.

eerie, a. Étrange, mystérieux.

efface, v.tr. Effacer; oblitérer.

effect¹, s. 1. (a) Effet m, influence f; résultat m. **To take e.,** (i) opérer; (ii) entrer en vigueur. **To no e.,** en vain. **To carry into e.,** mettre à exécution. (b) Sens m, teneur f. 2. **In e.,** en fait, en réalité. 3. pl. Effets.

effect², v.tr. Effectuer, accomplir.

effective. 1. a. (a) Efficace. (b) Frappant. 2. s.pl. Effectifs m.

effectively, adv. 1. Avec effet, efficacement. 2. Effectivement; en réalité.

effectual, a. Efficace.

effectually, adv. Efficacement.

effeminacy, s. Caractère efféminé; mollesse f.

effeminate, a. Efféminé.

effervesce, v.i. Être en effervescence.

effervescence, s. Effervescence f.

effete, a. Caduc, -uque

efficacious, a. Efficace.

efficaciously, adv. Efficacement; avec efficacité.

efficacy, s. Efficacité f.

efficiency, s. 1. Efficacité f. 2. Capacité f; valeur f.

efficient, a. (a) Effectif, efficace. (b) Capable, compétent.

efficiently, adv. 1. Efficacement. 2. Avec compétence.

effigy, s. Effigie f.

effort, s. Effort m. **He spares no e.,** il ne s'épargne pas.

effrontery, s. Effronterie f.

effulgence, s. Éclat m, sp en leur f.

effulgent, a Resplendissant, éclatant.

effusion, s. Effusion f.

effusive, a. Démonstratif, expansif.

effusively, adv Avec effusion, avec expansion.

effusiveness, s Effusion f.

egg¹, s. Œuf m.

egg², v.tr. **To egg on,** inciter.

egg-cup, s. Coquetier m.

egg-shell, s. Coquille f d'œuf.

egg-spoon, s. Cuiller f à œufs.

egoism, s. Égoïsme m.

egoist, s. Égoïste mf.

egotism, s. Égotisme m.

egotist, s. Égotiste mf.

egregious, a. Insigne.

egress, s. Sortie f, issue f.

Egypt. Pr.n L'Égypte f.

Egyptian, a. & s. Égyptien, -ienne.

eh, int. Eh! hé! hein?

eider-down, s. Édredon piqué.

eight. 1. num. a. & s. Huit (m). 2. s. Équipe f de huit rameurs.

eighteen, num. a. & s. Dix-huit (m).

eighteenth, num. a. & s. (a) Dixhuitième. (b) (On) the e., le dix-huit.

eighth, num. a. & s. (a) Huitième. (b) (On) the e., le huit.

eighty, num. a. & s. Quatre-vingts (m).

either. 1. a. & pron. (a) L'un(e) et l'autre. **On e. side,** de chaque côté. (b) L'un(e) ou l'autre; ni l'un ni l'autre. **E. of them,** soit l'un(e), soit l'autre. 2. conj. & adv. (a) **E. . . . or . . .,** ou . . ., ou . . .; soit . . ., soit . . . (b) **Not . . . e.,** ne . . . non plus.

ejaculate, v.tr. S'écrier.

ejaculation, s. Cri m, exclamation f.

eject, *v.tr* **1.** Jeter, émettre. **2.** Expulser.

ejection, *s.* Éviction *f* expulsion *f*.

eke, *v.tr.* To eke out, augmenter.

elaborate[1], *a.* Compliqué; minutieux.

elaborate[2], *v.tr.* Élaborer.

elaborately, *adv.* Avec soin; minutieusement.

elapse, *v.i.* S'écouler; (se) passer.

elastic, *a. & s.* Élastique (*m*).

elasticity, *s.* Élasticité *f*.

elate, *v.tr.* Exalter, transporter.

elation, *s.* **1.** Exaltation *f*. **2.** Joie *f*.

elbow[1], *s.* **1.** Coude *m* To lean on one's e., s'accouder. **2.** Coude, tournant *m*.

elbow[2], *v.tr. & i.* (*a*) Coudoyer. (*b*) To e. one's way, se frayer un passage.

elbow-room, *s.* To have e.-r., avoir ses coudées franches.

elder[1]. **1.** *a.* Aîné, plus âgé **2.** *s.* Aîné, -ée; plus âgé, -ée.

elder[2], *s.* E.(-tree), sureau *m*.

elder-berry, *s.* Baie *f* de sureau.

elderly, *a.* D'un certain âge; assez âgé.

eldest, *a.* Aîné.

elect[1], *a.* Élu.

elect[2], *v.tr.* **1.** Choisir. **2.** Élire.

election, *s.* Élection *f*.

elector, *s.* Électeur *m*, votant *m*.

electric, *a.* Électrique.

electrical, *a.* Électrique.

electrically, *adv.* Électriquement.

electrician, *s.* Électricien *m*.

electricity, *s.* Électricité *f*.

electrify, *v.tr.* Électriser.

electrocute, *v.tr.* Électrocuter.

electrocution, *s.* Électrocution *f*.

elegance, *s.* Élégance *f*

elegant, *a.* Élégant.

elegantly, *adv.* Élégamment

elegy, *s.* Élégie *f*.

element, *s.* **1.** Élément *m*; corps *m* simple. **2.** *pl.* Rudiments *m*.

elementary, *a.* Élémentaire.

elephant, *s.* Éléphant *m*.

elevate, *v.tr* Élever.

elevated, *a.* Élevé.

elevating, *a.* Qui élève l'esprit.

elevation, *s.* Élévation *f*.

eleven. 1. *num. a. & s.* Onze (*m*). **2.** *s.* Équipe *f* de onze joueurs.

eleventh, *num. a. & s.* Onzième. (On) the eleventh, le onze.

elf, *s.* Elfe *m*; lutin *m*, lutine *f*.

elfin, *a.* D'elfe, de lutin, de fée.

elfish, *a.* (*a*) Des elfes. (*b*) Espiègle.

elicit, *v.tr.* Tirer; découvrir.

elide, *v.tr.* Élider.

eligible, *a.* Éligible (*for*, à).

eliminate, *v.tr.* Éliminer.

elimination, *s.* Élimination *f*.

elision, *s.* Élision *f*.

elixir, *s.* Élixir *m*.

elk, *s.* Élan *m*.

ell, *s.* Aune *f*.

elm, *s.* Orme *m*.

elocution, *s.* Élocution *f*, diction *f*.

elongate, *v.tr.* Allonger, étendre.

elope, *v.i.* S'enfuir.

elopement, *s.* Fuite *f*.

eloquence, *s.* Éloquence *f*.

eloquent, *a.* Éloquent.

eloquently, *adv.* Éloquemment.

else. 1. *adv.* Autrement; ou bien. **2.** (*a*) *a.* or *adv.* Anyone e., tout autre; encore quelqu'un. Anything e., n'importe quoi d'autre; autre chose. Someone e., un autre. Nothing e., rien *m* d'autre. Everything e., tout le reste. (*b*) *adv.* Everywhere e., partout ailleurs.

elsewhere, *adv.* Ailleurs; autre part.

elucidate, *v.tr.* Élucider, éclaircir.

elucidation, *s.* Élucidation *f*.

elude, *v.tr.* Éluder; échapper à.

elusive, *a.* Insaisissable.

elusory, *a.* Évasif.

emaciated, *a.* Émacié, décharné.

emaciation, *s.* Émaciation *f*.

emanate, *v.i.* Émaner.

emanation, *s.* Émanation *f*.

emancipate, *v.tr.* Émanciper.

emancipation, *s.* Émancipation *f*.

embalm, *v.tr.* Embaumer.

embankment, *s.* (*a*) Digue *f*. (*b*) Remblai *m*.

embargo, *s.* Embargo *m*.

embark. 1. *v.tr.* Embarquer. **2.** *v.i.* S'embarquer.

embarkation, *s.* Embarquement *m*.

embarrass, *v.tr.* Embarrasser, gêner; déconcerter.

embarrassed, *a.* Embarrassé; gêné.

embarrassment, *s.* Embarras *m*.

embassy, *s.* Ambassade *f*.

embellish, *v.tr.* Embellir, orner.

embellishment, *s* Embellissement *m*, ornement *m*.

embers, *s.pl.* Braise *f*; cendres ardentes.

embezzle, *v.tr.* Détourner.

embezzlement, *s.* Détournement *m.*

embitter, *v.tr.* Remplir d'amertume ; aigrir ; envenimer, aggraver.

embittered, *a.* Aigri.

emblem, *s.* Emblème *m,* symbole *m.*

emblematic, *a.* Emblématique.

embodiment, *s.* Incorporation *f;* incarnation *f;* personnification *f.*

embody, *v.tr.* **1.** Personnifier. **2.** Incorporer.

embolden, *v.tr.* Enhardir.

emboss, *v.tr.* Repousser.

embrace¹, *s.* Étreinte *f.*

embrace², *v.tr.* Embrasser.

embroider, *v.tr.* Broder.

embroidery, *s.* Broderie *f.*

embroil, *v.tr.* Brouiller.

embryo, *s.* Embryon *m.*

emend, *v.tr.* Corriger.

emendation, *s.* Émendation *f.*

emerald, *s.* Émeraude *f.*

emerge, *v.i.* **1.** Émerger ; surgir. **2.** Déboucher ; sortir.

emergency, *s.* Circonstance *f* critique ; cas urgent. **In case of e.,** au besoin. **E. exit,** sortie *f* de secours.

emery, *s.* Émeri *m.*

emetic, *a. & s.* Émétique *(m).*

emigrant, *a. & s.* Émigrant, -ante.

emigrate, *v.i.* Émigrer.

emigration, *s.* Émigration *f.*

eminence, *s.* Éminence *f.* **1.** Élévation *f.* **2.** Grandeur *f.*

eminent, *a.* Éminent.

eminently, *adv.* Éminemment.

emissary, *s.* Émissaire *m.*

emission, *s.* Émission *f.*

emit, *v.tr.* Dégager, émettre.

emollient, *a. & s.* Émollient *(m).*

emoluments, *s.* Émoluments *mpl,* traitement *m.*

emotion, *s.* Émotion *f;* trouble *m.*

emperor, *s.* Empereur *m.*

emphasis, *s.* **1.** Force *f;* accentuation *f.* **2. To lay e. on,** souligner.

emphasize, *v.tr.* Accentuer, appuyer sur, souligner.

emphatic, *a.* Énergique ; autoritaire ; positif.

emphatically, *adv.* Énergiquement.

empire, *s.* Empire *m.*

emplane, *v.i.* Monter en avion.

employ¹, *s.* Emploi *m.*

employ², *v.tr.* Employer ; faire usage de.

employee, *s.* Employé, -ée.

employer, *s.* Patron, patronne ; maître, maîtresse.

employment, *s.* **1.** Emploi *m.* **2.** Emploi, travail *m;* occupation *f.*

empower, *v.tr.* Autoriser.

empress, *s.* Impératrice *f.*

emptiness, *s.* Vide *m.*

empty¹, *a.* *(a)* Vide ; creux. *(b)* **E. words,** vaines paroles.

empty², **1.** *v.tr.* Vider ; décharger. **2.** *v.i.* Se décharger.

empty-handed, *a.* Les mains vides.

emu, *s.* Émeu *m.*

emulate, *v.tr.* Être l'émule de ; rivaliser avec, imiter.

emulation, *s.* Émulation *f.*

emulsion, *s.* Émulsion *f.*

enable, *v.tr.* Mettre à même (de faire qch).

enact, *v.tr.* Ordonner, décréter.

enactment, *s.* Loi *f,* ordonnance *f.*

enamel¹, *s.* Émail *m, pl.* émaux.

enamel², *v.tr.* Émailler.

enamour, *v.tr.* **Enamoured,** amoureux ; féru.

encampment, *s.* Campement *m.*

enchant, *v.tr.* **1.** Enchanter, ensorceler. **2.** Enchanter, charmer.

enchanter, *s.* Enchanteur *m.*

enchanting, *a.* Enchanteur, -eresse ; ravissant, charmant.

enchantment, *s.* Enchantement *m.*

enchantress, *s.* Enchanteresse *f.*

encircle, *v.tr.* Ceindre, encercler

encircling, *s.* Encerclement *m.*

enclose, *v.tr.* **1.** Enclore, clôturer *(with,* de). **2.** Inclure, renfermer. **Enclosed (herewith),** ci-inclus.

enclosure, *s.* **1.** Enceinte *f,* clôture. **2.** Enclos *m,* clos *m.* **3.** Annexe *f.*

encompass, *v.tr.* **1.** Entourer, ceindre. **2.** Consommer.

encore¹, *s. & int.* Bis *m.*

encore², *v.tr.* Bisser.

encounter¹, *s.* Rencontre *f.*

encounter², *v.tr.* Rencontrer ; éprouver ; affronter.

encourage, *v.tr.* Encourager.

encouragement, *s.* Encouragement *m.*

encouraging, *a.* Encourageant.

encouragingly, *adv.* D'une manière encourageante.

encroach, *v.i.* Empiéter *(on,* sur). **To e. upon,** abuser de.

encroachment, *s.* Empiétement *m.*

encumber, *v.tr* Encombrer.
encumbrance. *s.* Embarras *m*, charge *f*
encyclopaedia, *s.* Encyclopédie *f.*
end¹, *s.* **1.** Bout *m*, extrémité *f*; fin *f* From end to end, d'un bout à l'autre. Two hours on end, deux heures de suite. **2.** Limite *f*, borne *f*. **3.** Bout, fin. To make an end of, en finir avec. To come to an end, prendre fin. In the end, à la longue; à la fin; enfin. To come to a bad end, mal finir. **4.** Fin, but *m*.
end². **1.** *v.tr.* Finir, achever, terminer. **2.** *v.i.* Finir, se terminer.
endanger, *v.tr.* Mettre en danger.
endear, *v.tr.* Rendre cher.
endearing, *a.* Tendre, affectueux.
endeavour¹, *s.* Effort *m*, tentative *f.*
endeavour², *v.i.* S'efforcer; essayer, tâcher.
ended, *a.* Fini, terminé.
ending, *s.* Fin *f*; conclusion *f.*
endless, *a.* **1.** (*a*) Sans fin. (*b*) Sans bornes; infini. **2.** Continuel.
endlessly, *adv.* Sans fin; sans cesse.
endorse, *v.tr.* **1.** Endosser. **2.** Appuyer; souscrire à.
endorsement, *s.* **1.** Endossement *m*. **2.** Approbation *f.*
endow, *v.tr.* Doter (*with*, de); douer (*with*, de).
endowment, *s.* **1.** (*a*) Dotation *f*. (*b*) Fondation *f*. **2.** Don (naturel).
endurance, *s.* **1.** Endurance *f*, résistance *f*. **Beyond e.,** insupportable **2.** Patience *f.*
endure. **1.** *v.tr.* Supporter, endurer. **2.** *v.i.* Durer, rester.
enduring, *a.* **1.** Durable. **2.** Patient.
enemy, *s.* Ennemi, -e.
energetic, *a.* Énergique.
energetically, *adv.* Énergiquement.
energy, *s.* Énergie *f*, force *f.*
enervate, *v.tr.* Affaiblir, énerver.
enervation, *s.* **1.** Affaiblissement *m* **2.** Mollesse *f.*
enfeeble, *v.tr.* Affaiblir.
enfold, *v.tr.* Envelopper.
enforce, *v.tr.* **1.** Faire valoir. **2.** Mettre en vigueur. **3.** Faire observer.
enforcement, *s* Mise *f* en vigueur, application *f.*
enfranchisement, *s.* Admission *f* au suffrage.
engage, *v.tr. & i.* **1.** (*a*) Engager,

prendre. (*b*) Retenir, réserver. **2.** Occuper **3.** Attaquer.
engaged, *a.* **1.** Fiancé. **2.** Occupé, pris. **3.** Retenu.
engagement, *s.* **1.** Engagement *m*. To have an e., être pris. **2.** Poste *m*, situation *f*. **3.** Fiançailles *fpl*. **4.** Combat *m*.
engaging, *a.* Engageant, attrayant.
engender, *v.tr.* Engendrer.
engine, *s* **1.** Machine *f*, appareil *m*. **2.** Locomotive *f* **3.** Moteur *m*.
engine-driver, *s.* Mécanicien *m*.
engineer¹, *s.* **1.** Ingénieur *m*. **2.** *Nau :* Mécanicien m. **3.** Soldat *m* du génie. **The Engineers,** le génie.
engineer², *v.tr.* Machiner.
engineering, *s* Le génie.
England. *Pr.n* L'Angleterre *f.*
English. **1.** *a. &* *s.* Anglais, -aise. **2.** *s.* L'anglais *m*.
Englishman, *s.* Anglais *m*.
Englishwoman, *s.* Anglaise *f.*
engrave, *v.tr.* Graver.
engraver, *s.* Graveur *m*.
engraving, *s.* Gravure *f*; (*print*) estampe *f.*
engross, *v.tr.* Absorber, occuper
engulf, *v.tr.* Engloutir, engouffrer.
enhance, *v.tr.* Rehausser.
enigma, *s.* Énigme *f.*
enigmatic, *a.* Énigmatique.
enjoin, *v.tr.* Enjoindre, prescrire.
enjoy, *v.tr.* **1.** Aimer, goûter; prendre plaisir à. To e. oneself, s'amuser. **2.** Jouir de.
enjoyable, *a.* Agréable.
enjoyably, *adv.* Agréablement.
enjoyment, *s.* Plaisir *m.*
enlarge. **1.** *v.tr.* (*a*) Agrandir. (*b*) Développer. **2.** *v.i* To e. upon, s'étendre sur.
enlargement, *s.* Agrandissement *m.*
enlighten, *v.tr.* Éclairer.
enlightened, *a.* Éclairé.
enlightenment. *s.* Éclaircissements *mpl.*
enlist. **1.** *v.tr.* (*a*) Enrôler. **2.** *v.i.* S'engager, s'enrôler.
enlistment, *s.* Engagement *m.* enrôlement *m.*
enliven, *v.tr.* (*a*) Animer; stimuler. (*b*) Égayer.
enmity, *s.* Inimitié *f*, hostilité *f.*
ennoble, *v.tr.* Anoblir.
enormity, *s.* Énormité *f.*

enormous, *a.* Énorme.

enormously, *adv.* Énormément.

enough. 1. *a.* & *s.* Assez. **That's e.,** en voilà assez ! **More than e.,** plus qu'il n'en faut. **It was e. to drive one crazy,** c'était à vous rendre fou. **2.** *adv.* (a) Assez. (b) **You know well e.,** vous savez très bien. **Well e.,** passablement.

enquire, *v.* = INQUIRE.

enquiry, *s.* = INQUIRY.

enrage, *v.tr.* Rendre furieux.

enrapture, *v.tr.* Ravir, enchanter.

enrich, *v.tr.* Enrichir.

enrichment, *s.* Enrichissement *m.*

enrol, *v.tr.* Enrôler.

ensconce, *v.tr.* **To e. oneself,** se camper.

ensign, *s.* Étendard *m,* drapeau *m.*

enslave, *v.tr.* Asservir.

enslavement, *s.* Asservissement *m.*

ensnare, *v.tr.* Prendre au piège.

ensue, *v.i.* S'ensuivre.

ensuing, *a.* Suivant ; subséquent.

ensure, *v.tr.* Assurer.

entail, *v.tr.* Amener ; occasionner.

entangle, *v.tr.* **1.** Empêtrer. **2.** Emmêler ; enchevêtrer.

entanglement, *s.* Embrouillement *m,* enchevêtrement *m.*

enter. I. *v.i.* Entrer.
II. enter, *v.tr.* **1.** Entrer, pénétrer, dans ; monter dans. **2. To e. the Army,** se faire soldat. **3.** (a) Inscrire. (b) **To e. a protest,** protester formellement. **enter into,** *v.i.* **1.** Fournir (des explications). **2.** Partager. **enter on, upon,** *v.i.* Entrer en : débuter dans ; entamer.

enterprise, *s.* **1.** Entreprise *f.* **2.** Esprit entreprenant.

enterprising, *a.* Entreprenant.

entertain, *v.tr.* **1.** Amuser, divertir. **2.** Régaler, fêter. **3.** Accueillir. **4.** Concevoir ; nourrir.

entertainer, *s.* Hôte *m,* hôtesse *f.*

entertaining, *a.* Amusant, divertissant.

entertainment, *s.* **1.** (a) Divertissement *m.* (b) Spectacle *m.* **2.** Hospitalité *f.*

enthral, *v.tr.* Captiver.

enthrone, *v.tr.* Mettre sur le trône.

enthusiasm, *s.* Enthousiasme *m.*

enthusiast, *s.* Enthousiaste *mf.*

enthusiastic, *a.* Enthousiaste. **To become e.,** s'enthousiasmer.

enthusiastically, *adv* Avec enthousiasme.

entice, *v.tr.* Attirer, séduire.

enticement, *s.* **1.** Séduction *f.* **2.** Attrait *m,* charme *m.* **3.** Appât *m.*

enticing, *a.* Séduisant, attrayant.

entire, *a.* (a) Entier, tout. (b) Entier, complet.

entirely, *adv.* Entièrement, tout à fait.

entirety, *s.* **In its e.,** en entier.

entitle, *v.tr.* Donner le droit.

entitled, *a.* **To be e.,** avoir droit ; avoir qualité.

entity, *s.* Entité *f.*

entomb, *v.tr.* Mettre au tombeau ; ensevelir.

entomology, *s.* Entomologie *f.*

entrails, *s.pl.* Entrailles *f.*

entrance¹, *s.* **1.** (a) Entrée *f.* (b) Admission *f,* accès *m.*

entrance², *v.tr.* Extasier, ravir.

entrance-fee, *s.* Prix *m* d'entrée.

entrancing, *a.* Enchanteur, -eresse ; ravissant.

entrap, *v.tr.* Prendre au piège.

entreat, *v.tr.* Prier, supplier.

entreating, *a.* Suppliant.

entreaty, *s.* Prière *f,* supplication *f.*

entrench, *v.tr.* Retrancher.

entrenchment, *s.* Retranchement *m.*

entrust, *v.tr.* Charger (*with,* de) ; confier.

entry, *s.* **1.** (a) Entrée *f.* 'No e.,' "sens interdit." (b) Début *m.* **2.** Enregistrement *m* ; inscription *f.*

entwine. I. *v.tr.* (a) Entrelacer. (b) Enlacer (*with,* de). **2.** *v.i.* S'entrelacer.

enumerate, *v.tr.* Énumérer.

enumeration, *s.* Énumération *f.*

enunciate, *v.tr.* **1.** Énoncer, exprimer. **2.** Prononcer, articuler.

envelop, *v.tr.* Envelopper.

envelope, *s.* Enveloppe *f.*

envenom, *v.tr.* Envenimer aigrir.

enviable, *a.* Enviable.

envious, *a.* Envieux.

enviously, *adv.* Avec envie.

environment, *s.* Milieu *m,* entourage *m* ; environnement *m.*

environs, *s.pl.* Environs *m.*

envisage, *v.tr.* Envisager.

envoy, *s.* Envoyé, -ée.

envy¹, *s.* Envie *f.*

envy[2], *v.tr.* Envier, porter envie à

epaulet(te), *s.* Épaulette *f.*

epic. **1.** *a.* Épique. **2.** *s.* Poème *m* épique ; épopée *f.*

epicure, *s.* Gourmet *m.*

epidemic. **1.** *a.* Épidémique. **2.** *s.* Épidémie *f.*

epigram, *s.* Épigramme *f.*

epilogue, *s.* Épilogue *m.*

episcopal, *a.* Épiscopal, -aux.

episode, *s.* Épisode *m.*

epistle, *s.* Épître *f.*

epitaph, *s.* Épitaphe *f.*

epithet, *s.* Épithète *f.*

epitome, *s.* Épitomé *m*, abrégé *m.*

epitomize, *v.tr.* Abréger, résumer.

epoch, *s.* Époque *f*, âge *m.*

Epsom. *Pr.n.* E. salts, sulfate *m* de magnésie.

equability, *s.* Uniformité *f* ; égalité *f*, régularité *f.*

equable, *a.* Uniforme, régulier.

equal[1]. **1.** *a.* (*a*) Égal, -aux. (*b*) **E. to the occasion**, à la hauteur de la situation. **2.** *s.* Égal, -ale ; pair *m.*

equal[2], *v.tr.* Égaler.

equality, *s.* Égalité *f.*

equalize, *v.tr.* Égaliser.

equally, *adv.* Également, pareillement.

equanimity, *s.* Tranquillité *f* d'esprit ; équanimité *f.*

equation, *s.* Équation *f.*

equator, *s.* Équateur *m.*

equatorial, *a.* Équatorial, -aux

equestrian, *a.* Équestre.

equilibrium, *s.* Équilibre *m* ; aplomb *m.*

equinox, *s.* Équinoxe *m.*

equip, *v.tr.* **1.** Équiper, armer. **2.** Monter ; munir (*with*, de).

equipage, *s.* Équipage *m.*

equipment, *s.* Équipement *m.*

equitable, *a.* Équitable, juste.

equitably, *adv.* Équitablement ; avec justice.

equity, *s.* Équité *f.*

equivalence, *s.* Équivalence *f.*

equivalent, *a.* & *s.* Équivalent (*m*).

equivocal, *a.* Équivoque. (*a*) Ambigu, -uë. (*b*) Incertain. (*c*) Suspect.

equivocally, *adv.* D'une manière équivoque.

equivocate, *v.i.* Équivoquer.

equivocation, *s.* Équivocation *f.*

era, *s.* Ère *f.*

eradicate, *v.tr.* Extirper, déraciner.

eradication, *s.* Extirpation *f.*

erase, *v.tr.* Effacer.

eraser, *s.* (*a*) Grattoir *m.* (*b*) Ink e., gomme *f* à encre.

erasure, *s.* Rature *f* ; grattage *m.*

erect[1], *a.* Droit. **With head e.**, la tête haute.

erect[2], *v.tr.* **1.** Dresser. **2.** Ériger, construire.

erection, *s.* (*a*) Dressage *m.* (*b*) Construction *f.*

ermine, *s.* Hermine *f.*

erode, *v.tr.* Éroder ; ronger.

erosion, *s.* Érosion *f.*

erotic, *a.* Érotique.

err, *v.i.* (*a*) Errer ; se tromper. (*b*) Pécher.

errand, *s.* Commission *f*, course *f.*

errand-boy, *s.* Garçon *m* de courses.

errant, *a.* Errant.

erratic, *a.* **1.** Irrégulier. **2.** Excentrique.

erratically, *adv.* Sans méthode, sans règle.

erring, *a.* Dévoyé, égaré.

erroneous, *a.* Erroné.

erroneously, *adv.* Erronément.

error, *s.* **1.** Erreur *f*, faute *f*, méprise *f.* **2.** **To be in e.**, être dans l'erreur ; avoir tort.

erudite, *a.* Érudit.

erudition, *s.* Érudition *f.*

erupt, *v.i.* Entrer en éruption.

eruption, *s.* (*a*) Éruption *f.* (*b*) Éclat *m.*

escalator, *s.* Escalier roulant.

escapade, *s.* Escapade *f.*

escape[1], *s.* (*a*) Fuite *f*, évasion *f.* **To make one's e.**, s'échapper. **To have a narrow e.**, l'échapper belle. (*b*) Échappement *m.*

escape[2]. **1.** *v.i.* (S')échapper ; s'évader. **2.** *v.tr.* Échapper à.

eschew, *v.tr.* Éviter ; renoncer à

escort[1], *s.* Escorte *f.*

escort[2], *v.tr.* Escorter.

especial, *a.* Spécial, -aux ; particulier. **In e.**, surtout ; en particulier.

especially, *adv.* Surtout, particulièrement.

espionage, *s.* Espionnage *m.*

esplanade, *s.* Esplanade *f.*

espouse, *v.tr.* Épouser.

espy, *v.tr.* Apercevoir, aviser.

esquire, *s.* = Monsieur.

essay¹. **1.** Essai *m*; tentative *f*. **2.** Essai; composition *f* (littéraire).

essay², *v.tr.* Essayer.

essence, *s.* Essence *f*.

essential. **1.** *a.* Essentiel, indispensable. **2.** *s.* Essentiel.

essentially, *adv.* Essentiellement.

establish, *v.tr.* Établir.

established, *a.* Établi; solide.

establishment, *s.* **1.** (*a*) Constatation *f*. (*b*) Établissement *m*; fondation *f*. **2.** Établissement, maison *f*.

estate, *s.* **1.** Rang *m*. **2.** Bien *m*, domaine *m*. **3.** Terre *f*, propriété *f*.

estate-agent, *s.* Agent *m* de location.

esteem¹, *s.* Estime *f*, considération *f*.

esteem², *v.tr.* Estimer.

estimable, *a.* Estimable.

estimate¹, *s.* **1.** Appréciation *f*, évaluation *f*. At the lowest e., au bas mot. **2.** Devis *m*; chiffre prévu (*of*, pour).

estimate², *v.tr.* Estimer, évaluer

estimation, *s.* Jugement *m*.

estrangement, *s.* Éloignement *m*.

estuary, *s.* Estuaire *m*.

etch, *v.tr.* Graver à l'eau-forte.

etching, *s.* **1.** Gravure *f* à l'eau-forte. **2.** Eau-forte *f.*, *pl.* eaux-fortes.

eternal, *a.* (*a*) Éternel. (*b*) Continuel; sans fin.

eternally, *adv.* Éternellement.

eternity, *s.* Éternité *f*.

ether, *s.* Éther *m*.

ethereal, *a.* Éthéré; impalpable

ethic(al), *a.* Moral, -aux.

ethics, *s.pl.* Éthique *f*, morale *f*

ethnology, *s.* Ethnologie *f*.

etiquette, *s.* Étiquette *f*.

etymological, *a.* Étymologique

etymology, *s.* Étymologie *f*.

eulogize, *v.tr.* Faire l'éloge de

eulogy, *s.* Panégyrique *m*.

eunuch, *s.* Eunuque *m*.

euphemism, *s.* Euphémisme *m*.

euphemistic, *a.* Euphémique.

euphony, *s.* Euphonie *f*.

Europe. *Pr.n.* L'Europe *f*.

European, *a. & s.* Européen, -enne.

evacuate, *v.tr.* Évacuer.

evacuation, *s.* Évacuation *f*.

evade, *v.tr.* **1.** Éviter; se soustraire à. **2.** Échapper à.

evanescent, *a.* Évanescent.

evaporate. **1.** *v.tr.* Faire évaporer. **2.** *v.i.* S'évaporer, se vaporiser.

evaporation, *s.* Évaporation *f*.

evasion, *s.* **1.** Évitement *m*. **2.** Échappatoire *f*.

evasive, *a.* Évasif.

evasively, *adv.* Évasivement.

eve, *s.* Veille *f*.

even¹, *a.* **1.** Uni; plan. **2.** Égal, régulier, uniforme. **3.** To get e. with, rendre la pareille à. **4.** (*a*) Pair. (*b*) E. money, compte rond. **5.** Of e. date, de même date.

even², *adv.* Même; encore; seulement. E. so, quand même.

even³, *v.tr.* **1.** Égaliser. **2.** Rendre égal.

evening, *s.* Soir *m*; soirée *f*. In the e., le soir, au soir; du soir. All the e., toute la soirée. E. performance, représentation de soirée.

evening-dress, *s.* Habit *m*; tenue *f* de soirée.

evenly, *adv.* **1.** Uniment. **2.** (*a*) Régulièrement; également. (*b*) E. matched, de force égale.

evenness, *s.* **1.** Égalité *f*; régularité *f*. **2.** Sérénité *f*, calme *m*.

event, *s.* **1.** Cas *m*. **2.** (*a*) Événement *m*. (*b*) Issue *f*, résultat *m*. At all events, en tout cas. **3.** Épreuve *f*.

eventful, *a.* Plein d'événements; mouvementé; mémorable.

eventual, *a.* **1.** Éventuel. **2.** Définitif; final, -aux.

eventuality, *s.* Éventualité *f*.

eventually, *adv.* En fin de compte; dans la suite.

ever, *adv.* **1.** Jamais. (*a*) More than e., de plus belle. (*b*) E. since, dès lors, depuis. (*c*) E. and again, de temps en temps. **2.** (*a*) Toujours. Yours e., tout(e) à vous. (*b*) For e., pour toujours; à jamais; sans cesse. Scotland for e.! vive l'Écosse! **3.** (*a*) E. so long, un temps infini. E. so many times, je ne sais combien de fois. E. so much, infiniment. (*b*) What e. shall we do? qu'est-ce que nous allons bien faire?

evergreen. **1.** *a.* Toujours vert. **2.** *s.* Evergreens, plantes vertes.

everlasting, *a.* (*a*) Éternel. (*b*) Perpétuel; sans fin.

every, *a.* (*a*) Chaque; tout. (*b*) E. one, chacun, chacune.

everybody, *indef.pron.* Chacun; tout le monde; tous.

everyday, *a.* **1.** Journalier, quotidien. **2.** Ordinaire, commun. **In e. use,** d'usage courant.

everyone, *indef.pron.* Chacun ; tout le monde ; tous.

everything, *indef.pron.* Tout.

everywhere, *adv.* Partout. **E. you go,** partout où vous allez.

evict, *v.tr.* Évincer, expulser.

eviction, *s.* Éviction *f,* expulsion *f.*

evidence, *s.* **1.** Évidence *f.* **2.** Signe *m,* marque *f.* **3.** *(a)* Preuve *f.* *(b)* Témoignage *m.* **To give e.,** témoigner.

evident, *a.* Évident.

evidently, *adv* Évidemment, manifestement.

evil. 1. *a.* Mauvais ; méchant. **2.** *s.* Mal *m,* *pl.* maux.

evil-doer, *s.* Malfaiteur, -trice.

evil-looking, *a.* De mauvaise mine.

evil-minded, *a.* Malintentionné, malveillant.

evince, *v.tr.* Montrer, témoigner

evocation, *s.* Évocation *f.*

evoke, *v.tr.* Évoquer.

evolution, *s.* Évolution *f.*

evolve. 1. *v.tr.* Développer. **2.** *v.i.* Se développer.

ewe, *s.* Brebis *f.*

exact¹, *a.* Exact. *(a)* Précis. *(b)* **The e. word,** le mot juste.

exact², *v.tr.* *(a)* Exiger. *(b)* Extorquer.

exacting, *a.* Exigeant.

exaction, *s.* Exaction *f.*

exactitude, *s.* Exactitude *f.*

exactly, *adv.* Exactement ; tout juste E.! parfaitement !

exactness, *s* Précision *f.*

exaggerate, *v.tr.* Exagérer ; grandir. *Abs.* Exagérer.

exaggerated, *a.* Exagéré.

exaggeration, *s.* Exagération *f.*

exalt, *v.tr.* **1.** Élever. **2.** Exalter louer. **3.** Exciter, exalter.

exaltation, *s.* Exaltation *f.*

exalted, *a.* Élevé ; haut placé.

examination, *s.* Examen *m* ; inspection *f,* visite *f.*

examine, *v.tr* Examiner ; visiter.

examiner, *s.* **1.** Inspecteur -trice. **2.** Examinateur, -trice.

example, *s.* Exemple *m.* **1. For e.,** par exemple. **2.** Précédent *m.*

exasperate, *v.tr.* Exaspérer.

exasperating, *a.* Exaspérant.

exasperation, *s.* Exaspération *f.*

excavate, *v.tr.* Excaver, creuser.

excavation, *s.* Excavation *f* ; fouille *f.*

exceed, *v.tr.* Excéder, dépasser.

exceedingly, *adv.* Très, extrêmement.

excel. 1. *v.i.* Exceller. **2.** *v.tr.* Surpasser.

excellence, *s.* Excellence *f.* **1.** Perfection *f.* **2.** Mérite *m,* qualité *f.*

excellency, *s.* Excellence *f.*

excellent, *a.* Excellent, parfait.

excellently, *adv.* Excellemment.

except¹, *v.tr.* Excepter, exclure.

except², *prep.* *(a)* Excepté ; à l'exception de ; sauf. *(b)* **E. for,** à part.

exception, *s.* **1.** Exception *f.* **With the e. of,** à l'exception de. **2.** Objection *f.* **To take e. to,** s'offenser de.

exceptionable, *a.* Répréhensible.

exceptional, *a.* Exceptionnel.

exceptionally, *adv.* Exceptionnellement.

excess, *s.* **1.** Excès *m.* **2.** Excédent *m.* **E. luggage,** bagages *mpl.* en surpoids *m.* **E. fare,** supplément *m.*

excessive, *a.* Excessif ; immodéré.

excessively, *adv.* Excessivement.

exchange¹, *s.* **1.** Échange *m.* **2. Rate of e.,** taux *m* du change. **3.** *(a)* Bourse *f.* *(b)* **Telephone e.,** central *m* téléphonique.

exchange², *v.tr.* Échanger.

excise, *s.* Régie *f.*

excision, *s.* Excision *f,* coupure *f.*

excitability, *s.* Promptitude *f* à s'émouvoir.

excitable, *a.* Émotionnable, surexcitable.

excite, *v.tr.* **1.** Provoquer, exciter. **2.** *(a)* Exciter, enflammer. *(b)* Surexciter.

excited, *a.* Agité, surexcité.

excitement, *s.* Agitation *f,* surexcitation *f.*

exciting, *a.* Passionnant, émouvant.

exclaim, *v.i.* S'écrier, s'exclamer.

exclamation, *s.* Exclamation *f.*

exclude, *v.tr.* *(a)* Exclure. **Excluding,** à l'exclusion de. *(b)* Écarter.

exclusion, *s.* **1.** Exclusion *f.* **2.** Refus *m* d'admission *(from,* à).

exclusive, *a.* **1.** Exclusif. **2.** *(a)* Seul, unique. *(b)* Fermé. **3. E. of wine,** vin non compris.

exclusively, *adv.* Exclusivement.
excommunicate, *v.tr.* Excommunier.
excommunication, *s.* Excommunication *f.*
excrescence, *s.* Excroissance *f.*
excretion, *s.* Excrétion *f.*
excruciating, *a.* Atroce, affreux.
exculpate, *v.tr.* Disculper.
exculpation, *s.* Disculpation *f.*
excursion, *s.* Excursion *f;* voyage *m* d'agrément ; partie *f* de plaisir.
excusable, *a.* Excusable, pardonnable.
excusably, *adv.* Excusablement.
excuse¹, *s.* Excuse *f.*
excuse², *v.tr* (*a*) Excuser, pardonner. (*b*) Excuser, dispenser.
execrable, *a.* Exécrable, détestable.
execrably, *adv.* Détestablement.
execrate, *v.tr.* Exécrer, détester.
execration, *s.* Exécration *f.*
execute, *v.tr.* Exécuter.
execution, *s.* Exécution *f.*
executioner, *s.* Bourreau *m.*
executive. 1. *a.* Exécutif. **2.** *s.* Pouvoir exécutif, exécutif *m.*
executor, *s.* Exécuteur *m* testamentaire.
executrix, *s.* Exécutrice *f* testamentaire.
exemplary, *a.* Exemplaire.
exemplify, *v.tr.* Servir d'exemple à.
exempt¹, *a.* Exempt, dispensé.
exempt², *v.tr.* Exempter, dispenser.
exemption, *s.* Exemption *f.*
exercise¹, *s.* Exercice *m.*
exercise², *v.tr.* **1.** Exercer ; user de. **2.** *v.i.* S'entraîner. **3.** Mettre à l'épreuve.
exert, *v.tr.* **1.** Employer ; exercer. **2.** To e. oneself, se dépenser.
exertion, *s.* Effort *m,* efforts.
exhale, *v.tr.* Exhaler.
exhaust, *v.tr.* (*a*) Épuiser, tarir. (*b*) Épuiser, exténuer.
exhausted, *a.* Épuisé.
exhausting, *a.* Épuisant.
exhaustion, *s.* Épuisement *m.*
exhaustive, *a.* Approfondi.
exhaustively, *adv.* A fond.
exhibit, *v.tr.* **1.** Exhiber montrer. **2.** Offrir. **3.** Exposer.
exhibition, *s.* **1.** Exposition *f* étalage *m.* **2.** Exposition.
exhilarate, *v.tr.* Vivifier.
exhilarated, *a.* Ragaillardi.

exhilarating, *a.* Vivifiant.
exhilaration, *s.* Gaieté *f.*
exhort, *v.tr.* Exhorter.
exhortation, *s.* Exhortation *f.*
exhume, *v.tr.* Exhumer.
exigency, *s.* **1.** Exigence *f,* nécessité *f.* **2.** Situation *f* critique.
exigent, *a.* **1.** Urgent. **2.** Exigeant.
exiguous, *a.* Exigu, -uë.
exile¹, *s.* Exil *m,* bannissement *m.*
exile², *s.* Exilé, -ée ; banni, -ie.
exile³, *v.tr.* Exiler, bannir.
exist, *v.i.* Exister.
existence, *s.* Existence *f;* vie *f.*
existent, *a.* Existant.
existing, *a.* Existant, actuel, présent.
exit¹, *s.* Sortie *f.*
exit², *v.i.* E. Macbeth, Macbeth sort.
exodus, *s.* Exode *m.*
exonerate, *v.tr.* Exonérer.
exoneration, *s.* Exonération *f.*
exorbitant, *a.* Exorbitant.
exorcism, *s.* Exorcisme *m.*
exorcize, *v.tr.* Exorciser.
exotic, *a* Exotique.
expand. 1. *v.tr.* Dilater ; élargir. **2.** *v.i.* Se dilater.
expanse, *s.* Étendue *f.*
expansion, *s.* Expansion *f.*
expansive, *a.* Expansif.
expatiate, *v.i.* S'étendre.
expatriate, *v.tr.* Expatrier.
expect, *v.tr.* **1.** Attendre ; s'attendre à ; compter (sur). As one might e., comme de raison. How do you e. me to do it? comment voulez-vous que je le fasse ? **3.** I e. so, je pense que oui.
expectancy, *s.* Attente *f.*
expectant, *a.* Qui attend ; expectant.
expectantly, *adv.* Avec un air d'attente.
expectation, *s.* **1.** (*a*) Attente *f,* espérance *f.* **2.** *pl.* Espérances.
expected, *a.* Attendu, espéré.
expediency, *s.* Convenance *f.*
expedient. 1. *a.* Expédient, convenable. **2.** *s.* Expédient *m,* moyen *m.*
expedite, *v.tr.* **1.** Accélérer. **2.** Expédier, dépêcher.
expedition, *s.* **1.** (*a*) Expédition *f.* (*b*) Excursion *f.* **2.** Célérité *f.*
expeditious, *a.* Rapide ; prompt.
expeditiously, *adv.* Avec célérité ; promptement.
expel, *v.tr.* Expulser.

expend, *v.tr.* **1.** Dépenser. **2.** (a) Épuiser. (b) Consommer.

expenditure, *s.* Dépense *f.*

expense, *s.* **1.** Dépense *f*, frais *mpl.* **2.** Dépens *mpl.* **3.** *pl.* Indemnité *f.*

expensive, *a.* Coûteux, cher. **To be e.,** coûter cher *inv.*

experience[1], *s.* Expérience *f.* **1.** Épreuve personnelle. **2.** Pratique *f.*

experience[2], *v.tr.* Éprouver; faire l'expérience de.

experienced, *a.* Qui a de l'expérience; expérimenté; exercé.

experiment[1], *s.* Expérience *f.*

experiment[2], *v.i.* Expérimenter. faire des expériences.

expert[1], *a.* Habile, expert.

expert[2], *s.* Expert *m*; spécialiste *m.*

expiate, *v.tr.* Expier.

expiation, *s.* Expiation *f.*

expiration, *s.* Expiration *f.*

expire, *v.i.* (a) Expirer. mourir. (b) Expirer, cesser.

expiry, *s.* Expiration *f*, terme *m.*

explain, *v.tr.* Expliquer, éclaircir.

explain away, *v.tr.* Donner une explication satisfaisante de.

explanation, *s.* Explication *f.*

explanatory, *a.* Explicatif.

explicable, *a.* Explicable.

explicit, *a.* Explicite; catégorique.

explicitly, *adv.* Explicitement; catégoriquement.

explode. **1.** *v.tr.* Faire éclater; faire sauter. **2.** *v.i.* Faire explosion; éclater; sauter.

exploit[1], *s.* Exploit *m*; haut fait.

exploit[2], *v.tr.* Exploiter.

exploitation, *s.* Exploitation *f.*

exploration, *s.* Exploration *f.*

explore, *v.tr.* Explorer.

explorer, *s.* Explorateur, -trice.

explosion, *s.* Explosion *f.*

explosive, *a. & s.* Explosif (*m*).

exponent, *s.* Interprète *mf.*

export, *v.tr.* Exporter.

exportation, *s.* Exportation *f.*

exporter, *s.* Exportateur, -trice.

exports, *s.pl.* (i) Articles *m* d'exportation; (ii) exportations *f.*

expose, *v.tr.* **1.** Exposer. **2.** Démasquer.

exposed, *a.* (a) Exposé. (b) A nu.

exposition, *s.* Exposition *f.*

expostulate, *v.i.* Faire des remontrances (*with*, à).

expostulation, *s.* Remontrance *f.*

exposure, *s.* **1.** (a) Exposition *f.* (b) (Temps *m* de) pose *f.* **2.** Dévoilement *m.*

expound, *v.tr.* **1.** Exposer. **2.** Expliquer, interpréter.

express[1]. **1.** *a.* Exprès, -esse, formel. **For this e. purpose,** pour ce but même. **2.** *s.* Express *m*, rapide *m.*

express[2], *v.tr.* Exprimer.

expression, *s.* Expression *f.* **Beyond e.,** inexprimable.

expressive, *a.* Expressif.

expressly, *adv.* **1.** Expressément, formellement. **2.** Avec le seul but de.

expulsion, *s.* Expulsion *f.*

expunge, *v.tr.* Effacer, rayer.

expurgate, *v.tr.* Expurger.

expurgation, *s.* Expurgation *f.*

exquisite, *a.* (a) Exquis. (b) Vif; atroce.

exquisitely, *adv.* D'une manière exquise.

ex-service-man, *s.* Ancien combattant.

extempore. **1.** *adv.* D'abondance, impromptu. **2.** *a.* Improvisé. impromptu *inv.*

extemporize, *v.tr. & i.* Improviser.

extend. **I.** *v.tr.* **1.** Étendre, allonger. **2.** Prolonger. **3.** Étendre, porter plus loin. **4.** Tendre.

 II. extend, *v.i.* **1.** S'étendre, s'allonger. **2.** Se prolonger, continuer.

extension, *s.* **1.** Extension *f*; accroissement *m.* **2.** (R)allonge *f.* **3.** Prolongation *f.* **E. of time,** délai *m.*

extensive, *a.* Étendu, vaste, ample.

extensively, *adv.* Beaucoup; considérablement.

extent, *s.* Étendue *f*; importance *f.* **To a certain e.,** dans une certaine mesure.

extenuating, *a.* Atténuant.

extenuation, *s.* Atténuation *f.*

exterior. **1.** *a.* Extérieur. **2.** *s.* Extérieur *m*, dehors *mpl.*

exterminate, *v.tr.* Exterminer.

extermination, *s.* Extermination *f.*

external, *a.* (a) Externe. (b) Extérieur; du dehors.

externally, *adv.* Extérieurement; à l'extérieur.

extinct, *a.* (a) Éteint. (b) Disparu.

extinction, *s.* Extinction *f.*

extinguish, *v.tr.* Éteindre.

extirpate, *v.tr.* Extirper.

extirpation, *s.* Extirpation *f.*

extol, *v.tr.* Exalter, prôner.

extort, *v.tr.* Extorquer ; arracher.

extortion, *s.* Extorsion *f.*

extortionate, *a.* Exorbitant.

extra. 1. *a.* En sus, de plus ; supplémentaire. **E. charge,** supplément *m* de prix. 2. *adv.* (*a*) Plus que d'ordinaire. (*b*) En plus. 3. *s.* (*a*) Supplément *m.* (*b*) *pl.* Frais *m* supplémentaires.

extract¹, *s.* Extrait *m.*

extract², *v.tr.* Extraire ; arracher.

extraction, *s* 1. Extraction *f* 2. Origine *f.*

extradition, *s.* Extradition *f.*

extraneous, *a.* Étranger.

extraordinary, *a.* Extraordinaire.

extravagance, *s.* 1. Extravagance *f.* 2. Prodigalités *fpl.*

extravagant, *a.* 1. Extravagant. 2. Dépensier. 3. Exorbitant.

extravagantly, *adv.* 1. D'une façon extravagante. 2. Excessivement ; à l'excès.

extreme. 1. *a.* Extrême. 2. *s.* In the e., au dernier degré. **To drive to extremes,** pousser à bout.

extremely, *adv.* Extrêmement ; au dernier point.

extremity, *s.* 1. Extrémité *f* ; point *m* extrême ; bout *m.* 2. Gêne *f.*

extricate, *v.tr.* Dégager.

exuberance, *s.* Exubérance *f.*

exuberant, *a.* Exubérant.

exude, *v.tr. & i.* Exsuder.

exult, *v.i.* Exulter.

exultant, *a.* Triomphant, exultant.

exultation, *s.* Exultation *f.*

eye¹, *s.* 1. Œil *m, pl.* yeux. (*a*) To have blue eyes, avoir les yeux bleus. To open one's eyes wide, écarquiller les yeux. **To open s.o.'s eyes,** éclairer qn. To shut one's eyes to, être aveugle sur. (*b*) **To catch the eye,** frapper les regards. **To set eyes on,** apercevoir, voir. (*c*) **To see eye to eye with,** voir les choses du même œil que. (*d*) **To give an eye to,** veiller à. 2. Chas *m,* trou *m.*

eye², *v.tr.* Regarder observer.

eye-ball, *s.* Globe *m* de l'œil.

eyebrow, *s.* Sourcil *m.*

eye-glass, *s.* (*a*) Monocle *m.* (*b*) **Eye-glasses,** binocle *m,* lorgnon *m,* pince-nez *m inv.*

eye-lash, *s.* Cil *m.*

eyelet, *s.* Œillet *m.*

eyelid, *s.* Paupière *f.*

eye-opener, *s.* Révélation *f* ; surprise *f.*

eyepiece, *s.* Oculaire *m.*

eyesight, *s.* Vue *f.*

eyesore, *s.* Ce qui blesse la vue.

eyewitness, *s.* Témoin *m* oculaire.

eyrie, *s.* Aire *f.*

F

F, f, *s.* (La lettre) F, f, *f.*

fable, *s.* Fable *f,* conte *m.*

fabled, *a.* Légendaire, fabuleux.

fabric, *s.* 1. Édifice *m.* 2. Tissu *m* ; étoffe *f.* 3. Structure *f.*

fabrication, *s.* Invention *f.*

fabulous, *a.* Fabuleux ; légendaire.

fabulously, *adv.* Fabuleusement.

façade, *s.* Façade *f.*

face¹, *s.* 1. Figure *f,* visage *m,* face *f.* **To set one's f. against,** s'opposer résolument à. **In the f. of danger,** en présence du danger. 2. (*a*) Mine *f,* physionomie *f.* **To save f.,** sauver la face. **To make faces,** faire des grimaces. **To keep a straight f.,** garder son sérieux. (*b*) Audace *f,* front *m.* 3. Apparence *f,* aspect *m.*

On the f. of things, au premier aspect. 4. Surface *f.* 5. (*a*) Devant *m,* façade *f.* (*b*) Cadran *m.*

face², 1. *v.tr.* Affronter, faire face à ; envisager. 2. *v.i.* Être exposé à.

face-cream, *s.* Crème *f* de beauté.

face-powder, *s.* Poudre *f* de riz.

facet, *s.* Facette *f.*

facetious, *a.* Facétieux, plaisant.

facetiously, *adv.* Facétieusement.

face-value, *s.* Valeur nominale.

facilitate, *v.tr.* Faciliter.

facility, *s.* Facilité *f.*

facing, *s.* Revers *m,* parement *m.*

facsimile, *s.* Fac-similé *m.*

fact, *s.* 1. Fait *m,* action *f.* 2. **It is a f. that,** il est de fait que. **To know for a f.,** savoir de science certaine.

The f. is, c'est que. In f., de fait. In point of f., par le fait.

faction, s Faction f.

factor, s. Facteur m.

factory, s. Fabrique f, usine f.

faculty, s. (a) Faculté f. (b) Talent m.

fad, s. Marotte f, dada m.

fade. 1. v.i. (a) Se faner, se flétrir. (b) To f. away, s'évanouir. 2. v.tr Faner.

faggot, s. Fagot m.

Fahrenheit, a. Fahrenheit.

fail¹. Adv.phr. **Without** 1., sans faute ; à coup sûr.

fail², v.i. (a) Manquer, faillir, faire défaut. (b) Rester en panne. (c) Baisser. (d) Ne pas réussir ; échouer. I **f. to see why,** je ne vois pas pourquoi. (e) Faire faillite.

failing¹, s. Faible m, faiblesse f.

failing², prep. A défaut de ; faute de.

failure, s. 1. (a) Manque m, défaut m (b) Panne f. 2. (a) Insuccès m. (b) Faillite f. 3. (a) Raté, -ée. (b) Fiasco m.

faint¹, a. 1. (a) Faible, affaibli. (b) Léger ; vague. 2. **To feel f.,** se sentir mal.

faint², s. Évanouissement m. défaillance f.

faint³, v.i. S'évanouir, défaillir.

faintly, adv. 1. Faiblement. 2. Légèrement.

faintness, s. Faiblesse f.

fair¹, s. Foire f.

fair². I. a. 1. Beau, f. belle. 2. Blond. 3. Juste, équitable. **F. play,** franc jeu. 4. Passable ; assez bon. 5. Propice.
II. **fair,** adv. Loyalement, de bonne foi. **To play f.,** jouer beau jeu.

fair and square. 1. a. Loyal, honnête. 2. adv. (a) Au plein milieu. (b) Loyalement

fair-haired, a. Blond ; aux cheveux blonds.

fairly, adv. 1. Impartialement. 2. Honnêtement. 3. Passablement ; assez.

fairness, s. 1. Couleur blonde ; blancheur f. 2. Équité f, impartialité f.

fairy. 1. s. Fée f. 2. a. Féerique ; de(s) fée(s).

fairyland, s. (a) Le royaume des fées. (b) Féerie f.

fairy-like, a. Féerique.

fairy-tale, s. 1. Conte m de fées. 2. Mensonge m.

faith, s. Foi f ; confiance f, croyance f.

faithful, a. Fidèle (a) Loyal. -aux. (b) Exact, juste.

faithfully, adv. Fidèlement.

faithfulness, s. Fidélité f. 1. Loyauté f (to, envers). 2. Exactitude f.

faithless, a. 1. Infidèle ; sans foi. 2. Déloyal, -aux ; perfide.

faithlessness, s. Déloyauté f.

falcon, s. Faucon m.

fall¹, s. 1. Chute f ; descente f. 2. Chute ; cascade f, cataracte f. 3. Baisse f. 4. Perte f, ruine f.

fall², v.i. 1. Tomber. **To f. into a trap,** donner dans un piège. 2. (a) Descendre, baisser. (b) Aller en pente ; descendre. **His face fell,** sa figure s'allongea. 3. (a) A sound fell on my ear, un son frappa mon oreille. (b) Se jeter. 4. (a) Retomber. (b) **To f. under suspicion,** devenir suspect. 5. **To f. a victim,** devenir victime (to, de). **fall back,** v.i. Tomber en arrière. **fall behind,** v.i. Rester en arrière. **fall down,** v.i. 1. Tomber à terre, par terre. 2. Crouler, s'effondrer. **fall in,** v.i. 1. S'écrouler, s'effondrer. 2. Former les rangs. 3. **To f. in with,** rencontrer. **fall off,** v.i. 1. Tomber. 2. Diminuer. **fall out,** v.i. 1. Tomber dehors. 2. Se brouiller. **fall over,** v.i. Tomber à la renverse ; se renverser. **fall through,** v.i. Ne pas aboutir. **fall to,** v.i. Se mettre à l'œuvre.

fallacious, a. Fallacieux.

fallacy, s. Erreur f.

fallen, a. (a) Tombé. (b) Déchu.

fallible, a. Faillible.

false, a. 1. Faux, f. fausse. 2. Perfide. **To play s.o. f.,** trahir qn. 3. Artificiel, postiche ; contrefait.

falsehood, s. Mensonge m.

falsely, adv. Faussement.

falseness, s. Fausseté f.

falsify, v.tr. Falsifier.

falsity, s. Fausseté f.

falter, v.i. (a) Hésiter, trembler. (b) Vaciller.

faltering, a. 1. Hésitant, tremblant. 2. Vacillant.

fame, s. Renom m, renommée f.

famed, a. Célèbre, renommé.

familiar, a. Familier.

familiarity, s. Familiarité f.

familiarly, *adv.* Familièrement, intimement.

family, *s.* Famille *f.* **F. life,** vie familiale.

famine, *s.* (*a*) Famine *f.* (*b*) Disette *f.*

famished, *a.* Affamé.

famous, *a.* Célèbre, fameux.

fan[1], *s.* **1.** Éventail *m.* **2.** Ventilateur *m.*

fan[2], *s.* Passionné, -ée, enragé, -ée.

fanatic, *a. & s.* Fanatique (*mf*).

fanatical, *a.* Fanatique.

fanatically, *adv.* Fanatiquement.

fanaticism, *s.* Fanatisme *m.*

fancied, *a.* Imaginaire, imaginé.

fanciful, *a.* **1.** Capricieux, fantasque **2.** Chimérique ; imaginaire.

fancy[1]. I. *s.* **1.** Imagination *f*, fantaisie *f.* **2.** (*a*) Fantaisie, caprice *m.* (*b*) Fantaisie, goût *m.*

   II. **fancy,** *a.* De fantaisie. **F. goods,** nouveautés *f.* **F. dress,** travesti *m.*

fancy[2], *v.tr.* **1.** (*a*) S'imaginer, se figurer. (*b*) Croire, penser. **2.** Se sentir attiré vers.

fang, *s.* (*a*) Croc *m.* (*b*) Crochet *m.*

fan-light, *s.* Vasistas *m.*

fantastic, *a.* Fantasque, bizarre.

fantasy, *s.* Fantaisie *f.*

far[1], *adv.* Loin. **1.** (*a*) As far as the eye can reach, à perte de vue. **Far and wide,** de tous côtés. (*b*) To go so far as, aller jusqu'à. **As far as I know,** autant que je sache. **In so far as,** dans la mesure où. **Far from it,** tant s'en faut. **By far,** de beaucoup. **2. So far,** jusqu'ici. **3.** Beaucoup

far[2], *a.* Lointain, éloigné, reculé.

far-away, *a.* Lointain, éloigné.

farce, *s.* Farce *f.*

farcical, *a.* Risible, grotesque.

fare[1], *s.* **1.** Prix *m* du voyage, de la place, de la course. **2.** Chère *f.*

fare[2], *v.i.* Manger, se nourrir.

farewell, *int. & s.* Adieu (*m*).

far-fetched, *a.* Forcé, outré.

farm[1], *s.* Ferme *f.*

farm[2], *v.tr.* (*a*) Cultiver. (*b*) *Abs.* Être fermier.

farmer, *s.* Fermier, -ière.

farming, *s.* Agriculture *f.*

farm-yard, *s.* Basse-cour *f.*

far-off, *a.* Lointain, éloigné.

far-reaching, *a.* D'une grande portée.

far-seeing, *a.* Prévoyant ; perspicace.

far-sighted, *a.* Prévoyant ; perspicace.

farther. 1. *adv.* Plus loin. **F. off,** plus éloigné. **2.** *a.* Plus lointain, plus éloigné.

farthest. 1. *a.* (*a*) Le plus lointain, le plus éloigné. (*b*) Le plus long. **2.** *adv.* Le plus loin.

fascinate, *v.tr.* Fasciner, charmer.

fascinating, *a.* Enchanteur, -eresse ; séduisant.

fascination, *s.* Fascination *f.*

fashion[1], *s.* **1.** Façon *f* ; manière *f.* **French f.,** à la française. **After a f.,** tant bien que mal. **2.** Mode *f*, vogue *f.* **In (the) f.,** à la mode. **Out of f.,** démodé.

fashion[2], *v.tr.* Façonner, former.

fashionable, *a.* A la mode, élégant. **A f. resort,** un endroit mondain.

fashionably, *adv.* Élégamment ; à la mode.

fast[1] *s.* Jeûne *m.*

fast[2], *v.i.* Jeûner ; faire maigre.

fast[3]. I. *a.* **1.** (*a*) Ferme, fixe, solide. (*b*) Résistant ; bon teint *inv.* **2.** Rapide, vite. **F. train,** rapide *m.* **3.** En avance. **4.** Dissipé.

   II. **fast,** *adv.* **1.** Ferme, solidement. **To stand f.,** tenir bon. **2.** Vite, rapidement. **It is raining f.,** il pleut à verse.

fasten. 1. *v.tr.* (*a*) Attacher. (*b*) Fixer, assurer. **2.** *v.i.* S'attacher, se fixer.

fastener, *s.* Attache *f* ; fermeture *f.*

fastening, *s.* **1.** Attache *f*, attachement *m.* **2.** Fermeture *f.*

fastidious, *a.* Difficile ; délicat.

fasting, *s.* Jeûne *m.*

fat[1], *a.* Gras, *f.* grasse.

fat[2], *s.* **1.** Graisse *f.* **2.** Gras *m* (de viande).

fatal, *a.* Fatal, -als.

fatalism, *s.* Fatalisme *m.*

fatalist, *s.* Fataliste *mf.*

fatality, *s.* Accident mortel.

fatally, *adv.* **1.** Fatalement, inévitablement. **2.** Mortellement.

fate, *s.* Destin *m*, sort *m.*

fated, *a.* **1.** Fatal, -als ; inévitable. **2.** Destiné, condamné.

fateful, *a.* Décisif, fatal, -als.

father, *s.* Père *m.*

father-in-law, *s.* Beau-père *m, pl.* beaux-pères.

fatherland, s. Patrie f.
fatherless, a. Sans père.
fatherly, a. Paternel.
fathom[1], s. Brasse f.
fathom[2], v.tr. Approfondir, sonder.
fatigue[1], s. **1.** Fatigue f. **2.** Corvée f.
fatigue[2], v.tr. Fatiguer, lasser.
fatiguing, a. Fatigant, épuisant.
fatten. 1. v.tr. Engraisser. **2.** v.i.
Engraisser ; devenir gras.
fatty, a. Graisseux, oléagineux.
fatuity, s. Sottise f ; imbécillité f.
fatuous, a. Sot, f. sotte, imbécile.
fatuously, adv. Sottement.
fault, s. **1.** Défaut m ; imperfection f.
To a f., à l'excès. To find f. with,
trouver à redire contre. **2.** Faute f.
To be in f., être en défaut. **3.** At f.,
en défaut.
fault-finding, s. Disposition f à
critiquer.
faultless, a. Sans défaut ; impeccable.
faulty, a. Défectueux, imparfait ;
erroné, inexact.
favour[1], s. **1.** Faveur f. **2.** Grâce f,
bonté f. **3.** (a) Partialité f. (b) Protection f. **4.** Prep.phr. In f. of, partisan de.
favour[2], v.tr. Favoriser. **1.** Approuver ; préférer. **2.** Gratifier,
obliger. **3.** (a) Avantager. (b)
Faciliter.
favourable, a. Favorable ; propice.
favourably, adv. Favorablement,
avantageusement.
favoured, a. Favorisé.
favourite, s. **1.** s. Favori, f. favorite.
2. a. Favori, préféré.
favouritism, s. Favoritisme m.
fawn[1], s. Faon m.
fawn[2], v.ind.tr. To f. on, caresser ;
aduler.
fawning, a. Caressant ; servile.
fealty, s. Fidélité f.
fear[1], s. Crainte f, peur f.
fear[2], v.tr. **1.** Craindre, avoir peur de,
redouter. **2.** Appréhender, craindre.
fearful, a. **1.** Affreux, effrayant.
2. Peureux, craintif.
fearfully, adv. Affreusement.
fearless, a. Intrépide, courageux.
fearlessly, adv. Intrépidement ; sans
peur.
fearlessness, s. Intrépidité f.
fearsome, a. Redoutable.
feasibility, s. Praticabilité f.

feasible, a. Faisable, possible.
feast[1], s. **1.** Fête f. **2.** Festin m.
feast[2]. **1.** v.i. Faire festin. **2.** v.tr.
Régaler, fêter.
feat, s. **1.** Exploit m, haut fait. **2.**
Tour m de force.
feather, s. Plume f.
feature, s. **1.** Trait m. The features,
la physionomie. **2.** Trait, caractéristique f.
February, s. Février m.
federation, s. Fédération f.
fee, s. (a) Honoraires mpl. (b) Frais
mpl ; droit m.
feeble, a. Faible, infirme, débile.
feeble-minded, a. D'esprit faible.
feebleness, s. Faiblesse f.
feebly, adv. Faiblement.
feed. 1. v.tr. **1.** Nourrir ; donner à
manger à. **2.** Alimenter.
  II. v.i. Manger ; paître. **feed up,**
v.tr. Engraisser ; suralimenter.
feeding, s. Alimentation f.
feeding-bottle, s. Biberon m.
feel[1], s. **1.** Toucher m, tact m.
2. Sensation f.
feel[2]. **1.** (a) v.tr. Toucher, palper ;
tâter. (b) v.tr. & i. To f. in one's
pockets, fouiller dans ses poches.
2. (a) v.tr. Sentir. (b) v.tr. & i.
(Res)sentir, éprouver. To f. the
cold, être sensible au froid. To f.
for, être plein de pitié pour. (c) v.tr.
Avoir conscience de (qch.). **3.** v.i.
Pred. To f. cold, avoir froid. To f.
ill, se sentir malade. To f. certain,
être certain.
feeler, s. Antenne f, palpe f.
feeling[1], a. **1.** Sensible. **2.** Ému.
feeling[2], s. **1.** Toucher m, tact m.
2. Sensation f. **3.** Sentiment m ;
sensibilité f.
feign, v.tr. Feindre, simuler.
feigned, a. Feint, simulé.
feint, s. Feinte f.
felicity, s. Félicité f, bonheur m.
feline. 1. a. Félin. **2.** s. Félin m.
fell, v.tr. Abattre ; assommer.
fellow, s. **1.** Camarade m, compagnon
m. **2.** Semblable m, pareil m.
3. Membre m, associé, -ée. **4.** (a)
Homme m, garçon m. A queer f.,
un drôle de type. (b) Individu m.
fellow-citizen, s. Concitoyen, -enne.
fellow-countryman, -woman, s.
Compatriote mf.

fellow-creature, s. Semblable m.

fellow-feeling, s. Sympathie f.

fellowship, s. **1.** Communion f, communauté f. **2.** Association f.

felon, s. Criminel, -elle.

felony, s. Crime m.

felt, s. Feutre m.

female. 1. a. (a) Féminin; (de) femme. (b) Femelle. **2.** s. (a) Femme f. (b) Femelle f.

feminine, a. Féminin.

fence[1], s. Clôture f, palissade f.

fence[2]. **1.** v.i. Faire de l'escrime. **2.** v.tr. Clôturer.

fencing, s. Escrime f.

fencing-master, s. Maître m d'armes.

fend. 1. v.tr. To f. off, détourner. **2.** v.i. To f. for oneself, se débrouiller.

fender, s. Garde-feu m inv.

ferment[1], s. **1.** Ferment m. **2.** Fermentation f; agitation f.

ferment[2], v.i. Fermenter.

fermentation, s. Fermentation f.

fern, s. Fougère f.

ferocious, a. Féroce.

ferociously, adv. Avec férocité.

ferocity, s. Férocité f.

ferret[1], s. Furet m.

ferret[2], v.tr. To f. out, dénicher.

ferrule, s. Bout ferré, embout m.

ferry[1], s. **1.** Endroit m où l'on peut passer la rivière en bac. To cross the f., passer le bac. **2.** Bac.

ferry[2], v.tr. To f. across, passer en bac.

ferry-boat, s. Bac m.

ferryman, s. Passeur m.

fertile, a. Fertile, fécond.

fertility, s. Fertilité f, fécondité f.

fertilization, s. Fertilisation f.

fertilize, v.tr. Fertiliser.

fervency, s. Ferveur f.

fervent, a. Ardent, fervent.

fervently, adv. Avec ferveur.

fervid, a. Fervent.

fervour, s. Passion f, ferveur f

fester, v.i. Suppurer.

festival, s. Fête f.

festivity, s. Fête f, réjouissance f.

fetch, v.tr. **1.** (a) Aller chercher. (b) Apporter; amener. **2.** Rapporter.

fête[1], s. Fête f.

fête[2], v.tr. Fêter; faire fête à.

fetid, a. Fétide, puant.

fetish, s. Fétiche m.

fetter, v.tr. Enchaîner; charger de fers; entraver.

fetters, s. pl. Chaînes f, fers m.

feud, s. Inimitié f.

feudal, a. Féodal, -aux.

fever, s. Fièvre f.

fevered, a. Enfiévré, fiévreux.

feverish, a. Fiévreux, fébrile.

feverishly, adv. Fiévreusement, fébrilement.

feverishness, s. État fiévreux.

few, a. **1.** (a) Peu de. (b) A few, quelques; quelques-uns, -unes. (c) Peu nombreux. **2.** Few of them, peu d'entre eux.

fewer, a. **1.** Moins (de). **2.** Moins nombreux.

fewest, a. Le moins (de).

fewness, s. Rareté f; petit nombre.

fiasco, s. Fiasco m.

fiat, s. Décret m, ordre m.

fib[1], s. Petit mensonge; blague f.

fib[2], v.i. Blaguer, craquer.

fibre, s. Fibre f; filament m.

fibrous, a. Fibreux.

fickle, a. Inconstant, volage.

fickleness, s. Inconstance f.

fiction, s. **1.** Fiction f. **2.** Romans m.

fictitious, a. Fictif; imaginaire.

fiddle[1], s. **1.** Violon m. **2.** Violon de mer.

fiddle[2], v.i. **1.** Jouer du violon. **2.** Tripoter, patiner.

fiddler, s. Joueur m de violon.

fiddling, a. Futile, insignifiant.

fidelity, s. Fidélité f, loyauté f.

fidget, v.i. (a) Remuer continuellement. (b) S'inquiéter.

fidgeting, s. Agitation nerveuse.

fidgety, a. Nerveux, impatient.

field, s. **1.** Champ m. (a) In the fields, aux champs. (b) To take the f., entrer en campagne. **2.** Étendue f. **3.** Théâtre m, champ.

field-glass, s. (a) Lunette f d'approche. (b) Usu. pl. Jumelle(s) f.

field-marshal, s. (Feld-)maréchal m, pl. -aux.

field-mouse, s. Mulot m.

fiend, s. Démon m, diable m.

fiendish, a. Diabolique.

fiendishly, adv. Diaboliquement.

fierce, a. Féroce; acharné; violent.

fiercely, adv. **1.** Férocement. **2.** Violemment; avec acharnement.

fierceness, s. Violence f; férocité f; acharnement m.

fiery, *a.* **1.** Ardent, brûlant, enflammé. **2.** Fougueux emporté.

fife, *s.* Fifre *m.*

fifteen, *num. a. & s.* Quinze (*m*).

fifteenth. 1. *num. a. & s.* Quinzième. **On the f. of August,** le quinze août. **2.** *s.* Quinzième *m.*

fifth. 1. *num. a. & s.* Cinquième **Henry the Fifth,** Henri Cinq. **2.** *s.* Cinquième *m.*

fifty, *num. a. & s.* Cinquante (*m*). **About f.,** une cinquantaine de.

fig, *s.* Figue *f.*

fight[1], *s.* **1.** (*a*) Combat *m,* bataille *f.* (*b*) Assaut *m.* **Free f.,** mêlée générale. **2.** (*a*) Lutte *f.* (*b*) **To show f.,** résister.

fight[2]. 1. *v.i.* Se battre; combattre; lutter. **2.** *v.tr.* Se battre avec; combattre. **fight down,** *v.tr.* Vaincre. **fight off,** *v.tr.* Résister à.

fighter, *s.* **1.** Combattant *m.* **2.** Chasseur *m.*

fighting, *s.* Combat *m.*

fighting-cock, *s.* Coq *m* de combat

fig-tree, *s.* Figuier *m.*

figurative, *a.* **1.** Figuratif. **2.** Figuré.

figuratively, *adv.* **1.** Figurativement **2.** Au figuré.

figure, *s.* **1.** (*a*) Figure *f;* forme extérieure. (*b*) Taille *f.* **2.** Figure, apparence *f.* **3.** Chiffre *m.* **4.** F. of speech, façon *f* de parler.

filament, *s.* Filament *m.*

filch, *v.tr.* Chiper, escamoter.

file[1], *s.* Lime *f.*

file[2], *v.tr.* Limer.

file[3], *s.* **1.** (*a*) Spike *t.,* pique-notes *m inv.* (*b*) Classeur *m.* **2.** Dossier *m.*

file[4], *v.tr.* Enfiler; classer; ranger.

file[5], *s.* File *f.* **In single f.,** à la file.

filial, *a.* Filial, -aux.

filigree, *s.* Filigrane *m.*

filing, *s.* Classement *m.*

filing-cabinet, *s.* Classeur *m*

filings, *s.pl.* Limaille *f.*

fill. I. *v.tr.* **1.** Remplir, emplir (*with,* de); charger. **2.** (*a*) Combler. (*b*) Suppléer, pourvoir, à. **3.** Occuper. **II. fill,** *v.i.* Se remplir, s'emplir. **fill in,** *v.tr.* Remplir; insérer. **fill out. 1.** *v.tr.* Enfler. gonfler. **2.** *v.i.* S'enfler, se gonfler. **fill up. 1.** *v.tr.* (*a*) Combler. *Abs.* Faire le plein (*with,* de). (*b*) Boucher. (*c*) Remplir. **2.** *v.i.* Se remplir, se combler.

fillet, *s.* (*a*) Filet (de bœuf). (*b*) Rouelle *f* (de veau).

filling[1], *a.* Rassasiant.

filling[2], *s.* **1.** (R)emplissage *m.* **2.** Occupation *f.*

filly, *s.* Pouliche *f.*

film, *s.* **1.** Pellicule *f.* **2.** (*a*) Film *m,* bande *f.* (*b*) **The films,** le cinématographe.

filter[1], *s.* Filtre *m.*

filter[2], *v.tr. & i.* Filtrer.

filth, *s.* Ordure *f;* immondices *mpl.*

filthiness, *s.* Saleté *f.*

filthy, *a.* Sale, immonde, dégoûtant.

fin, *s.* Nageoire *f;* aileron *m.*

final, *a.* Final, -als. (*a*) Dernier. (*b*) Définitif, décisif.

finale, *s.* Finale *m.*

finality, *s.* Finalité *f.*

finally, *adv.* Finalement. **1.** Enfin. **2.** Définitivement. **3.** En somme.

finance[1], *s.* Finance *f.*

finance[2], *v.tr.* Financer.

financial, *a.* Financier.

financier, *s.* Financier *m.*

finch, *s.* Pinson *m.*

find[1], *s.* **1.** Découverte *f.* **2.** Trouvaille *f.*

find[2], *v.tr.* Trouver. **1.** Rencontrer, découvrir. **2.** (*a*) Retrouver. **I can't f. time to,** je n'ai pas le temps de. (*b*) Obtenir. **3.** Constater. **4.** (*a*) **To f. guilty,** déclarer coupable. (*b*) Rendre (un verdict). **5.** All found, tout fourni. **find out,** *v.tr.* (*a*) Deviner; découvrir; constater. *Abs.* **To f. out about,** se renseigner sur. (*b*) **To f. s.o. out,** trouver qn en défaut.

finding, *s.* **1.** Découverte *f.* **2.** Constatation *f.*

fine[1], *s.* **1.** In f., enfin. **2.** Amende *f.*

fine[2], *v.tr.* Frapper d'une amende.

fine[3], *a.* **1.** (*a*) Fin, pur. (*b*) Fin, subtil. **2.** Beau, bel, belle, beaux. **The f. arts,** les beaux-arts *m.* **3.** (*a*) Of the finest quality, de premier choix. (*b*) Excellent, magnifique. **That's f.!** voilà qui est parfait. (*c*) **That's all very f.,** tout cela est bel et bon. **4.** Beau. **5.** (*a*) Fin; menu. (*b*) **F. nib,** plume pointue. **6. To cut it f.,** faire qch. tout juste.

finely, *adv.* **1.** (*a*) Finement. (*b*) Délicatement. **2.** Admirablement.

finery, *s.* Parure *f;* fanfreluches *fpl.*

finesse, s. Finesse f.

finger[1], s. Doigt m. **First f.**, index m.

finger[2], v.tr. Manier, tâter

finger-nail, s. Ongle m.

finger-print, s. Empreinte digitale.

finish[1], s. **1.** Fin f; arrivée f. **2.** (a) Fini m, achevé m. (b) Apprêt m.

finish[2]. **1.** v.tr. Finir; terminer, achever. **2.** v.i. Finir; cesser se terminer.

finished, a. **1.** Fini; apprêté. **2.** Soigné, parfait; accompli.

finite, a. Fini, limité, borné.

fiord, s. Fiord m.

fir, s. **1.** Fir(-tree), sapin m. **Fir plantation,** sapinière f. **2.** (Bois m de) sapin.

fir-cone, s. Pomme f de pin.

fire[1], s. **1.** Feu m. (a) **To light a f.**, faire du feu. **Electric f.**, radiateur m électrique. (b) Incendie m, sinistre m. **On f.**, en feu, en flammes. (c) Lumière f, éclat m. **2.** Ardeur f, zèle m. **3.** Feu, tir m. **To be under f.**, essuyer le feu.

fire[2], v.tr. **1.** (a) Mettre feu à, embraser. (b) Animer **2.** Tirer; décharger.

fire-alarm, s. Avertisseur m d'incendie.

fire-arm, s. Arme f à feu.

fire-brand, s. Brandon m (de discorde).

fire-brigade, s. Sapeurs-pompiers mpl.

fire-engine, s. Pompe f à incendie.

fire-escape, s. Échelle f de sauvetage.

fire-extinguisher, s. Extincteur m d'incendie.

fire-fly, s. Luciole f.

fire-guard, s. Garde-feu m inv.

fire-insurance, s. Assurance f contre l'incendie.

fire-irons, s.pl. Garniture f de foyer.

fire-lighter, s. Allume-feu m inv.

fireman, s. Pompier m.

fire-place, s. Cheminée f, foyer m.

fire-proof, a. (a) Incombustible, ignifuge. (b) Réfractaire. **F.-p. dish,** plat allant au feu.

fireside, s. Foyer m; coin m du feu.

fire-wood, s. Bois m à brûler.

firework, s. **1.** Pièce f d'artifice. **2.** pl. Feu m d'artifice.

firm[1], s. **1.** Raison sociale. **2.** Maison f (de commerce).

firm[2], a. Ferme. **1.** Compact; solide. **2.** Constant; résolu **3.** adv. **To stand f.**, tenir bon.

firmament, s. Firmament m.

firmly, adv. **1.** Fermement, solidement. **2.** D'un ton ferme.

firmness, s. Fermeté f; solidité f.

first. I. a. Premier. (a) **At f. sight,** de prime abord; au premier abord. **In the f. place,** d'abord. **Head f.,** la tête la première. **F. night,** première f. **F. edition,** édition princeps. (b) **At f. hand,** de première main.

II. first, s. **1.** (Le) premier, (la) première. **2.** Commencement m. **At f.,** d'abord. **3. To travel f.,** voyager en première.

III. first, adv. **1.** Premièrement, au commencement, d'abord. **F. of all,** en premier lieu. **2.** Pour la première fois. **3.** Plutôt. **4. He arrived f.,** il arriva le premier. **You go f.!** allez devant! **Ladies f.!** place aux dames!

first-aid, s. Premiers secours.

first-born, a. & s. Premier-né, pl. premiers-nés, f. première(s)-née(s).

first-class, a. De première classe; de première qualité.

firstly, adv. Premièrement; en premier lieu.

first-rate, a. Excellent; de première classe.

fish[1], s. Poisson m.

fish[2], v.i. Pêcher. **To f. for trout,** pêcher la truite.

fish-bone, s. Arête f.

fisherman, s. Pêcheur m.

fishery, s. Pêche f.

fish-hook, s. Hameçon m.

fishing, s. La pêche.

fishing-boat, s. Bateau m de pêche.

fishing-line, s. Ligne f de pêche.

fishing-rod, s. Canne f à pêche.

fishing-tackle, s. Appareil m de pêche.

fish-knife, s. Couteau m. à poisson.

fishmonger, s. Marchand, -ande, de poisson.

fishy, a. **1.** De poisson. **2.** Louche.

fission, s. Fission f.

fissure, s. Fissure f, fente f.

fist, s. Poing m.

fit[1], s. **1.** Accès m, attaque f. **2.** Accès; crise f.

fit[2], a. **1.** Bon. propre (for, à). **To**

think fit, juger convenable. **2.** Capable. **Fit for nothing,** propre à rien. **3.** En bonne santé.

fit³, s. Ajustement m.

fit⁴. I. v.tr. **1.** Aller à. **2.** Adapter, ajuster.
II. **fit,** v.i. (a) S'ajuster, se raccorder. (b) Aller. **fit in,** v.i. Être en harmonie **fit on,** v.tr. Essayer. **fit out,** v.tr. Équiper (with, de).

fitful, a. Irrégulier, capricieux.

fitfully, adv. Irrégulièrement.

fitly, adv. Convenablement.

fitness, s. **1.** Aptitude f. **2.** (a) A-propos m, justesse f. (b) Convenance f. **3.** Santé f.

fitted, a. **1.** Ajusté, monté. **2.** F. for. apte à.

fitting¹, a. Convenable.

fitting², s. **1.** Ajustage m. **2.** pl. Garniture f.

five, num. a. & s. Cinq (m).

fix¹, s. Embarras m, difficulté f.

fix², v.tr. Fixer. **1.** Assurer. **2.** (a) Fixer; établir; arrêter. (b) **To fix (up)on,** se décider pour.

fixed, a. Fixe, arrêté.

fixedly, adv. Fixement.

fixity, s. Fixité f.

fixture, s. **1.** Appareil m fixe. **2.** Engagement m.

fizz, v.i. Pétiller.

fizzle, v.i. Pétiller.

fizzy, a. Gazeux, effervescent.

flabbiness, s. Flaccidité f; mollesse f.

flabby, a. Flasque; mou, f. molle.

flag¹, s. (a) Drapeau m. (b) Pavillon m.

flag², v.i. S'alanguir: traîner; se relâcher.

flagon, s. Flacon m.

flagrant, a. Flagrant, énorme.

flagrantly, adv. Scandaleusement.

flagship, s. (Vaisseau m) amiral m.

flagstaff, s. (a) Mât m de drapeau; (b) Hampe f de drapeau.

flagstone, s. Carreau m, dalle f.

flail, s. Fléau m.

flair, s. Flair m, perspicacité f.

flake, s. (a) Flocon m. (b) Écaille f, éclat m.

flame¹, s. Flamme f. **To burst into f.,** s'enflammer brusquement.

flame², v.i. Flamber, jeter des flammes. **flame up,** v.i. S'enflammer.

flaming, a. Flambant; en flammes.

flamingo, s. Flamant m.

flank, s. Flanc m.

flannel, s. Flanelle f.

flannelette, s. Flanelle f de coton

flap¹, s. **1.** Battement m, coup m. **2.** (a) Patte f (d'une enveloppe). (b) Abattant m (de table).

flap², v.tr. Battre (des ailes).

flare¹, s. **Landing f.,** feu m d'atterrissage.

flare², v.i. Flamboyer. **flare up,** v.i. S'enflammer brusquement.

flash¹, s. Éclair m. **In a f.,** en un rien de temps.

flash². I. v.i. (a) Jeter des éclairs; étinceler. (b) **To f. past,** passer comme un éclair. **2.** v.tr. (a) Faire étinceler. (b) Projeter.

flashing, a. Éclatant, flamboyant.

flashy, a. Voyant, éclatant.

flask, s. Flacon m.

flat¹, s. Appartement m.

flat². I. a. Plat. **1.** (a) Étendu à plat. (b) Plat, uni. **F. tyre,** pneu à plat. **2.** (a) Monotone. (b) Éventé, plat. **3.** Invariable, uniforme. **4.** (a) Sourd. (b) Bémol inv.
II. **flat,** adv. Nettement, positivement.
III. **flat,** s. **1.** Plat m. **2.** Bémol m.

flatly, adv. Nettement, carrément.

flatness, s. **1.** Égalité f; manque m de relief. **2.** Monotonie f.

flatten. 1. v.tr. Aplatir. **2.** v.i. (a) S'aplatir. (b) **To f. out,** se redresser.

flatter, v.tr. Flatter.

flatterer, s. Flatteur, -euse.

flattering, a. Flatteur, -euse.

flattery, s. Flatterie f.

flaunt, v.tr. Faire étalage de.

flavour¹, s. Saveur f, goût m.

flavour², v.tr. Assaisonner, parfumer.

flavouring, s. Assaisonnement m, condiment m.

flavourless, a. Sans saveur; insipide.

flaw, s. Défaut m, imperfection f

flawless, a. Sans défaut.

flax, s. Lin m.

flaxen, a. Blond filasse inv.

flaxen-haired, a. Blondasse

flay, v.tr. Écorcher.

flea, s. Puce f.

flea-bite, s. **1.** Morsure f de puce. **2.** Vétille f, bagatelle f.

fleck¹, s. **1.** Petite tache; moucheture f. **2.** Particule f.

fleck[2], *v.tr.* Tacheter (*with*, de).

fledgeling, *s.* Oisillon *m.*

flee. I. *v.i.* Fuir, s'enfuir, se sauver. 2. *v.tr.* S'enfuir de; fuir.

fleece[1], *s.* Toison *f.*

fleece[2], *v.tr.* Tondre, écorcher.

fleecy, *a.* Floconneux.

fleet[1], *s.* Flotte *f.*

fleet[2], *a.* Rapide.

fleeting, *a.* Fugitif; passager.

fleetness, *s.* Vitesse *f*, rapidité *f.*

Flemish, *a.* Flamand.

flesh, *s.* Chair *f.* **In the f.**, en chair et en os.

fleshless, *a.* Décharné.

flesh-wound, *s.* Blessure *f* dans les chairs.

fleshy, *a.* Charnu.

flexibility, *s.* Flexibilité *f.*

flexible, *a.* Flexible, souple, pliant.

flick[1], *s.* Chiquenaude *f*; petit coup.

flick[2], *v.tr.* Effleurer; (*with finger*) donner une chiquenaude à.

flicker[1], *s.* Tremblotement *m*; battement *m*, clignement *m.*

flicker[2], *v.i.* Trembloter, vaciller; clignoter.

flickering, *a.* Tremblotant; vacillant.

flight[1], *s.* I. (*a*) Vol *m.* (*b*) Course *f.* (*c*) Envol. **F. of fancy**, essor *m* de l'imagination. (*d*) Migration *f.* 2. Volée *f*, distance parcourue. 3. **F. of stairs**, escalier *m.* 4. (*a*) Bande *f*, vol. (*b*) *Av*: Escadrille *f.*

flight[2], *s.* Fuite *f.*

flighty, *a.* Frivole, écervelé, étourdi.

flimsiness, *s.* Manque *m* de solidité. (*a*) Légèreté *f.* (*b*) Futilité *f.*

flimsy, *a.* Sans solidité; faible.

flinch, *v.i.* I. Reculer, fléchir. 2. **Without flinching**, sans broncher.

fling, *v.tr.* Jeter; lancer. **fling aside**, *v.tr.* Rejeter; jeter de côté. **fling away**, *v.tr.* Jeter de côté. **fling down**, *v.tr.* Jeter à terre. **fling out**, *v.tr.* (*a*) Jeter dehors. (*b*) Étendre.

flint, *s.* I. Silex *m.* 2. Pierre *f* à briquet.

flippancy, *s.* Légèreté *f.*

flippant, *a.* Léger, désinvolte.

flippantly, *adv.* Légèrement.

flirt[1], *s.* Flirteur *m*; coquette *f.*

flirt[2], *v.i.* Flirter.

flirtation, *s.* Flirt *m.*

flirting, *s.* Flirt *m.*

flit, *v.i.* **To f. by**, passer comme une ombre. **To f. about**, aller et venir sans bruit.

flitter, *v.i.* Voleter, voltiger

float[1], *s.* Flotteur *m.*

float[2], *v.i.* (*a*) Flotter, nager; surnager. (*b*) Faire la planche.

floating, *a.* Flottant; à flot.

flock[1], *s.* Troupe *f*; troupeau *m*

flock[2], *v.i.* S'attrouper.

flog, *v.tr.* Fouetter.

flogging, *s.* Flagellation *f.*

flood[1], *s.* I. Flot *m*, flux *m.* 2. (*a*) Déluge *m*, inondation *f* (*b*) Crue *f.*

flood[2]. I. *v.tr.* Inonder, submerger. 2. *v.i.* Déborder.

flooding, *s.* I. Inondation *f* 2. Débordement *m.*

flood-light, *v.tr.* Illuminer par projecteurs.

flood-lighting, *s.* Éclairage diffusé.

flood-tide, *s.* Marée montante; flux *m.*

floor[1], *s.* I. Plancher *m.* 2. Étage *m.*

floor[2], *v.tr.* Terrasser.

flora, *s.* Flore *f.*

floral, *a.* Floral, -aux.

florid, *a.* Fleuri; orné à l'excès

florist, *s.* Fleuriste *mf*

flotilla, *s.* Flotille *f.*

flounce, *s.* Volant *m.*

flounder, *v.i.* Patauger, barboter.

flour, *s.* Farine *f.*

flourish[1], *s.* I. Geste prétentieux; brandissement *m.* 2. (*a*) Fanfare *f.* (*b*) Fioriture *f.*

flourish[2]. I. *v.i.* (*a*) Prospérer. (*b*) Fleurir. 2. *v.tr.* Brandir.

flourishing, *a.* Florissant; prospère.

flout, *v.tr.* Se moquer de.

flow[1], *s.* (*a*) Coulement *m*; écoulement *m.* (*b*) Passage *m.* (*c*) Courant *m.* affluence *f.* (*d*) Flot *m*, flux *m.*

flow[2], *v.i.* (*a*) Couler; se verser. (*b*) Monter. (*c*) Circuler.

flower[1], *s.* I. Fleur *f.* **Bunch of flowers**, bouquet *m.* 2. **Fine fleur**, élite *f.*

flower[2], *v.i.* Fleurir.

flower-bed, *s.* Parterre *m.*

flower-garden, *s.* Jardin *m* d'agrément.

flower-girl, *s.f.* Bouquetière.

flowering[1], *a.* Fleuri; en fleur

flowering[2], *s.* Fleuraison *f.*

flower-pot, *s.* Pot *m* à fleurs.

flowing, *a.* **1.** Coulant; montant. **2.** Flottant.

fluctuate, *v.i.* Fluctuer.

fluctuating, *a.* Variable.

fluctuation, *s.* Fluctuation *f.*

fluency, *s.* Facilité *f.*

fluent, *a.* Coulant, facile.

fluently, *adv.* Couramment.

fluff, *s.* Duvet *m*; peluche *f.*

fluffy, *a.* Pelucheux; duveteux. F. hair, cheveux flous.

fluid, *a. & s.* Fluide (*m*).

fluke, *s.* Coup de veine, de hasard.

flurry[1], *s.* Agitation *f*, émoi *m.*

flurry[2], *v.tr.* Agiter, effarer. To get flurried, perdre la tête.

flush[1], *s.* **1.** Chasse *f.* **2.** (*a*) Éclat *m.* (*b*) Rougeur *f.*

flush[2], *v.i.* Rougir.

flush[3], *a.* F. with, à fleur, au ras, de.

flushed, *a.* Enfiévré; rouge. F. with success, ivre de succès.

Flushing. *Pr.n.* Flessingue *f.*

fluster[1], *s.* Agitation *f*, trouble *m.*

fluster[2], *v.tr.* Agiter, bouleverser.

flute, *s.* Flûte *f.*

flutter[1], *s.* **1.** Battement *m*; palpitation *f.* **2.** Agitation *f*, émoi *m.*

flutter[2], *v.i. & tr.* Battre des ailes : flotter ; palpiter.

fly[1], *s.* Mouche *f.*

fly[2]. I. *v.i.* **1.** Voler. To fly to Paris, se rendre à Paris en avion. **2.** (*a*) Aller à toute vitesse; fuir. To fly at, s'élancer sur. To fly into a rage, s'emporter. The door flew open, la porte s'ouvrit en coup de vent. (*b*) Jaillir. **3.** To let fly, lancer. **4.** (*a*) Fuir, s'enfuir. To fly from danger, fuir le danger. (*b*) *v.tr.* To fly the country, s'enfuir du pays.

II. **fly,** *v.tr.* **1.** To fly a flag, battre (un) pavillon. **2.** Faire voler. **3.** Piloter. **fly away,** *v.i.* S'envoler. **fly back,** *v.i.* Faire ressort. **fly off,** *v.i.* S'envoler.

flyer, *s.* Aviateur, -trice.

flying[1], *a.* **1.** Volant, flottant. **2.** Court, passager.

flying[2], *s.* (*a*) Vol *m.* (*b*) Aviation *f.* F. ground, terrain *m* d'aviation.

flying-boat, *s.* Hydravion *m* à coque.

fly-paper, *s.* Papier *m* attrape-mouches.

foal, *s.* Poulain *m.*

foam[1], *s* Écume *f*; mousse *f.*

foam[2], *v.i.* Écumer.

focus[1], *s.* Foyer *m.* In f., au point.

focus[2], *v.tr.* **1.** Concentrer. **2.** Mettre au point.

focusing, *s.* Mise *f* au point.

fodder, *s.* Fourrage *m.*

foe, *s.* Ennemi *m.*

fog[1], *s.* Brouillard *m*; brume *f*

fog[2], *v.tr.* Embrouiller.

foggy, *a.* **1.** Brumeux. It is f., il fait du brouillard. **2.** Voilé; confus.

fog-horn, *s.* Sirène *f.*

foible, *s.* Côté *m* faible; faible *m.*

foil[1], *s.* **1.** Feuille *f.* clinquant *m.* **2.** Repoussoir *m.*

foil[2], *s.* Fleuret *m.*

foil[3], *v.tr.* Faire échouer; déjouer.

foist, *v.tr.* Refiler; imposer

fold[1], *s.* Pli *m*, repli *m.*

fold[2]. **1.** *v.tr.* (*a*) Plier. To f. back, rabattre. (*b*) Enlacer. (*c*) To f. one's arms, (se) croiser les bras. **2.** *v.i.* Se (re)plier.

folding, *a.* Pliant.

folding-chair, *s.* Chaise pliante.

foliage, *s.* Feuillage *m.*

folio, *s.* **1.** Folio *m*, feuille *f.* **2.** In-folio *m inv.*

folk, *s.pl.* Gens *mf*, personnes *f.* My f., les miens, ma famille.

folk-lore, *s.* Folklore *m.*

folk-song, *s.* Chanson *f* populaire.

follow. I. *v.tr.* **1.** Suivre. (*a*) To f. about, suivre partout. (*b*) Succéder à. **2.** Être le partisan de. **3.** Suivre, se conformer à. **4.** Exercer suivre. **5.** Suivre, comprendre.

II. **follow,** *v.i.* **1.** Suivre. As follows, ainsi qu'il suit. **2.** S'ensuivre, résulter. **follow up,** *v.tr.* **1.** Suivre de près. **2.** Poursuivre.

follower, *s.* (*a*) Serviteur *m*, satellite *m.* (*b*) Partisan *m*, disciple *mf.*

following[1], *a.* **1.** Qui suit. **2.** (*a*) Suivant. On the f. day, le jour suivant; le lendemain. (*b*) The f. resolution, la résolution que voici. (*c*) De suite.

following[2], *s.* (*a*) Suite *f.* (*b*) Parti *m.*

folly, *s.* Folie *f*, sottise *f.*

foment, *v.tr.* Fomenter.

fomentation, *s.* Fomentation *f.*

fond, *a.* **1.** Affectueux, tendre. **2.** To be f. of, aimer; être amateur de. F. of sweets, friand de sucreries.

fondle, *v.tr.* Caresser, câliner

fondly, *adv.* Tendrement.

fondness, *s.* **1.** Affection *f*, tendresse *f*. **2.** Penchant *m*, prédilection *f*.

food, *s.* **1.** Nourriture *f*; aliments *mpl*; vivres *mpl*. **2. F. and drink**, le boire et le manger.

food-stuffs, denrées *f*.

fool[1], *s.* **1.** Imbécile *mf*; idiot, -ote. **To make a f. of oneself**, se rendre ridicule. **2.** Dupe *f*.

fool[2]. **1.** *v.i.* Faire la bête. **2.** *v.tr.* Berner, duper.

foolery, *s.* Sottise *f*, bêtise *f*.

foolhardiness, *s.* Témérité *f*.

foolhardy, *a.* Téméraire.

fooling, *s.* **1.** Bouffonnerie *f*. **2.** Duperie *f*.

foolish, *a.* **1.** Sot, *f.* sotte; bête. **2.** Absurde, ridicule.

foolishly, *adv.* Sottement, bêtement.

foolishness, *s.* Sottise *f*, bêtise *f*.

foolscap, *s.* Papier *m* ministre.

foot[1], *s.* **1.** Pied *m*. (*a*) **To keep one's feet**, rester debout. **To put one's f. down**, faire acte d'autorité. (*b*) **Swift of f.**, léger à la course. (*c*) *Adv.phr.* **On foot.** (i) A pied. (ii) Debout. (iii) Sur pied, en train. **2.** Pied; patte *f* (de chien). **3.** Infanterie *f*. **4.** (*a*) Bas bout (d'une table). (*b*) Base *f*.

football, *s.* **1.** Ballon *m*. **2.** Le football.

footballer, *s.* Joueur *m* de football.

foot-bridge, *s.* Passerelle *f*; pont *m* pour piétons.

footfall, *s.* (Bruit *m* de) pas *m*.

foot-hills, *s.pl.* Contreforts *m*.

foothold, *s.* Assiette *f* de pied. To get a f., prendre pied.

footing, *s.* **1.** I missed my f., le pied me manqua. **2.** (*a*) **To gain a f.**, s'implanter. (*b*) **On a war f.**, sur le pied de guerre.

footlights, *s.pl.* Rampe *f*.

footman, *s.* Valet de pied *m*.

foot-note, *s.* Note *f* au bas de la page.

foot-passenger, *s.* Piéton *m*.

footpath, *s.* Sentier *m*; trottoir *m*.

footprint, *s.* Empreinte *f* de pas.

foot-soldier, *s.* Fantassin *m*.

footsore, *a.* Aux pieds endoloris.

footstep, *s.* Pas *m*; trace *f*.

footstool, *s.* Tabouret *m*.

foot-wear, *s.* Chaussures *fpl*.

foppish, *a.* Bellâtre, fat.

foppishness, *s.* Élégance affectée.

for[1], *prep.* Pour. I. **1.** (*a*) **Member for Liverpool**, député de Liverpool. (*b*) **To exchange for**, échanger contre. **To sell for ten francs**, vendre dix francs. **2.** (*a*) **What for?** pourquoi (faire)? **For sale**, à vendre. **For example**, par exemple. (*b*) **To jump for joy**, sauter de joie. **3. His feelings for you**, ses sentiments envers vous. **4.** Pendant; depuis. **5. To care for**, aimer. **Fit for nothing**, bon à rien. **6.** (*a*) **As for**, quant à. (*b*) **For all that**, malgré tout. (*c*) **But for her**, sans elle. (*d*) **Word for word**, mot à mot.

II. **1. It is easy for him**, il lui est facile (de). **2. It is not for me**, ce n'est pas à moi (de).

for[2], *conj.* Car.

forage[1], *s.* Fourrage *m*.

forage[2], *v.i.* Fourrager.

forbear, *v.i.* S'abstenir.

forbearance, *s.* Patience *f*.

forbearing, *a.* Patient, endurant.

forbid, *v.tr.* **1.** Défendre, interdire. 'Smoking forbidden'', ''défense de fumer.'' **To f. s.o. to**, défendre à qn de. **2.** Empêcher.

forbidding, *a.* Sinistre, rébarbatif.

force[1], *s.* Force *f*. **1.** (*a*) Violence *f*, contrainte *f*. (*b*) Influence *f*, autorité *f*. **2.** (*a*) Énergie *f*; intensité *f*. (*b*) Force, effort *m*. **3.** Puissance *f*; force. **4. To be in force**, être en vigueur.

force[2], *v.tr.* Forcer. **1.** (*a*) **She forced a smile**, elle eut un sourire contraint. (*b*) **To f. one's way**, se frayer un chemin. **2.** Contraindre, obliger.

force back, *v.tr.* Repousser; faire reculer.

forced, *a.* Forcé **1.** Obligatoire. **2.** Contraint.

forceful, *a.* Plein de force; énergique.

forceps, *s.sg. & pl.* Pince *f*; davier *m*.

forcible, *a.* **1.** De, par, force. **2.** Énergique, vigoureux.

forcibly, *adv.* **1.** Par force, de force. **2.** Énergiquement.

ford[1], *s.* Gué *m*.

ford[2], *v.tr.* Guéer, traverser à gué.

fore[1]. I. *a.* Antérieur, -e; de devant. II. **fore**, *s.* (*a*) Avant *m*. (*b*) **To the f.**, en évidence.

fore², *int.* Attention, gare, devant !

forearm, *s.* Avant-bras *m inv.*

forebode, *v.tr.* Présager, augurer.

foreboding, *s.* **1.** Présage *m.* **2.** Pressentiment.

forecast¹, *s.* Prévision *f.*

forecast², *v.tr.* Calculer, prévoir.

forecastle, *s.* Poste *m* de l'équipage.

forefather, *s.* Ancêtre *m.*

forefinger, *s.* Index *m.*

fore-foot, *s.* Pied antérieur ; patte *f* de devant.

forefront, *s.* Premier rang.

foregoing, *a.* Précédent, antérieur, -e. **The f.**, ce qui précède.

foregone, *a.* Prévu.

foreground, *s.* Premier plan.

forehead, *s.* Front *m.*

foreign, *a.* Étranger. **F. trade**, commerce extérieur. **The F. Office** = le Ministère des Affaires étrangères.

foreigner, *s.* Étranger, -ère.

foreland, *s.* Cap *m*, promontoire *m.*

foreleg, *s.* Jambe *f* de devant ; patte *f* de devant.

foreman, *s.* Contremaître *m* ; chef d'équipe.

foremost. 1. *a.* Premier ; le plus avancé. **2.** *adv.* **First and f.**, tout d'abord.

forenoon, *s.* Matinée *f.*

forerunner, *s.* Avant-coureur *m.*

foresee, *v.tr.* Prévoir, entrevoir.

foreseeing, *a.* Prévoyant.

foreshadow, *v.tr.* Annoncer.

foresight, *s.* Prévoyance *f.*

forest, *s.* Forêt *f.*

forestall, *v.tr.* Anticiper, devancer.

forestry, *s.* Sylviculture *f.*

foretaste, *s.* Avant-goût *m.*

foretell, *v.tr.* **1.** Prédire. **2.** Présager.

forethought, *s.* **1.** Préméditation *f.* **2.** Prévoyance *f.*

forewarn, *v.tr.* Prévenir, avertir.

foreword, *s.* Avant-propos *m inv.*

forfeit, *v.tr.* Perdre ; payer de.

forfeiture, *s.* Perte *f.*

forge¹, *s.* Forge *f.*

forge², *v.tr.* **1.** Forger. **2.** Contrefaire.

forged, *a.* **1.** Forgé. **2.** Faux, *f.* fausse, contrefait.

forger, *s.* Faussaire *mf.*

forgery, *s.* **1.** Contrefaçon *f* ; falsification *f.* **2.** Faux *m*

forget, *v.tr.* Oublier. **1. F. about it!** n'y pensez plus ! **2.** *(a)* Omettre, oublier. **Don't f. to**, ne manquez pas de *(b)* Négliger.

forgetful, *a.* **1.** Oublieux. **2.** Négligent.

forgetfulness, *s.* **1.** *(a)* Manque *m* de mémoire. *(b)* Oubli *m.* **2.** Négligence *f.*

forget-me-not, *s.* Myosotis *m.*

forgivable, *a.* Pardonnable.

forgive, *v.tr* **1.** Pardonner. **2.** Pardonner à.

forgiveness, *s.* **1.** Pardon *m.* **2.** Indulgence *f*, clémence *f.*

forgiving, *a.* Indulgent ; peu rancunier.

forgo, *v.tr.* Renoncer à ; s'abstenir de.

fork¹, *s.* **1.** Fourchette *f.* **2.** Fourche *f.* **3.** Bifurcation *f*, fourche.

fork², *v.i.* Fourcher.

forked, *a.* Fourchu, bifurqué.

forlorn, *a.* *(a)* Abandonné, délaissé. *(b)* Triste.

form¹, *s.* **1.** *(a)* Forme *f.* *(b)* Figure *f*, silhouette *f.* **2.** *(a)* Forme, formalité *f.* *(b)* **It is bad f.**, c'est de mauvais ton. **3.** Formule *f.* **4.** Forme ; condition *f.* **5.** Classe *f.* **6.** Banc *m*, banquette *f.*

form². I. *v.tr.* Former.
    II. **form**, *v.i.* Prendre forme ; se former.

formal, *a.* **1.** Formel. **2.** Cérémonieux.

formality, *s.* **1.** Formalité *f* **2.** Cérémonie *f.*

formally, *adv.* **1.** Formellement. **2.** Cérémonieusement.

formation, *s.* Formation *f.*

former, *a.* **1.** Antérieur, -e, précédent, ancien. **In f. times**, autrefois. **2. The f.**, *pron.* Celui-là, celle-là, ceux-là, celles-là.

formerly, *adv.* Autrefois, jadis.

formidable, *a.* Formidable, redoutable.

formula, *s.* Formule *f.*

formulate, *v.tr.* Formuler.

forsake, *v.tr.* Abandonner.

fort, *s.* Fort *m.*

forth, *adv.* **And so f.**, en ainsi de suite.

forthcoming, *a.* **1.** *(a)* Qui arrive. *(b)* Prochain, à venir. **2. To be f.**, ne pas se faire attendre.

forthwith, *adv.* Sur-le-champ ; tout de suite.

fortification, *s.* Fortification *f.*

fortify, *v.tr.* Fortifier.

fortitude, *s.* Force *f* d'âme.

fortnight, *s.* Quinzaine *f* ; quinze jours *m.*

fortnightly. **1.** *a.* Bimensuel. **2.** *adv.* Tous les quinze jours.

fortress, *s.* Forteresse *f.*

fortuitous, *a.* Fortuit, imprévu.

fortuitously, *adv.* Fortuitement ; par hasard.

fortunate, *a.* **1.** Heureux, fortuné. **To be f.,** avoir de la chance. **2.** Propice, heureux.

fortunately, *adv.* **1.** Heureusement. **2.** Par bonheur.

fortune, *s.* Fortune *f.* **1.** (*a*) Hasard *m,* chance *f.* (*b*) Sort *m.* **2.** (*a*) Bonne chance ; bonheur *m.* (*b*) Richesses *fpl,* biens *mpl.* **To make a f.,** faire fortune.

fortune-teller, *s.* Diseur, -euse, de bonne aventure.

fortune-telling, *s.* La bonne aventure.

forty, *num. a. & s.* Quarante (*m*). **About f.,** une quarantaine de.

forward[1]. **I.** *a.* **1.** Progressif, en avant. **2.** Avancé ; précoce. **3.** Effronté.
II. forward, *adv.* **1.** From that day **f.,** à partir de ce jour-là. **To look f. to,** attendre avec plaisir. **2.** (*a*) En avant. **To move f.,** avancer. **Straight f.,** tout droit. (*b*) A l'avant. **3. To come f.,** se proposer.

forward[2], *v.tr.* **1.** Avancer, favoriser. **2.** (*a*) Expédier, envoyer. (*b*) 'Please **f.,**' "prière de faire suivre."

forwarding, *s.* **1.** Avancement *m.* **2.** Expédition *f.*

forwardness, *s.* **1.** Avancement *m.* **2.** Effronterie *f.*

fossil, *a. & s.* Fossile (*m*).

foster, *v.tr.* Entretenir.

foster-brother, *s.* Frère *m* de lait.

foster-child, *s.* Nourrisson, -onne.

foster-mother, *s.* (Mère) nourrice.

foster-sister, *s.* Sœur *f* de lait.

foul[1]. **I.** *a.* **1.** Infect, nauséabond. **2.** (*a*) **To fall f. of,** se brouiller avec. (*b*) **F. weather,** gros temps. **3.** Déloyal, -aux.
II. foul, *s.* Faute *f.*

foul[2], *v.tr.* **1.** Salir, souiller. **2.** Obstruer.

foully, *adv.* Abominablement.

found, *v.tr.* Fonder.

foundation, *s.* **1.** Fondation *f.* **2.** Fondement *m.*

founder[1], *s.* Fondateur *m.*

founder[2], *v.i.* Sombrer.

foundling, *s.* Enfant trouvé, -ée

foundry, *s.* Fonderie *f.*

fount[1], *s.* Source *f.*

fount[2], *s.* Fonte *f.*

fountain, *s.* Fontaine *f.*

fountain-head, *s.* Source *f.*

fountain-pen, *s.* Porte-plume *m inv* (à) réservoir.

four, *num. a. & s.* Quatre (*m*). **On all fours,** à quatre pattes.

fourfold. **1.** *a.* Quadruple. **2.** *adv.* Quatre fois autant ; au quadruple.

four-footed, *a.* Quadrupède ; à quatre pattes.

fourteen, *num. a. & s.* Quatorze (*m*).

fourteenth, *num. a. & s.* Quatorzième. **(On) the f. of March,** le quatorze mars.

fourth. **1.** *num. a. & s* Quatrième. **(On) the f. of June,** le quatre juin. **2.** *s.* Quart *m.*

fowl, *s.* **1.** (*a*) Volatile *m.* (*b*) *Coll:* Oiseaux. **Wild f.,** gibier *m* d'eau. **2.** Poule *f,* coq *m* ; volaille *f.*

fowler, *s.* Oiseleur *m.*

fowl-house, *s.* Poulailler *m.*

fox, *s.* Renard *m.*

fox-cub, *s.* Renardeau *m.*

fox-glove, *s.* Digitale *f.*

fox-hound, *s.* Chien courant.

fox-hunting, *s.* La chasse au renard.

foxiness, *s.* Astuce *f,* roublardise *f.*

fox-terrier, *s.* Fox *m.*

fraction, *s.* **1.** Petite portion ; fragment *m.* **2.** Fraction *f.*

fractious, *a.* (*a*) Revêche. (*b*) Pleurnicheur, -euse.

fracture[1], *s.* Fracture *f.*

fracture[2], *v.tr.* Casser, briser.

fragile, *a.* Fragile ; faible.

fragility, *s.* Fragilité *f.*

fragment, *s.* Fragment *m* ; éclat *m.*

fragrance, *s.* Parfum *m.*

fragrant, *a.* Parfumé, odorant.

frail, *a.* **1.** Fragile ; frêle **2.** Faible, délicat.

frailty, *s.* Faiblesse *f.*

frame[1], *s.* **1.** Construction *f,* forme *f.*

F. of mind, disposition *f* d'esprit.
2. Cadre *m*.

frame[2], *v.tr.* **1.** Former. **2.** Projeter
3. Imaginer. **4.** Encadrer.

framework, *s.* Charpente *f* ossature
f, carcasse *f*.

France. *Pr.n.* La France.

franchise, *s.* Droit *m* de vote.

Francis. *Pr.n.* François *m*.

frank, *a.* Franc. *f.* franche.

frankly, *adv.* Franchement ; ouvertement.

frankness, *s.* Franchise *f*, sincérité *f*.

frantic, *a.* Frénétique, forcené ; fou
f. folle.

frantically, *adv.* Frénétiquement.

fraternal, *a.* Fraternel.

fraternity, *s.* **1.** Fraternité *f.* **2.**
Confrérie *f*.

fraternize, *v.i.* Fraterniser.

fraud, *s.* **1.** (*a*) Fraude *f.* (*b*) Supercherie *f.* **2.** Imposteur *m*.

fraudulent, *a.* Frauduleux.

fraudulently, *adv.* Frauduleusement

fray[1], *s.* Bagarre *f*, échauffourée *f*

fray[2], *v.i.* S'érailler, s'effiler.

freak, *s.* **1.** Caprice *m*; lubie *f*.
2. F. (of nature) phénomène *m*,
curiosité *f*.

freakish, *a.* Capricieux, fantasque.

freckle, *s.* Tache *f* de rousseur.

freckled, *a.* Taché de rousseur.

free[1], *a. & adv.* **1.** (*a*) Libre. (*b*) En
liberté. **2.** (*a*) **F. speech,** libre
parole. (*b*) Franc, *f.* franche. (*c*) **F.
from,** débarrassé de. (*d*) Exempt.
3. (*a*) **F. choice,** choix arbitraire.
(*b*) Libéral, -aux. (*c*) Franc, ouvert,
aisé. **F. and easy,** sans gêne. (*d*) **To
make f.,** prendre des libertés. **4.**
Gratuit ; franco *inv.* **Post f.,** franco
de port.

free[2], *v.tr.* (*a*) Affranchir ; libérer
(*b*) Débarrasser.

freedom, *s.* **1.** (*a*) Liberté *f*, indépendance *f*. (*b*) **F. of speech,** le
franc-parler. **2.** (*a*) Franchise *f*,
familiarité *f*. (*b*) Sans-gêne *m*.
3. Exemption *f*, immunité *f*

freely, *adv.* **1.** Librement, volontairement. **2.** Franchement.

freemason, *s.* Franc-maçon *m*. *pl.*
francs-maçons.

freemasonry, *s.* Franc-maçonnerie *f*.

free-thinker, *s.* Libre penseur ;
esprit fort.

free trade, *s.* Libre-échange *m*.

free will, *s.* Libre arbitre *m*. **Of one's
own f. w.,** de son propre gré.

freeze. **1.** *v.i.* (*a*) Geler. (*b*) (Se)
geler ; prendre. (*c*) **To f. to death,**
mourir de froid. **2.** *v.tr.* Geler,
congeler ; glacer.

freight, *s.* **1.** (*a*) Fret *m*. (*b*) Transport *m*. **2.** Fret, cargaison *f*.

French, I. *a.*(*a*) Français. (*b*) **F. lesson,**
leçon de français.
II. **French,** *s.* **1.** Le français. **To
speak F.,** parler français. **2.** *pl.* **The
F.,** les Français.

Frenchman, *s.* Français *m*.

French window, *s.* Porte-fenêtre *f*,
pl. portes-fenêtres.

Frenchwoman, *s.* Française *f*.

frenzied, *a.* Affolé, forcené.

frenzy, *s.* Frénésie *f*; transport *m*.

frequent[1], *a.* **1.** Nombreux. **2.**
Fréquent ; qui arrive souvent.

frequent[2], *v.tr.* Fréquenter, hanter.

frequently, *adv.* Fréquemment.

fresh. I. *a.* **1.** (*a*) Nouveau, -el, -elle.
(*b*) Frais, *f.* fraîche ; récent. **2.** Inexpérimenté. **3. F. water,** eau douce.
In the f. air, en plein air. **4.** Frais,
fleuri.
II. **fresh,** *adv.* Fraîchement,
nouvellement.

freshen. **1.** *v.i.* (Of wind) Fraîchir.
2. *v.tr.* Rafraîchir.

freshly, *adv.* Fraîchement, nouvellement.

freshness, *s.* **1.** Fraîcheur *f.* **2.** (*a*)
Vivacité *f.* (*b*) Inexpérience *f*.

fret. **1.** *v.tr.* (*a*) Ronger. (*b*) Inquiéter. **2.** *v.pr. & i.* Se tourmenter.

fretful, *a.* Chagrin ; irritable.

fretfully, *adv.* Avec irritation

fretfulness, *s.* Irritabilité *f*.

fret-saw, *s.* Scie *f* à découper.

fretwork, *s.* Travail ajouré.

friable, *a.* Friable.

friar, *s.* Moine *m*, frère *m*.

friction, *s.* **1.** Frottement *m*. **2.** Désaccord *m*.

Friday, *s.* Vendredi *m.* **Good F.,**
(le) Vendredi saint.

friend, *s.* **1.** Ami, *f.* amie. **To make
friends with,** se lier d'amitié avec.
2. Connaissance *f*.

friendless, *a.* Délaissé ; sans amis.

friendliness, *s.* Bienveillance *f*,
bonté *f* (towards, envers).

friendly, *a.* **1.** Amical, -aux ; sympathique. **On f. terms,** en bons rapports. **2.** Bienveillant, favorablement disposé. **3.** F. **society,** association *f* de bienfaisance.

friendship, *s.* Amitié *f.*

frieze, *s.* **1.** Frise *f.* **2.** Bordure *f.*

frigate, *s.* Frégate *f.*

fright, *s.* Peur *f,* effroi *m* **To take f.,** s'effrayer (*at,* de).

frighten, *v.tr.* Effrayer ; faire peur à.

frightened, *a.* Apeuré, épeuré **To be f.,** avoir peur.

frightening, *a.* Effrayant.

frightful, *a.* Affreux, épouvantable.

frightfulness, *s.* **1.** Horreur *f,* atrocité *f.* **2.** Terrorisme *m.*

frigid, *a.* Glacial, -als ; froid

frigidity, *s.* Frigidité *f.*

frill, *s.* Volant *m,* ruche *f.*

ʹringe, *s.* **1.** Frange *f.* **2.** (*a*) Bordure *f.* (*b*) Cheveux *mpl* à la chien

frisk, *v.i.* S'ébattre.

frisky, *a.* Vif, folâtre ; fringant.

fritter¹, *s.* Beignet *m.*

fritter², *v.tr.* **To f. away,** gaspiller

frivolity, *s.* Frivolité *f.*

frivolous, *a.* Frivole ; vain, futile.

frivolously, *adv.* Frivolement.

frizzle, *v.i.* Grésiller.

frizzy, *a.* Crêpelé, frisotté

frock, *s.* **1.** Robe *f.* **2.** Froc *m.*

frock-coat, *s.* Redingote *f.*

frog, *s.* Grenouille *f.*

frolic¹, *s.* (*a*) Ébats *mpl.* gambades *fpl.* (*b*) Fredaine *f.*

frolic², *v.i.* S'ébattre, folâtrer.

frolicsome, *a.* Gai, joyeux, folâtre.

from, *prep.* **1.** De. **2.** Depuis, dès, à partir de. **As f.,** à partir de. **3.** (*a*) De, à. **He stole a book f.,** il a volé un livre à. (*b*) **To shelter f.,** s'abriter contre. **4.** (*a*) D'avec, de. (*b*) **To drink f. the brook,** boire au ruisseau. **5. Tell him that f. me,** dites-lui cela de ma part. **6.** D'après. **F. what I can see,** à ce que je vois.

front¹, I. *s.* **1.** Front *m.* **2.** Devant *m* ; façade *f* ; plastron *m* (de chemise). **3. To come to the f.,** arriver au premier rang. **4.** *Adv.phr.* **In f.,** devant, en avant. **In f. of,** (i) en face de ; (ii) devant. II. **front,** *a.* Antérieur, -e, de devant, de face **F. seat,** siège au premier rang.

front², *v.tr. & i.* Faire face à.

frontage, *s.* (*a*) Étendue *f* du devant. (*b*) Façade *f.*

front-door, *s.* Porte *f* sur la rue.

frontier, *s.* Frontière *f.*

frontispiece, *s.* Frontispice *m.*

frost, *s.* Gelée *f,* gel *m.* **Ten degrees of f.,** dix degrés de froid.

frost-bite, *s.* Gelure *f.*

frost-bitten, *a.* Gelé.

frosted, *a.* **1.** Givré. **2.** Dépoli.

frosty, *a.* **1.** Gelé ; glacial, -als. **2.** Couvert de givre.

froth¹, *s.* Écume *f* ; mousse *f*

froth², *v.i.* Écumer, mousser.

frothy, *a.* Écumeux ; mousseux.

frown¹, *s.* Froncement *m* de sourcils ; regard sévère.

frown², *v.i.* Froncer les sourcils. **To f. upon,** désapprouver.

frowning, *a.* Renfrogné : sourcilleux ; menaçant.

frozen, *a* (*a*) Gelé, glacé. (*b*) Congelé.

frugal, *a.* **1.** Frugal, -aux ; économe. **2.** Frugal, simple.

frugality, *s.* Frugalité *f.*

frugally, *adv.* Frugalement

fruit, *s.* Fruit *m.*

fruiterer, *s.* Fruitier, -ière.

fruitful, *a.* Fructueux ; fertile.

fruitfully, *adv.* Fructueusement, utilement.

fruitfulness, *s.* Fertilité *f.*

fruition, *s.* **To come to f.,** fructifier.

fruitless, *a.* Vain.

fruitlessly, *adv.* Vainement

fruit-tree, *s.* Arbre fruitier.

frustrate, *v.tr.* (*a*) Faire échouer ; frustrer. (*b*) Contrecarrer.

frustration, *s.* Frustration *f.*

fry. **1.** *v.tr.* (Faire) frire. **Fried eggs,** œufs sur le plat. **2.** *v.i.* Frire.

frying-pan, *s.* Poêle *f.*

fuddle, *v.tr.* Brouiller les idées de.

fuddled, *a.* Brouillé.

fuel, *s.* Combustible *m.*

fugitive, *a. & s.* Fugitif, -ive.

fulcrum, *s.* Point *m* d'appui *m.*

fulfil, *v.tr.* (*a*) Répondre à, remplir. (*b*) Satisfaire. (*c*) Accomplir.

fulfilment, *s.* (*a*) Accomplissement *m.* (*b*) Exécution *f.*

full. I. *a.* **1.** Plein, rempli, comble. **2.** Plein, complet, -ète. **To be f. up,** avoir son plein. **F. up !** complet !

3. F. **particulars,** tous les détails.
4. Complet, entier. **In f. flight,** en pleine déroute.
II. **full,** s. **1.** Plein. **2.** *adv.phr.* (a) **In f.,** en toutes lettres. (b) **To the f.,** complètement, tout à fait.
III. **full,** *adv.* Justement. en plein.
fullness, s. **1.** Plénitude *f,* totalité *f.* **2.** Ampleur *f* ; abondance *f.*
full stop, s. Point.
fully, *adv.* **1.** Pleinement, entièrement, complètement. **2.** Au moins.
fulminate, *v.i.* Fulminer.
fulsome, *a.* Écœurant.
fumble, *v.i.* Fouiller ; tâtonner.
fumbling, *a.* Maladroit, gauche.
fume, s. Fumée *f,* vapeur *f.*
fumigate, *v.tr.* Fumiger.
fun, s. Amusement *m,* gaieté *f* ; plaisanterie *f.* **To make fun of,** se moquer de. **For fun, in fun,** pour rire.
function[1], s. **1.** Fonction *f.* **2.** Cérémonie publique ; solennité *f.*
function[2], *v.i.* Fonctionner.
functionary, s. Fonctionnaire *m.*
fund, s. **1.** Fonds *m.* **2.** *pl.* **To be in funds,** être en fonds.
fundamental, *a.* Fondamental, -aux ; essentiel.
fundamentally, *adv.* Fondamentalement, foncièrement.
funeral, s. (a) Funérailles *fpl* ; obsèques *fpl* (b) Convoi *m* funèbre.
funereal. *a.* Lugubre ; sépulcral, -aux.
fungus, s. Champignon *m.*
funnel, s. **1** Entonnoir *m.* **2.** Cheminée *f.*
funnily, *adv.* **1.** Drôlement. **2.** Curieusement. **F. enough,** chose curieuse.
funny, *a* Drôle. **1.** Comique, amusant, facétieux **2.** Curieux, bizarre.
funny-bone, s. Le petit juif.
fur, s. (a) Fourrure *f.* (b) Poil *m,* pelage *m.* (c) *pl* Peaux *fpl.*
furbish, *v.tr.* **1.** Fourbir, polir. **2.** (Re)mettre à neuf, retaper.
furious, *a.* Furieux ; furibond. **F. driving,** conduite folle.
furiously, *adv.* Furieusement.
furl, *v.tr.* Serrer, ferler.

furlough, s. Congé *m,* permission *f.*
furnace, s. **1.** Fourneau *m,* four *m.* **2.** Calorifère *m.*
furnish, *v.tr.* **1.** Fournir, pourvoir (*with,* de). **2.** Meubler, garnir.
furnishings, *s.pl.* Ameublement *m.*
furniture, s. Meubles *mpl,* ameublement *m.* **Piece of f.,** meuble.
furrier, s. Fourreur *m.*
furrow[1], s. **1.** Sillon *m.* **2.** Cannelure *f,* rainure *f.*
furrow[2], *v.tr.* Sillonner.
further[1]. I. *adv.* **1.** Plus loin. **F. off,** plus éloigné. **2.** (a) Davantage, plus. (b) Plus avant. (c) D'ailleurs, de plus.
II. **further,** *a.* **1.** Plus lointain, plus éloigné. **2.** Nouveau, -el, -elle, -eaux, additionnel.
further[2], *v.tr.* Avancer, favoriser.
furthermore, *adv.* En outre, de plus.
furthest. **1.** *a.* (a) Le plus lointain, le plus éloigné. (b) Le plus long. **2.** *adv.* Le plus loin.
furtive, *a.* Furtif ; sournois.
furtively, *adv.* Furtivement.
fury, s. Furie *f.* fureur *f* ; acharnement *m.*
furze, s. Ajonc *m.*
fuse[1], s. Fusée *f* ; amorce *f.*
fuse[2], s. Fusible *m* ; plomb *m.*
fuse[3]. **1.** *v.tr.* (a) Fondre (b) Amalgamer. **2.** *v.i.* Fondre.
fusible, *a.* Fusible.
fusilier, s. Fusilier *m.*
fusillade, s. Fusillade *f.*
fusion, s. Fusion *f.*
fuss[1], s. **1.** Bruit exagéré. **2.** Embarras *mpl* ; façons *fpl.* **To make a f. of,** être aux petits soins pour.
fuss[2]. **1.** *v.i.* Tatillonner. **To f. about,** faire l'affairé. **2.** *v.tr.* Tracasser, agiter.
fussily, *adv.* D'un air important.
fussiness, s. Façons *fpl.*
fussy, *a.* Tracassier, méticuleux.
fusty, *a.* **F. smell,** odeur de renfermé.
futile, *a.* **1.** Futile, vain. **2.** Puéril.
futility, s. **1.** Futilité *f.* **2.** Puérilité *f.*
future. **1.** *a.* Futur ; à venir ; d'avenir. **2.** s. Avenir *m.* **In (the) f.,** à l'avenir.
fuzzy, *a* (i) Bouffant, flou ; (ii) crêpelu, frisotté.

G

G, g, *s.* (La lettre) G, g *m.*
gabble¹, *s.* **1.** Bredouillement *m.*
2. Caquet *m,* jacasserie *f.*
gabble², *v.i.* (*a*) Bredouiller. (*b*) Caqueter, jacasser.
gable, *s.* Pignon *m.*
gad-fly, *s.* Taon *m.*
gadget, *s.* Chose *m,* machin *m.*
Gaelic, *a. & s.* Gaélique (*m*).
gaff¹, *s.* Gaffe *f.*
gaff², *v.tr.* Gaffer.
gag¹, *s.* Bâillon *m.*
gag², *v.tr.* Bâillonner.
gaiety, *s.* Gaîté *f,* gaieté *f.*
gaily, *adv.* Gaiement, allégrement.
gain¹, *s.* **1.** Gain *m,* profit *m.* **2.** Augmentation *f.*
gain², *v.tr.* Gagner. **1.** Acquérir. **2.** Avancer de. *Abs.* Avancer.
gainsay, *v.tr.* Contredire.
gait, *s.* Allure *f,* démarche *f.*
gaiter, *s.* Guêtre *f.*
gala, *s.* Fête *f,* gala *m.*
galantine, *s.* Galantine *f.*
gale, *s.* **1.** Coup *m* de vent ; vent fort. **2.** Tempête *f.*
gall¹, *s.* Fiel *m.*
gall², *s.* Écorchure *f,* excoriation *f.*
gall³, *v.tr* (*a*) Écorcher. (*b*) Irriter
gallant, *a.* **1.** Vaillant. **2.** Galant.
gallantly, *adv.* Galamment.
gallantry, *s.* **1.** Vaillance *f,* bravoure *f.* **2.** Galanterie *f.*
gallery, *s.* (*a*) Galerie *f.* (*b*) (Troisième) galerie ; paradis *m.*
galley, *s.* **1.** Yole *f.* **2.** Cuisine *f*
galley-slave, *s.* Galérien *m.*
galling, *a.* Irritant, exaspérant
gallop¹, *s.* Galop *m.*
gallop², *v.i. & tr.* Galoper.
galloping, *a.* Au galop.
gallows, *s* Potence *f,* gibet *m*
galosh, *s.* Caoutchouc *m.*
galvanic, *a.* Galvanique.
galvanize, *v.tr.* Galvaniser.
gamble¹, *s.* Jeu *m* de hasard
gamble², *v.i.* Jouer.
gambler, *s.* Joueur, -euse.
gambling, *s.* Le jeu.
gambol¹, *s.* Gambade *f.*
gambol², *v.i.* Gambader.
game, *s.* **1.** (*a*) Amusement *m,* jeu *m.* (*b*) Jeu. (*c*) **To play the g.,** jouer franc jeu. (*d*) Partie *f* ; manche *f.* **The deciding g.,** la belle. **2.** Gibier *m.* **Big g.,** les grands fauves.
game-bag, *s.* Carnassière *f* gibecière *f.*
game-cock, *s.* Coq *m* de combat.
gamekeeper, *s.* Garde-chasse *m, pl.* gardes-chasse(s).
gaming-table, *s.* Table *f* de jeu
gamut, *s.* Gamme *f.*
gander, *s.* Jars *m.*
gang, *s.* (*a*) Équipe *f.* (*b*) Bande *f.*
gangway, *s.* **1.** Passage *m.* **2.** Passerelle *f* de service.
gaol, *s.* Prison *f.*
gap, *s.* (*a*) Trou *m* ; trouée *f.* (*b*) Interstice *m* ; intervalle *m.* (*c*) Trou, lacune *f* vide *m.*
gape, *v.i.* **1.** (*a*) Bâiller (*b*) S'ouvrir (tout grand). **2.** Rester bouche bée.
gaping, *a.* Béant.
garage¹, *s.* Garage *m.* **G. keeper,** garagiste *m.*
garage², *v.tr.* Garer ; remiser.
garb, *s.* Vêtement *m,* costume *m.*
garbage, *s.* Immondices *fpl.*
garble, *v.tr.* Tronquer ; dénaturer.
garden, *s.* (*a*) Jardin *m* **Winter g.,** hall vitré. (*b*) *pl.* Jardin public.
garden-city, *s.* Cité-jardin *f, pl.* cités-jardins.
gardener, *s.* Jardinier, -ière.
gardening, *s.* Jardinage *m* ; horticulture *f*
garden-party, *s* Réception en plein air.
gargle, *v.i.* Se gargariser.
gargoyle, *s.* Gargouille *f.*
garland, *s.* Guirlande *f.*
garlic, *s.* Ail *m.*
garment, *s.* Vêtement *m.*
garnish, *v.tr.* Garnir, orner.
garnishing, *s.* Garniture *f.*
garret, *s.* Mansarde *f.* galetas *m*
garrison, *s.* Garnison *f.*
garrulous, *a.* Loquace, bavard
garter, *s.* Jarretière *f.*
gas, *s.* Gaz *m.* **To have gas,** se faire anesthésier.
gaseous, *a.* Gazeux.
gas-fire, *s.* Radiateur *m* à gaz.
gash¹, *s.* Coupure *f,* entaille *f.*
gash², *v.tr.* Entailler, couper.

gas-light, s. Lumière *f* du gaz.

gas-mask, s. Masque *m* à gaz.

gas-meter, s. Compteur *m* (à gaz).

gasometer, s. Gazomètre *m*.

gasp[1], s. (a) Hoquet *m* (b) Soupir *m*.

gasp[2], v.i. (a) Avoir un hoquet. (b) **To g. for breath,** haleter, suffoquer.

gas-pipe, s. Tuyau *m* à gaz.

gas-ring, s. (Brûleur *m* à) couronne *f*.

gas-stove, s. Fourneau *m* à gaz.

gastric, a. Gastrique.

gate, s. **I.** Porte *f* **2. (Wooden) g.,** barrière *f*.

gateway, s. Porte *f*, entrée *f*.

gather. I. v.tr. **I.** (a) Assembler, rassembler. (b) Ramasser. (c) Cueillir. **To g.** (in) **the harvest,** rentrer la récolte. **2. To g. speed,** prendre de la vitesse. **3.** Conclure.

II. gather, v.i. **I.** (a) Se réunir, se rassembler. (b) S'attrouper. **2.** S'accumuler.

gathering, s. **I.** (a) Rassemblement *m*. (b) Cueillette *f*. **2.** (a) Assemblée *f*. (b) Abcès *m*.

gaudily, adv. De manière voyante.

gaudiness, s. Clinquant *m*.

gaudy, a. Voyant, criard.

gauge[1], s. **I.** Calibre *m*. **2.** Indicateur *m*.

gauge[2], v.tr. Jauger, mesurer.

gaunt, a. Maigre, décharné.

gauze, s. Gaze *f*.

gawky, a. Dégingandé, gauche.

gay, a. **I.** Gai, allègre. **2.** Gai, brillant.

gaze[1], s. Regard *m* fixe.

gaze[2], v.i. Regarder fixement.

gazelle, s. Gazelle *f*.

gazette, s. **I.** Journal officiel. **2.** *Cin :* Topical G., actualités *fpl*.

gazetteer, s. Répertoire *m* géographique.

gear, s. **I.** (a) Effets, (b) Attirail *m*, appareil *m*. **2.** (a) **In g.,** engrené. **Out of g.,** désengrené. (b) Vitesse *f*.

gear-box, s. Boîte *f* de vitesses.

gelatine, s. Gélatine *f*.

gelatinous, a. Gélatineux.

gem, s. Pierre précieuse ; gemme *f*. joyau *m*.

gender, s. Genre *m*.

genealogical, a. Généalogique.

genealogy, s. Généalogie *f*.

general. I. a. Général, -aux **I.** (a) **The g. public,** le grand public. (b) **G. servant,** bonne *f* à tout faire.

2. adv.phr. **In g.,** en général ; généralement.

II. general, s. Général *m*.

generalization, s. Généralisation *f*.

generalize, v.tr. Généraliser.

generally, adv. Généralement ; en général.

generate, v.tr. Générer, produire

generating, a. Générateur, -trice.

generation, s. Génération *f*.

generosity, s. Générosité *f*

generous, a. Généreux.

generously, adv. Généreusement.

Geneva. Pr.n. Genève *f*. **The Lake of G.,** le lac Léman.

genial, a. (a) Doux, *f*. douce ; clément. (b) Plein de bonne humeur.

geniality, s. (a) Douceur *f*. (b) Bienveillance *f* ; bonne humeur.

genially, adv. Affablement, cordialement.

genius, s. **I.** Génie *m* **2.** Aptitudes naturelles.

Genoa. Pr.n. Gênes *f*.

genteel, a. Comme il faut.

gentility, s. Prétention *f* à la distinction, au bon ton.

gentle, a. **I.** Bien né **2.** Doux. *f*. douce

gentlefolk, s.pl. (a) Gens *m* comme il faut. (b) Personnes *f* de bonne famille

gentleman, s.m. **I.** Galant homme ; homme comme il faut. **2.** Monsieur *m*. **Ladies and gentlemen!** mesdames et messieurs ! **Gentlemen's hairdresser,** coiffeur pour hommes. **3.** Cavalier *m*.

gentlemanly, a. Comme il faut ; bien élevé.

gentleness, s. Douceur *f*.

gently, adv. Doucement.

genuine, a. (a) Authentique, véritable. (b) Véritable, sincère.

genuinely, adv. **I.** Authentiquement. **2.** Franchement, véritablement.

genuineness, s. **I.** Authenticité *f*. **2.** Sincérité *f*.

geographical, a. Géographique.

geography, s. Géographie *f*

geological, a. Géologique.

geologist, s. Géologue *m*

geology, s. Géologie *f*.

geometrical, a. Géométrique.

geometry, s. Géométrie *f*

geranium, s. Géranium *m*.

germ, *s.* Germe *m.*

German, *a. & s.* **1.** Allemand, -ande. **2.** *s.* L'allemand *m.*

germane, *a.* Se rapportant.

Germany. *Pr.n.* L'Allemagne *f.*

germinate, *v.i.* Germer.

gesticulate, *v.i.* Gesticuler.

gesticulation, *s.* Gesticulation *f.*

gesture, *s.* Geste *m*, signe *m.*

get. I. *v.tr.* **1.** (*a*) Procurer, obtenir. (*b*) Acquérir, gagner. (*c*) If I get the time, si j'ai le temps. **2.** (*a*) Recevoir. (*b*) Attraper. **3.** Aller chercher. **4. To get sth. ready,** préparer qch. **5. To get sth. done,** faire faire qch. **6.** I haven't got any, je n'en ai pas. **II. get,** *v.i.* **1.** Devenir. **To get angry,** se mettre en colère. (*b*) **To get killed,** se faire tuer. **2.** (*a*) Aller, arriver, se rendre. (*b*) Se mettre. (*c*) **To get to know,** apprendre. **get at,** *v.i.* Parvenir à, atteindre. **get away. 1.** *v.i.* (*a*) Partir. (*b*) S'échapper, se sauver. **2.** *v.tr.* Arracher. **get back. 1.** *v.i.* (*a*) Reculer. (*b*) Revenir, retourner. **2.** *v.tr.* Se faire rendre. **get by,** *v.i.* Passer. **get down. 1.** *v.i.* Descendre. **2.** *v.tr.* Descendre; décrocher. **get in,** *v.i.* Entrer; monter. **get into,** *v.i.* (*a*) Entrer dans; monter dans. (*b*) **To get into a rage,** se mettre en rage. **get off. I.** *v.i* **1.** (*a*) Descendre de. (*b*) Se faire exempter de. **2.** (*a*) Se tirer d'affaire; en être quitte (*with,* pour). (*b*) **To get off to sleep,** s'endormir. **II. get off,** *v.tr.* **1.** Ôter. **2.** Expédier. **get on. I.** *v.tr* Mettre. **II. get on,** *v.i.* **1.** Monter sur. **2.** Faire des progrès; réussir. **How are you getting on?** comment allez-vous? **get out. 1.** *v.tr.* (*a*) Tirer, retirer. (*b*) (Faire) sortir. **2.** *v.i.* (*a*) Sortir. (*b*) **To get out of a difficulty,** se débrouiller. **get over. 1.** *v.i.* (*a*) Franchir. (*b*) Se remettre de. **2.** *v.tr.* Faire passer par-dessus. **get through,** *v.i.* **1.** (*a*) Passer par. (*b*) Accomplir. **To g. t. the day,** faire passer la journée. **2.** Passer; être reçu. **get together. 1.** *v.i.* Se réunir, se rassembler. **2.** *v.tr.* Rassembler. **get up. I.** *v.i.* **1.** Monter à. **2.** Se lever. **II. get up,** *v.tr.* (*a*) Monter. (*b*) Faire lever. (*c*) Organiser.

geyser, *s.* **1.** Geyser *m.* **2.** Chauffe-bain *m,* *pl.* chauffe-bains.

ghastly, *a.* (*a*) Horrible, affreux. (*b*) Blême.

gherkin, *s.* Cornichon *m.*

ghost, *s.* Fantôme *m.* revenant *m.*

ghostly, *a.* Spectral, -aux.

ghost-story, *s.* Histoire *f* de revenants.

giant, *a. & s.* Géant (*m*)

giantess, *s.f.* Géante.

gibe[1]**,** *s.* Raillerie *f*; sarcasme *m.*

gibe[2]**,** *v.i.* **To g. at,** railler.

gibing, *a.* Moqueur, -euse.

giblets, *s.pl.* Abatis *m.*

giddiness, *s.* **1.** Étourdissement *m,* vertige *m.* **2.** Frivolité *f.*

giddy, *a.* **1.** (*a*) Étourdi. **I feel g.,** la tête me tourne. (*b*) Vertigineux. **2.** Frivole.

gift, *s.* Don *m*; cadeau *m.*

gifted, *a.* Bien doué.

gigantic, *a.* Géant, gigantesque.

giggle, *v.i.* Rire bêtement.

gild, *v.tr.* Dorer.

gilded, *a.* Doré.

gilding, *s.* Dorure *f.*

gills, *s.* *pl.* Ouïes *f,* branchies *f*

gilt, *s.* Dorure *f.*

gilt-edged, *a.* Doré sur tranche.

gimlet, *s.* Vrille *f*; foret *m.*

gin, *s.* Gin *m.*

ginger. 1. *s.* Gingembre *m.* **2.** *a.* Roux, *f.* rousse.

gingerbread, *s.* Pain *m* d'épice.

gipsy, *s.* Bohémien, enne; nomade *mf.*

giraffe, *s.* Girafe *f.*

girder, *s.* (*a*) Solive *f.* (*b*) Poutre *f.*

girdle, *s.* Ceinture *f.*

girl, *s.* **1.** Jeune fille *f.* **Little g.,** fillette *f.* **2.** Jeune personne *f.* **My eldest g.,** ma fille aînée.

girlish, *a.* **1.** De jeune fille. **2.** Efféminé.

girth, *s.* Circonférence *f.*

gist, *s.* Fond *m,* essence *f.*

give. I. *v.tr.* **1.** Donner. **2.** (*a*) Remettre. (*b*) Engager. **3. What did you g. for it?** combien l'avez-vous payé? **4. To g. a jump,** faire un saut; tressauter. **To g. a sigh,** pousser un soupir. **5. To g. s.o. one's hand,** tendre la main à qn. **6. To g. a toast,** porter un toast. **7.** (*a*) **To g. pleasure,** faire du plaisir. (*b*) Rendre. **8. To g. way.** (*a*) Céder; se casser;

s'affaisser. (b) Lâcher pied; s'abandonner.

II. **give**, v.i. Prêter, donner.

give away, v.tr. Donner. **give back**, v.tr. Rendre, restituer. **give in**, v.i. Céder; se rendre. **give off**, v.tr. Dégager, exhaler. **give out.** **1.** v.tr. (a) Distribuer. (b) Dégager. (c) Annoncer. **2.** v.i. Manquer; faire défaut. **give up**, v.tr. **1.** Rendre; abandonner; céder. **2.** (a) Renoncer à; abandonner. (b) Considérer comme perdu. **3.** Livrer.

given, a. **1.** Donné, convenu. **2.** Porté, enclin.

glacial, a. Glacial, -als.

glacier, s. Glacier m.

glad, a. Heureux; bien aise; content.

gladden, v.tr. Réjouir.

glade, s. Clairière f, éclaircie f.

gladly, adv. (a) Avec plaisir, volontiers. (b) Avec joie.

gladness, s. Joie f, allégresse f.

glamour, s. **1.** Enchantement m, charme m. **2.** Fascination f; éclat m.

glance[1], s. Regard m; coup d'œil. At a g., d'un coup d'œil.

glance[2], v.i. **1.** Jeter un regard (at, sur). To g. through, parcourir. **2.** To g. off, ricocher.

gland, s. Glande f.

glare[1], s. **1.** (a) Éclat m, clarté f. (b) Éblouissement m. **2.** Regard irrité.

glare[2], v.i. **1.** Briller d'un éclat éblouissant. **2.** Lancer un regard furieux.

glaring, a. **1.** Éblouissant. **2.** Manifeste.

glass, s. **1.** Verre m. **2.** pl. Lunettes f. **3.** The g. is falling, le baromètre baisse. **4.** Attrib. De, en, verre. G. door, porte vitrée.

glass-case, s. Vitrine f.

glassful, s. (Plein) verre.

glass-house, s. Serre f.

glass-ware, s. Verrerie f.

glassy, a. Vitreux.

glaucous, a. Glauque.

glaze. **I.** v.tr. Vitrer.

II. glaze, v.i. Devenir vitreux.

glazed, a. **1.** Vitré. **2.** Glacé.

glazier, s. Vitrier m.

gleam[1], s. (a) Rayon m, lueur f. (b) Reflet m.

gleam[2], v.i. Luire, reluire.

gleaming, a. Luisant.

glean, v.tr. Glaner.

glee, s. Joie f, allégresse f.

gleeful, a. Joyeux, allègre.

gleefully, adv. Joyeusement; allégrement.

glen, s. Vallée étroite; vallon m.

glide, v.i. (a) (Se) glisser, couler. (b) Planer.

glider, s. Planeur m, glisseur m.

gliding, s. (a) Glissement m. (b) Vol plané.

glimmer[1], s. Faible lueur f; miroitement m.

glimmer[2], v.i. Jeter une faible lueur; miroiter.

glimpse, s. Vision momentanée. To catch a g. of, entrevoir.

glint, s. Éclair m; reflet m.

glisten, v.i. Étinceler, scintiller.

glistening, a. Étincelant, scintillant.

glitter[1], s. Scintillement m.

glitter[2], v.i. Scintiller, étinceler.

glittering, a. Brillant, étincelant.

gloat, v.i. To g. over, savourer.

gloating, a. Avide.

globe, s. Globe m. (a) Sphère f. (b) Bocal m, -aux.

globular, a. Globulaire.

globule, s. Globule m, gouttelette f.

gloom, s. **1.** Obscurité f. **2.** Assombrissement m, mélancolie f.

gloomy, a. **1.** Sombre, obscur. **2.** Lugubre, morne, sombre.

glorious, a. **1.** Glorieux. **2.** (a) Resplendissant. (b) Superbe.

glory[1], s. Gloire f.

glory[2], v.i. To g. in, se glorifier de.

gloss, s. Lustre m, vernis m.

glossary, s. Glossaire m, lexique m.

glossy, a. Lustré, glacé, brillant.

glove, s. Gant m. The g. counter, la ganterie.

glow[1], s. **1.** Lueur f rouge; incandescence f. **2.** (a) Sensation f de chaleur. (b) Ardeur f, chaleur f.

glow[2], v.i. **1.** Rougeoyer. **2.** Rayonner.

glowing, a. **1.** Rougeoyant. **2.** Embrasé. **3.** Rayonnant. **4.** Chaleureux.

glow-worm, s. Ver luisant.

glue[1], s. Colle (forte)

glue[2], v.tr. Coller.

glum, a. Renfrogné, maussade.

glut, s. Surabondance f.

glutinous, *a.* Glutineux.

glutton, *s.* Gourmand, -ande ; glouton, -onne.

gluttonous, *a.* Glouton.

glycerine, *s.* Glycérine *f.*

gnarled, *a.* Noueux.

gnash, *v.tr.* Grincer (des dents).

gnat, *s.* Cousin *m.*

gnaw, *v.tr. & i.* Ronger.

go[1], *s.* **1.** Aller *m.* **2.** Entrain *m.* **3.** Coup *m,* essai *m.* **At one go,** d'un coup.

go[2], *v.i.* Aller. **1.** (*a*) **To come and go,** aller et venir. **To go a journey,** faire un voyage. **You go first!** à vous d'abord. (*b*) **To go to the head,** monter à la tête. (*c*) **To go hungry,** souffrir de la faim. (*d*) **To go one's own way,** faire à sa guise. **2.** Marcher. (*a*) **It has just gone twelve,** midi vient de sonner. (*b*) Aboutir ; tourner. **3.** Passer. **4.** (*a*) Partir ; s'en aller. **After I have gone,** après mon départ. (*b*) Disparaître. **It has all gone,** il n'y en a plus. **5.** (*a*) **To go and see s.o.,** aller trouver qn. (*b*) **He is going to see about it,** il va s'en occuper. (*c*) **To go fishing,** aller à la pêche. **6. To go to war,** se mettre en guerre. **7. To go to prove,** servir à prouver. **8.** S'étendre. **9.** (*a*) Devenir. (*b*) **To go to ruin,** tomber en ruine. **10.** (*a*) **Let me go!** lâchez-moi ! (*b*) **To let oneself go,** se laisser aller. **go about,** *v.i.* **How to go a. it,** comment s'y prendre. **go across,** *v.i.* Traverser ; franchir. **go along,** *v.i.* Passer par. **go away,** *v.i.* S'en aller, partir. **go back,** *v.i.* (*a*) Retourner. (*b*) Revenir (sur un sujet). **go by,** *v.i.* **1.** Passer. **2.** Suivre ; juger d'après. **go down,** *v.i.* **1.** Descendre. **2.** (*a*) Se coucher. (*b*) Couler à fond. (*c*) Tomber. (*d*) Baisser. **go for,** *v.i.* Aller chercher. **go forward,** *v.i.* Avancer. **go in,** *v.i.* (*a*) Entrer. (*b*) S'occuper (*for,* de). **go into,** *v.i.* **1.** Entrer dans. **2.** Examiner, étudier. **go off,** *v.i.* **1.** (*a*) Partir. (*b*) Se passer. **2. To go off the rails,** dérailler. **go on,** *v.i.* **1.** (*a*) Marcher ; continuer sa route. (*b*) Continuer ; reprendre la parole. (*c*) Se passer. **How are you going on?** comment allez-vous ? **2.** Se fonder sur, **go**

out, *v.i.* **1.** Sortir. **2.** Passer. **3. To go out of one's way,** s'écarter de son chemin. **4.** S'éteindre. **5.** Se retirer. **go over,** *v.i.* (*a*) Traverser, passer. (*b*) Examiner. **go round,** *v.i.* (*a*) Faire un détour. (*b*) Tourner. (*c*) Circuler. **go through,** *v.i.* **1.** (*a*) Passer par ; traverser. (*b*) Remplir ; subir, essuyer. (*c*) Percer. (*d*) Examiner en détail. **2.** Aller jusqu'au bout (*with,* de). **go under,** *v.i.* Succomber, sombrer. **go up,** *v.i.* **1.** (*a*) Monter. (*b*) **To go up to,** aborder. (*c*) Monter, hausser. **2.** Monter à. **go with,** *v.i.* **1.** (*a*) Accompagner. (*b*) Marcher avec. **2.** S'accorder avec. **go without,** *v.i.* (*a*) Se passer de. (*b*) Manquer de.

goad[1], *s.* Aiguillon *m.*

goad[2], *v.tr.* Aiguillonner, piquer.

go-ahead, *a.* Plein d'allant ; entreprenant.

goal, *s.* But *m.*

goat, *s.* Chèvre *f* ; bouc *m.*

goatherd, *s.* Chevrier, -ière.

go-between, *s.* Intermédiaire *mf*

goblet, *s.* Verre *m* à pied.

goblin, *s* Lutin *m.*

god, *s.* **1.** Dieu *m.* **2. Thank God!** Dieu merci ! grâce au ciel !

god-child, *s.* Filleul, *f.* filleule.

god-daughter, *s.* Filleule *f.*

goddess, *s.* Déesse *f.*

godfather, *s.* Parrain *m.*

godless, *a.* Athée, impie.

godliness, *s.* Piété *f.*

godly, *a.* Dévot, pieux, saint.

godmother, *s.* Marraine *f.*

god-parent, *s.* Parent spirituel.

godsend, *s.* Aubaine *f.*

godson, *s.* Filleul *m.*

goggles, *s.pl.* Lunettes *fpl.*

gold, *s.* (*a*) Or *m.* (*b*) Couleur *f* de l'or.

gold-dust, *s.* Poudre *f,* poussière *f,* d'or.

golden, *a.* D'or.

gold-field, *s.* Champ *m* aurifère.

goldfinch, *s.* Chardonneret *m.*

gold-fish, *s.* Poisson *m* rouge.

gold-laced, *a.* Galonné d'or ; chamarré d'or.

gold-leaf, *s.* Feuille *f* d'or ; or *m* en feuille.

gold-mine, *s.* Mine *f* d'or.

gold-plated, *a.* Doublé d'or.

goldsmith, s. Orfèvre m.

golf, s. Golf m.

golf-club, s. 1. Crosse ƒ de golf.
2. Club m de golf.

golf-course, s. Terrain m de golf

golfer, s. Golfeur, -euse.

golosh, s. Caoutchouc m.

gondola, s. Gondole ƒ.

gondolier, s. Gondolier m

gong, s. Gong m.

good. I. a. Bon. 1. (a) G. handwriting, belle écriture. (b) G. reason,
raison valable. (c) That's a g. thing!
tant mieux ! à la bonne heure ! Very
g.! très bien ! (d) G. day! bonjour !
G. evening! bonsoir ! 2. (a) G.
man, homme de bien. (b) Sage.
(c) Aimable. 3. A g. while, pas mal
de temps. A g. deal, beaucoup. 4.
It is as g. as new, c'est comme neuf.
II. good, s. 1. Bien m. (a) That
won't be much g., ça ne servira pas
à grand'chose. (b) It is all to the g.,
c'est autant de gagné. (c) Adv.phr.
He is gone for g., il est parti pour
de bon. 2. pl. (a) Biens, effets m.
(b) By goods train, en petite vitesse.

good-bye, int. & s. Adieu m.

good-class, a. De choix.

good-feeling, s. Bonne entente.

good-humoured, a. De bonne
humeur.

good-looking, a. Beau, ƒ belle.

good nature, s. Bonté ƒ.

good-natured, a. Bon.

goodness, s. 1. (a) Bonté ƒ. 2. Thank
g.! Dieu merci !

goose, s. Oie ƒ.

gooseberry, s. (a) Groseille ƒ à
maquereau, groseille verte. (b) G.
(-bush), groseillier m (à maquereau).

gore, v.tr. Blesser avec les cornes.

gorge, s. Gorge ƒ, défilé m.

gorgeous, a. Magnifique splendide.

gorilla, s. Gorille m.

gorse, s. Ajonc(s) m(pl).

gory, a. Sanglant, ensanglanté.

gosling, s. Oison m.

gospel, s. Évangile m.

gossamer, s. Gaze légère.

gossip¹, s. (a) Causerie ƒ. (b) Cancans m(pl).

gossip², v.i. Bavarder.

Gothic, a. Gothique.

gourd, s. Gourde ƒ, calebasse ƒ.

gourmand, s. Gourmand m.

gourmet, s. Gourmet m.

gout, s. Goutte ƒ.

gouty, a. Goutteux.

govern, v.tr. 1. Gouverner ; administrer. 2. Maîtriser.

governess, s. Institutrice ƒ.

government, s. Gouvernement m.

governor, s. Gouverneur m.

gown, s. Robe ƒ

grace¹, s. 1. Grâce ƒ. 2. Bénédicité m.

grace², v.tr. Embellir, orner.

graceful, a. Gracieux.

gracefully, adv. Avec grâce.

gracefulness, s. Grâce ƒ, élégance ƒ.

gracious, a. Gracieux.

graciously, adv. Avec bienveillance.

grade, s. (a) Grade m, rang m,
degré m. (b) Qualité ƒ; classe ƒ.

gradient, s. Rampe ƒ; pente ƒ.

gradual, a. Graduel, progressif.

gradually, adv. Graduellement ;
peu à peu.

graft, v.tr. Greffer, enter.

grain, s. 1. Grain m. 2. Fil m.
Against the g., à contre-fil.

grammar, s. Grammaire ƒ.

grammatical, a. Grammatical, -aux.

grammatically, adv. Grammaticalement.

gramophone, s. Gramophone m

granary, s. Grenier m.

grand, a. 1. (a) Grand ; principal,
-aux. G. stand, tribune ƒ. (b) G.
total, total global. 2. Grandiose,
magnifique.

grandchild, s. Petit-fils m ; petite-
fille ƒ, pl. petits-enfants m.

grand-daughter, s. ƒ. Petite-fille, pl.
petites-filles.

grandeur, s. Grandeur ƒ.

grandfather, s. Grand-père m, pl.
grands-pères.

grandmother, s. Grand'mère ƒ, pl.
grand'mères.

grandparent, s. Grand-père m,
grand'mère ƒ; pl. grands-parents m.

grandson, s. Petit-fils m, pl. petits-
fils.

granite, s. Granit m.

grant¹, s. 1. (a) Concession ƒ. (b)
Don m, cession ƒ. 2. Subvention ƒ.

grant², v.tr. 1. (a) Accorder, concéder. (b) Exaucer ; accéder à.
2. To take for granted, présumer ;
prendre pour admis.

granular, a. Granulaire, granuleux.

granulated, *a.* Granulé.

grape, *s.* (a) Grain *m* de raisin. (b) *pl.* Raisin *m.*

grape-fruit, *s.* Pamplemousse *f.*

graphic, *a.* Pittoresque, vivant.

grapple, *v.i.* En venir aux prises.

grasp[1], *s.* (a) Poigne *f.* (b) Prise *f;* étreinte *f.* (c) Compréhension *f.*

grasp[2], *v.tr.* 1. (a) Saisir; empoigner; serrer. (b) S'emparer, se saisir, de. 2. Comprendre.

grasping, *a.* Apre au gain.

grass, *s.* 1. Herbe *f.* 2. Gazon *m.*

grasshopper, *s.* Sauterelle *f.*

grassy, *a.* Herbeux.

grate[1], *s.* Foyer *m,* âtre *m.*

grate[2], *v.i.* To g. on, choquer.

grateful, *a.* 1. Reconnaissant 2. Agréable; réconfortant.

gratefully, *adv.* Avec reconnaissance

gratefulness, *s.* Reconnaissance *f.*

grater, *s.* Râpe *f.*

gratification, *s.* Satisfaction *f.*

gratified, *a.* Satisfait, content (*with*, de); flatté.

gratify, *v.tr.* 1. Faire plaisir, être agréable, à. 2. Satisfaire.

gratifying, *a.* Agréable; flatteur, -euse.

grating[1], *a.* Discordant, grinçant.

grating[2], *s.* Grille *f,* grillage *m.*

gratis. 1. *a.* Gratis, gratuit. 2. *adv.* Gratis, gratuitement.

gratitude, *s.* Gratitude *f,* reconnaissance *f* (*to,* envers).

gratuitous, *a.* Gratuit.

gratuity, *s.* Gratification *f;* pourboire *m*

grave[1], *s.* Tombe *f,* tombeau *m.*

grave[2], *a.* Grave, sérieux.

grave-digger, *s.* Fossoyeur *m.*

gravel, *s.* Gravier *m.*

gravely, *adv.* Gravement, sérieusement.

gravity, *s.* Gravité *f.*

gravy, *s.* Jus *m.*

gray, *a.* & *s.* Gris (*m*).

graze[1], *v.i.* Paître, brouter.

graze[2], *s.* Écorchure *f,* éraflure *f.*

graze[3], *v.tr.* 1. Écorcher, érafler. 2. Effleurer, raser.

grease[1], *s.* Graisse *f.*

grease[2], *v.tr.* Graisser.

greasy, *a.* 1. Graisseux. 2. Gras, *f.* grasse.

great, *a.* Grand. (a) A g. many,

beaucoup de. **The greater part,** la plupart. **To a g. extent,** en grande partie. (b) It is no g. **matter,** ce n'est pas une grosse affaire.

great-coat, *s.* Pardessus *m.*

greatly, *adv.* Grandement; beaucoup; très

greatness, *s.* Grandeur *f.*

Greece. *Pr.n.* La Grèce.

greed, *s.* Avidité *f,* cupidité *f.*

greedily, *adv.* 1. Avidement. 2. Avec gourmandise.

greedy, *a.* 1. Avide cupide. 2. Gourmand.

Greek. 1. *a.* & *s.* Grec, *f.* grecque. 2. *s.* Le grec.

green. 1. *a.* Vert. (a) To grow g., verdir. (b) Naïf, *f.* naïve. 2. *s.* (a) Vert *m.* (b) *pl.* Légumes verts. (c) Pelouse *f.*

greenery, *s.* Verdure *f,* feuillage *m.*

greengage, *s.* Reine-Claude *f, pl.* reines-Claude.

greengrocer, *s.* Marchand -ande, de légumes; fruitier, -ière.

greenhouse, *s.* Serre *f.*

greenish, *a.* Verdâtre.

greet, *v.tr.* Saluer, aborder.

greeting, *s.* Salutation *f,* salut *m; pl.* compliments *m.*

gregarious, *a.* Grégaire.

grenade, *s.* Grenade *f.*

grey, *a.* & *s.* Gris (*m*).

grey-haired, *a.* Aux cheveux gris

greyhound, *s.* Lévrier *m.*

greyish, *a.* Grisâtre.

gridiron, *s.* Gril *m.*

grief, *s.* Chagrin *m,* douleur *f.* **To come to g.,** avoir un accident.

grievance, *s.* 1. Grief *m.* 2. Injustice *f.*

grieve. 1. *v.tr.* Chagriner, affliger. 2. *v.i.* Se chagriner, s'affliger.

grieved, *a.* Chagriné, affligé.

grievous, *a.* 1. Douloureux, pénible. 2. Grave, lamentable.

grill[1], *s.* Grillade *f.*

grill[2], *s.* Gril *m.*

grill[3], *v.tr.* Griller, brasiller.

grille, *s.* Grille *f.*

grim, *a.* Sinistre; sévère.

grimace[1], *s.* Grimace *f.*

grimace[2], *v.i.* Grimacer.

grime, *s.* Saleté *f.*

grimly, *adv.* Sinistrement, sévèrement.

grimy, *a.* Sale, encrassé, noirci.

grin[1], *s.* **1.** Grimace *f* **2.** Large sourire.

grin[2], *v.i.* Grimacer.

grind. 1. *v.tr.* (*a*) Moudre. **To g. to dust,** réduire en poudre. (*b*) Repasser. (*c*) **To g. one's teeth,** grincer des dents. **2.** *v.i.* Grincer.

grinder, *s.* Rémouleur *m.*

grindstone, *s.* Meule *f* à aiguiser.

grip[1], *s.* **1.** Prise *f*; étreinte *f.* **To come to grips,** en venir aux mains. **2.** Poignée *f.*

grip[2], *v.tr.* Saisir, empoigner.

gristle, *s.* Cartilage *m,* croquant *m.*

grit, *s.* Grès *m,* sable *m.*

grizzled, *a.* Grisonnant.

groan[1], *s.* Gémissement *m.*

groan[2], *v.i.* Gémir.

grocer, *s.* Épicier, -ière.

grocery, *s.* Épicerie *f.*

groin, *s.* **1.** Aine *f.* **2.** (*a*) Arête *f.* (*b*) Nervure *f.*

groom, *s.* Valet *m* d'écurie.

groove, *s.* **1.** Rainure *f.* **2.** **To get into a g.,** devenir routinier.

grope, *v.i.* Tâtonner. **To g. one's way,** avancer à tâtons.

groping, *a.* Tâtonnant.

gross, *a.* **1.** Gras, *f.* grasse; gros, *f.* grosse. **2.** Grossier; crasse. **G. injustice,** injustice flagrante. **3.** Brut.

grossly, *adv.* Grossièrement; outre mesure.

grotesque, *a.* Grotesque; absurde.

grotto, *s.* Grotte *f.*

ground[1], *a.* Moulu, broyé, pilé.

ground[2], *s.* **1.** Fond *m.* **2.** *pl.* Marc *m.* **3.** Raison *f,* cause *f.* **4.** (*a*) Sol *m,* terre *f.* **Above g.,** sur terre. (*b*) Terrain *m.* **To stand one's g.,** tenir bon. (*c*) *pl.* Terrains, parc *m,* jardin *m.*

ground-floor, *s.* Rez-de-chaussée *m.*

groundless, *a.* Sans fondement.

group[1], *s.* Groupe *m.*

group[2], **1.** *v.tr.* Grouper. **2.** *v.i.* Se grouper.

grove, *s.* Bocage *m,* bosquet *m.*

grovel, *v.i.* Ramper.

grovelling, *a.* Rampant.

grow. 1. *v.i.* **1.** (*a*) Croître, pousser. (*b*) Germer. **2.** Grandir. **To g. up,** grandir. **3.** S'accroître, croître. **4.** Devenir.
II. **grow,** *v.tr.* **1.** Cultiver; planter. **2.** Laisser pousser.

growing, *a.* **1.** Croissant. **2.** Grandissant.

growl[1], *s.* Grognement *m.*

growl[2], *v.i.* & *tr.* Grogner.

grown-up, *a.* Grand.

growth, *s.* **1.** Croissance *f.* **2.** Accroissement *m*; augmentation *f.*

grub, *s.* (*a*) Larve *f.* (*b*) Ver *m.*

grubby, *a.* Sale, malpropre.

grudge[1], *s.* Rancune *f.*

grudge[2], *v.tr.* Donner, accorder, à contre-cœur.

grudging, *a.* **1.** Donné à contre-cœur. **2.** Avare.

gruesome, *a.* Macabre, affreux.

gruff, *a.* Bourru, revêche, rude.

gruffly, *adv.* D'un ton bourru.

grumble, *v.i.* & *tr.* Grommeler, grogner, murmurer.

grumbler, *s.* **1.** Grognard. -arde. **2.** Mécontent, -ente.

grumbling[1], *a.* Grondeur, -euse.

grumbling[2], *s.* Mécontentement *m.*

grumpy, *a.* Maussade, grincheux.

grunt[1], *s.* Grognement *m.*

grunt[2], *v.i.* Grogner, grognonner.

guarantee[1], *s.* Garantie *f*; caution *f.*

guarantee[2], *v.tr.* Garantir.

guaranteed, *a.* Avec garantie.

guard[1], *s.* **1.** Garde *f.* (*a*) **To be on one's g.,** être sur ses gardes. (*b*) **To be on g.,** être en faction. **2.** *Coll.* Garde *f.* **3.** Chef *m* de train. **4.** Corps-de-garde *m inv.*

guard[2]. **1.** *v.tr.* (*a*) Garder. (*b*) Protéger. **2.** *v.i* **To g. against,** se garder de.

guarded, *a.* Prudent, mesuré.

guardian, *s.* **1.** Gardien, -ienne. **2.** Tuteur, -trice.

guard-room, *s.* Corps-de-garde *m.*

Guernsey, *Pr.n.* Guernesey *m.*

guess[1], *s.* Conjecture *f,* estimation *f.*

guess[2], *v.tr.* & *i.* **1.** **To g. at,** deviner, conjecturer. **2.** **To g. right,** bien deviner.

guest, *s.* **1.** Convive *mf*; invité, -ée; hôte, -esse. **2.** Pensionnaire *mf*; client, -ente.

guest-house, *s.* Pension *f* de famille.

guidance, *s.* Direction *f,* gouverne *f,* conduite *f.*

guide[1], *s.* **1.** Guide *m.* **2.** **G.(-book),** (livret-)guide *m.* **Railway g.,** indicateur *m* des chemins de fer. **3.** Indication *f,* exemple *m.*

guide², *v.tr.* Guider, conduire.
guile, *s.* Artifice *m*, ruse *f*, astuce *f*.
guileless, *a.* **1.** Franc, *f.* franche. **2.** Candide.
guillotine¹, *s.* Guillotine *f*.
guillotine², *v.tr.* Guillotiner.
guilt, *s.* Culpabilité *f*.
guiltily, *adv.* D'un air coupable.
guiltless, *a.* Innocent.
guilty, *a.* Coupable.
guinea-fowl, *s.* Pintade *f*.
guinea-pig, *s.* Cochon *m* d'Inde.
guise, *s.* Apparence *f*.
guitar, *s.* Guitare *f*.
gulf, *s.* **1.** Golfe *m*. **2.** Gouffre *m*, abîme *m*.
gull, *s.* Mouette *f*, goéland *m*.
gullible, *a.* Facile à duper.
gully, *s.* (Petit) ravin ; couloir *m*.
gulp, *s.* **At one g.,** d'un coup.
gum¹, *s.* Gomme *f*.

gum², *v.tr.* Coller.
gum³, *s.* Gencive *f*.
gum-arabic, *s.* Gomme *f* arabique.
gun, *s.* **1.** Canon *m*. **2.** Fusil *m*.
gunboat, *s.* Canonnière *f*.
gunpowder, *s.* Poudre *f* (à canon).
gunwale, *s.* Plat-bord *m*, *pl.* plats-bords.
gurgle, *v.i.* Glouglouter.
gush, *v.i.* Jaillir, couler à flots.
gust, *s.* **G. of wind,** coup *m* de vent ; rafale *f*.
gusty, *a.* Venteux.
gutter, *s.* **1.** Gouttière *f*. **2.** Ruisseau *m*.
guttural, *a.* Guttural, -aux.
gymnasium, *s.* Gymnase *m*.
gymnast, *s.* Gymnaste *m*.
gymnastic. **1.** *a.* Gymnastique. **2.** *s.pl.* Gymnastique *f*.
gyrate, *v.i.* Tourner ; tournoyer.
gyroscope, *s.* Gyroscope *m*.

H

H, h, *s.* (La lettre) H, h *mf*.
ha, *int.* Ha ! ah !
haberdasher, *s.* **1.** Chemisier *m*. **2.** Mercier *m*.
haberdashery, *s.* **1.** Chemiserie *f*. **2.** Mercerie *f*.
habit, *s.* Habitude *f*, coutume *f*.
habitable, *a.* Habitable.
habitation, *s.* Habitation *f*.
habitual, *a.* Habituel, d'habitude.
habitually, *adv.* Habituellement, d'habitude.
habituate, *v.tr.* Habituer.
hack, *v.tr. & i.* Hacher ; tailler.
hackneyed, *a.* Rebattu, usé.
haddock, *s.* Aiglefin *m*.
haggard, *a.* (a) Hâve. (b) Hagard.
haggle, *v.i.* Marchander.
Hague (the). *Pr.n.* La Haye.
hail¹, *s.* Grêle *f*.
hail², *v.i. & tr.* It is hailing, il grêle.
hail³, *s.* Appel *m*. **Within h.,** à portée de voix.
hail⁴, *v.tr.* (a) Saluer. (b) Héler.
hail-stone, *s.* Grêlon *m*.
hail-storm, *s.* Orage accompagné de grêle.
hair, *s.* **1.** (a) Cheveu *m*. (b) *Coll.* The hair, les cheveux, la chevelure. To do one's h., se coiffer. **2.** (a)

Poil *m*. (b) *Coll.* Poil, pelage *m*. (c) Crin *m*.
hairbreadth, *a.* **To have a h. escape,** l'échapper belle.
hairbrush, *s.* Brosse *f* à cheveux.
hair-cut, *s.* Taille *f*, coupe *f*, de cheveux. To have a h.-c., se faire couper les cheveux.
hairdresser, *s.* Coiffeur, -euse.
hairdressing, *s.* Coiffure *f*.
hairpin, *s.* Épingle *f* à cheveux. H. bend, lacet *m*.
hair-restorer, *s.* Régénérateur *m* des cheveux.
hairy, *a.* Velu, poilu.
hake, *s.* Merluche *f*.
hale, *a.* Vigoureux.
half. **1.** *s.* (a) Moitié *f*. To cut in h., couper par moitié. (b) Demi *m*, demie *f*. Three and a half, trois et demi. (c) Return h., coupon *m* de retour. **2.** Demi. H. an hour, une demi-heure. **3.** *adv.* (a) A moitié. (b) It is h. past two, il est deux heures et demie. (c) H. as big, moitié aussi grand. H. as big again, plus grand de moitié.
half-breed, *s.* Métis, -isse.
half-brother, *s.* Demi-frère *m*, *pl.* demi-frères.
half-caste, *a. & s.* Métis, -isse.

half-closed, *a.* Entre-clos ; entr'ouvert.

half-dead, *a.* A moitié mort.

half-dozen, *s.* Demi-douzaine *f.*

half-fare, *s.* Demi-place *f.*

half-holiday, *s.* Après-midi *m or f*
libre.

half-hour, *s.* Demi-heure *f.*

half-sister, *s.* Demi-sœur *f, pl.*
demi-sœurs.

half-way, *adv.* A mi-chemin.

halibut, *s.* Flétan *m.*

hall, *s.* **1.** (Grande) salle. **2.** Château
m. **3.** Vestibule *m.* **H. porter,**
concierge *m.*

hall-mark, *s.* Poinçon *m.*

hallo, *int. & s.* Holà ! ohé !

hallucination, *s.* Hallucination *f.*

halo, *s.* Auréole *f.*

halt¹, *s.* Halte *f* ; arrêt *m.*

halt², *v.i.* S'arrêter. **H.!** halte !

halter, *s.* Licou *m,* longe *f.*

halting, *a.* Hésitant.

halve, *v.tr.* (*a*) Diviser en deux.
(*b*) Réduire de moitié.

ham, *s.* Jambon *m.* **Ham and eggs,**
œufs au jambon.

hamlet, *s.* Hameau *m.*

hammer¹, *s.* Marteau *m.*

hammer², *v.tr.* Marteler ; battre

hammock, *s.* Hamac *m.*

hamper¹, *s.* Manne *f,* banne *f.*

hamper², *v.tr.* Embarrasser, gêner.

hand¹, *s.* **1.** Main *f.* (*a*) On one's
hands and knees, à quatre pattes.
To take s.o.'s h., donner la main à
qn. Hands up! haut les mains !
(*b*) To have a h. in, se mêler de ;
tremper dans. (*c*) To have one's
hands full, avoir fort à faire. On
one's hands, à sa charge, sur les bras.
To change hands, changer de propriétaire, de mains. **2.** *Adv.phrs.* (*a*)
(Near) at h., sous la main. (*b*) Hat
in h., chapeau bas. **Revolver in
h.,** revolver au poing. **The matter
in h.,** la chose en question. (*c*) **Work
on h.,** travail en cours. (*d*) **On the
right h.,** du côté droit. On all hands,
partout. **On the one h.,** d'une part.
(*e*) **To come to h.,** arriver (à destination). (*f*) **H. in h.,** la main dans
la main. (*g*) **H. to h.,** corps *m* à corps.
(*h*) **From h. to mouth,** au jour le jour.
3. (*a*) Ouvrier, -ière ; manœuvre *m.*
(*b*) *pl.* Équipage *m.* **4.** *Cards :* Jeu *m.*

5. Aiguille *f* (de montre)　**6. H.
luggage,** bagages à main.

hand², *v.tr.* Passer, remettre. **hand
down,** *v.tr.* **1.** Descendre. **2.** Transmettre. **hand in,** *v.tr.* Remettre.
hand on, *v.tr.* Transmettre. **hand
out,** *v.tr.* Tendre, remettre. **hand
over,** *v.tr.* Remettre. **hand round,**
v.tr. Faire passer à la ronde.

hand-bag, *s.* Sac *m* à main ;
pochette *f.*

handbell, *s.* Sonnette *f,* clochette *f*

handbook, *s.* Guide *m* ; livret *m.*

handcuff, *v.tr.* Mettre les menottes à.

handcuffs, *s.pl.* Menottes *f.*

handful, *s.* Poignée *f.*

handicap¹, *s.* (*a*) Handicap *m.*
(*b*) Désavantage *m.*

handicap², *v.tr.* Handicaper.

handicapped, *a.* Désavantagé.

handicraft, *s.* Travail manuel.

handiwork, *s.* Ouvrage *m,* œuvre *f.*

handkerchief, *s.* Mouchoir *m.*

handle¹, *s.* (*a*) Manche *m* ; bras *m* ;
queue *f* ; poignée *f.* (*b*) Anse *f* ;
portant *m.*

handle², *v.tr.* **1.** Tâter des mains.
2. Manier.

handle-bar, *s.* Guidon *m.*

handling, *s.* (*a*) Maniement *m.* (*b*)
Rough h., traitement brutal.

hand-made, *a* Fait, fabriqué, à la
main.

hand-rail, *s.* Garde-fou *m, pl*
garde-fous.

hand-sewn, *a.inv.* Cousu à la main.

handshake, *s.* Poignée *f* de main.

handsome, *a.* (*a*) Beau, bel, beaux,
f. belle. (*b*) Gracieux, généreux.

handwriting, *s.* Écriture *f.*

handy, *a.* **1.** Adroit **2.** Maniable.
3. Commode. **4.** A portée (de la
main).

hang. I. *v.tr.* **1.** Pendre, suspendre
(*on,* à). **2.** To h. (down) one's head,
baisser la tête. **3.** To h. fire, traîner.
II. **hang,** *v.i.* **1.** Pendre, être
suspendu (*from,* à). **2.** Être pendu.
hang back, *v.i.* **1.** Rester en arrière.
2. Hésiter. **hang down,** *v.i.* **1.**
Pendre. **2.** Pencher. **hang out,**
v.tr. Pendre au dehors ; étendre.
hang up, *v.tr.* Accrocher pendre.

hangar, *s.* Hangar *m.*

hanging¹, *a.* Suspendu ; pendant.

hanging², *s.* **1.** (*a*) Suspension *f.*

(b) Pendaison f. **2.** pl. Tenture f; tapisserie f.

hangman, s. Bourreau m.

hank, s. Écheveau m.

haphazard. I. s. At h., au hasard. **2.** a. Fortuit. **3.** adv. A l'aventure.

happen, v.i. Arriver ; se passer, se produire. **Whatever happens,** quoi qu'il arrive. **It so happened,** le hasard a voulu. **As it happens,** justement.

happening, s. Événement m.

happily, adv. Heureusement.

happiness, s. Bonheur m, félicité f.

happy, a. Heureux. **1.** Heureux, bien aise, content. **2. H. thought!** bonne inspiration !

harangue[1], s. Harangue f.

harangue[2], v.tr. Haranguer.

harass, v.tr. Harasser, tracasser.

harbour[1], s. Port m.

harbour[2], v.tr. Héberger.

hard. I. a. **1.** Dur. **To get h.,** durcir. **2.** Difficile ; pénible. **3.** (a) Dur, sévère (to, envers). (b) H. fact, fait brutal. **4. To try one's hardest,** faire tout son possible. **5. H. frost,** forte gelée. **H. winter,** hiver rigoureux.

II. hard, adv. **1.** (a) Fort. **As h. as one can,** de toutes ses forces. **To look h. at,** regarder fixement. **To think h.,** réfléchir profondément. **It is raining h.,** il pleut à verse. (b) **To be h. up,** être à court. **2.** Difficilement. **3. H. by,** tout près.

hard-boiled, a. (Œuf) dur.

harden, v.tr. & i. Durcir.

hardened, a. Durci ; endurci.

hard-headed, a. Positif, pratique.

hard-hearted, a. Insensible, au cœur dur.

hardihood, s. Hardiesse f.

hardly, adv. **1.** (a) Sévèrement. (b) Péniblement. **2.** A peine ; ne . . . guère. **I h. know,** je n'en sais trop rien. **I need h. say,** point besoin de dire. **H. anyone,** presque personne.

hardness, s. **1.** Dureté f. **2.** (a) Difficulté f. (b) **H. of hearing,** dureté d'oreille. **3.** Sévérité f, rigueur f, dureté.

hardship, s. Privation f, fatigue f.

hardware, s. Quincaillerie f.

hard-working, a. Laborieux, assidu.

hardy, a. **1.** Hardi ; audacieux. **2.** Robuste ; endurci.

hare, s. Lièvre m. **Jugged h.,** civet m de lièvre.

haricot, s. Haricot blanc.

harlequin, s. Arlequin m.

harm[1], s. Mal m, tort m. **Out of harm's way,** à l'abri du danger.

harm[2], v.tr. Faire du mal à ; nuire à.

harmful, a. Malfaisant ; nuisible.

harmless, a. Inoffensif ; innocent.

harmonious, a. Harmonieux.

harmonize, v.i. S'harmoniser ; s'accorder.

harmony, s. Harmonie f.

harness[1], s. Harnais m.

harness[2], v.tr. **1.** (a) Harnacher. (b) Atteler. **2.** Aménager.

harpoon[1], s. Harpon m.

harpoon[2], v.tr. Harponner.

harrow[1], s. Herse f.

harrow[2], v.tr. Herser. **To h. s.o.'s feelings,** déchirer le cœur à qn.

harrowing, a. Poignant, navrant.

harry, v.tr. **1.** Dévaster. **2.** Harceler.

harsh, a. Dur, rude ; aigre, strident.

harshly, adv. Avec dureté.

harshness, s. **1.** Dureté f, rudesse f ; aigreur f. **2.** Sévérité f.

harvest[1], s. Moisson f.

harvest[2], v.tr. Moissonner. Abs. Rentrer, faire, la moisson.

harvester, s. **1.** Moissonneur, -euse. **2.** (Machine) Moissonneuse f.

hash, s. Hachis m.

haste, s. Hâte f, diligence f. **Make h.!** dépêchez-vous !

hasten. 1. v.tr. Accélérer, hâter. **2.** v.i. Se hâter, se dépêcher.

hastily, adv. **1.** A la hâte ; précipitamment. **2.** Sans réfléchir.

hastiness, s. **1.** Précipitation f, hâte f. **2.** Emportement m, vivacité f.

hasty, a. **1.** Précipité ; sommaire. **2.** Emporté, vif.

hat, s. Chapeau m.

hatch[1], s. Écoutille f.

hatch[2]. **1.** v.tr. Faire éclore ; ourdir (un complot). **2.** v.i. Éclore.

hatchet, s. Hachette f.

hate[1], s. Haine f.

hate[2], v.tr. Haïr, détester.

hateful, a. Odieux, détestable.

hat-peg, s. Patère f.

hatred, s. Haine f.

hat-stand, s. Porte-chapeaux m inv.

hatter, *s.* Chapelier, -ière.

haughtily, *adv.* Hautainement ; avec hauteur.

haughtiness, *s.* Hauteur *f.*

haughty, *a.* Hautain, altier.

haul, *v.tr.* Tirer ; traîner.

haunch, *s.* (*a*) Hanche *f.* (*b*) Cuissot *m*, quartier *m.*

haunt[1], *s.* Lieu fréquenté ; repaire *m.*

haunt[2], *v.tr.* (*a*) Fréquenter, hanter. (*b*) Obséder.

haunting, *a.* Obsédant.

have, *v.tr.* **1.** Avoir, posséder. **2.** (*a*) To h. news, recevoir des nouvelles. (*b*) Let me h. your keys, donnez-moi vos clefs. **3.** To h. tea with s.o., prendre le thé avec qn. **4.** (*a*) To h. a dream, faire un rêve. (*b*) To h. a pleasant evening, passer une soirée agréable. **5.** To h. sth. done, faire faire qch. **6.** Which one will you h.? lequel voulez-vous ? **7.** To h. to do sth., devoir faire qch. ; être obligé de faire qch. **8.** So I h.! En effet ! tiens, c'est vrai ! You haven't . . . —I have! vous n'avez pas . . .— Si ! Mais si !

haven, *s.* Havre *m*, port *m.*

haversack, *s.* Havresac *m.*

havoc, *s.* Ravage *m*, dégâts *mpl.*

hawk, *s.* Faucon *m.*

hawker, *s.* Colporteur *m.*

hawser, *s.* Haussière *f.*

hawthorn, *s.* Aubépine *f.*

hay, *s.* Foin *m.*

haymaker, *s.* Faneur, -euse.

haymaking, *s.* Fenaison *f.*

haystack, *s.* Meule *f* de foin.

hazard, *s.* **1.** (*a*) Hasard *m.* (*b*) Risque *m*, péril *m.* **2.** Accident *m* de terrain.

hazardous, *a.* Hasardeux, risqué.

haze, *s.* Brume légère.

hazel, *s.* Noisetier *m.*

hazel-nut, *s.* Noisette *f.*

hazy, *a.* **1.** Brumeux, embrumé. **2.** Nébuleux, fumeux, vague.

he, *pers.pron.* **1.** Il. Here he comes, le voici qui vient. He is an honest man, c'est un honnête homme. **2.** (*a*) Lui. It is he, c'est lui. (*b*) Celui. He that believes, celui qui croit.

head[1], *s.* **1.** Tête *f.* H. downwards, la tête en bas. H. first, h. foremost, la tête la première. To win by a h.,

gagner d'une tête. **2.** To take it into one's h., s'aviser, se mettre en tête. To keep one's h., conserver sa tête. To go off one's h., devenir fou. **3.** To come to a h., aboutir. **4.** (*a*) Chef *m.* (*b*) *Attrib.* H. clerk, premier commis. H. office, bureau principal. **5.** H. of a coin, face *f.*

head[2], *v.tr. & i.* Conduire, mener ; être à la tête de.

headache, *s.* Mal *m* de tête.

head-dress, *s.* Coiffure *f.*

heading, *s.* Rubrique *f* ; en-tête *m*, *pl.* en-têtes.

headland, *s* Cap *m*, promontoire *m.*

head-light, *s.* Phare *m.*

headlong. 1. *adv.* La tête la première ; tête baissée. **2.** *a.* Précipité. irréfléchi.

head-master, *s.* Principal *m* ; proviseur *m.*

head-mistress, *s.* Directrice *f.*

head-quarters, *s.pl.* Centre *m* ; bureau principal.

headstrong, *a.* Volontaire, têtu.

headway, *s.* Progrès *m.*

heal. 1. *v.tr.* Guérir. **2.** *v.i.* Se guérir.

health, *s.* Santé *f.*

healthy, *a.* (*a*) Sain ; en bonne santé ; bien portant. (*b*) Salubre.

heap[1], *s.* (*a*) Tas *m*, monceau *m.* (*b*) Heaps of times, bien des fois.

heap[2], *v.tr.* **1.** To h. (up), entasser, amonceler. **2.** Combler. remplir (*with*, de).

hear, *v.tr.* **1.** Entendre. To h. s.o. say sth., entendre dire qch. à qn. **2.** Écouter. H.! h.! très bien ! très bien ! **3.** Apprendre. **4.** Hoping to h. from you, dans l'attente de vous lire.

hearer, *s.* Auditeur, -trice.

hearing, *s.* **1.** Audition *f*, audience *f.* **2.** Ouïe *f.*

hearsay, *s.* Ouï-dire *m inv.*

hearse, *s.* Corbillard *m.*

heart, *s.* Cœur *m.* **1.** H. failure, défaillance *f* cardiaque. **2.** (*a*) Set your h. at rest, soyez tranquille. From the bottom of my h., de tout mon cœur. At h., au fond. (*b*) With all one's h., de tout son cœur. (*c*) To lose h., perdre courage. **3.** The h. of the matter, le vif de l'affaire. **4.** Queen of hearts, dame *f* de cœur.

heart-broken, *a.* Navré.

heart-disease, s. Maladie f de cœur.

hearten, v.tr. Ranimer le courage de.

heart-felt, a. Sincère.

hearth, s. Foyer m, âtre m.

hearth-rug, s. Tapis m de foyer.

heartily, adv. **I.** Cordialement ; sincèrement. **2.** De bon appétit.

heartiness, s. Cordialité f, chaleur f.

heartless, a. Sans cœur, sans pitié.

heart-rending, a. Navrant. **H.-r.** cries, cris déchirants.

hearty, a. **I.** Cordial, -aux. **2.** (a) Vigoureux, robuste. (b) Abondant.

heat¹, s. **I.** Chaleur f ; ardeur f. **2.** Épreuve f, manche f. **Dead h.,** course nulle.

heat², v.tr. (a) Chauffer. (b) Échauffer.

heated, a. **I.** Chaud, chauffé. **2.** To get h., s'échauffer.

heater, s. Radiateur m.

heath, s. **I.** Bruyère f. **2.** Lande f.

heathen, a. & s. Païen, -ïenne.

heather, s. Bruyère f.

heating, s. **Central h.,** chauffage central.

heat-wave, s. Vague f de chaleur.

heave¹, s. Soulèvement m.

heave², **I.** v.tr. **I.** Lever, soulever. **2.** Pousser (un soupir). **3.** Lancer, jeter. **II. heave,** v.i. Se soulever ; palpiter.

heaven, s. Ciel m, pl. cieux. **Thank H.!** Dieu merci !

heavenly, a. Céleste.

heavily, adv. **I.** Lourdement. **2.** To lose h., perdre une forte somme.

heaviness, s. (a) Lourdeur f, pesanteur f. (b) Engourdissement m.

heavy, a. **I.** Lourd. **2. H. baggage,** gros bagages. **H. shower,** grosse averse. **3.** (a) Pénible, laborieux. (b) **H. weather,** gros temps.

Hebrew, (a) a. & s. Hébreu, f. hébraïque. (b) s. L'hébreu m.

hectic, a. Agité, fiévreux.

hectogramme, s. = ·22 lb.

hedge, s. Haie f.

hedgehog, s. Hérisson m.

hedgerow, s. Bordure f de haies.

heed¹, s. Attention f garde f.

heed², v.tr. Faire attention à.

heedful, a. Vigilant, prudent.

heedless, a. Étourdi, insouciant.

heedlessly, adv. Étourdiment.

heel, s. Talon m. **To take to one's heels,** prendre la fuite.

heifer, s. Génisse f.

height, s. **I.** (a) Hauteur f, élévation f. (b) Taille f, grandeur f. **2.** Altitude f. **3.** Hauteur ; éminence f. **4.** Apogée m ; comble m. **In the h. of fashion,** à la dernière mode.

heighten, v.tr. Accroître, augmenter.

heinous, a. Odieux, atroce.

heir, s. Héritier m.

heiress, s. Héritière f.

Helen. Pr.n. Hélène f.

heliotrope. **I.** s. Héliotrope m. **2.** a. Héliotrope inv.

hell, s. L'enfer.

hellish, a. Infernal, -aux ; diabolique.

helm, s. Barre f ; gouvernail m.

helmet, s. Casque m.

helmsman, s. Homme m de barre ; timonier m.

help¹, s. **I.** Aide f, secours m. **To cry for h.,** crier au secours. **2. There's no h. for it,** il n'y a rien à faire.

help², v.tr. **I.** (a) Aider, secourir. **H.!** au secours ! (b) Faciliter. **2.** Servir. **H. yourself,** servez-vous. **3.** (a) Empêcher. **I can't h. it,** je n'y peux rien. **It can't be helped,** tant pis ! (b) S'empêcher. **I can't h. it,** c'est plus fort que moi.

helper, s. Aide mf.

helpful, a. **I.** Secourable, serviable. **2.** Utile.

helping¹, a. **To lend a h. hand,** prêter son aide.

helping², s. Portion f.

helpless, a. **I.** Sans ressource, sans appui. **2.** Faible. impuissant.

helplessness, s. **I.** Abandon m, délaissement m. **2.** Faiblesse f.

hem¹, s. **I.** Bord m. **2.** Ourlet m.

hem², v.tr. **I.** Ourler. **2. To hem in,** entourer, cerner.

hemisphere, s. Hémisphère m.

hemp, s. Chanvre m.

hen, s. Poule f.

hence, adv. **I.** D'ici. **2. Five years h.,** dans cinq ans (d'ici). **3.** De là.

henceforth, adv. Désormais.

henna, s. Henné m.

her¹, pers. pron. (a) La ; lui. **Have you seen her?** l'avez-vous vue ? **Look at her,** regardez-la. **Tell her,** dites-lui. (b) **I am thinking of her,** je pense à elle.

her², poss.a. Son, f. sa, pl. ses.

heraldry, s. Le blason.

herb, s. (a) Herbe f. (b) **Sweet herbs,** fines herbes.

herbal, a. D'herbes.

herbalist, s. Herboriste mf.

herd¹, s. (a) Troupeau m; troupe f, bande f.

herd², s. Pâtre m, gardien m.

herdsman, s. Bouvier m, pâtre m.

here, adv. **1.** (a) Ici. In h., ici. H. goes! allons-y! (b) **H. below,** ici-bas. **2.** Here's your hat, voici votre chapeau. **H. you are,** vous voici! **3.** (a) **H. and there,** par-ci par-là; çà et là. (b) **That's neither h. nor there,** cela ne fait rien.

hereabouts, adv. Près d'ici, par ici, dans ces parages.

hereafter, adv. Dorénavant à l'avenir.

hereby, adv. Par ceci.

hereditary, a. Héréditaire.

heredity, s. Hérédité f.

herein, adv. **1.** Ici; ci-inclus. **2.** En ceci.

heresy, s. Hérésie f.

heretic, s. Hérétique mf.

heretofore, adv. Jadis; jusqu'ici.

hereupon, adv. Là-dessus.

herewith, adv. Avec ceci; ci-joint.

heritage, s. Héritage m.

hermetically, adv. Hermétiquement

hermit, s. Ermite m.

hermitage, s. Ermitage m.

hero, s. Héros m.

heroic, a. Héroïque.

heroically, adv. Héroïquement.

heroine, s. Héroïne f.

heroism, s. Héroïsme m.

heron, s. Héron m.

hero-worship, s. Culte m des héros.

herring, s. Hareng m. **Red h.,** hareng saur.

hers, poss.pron. Le sien, la sienne, les siens, les siennes. **This book is h.,** ce livre est à elle.

herself, pers.pron. Elle-même; se.

hesitant, a. Hésitant, irrésolu.

hesitate, v.i. Hésiter.

hesitating, a. Hésitant, incertain

hesitation, s. Hésitation f

hew, v.tr. Couper, tailler.

hi, int. Hé, là-bas! ohé!

hibernate, v.i. Hiberner.

hiccough¹, s. Hoquet m.

hiccough², v.i. Avoir le hoquet.

hide¹. **1.** v.tr (a) Cacher (from, à).

To h. one's face, se cacher la figure. (b) **To h. sth. from sight,** dérober qch. aux regards **2.** v.i Se cacher

hide², s. Peau f. dépouille f; cuir m.

hide-and-seek, s. Cache-cache m.

hide-bound, a. Aux vues étroites.

hideous, a. **1.** Hideux, affreux, effroyable **2.** D'une laideur repoussante.

hideously, adv. Hideusement, affreusement.

hideousness, s. Hideur f, horreur f.

hiding¹, s. To go into h., se cacher.

hiding², s. Raclée f.

hiding-place, s Cachette f; retraite f.

high. I. a. **1.** Haut. How h. is that tree? quelle est la hauteur de cet arbre? **2.** Élevé. (a) **To play for h.** stakes, jouer gros (jeu) **H. speed,** grande vitesse. (b) **H. wind,** vent fort. **3.** Higher, supérieur. **4. H.** time, grand temps. **5. H. and dry,** à sec. **6.** On h., en haut.

II. **high,** adv. **1.** Haut; en haut. **2.** Fort, fortement, très.

high-class, a. De premier ordre.

high-handed, a. Arbitraire.

highly, adv. **1.** To think h. of, avoir une haute opinion de. **2.** Fort, très.

high-priced, a. De grand prix; cher.

high-spirited, a. Intrépide; plein d'ardeur; fougueux.

high-strung, a. Nerveux.

highway, s. Chemin m de grande communication.

hike¹, s. Excursion f à pied.

hike², v.i. Faire du tourisme à pied. To h. it, faire le trajet à pied.

hiker, s. Excursionniste mf à pied

hiking, s. Excursions fpl à pied.

hilarious, a. Gai, joyeux, hilare.

hilarity, s. Hilarité f, gaieté f.

hill, s. **1.** (a) Colline f, coteau m. (b) Éminence f. **2.** Côte f.

hillock, s. Petite colline; butte f.

hill-side, s. Flanc m de coteau; coteau m.

hilly, a. Montagneux; accidenté; montueux.

hilt, s. Poignée f, garde f.

him, pers. pron. **1.** Le; lui. I obey him, je lui obéis Call him, appelez-le. **2.** Celui.

himself, pers.pron. Lui-même; se

hind, *a.* H. legs, jambes de derrière.
H. quarters, arrière-train *m.*

hinder, *v.tr.* **1.** Gêner, embarrasser ;
retarder. **2.** Empêcher.

hindmost, *a.* Dernier.

hindrance, *s.* Empêchement *m*,
obstacle *m.*

Hindu, *a. & s.* Hindou, -oue.

hinge, *s.* **1.** Gond *m.* **2.** Charnière *f.*

hint[1], *s.* (*a*) Insinuation *f.* To give
s.o. a h., toucher un mot à qn.
(*b*) Signe *m*, indication *f.*

hint[2], *v.tr. & i.* Insinuer. To h. at,
laisser entendre.

hip, *s.* Hanche *f.*

hip-bath, *s.* Bain *m* de siège.

hippopotamus, *s.* Hippopotame *m.*

hire[1], *s.* **1.** Louage *m.* To let on h.,
louer. **2.** Salaire *m*, gages *mpl.*

hire[2], *v.tr.* **1.** Louer. **2.** To h. out,
louer.

hire-purchase, *s.* Location-vente *f.*

his[1], *poss.a.* Son, *f.* sa, *pl.* ses. He
fell on his back, il tomba sur le dos.

his[2], *poss.pron.* Le sien, la sienne, les
siens, les siennes. This book is his,
ce livre est à lui.

hiss[1], *s.* (*a*) Sifflement *m.* (*b*) Sifflet *m.*

hiss[2], *v.i. & tr.* Siffler.

historical, *a.* Historique.

history, *s.* (L')histoire *f.*

hit[1], *s.* **1.** (*a*) Coup *m.* (*b*) Touche *f*
2. Succès *m.*

hit[2]. (*a*) *v.tr.* Frapper. To hit s.o.
a blow, porter un coup à qn. (*b*) *v.i.*
To hit against, se cogner contre.
(*c*) Atteindre ; toucher. **hit out**,
v.i. Décocher un coup.

hitch, *s.* Anicroche *f*, contretemps *m.*
Without a h., sans à-coup.

hither, *adv.* Ici. H. and thither, çà
et là.

hitherto, *adv.* Jusqu'ici.

hive, *s.* Ruche *f.*

hoard[1], *s.* Amas *m*, accumulation *f.*

hoard[2], *v.tr.* Amasser ; accumuler.

hoarding, *s.* Palissade *f.*

hoarse, *a.* Enroué, rauque.

hoarsely, *adv.* D'une voix rauque.

hoarseness, *s.* Enrouement *m.*

hoary, *a.* **1.** Blanchi, chenu. **2.**
Vénérable, séculaire.

hoax[1], *s.* Mystification *f.*

hoax[2], *v.tr.* Mystifier, attraper.

hobble. **1.** *v.i.* Clocher, clopiner.
2. *v.tr.* Entraver.

hobby, *s.* Passetemps favori.

hobgoblin, *s.* Lutin *m*, farfadet *m.*

hock, *s.* Vin *m* du Rhin.

hockey, *s.* (Jeu *m* de) hockey *m.*

hoe[1], *s.* Houe *f*, binette *f.*

hoe[2], *v.tr.* Houer, biner ; sarcler.

hog, *s.* **1.** Porc *m*, pourceau *m.*

hogshead, *s.* Tonneau *m*, barrique *f.*

hoist, *v.tr.* Hisser.

hold[1], *s.* **1.** Prise *f*, étreinte *f.* To
take h. of, saisir, empoigner. To
keep h. of, ne pas lâcher. **2.** Soutien
m ; point *m* d'appui.

hold[2]. **I.** *v.tr.* **1.** Tenir. To h.
tight, serrer. **2.** To h. one's ground,
tenir ferme. To h. one's own, maintenir sa position. H. the line! ne
quittez pas ! **3.** Contenir, renfermer.
4. Retenir. **5.** Avoir ; posséder.
    II. hold, *v.i.* Tenir (bon). **hold
back.** **1.** *v.tr.* (*a*) Retenir. (*b*)
Cacher, dissimuler. **2.** *v.i.* Rester
en arrière ; hésiter. **hold forth**,
v.i. Pérorer. **hold in**, *v.tr.* To h.
oneself in, se contenir. **hold off.**
1. *v.tr.* Tenir à distance. **2.** *v.i.* Se
tenir à distance. **hold on**, *v.i.* To
h. on to, ne pas lâcher. **hold out.**
1. *v.tr.* Tendre, offrir. **2.** *v.i.* Durer ;
tenir. **hold over**, *v.tr.* Remettre.
hold together, *v.i.* Tenir (ensemble). **hold up**, *v.tr.* (*a*) Soutenir. (*b*) Lever. (*c*) Arrêter ; entraver.

hold[3], *s.* Nau : Cale *f.*

holder, *s.* **1.** Titulaire *mf* ; propriétaire *mf.* **2.** Support *m*, monture *f.*
3. Récipient *m.*

hole, *s.* Trou *m.* **1.** (*a*) Creux *m*,
cavité *f.* (*b*) Terrier *m.* **2.** Orifice *m*,
ouverture *f.*

holiday, *s.* (*a*) (Jour *m* de) fête *f* ;
jour férié. (*b*) Congé *m.* (*c*) The
holidays, les vacances.

holiness, *s.* Sainteté *f.*

Holland. *Pr.n.* La Hollande.

hollow[1]. **I.** *a.* **1.** Creux, caverneux,
évidé. **2.** Sourd.
    II. hollow, *adv.* Creux.
    III. hollow, *s* Creux *m* ; cavité
f ; excavation *f.*

hollow[2], *v.tr.* Creuser, évider.

hollow-cheeked, *a.* Aux joues
creuses.

hollow-eyed, *a.* Aux yeux caves.

holly, *s.* Houx *m.*

hollyhock, *s.* Rose trémière.

holster, *s.* Étui *m* de revolver.

holy, *a.* (*a*) Saint, sacré. **H. water,** eau bénite (*b*) Saint, pieux.

homage, *s.* Hommage *m.*

home. I. *s.* **1.** (*a*) Chez-soi *m inv* ; foyer *m.* (*b*) **At h.,** à la maison, chez soi. **To stay at h.,** garder la maison. **To feel at h.,** se sentir à l'aise. **To make oneself at h.,** faire comme chez soi. **2.** Patrie *f* ; pays (natal). **3.** Asile *m,* refuge *m.*
    II. **home,** *adv.* **1.** A la maison ; chez soi. **To go h.,** rentrer. **2.** (*a*) **To bring h.,** faire sentir. (*b*) **A fond.**
    III. **home,** *attrib.a.* **1. H. address,** adresse personnelle. **2. The H. Office** = le Ministère de l'Intérieur.

homeless, *a.* Sans foyer ; sans abri.

homely, *a.* **1.** Simple ordinaire. **2.** Sans beauté.

homesick, *a.* Nostalgique.

homesickness, *s.* Nostalgie *f.*

homestead, *s.* Ferme *f.*

homeward-bound, *a.* Sur le retour.

homewards, *adv.* Vers sa demeure ; vers son pays.

homicidal, *a.* Homicide.

homicide, *s.* Homicide *m*

homily, *s.* Homélie *f.*

homoeopathic, *a.* Homéopathique.

hone, *s.* Pierre *f* à aiguiser.

honest, *a.* (*a*) Honnête, probe. (*b*) Vrai, sincère.

honestly, *adv.* (*a*) Honnêtement, loyalement. (*b*) Sincèrement.

honesty, *s.* (*a*) Honnêteté *f,* probité *f.* (*b*) Véracité *f,* sincérité *f.*

honey, *s.* Miel *m.*

honey-bee, *s.* Abeille *f* ; mouche *f* à miel.

honeycomb¹, *s.* Rayon *m* de miel.

honeycomb², *v.tr.* Cribler.

honeymoon, *s.* Lune *f* de miel.

honeysuckle, *s.* Chèvrefeuille *m.*

honorary, *a.* Honoraire ; non rétribué, bénévole.

honour¹, *s.* Honneur *m.* **1. In h. bound,** obligé par l'honneur. **On one's h.,** engagé d'honneur. **2.** Distinction *f* honorifique. **3. Your H.,** Monsieur le juge.

honour², *v.tr.* Honorer.

honourable, *a.* Honorable.

honourably, *adv.* Honorablement.

honoured, *a.* Honoré.

hood, *s.* **1.** Capuchon *m* ; capeline *f.* **2.** Capote *f.*

hooded, *a.* Encapuchonné.

hoodwink, *v.tr.* Tromper.

hoof, *s.* Sabot *m.*

hook¹, *s.* **1.** Crochet *m,* croc *m.* (*a*) **Hat and coat h.,** patère *f.* (*b*) Agrafe *f.* **H. and eye,** agrafe et œillet *m.* **2.** Hameçon *m.*

hook², *v.tr.* Prendre à l'hameçon ; accrocher.

hooked, *a.* Crochu, recourbé.

hooligan, *s.* Voyou *m* ; gouape *f.*

hoop, *s.* **1.** Cercle *m.* **2.** Cerceau *m.*

hoot¹, *s.* **1.** Ululation *f.* **2.** Huée *f.* **3.** Cornement *m.*

hoot², *v.i.* (*a*) Ululer. (*b*) Huer. (*c*) Corner, klaxonner.

hooter, *s.* **1.** Sirène *f.* **2.** Trompe *f.*

hop¹, *s.* Houblon *m.*

hop², *v.i.* Sauter, sautiller.

hop-field, *s.* Houblonnière *f.*

hop-picker, *s.* Cueilleur, -euse, de houblon.

hope¹, *s.* **1.** Espérance *f,* espoir *m.* **2. To have hopes of sth.,** avoir qch. en vue.

hope². **1.** *v.i.* Espérer. **To h. for sth.,** espérer qch. **2.** *v.tr.* **Hoping to hear from you,** dans l'espoir de vous lire.

hopeful, *a.* Plein d'espoir.

hopefully, *adv.* Avec bon espoir.

hopefulness, *s.* Bon espoir.

hopeless, *a.* Sans espoir ; désespéré.

hopelessly, *adv.* **1.** Sans espoir. **2.** Irrémédiablement.

hopelessness, *s.* État désespéré.

horde, *s.* Horde *f.*

horizon, *s.* Horizon *m* **On the h.,** à l'horizon.

horizontal, *a.* Horizontal, -aux.

horizontally, *adv.* Horizontalement.

horn, *s.* **1.** Corne *f* ; bois *m* (d'un cerf). **2.** Cor *m.* **French h.,** cor d'harmonie. **3.** Trompe.

horned, *a.* A cornes, cornu.

hornet, *s.* Frelon *m.*

horn-rimmed, *a.* A monture en corne.

horny, *a.* (*a*) En corne. (*b*) Calleux.

horrible, *a.* Horrible, affreux.

horribly, *adv.* Horriblement. affreusement.

horrid, *a.* Horrible, affreux.

horrify, *v.tr.* (*a*) Horrifier. (*b*) Scandaliser.

horror, s. Horreur f.

horror-struck, a. Saisi d'horreur.

horse, s. **1.** Cheval m, -aux. **2.** Coll: Cavalerie f; troupes montées.

horse-artillery, s. Artillerie montée.

horseback, s. On h., à cheval.

horse-chestnut, s. **1.** Marron m d'Inde. **2.** Marronnier m d'Inde.

horse-dealer, s. Maquignon m.

horsehair, s. Crin m.

horseman, s. Cavalier m, écuyer m.

horse-play, s. Jeu brutal.

horse-pond, s. Abreuvoir m.

horse-power, s. Cheval-vapeur m, pl. chevaux-vapeur. **A forty h.-p. car,** une automobile de quarante chevaux.

horse-race, s. Course f de chevaux.

horse-racing, s. Hippisme m; courses fpl de chevaux.

horse-radish, s. Raifort m.

horseshoe, s. Fer m à cheval.

horsewhip[1], s. Cravache f.

horsewhip[2], v.tr. Cravacher, sangler.

horticulture, s. Horticulture f.

hose, s. **1.** Bas mpl. **2.** Tuyau m.

hosier, s. Bonnetier, -ière.

hosiery, s. Bonneterie f.

hospitable, a. Hospitalier.

hospitably, adv. Hospitalièrement.

hospital, s. Hôpital m, -aux. **H. nurse,** infirmière f.

hospitality, s. Hospitalité f.

host, s. (a) Hôte m. (b) Hôtelier m.

hostage, s. Otage m.

hostel, s. (a) Pension f, foyer m. (b) **Youth hostels,** auberges f de la jeunesse.

hostess, s. (a) Hôtesse f. (b) Hôtelière f.

hostile, a. (a) Hostile, ennemi. (b) Hostile, opposé.

hostility, s. **1.** Hostilité f (to, contre); animosité f. **2.** pl. Hostilités.

hot, a. **1.** (a) Chaud. **Boiling hot,** bouillant. **To be hot,** avoir chaud; faire chaud. (b) Brûlant, cuisant. **2.** (a) Violent. **To have a hot temper,** s'emporter facilement. (b) **Hot contest,** chaude dispute. **To be in hot pursuit of,** presser de près.

hot-blooded, a. Emporté, ardent.

hotel, s. Hôtel m. **Private h.,** hôtel de famille. **Residential h.,** pension f de famille.

hotel-keeper, s. Hôtelier, -ière.

hot-headed, a. **1.** Exalté, impétueux. **2.** Emporté violent.

hothouse, s. Serre chaude.

hotly, adv. **1.** Avec chaleur. **2.** Avec acharnement.

hot-tempered, a. Colérique; emporté, vif.

hot-water bottle, s. Bouillotte f.

hound[1], s. Chien courant. **The hounds,** la meute.

hound[2], v.tr. **To h. down,** poursuivre avec acharnement.

hour, s. Heure f. **Half an h.,** une demi-heure. **A quarter of an h.,** un quart d'heure. **H. by h.,** d'une heure à l'autre. **By the h.,** à l'heure. **Five miles an h.,** cinq milles à l'heure.

hour-hand, s. Petite aiguille.

hourly, adv. Toutes les heures; d'heure en heure.

house[1], s. **1.** Maison f, demeure f. **Town h.,** hôtel (particulier). **Country h.,** château m; maison de campagne. **Small h.,** maisonnette f. **At, to, in, my house,** chez moi. **To keep h. for,** tenir le ménage de. Attrib: **H. work,** travaux de ménage. **2.** Auditoire m, assistance f. **A good h.,** une salle pleine.

house[2], v.tr. Loger, héberger.

house-agent, s. Agent m de location.

housebreaker, s. Cambrioleur m.

housebreaking, s. Cambriolage m.

house-dog, s. Chien m de garde.

house-fly, s. Mouche f domestique.

household, s. **1.** Ménage f; famille f. **H. expenses,** frais de ménage. **2.** Domestiques.

householder, s. Chef m de famille, de maison; locataire.

housekeeper, s. **1.** Concierge mf. **2.** Femme f de charge.

housekeeping, s. Le ménage.

housemaid, s. Bonne f; femme f de chambre.

house-property, s. Immeubles mpl.

housewife, s. **1.** Maîtresse f de maison; ménagère f **2.** Nécessaire m à ouvrage.

housing, s. Logement m. **The h. problem,** la crise du logement.

hovel, s. Taudis m, masure f.

hover, v.i. Planer.

how, adv. **1.** Comment. **How are you?** comment allez-vous ? **2.** (a)

How much, how many, combien (de). **How old are you?** quel âge avez-vous? (b) **How pretty she is!** comme elle est jolie! **How I wish I could!** si seulement je pouvais!

however, adv. **1.** (a) De quelque manière que. **H. that may be,** quoi qu'il en soit (b) **H. good,** quelque excellent que. **H. little,** si peu que ce soit. **2.** Toutefois cependant, pourtant.

howl[1], s. Hurlement m.

howl[2], v.i. & tr. Hurler; mugir.

howling, s. Hurlement m; mugissement m.

hub, s. **1.** Moyeu m. **2.** Centre m d'activité.

hubbub, s. Clameur f; vacarme m.

huddle, v.tr. & i. **1.** Entasser pêle-mêle. **To h. together,** se tasser. **2.** Huddled (up) in a **corner,** blotti dans un coin.

hue, s. Teinte f, nuance f.

huff[1], s. **To be in a h.,** être troissé.

huff[2], v.tr. (a) Froisser. (b) Souffler.

huffy, a. **1.** Susceptible. **2.** Fâché, vexé.

hug[1], s. Étreinte f.

hug[2], v.tr. **1.** Étreindre, embrasser. **2. To hug the shore,** serrer la terre.

huge, a. Énorme, vaste; immense.

hulking, a. Gros, lourd.

hull, s. Coque f.

hullo, int. Ohé! holà!

hum[1], s. Bourdonnement m; ronflement m; ronron m.

hum[2]. **1.** v.i. Bourdonner; ronfler. **2.** v.tr. Fredonner.

human. **1.** a Humain. **2.** s. Être humain.

humane, a. (a) Humain, compatissant. (b) Clément.

humanely, adv. Humainement; avec humanité.

humanity, s. Humanité f.

humble[1], a. Humble.

humble[2], v.tr. Humilier mortifier. **To h. oneself,** s'abaisser.

humbly, adv. **1.** Humblement avec humilité. **2.** (Vivre) modestement.

humbug[1], s. **1.** Charlatanisme m; blague f. **2.** Charlatan m; blagueur m.

humbug[2], v.tr. Mystifier.

humdrum, a. Monotone.

humid, a. Humide.

humidity, s. Humidité f.

humiliate, v.tr. Humilier.

humiliation, s. Humiliation f.

humility, s. Humilité f.

humming-bird, s. Oiseau-mouche m, pl. oiseaux-mouches; colibri m.

humorist, s. **1.** Farceur m. **2.** Comique m.

humorous, a. Plein d'humour; drôle; humoriste.

humour[1], s. **1.** Humeur f, disposition f. **In a good h.,** de bonne humeur. **2.** Humour m.

humour[2], v.tr. Ménager.

hump, s. Bosse f.

humpback, s. Bossu, -ue.

humpbacked, a. Bossu.

humped, a. Bossu.

hunch, s. Gros morceau.

hunchback, s Bossu, -ue.

hundred, num. a. & s. Cent (m). About a h., une centaine de.

Hungarian, a. & s. Hongrois, -oise.

Hungary. Pr.n. La Hongrie.

hunger, s. Faim f.

hungrily, adv. Avidement, voracement.

hungry, a. **1.** Affamé. **To be h.,** avoir faim. **2.** Avide.

hunt[1], s. **1.** Chasse f. **2.** Recherche f.

hunt[2]. **1.** v.i. (a) Chasser. (b) **To h. for,** chercher. **2.** v.tr. Chasser. **hunt down,** v.tr. Traquer. **hunt up,** v.tr. Déterrer.

hunter, s. **1.** Chasseur m. **2.** Cheval m de chasse.

hunting, s. Chasse f.

huntsman, s. **1.** Chasseur m **2.** Veneur m, piqueur m.

hurdle, s. **1.** Claie f. **2.** Barrière f.

hurl, v.tr Lancer avec violence (at, contre).

hurrah, int. & s. Hourra (m).

hurricane, s. Ouragan m.

hurried, a. Pressé, précipité; fait à la hâte.

hurriedly, adv A la hâte.

hurry[1], s. Hâte f, précipitation f. **To be in a h.,** être pressé.

hurry[2]. **1.** v.tr. Hâter, presser **2.** v.i. (a) Se hâter, se presser. (b) Presser le pas. **hurry up,** v.i. Se dépêcher, se hâter.

hurt, v.tr. **1.** Faire (du) mal à, blesser. **2.** Faire de la peine à. **3.** Nuire à.

hurtful, a. (a) Nuisible, nocif. (b) Préjudiciable.

husband[1], s. Mari m, époux m.
husband[2], v.tr. Ménager.
hush[1], s. Silence m, calme m.
hush[2]. **1.** v.tr. Apaiser, faire taire.
2. v.i. Se taire ; faire silence.
hush up, v.tr. Étouffer.
hush[3], int. Chut ! silence !
hush-hush, a. Secret, -ète.
husk, s. Cosse f, gousse f.
huskiness, s. Enrouement m.
husky, a. Enroué.
hussar, s. Hussard m.
hustle. **1.** v.tr. Bousculer ; presser.
2. v.i. Se dépêcher, se presser.
hut, s. Hutte f, cabane f.
hutch, s. Coffre m, huche f.
hyacinth, s. Jacinthe f.
hybrid, a. & s. Hybride (m).
hydrant, s. Prise f d'eau.
hydraulic, a. Hydraulique.
hydrochloric, a Chlorhydrique.
hydrogen, s. Hydrogène m

hydroplane, s. Hydravion m
hyena, s. Hyène f.
hygiene, s. Hygiène f.
hygienic, a. Hygiénique.
hymn, s. Hymne f, cantique m.
hyphen, s. Trait m d'union.
hypnotic, a. Hypnotique.
hypnotism, s. Hypnotisme m.
hypnotist, s. Hypnotiste mf.
hypnotize, v.tr. Hypnotiser.
hypocrisy, s. Hypocrisie f.
hypocrite, s. Hypocrite mf.
hypocritical, a. Hypocrite.
hypocritically, adv. Hypocritement.
hypothesis, s. Hypothèse f.
hypothetic, a. Hypothétique, supposé.
hysterical, a. **1.** Hystérique. **2.** To become h., avoir une attaque de nerfs.
hysterics, s.pl. Attaque f de nerfs ; crise f de nerfs.

I

I[1], **i**, s. (La lettre) I, ı m.
I[2], pers. pron. (a) Je. **I accuse,** j'accuse. **Here I am,** me voici. (b) Moi mf. **It is I,** c'est moi.
ice[1], s. Glace f. **My feet are like ice,** j'ai les pieds glacés. **2. Strawberry ice,** glace à la fraise.
ice[2], v.tr. **1.** Rafraîchir avec de la glace ; frapper. **2.** Glacer.
ice-axe, s. Piolet m.
iceberg, s. Iceberg m ; montagne f de glace.
ice-cream, s. Glace f.
ice-floe, s. Banquise f ; banc m de glace.
Iceland, Pr.n. L'Islande f.
ice-pudding, s. Bombe glacée.
icicle, s. Glaçon.
icy, a. Glacial, -als.
idea, s. Idée f. **To get ideas into one's head,** se faire des idées.
ideal, a. & s. Idéal m, -aux.
idealist, s. Idéaliste mf.
idealize, v.tr. Idéaliser.
ideally, adv. Idéalement.
identical, a. Identique (with, à).
identically, adv. Identiquement.
identification, s. Identification f.
identify, v.tr. **1.** Identifier. **2.** Constater, établir, l'identité de.

identity, s. Identité f. **Mistaken i.,** erreur f sur la personne.
idiocy, s. Idiotie f.
idiom, s. **1.** Idiome m. **2.** Idiotisme m, locution f.
idiomatic, a. Idiomatique. **I. phrase,** idiotisme m.
idiot, s. (a) Idiot, -ote. (b) Imbécile mf.
idiotic, a. Bête.
idiotically, adv. Bêtement.
idle[1], a. **1.** (a) Inoccupé, oisif. (b) En chômage. **2.** Paresseux. **3.** Inutile, oiseux.
idle[2], v.i. Fainéanter.
idleness, s. **1.** (a) Oisiveté f, désœuvrement m. (b) Chômage m. **2.** Futilité f. **3.** Paresse f.
idler, s. (a) Oisif, -ive ; désœuvré, -ée. (b) Fainéant, -ante.
idly, adv. **1.** Inutilement. **2.** Paresseusement.
idol, s. Idole f.
idolize, v.tr. Idolâtrer, adorer.
idyll, s. Idylle f.
idyllic, a. Idyllique.
if, conj. **1.** Si. **If (it be) so,** s'il en est ainsi. **2.** (a) **If not,** sinon ; si ce n'est. **If only,** ne fût-ce que. (b) **Even if,** quand même. (c) **If only,** pourvu que. (d) **As if by chance,** comme par hasard.

ignite. I. *v.tr.* Mettre le feu à. **2.** *v.i.* Prendre feu.

ignition, *s.* **I.** Ignition *f.* **2.** Allumage *m.*

ignoble, *a.* Ignoble ; infâme, vil.

ignominious, *a.* Ignominieux.

ignominiously, *adv.* Ignominieusement ; avec ignominie.

ignominy, *s.* Ignominie *f,* honte *f.*

ignorance, *s.* Ignorance *f.*

ignorant, *a.* Ignorant. **To be i. of,** ignorer.

ignore, *v.tr.* Ne tenir aucun compte de.

ill. I. *a.* **I.** Mauvais. Ill effects, effets pernicieux. **2.** Malade, souffrant.
II. **ill,** *s.* **I.** Mal *m.* **2.** Dommage *m,* tort *m.*
III. **ill,** *adv.* Mal. **I. To take sth. ill,** prendre qch. en mauvaise part. **2.** Difficilement. **3. To be ill at ease,** être inquiet.

ill-advised, *a.* **I.** Malavisé. **2.** Peu judicieux.

ill-bred, *a.* Mal élevé.

ill-considered, *a.* Peu réfléchi.

ill-disposed, *a.* Malintentionné, malveillant.

illegal, *a.* Illégal, -aux.

illegality, *s.* Illégalité *f.*

illegally, *adv.* Illégalement.

illegible, *a.* Illisible.

illegitimate, *a.* Illégitime.

ill-fated, *a.* Infortuné.

ill-feeling, *s.* Ressentiment *m,* rancune *f.*

ill-health, *s.* Mauvaise santé.

ill-humoured, *a* De mauvaise humeur.

illicit, *a.* Illicite.

ill-informed, *a.* Mal renseigné.

illiterate, *a. & s.* Illettré, -ée.

ill-judged, *a.* Malavisé.

ill-luck, *s.* Mauvaise fortune.

ill-mannered, *a.* Malhonnête, grossier.

ill-natured, *a.* Méchant ; désagréable.

illness, *s.* Maladie *f.*

illogical, *a.* Illogique ; peu logique.

ill-omened, *a.* De mauvais présage.

ill-pleased, *a.* Mécontent.

ill-temper, *s.* Mauvais caractère.

ill-tempered, *a.* Maussade.

ill-timed, *a.* Mal à propos.

ill-treat, *v.tr.* Maltraiter.

ill-treatment, *s.* Mauvais traitements.

illuminate, *v.tr.* Éclairer.

illumination, *s.* Éclairage *m.*

ill-use, *v.tr.* Maltraiter.

illusion, *s.* Illusion *f.*

illusory, *a.* Illusoire.

illustrate, *v.tr.* **I.** Éclairer, expliquer. **2.** Illustrer.

illustration, *s.* **I.** Exemple *m.* **2.** Illustration *f,* gravure *f,* image *f.*

illustrious, *a.* Illustre, célèbre.

ill-will, *s.* Malveillance *f,* rancune *f.*

image, *s.* Image *f.*

imaginable, *a.* Imaginable.

imaginary, *a.* Imaginaire.

imagination, *s.* Imagination *f.*

imaginative, *a.* Imaginatif.

imagine, *v.tr.* (*a*) Imaginer, concevoir ; se figurer. (*b*) Croire.

imbecile, *a. & s.* Imbécile (*mf*).

imbecility, *s.* Imbécillité *f.*

imbibe, *v.tr.* (*a*) Absorber. (*b*) Boire.

imitate, *v.tr.* Imiter, copier.

imitation, *s.* **I.** Imitation *f.* **2.** (*a*) Beware of imitations, méfiez-vous des contrefaçons *f.* (*b*) Factice. I. jewellery, bijouterie fausse.

imitative, *a.* Imitatif.

imitator, *s.* Imitateur, -trice.

immaculate, *a.* Immaculé.

immaterial, *a.* **I.** Immatériel. **2.** Peu important.

immature, *a.* Pas mûr.

immeasurable, *a.* Incommensurable.

immediate, *a.* Immédiat. **I.** Sans intermédiaire ; direct. **2.** Instantané. **3.** Pressant, urgent.

immediately. **I.** *adv.* Immédiatement. (*a*) Directement. (*b*) Tout de suite. I. on his return, dès son retour. **2.** *conj.* Dès que.

immense, *a.* Immense, vaste.

immensely, *adv.* Immensément.

immerse, *v.tr.* **I.** Immerger, submerger. **2.** Plonger.

imminence, *s.* Imminence *f.*

imminent, *a.* Imminent.

immobility, *s.* Immobilité *f.*

immoderate, *a.* Immodéré.

immodest, *a.* Immodeste, impudique.

immoral, *a.* Immoral -aux. (*Of pers.*) Dissolu.

immorality, *s.* Immoralité *f.*

immortal, *a. & s.* Immortel (*m*).

immovable, *a* **I.** Fixe ; à demeure.

2. (Volonté) inébranlable. **3.** (Visage) impassible.

immovably, *adv.* **1.** Sans bouger. **2.** Immuablement. **3.** Sans s'émouvoir.

immune, *a.* A l'abri ; immunisé.

immunity, *s.* Exemption *f.*

immutable, *a.* Immuable.

imp, *s.* Diablotin *m*, lutin *m.*

impact, *s.* Choc *m*, impact *m.*

impair, *v.tr.* Affaiblir ; altérer

impale, *v.tr.* Empaler.

impalpable, *a.* Impalpable.

impart, *v.tr.* Communiquer.

impartial, *a.* Impartial, -aux.

impartiality, *s.* Impartialité *f.*

impartially, *adv.* Impartialement.

impassable, *a.* Infranchissable.

impassioned, *a.* Passionné, exalté.

impassive, *a.* Impassible.

impatience, *s.* Impatience *f.*

impatient, *a.* Impatient.

impatiently, *adv.* Avec impatience ; impatiemment.

impeccable, *a.* Impeccable.

impecunious, *a.* Impécunieux.

impede, *v.tr.* Empêcher, entraver.

impediment, *s.* Empêchement *m*, obstacle *m.*

impel, *v.tr.* **1.** Pousser, forcer. **2.** Pousser.

impend, *v.i.* Être imminent ; menacer.

impending, *a.* Imminent.

impenetrability, *s.* Impénétrabilité *f.*

impenetrable, *a.* Impénétrable.

imperative, *a.* (*a*) Impératif, péremptoire. (*b*) Urgent, impérieux.

imperatively, *adv.* Impérativement.

imperceptible, *a.* Imperceptible ; insaisissable.

imperceptibly, *adv.* Imperceptiblement, insensiblement.

imperfect, *a.* Imparfait, incomplet défectueux.

imperfectly, *adv.* Imparfaitement.

imperial, *a.* Impérial, -aux.

imperil, *v.tr.* Mettre en péril.

imperious, *a.* **1.** Impérieux, arrogant. **2.** Urgent.

imperiously, *adv.* Impérieusement.

impermeable, *a.* Imperméable.

impersonal, *a.* Impersonnel.

impersonate, *v.tr.* Se faire passer pour.

impertinence, *s.* Impertinence *f*, insolence *f.*

impertinent, *a.* Impertinent, insolent.

impertinently, *adv.* Avec impertinence ; d'un ton insolent.

imperturbability, *s.* Imperturbabilité *f.*

imperturbable, *a.* Imperturbable.

imperturbably, *adv.* Imperturbablement.

impervious, *a.* Inaccessible.

impetuosity, *s.* Impétuosité *f.*

impetuous, *a.* Impétueux.

impetuously, *adv.* Impétueusement.

impetus, *s.* Impulsion *f.*

impinge, *v.ind.tr.* **To i. on,** se heurter à.

impious, *a.* Impie.

implacability, *s.* Implacabilité *f.*

implacable, *a.* Implacable.

implacably, *adv.* Implacablement.

implant, *v.tr.* Implanter.

implement, *s.* Outil *m*, instrument *m*, ustensile *m.*

implicate, *v.tr.* Impliquer.

implication, *s.* Implication *f.*

implicit, *a.* Implicite ; absolu.

implicitly, *adv.* Implicitement.

implied, *a.* Implicite, tacite.

implore, *v.tr.* Implorer, supplier.

imploring, *a.* Suppliant.

imply, *v.tr.* Impliquer.

impolite, *a.* Impoli (**to,** envers).

impolitely, *adv.* Impoliment.

impoliteness, *s.* Impolitesse *f.*

import[1], *s.* **1.** Sens *m*, signification *f.* **2.** Imports, importations *f.* **I. duty,** droit *m* d'entrée.

import[2], *v.tr.* Importer.

importance, *s.* Importance *f.*

important, *a.* Important.

importation, *s.* Importation *f.*

importer, *s.* Importateur, -trice

importunate, *a.* Importun.

importune, *v.tr.* Importuner.

impose. 1. *v.tr.* Imposer. **2.** *v.i.* **To i. upon,** en imposer à.

imposing, *a.* Imposant ; grandiose.

impossibility, *s.* **1.** Impossibilité *f.* **2.** Chose *f* impossible.

impossible, *a.* Impossible.

impostor, *s.* Imposteur *m.*

imposture, *s.* Imposture *f.*

impotence, *s.* (*a*) Impuissance *f.* (*b*) Impotence *f.*

impotent, *a.* (*a*) Impuissant (*b*) Impotent.

impoverish, *v.tr.* Appauvrir.

impracticable, *a.* Infaisable, impraticable.

impregnable, *a* Imprenable, inexpugnable.

impregnate, *v.tr* Imprégner imbiber (*with*, de).

impress, *v.tr.* **1.** Imprimer. **2.** Faire sentir (*upon*, à). **3.** Faire une impression à.

impression, *s.* Impression *f.*

impressive, *a.* Impressionnant.

imprint¹, *s.* Empreinte *f.*

imprint², *v.tr.* Imprimer.

imprison, *v.tr.* Emprisonner.

imprisonment, *s.* Emprisonnement *m.*

improbability, *s.* Improbabilité *f*; invraisemblance *f.*

mprobable, *a* Improbable invraisemblable.

impromptu. 1. *adv.* Impromptu. **2.** *a.* Impromptu *inv.* **3.** *s.* Impromptu *m.*

improper, *a.* **1.** Impropre. **2.** Inconvenant. **3.** Déplacé.

improperly, *adv* Incorrectement.

impropriety, *s.* (*a*) Impropriété *f.* (*b*) Inconvenance *f.*

improve. 1. *v.tr.* (*a*) Améliorer; perfectionner. (*b*) *v.ind.tr.* To i. upon, améliorer. **2.** *v.i.* S'améliorer.

improvement, *s.* **1.** Amélioration *f*; perfectionnement *m* **2.** To be an i. on, surpasser.

improvident, *a.* (*a*) Imprévoyant. (*b*) Prodigue.

improvise, *v.tr.* Improviser.

imprudence, *s.* Imprudence *f.*

imprudent, *a.* Imprudent.

imprudently, *adv.* Imprudemment.

impudence, *s.* Impudence *f.* effronterie *f.*

impudent, *a.* Effronté, insolent.

impudently, *adv.* Effrontément.

impugn, *v.tr.* Mettre en doute.

impulse, *s.* Impulsion *f.*

impulsive, *a.* Impulsif.

impulsively, *adv.* Par impulsion.

impunity, *s.* Impunité *f* With i., impunément.

impure, *a.* Impur.

impurity, *s.* Impureté *f.*

imputation, *s.* Imputation *f.*

impute, *v.tr.* Imputer.

in. I. *prep.* **1.** (*a*) En, à, dans In Europe, en Europe In Japan, au Japon. In Paris, à Paris. (*b*) In the crowd, dans la foule. **2.** Blind in one eye, aveugle d'un œil. Two feet in length, long de deux pieds. **3.** One in ten, un sur dix. **4.** (*a*) In the evening, le soir, pendant la soirée. In August, au mois d'août. In the past, par le passé. Never in my life, jamais de ma vie. (*b*) In a little while, sous peu. **5.** In tears, en larmes. In despair, au désespoir. **6.** Dressed in white, habillé de blanc. **7.** (*a*) In a gentle voice, d'une voix douce. (*b*) In alphabetical order, par ordre alphabétique. (*c*) In the form of, sous forme de.

II. in, *adv.* **1.** (*a*) A la maison, chez soi. (*b*) The train is in, le train est en gare. (*c*) Is the fire still in? est-ce que le feu brûle encore? **2.** (*a*) To be in with, être en bons termes avec. (*b*) My luck is in, je suis en veine. **3.** All in, tout compris.

inability, *s* Incapacité *f*: impuissance *f.*

inaccessible, *a.* Inaccessible.

inaccuracy, *s.* Inexactitude *f*

inaccurate, *a.* Inexact.

inaccurately, *adv.* Inexactement.

inaction, *s.* Inaction *f.*

inactive, *a.* Inactif.

inadequate, *a.* Insuffisant.

inadmissible, *a.* Inadmissible.

inadvertence, *s.* Inadvertance *f.*

inadvertently, *adv* Par inadvertance.

inane, *a.* Inepte, stupide.

inanimate, *a.* Inanimé.

inappropriate, *a* Qui ne convient pas; impropre.

inaptitude, *s.* Inaptitude *f* (*for*, à).

inarticulate, *a.* (*a*) Inarticulé. (*b*) Muet, -ette; incapable de parler.

inarticulately, *adv.* Indistinctement.

inattentive, *a.* **1.** Inattentif. **2.** Négligent (*to*, de).

inaudible, *a.* Imperceptible.

inaugurate, *v.tr.* Inaugurer.

inauguration, *s.* Inauguration *f.*

inbred, *a.* Inné, naturel.

incalculable, *a.* Incalculable.

incandescence, *s.* Incandescence *f.*

incandescent, *a.* Incandescent.

incapability, *s.* Incapacité *f.*

incapable, *a.* Incapable.

incapacitate, *v.tr.* Rendre incapable.
incapacity, *s.* Incapacité *f.*
incarnate, *a.* Incarné.
incautious, *a.* Imprudent; inconsidéré.
incautiously, *adv.* Imprudemment.
incense¹, *s.* Encens *m.*
incense², *v.tr.* Exaspérer.
incensed, *a.* Exaspéré.
incentive, *s.* Stimulant *m.*
incessant, *a.* Incessant, continuel.
incessantly, *adv.* Sans cesse; incessamment.
inch, *s.* Pouce *m.* **By inches,** peu à peu.
incident, *s.* Incident *m.*
incidental. 1. *a.* (a) Fortuit, accidentel. (b) I. to, inséparable de.
incidentally, *adv.* En passant.
incision, *s.* Incision *f,* entaille *f.*
incisive, *a.* Incisif.
incite, *v.tr.* Inciter.
incitement, *s.* Incitation.
incivility, *s.* Incivilité *f.*
inclement, *a.* Rigoureux, rude.
inclination, *s.* **1.** Inclination *f.* **2.** Inclinaison *f,* pente *f.* **3.** (a) Penchant *m.* (b) Tendance *f.*
incline¹, *s.* Pente *f,* déclivité *f.*
incline². 1. *v.tr.* Incliner, pencher. **2.** *v.i.* (a) Incliner, pencher. (b) Être enclin.
inclined, *a.* **1.** Incliné. **2.** Enclin, porté. **To be i..** avoir de l'inclination.
include, *v.tr.* Comprendre, renfermer, embrasser.
inclusion, *s.* Inclusion *f.*
inclusive, *a.* Inclusif; global; tout compris; inclusivement.
incoherence, *s.* Incohérence *f.*
incoherent, *a.* Incohérent.
incoherently, *adv.* Sans cohérence, sans suite.
income, *s.* Revenu *m,* revenus *mpl.*
income-tax, *s.* Impôt *m* sur le revenu.
incommode, *v.tr.* Incommoder, gêner.
incomparable, *a.* Incomparable.
incompatible, *a.* Incompatible.
incompetence, *s.* Incompétence *f*
incompetent, *a.* Incapable.
incomplete, *a.* Incomplet, -ète.
incomprehensible, *a.* Incompréhensible.

inconceivable, *a.* Inconcevable.
inconclusive, *a.* Peu concluant.
inconclusively, *adv.* D'une manière peu concluante.
incongruous, *a.* **1.** Inassociable. **2.** Incongru, déplacé.
inconsequent, *a.* Inconséquent.
inconsiderable, *a.* Insignifiant.
inconsiderate, *a.* Sans égards pour les autres.
inconsistency, *s.* Inconsistance *f.*
inconsistent, *a.* **1.** Incompatible. **2.** Inconsistant, inconséquent.
inconsolable, *a.* Inconsolable.
inconspicuous, *a.* Peu apparent.
inconstancy, *s.* Inconstance *f.*
inconstant, *a.* Inconstant, volage.
incontestable, *a.* Incontestable.
inconvenience¹, *s.* Incommodité *f,* contretemps *m;* inconvénient *m.*
inconvenience², *v.tr.* Déranger.
inconvenient, *a.* Incommode; inopportun; gênant.
inconveniently, *adv* Incommodément.
incorporate, *v.tr.* Incorporer.
incorrect, *a.* **1.** Inexact. **2.** Incorrect.
incorrigible, *a.* Incorrigible.
incorruptible, *a.* Incorruptible
increase¹, *s.* Augmentation *f;* accroissement *m.*
increase². 1. *v.i.* (a) Augmenter; grandir, s'agrandir; s'accroître. (b) Se multiplier. **2.** *v.tr.* Augmenter; accroître.
increasing, *a.* Croissant.
incredible, *a.* Incroyable.
incredibly, *adv.* Incroyablement.
incredulity, *s.* Incrédulité *f.*
incredulous, *a.* Incrédule.
increment, *s.* Augmentation *f.*
incriminate, *v.tr.* Incriminer.
incubation, *s.* Incubation *f.*
incubator, *s.* Couveuse artificielle.
inculcate, *v.tr.* Inculquer.
inculpate, *v.tr.* Inculper.
incumbent, *a.* **To be i. on,** incomber à.
incur, *v.tr.* Courir; encourir; contracter.
incurable, *a.* Incurable.
incursion, *s.* Incursion *f.*
indebted, *a.* **1.** Endetté. **2.** Redevable.
indecent, *a.* Peu décent, indécent.

indecision, s. Indécision f.

indecisive, a. Indécisif; indécis.

indeed, adv. **1.** En effet; vraiment. **Very much i.,** infiniment. **2.** Même; à vrai dire. **If i.,** si tant est que. **3. Yes i.!** mais certainement!

indefatigable, a. Infatigable.

indefatigably, adv. Infatigablement.

indefensible, a. Indéfendable; insoutenable.

indefinite, a. Indéfini. **1.** Vague. **2.** Indéterminé.

indefinitely, adv. **1.** Vaguement. **2.** Indéfiniment.

indelible, a. Indélébile, ineffaçable.

indelicate, a. Indélicat; peu délicat.

indemnify, v.tr. **1.** Garantir. **2.** Indemniser.

indemnity, s. **1.** Garantie f. **2.** Indemnité f, dédommagement m.

indentation, s. **1.** Impression f. **2.** Denteture f; découpure f.

independence, s. Indépendance f

independent, a. Indépendant.

independently, adv. **1.** Indépendamment. **2.** Avec indépendance.

indescribable, a. Indescriptible.

indestructible, a. Indestructible.

index, s. **1.** Indice m. **2.** Index m table f alphabétique.

India. Pr.n. L'Inde f.

Indian. 1. (a) a. De l'Inde; indien. (b) s. Indien, -ienne. **2. Red Indians,** Peaux-Rouges m.

india-rubber, s. Caoutchouc m.

indicate, v.tr. Indiquer.

indication, s. Indice m, signe m.

indicative, a. Indicatif.

indicator, s. (a) Index m, aiguille f. (b) Tableau indicateur.

indict, v.tr. Accuser, inculper.

indictment, s. Accusation f.

Indies (the). Pr.n.pl. Les Indes f. **The East I.,** les Indes. **The West I.,** les Antilles f.

indifference, s. Indifférence f, manque m d'intérêt.

indifferent, a. **1.** Indifférent. **2.** Médiocre, passable.

indigent, a. & s. Indigent, pauvre.

indigestible, a. Indigeste.

indigestion, s. Dyspepsie f.

indignant, a. Indigné.

indignantly, adv. Avec indignation.

indignation, s. Indignation f.

indignity, s. Indignité f, affront m.

indigo, s. Indigo m.

indirect, a. Indirect.

indirectly, adv. Indirectement.

indiscreet, a. Indiscret, -ète.

indiscreetly, adv. Indiscrètement.

indiscretion, s. (a) Manque m de discrétion. (b) Indiscrétion f.

indiscriminately, adv. Sans faire de distinction; au hasard.

indispensable, a. Indispensable.

indisposed, a. **1.** Peu enclin. **2.** Souffrant.

indisposition, s. Indisposition f.

indisputable, a. Incontestable.

indistinct, a. Indistinct; confus; vague.

indistinctly, adv. Indistinctement.

indistinguishable, a. Indistinguible.

individual. 1. a. (a) Individuel. (b) Particulier. **2.** s. Individu m; particulier m.

individuality, s. Individualité f.

indivisible, a. Indivisible.

indolence, s. Indolence f, paresse f.

indolent, a. Indolent, paresseux.

indomitable, a. Indomptable.

indomitably, adv. Indomptablement.

indoors, adv. A la maison. **To keep i.,** garder la maison.

indubitable, a. Indubitable.

induce, v.tr. **1.** Persuader à. **2.** Amener, produire, occasionner.

inducement, s. Attrait m.

indulge. 1. v.tr. (a) Gâter. **To i. in,** permettre (qch) à. (b) S'abandonner à. **2.** v.i. **To i. in,** s'adonner à.

indulgence, s. **1.** Indulgence f. **2.** Douceur f.

indulgent, a. Indulgent.

industrial, a. Industriel.

industrious, a. Assidu, industrieux.

industry, s. **1.** Application f; diligence f. **2.** Industrie f.

inebriated, a. Ivre, gris.

ineffectual, a. Inefficace.

inefficacy, s. Inefficacité f.

inefficient, a. Incompétent.

ineligible, a. Inéligible.

inept, a. **1.** Déplacé; mal à propos. **2.** Inepte, absurde.

inequality, s. Inégalité f.

inequitable, a. Inéquitable.

inert, a. Inerte.

inertia, s. Inertie f.

inestimable, a. Inestimable.

inevitable, *a.* (*a*) Inévitable. (*b*) Fatal, -als ; obligé.

inevitably, *adv.* Inévitablement.

inexact, *a.* Inexact.

inexcusable, *a.* Inexcusable.

inexhaustible, *a.* Inépuisable

inexorable, *a.* Inexorable.

inexorably, *adv.* Inexorablement

inexpedient, *a.* Inopportun.

inexpensive, *a.* Pas cher.

inexperienced, *a.* Inexpérimenté

inexplicable, *a.* Inexplicable.

inexplicably, *adv.* Inexplicablement

inexpressibly, *adv.* Indiciblement.

inextricable, *a.* Inextricable.

infallible, *a.* Infaillible.

infallibly, *adv.* Infailliblement.

infamous, *a.* Infâme ; abominable

infamy, *s.* Infamie *f.*

infancy, *s.* (*a*) Première enfance : bas âge. (*b*) Débuts *mpl,* enfance.

infant, *s.* Enfant *mf* (en bas âge).

infantile, *a.* **1.** D'enfant ; enfantin **2.** Infantile.

infantry, *s.* Infanterie *f.*

infatuate, *v.tr.* Infatuer, affoler.

infatuated, *a.* Infatué.

infatuation, *s.* Infatuation *f,* engouement *m.*

infect, *v.tr.* **1.** Infecter, corrompre. **2.** Atteindre.

infection, *s.* Infection *f,* contagion *f.*

infectious, *a.* (*a*) Infectieux (*b*) Contagieux.

infer, *v.tr.* **1.** Inférer. **2.** Impliquer.

inference, *s.* Déduction *f.*

inferior. **1.** *a.* Inférieur, -e. **2.** *s.* (*a*) Inférieur, -e. (*b*) Subordonné, -ée.

inferiority, *s.* Infériorité *f.*

infernal, *a.* Infernal, -aux.

inferno, *s.* Enfer *m.*

infest, *v.tr.* Infester.

infidel, *a. & s.* Incroyant, -ante

infidelity, *s.* Infidélité *f.*

infinite, *a.* Infini.

infinitely, *adv.* Infiniment.

infinity, *s.* Infinité *f.*

infirm, *a.* Infirme, débile.

infirmary, *s.* Hôpital *m,* -aux.

infirmity, *s.* Infirmité *f.*

inflame, *v.tr.* Mettre le feu à, enflammer ; allumer.

inflammable, *a.* Inflammable.

inflammation, *s.* Inflammation *f.*

inflate, *v.tr.* Gonfler.

inflated, *a.* Gonflé

inflation, *s.* (*a*) Gonflement *m* (*b*) Hausse *f.*

inflexibility, *s.* Inflexibilité *f*

inflexible, *a.* Inflexible.

inflexibly, *adv.* Inflexiblement

inflexion, *s.* Inflexion *f.*

inflict, *v.tr.* Infliger ; donner, faire.

infliction, *s.* **1.** Infliction *f.* **2.** Peine infligée ; châtiment *m.*

influence¹, *s.* Influence *f.*

influence², *v.tr.* Influencer

influential, *a.* Influent.

influenza, *s.* Grippe *f.*

influx, *s.* Entrée *f,* affluence *f.*

inform. **1.** *v.tr.* (*a*) Informer, avertir. (*b*) Renseigner. **2.** *v.i.* To i. against, dénoncer.

informal, *a.* Sans cérémonie.

informally, *adv.* Sans cérémonie ; sans formalités.

informant, *s.* Informateur, -trice.

information, *s.* **1.** Renseignements *mpl,* informations *fpl.* **2.** Instruction *f,* savoir *m.* **3.** Dénonciation *f.*

informative, *a.* Instructif.

informer, *s.* Dénonciateur, -trice.

infrequent, *a.* Rare ; peu fréquent

infringe, *v.tr.* Enfreindre, violer

infringement, *s.* Infraction *f.*

infuriate, *v.tr.* Rendre furieux

infuriated, *a.* Furieux.

infuse, *v.tr.* Infuser.

infusion, *s.* Infusion *f.*

ingenious, *a.* Ingénieux.

ingeniously, *adv.* Ingénieusement.

ingenuity, *s.* Ingéniosité *f.*

ingenuous, *a.* Ingénu ; naïf, *f.* naïve.

ingenuously, *adv.* Ingénument, naïvement.

ingot, *s.* Lingot *m.*

ingratiate, *v.tr.* To i. oneself with, s'insinuer dans les bonnes grâces de.

ingratiating, *a.* Insinuant.

ingratitude, *s.* Ingratitude *f.*

ingredient, *s.* Ingrédient *m.*

inhabit, *v.tr.* Habiter, habiter dans.

inhabitable, *a.* Habitable.

inhabitant, *s.* Habitant, -ante.

inhale, *v.tr.* Aspirer, humer.

inherent, *a.* Inhérent, naturel.

inherit, *v.tr.* (*a*) Hériter de ; succéder à. (*b*) Hériter.

inheritance, *s.* Patrimoine *m,* héritage *m.*

inhospitable, *a.* Inhospitalier.

inhuman, *a.* Inhumain.

inhumanity, s. Inhumanité f.

inimical, a. Ennemi, hostile.

iniquitous, a. Inique.

iniquity, s. Iniquité f.

initial[1]. **I.** a. Initial, -aux ; premier. **2.** s.pl. Initiales fpl.

initial[2], v.tr. Parafer.

initiate[1], a. & s. Initié, -ée.

initiate[2], v.tr **I.** Commencer. **2.** Initier.

initiation, s. **I.** Commencement m. **2.** Initiation f.

initiative, s. Initiative f.

inject, v.tr. Injecter.

injection, s. Injection f.

injudicious, a. Peu judicieux.

injunction, s. Injonction f, ordre m

injure, v.tr. **I.** Nuire à, faire tort à **2.** (a) Blesser ; faire mal à. (b) Endommager, gâter.

injured, a. **I.** Offensé. **2.** Blessé s. The i., les accidentés m.

injurious, a. Nuisible, pernicieux.

injury, s.. **I.** Tort m, mal m. **2.** (a) Blessure f. (b) Dommage m, dégât m.

injustice, s. Injustice f.

ink, s. Encre f. In ink, à l'encre

inkling, s. Soupçon m.

inkpot, s. Encrier m.

inkstand, s. Encrier m.

ink-well, s. Encrier m.

inky, a. **I.** Taché d'encre. **2.** Noir comme (de) l'encre.

inland. I. s. (L')intérieur m. **2.** Attrib. Intérieur, -e. **3.** adv. To go i., pénétrer dans les terres.

inlay, v.tr. Incruster (with, de).

inlet, s. Petit bras de mer.

inmate, s. Habitant. -ante.

inn, s. Auberge f.

innate, a. Inné, naturel.

inner, a. Intérieur, -e ; de dedans. I. meaning, sens intime.

innings, s. Tour m de batte.

innkeeper, s. Aubergiste mf.

innocence, s. Innocence f.

innocent, a. Innocent.

innocently, adv. Innocemment.

innocuous, a. Inoffensif.

innovation, s. Innovation f

innuendo, s. Allusion f.

innumerable, a. Innombrable.

inoculate, v.tr. Inoculer.

inoculation, s. Inoculation f.

inoffensive, a. Inoffensif.

inopportune, a. Inopportun.

inordinate, a. Démesuré.

inquest, s. Enquête f.

inquire, v.tr. & i. **I.** S'informer de ; demander. **2.** To i. about, s'enquérir de, se renseigner sur. To i. for, demander. To i. into, examiner.

inquiring, a. Curieux.

inquiry, s. **I.** Enquête f. **2.** Demande f de renseignements. To make inquiries, s'informer (about, de). I. office, bureau m de renseignements.

inquisitive, a. Curieux.

inquisitively, adv. Avec curiosité.

inrush, s. Irruption f.

insane, a. Fou, f. folle.

insanity, s. Folie f, démence f.

insatiable, a. Insatiable.

insatiably, adv. Insatiablement.

inscribe, v.tr. Inscrire.

inscription, s. Inscription f.

inscrutable, a. Impénétrable.

insect, s. Insecte m.

insect-powder, s. Poudre f insecticide.

insecure, a. **I.** Peu sûr ; peu solide ; mal affermi. **2.** Exposé au danger.

insecurely, adv. Peu solidement ; sans sécurité.

insecurity, s. Insécurité f.

insensate, a. Insensé.

insensibility, s. **I.** Défaillance f. **2.** Insensibilité f.

insensible, a. **I.** Insensible. **2.** Sans connaissance.

insensitive, a. Insensible.

inseparable, a. Inséparable.

insert, v.tr. **I.** Insérer. **2.** Introduire, enfoncer.

insertion, s. Insertion f, introduction f.

inside. I. s. Dedans m, intérieur m. On the i., au dedans. **I.** out, sens dessus dessous. **2.** a. Intérieur, -eure, d'intérieur. **3.** adv. Intérieurement ; en dedans. **4.** prep. A l'intérieur de ; dans.

insidious, a. Insidieux.

insight, s. **I.** Perspicacité f ; pénétration f. **2.** Aperçu m.

insignificance, s. Insignifiance f.

insignificant, a. Insignifiant.

insincere, a. (a) Peu sincère. (b) Faux, f. fausse.

insincerity, s. Manque m de sincérité.

insinuate, v.tr. Insinuer. **I.** S'insinuer. **2.** Donner adroitement à entendre.

insinuating, a. Insinuant.

insinuation, s. Insinuation f.

insipid, a. Insipide, fade.

insist, v.i. Insister.

insistent, a. Qui insiste ; importun.

insistently, adv. Instamment ; avec insistance.

insolence, s. Insolence f.

insolent, a. Insolent (to, envers).

insolently, adv. Insolemment.

insoluble, a. Insoluble.

insolvency, s. (a) Insolvabilité f. (b) Faillite f.

insolvent, a. Insolvable.

insomnia, s. Insomnie f.

inspect, v.tr. Inspecter ; contrôler.

inspection, s. Inspection f ; vérification f ; contrôle m.

inspector, s. Inspecteur, -trice.

inspiration, s. Inspiration f.

inspire, v.tr. Inspirer.

inspiriting, a. Encourageant.

instability, s. Instabilité f.

install, v.tr. Installer.

installation, s. Installation f.

instalment, s. Acompte m.

instance, s. **1.** Exemple m, cas m. **2.** For i., par exemple. **3.** In the first i., en premier lieu.

instant¹, a. **1.** Instant, urgent. **2.** Courant ; de ce mois.

instant², s. Instant m, moment m.

instantaneous, a. Instantané.

instantaneously, adv. Instantanément.

instantly, adv. Tout de suite ; sur-le-champ.

instead. 1. Prep.phr. I. of, au lieu de ; à la place de. **2.** adv. Au lieu de cela ; plutôt.

instep, s. Cou-de-pied m.

instigate, v.tr. Instiguer, inciter.

instigation, s. Instigation f.

instigator, s. Instigateur, -trice.

instil, v.tr. Infiltrer.

instinct, s. Instinct m.

instinctive, a. Instinctif.

instinctively, adv. D'instinct ; instinctivement.

institute¹, s. Institut m.

institute², v.tr. Instituer établir.

institution, s. Institution f.

instruct, v.tr. **1.** Instruire. **2.** Charger.

instruction, s. **1.** Instruction f, enseignement m. **2.** pl. Indications f, instructions.

instructive, a. Instructif.

instructor, s. Maître.

instrument, s. Instrument m.

instrumental, a. **1.** Contributif. **2.** Instrumental.

insubordinate, a. Insubordonné.

insubordination, s. Insubordination f.

insufferable, a. Insupportable.

insufficient, a. Insuffisant.

insufficiently, adv. Insuffisamment.

insulate, v.tr. Isoler.

insulation, s. Isolement m.

insulator, s. Isolateur m.

insult¹, s. Insulte f, affront m.

insult², v.tr. Insulter.

insulting, a. Offensant, injurieux.

insuperable, a. Insurmontable.

insurance, s. (a) Assurance f. (b) Prime f d'assurance.

insure, v.tr. **1.** (i) Assurer, (ii) faire assurer. **2.** Garantir, assurer.

insurgent, a. & s. Insurgé, -ée.

insurmountable, a. Insurmontable.

insurrection, s. Insurrection f, soulèvement m.

intact, a. Intact.

intangible, a. Intangible, impalpable.

integral, a. Intégrant.

integrity, s. Intégrité f.

intellect, s. Intelligence f, esprit m.

intellectual, a. & s. Intellectuel, -elle.

intelligence, s. **1.** Intelligence f. **2.** Renseignement(s) m(pl).

intelligent, a. Intelligent ; avisé.

intelligently, adv. Intelligemment.

intelligible, a. Intelligible.

intelligibly, adv. Intelligiblement.

intemperate, a. **1.** Intempérant, immodéré. **2.** Adonné à la boisson.

intend, v.tr. **1.** Avoir l'intention (de). **2.** Destiner (for, à). **3.** Vouloir dire ; entendre.

intended, a. **1.** (a) Projeté. (b) Voulu. **2.** Intentionnel.

intense, a. Vif, f. vive ; fort, intense.

intensely, adv. Excessivement ; profondément.

intensify. 1. v.tr. Intensifier, augmenter ; renforcer. **2.** v.i. Devenir plus intense.

intensity, s. Intensité f ; violence f.

intensive, a. Intensif.

intent¹, s. Intention f, dessein m. To all intents and purposes, virtuellement.

intent², *a.* **1.** (*a*) **1. on,** tout entier à ; absorbé dans ; résolu à. (*b*) Attentif. **2.** Fixe.

intention, *s.* Intention *f.* (*a*) Dessein *m.* (*b*) But *m.*

intentional, *a.* Intentionnel, voulu.

intentionally, *adv.* A dessein ; exprès ; intentionnellement.

intently, *adv.* Attentivement ; fixement.

inter, *v.tr.* Enterrer, ensevelir.

intercede, *v.i.* Intercéder (*with,* auprès de).

intercept, *v.tr.* Intercepter.

intercourse, *s.* Commerce *m,* relations *fpl,* rapports *mpl.*

interest¹, *s.* **1.** Intérêt *m.* **2.** Avantage *m,* profit *m.* **3. To take an i. in,** s'intéresser à.

interest², *v.tr.* **1.** Intéresser. **2.** Éveiller l'intérêt de. **To be interested in,** s'intéresser à.

interested, *a.* Intéressé.

interesting, *a.* Intéressant.

interfere, *v.i.* (*a*) Intervenir ; s'interposer. (*b*) Toucher (*with,* à). (*c*) **To i. with,** gêner ; entraver.

interference, *s.* **1.** Intervention *f* ; intrusion *f.* **2.** Effet *m* parasitaire.

interfering, *a.* Importun.

interior. 1. *a.* Intérieur, -e. **2.** *s.* Intérieur *m.*

interlace. 1. *v.tr.* Entrelacer. **2.** *v.i.* S'entrelacer.

interloper, *s.* Intrus, -use.

interlude, *s.* Intermède *m.*

intermediary, *s.* Intermédiaire (*m*).

intermediate, *a.* Intermédiaire (*m*).

interminable, *a.* Interminable.

interminably, *adv.* Interminablement.

intermingle, *v.i.* S'entremêler.

intermission, *s.* Interruption *f.*

intermittent, *a.* Intermittent.

intern, *v.tr.* Interner.

internal, *a.* Intérieur, -e.

internally, *adv.* Intérieurement.

international, *a.* International, -aux.

internment, *s.* Internement *m.*

interpolation, *s.* Interpolation *f.*

interpose. 1. *v.tr.* Interposer. **2.** *v.i.* S'interposer, intervenir.

interposition, *s.* **1.** Interposition *f.* **2.** Intervention *f.*

interpret, *v.tr.* Interpréter.

interpretation, *s.* Interprétation *f.*

interpreter, *s.* Interprète *mf.*

interrogate, *v.tr.* Interroger.

interrogation, *s.* Interrogation *f* ; interrogatoire *m.*

interrupt, *v.tr.* Interrompre.

interruption, *s.* Interruption *f* ; dérangement *m.*

intersect. 1. *v.tr.* Entrecouper, intersecter. **2.** *v.i.* Se couper, se croiser.

intersperse, *v.tr.* Entremêler.

interstice, *s.* Interstice *m.*

interval, *s.* Intervalle *m.* **1.** (*a*) **At intervals,** par intervalles. (*b*) Entr'acte *m.* **2.** Écartement *m.*

intervene, *v.i.* **1.** Intervenir, s'interposer. **2.** Survenir, arriver.

intervening, *a.* Intermédiaire.

intervention, *s.* Intervention *f.*

interview¹, *s.* Entrevue *f.*

interview², *v.tr.* Interviewer.

intimacy, *s.* Intimité *f.*

intimate¹. 1. *a.* Intime. (*a*) **To become i.,** se lier. (*b*) Approfondi. **2.** *s.* Intime *mf.*

intimate², *v.tr.* **1.** Signifier, notifier. **2.** Donner à entendre, indiquer.

intimately, *adv.* Intimement ; à fond.

intimation, *s.* **1.** Avis *m.* **2.** Suggestion *f.*

intimidate, *v.tr.* Intimider.

intimidating, *a.* Intimidant.

intimidation, *s.* Intimidation *f.*

intimity, *s.* Intimité *f.*

into, *prep.* Dans, en. **To fall i. the hands of,** tomber entre les mains de.

intolerable, *a.* Intolérable, insupportable.

intolerant, *a.* Intolérant.

intoxicant, *s.* Boisson *f* alcoolique.

intoxicate, *v.tr.* Enivrer, griser.

intoxicated, *a.* Ivre ; gris.

intoxicating, *a.* Enivrant, grisant.

intoxication, *s.* Ivresse *f.*

intractable, *a.* Intraitable.

intrepid, *a.* Intrépide.

intrepidity, *s.* Intrépidité *f.*

intricacy, *s.* Complexité *f.*

intricate, *a.* Compliqué.

intrigue¹, *s.* Intrigue *f.*

intrigue², *v.i. & tr.* Intriguer.

intriguing, *a.* Intrigant.

intrinsic, *a.* Intrinsèque.

introduce, *v.tr.* **1.** Introduire. **2.** Présenter.

introduction, *s.* **1.** Introduction *f.* **2.** Présentation *f.* **3.** Avant-propos *m inv.*

introductory, *a.* Introductoire.
introspective, *a.* Introspectif.
intrude, *v.i.* Faire intrusion ; être importun ; empiéter.
intruder, *s.* Intrus, -use.
intrusion, *s.* Intrusion *f.*
intrusive, *a.* Importun, indiscret.
intuition, *s.* Intuition *f.*
inundate, *v.tr.* Inonder (*with*, de).
inundation, *s.* Inondation *f.*
inure, *v.tr.* Accoutumer, habituer.
invade, *v.tr.* **1.** Envahir. **2.** Empiéter sur.
invader, *s.* Envahisseur *m.*
invalid, *a. & s.* Malade (*mf*)
invaluable, *a.* Inestimable.
invariable, *a.* Invariable.
invariably, *adv.* Invariablement.
invasion, *s.* Invasion *f.* envahissement *m.*
invective, *s.* Invective *f.*
inveigh, *v.i.* Invectiver, fulminer.
inveigle, *v.tr.* Attirer, séduire.
invent, *v.tr.* Inventer.
invention, *s.* Invention *f.*
inventive, *a.* Inventif.
inventor, *s.* Inventeur, -trice.
inventory, *s.* Inventaire *m.*
inverse, *a. & s.* Inverse (*m*).
inversely, *adv.* Inversement.
invert, *v.tr.* Renverser, retourner.
invest, *v.tr.* **1.** Revêtir (*with*, de). **2.** Placer, investir.
investigate, *v.tr.* Examiner, étudier ; enquêter sur.
investigation, *s.* Investigation *f* ; enquête *f.*
investment, *s.* Placement *m.*
inveterate, *a.* Invétéré.
invidious, *a.* **1.** Odieux ; ingrat. **2.** Désobligeant.
invigorate, *v.tr.* Fortifier.
invincible, *a.* Invincible.
invisibility, *s.* Invisibilité *f.*
invisible, *a.* Invisible.
invitation, *s.* Invitation *f.*
invite, *v.tr.* **1.** Inviter ; convier. **2.** Engager, inviter. **3.** Provoquer.
inviting, *a.* Invitant, attrayant ; appétissant.
invocation, *s.* Invocation *f.*
invoice¹, *s.* Facture *f.*
invoice², *v.tr.* Facturer.
invoke, *v.tr.* Invoquer.
involuntarily, *adv.* Involontairement.

involuntary, *a.* Involontaire.
involve, *v.tr.* **1.** (*a*) Envelopper. (*b*) Compliquer. **2.** Engager. **3.** Comporter, entraîner.
involved, *a.* Embrouillé, compliqué.
invulnerable, *a.* Invulnérable.
inward, *a.* (*a*) Intérieur, -e. interne. (*b*) Vers l'intérieur.
inwardly, *adv.* En dedans ; intérieurement.
inwards, *adv.* Vers l'intérieur.
iodide, *s.* Iodure *m.*
iodine, *s.* Iode *m.*
iodoform, *s.* Iodoforme *m.*
ipecacuanha, *s.* Ipécacuana *m.*
irascible, *a.* Irascible, coléreux.
irate, *a.* Courroucé ; en colère.
ire, *s.* Courroux *m*, colère *f.*
iridescent, *a.* Irisé. iridescent.
iris, *s.* Iris *m.*
Irish, *a.* Irlandais ; d'Irlande
Irishman, *s.* Irlandais *m.*
Irishwoman, *s.* Irlandaise *f.*
irksome, *a.* Ennuyeux, ingrat.
iron¹, *s.* **1.** Fer *m.* Cast i., fonte *f.* **2.** Fer à repasser. **3.** *pl.* Fers, chaînes *f.*
iron², *v.tr.* Repasser.
ironical, *a.* Ironique.
ironically, *adv.* Ironiquement.
ironing, *s.* Repassage *m.*
ironmonger, *s.* Quincaillier *m.*
ironware, *s.* Quincaillerie *f.*
irony, *s.* Ironie *f.*
irradiate, *v.tr.* Illuminer.
irrational, *a.* Déraisonnable, absurde.
irreconcilable, *a.* **1.** Irréconciliable ; implacable. **2.** Incompatible.
irrecoverable, *a.* Irrécouvrable.
irredeemable, *a.* Incorrigible.
irrefutable, *a.* Irréfutable.
irregular, *a.* Irrégulier.
irregularity, *s.* Irrégularité *f.*
irregularly, *adv.* Irrégulièrement.
irrelevant, *a.* Non pertinent ; hors de propos.
irremediable, *a.* Irrémédiable.
irremediably, *adv.* Irrémédiablement.
irreparable, *a.* Irréparable.
irrepressible, *a.* Irrésistible, irréprimable.
irreproachable, *a.* Irréprochable.
irresistible, *a.* Irrésistible.
irresolute, *a.* Indécis.

irresolutely, *adv.* Irrésolument.
irrespective, *adv.* **1.** of, indépendamment de.
irresponsible, *a.* Étourdi.
irretrievably, *adv.* Irréparablement, irrémédiablement.
irreverence, *s.* Irrévérence *f.*
irreverent, *a.* Irrévérencieux.
irrevocable, *a.* Irrévocable.
irrigation, *s.* Irrigation *f.*
irritable, *a.* Irritable, irascible.
irritate, *v.tr.* Irriter, agacer.
irritating, *a.* Irritant, agaçant.
irritation, *s.* Irritation *f.*
irruption, *s.* Irruption *f.*
isinglass, *s.* Gélatine *f.*
island, *s.* Ile *f.* Small i. îlot *m.*
isle, *s.* Ile *f.*
islet, *s.* Ilot *m.*
isolate, *v.tr.* Isoler.
isolated, *a.* Isolé, écarté.
isolation, *s.* Isolement *m.*
issue¹, *s.* **1.** Issue *f*, sortie *f.* **2.** Issue, résultat *m.* **3.** Descendance *f.* **4.** The point at i., la question pendante. **5.** (*a*) Émission *f.* (*b*) Publication *f.* (*c*) Délivrance *f.*
issue². **1.** *v.i.* (*a*) Jaillir, s'écouler. (*b*) Provenir. **2.** *v.tr.* (*a*) Émettre. (*b*) Publier. (*c*) Distribuer.

isthmus, *s.* Isthme *m.*
it, *pers.pron.* **1.** (*a*) Il, *f.* elle. (*b*) Le, *f.* la. (*c*) Lui *mf.* **2. The worst of** it is, le plus mauvais de la chose c'est. **3.** Ce, cela, il. **Who is it?** qui est-ce ? **It doesn't matter,** cela ne fait rien. **4. How is it?** d'où vient ? **It is said that,** on dit que. **5. At** it, in it, to it, y. **Above it,** over it, au-dessus ; dessus. **For it,** en ; pour lui, pour elle, pour cela. **From it,** en. **Far from it,** tant s'en faut. **Of it,** en. **On it,** y, dessus.
Italian. 1. *a.* Italien, d'Italie. **2.** *s.* (*a*) Italien, -ienne. (*b*) L'italien *m.*
italics, *s.pl.* Italiques *m.*
Italy. *Pr.n.* L'Italie *f.*
itch, *v.i.* Démanger ; éprouver des démangeaisons.
itching, *s.* Démangeaison *f.*
item, *s.* Article *m* ; détail *m* ; numéro *m.*
itinerant, *a.* Ambulant.
itinerary, *s.* Itinéraire *m.*
its, *poss.a.* Son ; *f.* sa ; *pl.* ses.
itself, *pers.pron.* Lui-même, elle-même ; se ; même.
ivory, *s.* **1.** Ivoire *m.* **2.** *Attrib.* D'ivoire, en ivoire.
ivy, *s.* Lierre *m.*

J

J, j, *s.* (La lettre) J, j *m.*
jabber, *v.i.* Jacasser.
Jack¹. **I.** *Pr.n.* **1.** Jean, *m.* **2.** Le marin. **II. jack,** *s.* **1.** *Cards :* Valet *m.* **2.** Brochet *m.* **III. jack,** *s.* **1.** Cric *m*, vérin *m.* **2.** Cochonnet *m.*
jack² **up,** *v.tr.* Soulever avec un cric
jackal, *s.* Chacal *m*, -als.
jackass, *s.* (*a*) Ane (mâle) *m.* (*b*) Idiot *m*, imbécile *m.*
jackdaw, *s.* Choucas *m.*
jacket, *s.* (*a*) Veston *m* ; jaquette *f* ; casaque *f.*
jade, *s.* Jade *m.*
jaded, *a.* Excédé.
jagged, *a.* Déchiqueté, ébréché.
jaguar, *s.* Jaguar *m.*
jam¹, *s.* (*a*) Foule *f*, presse *f* (*b*) Embouteillage *m.*
jam². **1.** *v.tr.* Serrer, presser. **2.** *v.i.* Se coincer.

jam², *s.* Confiture *f.*
Jamaica. *Pr.n.* La Jamaïque.
jamb, *s.* Jambage *m*, montant *m.*
james. *Pr.n.* Jacques *m.*
jam-jar, *s.* Pot *m* à confitures.
Jane. *Pr.n.* Jeanne *f.*
jangle, *v.i.* Cliqueter ; s'entrechoquer.
January, *s.* Janvier *m.*
Japan. 1. *Pr.n.* Le Japon. **In J.,** au Japon. **2.** *s.* Laque *m* (de Chine).
japan², *v.tr.* Laquer.
Japanese. 1. *a. & s.* Japonais, -aise. nippon, -one. **2.** *s.* Le japonais.
jar¹, *s.* Choc *m* ; secousse *f.*
jar², *v.i.* Heurter, cogner. **To jar on,** froisser ; agacer.
jar³, *s.* Récipient *m* ; pot *m.*
jarring, *a.* Discordant.
jasmine, *s.* Jasmin *m.*
jaundice, *s.* Jaunisse *f.*
jaunt, *s.* Randonnée *f.*

jauntiness, s. Désinvolture f.

jaunty, a. **1.** Insouciant, désinvolte. **2.** Enjoué, vif.

jaw, s. Mâchoire f.

jay, s. Geai m.

jazz¹, s. Jazz m.

jazz², v.i. Danser le jazz.

jazz-band, s. Jazz-band m.

jealous, a. Jaloux.

jealously, adv. Jalousement.

jealousy, s. Jalousie f.

jeer¹, s. **1.** Raillerie f. **2.** Huée f.

jeer², v.i. Se moquer (at, de).

jeering¹, a. Railleur, -euse.

jeering², s. Raillerie f, moquerie f.

jelly, s. Gelée f.

jelly-fish, s. Méduse f.

jeopardize, v.tr. Mettre en péril.

jeopardy, s. Danger m, péril m.

jerk¹, s. Saccade f, secousse f.

jerk², **1.** v.tr. (a) Donner une secousse à. (b) Lancer brusquement. **2.** v.i. Se mouvoir par saccades.

jerkily, adv. Par saccades; par à-coups.

jerky, a. Saccadé.

jersey, s. Jersey m ; vareuse f ; maillot m.

jest¹, s. Raillerie f, plaisanterie f. In j., en plaisantant.

jest², v.i. Plaisanter; badiner.

jesting, s. Raillerie f, badinage m.

Jesuit, s. Jésuite m.

Jesus. Pr.n. Jésus m.

jet¹, s. Jais m.

jet², s. **1.** Jet m. **Jet plane,** avion à réaction. **2.** (a) Ajutage m. (b) Brûleur m.

jet-black, a. Noir comme du jais.

jet-propelled, a. (Avion) à réaction.

jettison, v.tr. Jeter à la mer.

jetty, s. Jetée f, digue f.

Jew, s. Juif m.

jewel, s. (a) Bijou m, joyau m. (b) pl. Pierres précieuses ; pierreries f.

jewel-case, s. Coffret m à bijoux ; écrin m.

jeweller, s. Bijoutier m, joaillier m.

jewellery, s. Bijouterie f, joaillerie f.

Jewess, s. Juive f.

Jewish, a. Juif, f. juive.

jib, v.i. (a) Refuser. (b) Regimber.

jig, s. Gigue f.

jilt¹, s. Coquette f.

jilt², v.tr. Planter (là).

jingle. **1.** v.i. Tinter ; cliqueter. **2.** v.tr. Faire tinter ; faire sonner.

jingling, s. Tintement m ; cliquetis m.

job, s. **1.** (a) Tâche f, besogne f, travail m. **Odd jobs,** petits travaux. **That's a good job!** ce n'est pas malheureux ! (b) Tâche difficile ; corvée f. **2.** Emploi m. **3.** Intrigue f, tripotage m.

jobbery, s. Tripotages mpl.

job lot, s. (Lot m de) soldes mpl.

jockey, s. Jockey m.

jocose, a. Facétieux ; goguenard.

jocular, a. Facétieux.

jocularity, s. Jovialité f.

jocularly, adv. Facétieusement.

jog¹, s. Secousse f ; cahot m.

jog², v.tr. Pousser ; rafraîchir.

John. Pr.n. Jean m.

join¹, s. Joint m, jointure f.

join². **I.** v.tr. **1.** (a) Joindre, unir. (b) Ajouter. **2.** (a) Se (re)joindre. (b) Entrer dans. **To j. a party,** s'affilier à un parti. **3.** Se joindre, s'unir, à.   **II. join,** v.i. Se (re)joindre, s'unir (with, à). **join in,** v.i. **1.** Prendre part à. **2.** Se mettre de la partie. **join up.** **1.** v.tr. Assembler. **2.** v.i. S'engager.

joiner, s. Menuisier m.

joint¹, s. **1.** (a) Joint m, jointure f. **Out of j.,** disloqué, déboîté. (b) Assemblage m. **2.** Morceau de viande. **Cut off the j.,** tranche f de rôti.

joint², a. (En) commun ; combiné.

jointed, a. Articulé.

jointly, adv. Ensemble, conjointement.

jointure, s. Douaire m.

joist, s. Solive f, poutre f.

joke¹, s. (a) Plaisanterie f, farce f. **Practical j.,** farce. (b) Bon mot ; plaisanterie.

joke², v.i. Plaisanter, badiner.

joker, s. **1.** Farceur, -euse ; plaisant m. **Practical j.,** mauvais plaisant. **2.** Cards : Joker m.

joking, s. Plaisanterie f, badinage m.

jokingly, adv. En plaisantant, pour rire.

jolly. **1.** a. Joyeux, gai. **2.** adv. Rudement.

jolt¹, s. Cahot m, secousse f.

jolt², v.tr. & i. Cahoter.

jostle, v.tr. Bousculer, coudoyer.

jot, v.tr. **To jot down,** noter.

journal, s. Journal m, -aux.
journalism, s. Journalisme m.
journalist, s. Journaliste mf.
journey, s. Voyage m; trajet m.
jovial, a. Jovial, -aux.
joviality, s. Jovialité f, gaîté f.
jovially, adv. Jovialement.
joy, s. Joie f, allégresse f.
joyful, a. Joyeux, heureux.
joyfully, adv. Joyeusement.
joyous, a. Joyeux.
joy-ride, s. **1.** Balade f en auto. **2.** Av : Vol m de plaisir.
joy-stick, s. Manche m à balai.
jubilant, a. (a) Réjoui. (b) Joyeux.
jubilantly, adv. Avec joie.
jubilation, s. Joie f, allégresse f.
jubilee, s. Jubilé m.
judge[1], s. **1.** Juge m. **2.** Arbitre m. **3.** Connaisseur, -euse.
judge[2], v.tr. **1.** (a) Juger. (b) Judging by, à en juger par. (c) Arbitrer. **2.** Apprécier, estimer.
judgement, s. **1.** (a) Jugement m. (b) Décision f judiciaire; arrêt m. **2.** Opinion f, avis m. **3.** Bon sens; discernement m.
judicial, a. Judiciaire.
judicially, adv. Judiciairement.
judicious, a. Judicieux.
judiciously, adv. Judicieusement.
jug, s. Cruche f, broc m; pot m.
juggle, v.i. (a) Jongler. (b) Faire des tours de passe-passe.
juggler, s. (a) Jongleur, -euse. (b) Prestidigitateur m.
jugglery, s. (a) Jonglerie f. (b) Tours mpl de passe-passe.
Jugoslav, a. & s. Yougoslave (mf).
Jugoslavia. Pr.n. La Yougoslavie.
juice, s. Jus m, suc m.
juicy, a. Succulent, juteux.
July, s. Juillet m.
jumble, v.tr. Brouiller, mêler.
jump[1], s. **1.** Saut m, bond m. J. in prices, saute f dans les prix. **2.** Sursaut m, haut-le-corps m inv.
jump[2]. I. v.i. **1.** Sauter, bondir. To j. to a conclusion, conclure à la légère. **2.** Sursauter, tressauter.
II. **jump,** v.tr. Franchir, sauter. To j. the metals, sortir des rails.
jump about, v.i. Sautiller. **jump across,** v.tr. Franchir d'un bond.

jump in, v.i. Entrer d'un bond.
jump out, v.i. Sortir d'un bond. To j. out of bed, sauter à bas du lit.
jump up, v.i. **1.** Sauter sur ses pieds. **2.** Bondir.
jumper, s. Casaquin m, casaque f.
junction, s. **1.** Jonction f, confluent m. **2.** (a) (Em)branchement m. (b) Gare f d'embranchement.
juncture, s. Conjoncture f.
June, s. Juin m.
jungle, s. Jungle f, fourré m.
junior, a. & s. **1.** Cadet, -ette; plus jeune. W. Smith J., W. Smith fils. **2.** Subalterne (m).
junk, s. Jonque f.
junket, s. Lait caillé.
jurisdiction, s. Juridiction f.
jury, s. Jury m; jurés mpl.
jury-box, s. Banc(s) m(pl) du jury.
juryman, s. Juré m, membre m du jury.
just. I. a. Juste, équitable.
II. **just,** adv. **1.** (a) Juste, justement; au juste. J. by the gate, tout près de la porte. Not ready j. yet, pas encore tout à fait prêt. That's j. it, c'est bien cela. J. so! c'est cela ! parfaitement ! It's j. the same, c'est tout un. (b) J. as you please! comme vous voudrez! J. as, au moment où (il partait). (c) J. now, actuellement; pour le moment; tout à l'heure. **2.** (a) Immédiatement. (b) He has j. written to you, il vient de vous écrire. He has j. come, il ne fait que d'arriver. J. out, vient de paraître. **3.** Sur le point de. **4.** J. in time to, juste à temps pour. **5.** (a) Seulement. J. once, rien qu'une fois. J. one, un seul. (b) J. listen! écoutez donc !
justice, s. Justice f.
justifiable, a. Justifiable; légitime.
justifiably, adv. Justifiablement, légitimement.
justification, s. Justification f.
justified, a. Justifié.
justify, v.tr. Justifier; motiver.
justly, adv. **1.** Avec justice. **2.** Avec justesse.
jut, v.i. Faire saillie.
juvenile, a. Juvénile.

K

K, k, *s.* (La lettre) K, k *m.*
kale, *s.* Chou frisé.
kangaroo, *s.* Kangourou *m.*
keel, *s.* Quille *f.*
keen, *a.* **1.** Affilé, aiguisé. **K.** edge, fil tranchant. **2.** Vif, perçant. **3.** (*a*) Ardent, zélé. (*b*) Acharné. **4.** Fin.
keenly, *adv.* Aprement, vivement.
keenness, *s.* **1.** Finesse *f*, acuité *f.* **2.** Apreté *f.* **3.** Ardeur *f*, zèle *m.*
keep¹, *s.* Nourriture *f*; frais *mpl* de subsistance.
keep². I. *v.tr.* **1.** Observer, suivre; tenir. **2.** Célébrer. **3.** Préserver. **4.** (*a*) Garder. (*b*) Entretenir. **5.** Maintenir. **6.** Retenir. **7.** Empêcher. **8.** **To k.** waiting, faire attendre.
II. **keep,** *v.i.* **1.** Rester, se tenir. **How are you keeping?** comment allez-vous? **2.** Continuer. **3.** Se conserver. **keep away.** **1.** *v.tr.* Éloigner; tenir éloigné. **2.** *v.i.* Se tenir à l'écart. **keep back.** **1.** *v.tr.* (*a*) Arrêter; retenir. (*b*) Dissimuler. **2.** *v.i.* Se tenir en arrière. **keep from,** *v.i.* S'abstenir de. **keep in,** *v.tr.* (*a*) Retenir à la maison. (*b*) Contenir. **keep off.** **1.** *v.tr.* (*a*) Éloigner. **2.** *v.i.* Se tenir éloigné. **keep on.** **1.** *v.tr.* Garder. **2.** *v.i.* (*a*) Avancer. (*b*) Continuer (de). **keep out.** (*a*) *v.tr.* Empêcher d'entrer. (*b*) *v.i.* Se tenir dehors. **keep to,** *v.i.* S'en tenir à; garder. **To k.** to the left, tenir la gauche. **keep together,** *v.i.* (*a*) Rester ensemble. (*b*) Rester unis. **keep up.** **1.** *v.tr.* (*a*) Entretenir. (*b*) Conserver. (*c*) Soutenir. (*d*) Faire veiller. **2.** *v.i.* **To k.** up with the times, se maintenir à la page.
keeper, *s.* (*a*) Garde *m*, gardien *m*; conservateur *m.* (*b*) Patron, -onne.
keeping, *s.* **1.** (*a*) Observation *f.* (*b*) Célébration *f.* **2.** Garde *f.* **3.** In k. with, en accord, en rapport, avec.
keepsake, *s.* Souvenir *m.*
kennel, *s.* Niche *f.*
kernel, *s.* Amande *f.*
kettle, *s.* Bouilloire *f.*
kettle-drum, *s.* Timbale *f.*
key, *s.* **1.** Clef *f*, clé *f.* **2.** Ton *m.* **3.** Touche *f.*

keyhole, *s.* Trou *m* de (la) serrure.
key-note, *s.* Note dominante.
khaki. **1.** *s.* Kaki *m.* **2.** *a.* Kaki *inv.*
kick¹, *s.* (*a*) Coup *m* de pied. (*b*) Ruade *f.*
kick². **1.** *v.i.* Donner un coup de pied; ruer. **2.** *v.tr.* (*a*) Donner un coup de pied à. (*b*) **To k. a** {goal, marquer un but. **kick off,** *v.tr.* *Abs.* Donner le coup d'envoi.
kick-off, *s.* Coup *m* d'envoi.
kid, *s.* **1.** (*a*) Chevreau, *f.* chevrette. (*b*) (Peau *f* de) chevreau. **2.** Mioche *mf*, gosse *mf.*
kidnap, *v.tr.* Enlever de vive force.
kidnapper, *s.* Auteur *m* d'un enlèvement.
kidney, *s.* **1.** Rein *m.* **2.** Rognon *m.*
kill, *v.tr.* (*a*) Tuer; faire mourir. (*b*) Abattre, tuer. **kill off,** *v.tr.* Exterminer.
killer, *s.* Tueur, -euse; meurtrier *m.*
kill-joy, *s.* Rabat-joie *m inv.*
kiln, *s.* Four *m.*
kilogramme, *s.* = 2.2 lbs.
kilometre, *s.* Kilomètre *m.* = ⅝ mile.
kilt, *s.* Kilt *m.*
kimono, *s.* Kimono *m.*
kin, *s.* (*a*) Parents *mpl.* (*b*) **To inform the next of kin,** prévenir la famille.
kind¹, *s.* **1.** Genre *m*, espèce *f*, sorte *f.* Nothing of the k., rien de la sorte. **2.** In k., en nature; de la même monnaie.
kind², *a.* Bon, aimable, bienveillant.
kind-hearted, *a.* Bon, bienveillant.
kindle, *v.tr.* Allumer.
kindliness, *s.* Bonté *f*, bienveillance *f.*
kindly¹, *adv.* Avec bonté, avec bienveillance. Will you k.? voulez-vous avoir la bonté de?
kindly², *a.* Bon, bienveillant.
kindness, *s.* **1.** Bonté *f*; bienveillance *f.* **2.** To do a k., rendre service.
king, *s.* **1.** Roi *m.* **2.** (*At draughts*) = Dame *f.*
kingdom, *s.* **1.** Royaume *m.* The United K., le Royaume-Uni. **2.** Règne *m.*
kingfisher, *s.* Martin-pêcheur *m*, *pl.* martins-pêcheurs.
kingly, *a.* De roi; royal, -aux.
kink, *s.* Nœud *m*; faux pli.

kiosk, s. Kiosque m.

kipper, s. Hareng salé et fumé.

kiss¹, s. Baiser m.

kiss², v.tr. Donner un baiser à, embrasser.

kit, s. **1.** (a) Petit équipement; fourniment m; effets mpl. **2.** Trousseau m, trousse f. **Repair kit,** nécessaire m de réparation.

kit-bag, s. **1.** Sac m (de voyage). **2.** Ballot m, musette f.

kitchen, s. Cuisine f.

kitchen-garden, s. (Jardin m) potager m.

Kitchen-utensils, s.pl. Batterie f de cuisine.

kite, s. **1.** Milan m. **2.** Cerf-volant m, pl. cerfs-volants.

kitten, s. Petit(e) chat(te).

kitty, s. Cagnotte f.

knack, s. Tour m de main; truc m.

knapsack, s. Havresac m; sac m.

knave, s. **1.** Coquin m. **2.** Cards: Valet m.

knavery, s. Coquinerie f.

knavish, a. De coquin; fourbe.

knead, v.tr. Pétrir.

knee, s. Genou m, -oux.

knee-cap, s. Rotule f.

knee-deep, a. Jusqu'aux genoux.

kneel, v.i. S'agenouiller; se mettre à genoux.

kneeling, a. Agenouillé; à genoux.

knell, s. Glas m. **Death k.,** glas funèbre.

knickerbockers, s.pl. Culotte f.

knick-knack, s. Bibelot m.

knife¹, s. Couteau m.

knife², v.tr. Donner un coup de couteau à; poignarder.

knife-grinder, s. Rémouleur m.

knight¹, s. **1.** Chevalier m. **2.** (At chess) Cavalier m.

knight², v.tr. Faire, créer, chevalier.

knight-errant, s. Chevalier errant.

knighthood, s. Titre m de chevalier.

knit, v.tr. (a) Tricoter. (b) To k. one's brows, froncer les sourcils. (c) Lier.

knitting, s. **1.** Tricotage m. **2.** Tricot m.

knitting-needle, s. Aiguille f à tricoter.

knob, s. (a) Bosse f, protubérance f. (b) Pomme f; bouton m.

knock¹, s. **1.** Coup m, heurt m. **2.** Coup de marteau.

knock². **1.** v.tr. Frapper, heurter, cogner. **2.** v.i. (a) Frapper, heurter. (b) Se heurter. **knock about,** v.tr. Maltraiter, malmener. **knock down,** v.tr. **1.** Renverser; jeter par terre. **2.** Adjuger. **knock off.** I. v.tr. **1.** (a) Faire sauter. (b) Rabattre. **2.** Faire tomber. II. **knock off,** v.i. Cesser le travail. **knock out,** v.tr. Faire sortir; chasser. **knock up.** I. v.tr. Éreinter, épuiser. **2.** v.i. S'effondrer.

knock-down, attrib.a. **K.-d. blow,** coup d'assommoir.

knocker, s. Marteau m.

knocking, s. Coups mpl.

knoll, s. Tertre m, butte f.

knot¹, s. **1.** Nœud m. **2.** Groupe m

knot², v.tr. Nouer.

knotty, a. **1.** Plein de nœuds. **2. K. point,** question difficile. **3.** Noueux.

know¹, s. To be in the k., être au courant.

know², v.tr. **1.** (a) Reconnaître. (b) Distinguer. **2.** Connaître. **3.** Savoir. To k. how to do sth., savoir faire qch. **4.** To get to k., apprendre. **Please let us k.,** veuillez nous faire savoir. **5.** To k. better than to, se bien garder de. **You k. best,** vous en êtes le meilleur juge. **know about,** v.i. Être informé de. **I k. nothing about it,** je n'en sais rien.

knowing¹, a. Fin, rusé. **A k. smile,** un sourire entendu.

knowing², s. **There is no k.,** il n'y a pas moyen de savoir.

knowledge, s. **1.** Connaissance f. **I had no k. of it,** je l'ignorais. **To the best of my k.,** autant que je sache. **To my certain k.,** à mon vu et su. **Without my k.,** à mon insu. **2.** Savoir m, connaissances.

known, a. Connu, reconnu, su. **To make k.,** faire connaître; déclarer.

knuckle, s. Articulation f, jointure f, du doigt.

kudos, s. Gloire f.

L

L, l, s. (La lettre) L, l m or f.
label¹, s. Étiquette f.
label², v.tr. Étiqueter.
laboratory, s. Laboratoire m.
laborious, a. Laborieux.
laboriously, adv. Laborieusement.
labour¹, s. **1.** Travail m, labeur m, peine f. **2.** (a) Main-d'œuvre f, Capital and l., le capital et le travail. (b) The L. party, le parti travailliste.
labour², v.i. (a) Travailler, peiner. (b) To l. under a delusion, se faire illusion.
laboured, a. **1.** Travaillé. **2.** Pénible.
labourer, s. (a) Travailleur m. (b) Manœuvre m. (c) Agricultural l., ouvrier m agricole.
labyrinth, s. Labyrinthe m.
lace¹, s. **1.** Lacet m; cordon m. **2.** Gold l., galon m, passement m d'or. **3.** Dentelle f, point m.
lace², v.tr. Lacer.
lacerate, v.tr. Lacérer; déchirer.
laceration, s. Lacération f.
lack¹, s. Manque m, défaut m. For l. of, faute de.
lack², v.tr. Manquer de; ne pas avoir.
lacking, a. Qui manque; manquant.
laconic, a. Laconique.
laconically, adv. Laconiquement.
lacquer¹, s. Laque m.
lacquer², v.tr. Laquer.
lad, s. Jeune homme m; (jeune) garçon m.
ladder¹, s. **1.** Échelle f. **2.** Éraillure f.
ladder², v.i. Se démailler.
laden, a. Chargé.
ladle, s. Cuiller f à pot. Soup l., cuiller à potage.
lady, s. Dame f. **1.** (a) Femme bien élevée. (b) Young l., demoiselle f, jeune fille f. (c) Ladies' tailor, tailleur pour dames. L. doctor, doctoresse f. **2.** My l., madame f.
ladyship, s. Her l., madame f.
lag, v.i. Traîner.
lager, s. Bière allemande.
laggard, s. Traînard m.
lagoon, s. Lagune f.
lair, s. Tanière f, repaire m.
lake, s. Lac m.
lamb, s. Agneau m.
lambent, a. Blafard.

lame¹, a. **1.** Boiteux. **2.** Faible.
lame², v.tr. Estropier.
lameness, s. **1.** Boitement m. **2.** Faiblesse f.
lament¹, s. Lamentation f.
lament², v.tr. & i. Se lamenter; pleurer.
lamentable, a. Lamentable déplorable.
lamentably, adv. Lamentablement, déplorablement.
lamentation, s. Lamentation f.
lamp, s. (a) Lampe f. (b) Lanterne. Side lamps, feux m de côté.
lamp-post, s. Réverbère m.
lamp-shade, s. Abat-jour m inv.
lance, s. Lance f.
lance-corporal, s. Soldat m de première classe.
lancer, s. Lancier m.
lancet, s. Lancette f.
land¹, s. **1.** (a) Terre f. Dry l., terre ferme. To see how the l. lies, sonder le terrain. (b) Terre, sol m. **2.** Terre, pays m.
land². **1.** v.tr. (a) Mettre à terre; débarquer. (b) To l. a fish, amener un poisson à terre. **2.** v.i. Descendre à terre; débarquer; atterrir.
landing¹, a. L. force, troupes fpl de débarquement.
landing², s. **1.** (a) Débarquement m; mise f à terre. (b) Atterrissage m. **2.** Palier m.
landing-ground, s. Terrain m d'atterrissage.
landlady, s. **1.** Logeuse f. **2.** Hôtelière f, hôtesse f.
landlord, s. **1.** Propriétaire m. **2.** Aubergiste m, hôtelier m, hôte m.
landmark, s. **1.** (Point m de) repère m. **2.** Événement marquant.
landowner, s. Propriétaire foncier.
landscape, s. Paysage m.
land-slide, s. Éboulement m de terrain.
lane, s. Chemin vicinal.
language, s. **1.** Langue f. **2.** Langage m.
languid, a. Languissant.
languish, v.i. Languir.
languishing, a. Languissant.
languor, s. Langueur f.

lanky, *a.* Grand et maigre.

lantern, *s.* (*a*) Lanterne *f*, falot *m*; fanal *m*, -aux. **Chinese l.**, lanterne vénitienne. (*b*) **Magic l.**, lanterne magique.

lap[1], *s.* **1.** Pan *m*, basque *f* (d'un vêtement). **2.** Genoux *mpl*.

lap[2], *s.* Tour *m*; circuit *m*.

lap[3]. **1.** *v.tr.* Laper. **2.** *v.i.* Clapoter.

lap-dog, *s.* Bichon *m*.

lapel, *s.* Revers *m*.

Lapp, *a. & s.* Lapon, -one.

lapse[1], *s.* **1.** Erreur *f*, faute *f*; défaillance *f*. **2.** Cours *m*, marche *f*; laps *m*.

lapse[2], *v.i.* **1.** Déchoir. **2.** (Se) périmer; cesser d'être en vigueur.

lapsed, *a.* **1.** Déchu. **2.** Périmé.

lapwing, *s.* Vanneau *m*.

larceny, *s.* Larcin *m*.

larch, *s.* Mélèze *m*.

lard, *s.* Saindoux *m*.

larder, *s.* Garde-manger *m inv.*

large. **I.** *a.* (*a*) Grand; gros, *f.* grosse. (*b*) Considérable; fort. **II. large**, *s.* **To set at l.**, élargir. **To be at l.**, être libre.

lark[1], *s.* Alouette *f*.

lark[2], *s.* Farce *f*, blague *f*.

larkspur, *s.* Pied-d'alouette *m*.

larva, *s.* Larve *f*.

lascivious, *a.* Lascif.

lash[1], *s.* **1.** (*a*) Coup *m* de fouet. (*b*) Lanière *f*. **2.** Cil *m*.

lash[2], *v.tr. & i.* (*a*) Cingler. (*b*) Battre. **lash out**, *v.i.* Ruer.

lash[3], *v.tr.* Lier, attacher.

lashing, *s.* Fouettée *f*.

lass, *s.* Jeune fille *f*.

lassitude, *s.* Lassitude *f*.

lasso[1], *s.* Lasso *m*.

lasso[2], *v.tr.* Prendre au lasso.

last[1], *s.* Forme *f* (à chaussure).

last[2]. **I.** *a.* Dernier. **1. The l. but one**, l'avant dernier. **2. L. week**, la semaine dernière. **II. last**, *s.* **1. This l.**, ce dernier, cette dernière. **2.** (*a*) **To, till, the l.**, jusqu'au bout. (*b*) **At l.**, enfin. **III. last**, *adv.* Le dernier.

last[3], *v.i.* Durer, se maintenir.

lasting, *a.* Durable.

lastly, *adv.* Pour finir; en dernier lieu.

latch[1], *s.* (*a*) Loquet *m*. (*b*) Serrure *f* de sûreté.

latch[2], *v.tr.* Fermer à demi-tour.

latch-key, *s.* Clef *f* de maison.

late. **I.** *a.* **1.** (*a*) En retard. (*b*) Retardé. **2.** Tard. **In l. summer**, vers la fin de l'été. **3.** Tardif. **4.** (*a*) Ancien. (*b*) **My l. father**, feu mon père. **5.** Récent, dernier. **Of l.**, dernièrement.

II. late, *adv.* **1.** En retard. **To arrive too l.**, arriver trop tard. **2.** Tard. **To keep s.o. l.**, attarder qn. **L. in life**, à un âge avancé. **A moment later**, l'instant d'après.

late-comer, *s.* Retardataire *mf*.

lately, *adv.* Dernièrement, récemment.

lateness, *s.* **The l. of the hour**, l'heure avancée.

latent, *a.* Latent; caché.

lateral, *a.* Latéral. -aux.

lath, *s.* Latte *f*.

lathe, *s.* Tour *m*.

lather[1], *s.* **1.** Mousse *f* de savon. **2.** Écume *f*.

lather[2]. **1.** *v.tr.* Savonner. **2.** *v.i.* Mousser.

latitude, *s.* Latitude *f*.

latter, *a.* Dernier. **The l.**, celui-ci, ceux-ci, celle(s)-ci.

lattice, *s.* Treillis *m*, treillage *m*.

laudable, *a.* Louable.

laudably, *adv.* Louablement.

laudanum, *s.* Laudanum *m*.

laudatory, *a.* Élogieux.

laugh[1], *s.* Rire *m*. **With a l.**, en riant.

laugh[2]. **1.** *v.i.* Rire. (*a*) **To l. to oneself**, rire en soi-même. **To l. up one's sleeve**, rire sous cape. (*b*) **To l. at**, rire de. **2.** *v.tr.* **To l. s.o. to scorn**, accabler qn de ridicule.

laughable, *a.* Risible, ridicule.

laughing[1], *a.* Riant; rieur, -euse.

laughing[2], *s.* **It is no l. matter**, il n'y a pas de quoi rire.

laughingly, *adv.* En riant.

laughing-stock, *s.* Risée *f*.

laughter, *s.* Rire(s) *m(pl)*. **To roar with l.**, rire aux éclats.

launch[1], *s.* Chaloupe *f*. **Motor l.**, vedette *f*.

launch[2], *v.tr.* (*a*) Lancer. (*b*) Déclencher (une offensive).

launching, *s.* Lancement *m*.

laundress, *s.* Blanchisseuse *f*.

laundry, *s.* Blanchisserie *f*.

laurel, *s.* Laurier *m*.

lava, *s.* Lave *f*.

lavatory, s. Cabinet m de toilette ; lavabo m.

lavender, s. & a. Lavande (f).

lavender-water, s. Eau f de lavande.

lavish[1], a. 1. Prodigue. 2. Somptueux ; abondant.

lavish[2], v.tr. Prodiguer.

lavishly, adv. Avec prodigalité.

lavishness, s. Prodigalité f.

law, s. 1. Loi f. Laws of a game, règles f d'un jeu. 2. To lay down the law, faire la loi. 3. Droit m. 4. Court of law, cour f de justice ; tribunal m, -aux.

law-abiding, a. Respectueux des lois ; ami de l'ordre.

lawful, a. Légal, -aux. 1. Permis, licite. 2. Légitime.

lawfully, adv. Légalement, légitimement.

lawless, a. Déréglé, désordonné.

lawlessness, s. Dérèglement m.

lawn, s. Pelouse f.

lawn-mower, s. Tondeuse f (de gazon).

lawn-tennis, s. (Lawn-)tennis m.

lawsuit, s. Procès m.

lawyer, s. 1. Homme m de loi. 2. (a) Avocat m. (b) Avoué m.

lax, a. 1. (a) Relâché ; négligent. (b) Vague. 2. Flasque.

laxity, s. (a) Relâchement m ; mollesse f. (b) Imprécision f.

lay[1], a. Laïque, lai.

lay[2], v.tr. 1. Coucher. 2. (a) Abattre. (b) Exorciser, conjurer. 3. Mettre, poser. 4. Pondre. 5. Parier. 6. Poser, asseoir ; ranger. To lay the cloth, mettre le couvert. To lay for three, mettre trois couverts. To lay the fire, préparer le feu. lay aside, v.tr. Mettre de côté. lay by, v.tr. Mettre de côté ; réserver. lay down, v.tr. 1. (a) Déposer, poser ; mettre bas. (b) Coucher, étendre. 2. Poser, établir. lay in, v.tr. Faire provision de. lay on, v.tr. 1. (a) Appliquer. (b) Abs. Frapper. 2. Installer. lay out, v.tr. 1. Arranger, disposer. 2. Dépenser. 3. To lay oneself out, se mettre en frais. lay up, v.tr. 1. Remiser. 2. To be laid up, être alité.

layer, s. Couche f.

lazily, adv. Paresseusement.

laziness, s. Paresse f, fainéantise f.

lazy, a. Paresseux, fainéant.

lead[1], s. 1. Plomb m. 2. Mine f. 3. Sonde f.

lead[2], s. 1. Conduite f. (a) To follow s.o.'s l., suivre l'exemple de qn. (b) To take the l., prendre la direction. 2. Your l.! à vous de jouer. 3. Laisse f.

lead[3]. I. v.tr. 1. (a) Mener ; conduire. (b) To l. the way, aller devant. 2. Commander. 3. Abs. Tenir la tête. 4. Abs. Ouvrir le jeu.
II. **lead,** v.i. Mener, conduire.

lead away, v.tr. 1. Emmener. 2. Entraîner, détourner. **lead back,** v.tr. Ramener, reconduire. **lead on,** v.tr. Conduire, entraîner.

leaden, a. De plomb.

leader, s. (a) Conducteur, -trice ; guide m. (b) Chef m.

leadership, s. Conduite f.

leading, a. Premier ; principal, -aux. L. article, article principal.

leaf, s. 1. Feuille f. 2. Feuillet m. To turn over a new l., changer de conduite. 3. Battant m.

leaflet, s. Feuillet m ; papillon m.

leafy, a. Feuillu ; couvert de feuilles.

league[1], s. Lieue f.

league[2], s. Ligue f.

leak[1], s. (a) Fuite f. (b) Voie f d'eau.

leak[2], v.i. 1. Avoir une fuite ; fuir. 2. Faire eau. **leak out,** v.i. S'ébruiter, transpirer.

leakage, s. Fuite f.

lean[1]. 1. a. Maigre ; amaigri, décharné. 2. s. Maigre m.

lean[2]. 1. v.i. (a) S'appuyer. To l. on one's elbow, s'accouder. (b) Se pencher ; incliner, pencher. 2. v.tr. Appuyer.

leaning[1], a. Penché, penchant.

leaning[2], s. Inclination f ; tendance f (towards, à).

leanness, s. Maigreur f.

leap[1], s. Saut m, bond m.

leap[2]. 1. v.i. (a) Sauter, bondir. (b) To l. (up), jaillir. 2. v.tr. Sauter.

leap-frog, s. Saute-mouton m.

leap-year, s. Année f bissextile.

learn, v.tr. Apprendre.

learned, a. Savant, instruit.

learner, s. Élève mf, débutant, -ante.

learning, s. 1. Étude f. 2. Science f, instruction f.

lease[1], s. Bail m, pl. baux.

lease², *v.tr.* **1.** Louer ; donner à bail. **2.** Prendre à bail ; louer.

leasehold, *a.* Tenu à bail.

leaseholder, *s.* Locataire *mf* à bail.

leash, *s.* Laisse *f*, attache *f*.

least. 1. *a.* (Le. la) moindre ; (le, la) plus petit(e). **2.** *s.* (The) l., (le) moins. **To say the l.**, pour ne pas dire plus. **At l.**, (tout) au moins. **I can at l. try**, je peux toujours essayer. **Not in the l.**, pas le moins du monde. **3.** *adv.* Moins.

leather, *s.* Cuir *m*.

leave¹, *s.* **1.** Permission *f*, permis *m*. **2.** To take one's l., prendre congé ; faire ses adieux.

leave², *v.tr.* **1.** Laisser. (*a*) Left to oneself, livré à soi-même. (*b*) To l. go of, lâcher. (*c*) Déposer. (*d*) L it to me, laissez-moi faire. (*e*) To be left, rester. **2.** (*a*) Quitter ; sortir de ; *abs.* partir. (*b*) Abandonner. **leave behind**, *v.tr.* Laisser. **leave off. 1.** *v.tr.* (*a*) Quitter. (*b*) Cesser. **2.** *v.i.* Cesser, s'arrêter. **leave out**, *v.tr.* **1.** Exclure. **2.** (*a*) Omettre. (*b*) Oublier. **leave over**, *v.tr.* **1.** Remettre à plus tard. **2.** To be left over, rester.

leaving, *s.* **1.** Départ *m* **2.** *pl.* Restes *m*.

lecture¹, *s.* **1.** Conférence *f*. **2.** Semonce *f*.

lecture². **1.** *v.i.* Faire une conférence. **2.** *v.tr.* Semoncer.

lecturer, *s.* Conférencier, -ière.

ledge, *s.* Rebord *m* ; corniche *f*.

ledger, *s.* Grand livre.

lee, *s.* (*a*) Côté *m* sous le vent. (*b*) Abri *m* (contre le vent).

leech, *s.* Sangsue *f*.

leek, *s.* Poireau *m*.

leeward, *a. & adv.* Sous le vent.

left. 1. *a.* Gauche. **On my l. hand**, à ma gauche. **2.** *s.* Gauche *f* On the l., à gauche.

leg, *s.* **1.** Jambe *f* ; patte *f*. **To pull s.o.'s leg**, se payer la tête de qn. **2.** Cuisse *f* (de volaille). **Leg of mutton**, gigot *m*. **3.** Pied *m* (de table).

legacy, *s.* Legs *m*.

legal, *a.* Légal, -aux. **To take l. advice**, consulter un avocat.

legality, *s.* Légalité *f*.

legally, *adv.* Légalement.

legate, *s.* Légat *m*.

legatee, *s.* Légataire *mf*.

legation, *s.* Légation *f*.

legend, *s.* Légende *f*, fable *f*.

legendary, *a.* Légendaire.

leggings, *s.pl.* Jambières *f* ; guêtres *f*.

legibility, *s.* Lisibilité *f*, netteté *f*.

legible, *a.* Lisible, net, *f.* nette.

legibly, *adv.* Lisiblement.

legion, *s.* Légion *f*.

legislation, *s.* Législation *f*.

legislative, *a.* Législatif.

legislator, *s.* Législateur *m*.

legitimate, *a.* Légitime.

legitimately, *adv.* Légitimement.

leisure, *s.* Loisir *m*.

leisurely, *adv.* Posément ; sans se presser.

lemon. 1. *s.* Citron *m*. **2.** *a.* Jaune citron *inv.*

lemonade, *s.* Limonade *f* ; citronnade *f* ; citron pressé.

lemon-squash, *s.* Citron pressé ; citronnade *f*.

lemon-squeezer, *s.* Presse-citrons *m*.

lemon-tree, *s.* Citronnier *m*.

lend, *v.tr.* Prêter.

lender, *s.* Prêteur, -euse.

length, *s.* **1.** Longueur *f*. **2.** L. of service, ancienneté *f*. **At l.**, tout au long ; enfin, à la fin. **At some l.**, assez longuement. **3.** To go to the l. of, aller jusqu'à. **4.** Morceau *m*, bout *m*. **Dress l.**, coupon de robe.

lengthen. 1. *v.tr.* Allonger, rallonger ; prolonger. **2.** *v.i.* S'allonger, se rallonger.

lengthening, *s.* **1.** Allongement *m*, prolongation *f*. **2.** Augmentation *f*.

lengthily, *adv.* Longuement, avec prolixité.

lengthy, *a.* Assez long, prolixe.

leniency, *s.* Clémence *f*.

lenient, *a.* Clément ; indulgent.

leniently, *adv.* Avec clémence.

lens, *s.* (*a*) Lentille *f*. (*b*) Loupe *f* ; verre grossissant.

Lent, *s.* Le carême.

lentil, *s.* Lentille *f*.

leopard, *s.* Léopard *m*.

leper, *s.* Lépreux, -euse.

leprosy, *s.* Lèpre *f*.

less. 1. *a.* (*a*) Moindre. **L. than**, au-dessous de. (*b*) Moins de. **2.** *prep.* Moins. **3.** *s.* Moins *m*. **4.** *adv.* Moins. **One man l.**, un homme de moins. **L. than six**, moins de six.

L. and l., de moins en moins. **None the l.,** néanmoins.

lessee, *s.* Locataire *mf* (à bail).

lessen. 1. *v.i.* S'amoindrir, diminuer. **2.** *v.tr.* Amoindrir, diminuer.

lesson, *s.* Leçon *f.*

lessor, *s.* Bailleur, -eresse.

lest, *conj.* De peur que . . . ne.

let. I. *v.tr.* **1.** (*a*) Permettre ; laisser. **To let go,** lâcher. (*b*) **To let s.o. know sth.,** faire savoir qch. à qn. **2. House to let,** maison à louer.

II. let, *v.aux.* **Let us make haste!** dépêchons-nous ! **Let me see!** attendez un peu ! **let down,** *v.tr.* Baisser ; défaire. **let in,** *v.tr.* Laisser entrer. **let into,** *v.tr.* **To let i. a secret,** mettre dans le secret. **let off,** *v.tr.* **1.** Tirer, faire partir. **2.** Lâcher, laisser échapper. **3.** Faire grâce à. **let out,** *v.tr.* Laisser sortir.

lethal, *a.* Mortel. **L. weapon,** arme léthifère.

lethargic, *a.* Léthargique.

lethargy, *s.* Léthargie *f.*

letter[1], *s.* **1.** Lettre *f,* caractère *m.* **To the l.,** au pied de la lettre. **2.** Lettre, missive *f.* **To open the letters,** dépouiller le courrier. **3.** *pl.* Belles-lettres *f* ; littérature *f.*

letter[2], *v.tr.* Marquer avec des lettres.

letter-balance, *s.* Pèse-lettres *m inv.*

letter-box, *s.* Boîte *f* aux lettres.

letter-card, *s.* Carte-lettre *f,* pl. cartes-lettres.

letter-opener, *s.* Ouvre-lettres *m inv.*

letter-paper, *s.* Papier *m* à lettres.

letting, *s.* Louage *m.*

lettuce, *s.* Laitue *f.* **Cos l.,** laitue romaine.

level[1]. **I.** *s.* **1.** Niveau *m.* **On a l. with,** à la hauteur de. **2.** (*a*) Surface *f* de niveau. (*b*) Niveau, étage *m.*

II. level, *a.* (*a*) De niveau, à niveau. (*b*) Égal, -aux ; uni. (*c*) **L. with,** de niveau avec ; à hauteur de.

level[2], *v.tr.* **1.** Niveler. **2.** Pointer ; diriger (*at*, sur).

level-headed, *a.* Qui a la tête bien équilibrée.

levelling, *s.* **1.** Nivellement *m.* **2.** Pointage *m.*

lever, *s.* Levier *m.*

leveret, *s.* Levraut *m.*

levity, *s.* Légèreté *f.*

levy[1], *s.* Levée *f.*

levy[2], *v.tr.* Lever, percevoir.

lewd, *a.* Impudique, lascif.

lexicon, *s.* Lexique *m.*

liability, *s.* **1.** Responsabilité *f.* **2.** *pl.* Engagements *m.* **3.** (*a*) **L. to,** risque *m* de. (*b*) Disposition *f,* tendance *f.*

liable, *a.* **1.** Responsable (*for,* de). **2. L. to a fine,** passible d'une amende. **3.** Sujet, -ette, exposé. **4.** Susceptible (*to,* de).

liaison, *s.* Liaison *f.*

liar, *s.* Menteur, -euse.

libel[1], *s.* Diffamation *f* calomnie *f.*

libel[2], *v.tr.* Diffamer ; calomnier.

libellous, *a.* Diffamatoire.

liberal, *a.* **1.** (*a*) Libéral, -aux. (*b*) D'esprit large. **2.** (*a*) Libéral, généreux. (*b*) Libéral, abondant. **3.** *a. & s.* Libéral (*m*).

liberality, *s.* Libéralité *f.*

liberally, *adv.* Libéralement

liberate, *v.tr.* Libérer.

liberation, *s.* Libération *f.*

liberty, *s.* Liberté *f.* (*a*) **To be at l. to,** être libre de. (*b*) **To take the l. of,** se permettre de. (*c*) **To take liberties,** prendre des libertés.

librarian, *s.* Bibliothécaire *m.*

library, *s.* Bibliothèque *f.* **Lending l.,** cabinet *m* de lecture. **Reference l.,** salle *f* de lecture.

licence, *s.* **1.** Permis *m,* autorisation. **Marriage l.,** dispense *f* de bans. **Driving l.,** permis de conduire. **2.** Licence *f.*

license, *v.tr.* Accorder un permis à.

licensee, *s.* Patenté, -ée.

licentious, *a.* Licencieux.

lichen, *s.* Lichen *m.*

lick[1], *s.* Coup *m* de langue.

lick[2], *v.tr.* Lécher.

lid, *s.* Couvercle *m.*

lie[1], *s.* Mensonge *m.* **To tell lies,** mentir.

lie[2], *v.i.* Mentir.

lie[3], *s.* **1.** Disposition *f.* **2.** Position *f,* assiette *f.*

lie[4], *v.i.* **1.** (*a*) Être couché. **Here lies,** ci-gît. (*b*) Être, rester, se tenir. **To lie still,** rester tranquille. **2. The difference lies in this,** la différence réside en ceci. **lie about,** *v.i.* Traîner. **lie back,** *v.i.* Se laisser retomber. **lie down,** *v.i.* Se coucher, s'étendre. **lie up,** *v.i.* Garder le lit.

lieu, *s.* In l. of, au lieu de.

lieutenant, *s.* Lieutenant *m*; lieutenant de vaisseau.

life, *s.* **1.** Vie *f.* To take s.o.'s l., tuer qn. To take one's own l., se suicider. To save s.o.'s l., sauver la vie à qn. To fly for one's l., s'enfuir à toutes jambes. To put new l. into, ranimer. **2.** (*a*) Vie, vivant *m.* Never in my l., jamais de la vie. Tired of l., las de vivre. L. annuity, rente viagère. (*b*) Biographie *f.* (*c*) Durée *f.* He has seen l., il a beaucoup vécu.

life-belt, *s.* Ceinture *f* de sauvetage.

life-boat, *s.* Canot *m* de sauvetage.

life-buoy, *s.* Bouée *f* de sauvetage.

life-guard, *s.* Garde *f* du corps.

lifeless, *a.* Sans vie; inanimé.

lifelike, *a.* Vivant.

lifelong, *a.* De toute la vie.

life-size, *a.* De grandeur naturelle.

lifetime, *s.* Vie *f.* In his l., de son vivant.

lift¹, *s.* **1.** Haussement *m*; levée *f.* **2.** Ascenseur *m.*

lift², *v.tr.* (*a*) Lever; soulever. To l. up one's head, redresser la tête. To l. down, descendre. (*b*) Dresser.

lift-attendant, *s.* Liftier, -ière.

light¹, *s.* **1.** Lumière *f.* (*a*) By the l. of, à la lumière de. (*b*) It is l., il fait jour. To come to l., se découvrir. To bring to l., mettre au jour. (*c*) Éclairage *m*; jour *m.* (*d*) To throw l. on, jeter le jour sur; éclairer. **2.** (*a*) Lumière, lampe *f.* (*b*) Feu *m.* (**Traffic**) lights, feux de circulation.

light². **1.** *v.tr.* (*a*) Allumer. *Abs.* To l. up, allumer. (*b*) Éclairer, illuminer. **2.** *v.i.* (*a*) S'allumer; prendre feu. (*b*) S'éclairer, s'illuminer.

light³, *a.* **1.** Clair; éclairé. **2.** Blond; clair.

light⁴, *a.* **1.** Léger. **2.** To travel l., voyager avec peu de bagages. **3.** To make l. of, traiter à la légère.

lighten. **1.** *v.tr.* Alléger. **2.** *v.i.* Être soulagé.

lighter, *s.* Briquet *m* (à essence).

light-hearted, *a.* Allègre.

lighthouse, *s.* Phare *m.*

lighting, *s.* **1.** Allumage *m.* **2.** Éclairage *m.*

lightly, *adv.* **1.** Légèrement. **2.** To get off l., s'en tirer à bon compte. **3.** To speak l., parler à la légère.

lightness, *s.* Légèreté *f.*

lightning, *s.* Éclairs *mpl*, foudre *f.* A flash of l., un éclair.

lightning-conductor, *s.* Paratonnerre *m.*

like¹. I. *a.* **1.** Semblable, pareil, -eille; tel; ressemblant. **2.** (*a*) One l. it, le pareil, la pareille. A critic l. you, un critique tel que vous. What is he l.? comment est-il? (*b*) That's l. a woman! voilà bien les femmes! II. **like,** *prep.* Comme. III. **like,** *s.* Semblable *mf*; pareil, -eille.

like², *v.tr.* **1.** Aimer. How do you l. him? comment le trouvez-vous? As much as you l., tant que vous voudrez. **2.** (*a*) I l. to see them, j'aime à les voir. (*b*) As you l., comme vous voudrez. To do as one likes, en faire à sa tête.

likeable, *a.* Agréable, sympathique.

likelihood, *s.* Vraisemblance *f.*

likely. I. *a.* **1.** Vraisemblable, probable. **2.** Susceptible (*to*, de). II. **likely,** *adv.* Very l., vraisemblablement; très probablement. As l. as not, autant que je sache.

likeness, *s.* **1.** Ressemblance *f.* **2.** Apparence *f.* **3.** Portrait *m.*

likewise, *adv.* De plus, aussi.

liking, *s.* Goût *m*, penchant *m.* To one's l., à souhait. To take a l. to, prendre en affection.

lilac. **1.** *s.* Lilas *m.* **2.** *a.* Lilas *inv.*

lily, *s.* **1.** Lis *m.* **2.** L. of the valley, muguet *m.*

limb *s.* **1.** Membre *m.* **2.** Branche *f* (d'un arbre).

lime¹, *s.* Chaux *f.*

lime², *s.* Lime *f.* Sweet l., limette *f.* Sour l., limon *m.*

lime³, *s.* L.(-tree), tilleul *m.*

lime-juice, *s.* Jus *m* de limon.

lime-kiln, *s.* Four *m* à chaux.

limelight, *s.* Lumière *f* oxhydrique. In the l., très en vue.

limestone, *s.* Pierre *f* à chaux; calcaire *m.*

limit¹, *s.* Limite *f*, borne *f.*

limit², *v.tr.* Limiter, borner.

limitation, *s.* Limitation *f.*

limitless, *a.* Sans bornes ; illimité.

limp¹, *s.* Boitement *m*, clochement *m.* To walk with a l., boiter.

limp², *v.i.* Boiter, clocher, clopiner.

limp³, *a.* Mou, *f.* molle ; flasque.

limpet, *s.* Patelle *f.*

limpid, *a.* Limpide, clair.

limpidity, *s.* Limpidité *f*, clarté *f.*

limping, *a.* Boiteux.

linden(-tree), *s.* Tilleul *m.*

line¹, *s.* **1.** (*a*) Ligne *f*, corde *f.* (*b*) Ligne, fil *m.* **2.** (*a*) Ligne, trait *m*, raie *f.* (*b*) Ride *f.* (*c*) **I draw the l. at,** je ne vais pas jusqu'à. **3.** (*a*) Ligne, rangée *f.* (*b*) File *f* ; queue *f.* (*c*) **L. of poetry,** vers *m.* **Marriage lines,** acte *m* de mariage. **4.** Ligne, compagnie *f.* **5.** Voie *f*, ligne.

line², *v.tr.* Border. **line up,** *v.i.* S'aligner.

line³, *v.tr.* Doubler (*with*, de).

lineage, *s.* Lignée *f*, lignage *m.*

lineal, *a.* Linéal, -aux.

lineament, *s.* Trait *m*, linéament *m.*

lined, *a.* Doublé ; fourré.

linen, *s.* **1.** Toile *f* (de lin). **2.** Linge *m*, lingerie *f.*

linen-draper, *s.* Marchand de blanc, de nouveautés.

liner, *s.* Paquebot *m.* **Atlantic l.,** transatlantique *m.*

ling¹, *s.* Morue longue.

ling², *s.* Bruyère commune.

linger, *v.i.* (*a*) Tarder, s'attarder. (*b*) **To l.** (on), traîner.

lingering, *a.* **1.** **L.** look, regard prolongé. **2. L. death,** mort lente.

linguist, *s.* Linguiste *mf.*

liniment, *s.* Liniment *m.*

lining, *s.* Doublure *f* ; coiffe *f.*

link¹, *s.* **1.** (*a*) Chaînon *m*, maillon *m*, anneau *m.* (*b*) *pl.* Boutons jumelés, à chaînettes. **2.** Lien *m*, trait *m* d'union.

link², *v.tr.* Enchaîner, (re)lier.

links, *s.pl.* Terrain *m* de golf.

linnet, *s.* Linotte *f.*

linoleum, *s.* Linoléum *m.*

linseed, *s.* Graine *f* de lin.

lint, *s.* Charpie *f.*

lintel, *s.* Linteau *m.*

lion, *s.* **1.** Lion *m.* **Lion's cub,** lionceau *m.* **2. The Gulf of Lions,** le golfe du Lion.

lioness, *s.* Lionne *f.*

lip, *s.* **1.** Lèvre *f.* **2.** (*a*) Bord *m*, rebord *m.* (*b*) Rebord, saillie *f.*

lipstick, *s.* Bâton *m* de rouge.

liquefy. **1.** *v.tr.* Liquéfier. **2.** *v.i.* Se liquéfier.

liqueur, *s.* Liqueur *f.* **L. brandy,** fine champagne.

liquid. **1.** *a.* (*a*) Liquide. (*b*) Limpide. (*c*) Disponible. **2.** *s.* Liquide *m.*

liquidate, *v.tr.* Liquider.

liquor, *s.* Boisson *f* alcoolique.

liquorice, *s.* Réglisse *f.*

Lisbon. *Pr.n.* Lisbonne *f.*

lisp¹, *s.* Zézaiement *m.*

lisp², *v.i. & tr.* Zézayer.

lissom, *a.* Souple, agile, leste.

list¹, *s.* Liste *f*, rôle *m*, tableau *m*, état *m.* **Wine l.,** carte *f* des vins.

list², *s.* Faux bord ; bande *f.*

listen, *v.ind.tr.* **1.** Écouter. **To l. to,** écouter. **2.** Faire attention ; écouter. **listen in,** *v.i.* Se mettre à l'écoute.

listener, *s.* Auditeur, -trice.

listless, *a.* Nonchalant ; apathique.

literal, *a.* (*a*) Littéral, -aux. (*b*) Positif ; sans imagination.

literally, *adv.* Littéralement.

literary, *a.* Littéraire.

literature, *s.* Littérature *f.* **Light l.,** lectures amusantes.

lithe, *a.* Souple, agile.

lithograph, *s.* Lithographie *f.*

lithography, *s.* Lithographie *f.*

litigation, *s.* Litige *m.*

litter, *s.* **1.** Litière *f.* **2.** Fouillis *m*, désordre *m.* **3.** Portée *f.*

little. **I.** *a.* **1.** Petit. **2.** Peu (de). **3.** Mesquin.

II. little, *s.* **1.** Peu *m* ; peu de chose. **L. by l.,** peu à peu. **2.** **A l. more,** encore un peu.

III. little, *adv.* Peu.

littleness, *s.* Petitesse *f.*

live¹, *a.* **1.** (*a*) Vivant ; en vie. (*b*) **L. coals,** charbons ardents. **2. L. wire,** fil en charge.

live², *v.i.* Vivre. (*a*) **To l. on vegetables,** se nourrir de légumes. **He earns enough to l. upon,** il gagne de quoi vivre. (*b*) **To l. well,** faire bonne chère. (*c*) **Where do you l.?** où demeurez-vous?

livelihood, *s.* Vie *f* ; gagne-pain *m inv.*

liveliness, *s.* Vivacité *f*, animation *f.*

lively, *a.* (*a*) Vif, animé. (*b*) **To take a l. interest in,** s'intéresser vivement à.

liven. **1.** *v.tr.* Animer. **2.** *v.i.* To l. up, s'animer.

liver, *s.* Foie *m.*

livery, *s.* Livrée *f.*

livid, *a.* Livide, blême.

living[1], *a.* Vivant, vif ; en vie.

living[2], *s.* **1.** Vie *f.* **2. To earn one's l.,** gagner sa vie. **To make a l.,** gagner de quoi vivre. **3.** Bénéfice *m,* cure *f.*

lizard, *s.* Lézard *m.*

load[1], *s.* **1.** (*a*) Fardeau *m.* (*b*) Charretée *f.* **2.** Charge *f.*

load[2], *v.tr.* Charger (*with,* de).

loaded, *a.* **1.** Chargé. **2.** L. dice, dés pipés.

loaf[1], *s.* Pain *m* ; miche *f.*

loaf[2], *v.i.* Flâner.

loafer, *s.* Flâneur *m.*

loaf-sugar, *s.* Sucre *m* en pains.

loam, *s.* Terre grasse.

loan, *s.* **1.** Prêt *m.* **2.** Emprunt *m.*

loath, *a.* To be l., répugner à.

loathe, *v.tr.* Détester, exécrer.

loathing, *s.* Dégoût *m,* répugnance *f.*

loathsome, *a.* Repoussant, écœurant, répugnant.

lobby, *s.* Vestibule *m.*

lobe, *s.* Lobe *m.*

lobster, *s.* Homard *m.*

local, *a.* Local, régional.

locality, *s.* Localité *f* ; voisinage *m.*

locally, *adv.* Localement ; dans la région.

locate, *v.tr.* **1.** Localiser ; découvrir **2.** To be located, être situé.

location, *s.* Situation *f.*

lock[1], *s.* Mèche *f,* boucle *f.*

lock[2], *s.* **1.** Serrure *f,* fermeture *f.* Under l. and key, sous clef. **2.** Platine *f.* **3.** Écluse *f.*

lock[3], *v.tr.* **1.** Fermer à clef. **2.** (*a*) Enfermer. (*b*) Serrer. **lock in,** *v.tr.* Mettre sous clef. **lock up,** *v.tr.* (*a*) Mettre sous clef. (*b*) Enfermer.

locker, *s.* Armoire *f* ; coffre *m.*

locket, *s.* Médaillon *m.*

lock-gate, *s.* Porte *f* d'écluse.

lock-keeper, *s.* Gardien *m* d'écluse ; éclusier *m.*

locksmith, *s.* Serrurier *m.*

locomotion, *s.* Locomotion *f.*

locomotive, *s.* Locomotive *f.*

locust, *s.* Grande sauterelle.

locution, *s.* Locution *f.*

lode, *s.* Filon *m,* veine *f.*

lodge[1], *s.* **1.** Loge *f* ; pavillon *m* d'entrée. **2.** Loge, atelier *m.*

lodge[2]. **I.** *v.tr.* **1.** Loger. **2.** To l. a complaint, porter plainte. **II. lodge,** *v.i.* (Se) loger. To l. with, demeurer chez.

lodger, *s.* Locataire *mf.*

lodging, *s.* Logement *m,* logis *m,* appartement *m.* **To let lodgings,** louer des chambres.

lodging-house, *s.* Hôtel garni ; maison meublée.

loft, *s.* Grenier *m,* soupente *f.*

lofty, *a.* **1.** Haut, élevé. **2.** Condescendant. **3.** Sublime.

log, *s.* **1.** Bûche *f.* **2.** Loch *m.* **3.** Livre *m* de loch.

log-book, *s.* **1.** (*a*) Livre *m* de loch. (*b*) Journal *m* de navigation. **2.** Livre de vol.

logic, *s.* Logique *f.*

logical, *a.* Logique.

logically, *adv.* Logiquement.

loin, *s.* **1.** *pl.* Reins *m.* **2.** Filet *m.*

loiter, *v.i.* Flâner, traîner.

loiterer, *s.* Flâneur, -euse.

loll, *v.i.* Être étendu.

London. *Pr.n.* Londres *f.*

loneliness, *s.* **1.** Solitude *f,* isolement *m.* **2.** Sentiment *m* d'abandon.

lonely, *a.* Solitaire, isolé. **To feel very l.,** se sentir bien seul.

long[1]. **I.** *a.* Long, *f.* longue. **1.** To be six feet l., être long de six pieds. **2. The days are getting longer,** les jours croissent. **It will take a l. time,** ce sera long. **A l. time ago,** il y a longtemps. **At the longest,** au plus. **II. long,** *s.* Before l., avant peu ; sous peu. For l., pendant longtemps. **III. long,** *adv.* **1.** (*a*) Longtemps. As l. as I live, tant que je vivrai. So l. as, pourvu que. **He won't be l.,** il ne tardera pas. (*b*) **How l. ?** combien de temps ? **2. Not l. before,** peu de temps avant. **3. All day l.,** pendant toute la journée. **4. No longer,** ne . . . plus.

long[2], *v.i.* To l. for, désirer ardemment ; avoir grande envie de.

long-drawn-out, *a.* Long ; prolongé.

long-headed, *a.* Perspicace, avisé.

longing, *s.* Désir ardent, grande envie.

longitude, *s.* Longitude *f.*

long-lived, *a.* Qui a la vie longue.

long-standing, *attrib.a.* Ancien ; de longue date.

long-suffering, *a.* Patient, endurant.

look¹, *s.* **1.** Regard *m.* **2.** (*a*) Aspect *m*, air *m*, apparence *f* ; mine *f.* (*b*) *pl.* (Good) looks, belle mine.

look², *v.i. & tr.* **1.** *v.i.* Regarder. To l. the other way, détourner les yeux. **2.** *v.tr.* To l. s.o. up and down, toiser qn. **3.** *Pred.* Avoir l'air, paraître, sembler. What does he l. like? comment est-il ? It looks like it, cela en a l'air. **look after,** *v.ind.tr.* Soigner ; s'occuper de ; veiller à. **look at,** *v.ind.tr.* Regarder, considérer. To l. at one's watch, regarder à sa montre. To l. at him, à le voir. **look away,** *v.i.* Détourner les yeux. **look back,** *v.i.* Regarder en arrière ; se retourner. **look down,** *v.i.* Regarder en bas ; baisser les yeux. To l. d. on, regarder de haut en bas ; dédaigner. **look for,** *v.ind.tr.* **1.** Chercher. **2.** S'attendre à. **look forward,** *v.i.* To l. f. to, s'attendre à ; attendre avec plaisir. **look into,** *v.ind.tr.* Examiner, étudier. **look out. 1.** *v.i.* (*a*) Regarder au dehors. (*b*) Veiller. To l. out for, être à la recherche de. (*c*) Prendre garde. **2.** *v.tr.* Chercher. **look over,** *v.tr.* Parcourir des yeux ; examiner. **look round,** *v.i.* **1.** Regarder autour de soi. **2.** Tourner la tête. **look through,** *v.tr.* Parcourir, examiner. **look up. 1.** *v.i.* (*a*) Regarder en haut ; lever les yeux. (*b*) To l. up to, respecter. **2.** *v.tr.* Consulter ; (re)chercher.

looking-glass, *s.* Miroir *m*, glace *f.*

look-out, *s.* **1.** Veille *f.* **2.** Affaire *f.*

loom¹, *s.* Métier *m* à tisser.

loom², *v.i.* Apparaître indistinctement.

loop¹, *s.* Boucle *f.*

loop², *v.tr.* Boucler.

loop-hole, *s.* **1.** Meurtrière *f.* **2.** Échappatoire *f.*

loose, *a.* **1.** (*a*) Mal assujetti ; branlant ; détaché. (*b*) Déchaîné, lâché. (*c*) Mobile. L. sheets, feuilles volantes. (*d*) L. cash, menue monnaie. **2.** Vague, peu exact.

loose-leaf, *attrib.a.* A feuilles mobiles.

loosen. 1. *v.tr.* Relâcher. **2.** *v.i.* Se délier, se défaire.

looseness, *s.* **1.** Relâchement *m* ; ampleur *f.* **2.** (*a*) Vague *m.* (*b*) Licence *f.*

loot¹, *s.* **1.** Pillage *m.* **2.** Butin *m.*

loot², *v.tr.* Piller, saccager.

looting, *s.* Pillage *m* ; sac *m.*

lop, *v.tr.* Élaguer, tailler.

loquacious, *a.* Loquace.

loquacity, *s.* Loquacité *f.*

lord, *s.* **1.** Seigneur *m* maître *m.* **2.** Lord *m.*

lordly, *a.* **1.** Noble majestueux. **2.** Hautain, altier.

lordship, *s.* Suzeraineté *f* (over, de).

lore, *s.* Science *f*, savoir *m.*

lorgnette, *s.* Face-à-main *m*, *pl.* faces-à-main.

lorry, *s.* Camion *m.*

lose, *v.tr.* **1.** (*a*) Perdre. (*b*) He has lost an arm, il lui manque un bras. (*c*) To be lost at sea, périr en mer. **2.** To l. one's way, s'égarer. To l. sight of, perdre de vue. **3.** Retarder. **4.** Manquer.

loser, *s.* Perdant, -ante.

losing, *a.* Perdant.

loss, *s.* **1.** Perte *f.* **2.** Dead l., perte sèche. **3.** Déperdition *f.* **4.** To be at a l., être embarrassé, désorienté.

lost, *a.* Perdu. L. property office, service *m* des objets trouvés.

lot, *s.* **1.** To draw lots, tirer au sort. **2.** (*a*) Sort, part *f*, partage *m.* (*b*) Destin *m*, destinée *f.* **3.** Lot *m.* **4.** Beaucoup. What a lot of people ! que de gens ! Such a lot, tellement.

lotion, *s.* Lotion *f.*

lottery, *s.* Loterie *f.*

loud. 1. *a.* (*a*) Bruyant, retentissant. L. laugh, gros rire. In a l. voice, à haute voix. (*b*) Criard, voyant. **2.** *adv.* Haut, à haute voix.

loudly, *adv.* Haut, fort, à voix haute ; bruyamment.

loudness, *s.* Force *f* ; grand bruit.

loud-speaker, *s.* Haut-parleur *m*, *pl.* haut-parleurs.

lounge¹, *s.* (*a*) Promenoir *m* ; hall *m.* (*b*) Foyer *m.*

lounge², *v.i.* Flâner.

lounge-chair, *s.* Chaise-longue *f*, *pl.* chaises-longues.

lounge-suit, *s.* Complet veston *m.*

louring, *a.* **1.** Renfrogné. **2.** Sombre, menaçant.

lout, *s.* Rustre *m*, lourdaud *m.*

lovable, *a.* Aimable ; sympathique.

love[1], *s.* **1.** Amour *m.* (*a*) Affection *f*, tendresse *f.* (*b*) Amour. **To fall in l. with,** s'éprendre, tomber amoureux, de. **To make l.,** faire la cour. **2.** Zéro *m*, rien *m.* **L. all,** égalité *f* à rien. **L. game,** jeu blanc.

love[2], *v.tr.* (*a*) Aimer, affectionner. (*b*) Aimer d'amour.

love-letter, *s.* Billet doux.

loveliness, *s.* Beauté *f.*

lovely, *a.* Beau, *f.* belle ; ravissant.

lover, *s.* **1.** (*a*) Amoureux *m*, prétendant *m.* (*b*) Fiancé *m.* **2.** Her l., son amant. **3.** Amateur *m*, ami(e).

loving, *a.* Affectueux, affectionné.

low[1]. **I.** *a.* **1.** Bas, *f.* basse. **2.** (*a*) Profond. (*b*) **To lie low,** se tenir coi. **3. Lower,** inférieur, -e. **4. Low diet,** régime peu substantiel. **To be in low spirits,** être abattu. **5. Low speed,** petite vitesse. **6. In a low voice,** à mi-voix.
II. low, *adv.* Bas.

low[2], *v.i.* Meugler.

lower, *v.tr.* (*a*) Baisser ; abaisser. (*b*) Réduire.

lowering[1], *a.* Abaissant.

lowering[2], *a.* **1.** Renfrogné. **2.** Sombre, menaçant.

lowly, *a.* Humble, modeste.

low-lying, *a.* Situé en bas ; enfoncé

low-necked, *a.* Décolleté.

low-spirited, *a.* Abattu, triste.

loyal, *a.* Fidèle, dévoué ; loyal, -aux (*to*, envers).

loyally, *adv.* Fidèlement.

loyalty, *s.* Fidélité *f.*

lozenge, *s.* Pastille *f*, tablette *f.*

lubricant, *a. & s.* Lubrifiant (*m*).

lubricate, *v.tr.* Lubrifier ; graisser.

Lucerne. *Pr.n.* Lucerne *f.* **The Lake of L.,** le lac des Quatre-Cantons.

lucid, *a.* **1.** Brillant, lumineux. **2.** (*a*) Lucide. (*b*) Clair, transparent.

luck, *s.* **1.** Hasard *m*, chance *f*, fortune *f.* **Worse l.!** tant pis ! **Hard l.!** pas de chance ! **2.** Bonheur *m*, (bonne) chance. **To be in l.,** avoir de la chance.

luckily, *adv.* Heureusement ; par bonheur.

lucky, *a.* Heureux, fortuné. **To be l.,** avoir de la chance.

lucrative, *a.* Lucratif.

ludicrous, *a.* Risible, grotesque.

luggage, *s.* Bagage(s) *m(pl).*

luggage-carrier, *s.* Porte-bagages *m inv.*

luggage-label, *s.* Étiquette *f* à bagages.

luggage-van, *s.* Fourgon *m* (aux bagages).

lugubrious, *a.* Lugubre.

lukewarm, *a.* Tiède.

lull[1], *s.* Moment *m* de calme ; accalmie *f.*

lull[2], *v.tr.* Bercer, endormir.

lullaby, *s.* Berceuse *f.*

lumber[1], *s.* Vieux meubles ; fatras *m.*

lumber[2], *v.tr.* Encombrer.

lumbering, *a.* Lourd, pesant.

luminous, *a.* Lumineux.

lump, *s.* (*a*) Morceau *m* ; motte *f.* **L. sum,** somme globale. (*b*) Bosse *f.*

lunacy, *s.* Démence *f* ; folie *f.*

lunar, *a.* Lunaire ; de (la) lune.

lunatic, *a. & s.* Fou, *f.* folle.

lunch[1], *s.* Déjeuner *m.*

lunch[2], *v.i.* Déjeuner.

luncheon, *s.* Déjeuner *m.*

lung, *s.* Poumon *m.*

lurch[1], *s.* **1.** Embardée *f.* **2.** Pas titubant.

lurch[2], *v.i.* **1.** Embarder. **2.** Tituber.

lure[1], *s.* **1.** Leurre *m.* **2.** (*a*) Piège *m* (*b*) Attrait *m.*

lure[2], *v.tr.* Attirer, séduire.

lurid, *a.* Blafard, sinistre.

lurk, *v.i.* Se cacher ; rester tapi.

lurking, *a.* Caché. **A. l. suspicion,** un vague soupçon.

luscious, *a.* Succulent, savoureux.

lust, *s.* Appétit *m* ; convoitise *f.*

lustily, *adv.* Vigoureusement.

lustre, *s.* **1.** Éclat *m*, brillant *m.* **2.** Lustre *m.*

lustrous, *a.* Brillant, éclatant.

lusty, *a.* Vigoureux, fort, robuste

luxuriance, *s.* Luxuriance *f.*

luxuriant, *a.* Luxuriant.

luxurious, *a.* Luxueux.

luxury, *s.* **1.** Luxe *m.* **2.** (Objet *m* de) luxe.

lying[1], *a.* Faux, *f.* fausse.

lying[2], *s.* Le mensonge.

lying[3], *a.* Couché, étendu.

lynx, *s.* Lynx *m.*

Lyons. *Pr.n.* Lyon *m.*

lyric. **1.** *a.* Lyrique. **2.** *s.* Poème *m* lyrique.

lyrical, *a.* Lyrique.

M

M, m, *s.* (La lettre) M, m *f.*

macaroni, *s.* Macaroni *m.*

macaroon, *s.* Macaron *m.*

machine, *s.* Machine *f.*

machine-gun, *s.* Mitrailleuse *f.*

machinery, *s.* Mécanisme *m* ; machines *fpl,* machinerie *f.*

mackerel, *s.* Maquereau *m.*

mackintosh, *s.* Caoutchouc *m* ; imperméable *m.*

mad, *a.* **1.** Fou, *f.* folle. **Raving mad,** fou furieux. **2. Mad for revenge,** assoiffé de revanche. **3. Mad dog,** chien enragé.

madam, *s.* Madame *f,* mademoiselle *f.*

madden, *v.tr.* Rendre fou ; exaspérer.

maddening, *a.* A rendre fou ; exaspérant.

made, *a.* Fait, fabriqué, confectionné.

Madeira. *Pr.n.* Vin *m.* de Madère. **M. cake,** gâteau *m* de Savoie.

madly, *adv.* **1.** Follement ; en fou ; comme un fou. **2.** Éperdument. **3.** Furieusement.

madman, *s.* Fou *m.*

madness, *s.* **1.** Folie *f.* **2.** Rage *f.*

magazine, *s.* **1.** Magasin *m.* **2.** Revue *f* périodique ; magazine *m.*

maggot, *s.* Ver *m,* asticot *m.*

magic, *s.* **1.** *s.* Magie *f,* enchantement *m.* **2.** *a.* Magique, enchanté.

magical, *a.* Magique.

magician, *s.* Magicien, -ienne.

magistrate, *s.* Magistrat *m,* juge *m.*

magnanimity, *s.* Magnanimité *f.*

magnanimous, *a.* Magnanime.

magnate, *s.* Magnat *m.*

magnesia, *s.* Magnésie *f.*

magnet, *s.* Aimant *m.*

magnetic, *a.* Magnétique ; aimanté.

magnetism, *s.* Magnétisme *m.*

magneto, *s.* Magnéto *f.*

magnificence, *s.* Magnificence *f.*

magnificent, *a.* Magnifique.

magnificently, *adv.* Magnifiquement.

magnify, *v.tr.* Grossir, agrandir **Magnifying glass,** loupe *f.*

magnitude, *s.* Grandeur *f.*

magpie, *s.* Pie *f.*

mahogany, *s.* Acajou *m.*

Mahometan, *a. & s.* Mahométan, -e.

maid, *s.* **1.** Jeune fille. **2.** Vierge. **3. Old m.,** vieille fille. **4.** Bonne *f,* domestique *f.* **Lady's m.,** femme *f* de chambre.

maiden, *s.* **1.** (*a*) Jeune fille *f.* (*b*) Vierge *f.* **2.** *Attrib.* (*a*) **M. lady,** demoiselle *f.* (*b*) **M. name,** nom de jeune fille. (*c*) **M. voyage,** premier voyage.

maidservant, *s.* Servante *f* ; bonne *f.*

mail, *s.* Courrier *m.*

mail-bag, *s.* Sac *m* de poste.

mail-boat, *s.* Paquebot-poste *m, pl.* paquebots-poste.

mail-order, *s.* Commande faite par l'entremise de la poste.

mail-train, *s.* Train-poste *m pl.* trains-poste.

mail-van, *s.* Wagon-poste *m pl.* wagons-poste.

maim, *v.tr.* Estropier, mutiler.

main[1]**,** *s.* **1. In the m.,** en général. **2.** Canalisation maîtresse ; conducteur principal.

main[2]**,** *a.* **1. By m. force,** de vive force. **2.** Principal, -aux ; premier. (*a*) **The m. body,** le gros. (*b*) **The m. point,** le principal. (*c*) **M. line,** voie principale.

mainland, *s.* Continent *m* ; terre *f* ferme.

mainly, *adv.* **1.** Principalement, surtout. **2.** En grande partie.

mainspring, *s.* Grand ressort.

mainstay, *s.* Soutien principal.

maintain, *v.tr.* **1.** Maintenir ; soutenir. **2.** Entretenir, soutenir.

maintenance, *s.* **1.** Maintien *m.* **2.** Entretien *m.*

maize, *s.* Maïs *m.*

majestic, *a.* Majestueux.

majestically, *adv.* Majestueusement.

majesty, *s.* Majesté *f.*

major[1]**,** *s.* Commandant *m.*

major[2]**,** *a.* (*a*) Majeur, -e. **M. road,** route de priorité. (*b*) Aîné.

majority, *s.* Majorité *f.*

make[1]**,** *s.* (*a*) Façon *f,* fabrication *f.* (*b*) Marque *f.*

make[2]**.** **I.** *v.tr.* **1.** Faire ; construire ; fabriquer ; confectionner. **What is it made of?** en quoi est-ce ? **To m.**

a noise, faire du bruit. To m. one's escape, s'échapper, se sauver. 2. Gagner. 3. *Pred.* Rendre. To m. known, faire connaître. To m. oneself comfortable, se mettre à l'aise. 4. You should m. him do it, vous devriez le lui faire faire.

II. **make**, *v.i.* To m. for, se diriger vers (un endroit). **make away**, *v.i.* To m. a. with, enlever. **make off**, *v.i.* Se sauver. **make out**, *v.tr.* 1. Faire, dresser ; tirer. 2. Établir, prouver. 3. *(a)* Comprendre ; déchiffrer. I can't m. it out, je n'y comprends rien. *(b)* Distinguer. **make over**, *v.tr.* Céder. **make up.** I. *v.tr.* 1. Compléter ; combler. 2. Regagner. 3. Faire ; composer. 4.*(a)* Faire, confectionner. *(b)* Dresser. *(c)* Inventer. 5. Former, composer (un ensemble). 6. Se farder. 7. To m. up one's mind, prendre son parti. 8. Arranger. To m. it up, se réconcilier. II. **make up**, *v.i.* To m. up for, rattraper (le temps perdu).

maker, *s.* Faiseur, -euse ; fabricant *m* ; constructeur *m*.

makeshift, *s.* Pis aller *m inv*, expédient *m*.

make-up, *s.* Maquillage *m*, fard *m*.

make-weight, *s.* Complément *m* de poids.

making, *s.* Fabrication *f* ; confection *f* ; construction *f*.

maladroit, *a.* Maladroit.

malady, *s.* Maladie *f*, mal *m*.

malaria, *s.* Malaria *f*.

male. 1. *a* Mâle ; masculin. 2. *s.* Mâle *m*.

malefactor, *s.* Malfaiteur, -trice.

malevolence, *s.* Malveillance *f*.

malevolent, *a.* Malveillant.

malice, *s.* Malice *f*, malveillance *f*.

malicious, *a.* *(a)* Méchant, malveillant. *(b)* Rancunier.

maliciously, *adv.* *(a)* Avec malveillance. *(b)* Par rancune.

malign[1], *a.* Pernicieux, nuisible.

malign[2], *v.tr.* Calomnier, diffamer.

malignant, *a.* Malin, *f.* maligne ; méchant.

mallet, *s.* Maillet *m*.

malt, *s.* Malt *m*.

Malta. *Pr.n.* Malte *f*.

maltreat, *v.tr* Maltraiter.

maltreatment, *s.* Mauvais traitement.

mamma, *s.* Maman *f*.

mammal, *s.* Mammifère *m*.

mammoth. 1. *s.* Mammouth *m*. 2. *Attrib. a.* Géant, monstre.

man[1], *s.* 1. Homme *m*. 2. *(a)* To a man, jusqu'au dernier. *(b)* An old man, un vieillard. The dead man, le mort. 3. Man and wife, mari *m* et femme. 4. *(a)* Domestique *m*, valet *m*. *(b)* Employé *m*, garçon *m*.

man[2], *v.tr.* Garnir d'hommes.

manage, *v.tr.* 1. Diriger, gérer. 2. Gouverner ; tenir. 3. Arranger, conduire. 4. *Abs.* S'arranger.

manageable, *a* 1. Maniable. 2. Traitable.

management, *s.* 1. *(a)* Maniement *m*. *(b)* Direction *f*, conduite *f*. 2. Adresse *f*. 3. *Coll :* Administration *f*.

manager, *s.* 1. Directeur *m*, administrateur *m*. 2. Ménagère *f*.

manageress, *s.* Directrice *f*.

managing, *a.* Directeur, -trice ; gérant.

mandarine, *s.* Mandarine *f*.

mandate, *s.* Mandat *m*.

mandoline, *s.* Mandoline *f*.

mane, *s.* Crinière *f*.

manful, *a.* Vaillant, hardi, viril.

manfully, *adv.* Vaillamment, hardiment.

manger, *s.* Mangeoire *f*, crèche *f*.

mangle[1], *s.* Calandreuse *f*.

mangle[2], *v.tr.* Calandrer.

mangle[3], *v.tr.* Déchirer, mutiler.

mangling[1], *s.* Calandrage *m*.

mangling[2], *s.* Lacération *f* ; mutilation *f*.

mango, *s.* Mangue *f*.

mangy, *a.* Galeux.

manhood, *s.* Age *m* d'homme ; virilité *f*.

mania, *s.* Manie *f* ; folie *f*.

maniac, *a. & s.* Fou furieux, folle furieuse.

maniacal, *a.* Fou, *f.* folle.

manicure[1], *s.* 1. Soin *m* des mains. M. set, trousse *f* de manucure. 2. Manucure *mf*.

manicure[2], *v.tr.* Soigner les mains.

manicurist, *s.* Manucure *mf*.

manifest[1], *a.* Manifeste, évident.

manifest[2], *v.tr.* Manifester, témoigner.

manifestation, s. Manifestation f.

manifesto, s. Manifeste m.

manifold, a. (a) Divers, varié. (b) Multiple, nombreux.

manipulate, v.tr. Manipuler.

manipulation, s. Manipulation f.

mankind, s.inv. 1. Le genre humain. 2. Les hommes.

manliness, s. Caractère m mâle; virilité f.

manly, a. D'homme; mâle, viril.

mannequin, s. Mannequin m.

manner, s. 1. Manière f, façon f. In such a m., de manière. 2. pl. Mœurs f. 3. Maintien m, air m. 4. pl. Manières. To forget one's manners, oublier les convenances. 5. Espèce f, sorte f.

manœuvre[1], s. Manœuvre f.

manœuvre[2], v.tr. & i. Manœuvrer.

man-power, s. Main-d'œuvre f.

man-servant, s. Domestique m; valet m.

mansion, s. 1. Château m; hôtel (particulier). 2. pl. Maison f de rapport.

manslaughter, s. Homicide m involontaire.

mantelpiece, s. Manteau m de cheminée.

mantle, s. 1. (a) Manteau m. (b) Mante f, pèlerine f. 2. Manchon m.

manual. 1. a. Manuel. 2. s. Manuel m; aide-mémoire m inv.

manufactory, s. Fabrique f, usine f.

manufacture[1], s. Fabrication f; confection f.

manufacture[2], v.tr. Fabriquer, manufacturer; confectionner.

manufacturer, s. Fabricant m, industriel m, manufacturier m.

manure[1], s. Engrais m; fumier m.

manure[2], v.tr. Fumer, engraisser.

manuscript, a. & s. Manuscrit (m).

many, a. & s. Un grand nombre (de); beaucoup (de); bien des; plusieurs. Ever so m. times, je ne sais combien de fois. M. of us, beaucoup d'entre nous. In so m. words, en propres termes. Too m., trop de. How m.? combien de. As m. . . . as, autant de . . . que.

map[1], s. Carte f.

map[2], v.tr. To map out, tracer.

maple, s. Érable m.

mar, v.tr. Gâter; troubler.

marauder, s. Maraudeur m.

marauding, a. Maraudeur, -euse.

marble, s. 1. Marbre m. 2. Bille f

March[1], s. Mars m.

march[2], s. 1. (a) Marche f. On the m., en marche. M. past, défilé m. (b) Pas m, allure f. 2. Marche, progrès m.

march[3], v.i. Marcher. To m. past, défiler.

marchioness, s. Marquise f.

mare, s. Jument f.

Margaret. Pr.n. Marguerite f.

margarine, s. Margarine f.

margin, s. Marge f.

marginal, a. Marginal, -aux; en marge.

marigold, s. Souci m.

marine. 1. a. Marin. 2. s. (a) Marine f. (b) Soldat m de l'infanterie de marine.

mariner, s. Marin m.

marionette, s. Marionnette f.

maritime, a. Maritime.

mark[1], s. 1. But m, cible f. 2. Marque f, signe m. 3. Marque f, tache f 4. Marque, trace f.

mark[2], v.tr. 1. Marquer, chiffrer. 2. Marquer; repérer; indiquer. 3. To m. time, piétiner sur place. 4. Observer, noter.

marked, a. Marqué; sensible.

market, s. (a) Marché m; halles fpl. (b) Débouché m. On the m., mis en vente. (c) Black m., marché noir.

market-day, s. Jour m de marché.

market-garden, s. Jardin maraîcher.

market-gardener, s. Maraîcher, -ère.

marketing, s. To go m., aller aux provisions.

market-place, s. Place f du marché.

market-price, s. Prix courant.

marking, s. 1. Marquage m. 2. pl. Marques f; taches f, rayures f.

marking-ink, s. Encre f à marquer.

marksman, s. Tireur m d'élite.

marksmanship, s. Adresse f au tir.

marmalade, s. Confiture f d'oranges.

marquee, s. Marquise f.

marquess, marquis, s. Marquis m.

marriage, s. Mariage m. The m. service, la bénédiction nuptiale.

marrow, s. 1. Moelle f. 2. Vegetable m., courge f à la moelle.

marry, v.tr. 1. Marier. 2. (a) Se

marier avec; épouser. (b) *Abs.* Se marier.

Marseilles. *Pr.n.* Marseille *f*.

marsh, *s.* Marais *m*, marécage *m*.

marshal[1], *s.* **Air M.,** général *m*, *pl*. -aux, de corps aérien.

marshal[2], *v.tr.* Placer en ordre.

marshalling, *s.* Disposition *f* en ordre.

marshy, *a.* Marécageux.

marten, *s.* Marte *f*.

martial, *a.* Martial, -aux; guerrier.

martin, *s.* Martinet *m*.

martyr, *s.* Martyr, *f.* martyre.

martyrdom, *s.* Martyre *m*.

marvel[1], *s.* Merveille *f*.

marvel[2], *v.i.* S'émerveiller (*at, de*).

marvellous, *a.* Merveilleux, étonnant.

marvellously, *adv.* A merveille; merveilleusement.

Mary. *Pr.n.* Marie *f*.

marzipan, *s.* Massepain *m*.

mascot, *s.* Mascotte *f*.

masculine, *a.* Masculin, mâle.

mash, *v.tr.* Brasser, écraser. **Mashed potatoes,** pommes *f* mousseline.

mask[1], *s.* Masque *m*; loup *m*.

mask[2], *v.tr.* Masquer.

mason, *s.* **1.** Maçon *m*. **2.** Franc-maçon *m*, *pl.* francs-maçons.

masonry, *s.* Maçonnerie *f*.

masquerade, *v.i.* Se masquer. **To m. as,** se déguiser en.

mass[1], *s.* Messe *f*. **High m.,** la grand'messe.

mass[2], *s.* **1.** Masse *f*, amas *m*. **2.** (a) Multitude *f*. (b) **The masses,** les masses; la foule. **M. meeting,** réunion *f* en masse. **M. production,** fabrication *f* en série.

massacre[1], *s.* Massacre *m*, tuerie *f*.

massacre[2], *v.tr.* Massacrer.

massage[1], *s.* Massage *m*.

massage[2], *v.tr.* Masser.

masseur, *f.* **masseuse,** *s.* Masseur, -euse.

massive, *a.* Massif.

mast, *s.* **1.** Mât *m*. **2.** Pylône *m*.

master[1], *s.* **1.** (a) Maître *m*. **To be one's own m.,** s'appartenir. (b) Maître, patron *m*, chef *m*. **2.** Maître; professeur *m*. **3. M. John,** Monsieur Jean. **4.** *Attrib.* (a) **M. mariner,** capitaine au long cours. (b) **M. mind,** esprit supérieur.

master[2], *v.tr.* Dompter, maîtriser.

masterful, *a.* Impérieux, autoritaire.

masterly, *a.* De maître. **In a m. manner,** magistralement.

masterpiece, *s.* Chef-d'œuvre *m*, *pl.* chefs-d'œuvre.

mastery, *s.* Maîtrise *f*; domination *f*.

masticate, *v.tr.* Mâcher, mastiquer.

mastiff, *s.* Mâtin *m*.

mat, *s.* (a) Natte *f*. (b) Paillasson *m*.

match[1], *s.* **1.** Égal, -ale; pareil, -eille. **2.** Lutte *f*, partie *f*, match *m*. **3.** Mariage *m*, alliance *f*.

match[2]. **1.** *v.tr.* (a) Égaler; être l'égal de. (b) Apparier; assortir. **2.** *v.i.* S'assortir; s'harmoniser.

match[3], *s.* Allumette *f*.

match-box, *s.* Boîte *f* à allumettes.

matching, *s.* Assortiment *m*; appariement *m*.

matchless, *a.* Incomparable.

mate[1], *s.* Échec *m* et mat *m*.

mate[2], *v.tr.* Faire échec et mat.

mate[3], *s.* **1.** Camarade *mf*; compagnon, *f.* compagne. **2.** Officier *m*.

mate[4], *v.i.* S'accoupler.

material. I. *a.* **1.** Matériel, grossier. **2.** Important; essentiel. **II.** **material,** *s.* **1.** (a) Matière *f*, matériaux *mpl.* (b) *pl.* Fournitures *f*, accessoires *m*. **Writing materials,** de quoi écrire. **2.** Étoffe *f*, tissu *m*.

materialist, *s.* Matérialiste *m*.

materially, *adv.* **1.** Matériellement. **2.** Sensiblement.

maternal, *a.* Maternel.

maternity, *s.* Maternité *f*.

mathematical, *a.* Mathématique.

mathematics, *s.pl.* Mathématiques *f*.

matinée, *s.* Matinée *f*.

matins, *s.pl.* Matines *f*.

matrimonial, *a.* Matrimonial, -aux.

matrimony, *s.* Le mariage.

matron, *s.* **1.** Matrone *f*. **2.** (a) Intendante *f*. (b) Infirmière *f* en chef.

matter[1], *s.* **1.** Matière *f*; substance *f*. **2.** Matière, sujet *m*. **Reading m.,** choses *f* à lire. **3.** No m., n'importe. **4.** Affaire *f*, chose, cas *m*. **In this m.,** à cet égard. **For that m.,** d'ailleurs. **What is the m.?** qu'y a-t-il?

matter[2], *v.i.* Importer; avoir de l'importance. **It does not m.,** n'importe; cela ne fait rien.

Matterhorn (the). *Pr.n.* Le Mont Cervin.

matter-of-fact, *a.* Pratique.

mattress, *s.* Matelas *m.*

mature[1], *a.* Mûr.

mature[2], *v.i.* Mûrir.

maturely, *adv.* Mûrement.

maturity, *s.* Maturité *f.*

maudlin, *a.* Larmoyant, pleurard.

maul, *v.tr.* Meurtrir, malmener.

maunder, *v.i.* Divaguer, radoter.

maunderings, *s.* Divagations *f.*

Maundy Thursday, *s.* Le jeudi saint.

Mauritius, *Pr.n.* L'île *f* Maurice.

mausoleum, *s.* Mausolée *m.*

mauve, *a. & s.* Mauve (*m*).

mawkish, *a.* Fade, insipide.

maxim, *s.* Maxime *f,* dicton *m.*

maximum, *a. & s.* Maximum (*m*).

may[1], *v.aux.* **1.** (*a*) I may, je peux. (*b*) It may be, il se peut bien. **Be that as it may,** quoi qu'il en soit. That's as may be, c'est selon. Run as he might, il a eu beau courir. (*c*) We may as well, autant vaut. **2. May I?** vous permettez? **May I come in?—You may,** puis-je entrer? —Mais parfaitement. **3.** I hope it may be true, pourvu que cela soit vrai! **4.** Much good may it do you! grand bien vous fasse!

May[2], *s.* **1.** Mai *m.* **2.** May(-tree), aubépine *f.*

maybe, *adv.* Peut-être.

May-day, *s.* Le premier mai.

mayor, *s.* Maire *m.*

mayoress, *s.* Femme *f* du maire; mairesse *f.*

maze, *s.* Labyrinthe *m,* dédale *m.*

me, *pers.pron.* **1.** Me; moi. They hear me, ils m'entendent. **2.** Moi. Come to me, venez à moi.

meadow, *s.* Pré *m,* prairie *f.*

meagre, *a.* Maigre; peu copieux.

meal[1], *s.* Farine *f.*

meal[2], *s.* Repas *m.*

mean[1], *s.* **1.** (*a*) Milieu *m.* (*b*) Moyenne *f.* **2.** *pl.* Moyen(s) *m(pl),* voie(s) *f(pl).* **By all means!** mais certainement! **By means of,** au moyen de. **3.** *pl.* Moyens; ressources *f.*

mean[2], *a.* Moyen.

mean[3], *a.* **1.** Misérable. **2.** Bas, méprisable. **A m. trick,** un vilain tour. **3.** Avare, mesquin.

mean[4], *v.tr.* **1.** (*a*) Avoir l'intention; se proposer. **He didn't m. it,** il ne

l'a pas fait exprès. (*b*) **He means well,** il a de bonnes intentions. **2.** Destiner (*for,* à). **3.** (*a*) Vouloir dire; signifier. (*b*) **What do you m. by that?** qu'entendez-vous par là? **You don't m. it!** vous plaisantez! **I m. it,** c'est sérieux.

meander, *v.i.* Serpenter.

meaning[1], *a.* Significatif.

meaning[2], *s.* (*a*) Signification *f,* sens *m.* (*b*) Pensée *f.*

meaningless, *a.* Dénué de sens.

meanly, *adv.* **1.** Misérablement, pauvrement. **2.** Bassement.

meanness, *s.* **1.** Pauvreté *f.* **2.** (*a*) Mesquinerie *f.* (*b*) Vilenie *f.*

meantime, meanwhile, *s. & adv.* Dans l'intervalle; en attendant.

measles, *s.pl.* Rougeole *f.*

measure[1], *s.* **1.** Made to m., fait sur mesure. **2.** (*a*) Mesure. (*b*) Mètre *m.* **3.** Mesure, limite *f.* **4.** Mesure, démarche *f.*

measure[2], *v.tr.* (*a*) Mesurer; métrer. (*b*) Mesurer; prendre la mesure de.

measured, *a.* **1.** Mesuré, déterminé. **2.** (*a*) Cadencé. (*b*) **With m. steps,** à pas comptés.

measurement, *s.* **1.** Mesurage *m.* **2.** Mesure *f,* dimension *f.*

meat, *s.* **1.** Viande *f.* **2.** Aliment *m,* nourriture *f.*

mechanic, *s.* **1.** Artisan *m,* ouvrier *m.* **2.** Mécanicien *m.*

mechanical, *a.* **1.** Mécanique. **2.** Machinal, -aux; automatique.

mechanically, *adv.* Machinalement.

mechanism, *s.* Appareil *m,* dispositif *m;* mécanisme *m.*

medal, *s.* Médaille *f.*

medallion, *s.* Médaillon *m.*

meddle, *v.i.* Se mêler (*with,* de). To m. with, toucher à.

meddler, *s.* Officieux, -euse.

meddlesome, *a.* Officieux.

meddling, *s.* Intervention *f,* ingérence *f.*

mediate, *v.i.* S'entremettre.

mediation, *s.* Médiation *f.*

medical, *a.* Médical, -aux. **M. officer,** médecin *m* sanitaire; major *m.*

medicinal, *a.* Médicinal, -aux.'

medicine, *s.* **1.** La médecine. **2.** Médicament *m,* médecine *f.*

medicine-chest, *s.* (Coffret *m* de) pharmacie *f.*

medieval, *a.* Du moyen âge ; médiéval, -aux.

mediocre, *a.* Médiocre.

mediocrity, *s.* Médiocrité *f.*

meditate. I. *v.tr.* Méditer. **2.** *v.i.* (*a*) Méditer. (*b*) Se recueillir.

meditation, *s.* Méditation *f* ; recueillement *m.*

meditative, *a.* Méditatif, recueilli.

Mediterranean, *a.* The M. (Sea), la (mer) Méditerranée.

medium. I. *s.* **1.** Milieu *m.* **Happy m.,** juste milieu. **2.** Milieu, véhicule *m.* **3.** Intermédiaire *m.* entremise *f.* **4.** Médium *m.*
  II. **medium,** *a.* Moyen.

medley, *s.* Mélange *m* ; pot pourri.

meek, *a.* Doux, *f.* douce ; humble.

meekly, *adv.* Avec douceur ; humblement.

meekness, *s.* Soumission *f.*

meerschaum, *s.* Écume *f* de mer.

meet[1], *a.* Convenable ; séant.

meet[2]. **I.** *v.tr.* **1.** Rencontrer ; se rencontrer avec. **2.** Faire face à. **3.** Rejoindre. **To go to m.,** aller au-devant de ; aller à la rencontre de. **4.** Faire la connaissance de. **5.** Frapper. **6.** (*a*) Se conformer à. (*b*) Satisfaire à.
  II. **meet,** *v.i.* (*a*) Se rencontrer, se voir. (*b*) Se réunir. (*c*) Se joindre. (*d*) To m. with, rencontrer, trouver. **To m. with a refusal,** essuyer un refus.

meeting, *s.* **1.** Rencontre *f.* **2.** Assemblée *f,* réunion *f.*

melancholy. 1. *s.* Mélancolie *f.* **2.** *a.* Mélancolique ; triste.

mellow, *a.* **1.** Fondant, mûr. **2.** Moelleux ; doux, *f.* douce.

melodious, *a.* Mélodieux.

melodrama, *s.* Mélodrame *m.*

melodramatic, *a.* Mélodramatique.

melody, *s.* Mélodie *f,* air *m,* chant *m.*

melon, *s.* Melon *m.*

melt. I. *v.i.* Fondre ; se fondre.
  II. **melt,** *v.tr.* **1.** (Faire) fondre. **2.** Attendrir, émouvoir.

melting, *a.* (*a*) Fondant. (*b*) Attendri.

member, *s.* Membre *m.* **M. of the audience,** assistant, -ante.

membrane, *s.* Membrane *f.*

memento, *s.* Mémento *m.*

memoir, *s.* (*a*) Mémoire *m.* étude *f.*

(*b*) Notice *f* biographique. (*c*) *pl.* Mémoires.

memorable, *a.* Mémorable.

memorandum, *s.* Mémorandum *m.*

memorial. I. *a.* Commémoratif. **2.** *s.* (*a*) Monument *m.* (*b*) Pétition *f.*

memory, *s.* **1.** Mémoire *f.* **2.** Souvenir *m.*

menace[1], *s.* Menace *f.*

menace[2], *v.tr.* Menacer.

menacing, *a.* Menaçant.

menagerie, *s.* Ménagerie *f.*

mend[1], *s.* **1.** Reprise *f,* raccommodage *m.* **2.** Amélioration *f.*

mend[2]. **I.** *v.tr.* **1.** Raccommoder. **2.** Rectifier, corriger. **3.** (*a*) To m. matters, arranger les choses. (*b*) To m. one's pace, hâter le pas.
  II. **mend,** *v.i.* **1.** Se remettre. **2.** S'amender, se corriger. **3.** S'améliorer.

mendicant, *s.* Mendiant, -ante.

menial. 1. *a.* Servile ; bas, *f.* basse. **2.** *s.* Domestique *mf.*

mental, *a.* Mental, -aux ; de l'esprit. **M. home,** asile *m* d'aliénés.

mentality, *s.* Mentalité *f.*

mentally, *adv.* Mentalement.

mention[1], *s.* Mention *f.*

mention[2], *v.tr.* Mentionner, citer. Not to m., sans parler de. **Don't m. it!** il n'y a pas de quoi !

menu, *s.* Menu *m.*

mercantile, *a.* Mercantile.

mercenary, *a. & s.* Mercenaire (*m*).

merchandise, *s.* Marchandise *f.*

merchant. 1. *s.* Négociant *m* ; commerçant *m.* **2.** *a.* Marchand.

merchantman, *s.* Navire marchand.

merciful, *a.* Miséricordieux (*to* pour) ; clément (*to,* envers).

merciless, *a.* Impitoyable ; sans pitié.

mercilessly, *adv* Impitoyablement ; sans merci.

mercury, *s.* Mercure *m.*

mercy, *s.* Miséricorde *f,* grâce *f,* merci *f.* **At the m. of,** au gré de.

mere[1], *s.* Lac *m,* étang *m.*

mere[2], *a.* Simple, pur, seul. **He's a m. boy,** ce n'est qu'un enfant.

merely, *adv.* Simplement, seulement.

merge. 1. *v.tr.* Fondre, fusionner. **2.** *v.i.* Se confondre.

meringue, *s.* Meringue *f.*

miscalculate, *v.tr.* Mal calculer.

miscalculation, *s.* Faux calcul; mécompte *m.*

miscellaneous, *a.* Varié, divers.

miscellany, *s.* Mélange *m.*

mischance, *s.* **1.** Mauvaise chance. **2.** Malheur *m,* mésaventure *f.*

mischief, *s.* **1.** Mal *m,* tort *m,* dommage *m.* **To make m.,** apporter le trouble. **2.** Malice *f.* **To get into m.,** faire des sottises.

mischief-maker, *s* Brandon *m* de discorde.

mischievous, *a.* **1.** Méchant, malfaisant. **2.** Espiègle; malicieux.

mischievously, *adv.* **1.** Méchamment. **2.** Malicieusement; par espièglerie.

misconduct[1], *s.* Mauvaise conduite.

misconduct[2], *v.tr.* **To m. oneself,** se mal conduire.

misconstrue, *v.tr.* Mal interpréter.

miscreant, *s.* Scélérat *m.*

misdeed, *s.* Méfait *m.*

misdemeanour, *s.* Délit.

misdirect, *v.tr.* **1.** Mal adresser. **2.** Mal diriger. **3.** Mal renseigner.

misdoing, *s.* Méfait *m,* faute *f.*

miser, *s.* Avare *mf.*

miserable, *a.* **1.** Malheureux, triste. **2.** Misérable.

miserably, *adv.* Misérablement.

miserliness, *s.* Avarice *f.*

miserly, *a.* **1.** Avare. **2.** D'avare; sordide.

misery, *s.* **1.** Souffrance *f,* supplice *m.* **2.** Misère *f,* détresse *f.*

misfire, *v.i.* Rater.

misfortune, *s.* Infortune *f,* malheur *m,* calamité *f.*

misgiving, *s.* Doute *m,* crainte *f.*

misguided, *a.* Peu judicieux; malencontreux.

mishap, *s.* Contretemps *m.*

misinform, *v.tr.* Mal renseigner.

misinterpret, *v.tr.* Mal interpréter.

misjudge, *v.tr.* Mal juger; méconnaître.

misjudged, *a.* Erroné; peu judicieux.

mislay, *v.tr.* Égarer.

mislead, *v.tr.* (*a*) Induire en erreur; tromper. (*b*) Égarer, fourvoyer.

misleading, *a.* Trompeur, -euse; fallacieux.

mismanage, *v.tr.* Mal administrer

mismanagement, *s.* Mauvaise administration.

misplace, *v.tr.* **1.** Placer a faux. **2.** Mal placer.

misplaced, *a.* **1.** Mal placé. **2.** Hors de propos.

misprint, *s.* Faute *f* d'impression.

mispronounce, *v.tr.* Mal prononcer.

misquote, *v.tr.* Citer à faux.

misread, *v.tr.* Mal lire, mal interpréter.

misrepresent, *v.tr.* Mal représenter; dénaturer, travestir.

misrepresentation, *s.* Faux rapport.

miss[1], *s.* Coup manqué.

miss[2], *v.tr.* **1.** (*a*) Manquer. **To m. the point,** répondre à côté. (*b*) **To m. one's way,** se tromper de route. **He missed his footing,** le pied lui manqua. (*c*) Ne pas trouver. (*d*) Manquer, laisser échapper. **2. To m. (out),** passer, sauter. **3.** (*a*) Remarquer l'absence de. (*b*) Regretter.

miss[3], *s.* Mademoiselle *f.*

mis-shapen, *a.* Difforme.

missile, *s.* Projectile *m.*

missing, *a.* Absent; perdu; manquant.

mission, *s.* Mission *f.*

missionary, *s.* Missionnaire *m.*

missive, *s.* Lettre *f,* missive *f.*

mis-statement, *s.* Exposé inexact; erreur *f* de fait.

mist, *s.* **1.** Brume *f.* **2.** Buée *f;* voile *m.*

mistake[1], *s.* **1.** Erreur *f,* méprise *f,* faute *f.* **To make a m.,** se tromper.

mistake[2], *v.tr.* **1.** Comprendre mal; se méprendre sur. **2.** Confondre (*for,* avec).

mistaken, *a.* **1. To be m.** faire erreur. **2.** Erroné.

mister, *s.* Monsieur *m.*

mistletoe, *s.* Gui *m.*

mistress, *s.* (*a*) Maîtresse *f* (*b*) Patronne *f.*

misty, *a.* Brumeux, embrumé.

misunderstand, *v.tr.* **1.** Mal comprendre. **2.** Se méprendre sur le compte de.

misunderstanding, *s.* **1.** Malentendu *m.* **2.** Mésintelligence *f.*

misunderstood, *a.* **1.** Mal compris. **2.** Incompris.

misuse[1], *s.* Abus *m.*

misuse[2], *v.tr.* Maltraiter.

mitigate, *v.tr.* Adoucir; atténuer.

mitigation, *s.* Atténuation *f*
mitre, *s.* Mitre *f*.
mix. **1.** *v.tr.* (*a*) Mêler, mélanger. (*b*) Confondre. **2.** *v.i.* Se mêler, se mélanger. To mix with people, fréquenter les gens. **mix up**, *v.tr.* Mêler, mélanger ; embrouiller.
mixed, *a.* **1.** Mêlé, mélangé, mixte. M. ice, glace panachée. M. feelings, sentiments mixtes **2.** To get m., s'embrouiller.
mixture, *s.* Mélange *m.*
moan[1], *s.* Gémissement *m*, plainte *f*.
moan[2], *v.i.* Gémir ; se lamenter.
moaning, *s.* Gémissement *m.*
moat, *s.* Fossé *m*, douve *f*.
mob, *s.* Foule *f* ; ameutement *m.*
mobile, *a.* Mobile.
mobility, *s* Mobilité *f*.
mobilization, *s.* Mobilisation *f*.
mobilize. **1.** *v.tr.* Mobiliser. **2.** *v.i.* Entrer en mobilisation.
moccasin, *s.* Mocassin *m.*
mock[1], *attrib.a.* Feint, contrefait ; faux, *f.* fausse. **M.** turtle soup, potage *m* à la tête de veau.
mock[2], *s.* To make a m. of, se moquer de.
mock[3], *v.tr.* **1.** Se moquer de ; railler. **2.** (*a*) Narguer. (*b*) Imiter singer.
mockery, *s.* Moquerie *f*, raillerie *f.*
mocking, *a* Moqueur, -euse. railleur, -euse.
mode, *s.* Mode *m*, méthode *f.*
model[1], *s.* **1.** Modèle *m.* **2.** *Art :* Modèle *mf.* **3.** *Dressm :* Modèle *m*, patron *m.*
model[2], *v.tr* Modeler.
moderate[1], *a* Modéré ; médiocre ; modique.
moderate[2]. (*a*) *v.tr.* Modérer ; tempérer. (*b*) *v.i.* Se modérer.
moderately, *adv* Modérément ; avec modération.
moderation, *s* Modération *f*, mesure *f.* In m., modérément.
modern, *a.* Moderne. **M** languages, langues vivantes
modest, *a.* Modeste.
modestly, *adv.* Modestement.
modesty, *s.* Modestie *f*.
modification, *s* Modification *f.*
modify, *v.tr.* (*a*) Modifier. (*b*) Mitiger, atténuer.
modulation, *s.* Modulation *f.*

Mohammedan. *a. & s.* Mahométan,-ane.
moiety, *s.* Moitié *f.*
moist, *a.* Humide ; moite.
moisten, *v.tr.* Humecter, mouiller
moisture, *s.* Humidité *f.*
molasses, *s.pl.* Mélasse *f.*
mole[1], *s.* Grain *m* de beauté
mole[2], *s.* Taupe *f.*
mole[3], *s.* Môle *m* ; brise-lames *m inv.*
molecule, *s* Molécule *f.*
mole-hill, *s.* Taupinière *f.*
moleskin, *s.* (Peau *f* de) taupe *f.*
molest, *v.tr.* Rudoyer.
molestation, *s.* Molestation *f.*
mollify, *v.tr.* Adoucir, apaiser.
mollusc, *s.* Mollusque *m.*
moment, *s.* **1.** Moment *m*, instant *m.* At this m., en ce moment ; actuellement **2.** To be of m., être important.
momentarily, *adv.* **1.** Momentanément. **2.** D'un moment à l'autre.
momentary. *a.* Momentané, passager.
momentous, *a.* Important.
monarch, *s.* Monarque *m.*
monarchy, *s* Monarchie *f.*
monastery, *s.* Monastère *m.*
monastic, *a.* Monastique.
Monday, *s.* Lundi *m.*
monetary, *a.* Monétaire.
money, *s.* Monnaie *f* ; argent *m.* There is m. in it, c'est une bonne affaire.
money-box, *s* **1.** Tirelire *f.* **2.** Caisse *f.*
money-changer, *s* Changeur *m.* cambiste *m.*
moneyed, *a.* Riche.
money-lender, *s.* Prêteur *m* d'argent.
mongrel, *s & a.* Métis. -isse **M.** cur, roquet *m.*
monitor, *s.* Moniteur, -trice.
monk, *s.* Moine *m*, religieux *m.*
monkey, *s.* Singe *m.* Female m. guenon *f.*
monkey-wrench, *s.* Clé anglaise
monocle, *s.* Monocle *m.*
monogamy, *s.* Monogamie *f*
monogram, *s.* Monogramme *m.*
monograph, *s.* Monographie *f.*
monologue, *s.* Monologue *m.*
monomania, *s.* Monomanie *f.*
monopolize, *v.tr.* **1.** Monopoliser. **2.** Accaparer ; s'emparer de.

monopoly, *s.* Monopole *m.*

monosyllable, *s.* Monosyllabe *m.*

monotonous, *a.* Monotone.

monotonously, *adv.* Monotonement.

monotony, *s.* Monotonie *f.*

monster. 1. *s.* Monstre *m.* 2. *a.* Monstre ; énorme.

monstrosity, *s.* Monstruosité *f.*

monstrous, *a.* Monstrueux.

month, *s.* Mois *m.* By the m., au mois.

monthly[1]. 1. *a.* Mensuel 2. *s.* Publication mensuelle.

monthly[2], *adv.* Mensuellement ; tous les mois.

monument, *s.* Monument *m.*

monumental, *a.* Monumental, -aux.

moo, *v.i.* Meugler, beugler.

mood, *s.* Humeur *f*, disposition *f.*

moody, *a.* Maussade.

moon, *s.* Lune *f.*

moonbeam, *s* Rayon *m* de lune.

moonlight, *s.* Clair *m* de lune.

moor[1], *s.* Lande *f*, bruyère *f.*

moor[2]. 1. *v.tr.* Amarrer ; mouiller. 2. *v.i.* S'amarrer.

Moor[3], *s.* Maure *m*, Mauresque *f.*

mooring, *s.* Amarrage *m.*

Moorish, *a.* Mauresque, maure.

moose, *s.* Élan *m*, orignac *m.*

moot, *a.* **M. point,** point *m* de droit.

mop[1], *s.* Balai *m* à franges.

mop[2], *v.tr.* Éponger, essuyer. **mop up,** *v.tr.* Éponger ; essuyer.

mope, *v.i.* Être triste.

moraine, *s.* Moraine *f.*

moral. I. *a.* Moral. -aux.
II. **moral,** *s.* 1. Morale *f.* moralité *f.* 2. *pl.* Mœurs *fpl.*

morale, *s.* Moral *m.*

moralist, *s.* Moraliste *mf.*

morality, *s.* (*a*) Moralité *f.* (*b*) Bonnes mœurs.

moralize, *v.i.* Moraliser.

morally, *adv.* Moralement.

morass, *s.* Marais *m* ; fondrière *f.*

morbid, *a.* Morbide.

morbidity, *s.* Morbidité *f.*

morbidly, *adv.* Morbidement, maladivement.

mordant, *a.* Mordant, caustique.

more. 1. *a.* Plus (de). **M. than ten men,** plus de dix hommes. **One m.,** encore un. **Is there any m.?** y en a-t-il encore ? 2. *s. or indef. pron.* Davantage. **That's m. than enough,**

c'est plus qu'il n'en faut. **What is m.,** qui plus est. 3. *adv.* (*a*) Plus, davantage. **M. and m.,** de plus en plus. (*b*) Once m., encore une fois. 4. *adv.* **All the m.,** d'autant plus. 5. **No m.** (*a*) **I have no m. money,** je n'ai plus d'argent. **No m. soup,** thank you, plus de potage, merci. (*b*) *s.* **I have no m.,** je n'en ai plus. (*c*) *adv.* Ne . . plus.

moreover, *adv.* D'ailleurs ; du reste ; et qui plus est.

moribund, *a.* Moribond.

Mormon, *a. & s* Mormon, -one.

morning, *s.* (*a*) Matin *m.* **The m.** before, la veille au matin. **Four o'clock in the m.,** quatre heures du matin. **Early in the m.,** matinalement. **Good m.,** bonjour. (*b*) Matinée *f.*

morning-coat, *s.* Jaquette *f.*

Morocco. 1. *Pr.n.* Le Maroc. 2. *s.* M. (leather), maroquin *m.*

morose, *a.* Chagrin, morose.

morosely, *adv.* D'un air chagrin, morose.

moroseness, *s.* Morosité *f.*

morphia, *s.* Morphine *f.*

Morse. *Pr.n.* **The M.** alphabet, l'alphabet *m* Morse.

morsel, *s.* Petit morceau.

mortal, *a.* Mortel.

mortality, *s.* Mortalité *f.*

mortally, *adv.* Mortellement. **M.** wounded, blessé à mort.

mortar, *s.* Mortier *m.*

mortgage[1], *s.* Hypothèque *f.*

mortgage[2], *v.tr.* Hypothéquer.

mortification, *s.* Mortification *f.*

mortify, *v.tr.* Mortifier.

mortuary, *s.* Morgue *f.*

mosaic. 1. *a.* En mosaïque. 2. *s.* Mosaïque *f.*

Moscow. *Pr.n.* Moscou *m.*

Moslem, *a. & s.* Mahométan, -ane.

mosque, *s.* Mosquée *f.*

mosquito, *s.* Moustique *m.*

moss, *s.* Mousse *f.* M. rose, rose moussue.

mossy, *a.* Moussu.

most. 1. *a.* (*a*) Le plus (de). (*b*) **M.** men, la plupart des hommes. 2. *s. & indef. pron.* At (the) m., au plus. 3. *adv.* (*a*) Le plus. (*b*) Le plus, la plus, les plus. 4. *adv.* Très, fort, bien. **M. likely,** très probablement.

mostly, *adv.* **1.** Pour la plupart. **2.** Le plus souvent.

moth, *s.* Papillon *m* de nuit; phalène *f.*

moth-balls, *s.pl.* Boules *f* de naphtaline.

moth-eaten, *a.* Rongé des mites, mité.

mother, *s.* Mère *f.*

mother country, *s.* Mère-patrie *f,* *pl.* mères-patries; métropole *f* (d'une colonie).

motherhood, *s.* Maternité *f.*

mother-in-law, *s.* Belle-mère *f,* *pl.* belles-mères.

motherless, *a.* Sans mère.

motherly, *a.* Maternel.

mother of pearl, *s.* Nacre *f.*

mother tongue, *s.* Langue maternelle.

motion, *s.* **1.** Mouvement *m,* déplacement *m.* **2.** Signe *m,* geste *m.* **3.** Motion *f,* proposition *f.*

motionless, *a.* Immobile.

motive. 1. *a.* Moteur, -trice. **2.** *s.* (*a*) Motif *m.* (*b*) Mobile *m.*

motley, *a.* (*a*) Bariolé, bigarré. (*b*) Divers, mêlé.

motor[1]. 1. *a.* Moteur, -trice. **2.** *s.* Moteur *m.*

motor[2]. 1. *v.i.* Aller, voyager, en auto(mobile). **2.** *v.tr.* Conduire en auto(mobile).

motor boat, *s.* Canot *m* automobile.

motor bus, *s.* Autobus *m.*

motor car, *s.* Auto(mobile) *f,* voiture *f.*

motor coach, *s.* Autocar *m.*

motor cycle, *s.* Motocyclette *f.*

motor cyclist, *s.* Motocycliste *mf.*

motoring, *s.* To go in for m., faire de l'automobile.

motorist, *s.* Automobiliste *mf.*

motor lorry, *s.* Camion *m* automobile.

motor show, *s.* Salon *m* de l'automobile.

mottle, *v.tr.* Tacheter, marbrer.

motto, *s.* Devise *f.*

mould[1], *s.* Terre végétale.

mould[2], *s.* Moule *m.*

mould[3], *v.tr.* Mouler; pétrir.

mould[4], *s.* Moisi *m,* moisissure *f.*

moulder, *v.i.* Tomber en poussière; s'effriter.

mouldy, *a.* Moisi.

moult, *v.i.* Muer.

mound, *s.* Tertre *m,* butte *f.*

mount[1], *s.* Mont *m,* montagne *f.*

mount[2], *s.* (*a*) Montage *m,* support *m;* monture *f.* (*b*) **Stamp m.,** charnière *f.*

mount[3]. I. *v.i.* Se mettre en selle; monter à cheval.
　II. **mount,** *v.tr. & i.* Monter sur.
　III. **mount,** *v.tr.* Monter.

mount up, *v.i.* Croître, monter.

mountain, *s.* Montagne *f.* **M. scenery,** paysage montagneux.

mountain ash, *s.* Sorbier *m* des oiseaux.

mountaineer, *s.* **1.** Montagnard *m.* **2.** Alpiniste *mf,* ascensionniste *mf.*

mountaineering, *s.* Alpinisme *m.*

mountainous, *a.* Montagneux.

mountain range, *s.* Chaîne *f* de montagnes.

mountebank, *s.* (*a*) Saltimbanque *m.* (*b*) Charlatan *m.*

mourn, *v.i. & tr.* Pleurer, (se) lamenter. **To m. for,** pleurer.

mourner, *s.* **1.** Affligé, -ée. **2. The mourners,** le cortège funèbre.

mournful, *a.* Lugubre mélancolique.

mournfully, *adv.* Lugubrement.

mourning, *s.* **1.** Affliction *f,* deuil *m.* **2.** Habits *mpl* de deuil. **To go into m.,** prendre le deuil.

mouse, *s.* Souris.

mouse-hole, *s.* Trou *m* de souris.

mousetrap, *s.* Souricière *f.*

moustache, *s.* Moustache.

mouth, *s.* **1.** Bouche *f.* **2.** Gueule *f.* **3.** (*a*) Ouverture *f,* entrée *f.* (*b*) Embouchure *f.*

mouthful, *s.* Bouchée *f.*

mouthpiece, *s.* **1.** Embouchure *f.* **2.** Porte-parole *m.*

movable, *a.* Mobile.

move[1], *s.* **1.** Coup; démarche *f.* **2.** Mouvement *m.*

move[2]. I. *v.tr.* **1.** (*a*) Déplacer; changer de place. **To m. a piece,** jouer une pièce. (*b*) Déménager. **2.** (*a*) Remuer, bouger. (*b*) Mouvoir; mettre en mouvement. **3.** Émouvoir, toucher. **4. To m. a resolution,** proposer une motion.
　II. **move,** *v.i.* (*a*) Se mouvoir, se déplacer. **Keep moving!** circulez! (*b*) Faire un mouvement; bouger,

(se) remuer. (c) Marcher, aller.
move back. 1. *v.tr.* (a) Faire
reculer. (b) Ramener en arrière.
2. *v.i.* (Se) reculer. **move forward.**
1. *v.tr.* Avancer; faire avancer
2. *v.i.* (S')avancer.
movement, *s.* Mouvement *m.*
moving, *a.* **1.** (a) En mouvement.
(b) Mobile. **2.** Moteur, -trice.
3. Émouvant.
mow, *v.tr.* **1.** Faucher. **2.** Tondre.
Mr, *s.* Monsieur *m.*
Mrs, *s.* Madame *f.*
much. 1. *a.* (a) Beaucoup (de); bien
(du, de la, des). (b) How m.? combien (de)? **2.** *adv.* Beaucoup, bien.
M. to my astonishment, à mon
grand étonnement. **3.** *s.* (a) This
m., autant que ceci. (b) To make
m. of, faire fête à. **4.** (a) As m.,
autant (de). (b) As m. as, autant que.
(c) So m., tant (de), autant (de).
So m. the better, tant mieux. So
m. so, à tel point. (d) Too m.,
trop (de).
muck, *s.* Fange *f*; ordures *fpl.*
mud, *s.* Boue *f*, bourbe *f.*
muddied, *a.* Couvert de boue.
muddle[1], *s.* Confusion *f*, emmêlement *m*, fouillis *m.*
muddle[2], *v.tr.* Embrouiller.
muddler, *s.* Brouillon, -onne.
muddy, *a.* (a) Boueux, bourbeux.
(b) Couvert de boue.
mudguard, *s.* Garde-boue *m inv.*
muffle, *v.tr.* **1.** Emmitoufler (*in*, de).
2. Assourdir.
mug, *s.* Chope *f*; (grosse) tasse.
Tin mug, timbale *f.*
muggy, *a.* Chaud et humide.
mulatto, *s.* Mulâtre, -esse.
mulberry, *s.* Mûre *f.*
mulberry-tree, *s.* Mûrier *m.*
mule, *s.* **1.** Mulet *m*; mule *f.*
2. Métis, -isse; hybride *m.*
muleteer, *s.* Muletier *m.*
multiple, *a. & s.* Multiple (*m*).
M. store, maison *f* à succursales.
multiplication, *s.* Multiplication *f.*
multiply. 1. *v.tr.* Multiplier. **2.** *v.i.*
Se multiplier.
multitude, *s.* Mult.tude *f*; foule *f.*
mumble, *v.tr.* Marmotter.
mummy, *s.* Momie *f.*
mumps, *s.pl.* Oreillons *mpl.*
munch, *v.tr.* Mâcher, mâchonner.

mundane, *a.* Mondain.
municipal, *a.* Municipal, -aux. **M.**
buildings, hôtel *m* de ville.
municipality, *s.* Municipalité *f*
munificence, *s.* Munificence *f.*
munificent, *a.* Munificent.
munitions, *s.pl.* Munitions *f.*
mural, *a.* Mural, -aux.
murder[1], *s.* Meurtre *m.*
murder[2], *v.tr.* Assassiner.
murderer, *s.* Meurtrier *m*, assassin *m.*
murderess, *s* Meurtrière *f*, assas-
sine *f.*
murderous, *a.* Meurtrier assassin
murky, *a.* Ténébreux.
murmur[1], *s.* Murmure *m.*
murmur[2], *v.i. & tr.* Murmurer
muscle, *s.* Muscle *m.*
muscular, *a.* **1.** Musculaire. **2.**
Musculeux, musclé.
muse[1], *s.* Muse *f.*
muse[2], *v.i.* Méditer, rêver.
museum, *s.* Musée *m.*
mushroom, *s.* Champignon *m.*
music, *s.* Musique *f*
musical, *a.* **1.** Musical. -aux. **M.**
instrument, instrument *m* de musique. **2.** Harmonieux, mélodieux
music-hall, *s.* Music-hall *m.*
musician, *s.* Musicien, -ienne.
music-stand, *s.* Pupitre *m* à musique.
musing[1], *a.* Rêveur, -euse.
musing[2], *s.* Rêverie *f*; méditation *f.*
musk, *s.* Musc *m.*
musket, *s.* Mousquet *m.*
musky, *a.* Musqué.
muslin, *s.* Mousseline *f.*
mussel, *s.* Moule *f.*
must, *modal aux. v.* (a) Do so if you
m., faites-le s'il le faut. (b) It
must be the doctor, ce doit être le
médecin.
mustard, *s.* Moutarde *f.*
mustard-plaster, *s.* Sinapisme *m.*
mustard-pot, *s.* Moutardier *m.*
muster. 1. *v.tr.* Rassembler. **2.** *v.i.*
Se réunir, se rassembler.
mustiness, *s.* Relent *m.*
musty, *a.* Moisi.
mutable, *a.* Muable, variable
mute. I. *a.* Muet, -ette.
II. **mute,** *s.* **1.** Muet. -ette.
2. Sourdine *f.*
mutilate, *v.tr.* Mutiler, estropier.
mutilation, *s.* Mutilation *f.*
mutineer, *s.* Révolté *m*, mutiné *m.*

mutinous, *a.* Rebelle, mutin.

mutiny[1], *s.* Revolte *f*, mutinerie *f*.

mutiny[2], *v.i.* Se révolter, se mutiner.

mutter, *v.tr. & i.* Marmotter ; murmurer.

muttering, *s.* Marmottage *m* ; murmures *mpl* ; grondement *m*.

mutton, *s.* Mouton *m*. **Leg of m.** gigot *m*.

mutton-chop, *s.* Côtelette *f* de mouton.

mutual, *a.* **1.** Mutuel, réciproque. **2. M. friend,** ami commun.

mutually, *adv.* Mutuellement, réciproquement.

muzzle[1], *s.* **1.** Museau *m*. **2.** Bouche *f*, gueule *f*. **3.** Muselière *f*.

muzzle[2], *v.tr.* Museler.

my, *poss.a.* Mon ; *f.* ma, *pl* mes.

myopia, *s.* Myopie *f*.

myriad, *s.* Myriade *f*

myrrh, *s.* Myrrhe *f*.

myrtle, *s.* Myrte *m*.

myself, *pers.pron.* Moi-même ; me.

mysterious, *a* Mystérieux.

mysteriously, *adv.* Mystérieusement.

mystery, *s.* Mystère *m*

mystic, *a.* (*a*) Ésotérique, mystique. (*b*) Occulte.

mystical, *a.* Mystique.

mysticism, *s.* Mysticisme *m*.

mystification, *s.* Mystification *f*.

mystify, *v.tr.* Mystifier.

myth, *s.* Mythe *m*.

mythical, *a.* Mythique.

mythological, *a.* Mythologique.

mythology, *s* Mythologie *f*.

N

N, n, *s.* (La lettre) N, n *m*.

nag[1], *s.* Bidet *m*.

nag[2], *v.tr & i.* Gronder.

nagging, *a.* Grondeur, -euse.

nail[1], *s.* **1.** Ongle *m*. **2.** Clou *m*, *pl*. clous.

nail[2], *v.tr.* Clouer.

nail-brush, *s.* Brosse *f* à ongles

nailed, *a.* (*a*) Cloué. (*b*) Clouté.

nail-file, *s.* Lime *f* à ongles.

naïve, *a.* Naïf, *f.* naïve ; ingénu.

naïvely, *adv.* Naïvement, ingénument.

naïvety, *s.* Naïveté *f*.

naked, *a.* Nu.

nakedness, *s.* Nudité *f*.

name[1], *s.* **1.** Nom *m*. (*a*) **Full n.,** nom et prénoms. **Christian n.,** nom de baptême. **My n. is,** je m'appelle. (*b*) Terme *m*. **2.** Réputation *f* renommée *f*.

name[2], *v.tr.* **1.** Nommer ; dénommer. **2.** Désigner par son nom **3.** Citer.

nameless, *a.* **1.** Sans nom ; inconnu. **2.** Anonyme. **3.** Indicible.

namely, *adv.* À savoir ; c'est-à-dire.

namesake, *s.* Homonyme *m*.

nap[1], *s.* Petit somme.

nap[2], *s.* Napoléon *m* ; nap *m*.

nape, *s.* **The n. of the neck,** la nuque.

naphtha, *s.* (Huile *f* de) naphte *m*.

napkin, *s.* Serviette *f*.

Napoleon. *Pr.n.* Napoléon *m*.

narcissus, *s.* Narcisse *m*.

narcotic, *a. & s.* Narcotique (*m*).

narrate, *v.tr* Narrer, raconter.

narration, *s.* Narration *f*.

narrative, *s.* Récit *m*, narration *f*

narrator, *s.* Narrateur, -trice.

narrow[1], *a.* (*a*) Étroit. (*b*) Minutieux.

narrow[2]. **1.** *v.tr.* Restreindre, borner. **2.** *v.i.* Devenir plus étroit.

narrowly, *adv.* **1.** (*a*) Étroitement. (*b*) De près. **2.** Tout juste.

narrow-minded. *a* Borné : à l'esprit étroit.

narrowness, *s.* (*a*) Étroitesse *f*. (*b*) Petitesse *f* ; limitation *f*.

nasal, *a.* Nasal, -aux. **N. accent,** accent nasillard.

nasturtium, *s.* Capucine *f*.

nasty, *a.* **1.** Désagréable ; dégoûtant. **2.** Méchant, désagréable

nation, *s.* Nation *f*.

national, *a.* National, -aux.

nationality, *s.* Nationalité *f*.

native. **I.** *s.* (*a*) Natif, -ive. (*b*) Indigène *mf*. **II. native,** *a.* **1.** Naturel, inné. **2.** Natal, -aux. **N. language,** langue maternelle.

natural, *a.* Naturel. **1. N. law,** loi de la nature. **2.** (*a*) Natif, inné. (*b*) **As is n.,** comme de raison.

naturalist, *s.* Naturaliste *mf*

naturalization, s. Naturalisation f.

naturalize, v.tr. Naturaliser.

naturally, adv. Naturellement.

nature, s. Nature f. **1.** (a) Essence f, caractère m. (b) Naturel m, caractère. By n., naturellement. **2.** Espèce f. **3.** (La) nature.

naught, s. **1.** Rien m, néant m To come to n., échouer. **2.** Zéro m.

naughty, a. Vilain, méchant.

nausea, s. Nausée f.

nauseate, v.tr. Écœurer, dégoûter.

nauseating, a. Écœurant.

nauseous, a. Dégoûtant.

nautical, a. Nautique, marin.

naval, a. Naval, -als N. officer, officier de marine.

nave, s. Nef f, vaisseau m

navigable, a. Navigable.

navigate. 1. v.i. Naviguer. **2.** v.tr Gouverner, diriger.

navigation, s. Navigation f.

navigator, s Navigateur m

navvy, s. Terrassier m.

navy, s. Marine f de guerre.

navy blue, s. Bleu m marine inv.

naze, s. Promontoire m, pointe f.

near¹. I. adv. Près, proche. To draw n., s'approcher (to, de). N at hand, tout près.

II. near, prep. Près de, auprès de.

III. near, a. **1.** Proche; intime, cher. **2.** The nearest road, le plus court. **3.** Chiche, parcimonieux.

near², v.tr. (S')approcher de.

near by, adv. & prep Tout près (de), tout proche (de).

nearly, adv. **1.** (De) près. **2.** Presque, à peu près, près de. Very n., peu s'en faut. I n. fell, je faillis tomber.

nearness, s. Proximité f.

near-sighted, a. Myope.

neat, a. **1.** Pur; sans eau. **2.** Simple et de bon goût : bien rangé, en ordre.

neatly, adv. Avec ordre.

neatness, s. **1.** Simplicité f, bon goût. **2.** Ordre m.

nebulous, a. Nébuleux.

necessarily, adv. Nécessairement. de (toute) nécessité.

necessary. 1. a. (a) Nécessaire, indispensable. It is n. to, il faut. If n., s'il le faut ; au besoin. (b) Inévitable. **2.** s. pl. Nécessités f.

necessitate, v.tr. Nécessiter.

necessity, s. Nécessité f. (a) Obligation f, contrainte f. (b) Besoin m.

neck, s. **1.** (a) Cou m. To win by a n., gagner par une encolure. (b) Encolure f. Low n., décolleté m. **2.** (a) Goulot m. (b) Langue f.

necklace, s. Collier m.

necklet, s. Collier m Fur n., tour m de cou.

neck-tie, s. Cravate f.

nectar, s. Nectar m.

nectarine, s. Brugnon m.

need¹, s. **1.** Besoin m. To be in n. of, avoir besoin de. **2.** Adversité f ; embarras m.

need². 1. v.tr. (a) Avoir besoin de ; réclamer, exiger. That needs no saying, cela va sans dire. (b) Être obligé de. **2.** Modal aux. N. he go? a-t-il besoin, est-il obligé, d'y aller ? You n. not wait, inutile d'attendre.

needful, a Nécessaire.

needle, s. Aiguille f.

needle-case, s. Étui m à aiguilles

needless, a. Inutile, superflu.

needlewoman, s. Couturière f.

needlework, s Travaux mpl à l'aiguille.

needy, a. Nécessiteux, besogneux.

nefarious, a. Infâme, scélérat.

negation, s. Négation f.

negative¹. I. a. Négatif.

II. **negative,** s. **1.** Négative f. **2.** Négatif m, cliché m.

negative², v.tr. Rejeter.

neglect¹, s. **1.** (a) Manque m d'égards. (b) Manque de soin(s). **2.** Négligence f.

neglect², v.tr **1.** (a) Manquer d'égards envers. (b) Manquer de soins pour. **2.** Négliger

neglected, a. Négligé.

neglectful, a. Négligent.

negligence, s. Négligence f.

negligent, a. **1.** Négligent. **2.** Nonchalant, insouciant

negligently, adv Négligemment ; avec négligence.

negligible, a. Négligeable

negotiable, a. Négociable.

negotiate. 1. v.tr Négocier **2.** v.i Traiter.

negotiation, s. Négociation f Under n., en négociation.

negotiator, s Négociateur -trice

negress, s. Négresse f.

negro, a. & s. Nègre (m).

neigh[1]**,** s. Hennissement m

neigh[2]**,** v.i. Hennir.

neighbour, s. Voisin, -ine.

neighbourhood, s. **1.** Voisinage m, proximité f. **2.** Alentours mpl.

neighbouring, a. Avoisinant, voisin ; proche.

neighing, s. Hennissement m.

neither. 1. adv. & conj. (a) N. . . . nor, ni . . . ni. (b) Non plus. **2.** a. & pron. Ni l'un(e) ni l'autre ; aucun(e).

neon, s. Néon m.

neophyte, s. Néophyte mf.

nephew, s. Neveu m.

nerve, s. **1.** (a) Nerf m. (b) Assurance f. (c) Audace f. **2.** Nervure f. **3. To strain every n.,** déployer tous ses efforts

nerveless, a. Inerte, sans force.

nervous, a. **1.** (a) Excitable. (b) Inquiet, -ète. (c) Timide. **2.** Nerveux.

nervously, adv. **1.** Timidement. **2.** Craintivement.

nervousness, s. (a) Nervosité f. (b) Timidité f.

ness, s. Promontoire m, cap m.

nest, s. Nid m.

nestle, v.i. Se serrer ; se blottir

nestling, s. Oisillon m.

net[1]**,** s. Filet m.

net[2]**,** v.tr. Prendre au filet.

net[3]**,** a. Net, f. nette.

nether, a. Inférieur, -e, bas, f. basse. **The n. regions,** l'enfer m.

nettle, s. Ortie f.

network, s. Réseau m.

neuralgia, s. Névralgie f.

neuritis, s. Névrite f.

neurotic, a. Névrosé, neurotique.

neuter, a. Neutre.

neutral, a. & s. Neutre (m)

neutrality, s. Neutralité f.

neutralize, v.tr. Neutraliser

never, adv. (a) (Ne . . .) jamais. (b) **Well I n.!** par exemple !

nevertheless, adv. Néanmoins, quand même, toutefois, pourtant.

new, a. **1.** Nouveau, -elle. **2.** Neuf, f. neuve ; non usagé. **3.** Frais. **New potatoes.** pommes de terre nouvelles.

new-comer, s. Nouveau venu. f. nouvelle venue.

Newfoundland. 1. Pr.n. Terre-Neuve f. **2.** s. Terre-neuve m inv.

new-laid, a. Frais pondu

newly, adv. Récemment, nouvellement.

newness, s. **1.** (a) Nouveauté f. (b) Inexpérience f. **2.** État neuf.

news, s. Nouvelles f. **1. A piece ot n.,** une nouvelle. **2. N. film, reel,** film m d'actualité.

news-agent, s. Marchand m de journaux.

news-boy, s. Vendeur m de journaux.

newspaper, s. Journal m, -aux.

newt, s. Triton m.

New Year, s. Nouvel an ; nouvelle année. **New-Year's Day,** le jour de l'an.

next. 1. a. **1.** Prochain ; le plus proche. **The n. room,** la chambre voisine. **Seated n. to me,** assis à côté de moi. **2.** (a) Prochain, suivant. **The n. day,** le lendemain. **The n. day but one,** le surlendemain **The n. instant,** l'instant d'après. (b) **Who comes n.?** à qui le tour ? II. **next,** adv. **1.** Ensuite, après. **2. When n.,** la prochaine fois que. III. **next,** prep. Auprès de. à côté de.

next door. 1. adv. **The people n. d.,** les gens d'à côté. **2.** Attrib. **N.-d. neighbours,** voisins d'à côté.

nib, s. (Bec m de) plume f.

nibble, v.tr. & i. Grignoter.

nice, a. **1.** Délicat ; subtil, fin. **2.** (a) Gentil, f. gentille ; sympathique. (b) Joli, bon (c) **N. people,** des gens bien.

nicely, adv. Joliment, gentiment, bien.

nicety, s. **1.** (a) **To a n.,** exactement. (b) Subtilité f. **2.** pl. Minuties f

niche, s. Niche f.

nick[1]**,** s. **1.** Entaille f, encoche f. **2. In the n. of time,** juste à temps.

nick[2]**,** v.tr. Entailler encocher.

nickel, s. Nickel m.

nickname[1]**,** s. Surnom m ; sobriquet m.

nickname[2]**,** v.tr. Surnommer.

nicotine, s. Nicotine f.

niece, s. Nièce f.

niggard, s. Grippe-sou m.

niggardly, a. Chiche, ladre.

nigger, s. Nègre, f. négresse.

niggle, v.i. Vétiller ; tatillonner.

night, s. **1.** (a) Nuit f, soir m. **The n. before,** la veille (au soir). **Good n.!** bonsoir ! bonne nuit ! **At n.,**

la nuit. **By n.**, de nuit. (b) **First n.**, première f. **2.** Obscurité f.

night-club, s. Boîte f de nuit.

night-dress, s. Chemise f de nuit.

nightfall, s. Tombée f du jour, de la nuit. **At n.**, à la nuit tombante.

nightingale, s. Rossignol m.

nightjar, s. Engoulevent m.

night-light, s. Veilleuse f.

nightly. 1. a. De nuit, nocturne. **2.** adv. Tous les soirs.

nightmare, s. Cauchemar m.

nightshade, s. **Deadly n.**, belladone f.

night-time, s. La nuit.

nihilist, s. Nihiliste mf

nil, s. Rien m, zéro m.

Nile (the). Pr.n. Le Nil.

nimble, a. Agile, leste ; prompt.

nimbly, adv. Agilement ; lestement.

nimbus, s. **1.** Nimbe m, auréole f. gloire f. **2.** Nimbus m.

nine, num. a. & s. Neuf (m).

ninepin, s. Quille f.

nineteen, num. a. & s. Dix-neuf (m).

nineteenth, num. a & s Dix-neuvième (m).

ninety, num. a. & s. Quatre-vingt-dix (m). **N.-one**, quatre-vingt-onze

ninth, num. a. & s. Neuvième (m).

nip[1], s. **1.** Pincement m. **To give s.o. a nip**, pincer qn. **2.** Morsure f

nip[2], v.tr. Pincer.

nipper, s. **1.** pl. Pinces fpl ; tenailles fpl. **2.** Gamin m.

nitrate, s. Nitrate m, azotate m

nitre, s. Nitre m, salpêtre m.

nitric, a. **N. acid**, acide m nitrique azotique ; eau-forte f

nitrogen, s. Azote m.

no. I. a. **1.** Nul, pas de, point de aucun. **Of no interest**, sans intérêt. **No nonsense!** pas de bêtises ! **No admittance**, entrée interdite. **No smoking**, défense de fumer. **2.** Peu ; ne . . . pas. **3. No one**, pron. Personne m, nul m, aucun m.

II. no, adv. **1. Whether or no**, dans tous les cas. **2. He is no longer here**, il n'est plus ici.

III. no. 1. a. v.tr. Non. **2.** s. Non m.

Noah. Pr.n. Noé m.

nobility, s. Noblesse f.

noble, a. & s. Noble (m).

nobleman, s. Noble m.

nobly, adv. **1.** Noblement. **2.** Magnifiquement, superbement.

nobody. 1. pron. Personne m, nul m, aucun m. **2.** s. Nullité f, zéro m

nocturnal, a. Nocturne.

nocturne, s. Nocturne m.

nod[1], s. Inclination f de la tête.

nod[2], v.tr. & i. **1.** Faire un signe de tête ; incliner la tête. **2.** Somnoler.

noise, s. Bruit m. **1.** Tapage m, vacarme m, fracas m. **2.** Son m.

noiseless, a. Sans bruit.

noiselessly, adv. Silencieusement ; sans bruit.

noisily, adv. Bruyamment.

noisome, a. Fétide, infect.

noisy, a. Bruyant, tapageur, -euse. **To be n.**, faire du bruit, du tapage.

nomad, a. & s. Nomade (mf).

nomadic, a. Nomade.

nomenclature, s. Nomenclature f.

nominal, a. Nominal, -aux.

nominally, adv. Nominalement ; de nom.

nominate, v.tr. (a) Nommer, choisir. (b) Proposer, présenter.

nomination, s. **1.** Nomination f. **2.** Présentation f.

nominee, s. Candidat désigné.

nonchalance, s. Nonchalance f.

nonchalant, a. Nonchalant ; indifférent.

non-combatant, a. & s. Non-combattant (m).

non-commissioned, a. Sans brevet. **Non-c. officer**, sous-officier m.

non-committal, a. Qui n'engage à rien.

non-conductor, s. Non-conducteur m ; calorifuge m ; isolant m.

nondescript, a. Indéfinissable, inclassable.

none. 1. pron. (a) Aucun. **N. at all**, pas un(e) seul(e). (b) Personne. **N. can tell**, nul ne le sait. **2.** adv. **He was n. too soon**, il arriva juste à temps.

nonentity, s. Non-valeur f ; nullité f.

non-freezing, a. Incongelable.

non-inflammable, a Ininflammable, ignifuge.

nonplus, v.tr. Embarrasser interdire, interloquer.

nonsense, s. **1.** Non-sens m **2.** Absurdité f, déraison f. **To talk n.**, dire des bêtises. **Nonsense!** pas possible !

nonsensical, a. Absurde

non-stop, *attrib.a. & adv.* Sans arrêt ; sans escale.

noodles, *s.pl.* Nouilles *f.*

nook, *s.* Coin *m,* recoin *m.*

noon, *s.* Midi *m.*

noose, *s.* Nœud coulant ; lacet *m.*

nor, *conj.* (Ne, ni ...) ni. **Neither you nor I,** ni vous ni moi. **Nor you either,** ni vous non plus.

normal. 1. *a.* Normal, -aux, régulier, ordinaire. **2.** *s.* Normale *f.*

normally, *adv.* Normalement.

Norman, *a. & s.* Normand, -ande.

Normandy. *Pr.n.* La Normandie.

north. 1. *s.* Nord *m.* **2.** *adv.* Au nord ; vers le nord. **3.** *a.* Nord *inv* ; septentrional, -aux.

north-east. 1. *s.* Nord-est *m.* **2.** *a.* (Du) nord-est *inv.* **3.** *adv* Vers le nord-est.

northerly, *a.* Du nord ; vers le nord ; au nord.

northern, *a.* (Du) nord ; septentrional, -aux. **N. lights,** aurore boréale.

North Sea (the), *s.* La mer du Nord.

northward. 1. *s.* **To the n.,** au nord. **2.** *a.* Au, du, nord.

northwards, *adv.* Vers le nord.

north-west. 1. *s.* Nord-ouest *m.* **2.** *a.* (Du) nord-ouest *inv.* **3.** *adv.* Vers le nord-ouest.

Norway. *Pr.n.* La Norvège.

Norwegian. 1. *a. & s.* Norvégien, -ienne. **2.** *s.* Le norvégien.

nose, *s.* Nez *m* ; museau *m.* **To blow one's n.,** se moucher.

nose-dive[1], *s.* Vol piqué.

nose-dive[2], *v.i.* Piquer du nez.

nosegay, *s.* Bouquet *m.*

nostalgia, *s.* Nostalgie *f.*

nostril, *s.* Narine *f* ; naseau *m.*

not, *adv.* (Ne) pas, (ne) point. **1.** (*a*) **Not at all,** pas du tout. (*b*) **I think not,** je crois que non. **Not negotiable,** non-négociable. **2. Not including,** sans compter.

notability, *s* Notabilité *f.*

notable. *a.* (*a*) Notable, insigne. (*b*) *s.* Notable *m.*

notably, *adv.* **1.** Notablement **2.** Notamment, particulièrement

notary, *s.* Notaire *m*

notch[1], *s.* Entaille *f,* encoche *f.*

notch[2], *v.tr.* Entailler, encocher.

note[1], *s* **1.** (*a*) Note *f* ; caractère *m*

de musique. (*b*) Touche *f.* (*c*) Note, son *m.* **2.** Marque *f,* signe *m.* **3.** (*a*) Note, mémorandum *m.* (*b*) Note, annotation *f.* (*c*) Billet *m.* **4.** Bank n., billet de banque. **5.** (*a*) **Man of n.,** homme marquant. (*b*) **Nothing of n.,** rien d'important. **To take n. of,** remarquer.

note[2], *v.tr.* **1.** Noter, constater, remarquer. **2. To n. down,** inscrire.

note-book, *s* Carnet *m,* calepin *m.*

note-case, *s.* Porte-billets *m inv.*

noted, *a.* Distingué, éminent ; célèbre.

note-paper, *s.* Papier *m* à écrire.

noteworthy, *a.* Remarquable ; digne d'attention.

nothing. I. *s.* or *pron.* Rien ... ne. (*a*) **To say n. of,** sans parler de. (*b*) **N. new,** rien de nouveau. **N. much,** pas grand'chose. (*c*) **That is n. to do with you,** cela ne vous regarde pas. (*d*) **N. else,** rien d'autre. (*e*) **To think n. of** ne faire aucun cas de.

  II. nothing, *s* **1.** Zéro *m.* **2.** Néant *m* ; rien *m.* **To come to n.,** ne pas aboutir.

  III. nothing, *adv.* Aucunement, nullement ; pas du tout.

notice[1], *s.* **1.** (*a*) Avis *m.* (*b*) Avertissement *m.* (*c*) Avis formel, instructions formelles. (*d*) **At short n.,** à court délai. (*e*) **N. to quit,** congé *m* **2.** (*a*) Affiche *f.* (*b*) Annonce *f.* (*c*) Revue *f.* **3. To take n. of,** tenir compte, prendre connaissance de.

notice[2], *v.tr.* Observer, remarquer, s'apercevoir de.

noticeable, *a.* Perceptible, sensible.

noticeably, *adv.* Perceptiblement, sensiblement.

notice-board, *s.* Tableau *m* d'annonces.

notification, *s.* Avis *m,* notification *f,* annonce *f.*

notify, *v.tr.* Annoncer, notifier.

notion, *s.* (*a*) Notion *f,* idée *f.* (*b*) Opinion *f,* pensée *f.* (*c*) Caprice *m.*

notoriety, *s.* Notoriété *f.*

notorious, *a.* **1.** Notoire **2.** Insigne ; mal famé.

notoriously, *adv.* Notoirement.

notwithstanding. 1. *prep.* Malgré ; en dépit de. **2.** *adv.* Quand même, tout de même ; néanmoins.

nought, s. 1. Rien m. 2. Zéro m.

noun, s. Substantif m, nom m.

nourish, v.tr. 1. Nourrir; alimenter. 2. Nourrir, entretenir.

nourishing, a. Nourrissant, nutritif.

nourishment, s. 1. Alimentation f. 2. Nourriture f.

novel[1], s. Roman m.

novel[2], a. Nouveau -elle; original -aux; singulier.

novelist, s. Romancier, -ière

novelty, s. Nouveauté f.

November, s. Novembre m.

novice, s. Novice mf; débutant, -ante.

now. I. adv. 1. Maintenant. (a) En ce moment, actuellement. (b) Tout de suite. (c) Now and then, de temps en temps. Now . . now . . ., tantôt . . . tantôt. . . . 2. (a) Or; déjà. (b) Donc. Well now! eh bien!
II. **now**, conj. Maintenant que, à présent que.
III **now**, s. In three days from now, d'ici trois jours. Until now, jusqu'ici. From now, dès maintenant.

nowadays, adv. Aujourd'hui; de nos jours.

nowhere, adv. Nulle part.

noxious, a. Nuisible, nocif.

nozzle, s. Ajutage m; jet m; bec m.

nucleus, s. Noyau m.

nude, a. & s. Nu (m).

nudge[1], s. Coup m de coude.

nudge[2], v.tr. Pousser du coude.

nudist, s. Nudiste mf.

nudity, s. Nudité f.

nugget, s. Pépite f (d'or).

nuisance, s. (a) Peste f; fléau m. (b) What a n.! quel ennui!

null, a. N. and void, nul et non avenu.

nullify, v.tr. Annuler, nullifier.

numb[1], a. Engourdi.

numb[2], v.tr. Engourdir.

number[1], s. 1. (a) Nombre m. (b) Books without n., des livres innombrables. (c) pl. In small numbers, en petit nombre. (d) One of their n., (l')un d'entre eux. 2. Chiffre m. 3. Numéro m.

number[2], v.tr. 1. Compter, dénombrer. 2. Numéroter.

numbering-machine, s. Numéroteur m.

numberless, a. Innombrable

numbness, s. Engourdissement m.

numeral. 1. a. Numéral, -aux. 2. s. Chiffre m, nombre m.

numerical, a. Numérique.

numerically, adv. Numériquement.

numerous, a. Nombreux.

nun, s. Religieuse f, nonne f.

nunnery, s. Couvent m.

nuptial. 1. a. Nuptial -aux 2. s.pl. Noces f.

nurse[1], s. 1. (a) Nourrice f. (b) Bonne f. 2. (Sick-)n., garde-malade f, pl. gardes-malades Hospital n., infirmière f

nurse[2], v.tr 1. Soigner. 2. Nourrir, entretenir. 3. Bercer.

nursemaid, s. Bonne f d'enfants.

nursery, s. 1. Chambre f des enfants; nursery f. N. rhyme, chanson f de nourrice. 2. Pépinière f

nurseryman, s. Pépiniériste m.

nursing, s. (a) Soins mpl. (b) Profession f de garde-malade.

nursing home, s Clinique f; hôpital privé.

nut, s. 1. (a) Noix f. 2. Écrou m.

nut-crackers, s. Casse-noisettes mim.

nutmeg, s. Muscade f.

nutriment, s. Nourriture f

nutrition, s. Nutrition f

nutritious, a. Nutritif, nourrissant

nutritive, a. Nutritif, nourrissant.

nutshell, s. Coquille f de noix. In a n., en un mot.

nymph, s. Nymphe f.

O

O[1], **o**, s. (La lettre) O. o m.

O[2], int. O, oh.

oaf, s. Lourdaud m.

oak, s. (a) **Oak(-tree)**, chêne m (b) (Bois m de) chêne.

oak-apple, s. Pomme f de chêne.

oar, s. Aviron m, rame f.

oarsman, s. Rameur m.

oasis, s. Oasis f.

oaten, a. D'avoine.

oath, s. 1. Serment m. On o., sous serment. 2. Juron m; gros mot.

oatmeal, *s.* Farine *f* d'avoine.

oats, *s.pl.* Avoine *f.*

obduracy, *s.* (*a*) Endurcissement *m*; opiniâtreté *f.* (*b*) Inflexibilité *f.*

obdurate, *a.* (*a*) Endurci; opiniâtre. (*b*) Inflexible.

obedience, *s.* Obéissance *f.*

obedient, *a.* Obéissant. soumis docile. **To be o.**, obéir.

obediently, *adv.* Avec obéissance.

obeisance, *s.* Salut *m*, révérence *f.*

obelisk, *s.* Obélisque *m.*

obese, *a.* Obèse.

obey, *v.tr.* Obéir à.

obituary, *a. & s.* Nécrologe *m.* **O. notice**, notice nécrologique.

object[1], *s.* **I.** Objet *m*; chose *f.* **2.** But *m*, objectif *m.*

object[2], *v.i.* Faire objection, trouver à redire. **Do you o. to my smoking?** la fumée vous gêne-t-elle?

objection, *s* **I.** Objection *f.* **To take o. to**, se fâcher de. **If you have no o.**, si cela ne vous fait rien. **2.** Inconvénient *m.*

objectionable, *a.* **I.** Répréhensible. **2.** Désagréable.

objective, *s.* But *m*, objectif *m.*

obligation, *s.* Obligation *f.* (*a*) Dette *f* de reconnaissance (*b*) *pl.* Engagements *mpl.*

obligatory, *a.* Obligatoire.

oblige, *v.tr.* **I.** Obliger, astreindre. **2.** (*a*) Rendre service à. (*b*) **To be obliged to s.o.**, être obligé à qn.

obliging, *a.* Obligeant, serviable.

obligingness, *s.* Obligeance *f.*

oblique, *a.* Oblique; de biais.

obliquely, *adv.* Obliquement de biais.

obliterate, *v.tr.* (*a*) Effacer. (*b*) Oblitérer.

obliteration, *s.* **I.** (*a*) Effaçage *m.* (*b*) Rature *f.* **2.** Oblitération *f.*

oblivion, *s.* Oubli *m.*

oblivious, *a.* **I.** Oublieux. **2.** **To be o. of**, ignorer.

oblong. **I.** *a.* Oblong, -ongue. **2.** *s.* Rectangle *m.*

obloquy, *s.* (*a*) Calomnie *f* (*b*) Honte *f*, opprobre *m.*

obnoxious, *a.* (*a*) Odieux: antipathique. (*b*) Repoussant.

oboe, *s.* Hautbois *m.*

obscene, *a.* Obscène.

obscenity, *s.* Obscénité *f.*

obscure[1], *a.* **I.** Obscur, ténébreux, sombre. **2.** Obscur; peu clair. **3.** Peu connu.

obscure[2], *v.tr.* Obscurcir.

obscurely, *adv.* Obscurément

obscurity, *s.* Obscurité *f.*

obsequies, *s.pl.* Obsèques *f.*

obsequious, *a.* Obséquieux.

obsequiously, *adv.* Obséquieusement.

obsequiousness, *s.* Obséquiosité *f.*

observable, *a.* Visible; perceptible.

observance, *s.* **I.** Observance *f.* **2.** *pl.* Pratiques *f.*

observant, *a.* **I.** Observateur, -trice. **2.** **He is very o.**, rien ne lui échappe.

observation, *s.* **I.** (*a*) Observation *f.* (*b*) **To take an o.**, faire le point. **2.** Remarque *f.*

observatory, *s.* Observatoire *m.*

observe, *v.tr.* **I.** Observer; se conformer à. **2.** Observer, regarder. **3.** Remarquer, noter. **4.** Dire.

observer, *s.* Observateur, -trice

obsess, *v.tr.* Obséder.

obsession, *s.* Obsession *f.*

obsolete, *a.* Désuet, -ète; hors d'usage; suranné.

obstacle, *s.* Obstacle *m.*

obstinacy, *s.* Obstination *f.*, entêtement *m*, opiniâtreté *f.*

obstinate, *a.* Obstiné: entêté; opiniâtre.

obstinately, *adv.* Obstinément opiniâtrement.

obstruct, *v.tr.* (*a*) Obstruer; encombrer. (*b*) Gêner, entraver.

obstruction, *s.* **I.** (*a*) Engorgement *m.* (*b*) Empêchement *m* **2.** Encombrement *m*; obstacle *m.*

obstructive, *a.* Obstructif.

obtain. **I.** *v.tr.* Obtenir; se procurer. **2.** *v.i.* Avoir cours.

obtainable, *a.* Procurable.

obtrude, *v.tr. & i.* Mettre en avant. **To o. on**, importuner.

obtrusion, *s.* Intrusion *f*; importunité *f.*

obtrusive, *a.* Importun; indiscret, -ète.

obtuse, *a.* Obtus.

obviate, *v.tr.* Éviter, obvier à.

obvious, *a.* Évident, manifeste.

obviously, *adv.* Évidemment, manifestement.

occasion[1], *s.* **I.** Cause *f*, occasion *f.* **Should the o. arise**, le cas échéant.

2. Occasion. On one o., une fois.
As o. requires, au besoin.

occasion[2], *v.tr.* Occasionner.

occasional, *a.* Qui vient de temps
en temps.

occasionally, *adv.* De temps en
temps.

occult, *a.* Occulte.

occupancy, *s.* Occupation *f.*

occupant, *s.* Occupant, -ante.

occupation, *s.* Occupation *f.* **1.** To
be in o. of, occuper. **2.** (*a*) Occupation. (*b*) Emploi *m.*

occupier, *s.* Occupant, -ante ; locataire *mf* ; habitant, -ante.

occupy, *v.tr.* Occuper.

occur, *v.i.* **1.** Avoir lieu ; arriver ; se
produire. **2.** Se rencontrer, se
trouver. **3. It occurs to me**, il me
vient à l'idée

occurrence, *s.* **1.** To be of frequent
o., arriver souvent. **2.** Événement *m.*

ocean, *s.* Océan *m.*

ochre, *s.* Ocre *f.*

o'clock, *adv.phr.* **Two o'c.**, deux
heures. **Twelve o'c.**, midi *m* ;
minuit *m.*

octagon, *s.* Octogone *m.*

octagonal, *a.* Octogonal. -aux

octave, *s.* Octave *f.*

octavo, *a. & s.* In-octavo (*m*).

October, *s.* Octobre *m.*

octogenarian, *a. & s.* Octogénaire (*mf*).

octopus, *s.* Poulpe *m* : pieuvre *f.*

ocular, *a.* Oculaire.

oculist, *s.* Oculiste *m.*

odd, *a.* **1.** (*a*) Impair. (*b*) **The odd
game**, la belle. **2.** (*a*) Dépareillé.
(*b*) **At odd times**, par-ci par-là.
Odd lot, solde *m.* **3.** Singulier
drôle ; excentrique.

oddity, *s.* Singularité *f,* bizarrerie *f.*

oddly, *adv.* Bizarrement, singulièrement. **O. enough**, chose curieuse.

oddness, *s.* Singularité *f,* bizarrerie *f.*

odds, *s.pl.* **1.** (*a*) Avantage *m* ;
chances *fpl.* (*b*) Différence *f.* (*c*)
Long o., forte cote. **2. To be at o.**,
être brouillé. **3. O. and ends**, petits
bouts.

ode, *s.* Ode *f.*

odious, *a.* Odieux ; détestable.

odium, *s.* Réprobation *f* ; haine *f.*

odorous, *a.* Odorant.

odour, *s.* (*a*) Odeur *f.* (*b*) Parfum *m.*

odourless, *a.* Inodore : sans odeur.

of, *prep.* De. **1.** (*a*) **To buy sth. of
s.o.**, acheter qch. à, chez, qn. (*b*) **Of
necessity**, par nécessité. **2. It is very
kind of you**, c'est bien aimable de
votre part. **3. Made of wood**, fait
de, en, bois. **4. What of it?** et
après ? **5.** (*a*) **Swift of foot**, aux pieds
légers. (*b*) **All of a tremble**, tout
tremblant. **6. How much of it do
you want?** combien en voulez-vous ?
Two of them, deux d'entre eux.
7. (*a*) **The first of June**, le premier
juin. (*b*) **It's no business of yours**,
ce n'est pas votre affaire.

off. I. *adv.* **1.** (*a*) **A mile off**, à un
mille de distance. (*b*) **To go off**, s'en
aller, partir. **To go off (to sleep)**.
s'endormir (*c*) **A la cantonade**.
2. (*a*) **Hats off!** chapeaux bas ! **Dish
that is off**, plat qui est épuisé. (*b*) **To
finish off**, parachever. **3. To be
badly off**, être dans la gêne. **4.** *Adv.
phr.* **Off and on**, par intervalles
II. off, *prep.* **1.** (*a*) De. (*b*)
Écarté de, éloigné de. **A day off**.
un jour de congé. **2. Au large de**.
III. off, *a.* **Off season**. morte-
saison *f.*

offal, *s.* Rebut *m,* déchets *mpl.*

offence, *s.* **1. To take o. at**, se froisser
de. **To give o. to**, offenser froisser.
2. Offense *f,* faute *f.*

offend. 1. *v.i.* Pécher. **2.** *v.tr.* (*a*)
Offenser, froisser. **To be offended
at sth.**, se piquer de qch. (*b*) **To o.
the eye**, choquer les regards.

offender, *s.* Coupable *m,* offenseur *m.*

offending, *a.* Offensant, fautif.

offensive. I. *a.* (*a*) Offensif. (*b*)
Offensant, choquant : nauséabond.
2. *s.* Offensive *f.*

offensively, *adv.* Désagréablement.

offer[1], *s.* Offre *f.* **O. of marriage**,
demande *f* en mariage.

offer[2]. **1.** *v.tr.* (*a*) Offrir à. (*b*) Présenter, offrir. **2.** *v.i.* S'offrir. se
présenter.

offering, *s.* Offre *f.*

off-hand. 1. *adv.* (*a*) Sans préparation ; au pied levé. (*b*) Sans cérémonie, sans façon. **2.** *a.* (*a*) Spontané. (*b*) Brusque, cavalier.

office, *s.* **1.** Office *m,* service *m.*
2. (*a*) Fonctions *fpl.* (*b*) Charge *f,*
emploi *m.* **To be in o.**, être au
pouvoir. **3.** (*a*) Bureau *m* : étude *f.*

(b) **Government o.**, ministère m. (c) pl. Communs m et dépendances f.

officer, s. **1.** Officier m. **2.** Fonctionnaire m.

official. **1.** a. Officiel **2.** s. Fonctionnaire m.

officially, adv. Officiellement.

officiate, v.i. Officier.

officious, a. Empressé ; trop zélé

officiousness, s. Excès m de zèle

offset[1], s. Compensation f

offset[2], v.tr Compenser.

offshoot, s. Rejeton m.

offspring, s. Coll. Progéniture f, descendance f ; descendants mpl.

often, adv. Souvent, fréquemment. How o.? combien de fois ?

ogive, s. Ogive f.

ogle, v.tr. Lancer des œillades a.

ogre, f. **ogress,** s. Ogre, f. ogresse

oh, int. O, oh.

oil[1], s. Huile f. **Fuel oil,** mazout m.

oil[2], v.tr. Huiler, graisser.

oil-can, s. Burette f à huile.

oilcloth, s. Linoléum imprimé.

oil-colour, s. Couleur f à l'huile.

oiliness, s. Aspect graisseux ; onctuosité f.

oiling, s. Graissage m, huilage m.

oilman, s. Marchand m de couleurs.

oil-painting, s. Tableau peint à l'huile.

oilskin, s. Toile cirée.

oilstone, s. Pierre f à huile.

oil-stove, s. Fourneau m à pétrole.

oily, a. **1.** Huileux. **2.** Onctueux.

ointment, s. Onguent m.

O.K., a. (a) Très bien ! d'accord ! (b) En règle.

old, a. **1.** Vieux, f. vieille ; âgé. An old man, un vieillard. An old woman, une vieille. **Old age,** la vieillesse. **2. How old are you?** quel âge avez-vous ? To be five years old, avoir cinq ans. **3.** Ancien. Old boy, ancien élève. **4.** Of old, adv.phr. Jadis, autrefois.

old-fashioned, a. **1.** Démodé ; suranné. **2.** Arriéré.

olive, s. **1.** O.(-tree), olivier m. **2.** Olive f.

olive-oil, s. Huile f d'olive.

omelet, s. Omelette f.

omen, s. Présage m, augure m.

ominous, a. De mauvais augure ; sinistre ; inquiétant.

ominously, adv. Sinistrement.

omission, s **1.** Omission f. **2.** Négligence f.

omit, v.tr. Omettre.

omnibus, s. Autobus m.

omnipotence, s Omnipotence f.

omnipotent, a. Omnipotent.

omnivorous, a. Omnivore.

on. I. prep. **1.** (a) Sur. **Do not tread on it,** ne marchez pas dessus. (b) On foot, à pied. (c) To be on the staff, faire partie du personnel. **2.** Hanging on the wall, pendu au mur. On page four, à la page quatre. **3.** On the right, à droite. On this side, de ce côté. **4.** (a) On Sundays, le(s) dimanche(s). On April 3rd, le trois avril. (b) On and after, à partir de. On application, sur demande. On examination, après examen. **5.** On the sly, en sourdine. **6.** On sale, en vente. **7.** On business, pour affaires. On holiday, en vacances. **8.** To have pity on, avoir pitié de

II. on, adv. **1.** Go on! continuez ! And so on, et ainsi de suite. **2.** Later on plus tard.

once, adv. **1.** Une fois. O. only, une seule fois. O. a week, tous les huit jours. O. for all, une fois pour toutes. **2.** Autrefois. **3.** At o. (a) Tout de suite : sur-le-champ. (b) A la fois.

one. I. num.a. **1.** Un That's one comfort, c'est déjà une consolation. **2.** (a) Seul, unique. (b) Même. It's all one, cela revient au même.

II. one, s There is only one left, il n'en reste qu'un. To be at one with, être d'accord avec.

III. one, dem.pron. (a) This one, celui-ci, f. celle-ci. Which one do you prefer? lequel, laquelle, préférez-vous ? Our dear ones, ceux qui nous sont chers.

IV one. indef.a. One day, un jour.

V. one, indef.pron. **1.** One of them, l'un d'eux. One and all, tous sans exception. One after the other, l'un après l'autre. One by one, un à un. **2.** Quelqu'un. **3.** (a) On. (b) Vous. It is enough to kill one, il y a de quoi vous faire mourir. **4.** One's, son, f. sa, pl. ses.

one-armed, a. Manchot, -ote.

one-eyed, *a.* Borgne.

onerous, *a.* Onéreux ; pénible.

oneself, *pron.* Soi(-même) ; se.

one-sided, *a.* (a) Inégal -aux (b) Partial, -aux.

one-way, *attrib.a.* A sens unique.

onion, *s.* Oignon *m.* **Spring o.,** ciboule *f.*

onion-sauce, *s.* Sauce blanche à l'oignon.

onlooker, *s.* Spectateur, -trice The onlookers, les assistants *m.*

only. I. *a.* Seul, unique.
II. **only,** *adv.* Seulement, ne . . que. **O.** he can say, lui seul saurait le dire. **O.** to think of it, rien que d'y penser. **O.** yesterday, pas plus tard qu'hier.
III. **only,** *conj* Mais, seulement.

onset, *s.* Assaut *m,* attaque *f.*

onslaught, *s.* Assaut *m,* attaque *f.*

onus, *s.* Responsabilité *f,* charge *f.*

onward, *adv. & a.* En avant.

onwards, *adv.* En avant.

ooze[1]**,** *s.* Vase *f,* limon *m.*

ooze[2]**,** *v.i.* Suinter ; dégoutter.

opal, *s.* Opale *f.*

opaque, *a.* Opaque.

open[1]**,** *a.* Ouvert. **1.** (a) Half o., entr'ouvert, entrebâillé. (b) Ouvert ; débouché. (c) **O.** to the public, ouvert, accessible, au public. **2.** Sans bornes. **In the o. air,** en plein air. **The o. sea,** le large. **3.** (a) Découvert. (b) **O.** to every wind, exposé à tous les vents. (c) **O.** to conviction, accessible à la conviction. **4.** (a) Manifeste ; public, -ique. (b) Franc, *f.* franche. **5. O.** wound, plaie béante. **Dress o.** at the neck, robe échancrée au col. **6.** Vacant. **7.** Non résolu. **O.** question, question discutable. **To keep an o.** mind, rester sans parti pris.

open[2]**.** I. *v.tr.* **1.** (a) Ouvrir. (b) Déboucher ; décacheter ; défaire. (c) Inaugurer. **2.** Découvrir, exposer, révéler. **3.** Commencer ; entamer.
II. **open,** *v.i.* **1.** S'ouvrir. **2.** Commencer. **open out.** I. *v.tr.* (a) Ouvrir, déplier. (b) Développer. **2.** *v.i.* S'ouvrir, s'étendre. **open up,** *v.tr.* Ouvrir ; exposer ; frayer.

open-handed, *a.* Généreux.

opening, *s.* **1.** (a) Ouverture *f.* (b) Inauguration *f.* **2.** Trou *m,* ouver-

ture ; clairière *f.* **3.** Occasion *f* favorable. **4.** *Attrib.* Inaugural, -aux. **O. sentence,** phrase de début.

openly, *adv.* Ouvertement, franchement.

open-mouthed, *a.* Bouche bée

openness, *s.* Franchise *f.*

opera, *s.* Opéra *m.*

opera-glass, *s.* Jumelle *f.*

operate. I. *v.i.* **1.** Opérer. **2. To o. on s.o.,** opérer qn.
II. **operate,** *v.tr.* Opérer, effectuer.

operatic, *a.* D'opéra.

operation, *s.* **1.** Fonctionnement *m* action *f.* **2.** Opération *f.*

operative. I. *a.* Opératif, actif. **To become o.,** prendre effet. **2.** *a. & s.* Ouvrier, -ière.

operator, *s.* Opérateur, -trice. **Wireless o.,** sans-filiste *mf*

opiate, *s.* Opiat *m.*

opinion, *s.* Opinion *f,* avis *m.* **In my o.,** à mon avis **To ask s.o.'s o.,** consulter qn.

opium, *s.* Opium *m.*

opponent, *s.* Adversaire *m.*

opportune, *a.* Opportun, convenable, commode ; à propos.

opportunely, *adv.* Opportunément

opportunity, *s.* Occasion *f.*

oppose, *v.tr.* S'opposer à ; résister à.

opposed, *a.* Opposé, hostile.

opposing, *a.* Opposé.

opposite. I. *a.* (a) Opposé ; vis-à-vis (to, de) ; en face (to, de). (b) Contraire. **The o. sex,** l'autre sexe. **In the o. direction,** en sens inverse. **2.** *s.* Opposé *m.* **Just the o.,** tout le contraire. **3.** *adv.* Vis-à-vis ; en face **4.** *prep.* En face de, vis-à-vis (de).

opposition, *s.* Opposition *f.*

oppress, *v.tr.* (a) Opprimer. (b) Oppresser, accabler.

oppression, *s.* (a) Oppression *f.* (b) Accablement *m.*

oppressive, *a.* **1.** Oppressif, opprimant. **2.** (a) Lourd, étouffant. (b) Accablant.

oppressor, *s.* Oppresseur *m.*

opprobrious, *a.* Injurieux, outrageant.

opprobrium, *s.* Opprobre *m.*

optical, *a.* **1.** Optique. **2. O. illusion,** illusion d'optique.

optician, *s.* Opticien *m.*

optimism, s. Optimisme m.
optimist, s. Optimiste mf.
optimistic, a. Optimiste.
optimistically, adv. Avec optimisme.
option, s. Option f, choix m.
optional, a. Facultatif.
opulence, s. Opulence f, richesse f.
opulent, a. Opulent.
or, conj. (a) Ou ; ni. **Without money or luggage,** sans argent ni bagages. **A mile or so,** environ un mille. (b) Sinon.
oracle, s. Oracle m.
oracular, a. Équivoque, obscur.
oral, a. Oral, -aux.
orally, adv. Oralement ; de vive voix.
orange, s. **1.** Orange f. **2.** O.(-tree), oranger m. **3.** a. & s. Orangé (m) ; orange (m) inv.
orange-blossom, s. Fleurs fpl d'oranger.
orange-lily, s. Lis orangé.
oration, s. Allocution f, discours m.
orator, s. Orateur m.
oratorio, s. Oratorio m.
oratory, s. L'art m oratoire ; l'éloquence f.
orb, s. Orbe m ; globe m sphère f.
orbit, s. Orbite f.
orchard, s. Verger m.
orchestra, s. Orchestre m.
orchestral, a. Orchestral, -aux.
orchid, s. Orchidée f.
ordain, v.tr. Ordonner.
ordeal, s. Épreuve f.
order[1], s. **1.** Ordre m. **2.** Succession f, suite f. **3. Is your passport in o.?** votre passeport est-il en règle ? **Out of o.,** en mauvais état. **4. Law and o.,** l'ordre public. **5. In o. to do sth.,** afin de, pour, faire qch. **In o. that,** afin que, pour que. **6.** (a) Commandement m, instruction f. **Until further orders,** jusqu'à nouvel ordre. (b) Commande f. **Suit made to o.,** complet fait sur mesure. **7.** (a) Arrêt m. (b) **Money o.,** mandatposte m, pl. mandats-poste. **Postal o.,** bon m de poste.
order[2], v.tr. (a) Ordonner, commander, à. (b) Prescrire, ordonner. (c) Commander.
orderly. **1.** a. (a) Ordonné, méthodique ; rangé. (b) Tranquille, discipliné. **2.** s. **Street o.,** balayeur m.
ordinal, a. & s. Ordinal, -aux.

ordinance, s. Ordonnance f. décret m, règlement m.
ordinarily, adv. Ordinairement, normalement ; d'ordinaire, d'habitude.
ordinary. **I.** a. Ordinaire ; coutumier ; normal, -aux.
 II. ordinary, s. Ordinaire m. **Out of the o.,** exceptionnel ; peu ordinaire.
ordnance, s. **1.** Artillerie f. **2. O. Survey,** service topographique.
ore, s. Minerai m.
organ, s. **1.** (a) Orgue m. (b) **Street o.,** orgue de Barbarie. **2.** Organe m.
organic, a. Organique.
organism, s. Organisme m.
organist, s. Organiste mf.
organization, s. Organisation f.
organize, v.tr. Organiser.
organizer, s. Organisateur, -trice.
orgy, s. Orgie f.
orient, s. Orient m.
oriental. **1.** a. Oriental, -aux ; d'Orient. **2.** s. Oriental, -ale.
orifice, s. Orifice m, ouverture f.
origin, s. Origine f.
original. **1.** a. (a) Originaire, primitif. (b) Original, -aux. **2.** s Original m.
originality, s. Originalité f.
originally, adv. (a) Originairement ; à l'origine. (b) Originellement ; dès l'origine.
originate, v.i. Dériver, provenir.
originator, s. Auteur m.
ornament[1], s. Ornement m.
ornament[2], v.tr. Orner, décorer.
ornamental, a. Ornemental, -aux.
ornamentation, s. Ornementation f, décoration f.
ornate, a. Orné.
ornithology, s. Ornithologie f.
orphan, s. Orphelin, -ine.
orphanage, s. Orphelinat m.
orthodox, a. Orthodoxe.
orthography, s. Orthographe f
oscillate, v.i. Osciller.
oscillation, s. Oscillation f.
osier, s. Osier m.
osprey, s. **1.** Orfraie f. **2.** Aigrette f.
ossuary, s. Ossuaire m.
Ostend. Pr.n. Ostende.
ostensible, a. Prétendu ; soi-disant ; feint.
ostensibly, adv. En apparence ; censément.
ostentation, s. Ostentation f.

ostentatious, *a.* Fastueux ; plein d'ostentation.

ostentatiously, *adv.* Avec ostentation.

ostler, *s.* Valet *m* d'écurie.

ostracize, *v.tr.* Ostraciser.

ostrich, *s.* Autruche *f.*

ostrich-feather, *s.* Plume *f* d'autruche.

other. 1. *a.* Autre. (*a*) O. things being equal, toutes choses égales. (*b*) O. people, d'autres ; autrui *m.* **2.** *pron.* Autre. (*a*) I have no o., je n'en ai pas d'autre. One or o. of us, l'un de nous. (*b*) *pl.* D'autres ; autrui. **3.** *adv.* Autrement.

otherwise, *adv.* **1.** Autrement. Except where o. stated, sauf indication contraire. **2.** Autrement ; sans quoi, sans cela. **3.** Sous d'autres rapports ; par ailleurs.

otter, *s.* Loutre *f.*

ottoman, *s.* Divan *m*, ottomane *f.*

ought, *v.aux.* Devoir, falloir. **1.** One o. not, il ne faut, on ne doit, pas. As one o., comme il convient. **2.** You o. not to have waited, vous n'auriez pas dû attendre.

our, *poss.a.* Notre, *pl.* nos.

ours, *poss.pron.* Le nôtre, la nôtre, les nôtres. This is o., ceci est à nous ; ceci nous appartient. A friend of o., un(e) de nos ami(e)s.

ourselves, *pers.pron.pl.* Nous(-mêmes).

oust, *v.tr.* **1.** Déloger. **2.** Évincer.

out. 1. *adv.* **1.** Dehors. (*a*) The voyage out, l'aller *m.* (*b*) My father is out, mon père est sorti. Out at sea, au large. Out there, là-bas. The tide is out, la marée est basse. **2.** To lean out, se pencher au dehors. **3.** (*a*) Découvert, exposé. The sun is out, il fait du soleil. The book is just out, le livre vient de paraître. (*b*) Out loud, tout haut, à haute voix. **4.** Hors jeu. **5.** Éteint. **6.** (*a*) A bout ; achevé. (*b*) Hear me out, écoutez-moi jusqu'au bout. **7.** Out of, hors de ; dans ; par ; parmi ; d'entre. To be out of one's mind, avoir perdu la raison. To throw sth. out of the window, jeter qch. par la fenêtre. To drink out of a glass, boire dans un verre. One out of three, un sur trois. Out of respect, par respect. To be out of tea, ne plus avoir de thé.

    II. **out,** *attrib.a.* **1.** Extérieur, à l'extérieur. **2.** Hors de l'ordinaire.

outbreak, *s.* **1.** Éruption *f.* **2.** Révolte *f*, émeute *f.*

out-building, *s.* Bâtiment extérieur ; annexe *f.* **Out-buildings,** communs *m*, dépendances *f.*

outburst, *s.* Éruption *f.* explosion *f* ; éclat *m.*

outcast, *a. & s.* Proscrit, -ite.

outcome, *s.* Issue *f* ; dénouement *m.*

outcry, *s.* Réclamations indignées.

outdo, *v.tr.* Surpasser ; l'emporter sur.

outdoor, *a.* Extérieur, -eure ; au dehors ; au grand air. **O. clothes,** vêtements de ville.

outdoors, *adv.* Dehors ; hors de la maison ; en plein air.

outer, *a.* Extérieur, -eure ; externe. **O. garments,** vêtements de dessus.

outfit, *s.* **1.** Équipement *m*, équipage *m* ; attirail *m.* **Repairing o.,** nécessaire *m*, trousse *f*, à réparations **2.** Trousseau *m* ; effets *mpl.*

outfitter, *s.* Fournisseur *m* d'articles d'habillement.

outflow, *s.* Écoulement *m.*

outgoing, *a.* Sortant. **O. tide,** marée descendante.

outgoings, *s.pl.* Dépenses *f.*

outing, *s.* (*a*) Promenade *f.* (*b*) Excursion *f*, sortie *f* ; partie *f* de plaisir.

outlandish, *a.* Baroque, bizarre

outlaw, *s.* Proscrit, -ite.

outlay, *s.* Débours *mpl*, frais *mpl.*

outlet, *s.* Issue *f.*

outline¹, *s.* **1.** Contour *m*, profil *m.* **2.** Dessin *m* au trait ; tracé *m* ; aperçu *m.*

outline², *v.tr.* **1.** Silhouetter **2.** Esquisser ; ébaucher.

outlive, *v.tr.* Survivre à.

outlook, *s.* Vue *f*, perspective *f.*

outlying, *a.* Éloigné, écarté.

out-of-date, *adj.phr.* **1.** Suranné, vieilli ; démodé. **2.** Périmé.

out-of-the-way, *a.* **1.** Écarté. **2.** Peu ordinaire.

output, *s.* Rendement *m* ; débit *m*

outrage¹, *s.* Outrage *m*, atteinte *f.*

outrage², *v.tr.* Outrager.

outrageous, *a.* (*a*) Immodéré, indigne ; excessif. (*b*) Outrageux.

outright. 1. *adv.* **1.** (*a*) Complètement. (*b*) Du premier coup ; sur

le coup. **To kill s.o. o.**, tuer qn raide.
2. Sans ménagement ; carrément.
II. outright, a Franc, f. franche ;
carré.

outset, s Commencement m.

outside. I. s. (a) Extérieur m, dehors
m. (b) **At the o.**, tout au plus.
(c) Impériale f. **2.** *Attrib.a.* Du
dehors ; extérieur, -e. **3.** adv.
Dehors, à l'extérieur, en dehors.
4. prep. En dehors de, à l'extérieur
de.

outsize, s. **1.** Dimension f hors série
2. *Attrib :* En taille exceptionnelle.

outskirts, s.pl. Abords m ; lisière f ;
faubourgs m.

outspoken, a Franc, f. franche ;
carré, rond **To be o.**, avoir son
franc-parler.

outspread, a Étendu ; déployé.

outstanding, a. **1.** Saillant ; marquant. **2.** En suspens ; dû ; arriéré.

outstretched, a Déployé, étendu.

outstrip, v.tr. (a) Devancer dépasser. (b) Surpasser.

outward. I. a (a) En dehors. (b)
Extérieur, -e ; de dehors. **2.** adv.
Au dehors ; vers l'extérieur.

outwardly, adv. **1.** A l'extérieur, au
dehors. **2.** En apparence.

outwards, adv Au dehors ; vers
l'extérieur.

outwit, v.tr. Circonvenir.

oval. I. a. Ovale ; en ovale. **2.** s
Ovale m.

ovation, s. Ovation f.

oven, s. Four m. **Dutch o.**, rôtis-
soire f.

over. I. prep **1.** (a) Sur, dessus, par-
dessus. (b) **All o. the world**, par
tout le monde. **2.** Au-dessus de.
3. O. the border, au delà de la
frontière. **4.** Plus de ; au-dessus de.
O. and above, en sus de.

II. over, adv **1.** (a) **To be all o.
dust**, être tout couvert de poussière.
(b) **O. and o. again**, à plusieurs
reprises. **2.** (a) Par-dessus. (b) **To
lean o.**, se pencher ; pencher. **3. To
fall o.**, tomber à la renverse ; se
renverser. **To knock o.**, renverser.
4. To cross o., traverser. **O. there,**
là-bas. **5.** En plus, en excès. (a) **I
have a card o.**, j'ai une carte de trop.
O. and above, en outre. (b) Trop ;
à l'excès **6.** Fini, achevé.

III. over, s. Série f.

overall, s (a) Blouse f. (b) pl.
Salopette f ; bleus mpl.

overawe, v.tr Intimider.

overbalance. 1. v.i. & pr. Perdre
l'équilibre. **2.** v.i. Se renverser ;
tomber.

overbearing, a. Arrogant. impérieux, autoritaire.

overboard, adv. A la mer.

over-bold, a. **1.** Téméraire **2.** Présomptueux.

overburden, v.tr Surcharger, accabler (with, de).

overcast, a Assombri, couvert.

overcharge, v.tr. Écorcher.

overcoat, s. Pardessus m.

overcome[1], v.tr. Triompher de,
vaincre ; surmonter.

overcome[2], a. Accablé.

over-confidence, s. **1.** Confiance
exagérée. **2.** Suffisance f.

over-confident, a. **1.** Trop confiant.
2. Suffisant.

overcrowded, a. (a) Bondé. (b) Surpeuplé.

overdo, v.tr. **1.** Outrer ; charger.
2. Trop cuire.

overdose, s. Trop forte dose.

overdue, a. Arriéré, en retard.

overeat, v.pr. & i. Trop manger.

over-estimate, v.tr. Surestimer ;
exagérer.

overexcite, v.tr. Surexciter.

overexcitement, s. Surexcitation f.

overexertion, s. Surmenage m.

over-fatigue[1], s. Surmenage m.

over-fatigue[2], v.tr. Surmener.

overfed, a. Suralimenté.

overflow[1], s. **1.** (a) Débordement m.
(b) Inondation f. **2.** Trop-plein m inv.

overflow[2], v.i. Déborder.

overgrown, a. Couvert.

overhang, v.tr Surplomber.

overhanging, a. Surplombant.

overhaul, v.tr. **1.** Examiner en
détail. **2.** Rattraper, dépasser.

overhead, adv. Au-dessus ; en haut,
en l'air.

overhear, v.tr. Surprendre.

overheat, v.tr. Surchauffer.

overjoyed, a. Ravi.

overlap, v.tr & i. **1.** Chevaucher.
2. Dépasser.

overleaf, adv. Au dos, au verso.

overload, v.tr. Surcharger.

overlook, *v.tr.* **1.** Dominer ; donner sur. **2.** (*a*) Oublier, laisser passer. (*b*) Fermer les yeux sur **3.** Surveiller.

overnight, *adv.* **1.** Pendant la nuit. **2.** Jusqu'au lendemain.

overpayment, *s.* Surpaye *f* ; paiement *m* en trop.

overpower, *v.tr.* Maîtriser, dominer, accabler.

overpowering, *a* Irrésistible ; accablant.

overrate, *v.tr.* Surestimer.

override, *v.tr.* Outrepasser.

over-ripe, *a.* Trop mûr.

overrule, *v.tr.* Décider contre.

overrun, *v.tr.* **1.** Se répandre sur, envahir. **2.** Dépasser.

overseas, *adv.* Outre-mer.

oversee, *v.tr.* Surveiller.

overseer, *s.* Surveillant, -ante ; contremaître, -tresse.

overshadow, *v.tr.* **1.** Ombrager. **2.** Éclipser.

overshoot, *v.tr.* Dépasser.

oversight, *s.* Oubli *m*, omission *f*.

oversleep, *v.i. & pron.* Dormir trop longtemps.

overstatement, *s.* Exagération *f*.

overt, *a.* Patent, évident.

overtake, *v.tr.* **1.** (*a*) Rattraper. (*b*) Dépasser. **2.** Arriver à ; surprendre.

overtax, *v.tr.* Trop exiger de. **To o. one's strength,** se surmener.

overthrow[1], *s.* Renversement *m* ; défaite *f*.

overthrow[2], *v.tr.* **1.** Renverser. **2.** Défaire, vaincre.

overtime, *s.* Heures *f* supplémentaires.

overture, *s.* Ouverture *f*.

overturn. 1. *v.tr.* Renverser. **2.** *v.i.* Se renverser ; chavirer.

overwhelm, *v.tr.* **1.** Submerger. **2.** (*a*) Écraser, accabler (*b*) Déborder. (*c*) Combler.

overwhelming, *a* Irrésistible ; accablant.

overwork. 1. *v.tr.* Surmener. **2.** *v.i.* Se surmener.

overwrought, *a.* Excédé.

owe, *v.tr.* Devoir.

owing. 1. *Pred.a.* Dû, *f.* due **2. O. to,** à cause de, par suite de

owl, *s.* Hibou *m*, -oux.

owlet, *s.* Jeune hibou *m*.

own[1], *v.tr.* **1.** Posséder **2.** Reconnaître ; avouer.

own[2]. **1.** *a.* (*a*) *Attrib.* Propre. (*b*) *Pred.* Le mien, le tien, *etc.* ; à moi, à toi, *etc.* **2.** *s.* **My own, his own,** *etc.* (*a*) Le mien, le sien, *etc.* **For reasons of his own,** pour des raisons particulières. (*b*) **On one's own,** de sa propre initiative.

owner, *s.* Propriétaire *mf*, possesseur *m* ; patron, -onne.

ox, *s.* Bœuf *m*.

oxalic, *a.* Oxalique.

oxide, *s.* Oxyde *m*.

ox-tail, *s.* Queue *f* de bœuf.

ox-tongue, *s.* Langue *f* de bœuf

oxygen, *s.* Oxygène *m*.

oyster, *s.* Huître *f*.

oyster-bed, *s.* Huîtrière *f*.

oyster-shell, *s.* Écaille *f* d'huître.

ozone, *s.* Ozone *m*.

P

P, p, *s.* (La lettre) P, p *m*.

pace[1], *s.* **1.** Pas *m*. **2.** Vitesse *f*, train *m*, allure *f*.

pace[2], *v.i.* **To p. up and down,** faire les cent pas.

pacific, *a.* (*a*) Pacifique. (*b*) Paisible.

pacifist, *s. & a.* Pacifiste (*mf*)

pacify, *v.tr.* Pacifier ; apaiser.

pack[1], *s.* **1.** (*a*) Paquet *m*. **2.** (*a*) Bande *f.* (*b*) **P. of hounds,** meute *f.* **3.** Jeu *m*.

pack[2], *v.tr.* **1.** Emballer, empaqueter ; *abs.* faire ses malles. **2.** Tasser ;

serrer. **3.** Remplir, bourrer. **The train was packed,** le train était bondé. **Packed hall,** salle comble.

package, *s.* Paquet *m*, colis *m*

packer, *s.* Emballeur *m*.

packet, *s.* Paquet *m*.

packing, *s.* Emballage *m*, empaquetage *m*. **To do one's p.,** faire ses malles.

packing-case, *s.* Caisse *f* d'emballage.

packing-paper, *s.* Papier *m* d'emballage.

pact, *s.* Pacte *m,* convention *f*

pad¹, *s.* **1.** (*a*) Bourrelet *m,* coussinet *m.* (*b*) Tampon *m.* **2.** Bloc *m.*

pad², *v.tr.* Rembourrer.

padding, *s.* **1.** Rembourrage *m.* **2.** Ouate *f,* bourre *f.*

paddle¹, *s.* **1.** Pagaie *f.* **2.** Aube *f.*

paddle², *v.tr.* Pagayer.

paddle³, *v.i.* Barboter.

padlock¹, *s.* Cadenas *m.*

padlock², *v.tr.* Cadenasser.

pagan, *a. & s.* Païen, -ïenne

paganism, *s.* Paganisme *m.*

page¹, *s.* **1.** Page *m.* **2.** Chasseur *m*

page², *s.* Page *f.*

pagoda, *s.* Pagode *f.*

paid, *a.* A gages ; rétribué.

pail, *s.* Seau *m.*

pailful, *s.* (Plein) seau.

pain¹. **1.** (*a*) Douleur *f,* souffrance *f* ; peine *f.* (*b*) **To have a p. in one's head,** souffrir de la tête. **2.** *pl.* Peine. **To take pains,** se donner du mal. **3. On p. of,** sous peine de.

pain², *v.tr.* Faire souffrir ; peiner, affliger. **It pains me,** il m'en coûte.

pained, *a.* Attristé, peiné (*at.* de).

painful, *a.* **1.** Douloureux. **2.** Pénible.

painfully, *adv.* Douloureusement ; péniblement.

painless, *a.* Sans douleur.

painstaking, *a.* Soigneux, assidu.

paint¹, *s.* (*a*) Peinture *f.* (*b*) **Box of paints,** boîte de couleurs.

paint², *v.tr.* **1.** (*a*) Peindre. (*b*) *Abs.* Faire de la peinture. **2.** Dépeindre.

paint-brush, *s.* Pinceau *m.*

painter¹, *s.* Peintre *m.*

painter², *s.* Amarre *f.*

painting, *s.* **1.** Peinture *f.* **2.** Tableau *m.*

pair¹, *s.* (*a*) Paire *f.* (*b*) Couple *m.*

pair², *v.i.* S'accoupler, s'apparier

pal, *s.* Camarade *mf.*

palace, *s.* Palais *m.*

palatable, *a.* Agréable au goût.

palate, *s.* Palais *m.*

palatial, *a.* Magnifique, grandiose.

pale, *a.* (*a*) Pâle, blême. **To turn p.,** pâlir. (*b*) Clair.

paleness, *s.* Pâleur *f.*

palette, *s.* Palette *f.*

paling, *s.* Palissade *f.*

palisade, *s.* Palissade *f.*

pall¹, *s.* Drap *m* mortuaire.

pall², *v.i.* S'affadir ; devenir fade.

palliate, *v.tr.* Pallier ; atténuer.

palliative, *s.* Palliatif *m,* lénitif *m.*

pallid, *a.* (*a*) Pâle, décoloré. (*b*) Blafard. (*c*) Blême.

pallor, *s.* Pâleur *f.*

palm¹, *s.* **1.** Palmier *m.* **2. P. Sunday,** le dimanche des Rameaux.

palm², *s.* Paume *f.*

palmist, *s.* Chiromancien, -ienne

palmistry, *s.* Chiromancie *f.*

palm-oil, *s.* Huile *f* de palme, de palmier.

palpable, *a.* Palpable.

palpitate, *v.tr.* Palpiter.

palpitation, *s.* Palpitation *f.*

paltriness, *s.* Mesquinerie *f.*

paltry, *a.* Misérable, mesquin.

pamper, *v.tr.* Choyer, dorloter.

pamphlet, *s.* Brochure *f.*

pan, *s.* Casserole *f,* poêlon *m.*

Panama, *s.* **P.** (hat), panama *m*

pancake, *s.* Crêpe *f.*

pane, *s.* Vitre *f,* carreau *m*

panel, *s.* Panneau *m.*

panelled, *a.* Boisé, lambrissé.

panelling, *s.* Lambris *m,* boiserie *f.*

pang, *s.* Angoisse subite ; douleur *f.*

panic, *s.* Panique *f* ; affolement *m.*

panic-stricken, *a.* Pris de panique ; affolé.

panorama, *s.* Panorama *m.*

panoramic, *a.* Panoramique.

pansy, *s.* Pensée *f.*

pant, *v.i.* (*a*) Panteler. (*b*) Haleter.

panther, *s.* Panthère *f.*

pantomime, *s.* Revue-féerie *f.*

pantry, *s.* Garde-manger *m inv.*

pants, *s.pl.* Caleçon *m.*

papa, *s.* Papa *m.*

papacy, *s.* Papauté *f.*

papal, *a.* Papal, -aux.

paper¹, *s.* **1.** Papier *m.* **Brown p.,** papier gris. **Cigarette p.,** papier à cigarettes. **2.** Document *m,* pièce *f.* **3.** Étude *f,* mémoire *m.* **4.** Journal *m,* -aux.

paper², *v.tr.* Tapisser.

paper-fastener, *s.* Attache *f* métallique.

paper-knife, *s.* Coupe-papier *m inv.*

paper-weight, *s.* Presse-papiers *m inv.*

par, *s.* Pair *m,* égalité *f.*

parachute, *s.* Parachute *m.*

parachutist, *s.* Parachutiste *mf.*

parade¹, *s.* **1.** Parade *f.* **2.** (*a*)

Rassemblement *m.* (*b*) Exercice *m.*
3. Défilé *m.* **4.** Esplanade *f.*

parade². **I.** *v.tr.* (*a*) Faire parade de ; afficher. (*b*) Faire parader. **2.** *v.i.* Parader.

parade-ground. Place *f* d'armes.

paradise, *s.* Paradis *m.* **Bird of p.,** oiseau *m* de paradis.

paradox, *s.* Paradoxe *m.*

paradoxically, *adv.* Paradoxalement.

paraffin, *s.* **1.** Paraffine *f.* **Liquid p.,** huile *f* de vaseline. **2.** Pétrole *m.*

paraffin-oil, *s.* Pétrole *m* ; pétrole lampant.

paragon, *s.* Parangon *m*, modèle *m.*

paragraph, *s.* **1.** Paragraphe *m*, alinéa *m.* **2.** Entrefilet *m.*

parakeet, *s.* Perruche *f.*

parallel. I. *a.* **1.** Parallèle. **2.** Analogue.
II. parallel, *s.* **1.** Parallèle *f.*
2. Parallèle *m*, comparaison *f.*

paralyse, *v.tr.* Paralyser.

paralysing, *a.* Paralysant.

paralysis, *s.* Paralysie *f.*

paramount, *a.* **1.** Souverain **2.** Suprême.

parapet, *s.* Parapet *m* ; garde-fou *m* *pl.* garde-fous.

paraphernalia, *s.pl.* (*a*) Effets *m* ; affaires *f.* (*b*) Attirail *m*, appareil *m.*

paraphrase, *v.tr.* Paraphraser.

parasite, *s.* Parasite *m.*

parcel, *s.* Paquet *m*, colis *m.*

parcel post, *s.* Service *m* des colis postaux.

parch, *v.tr.* Rôtir, griller. **To be parched with thirst**, avoir une soif ardente.

parchment, *s.* Parchemin *m.*

pardon¹, *s.* Pardon *m.* **I beg your p.!** je vous demande pardon !

pardon², *v.tr.* **1.** Pardonner. **2.** Pardonner à. **3.** Gracier.

pardonable, *a.* Pardonnable.

pare, *v.tr.* **1.** Rogner. **2.** Peler

paregoric, *s.* Parégorique *m.*

parent, *s.* Père *m*, mère *f* ; *pl.* parents *m*, les père et mère.

parental, *a.* Des parents ; paternel.

parenthesis, *s.* Parenthèse *f.* **In parentheses**, entre parenthèses.

pariah, *s.* Paria *m.*

Paris. *Pr.n.* Paris *m.*

parish, *s.* Paroisse *f.* **P. church,** église paroissiale.

parishioner, *s.* Paroissien, -ienne.

Parisian, *a. & s.* Parisien, -ienne.

park¹, *s.* **1.** Parc *m.* **2.** Car p., parc de stationnement.

park², *v.tr.* Parquer garer ; *abs.* stationner.

parking, *s.* Parcage *m.* *Aut :* 'No p.,' "défense de stationner."

parley¹, *s.* Conférence *f* ; pourparlers *mpl.*

parley², *v.i.* Parlementer.

parliament, *s.* Le Parlement. **The Houses of P.,** le palais du Parlement.

parliamentary, *a.* Parlementaire.

parochial, *a.* Paroissial, -aux.

parody¹, *s.* Parodie *f*, pastiche *m.*

parody², *v.tr.* Parodier, pasticher

parole, *s.* Parole *f.*

paroxysm, *s.* (*a*) Paroxysme *m.* (*b*) Crise *f* ; accès *m.*

parrot, *s.* Perroquet *m.*

parry, *v.tr.* Parer, détourner.

parsimonious, *a.* Parcimonieux.

parsley, *s.* Persil *m.*

parsnip, *s.* Panais *m.*

parson, *s.* Prêtre *m.*

parsonage, *s.* Presbytère *m*, cure *f.*

part¹. I. *s.* **1.** Partie *f.* (*a*) Pièce *f*, organe *m.* (*b*) **Parts of speech,** parties du discours. (*c*) Fascicule *m*, livraison *f.* **2.** Part *f.* (*a*) **To take p. in,** prendre part à. (*b*) Rôle *m*, personnage *m.* **3.** (*a*) **To take s.o.'s p.,** prendre le parti de qn. (*b*) **On the p. of,** de la part de. **For my p.,** quant à moi. **4. To take in good p.,** prendre en bonne part.
II. part, *adv.* Partiellement ; en partie.

part². I. *v.tr.* (*a*) **To p. one's hair,** se faire une raie. (*b*) Séparer. **2.** *v.i.* (*a*) Se diviser. (*b*) Se quitter, se séparer. (*c*) (Se) rompre ; céder.

part with, *v.i.* Céder ; se dessaisir de.

partake, *v.i.* **To p. of,** prendre.

partial, *a.* **1.** Partial, -aux. **2.** Partiel ; en partie.

partiality, *s.* **1.** Partialité *f.* **2.** Prédilection *f.*

partially, *adv.* **1.** Avec partialité. **2.** En partie.

participate, *v.i.* Participer (*in*, à).

participation, *s.* Participation *f.*

participle, *s.* Participe *m.*

particle, *s.* Particule *f*, parcelle *f.*

particular. I. *a.* **1.** Particulier ; spécial. -aux. **For no p. reason,** sans raison précise. **2.** Méticuleux : pointilleux.

II. **particular,** Détail *m.* particularité *f.*

particularly, *adv.* Particulièrement.

parting, *s* **1.** (*a*) Séparation *f.* (*b*) Départ *m.* **2.** Rupture *f.* **3.** Raie *f*

partisan, *s.* Partisan *m.*

partition, *s.* (*a*) Cloison *t.* (*b*) Compartiment *m.*

partly, *adv* Partiellement ; en partie.

partner, *s.* (*a*) Associé, -ée. (*b*) Partenaire *mf.* (*c*) Cavalier *m* ; dame *f* ; danseur, -euse.

partnership, *s.* **1.** Association *f* **2.** Société *f.*

partridge, *s.* (*a*) Perdrix *f.* (*b*) Perdreau *m.*

party, *s.* **1.** Parti *m.* **2.** (*a*) Partie *f.* (*b*) Evening p., soirée *f.* **3.** Bande *f,* groupe *m.*

pass¹, *s.* Col *m,* défilé *m.*

pass², *s.* Passe, permission *f.*

pass³. I. *v.i.* **1.** Passer. **To let s.o. p.,** livrer passage à qn **2.** (Se) passer, s'écouler.

II. **pass,** *v.tr* **1.** (*a*) Passer devant, près de ; croiser. (*b*) Passer, franchir. (*c*) Dépasser. (*d*) Passer ; réussir à. (*e*) Être accepté par. **2.** Approuver. **3.** Transmettre, donner. **4.** (*a*) **To p. sentence,** prononcer le jugement. (*b*) **To p. remarks,** faire des remarques. **pass off,** *v.i.* Se passer. **pass on.** I. *v.i.* **1.** Passer son chemin. **2.** *v.tr.* Faire circuler. **pass over.** I. *v.i.* **1.** Passer sous silence. **2.** Se dissiper, finir. II. **pass over,** *v.tr.* Donner, transmettre. **pass round,** *v.tr.* Faire circuler. **pass through,** *v.i.* Traverser.

passable, *a.* Passable ; assez bon.

passage, *s.* **1.** Passage *m.* **2.** (*a*) Couloir *m,* corridor *m.* (*b*) Passage, ruelle *f.*

pass-book, *s.* Carnet *m* de banque.

passenger, *s.* Voyageur, -euse ; passager, -ère. **passenger coach,** *s.* Wagon *m* à voyageurs. **passenger train.** Train *m* de voyageurs. **By p. t.,** par grande vitesse.

passer(-by), *s.* Passant, -ante.

passing, *a.* (*a*) Passant. (*b*) Passager, éphémère

passion, *s.* **1.** Passion *f.* **2.** Colère *f,* emportement *m.*

passionate, *a.* **1.** Emporté ; véhément. **2.** Passionné

passionately, *adv.* **1.** Passionnément. **2.** Avec colère.

passive, *a.* Passif.

passively, *adv.* Passivement.

passport, *s.* Passeport *m.*

password, *s.* Mot *m* de passe.

past¹. I. *a.* Passé, ancien. **In times p.,** autrefois. **For some time p.,** depuis quelque temps. **2.** *s.* Passé *m.* **In the p.,** autrefois.

past². **1.** *prep.* Au delà de. (*a*) **To walk p. s.o.,** passer qn. (*b*) Plus de. **A quarter p. four,** quatre heures un quart. **2.** *adv.* **To walk, go, p.,** passer.

paste¹, *s.* **1.** Pâte *f.* **2.** Strass *m.*

paste², *v.tr.* Coller.

pasteboard, *s.* Carton *m.* **P. box,** carton.

pastime, *s.* Passe-temps *m inv.*

pastry, *s.* Pâtisserie *f.*

pastry-cook, *s.* Pâtissier, -ière

pasturage, *s.* Pâturage *m.*

pasture¹, *s.* Pâturage *m.*

pasture². **1.** *v.i.* Paître. **2.** *v.tr.* (Faire) paître.

pasty¹, *a.* **1.** Pâteux. **2. P. face,** visage terreux.

pasty², *s.* Pâté *m.*

pat¹, *s.* **1.** (*a*) Coup léger (*b*) Caresse *f.* **2.** Rondelle *f.*

pat², *v.tr.* (*a*) Taper, tapoter (*b*) Caresser.

patch¹, *s.* **1.** Pièce *f.* **2.** (Rubber) p., pastille *f.* **3.** Tache *f.* **P. of snow,** flaque *f* de neige. **4.** (*a*) Morceau *m* parcelle *f.* (*b*) Carré *m,* plant *m.*

patch², *v.tr.* Rapiécer, raccommoder. **patch up,** *v.tr.* Rapetasser ; rafistoler.

patchy, *a.* Inégal.

patent¹. I. *a.* **1.** Breveté. **P. medicine,** spécialité pharmaceutique. **P. leather,** cuir verni. **2.** Patent, manifeste.

II. **patent,** *s.* (*a*) Brevet *m* d'invention. (*b*) Invention brevetée.

patent², *v.tr.* Faire breveter.

paternal, *a.* Paternel.

paternity, *s.* Paternité *f.*

path, *s.* **1.** Chemin *m* ; sentier *m* ; allée *f.* **2.** Course *f* ; route *f.*

pathetic, *a.* Pathétique.
pathetically, *adv.* Pathétiquement.
pathos, *s.* Pathétique *m.*
pathway, *s.* (*a*) Sentier *m.* (*b*) Trottoir *m.*
patience, *s.* 1. Patience *f.* 2. Réussite *f.*
patient. I. *a.* Patient, endurant.
II. **patient,** *s.* Malade *mf.*
patiently, *adv.* Patiemment.
patriarch, *s.* Patriarche *m.*
patrimony, *s.* Patrimoine *m.*
patriot, *s.* Patriote *mf.*
patriotic, *a.* 1. Patriote. 2. Patriotique.
patriotically, *adv.* Patriotiquement; en patriote.
patriotism, *s.* Patriotisme *m.*
patrol[1], *s.* Patrouille *f.*
patrol[2]. 1. *v.i.* Patrouiller. 2. *v.tr.* Faire la patrouille dans.
patron. 1. *s.* Patron -onne. 2. Client, -ente.
patronage, *s.* Patronage *m.*
patronize, *v.tr.* 1. Traiter d'un air protecteur. 2. Accorder sa clientèle à.
patronizing, *a.* Protecteur, -trice.
patter[1], *s.* Petit bruit ; fouettement *m.*
patter[2], *v.i.* Sonner par petits coups ; fouetter.
pattern, *s.* 1. Modèle *m,* type *m.* 2. (*a*) Modèle ; dessin *m.* (*b*) Patron *m.*
patty, *s.* Bouchée *f* à la reine.
pauper, *s.* 1. Indigent, -ente 2. Pauvre, -esse.
pause[1], *s.* Pause *f,* arrêt *m.*
pause[2], *v.i.* 1. Faire une pause ; marquer un temps. 2. Hésiter.
pave, *v.tr.* Paver.
pavement, *s.* (*a*) Pavé *m,* pavage *m.* (*b*) Trottoir *m.*
pavilion, *s.* Pavillon *m.*
paving, *s.* Pavé *m,* dalles *fpl*
paving-stone, *s.* Pavé *m.*
paw, *s.* Patte *f.*
pawn[1], *s.* In p., en gage.
pawn[2], *v.tr.* Engager.
pawn[3], *s.* Pion *m.*
pawnbroker, *s.* Prêteur, -euse, sur gages.
pawnshop, *s.* Bureau *m* de prêt sur gages.
pay[1], *s.* Paie *f,* salaire *m* ; gages *mpl* ; traitement *m* ; solde *f.*
pay[2], *v.tr.* 1. Payer. 2. (*a*) Solder, régler. 'Paid,' "pour acquit."

(*b*) To pay honour to, faire honneur à. To pay one's respects, présenter ses respects. To pay s.o. a visit, faire une visite à qn. **pay away,** *v.tr.* Dépenser. **pay back,** *v.tr.* 1. Rendre. 2. Rembourser. **pay down,** *v.tr.* (*a*) Payer comptant. (*b*) To pay something d., verser une provision. **pay for,** *v.tr.* Payer. To pay s.o. for his trouble, dédommager qn de sa peine. **pay off,** *v.tr.* 1. Solder, régler, acquitter. 2. Rembourser. **pay out,** *v.tr.* Payer ; débourser.
payable, *a.* Payable, acquittable.
paying, *a.* 1. Payant. P. guest, pensionnaire *mf.* 2. Qui rapporte.
paymaster, *s.* Payeur *m* ; trésorier *m* ; commissaire *m.*
payment, *s.* (*a*) Paiement *m* ; versement *m.* Cash p., paiement comptant. (*b*) Rémunération *f.*
pea, *s.* 1. Pois *m.* Green peas, petits pois. 2. Sweet pea, pois de senteur.
peace, *s.* 1. Paix *f.* At p., en paix. 2. Ordre public. Justice of the p., juge *m* de paix. 3. Tranquillité *f.*
peaceable, *a.* Pacifique.
peaceably, *adv.* Pacifiquement.
peaceful, *a.* 1. Paisible calme, tranquille. 2. Pacifique.
peacefully, *adv.* 1. Paisiblement. 2. Pacifiquement.
peacefulness, *s.* Tranquillité *f.*
peacemaker, *s.* Pacificateur, -trice.
peach, *s.* 1. Pêche *f.* 2. P.(-tree), pêcher *m.*
peacock, *s.* Paon *m.*
peahen, *s.* Paonne *f.*
peak, *s.* 1. Visière *f.* 2. Pic *m,* cime *f.*
peal[1], *s.* 1. Carillon *m.* 2. Coup *m.*
peal[2], *v.i.* (*a*) Carillonner. (*b*) Retentir.
peanut, *s.* Arachide *f,* cacahuète *f.*
pear, *s.* 1. Poire *f.* 2. P.(-tree), poirier *m.*
pearl, *s.* 1. Perle *f.* 2. P. button, bouton de nacre.
pearl-barley, *s.* Orge perlé.
peasant, *s.* Paysan, -anne.
pea-soup, *s.* Soupe *f* aux pois.
peat, *s.* Tourbe *f.*
pebble, *s.* 1. Caillou *m,* -oux ; galet *m.* 2. Cristal *m* de roche.
pebbly, *a.* Cailouteux ; à galets.
peck[1], *s.* Coup *m* de bec.

peck², *v.tr.* Picoter, becqueter; donner un coup de bec à.

peculiar, *a.* (*a*) Particulier. (*b*) Spécial, -aux; particulier. (*c*) Étrange; bizarre, singulier.

peculiarity, *s.* 1. Trait distinctif; particularité *f.* 2. Bizarrerie *f.*

peculiarly, *adv.* (*a*) Particulièrement. (*b*) Étrangement; singulièrement.

pecuniary, *a.* Pécuniaire.

pedagogue, *s.* Pédagogue *m.*

pedal¹, *s.* Pédale *f.*

pedal², *v.i.* Pédaler.

pedant, *s.* Pédant, -ante.

pedantic, *a.* Pédant, pédantesque.

pedestal, *s.* Piédestal *m*, -aux.

pedestrian. 1. *a.* Pédestre. 2. *s.* Piéton *m.*

pedigree, *s.* (*a*) Ascendance *f*, généalogie *f.* (*b*) **P. dog**, chien de race.

pedlar, *s.* Colporteur *m.*

peel¹, *s.* Pelure *f*; écorce *f*, peau *f.* Candied **p.**, zeste confit.

peel². 1. *v.tr.* Peler; éplucher. 2. *v.i.* (*a*) **To p. (off)**, s'écailler. (*b*) Peler.

peelings, *s.pl.* Épluchures *f.*

peep¹, *s.* Coup *m* d'œil.

peep², *v.i.* 1. **To p. at**, regarder à la dérobée. 2. **To p. (out)**, se laisser entrevoir.

peer¹, *s.* Pair *m.*

peer², *v.i.* **To p. at**, scruter du regard.

peerage, *s.* Pairie *f.*

peeress, *s.* Pairesse *f.*

peerless, *a.* Sans pareil, sans pair.

peevish, *a.* Irritable, geignard.

peg, *s.* (*a*) Cheville *f*; fiche *f.* (*b*) Patère *f.*

pelican, *s.* Pélican *m.*

pellet, *s.* (*a*) Boulette *f.* (*b*) Grain *m* de plomb.

pell-mell. 1. *adv.* Pêle-mêle. 2. *a.* En confusion.

pellucid, *a.* Pellucide, transparent.

pelt. 1. *v.tr.* Lancer une volée (de pierres) à. 2. *v.i.* **Pelting rain**, pluie battante.

pen¹, *s.* Parc *m*, enclos *m.*

pen², *s.* 1. Plume *f.* 2. **Steel pen**, plume métallique.

penal, *a.* Pénal, -aux. **P. servitude**, travaux forcés.

penalize, *v.tr.* (*a*) Infliger une peine à. (*b*) Pénaliser.

penalty, *s.* 1. (*a*) Peine *f*, pénalité *f.* (*b*) Désavantage *m.* 2. Pénalité.

penance, *s.* Pénitence *f.*

pencil, *s.* Crayon *m.* **Lead p.**, crayon à mine de plomb. **Coloured p.**, crayon de couleur.

pencil-case, *s.* (*a*) Porte-crayon *m inv.* (*b*) Porte-mine *m inv.*

pencil-holder, *s.* Porte-crayon *m inv.*

pencil-sharpener, *s.* Taille-crayon *m inv.*

pendant, *s.* Pendentif *m*; pendeloque *f* (de lustre).

pendent, *a.* Pendant; retombant.

pending. 1. *a.* Pendant. 2. *prep.* (*a*) Pendant. (*b*) En attendant.

pendulum, *s.* Pendule *m*, balancier *m.*

penetrate. 1. *v.tr.* Pénétrer, percer. 2. *v.i.* Pénétrer.

penetrating, *a.* Pénétrant; mordant.

penetration, *s.* Pénétration *f.*

penguin, *s.* Manchot *m.*

penholder, *s.* Porte-plume *m inv.*

penicillin, *s.* Pénicilline *f.*

peninsula, *s.* Péninsule *f*; presqu'île *f.*

penitence, *s.* Pénitence *f.*

penitent. 1. *a.* Pénitent, contrit. 2. *s.* Pénitent, -ente.

penitently, *adv.* D'un air contrit.

penknife, *s.* Canif *m.*

pennant, *s.* Flamme *f*, guidon *m.*

penniless, *a.* Sans le sou.

pennon, *s.* Flamme *f*, banderole *f.*

pension¹, *s.* 1. Pension *f*, retraite *f.* **Old age p.**, retraite de vieillesse. 2. Pension de famille.

pension², *v.tr.* Pensionner. **To p. off**, mettre à la retraite.

pensioner, *s.* Titulaire *mf* d'une pension; retraité, -ée.

pensive, *a.* Pensif, songeur, -euse.

pensively, *adv.* Pensivement; d'un air pensif.

penurious, *a.* 1. Pauvre. 2. (*a*) Parcimonieux. (*b*) Mesquin.

penury, *s.* Pénurie *f.*

people¹, *s.* I. Peuple *m*, nation *f.* II. **people**. *Coll:* 1. (*a*) Peuple, habitants *mpl.* (*b*) Parents *mpl.* 2. Populace. 3. (*a*) Gens *mpl*, monde *m.* (*b*) Personnes *fpl.*

people², *v.tr.* Peupler.

pepper¹, *s.* Poivre *m.*

pepper², *v.tr.* Poivrer.

pepper-castor, *s.* Poivrière *f.*

peppermint, *s.* 1. Menthe poivrée. 2. Pastille *f* de menthe.

peppery, *a.* 1. Poivré. 2. Irascible.

per, *prep.* **1.** (*a*) Par. (*b*) **Fifty francs per pound,** cinquante francs la livre. **2.** Per annum, par an. **Per cent,** pour cent.

perambulator, *s.* Voiture *f* d'enfant.

perceive, *v.tr.* **1.** S'apercevoir de. **2.** Apercevoir.

percentage, *s.* Pourcentage *m.*

perceptible, *a.* Perceptible.

perceptibly, *adv.* Sensiblement.

perception, *s.* Perception *f.*

perceptive, *a.* Perceptif.

perch[1], *s.* Perchoir *m.*

perch[2], *v.i.* (Se) percher ; jucher

perch[3], *s.* Perche *f.*

percolator, *s.* Filtre *m.*

percussion, *s.* Percussion *f* ; choc *m.*

perdition, *s.* Perte *f.* ruine *f.*

peremptorily, *adv.* Péremptoirement.

peremptory, *a.* Péremptoire.

perfect[1], *a.* Parfait.

perfect[2], *v.tr.* **1.** Achever, parachever. **2.** Rendre parfait.

perfection, *s.* Perfection *f.* **To succeed to p.,** réussir à souhait.

perfectly, *adv.* Parfaitement.

perfidious, *a.* Perfide.

perfidy, *s.* Perfidie *f.*

perforate, *v.tr.* Perforer, percer, transpercer.

perforated, *a.* Perforé.

perforation, *s.* Perforation *f.*

perform, *v.tr.* **1.** Exécuter ; accomplir ; s'acquitter de. **2.** Jouer, représenter.

performance, *s.* **1.** Exécution *f* ; accomplissement *m.* **2.** Acte *m,* exploit *m.* **3.** Représentation *f* ; séance *f* (de cinéma). **Evening p.,** soirée *f.* **Afternoon p.,** matinée *f.*

performer, *s.* Artiste *mf.* **1.** Exécutant, -ante. **2.** Acteur, -trice.

perfume[1], *s.* Parfum *m.*

perfume[2], *v.tr.* Parfumer.

perfunctory, *a.* **1.** Superficiel. **2.** Négligent ; peu zélé.

pergola, *s.* Tonnelle *f.*

perhaps, *adv.* Peut-être.

peril, *s.* Péril *m,* danger *m.*

perilous, *a.* Périlleux, dangereux.

perilously, *adv.* Périlleusement, dangereusement.

period, *s.* Période *f.* **1.** Durée *f,* délai *m.* **2.** Époque *f,* âge *m.*

periodical, *a. & s.* Périodique (*m*).

periodically, *adv.* Périodiquement.

periscope, *s.* Périscope *m.*

perish, *v.i.* (*a*) Périr, mourir (*b*) Se détériorer.

perishable, *a.* Périssable.

perjurer, *s.* Parjure *mf.*

perjury, *s.* Faux témoignage.

perky, *a.* (*a*) Éveillé, guilleret. (*b*) Dégagé, désinvolte.

perm[1], *s.* Permanente *f,* indéfrisable *f.*

perm[2], *v.tr.* **To have one's hair permed,** se faire faire une indéfrisable.

permanency, *s.* **1.** Permanence *f.* **2.** Emploi permanent.

permanent, *a.* Permanent. **P. address,** résidence fixe. **P. wave,** ondulation permanente.

permanently, *adv.* D'une façon permanente.

permeate, *v.tr. & i.* Filtrer à travers.

permissible, *a.* Tolérable, permis.

permission, *s.* Permission *f.*

permit[1], *s.* Permis *m,* autorisation *f.*

permit[2], *v.tr.* Permettre.

pernicious, *a.* Pernicieux.

peroxide, *s.* **Hydrogen p.,** eau oxygénée.

perpendicular, *a. & s.* Perpendiculaire (*f*).

perpendicularly, *adv.* Perpendiculairement.

perpetrate, *v.tr.* Commettre, perpétrer.

perpetrator, *s.* Auteur *m.*

perpetual, *a.* (*a*) Perpétuel, éternel. (*b*) Sans fin ; continuel.

perpetually, *adv.* (*a*) Perpétuellement. (*b*) Sans cesse.

perpetuate, *v.tr.* Perpétuer.

perpetuation, *s.* Perpétuation *f.*

perpetuity, *s.* Perpétuité *f.*

perplex, *v.tr.* Embarrasser ; mettre dans la perplexité.

perplexed, *a.* Perplexe, embarrassé.

perplexing, *a.* Embarrassant, troublant.

perplexity, *s.* Perplexité *f* embarras *m.*

perquisite, *s.* Casuel *m.*

persecute, *v.tr.* **1.** Persécuter. **2.** Tourmenter ; harceler.

persecution, *s.* Persécution *f.*

persecutor, *s.* Persécuteur, -trice.

perseverance, *s.* Persévérance *f.*

persevere, *v.i.* Persévérer.

persevering, *a.* Persévérant, assidu.
Persian. **1.** *a. & s.* Persan -ane.
P. **carpet**, tapis *m* de Perse. **2.** *s.*
Le persan.
persist, *v.i.* Persister.
persistency, *s.* Persistance *f.* **1.**
Obstination *f.* **2.** Continuité *f.*
persistent, *a.* Persistant.
persistently, *adv.* Avec persistance.
person, *s.* Personne *f*, individu *m*;
pl. gens *m.*
personage, *s.* Personnage *m* personne *f*, personnalité *f.*
personal, *a.* Personnel. (*a*) **Don't be**
p., ne faites pas de personnalités.
(*b*) **To make a p. application**, se
présenter en personne.
personality, *s.* (*a*) Personnalité *f.*
(*b*) Caractère *m* propre.
personally, *adv.* Personnellement.
personify, *v.tr.* Personnifier.
perspective, *s.* Perspective *f.*
perspicacious, *a.* Perspicace.
perspicacity, *s.* Perspicacité *f.*
perspicuous, *a.* Clair, lucide.
perspiration, *s.* (*a*) Transpiration *f.*
(*b*) Sueur *f.*
perspire, *v.i.* Transpirer, suer.
perspiring, *a.* En sueur.
persuade, *v.tr.* (*a*) Persuader. (*b*)
Persuader à. **P. your brother to
come!** déterminez votre frère à
venir !
persuasion, *s.* (*a*) Persuasion *f.* (*b*)
Conviction *f.*
persuasive, *a.* Persuasif.
pert, *a.* Mutin ; effronté, hardi.
pertinacious, *a.* Obstiné, entêté.
pertinacity, *s.* Obstination *f*, opiniâtreté *f*, entêtement *m.*
pertinent, *a.* Pertinent ; à propos
perturb, *v.tr.* Troubler, inquiéter.
perturbation, *s.* Inquiétude *f.*
Peru. *Pr.n.* Le Pérou.
perusal, *s.* Lecture *f.*
peruse, *v.tr.* Lire attentivement.
pervade, *v.tr.* S'infiltrer dans.
pervasive, *a.* Pénétrant.
perverse, *a.* (*a*) Pervers méchant.
(*b*) Contrariant.
perversely, *adv.* Perversement.
perverseness, *s.* (*a*) Perversité *f.*
(*b*) Esprit *m* contraire.
perversion, *s.* Perversion *f.*
perversity, *s.* (*a*) Perversité *f.* (*b*)
Esprit *m* contraire.

pervert[1], *s.* Perverti, -ie.
pervert[2], *v.tr.* **1.** Détourner. **2.** Pervertir. **3.** Fausser.
pessimism, *s.* Pessimisme *m*
pessimist, *s.* Pessimiste *mf.*
pessimistic, *a.* Pessimiste.
pessimistically, *adv.* Avec pessimisme.
pest, *s.* Peste *f*, fléau *m.*
pester, *v.tr.* Tourmenter, importuner.
pestilence, *s.* Peste *f.*
pestilent, *a.* Pestilentiel.
pestilential, *a.* Pestilentiel.
pestle, *s.* Pilon *m.*
pet[1]. **1.** *s.* (*a*) Animal familier, favori.
(*b*) Enfant gâté. **2.** *Attrib.* Choyé,
favori.
pet[2], *v.tr.* Choyer, mignoter.
petal, *s.* Pétale *m.*
Peter. **1.** *Pr.n.* Pierre *m.* **2.** *s.* **Blue**
P., pavillon *m* de partance.
petition[1], *s.* Pétition *f*, requête *f.*
petition[2], *v.tr.* Adresser présenter,
une pétition à.
petitioner, *s.* Pétitionnaire *mf.*
petrify, *v.tr.* Pétrifier
petrol, *s.* Essence *f.*
petrol-can, *s.* Bidon *m* à essence.
petroleum, *s.* Pétrole *m.*
petticoat, *s.* Jupe *f* de dessous ;
jupon *m.*
pettiness, *s.* Petitesse *f*, mesquinerie *f.*
pettish, *a.* De mauvaise humeur ;
maussade ; irritable.
petty, *a.* **1.** (*a*) Petit, insignifiant.
(*b*) Mesquin. **2.** **P. cash**, petite
caisse.
petulance, *s.* Irritabilité *f.*
petulant, *a.* Irritable.
pewter, *s.* Étain *m.*
phantasm, *s.* Chimère *f*, illusion *f.*
phantom, *s.* Fantôme *m*, spectre *m.*
pharmaceutical, *a.* Pharmaceutique.
pharmacopœia, *s.* Pharmacopée *f.*
pharmacy, *s.* Pharmacie *f.*
phase, *s.* Phase *f.*
pheasant, *s.* Faisan, -ane.
phenacetin, *s.* Phénacétine *f.*
phenomenal, *a.* Phénoménal, -aux.
phenomenon, *s.* Phénomène *m.*
phew, *int.* Pouf !
phial, *s.* Fiole *f*, flacon *m.*
philanthropic, *a.* Philanthropique ;
philanthrope.
philanthropist, *s.* Philanthrope *m.*

philanthropy, *s.* Philanthropie *f.*
philatelic, *a.* Philatélique.
philatelist, *s.* Philatéliste *mf*
philately, *s.* Philatélie *f.*
Philip. *Pr.n.* Philippe *m.*
philological, *a.* Philologique.
philologist, *s.* Philologue *m.*
philology, *s.* Philologie *f.*
philosopher, *s.* Philosophe *m.*
philosophical, *a.* **1.** Philosophique. **2.** Philosophe, calme, modéré.
philosophically, *adv.* Philosophiquement.
philosophy, *s.* Philosophie *f.*
phlegm, *s.* Flegme *m.*
phlegmatic, *a.* Flegmatique.
phone[1], *s.* Téléphone *m.*
phone[2], *v.tr. & i.* Téléphoner (à).
phonetic, *a.* Phonétique.
phonetically, *adv.* Phonétiquement.
phonetics, *s.pl.* Phonétique *f.*
phosphate, *s.* Phosphate *m.*
phosphorescent, *a.* Phosphorescent.
phosphorus, *s.* Phosphore *m.*
photograph[1], *s.* Photographie *f.* To have one's p. taken, se faire photographier.
photograph[2], *v.tr.* Photographier.
photographer, *s.* Photographe *m.*
photographic, *a.* Photographique.
photography, *s.* Photographie *f.*
phrase, *s.* Locution *f.*
phthisis, *s.* Phtisie *f.*
physic, *s.* Médecine *f.*
physical, *a.* Physique.
physically, *adv.* Physiquement.
physician, *s.* Médecin *m.*
physics, *s.pl.* La physique.
physiognomy, *s.* Physionomie *f.*
physiological, *a.* Physiologique.
physiology, *s.* Physiologie *f.*
physique, *s.* Physique *m.*
pianiste, *s.* Pianiste *mf.*
piano, pianoforte, *s.* Piano *m.* Grand p., piano à queue.
piastre, *s.* Piastre *f.*
pick[1], *s.* Choix *m*, élite *f.*
pick[2], *v.tr.* **1.** To p. holes in, trouver à redire à. **2.** To p. one's teeth, se curer les dents. **3.** Picoter, becqueter. **4.** Choisir. To p. and choose, se montrer difficile. **5.** Cueillir. **6.** To p. pockets, pratiquer le vol à la tire. **pick out,** *v.tr.* Choisir. **pick over,** *v.tr.* Trier. **pick up.** I. *v.tr.* **1.** Ramasser. **2.**

Apprendre. **3.** Trouver. **4.** (*a*) Repérer. (*b*) Capter II. **pick up,** *v.i.* Se rétablir.
pickaxe, *s.* Pioche *f.*
picket, *s.* Piquet *m.*
pickle[1], *s.* **1.** Marinade *f* ; saumure *f.* **2.** *pl.* Conserves *f* au vinaigre.
pickle[2], *v.tr.* Mariner ; conserver.
pick-me-up, *s.* Cordial *m*, -aux.
pickpocket, *s.* Voleur *m* à la tire ; pickpocket *m.*
picnic[1], *s.* Partie *f* de plaisir ; pique-nique *m.*
picnic[2], *v.i.* Faire un pique-nique.
pictorial, *a.* (*a*) En images. (*b*) Illustré.
picture[1], *s.* **1.** Image *f* ; tableau *m* ; peinture *f* ; gravure *f.* **2.** The pictures, le ciné.
picture[2], *v.tr.* **1.** Dépeindre, représenter. **2.** To p. to oneself, se figurer.
picture-book, *s.* Livre *m* d'images
picture-card, *s.* Figure *f.*
picturesque, *a.* Pittoresque.
pie, *s.* (*a*) Meat pie, pâté *m.* (*b*) Fruit pie, tourte *f.*
piebald, *a.* (*a*) Pie. (*b*) Bigarré.
piece[1], *s.* Pièce *f.* **1.** (*a*) Morceau *m* ; bout *m.* (*b*) Fragment *m.* To come to pieces, s'en aller en morceaux. **2.** Partie *f.* To take to pieces, démonter, défaire. **3.** All in one p., tout d'une pièce. **4.** P. of advice, conseil *m.*
piecemeal, *adv.* Par morceaux.
piecrust, *s.* Croûte *f* de pâté.
pied, *a.* Mi-parti ; bariolé, bigarré.
pie-dish, *s.* Terrine *f* ; tourtière *f.*
pier, *s.* **1.** Jetée *f*, digue *f* ; quai *m.* **2.** Pilier *m.*
pierce, *v.tr.* Percer, transpercer.
piercing, *a.* Aigu, -uë, perçant ; pénétrant.
piety, *s.* Piété *f.*
pig, *s.* Porc *m*, cochon *m.*
pigeon, *s.* Pigeon *m.*
pigeon-hole[1], *s.* Case *f.*
pigeon-hole[2], *v.tr.* Caser, classer.
pigeon-house, *s.* Colombier *m*, pigeonnier *m.*
pigheaded, *a.* Obstiné, entêté.
pigment, *s.* Matière colorante ; colorant *m.*
pigskin, *s.* Peau *f* de porc.
pigsty, *s.* Porcherie *f* ; étable *f* à porcs.

pike, s. Brochet m.
pile[1], s. Pieu m. **Built on piles,** bâti sur pilotis.
pile[2], s. Tas m, monceau m.
pile[3]. I. v.tr. (a) **To p. (up),** entasser, amasser. 2. v.i. **To p. up,** s'amonceler, s'entasser.
pilgrim, s. Pèlerin, -ine.
pilgrimage, s. Pèlerinage m.
pill, s. Pilule f.
pillage[1], s. Pillage m.
pillage[2], v.tr. Piller, saccager.
pillar, s. Pilier m; colonne f.
pillar-box, s. Borne postale.
pillion, s. Siège m arrière. **To ride p.,** monter derrière.
pillow, s. Oreiller m.
pillow-case, s. Taie f d'oreiller.
pilot[1], s. (a) Pilote m. (b) Guide m.
pilot[2], v.tr. (a) Piloter. (b) Conduire.
pilot-lamp, s. Lampe f témoin.
pimento, s. Piment m.
pimple, s. Bouton m.
pin[1], s. I. Épingle f. 2. Goupille f, cheville f.
pin[2], v.tr. I. Épingler; attacher avec une épingle. 2. Fixer, clouer.
pinafore, s. Tablier m.
pincers, s.pl. Pince f, tenailles fpl.
pinch[1], s. I. (a) **To give s.o. a p.,** pincer qn. (b) **At a p.,** au besoin 2. Pincée f.
pinch[2], v.tr. I. Pincer. 2. Serrer, gêner.
pinched, a. I. Tiré, hâve. 2. Étroit.
pincushion, s. Pelote f à épingles.
pine[1], s. Pin m.
pine[2], v.i. Languir.
pine-apple, s. Ananas m.
pine-cone, s. Pomme f de pin
pin-hole, s. Trou m d'épingle.
pinion[1], s. I. Aileron m. 2. Penne f rémige f.
pinion[2], v.tr. Ligoter.
pink. I. s. Œillet m. 2. a. & s. Rose (m).
pinkish, a. Rosé, rosâtre.
pinnacle, s. I. (a) Cime f; pic m. (b) **Rock p,** gendarme m. 2. Sommet m; faîte m.
pin-prick, s. Coup m d'épingle.
pioneer, s. Pionnier m.
pious, a. Pieux.
pip[1], s. Point m.
pip[2], s. Pépin m.
pipe, s. I. Tuyau m. 2. Chalumeau m. 3. Pipe f.

piper, s. Joueur m de cornemuse.
piquancy, s. Sel m, piquant m.
piquant, a. Piquant.
pique[1], s. Pique f, ressentiment m.
pique[2], v.tr. I. Piquer, dépiter. 2. Piquer, exciter.
piracy, s. Piraterie f.
pirate, s. Pirate m.
piratical, a. De pirate.
pistachio, s. Pistache f.
pistol, s. Pistolet m.
pistol-shot, s. Coup m de pistolet.
piston, s. Piston m.
pit, s. I. (a) Fosse f, trou m. (b) Mine f. 2. Parterre m. 3. Petite cavité, piqûre f.
pitch[1], s. Poix f; brai m.
pitch[2], s. I. Terrain m entre les guichets. 2. (a) Hauteur f; diapason m. (b) Degré m. **To such a p.,** à tel point.
pitch[3]. I. v.tr. I. Dresser. 2. Lancer; jeter.
 II. **pitch,** v.i. Tanguer.
pitch-dark, a. **It is p.-d.,** il fait nuit noire.
pitcher, s. Cruche f; broc m
pitchfork, s. Fourche f.
piteous, a. Pitoyable, piteux.
piteously, adv. Pitoyablement.
pitfall, s. Trappe f; piège m.
pith, s. I. Moelle f. 2. (a) Sève f ardeur f. (b) Essence f.
pithy, a. Concis; substantiel.
pitiable, a. Pitoyable, piteux.
pitiably, adv. Pitoyablement.
pitiful, a. I. Compatissant; plein de pitié. 2. (a) Pitoyable, lamentable. (b) Lamentable.
pitifully, adv. I. Avec compassion. 2. Pitoyablement.
pitiless, a. Impitoyable; sans pitié.
pitilessly, adv. Sans pitié.
pittance, s. Maigre salaire m.
pity[1], s. Pitié f. (a) Compassion f. (b) **What a p.!** quel dommage !
pity[2], v.tr. Plaindre; avoir pitié de.
pitying, a. Compatissant.
pivot, s. Pivot m; axe m.
placard, s. Écriteau m; affiche f
placate, v.tr. Apaiser, calmer.
place[1], s. I. (a) Lieu m, endroit m, localité f. **In another p.,** autre part; ailleurs. **This is no p. for you,** vous n'avez que faire ici. (b) **P. of residence,** demeure f. (c) Cour f, ruelle f.

2. Place *f*. **To lay a p.**, mettre un couvert. **Remark out of p.**, observation hors de propos, déplacée. **To take p.**, avoir lieu ; se passer. **3.** Place, rang *m*. **To keep one's p.**, observer les distances. **4.** Place, poste *m*, emploi *m*.

place², *v.tr.* **1.** Placer ; mettre **2.** Donner un rang à.

placid, *a.* Placide, calme, tranquille.

placidity, *s.* Placidité *f*, calme *m*.

placidly, *adv.* Avec calme ; tranquillement.

plague¹, *s.* **1.** Fléau *m*. **2.** Peste *f*.

plague², *v.tr.* Tourmenter.

plaice, *s.* Carrelet *m* ; plie *f*.

plain. I. *a.* **1.** Clair, évident. **In p. figures**, en chiffres connus. **2.** (*a*) **In p. clothes**, en civil. (*b*) Uni, lisse. (*c*) **P. cooking**, cuisine bourgeoise. **3.** Laid ; sans beauté.
II. **plain**, *adv.* Clairement, distinctement.
III. **plain**, *s.* Plaine *f*.

plainly, *adv.* **1.** Clairement, manifestement, évidemment. **2.** (*a*) Simplement. (*b*) Franchement, carrément. **To speak p.**, user du franc-parler.

plainness, *s.* **1.** Clarté *f* ; netteté *f*. **2.** (*a*) Simplicité *f*. (*b*) Franchise *f*. **3.** Manque *m* de beauté ; laideur *f*.

plain-speaking, *s.* Franchise *f* ; franc-parler *m*.

plaintiff, *s.* Plaignant, -ante.

plaintive, *a.* Plaintif.

plaintively, *adv.* Plaintivement ; d'un ton plaintif.

plait¹, *s.* Natte *f*, tresse *f*.

plait², *v.tr.* Natter, tresser.

plan¹, *s.* **1.** Plan *m* ; cadre *m*. **2.** Projet *m*, plan. **According to p.**, selon les prévisions.

plan², *v.tr.* Projeter, se proposer

plane¹, *a.* Plan, uni ; plat.

plane², *s.* **1.** Plan *m*. **2.** Avion *m*

plane³, *s.* Rabot *m*.

plane⁴, *v.tr.* Raboter ; aplanir.

plane⁵, *s.* **P.(-tree)**, platane *m*.

planet, *s.* Planète *f*.

plank, *s.* Planche *f*.

plant¹, *s.* **1.** Plante *f*. **2.** Appareil(s) *m*(*pl*) ; installation *f*.

plant², *v.tr.* Planter.

plantain, *s.* Banane *f*.

plantation, *s.* Plantation *f*.

planter, *s.* Planteur *m*.

plaque, *s.* Plaque *f*.

plaster¹, *s.* **1.** Emplâtre *m*. **Adhesive p.**, sparadrap *m*. **Court p.**, taffetas gommé. **2.** Plâtre *m* **P. of Paris**, plâtre de moulage.

plaster², *v.tr.* Plâtrer.

plastic, *a.* **1.** Plastique. **2.** *s.pl.* Plastique(s) *m*.

plate, *s.* **1.** Plaque *f*. **2.** (*a*) **Hot p.**, plaque chauffante. (*b*) **Number p.**, plaque matricule. (*c*) Dentier *m*. **3.** Gravure *f*. **4.** Vaisselle *f* d'or, d'argent. **5.** Assiette *f*.

plateau, *s.* Plateau *m*.

plateful, *s.* Assiettée *f*.

plate-glass, *s.* Glace *f* sans tain ; glace de vitrage.

plate-rack, *s.* Porte-assiettes *m inv.*

platform, *s.* **1.** Terrasse *f*. **2.** (*a*) Plateforme *f*. (*b*) Quai *m*, trottoir *m*. **3.** Estrade *f*, tribune *f*.

platinum, *s.* Platine *m*.

platitude, *s.* Platitude *f*.

platter, *s.* Plat *m* (de bois).

plausibility, *s.* Plausibilité *f*.

plausible, *a.* **1.** (*a*) Plausible. (*b*) Spécieux. **2.** Enjôleur, -euse.

plausibly, *adv.* Plausiblement.

play¹, *s.* **1.** Jeu *m*. **In full p.**, en pleine activité. **2.** Jeu, amusement *m*. **3.** (*a*) Pièce *f* de théâtre. (*b*) Spectacle *m*.

play². I. *v.i.* **1.** Gambader, folâtrer. **2.** Jouer.
II. **play**, *v.tr. or ind.tr.* **1.** **To p. (at) billiards**, jouer au billard. **2.** **To p. the piano**, jouer du piano.
III. **play**, *v.tr.* **1.** Jouer. **2.** **To p. a game of tennis**, faire une partie de tennis. **To p. a match**, disputer un match. **3.** **To p. s.o. false**, trahir qn.

player, *s.* Joueur, -euse.

playfellow, *s.* Camarade *mf* de jeu.

playful, *a.* Enjoué, badin, folâtre.

playfully, *adv.* Gaiement ; en badinant.

playfulness, *s.* Enjouement *m*, badinage *m*.

playgoer, *s.* Habitué, -ée, des spectacles.

playground, *s.* Cour *f* de récréation.

playing-card, *s.* Carte *f* à jouer.

playmate, *s.* Camarade *mf* de jeu.

plaything, *s.* Jouet *m*.

playtime, s. Récréation f.

playwright, s. Auteur m dramatique.

plea, s. **1.** Défense f. **2.** (a) Excuse f, prétexte m. (b) Appel m (for, à).

plead. 1. v.i. Plaider. **To p. guilty,** s'avouer coupable. **2.** v.tr (a) Plaider. (b) Prétexter.

pleasant, a **1.** Agréable aimable. **2.** Affable.

pleasantly, adv. **1.** Agréablement **2.** Avec affabilité.

pleasantry, s. Plaisanterie f.

please, v.tr. **1.** Plaire à ; faire plaisir à ; contenter! **Hard to p.,** difficile. **P. yourself!** faites à votre guise. **2.** (If you) p., s'il vous plaît. **P. be seated,** veuillez vous asseoir. **3.** Abs. Do as you p., faites comme vous voudrez.

pleased, a. Satisfait, content.

pleasing, a. Agréable.

pleasurable, a. Agréable.

pleasure, s. **1.** Plaisir m. **P. trip,** voyage d'agrément. **2.** Volonté f; bon plaisir.

pleat[1], s. Pli m.

pleat[2], v.tr Plisser.

pledge[1], s. **1.** Gage m. **2.** Promesse f, vœu m.

pledge[2], v.tr. **1.** Mettre en gage **2.** Engager. **3.** Boire à la santé de.

plentiful, a Abondant, copieux.

plentifully, adv Abondamment ; copieusement.

plenty, s. Abondance f. **You have p. of time,** vous avez largement le temps.

pliable, a. **1.** Flexible ; souple. **2.** Docile, complaisant.

pliers, s.pl. Pince f, tenaille f.

plight, s. Condition f, état m.

plinth, s. Plinthe f ; socle m.

plod, v.i. **1.** Marcher péniblement. **2.** Travailler laborieusement.

plot[1], s. **1.** Parcelle f (de terrain). **2.** Intrigue f. **3.** Complot m, conspiration f.

plot[2], v.tr. & i. Comploter, conspirer.

plotter, s. Conspirateur, -trice.

plough[1], s. Charrue f.

plough[2], v.tr. (a) Labourer. Abs. Labourer la terre. **Ploughed lands,** labours m. (b) Fendre, sillonner.

ploughman, s. Laboureur m.

ploughshare, s. Soc m de charrue.

plover, s. Pluvier m.

pluck[1], s. Courage m, cran m.

pluck[2], v.tr **1.** Arracher ; cueillir. **2.** Plumer.

pluckily, adv. Courageusement.

plucky, a. Courageux.

plug[1], s. **1.** Tampon m, bouchon m. **2.** Cheville f ; fiche f de connexion. **Wall p.,** prise f de courant.

plug[2], v.tr. Boucher, tamponner.

plum, s. Prune f. **P.(-tree),** prunier m.

plumage, s. Plumage m.

plumb, v.tr. Sonder.

plumber, s. Plombier m.

plumbing, s. **1.** Plomberie f. **2.** Coll. Tuyauterie f.

plum-cake, s. Gâteau m aux raisins

plume, s. Panache m, plumet m.

plump, a. Rebondi, grassouillet, -ette, dodu ; bien en chair.

plumpness, s. Embonpoint m

plunder[1], s. Butin m.

plunder[2], v.tr. Piller, dépouiller.

plunge[1], s. Plongeon m.

plunge[2]. **1.** v.tr. Plonger, immerger. **2.** v.i. (a) Plonger (b) Ruer. (c) Jouer sans compter.

plural, a. & s. Pluriel (m).

plus. 1. prep. Plus. **2.** s. Plus m.

plus-fours, s.pl. Culotte f de golf.

plush, s. Peluche f.

plutocrat, s. Ploutocrate m.

ply. 1. v.tr. (a) Manier vigoureusement. (b) Exercer. (c) **To ply with questions,** presser de questions. **2.** v.i. Faire le service.

plywood, s (Bois) contre-plaqué m.

p.m. De l'après-midi, du soir.

pneumatic, a. Pneumatique.

pneumonia, s. Pneumonie f.

poach[1], v.tr. Pocher.

poach[2], v.tr. & i Braconner.

poacher, s. Braconnier m.

poaching, s. Braconnage m.

pocket[1], s. **1.** (a) Poche f. **P. edition,** édition de poche. (b) **To be in p.,** être en bénéfice. **I am out of p. by it,** j'y suis de ma poche. **2.** Blouse f.

pocket[2], v.tr. **1.** Empocher ; mettre dans sa poche. **2.** Blouser.

pocket-book, s. (a) Carnet m de poche ; calepin m. (b) Portefeuille m.

pocketful, s. Pleine poche ; pochée f.

pocket-handkerchief, s. Mouchoir m de poche.

pocket-knife, s. Couteau m de poche.

pocket-money, *s.* Argent *m* de poche.
pod, *s.* Cosse *f*, gousse *f*.
poem, *s.* Poème *m*; poésie *f*.
poet, *s.* Poète *m*.
poetic(al), *a.* Poétique.
poetically, *adv.* Poétiquement.
poetry, *s.* Poésie *f*. **To write** p.,
écrire des vers. **Piece of** p., poésie.
poignant, *a.* Poignant, vif; angoissant.
point[1], *s.* I. Point *m*. **1. Decimal** p.,
virgule *f*. **2. From all points of view,**
sous tous ses aspects. **3.** (*a*) Point,
détail *m*. **To make a** p. **of,** se faire
un devoir de. **In** p. **of fact,** par le
fait. (*b*) **Here is the** p., voici ce dont
il s'agit. (*c*) Qualité *f*. **4.** (*a*) **I was
on the** p. **of jumping,** j'allais sauter.
(*b*) **To come to the** p., arriver au fait.
    II. **point,** *s.* **1.** Pointe *f*. **2.** *pl.*
Aiguillage *m*; aiguille *f*. **3. P. of
the compass,** aire *f* de vent.
point[2]. I. *v.tr.* Tailler en pointe.
    II. **point,** *v.i.* **To** p. **at,** montrer
du doigt. **point out,** *v.tr.* **1.**
Montrer du doigt. **2.** Signaler.
point-blank. 1. *a.* De but en blanc;
net, *f.* nette. **2.** *adv.* A bout
portant. **To refuse** p.-b., refuser net.
pointed, *a.* **1.** Pointu; à pointe.
2. Peu équivoque.
pointedly, *adv.* D'une manière
marquée.
pointer, *s.* (*a*) Aiguille *f*, index *m*.
(*b*) Baguette *f*.
pointless, *a.* (*a*) Fade. (*b*) Qui ne
rime à rien.
pointsman, *s.* Aiguilleur *m*.
poise[1], *s.* Équilibre *m*, aplomb *m*.
poise[2], *v.tr.* (*a*) Équilibrer. (*b*) Balancer.
poison[1], *s.* Poison *m*. **To take** p.,
s'empoisonner.
poison[2], *v.tr.* (*a*) Empoisonner.
(*b*) Corrompre.
poisoner, *s.* Empoisonneur, -euse.
poisoning, *s.* Empoisonnement *m*;
intoxication *f*.
poisonous, *a.* Toxique; em-
poisonné; venimeux; vénéneux.
poke[1], *s.* Poussée *f*.
poke[2]. I. *v.tr.* **1.** Pousser. **2.** Tisonner. **3. To** p. **fun at,** se moquer de.
    II. **poke,** *v.i.* **To** p. (**about**),
fouiller.
poker[1], *s.* Tisonnier *m*.
poker[2], *s.* Poker *m*.

Poland. *Pr.n.* La Pologne.
polar, *a.* Polaire. **P. bear,** ours blanc.
pole[1], *s.* (*a*) Perche *f*. **Tent** p., mât *m*,
montant *m*, de tente. (*b*) Timon *m*.
flèche *f*.
pole[2], *s.* Pôle *m*.
Pole[3], *s.* Polonais, -aise.
pole-axe, *s.* Merlin *m*; assommoir *m*.
polecat, *s.* Putois *m*.
pole-star (the), *s.* L'étoile *f* polaire.
police, *s.* Police *f*. (*a*) **P. station,**
poste *m* de police. (*b*) **The** p., la
Sûreté.
policeman, *s.* Agent *m* (de police).
sergent *m* de ville.
policewoman, *s.* Femme-agent *f* (de
police), *pl.* femmes-agents.
policy[1], *s.* **1.** Politique *f*; ligne *f* de
conduite. **2.** Diplomatie *f*.
policy[2], *s.* Police *f* (d'assurance).
polish[1], *s.* **1.** Poli *m*, brillant *m*, lustre
m. **2. Nail** p., vernis *m* pour les
ongles. **3.** Belles manières.
polish[2], *v.tr.* Polir; cirer; faire
reluire.
Polish[3], *a.* Polonais.
polished, *a.* Poli, brillant.
polite, *a.* Poli, courtois.
politely, *adv.* Poliment.
politeness, *s.* Politesse *f*, civilité *f*.
politic, *a.* Politique, avisé.
political, *a.* Politique.
politician, *s.* Homme *m* politique.
politics, *s.pl.* La politique.
poll, *s.* Vote *m*; scrutin *m*.
polling, *s.* Vote *m*; élections *fpl.*
pollute, *v.tr.* Polluer, corrompre.
pollution, *s.* Pollution *f*, souillure *f*.
polygamist, Polygame *mf*.
polygamy, *s.* Polygamie *f*.
polyglot, *a.* & *s.* Polyglotte (*mf*).
polygon, *s.* Polygone *m*.
polytechnic. 1. *a.* Polytechnique.
2. *s.* École professionnelle.
pomade, *s.* Pommade *f*.
pomegranate, *s.* Grenade *f*.
pomp, *s.* Pompe *f*, éclat *m*, splendeur *f*.
pompon, *s.* Pompon *m*.
pomposity, *s.* Emphase *f*, suffisance *f*.
pompous, *a.* **1.** Pompeux, fastueux.
2. Suffisant.
pompously, *adv.* Pompeusement.
pond, *s.* Étang *m*; mare *f*.
ponder. 1. *v.tr.* Réfléchir sur;
ruminer. **2.** *v.i.* Méditer.

14

ponderous, *a.* Lourd, pesant.

pontiff, *s.* Pontife *m*; pape *m*; évêque *m*.

pontifical, *a.* Pontifical, -aux.

pontoon, *s.* Ponton.

pontoon-bridge, *s.* Pont *m* de bateaux.

pony, *s.* Poney *m*.

pony-carriage, *s.* Panier *m*.

poodle, *s.* Caniche *mf*.

pool¹, *s.* **1.** Mare *f*. **2.** Trou *m* d'eau.

pool², *s.* Fonds communs; masse commune.

pool³, *v.tr.* Mettre en commun.

poop, *s.* Poupe *f*.

poor, *a.* Pauvre. **1.** (*a*) Besogneux, malheureux. (*b*) *s.pl.* **The p.,** les pauvres *m*, les indigents. **2.** De piètre qualité. **P. quality,** basse qualité. **P. health,** santé débile.

poorly. **1.** *adv.* Pauvrement, médiocrement. **2.** *pred.a.* Indisposé.

poorness, *s.* **1.** Pauvreté *f*, insuffisance *f*. **2.** Infériorité *f*.

pop. **1.** *int.* Crac! pan! **To go pop,** éclater, crever. **2.** *s.* Bruit sec.

pope, *s.* Pape *m*.

popish, *a.* Papiste.

poplar, *s.* Peuplier *m*.

poppy, *s.* Pavot *m*. **Corn p.,** coquelicot *m*.

populace, *s.* Populace *f*.

popular, *a.* Populaire.

popularity, *s.* Popularité *f*.

popularize, *v.tr.* (*a*) Populariser. (*b*) Rendre populaire.

popularly, *adv.* Populairement

populate, *v.tr.* Peupler.

population, *s.* Population *f*.

populous, *a.* Populeux; très peuplé.

porcelain, *s.* Porcelaine *f*.

porch, *s.* (*a*) Porche *m*. portique *m*. (*b*) Marquise *f*.

porcupine, *s.* Porc-épic *m*, *pl.* porcs-épics.

pore¹, *s.* Pore *m*.

pore², *v.i.* **To p. over a book,** être plongé dans un livre.

pork, *s.* Porc *m*. **Salt p.,** petit salé.

pork-butcher, *s.* Charcutier, -ière.

pork-pie, *s.* Pâté *m* de porc.

porous, *a.* Poreux, perméable.

porpoise, *s.* Marsouin *m*.

porridge, *s.* Bouillie *f* d'avoine.

port¹, *s.* Port *m*.

port², *s. Nau:* Bâbord *m*.

port³, *s.* Vin *m* de Porto; porto *m*.

portable, *a.* Portatif; mobile. **P. wireless set,** poste transportable.

portal, *s.* (*a*) Portail *m*. (*b*) Portique *m*.

portend, *v.tr.* Présager, augurer.

portent, *s.* **1.** Présage *m* de malheur. **2.** Prodige *m*.

portentous, *a.* **1.** Menaçant. **2.** Prodigieux. **3.** Solennel.

porter¹, *s.* Portier *m*, concierge *m*.

porter², *s.* **1.** Portefaix *m*; chasseur *m*; porteur *m*. **2.** Bière brune.

porterage, *s.* **1.** Transport *m*. **2.** Prix *m* de transport.

portfolio, *s.* (*a*) Serviette *f*. (*b*) Chemise *f* de carton. (*c*) Portefeuille *m*.

port-hole, *s.* Sabord *m*, hublot *m*.

portico, *s.* Portique *m*.

portion, *s.* (*a*) Partie *f*; part *f*. (*b*) Portion *f*, ration *f*.

portly, *a.* **1.** Majestueux. **2.** Corpulent, ventru.

portmanteau, *s.* Valise *f*.

portrait, *s.* Portrait *m*.

portray, *v.tr.* Dépeindre, décrire.

portrayal, *s.* Peinture *f*, description *f*.

Portugal. *Pr.n.* Le Portugal.

Portuguese. **1.** *a. & s.* Portugais, -aise. **2.** *s.* Le portugais.

pose¹, *s.* **1.** Pose *f*, attitude *f*. **2.** Affectation *f*.

pose². I. *v.tr.* Poser.
II. **pose.** *v.i.* **1.** Poser. **2.** **To p. as,** se faire passer pour.

posing, *s.* Pose *f*.

position, *s.* **1.** Posture *f*, attitude *f*. **2.** Position *f*; place *f*; situation *f*. **3.** (*a*) État *m*, condition *f*. **To be in a p. to do sth.,** être à même de faire qch. (*b*) Rang social. **4.** Emploi *m*, poste *m*.

positive, *a.* **1.** Positif, affirmatif. **2.** (*a*) Convaincu, certain. (*b*) Absolu, tranchant.

positively, *adv.* **1.** Positivement, affirmativement. **2.** Assurément.

possess, *v.tr.* **1.** Avoir, posséder. **2.** **To p. oneself of,** s'emparer de. **3.** **What possessed you?** qu'est-ce qui vous a pris.

possession, *s.* **1.** Possession *f*, jouissance *f*. **To take p. of,** s'emparer de. **2.** Objet possédé; possession.

possibility, *s.* **1.** Possibilité *f*. **2.** Événement *m* possible; éventualité *f*.

possible, *a.* Possible. **As far as p.,** dans la mesure du possible. **As early as p.,** le plus tôt possible.

possibly, *adv.* **1.** I cannot p. do it, il ne m'est pas possible de le faire. **2.** Peut-être; c'est possible; cela se peut.

post¹, *s.* Poteau *m*, montant *m*.

post², *v.tr.* Placarder; afficher.

post³, *s.* **1.** Courrier *m*. **By return of p.,** par retour du courrier. **2.** Poste *f*. **To send by post,** envoyer par la poste.

post⁴, *v.tr.* Mettre à la poste.

post⁵, *s.* Poste *m*; situation *f*.

postage, *s.* Port *m*, affranchissement *m*.

postal, *a.* Postal, -aux.

postcard, *s.* Carte postale. **Picture p.,** carte postale illustrée.

poster, *s.* Affiche murale.

posterity, *s.* Postérité *f*.

post-free, *attrib. a.* Franc de port; en franchise; franco *inv.*

post-haste, *adv.* En toute hâte.

posthumous, *a.* Posthume.

postman, *s.* Facteur *m*.

postmark, *s.* Timbre *m* d'oblitération.

postmaster, *s.* Receveur *m* des Postes.

postmistress, *s.* Receveuse *f* des Postes.

post-mortem, *s.* Autopsie *f*.

post-office, *s.* Bureau *m* de(s) poste(s); poste *f*.

post-paid, *a.* Affranchi; port payé.

postpone, *v.tr.* Remettre, différer.

postponement, *s.* Remise *f* à plus tard; renvoi *m*; ajournement *m*.

postscript, *s.* Post-scriptum *m inv.*

posture, *s.* Posture *f*, attitude *f*.

post-war, *attrib.a.* D'après guerre.

pot, *s.* (*a*) Pot *m*. (*b*) Marmite *f*. **Pots and pans,** batterie *f* de cuisine

potash, *s.* Potasse *f*.

potassium, *s.* Potassium *m*.

potato, *s.* Pomme *f* de terre. **Boiled potatoes,** pommes de terre à l'eau. **Baked potatoes,** pommes de terre au four.

potency, *s.* Force *f*, puissance *f*.

potent, *a.* Efficace; puissant.

potentate, *s.* Potentat *m*.

potential. *a.* (*a*) En puissance; virtuel; latent. (*b*) Potentiel.

potentially, *adv.* Potentiellement, virtuellement.

potion, *s.* Potion *f*; dose *f*.

potted, *a.* En pot, en terrine.

potter, *s.* Potier *m*.

pottery, *s.* **1.** Poterie *f*. **2.** Vaisselle *f* de terre.

pouch, *s.* Petit sac; bourse *f*.

poulterer, *s.* Marchand *m* de volaille.

poultice¹, *s.* Cataplasme *m*.

poultice², *v.tr.* Mettre un cataplasme sur.

poultry, *s.* *Coll.* Volaille *f*.

poultry-yard, *s.* Basse-cour *f*, *pl.* basses-cours.

pounce, *v.i.* (*a*) Fondre, s'abattre. (*b*) Se jeter.

pound¹, *s.* Livre *f*.

pound², *v.tr.* Broyer, piler.

pour. **1.** *v.tr.* Verser. **2.** *v.i.* Tomber à verse. **pour out. 1.** *v.tr.* Verser. **2.** *v.i.* Sortir à flots.

pouring, *a.* Torrentiel; battant.

pout¹, *s.* Moue *f*.

pout², *v.i.* (*a*) Faire la moue. (*b*) Bouder.

poverty, *s.* Pauvreté *f*.

poverty-stricken, *a.* Dans la misère.

powder¹, *s.* Poudre *f*.

powder², *v.tr.* **1.** Saupoudrer (*with*, de). **2.** To p. (one's face), se poudrer le visage. **3.** Réduire en poudre.

powder-puff, *s.* Houppe *f*.

power, *s.* **1.** Pouvoir *m*. **2.** Faculté *f*, capacité *f*. **3.** Vigueur *f*, force *f*. **4.** Puissance *f*; force. **5.** Pouvoir, influence *f*, autorité *f*.

powerful, *a.* (*a*) Puissant. (*b*) Fort, vigoureux.

powerfully, *adv.* Puissamment; fortement.

powerless, *a.* Impuissant.

powerlessness, *s.* Impuissance *f*.

power station, *s.* Station génératrice.

practicability, *s.* Praticabilité *f*.

practicable, *a.* Praticable.

practical, *a.* Pratique.

practically, *adv.* **1.** Pratiquement, en pratique. **2.** Pour ainsi dire.

practice, *s.* **1.** Pratique *f*. **2.** Habitude *f*, coutume *f*. **3.** Exercice *m*; usage *m*. **4.** Pratique, clientèle *f* **5.** *pl.* Pratiques, menées *fpl.*

practise, *v.tr.* **1.** Pratiquer; mettre en pratique. **2.** Pratiquer, exercer.

practised, *a.* Exercé, expérimenté.

practitioner, *s.* Praticien *m.* **Medical p.,** médecin *m.* **General p.,** médecin et chirurgien.

prairie, *s.* Prairie *f.*

praise[1], *s.* Éloge *m* ; louange *f.*

praise[2], *v.tr.* Louer, faire l'éloge de.

praiseworthy, *a.* Digne d'éloges ; méritoire.

prance, *v.i.* **1.** Fringuer ; piaffer. **2.** Se pavaner ; se carrer.

prank, *s.* **1.** Escapade *f*, frasque *f*, fredaine *f.* **2.** Tour *m*, farce *f.*

prattle[1], *s.* Babil *m*, babillage *m.*

prattle[2], *v.i.* Babiller.

prawn, *s.* Grande crevette.

pray, *v.tr. & i.* **1.** Prier, implorer, supplier. **2. P. take a seat,** veuillez vous asseoir.

prayer, *s.* **1.** Prière *f.* **To say one's prayers,** faire ses dévotions. **2.** Demande instante.

prayer-book, *s.* Livre *m* de prières.

preach, *v.i. & tr.* Prêcher.

preacher, *s.* Prédicateur *m.*

preamble, *s.* Préambule *m.*

precarious, *a.* Précaire, incertain.

precariously, *adv.* Précairement.

precaution, *s.* Précaution *f.*

precautionary, *a.* De précaution.

precede, *v.tr.* **1.** Précéder. **2.** Avoir le pas, la préséance, sur.

precedence, *s.* (*a*) Préséance *f* ; priorité *f.* (*b*) Droit *m* de priorité.

precedent, *s.* Précédent *m.*

preceding, *a.* Précédent.

precept, *s.* Précepte *m.*

preceptor, *s.* Précepteur *m.*

precinct, *s.* (*a*) Enceinte *f*, enclos *m.* (*b*) *pl.* Pourtour *m.*

precious, *a.* Précieux.

precipice, *s.* Précipice *m.*

precipitancy, *s.* Précipitation *f.*

precipitate[1], *a.* Précipité.

precipitate[2], *v.tr.* (*a*) Précipiter. (*b*) Accélérer, hâter, précipiter.

precipitately, *adv.* Précipitamment ; avec précipitation.

precipitation, *s.* Précipitation *f.*

precipitous, *a.* Escarpé, abrupt ; à pic.

precipitously, *adv.* A pic.

précis, *s.* Précis *m*, résumé *m.*

precise, *a.* **1.** Précis ; exact. **2.** Méticuleux.

precisely, *adv.* **1.** (*a*) Avec précision. (*b*) **At six o'clock p.,** à six heures précises. **2.** Parfaitement !

preciseness, *s.* **1.** Précision *f.* **2.** Méticulosité *f.*

precision, *s.* Précision *f.*

preclude, *v.tr.* Empêcher, prévenir.

precocious, *a.* Précoce.

precursor, *s.* Précurseur *m.*

predatory, *a.* Rapace, pillard.

predecease, *v.tr.* Mourir avant (qn).

predecessor, *s.* Prédécesseur *m.*

predicament, *s.* Situation *f* difficile

predict, *v.tr.* Prédire.

prediction, *s.* Prédiction *f.*

predilection, *s.* Prédilection *f.*

predisposition, *s.* Prédisposition *f.*

predominant, *a.* Prédominant.

predominate, *v.i.* Prédominer.

predominating, *a.* Prédominant.

pre-eminent, *a.* (*a*) Prééminent. (*b*) Remarquable.

preface, *s.* **1.** Préface *f* ; avant-propos *m inv.* **2.** Introduction *f.*

prefect, *s.* Préfet *m.*

prefer, *v.tr.* **1. To p. a complaint,** porter plainte. **2.** Préférer, aimer mieux.

preferable, *a.* Préférable.

preferably, *adv.* Préférablement.

preference, *s.* Préférence *f.* **In p.,** préférablement.

preferential, *a.* Préférentiel.

preferment, *s.* Avancement *m.*

prefix[1], *s.* Préfixe *m.*

prefix[2], *v.tr.* Mettre comme introduction.

prehensile, *a.* Préhensile.

prehistoric, *a.* Préhistorique.

prejudge, *v.tr.* Préjuger.

prejudice[1], *s.* **1.** Préjudice *m*, tort *m.* dommage *m.* **2.** Préjugé *m.*

prejudice[2], *v.tr.* **1.** Nuire, porter préjudice, à. **2.** Prévenir, prédisposer.

prejudiced, *a.* (i) Prévenu ; (ii) à préjugés. **To be p.,** avoir des préjugés.

prejudicial, *a.* Préjudiciable.

prelate, *s.* Prélat *m.*

preliminary, **1.** *a.* Préliminaire, préalable. **2.** *s.* (*a*) Prélude *m.* (*b*) *pl.* Préliminaires *m.*

prelude, *s.* Prélude *m* (*to*, de).

premature, *a.* Prématuré.

prematurely, *adv.* Prématurément.

premeditate, *v.tr.* Préméditer.

premeditated, *a.* Prémédité ; réfléchi.

premeditation, s. Préméditation f.

premier. **1.** a. Premier. **2.** s. Premier ministre.

premises, s.pl. Local, -aux. On the p., sur les lieux.

premium, s. **1.** Prix m, récompense f; prime f. **2.** Prix convenu, indemnité f. **3.** To be at a p., faire prime.

premonition, s. Prémonition f.

premonitory, a. Prémonitoire.

preoccupation, s. Préoccupation f.

preoccupied, a. Préoccupé.

preoccupy, v.tr. Préoccuper.

preparation, s. **1.** Préparation f. **2.** pl. Préparatifs m.

preparatory. **1.** a. Préparatoire, préalable. **2.** adv. Préalablement.

prepare. **1.** v.tr. Préparer. **2.** v.i. Se préparer, se disposer.

prepared, a. Préparé, prêt.

prepay, v.tr. Payer d'avance; affranchir.

preponderant, a. Prépondérant.

preponderating, a. Prépondérant.

preposition, s. Préposition f.

prepossessed, a. **1.** Imbu, imprégné (with, de); pénétré. **2.** Prévenu.

prepossessing, a. Agréable, prévenant.

prepossession, s. Prévention f; préjugé m.

preposterous, a. Absurde.

prerogative, s. Prérogative f.

presage[1], s. (a) Présage m. (b) Pressentiment m.

presage[2], v.tr. Présager, annoncer.

prescribe, v.tr. Prescrire, ordonner.

prescription, s. Ordonnance f.

presence, s. **1.** Présence f. **2.** Air m, mine f.

present[1]. **I.** a. **1.** Présent. All p., toute l'assistance. **2.** (a) Présent. At the p. time, à présent. (b) En question; que voici.

II. **present,** s. Up to the p., jusqu'à présent. At p., à présent; actuellement. For the p., pour le moment.

present[2], s. Cadeau m, présent m.

present[3], v.tr. **1.** Présenter. **2.** Donner.

presentable, a. Présentable.

presentation, s. Présentation f.

present-day, attrib.a. Actuel; d'aujourd'hui.

presentiment, s. Pressentiment m.

presently, adv. Tout à l'heure; dans un instant.

preservation, s. **1.** Conservation f. **2.** Préservation f.

preservative, a. & s. Préservatif (m).

preserve[1], s. **1.** Confiture f. **2.** (a) Réserve f. (b) Game p., chasse gardée.

preserve[2], v.tr. **1.** Préserver, garantir. **2.** Conserver.

preserved, a. **1.** Conservé; confit. **2.** Well p., en bon état de conservation.

preserver, s. Préservateur. -trice; sauveur m.

preside, v.i. Présider.

president, s. Président, -ente.

press[1], s. **1.** Presse f. **2.** The p., la presse, les journaux m.

press[2]. **I.** v.tr. Presser. **1.** (a) Appuyer, peser, sur. (b) Serrer. **2.** Insister sur. To p. one's advantage, poursuivre son avantage. **3.** Abs. Time presses, le temps presse.

II. **press,** v.i. Se serrer, se presser. **press forward, press on.** **1.** v.i. Presser, forcer, le pas. **2.** v.tr. Activer, hâter.

pressed, a. **1.** Pressé, serré, comprimé. **2.** To be hard p., être aux abois. P. for time, très pressé.

pressing, a. Pressant; pressé, urgent. P. invitation, invitation instante.

pressure, s. **1.** (a) Pression f; poussée f. (b) Blood p., tension artérielle. **2.** To bring p. to bear, exercer une pression. P. of business, presse f des affaires.

prestige, s. Prestige m.

presumably, adv. Probablement.

presume. **1.** v.tr. (a) Présumer; supposer. (b) Prendre la liberté, présumer. **2.** v.i. (a) To p. too much, trop présumer de soi. (b) Abs. Se montrer présomptueux. (c) To p. on, abuser de.

presumption, s. Présomption f.

presumptuous, a. Présomptueux.

pretence, s. **1.** Semblant m; simulation f; prétexte m. **2.** Prétention f.

pretend, v.tr. (a) Feindre, simuler. (b) Prétendre.

pretension, s. **1.** Prétention f. **2.** Droit m, titre m.

pretentious, a. Prétentieux.

pretext[1], s. Prétexte m.

pretext², *v.tr.* Alléguer comme prétexte ; prétexter.

prettily, *adv.* Joliment ; gentiment.

prettiness, *s.* Gentillesse *f.*

pretty. **1.** *a.* Joli ; beau, *f.* belle ;
gentil, -ille. **2.** *adv.* Assez. passablement.

prevail, *v.i.* **1.** Prévaloir ; l'emporter. **2.** To p. (up)on, amener,
décider. **3.** Prédominer, régner.

prevailing, *a.* Dominant. P. fashion,
mode en vogue.

prevalence, *s.* Prédominance *f* ;
généralité *f.*

prevalent, *a.* (Pré)dominant, répandu, général.

prevaricate, *v.i.* **1.** Équivoquer,
tergiverser. **2.** Mentir.

prevarication, *s.* **1.** Équivoques *fpl* ;
tergiversation *f.* **2.** Mensonge *m.*

prevent, *v.tr.* **1.** Empêcher, mettre
obstacle à. **2.** (*a*) Prévenir, détourner. (*b*) Éviter.

prevention, *s.* Empêchement *m.*

preventive. **1.** *a.* Préventif. **2.** *s.*
Empêchement *m.*

previous. **1.** *a.* Préalable ; antérieur,
-e ; précédent. **2.** *adv.* P. to, avant.

previously, *adv.* Préalablement ;
auparavant.

prevision, *s.* Prévision *f.*

pre-war, *attrib.a.* D'avant-guerre.

prey¹, *s.* Proie *f.*

prey², *v.i.* To p. upon, faire sa proie
de ; ronger, miner.

price¹, *s.* Prix *m.*

price², *v.tr.* **1.** Mettre un prix à.
2. Estimer, évaluer.

priceless, *a.* Hors de prix ; inestimable.

price-list, *s.* Prix-courant *m*, *pl.*
prix-courants.

prick¹, *s.* Piqûre *f.*

prick², *v.tr.* Piquer.

prickle, *s.* Piquant *m* ; épine *f.*

prickly, *a.* Hérissé ; armé de
piquants ; épineux.

pride¹, *s.* Orgueil *m.* (*a*) Fierté *f*,
morgue *f.* False p., vanité *f.*
(*b*) Amour-propre *m.*

pride², *v.pr.* To p. oneself (up)on,
s'enorgueillir de.

priest, *s.* Prêtre *m.*

priesthood, *s.* *Coll.* Clergé *m.*

priestly, *a.* Sacerdotal, -aux.

prig, *s.* Poseur *m.*

priggish, *a.* Poseur, suffisant.

prim, *a.* Collet monté *inv* ; guindé.

prima facie, *adv. & a.* De prime
abord, à première vue.

primary, *a.* **1.** Premier, primitif ;
primaire. **2.** Premier, essentiel.

prime¹, *a.* **1.** Premier ; principal,
-aux. **2.** De première qualité.
3. Premier, originel.

prime², *s.* In the p. of life, dans la
force de l'âge.

primitive, *a.* Primitif.

primly, *adv.* D'un air collet monté.

primness, *s.* Air *m* collet monté.

primrose, *s.* Primevère *f.*

prince, *s.* Prince *m.*

princely, *a.* Princier ; royal, -aux

princess, *s.* Princesse *f.*

principal. **I.** *a.* Principal, -aux　P.
clerk, premier commis.
　　II. **principal**, *s.* **1.** Directeur *m*,
chef *m*, patron *m.* **2.** Capital *m*,
principal *m.*

principality, *s.* Principauté *f.*

principally, *adv.* Principalement.

principle, *s.* Principe *m.* On p., par
principe.

print¹, *s.* **1.** Empreinte *f*, impression
f. **2.** (*a*) Out of p., épuisé. (*b*) Large
p., gros caractères. **3.** Gravure *f*,
image *f.* **4.** (*a*) Épreuve *f* ; copie *f.*
(*b*) Blue p., dessin négatif. **5.**
Indienne *f*, cotonnade *f.*

print², *v.tr.* Imprimer. 'Printed
matter,' "imprimés" *mpl.*

printer, *s.* Imprimeur *m.* Printer's
error, faute *f* d'impression.

printing, *s.* (*a*) Impression *f*, tirage
m. (*b*) Imprimerie *f.*

printing-press, *s.* Presse *f* d'imprimerie.

prior¹. **1.** *a.* Préalable, précédent ;
antérieur, -e. **2.** *adv.* Antérieurement.

prior², *s.* Prieur *m.*

prioress, *s.* Prieure *f.*

priority, *s.* Priorité *f*, antériorité *f.*

priory, *s.* Prieuré *f.*

prism, *s.* Prisme *m.*

prismatic, *a.* Prismatique.

prison, *s.* Prison *f.*

prisoner, *s.* Prisonnier, -ière.

pristine, *a.* Premier, primitif.

privacy, *s.* Intimité *f* ; retraite *f.*

private. **I.** *a.* Privé, particulier.
1. P. persons, (simples) particuliers.
2. Secret, -ète. **3.** In my p. opinion,

à mon avis personnel. **4. 'P.,'** "entrée interdite au public." P. **income**, rentes *fpl.*

II. **private**, *s.* **1.** *Adv.phr.* In p., sans témoins. **2.** Simple soldat *m.*

privately, *adv.* **1.** Privément; en simple particulier. **2.** En particulier.

privation, *s.* Privation *f.*

privet, *s.* Troène *m.*

privilege[1], *s.* Privilège *m.*

privilege[2], *v.tr.* Privilégier.

prize[1], *s.* **1.** Prix *m.* **2.** Lot *m.*

prize[2], *v.tr.* Évaluer, priser. To p. highly, faire grand cas de.

prize[3], *s.* Prise *f*, capture *f.*

prize-fighter, *s.* Boxeur professionnel.

prize-fighting, *s.* Boxe professionnelle.

prize-money, *s.* Part *f* de prise.

pro, *Lt. prep.* **1.** Pro forma, pour la forme. **2.** Pro tem(pore), *adv.phr.* temporairement. **3.** The pros and cons, le pour et le contre.

probability, *s.* Probabilité *f*; vraisemblance *f.*

probable, *a.* Probable.

probably, *adv.* Probablement; vraisemblablement.

probation, *s.* Épreuve *f*, stage *m.*

probationer, *s.* Stagiaire *mf.*

probe[1], *s.* Sonde *f.*

probe[2], *v.tr.* **1.** Sonder, explorer. **2.** Approfondir, fouiller. **3.** *v.i.* To p. into, sonder.

probity, *s.* Probité *f.*

problem, *s.* Problème *m.* P. play, pièce à thèse.

problematical, *a.* Problématique; douteux, incertain.

procedure, *s.* **1.** Procédé *m.* **2.** Procédure *f.*

proceed, *v.i.* **1.** (*a*) Continuer. Before we p. any farther, avant d'aller plus loin. (*b*) Se rendre. (*c*) How shall we p.? quelle est la marche à suivre? (*d*) Se mettre (à). **2.** (Se) continuer, se poursuivre. **3.** Procéder. **4.** Sortir, provenir.

proceeding, *s.* **1.** Façon *f* d'agir. **2.** (*a*) Procédé *m*, action *f.* (*b*) *pl.* Débats *m.*

proceeds, *s.pl.* Produit *m.*

process, *s.* **1.** (*a*) Processus *m.* It's a slow p., c'est un travail long. (*b*) Cours *m*, avancement *m.* **2.** Méthode *f*; procédé *m.*

procession, *s.* Cortège *m*; défilé *m.*

proclaim, *v.tr.* Proclamer; déclarer.

proclamation, *s.* Proclamation *f.*

proclivity, *s.* Penchant *m*, tendance *f*, inclination *f.*

procrastinate, *v.i.* Remettre les affaires à plus tard.

procrastination, *s.* Remise *f* des affaires à plus tard.

procreate, *v.tr.* Procréer, engendrer.

procurable, *a.* Procurable.

procuration, *s.* Procuration *f.*

procure, *v.tr.* Obtenir, procurer.

prod, *v.tr.* **1.** Pousser. **2.** Aiguillonner, stimuler.

prodigal, *a. & s.* Prodigue (*mf*).

prodigality, *s.* Prodigalité *f.*

prodigally, *adv.* En prodigue.

prodigious, *a.* Prodigieux.

prodigy, *s.* Prodige *m.*

produce[1], *s.* **1.** (*a*) Rendement *m.* (*b*) Produit *m.* **2.** Coll. Denrées *fpl.*

produce[2], *v.tr.* **1.** (*a*) Présenter. (*b*) Mettre en scène. **2.** (*a*) Créer. (*b*) Fabriquer. (*c*) Produire. **3.** Rapporter, rendre.

producer, *s.* Producteur. -trice; metteur *m* en scène.

product, *s.* Produit *m.*

production, *s.* **1.** (*a*) Production *f*; présentation *f.* (*b*) Mise *f* en scène. **2.** (*a*) Génération *f*; production. (*b*) Fabrication *f.* **3.** Produit *m.*

productive, *a.* Productif.

profane[1], *a.* Profane; impie.

profane[2], *v.tr.* Profaner.

profanity, *s.* Impiété *f.*

profess, *v.tr.* Professer. To p. oneself satisfied, se déclarer satisfait.

professed, *a.* (*a*) Déclaré. (*b*) Prétendu, soi-disant.

professedly, *adv.* De son propre aveu; ouvertement.

profession, *s.* **1.** Profession *f*, déclaration *f.* **2.** Profession, métier *m.*

professional. **1.** *a.* Professionnel. **2.** *s.* (*a*) Expert *m.* *pl.* Gens *m* de métier. (*b*) Professionnel, -elle.

professor, *s.* Professeur *m.*

proffer, *v.tr.* Offrir, présenter.

proficiency, *s.* Capacité *f*, compétence *f.*

proficient, *a.* Capable, compétent.

profile, *s.* Profil *m.*

profit[1], *s.* Profit *m*, bénéfice *m*; avantage *m.*

profit[2]. **I.** *v.tr.* Profiter à; être avantageux à. **2.** *v.i.* Profiter, bénéficier (*by*, de).

profitable, *a.* Profitable, avantageux.

profitably, *adv.* Profitablement, avantageusement.

profiteer[1], *s.* Profiteur, -euse; mercanti *m.*

profiteer[2], *v.i.* Faire des bénéfices excessifs.

profiteering, *s.* Mercantilisme *m*

profitless, *a.* Sans profit.

profligate, *a. & s.* **I.** Prodigue (-ée; libertin, -ine. **2.** Prodigue (*mf*).

profound, *a.* Profond.

profoundly, *adv.* Profondément.

profundity, *s.* Profondeur *f.*

profuse, *a.* **I.** To be p. in, se confondre en. **2.** Profus, abondant.

profusely, *adv.* Profusément.

profusion, *s.* Profusion *f.*

progeny, *s.* **I.** Progéniture *f.* **2.** Descendants *mpl.*

prognostic, *s.* Pronostic *m.*

prognosticate, *v.tr.* Pronostiquer.

programme, *s.* Programme *m.*

progress[1], *s.* (*a*) Marche *f* en avant; avancement *m*; cours *m.* (*b*) Progrès *m.*

progress[2], *v.i.* (*a*) S'avancer. (*b*) Faire des progrès.

progression, *s.* Progression *f.*

progressive, *a.* Progressif.

progressively, *adv.* Progressivement.

prohibit, *v.tr.* **I.** Prohiber, défendre, interdire. **2.** Empêcher.

prohibition, *s.* Prohibition *f*, interdiction *f*, défense *f.*

prohibitive, *a.* Prohibitif.

project[1], *s.* Projet *m.*

project[2]. **I.** *v.tr.* Projeter. **II. project**, *v.i.* Faire saillie.

projectile, *a. & s.* Projectile (*m*).

projecting, *a.* Saillant, en saillie.

projection, *s.* **I.** (*a*) Projection *f.* (*b*) Conception *f.* **2.** Saillie *f.*

prolific, *a.* Prolifique; fécond.

prolix, *a.* Prolixe, diffus.

prolixity, *s.* Prolixité *f.*

prologue, *s.* Prologue *m.*

prolong, *v.tr.* Prolonger.

prolongation, *s.* Prolongation *f.*

promenade[1], *s.* **I.** Promenade *f.* **2.** (*a*) Esplanade *f.* (*b*) Promenoir *m.*

promenade[2], *v.i.* Se promener.

prominence, *s.* (*a*) Proéminence *f*; relief *m.* (*b*) Saillie *f.*

prominent, *a.* **I.** Saillant; proéminent. **2.** (*a*) Remarquable. (*b*) Éminent.

prominently, *adv.* Éminemment.

promiscuity, *s.* Promiscuité *f.*

promiscuous, *a.* **I.** Confus, mêlé. **2.** Casuel, fortuit.

promiscuously, *adv.* **I.** Confusément. **2.** Casuellement.

promise[1], *s.* Promesse *f.* To show great p., donner de belles espérances.

promise[2], *v.tr.* (*a*) Promettre. (*b*) To p. well, s'annoncer bien.

promising, *a.* Plein de promesses.

promontory, *s.* Promontoire *m.*

promote, *v.tr.* **I.** Donner de l'avancement à. To be promoted, être promu. **2.** (*a*) Encourager; favoriser. (*b*) Lancer.

promoter, *s.* Instigateur, -trice.

promotion, *s.* Promotion *f*, avancement *m.*

prompt[1], *a.* Prompt. (*a*) Vif, rapide. (*b*) Immédiat.

prompt[2], *v.tr.* **I.** Inciter. **2.** Souffler.

prompter, *s.* Souffleur, -euse.

prompting, *s.* Suggestion *f*; incitation *f.*

promptitude, *s.* Promptitude *f*, empressement *m.*

promptly, *adv.* Promptement.

promulgate, *v.tr.* **I.** Promulguer. **2.** Disséminer, répandre.

promulgation, *s.* **I.** Promulgation *f.* **2.** Dissémination *f.*

prone, *a.* **I.** Couché sur le ventre. **2.** Enclin.

proneness, *s* Disposition *f* inclination *f.*

prong, *s.* Fourchon *m*, dent *f.*

pronged, *a.* A fourchons, à dents.

pronoun, *s.* Pronom *m.*

pronounce, *v.tr.* **I.** (*a*) Déclarer. (*b*) Prononcer.

pronounced, *a.* Prononcé, marqué.

pronouncement, *s.* Déclaration *f.*

pronunciation, *s.* Prononciation *f.*

proof[1], *s.* **I.** Preuve *f.* To give p. of, témoigner. **2.** Épreuve *f.*

proof[2], *a.* P. against, résistant à; à l'épreuve de.

prop[1], *s.* Appui *m*, support *m.*

prop[2], *v.tr.* Appuyer, soutenir.

propaganda, *s.* Propagande *f.*

propagate. I. *v.tr.* Propager. 2. *v.pr. & i.* Se propager, se reproduire.

propagation, *s.* Propagation *f* reproduction *f*.

propel, *v.tr.* Propulser ; pousser en avant.

propeller, *s.* I. Propulseur *m.* 2. Hélice *f*.

propensity, *s.* Propension *f*, penchant *m*, inclination *f*, tendance *f*.

proper, *a.* I. Propre. 2. Vrai, juste, approprié. 3. (*a*) Convenable. At the p. time, en temps opportun. To deem it p. to, juger bon de. (*b*) Comme il faut ; bienséant, correct.

properly, *adv.* I. (*a*) Proprement. (*b*) Bien ; de la bonne façon. 2. Convenablement ; comme il faut.

property, *s.* I. (*a*) Propriété *f*, biens *mpl*, avoir *m.* That's my p., cela m'appartient. (*b*) Immeuble *m*, immeubles. 2. Accessoire *m*. 3. Propriété ; qualité *f*.

prophecy, *s.* Prophétie *f*.

prophesy. I. *v.i.* Prophétiser. 2. *v.tr.* Prophétiser, prédire.

prophet, *s.* Prophète *m*.

prophetic, *a.* Prophétique.

prophetically, *adv.* Prophétiquement.

propitiate, *v.tr.* I. Rendre propice, favorable. 2. Apaiser.

propitiation, *s.* I. Propitiation *f*. 2. Apaisement *m*.

propitious, *a.* Propice, favorable.

proportion, *s.* I. Partie *f* ; portion *f* ; part *f*. 2. Rapport *m*, proportion *f*. (*a*) In p. as, à mesure que. (*b*) Out of p., mal proportionné. 3. *pl.* Proportions ; dimensions *f*.

proportional, *a.* Proportionnel ; en proportion (*to*, de).

proportionate, *a.* Proportionné.

proposal, *s.* I. (*a*) Proposition *f*, offre *f*. (*b*) Demande *f* en mariage. 2. Dessein *m*, projet *m*.

propose, *v.tr.* I. (*a*) Proposer. (*b*) To p. a toast, porter un toast. (*c*) Se proposer. What do you p. to do? que comptez-vous faire ? 2. *Abs.* Faire la demande en mariage.

proposer, *s.* Proposeur, -euse.

proposition, *s.* Proposition *f*, offre *f*.

propound, *v.tr.* Proposer.

proprietary, *a.* (*a*) De propriétaire. (*b*) P. article, spécialité *f*.

proprietor, *s.* Propriétaire *mf*.

propriety, *s.* I. Propriété *f*, justesse *f*, rectitude *f*. 2. Bienséance *f*.

propulsion, *s.* Propulsion *f*.

propulsive, *a.* Propulsif.

prorogue, *v.tr.* Proroger.

prosaic, *a.* Prosaïque.

proscribe, *v.tr.* Proscrire.

proscription, *s.* Proscription *f*.

prose, *s.* Prose *f*.

prosecute, *v.tr.* Poursuivre.

prosecution, *s.* I. Poursuites *fpl*. Witness for the p., témoin à charge. 2. Continuation *f*.

prosecutor, *s.* Plaignant, -e, demandeur, -eresse.

proselyte, *s.* Prosélyte *mf*.

prose-writer, *s.* Prosateur *m*.

prosody, *s.* Prosodie *f*.

prospect, *s.* I. Vue *f* ; perspective *f*. 2. Perspective ; expectative *f*. 3. *pl.* Avenir *m*, espérances *fpl*.

prospective, *a.* En perspective.

prospector, *s.* Prospecteur *m*.

prospectus, *s.* Prospectus *m*.

prosper, *v.i.* Prospérer, réussir.

prosperity, *s.* Prospérité *f*.

prosperous, *a.* Prospère, florissant.

prostrate[1]**,** *a.* I. Prosterné ; couché ; étendu. 2. Abattu.

prostrate[2]**,** *v.tr.* Accabler To p. oneself, se prosterner.

prostration, *s.* Abattement *m*.

prosy, *a.* Prosaïque ; verbeux.

protect, *v.tr.* (*a*) Protéger. (*b*) Sauvegarder.

protecting, *a.* Protecteur, -trice.

protection, *s.* I. (*a*) Protection *f* ; sauvegarde *f*. (*b*) Patronage *m*. 2. Abri *m*, protection.

protective, *a.* Protecteur, -trice.

protector, *s.* Protecteur *m*.

protectorate, *s.* Protectorat *m*.

protest[1]**,** *s.* Protestation *f*. Under p., en protestant.

protest[2]**.** I. *v.tr.* Protester. 2. *v.i.* Protester, réclamer.

protestant, *a. & s.* Protestant, -ante.

protestation, *s.* Protestation *f*.

protract, *v.tr.* Prolonger, allonger.

protrude, *v.i.* S'avancer, faire saillie.

protruding, *a.* En saillie ; saillant ; bombé.

protrusion, *s.* Saillie *f*.

protuberance, *s.* Protubérance *f*.

protuberant, *a.* Protubérant.

proud, *a.* Fier, orgueilleux.

proudly, *adv.* Fièrement ; avec fierté.

prove. I. *v.tr.* **1.** (*a*) Éprouver. (*b*) Vérifier. **2.** (*a*) Prouver, démontrer. (*b*) Homologuer.
II. **prove,** *v.i.* Se montrer.

proverb, *s.* Proverbe *m.*

proverbial, *a.* Proverbial, -aux.

proverbially, *adv.* Proverbialement.

provide. I. (*a*) *v.i.* To p. against, se pourvoir contre. (*b*) *v.tr.* Stipuler. **2.** (*a*) *v.tr.* Fournir. (*b*) *v.i.* Pourvoir à l'entretien (*for*, de). (*c*) *v.i.* Subvenir (*for*, à).

provided. I. **1.** *a.* Pourvu, muni (*with*, de). **2.** *conj.* P. (*that*), pourvu que ; à condition que.

providence, *s.* **1.** Prévoyance *f*, prudence *f.* **2.** Providence *f.*

provident, *a.* Prévoyant.

providential, *a.* Providentiel.

province, *s.* **1.** Province *f.* In the provinces, en province. **2.** Ressort *m.*

provincial, *a.* Provincial, -aux.

provision[1], *s.* **1.** To make p. for, pourvoir à. **2.** (*a*) Provision *f.* (*b*) *pl.* Provisions ; vivres *m.* P. merchant, marchand *m* de comestibles. **3.** Article *m* ; stipulation *f.*

provision[2], *v.tr.* Approvisionner.

provisional, *a.* Provisoire.

provisionally, *adv.* Provisoirement.

proviso, *s.* Clause conditionnelle.

provocation, *s.* Provocation *f.*

provocative, *a.* Provocant.

provoke, *v.tr.* **1.** (*a*) Provoquer, inciter. (*b*) Irriter, agacer. **2.** Exciter.

provoking, *a.* Irritant, contrariant

prow, *s.* Proue *f.*

prowess, *s.* Prouesse *f*, vaillance *f.*

prowl, *v.i.* Rôder.

prowler, *s.* Rôdeur, -euse.

proximity, *s.* Proximité *f.*

proximo, *adv.* Prochain.

proxy, *s.* **1.** Procuration *f* ; mandat *m.* **2.** Mandataire *mf.*

prude, *s.* Prude *f.*

prudence, *s.* Prudence *f*, sagesse *f.*

prudent, *a.* Prudent, sage.

prudently, *adv.* Prudemment, sagement.

prudish, *a.* Prude.

prudishness, *s.* Pruderie *f.*

prune[1], *s.* Pruneau *m.*

prune[2], *v.tr.* Tailler.

pruning, *s.* Taille *f.*

pruning-knife, *s.* Serpette *f.*

pry, *v.i.* Fureter ; fouiller.

prying, *a.* Curieux, indiscret, -ète.

psalm, *s.* Psaume *m.*

pseudonym, *s.* Pseudonyme *m.*

pshaw, *int.* Fi ! peuh !

psychiatrist, *s.* Psychiatre *mf.*

psychiatry, *s.* Psychiatrie *f.*

psychic, *a.* Psychique.

psychological, *a.* Psychologique.

psychologist, *s.* Psychologue *m.*

psychology, *s.* Psychologie *f.*

public. I. *a.* Public, *f.* publique. P. holiday, fête légale. **2.** *s.* (*a*) Public *m.* (*b*) In p., en public ; publiquement.

publican, *s.* (*a*) Aubergiste *mf.* (*b*) Débitant, -ante, de boissons.

publication, *s.* Publication *f.*

public house, *s.* **1.** Auberge *f.* **2.** Débit *m* de boissons.

publicity, *s.* **1.** Publicité *f.* **2.** Réclame *f.*

publicly, *adv.* Publiquement ; en public.

publish, *v.tr.* Publier. **Just published,** vient de paraître.

publisher, *s.* Éditeur *m.*

publishing, *s.* Publication *f.*

pucker[1], *s.* Ride *f*, pli *m.*

pucker[2], *v.tr.* Rider ; plisser.

pudding, *s.* (*a*) Pudding *m*, pouding *m.* (*b*) Rice *f*., riz *m* au lait.

puddle, *s.* Flaque *f* d'eau.

puerile, *a.* Puéril.

puff[1], *s.* **1.** Souffle *m* ; bouffée *f.* **2.** Réclame *f* ; puff *m.*

puff[2], *v.i.* Souffler. **To p. and blow,** haleter. **puff out,** *v.tr.* (*a*) Gonfler. (*b*) Lancer.

puff-box, *s.* Boîte *f* à houppe.

puffed, *a.* Essoufflé ; à bout de souffle. P. up, gonflé.

puff-pastry, *s.* Pâte feuilletée.

puffy, *a.* Bouffi, boursouflé.

pug, *s.* Carlin *m* ; roquet *m.*

pugilism, *s.* Pugilat *m* ; la boxe.

pugilist, *s.* Pugiliste *m* ; boxeur *m.*

pugnacious, *a.* Querelleur, -euse.

pug-nosed, *a.* Au nez épaté.

pull[1], *s.* **1.** (*a*) Traction *f.* **To give a p.,** tirer. (*b*) Effort *m* de traction. **2.** Avantage *m.*

pull[2], *v.tr.* **1.** (*a*) Tirer. **To p. the**

trigger, presser la détente. (b) Manier. *Abs.* Ramer. (c) *v.i.* **To p. at** a rope, tirer sur un cordage. **2.** Traîner, tirer. **3. To p. a face,** faire une grimace. **pull apart,** *v.tr.* Séparer. **pull down,** *v.tr.* **1.** Baisser ; rabattre (son voile). **2.** Démolir, abattre. **pull in,** *v.tr.* (a) Rentrer. (b) Retenir. **pull off,** *v.tr.* Retirer, ôter. **pull on,** *v.tr.* Enfiler, mettre. **pull out,** *v.tr.* (a) Sortir, (re)tirer. (b) Arracher. **pull through,** *v.i.* Se tirer d'affaire. **pull to,** *v.tr.* Tirer, fermer. **pull together,** *v.tr.* **1. To p.** oneself t., se reprendre. **2.** *Abs.* Tirer ensemble. **pull up. 1.** *v.tr.* (a) (Re)monter, hisser. (b) Hausser, lever ; retrousser. (c) Arracher. (d) Arrêter. **2.** *v.i.* S'arrêter.

pullet, *s.* Poulette *f.*

pulley, *s.* Poulie *f.*

Pullman. *Pr.n.* **P. car,** voiture *f* Pullman.

pull-over, *s.* Pull-over *m.*

pulp, *s.* Pulpe *f.*

pulpit, *s.* Chaire *f.*

pulsate, *v.i.* (a) Battre. (b) Palpiter.

pulsation, *s.* Pulsation *f*, battement *m.*

pulse, *s.* Pouls *m.*

pulverize, *v.tr.* Pulvériser ; broyer.

pumice, *s.* Ponce *f.*

pump[1], *s.* Pompe *f.*

pump[2], *v.tr. & i.* Pomper.

pump[3], *s.* Escarpin *m.*

pump-handle, *s.* Bras *m* de pompe.

pumpkin, *s.* Potiron *m*, citrouille *f.*

pun, *s.* Calembour *m* ; jeu *m* de mots.

punch[1], *s.* **1.** (a) Pointeau *m.* (b) Perçoir *m.* **2.** Poinçon *m* ; pince *f* de contrôle.

punch[2], *s.* Coup *m* de poing.

punch[3], *v.tr.* **1.** Percer ; découper ; poinçonner. **2.** Donner un coup de poing à.

Punch[4]. *Pr.n.* = Polichinelle *m* ou Guignol *m.*

punctilious, *a.* Pointilleux.

punctual, *a.* Ponctuel, exact.

punctuality, *s.* Ponctualité *f.*

punctually, *adv.* Ponctuellement.

punctuate, *v.tr.* Ponctuer.

punctuation, *s.* Ponctuation *f.*

puncture[1], *s.* **1.** Crevaison *f.* **2.** Piqûre *f*, perforation *f.*

puncture[2], *v.tr.* Crever, perforer.

pungency, *s.* **1.** Goût piquant ; odeur forte. **2.** Acreté *f.*

pungent, *a.* **1.** Mordant, caustique. **2.** Acre, irritant.

punish, *v.tr.* Punir ; châtier.

punishment, *s.* **1.** Punition *f*, châtiment *m.* **Capital p.,** peine capitale

punitive, *a.* Punitif ; répressif.

punt, *s.* Bachot *m.*

punt-pole, *s.* Gaffe *f*, perche *f.*

puny, *a.* **1.** (a) Petit, menu (b) Mesquin. **2.** Chétif, faible.

pup, *s.* Petit chien, jeune chien.

pupil[1], *s.* Élève *mf* ; écolier, -ière.

pupil[2], *s.* Pupille *f.*

puppet, *s.* Marionnette *f* ; pantin *m.*

puppy, *s.* Jeune chien *m.*

purchase[1], *s.* **1.** Achat *m*, acquisition *f.* **2.** Prise *f.*

purchase[2], *v.tr.* Acheter, acquérir.

purchase-price, *s.* Prix *m* d'achat

purchaser, *s.* Acheteur. -euse.

pure, *a.* Pur.

purely, *adv.* Purement.

purgative, *a. & s.* Purgatif (*m*).

purgatory, *s.* Le purgatoire.

purge[1], *s.* Purgation *f.*

purge[2], *v.tr.* **1.** Purger. **2.** Purifier.

purification, *s.* Purification *f.*

purify, *v.tr.* Purifier.

puritanical, *a.* De puritain.

purity, *s.* Pureté *f.*

purlieus, *s.pl.* Alentours *mpl.*

purloin, *v.tr.* Soustraire ; voler.

purple. I. *a.* Violet ; pourpre.

II. purple, *s.* Pourpre *f.*

purport[1], *s.* (a) Sens *m*, signification *f.* (b) Portée *f*, valeur *f*, force *f.*

purport[2], *v.tr.* **1.** Avoir la prétention. **2.** Impliquer.

purpose[1], *s.* **1.** (a) Dessein *m*, objet *m* ; but *m*, intention *f.* **On p.,** exprès, à dessein. (b) Résolution *f.* **2.** Destination *f*, fin *f.* **To answer the p.,** répondre au but. **For this p.,** à cet effet. **3. To the p.,** à propos. **4. To some p.,** utilement.

purpose[2], *v.tr.* Se proposer, avoir l'intention.

purposeful, *a.* (a) Prémédité. (b) Avisé. (c) Tenace.

purposeless, *a.* Sans but ; inutile.

purposely, *adv.* **1.** A dessein. **2.** Exprès.

purr, *v.i.* Ronronner.

purse[1], *s.* Bourse *f*, porte-monnaie *m inv.*

purse², *v.tr.* To p. (up) one's lips, pincer les lèvres ; faire la moue.

purser, *s.* Commissaire *m.*

pursuance, *s.* In p of. conformément à ; suivant.

pursue, *v.tr.* **1.** (*a*) Poursuivre. (*b*) Rechercher. **2.** Continuer, suivre.

pursuer, *s.* Poursuivant, -ante.

pursuit, *s.* **1.** (*a*) Poursuite *f.* (*b*) In p. of, à la recherche, en quête, de. **2.** (*a*) Carrière *f* profession *f.* (*b*) Occupation *f.*

purveyor, *s.* Fournisseur, -euse.

push¹, *s.* **1.** Poussée *f*, impulsion *f.* **2.** At a p., au besoin.

push². I. *v.tr.* Pousser. **1.** To p. oneself forward, se mettre en avant. **2.** (*a*) Poursuivre. (*b*) Pousser la vente de.
II. **push**, *v.i.* **1.** To p. (one's way), se frayer un chemin. **2.** Pousser. **push aside**, *v.tr.* Écarter. **push back**, *v.tr.* Repousser ; faire reculer. **push in**. I. *v.tr.* Enfoncer. **2.** *v.i.* Entrer à toute force. **push on**. **1.** *v.tr.* Pousser en avant. **2.** *v.i.* Pousser. **push out**, *v.tr.* Pousser dehors ; faire sortir.

pushing, *a.* (*a*) Entreprenant. (*b*) A p man, un ambitieux. (*c*) Indiscret, -ète.

pusillanimous, *a.* Pusillanime.

put. I. *v.tr.* Mettre. **1.** (*a*) To put s.o. in his place, remettre qn à sa place. (*b*) To put the matter right, arranger l'affaire. **2.** Poser, faire. To put it bluntly, pour parler franc. **3.** (*a*) To put to bed, mettre au lit ; coucher. (*b*) **To put to sleep.** endormir.
II. **put**, *v.i.* To put to sea, prendre le large. **To put into port,** faire relâche. **put away**, *v.tr.* **1.** (*a*) Serrer ; ranger. (*b*) Mettre de côté. **2.** Écarter. **put back**, *v.tr.* (*a*) Remettre à sa place. (*b*) Retarder. **put by**, *v.tr.* Mettre en réserve. **put down**, *v.tr.* **1.** Déposer, poser. **2.** Supprimer. **3.** (*a*) Noter. To put d. one's name, s'inscrire ; se faire inscrire. (*b*) Attribuer. **put forward**, *v.tr.* **1.** (*a*) Émettre, avancer

proposer. (*b*) Mettre en avant. **2.** Avancer. **put in**, *v.i.* Faire escale. **put off**. **1.** *v.tr.* (*a*) Retirer, ôter. (*b*) Remettre, différer. (*c*) Se débarrasser de. **2.** *v.i.* Démarrer. **put on**, *v.tr.* **1.** Monter. **2.** (*a*) Mettre ; chausser. Put on your hat, couvrez-vous. (*b*) Prendre. **3.** Avancer. **To put on the light,** mettre la lumière ; allumer. **put out**, *v.tr.* **1.** Avancer ; étendre. **2.** Mettre dehors. **3.** Démettre, déboîter. **4.** Éteindre. **5.** (*a*) Déconcerter. (*b*) Ennuyer, contrarier. (*c*) Incommoder, gêner. **put through**, *v.tr.* **1.** Mener à bien. **2.** Mettre en communication (*to*, avec). **put together**, *v.tr.* **1.** Joindre ; monter, assembler. **2.** Rapprocher. **put up**, *v.tr.* **1.** (*a*) Lever ; dresser. **To put up one's hands,** mettre haut les mains. (*b*) Apposer. **2.** Augmenter. **3.** Offrir, faire ; présenter. **4.** To put up for sale, mettre en vente. **5.** (*a*) Héberger ; loger. (*b*) Remiser. **6.** *Abs.* To put up with, s'accommoder de ; endurer. **7.** Construire ; ériger.

putrefy, *v.i.* Se putréfier, pourrir.

putrid, *a.* Putride ; infect.

putt¹, *s.* Coup roulé

putt², *v.tr.* Poter.

puttee, *s.* Bande molletière.

putting-green, *s.* Pelouse *f* du trou.

putty, *s.* Mastic *m*, enduit *m.*

puzzle¹, *s.* **1.** Énigme *f.* **2.** Devinette *f*, problème *m.*

puzzle². **1.** *v.tr.* Embarrasser, intriguer. **2.** *v.i.* Se creuser la tête. **puzzle out**, *v.tr.* Débrouiller. éclaircir.

puzzling, *a.* Embarrassant, intriguant.

pygmy. **1.** *s.* Pygmée *m.* **2.** *Attrib.* Pygméen.

pyjamas, *s.* Pyjama *m.*

pylon, *s.* Pylône *m.*

pyramid, *s.* Pyramide *f.*

Pyrenees (the). *Pr.n.* Les Pyrénées *f.*

python, *s.* Python *m.*

Q

Q, q, *s.* (La lettre) Q, q *m.*

quack¹, *s. & int.* Couin-couin (*m*).

quack², *v.i.* Faire couin-couin.

quack³, *s.* Charlatan *m.*

quadrangle, s. Cour (carrée).

quadrille, s. Quadrille m.

quadroon, a. & s. Quarteron, -onne.

quadruped, s. Quadrupède m.

quagmire, s. Fondrière f.

quail[1], s. Caille f.

quail[2], v.i. Fléchir, faiblir.

quaint, a. Étrange, bizarre.

quaintness, s. Bizarrerie f.

quake, v.i. Trembler (*with*, de).

quaker, s. Quaker m.

qualification, s. **1.** Réserve f, restriction f. **2.** Capacité f; aptitude f.

qualified, a. **1.** (a) To be q. to, avoir les capacités pour. (b) Autorisé. **2.** Restreint, modéré.

qualify. I. v.tr. **1.** Qualifier. **2.** Modifier. II. **qualify**, v.i. Se qualifier.

quality, s. Qualité f.

qualm, s. Scrupule m, remords m.

quandary, s. To be in a q., ne trop savoir que faire.

quantity, s. Quantité f.

quarantine[1], s. Quarantaine f.

quarantine[2], v.tr. Mettre en quarantaine.

quarrel[1], s. Querelle f, dispute f.

quarrel[2], v.i. **1.** Se quereller, se disputer. **2.** To q. with sth., trouver à redire à qch.

quarrelling, s. Querelles fpl, disputes fpl.

quarrelsome, a. Querelleur, -euse.

quarry[1], s. Proie f.

quarry[2], s. Carrière f.

quarry[3], v.tr. Extraire de la carrière.

quarryman, s. Carrier m.

quarter[1], s. **1.** (a) Quart m. (b) Quartier m. **2.** (a) Trimestre m; terme m. (b) A q. to six, six heures moins le quart. **3.** From all quarters, de tous côtés. In high quarters, en haut lieu. **4.** pl. Résidence f; quartier. **5.** pl. Postes de combat. **6.** To give q., faire quartier.

quarter[2], v.tr. **1.** Diviser en quatre. **2.** Cantonner, caserner.

quarter-day, s. Le jour du terme; le terme.

quarter-deck, s. Plage f arrière.

quarterly. 1. a. Trimestriel. **2.** s. Publication trimestrielle. **3.** adv. Trimestriellement; par trimestre.

quartet(te), s. Quatuor m.

quartz, s. Quartz m.

quash, v.tr. Casser, annuler.

quatrain, s. Quatrain m.

quaver[1], s. **1.** Croche f. **2.** (a) Trille m. (b) Tremblement m.

quaver[2], v.i. Chevroter, trembloter.

quavering, a. Tremblotant, chevrotant.

quay, s. Quai m.

queen, s. **1.** Reine f. **2.** Dame f.

queen-bee, s. Abeille f mère.

queer, a. **1.** (a) Étrange, singulier. (b) Suspect. **2.** I feel very q., je me sens tout chose.

queerly, adv. Étrangement, bizarrement.

queerness, s. Étrangeté f, bizarrerie f.

quell, v.tr. Calmer; dompter.

quench, v.tr. **1.** Éteindre. **2.** To q. one's thirst, se désaltérer.

querulous, a. Plaintif et maussade.

query[1], s. Question f.

query[2], v.tr. Mettre en question.

quest, s. Recherche f.

question[1], s. Question f. **1.** Without q., sans aucun doute. **2.** That is not the q., il ne s'agit pas de cela. It is out of the q., il ne faut pas y songer.

question[2], v.tr. **1.** Questionner, interroger. **2.** Mettre en doute.

questionable, a. **1.** Contestable, discutable. **2.** Équivoque.

questioner, s. Interrogateur, -trice.

questioning[1], a. Interrogateur, -trice.

questioning[2], s. Questions fpl, interrogation f.

queue[1], s. Queue f.

queue[2], v.i. To q. (up), faire queue.

quibble[1], s. Chicane f de mots; faux-fuyant m, pl. faux-fuyants.

quibble[2], v.i. Chicaner sur les mots.

quibbler, s. Chicaneur, -euse.

quibbling, s. Chicane f de mots.

quick. 1. a. (a) Rapide. Be q.! faites vite! dépêchez-vous! (b) Prompt, vif. Q. ear, oreille fine. **2.** s. Vif m. **3.** adv. Vite, rapidement.

quicken, v.tr. (a) Exciter, stimuler. (b) Hâter, accélérer.

quicklime, s. Chaux vive.

quickly, adv. Vite, rapidement, vivement.

quickness, s. **1.** Vitesse f, rapidité f. **2.** Finesse f; promptitude f.

quicksand, s. Sable mouvant.

quicksilver, *s.* Vif-argent *m*, mercure *m*.

quick-tempered, *a* Emporté, irascible.

quick-witted, *a.* Vif, éveillé.

quid pro quo, *s.* Équivalent *m*.

quiescence, *s.* Repos *m*, quiétude *f*.

quiescent, *a.* En repos ; tranquille.

quiet[1], *s.* Tranquillité *f*, repos *m*.

quiet[2], *a.* **1.** Tranquille, calme ; silencieux. **Be q.!** taisez-vous ! **2.** (*a*) Simple ; sobre. (*b*) *s.* **On the q.,** à la dérobée. **3.** Calme, tranquille, paisible.

quiet[3]. **1.** *v.tr.* Apaiser, calmer. **2.** *v.i.* **To q. down,** s'apaiser, se calmer.

quieten, *v.tr. & i.* = QUIET[3].

quietly, *adv.* (*a*) Tranquillement, doucement. (*b*) Silencieusement, sans bruit.

quietness, *s.* **1.** Tranquillité *f*, repos *m*, calme *m*. **2.** Sobriété *f*.

quietude, *s.* Quiétude *f*.

quill, *s.* **1.** Tuyau *m* (de plume). **2.** Piquant *m*.

quilt[1], *s.* Couverture piquée, ouatée.

quilt[2], *v.tr.* Piquer, ouater.

quince, *s.* Coing *m*.

quinine, *s.* Quinine *f*.

quintessence, *s.* Quintessence *f*.

quintet(te), *s.* *Mus :* Quintette *m*.

quip, *s.* Sarcasme *m*, repartie *f*.

quire, *s.* Main *f* (de papier).

quit[1], *a.* Quitte. **Q. of,** débarrassé de.

quit[2], *v.tr.* Quitter. *Abs.* Vider les lieux.

quite, *adv.* **1.** Tout à fait ; entièrement ; tout. **Q. enough,** bien assez. **Q. right,** très bien. **Q. so!** parfaitement ! **2. Q. a surprise,** une véritable surprise.

quiver[1], *s.* Carquois *m*.

quiver[2], *s.* Tremblement *m*.

quiver[3], *v.i.* Trembler ; frémir ; trembloter.

quixotic, *a.* Exalté, visionnaire.

quiz, *v.tr.* **1.** Railler, persifler. **2.** Lorgner.

quizzical, *a.* **1.** Risible, cocasse. **2.** Railleur, -euse ; plaisant.

quoit, *s.* Palet *m*.

quota, *s.* Quote-part *f*, *pl.* quotesparts.

quotation, *s.* **1.** Citation *f*. **2.** Cote *f*, cours *m*, prix *m*.

quotation-marks, *s.pl.* Guillemets *m*.

quote, *v.tr.* **1.** (*a*) Citer. (*b*) Rappeler. **2.** Établir, faire (un prix).

R

R, r, *s.* (La lettre) R, r *f*.

rabbi, *s.* Rabbin *m*.

rabbit, *s.* **1.** Lapin *m*. **Wild r.,** lapin de garenne. **2. Welsh r.,** fondue *f* au fromage sur canapé.

rabbit-hole, *s.* Terrier *m* de lapin.

rabbit-hutch, *s.* Clapier *m*.

rabbit-warren, *s.* Garenne *f*.

rabble, *s.* **1.** Cohue *f* ; foule *f*. **2. The r.,** la canaille.

rabid, *a.* (*a*) Furieux. (*b*) Outrancier.

race[1], *s.* Course *f*. **To run a r.,** disputer une course.

race[2]. **1.** *v.i.* (*a*) Lutter de vitesse. (*b*) **To r. along,** filer à toute vitesse. **2.** *v.tr.* Lutter de vitesse avec.

race[3], *s.* Race *f*.

race-course, *s.* Champ *m* de courses.

race-horse, *s.* Cheval *m*, -aux, de course.

racer, *s.* Cheval *m*, -aux, de course.

racial, *a.* De (la) race.

racing, *s.* Courses *fpl*.

rack[1], *s.* (*a*) Râtelier *m*. (*b*) **Bomb r.,** lance-bombes *m inv*. **Luggage r.,** porte-bagages *m inv* ; filet *m* (à bagages).

rack[2], *v.tr.* Tourmenter, torturer.

racket[1], *s.* Raquette *f*.

racket[2], *s.* **1.** Tapage *m*, vacarme *m*. **To stand the r.,** subvenir aux dépenses. **2.** Affaire véreuse.

racketeer, *s.* Trafiquant *m*.

rack-railway, *s.* Chemin *m* de fer à crémaillère.

racy, *a.* Vif, piquant.

radar, *s.* Radar *m*.

radiance, Rayonnement *m*.

radiant, *a.* Radieux ; rayonnant.

radiate. 1. *v.i.* Rayonner ; irradier. **2.** *v.tr.* Émettre, dégager.

radiation, *s.* Irradiation *f* ; rayonnement *m*.

radiator, *s.* Radiateur *m*.

radical, *a.* Radical, -aux.

radically, *adv.* Radicalement. foncièrement.

radio, *s.* Télégraphie *f* sans fil ; radio *f.*

radiogram, *s.* Radiogramme *m.*

radiograph[1], *s.* Radiogramme *m.*

radiograph[2], *v.tr.* Radiographier.

radish, *s.* Radis *m.*

radium, *s.* Radium, *m.*

radius, *s.* Rayon *m.*

raffle[1], *s.* Tombola *f.*

raffle[2], *v.tr.* Mettre en tombola.

raft, *s.* Radeau *m.*

rag[1], *s.* **I.** Chiffon *m* ; lambeau *m.*
2. *pl.* Haillons *m*, guenilles *f*, loques *f.*

ragamuffin, *s.* **I.** Gueux *m.* **2.**
Gamin *m* des rues.

rage[1], *s.* **I.** Rage *f*, fureur *f.* **To fly
into a r.**, s'emporter. **2.** Manie *f.*
To be all the r., faire fureur.

rage[2], *v.i.* **I.** Être furieux ; rager.
2. Faire rage ; sévir.

ragged, *a.* (*a*) En lambeaux. (*b*) En
haillons ; déguenillé.

raging, *a.* Furieux ; en fureur.

raid[1], *s.* Raid *m.*

raid[2], **I.** *v.i.* Faire un raid. **2.** *v.tr.*
Faire une descente dans.

raider, *s.* **I.** Maraudeur *m.* **2.** Avion
m en raid.

rail[1], *s.* **I.** (*a*) Barre *f.* (*b*) Barre
d'appui ; rampe *f.* **2.** *pl.* Grille *f.*
3. (*a*) Rail *m.* **Live r.**, rail de contact.
To leave the rails, dérailler. (*b*) **By
rail**, en chemin de fer.

rail[2], *v.tr.* **To r. round**, entourer
d'une grille.

rail[3], *v.i.* **To r. at**, crier contre.

rail-car, *s.* Micheline *f.*

railing(s), *s.(pl.)* **I.** Grille *f.* **2.**
Balustrade *f* ; rampe *f.*

raillery, *s.* Raillerie *f.*

railway, *s.* Chemin *m* de fer ; voie
ferrée. **R. station**, station *f* de
chemin de fer ; gare *f.*

raiment, *s.* Habillement *m.*

rain[1], *s.* Pluie *f.*

rain[2], *v.tr. & i.* Pleuvoir. **It is raining fast**, il pleut à verse.

rainbow, *s.* Arc-en-ciel *m*, *pl.* arcs-
en-ciel.

rain-coat, *s.* Imperméable *m.*

raindrop, *s.* Goutte *f* de pluie.

rainfall, *s.* Chute *f* de pluie.

rainproof, *a.* Imperméable.

rainy, *a.* Pluvieux.

raise, *v.tr.* **I.** (*a*) Dresser, mettre

debout ; relever. (*b*) Soulever. **2.**
Ériger. **3.** Élever ; cultiver. **4.** (*a*)
Lever. (*b*) **To r. s.o.'s hopes**, exalter
l'espoir de qn. **5.** (*a*) Hausser.
(*b*) Augmenter. **6. To r. money**, se
procurer de l'argent. **To r. a loan**,
émettre un emprunt.

raisin, *s.* Raisin sec.

rake[1], *s.* Râteau *m.*

rake[2], *v.tr.* **I.** Ratisser. **2.** (*a*)
Râteler. (*b*) Gratter, racler.

rake[3], *s.* Viveur *m*, roué *m.*

rally[1], *s.* (*a*) Ralliement *m* (*b*) Réunion *f.*

rally[2]. **I.** *v.tr.* Rallier. **2.** *v.i.* (*a*) Se
reformer. (*b*) Se rallier. (*c*) Re-
prendre des forces.

Ralph. *Pr.n.* Raoul *m*, Rodolphe *m.*

ram[1], *s.* **I.** Bélier *m.* **2.** Éperon *m.*

ram[2], *v.tr.* **I.** Battre, tasser. **2.**
Éperonner.

ramble[1], *s.* Promenade *f.*

ramble[2], *v.i.* **I.** Errer à l'aventure.
2. Parler sans suite.

rambling, *a.* **I.** Errant. vagabond.
2. Décousu.

ramify, *v.i.* Se ramifier.

ramp, *s.* Rampe *f* ; pente *f.*

rampant, *a.* **I.** Violent, effréné. **To
be r.**, s'étaler. **2.** Exubérant.

rampart, *s.* Rempart *m.*

ramshackle, *a.* Délabré.

rancid, *a.* Rance.

rancidity, *s.* Rancidité *f.*

rancour, *s.* Rancune *f*, rancœur *f.*

random. **I.** *s.* **At r.**, au hasard.
2. *a.* **R. shot**, coup tiré au hasard.

range[1], *s.* **I.** (*a*) Rangée *f.* (*b*) Chaîne
f. **2.** (*a*) Étendue *f.* **R. of action**,
champ d'activité. (*b*) **R. of colours**,
gamme *f* de couleurs. **3.** (*a*) Distance *f.* (*b*) Portée *f.* **4.** Fourneau *m*
de cuisine.

range[2]. **I.** *v.tr.* Ranger ; classer.
     II. range, *v.i.* S'étendre.

rank[1], *s.* **I.** (*a*) Rang *m.* (*b*) *pl.* **To
rise from the ranks**, sortir du rang.
2. (*a*) Rang ; classe *f.* (*b*) Grade *m.*
3. Station *f.*

rank[2]. **I.** *v.tr.* Ranger, compter.
2. *v.i.* Se ranger, être classé.

rank[3], *a.* **I.** Luxuriant ; exubérant.
2. (*a*) Rance. (*b*) Grossier. **3. R.
poison**, poison violent.

rankle, *v.i.* **To r. in s.o.'s mind**,
rester sur le cœur de qn.

rankling, *a.* Envenimé.

ransack, *v.tr* **1.** Fouiller. **2.** Saccager, piller.

ransom¹, *s.* Rançon *f.*

ransom², *v.tr.* **1.** Payer la rançon de. **2.** Mettre à rançon.

rant¹, *s.* Rodomontades *fpl.*

rant², *v.i.* Déclamer.

rap¹, *s.* Petit coup sec et dur.

rap², *v.tr. & i.* Frapper

rapacious, *a.* Rapace.

rapacity, *s.* Rapacité *f.*

rapid, *a. & s.* Rapide (*m*).

rapidity, *s.* Rapidité *f.*

rapidly, *adv.* Rapidement.

rapier, *s.* Rapière *f.*

rapt. **1.** *p.p.* (*a*) Ravi, extasié. (*b*) Absorbé. **2.** *a.* Profond.

rapture, *s.* Ravissement *m*, extase *m*. To go into raptures, s'extasier.

rapturous, *a.* De ravissement. d'extase ; frénétique.

rare, *a.* Rare.

rarefied, *a.* Raréfié.

rarely, *adv.* Rarement.

rareness, *s.* Rareté *f.*

rarity, *s.* **1.** Rareté *f.* **2.** Objet *m* rare.

rascal, *s.* Coquin, -ine.

rascality, *s.* Coquinerie *f.*

rascally, *a.* De coquin ; méchant ; misérable.

rash¹, *s.* Éruption *f.*

rash², *a.* Téméraire ; irréfléchi.

rasher, *s.* Tranche *f* (de lard).

rashly, *adv.* Témérairement.

rashness, *s.* Témérité *f* ; étourderie *f.*

rasp. **1.** *v.tr.* Râper. **2.** *v.i.* Grincer.

raspberry, *s.* Framboise *f.* R. bush. framboisier *m.*

rasping, *a.* Apre.

rat¹, *s.* **1.** Rat *m.* **2.** Jaune *m* ; renard *m.*

rat², *v.i.* (*a*) Tourner casaque (*b*) Faire le renard.

ratchet, *s.* Cliquet *m.*

rate¹, *s.* **1.** R. per cent, pourcentage *m.* **2.** (*a*) Taux *m* ; raison *f.* (*b*) Allure *f*, vitesse *f.* (*c*) Taux, cours *m.* At that r., à ce compte-là. At any r., dans tous les cas. **3.** Impôt local. Rates and taxes, impôts et contributions. **4.** Estimation *f*, évaluation *f.*

rate². **1.** *v.tr.* (*a*) Estimer, évaluer. (*b*) Considérer. **2.** *v.i.* Être classé.

rate³, *v.tr.* Tancer, semoncer.

rate-collector, *s.* Percepteur *m* des impôts locaux.

ratepayer, *s.* Contribuable *mf.*

rather, *adv.* **1.** Plutôt. **2.** Un peu ; assez. R. plain, plutôt laid. I r. think, je crois bien que.

ratification, *s.* Ratification *f.*

ratify, *v.tr.* Ratifier.

rating¹, *s.* (*a*) Estimation *f.* (*b*) Classement *m.*

rating², *s.* Semonce *f.*

ratio, *s.* Raison *f*, proportion *f.*

ration¹, *s.* Ration *f.* R. book, carnet *m* de rations.

ration², *v.tr.* Rationner.

rational, *a.* (*a*) Raisonnable ; doué de raison. (*b*) Raisonné.

rationally, *adv.* Raisonnablement.

rationing, *s.* Rationnement *m.*

rat-poison, *s.* Mort *f* aux rats.

rattan, *s.* Rotin *m* ; jonc *m* d'Inde.

rattle¹, *s.* **1.** (*a*) Hochet *m.* (*b*) Crécelle *f.* **2.** Bruit *m*, fracas *m* ; trictrac *m* (de dés).

rattle². **1.** *v.i.* Cliqueter ; branler. **2.** *v.tr.* (*a*) Agiter avec bruit ; faire cliqueter. (*b*) Consterner.

rattlesnake, *s.* Serpent *m* à sonnettes, crotale *m.*

rat-trap, *s.* Ratière *f.*

raucous, *a.* Rauque.

raucously, *adv.* D'une voix rauque, éraillée.

ravage, *v.tr.* Ravager, dévaster.

ravaging¹, *a.* Ravageur.

ravaging², *s.* Ravagement *m.*

rave, *v.i.* (*a*) Être en délire ; battre la campagne. (*b*) To r. at, pester contre. Raving lunatic, fou furieux. (*c*) Être en furie.

raven, *s.* (Grand) corbeau.

ravening, *a.* Vorace, rapace.

ravenous, *a.* Vorace.

ravenously, *adv.* Voracement.

ravine, *s.* Ravin *m.*

raving, *s.* **1.** Délire *m*, divagation *f.* **2.** *pl.* Paroles incohérentes.

ravish, *v.tr.* Ravir.

ravishing, *a.* Ravissant.

raw, *a.* **1.** Cru. **2.** Raw material, matière première. **3.** Sans expérience. A raw hand, un novice. **4.** A vif.

rawness, *s.* **1.** Crudité *f.* **2.** Inexpérience *f.* **3.** Froid *m* humide.

ray, *s.* Rayon *m.*

rayon, *s.* Rayonne *f.*

raze, *v.tr.* Raser.

razor, *s.* Rasoir *m.* **Safety r.,** rasoir de sûreté.

re, *prep. phr.* Relativement à.

reach[1], *s.* (*a*) Portée *f*, atteinte *f*. (*b*) **Within easy r.,** à proximité.

reach[2]. I. *v.tr.* **1. To r. out,** étendre ; tendre. **2.** Atteindre. **3.** Arriver à, parvenir à. **4.** Passer.
II. **reach,** *v.tr. & i.* Arriver à ; atteindre.
III. **reach,** *v.i.* **1.** S'étendre. As far as the eye could r., à perte de vue. **2. To r. out,** tendre la main.

react, *v.i.* Réagir.

reaction, *s.* Réaction *f*.

reactionary, *a. & s.* Réactionnaire(*mf*).

read, *v.tr.* **1.** (*a*) Lire. (*b*) Corriger (des épreuves). (*c*) **To r. up,** étudier. **2.** Faire la lecture. **read out,** *v.tr.* Lire à haute voix. **read through,** *v.tr.* **1.** Parcourir. **2.** Lire en entier.

readable, *a.* Lisible.

reader, *s.* Lecteur, -trice.

readily, *adv.* **1.** Volontiers, avec empressement. **2.** Facilement.

readiness, *s.* **1.** (*a*) Empressement *m*, alacrité *f*. (*b*) Bonne volonté. **2.** Facilité *f*. **3. To be in r.,** être prêt.

reading, *s.* (La) lecture.

reading-book, *s.* Livre *m* de lecture.

reading-desk, *s.* Pupitre *m*.

reading-glass, *s.* Loupe *f*.

reading-room, *s.* Salle *f* de lecture.

readjust, *v.tr.* Rajuster.

readjustment, *s.* Rajustement *m*.

ready. I. *a.* **1.** (*a*) Prêt. **To get r.,** se préparer. (*b*) **R. to hand,** sous la main. **R. money,** argent comptant. **2.** Prêt, disposé. **3.** Prompt, facile.
II. **ready,** *adv.* **R. dressed,** tout habillé.

ready-made, *a.* Tout fait. **R.-m.** clothes, vêtements de confection.

ready-reckoner, *s.* Barème *m*.

real, *a.* **1.** (*a*) Vrai. **R. silk,** soie naturelle. (*b*) Véritable, réel. **2. R.** property, propriété immobilière.

realism, *s.* Réalisme *m*.

realist, *a. & s.* Réaliste (*mf*).

realistic, *a.* Réaliste.

realistically, *adv.* Avec réalisme

reality, *s.* (La) réalité.

realization, *s.* Réalisation *f*.

realize, *v.tr.* **1.** Réaliser. **2.** Se rendre compte de.

really, *adv.* Vraiment ; réellement ;

en effet. **Is it r. true?** est-ce bien vrai ? **Not r.!** pas possible !

realm, *s.* Royaume *m*.

ream, *s.* Rame *f*.

reanimate, *v.tr.* Ranimer, réanimer.

reap, *v.tr.* (*a*) Moissonner. (*b*) Recueillir.

reaper, *s.* **1.** Moissonneur, -euse. **2.** Moissonneuse *f*.

reappear, *v.i.* Reparaître.

reappearance, *s.* Réapparition *f*.

rear[1]. I. *s.* (*a*) Arrière *m*, derrière *m*. (*b*) Dernier rang, queue *f*.
II. **rear,** *a.* D'arrière, de queue ; postérieur, -eure.

rear[2]. **1.** *v.tr.* Élever ; cultiver. **2.** *v.i.* Se cabrer.

rear-admiral, *s.* Contre-amiral *m*, *pl.* contre-amiraux.

rearm, *v.tr.* Réarmer.

rearmament, *s.* Réarmement *m*.

rearmost, *a.* Dernier.

re-arrange, *v.tr.* Arranger de nouveau.

re-arrangement, *s.* Nouvel arrangement.

reason[1], *s.* **1.** Raison *f*, cause *f*. For no r., sans motif. **The r. why,** le pourquoi. **I have r. to believe,** j'ai lieu de croire. **With r.,** à bon droit. **2.** Raison ; faculté *f* de raisonner. **3.** Raison ; bon sens. **It stands to r.,** cela va sans dire.

reason[2]. **1.** *v.i.* Raisonner. **2.** *v.tr.* Arguer.

reasonable, *a.* Raisonnable.

reasonably, *adv.* Raisonnablement.

reasoned, *a.* **1.** Raisonné ; motivé. **2.** Raisonnable.

reasoner, *s.* Raisonneur, -euse.

reasoning[1], *a.* Doué de raison.

reasoning[2], *s.* Raisonnement *m*.

reassure, *v.tr.* Rassurer.

reassuring, *a.* Rassurant.

reawaken. **1.** *v.tr.* Réveiller. **2.** *v.i.* Se réveiller.

rebate, *s.* Rabais *m*, escompte *m*.

rebel[1]. **1.** *a.* Insurgé. **2.** *s.* Rebelle *mf*., insurgé *m*.

rebel[2], *v.i.* Se rebeller.

rebellion, *s.* Rébellion *f*, révolte *f*

rebellious, *a.* Rebelle.

rebound, *v.i.* Rebondir.

rebuff[1], *s.* Rebuffade *f* ; échec *m*.

rebuff[2], *v.tr.* Repousser, rebuter.

rebuild, *v.tr.* Rebâtir, reconstruire.

rebuke[1], *s.* Réprimande *f*, blâme *m*.

rebuke[2], *v.tr.* Réprimander, blâmer.

rebut, *v.tr.* Réfuter.

recalcitrance, *s.* Récalcitrance *f*.

recalcitrant, *a.* Récalcitrant.

recall[1], *s.* 1. Rappel *m*. 2. Rétractation *f*, révocation *f*.

recall[2], *v.tr.* 1. Rappeler. 2. Rétracter.

recant. 1. *v.tr.* Rétracter; abjurer. 2. *v.i.* Se rétracter.

recapitulate, *v.tr.* Récapituler.

recapitulation, *s.* Récapitulation *f*.

recapture, *v.tr.* Reprendre.

recede, *v.i.* S'éloigner, reculer.

receding, *a.* (*a*) Qui s'éloigne. (*b*) Fuyant.

receipt[1], *s.* 1. (*a*) Recette *f*. (*b*) Perception *f*. (*c*) Réception *f*; reçu *m*. 2. Reçu, quittance *f*.

receipt[2], *v.tr.* Acquitter.

receive, *v.tr.* 1. (*a*) Recevoir. Received with thanks, pour acquit. (*b*) Recéler. 2. Recevoir; accueillir.

receiver, *s.* 1. (*a*) Personne *f* qui reçoit. (*b*) Receveur *m*. (*c*) Receleur -euse. 2. Récepteur *m*.

recent, *a.* Récent.

recently, *adv.* Récemment : tout dernièrement.

receptacle, *s.* 1. Réceptacle *m*. 2. Récipient *m*.

reception, *s.* 1. (*a*) Réception *f*. (*b*) R. desk, la réception. 2. Accueil *m*.

receptive, *a.* Réceptif.

recess, *s.* 1. Vacances *fpl*. 2. (*a*) Recoin *m*. (*b*) Embrasure *f*; niche *f*.

recipe, *s.* Recette *f*.

recipient, *s.* Donataire *mf*.

reciprocal, *a.* Réciproque, mutuel.

reciprocally, *adv.* Réciproquement, mutuellement.

reciprocate. 1. *v.tr.* Payer de retour. 2. *v.i.* Retourner le compliment.

reciprocity, *s.* Réciprocité *f*.

recital, *s.* 1. Récit *m*, narration *f*. 2. Audition *f*.

recitation, *s.* Récitation *f*.

recite, *v.tr. & i.* Réciter, déclamer.

reckless, *a.* Insouciant; téméraire. R. driving, conduite imprudente.

recklessly, *adv.* Témérairement; avec insouciance.

recklessness, *s.* Insouciance *f*; imprudence *f*, témérité *f*.

reckon. (*a*) *v.tr. & i.* Compter,

calculer. (*b*) *v.tr.* Estimer, juger.

reckon up, *v.tr.* Compter, calculer.

reckoning, *s.* 1. Compte *m*, calcul *m*. 2. Note *f*; addition *f*.

reclaim, *v.tr.* (*a*) Réformer, corriger. (*b*) Amender.

reclamation, *s.* 1. Réforme *f*. 2. Réclamation *f*.

recline. 1. *v.tr.* Reposer, appuyer 2. *v.i.* Être couché; reposer.

recluse, *s.* Reclus, -use.

recognition, *s.* Reconnaissance *f*.

recognizable, *a.* Reconnaissable.

recognizance, *s.* Caution *f*.

recognize, *v.tr.* Reconnaître.

recognized, *a.* Reconnu, admis, reçu.

recoil[1], *s.* (*a*) Rebondissement *m*, détente *f*. (*b*) Recul *m*.

recoil[2], *v.i.* 1. (*a*) Se détendre. (*b*) Reculer. 2. Retomber.

recollect, *v.tr.* 1. Se rappeler; se souvenir de. 2. To r. oneself, se recueillir.

recollection, *s.* Souvenir *m*.

recommence, *v.tr. & i.* Recommencer.

recommend, *v.tr.* Recommander.

recommendation, *s.* Recommandation *f*.

recompense[1], *s.* 1. Récompense *f* (*for*, de). 2. Dédommagement *m* (*for*, de).

recompense[2], *v.tr.* 1. Récompenser (*for*, de). 2. Dédommager (*for*, de).

reconcilable, *a.* Conciliable.

reconcile, *v.tr.* 1. Réconcilier. 2. To r. oneself, se résigner. 3. Concilier.

reconciliation, *s.* 1. Réconciliation *f*. 2. Conciliation *f*.

recondite, *a.* Abstrus, profond.

reconnaissance, *s.* Reconnaissance *f*.

reconnoitre, *v.tr.* Reconnaître. *Abs.* Faire une reconnaissance.

reconsider, *v.tr.* 1. Considérer de nouveau. 2. Revenir sur.

reconsideration, *s.* Examen *m* à nouveau.

reconstruct, *v.tr.* 1. Reconstruire. 2. Reconstituer.

reconstruction, *s.* 1. Reconstruction *f*. 2. Reconstitution *f*.

record[1], *s.* 1. Minute *f*. 2. (*a*) Note *f*, mention *f*. (*b*) Registre *m*. 3. *pl*. Archives *f*, annales *f*. 4. Monument *m*, document *m*. 5. Record *m*. 6. Disque *m*.

record², *v.tr.* (*a*) Enregistrer. (*b*) Narrer, rapporter.

recorder, *s.* **1.** Archiviste *m.* **2.** Appareil enregistreur.

recording¹, *a.* Enregistreur, -euse.

recording², *s.* (*a*) Enregistrement *m.* (*b*) Narration *f.*

recount, *v.tr.* Raconter.

recoup, *v.tr.* Dédommager.

recourse, *s.* **1.** Recours *m.* **2.** Expédient *m.*

recover¹, *v.tr.* **1.** Recouvrer, retrouver. **To r. one's breath**, reprendre haleine. **2.** Regagner ; rattraper. **3.** *v.i.* Guérir ; se remettre.

recover², *v.tr.* Recouvrir.

recovery, *s.* **1.** Recouvrement *m.* **2.** (*a*) Rétablissement *m*, guérison *f.* (*b*) Redressement *m.*

recreant. **1.** *a.* Lâche. **2.** *s.* (*a*) Lâche *m.* (*b*) Traître *m.*

recreation, *s.* Récréation *f*, divertissement *m.*

recreation-ground, *s.* Terrain *m* de jeux.

recriminate, *v.i.* Récriminer.

recrimination, *s.* Récrimination *f.*

recrudescence, *s.* Recrudescence *f.*

recruit¹, *s.* Recrue *f.*

recruit², *v.tr.* Recruter.

recruiting, *s.* Recrutement *m.*

rectangle, *s.* Rectangle *m.*

rectangular, *a.* Rectangulaire.

rectification, *s.* Rectification *f.*

rectify, *v.tr.* Rectifier, corriger.

rectitude, *s.* Rectitude *f.*

rector, *s.* **1.** Curé *m.* **2.** Recteur *m.*

rectory, *s.* Presbytère *m.*

recumbent, *a.* Couché, étendu.

recuperate, *v.i.* Se remettre.

recuperation, *s.* Rétablissement *m.*

recur, *v.i.* **1.** Revenir. **2.** Se renouveler.

recurrence, *s.* Réapparition *f*, renouvellement *m*, retour *m.*

recurrent, *a.* Périodique.

recurring, *a.* Périodique.

red. **1.** *a.* (*a*) Rouge. **To turn red**, rougir. (*b*) Roux, *f.* rousse. **2.** *s.* Rouge *m.*

redden, *v.tr. & i.* Rougir.

reddish, *a.* (*a*) Rougeâtre. (*b*) Roussâtre.

redeem, *v.tr.* **1.** Racheter ; amortir. **2.** Libérer, racheter.

redemption, *s.* **1.** Remboursement *m*, amortissement *m.* **2.** Rachat *m.*

red-faced, *a.* Rougeaud, sanguin.

red-haired, *a.* Roux, *f.* rousse.

red-handed, *a.* En flagrant délit.

red-hot, *a.* **1.** (Chauffé au) rouge. **2.** Ardent.

redness, *s.* Rougeur *f.*

redolent, *a.* **1.** Odorant, parfumé. **2.** Qui a une forte odeur.

redouble, *v.tr. & i.* Redoubler.

redoubtable, *a.* Redoutable, formidable.

redound, *v.i.* Contribuer.

redress¹, *s.* Réparation *f.*

redress², *v.tr.* **1.** Rétablir **2.** Redresser, réparer.

red-tape, *s.* **1.** Bureaucratie *f.* **2.** Surabondance *f.*

reduce, *v.tr.* **1.** Réduire ; diminuer. **To r. speed**, ralentir la marche. **2. To r. to ashes**, réduire en cendres. **3. To r. to silence**, faire taire.

reduced, *a.* Réduit.

reduction, *s.* (*a*) Réduction *f*, diminution *f.* (*b*) Rabais *m.*

redundancy, *s.* **1.** Redondance *f.* **2.** Surabondance *f.*

redundant, *a.* **1.** Redondant. **2.** Surabondant.

re-echo. **1.** *v.tr.* Répéter, renvoyer. **2.** *v.i.* Retentir, résonner.

reed, *s.* Roseau *m.*

reef, *s.* Récif *m.*

reek¹, *s.* Odeur forte, âcre.

reek², *v.i.* Sentir mauvais ; fumer.

reel¹, *s.* **1.** Dévidoir *m* ; bobine *f.* **2.** Moulinet.

reel², *v.i.* **1.** Tournoyer. **My head reels**, la tête me tourne. **2.** Chanceler.

reel³, *s.* Branle *f.*

re-embark, *v.tr. & i.* Rembarquer.

re-enter. **1.** *v.i.* Rentrer. **2.** *v.tr.* Rentrer dans.

refasten, *v.tr.* Rattacher ; ragrafer.

refer. **1.** *v.tr.* (*a*) Rapporter, rattacher. (*b*) Soumettre. (*c*) Renvoyer. **2.** *v.i.* (*a*) Se référer. (*b*) Se rapporter, avoir rapport. (*c*) Faire allusion.

referee, *s.* Arbitre *m.*

reference, *s.* **1.** Renvoi *m* ; référence *f.* **2. Work of r.**, ouvrage à consulter. **3.** Rapport *m.* **With r. to**, en ce qui concerne. **4. To make r. to**, signaler.

refill[1], *s.* Pile *f*, mine *f*, de rechange.

refill[2], *v.tr.* (*a*) Remplir. (*b*) *Abs.* Faire le plein.

refine, *v.tr.* Raffiner ; affiner.

refined, *a.* Raffiné.

refinement, *s.* Raffinement *m*.

reflect. 1. *v.tr.* Réfléchir, refléter. 2. *v.i.* (*a*) Méditer ; réfléchir. (*b*) Faire du tort (*on*, à).

reflection, *s.* 1. Réfléchissement *m*. 2. Réflexion *f*, reflet *m*. 3. To cast **reflections on,** critiquer. 4. On r., (toute) réflexion faite. 5. *pl.* Considérations *f*, pensées *f*.

reflector, *s.* Réflecteur *m*.

reform[1], *s.* Réforme *f*.

reform[2]. 1. *v.tr.* Réformer. 2. *v.i.* Se réformer.

reformation, *s.* Réformation *f*.

reformer, *s.* Réformateur, -trice.

refract, *v.tr.* Réfracter.

refractory, *a.* Réfractaire, indocile.

refrain[1], *s.* Refrain *m*.

refrain[2], *v.i.* Se retenir, s'abstenir.

refresh, *v.tr.* Rafraîchir.

refreshing, *a.* Rafraîchissant.

refreshment, *s.* Rafraîchissement *m*. R. room, buffet *m*.

refrigerator, *s.* Réfrigérateur *m*.

refuge, *s.* 1. Refuge *m*, abri *m* (*from*, contre). To take r., se réfugier. 2. Lieu de refuge, asile *m*.

refugee, *s.* Réfugié, -ée.

refund[1], *s.* Remboursement *m*.

refund[2], *v.tr.* (*a*) Rembourser. (*b*) Restituer.

refusal, *s.* Refus *m*.

refuse[1]. 1. *s.* Rebut *m* ; déchets *mpl*. 2. *a.* De rebut.

refuse[2], *v.tr.* 1. Refuser. 2. Rejeter, repousser.

refute, *v.tr.* Réfuter.

regain, *v.tr.* Regagner ; recouvrer.

regal, *a.* Royal, -aux.

regale, *v.tr.* Régaler.

regally, *adv.* Royalement ; en roi.

regard[1], *s.* 1. In this r., à cet égard. With r. to, quant à. 2. Égard *m* ; attention *f*. 3. (*a*) Égard, respect *m*. (*b*) *pl.* Amitiés *fpl*.

regard[2], *v.tr.* 1. Regarder. 2. Faire attention, prendre garde, à. 3. Concerner. As regards, pour ce qui regarde.

regardful, *a.* 1. Soigneux. 2. Plein d'égards.

regarding, *prep.* A l'égard de ; concernant ; quant à.

regardless, *a.* Peu soigneux. R. of, sans regarder à.

regatta, *s.* Régate *f*.

regeneration, *s.* Régénération *f*.

regent, *a. & s.* Régent, -ente.

regime, *s.* Régime *m*.

regimen, *s.* Régime *m*.

regiment, *s.* Régiment *m*.

regimental. 1. *a.* Du régiment, régimentaire. 2. *s.pl.* Uniforme *m*.

region, *s.* Région *f*.

register[1], *s.* Registre *m*.

register[2]. 1. *v.tr.* (*a*) Enregistrer ; inscrire. To r. a birth, déclarer une naissance. (*b*) Recommander. (*c*) Marquer. 2. *v.i.* S'inscrire.

registrar, *s.* 1. Greffier *m*. 2. Officier *m* de l'état civil.

registration, *s.* Enregistrement *m*, inscription *f*.

registry, *s.* 1. Enregistrement *m*. 2. (*a*) Bureau *m* de l'état civil. (*b*) Agence *f* de placement.

regret[1], *s.* Regret *m*.

regret[2], *v.tr.* Regretter.

regretful, *a.* Plein de regrets.

regretfully, *adv.* Avec regret, à regret.

regrettable, *a.* Regrettable.

regular, *a.* Régulier. 1. As r. as clockwork, exact comme une horloge. My r. time for going to bed, l'heure habituelle à laquelle je me couche. 2. Réglé, rangé. 3. (*a*) Dans les règles ; réglementaire. (*b*) Ordinaire. 4. Vrai, véritable.

regularity, *s.* Régularité *f*.

regularly, *adv.* 1. Régulièrement. 2. Véritablement, franchement.

regulate, *v.tr.* Régler.

regulation, *s.* 1. (*a*) Réglage *m*. (*b*) Règlement *m*. 2. Règlement, arrêté *m*.

regulator, *s.* Régulateur *m*.

rehearsal, *s.* 1. Récit détaillé, relation *f*. 2. Répétition *f*. Dress r., générale *f*.

rehearse, *v.tr.* 1. Raconter tout au long. 2. Répéter.

reign[1], *s.* Règne *m*.

reign[2], *v.i.* Régner.

reimburse, *v.tr.* Rembourser.

reimbursement, *s.* Remboursement *m*.

rein, *s.* Rêne *f* ; guide *f*.

reindeer, *s.* Renne *m*.

reinforce, *v.tr.* Renforcer ; appuyer.

reinforcements, *s.pl.* Renforts *m.*

reinstate, *v.tr.* **1.** Réintégrer ; rétablir. **2.** Remettre, rétablir.

reinstatement, *s.* **1.** Réintégration *f.* **2.** Rétablissement *m.*

reiterate, *v.tr.* Réitérer.

reiteration, *s.* Réitération *f.*

reject, *v.tr.* Rejeter, repousser.

rejection, *s.* Rejet *m* ; refus *m.*

rejoice. 1. *v.tr.* Réjouir. **2.** *v.i.* Se réjouir (*at, de*).

rejoicing, *s.* Réjouissance *f.*

rejoin[1], *v.i.* Répliquer, répondre.

rejoin[2], *v.tr.* Rejoindre.

rejoinder, *s.* Réplique *f,* repartie *f.*

rejuvenation, *s.* Rajeunissement *m*

relapse, *s.* Rechute *f.*

relate. 1. *v.tr.* Raconter, conter. **2.** *v.i.* Se rapporter. avoir rapport.

related, *a* **1.** Ayant rapport. **2.** Apparenté ; parent (*to, de*) ; (*by marriage*) allié (*to,* à).

relating, *a.* Relatif.

relation, *s.* **1.** Relation *f,* récit *m.* **2.** Relation, rapport *m.* **3.** Parent. -ente.

relationship, *s.* **1.** Rapport *m.* **2.** Parenté *f* ; lien *m* de parenté.

relative. 1. *a.* Relatif. **2.** *adv.* R. to, au sujet de. **3.** *s.* Parent, -ente.

relatively, *adv.* Relativement ; par rapport.

relax. 1. *v.tr.* (*a*) Relâcher ; détendre. (*b*) Mitiger. **2.** *v.i.* Se relâcher ; se détendre.

relaxation, *s.* (*a*) Relâchement *m* (*b*) Mitigation *f.* **2.** Délassement *m,* repos *m,* détente *f.*

relaxing, *a.* Énervant, débilitant

relay[1], *s.* Relais *m.*

relay[2], *v.tr.* Relayer.

release[1], *s.* **1.** (*a*) Délivrance *f* ; libération *f.* (*b*) Mise *f* en liberté. **2.** Lâchage *m.* **3.** Acquit *m.*

release[2], *v.tr.* (*a*) Décharger, libérer. (*b*) Libérer, élargir. (*c*) Lâcher.

relegate, *v.tr.* Reléguer.

relent, *v.i.* Se laisser attendrir.

relentless, *a.* Implacable, impitoyable.

relentlessly, *adv.* Implacablement. impitoyablement.

relentlessness, *s.* Inflexibilité *f,* implacabilité *f* ; acharnement *m.*

relevance, *s.* Pertinence *f.*

relevant, *a.* Pertinent ; à propos.

reliability, *s.* Sûreté *f* ; honnêteté *f.*

reliable, *a.* Sûr ; sérieux

reliance, *s.* Confiance *f.*

reliant, *a.* To be r. on, dépendre de.

relic, *s.* **1.** Relique *f.* **2.** *pl.* Restes *m.*

relief[1], *s.* **1.** (*a*) Soulagement *m* ; allégement *m.* (*b*) Décharge *f* **2.** Secours *m.* **3.** Relève *f.*

relief[2], *s.* Relief *m.* **To stand out in** r., ressortir, se détacher.

relieve, *v.tr.* **1.** (*a*) Soulager, alléger ; tranquilliser. **To r. one's feelings,** se décharger le cœur. (*b*) Tromper, dissiper. **2.** Secourir, aider. **3.** Débarrasser ; dégager ; relever.

religion, *s.* Religion *f* ; culte *m*

religious, *a.* Religieux.

religiously, *adv.* Religieusement

relinquish, *v.tr.* **1.** Abandonner ; renoncer à. **2.** Lâcher.

relinquishment, *s.* Abandon *m.*

reliquary, *s.* Reliquaire *m.*

relish[1], *s.* (*a*) Goût *m,* saveur *f.* (*b*) Assaisonnement *m.*

relish[2], *v.tr.* Goûter, savourer

reluctance, *s.* Répugnance *f* With r., à regret, à contre-cœur.

reluctant, *a.* **1.** Peu disposé **2.** Accordé à contre-cœur.

reluctantly, *adv.* A contre-cœur.

rely, *v.i.* Compter ; se fier (*upon.* à).

remain, *v.i.* Demeurer, rester.

remainder, *s.* **1.** Reste *m,* restant *m.* **2.** *Coll.* The r., les autres *mf.*

remaining, *a.* De reste.

remains, *s.pl.* Restes *m* ; vestiges *m.* Mortal r., dépouille mortelle.

remark[1], *s.* **1.** Remarque *f,* attention *f,* **2.** Remarque, observation *f.*

remark[2], **1.** *v.tr.* (*a*) Remarquer, observer. (*b*) Faire la remarque ; faire observer. **2.** *v.i.* Faire une remarque.

remarkable, *a.* Remarquable.

remarkably, *adv.* Remarquablement

remedy[1], *s.* Remède *m.*

remedy[2], *v.tr.* Remédier à.

remember, *v.tr.* **1.** (*a*) Se souvenir de ; se rappeler. **As far as I r.,** autant qu'il m'en souvient. (*b*) **That is worth remembering,** cela est à noter. (*c*) **To r. oneself,** se ressaisir. **2. R. me to them,** rappelez-moi à leur bon souvenir.

remembrance, s. Souvenir m, mémoire f.

remind, v.tr. To r. s.o. of sth., rappeler qch. à qn. That reminds me! à propos !

reminder, s. Mémento m. As a r., pour rappeler.

reminiscence, s. 1. Réminiscence f. 2. pl. Souvenirs m.

reminiscent, a. 1. Qui se souvient. 2. R. of, qui rappelle.

remiss, a. Négligent, insouciant.

remission, s. Remise f.

remissness, s. Négligence f.

remit, v.tr. 1. Remettre. 2. (R)envoyer.

remittal, s. Remise f.

remittance, s. Remise f ; envoi m de fonds.

remnant, s. 1. Reste m, restant m. 2. Vestige m. 3. Coupon m. 4. pl Soldes m.

remonstrance, s. Remontrance f.

remonstrate, v.i. Faire des remontrances (with, à) ; protester.

remorse, s. 1. Remords m. 2. Without r., sans aucune componction.

remorseful, a. Plein de remords ; repentant.

remorsefully, adv. Avec remords.

remorseless, a. 1. Sans remords. 2. Sans pitié ; impitoyable.

remorselessly, adv. 1. Sans remords. 2. Sans pitié.

remote, a. 1. Lointain ; éloigné, écarté. 2. Vague.

remotely, adv. 1. Loin ; au loin. 2. Vaguement.

remoteness, s. Éloignement m.

removable, a. 1. Détachable ; amovible. 2. Transportable.

removal, s. 1. (a) Enlèvement m ; suppression f. (b) Révocation f. 2. Déplacement m. 3. Déménagement m.

remove, v.tr. 1. (a) Enlever, ôter ; écarter ; supprimer. (b) Révoquer. 2. (a) Déplacer. Abs. Déménager. (b) Éloigner.

remunerate, v.tr. Rémunérer.

remuneration, s. Rémunération f.

remunerative, a. Rémunérateur -trice.

rend, v.tr. Déchirer.

render, v.tr. Rendre.

rendezvous, s. Rendez-vous m.

renegade, s. Renégat, -ate.

renew, v.tr. (a) Renouveler. (b) To r. acquaintance, renouer connaissance.

renewal, s. Renouvellement m.

renounce, v.tr. 1. Renoncer à, abandonner. 2. Répudier.

renouncement, s. Renoncement m.

renovate, v.tr Remettre à neuf.

renovation, s. Rénovation f.

renown, s. Renommée f, renom m.

renowned, a. Renommé.

rent¹, s. Déchirure f, accroc m.

rent², s. Loyer m ; location f.

rent³, v.tr. Louer.

rental, s. Loyer m.

renunciation, s. 1. Renoncement m, renonciation f. 2. Reniement m.

reopen, v.tr. & i. Rouvrir.

reorganization, s. Réorganisation f.

reorganize. 1. v.tr. Réorganiser. 2. v.i. Se réorganiser.

rep, s. Reps m.

repair¹, s. 1. Réparation f. 2. In good r., en bon état.

repair², v.tr. Réparer, remettre en état ; raccommoder.

reparation, s. Réparation f.

repartee, s. Repartie f.

repast, s. Repas m.

repatriate, v.tr. Rapatrier.

repay, v.tr. 1. Rendre. 2. Rembourser ; récompenser.

repayment, s. 1. Remboursement m. 2. Récompense f.

repeal¹, s. Abrogation f ; rappel m.

repeal², v.tr. Abroger ; révoquer.

repeat, v.tr. (a) Répéter ; réitérer. (b) Rapporter. (c) Renouveler.

repeated, a. Répété, réitéré, redoublé.

repeatedly, adv. A plusieurs reprises.

repel, v.tr. 1. Repousser 2. Répugner à.

repellent, a. Répugnant.

repent, v.i. Se repentir.

repentance, s. Repentir m.

repentant, a. Repentant, repenti.

repercussion, s. Répercussion f.

repertoire, s. Répertoire m.

repetition, s. Répétition f.

repine, v.i. Se chagriner.

replace, v.tr. 1. Replacer ; remettre en place. 2. Remplacer.

replenish, *v.tr.* Remplir (*with*, de).
replenishment, *s.* Remplissage *m.*
replete, *a.* Rempli, plein (*with*, de).
repletion, *s.* Réplétion *f.*
replica, *s.* Réplique *f.*, double *m.*
reply[1], *s.* Réponse *f.*
reply[2], *v.i. & tr.* Répondre, répliquer.
report[1], *s.* **1.** (*a*) Rapport *m* ; compte rendu. (*b*) **Weather r.,** bulletin *m* météorologique. **2.** Bruit *m* qui court ; rumeur *f.* **3.** Réputation *f.* **4.** Détonation *f* ; coup *m.*
report[2]. I. *v.tr.* **1.** (*a*) Rapporter ; rendre compte de. (*b*) Rapporter, dire. **2.** Signaler.
  II. **report,** *v.ind.tr.* Faire un rapport.
reporter, *s.* Journaliste *m*, reporter *m.*
reporting, *s.* Reportage *m.*
repose[1], *s.* Repos *m.*
repose[2], *v.i.* (*a*) Se reposer. (*b*) Reposer.
repository, *s.* Dépôt *m.* **Furniture r.,** garde-meuble *m*, *pl.* garde-meubles.
reprehend, *v.tr.* Blâmer, réprimander.
reprehensible, *a.* Répréhensible, blâmable.
represent, *v.tr.* **1.** Représenter. **2.** Faire remarquer.
representation, *s.* Représentation *f.*
representative. **I.** *a.* (*a*) Représentatif. (*b*) Qui représente. **2.** *s.* Représentant, -ante ; délégué, -ée.
repress, *v.tr.* Réprimer.
repressed, *a.* Réprimé, contenu.
repression, *s.* Répression *f.*
repressive, *a.* Répressif, réprimant.
reprieve[1], *s.* **1.** Commutation *f* de la peine capitale. **2.** Répit *m*, délai *m.*
reprieve[2], *v.tr.* Accorder une commutation de la peine capitale.
reprimand[1], *s.* Réprimande *f.*
reprimand[2], *v.tr.* Réprimander.
reprint[1], *s.* Réimpression *f.*
reprint[2], *v.tr.* Réimprimer.
reprisals, *s.pl.* Représailles *f.*
reproach[1], *s.* **1.** Honte *f* ; opprobre *m.* **2.** Reproche *m*, blâme *m.*
reproach[2], *v.tr.* Faire des reproches à. **To r. s.o. with sth.,** reprocher qch. à qn.
reproachful, *a.* Réprobateur, -trice ; plein de reproches.

reproachfully, *adv.* D'un air de reproche.
reprobate, *s.* Vaurien, -ienne.
reprobation, *s.* Réprobation *f.*
reproduce, *v.tr.* Reproduire.
reproduction, *s.* **1.** Reproduction *f.* **2.** Copie *f*, imitation *f.*
reproof, *s.* **1.** Reproche *m.* **2.** Réprimande *f.*
reprove, *v.tr.* Reprendre ; réprimander.
reproving, *a.* Réprobateur, -trice
reptile, *s.* Reptile *m.*
republic, *s.* République *f.*
republican, *a. & s.* Républicain, -aine.
repudiate, *v.tr.* Répudier.
repudiation, *s.* Répudiation *f.*
repugnance, *s.* Répugnance *f*, antipathie *f.*
repugnant, *a.* Répugnant. **To be r.,** répugner.
repulse[1], *s.* **1.** Échec *m* ; défaite *f.* **2.** Rebuffade *f*, refus *m.*
repulse[2], *v.tr.* Repousser.
repulsion, *s.* Répulsion *f*, aversion *f.*
repulsive, *a.* Répulsif, repoussant.
reputable, *a.* Honorable, estimable.
reputation, *s.* Réputation *f.*
repute, *s.* Réputation *f*, renom *m.*
reputed, *a.* Réputé, censé.
request[1], *s.* **1.** Demande *f*, requête *f.* **Earnest r.,** sollicitation *f.* **'Cars stop by r.,'** "arrêt facultatif." **2.** Recherche *f*, demande.
request[2], *v.tr.* **1.** Demander ; solliciter. **2.** Prier.
requiem, *s.* Requiem *m.*
require, *v.tr.* **1.** Demander, réclamer. **2.** Exiger, réclamer ; avoir besoin de. **If required,** au besoin.
required, *a.* Exigé, demandé, voulu.
requirement, *s.* **1.** Demande *f.* **2.** Besoin *m.* **3.** Condition requise.
requisite. **1.** *a.* Requis (*to*, pour) ; nécessaire. **2.** *s.* (*a*) Condition requise. (*b*) Chose *f* nécessaire ; accessoire *m.*
requisition[1], *s.* Demande *f.*
requisition[2], *v.tr.* Réquisitionner.
requital, *s.* **1.** Récompense *f*, retour *m.* **2.** Revanche *f*, représailles *fpl.*
requite, *v.tr.* Récompenser.
reredos, *s.* Retable *m.*
rescind, *v.tr.* Rescinder ; annuler.
rescission, *s.* Rescision *f.*
rescue[1], *s.* Délivrance *f* ; sauvetage *m.*

rescue², *v.tr.* Sauver, délivrer.
rescuer, *s.* **1.** Libérateur, -trice. **2.** Sauveteur *m.*
research, *s.* Recherche *f.*
resemblance, *s.* Ressemblance *f.*
resemble, *v.tr.* Ressembler à.
resent, *v.tr.* **1.** Être offensé de. **2.** S'offenser de ; ressentir.
resentful, *a.* **1.** Plein de ressentiment ; rancunier. **2.** Froissé.
resentfully, *adv.* Avec ressentiment.
resentment, *s.* Ressentiment *m.*
reservation, *s.* Réserve *f.*
reserve¹, *s.* Réserve *f.*
reserve², *v.tr.* Réserver ; retenir.
reserved, *a.* Réservé.
reservoir, *s.* Réservoir *m.*
reside, *v.i.* Résider.
residence, *s.* **1.** Résidence *f,* demeure *f,* séjour *m.* **2.** Demeure, maison *f.*
resident. **1.** *a.* Résidant. **2.** *s.* (*a*) Habitant, -ante. (*b*) Résident *m.*
residential, *a.* D'habitation.
residue, *s.* Reste *m.*
resign, *v.tr.* (*a*) Résigner ; *abs.* démissionner. (*b*) Abandonner.
resignation, *s.* **1.** Démission *f.* **2.** Résignation *f* ; soumission *f.*
resigned, *a.* Résigné.
resignedly, *adv.* Avec résignation.
resilient, *a.* Rebondissant, élastique.
resin, *s.* **1.** Résine *f.* **2.** Colophane *f.*
resinous, *a.* Résineux.
resist, *v.tr* **1.** Résister à. **2.** Repousser.
resistance, *s.* Résistance *f.*
resistless, *a.* Irrésistible.
resolute, *a.* Résolu, déterminé.
resolutely, *adv.* Résolument.
resolution, *s.* Résolution *f.*
resolve¹, *s.* Résolution *f.*
resolve². I. *v.tr.* Résoudre. II. **resolve**, *v.i* Se résoudre ; résoudre.
resolved, *a.* Résolu, décidé.
resonant, *a.* Résonnant.
resort¹, *s.* **1.** (*a*) Ressource *f.* (*b*) Recours *m.* **2.** (*a*) Lieu *m* de séjour, de rendez-vous. (*b*) **Health r.**, station thermale.
resort², *v.i.* **1.** Avoir recours, recourir. **2.** Se rendre, affluer (*to,* dans).
resound, *v.i.* Résonner ; retentir.
resounding, *a.* Résonnant, retentissant.

resource, *s.* Ressource *f.*
resourceful, *a.* Fertile en ressources.
respect¹, *s.* **1.** Rapport *m,* égard *m.* **2.** Respect *m* ; estime *f.* **3.** *pl.* Respects, hommages *m.*
respect², *v.tr.* Respecter. **1.** Honorer. **2.** Avoir égard à. **3.** Avoir rapport à ; concerner. **As respects,** quant à.
respectability, *s* Respectabilité *f.*
respectable, *a.* Respectable. **1.** Digne de respect. **2.** Honorable.
respectably, *adv.* Respectablement, convenablement.
respectful, *a.* Respectueux.
respectfully, *adv.* Respectueusement.
respecting, *prep.* Relativement à ; quant à.
respective, *a.* Respectif.
respectively, *adv.* Respectivement.
respiration, *s.* Respiration *f.*
respite, *s.* Répit *m,* relâche *m.*
resplendent, *a.* Resplendissant.
respond, *v.i.* Répondre.
response, *s.* Réponse *f.*
responsibility, *s.* Responsabilité *f.*
responsible, *a.* **1.** Responsable. **2.** Capable, compétent.
responsive, *a.* Impressionnable ; sensible.
rest¹, *s.* **1.** (*a*) Repos *m.* **At r.**, tranquille. (*b*) **To take a r.**, se reposer. (*c*) **To come to r.**, s'arrêter, s'immobiliser. **2.** Pause *f,* silence *m.* **3.** Support *m.*
rest². I. *v.i.* **1.** (*a*) Avoir du repos. (*b*) Se reposer. (*c*) Demeurer, rester. **2.** Se poser, s'appuyer. II. **rest**, *v.tr.* (*a*) Reposer, faire reposer. (*b*) Appuyer ; déposer.
rest³, *s.* **1.** Reste *m,* restant *m* **2.** **The r.,** les autres *mf.*
rest⁴, *v.i.* **1.** Rester, demeurer. **2.** **It rests with you,** il dépend de vous.
restaurant, *s.* Restaurant *m.*
restaurant-car, *s.* Wagon-restaurant *m,* *pl.* wagons-restaurants.
restful, *a.* Reposant ; paisible, tranquille.
restfulness, *s.* Tranquillité *f.*
restitution, *s.* Restitution *f.*
restive, *a.* Rétif.
restless, *a.* **1.** Sans repos **2.** (*a*) Agité. (*b*) Remuant. **3.** Inquiet, -ète, agité.

restlessness, s. **1.** (a) Inquiétude f,
agitation f. (b) Mouvement incessant. **2.** Nervosité f.

restoration, s. **1.** Restitution f. **2.**
Restauration f.

restorative, a. & s. Fortifiant (m).

restore, v.tr. **1.** Restituer, rendre
2. Restaurer. **3.** Rétablir. **4. To r.**
the circulation, réactiver la circulation.

restrain, v.tr. **1.** Retenir, empêcher.
2. Contenir, refréner.

restrained, a. Contenu.

restraint, s. (a) Contrainte f, frein m.
(b) Contrainte ; réserve f.

restrict, v.tr. Restreindre ; réduire

restricted, a. Restreint, limité

restriction, s. Restriction f.

restrictive, a. Restrictif.

result[1], s. Résultat m ; aboutissement m. **As a r. of,** par suite de.

result[2], v.i. Résulter.

resultant, a. Résultant.

resume, v.tr. **1.** Reprendre, regagner.
2. Reprendre ; renouer. **3.** Reprendre, récapituler.

résumé, s. Résumé m.

resumption, s. Reprise f.

resurrection, s. Résurrection f.

resuscitate, v.tr. & i. Ressusciter.

resuscitation, s. Ressuscitation f.

retail[1], s. Détail m ; vente f au détail.

retail[2], v.tr. **1.** Détailler, vendre au
détail. **2.** Répéter.

retailer, s. Marchand m au détail.

retain, v.tr. **1.** Retenir. **2.** Conserver,
garder.

retaliate, v.i. Rendre la pareille.

retaliation, s. Représailles fpl.

retard, v.tr. Retarder.

retention, s. Conservation f.

retentive, a. Tenace.

reticence, s. Réticence f.

reticent, a. Peu communicatif ;
taciturne.

reticule, s. Réticule m ; sac m à main.

retinue, s. Suite f.

retire, v.i. **1.** (a) Se retirer. (b) Aller
se coucher. **2.** Se démettre. **To r.**
on a pension, prendre sa retraite.
3. Reculer.

retired, a. **1.** Retiré. **2.** Retraité.

retirement, s. (a) La retraite. (b)
In r., retiré du monde.

retiring, a. **1.** Réservé. **2.** Sortant.

retort[1], s Réplique f ; riposte f.

retort[2], v.tr. Répliquer, riposter.

retort[3], s. Cornue f.

retrace, v.tr. **To r. one's steps,**
revenir sur ses pas.

retract, v.tr Rétracter ' Abs Se
rétracter.

retreat[1], s. **1.** Retraite f **2.** Abri m,
asile m ; retraite.

retreat[2], v.i. (a) Se retirer. (b) Battre
en retraite.

retribution, s. Châtiment m.

retrieve, v.tr. **1.** (a) Rapporter. (b)
Recouvrer. **2.** Rétablir. **3.** Réparer.

retrocession, s. Recul m.

retrograde, a. Rétrograde.

retrospect, s Coup d'œil rétrospectif.

retrospective, a. Rétrospectif.

return[1], s. **1.** Retour m. **R. ticket,**
billet d'aller et retour. **2.** (a) pl.
Recettes f. (b) Profit m ; rendement
m. **3.** (a) Renvoi m, retour. (b) Restitution f. (c) In r. for, en échange,
moyennant quoi. **4.** Récompense f.
In r. for, en retour de. **5.** État m,
exposé m.

return[2]. **I.** v.i. Revenir ; retourner.
To r. home, rentrer.
II. return, v.tr. **1.** (a) Rendre ;
restituer ; renvoyer. (b) Remettre.
2. Répondre. **3.** Déclarer, rapporter.
4. Élire.

reunion, s. Réunion f, assemblée f.

reveal, v.tr. (a) Révéler, découvrir.
(b) Laisser voir.

reveille, s. Le réveil ; la diane

revel, v.i. Se délecter (in, à).

revelation, s. Révélation f.

revelry, s. (a) Divertissements mpl.
(b) Orgie f.

revenge[1], s. Vengeance f ; revanche
f. In r., pour se venger.

revenge[2], v.tr. Venger.

revengeful, a. Vindicatif.

revenue, s. Revenu m, rentes fpl.

reverberate, v.i. (a) Retentir, résonner. (b) Réverbérer.

reverberation, s. (a) Renvoi m. (b)
Réverbération f.

revere, v.tr. Révérer, vénérer.

reverence[1], s. **1.** Révérence f, vénération f. **2.** Your R., monsieur l'abbé.

reverence[2], v.tr. Révérer.

reverend, a. **1.** Vénérable. **2.** Révérend.

reverent, a. Respectueux.

reverently, *adv.* Avec respect.

reverie, *s.* Rêverie *f.*

reverse[1], *a.* Inverse, contraire.

reverse[2], *s.* **1.** Inverse *m,* contraire *m.* **2.** Revers *m.*

reverse[3], *v.tr.* **1.** Renverser. **2.** (*a*) Invertir (l'ordre). (*b*) *Abs.* Faire marche arrière. **3.** Réformer.

reversed, *a.* **1.** Renversé. **2.** Inverse, contraire.

reversion, *s.* Retour *m.*

revert, *v.i.* Revenir, retourner.

review[1], *s.* **1.** Revue *f.* **2.** Examen *m,* revue. **3.** Compte rendu.

review[2], *v.tr.* **1.** Passer en revue. **2.** Faire le compte rendu de.

reviewer, *s.* Critique *m.*

revile, *v.tr.* Injurier.

revise, *v.tr.* Revoir, relire ; corriger, reviser.

revision, *s.* Revision *f.*

revisit, *v.tr.* Visiter de nouveau.

revival, *s.* **1.** Renaissance *f* ; reprise *f.* **2.** Retour *m* des forces.

revive. 1. *v.i.* (*a*) Ressusciter. (*b*) Se ranimer. (*c*) Reprendre ; renaître. **2.** *v.tr.* (*a*) Faire revivre ; ressusciter. (*b*) Ranimer ; renouveler.

revocation, *s.* Révocation *f.*

revoke[1], *s.* Fausse renonce.

revoke[2]. **1.** *v.tr.* Révoquer. **2.** *v.i.* Faire une fausse renonce.

revolt[1], *s.* Révolte *f.*

revolt[2], *v.i.* Se révolter, se soulever.

revolting, *a.* Révoltant.

revolution, *s.* **1.** (*a*) Rotation *f.* (*b*) Tour *m.* **2.** Révolution *f.*

revolutionary, *a. & s.* Révolutionnaire (*mf*).

revolve. 1. *v.tr.* (*a*) Retourner. (*b*) Faire tourner. **2.** *v.i.* Tourner.

revolver, *s.* Revolver *m.*

revolving, *a.* **1.** En rotation. **2.** Tournant.

revue, *s.* Revue *f.*

revulsion, *s.* Revirement *m.*

reward[1], *s.* Récompense *f.*

reward[2], *v.tr.* Récompenser (*for,* de).

rhapsody, *s.* Rapsodie *f.*

Rheims. *Pr.n.* Reims *m.*

rhetoric, *s.* Rhétorique *f.*

rhetorical, *a.* De rhétorique.

rheumatic, *a.* Rhumatismal, -aux.

rheumatism, *s.* Rhumatisme *m.*

Rhine (the). *Pr.n.* Le Rhin.

rhinoceros, *s.* Rhinocéros *m.*

rhubarb, *s.* Rhubarbe *f.*

rhyme[1], *s.* **1.** Rime *f.* **2.** *pl.* Vers (rimés) ; poésie *f.* **In r.,** en vers.

rhyme[2], *v.i.* Rimer.

rhythm, *s.* Rythme *m,* cadence *f.*

rhythmic, *a.* Rythmique, cadencé.

rib, *s.* Côte *f.*

ribald, *a.* Licencieux, impudique

ribbon, *s.* Ruban *m.*

rice, *s.* Riz *m.*

rice pudding, *s.* Riz *m* au lait.

rich, *a.* Riche. **To grow r.,** s'enrichir.

riches, *s.pl.* Richesses *fpl.*

richly, *adv.* **1.** Richement. **2.** Joliment.

richness, *s.* Richesse *f.*

rick, *s.* Meule *f.*

rickety, *a.* Branlant.

rid, *v.tr.* Débarrasser, délivrer. **To get rid of,** se débarrasser de.

riddance, *s.* Débarras *m.*

riddle[1], *s.* Énigme *f,* devinette *f.*

riddle[2], *s.* Crible *m.*

riddle[3], *v.tr.* Cribler.

ride[1], *s.* Course *f,* promenade *f* (à cheval, en automobile, *etc.*).

ride[2]. **I.** *v.i.* **1.** (*a*) Chevaucher ; se promener, monter, à cheval. (*b*) **To r. on a bicycle,** se promener à bicyclette. **2.** Se promener en voiture ; aller en autobus.

II. **ride,** *v.tr.* **1. To r. a race,** courir une course. **2. To r. a horse,** monter un cheval. **To r. a bicycle,** aller à bicyclette. **ride away,** *v.i.* Partir, s'éloigner (à cheval). **ride back,** *v.i.* (S'en) retourner, s'en revenir (à cheval). **ride behind,** *v.i.* Monter en croupe. **ride by,** *v.i.* Passer (à cheval). **ride off,** *v.i.* Partir, s'éloigner (à cheval).

rider, *s.* **1.** Cavalier, -ière. **2.** Ajouté *m,* annexe *f.*

ridge, *s.* Arête *f,* crête *f.*

ridicule[1], *s.* Moquerie *f,* raillerie *f.* **To hold up to r.,** se moquer de.

ridicule[2], *v.tr.* Se moquer de.

ridiculous, *a.* Ridicule.

riding, *s.* Équitation *f.*

riding-habit, *s.* Amazone *f.*

riding-whip, *s.* Cravache *f.*

rife, *pred.a.* **To be r.,** régner, sévir ; courir les rues.

rifle[1], *v.tr.* Piller.

rifle[2], *s.* Fusil *m.*

rifle-range, *s.* Champ *m* de tir.

rift, *s.* Fente *f*; fissure *f*.

rigging, *s.* Gréement *m*.

right[1]. **I.** *a.* **1.** Bon, honnête, droit. It is only r., il n'est que justice (*to*, de). **2.** (*a*) Correct, juste, exact. **To put r.,** corriger, rectifier. (*b*) **To be r.,** avoir raison. (*c*) **The r. thing to do,** ce qu'il y a de mieux à faire. **That's r.!** c'est bien cela! à la bonne heure! **Quite r.!** parfaitement! **3.** (*a*) **To be in one's r. mind,** avoir toute sa raison. **To set things r.,** rétablir les choses. (*b*) **All r.,** très bien. **4.** Droit. **II. right,** *s.* **1.** Le droit; le bien. **To be in the r.,** avoir raison. **2.** (*a*) Droit, titre *m*. **In one's own r.,** de son chef; en propre. (*b*) *pl.* **By rights,** en toute justice. **Within one's rights,** dans son droit. **3.** Droite *f*; côté droit. **On the r.,** à droite. **III. right,** *adv.* **1.** (*a*) Droit. **To go r. on,** continuer tout droit. (*b*) **R. away,** sur-le-champ. **2. R. at the top,** tout en haut. **R. in the middle,** au beau milieu. **3.** (*a*) **To do r.,** bien faire. (*b*) Correctement : juste. **4.** A droite.

right[2], *v.tr.* Redresser.

right-angled, *a.* A angle droit.

righteous, *a.* **1.** Droit, juste; vertueux. **2.** Juste, justifié.

righteousness, *s.* Droiture *f*, vertu *f*.

rightful, *a.* Légitime, juste.

rightfully, *adv.* Légitimement; à juste titre.

rightly, *adv.* Correctement. **R. or wrongly,** à tort ou à raison.

right-minded, *a.* Sain d'esprit.

rigid, *a.* Rigide, raide.

rigidity, *s.* Rigidité *f*.

rigidly, *adv.* Rigidement.

rigorous, *a.* Rigoureux.

rigorously, *adv.* Rigoureusement.

rigour, *s.* Rigueur *f*, sévérité *f*.

rim, *s.* **1.** Jante *f*. **2.** Bord *m*.

rime, *s.* Givre *m*; gelée blanche.

rimmed, *a.* A bord; bordé.

rind, *s.* Peau *f*; pelure *f*; couenne *f*.

ring[1], *s.* **1.** Anneau *m*; bague *f*. **2.** Rond *m*, anneau. **3.** Cercle *m*. **4.** Groupe *m*, petite coterie. **5.** Arène *f*, piste *f*. **6.** Enceinte *f*, ring *m*.

ring[2], *s.* **1.** Sonnerie *f*; tintement *m*; timbre *m*. **2.** (*a*) Coup *m* de son-

nette. (*b*) **R. on the telephone,** appel *m* téléphonique. **I'll give you a r.,** je vous téléphonerai.

ring[3]. **1.** *v.i.* (*a*) Sonner, tinter. (*b*) Résonner, retentir (*with*, de). **2.** *v.tr.* Sonner, faire sonner. *Abs.* **To r. for,** sonner **ring out,** *v.i.* Sonner; retentir. **ring up,** *v.tr.* Donner un coup de téléphone à.

ring-dove, *s.* Ramier *m*.

ringing[1], *a.* Sonore, retentissant.

ringing[2], *s.* Tintement *m*.

ringleader, *s.* Chef *m* d'émeute.

ringlet, *s.* Boucle *f* (de cheveux).

rinse, *v.tr.* Rincer.

riot[1], *s.* **1.** Émeute *f*. **2.** Orgie *f*. **3. To run r.,** se déchaîner; pulluler.

riot[2], *v.i.* S'ameuter.

rioter, *s.* Émeutier *m*, séditieux *m*.

rioting, *s.* Émeutes *fpl*; troubles *mpl*.

riotous, *a.* Tumultueux, turbulent.

rip, *v.tr.* Fendre; déchirer. **rip off,** *v.tr.* Arracher.

ripe, *a.* Mûr.

ripen, *v.tr. & i.* Mûrir.

ripeness, *s.* Maturité *f*.

ripple, *s.* (*a*) Ride *f*; ondulation *f*. (*b*) Gazouillement *m*.

rise[1], *s.* **1.** Ascension *f*. **2.** (*a*) Montée *f*, côte *f*; rampe *f*. (*b*) Éminence *f*. **3.** (*a*) Crue *f*; flot *m*; élévation *f*. (*b*) Augmentation *f*, hausse *f*. **4. To give r. to,** faire naître.

rise[2], *v.i.* **1.** Se lever; se mettre debout. **2.** Se soulever. **3.** Se lever; monter. **4.** (*a*) S'élever, se dresser. (*b*) Augmenter. **5. To r. to the occasion,** se montrer à la hauteur de la situation. **6.** Prendre sa source.

rising[1], *a.* **1.** Levant. **2.** Qui monte; en hausse. **R. tide,** marée montante.

rising[2], *s.* Ameutement *m*, soulèvement *m*.

risk[1], *s.* Risque *m*, péril *m*.

risk[2], *v.tr.* Risquer, aventurer.

risky, *a.* Hasardeux, chanceux

rissole, *s.* Rissole *f*.

rite, *s.* Rite *m*.

ritual. **1.** *a.* Rituel. **2.** *s.* Rites *mpl*.

rival[1], *a. & s.* (*a*) Rival, -ale, *pl.* -aux, -ales. (*b*) Émule *mf*.

rival[2], *v.tr.* (*a*) Rivaliser avec (*b*) Être l'émule de.

rivalry, *s.* (*a*) Rivalité *f*. (*b*) Émulation *f*.

river, *s.* Fleuve *m*; rivière *f*.

rivet[1], *s.* Rivet *m*.

rivet[2], *v.tr.* (*a*) River, riveter. (*b*) Fixer.

Riviera (the). *Pr.n.* La Côte d'Azur.

rivulet, *s.* Ruisseau *m*.

road, *s.* **1.** Route *f*, chemin *m*, voie *f*. **High r.,** main r., grand chemin, grande route. **R. transport,** transports routiers. **2.** Chaussée *f*.

roadside, *s.* Bord *m*, côté *m*, de la route, de la chaussée.

roadstead, *s.* Rade *f*.

roadway, *s.* Chaussée *f*.

roam, *v.i.* Errer, rôder.

roaming, *s.* Errant, vagabond.

roan, *a.* Rouan, -anne.

roar[1], *s.* Hurlement *m*; rugissement *m*. **Roars of laughter,** grands éclats de rire.

roar[2], *v.i.* Hurler, rugir.

roaring, *s.* Rugissement *m*.

roast[1], *s.* Rôti *m*.

roast[2]. **1.** *v.tr.* (*a*) Rôtir, faire rôtir. (*b*) Griller, torréfier. **2.** *v.i.* Rôtir.

roast[3], *a.* Rôti. **R. beef,** rôti *m* de bœuf; rosbif *m*.

rob, *v.tr.* Voler. **To rob s.o of th.,** voler qch. à qn.

robber, *s.* Voleur, -euse.

robbery, *s.* Vol *m*; brigandage *m*.

robe, *s.* **1.** Robe *f*. **2.** Vêtement *m*.

robin, *s.* Rouge-gorge *m*, *pl.* rouges-gorges.

robot, *s.* Automate *m*.

robust, *a.* Robuste, solide.

rock[1], *s.* (*a*) Rocher *m* roc *m*. (*b*) Roche *f*.

rock[2]. **1.** *v.tr.* (*a*) Bercer, balancer; basculer. (*b*) Ébranler. **2.** *v.i.* Balancer.

rockery, *s.* Rochers artificiels.

rocket, *s.* Fusée *f*.

rock-garden, *s.* Jardin *m* de rocaille.

rocking, *a.* **1.** Oscillant. **2.** Branlant.

rock-salt, *s.* Sel *m* gemme.

rocky, *a.* Rocheux.

rod, *s.* **1.** Baguette *f*. **2.** Verge *f*. **3. Rod and line,** ligne *f* de pêche. **4. Stair rod,** tringle *f* d'escalier.

rodent, *s.* Rongeur *m*.

roe, *s.* (*a*) **(Hard) roe,** œufs *mpl*. (*b*) **Soft roe,** laite *f*, laitance *f*.

roebuck, *s.* Chevreuil *m*.

rogue, *s.* **1.** Coquin, -ine; fripon, -onne. **2.** Malin, -igne.

roguery, *s.* Coquinerie *f*, friponnerie *f*.

roguish, *a.* Malin, -igne, espiègle.

roguishly, *adv.* Avec espièglerie.

roguishness, *s.* Malice *f*.

rôle, *s.* Rôle *m*.

roll[1], *s.* **1.** (*a*) Rouleau *m*. (*b*) Petit pain. **2.** Rôle *m*, liste *f*. **To call the r.,** faire l'appel.

roll[2]. I. *v.tr.* Rouler. II. **roll,** *v.i.* Rouler. **roll over.** **1.** *v.tr.* Retourner. **2.** *v.i.* Se retourner (en roulant). **roll up,** *v.tr.* (*a*) Rouler, enrouler: retrousser. (*b*) Envelopper.

roller, *s.* **1.** Rouleau *m*; enrouleur *m*. **2.** Lame *f* de houle.

roller-skates *s.pl.* Patins *m* à roulettes.

roller-towel, *s.* Essuie-main(s) *m* à rouleau.

rolling[1], *a.* Roulant.

rolling[2], *s.* **1.** Roulement *m*. **2.** Roulis *m*.

rolling-pin, *s.* Rouleau *m*.

rolling-stock, *s.* Matériel roulant.

Roman, *a. & s.* Romain, -aine. **R. nose,** nez aquilin. **R. Catholic,** *a. & s.* Catholique (*mf*).

romance, *s.* **1.** Histoire *f* romanesque. **It's quite a r.,** c'est tout un roman. **2.** Romance *f*.

romantic, *a.* (*a*) Romanesque (*b*) Romantique.

Rome. *Pr.n.* Rome *f*.

romp[1], *s.* Gambades *fpl*.

romp[2], *v.i.* S'ébattre.

roof, *s.* **1.** Toit *m*, toiture *f*, comble *m*. **2. R. of the mouth,** palais *m*.

rook[1], *s.* Freux *m*.

rook[2], *s.* *Chess:* Tour *f*.

rookery, *s.* Colonie *f* de freux.

room, *s.* **1.** Place *f*, espace *m*. **2. There is r. for improvement,** cela laisse à désirer. **3.** (*a*) Pièce *f*; salle *f*; chambre *f*. **Private r.,** cabinet particulier; salon réservé. (*b*) *pl.* Appartement *m*.

roomy, *a.* Spacieux; ample.

roost[1], *s.* Juchoir *m*, perchoir *m*.

roost[2], *v.i.* Se jucher.

rooster, *s.* Coq *m*.

root[1], *s.* **1.** Racine *f*. **2.** Source *f*, fondement *m*.

root[2], *v.tr.* Enraciner. **Rooted to the spot,** cloué sur place. **root out, up,** *v.tr.* Déraciner; extirper.

rooted, *a.* Enraciné, invétéré.

rope[1], *s.* **1.** Corde *f*, cordage *m*. **To know the ropes**, connaître son affaire. **2.** Grand collier.

rope[2], *v.tr.* **1.** Corder **2.** Roped **together**, en cordée.

rope-ladder, *s.* Échelle *f* de corde.

rosary, *s.* Rosaire *m.*

rose, *s.* **1.** Rose *f.* **2.** Pomme *f.* **3.** Rose *m.*

roseate, *a.* Rose, rosé.

rosebud, *s.* Bouton *m* de rose

rose-bush, *s.* Rosier *m.*

rose-coloured, *a.* Rose, rosé ; couleur de rose *inv.*

rosemary, *s.* Romarin *m.*

rose-tree, *s.* Rosier *m.*

rosette, *s.* Cocarde *f* ; rosette *f.*

rose-water, *s.* Eau *f* de rose.

rosewood, *s.* Palissandre *m.*

rosin, *s.* Colophane *f.*

rostrum, *s.* Tribune *f.*

rosy, *a.* Rose, rosé. **R. cheeks**, joues vermeilles.

rot[1], *s.* **1.** Pourriture *f*, carie *f.* **2.** Démoralisation *f.*

rot[2]. **I.** *v.i.* (Se) pourrir. **2.** *v.tr.* Pourrir, faire pourrir.

rota, *s.* Liste *f* ; tableau *m.*

rotary, *a.* Rotatif, rotatoire

rotate. **1.** *v.i.* Tourner. **2.** *v.tr.* Faire tourner.

rotation, *s.* **1.** Rotation *f.* **2. In r.**, à tour de rôle.

rotten, *a.* Pourri, carié.

rottenness, *s.* État *m* de pourriture.

rotund, *a.* Rond, arrondi.

rotunda, *s.* Rotonde *f.*

rotundity, *s.* Rondeur *f*, rotondité *f.*

rouge, *s.* Rouge *m*, fard *m.*

rough. **I.** *a.* **1.** (*a*) Rêche, rugueux ; rude. (*b*) Inégal, accidenté. **2.** Grossier ; brutal, -aux. **R. sea**, mer agitée. **R. weather**, gros temps. **3.** Grossier ; bourru, rude. **4.** Approximatif. **R. draft**, brouillon *m.* **II. rough**, *adv.* Rudement, grossièrement. **III. rough**, *s.* Voyou *m.*

roughen, *v.tr.* Rendre rude, rugueux.

roughly, *adv.* **1.** Rudement ; brutalement. **2.** Grossièrement. **3.** Approximativement ; à peu près. **R. speaking**, en général.

roughness, *s.* **1.** Aspérité *f*, rugosité *f.* **2.** (*a*) Grossièreté *f.* (*b*) Agitation *f.* **3.** Rudesse *f.*

roulette, *s.* Roulette *f.*

round[1]. **I.** *a.* **1.** Rond, circulaire. **R. shoulders**, épaules voûtées. **2. R. dance**, ronde *f.* **R. towel**, essuie-main(s) à rouleau. **3. In r. figures**, en chiffres ronds. **II. round**, *s.* **1.** Cercle *m*, rond *m.* **2. R. of beef**, tranche grasse. **R. of toast**, rôtie *f.* **3.** (*a*) Tour *m.* **To have a r. of golf**, faire une tournée de golf. (*b*) Tournée *f.* **4.** Round *m*, reprise *f.* **5. R. of applause**, salve *f* d'applaudissements.

round[2]. **I.** *adv.* **1.** (*a*) **To go r.**, tourner. **To turn r.**, se retourner. (*b*) **All the year r.**, toute l'année. **2.** Autour. **3. To hand r.**, faire circuler. **II. round**, *prep.* **1.** Autour de. **2. To go r.**, contourner.

round[3], *v.tr.* Doubler.

roundabout. I. *s.* **1.** Chevaux *mpl* de bois ; carrousel *m.* **2.** Sens *m* gyro ; circulation *f* giratoire. **II. roundabout**, *a.* Détourné, indirect.

rounded, *a.* Arrondi.

roundish, *a.* Rondelet, -ette.

roundness, *s.* Rondeur *f.*

round-shouldered, *a.* Au dos voûté.

rouse. **I.** *v.tr.* **1.** (*a*) Réveiller ; secouer ; inciter. (*b*) Mettre en colère. **2.** Susciter. **II. rouse**, *v.i.* Se réveiller ; se secouer.

rousing, *a.* Enlevant.

rout[1], *s.* Déroute *f.*

rout[2], *v.tr.* Mettre en déroute.

route, *s.* Itinéraire *m* ; route *f.*

routed, *a.* En déroute.

routine, *s.* Routine *f.*

rove, *v.i.* Rôder ; vagabonder.

roving[1], *a.* Vagabond, nomade.

roving[2], *s.* Vagabondage *m.*

row[1], *s.* Rang *m*, rangée *f* ; ligne *f.*

row[2], *s.* Promenade *f* en canot.

row[3]. **I.** *v.i.* (*a*) Ramer ; nager. **To row a race**, faire une course d'aviron. (*b*) Canoter. **2.** *v.tr.* Conduire à l'aviron.

row[4], *s.* **1.** Tapage *m*, vacarme *m.* **2.** Rixe *f*, scène *f.* **3.** Réprimande *f.*

rowdy. **I.** *a.* Tapageur, -euse. **2.** *s.* Voyou *m.*

rower, *s.* Rameur, -euse.

rowing, *s.* Conduite *f* à l'aviron ; nage *f* ; canotage *m.*

rowing-boat, s. Bateau m à rames ; canot m à l'aviron.

rowlocks, s.pl. Dames f de nage.

royal, a. (a) Royal, -aux. (b) Royal, princier.

royalist, a. & s. Royaliste (mf).

royally, adv. Royalement.

royalty, s. 1. Royauté f. 2. pl. Redevance f ; droits m d'auteur.

rub¹, s. Frottement m ; friction f.

rub², 1 v.tr. Frotter. 2. v.i. Frotter ; se frotter. **rub down,** v.tr. (a) Panser. (b) Frictionner. **rub out,** v.tr. Effacer. **rub up,** v.tr. Astiquer, fourbir.

rubber¹, s 1. Frottoir m. 2. (a) (India-)r., gomme f à effacer. (b) (India-)r., caoutchouc m.

rubber², s. Robre m. **The r. game,** la belle.

rubbing, s. Frottage m.

rubbish, s. 1. (a) Immondices fpl, détritus mpl. (b) Choses fpl sans valeur. (c) Camelote f. 2. Bêtises f.

rubbishy, a. Sans valeur ; de camelote.

rubble, s. Blocaille f.

rubicund, a. Rubicond ; rougeaud.

ruby, s. Rubis m.

rucksack, s. Sac m touriste.

rudder, s. Gouvernail m.

ruddiness s. Coloration f du teint.

ruddy, a. (a) Coloré, haut en couleur. (b) Rougeâtre.

rude, a. 1. (a) Primitif, rude. (b) Grossier. 2. Brusque. 3. Impoli ; mal élevé.

rudely, adv. 1. Grossièrement. 2. Brusquement. 3. Impoliment.

rudeness, s. Impolitesse f.

rudiment, s. Rudiment m.

rudimentary, a. Rudimentaire.

rue¹, v.tr. Se repentir de.

rue², s. Rue f.

rueful, a. Triste, lugubre.

ruffian, s. Bandit m, brute f.

ruffianly, a. Brutal.

ruffle, v.tr. Ébouriffer ; troubler, rider ; contrarier.

rug, s. 1. Couverture f. 2. Carpette f ; descente f de lit.

rugged, a. 1. Rugueux. 2. Rude, irrégulier. 3. Bourru, rude.

ruggedness, s. 1. Rugosité f. 2. Rudesse f.

ruin¹, s. Ruine f.

ruin², v.tr. Ruiner.

ruined, a. 1. En ruines. 2. Ruiné.

ruinous, a. 1. En ruines ; délabré. 2. Ruineux.

rule¹, s. 1. Règle f. (a) **As a r.,** en règle générale. (b) **Rules and regulations,** statuts m et règlements m. 2. Empire m, autorité f.

rule², v.tr. 1. Gouverner, régir. 2. Régler, rayer. **To r. a line,** tracer une ligne à la règle. **rule out,** v.tr. 1. Écarter, éliminer. 2. Biffer, rayer.

ruler, s. 1. Souverain, -aine. 2. Règle f, mètre m.

ruling¹, a. Souverain, dominant.

ruling², s. Décision f.

rum, s. Rhum m.

Rumania. Pr.n. La Roumanie.

Rumanian, a. & s. Roumain, -aine.

rumble¹, s. 1. Grondement m ; roulement m.

rumble², v.i. Gronder ; rouler.

ruminate, v.i. Ruminer.

rumination, s. Rumination f.

rummage, v.i. Fouiller.

rumour¹, s. Rumeur f, bruit m.

rumour², v.tr. **It is rumoured,** le bruit court.

rumple, v.tr. Chiffonner ; ébouriffer.

rump-steak, s. Romsteck m.

run¹, s. 1. Course f. 2. (a) Course, promenade f. (b) Trajet m. (c) Traversée f, parcours m. 3. Suite f. **In the long run,** à la longue. 4. Vogue f.

run². I. v.i. 1. Courir. 2. Fuir, s'enfuir, se sauver. 3. (a) Aller, marcher. (b) Circuler. 4. Fonctionner, marcher. 5. Déteindre. 6. Couler.

II. **run,** v.tr. 1. **To run s.o. close,** serrer qn de près. 2. **To run one's head against the door,** donner de la tête contre la porte. 3. Tenir. 4. Passer ; faire passer. **To run one's eye over,** parcourir des yeux. **run across,** v.i. Rencontrer par hasard. **run against,** v.i. Se heurter contre. **run along,** v.i. Longer. **run away,** v.i. (a) S'enfuir, se sauver. (b) S'emballer. (c) **To run away with s.o.,** enlever qn. **run down.** I. v.i. 1. Couler sur. 2. S'arrêter. II. **run down,** v.tr. 1. Dénigrer, déprécier. 2. Couler. **run into,** v.i. (a) To run into debt, s'endetter. (b) Entrer en collision avec. **run off.** I. v.i. Fuir, s'enfuir, se sauver. 2. v.tr. Faire écouler. **run on,** v.i. (a) Continuer sa course. (b) S'écouler. (c) Continuer à parler. **run out,** v.i. (a) Sortir en courant. (b) Se retirer. (c) Couler, fuir. (d) Se terminer, expirer. (e) Venir à manquer. **run over,** v.i. I. (a) Passer en revue. (b) Passer sur le corps de. 2. Déborder. **run round,** v.i. Faire le tour de. **run through.** I. v.i. (a) Traverser en courant. (b) Parcourir du regard. (c) Dissiper. 2. v.tr. Transpercer. **run up.** I. v.i. (a) Accourir. (b) Monter, s'élever. 2. v.tr. Hisser.

runaway, attrib. a. & s. (a) Fugitif. -ive. (b) **R. horse,** cheval emballé.

rung, s. Échelon m; bâton m.

runner, s. I. Coureur, -euse. 2. **Scarlet r.,** haricot m d'Espagne. 3. Patin m.

running[1], a. I. **R. jump,** saut avec élan. 2. **R. water,** eau courante. 3. (a) Continu. (b) Consécutif; de suite.

running[2], s. I. Course(s) f(pl). **To be in the r.,** avoir des chances d'arriver. 2. (a) Marche f, fonctionnement m. **In r. order,** prêt au service. (b) Direction f.

runway, s. Piste f d'envol.

rupture, s. Rupture f; brouille f.

rural, a. Rural, -aux; champêtre.

ruse, s. Ruse f, stratagème m.

rush[1], s. Jonc m.

rush[2], s. I. (a) Course précipitée. **To make a r. at,** se précipiter sur. (b) **R. hours,** heures d'affluence. 2. Hâte f.

rush[3]. I. v.t. (a) Se précipiter; s'élancer. (b) **T. r. at,** fondre sur. II. **rush,** v.tr. I. Pousser violemment; transporter d'urgence. 2. Dépêcher; exécuter d'urgence

russet, a. & s. Roussâtre.

Russia. Pr.n. La Russie.

Russian. I. s. (a) Russe mf. (b) Le russe. 2. a. De Russie; russe.

rust[1], s. Rouille f.

rust[2]. I. v.i. Se rouiller. 2. v.tr. Rouiller.

rustic. I. a. Rustique; agreste. 2. s. Paysan, -anne.

rustle[1], s. Bruissement m.

rustle[2]. I. v.i. Bruire; faire froufrou. 2. v.tr. Faire bruire.

rusty, a. Rouillé.

rut, s. Ornière f.

ruthless, a. Impitoyable.

ruthlessly, adv. Sans pitié.

ruthlessness, s. Cruauté f.

rye, Seigle m.

S

S, s, s. (La lettre) S, s f.

Sabbath, s. (a) Sabbat m. (b) Dimanche m.

sable[1], s. Zibeline f.

sable[2], a. Noir.

sabot, s. Sabot m.

sabotage[1], s. Sabotage m.

sabotage[2], v.tr. Saboter.

sabre, s. Sabre m.

saccharin, s. Saccharine f.

sachet, s. Sachet m.

sack[1], s. I. (Grand) sac. 2. **To give s.o. the s.,** congédier qn.

sack[2], v.tr. Congédier.

sack[3], s. Sac m, pillage m.

sack[4], v.tr. Saccager, mettre à sac.

sackcloth, s. Toile f à sacs.

sackful, a. Sachée f, plein sac.

sacrament, s. Sacrement m.

sacred, a. I. (a) Sacré. (b) Con-

sacré. 2. (a) Sacré, saint. (b) **S. music,** musique religieuse. 3. Sacré, inviolable.

sacredness, s. Inviolabilité f.

sacrifice[1], s. I. (a) Sacrifice m. (b) Victime f. 2. **At a s.,** à perte.

sacrifice[2], v.tr. Sacrifier.

sacrilege, s. Sacrilège m.

sacrilegious, a. Sacrilège.

sacristan, s. Sacristain m.

sacristy, s. Sacristie f.

sacrosanct, a. Sacro-saint.

sad, a. (a) Triste. **To make sad,** attrister. (b) Affligeant; morne.

sadden, v.tr. Attrister, affliger.

saddle[1], s. Selle f.

saddle[2], v.tr. (a) Seller. (b) Charger (with, de).

saddle-bag, s. I. Sacoche f. 2. Moquette f.

saddler, s. Sellier m.

sadist, s. Sadique mf.

sadistic, a. Sadique.

sadly, adv. Tristement.

sadness, s. Tristesse f, mélancolie f.

safe[1], s. Coffre-fort m, pl. coffres-forts.

safe[2], a. **1.** (a) En sûreté ; à l'abri. (b) S. and sound, sain et sauf. **2.** (a) Sans danger ; sûr (b) Is it s.? est-ce qu'il n'y a pas de danger ? (c) To be on the s. side, être du bon côté. It is s. to say, on peut dire à coup sûr.

safe-conduct, s. Sauf-conduit m, pl. sauf-conduits.

safeguard[1], s. Sauvegarde f.

safeguard[2], v.tr. Sauvegarder.

safe-keeping, s. Bonne garde.

safely, adv. **1.** Sans accident ; sain et sauf. **2.** Sûrement, sans danger.

safety, s. Sûreté f, sécurité f. In a place of s., en lieu sûr.

safety-pin, s. Épingle de sûrete.

safety-valve, s. Soupape f de sûreté.

saffron, s. Safran m.

sag, v.i. S'affaisser, fléchir.

sagacious, a. Sagace, avisé.

sagacity, s. Sagacité f ; sagesse f.

sage[1]. **1.** a. Sage, prudent. **2.** s. Philosophe m, sage m.

sage[2], s. Sauge f.

sago, s. Sagou m. **S. pudding,** sagou au lait.

sail[1], s. **1.** Voile f. To set s., mettre à la voile. **2.** Aile f, volant m.

sail[2], s. To go for a s., faire une promenade à la voile.

sail[3], v.i. (a) Aller à la voile ; naviguer. (b) Partir ; prendre la mer.

sailcloth, s. Toile f à voile(s).

sailing-ship, s. Voilier m.

sailor, s. Marin m, matelot m.

saint. (a) s. Saint, -e. **All Saints' (Day),** la Toussaint. (b) Attrib.a. Saint.

Saint Bernard, s. (Chien m) saint-bernard inv.

Saint Lawrence. Pr.n. Saint-Laurent.

saintliness, s. Sainteté f.

saintly, a. (De) saint.

sake, s. For the s. of, à cause de. For my s., pour moi.

salad, s. Salade f. **Mixed s.,** salade panachée. **Fruit s.,** macédoine f de fruits.

salad-bowl, s. Saladier m.

salad-oil, s. Huile f comestible.

salary, s. Traitement m, appointements mpl.

sale, s. **1.** Vente f ; débit m, mise f en vente. For s., à vendre. **2. S. price,** prix de solde.

saleable, a. De vente facile.

sale-room, s. Salle f de(s) vente(s).

salesman, s. Vendeur m.

salesmanship, s. L'art m de vendre.

saleswoman, s. Vendeuse f.

salient, a. Saillant.

saline, a. Salin, salé.

saliva, s. Salive f.

sallow, a. Jaunâtre, olivâtre.

sallowness, s. Ton m jaunâtre.

salmon, s. Saumon m.

salmon-trout, s. Truite saumonée.

salon, s. Salon m.

saloon, s. **1.** Salle f, salon m. **2. S. deck,** pont de première classe.

salt[1]. **I.** s. Sel m. **II. salt,** a. Salé.

salt[2], v.tr. (a) Saler. (b) Saupoudrer de sel.

salt-cellar, s. Salière f.

saltness, s. Salure f, salinité f.

saltpetre, s. Salpêtre m.

salt-spoon, s. Cuiller f à sel.

salubrious, a. Salubre, sain.

salubrity, s. Salubrité f.

salutary, a. Salutaire.

salutation, s. Salutation f.

salute[1], s. Salut m, salutation f.

salute[2], v.tr. Saluer.

salvage, s. **1.** Sauvetage m. **2.** Objets sauvés.

salvation, s. Salut m.

salve[1], s. Onguent m, baume m.

salve[2], v.tr. Sauver, relever (un vaisseau) ; effectuer le sauvetage de.

salver, s. Plateau m.

salvo, s. Salve f.

same. I. a. & pron. (Le, la) même, (les) mêmes. **Of the s. kind,** similaire. In the s. way, de même. At the s. time, (i) en même temps ; (ii) à la fois. It's all the s., c'est tout un. It is all the s. to me, ça m'est égal. **2.** adv. To think the s., penser de même. All the s., malgré tout ; quand même.

sameness, s. **1.** (a) Identité f. (b) Ressemblance f. **2.** Monotonie f.

sample[1], s. Échantillon m.

sample[2], *v.t*. Goûter ; essayer.

sanatorium, *s*. Sanatorium *m*.

sanctify, *v.tr*. Sanctifier ; consacrer.

sanctimonious, *a*. Béat.

sanction[1], *s*. Sanction *f*.

sanction[2], *v.tr*. Sanctionner.

sanctity, *s*. **1**. Sainteté *f*. **2**. Inviolabilité *f*.

sanctuary, *s*. Sanctuaire *m*.

sand, *s*. **1**. (*a*) Sable *m*. (*b*) *pl*. Banc *m* de sable. **2**. *pl*. Plage *f*, grève *f*

sandal, *s*. Sandale *f*.

sandbag[1], *s*. **1**. Sac *m* à terre. **2**. Assommoir *m* ; boudin *m*.

sandbag[2], *v.tr*. Assommer.

sand-bank, *s*. Banc *m* de sable.

sand-hill, *s*. Dune *f*.

sandpaper[1], *s*. Papier *m* de verre.

sandpaper[2], *v.tr*. Frotter au papier de verre.

sand-shoes, *s.pl*. Sandales *f*. espadrilles *f*.

sandstone, *s*. Grès *m*.

sandwich[1], *s*. Sandwich *m*. **Ham sandwiches**, sandwichs au jambon.

sandwich[2], *v.tr*. Serrer, intercaler.

sandy, *a*. **1**. Sableux, sablonneux ; sablé. **2**. Roux pâle *inv*.

sane, *a*. Sain d'esprit ; sensé.

sanely, *adv*. Raisonnablement.

sanguinary, *a*. (*a*) Sanguinaire, sanglant. (*b*) Altéré de sang.

sanguine, *a*. (*a*) Sanguin. (*b*) Confiant, optimiste.

sanitary, *a*. Hygiénique, sanitaire.

sanitation, *s*. Hygiène *f* ; système *m* sanitaire.

sanity, *s*. Santé *f* d'esprit ; jugement sain.

Santa Claus. *Pr.n*. Le Bonhomme Noël.

sap[1], *s*. Sève *f*.

sap[2], *v.tr. & i*. Saper, miner.

sapling, *s*. Jeune arbre *m* ; baliveau *m*.

sapphire, *s*. Saphir *m*.

sap-wood, *s*. Aubier *m*.

sarcasm, *s*. **1**. Ironie *f* ; esprit *m* sarcastique. **2**. Sarcasme *m*.

sarcastic, *a*. Sarcastique ; mordant. **S. remark**, sarcasme *m*.

sarcastically, *adv*. D'une manière sarcastique ; ironiquement.

sardine, *s*. Sardine *f*.

Sardinia. *Pr.n*. La Sardaigne.

Sardinian, *a. & s*. Sarde (*mf*).

sardonic, *a*. Sardonique.

sardonically, *adv*. Sardoniquement.

Sark. *Pr.n*. Sercq *m*.

sash[1], *s*. Écharpe *f* ; ceinture *f*.

sash[2], *s*. Cadre *m*.

Satan. *Pr.n*. Satan *m*.

satanic, *a*. Satanique, diabolique.

satchel, *s*. Sacoche *f* ; cartable *m*.

sate, *v.tr*. **1**. Assouvir ; rassasier **2**. Rassasier ; blaser (*with*, de).

sated, *a*. **1**. Rassasié (*with*, de). **2**. **To become s.**, se blaser (*with*, de).

satellite, *s*. Satellite *m*.

satiate, *v.tr*. Rassasier (*with*, de) ; blaser (*with*, de).

satiated, *a*. Rassasié.

satiety, *s*. Satiété *f*.

satin, *s*. Satin *m*.

satire, *s*. Satire *f*, sarcasme *m*.

satirical, *a*. **1**. Satirique **2**. Sarcastique, ironique.

satirically, *adv*. Satiriquement.

satisfaction, *s*. **1**. (*a*) Acquittement *m*, paiement *m*. (*b*) Réparation *f*. (*c*) Assouvissement *m*. **2**. Satisfaction *f*, contentement *m*.

satisfactorily, *adv*. De façon satisfaisante.

satisfactory, *a*. Satisfaisant

satisfied, *a*. **1**. Content, satisfait. **2**. Convaincu.

satisfy, *v.tr*. **1**. S'acquitter de ; remplir. **2**. Satisfaire. **3**. Convaincre.

satisfying, *a*. Satisfaisant ; nourrissant.

saturate, *v.tr*. Saturer (*with*, de)

saturation, *s*. Saturation *f*.

Saturday, *s*. Samedi *m*.

saturnine, *a*. Taciturne, sombre

satyr, *s*. Satyre *m*.

sauce, *s* (*a*) Sauce *f*. (*b*) Assaisonnement *m* ; condiment *m*.

sauce-boat, *s*. Saucière *f*

saucepan, *s*. Casserole *f*

saucer, *s*. Soucoupe *f*.

saucily, *adv*. D'un ton effronté

sauciness, *s*. Impertinence *f*.

saucy, *a*. Impertinent, effronté

saunter[1], *s*. Flânerie *f*

saunter[2], *v.i*. Flâner.

sausage, *s*. (*a*) Saucisse *f* (*b*) Saucisson *m*.

sausage-meat, *s*. Chair *f* à saucisse.

sausage-roll, *s*. Saucisse enrobée.

savage. **1**. *a*. (*a*) Sauvage, barbare. (*b*) Féroce. (*c*) Furieux ; en rage. **2**. *s*. Sauvage *mf*.

15

savagely, *adv.* Sauvagement féroce-ment; furieusement.

savageness, *s.* Férocité f.

save[1], *v.tr.* **1.** Sauver. **To s. appear-ances,** sauver les apparences. **2.** (*a*) Mettre de côté; réserver. (*b*) Éco-nomiser, épargner; *abs.* économiser pour l'avenir. **3.** Ménager; éviter. **To s. time,** gagner du temps. **4. To s. s.o. sth.,** éviter. épargner, qch. à qn.

save[2], *prep.* Sauf, excepté.

saveloy, *s.* Cervelas m.

saving[1]. I. *a.* **1.** Qui sauve; qui protège. **2.** Économe, ménager **3. S. clause,** réservation f.

  II. **saving** I. *prep. & conj.* Sauf, excepté. **2.** *prep.* Sauf.

saving[2], *s.* **1.** (*a*) Délivrance f, salut m. (*b*) Sauvetage *m.* (*c*) Protection f **2.** *pl.* Économies.

savings-bank, *s.* Caisse f d'épargne

saviour, *s.* Sauveur m.

savour, *s.* Saveur f, goût m.

savoury. I. *a.* (*a*) Savoureux appé-tissant; succulent. (*b*) **S. herbs,** plantes aromatiques. **S. omelette,** omelette aux fines herbes. **2.** *s.* Entremets non sucré.

Savoy. I. *Pr.n.* La Savoie **2.** *s.* Chou, *pl.* -oux, frisé.

saw[1], *s.* Scie f.

saw[2], *v.tr.* Scier. **To saw up wood,** débiter du bois.

sawdust, *s.* Sciure f.

sawmill, *s.* Scierie f.

saxophone, *s.* Saxophone m.

say[1], *s.* **To have one's say,** dire son mot.

say[2], *v.tr.* Dire. **1.** (*a*) **To say again,** répéter. **What did you say?** plaît-il? **So he says!** A l'en croire! **Said he,** fit-il. (*b*) **So to say,** pour ainsi dire. **One might as well say,** autant dire. **I must say,** j'avoue; franchement. **That is to say,** c'est-à-dire; à savoir. **To say nothing of,** sans parler de. (*c*) **I should say not,** je ne crois pas; je crois que non. **Didn't I say so!** quand je vous le disais! (*d*) **I say!** dites donc! **2.** Dire, réciter; faire.

saying, *s.* **1.** (*a*) **It goes without s.,** il va de soi. (*b*) **There is no s.,** im-possible de dire. **2.** Dit m; dicton m.

scab, *s.* Croûte f.

scabbard, *s.* Fourreau m

scaffold, *s.* Échafaud m.

scaffolding, *s.* Échafaudage m.

scald[1], *s.* Échaudure f.

scald[2], *v.tr.* Échauder.

scalding, *a.* **S. hot,** tout bouillant

scale[1], *s.* Écaille f.

scale[2], *v.tr.* Écailler.

scale[3], *s.* **1.** Plateau m, plat m (de balance). **To turn the s.,** emporter la balance. **2.** *pl.* Balance.

scale[4], *s.* **1.** (*a*) Échelle f. **On a large s.,** en grand. (*b*) Envergure f; étendue f. **2.** Gamme f.

scale[5], *v.tr.* Escalader.

scallop, *s.* **1.** Coquille f (de poisson au gratin). **2.** Feston m, dentelure f.

scalp[1], *s.* **1.** Cuir chevelu. **2.** Scalpe m.

scalp[2], *v.tr.* Scalper.

scalpel, *s.* Scalpel m.

scaly, *a.* Écailleux, squameux.

scamp[1], *s.* Vaurien, -enne; garne-ment m.

scamp[2], *v.tr.* Bâcler.

scamper[1], *s.* (*a*) Course f folâtre, allègre. (*b*) Course rapide.

scamper[2], *v.i.* (*a*) Courir allègre-ment. (*b*) **To s. off,** se sauver à toutes jambes.

scan, *v.tr.* **1.** (*a*) Scander, mesurer. (*b*) *v.i.* Se scander. **2.** Scruter.

scandal, *s.* **1.** Scandale m; honte f. **2.** Médisance f.

scandalize, *v.tr.* Scandaliser.

scandal-monger, *s.* Mauvaise langue.

scandalous, *a.* Scandaleux, infâme.

scandalously, *adv.* Scandaleuse-ment.

scant, *a.* Insuffisant, peu abondant

scantily, *adv.* Insuffisamment; peu abondamment.

scantiness, *s.* Insuffisance f, rareté f.

scanty, *a.* Insuffisant; peu abon-dant; étroit.

scapegoat, *s.* Bouc m émissaire.

scapegrace, *s* Polisson, -onne.

scar[1], *s.* Cicatrice f.

scar[2], *v.tr.* Laisser une cicatrice sur.

scarab, *s.* Scarabée m.

scarce. **1.** *a.* Rare; peu abondant. **2.** *adv.* A peine.

scarcely, *adv.* A peine; presque pas

scarcity, *s.* Rareté f; manque m.

scare[1], *s.* Panique f, alarme f.

scare[2], *v.tr.* Effrayer, effarer, alarmer. **To s. away,** effaroucher.

scarecrow, *s.* Épouvantail m.

scare-monger, s. Alarmiste mf.

scarf, s. Écharpe f; fichu m; cache-col m inv; foulard m.

scarlet, a. & s. Écarlate (f). **S. fever,** scarlatine f.

scarred, a. Couturé; balafré.

scatheless, a. Sain et sauf.

scathing, a. Acerbe, cinglant.

scatter. **1.** v.tr. (a) Disperser, mettre en fuite. (b) Éparpiller. **2.** v.i. se disperser; s'éparpiller.

scattered, a. Dispersé, éparpillé; épars.

scattering, s. **1.** Dispersion f; éparpillement m. **2.** Petit nombre.

scavenger, s. Boueur m; balayeur m des rues.

scenario, s. Scénario m.

scene, s. **1.** (a) Scène f. **The s. is laid in London,** l'action f se passe à Londres. (b) Théâtre m, lieu m. **2.** Scène, incident m, spectacle m. **3.** Décor m. **Behind the scenes,** dans la coulisse.

scenery, s. **1.** Décors mpl. **2.** Paysage m; vue f.

scent[1], s. **1.** Parfum m, senteur f; odeur f. **2.** (a) Fumet m. (b) Piste f, voie f. **3.** Odorat m, flair m.

scent[2], v.tr. **1.** Flairer. **2.** Parfumer, embaumer.

scent-bottle, s. Flacon m de parfum; flacon à odeur.

scented, a. **1.** Parfumé (with, de); embaumé (with, de). **2.** Odorant.

sceptic, s. Sceptique mf.

sceptical, a. Sceptique.

sceptically, adv. Avec scepticisme.

scepticism, s. Scepticisme m.

sceptre, s. Sceptre m.

schedule, s. **1.** (a) Annexe f. (b) Bordereau m. **2.** (a) Inventaire m; barème m. (b) Cédule f.

scheme[1], s. **1.** Arrangement m, combinaison f. **2.** Résumé m, exposé m. **3.** (a) Plan, projet m. (b) Machination f.

scheme[2]. **1.** v.i. Intriguer. **2.** v.tr. Machiner, combiner.

schemer, s. Intrigant, -ante.

scheming[1], a. Intrigant.

scheming[2], s. **1.** Plans mpl, projets mpl. **2.** Intrigues fpl.

schism, s. Schisme m.

scholar, s. **1.** Élève mf, écolier, -ière. **2.** Savant, -ante. **3.** Boursier, -ière.

scholarly, a. Savant, érudit.

scholarship, s. **1.** Savoir m, science f. **2.** Bourse f.

scholastic, a. Scolaire.

school[1], s. **1.** (a) École f. (b) **The upper s.,** les hautes classes. **2.** **To be in s.,** être en classe. **S. children,** écoliers m. **3.** École, institut m. **4.** Faculté f.

school[2], v.tr. **1.** Instruire; faire l'éducation de. **2.** Former; discipliner.

school[3], s. Banc m; bande f.

school-book, s. Livre m classique; livre de classe.

schoolboy, s. Écolier m; élève m.

schoolfellow, s. Camarade mf de classe.

schoolgirl, s. Écolière f; élève f.

schooling, s. Instruction f, éducation f.

schoolmaster, s. (a) Instituteur m; maître m d'école; professeur m. (b) Directeur m.

schoolmistress, s. (a) Institutrice f; maîtresse f d'école; professeur m. (b) Directrice f.

schoolroom, s. (Salle f de) classe f.

school-teacher, s. Instituteur, -trice.

schooner, s Goélette f.

science, s. Science f.

scientific, a. Scientifique. **S. instruments,** instruments de précision.

scientist, s. Savant, -ante; homme de science.

scimitar, s. Cimeterre m.

scintillate, v.i. Scintiller, étinceler.

scissors, s.pl. Ciseaux mpl.

scoff, v.i. Se moquer.

scoffer, s Moqueur, -euse; railleur, -euse.

scoffing[1], a. Moqueur, -euse.

scoffing[2], s. Moquerie f, raillerie f.

scold. **1.** v.i. Gronder. **2.** v.tr. Gronder, réprimander.

scolding[1], a. Grondeur, -euse.

scolding[2], s. Gronderie f, semonce f.

scone, s. Pain m au lait.

scoop[1], s. **1.** Pelle f à main. **2.** Seau m à charbon.

scoop[2], v.tr. **To s.** (out), excaver; évider. **To s. up,** ramasser avec la pelle.

scooter, s. Trottinette f, patinette f.

scope, s. (a) Portée f, étendue f. (b) Espace m, place f. **Full s.,** libre carrière.

scorch. 1. *v.tr.* Roussir ; rôtir, flétrir. **2.** *v.i.* Roussir. **3.** *v.i.* Brûler le pavé.

scorching[1]**. 1.** *a.* Brûlant, ardent. **2.** *adv.* S. hot, tout brûlant.

scorching[2]**,** *s.* **1.** Roussissement *m.* **2.** Allure excessive.

score[1]**,** *s.* **1.** Éraflure *f*, entaille *f.* **2.** Old scores, vieux comptes. **3.** Points *mpl.* What's the s. ? où en est le jeu ? **4.** Partition *f.* **5.** (*a*) Vingt, vingtaine *f.* (*b*) *pl.* Un grand nombre. **6.** Point *m*, sujet *m.* On the s. of, pour cause de.

score[2]**,** *v.tr.* **1.** Érafler ; strier ; rayer. **2.** (*a*) Compter, marquer. (*b*) Gagner.

scorer, *s.* Marqueur *m.*

scoring, *s.* Marque *f.* S. board, tableau *m*, boulier *m.*

scorn[1]**,** *s.* Dédain *m*, mépris *m.*

scorn[2]**,** *v.tr.* Dédaigner, mépriser.

scornful, *a.* Dédaigneux, méprisant.

scornfully, *adv* Dédaigneusement ; avec mépris.

scorpion, *s.* Scorpion *m.*

Scot[1]**,** *s.* Écossais, -aise.

scot[2]**,** *s.* Écot *m.*

Scotch. *a.* Écossais ; d'Écosse. S. terrier, terrier griffon.

Scotchman, *s.* Écossais *m.*

Scotchwoman, *s.* Écossaise *f.*

scot-free, *a.* **1.** Indemne. **2.** Sans frais.

Scotland. *Pr.n.* L'Écosse *f.*

Scots, *a.* Écossais.

Scotsman, *s.* Écossais *m.*

Scotswoman, *s.* Écossaise *f.*

Scottish, *a.* Écossais.

scoundrel, *s* Chenapan *m*, coquin *m*, scélérat *m.*

scoundrelly, *a.* Scélérat, vil.

scour[1]**,** *s.* Nettoyage *m*, récurage *m.*

scour[2]**,** *v.tr.* **1.** Nettoyer ; récurer. **2.** Donner une chasse d'eau à.

scour[3]**,** *v.tr.* Parcourir ; fouiller.

scourge[1]**,** *s.* Fléau *m.*

scourge[2]**,** *v.tr.* Châtier.

scout[1]**,** *s.* (*a*) Éclaireur *m* (*b*) Boy s., boy-scout *m*, *pl.* boy-scouts.

scout[2]**,** *v.i.* Aller en reconnaissance.

scout[3]**,** *v.tr.* Repousser avec mépris.

scoutmaster, *s.* Chef *m* éclaireur.

scowl[1]**,** *s.* Air menaçant, renfrogné ; froncement *m* de(s) sourcils.

scowl[2]**,** *v.i.* Se renfrogner ; froncer les sourcils.

scowling, *a.* Renfrogné, menaçant.

scraggy, *a.* Décharné, maigre.

scramble[1]**,** *s.* **1.** Marche *f* à quatre pattes. **2.** Mêlée *f*, bousculade *f.*

scramble[2]**. 1.** *v.i.* (*a*) To s. up, monter à quatre pattes. (*b*) To s. for, se bousculer pour avoir. **2.** *v.tr* Scrambled eggs, œufs brouillés.

scrap[1]**,** *s.* **1.** Petit morceau ; bout *m* chiffon *m.* **2.** *pl.* Restes *m* ; bribes *f.*

scrap[2]**,** *v.tr.* Mettre au rebut

scrap[3]**,** *s.* Querelle *f*, rixe *f.*

scrap-book, s Album *m* (de découpures).

scrape[1]**,** *s.* **1.** Coup *m* de grattoir **2.** Mauvais pas.

scrape[2]**.** I. *v.tr.* **1.** Érafler. écorcher. **2.** Racler, gratter.
II. **scrape,** *v.i.* (*a*) Gratter. (*b*) Grincer. **scrape away,** *v.tr.* Enlever en raclant. **scrape off,** *v.tr.* Enlever au racloir.

scrap-iron, *s.* Ferraille *f.*

scratch[1]**,** *s.* **1.** (*a*) Coup *m* d'ongle, de griffe. (*b*) Égratignure *f*, éraflure *f.* **2.** (*a*) Grattement *m.* (*b*) Grincement *m.* **3.** Scratch *m.*

scratch[2]**.** I. *v.tr.* **1.** Égratigner, griffer ; donner un coup de griffe à. **2.** Gratter. *v.i.* To s. at, gratter à. **3.** To s. off, rayer, biffer. de. *Abs* Déclarer forfait.
II. **scratch,** *v.i.* Grincer, gratter. **scratch out,** *v.tr.* Rayer biffer, raturer.

scratch[3]**,** *a.* Improvisé, sommaire

scrawl[1]**,** *s.* Griffonnage *m.*

scrawl[2]**,** *v.tr.* Griffonner.

scream[1]**,** *s.* (*a*) Cri perçant. (*b*) Éclat *m.*

scream[2]**,** *v.i.* (*a*) Pousser des cris. (*b*) To s. with laughter, rire aux éclats.

scree, *s.* Éboulis *m.*

screech[1]**,** s Cri perçant ; cri rauque.

screech[2]**,** *v.i.* Pousser des cris perçants, des cris rauques.

screen[1]**,** *s.* **1.** (*a*) Écran *m.* (*b*) S. of trees, rideau *m* d'arbres. Under s. of, à l'abri de *m* de. **2.** Crible *m.*

screen[2]**,** *v.tr.* **1.** (*a*) Cacher, dérober. (*b*) Abriter, protéger. **2.** Tamiser. **3.** Mettre à l'écran.

screw[1]**,** *s.* **1.** Vis *f.* **2.** Hélice *f.* **3.** Coup *m* de tournevis. **4.** Avare *m.*

screw[2]**,** *v.tr.* Visser. **screw down,**

v.tr. Fermer à vis. **screw up,** *v.tr*
1. Plisser (les yeux); pincer (les lèvres). **2. To s. up one's courage,** prendre son courage à deux mains.
screwdriver, *s.* Tournevis *m.*
scribble[1], *s.* Griffonnage *m.*
scribble[2], *v.tr.* Griffonner.
scribbling, *s.* Griffonnage *m.* **S. paper,** papier à brouillon. **S. block,** bloc *m* brouillon.
scrimmage, *s.* Mêlée *f*; bousculade *f.*
script, *s.* (*a*) Manuscrit *m.* (*b*) Scénario *m.*
scriptural, *a.* Scriptural, -aux.
scripture, *s.* Holy S., l'Écriture sainte.
scroll, *s.* Rouleau *m.*
scrub[1], *s.* Broussailles *fpl*; brousse *f.*
scrub[2], *s.* Friction *f*; nettoyage *m.*
scrub[3], *v.tr.* Laver, frotter (le plancher).
scrubbing-brush, *s.* Brosse *f* de chiendent.
scruff, *s.* Nuque *f.*
scruple[1], *s.* Scrupule *m.*
scruple[2], *v.i.* Avoir des scrupules (à).
scrupulous, *a.* Scrupuleux; exact. méticuleux.
scrupulously, *adv.* **1.** Scrupuleusement. **2.** Méticuleusement.
scrutinize, *v.tr.* Scruter.
scrutinizing, *a.* Scrutateur, -trice.
scrutiny, *s.* Examen minutieux.
scuffle[1], *s.* Mêlée *f*, bousculade *f.*
scuffle[2], *v.i.* Se bousculer.
scull[1], *s.* **1.** Aviron *m*, rame *f.* **2.** Godille *f.*
scull[2], *v.i.* (*a*) Ramer, nager. (*b*) Godiller.
scullery, *s.* Arrière-cuisine *f.*
sculptor, *s.* Sculpteur *m.*
sculpture, *s.* Sculpture *f.*
scum, *s.* **1.** Écume *f.* **2.** Rebut *m.*
scurrilous, *a.* Grossier, injurieux.
scurvy[1], *s.* Scorbut *m.*
scurvy[2], *a.* Bas, *f.* basse, vil. vilain.
scut, *s.* Couette *f.*
scutcheon, *s.* Écu *m*, écusson *m.*
scuttle[1], *s.* Seau *m* à charbon.
scuttle[2], *v.tr.* Saborder.
scuttle[3], *v.i.* **To s. off,** déguerpir.
scythe, *s.* Faux *f.*
sea, *s.* **1.** Mer *f.* **1.** (*a*) **By the sea,** au bord de la mer. **By sea,** par (voie de) mer. **Sea trip,** excursion *f* en mer. (*b*) **The open sea,** le large. **All at sea,**

désorienté. **2.** (*a*) Lame *f.* houle *f.* (*b*) Paquet *m* de mer.
sea-bathing, *s.* Bains *mpl* de mer
sea-breeze, *s.* Brise *f* du large.
sea-coast, *s.* Littoral *m*, -aux; côte *f.*
seafaring, *a.* **S. man,** marin *m.*
sea-front, *s.* Digue *f*, esplanade *f.* **On the s.-f.,** sur la mer.
sea-gull, *s.* Mouette *f*, goéland *m.*
seal[1], *s.* Phoque *m.*
seal[2], *s.* Sceau *m*; cachet *m.*
seal[3], *v.tr.* **1.** (*a*) Sceller; cacheter. **2.** Fermer.
sea-level, *s.* Niveau *m* de la mer.
sealing-wax, *s.* Cire *f* à cacheter.
sealskin, *s.* **1.** Peau *f* de phoque. **2.** Loutre *f.*
seam[1], *s.* **1.** Couture *f.* **2.** Couche *f* gisement *m.*
seam[2], *v.tr.* Couturer.
seaman, *s.* Marin *m*, matelot *m.*
seamanship, *s.* Manœuvre *f.*
séance, *s.* Séance *f* de spiritisme.
seaplane, *s.* Hydravion *m.*
seaport, *s.* Port *m* de mer.
sear, *v.tr.* Flétrir, dessécher.
search[1], *s.* **1.** Recherche(s) *f* (*pl*). **In s. of,** à la recherche de. **2.** Visite *f.*
search[2]. **1.** *v.tr.* Inspecter; chercher dans; fouiller; visiter. **2.** *v.i.* **To s. for,** (re)chercher.
searching, *a.* Minutieux; pénétrant.
searchlight, *s.* Projecteur *m.*
sea-shore, *s.* (*a*) Rivage *m*; bord *m* de la mer. (*b*) Plage *f.*
sea-sick, *a.* **To be s.-s.,** avoir le mal de mer.
sea-sickness, *s.* Mal *m* de mer.
seaside, *s.* **1.** Bord *m* de la mer. **2.** *Attrib.* **S. resort,** station *f* balnéaire; plage *f.*
season[1], *s.* **1.** Saison *f.* **The dead s.,** la morte-saison. **2.** Période *f*, temps *m.* **In due s.,** en temps voulu.
season[2], *v.tr.* (*a*) Assaisonner, relever. (*b*) Dessécher. (*c*) Acclimater.
seasonable, *a.* **1.** De (la) saison. **2.** Opportun, à propos.
seasoned, *a.* **1.** Assaisonné. **2.** Sec, *f.* sèche.
seasoning, *s.* Assaisonnement *m.*
season-ticket, *s.* Carte *f* d'abonnement. **S.-t. holder,** abonné, -ée.
seat[1], *s.* **1.** (*a*) Siège *m*; banquette *f.* (*b*) **To take a s.,** s'asseoir. **To keep**

one's s., rester assis. (c) Place f.
Take your seats! "en voiture!"
2. Siège; fond m. 3. Théâtre m;
siège, centre m.
seat², v.tr. 1. (Faire) asseoir 2.
Placer; trouver place pour.
sea-wall, s. Digue f.
sea-water, s. Eau f de mer.
seaweed, s. Algue f, goémon m
secede, v.i. Faire sécession.
seclude, v.tr. Tenir retiré.
secluded, a. Écarté, retiré.
seclusion, s. Solitude f, retraite f.
second¹, s. Seconde f.
second². I. a. 1. Second, deuxième.
(a) The s. of January, le deux janvier.
(b) The s. largest, le plus grand sauf
un. To travel s. class, voyager en
deuxième classe. 2. Second; autre;
nouveau, -elle. S sight, seconde
vue.
    II. **second**, s. 1. (Le) second, (la)
seconde; (le, la) deuxième. 2. (a)
Témoin m. 3. Second m.
second³, v.tr. Seconder; appuyer.
secondary, a. Secondaire.
second-class, a. De seconde (classe);
de deuxième qualité.
second-hand, a. D'occasion. S.-h.
car, voiture usagée.
secondly, adv. Deuxièmement; en
second lieu.
second-rate, a. Médiocre, inférieur.
secrecy, s. Discrétion f.
secret. 1. a. Secret, -ète; caché.
2. s. (a) Secret m. I make no s. of it,
je n'en fais pas mystère. (b) In s.,
en secret.
secretary, s. (a) Secrétaire m. (b) S.
of State, ministre m.
secrete, v.tr. Cacher.
secretive, a. Réservé, dissimulé.
secretly, adv. Secrètement; en
secret.
sect, s. Secte f.
section, s. 1. Sectionnement m, section f. 2. Tranche f. 3. Section;
partie f, division f.
sectional, a. En sections. S. bookcase, bibliothèque démontable.
sector, s. Secteur m.
secular, a. Séculier. S. music,
musique profane.
secure¹, a. 1. Sûr; assuré. 2. En
sûreté; sauf. 3. Fixé, assujetti;
ferme, sûr.

secure², v.tr. 1. Mettre en sûreté.
2. Fixer, retenir. 3. Obtenir,
acquérir.
securely, adv. 1. Sûrement; avec
sécurité. 2. Fermement, solidement.
security, s. 1. (a) Sécurité f, sûreté f.
(b) Solidité f. 2. (Moyen m de)
sécurité; sauvegarde f. 3. (a) Caution f; gage m. (b) Caution; garant
m. (c) pl. Titres m, valeurs f.
sedate, a. Posé, reposé; composé.
sedately, adv. Posément.
sedative, a. & s. Sédatif (m).
sedentary, a. Sédentaire.
sediment, s. Sédiment m, dépôt m.
sedition, s. Sédition f.
seditious, a. Séditieux.
seduce, v.tr. Séduire, corrompre.
seduction, s. 1. Séduction f, corruption f. 2. Attrait m, charme m.
seductive, a. Séduisant, attrayant.
sedulous, a. Assidu, appliqué
see, v.tr. 1. Voir. (a) Visiter; apercevoir. (b) Abs. As far as the eye
can see, à perte de vue. 2. (a) Comprendre, saisir. (b) Observer, remarquer; s'apercevoir de. (c) Voir,
juger, apprécier. 3. Examiner; regarder avec attention. Let me see,
(i) attendez un peu; (ii) faites voir !
4. (a) Fréquenter, avoir des rapports
avec. (b) To go and see s.o., aller
trouver qn. To see the doctor, consulter le médecin. (c) Recevoir.
see about, v.ind.tr. S'occuper de.
see after, v.ind.tr. S'occuper de;
se charger de. **see after**, v.ind.tr.
S'occuper de; veiller à. **see
through**. 1. v.i. (a) Voir à travers.
(b) Pénétrer les intentions de; pénétrer. 2. v.tr. Mener à bonne fin.
see to, v.ind.tr. S'occuper de;
veiller à.
seed, s. (a) Graine f. (b) Coll.
Semence f; graine(s).
seed-cake, s. Gâteau m au carvi.
seed-pearls, s.pl. Semence f de
perles.
seeing¹. 1. a. Voyant; qui voit.
2. Conj.phr. S. that, puisque, vu que.
seeing², s. Vue f; vision f. It is
worth s., cela vaut la peine d'être vu.
seek, v.tr. 1. Chercher; rechercher.
2. To s. to, essayer de, chercher à.
seek for, v.ind.tr. (Re)chercher.
seem, v.i. 1. Sembler, paraître.
2. Impers. It seems to me, il me

semble. **So it seems,** à ce qu'il
paraît.

seeming, a. Apparent ; soi-disant *inv.*

seemingly, *adv.* Apparemment ; en
apparence.

seemliness, s. Décorum m.

seemly, a. Convenable, bienséant.

seep, *v.i.* Suinter ; s'infiltrer.

seer, s. Prophète m.

see-saw[1], s. Bascule f, balançoire f.

see-saw[2], *v.i.* Basculer ; osciller.

seethe, *v.i.* (a) Bouillonner. (b)
S'agiter, grouiller.

segment, s. Segment m.

segregate, *v.tr.* Isoler.

segregation, s. Ségrégation f.

seize, *v.tr.* (a) Se saisir, s'emparer,
de. (b) **To s. by the throat,** prendre
à la gorge. (c) Saisir. (d) *v.ind.tr.*
To s. (up)on, saisir ; se saisir de.

seizure, s. **1.** Saisie f. **2.** Attaque f.

seldom, *adv.* Rarement.

select[1], a. **1.** Choisi. **2.** De (premier)
choix ; d'élite.

select[2], *v.tr.* Choisir (*from,* parmi).

selection, s. **1.** Choix m, sélection f.
2. *pl.* Morceaux choisis.

self. 1. s. Le moi. **2.** *pron.* **Pay s.,**
payez à moi-même.

self-apparent, a. Évident.

self-assertion, s. Outrecuidance f.

self-assertive, a. Outrecuidant.

self-assurance, s. Confiance f en
soi ; assurance f ; aplomb m.

self-command, s. Maîtrise f de soi.

self-conceit, s. Suffisance f.

self-confidence, s. Confiance f en
soi ; assurance f.

self-confident, a. Sûr de soi ; plein
d'assurance.

self-conscious, a. Embarrassé, gêné.

self-consciousness, s. Contrainte f,
embarras m, gêne f.

self-contained, a. **1.** Peu communicatif. **2.** **S.-c. flat,** appartement avec
entrée particulière.

self-control, s. Sang-froid m ; maîtrise f de soi.

self-deception, s. Illusion f ; déception f de soi-même.

self-defence, s. Défense personnelle.

self-denial, s. (a) Abnégation f de
soi ; renoncement(s) m(pl). (b)
Frugalité f.

self-esteem, s. Respect m de soi ;
amour-propre m.

self-evident, a. Évident en soi.

self-importance, s. Suffisance f,
présomption f.

self-important, a. Suffisant, présomptueux.

self-indulgence, s. Satisfaction f
égoïste de ses appétits.

self-indulgent, a. Qui ne se refuse
rien.

self-interest, s. Intérêt personnel.

selfish, a. Égoïste, intéressé.

selfishly, *adv.* Égoïstement ; en
égoïste.

selfishness, s. Égoïsme m.

self-possessed, a. Maître de soi.

self-possession, s. Aplomb m, sang-
froid m.

self-preservation, s. Conservation f
de soi-même.

self-reliance, s. Indépendance f.

self-reliant, a. Indépendant.

self-respect, s. Respect m de soi ;
amour-propre m.

self-respecting, a. Qui se respecte.

self-restraint, s. Retenue f ; modération f.

self-satisfied, a. Content de soi ;
suffisant.

self-starter, s. Démarreur m.

self-willed, a. Opiniâtre, volontaire.

sell, *v.tr.* **1.** (a) Vendre. **He sold it
for ten shillings,** il l'a vendu dix
shillings. (b) **To s. well,** être de
bonne vente. **2.** Vendre, trahir.

sell off, *v.tr.* Solder ; liquider.

seller, s. (a) Vendeur, -euse. (b)
Marchand, -ande ; débitant, -ante.

selling, s. Vente f ; placement m.
S. price, prix m de vente.

selling off, s. Liquidation f.

seltzer, s. Eau f de seltz.

semaphore, s. Sémaphore m.

semblance, s. Apparence f, semblant m.

semicircle, s. Demi-cercle m, *pl.*
demi-cercles.

semicircular, a. Demi-circulaire,
pl. demi-circulaires.

semicolon, s. Point m et virgule.

semi-conscious, a. A demi conscient.

semi-detached, a. **S.-d. house,**
maison jumelle.

seminary, s. Séminaire m.

Semitic, a. Sémitique.

semolina, s. Semoule f.

senate, s. Sénat m.

senator, s. Sénateur m.

send, v.tr. **1.** (a) Envoyer. (b) Envoyer; expédier **2.** Faire passer. **3.** Abs. To s. for, envoyer chercher. **I shall s. for it,** je vais l'envoyer prendre. **send away,** v.tr. (a) Renvoyer, congédier. (b) Expédier. **send back,** v.tr. Renvoyer. **send in,** v.tr. **1.** Faire (r)entrer. **2.** Livrer; remettre. **send off,** v.tr. (a) Envoyer. (b) Expédier. **send on,** v.tr. (a) Faire suivre. (b) Transmettre. **send out,** v.tr. (a) Faire sortir. (b) Lancer. (c) Émettre. **send round,** v.tr. Faire circuler.

sender, s. Envoyeur, -euse; expéditeur, -trice.

senile, a. Sénile.

senility, s. Sénilité f.

senior, **1.** a. (a) Aîné; père. (b) Supérieur, -e. **2.** s. (a) Aîné, -ée; doyen, -enne. (b) **To be s.o.'s s.,** être l'ancien, le doyen, de qn.

seniority, s. **1.** Priorité f d'âge; supériorité f d'âge. **2.** Ancienneté f.

senna, s. Séné m.

sensation, s. Sensation f. **1.** Sentiment m; impression f. **2.** Effet sensationnel.

sensational, a. Sensationnel.

sense, s. **1.** Sens m. **2.** pl. (a) **In one's senses,** sain d'esprit. (b) **To lose one's senses,** perdre connaissance f. **3.** (a) Sensation f. (b) Sentiment m, conscience f. **4.** Bon sens, intelligence f. **To talk s.,** parler raison. **5.** Sens, signification f. **In the full s.,** dans toute l'acception.

senseless, a. **1.** Sans connaissance; inanimé. **2.** Insensé, déraisonnable.

sensibility, s. Sensibilité f.

sensible, a. **1.** Sensible, perceptible. **2.** Sensible, appréciable. **3.** Conscient. **4.** Sensé, raisonnable.

sensibly, adv. **1.** Sensiblement. **2.** Sensément, raisonnablement.

sensitive, a. (a) Sensible sensitif. (b) Susceptible.

sensual, a. Sensuel; voluptueux.

sensuality, s. Sensualité f.

sensuous, a. Voluptueux.

sentence¹, s. **1.** (a) Jugement m; sentence f, condamnation f. (b) Peine f. **2.** Phrase f.

sentence², v.tr. Condamner.

sententious, a. Sentencieux.

sentient, a. Sentant, sensible.

sentiment, s. **1.** Sentiment m. **2.** Sentimentalité f.

sentimental, a. Sentimental, -aux.

sentimentality s. Sentimentalité f, sensiblerie f.

sentimentally, adv. Sentimentalement.

sentinel, s. Factionnaire m; sentinelle f.

sentry, s. **1.** (a) Factionnaire m. (b) Sentinelle f. **2.** Faction f.

sentry-box, s. Guérite f.

sepal, s. Sépale m.

separate¹, a. (a) Séparé, détaché. (b) Distinct, indépendant.

separate². **1.** v.tr. Séparer; désunir; détacher. **2.** v.i. Se séparer.

separately, adv. Séparément; à part.

separation, s. **1.** Séparation f (from, d'avec). **2.** Écart m, distance f.

sepia, s. Sépia f.

September, s. Septembre m.

septic, a. Septique.

sepulchral, a. Sépulcral, -aux.

sepulchre, s. Sépulcre m.

sequel, s. Suite f.

sequence, s. **1.** (a) Succession f; ordre naturel. **In s.,** en série. (b) Suite f, série f. **2.** Séquence f.

sequestered, a. Retiré.

sequin, s. Sequin m.

seraphic, a. Séraphique.

Serb, a. & s. Serbe (mf).

Serbian, a. & s. Serbe (mf).

serenade¹, s. Sérénade f.

serenade², v.tr. Donner une sérénade à (qn).

serene, a. Serein, calme.

serenely, adv. Tranquillement; avec sérénité.

serenity, s. Sérénité f, calme m.

serge, s. Serge f.

sergeant, s (a) Sergent m; maréchal m des logis. (b) **Police s.,** brigadier.

sergeant-major, s. Sergent m major; maréchal des logis chef.

serial, a. **1.** **S. number,** numéro de série. **2.** s. Feuilleton m.

series, s. Série f, suite f.

serious, a. **1.** Sérieux. **1.** Grave. **2.** Réfléchi. **I am s.,** je ne plaisante pas.

seriously, adv. Sérieusement. **1.** Gravement. **2.** Au sérieux.

seriousness, s. **1.** Gravité f. **2.** Sérieux m. **3.** In all s., sérieusement.
sermon, s. Sermon m.
serpent, s. Serpent m.
serpentine, a. Serpentin ; sinueux.
serrated, a. Dentelé.
serried, a. Serré.
servant, s. **1.** (a) Domestique mf ; servante f, bonne f. **Officer's s.,** ordonnance f. (b) Serviteur m, servante. **2.** Employé, -ée. **Civil s.,** fonctionnaire mf.
servant-girl, s Domestique f ; bonne f.
serve. I. v.tr. **1.** (a) Servir. (b) Faire. **2.** Être utile à, suffire à. **3.** Desservir. **4.** Traiter. **It serves you right!** c'est bien fait !
II. **serve,** v.i. **1.** To s. for, servir à. To s. as, servir de. **2.** When occasion serves, lorsque l'occasion est favorable. **serve out,** v.tr Distribuer.
service, s. **1.** Service m. **On active s.,** en activité. **2.** Distribution f, installation f. **3.** Emploi m. **4.** (a) I am at your s., je suis à votre disposition f. (b) Utilité f. **To be of s.,** être utile. **5.** Office m.
serviceable, a. **1.** Serviable. **2.** (a) Utilisable. (b) Utile ; avantageux. (c) Pratique.
serviette, s. Serviette f de table.
servile, a. Servile.
servility, s. Servilité f.
serving, a. Servant ; au service.
servitude, s. Servitude f.
session, s. Session f ; séance f.
set¹, s. Ensemble m. (a) Jeu m ; collection complète ; service m. (b) Wireless set, poste m de radio. (c) Manche f ; set m. (d) Groupe m.
set². I. v.tr. **1.** Asseoir, placer. **2.** Mettre, poser. **3.** Planter. **4.** Régler. **5.** Sertir, enchâsser. **6.** Dresser, tendre. **7.** Assigner. **8.** To set the fashion, fixer la mode. **9.** To set a bone, remettre un os. **10.** To set one's teeth, serrer les dents. **11.** To set going, mettre en train. **12.** Donner.
II. **set,** v.i. **1.** Se coucher. **2.** Se ressouder. **3.** (a) Se coaguler ; prendre. (b) Faire prise. **4.** To set to work, se mettre à l'œuvre. **set about,** v.i. Se mettre à. **set**

down, v.tr. Poser, déposer ; débarquer. **set forth. 1.** v.tr. Énoncer ; exposer. **2.** v.i. Se mettre en route. **set in,** v.i. Commencer. **set off. I.** v.tr. Faire ressortir, faire valoir. **II. set off,** v.i. Partir ; se mettre en route. **set out. I.** v.tr. **1.** Équiper. **2.** Arranger, disposer. **II. set out,** v.i. Se mettre en route. **set to,** v.i. Se mettre au travail. **set up. I.** v.tr. **1.** Élever, ériger. **2.** Établir ; fonder. **II. set up,** v.i. **1.** S'établir. **2.** v.i. & pr. Se poser. **set upon,** v.i. Attaquer.
set³, a. **1.** (a) Fixe ; immobile ; figé. (b) Bandé, tendu. **2. Set purpose,** ferme intention.
set-back, s. Déconvenue f.
set-off, s. Contraste m.
set square, s. Équerre f.
settee, s. Canapé m, causeuse f.
setting¹, a. Baissant, couchant.
setting², s. **1.** (a) Mise f, pose f. (b) Disposition f. **2.** (a) Coucher m. (b) Prise f ; coagulation f. **3.** (a) Cadre m. (b) Monture f. (c) Arrangement m.
settle. I. v.tr. **1.** (a) Établir, installer. (b) Coloniser. **2.** Mettre ordre à. **3.** Dissiper (les doutes de qn). **4.** Concerter ; calmer. **5.** Fixer, déterminer. **6.** (a) Résoudre, décider ; arranger. (b) Régler, solder ; payer.
II. **settle,** v.i. **1.** (a) S'établir. (b) Se percher. **2.** Se clarifier ; se précipiter. **settle down,** v.i. **1.** S'établir. **2.** Se ranger.
settled, a. **1.** Invariable, sûr ; fixe. **2.** Arrangé, décidé. **3.** Établi. **4.** Colonisé.
settlement, s. **1.** Colonisation f. **2.** Règlement m. **3.** Colonie f.
settler, s. Colon m.
seven, num. a. & s. Sept (m).
seventeen, num. a. & s. Dix-sept (m).
seventeenth, num. a. & s. Dix-septième (m). **(On) the s. of March,** le dix-sept mars.
seventh, num. a. & s. Septième (m). **(On) the s. of May,** le sept mai.
seventy, num. a. & s. Soixante-dix (m).
sever, v.tr. (a) Désunir, disjoindre ; rompre. (b) Couper.
several, a. **1.** Séparé ; différent. **2.** Plusieurs.
severe, a. **1.** Sévère, strict, rigoureux. **2.** (a) Rigoureux, dur. (b) Vif.

severely, *adv.* **1.** Sévèrement; avec sévérité. **2.** Grièvement.

severity, *s.* **1.** Sévérité *f,* rigueur *f.* **2.** (*a*) Rigueur, inclémence *f.* (*b*) Gravité *f.*

sew, *v.tr.* Coudre. **sew on,** *v.tr.* Coudre, attacher.

sewage, *s.* Eau *f* d'égout.

sewer, *s.* Égout *m.*

sewing, *s.* Couture *f.* **S. needle,** aiguille *f* à coudre.

sewing-cotton, *s.* Fil *m* à coudre.

sewing-machine, *s.* Machine *f* à coudre.

sex, *s.* Sexe *m.*

sextet, *s.* Sextuor *m.*

sexton, *s.* (*a*) Sacristain *m.* (*b*) Fossoyeur *m.*

sexual, *a.* Sexuel.

sh, *int.* Chut !

shabbily, *adv.* **1.** Pauvrement. **S. dressed,** miteux. **2.** Mesquinement.

shabbiness, *s.* **1.** État râpé; apparence *f* pauvre. **2.** Mesquinerie *f.*

shabby, *a.* **1.** Pauvre, minable. **To look s.,** avoir l'air râpé. **2.** Mesquin.

shackle, *v.tr.* Mettre les fers à, entraver.

shackles, *s.pl.* Fers *m.*

shade[1], *s.* **1.** Ombre *f.* **2.** Nuance *f;* teinte *f.* **3.** Abat-jour *m inv.*

shade[2], *v.tr.* Ombrager.

shadiness, *s.* Ombre *f,* ombrage *m.*

shadow[1], *s.* Ombre *f.*

shadow[2], *v.tr.* **1.** Ombrager. **2.** Filer.

shadowing, *s.* Filature *f.*

shadowy, *a.* Indécis, vague.

shady, *a.* **1.** (*a*) Ombreux. (*b*) Ombragé. **2.** Louche.

shaft[1], *s.* **1.** Hampe *f,* bois *m.* **2.** Flèche *f,* trait *m.* **3.** Rayon *m.* **4.** Tige *f.* **5.** Brancard *m,* limon *m.*

shaft[2], *s.* Puits *m.*

shaggy, *a.* Poilu; en broussailles.

shagreen, *s.* Chagrin *m.*

shake[1], *s.* (*a*) Secousse *f.* **A s. of the head,** un hochement de tête. (*b*) Tremblement *m.* (*c*) Trille *m.*

shake[2]. **I.** *v.tr.* **1.** Secouer; agiter. **To s. one's head,** faire non de la tête. **To s. hands with,** serrer la main à. **2.** Ébranler.

II. shake, *v.i.* Trembler; chanceler, branler. **shake down,** *v.tr.* Secouer, faire tomber. **shake off,** *v.tr.* Se débarrasser, se défaire, de.

shake up, *v.tr.* **1.** Secouer, brasser. **2.** Agiter.

shakiness, *s.* Manque *m* de stabilité; chevrotement *m.*

shaking, *s.* Secouement *m.*

shaky, *a.* Peu solide; chancelant, tremblant.

shall, *modal aux. v.* **I. 1.** (*a*) **All is as it should be,** tout est très bien. (*b*) **You s. do it!** vous le ferez, je le veux ! (*c*) **You should do it,** vous devriez le faire. **You should have seen him,** il fallait le voir ! (*d*) **I should think so!** je crois bien ! **2. S. I open the window?** voulez-vous que j'ouvre la fenêtre ? **3. If he should come,** si par hasard il vient. **Should I be free,** si je suis libre.

II. shall. 1. You shan't have any! tu n'en auras pas ! **2.** (*a*) **Will you be there?**—I s., y serez-vous ?—Oui (, j'y serai). (*b*) **S. you come to-morrow?** vous viendrez demain ? **3. We should come if we were invited,** nous viendrions si on nous invitait. **4. I should like a drink,** je prendrais bien quelque chose.

shallot, *s.* Échalote *f.*

shallow. I. *a.* (*a*) Peu profond; plat. (*b*) Superficiel, frivole. **2.** *s.* Basfond *m, pl.* bas-fonds.

shallowness, *s.* (Le) peu de profondeur.

sham[1]. **I.** *a.* Simulé, feint; faux, *f.* fausse.

II. sham, *s.* Feinte *f,* trompe-l'œil *m inv.*

sham[2], *v.tr.* Feindre, simuler.

shambles, *s.pl.* (*a*) Abattoir *m.* (*b*) Scène *f* de carnage.

shame[1], *s.* (*a*) Honte *f.* **For s.!** fi ! quelle honte ! (*b*) **It's a s.!** c'est honteux ! **What a s.!** quel dommage !

shame[2], *v.tr.* Faire honte à, humilier.

shamefaced, *a.* Honteux; penaud.

shameful, *a.* Honteux, scandaleux.

shamefully, *adv.* Honteusement, scandaleusement.

shamefulness, *s.* Honte *f,* infamie *f.*

shameless, *a.* **1.** Éhonté, effronté. **2.** Honteux, scandaleux.

shamelessly, *adv.* Effrontément.

shamelessness, *s.* **1.** Immodestie *f,* impudeur *f.* **2.** Effronterie *f.*

shampoo, *s.* Schampooing *m.* **Dry s.,** friction *f.*

shape[1], *s.* **1.** (*a*) Forme *f*; façon *f*, coupe *f*. (*b*) Taille *f*. (*c*) Forme indistincte; apparition *f*. **2.** Moule *m*.

shape[2]. **1.** *v.tr.* Façonner; tailler. **2.** *v.i.* Se développer.

shaped, *a.* Façonné, taillé.

shapeless, *a.* Informe; difforme.

shapelessness, *s.* Manque *m* de forme.

shapeliness, *s.* Beauté *f* de forme.

shapely, *a.* Bien fait, bien tourné.

share[1], *s.* **1.** Part *f*, portion *f*. **S.** in profits, participation *f* aux bénéfices. To go shares, partager. **S.** and s. alike, en partageant également. **2.** Contribution *f*, écot *m*; intérêt *m*. **3.** Action *f*, titre *m*.

share[2]. **1.** *v.tr.* Partager. **2.** *v.tr.* & *ind. tr.* Prendre part, participer (*in*, à). **share out**, *v.tr.* Partager, répartir.

shareholder, *s.* Actionnaire *mf*.

sharing, *s.* **1.** Partage *m*. **2.** Participation *f*.

shark, *s.* Requin *m*.

sharp. **I.** *a.* **1.** (*a*) Tranchant, aiguisé; aigu, uë, pointu. (*b*) Anguleux. (*c*) Net, *f.* nette. **2.** (*a*) Fin; éveillé; pénétrant. (*b*) Rusé, malin, -igne. **S.** practice, procédés peu honnêtes. **3.** **S.** tongue, langue acérée. **4.** Piquant; aigre, acide. **II. sharp**, *s.* Dièse *m*. **III. sharp**, *adv.* **1.** Brusquement. **2.** Ponctuellement. **3.** **Look s.!** faites vite!

sharp-edged, *a.* Tranchant, affilé.

sharpen, *v.tr.* **1.** (*a*) Affiler, affûter, aiguiser. (*b*) Tailler (en pointe). **2.** Dégourdir.

sharper, *s.* **1.** Aigrefin *m*. **2.** Tricheur *m*.

sharply, *adv.* **1.** Nettement. **2.** Brusquement.

sharpness, *s.* **1.** (*a*) Acuité *f*, finesse *f*. (*b*) Netteté *f*. **2.** Intelligence *f*. **3.** Sévérité *f*, acerbité *f*.

sharp-sighted, *a.* A la vue perçante.

shatter, *v.tr.* Fracasser; briser.

shattering, *a.* Écrasant.

shave[1], *s.* **1.** To have a s., se faire raser; se raser. **2.** To have a close s., l'échapper belle.

shave[2], *v.tr.* **1.** Raser; faire la barbe à. **2.** Friser, effleurer.

shaving, *s.* Copeau *m*.

shaving-brush, *s.* Blaireau *m*.

shaving-soap, *s.* Savon *m* à barbe.

shawl, *s.* Châle *m*.

she, *pers. pron.* **1.** Elle. **Here she comes**, la voici qui vient. **2.** She who believes, celle qui croit.

sheaf, *s.* **1.** Gerbe *f*. **2.** Liasse *f*.

shear, *v.tr.* **1.** Couper. **2.** Tondre.

shearer, *s.* Tondeur *m*.

shearing, *s.* Tonte *f*, tondaison *f*.

shears, *s.pl.* Cisailles *f*; (grands) ciseaux.

sheath, *s.* Fourreau *m*; gaine *f*.

sheathe, *v.tr.* Mettre au fourreau; rengainer.

shed[1], *s.* Hangar *m*; appentis *m*.

shed[2], *v.tr.* **1.** Perdre; jeter. **2.** Répandre, verser.

sheen, *s.* Luisant *m*, lustre *m*.

sheep, *s.* Mouton *m*.

sheep-dog, *s.* Chien *m* de berger.

sheepfold, *s.* Parc *m* à moutons.

sheepish, *a.* **1.** Penaud; interdit. **2.** Timide; gauche.

sheepishly, *adv.* **1.** D'un air penaud. **2.** D'un air timide.

sheepishness, *s.* **1.** Timidité *f*. **2.** Air penaud.

sheepskin, *s.* Peau *f* de mouton

sheer[1], *v.i.* Embarder. **sheer off**, *v.i.* **1.** Larguer les amarres **2.** S'écarter.

sheer[2]. **1.** *a.* (*a*) Pur, véritable; absolu. (*b*) A pic. **2.** *adv.* (*a*) Tout à fait. (*b*) A pic.

sheet, *s.* **1.** Drap *m* (de lit). **2.** Feuille *f*, feuillet *m*. **3.** Nappe *f*.

sheet-lightning, *s.* Éclairs *mpl* en nappe.

shelf, *s.* **1.** Tablette *f*; planche *f*; rayon *m*. **2.** Rebord *m*, corniche *f*.

shell[1], *s.* **1.** (*a*) Coquille *f*; carapace *f*; écaille *f*. (*b*) Coquille; coque *f*. **2.** Carcasse *f*; coque. **3.** Obus *m*.

shell[2], *v.tr.* **1.** Écaler; écosser. **2.** Bombarder.

shell-fish, *s.* (*a*) Coquillage *m*. (*b*) Crustacé *m*.

shelling, *s.* Bombardement *m*.

shelter[1], *s.* **1.** Abri *m*; asile *m*. **2.** Under s., à l'abri, à couvert.

shelter[2]. **1.** *v.tr.* (*a*) Abriter. (*b*) Donner asile à. **2.** *v.i.* & *pr.* Se mettre à l'abri, à couvert.

sheltered, *a.* Abrité.

sheltering, *a.* Protecteur, -trice.

shelving[1], *s* Rayons *mpl*; rayonnage *m*.

shelving[2], *a.* En pente; ncline

shepherd, *s.* Berger *m.*

shepherdess, *s.* Bergère *f*

sherbet, *s* Sorbet *m.*

sherry, *s.* Vin *m* de Xérès; xérès *m*.

shield[1], *s* Bouclier *m.*

shield[2], *v.tr.* Protéger.

shift[1], *s.* **1.** Changement *m* de position. **2.** Équipe *f* poste *m.* **To work in shifts**, se relayer. **3.** Expédient *m.*

shift[2]. I. *v.tr.* (*a*) Changer de place; déplacer. (*b*) Changer.
II. **shift**, *v.i.* **1.** (*a*) Changer de place; se déplacer. (*b*) Changer **2. To s. for oneself**, se débrouiller.

shifting, *a.* **1.** Qui se déplace. **2.** Changeant.

shiftless, *a.* **1.** Paresseux; sans énergie. **2.** Peu débrouillard.

shifty, *a.* Roublard; sournois

shimmer[1], *s.* Chatoiement *m.*

shimmer[2], *v.i.* Miroiter, chatoyer

shin, *s.* Devant de la jambe.

shine[1], *s.* **1.** Éclat *m*, lumière *f* **2.** Brillant *m*; luisant *m*

shine[2], *v.i.* **1.** Briller; reluire **2. To s. on**, illuminer.

shingle[1], *s.* Coupe *f* à la garçonne.

shingle[2], *v.tr.* Couper à la garçonne

shingle[3], *s.* Galets *mpl.*

shining, *a.* Brillant, (re)luisant

shiny, *a.* Brillant, luisant.

ship[1], *s.* Navire *m*; vaisseau *m*; bâtiment *m.* **On board s.**, à bord

ship[2]. I. *v.tr.* Embarquer.
II. **ship**, *v.i.* S'embarquer.

shipbuilding, *s.* Construction navale.

ship-mate, *s.* Camarade *m* de bord.

shipment, *s.* Chargement *m*

ship-owner, *s.* Armateur *m.*

shipping, *s.* **1.** Embarquement *m.* **2.** *Coll:* Navires *mpl*, vaisseaux *mpl.*

shipwreck[1], *s.* Naufrage *m.*

shipwreck[2], *v.tr* **To be shipwrecked** faire naufrage.

shipwrecked, *a.* Naufragé.

shipyard, *s* Chantier *m* de construction.

shirk, *v.tr.* Manquer à, se dérober à. *Abs.* Négliger son devoir.

shirker, *s.* Carotteur -euse.

shirt, *s.* Chemise *f.*

shirt-button, *s.* Bouton *m* de chemise.

shirt-collar, *s.* Col *m* de chemise

shirt-front, *s.* Plastron *m.*

shirt-sleeve, *s.* **In one's shirt-sleeves** en bras de chemise.

shiver[1]. **1.** *v.tr.* Fracasser; briser en éclats. **2.** *v.i.* Voler en éclats.

shiver[2], *s.* Frisson *m.*

shiver[3], *v.i* Frissonner. grelotter. trembler.

shoal[1]. I. *a.* Peu profond. **2.** *s.* Haut-fond *m*, *pl.* hauts-fonds.

shoal[2], *s.* Banc voyageur; grande quantité, tas *m.*

shock[1], *s.* **1.** Choc *m*, heurt *m.* **2.** (*a*) Coup *m*, atteinte *f.* (*b*) **Electric s.**, secousse *f* électrique.

shock[2], *v.tr.* (*a*) Choquer, scandaliser. (*b*) Bouleverser.

shocking, *a.* Choquant: révoltant, affreux.

shoddy[1], *s.* Camelote *f* pacotille *f.*

shoddy[2], *a.* De pacotille; camelote.

shoe[1], *s.* **1.** Soulier *m.* **To put on one's shoes**, se chausser. **2.** Fer *m*

shoe[2], *v.tr.* **1.** Chausser. **2.** Ferrer.

shoeblack, *s.* Décrotteur *m*, cireur *m.*

shoe-horn, *s.* Chausse-pied *m* *pl.* chausse-pieds, corne *f.*

shoe-lace, *s.* Lacet *m*; cordon *m* de soulier.

shoemaker, *s.* Cordonnier *m.*

shoot[1], *s.* **1.** Pousse *f*; rejeton *m.* **2.** Couloir *m*; glissière *f.*

shoot[2]. I. *v.i.* **1.** Se précipiter **2.** Lanciner.
II. **shoot**, *v.tr.* **1.** (*a*) Précipiter, lancer; pousser. (*b*) Verser, décharger. **2.** Darder. **3.** (*a*) Décocher; tirer (*b*) **To s. straight**, bien viser. **To s. at**; tirer, faire feu, sur. (*c*) Tuer, atteindre, d'un coup de fusil; fusiller. (*d*) Chasser; abattre. **4.** Tourner (un film).

shoot down, *v.tr* Abattre, descendre. **shoot up**, *v.i* (*a*) Jaillir. (*b*) Pousser.

shooting[1], *a.* Lancinant. **S. star**, étoile filante.

shooting[2], *s.* (*a*) **S. affray**, bagarre *f* avec coups de feu. (*b*) Tir *m.* **To go s.**, aller à la chasse.

shooting-range, *s.* Champ *m* de tir.

shop[1], *s.* **1.** Magasin *m*; boutique *f.* **2. To talk s.**, parler affaires.

shop[2], *v.i* Faire des achats des emplettes.

shop-assistant, *s.* Commis *m*, garçon *m*, demoiselle *f*, de magasin.

shop-front, *s.* Devanture *f* de magasin.

shopkeeper, *s.* Boutiquier -ière ; marchand, -ande.

shopper, *s.* Acheteur, -euse.

shopping, *s.* Achats *mpl*, emplettes *fpl*. **To go s.,** faire ses emplettes.

shop-soiled, *a.* Défraîchi.

shop-walker, *s.* Chef *m* de rayon.

shop-window, *s.* Vitrine *f* ; étalage *m* ; devanture *f*.

shore, *s.* (*a*) Rivage *m*, littoral *m* ; bord *m*. (*b*) **On s.,** à terre.

short. I. *a.* **1.** Court ; de petite taille. **A s. way off,** à peu de distance. **S. steps,** petits pas. **2.** Court, bref. (*a*) De peu de durée. **For a s. time,** pour peu de temps. **In a s. time,** sous peu ; bientôt. (*b*) **S.** story, nouvelle *f*, conte *m*. **In s.,** bref. (*c*) Brusque ; sec, *f.* sèche. **3.** (*a*) Insuffisant. (*b*) **S. of** à court de.
II. **short,** *adv.* **1.** **To stop s.,** s'arrêter court. **2.** **To fall s. of,** être au-dessous de. **S. of burning it,** à moins de le brûler.

shortage, *s.* **1.** Insuffisance *f*, manque *m*. **2.** Crise *f*, disette *f*. **Food s.,** disette.

short-circuit[1], *s.* Court-circuit *m*.

short-circuit[2], *v.tr.* Court-circuiter.

shortcoming, *s.* Défaut *m*, imperfection *f*.

shorten, *v.tr. & i.* Raccourcir.

shorthand, *s.* Sténographie *f.* **S. typist,** sténodactylographe *mf*.

short-handed, *a.* À court de personnel.

short-lived, *a.* Éphémère, de courte durée.

shortly, *adv.* **1.** Brièvement, en peu de mots. **2.** Brusquement, sèchement. **3.** Bientôt, prochainement. **S. after** (wards), peu (de temps) après.

shortness, *s.* **1.** (*a*) Brièveté *f*, courte durée. (*b*) Brusquerie *f*. **2.** Manque *m*, insuffisance *f*.

shorts, *s.pl.* Culotte *f* de sport.

short-sighted, *a.* **1.** Myope. **2.** Imprévoyant.

short-sightedness, *s.* **1.** Myopie *f*. **2.** Imprévoyance *f*.

short-tempered, *a* Vif ; d'un caractère emporté.

shot, *s.* **1.** *Coll.* Projectiles *mpl*. **2.** Plomb *m*. **3.** (*a*) Coup *m* (de feu). (*b*) Tireur, -euse.

shot-gun, *s.* Fusil *m* de chasse.

should. *See* SHALL.

shoulder, *s.* (*a*) Épaule *f*. **Slung across the s.,** en bandoulière. (*b*) Épaulement *m*.

shoulder-blade, *s.* Omoplate *f*.

shoulder-strap, *s.* Bretelle *f* ; épaulette *f*.

shout[1], *s.* (*a*) Cri *m* ; éclat *m* (*b*) Clameur *f*.

shout[2]. **1.** *v.i.* Crier ; pousser des cris. **2.** *v.tr.* Crier ; vociférer. **shout down,** *v.tr.* Huer. **shout out.** **1.** *v.i.* Crier, s'écrier. **2.** *v.tr.* Crier.

shouting, *s.* Cris *mpl* ; acclamations *fpl.*

shove[1], *s.* Poussée *f*.

shove[2], *v.tr.* Pousser.

shovel[1], *s.* Pelle *f*.

shovel[2], *v.tr.* Pelleter.

shovelful, *s.* Pellée *f*, pelletée *f*.

show[1], *s.* **1.** Mise *f* en vue ; étalage *m*. **2.** (*a*) Exposition *f* ; exhibition *f*. (*b*) Spectacle *m*. (*c*) Étalage. **3.** (*a*) Apparence *f* ; semblant *m*. (*b*) Parade *f*, ostentation *f*.

show[2]. I. *v.tr.* **1.** Montrer. (*a*) Faire voir, exhiber. **To s. itself,** devenir visible ; se révéler. (*b*) Représenter figurer. (*c*) Indiquer. **To s. a profit,** faire ressortir un bénéfice. **2.** Conduire. **To s. into a room,** faire entrer dans une pièce. **3.** (*a*) Faire preuve de ; témoigner de. (*b*) Révéler, montrer.
II. **show,** *v.i.* Se montrer, paraître ; se laisser voir. **show off.** **1.** *v.tr.* (*a*) Faire valoir. (*b*) Faire parade de. **2.** *v.i.* Parader, poser. **show through,** *v.i.* Transparaître. **show up.** I. *v.tr.* Démasquer ; dévoiler ; révéler. II. **show up,** *v.i.* Se détacher, ressortir.

show-case, *s.* Vitrine *f*.

shower, *s.* (*a*) Averse *f*. **Heavy s.,** ondée *f*. (*b*) Volée *f*. **S. of sparks,** gerbe *f* d'étincelles.

shower-bath, *s.* Douche *f*.

showery, *a.* Pluvieux.

showing, *s.* Exposition *f*, mise *f* en vue. **On your own s.,** à ce que vous dites vous-même.

showroom, s. Salle f, salon m d'exposition.

showy, a. Prétentieux, voyant.

shred, s. Brin m; lambeau m, fragment m.

shrew, s.f. Mégère f.

shrewd, a. Sagace, perspicace.

shrewdly, adv. Sagacement; avec perspicacité.

shrewdness, s. Sagacité f; finesse f.

shriek[1], s. Cri perçant. **Shrieks of laughter,** grands éclats de rire.

shriek[2], v.i. Pousser des cris aigus; crier.

shrieking, s. Cris stridents.

shrill, a. Aigu, -uë, strident.

shrillness, s. Stridence f.

shrilly, adv. D'un ton aigu, criard.

shrimp, s. Crevette (grise).

shrimping, s. Pêche f à la crevette.

shrine, s. 1. Châsse f, reliquaire m. 2. Tombeau m.

shrink, v.i. (a) Se contracter; (se) rétrécir. (b) Faire un mouvement de recul. **To s. from doing sth.,** répugner à faire qch.

shrinkage, s. Contraction f; rétrécissement m.

shrinking, a. Timide, craintif.

shrivel. 1. v.tr. Brûler. 2. v.i. Se rider, se ratatiner.

shroud, s. Linceul m, suaire m.

shrouded, a. Enveloppé, voilé.

shrub, s. Arbrisseau m, arbuste m.

shrubbery, s. Bosquet m; plantation f d'arbustes.

shrug[1], s. Haussement m d'épaules.

shrug[2], v.tr. Hausser les épaules.

shrunken, a. Contracté; ratatiné.

shudder[1], s. Frisson m; frémissement m.

shudder[2], v.i. Frissonner; frémir.

shuffle. 1. v.tr. & i. Traîner les pieds. 2. v.tr. Battre; mêler. 3. v.i. Équivoquer.

shun, v.tr. Fuir, éviter.

shunt, v.tr. Manœuvrer.

shunting, s. Manœuvre f; aiguillage m.

shut. 1. v.tr. Fermer. 2. v.i. (Se) fermer. **shut down,** v.tr. (a) Rabattre. (b) Fermer (une usine). **shut in,** v.tr. (a) Enfermer. (b) Entourer, encercler. **shut off,** v.tr. 1. Couper. 2. Séparer, isoler. **shut out,** v.tr. Exclure. **shut to.**

1. v.tr. Fermer. 2. v.i. Se fermer. **shut up,** v.tr. (a) Enfermer. (b) Clore.

shutter, s. 1. Volet m; contrevent m. 2. Obturateur m.

shutting, s. Fermeture f.

shuttle, s. 1. Navette f. 2. **S. service,** navettes.

shy[1], v.i. Faire un écart; broncher.

shy[2], a. Sauvage, farouche, timide.

shyly, adv. Timidement.

shyness, s. Timidité f; sauvagerie f.

sibilant, a. Sifflant.

Sicily. Pr.n. La Sicile.

sick, a. 1. Malade. 2. **To feel s.,** avoir mal au cœur. 3. **S. of,** las, dégoûté.

sick-bed, s. Lit m de douleur.

sicken. 1. v.i. (a) Tomber malade. (b) Se lasser. 2. v.tr. Dégoûter.

sickening, a. Écœurant, navrant.

sickle, s. Faucille f.

sickliness, s. 1. État maladif. 2. Pâleur f. 3. Fadeur f.

sickly, a. 1. (a) Maladif, souffreteux. (b) **S. smile,** sourire pâle. 2. Malsain, insalubre. 3. (Of taste) Fade.

sickness, s. 1. Maladie f. 2. Mal de cœur.

sick-nurse, s. Garde-malade mf, pl. gardes-malades.

sick-room, s. Chambre f de malade.

side[1], s. Côté m. 1. Flanc m. **By the s. of,** à côté de. **S. by s.,** côte à côte. 2. (a) **Wrong s. out,** à l'envers. (b) **To hear both sides,** entendre le pour et le contre. **On this s.,** de ce côté-ci. **To move to one s.,** se ranger. 4. (a) Parti m. (b) Section f, division f. (c) Camp m, équipe f. 5. Attrib. Latéral, de côté. **S. issue,** question d'intérêt secondaire.

side[2], v.i. **To s. with,** se ranger du côté de.

side-arms, s.pl. Armes blanches.

sideboard, s. Buffet m.

sidelong. 1. adv. Obliquement, de côté. 2. a. Oblique.

side-road, s. Chemin m de traverse.

side-slip, s. 1. Dérapage m. 2. Glissade f sur l'aile.

side-view, s. Vue f de profil, de côté.

side-walk, s. Trottoir m.

sideways. 1. a. De côté; latéralement. 2. a. Latéral, -aux; de côté.

siding, s. Voie f de garage.

sidle, v.i. S'avancer de côté.

siege, s. Siège m.

siesta, s. Sieste f.

sieve, s. Crible m ; tamis m.

sift, v.tr. Passer au tamis ; tamiser.

sifting, s. Tamisage m.

sigh¹, s. Soupir m.

sigh², v.i. Soupirer.

sight¹, s. **1.** Vue f. (a) Short s., myopie f. (b) To catch s. of, apercevoir. To lose s. of, perdre de vue. I can't bear the s. of him, je ne peux pas le sentir. At first s., au premier abord. **2.** To come into s., (ap)paraître. Out of s., caché aux regards. **3.** Visée f. **4.** (a) Spectacle m. (b) Chose digne d'être vue.

sight², v.tr. Apercevoir.

sightliness, s. Grâce f, beauté f.

sightly, a. Agréable à voir ; avenant.

sight-seeing, s. Visite f des monuments.

sight-seer, s. Curieux, -euse.

sign¹, s. **1.** Signe m. **2.** (a) Indice m, indication f. (b) Trace f. **3.** Enseigne f. **4.** Symbole m.

sign², v.tr. Signer.

signal¹, s. Signal, -aux m.

signal², **1.** v.i. Donner un signal ; signaler. **2.** v.tr. Signaler.

signal³, a. Signalé, insigne.

signal-box, s. Cabine f à signaux.

signalize, v.tr. Signaler, marquer.

signalling, s. Signalisation f; transmission f de signaux.

signally, adv. Remarquablement.

signalman, s. Signaleur m.

signature, s. Signature f. S. tune, s. Indicatif musical.

sign-board, s. Enseigne f.

signet, s. Sceau m, cachet m.

signet-ring, s. Chevalière f.

significance, s. **1.** Signification f. **2.** Importance f. conséquence f.

significant, a. **1.** Significatif. **2.** Important, de grande portée.

significantly, adv. D'une manière significative.

signification, s. Signification f.

signify. **1.** v.tr. Signifier. **2.** v.i. Importer. It does not s., cela ne fait rien.

signing, s. Signature f.

sign-post, s. Poteau indicateur.

silence¹, s. Silence m.

silence², v.tr. Réduire au silence ; faire taire.

silent, a. Silencieux. To keep s., se taire.

silently, adv. Silencieusement ; en silence.

silhouette, s. Silhouette f.

silk, s. Soie f. (a) S. stockings, bas de soie. (b) Oiled s., taffetas m imperméable.

silken, a. Soyeux.

silkworm, s. Ver m à soie.

silky, a. Soyeux.

sill, s. Tablette f de fenêtre.

silliness, s. Sottise f, niaiserie f.

silly, a. Sot, f. sotte ; niais. To do a s. thing, faire une bêtise.

silver, s. **1.** Argent m. **2.** Attrib. (a) D'argent, en argent. (b) S. hair, cheveux argentés. **3.** Argent monnayé. **4.** Argenterie f.

silver-haired, a. Aux cheveux argentés

silver-mounted, a. Monté en argent.

silver-plate, s. Coll: Argenterie f; vaisselle f d'argent.

silver-plated, a. Argenté.

silvery, a. (a) Argenté ; d'argent. (b) Argentin.

similar, a. Semblable, pareil, -eille.

similarity, s. Ressemblance f, similarité f.

similarly, adv. Pareillement, semblablement.

simile, s. Comparaison f, image f.

simmer, v.i. Mijoter, bouillotter.

simper¹, s. Sourire affecté.

simper², v.i. Minauder.

simple, a. (a) Simple, sans affectation. (b) Naïf ; crédule, niais.

simple-minded, a. Simple d'esprit ; naïf.

simple-mindedness, s. Simplicité f d'esprit ; naïveté f.

simpleton, s. Nigaud, -aude.

simplicity, s. **1.** Bêtise f, niaiserie f. **2.** Simplicité.

simplify, v.tr. Simplifier.

simply, adv. **1.** Simplement. **2.** (a) Absolument. (b) Uniquement ; tout simplement.

simulate, v.tr. Simuler, feindre.

simulation, s. Simulation f, feinte f.

simultaneous, a. Simultané.

simultaneously, adv. (a) Simultanément. (b) En même temps.

sin¹, s. Péché m.

sin², *v.i.* Pécher.

since. **1.** *adv.* Depuis. (*a*) **Ever s.**, depuis (lors). (*b*) Il y a. **2.** *prep.* Depuis. **3.** *conj.* (*a*) Depuis que ; que. (*b*) Puisque.

sincere, *a.* Sincère ; franc, -che.

sincerely, *adv.* Sincèrement. **Yours s.**, cordialement à vous.

sincerity, *s.* Sincérité *f* ; bonne foi *f*.

sinecure, *s.* Sinécure *f*.

sinew, *s.* **1.** Tendon *m.* **2.** *pl.* Nerf *m*, force *f*.

sinewy, *a.* Musclé, nerveux.

sinful, *a.* Coupable.

sinfully, *adv.* D'une façon coupable.

sinfulness, *s.* **1.** Culpabilité *f.* **2.** Le péché.

sing. **1.** *v.tr.* Chanter. **2.** *v.i.* Tinter, bourdonner.

singe, *v.tr.* **1.** Brûler légèrement ; roussir. **2.** Passer à la flamme.

singer, *s.* Chanteur, *f.* chanteuse, (*professional*) cantatrice.

singing¹, *a.* Chanteur, -euse ; chantant.

singing², *s.* **1.** Chant *m.* **2.** Bourdonnement *m*, tintement *m*.

single¹, *a.* **1.** (*a*) Seul, unique. **Not a s. one**, pas un seul ; pas un. (*b*) Individuel, particulier. **2.** (*a*) **S. bed**, lit pour une personne. **S. bedroom**, chambre à un lit. (*b*) Célibataire ; non marié(e).

single², *v.tr.* **To s. out**, choisir.

single-handed, *a.* Seul, sans aide.

singly, *adv.* **1.** Séparément ; un à un. **2.** Seul ; sans aide.

singular, *a.* Singulier.

singularly, *adv.* Singulièrement. (*a*) Remarquablement. (*b*) Bizarrement.

sinister, *a.* Sinistre.

sink¹, *s.* Évier *m*.

sink². **I.** *v.i.* **1.** Aller au fond ; couler. **2.** Tomber. **3.** (*a*) **To s. (down)**, s'affaisser. (*b*) Baisser. (*c*) Se laisser tomber. **His heart sank**, le cœur lui manqua. **His spirits sank**, son courage s'abattit. **4.** Descendre ; s'abaisser.

II. sink, *v.tr.* **1.** Couler, faire sombrer. **2.** Baisser ; enfoncer. **3.** Supprimer.

sinking, *s.* **1.** Enfoncement *m.* **2.** Affaissement *m.* **3.** Affaiblissement *m* ; abaissement *m*.

sinner, *s.* Pécheur, *f.* pécheresse

sinning, *s.* Le péché

sinuous, *a.* Sinueux.

sip¹, *s.* Petit coup ; petite gorgée.

sip², *v.tr* Boire à petits coups.

siphon, *s.* Siphon *m*.

sir, *s.* Monsieur *m*

siren, *s.* Sirène *f*.

sirloin, *s.* Aloyau *m*.

sister, *s.* **1.** Sœur *f.* **2.** (*a*) Religieuse *f* ; sœur. (*b*) Infirmière *f* en chef.

sister-in-law, *s* Belle-sœur *f*, *pl.* belles-sœurs.

sisterly, *a.* De sœur.

sit. **I.** *v.i.* **1.** (*a*) S'asseoir ; être assis. (*b*) Poser (pour son portrait). (*c*) Siéger (au parlement). **2.** Siéger ; être en séance.

II. sit, *v.tr.* Asseoir. **sit down**, *v.i.* S'asseoir ; prendre un siège.

sit up, *v.i.* **1.** (*a*) Se redresser. (*b*) Se mettre sur son séant. **2.** Veiller.

site, *s.* Emplacement *m*.

sitting¹, *a.* **1.** Assis. **2.** En séance.

sitting², *s.* Séance *f*.

sitting-room, *s.* Petit salon.

situate, *v.tr.* Situer.

situated, *a.* Situé.

situation, *s.* **1.** Situation *f.* **2.** Emploi *m*, place *f*.

six, *num. a. & s.* Six (*m*). **At sixes and sevens**, en désordre.

sixteen, *num. a. & s.* Seize (*m*).

sixteenth, *num. a. & s.* Seizième. **(On) the s. of August**, le seize août.

sixth, *num. a. & s.* Sixième (*m*). **(On) the s. of June**, le six juin.

sixty, *num. a. & s.* Soixante (*m*).

size, *s.* **1.** Grandeur *f*, dimension *f*, grosseur *f.* **2.** Numéro *m* ; taille *f* ; encolure *f* ; pointure *f*.

sizzle, *v.i.* Grésiller.

skate¹, *s.* Raie *f*.

skate², *s.* Patin *m*.

skate³, *v.i.* Patiner.

skater, *s.* Patineur, -euse.

skating, *s.* Patinage *m*.

skating-rink, *s.* Skating *m*.

skein, *s.* Écheveau *m*.

skeleton, *s.* **1.** Squelette *m.* **2.** Charpente *f*, carcasse *f*.

sketch¹, *s.* Croquis *m*, esquisse *f*.

sketch², *v.tr.* Esquisser.

sketch-book, *s.* Cahier *m* de croquis.

sketching, *s.* Prise *f* de croquis.

skewer¹, *s.* Brochette *f*.

skewer², *v.tr.* Brocheter.

ski[1], *s.* Ski *m.*

ski[2], *v.i.* Faire du ski.

skid, *v.i.* Déraper, patiner.

skidding, *s.* Dérapage *m* ; patinage *m.*

skiff, *s.* **1.** Esquif *m.* **2.** Skiff *m.*

skiing, *s.* Le ski.

skilful, *a.* Adroit, habile.

skilfully, *adv.* Habilement, adroitement.

skilfulness, *s.* Habileté *f*, adresse *f.*

skill, *s.* Habileté *f*, adresse *f.*

skilled, *a.* Habile.

skim, *v.tr. & i.* **1.** Écumer ; écrémer. **2.** Effleurer, raser.

skimpy, *a.* Maigre.

skin[1], *s.* **1.** Peau *f.* **Soaked to the s.**, trempé jusqu'aux os. **2.** Dépouille *f*, peau. **3.** Pelure *f.*

skin[2], *v.tr.* (*a*) Écorcher, dépouiller. (*b*) Peler, éplucher.

skin-deep, *a.* Superficiel.

skinflint, *s.* Ladre *m.*

skinny, *a.* Décharné ; maigre.

skip. **1.** *v.i.* Sauter, sautiller, gambader. **2.** *v.tr. & i.* Sauter, passer.

skipper, *s.* **1.** Patron *m.* **2.** Chef *m* d'équipe.

skirmish, *s.* Escarmouche *f.*

skirt[1], *s.* **1.** Jupe *f.* **2.** *pl.* Bord *m* ; lisière *f.*

skirt[2], *v.tr. & i.* Longer, serrer.

skit, *s.* Satire *f* (*on*, de).

skittle, *s.* **1.** Quille *f.* **2.** *pl.* Jeu *m* de quilles.

skulk, *v.i.* Se cacher ; se dérober.

skull, *s.* Crâne *m.*

skunk, *s.* **1.** Mouffette *f.* **2.** Skunks *m.*

sky, *s.* Ciel *m*, *pl.* cieux, ciels.

sky-blue. **1.** *s.* Bleu *m* céleste. **2.** *a.* Azuré.

skylark, *s.* Alouette *f.*

skylarking, *s.* Rigolade *f.*

skylight, *s.* Châssis vitré ; lucarne *f.*

sky-line, *s.* (Ligne *f* d')horizon *m.*

sky-rocket, *s.* Fusée volante.

sky-scraper, *s.* Gratte-ciel *m inv.*

sky-sign, *s.* Enseigne lumineuse.

slab, *s.* Plaque *f*, dalle *f.*

slack, *a.* **1.** (*a*) Mou, *f.* molle, lâche, flasque ; dégonflé. (*b*) Faible, sans force. **2.** Négligent. **3.** **S. time**, accalmie *f.* **The s. season**, la mortesaison *pl.* mortes-saisons.

slacken. **1.** *v.tr.* Ralentir. **To s. speed**, diminuer de vitesse. **2.** *v.i.* (*a*) To s. off, se relâcher. (*b*)

Prendre du mou. (*c*) Ralentir ; diminuer.

slackening, *s.* Ralentissement *m* ; diminution *f* ; relâchement *m.*

slackly, *adv.* **1.** Sans énergie **2.** Mollement.

slackness, *s.* **1.** (*a*) Manque *m* d'énergie ; mollesse *f.* (*b*) Désœuvrement *m.* **2.** Mou *m.* **3.** Stagnation *f.*

slam[1], *s.* Claquement *m.*

slam[2]. **1.** *v.tr.* Faire claquer. **2.** *v.i.* Claquer.

slam[3], *s.* Chelem *m.*

slander[1], *s.* Calomnie *f.*

slander[2], *v.tr.* Calomnier.

slanderer, *s.* Calomniateur, -trice.

slanderous, *a.* Calomnieux.

slang, *s.* Argot *m.*

slant[1], *s.* **1.** Pente *f*, inclinaison *f.* **2.** Biais *m*, biseau *m.*

slant[2]. **1.** *v.i.* (*a*) Être en pente. (*b*) Être oblique. **2.** *v.tr.* Incliner.

slanting, *a.* (*a*) En pente, incliné. (*b*) Oblique.

slap[1], *s.* Claque *f*, tape *f.* **S. in the face**, soufflet *m*, gifle *f.*

slap[2], *v.tr.* Frapper avec la main. **To s. s.o.'s face**, gifler qn.

slapping, *s.* Fouettée *f*, fessée *f.*

slash[1], *s.* Estafilade *f*, entaille *f.*

slash[2], *v.tr.* Taillader ; balafrer.

slashing, *a.* Mordant, cinglant.

slate, *s.* Ardoise *f.*

slate-quarry, *s.* Ardoisière *f.*

slattern, *s.* Femme mal soignée.

slatternly, *a.* Mal soignée.

slaughter[1], *s.* **1.** Abattage *m.* **2.** Tuerie *f*, carnage *m.*

slaughter[2], *v.tr.* **1.** Abattre. **2.** Tuer.

slaughter-house, *s.* Abattoir *m.*

Slav, *a. & s.* Slave (*mf*).

slave[1], *s.* Esclave *mf.*

slave[2], *v.i.* Peiner. **To s. away**, s'échiner.

slaver[1], *s.* Bave *f.*

slaver[2], *v.i.* Baver.

slavery, *s.* **1.** Esclavage *m.* **2.** Travail tuant.

slavish, *a.* D'esclave ; servile.

slavishly, *adv.* En esclave ; servilement.

slay, Tuer ; mettre à mort.

sledge, *s.* Traîneau *m.*

sledge-hammer, *s.* Mail *m.*

sleek, *a.* Lisse ; luisant.

sleekness, *s.* Luisant *m*

sleep[1], *s.* Sommeil *m.* **To go to s.,** s'endormir. **To send to s.,** endormir.

sleep[2], *v.i. & tr.* **1.** Dormir. **2.** Coucher. **sleep out,** *v.i.* Découcher.

sleeper, *s.* **1.** Dormeur, -euse. **To be a light s.,** avoir le sommeil léger. **2.** Traverse *f.* **3.** Wagon-lit *m, pl.* wagons-lits.

sleepily, *adv.* D'un air endormi, somnolent.

sleepiness, *s.* **1.** Somnolence *f.* **2.** Indolence *f,* léthargie *f.*

sleeping[1], *a.* Dormant, endormi.

sleeping[2], *s.* Sommeil *m.* **S. accommodation,** logement *m.*

sleeping apartments, *s.pl.* Chambres *f* à coucher.

sleeping-car, *s.* Wagon-lit *m, pl.* wagons-lits.

sleeping draught, *s.* Potion *f* soporifique.

sleeping-suit, *s.* Pyjama *m.*

sleepless, *a.* Sans sommeil. **S. night,** nuit blanche.

sleeplessness, *s.* Insomnie *f.*

sleepy, *a.* **1.** (*a*) Somnolent. **To feel s.,** avoir sommeil. (*b*) Endormi. **2.** Engourdi.

sleet, *s.* Neige à moitié fondue.

sleeve, *s.* Manche *f.*

sleigh, *s.* Traîneau *m.*

slender, *a.* **1.** Mince, ténu; svelte, élancé; fuselé. **2.** Faible; mince.

slenderness, *s.* **1.** Minceur *f;* sveltesse *f.* **2.** Exiguité *f.*

slice[1], *s.* Tranche *f.* **S. of bread and butter,** tartine *f* de beurre.

slice[2], *v.tr.* Découper en tranches. **slice off,** *v.tr.* Trancher, couper.

slide[1], *s.* **1.** Glissade *f;* glissement *m.* **2.** Dark s., châssis *m* porte-plaques. **3.** Barrette *f.*

slide[2]. **1.** *v.i.* (*a*) Glisser, coulisser. (*b*) Faire des glissades. **2.** *v.tr.* (Faire) glisser.

sliding[1], *a.* Glissant; coulissant. **S. door,** porte à glissières. **On a s. scale,** suivant une échelle mobile.

sliding[2], *s.* **1.** Glissade *f.* **2.** Coulissement *m,* glissement *m.*

slight[1], *a.* **1.** Mince, ténu; frêle. **2.** Léger. **To some s. extent,** quelque peu.

slight[2], *s.* Affront *m.*

slight[3], *v.tr.* Traiter sans considération.

slightingly, *adv.* Avec peu d'égards.

slightly, *adv.* **1.** S. built, à la taille mince. **2.** Légèrement; un peu.

slightness, *s.* **1.** Minceur *f.* **2.** Légèreté *f;* peu *m* d'importance.

slim, *a.* Svelte, élancé; mince.

slime, *s.* Limon *m,* vase *f.*

sliminess, *s.* État vaseux.

slimness, *s.* Taille *f* mince; sveltesse *f.*

slimy, *a.* **1.** (*a*) Vaseux. (*b*) Visqueux, gluant. (*b*) Couvert de vase.

sling[1], *s.* **1.** Fronde *f.* **2.** (*a*) Écharpe *f.* (*b*) Bandoulière *f.* (*c*) Élingue *f.*

sling[2], *v.tr.* **1.** Lancer, jeter. **2.** Suspendre. **3.** Élinguer.

slink, *v.i.* **To s. off,** partir furtivement.

slinking, *a.* Furtif.

slip[1], *s.* **1.** (*a*) Glissade *f,* glissement *m,* faux pas. (*b*) Inadvertance *f.* (*c*) Écart *m;* peccadille *f.* **2.** Taie *f* d'oreiller.

slip[2]. **I.** *v.i.* **1.** (*a*) Glisser. (*b*) Se glisser, se couler. **2.** (*a*) Faire une bévue. (*b*) Faire un écart de conduite. **3.** To let s., laisser échapper. **II.** slip, *v.tr.* **1.** Lâcher. **2.** Couler, glisser. **slip on,** *v.tr.* Enfiler, passer.

slip[3], *s.* Bande étroite; bout *m.*

slip-knot, *s.* Nœud coulant.

slipper, *s.* Pantoufle *f.*

slipper-bath, *s.* Baignoire *f* en sabot.

slippery, *a.* **1.** Glissant. **2.** Instable, incertain. **3.** Fin, rusé.

slit[1], *s.* Fente *f;* fissure *f.*

slit[2], *v.tr.* (*a*) Fendre. (*b*) Faire une incision dans.

sloe, *s.* Prunelle *f.*

sloop, *s.* **1.** Sloop *m.* **2.** Aviso *m.*

slop-basin, *s.* Vide-tasses *m inv.*

slope[1], *s.* **1.** Pente *f,* inclinaison *f.* **2.** Pente; talus *m;* versant *m.*

slope[2], *v.i.* (*a*) Être en pente; incliner, pencher. (*b*) Aller en pente.

sloping, *a.* En pente; incliné.

slot, *s.* Entaille *f,* rainure *f.*

sloth, *s.* Paresse *f,* fainéantise *f.*

slothful, *a.* Paresseux, indolent.

slouch, *v.i.* Manquer de tenue.

slough, *s.* Bourbier *m,* fondrière *f.*

sloven, *s.* Mal soigné, -ée.

slovenliness, *s.* **1.** Manque *m* de tenue. **2.** Manque de soin.

slovenly, *a.* **1.** Mal soigné. **2.**

(a) Négligent; sans soin. (b) Négligé.

slow[1]. I. a. **1.** (a) Lent. **S. train,** train omnibus. (b) **He was not s. to,** il ne tarda pas à. (c) A l'esprit lourd. (d) Ennuyeux. **2.** En retard.
II. **slow,** adv. Lentement. **To go slower,** ralentir sa marche.

slow[2]. **1.** v.i. **To s. down, up,** ralentir; diminuer de vitesse. **2.** v.tr. **To s. down, up,** ralentir.

slowly, adv. Lentement.

slowness, s. Lenteur f.

slug, s. Limace f.

sluggard, s. Paresseux m, fainéant m.

sluggish, s. Paresseux, léthargique.

sluggishness, s. **1.** (a) Paresse f. (b) Lourdeur f. **2.** Lenteur f.

sluice[1], s. Écluse f.

sluice[2], v.tr. Laver à grande eau.

slum, s. Bas quartier.

slumber[1], s. Sommeil m.

slumber[2], v.i. Sommeiller; dormir.

slump, s. Baisse soudaine.

slur, s. Affront m.

slush, s. Fange f, bourbe f.

slushy, a. Boueux.

sly, a. **1.** (a) Matois, rusé. (b) Sournois. (c) **On the sly,** furtivement. **2.** Malin, -igne.

slyly, adv. (a) Avec finesse. (b) Sournoisement.

slyness, s. (a) Finesse f. (b) Sournoiserie f.

smack[1], s. **1.** Claquement m. **2.** Claque f.

smack[2], v.tr. (a) Faire claquer. (b) Frapper, taper. **To s. s.o.'s face,** donner une gifle à qn.

smack[3], s. Bateau pêcheur.

small. I. a. Petit. **1.** Menu. **S. letters,** minuscules f. **2. S. voice,** voix fluette. **3. S. income,** mince revenu. **4.** Peu important; peu considérable. **5.** Mesquin, chétif.
II. **small,** adv. Menu, en petits morceaux.

small-arms, s.pl. Armes portatives.

small-minded, a. A l'esprit mesquin.

smallness, s. Petitesse f; exiguïté f.

smallpox, s. Petite vérole; variole f.

smart[1], s. Douleur cuisante.

smart[2], v.i. Cuire, brûler.

smart[3], a. **1.** Vif; alerte. **2.** (a) Habile; à l'esprit éveillé. (b) Malin, -igne. **3.** Élégant, distingué.

smarten. 1. v.tr. (a) **To s. up,** dégourdir. (b) **To s. oneself up,** se faire beau. **2.** v.i. **To s. up.** (a) S'animer. (b) Se dégourdir.

smartly, adv. **1.** Promptement, vivement. **2.** Habilement. **3.** Élégamment.

smartness, s. **1.** Vivacité f. **2.** Habileté. **3.** Élégance f.

smash[1], s. **1.** Coup écrasant. **2.** Désastre m. **3.** Débâcle f.

smash[2]. I. v.tr. (a) Briser. (b) Détruire; écraser.
II. **smash,** v.i. Éclater en morceaux.

smashing, a. Écrasant, assommant.

smattering, s. Légère connaissance.

smear[1], s. Tache f, souillure f.

smear[2], v.tr. (a) Barbouiller, salir (with, de). (b) Enduire (with, de).

smell[1], s. **1.** Odorat m; flair m. **2.** (a) Odeur f; parfum m. (b) Mauvaise odeur.

smell[2]. **1.** v.tr. & ind.tr. (a) Flairer; sentir. (b) Abs. Avoir de l'odorat. (c) Sentir l'odeur de; sentir. **2.** v.i. Sentir.

smelling-salts, s.pl. Sels volatils

smelt, v.tr. Fondre.

smelting, s. Fonte f.

smile[1], s. Sourire m.

smile[2], v.i. Sourire.

smiling, a. Souriant.

smirch, v.tr. Tacher; souiller.

smirk, v.i. Minauder.

smirking, a. Affecté; minaudier.

smite, v.tr. Frapper.

smith, s. Forgeron m.

smithereens, s.pl. Morceaux m.

smithy, s. Forge f.

smock, s. Blouse f, sarrau m.

smoke[1], s. Fumée f.

smoke[2]. **1.** v.i. Fumer. **2.** v.tr. (a) Fumer. (b) Noircir de fumée. Abs. **Do you mind if I s.?** la fumée vous gêne-t-elle?

smoker, s. Fumeur, -euse.

smoking[1], a. Fumant.

smoking[2], s. Habitude f de fumer. **No s.,** défense f de fumer.

smoking-compartment, s. Compartiment m pour fumeurs.

smoky, a. Fumeux; plein de fumée.

smooth[1], a. **1.** (a) Lisse; uni; poli; calme. (b) Glabre. **2.** Doux, f. douce; sans heurts.

smooth[2], *v.tr.* Lisser ; égaliser.

smoothly, *adv.* 1. Uniment ; sans inégalités. 2. (Marcher) doucement.

smoothness, *s.* 1. (*a*) Égalité *f* ; satiné *m.* (*b*) Calme *m.* 2. Douceur *f.*

smother, *v.tr.* Étouffer ; suffoquer.

smoulder, *v.i.* (*a*) Brûler lentement. (*b*) Couver.

smouldering, *a.* Qui couve.

smudge[1], *s.* Tache *f* ; noircissure *f.*

smudge[2], *v.tr.* Salir, barbouiller.

smug, *a.* Suffisant.

smuggle, *v.tr.* Passer en fraude. *Abs.* Faire la contrebande.

smuggler, *s.* Contrebandier *m.*

smuggling, *s.* Contrebande *f.*

smugness, *s.* Suffisance *f.*

smut, *s.* Parcelle *f* de suie.

smutty, *a.* Noirci ; sali.

snack, *s.* Léger repas ; casse-croûte *m inv.* To have a s., manger sur le pouce.

snag, *s.* (*a*) Chicot *m* ; souche *f* au ras d'eau. (*b*) Obstacle caché.

snail, *s.* Limaçon *m.* escargot *m,* colimaçon *m.*

snake, *s.* Serpent *m.*

snake-bite, *s.* Morsure *f* de serpent.

snap[1]. I. *s.* 1. (*a*) Coup *m* de dents. (*b*) Coup sec, claquement *m.* 2. Cassure *f.* 3. Fermoir *m* ; bouton *m* à pression. 4. Instantané *m.*

    II. **snap**, *attrib.a.* Instantané, imprévu.

    III. **snap**, *adv.* Crac.

snap[2]. I. *v.i.* 1. To s. at, chercher à mordre. 2. Claquer ; faire un bruit sec. 3. Se casser net.

    II. **snap**, *v.tr.* 1. Happer. 2. (*a*) Faire claquer. (*b*) Prendre un instantané de. 3. Casser, rompre.

snap up, *v.tr.* Saisir, happer.

snappish, *a.* Irritable ; hargneux.

snappy, *a.* 1. Irritable. 2. Vif.

snapshot[1], *s.* Instantané *m.*

snapshot[2], *v.tr.* Prendre un instantané de.

snare[1], *s.* (*a*) Lacet *m.* (*b*) Piège *m.*

snare[2], *v.tr.* Prendre au lacet ; attraper.

snarl[1], *s.* Grognement *m.*

snarl[2], *v.i.* Grogner.

snarling[1], *a.* Hargneux.

snarling[2], *s.* Grognement *m.*

snatch[1], *s.* 1. To make a s. at, chercher à saisir. 2. *pl.* Fragments *m.*

snatch[2], *v.tr. & i.* 1. Saisir, empoigner. To s. a meal, manger un morceau sur le pouce. 2. Arracher.

sneak[1], *s.* Pleutre *m* ; rapporteur, -euse.

sneak[2], *v.i.* (*a*) To s. off, partir furtivement. (*b*) Moucharder.

sneaking, *a.* (*a*) Furtif. (*b*) Sournois, dissimulé.

sneer[1], *s.* 1. Sourire *m* de mépris ; ricanement *m.* 2. Sarcasme *m.*

sneer[2], *v.i.* Ricaner ; lancer des sarcasmes.

sneering, *a.* Ricaneur, -euse ; moqueur, -euse.

sneeze[1], *s.* Éternuement *m.*

sneeze[2], *v.i.* Éternuer.

snick, *s.* Entaille *f,* encoche *f.*

sniff[1], *s.* Reniflement *m.*

sniff[2], *v.i. & tr.* Renifler.

snigger, *v.i.* Rire sous cape.

snip[1], *s.* (*a*) Petite entaille. (*b*) Coup *m* de ciseaux.

snip[2], *v.tr.* Couper avec des ciseaux.

snipe, *s.* Bécassine *f.*

sniper, *s.* Canardeur *m.*

sniping, *s.* Tir *m* en canardeur.

snippet, *s.* Bout *m,* morceau *m.*

snivel[1], *s.* Reniflement larmoyant.

snivel[2], *v.i.* Pleurnicher, larmoyer.

snivelling[1], *a.* Pleurnicheur, -euse ; larmoyant.

snivelling[2], *s.* Pleurnicherie *f.*

snob, *s.* Personne *f* qui admire les grands.

snobbish, *a.* Admirateur, -trice, des grands.

snobbishness, *s.* Admiration *f* des grands.

snooze[1], *s.* Petit somme.

snooze[2], *v.i.* Sommeiller.

snore[1], *s.* Ronflement *m.*

snore[2], *v.i.* Ronfler.

snoring, *s.* Ronflement *m.*

snort[1], *s.* Reniflement *m* ; ébrouement *m.*

snort[2], *v.i.* Renifler fortement ; s'ébrouer.

snout, *s.* Museau *m* ; groin *m.*

snow[1], *s.* Neige *f.*

snow[2]. 1. *v. impers.* Neiger. 2. Snowed up, retenu par la neige.

snowball, *s.* Boule *f* de neige.

snow-blindness, *s.* Cécité *f* des neiges.

snow-capped, *a.* Couronné de neige

snow-drift, s. Amoncellement m de neige.

snowdrop, s. Perce-neige m or f inv.

snow-flake, s. Flocon m de neige.

snow-line, s. Limite f des neiges perpétuelles.

snow-shoes, s.pl. Raquettes f.

snow-storm, s. Tempête f de neige.

snow-white, a. D'un blanc de neige.

snowy, a. Neigeux ; de neige.

snub[1], s. Mortification f, rebuffade f.

snub[2], v.tr. Infliger un affront à.

snub[3], a. Camus, retroussé.

snub-nosed, a. Camus.

snuff, s. Tabac m à priser. **To take s.,** priser **A pinch of s.,** une prise.

snuff-box, s. Tabatière f.

snuffling, a. Nasillard.

snug, a. Confortable.

snuggle, v.i. Se pelotonner.

snugly, adv. Confortablement, douillettement.

snugness, s. Confortable m.

so. I. adv. **I.** Si, tellement ; tant ; aussi. **So much,** tellement, tant. **2.** (a) Ainsi ; de cette manière. **So many,** tant de. **And so on,** et ainsi de suite. **So to speak,** pour ainsi dire. (b) **I think so,** je le crois. **So it seems,** à ce qu'il paraît. **I told you so!** je vous l'avais bien dit! **So much so,** à tel point. **Is that so?** vraiment ? (c) **How so?** comment cela ? **Perhaps so,** cela se peut. **Quite so!** parfaitement ! **A week or so,** une semaine environ. (d) **He's right and so are you,** il a raison et vous aussi. **3.** Conj.phr. **So that.** (a) Pour que. (b) De sorte que. **4.** Conj.phr. **So as to.** (a) Afin de. (b) De sorte que.

II. **so,** conj. Donc, c'est pourquoi.

soak. **I.** v.tr. Tremper. **2.** v.i. (a) Baigner, tremper. (b) S'infiltrer, s'imbiber.

soaked, a. Trempé.

soaking[1], a. Trempé.

soaking[2], s. (a) Trempe f. (b) Trempée f.

soap[1], s. Savon m.

soap[2], v.tr. Savonner.

soap-dish, s. Plateau m à savon.

soap flakes, s.pl. Savon m en paillettes.

soap-suds, s.pl. Eau f de savon.

soapy, a. Savonneux ; couvert de savon.

soar, v.i. Prendre son essor ; monter.

soaring[1], a. Qui monte.

soaring[2], s. **I.** (a) Essor m. (b) Hausse f. **2.** Planement m.

sob[1], s. Sanglot m.

sob[2], v.i. Sangloter.

sober[1], a. (a) Sobre, modéré, tempéré. (b) Calme, posé.

sober[2]. **I.** v.tr. Dégriser. **2.** v.i. **To s. down,** s'assagir.

soberly, adv. (a) Sobrement, modérément. (b) Avec calme ; tranquillement.

sober-minded, a. Sérieux ; pondéré.

soberness, s. (a) Sobriété f, tempérance f. (b) Calme m, tranquillité f.

sobriety, s. = SOBERNESS.

so-called, a. **I.** Ainsi nommé. **2.** Soi-disant ; prétendu.

sociability, s. Sociabilité f.

sociable, a. Sociable.

sociably, adv. Sociablement, amicalement.

social, a. Social, -aux.

socialism, s. Socialisme m.

socialist, a. & s. Socialiste (mf).

socially, adv. Socialement.

society, s. **I.** Société f. (a) Compagnie f. (b) **To go into s.,** aller dans le monde. **S. woman,** mondaine f. **2.** Société ; association f.

sock, s. **I.** Chaussette f. **2.** Semelle intérieure.

socket, s. **I.** Emboîture f, douille f. **2.** (a) Alvéole m or f. (b) Orbite f.

sod, s. **I.** Gazon m. **2.** Motte f de gazon.

soda, s. **I.** (a) Soude f. **Caustic s.,** soude caustique. (b) **Baking s.,** bicarbonate m de soude. **2.** Eau f de seltz ; soda m.

soda-water, s. Eau f de seltz ; soda m.

sofa, s. Sofa m, canapé m.

soft. **I.** a. **I.** Mou, f. molle. **2.** Doux, f. douce. **S. heart,** cœur tendre. **II. soft,** adv. Doucement.

soft-boiled, a. Mollet.

soften. **I.** v.tr. (a) Amollir. (b) Affaiblir. (c) Adoucir. (d) Attendrir. **2.** v.i. (a) S'amollir. (b) S'attendrir.

softening, s. (a) Amollissement m. (b) Attendrissement m.

soft-hearted, *a.* Au cœur tendre.

softly, *adv.* 1. (*a*) Doucement. **To tread s.,** marcher sans bruit. (*b*) Tendrement. 2. Mollement.

softness, *s.* 1. Douceur *f.* 2. Mollesse *f.*

soil¹, *s.* Sol *m*, terrain *m*, terre *f.*

soil², *v.tr.* Souiller, salir.

soiled, *a.* Souillé, sali. **S. linen,** linge sale.

sojourn, *s.* Séjour *m.*

solace¹, *s.* Consolation *f*, soulagement *m.*

solace², *v.tr.* Consoler ; soulager.

solar, *a.* Solaire.

solder¹, *s.* Soudure *f.*

solder², *v.tr.* Souder ; ressouder.

soldier, *s.* Soldat *m* ; militaire *m.*

sole¹, *s.* 1. Plante *f* (du pied). 2. Semelle *f.*

sole², *v.tr.* Ressemeler.

sole³, *s.* Sole *f.*

sole⁴, *a.* Seul, unique. **S. agent,** agent exclusif.

solecism, *s.* Solécisme *m.*

solely, *adv.* Uniquement.

solemn, *a.* 1. Solennel. 2. Grave, sérieux. **To keep a s. face,** composer son visage.

solemnity, *s.* Solennité *f.*

solemnize, *v.tr.* Solenniser.

solemnly, *adv.* 1. Solennellement. 2. Gravement.

solicit, *v.tr.* Solliciter.

solicitation, *s.* Sollicitation *f.*

solicitor, *s.* Avoué *m.*

solicitous, *a.* Soucieux, désireux. **S. about sth.,** préoccupé de qch.

solicitously, *adv.* Avec sollicitude.

solicitude, *s.* Sollicitude *f*, souci *m.*

solid. 1. *a.* Solide. (*a*) **In the s. rock,** dans la pierre vive. (*b*) Plein, massif. **S. vote,** vote unanime. (*c*) En une seule pièce. 2. *s.* Solide *m.*

solidarity, *s.* Solidarité *f.*

solidify. 1. *v.tr.* Solidifier. 2. *v.i.* Se solidifier.

solidity, *s.* Solidité *f.*

solidly, *adv.* Solidement.

soliloquize, *v.i.* Se parler à soi-même.

soliloquy, *s.* Soliloque *m.*

soling, *s.* Ressemelage *m.*

solitary, *a.* (*a*) Solitaire. (*b*) Solitaire, retiré.

solitude, *s.* 1. Solitude *f*, isolement *m.* 2. Lieu *m* solitaire.

solo, *s.* 1. Solo *m.* 2. Whist *m* de Gand.

soloist, *s.* Soliste *mf.*

Solomon. *Pr.n.* Salomon *m.*

solstice, *s.* Solstice *m.*

solubility, *s.* Solubilité *f.*

soluble, *a.* Soluble.

solution, *s.* Solution *f.*

solve, *v.tr.* Résoudre.

solvency, *s.* Solvabilité *f.*

solvent. 1. *a.* Solvable. 2. *s.* Dissolvant *m.*

sombre, *a.* Sombre, morne.

sombrely, *adv.* Sombrement.

some. I. *a.* 1. Quelque, quelconque. **S. day,** un de ces jours. **S. way or another,** d'une manière ou d'une autre. 2. De. **Can you give me s. lunch?** pouvez-vous me donner à déjeuner ? 3. Quelque. **After s. time,** après un certain temps.
  II. **some,** *pron.* 1. Certains. 2. I have s., j'en ai. **S. of them,** quelques-uns d'entre eux.
  III. **some,** *adv.* Environ, quelque.

somebody, *s. or pron.* Quelqu'un. **S. is knocking,** on frappe. **S. or other,** je ne sais qui.

somehow, *adv.* De façon ou d'autre, d'une manière ou d'une autre.

someone, *pron.* Quelqu'un ; on.

somersault, *s.* (*a*) Culbute *f.* (*b*) Saut périlleux.

something. I. *s. or pron.* Quelque chose *m.* 1. **S. or other,** je ne sais quoi. **S. to drink,** de quoi boire. **S. else,** autre chose. 2. (*a*) Un peu. (*b*) **There's s. in him,** il a du fond.
  II. **something,** *adv.* Quelque peu, tant soit peu.

sometimes, *adv.* Quelquefois, parfois.

somewhat, *adv.* Quelque peu ; un peu ; tant soit peu.

somewhere, *adv.* Quelque part. **S. else,** ailleurs ; autre part. **S. or other,** je ne sais où.

somnambulist, *s.* Somnambule *mf.*

somnolence, *s.* Somnolence *f.*

somnolent, *a.* Somnolent.

son, *s.* Fils *m.*

sonata, *s.* Sonate *f.*

song, *s.* 1. Chant *m.* 2. Chanson *f.*

song-bird, *s.* Oiseau chanteur.

son-in-law, *s.* Gendre *m.*

sonnet, *s.* Sonnet *m.*

sonorous, *a.* Sonore.

sonorously, *adv.* D'un ton sonore.

soon, *adv.* 1. (*a*) Bientôt, tôt. **See you again s.!** à bientôt! **How s.?** en combien de temps? (*b*) **As s. as,** aussitôt que, dès que. (*c*) **I would as s. stay,** j'aime autant rester. 2. (*a*) **No sooner had he finished,** à peine eut-il fini. (*b*) **I would sooner,** j'aimerais mieux.

soot, *s.* Suie *f.*

soothe, *v.tr.* Calmer, apaiser.

soothing, *a.* Calmant, apaisant.

sooty, *a.* Couvert de suie.

sophist, *s.* Sophiste *m.*

sophisticated, *a.* Blasé.

sophistry, *s.* 1. Sophistique *f.* 2. Sophisme *m.*

soporific, *a. & s.* Soporifique (*m*).

sopping, *a.* **S. wet,** tout trempé.

soprano, *s.* Soprano *mf.*

sorcerer, *s.* Sorcier *m*; magicien *m.*

sorceress, *s.* Sorcière *f.*

sorcery, *s.* Sorcellerie *f.*

sordid, *a.* Sordide. (*a*) Sale. (*b*) Bas, *f.* basse, vil.

sordidness, *s.* Sordidité *f.* (*a*) Saleté *f.* (*b*) Bassesse *f.*

sore[1], *a.* 1. (*a*) Douloureux, endolori. (*b*) Enflammé, irrité. **S. throat,** mal *m* de gorge. 2. Chagriné.

sore[2], *s.* Plaie *f*; blessure *f.*

sorely, *adv.* Fort.

soreness, *s.* 1. Endolorissement *m.* 2. Chagrin *m*, peine *f.*

sorrel, *s.* Oseille *f.*

sorrow[1], *s.* Peine *f*, chagrin *m*, tristesse *f.*

sorrow[2], *v.i.* S'affliger, être affligé.

sorrowful, *a.* Affligé, chagriné; triste; attristant, pénible.

sorrowfully, *adv.* Tristement; avec chagrin.

sorrowing, *a.* Affligé.

sorry, *a.* 1. (*a*) Fâché, désolé, peiné. **S.!** pardon! (*b*) **I am s. for him,** je le plains. 2. Mauvais; misérable.

sort[1], *s.* (*a*) Sorte *f*, genre *m*, espèce *f.* **Nothing of the s.,** pas du tout! **I shall do nothing of the s.,** je n'en ferai rien. (*b*) **To be out of sorts,** être indisposé.

sort[2], *v.tr.* Trier, assortir; débrouiller.

sorter, *s.* Trieur, -euse.

sortie, *s.* Sortie *f.*

sorting, *s.* Triage *m*, tri *m*; classement *m.*

so-so, *adv.* Comme ci comme ça.

sot, *s.* Ivrogne *m.*

soul, *s.* Ame *f.* **Ship lost with all souls,** navire perdu corps et biens. **Poor s.!** pauvre créature *f*!

sound[1], *s.* Son *m*, bruit *m.*

sound[2]. I. *v.i.* 1. Sonner, résonner; retentir. 2. Paraître, sembler. **That sounds well,** cela fait bon effet.

II. **sound,** *v.tr.* 1. Sonner. **To s. the horn,** corner. 2. Prononcer. 3. Ausculter.

sound[3]. I. *v.tr.* Sonder. *Abs.* Prendre le fond. 2. *v.i.* Faire la sonde; foncer.

sound[4], *s.* Détroit *m*; goulet *m.*

sound[5]. I. *a.* 1. (*a*) Sain. (*b*) En bon état. 2. (*a*) Solide. (*b*) Valide. 3. **S. sleep,** sommeil profond.

II. **sound,** *adv.* Profondément.

soundly, *adv.* 1. Sainement; judicieusement. 2. **To sleep s.,** dormir profondément. **To thrash s.o. s.,** rosser qn d'importance.

soundness, *s.* 1. Bon état. 2. Solidité *f.*

sound-wave, *s.* Onde *f* sonore.

soup, *s.* Soupe *f*, potage *m.* **Thick s.,** crème *f*, purée *f.* **Clear s.,** consommé *m.*

soup-ladle, *s.* Louche *f.*

soup-plate, *s.* Assiette creuse.

soup-tureen, *s.* Soupière *f.*

sour, *a.* 1. (*a*) Aigre, acide, sur. (*b*) **To turn s.,** tourner à l'aigre. 2. Revêche; aigre.

source, *s.* Source *f.*

sourly, *adv.* Avec aigreur.

sourness, *s.* Aigreur *f*; acidité *f.*

south. 1. *s.* Sud *m*, midi *m.* **The S. of France,** le Midi. 2. *adv.* Au sud; vers le sud. 3. *a.* Sud *inv*; du sud.

South Africa. *Pr.n.* L'Afrique australe.

south-east. 1. *s.* Sud-est *m.* 2. *adv.* Vers le sud-est. 3. *a.* Du sud-est.

south-easterly, *a.* Du sud-est.

south-eastern, *a.* Du sud-est.

southerly, *a.* (*a*) Du sud. (*b*) **S. aspect,** exposition au midi.

southern, *a.* (Du) sud; du midi; méridional, -aux.

southwards, *adv.* Vers le sud.

south-west. 1. *s.* Sud-ouest *m.* 2.

adv. Vers le sud-ouest. **3.** *a.* Du sud-ouest.

south-westerly, *a.* Du sud-ouest.

south-western, *a.* Du sud-ouest.

souvenir, *s.* Souvenir *m*, mémento *m*.

sovereign. I. *a.* Souverain ; suprême. **2.** *s.* Souverain, -aine.

sovereignty, *s.* Souveraineté *f*.

soviet, *s.* Soviet *m*. **S. union,** union soviétique.

sow[1], *v.tr.* Semer.

sow[2], *s.* (*a*) Truie *f*. (*b*) Laie *f*.

sower, *s.* Semeur, -euse.

sowing, *s.* Semailles *fpl*.

soya, *s.* Soya *m* ; pois chinois.

spa, *s.* Ville *f* d'eau ; station thermale.

space[1], *s.* **I.** Espace *m*, intervalle *m*. **2.** (*a*) L'espace. (*b*) Place *f*. (*c*) Étendue *f* ; surface *f*. **3.** Espace libre ; écartement *m*. **Blank s.,** blanc *m*.

space[2], *v.tr.* **To s.** (out), espacer.

spaced, *a.* Écarté ; espacé.

spacing, *s.* Espacement *m*, écartement *m*.

spacious, *a.* (*a*) Spacieux, vaste. (*b*) Ample.

spaciousness, *s.* Vaste étendue *f*.

spade[1], *s.* Bêche *f* ; pelle *f*.

spade[2], *s. Cards :* Pique *m*.

spaghetti, *s.* Spaghetti *mpl*.

Spain. *Pr.n.* L'Espagne *f*.

span[1], *s.* **I.** Empan *m*. **2.** (*a*) Portée *f* ; largeur *f*. (*b*) Travée *f*.

span[2], *v.tr.* **I.** Mesurer à l'empan. **2.** Franchir, enjamber.

spangle[1], *s.* Paillette *f*.

spangle[2], *v.tr.* Pailleter (*with*, de). **Spangled with silver,** lamé d'argent.

Spaniard, *s.* Espagnol, -ole

spaniel, *s.* Épagneul *m*.

Spanish. I. *a.* Espagnol ; d'Espagne. **2.** *s.* L'espagnol *m*.

spank, *v.tr.* Fesser.

spanking, *s.* Fessée *f*.

spanner, *s.* Clef *f* (à écrous).

spar[1], *s.* (*a*) Espar *m*. (*b*) *pl.* **The spars,** la mâture.

spar[2], *s.* Spath *m*.

spare[1], *a.* **I.** (*a*) Frugal. (*b*) Sec, *f*. sèche ; maigre. **2. S. time,** moments perdus ; loisir *m*. **S. bedroom,** chambre d'ami. **3.** **S. parts,** pièces *f* de rechange. **S. wheel,** roue de secours.

spare[2], *v.tr.* **I.** Épargner, ménager. **2.** (*a*) Se passer de. (*b*) **I cannot s.**

the time, je n'ai pas le temps. **3.** Faire grâce à ; épargner. **To s. s.o.'s feelings,** ménager qn.

sparing, *a.* **I.** Ménager ; économe. **To be s. with,** ménager. **S. of,** avare de. **2.** Modéré.

spark[1], *s.* (*a*) Étincelle *f*. (*b*) **Sparks,** le radio.

spark[2], *v.i.* Émettre des étincelles.

sparking-plug, *s.* Bougie *f*.

sparkle[1], *s.* **I.** Brève lueur. **2.** Étincellement *m* ; éclat *m*.

sparkle[2], *v.i.* Étinceler, scintiller.

sparkling[1], *a.* (*a*) Étincelant, brillant. (*b*) Mousseux.

sparkling[2], *s.* **I.** Étincellement *m* ; scintillement *m*. **2.** Pétillement *m*.

sparrow, *s.* Moineau *m*, passereau *m*.

sparse, *a.* Clairsemé, épars.

sparsely, *adv.* Peu abondamment.

spasm, *s.* Accès *m*.

spasmodic, *a.* **I.** Involontaire, convulsif. **2.** Fait par à-coups.

spasmodically, *adv.* Par à-coups.

spat, *s.* Demi-guêtre *f*.

spate, *s.* Crue *f*.

spatter, *v.tr.* Éclabousser.

spatula, *s.* Spatule *f*.

spawn[1], *s.* Frai *m*.

spawn[2], *v.i.* Frayer.

speak. I. *v.i.* **I.** (*a*) Parler. **Without speaking,** sans rien dire. (*b*) Causer. **To s. to,** parler à ; s'adresser à. **Speaking for myself,** pour ma part. **Roughly speaking,** approximativement. **2.** Faire un discours ; prendre la parole.

II. speak, *v.tr.* **I.** Dire. **2.** Parler. **speak of,** *v.i.* Parler de. **Speaking of,** à propos de. **To s. well of,** dire du bien de. **speak out,** *v.i.* (*a*) Parler à haute voix. (*b*) Parler franchement. **speak up,** *v.i.* **I.** Parler plus haut. **2. To s. up for,** parler en faveur de.

speaker, *s.* **I.** Parleur, -euse. **2.** Orateur *m*.

speaking[1], *a.* Expressif, éloquent.

speaking[2], *s.* Parler *m*, discours *m*, parole *f*.

speaking-trumpet, *s.* Porte-voix *m.inv.*

speaking-tube, *s.* Tube *m* acoustique.

spear[1], *s.* (*a*) Lance *f*. (*b*) Javelot *m*.

spear[2], *v.tr.* (Trans)percer d'un coup de lance.

spear-thrust, *s.* Coup *m* de lance.

special. 1. *a.* Spécial, -aux ; particulier. **2.** *s.* Train spécial.

specialist, *s.* Spécialiste *mf.*

speciality, *s.* **1.** Spécialité *f.* **2.** Particularité *f.*

specialize, *v.i.* Se spécialiser.

specially, *adv.* Spécialement, particulièrement ; surtout.

specie, *s.* Espèces monnayées.

species, *s.inv.* **1.** Espèce *f.* sorte *f.* **2.** Essence *f.*

specific, *a.* **1.** (*a*) Spécifique. (*b*) Explicite. **2.** *s.* Spécifique *m.*

specify, *v.tr.* Spécifier, déterminer.

specimen, *s.* (*a*) Spécimen *m.* (*b*) Exemple *m*, échantillon *m.*

specious, *a.* Spécieux.

speciousness, *s.* Spéciosité *f.*

speck, *s.* **1.** Petite tache ; moucheture *f.* **2.** Grain *m*, atome *m.*

speckled, *a.* Tacheté, moucheté.

spectacle, *s.* **1.** Spectacle *m.* **2.** *pl.* Lunettes *f.*

spectacle-case, *s.* Étui *m* à lunettes.

spectacular, *a.* Spectaculaire.

spectator, *s.* Spectateur, -trice ; assistant, -ante.

spectral, *a.* Spectral, -aux.

spectre, *s.* Spectre *m*, fantôme *m.*

speculate, *v.i.* **1.** Faire des conjectures (*about*, sur). **2.** Spéculer (*in*, sur).

speculation, *s.* (*a*) Spéculation *f.* (*b*) Conjecture *f.*

speculative, *a.* Spéculatif.

speech, *s.* **1.** (*a*) La parole. (*b*) Parts of s., parties *f* du discours. **2.** Langue *f* ; parler *m.* **3.** Discours *m.*

speechless, *a.* Interdit, interloqué. S. with surprise, muet de surprise.

speed¹, *s.* Vitesse *f* ; marche *f* ; rapidité *f.* At full s., à toute vitesse. Maximum s., vitesse limite.

speed², *v.i.* Se hâter, se presser.

speed³. 1. *v.tr.* To s. (up), accélérer. **2.** *v.i.* Faire de la vitesse.

speed-boat, *s.* Hors-bord *m.*

speedily, *adv.* Vite, promptement.

speed-indicator, *s.* Compteur *m.*

speediness, *s.* Rapidité *f*, célérité *f.*

speeding, *s.* **1.** Excès *m* de vitesse. **2.** S. (up), accélération *f.*

speedometer, *s.* Indicateur *m.* de vitesse ; compteur *m.*

speed-way, *s.* Autostrade *f.*

speedy, *a.* Rapide, prompt.

spell¹, *s.* Charme *m.* To cast a s., jeter un sort.

spell², *v.tr.* **1.** Épeler ; orthographier. How is it spelt? comment cela s'écrit-il ? **2.** Signifier.

spell³, *s.* **1.** Tour *m.* **2.** Période *f.*

spell-bound, *a.* Figé sur place ; sous le charme.

spelling, *s.* Épellation *f* ; orthographe *f.*

spelling-bee, *s.* Concours (oral) d'orthographe.

spend, *v.tr.* **1.** Dépenser. **2.** Passer employer.

spending, *s.* Dépense *f.*

spendthrift, *s.* Dépensier, -ière.

spent, *a.* Épuisé.

sphere, *s.* Sphère *f.*

spherical, *a.* Sphérique.

sphinx, *s.* Sphinx *m.*

spice¹, *s.* **1.** Épice *f.* **2.** Nuance *f* ; soupçon *m.*

spice², *v.tr.* Épicer.

spiciness, *s.* Goût épicé.

spicy, *a.* **1.** Épicé ; relevé **2.** Aromatique, parfumé.

spider, *s.* Araignée *f.*

spigot, *s.* Fausset *m.*

spike, *s.* **1.** Pointe *f* ; piquant *m.* **2.** Épi *m.*

spiked, *a.* Garni de pointes ; barbelé.

spill¹, *s.* To have a s., culbuter ; (*in motor car*) faire panache.

spill². I. *v.tr.* Répandre, renverser. **II. spill,** *v.i.* Se répandre.

spill³, *s.* Allume-feu *m inv.*

spin¹, *s.* (*a*) Tournoiement *m.* (*b*) To get into a s., descendre en vrille.

spin². 1. *v.tr.* (*a*) Filer. (*b*) Faire tourner. **2.** *v.i.* Tourner. To s. round and round, tournoyer. spin out, *v.tr.* Faire traîner en longueur.

spinach, *s.* Épinards *mpl.*

spinal, *a.* Spinal, -aux. S. column, colonne vertébrale.

spindle, *s.* Fuseau *m.*

spine, *s.* Épine dorsale ; colonne vertébrale.

spinning, *s.* **1.** Filage *m.* **2.** Tournoiement *m* ; rotation *f.*

spinning-wheel, *s.* Rouet *m.*

spinster, *s.* Fille non mariée.

spiny, *a.* Épineux.

spiral. 1. *s.* Spirale *f*, hélice *f.* **2.** *a.* Spiral, -aux ; en spirale.

spire, s. Aiguille f, flèche.
spirit, s. **1.** Esprit m, âme f. **2.** Evil s., esprit malin, mauvais génie. **3.** The leading s., l'âme, le chef. **4.** Esprit, disposition f. **5.** (a) Caractère m, courage m. (b) Ardeur f, entrain m. (c) In high spirits, en verve. In low spirits, abattu. **6.** (a) pl. Spiritueux mpl; alcool m. (b) Methylated s., alcool à brûler.
spirited, a. Vif, animé; fougueux.
spirit-lamp, s. Lampe f à alcool, à esprit de vin.
spiritless, a. **1.** Sans vie. **2.** Sans courage. **3.** Abattu.
spiritual, a. Spirituel.
spiritualism, s. Spiritisme m.
spiritualist, s. & a. Spirite (mf).
spirituous, a. Spiritueux.
spit[1], s. **1.** Broche f. **2.** Pointe f de terre.
spit[2], v.tr. Embrocher.
spit[3], **1.** v.i. Cracher; crachiner. **2.** v.tr. Cracher.
spite[1], s. **1.** (a) Rancune f. (b) Malveillance f. (c) Pique f, dépit m. **2.** Prep.phr. In s. of, en dépit de; malgré.
spite[2], v.tr. Vexer, contrarier.
spiteful, a. Rancunier, vindicatif.
spitefully, adv. **1.** Par dépit; par rancune. **2.** Méchamment.
spitefulness, s. Méchanceté f.
spittoon, s. Crachoir m.
splash[1], s. **1.** Éclaboussement m; clapotis m. **2.** (a) Éclaboussure f. (b) Tache f.
splash[2]. **1.** v.tr. Éclabousser (with, de). **2.** v.i. (a) Rejaillir en éclaboussures; clapoter. (b) Barboter.
spleen, s. **1.** Rate f. **2.** Mauvaise humeur.
splendid, a. Splendide; magnifique. That's s.! à la bonne heure!
splendidly, adv. Splendidement.
splendour, s. Splendeur f; éclat m.
splint, s. Éclisse f.
splinter[1], s. Éclat m.
splinter[2]. **1.** v.tr. Briser en éclats. **2.** v.i. Éclater.
split[1], s. **1.** Fente f; fissure f. **2.** Division f; rupture f.
split[2]. **1.** v.tr. (a) Fendre. To s. the atom, désintégrer l'atome. (b) Diviser. **2.** v.i. Se fendre.
split[3], a. Fendu.

splutter[1], s. Bredouillement m.
splutter[2]. **1.** v.tr. Bredouiller. **2.** v.i. (a) Cracher. (b) Bredouiller.
spoil[1], s. Dépouilles fpl; butin m.
spoil[2]. **1.** v.tr. Gâter; abîmer. **2.** v.i. Se gâter.
spoke, s. Rayon m.
spoken, a. Parlé.
spokesman, s. Porte-parole m inv.
sponge[1], s. Éponge f.
sponge[2], s. Coup m d'éponge.
sponge[3], v.tr. Éponger.
sponge-cake, s. **1.** Gâteau m mousseline. **2.** Madeleine f.
sponge-finger, s. Biscuit m à la cuiller.
spongy, a. Spongieux.
sponsor[1], s. **1.** Garant m, caution f. **2.** Parrain m, marraine f.
sponsor[2], v.tr. Être le garant de.
spontaneous, a. Spontané.
spontaneously, adv. Spontanément.
spool, s. Bobine f.
spoon, s. Cuiller f, cuillère f. S. and fork, couvert m.
spoonful, s. Cuillerée f.
sporadic, a. Sporadique.
spore, s. Spore f.
sport[1], s. **1.** Jeu m, divertissement m. To make s. of, se moquer de. **2.** Sport m. **3.** Jouet m.
sport[2], v.i. Jouer; se divertir.
sportive, a. Badin; folâtre.
sports-ground, s. Terrain m de jeux; stade m.
sportsman, s. **1.** Chasseur m; pêcheur m. **2.** Amateur m de sport.
spot[1], s. **1.** (a) Endroit m, lieu m. (b) Adv. phr: On the s., sur-le-champ; immédiatement. **2.** Tache f, macule f. **3.** Pois m.
spot[2], v.tr. **1.** (a) Tacher, souiller. (b) Tacheter, moucheter. **2.** (a) Repérer; apercevoir. (b) Reconnaître.
spotless, a. Sans tache; pur.
spotlessly, adv. S. clean, d'une propreté irréprochable.
spotlight, s. Feu m de projecteur.
spotted, a. (a) Tacheté, moucheté. (b) A pois.
spouse, s. Époux, f. épouse.
spout[1], s. (a) Tuyau m. (b) Bec m; jet m.
spout[2]. **1.** v.i. (a) Jaillir. (b) Souffler. **2.** v.tr. Faire jaillir.

spouting, s. Jaillissement m.

sprain¹, s. Entorse f, foulure f.

sprain², v.tr. **To s. one's wrist,** se fouler le poignet. **To s. one's ankle,** se donner une entorse.

sprat, s. Sprat m, harenguet m.

sprawl, v.i. S'étendre, s'étaler.

spray¹, s. **1.** Embrun m. **2.** (a) Poussière f d'eau. (b) Jet pulvérisé. **3.** Gicleur m; vaporisateur m.

spray², v.tr. **1.** Pulvériser, vaporiser, atomiser. **2.** Asperger, arroser.

spread¹, s. **1.** (a) Étendue f. (b) Envergure f. **2.** Diffusion f; expansion f.

spread². I. v.tr. **1.** Étendre; tendre. **2.** Répandre.
II. **spread,** v.i. **1.** S'étendre, s'étaler. **2.** Se répandre; se propager. **3.** Se disperser.

spreading, s. **1.** (a) Développement m. (b) Propagation f; diffusion f. **2.** (a) Extension f. (b) Dispersion f.

sprig, s. Brin m, brindille f.

sprightly, a. Éveillé, enjoué.

spring¹, s. **1.** Source f. **2.** Printemps m. **S.** flowers, fleurs printanières. **3.** Saut m, bond m. **4.** Élasticité f. **5.** (a) Ressort m. (b) pl. Suspension f.

spring². I. v.i. **1.** Bondir, sauter. **To s.**, s'élancer sur. **2.** Jaillir, sourdre.
II. **spring,** v.tr. Faire jouer; faire sauter. **spring up,** v.i. **1.** Se lever précipitamment. **2.** (a) Pousser. (b) Se lever; s'établir.

spring-balance, s. Peson m à ressort.

spring-board, s. Tremplin m.

spring-mattress, s. Sommier m élastique.

spring-tide, s. Grande marée.

springtime, s. Printemps m.

springy, a. Élastique; flexible.

sprinkle, v.tr. (a) Répandre, jeter. (b) Asperger; saupoudrer.

sprint¹, s. Pointe f de vitesse.

sprint², v.i. Faire une course de vitesse.

sprite, s. Lutin m; farfadet m.

sprout¹, s. **1.** (a) Rejeton m, pousse f. (b) Germe m, bourgeon m. **2. Brussels sprouts,** choux m de Bruxelles.

sprout². **1.** v.i. (a) Pousser, pointer. (b) Germer. **2.** v.tr. Pousser.

spruce¹, a. Pimpant; soigné.

spruce², s. Sapin m, épinette f.

spry, a. Vif, actif.

spur¹, s. **1.** Éperon m. **2.** Coup m d'éperon; stimulant m; aiguillon m. **On the s. of the moment,** sous l'impulsion du moment. **3.** Ergot m.

spur², v.tr. **1.** Éperonner. **2. To s. on,** aiguillonner, stimuler.

spurious, a. Faux, f. fausse; contrefait.

spurn, v.tr. **1.** Repousser du pied. **2.** Traiter avec mépris.

spurt¹, s. **1.** Jaillissement m; jet m. **2.** (a) Effort soudain. (b) **To put on a s.,** démarrer, emballer.

spurt², v.i. **1.** Jaillir, gicler. **2.** Emballer, démarrer.

sputter, v.i. (a) Bredouiller. (b) Grésiller, crépiter.

sputtering, s. **1.** Bredouillement m. **2.** Crépitement m.

spy¹, s. Espion, -onne.

spy². **1.** v.tr. Remarquer. **2.** v.i. Espionner.

spying, s. Espionnage m.

squabble¹, s. Querelle f.

squabble², v.i. Se quereller.

squabbling, s. Querelles fpl.

squad, s. **1.** Escouade f. **Firing s.,** peloton m d'exécution. **2.** Brigade f.

squadron, s. **1.** (a) Escadron m. (b) Escadrille f. **S. leader,** commandant m. **2.** Escadre f.

squalid, a. Sale; misérable.

squall¹, v.i. Crier, brailler.

squall², s. Grain m; bourrasque f.

squalling, a. Criard, braillard.

squalor, s. Saleté f; misère f.

squander, v.tr. Gaspiller.

squanderer, s. Gaspilleur, -euse.

squandering, s. Gaspillage m.

square¹. I. s. **1.** Carré m. **2.** (a) Carreau m; case f. (b) **Silk s.,** foulard m. **3.** Place f; square m. **4.** Équerre f.
II. **square,** a. **1.** Carré. **2. To get things s.,** mettre tout en ordre. **To be s. with,** être quitte envers.

square². I. v.tr. Balancer régler; arranger.
II. **square,** v.i. S'accorder. **square up,** v.tr. Régler ses comptes.

squash¹, s. Cohue f, presse f.

squash². **1.** v.tr. Écraser, aplatir. **2.** v.i. (a) S'écraser. (b) Se serrer.

squat¹, v.i. (a) S'accroupir. (b) Se tapir.

squat[2], *a.* Ramassé, trapu.

squatter, *s.* Squatter *m.*

squawk[1], *s.* Cri *m* rauque.

squawk[2], *v.i.* Pousser des cris rauques.

squeak[1], *s.* Cri aigu ; crissement *m.*

squeak[2], *v.i.* Pousser des cris aigus ; crier.

squeaking, *s.* Couics *mpl.*

squeal[1], *s.* Cri aigu ; cri perçant.

squeal[2], *v.i.* Pousser des cris aigus

squealing[1], *a.* Criard.

squealing[2], *s.* Cris aigus ; hauts cris.

squeeze[1], *s.* **1.** (*a*) Compression *f.* (*b*) Étreinte *f.* **2.** Presse *f*, cohue *f.*

squeeze[2], *v.tr.* **1.** (*a*) Presser. (*b*) Étreindre. **2.** Faire entrer de force. **To s. out**, exprimer. **3.** Exercer une pression sur.

squib, *s.* Crapaud *m.*

squint[1], *s.* Strabisme *m.*

squint[2], *v.i.* Loucher.

squirm, *v.i.* Se tortiller.

squirrel, *s.* Écureuil *m.*

squirt[1], *s.* **1.** Seringue *f.* **2.** Jet *m.*

squirt[2]. **1.** *v.tr.* Lancer en jet. **2.** *v.i.* Jaillir.

stab[1], *s.* Coup *m* de poignard. de couteau.

stab[2], *v.tr.* Poignarder.

stability, *s.* Stabilité *f*, solidité *f.*

stable[1], *s.* Écurie *f.*

stable[2], *v.tr.* Loger.

stable[3], *a.* **1.** Stable ; solide, fixe. **2.** Constant, ferme.

stabling, *s.* **1.** Logement *m.* **2.** *Coll:* Écuries *fpl.*

stack[1], *s.* **1.** (*a*) Meule *f.* (*b*) Pile *f*, tas *m.* **2.** Souche *f.*

stack[2], *v.tr.* **1.** Mettre en meule. **2.** Empiler, entasser.

stadium, *s.* Stade *m.*

staff, *s.* **1.** (*a*) Bâton *m.* (*b*) Hampe *f.* **2.** (*a*) État-major *m.* (*b*) Personnel *m.* **3.** Portée *f.*

staff-officer, *s.* Officier *m* d'état-major.

stag, *s.* Cerf *m.*

stage[1], *s.* **1.** Estrade *f*, échafaud *m.* **2.** (*a*) Scène *f.* **To come on the s.**, entrer en scène. **S. directions**, indications scéniques. (*b*) Champ *m* d'action. **3.** Phase *f*, période *f.* **4.** Étape *f.*

stage[2], *v.tr.* (*a*) Monter (une pièce). (*b*) Organiser.

stage-box, *s.* Loge *f* d'avant-scène.

stage-door, *s.* Entrée *f* des artistes.

stage-fright, *s.* Trac *m.*

stage-manager, *s.* Régisseur *m.*

stage-whisper, *s.* Aparté *m.*

stagger. **I.** *v.i.* Chanceler, tituber. **II.** **stagger**. *v.tr.* Confondre consterner.

staggering, *a.* **I.** Chancelant, titubant. **2.** Atterrant.

staging, *s.* Échafaud *m* échafaudage *m.*

stagnant, *a.* Stagnant.

stagnate, *v.i.* Être stagnant.

stagnation, *s.* Stagnation *f.*

staid, *a.* Posé, sérieux, sage.

stain[1], *s.* **1.** Tache *f*, souillure *f.* **2.** Couleur *f*, colorant *m.*

stain[2], *v.tr.* **1.** Tacher. **2.** Teindre.

stainless, *a.* **I.** Sans tache ; immaculé. pur. **2.** **S. steel**, acier *m* inoxydable.

stair, *s.* **I.** Marche *f*, degré *m.* **2.** *pl.* Escalier *m.*

staircase, *s.* Escalier *m.*

stake[1], *s.* **I.** Pieu *m*, poteau *m* ; tuteur *m.* **2.** Mise *f*, enjeu *m.* **At s.**, en jeu. **To have a s. in**, avoir des intérêts dans.

stake[2], *v.tr.* **I.** **To s. (out)**, jalonner. **2.** Ramer. **3.** Mettre en jeu ; jouer.

stalactite, *s.* Stalactite *f.*

stale, *a.* **I.** Rassis. **2.** Vieux, *f.* vieille ; passé.

stalemate, *s.* Pat *m.*

stalk[1]. **I.** *v.i.* **To s. (along)**, marcher d'un pas majestueux. **2.** *v.tr.* Traquer d'affût en affût

stalk[2], *s.* **I.** Tige *f* ; queue *f* ; trognon *m.* **2.** Pied *m.*

stall[1], *s.* **I.** (*a*) Stalle *f.* (*b*) Étable *f.* **2.** Étalage *m* ; échoppe *f* ; étal *m.* **3.** Fauteuil *m* d'orchestre.

stall[2]. **I.** *v.tr.* Caler. **2.** *v.i.* (Se) caler.

stallion, *s.* Étalon *m.*

stalwart, *a.* **I.** Robuste. **2.** Vaillant.

stamina, *s.* Vigueur *f*, résistance *f.*

stammer[1], *s.* (*a*) Bégaiement *m.* (*b*) Balbutiement *m.*

stammer[2], *v.i. & tr.* (*a*) Bégayer (*b*) Balbutier.

stammerer, *s.* Bègue *mf.*

stamp[1], *s.* **I.** Battement *m* de pied. **2.** (*a*) Timbre *m*, empreinte *f.* **Rubber s.**, tampon *m.* (*b*) Étampe *f*, poinçon *m.* **3.** **Postage s.**, timbre

(-poste) *m*, *pl.* timbres(-poste).
4. Pilon *m* ; broyeuse *f*.

stamp[2], *v.tr.* **1.** (*a*) To s. one's foot, frapper du pied. (*b*) Piétiner. **To s. on,** fouler aux pieds. **2.** Frapper ; estamper. **3.** Timbrer, affranchir.

stamp-album, *s.* Album *m* de timbres-poste.

stamp-collector, *s.* Collectionneur, -euse, de timbres-poste.

stamp-duty, *s.* Impôt *m* du timbre.

stamped, *a.* **S. paper,** papier timbré.

stampede[1], *s.* **1.** Fuite précipitée ; panique *f*. **2.** Ruée *f*.

stampede[2]. **1.** *v.i.* (*a*) Fuir à la débandade. (*b*) Se ruer. **2.** *v.tr.* Jeter la panique parmi.

stamping, *s.* **1.** Piétinement *m*. **2.** Timbrage *m*.

stance, *s.* Position *f* des pieds.

stanch, *v.tr.* Étancher.

stanchion, *s.* Étançon *m*, étai *m*.

stand[1], *s.* **1.** Arrêt *m*, halte *f*. **2.** Résistance *f*. **3.** Situation *f*, position *f*. **4.** Station *f*, stationnement *m*. **5.** Support *m*. **6.** Étalage *m*. **7.** (*a*) Tribune *f* ; stand *m*. (*b*) Estrade *f*.

stand[2]. **I.** *v.i.* **1.** (*a*) Être debout ; se tenir debout. (*b*) Se lever. **2.** Se trouver ; être. **3.** S'arrêter ; faire halte. **4.** Rester, durer. **To s. fast,** tenir bon. **5.** Tenir. **6.** (*a*) **To s. in need of,** avoir besoin de. (*b*) **To s. security,** assurer. **To s. as candidate,** se porter candidat. (*c*) **How do we s.?** où en sont nos comptes ? **As matters s.,** au point où en sont les choses. **To s. well with,** être estimé de. **7.** Reposer.

II. stand, *v.tr.* **1.** Mettre, poser. **2. To s. one's ground,** tenir bon. **3.** Supporter, subir. **I can't s. it any longer,** je n'y tiens plus. **4.** Payer, offrir. **stand aside,** *v.i.* (*a*) Se tenir à l'écart. (*b*) Se ranger. **stand by,** *v.i.* **1.** (*a*) Se tenir prêt. (*b*) Se tenir là. **2.** (*a*) Se tenir près de. (*b*) Soutenir. **stand for,** *v.ind.tr.* **1.** Défendre. **2.** Tenir lieu de. **3.** Signifier. **stand out,** *v.i.* **1.** Résister ; tenir bon. **2. To s. out for,** insister sur. **3.** Faire saillie. **stand over,** *v.i.* Rester en suspens. **stand up,** *v.i.* **1.** (*a*) Se lever ; se mettre debout. (*b*) Se dresser, se tenir droit. **2.** (*a*) **To s. up against,** résister à.

(*b*) **To s. up for,** défendre. (*c*) **To s. up to,** affronter.

standard, *s.* **1.** Bannière *f* ; étendard *m* ; pavillon *m*. **2.** Étalon *m*. **3.** Modèle *m*, type *m*. **S. of living,** niveau *m* de vie. **4.** Degré *m* ; qualité *f*. **5. S. size,** taille courante.

stand-by, *s.* Ressource *f*.

standing, *s.* **1.** Stationnement *m*. **2.** Durée *f*. **3.** Rang *m*, position *f* ; importance *f*.

standing room, *s.* Place *f* debout.

standpoint, *s.* Point *m* de vue.

standstill, *s.* Arrêt *m*, immobilisation *f*. **To come to a s.,** s'arrêter.

stanza, *s.* Stance *f*, strophe *f*.

staple, *s.* (*a*) Produit principal. (*b*) Matière première.

star[1], *s.* **1.** Étoile *f* ; astre *m*. **2.** Vedette *f*.

star[2], *v.i.* Être en vedette.

starboard, *s.* Tribord *m*.

starch[1], *s.* Amidon *m*.

starch[2], *v.tr.* Empeser, amidonner.

stare[1], *s.* Regard *m* fixe.

stare[2]. **1.** *v.i.* (*a*) Regarder fixement. (*b*) Écarquiller les yeux. **2.** *v.ind.tr* **To s. at,** regarder fixement ; dévisager. **3.** *v.tr.* **To s. s.o. in the face,** dévisager qn.

stark. 1. *a.* Raide, rigide. **2.** *adv.* **S. naked,** tout nu.

starlight, *s.* **1.** Lumière *f* des étoiles. **2.** *Attrib.* **A s. night,** une nuit étoilée.

starling, *s.* Étourneau *m*.

starry, *a.* Étoilé, (par)semé d'étoiles.

start[1], *s.* **1.** (*a*) Tressaillement *m*, sursaut *m*. **He gave a s.,** il sursauta. (*b*) Saut *m* ; mouvement *m* brusque. **2.** (*a*) Commencement *m*, début *m*. **To make a good s.,** bien commencer. (*b*) Départ *m*.

start[2]. **I.** *v.i.* **1.** (*a*) Tressaillir, tressauter, sursauter. (*b*) Jaillir ; sortir. **2.** (*a*) Commencer ; débuter. **To s. with,** en premier lieu. (*b*) Partir ; se mettre en route. (*c*) Démarrer ; s'ébranler.

II. start, *v.tr.* **1.** Commencer. **2.** Donner le signal du départ à. **3.** Lancer. **4.** Mettre en marche.

starting, *s.* **1.** Tressaillement *m* ; sursaut *m*. **2.** (*a*) Commencement *m*, début *m*. (*b*) Départ *m*. **3.** Mise *f* en train.

starting-handle, *s.* Manivelle *f* de mise en marche.

starting-point, *s.* Point *m* de départ.

starting-post, *s.* Poteau *m* de départ.

startle, *v.tr.* Effrayer, alarmer ; faire tressaillir.

startling, *a.* Effrayant, saisissant.

starvation, *s.* Privation *f* de nourriture. **To die of s.,** mourir de faim.

starve. I. *v.i.* (*a*) **To s. to death,** mourir de faim. (*b*) Manquer de nourriture. **2.** *v.tr.* (*a*) Faire mourir de faim. (*b*) Priver de nourriture.

starved, *a.* Affamé.

starving, *a.* Mourant de faim.

state¹, *s.* **I.** État *m*, condition *f*. **2.** (*a*) Rang *m*, dignité *f*. (*b*) Pompe *f*, parade *f*. **3.** État, nation *f*.

state², *v.tr.* **I.** (*a*) Énoncer, déclarer. (*b*) Exposer. **2.** Arrêter, fixer.

stateliness, *s.* Majesté *f* ; dignité *f*.

stately, *a.* **I.** Majestueux ; imposant. **2.** Plein de dignité.

statement, *s.* **I.** Exposition *f*, exposé *m* ; rapport *m*. **2. S. of account,** état *m* de compte.

state-room, *s.* Cabine *f* (de luxe).

statesman, *s.* Homme *m* d'État.

station¹, *s.* **I.** (*a*) Position *f*, place *f*. (*b*) Station *f*, poste *m*. **2.** Position, condition *f*. **3.** Gare *f*.

station², *v.tr.* Placer, mettre.

stationary, *a.* Stationnaire ; immobile.

stationer, *s.* Papetier, -ière. **Stationer's shop,** papeterie *f*.

stationery, *s.* Papeterie *f*.

stationmaster, *s.* Chef *m* de gare.

statistical, *a.* Statistique.

statistics, *s.pl.* La statistique.

statuary, *s.* Statues *fpl.*

statue, *s.* Statue *f*.

stature, *s.* Stature *f* ; taille *f*.

status, *s.* Condition *f*, rang *m*.

statute, *s.* **I.** Loi *f*. **2.** *pl.* Statuts *m*, règlements *m*.

statutory, *a.* **I.** Fixé par la loi. **2.** Statutaire.

staunch¹, *a.* Sûr, dévoué.

staunch², *v.tr.* Étancher.

staunchly, *adv.* Avec fermeté ; avec dévouement.

staunchness, *s.* Fermeté *f* ; dévouement *m*.

stave, *v.tr.* **To s. in,** Défoncer, enfoncer. **To s. off,** Détourner, écarter.

stay¹, *s.* Séjour *m*.

stay². **I.** *v.i.* **I.** (*a*) Rester ; demeurer. **To s. in bed,** garder le lit. (*b*) **To come to s.,** venir pour rester définitivement.

II. stay, *v.tr.* Arrêter ; retenir.

stay away, *v.i.* Ne pas venir ; s'absenter. **stay up,** *v.i.* Ne pas se coucher, veiller.

stay³, *s.* **I.** Support *m*, soutien *m*. **2.** *pl.* Corset *m*.

staying, *s.* **I.** Séjour *m*. **2. S. power,** endurance *f*.

steadfast, *a.* Ferme ; constant.

steadfastly, *adv.* Fermement ; avec constance.

steadfastness, *s.* Fermeté *f* ; constance *f*.

steadily, *adv.* **I.** Fermement. **2.** (*a*) Régulièrement. (*b*) Uniment. **3.** Assidûment. **4.** Avec sagesse.

steadiness, *s.* **I.** Fermeté *f*. **2.** Assiduité *f*. **3.** Stabilité *f*. **4.** Conduite rangée.

steady¹. **I.** *a.* (*a*) Ferme solide ; fixe, rigide. (*b*) Continu, soutenu ; régulier. (*c*) Assidu, régulier. (*d*) Rangé posé. **2.** *adv.* **S.!** ne bougez pas ! doucement !

steady². **I.** *v.tr.* Raffermir, affermir. **2.** *v.i.* Se raffermir.

steak, *s.* (*a*) Tranche *f*. (*b*) Bifteck *m*. Fillet s., tournedos *m*.

steal. I. *v.tr.* (*a*) Voler, dérober, soustraire (*from*, à). (*b*) **To s. a march on,** devancer. **2.** *v.i.* **To s. away,** s'en aller à la dérobée.

stealing, *s.* Vol *m*.

stealth, *s.* **By s.,** furtivement.

stealthily, *adv.* A la dérobée ; furtivement.

stealthiness, *s.* Caractère furtif.

stealthy, *a.* Furtif.

steam¹, *s.* (*a*) Vapeur *f* ; buée *f*. (*b*) **To get up s.,** chauffer.

steam². **I.** *v.tr.* Cuire à l'étuvée. **2.** *v.i.* (*a*) Fumer. (*b*) Marcher (à la vapeur).

steamboat, *s.* Bateau *m*, navire *m*, à vapeur ; vapeur *m*.

steam-engine, *s.* Machine *f* à vapeur.

steamer, *s.* **I.** Vapeur *m*. **2.** Marmite *f* à vapeur.

steam-roller, *s.* Rouleau *m* compresseur.

steamship, s. Navire m à vapeur ; vapeur m.

steel¹, s. **1.** Acier m. **S. pen,** plume métallique. **2.** Fusil m ; affiloir m.

steel², v.tr. **To s. oneself,** s'endurcir.

steel-engraving, s. Estampe f sur acier.

steep¹, a. Escarpé ; à pic ; raide.

steep², v.tr. Saturer, imbiber.

steeple, s. (a) Clocher m. (b) Flèche f.

steeply, adv. En pente rapide ; à pic.

steepness, s. Raideur f.

steer¹, v.tr. Gouverner ; diriger. Abs. Gouverner ; barrer. **To s. clear of,** éviter.

steer², s. Bœuf m.

steering, s. Direction f, conduite f.

steering-wheel, s. Volant m.

stellar, a. Stellaire.

stem¹, s. **1.** Tige f ; queue f ; tronc m. **2.** Pied m, patte f ; tuyau m. **3.** Étrave f, avant m.

stem², v.tr. **1.** Contenir, arrêter. **2.** Lutter contre ; refouler.

stench, s. Puanteur f.

stencil, v.tr. Marquer au patron.

stenographer, s. Sténographe mf

stenography, s. Sténographie f.

step¹, s. **1.** Pas m. **In the steps of,** sur les traces de. **2.** Pas, cadence f. **3.** Démarche f. **To take steps,** se préparer. **4.** Marche f, degré m ; marchepied m. **Flight of steps,** perron m. **5.** pl. Escabeau m.

step², v.i. **S. this way,** venez par ici. **step aside,** v.i. **1.** S'écarter, se ranger. **2.** Se détourner de son chemin. **step in,** v.i. **1.** Entrer ; monter. **2.** Intervenir. **step on,** v.i. Mettre le pied sur. **step out,** v.i. **1.** Sortir ; descendre. **2.** Allonger le pas. **step over,** v.i. Franchir ; enjamber.

stepbrother, s. Demi-frère m, pl. demi-frères.

stepchild, s. Enfant mf d'un autre lit.

stepdaughter, s. Belle-fille f, pl. belles-filles.

stepfather, s. Beau-père m, pl. beaux-pères.

Stephen, Pr.n. Étienne m.

step-ladder, s. Escabeau m.

stepmother, s. Belle-mère f, pl. belles-mères.

stepping-stones, s.pl. Pierres f de gué.

stepsister, s. Demi-sœur f, pl. demi-sœurs.

stepson, s. Beau-fils m, pl. beaux-fils

stereoscope, s. Stéréoscope m.

stereotype, v.tr. Stéréotyper.

stereotyped, a. **S. phrase,** cliché m

sterile, a. Stérile.

sterility, s. Stérilité f.

sterilization, s. Stérilisation f

sterilize, v.tr. Stériliser.

sterling, a. De bon aloi ; solide.

stern¹, a. Sévère, rigide, dur.

stern², s. Arrière m.

sternly, adv. Sévèrement, durement.

sternness, s. Sévérité f ; austérité f

stethoscope, s. Stéthoscope m.

stew¹, s. Ragoût m ; civet m.

stew². **1.** v.tr. Faire cuire en ragoût, en compote. **2.** v.i. Cuire à la casserole.

steward, s. **1.** Économe m, régisseur m. **2.** Garçon m ; steward m. **Chief s.,** maître m d'hôtel. **3.** Commissaire m.

stewardess, s. Femme f de chambre (de bord) ; stewardess.

stewed, a. **S. fruit,** compote f de fruits. **S. prunes,** pruneaux au jus.

stick¹, s. **1.** (a) Bâton m. (b) Manche m. (c) Crosse f. (d) Morceau m de bois. **2.** Bâton ; barre f.

stick². **I.** v.tr. **1.** Piquer, enfoncer **2.** Mettre. **3.** Coller.
II. **stick,** v.i. **1.** Se piquer, s'enfoncer. **2.** (Se) coller, adhérer. **To s. to,** ne pas abandonner ; garder pour soi. **S. to it!** persévérez ! **3.** Être pris, engagé ; s'embourber.

stick down, v.tr. Fermer, coller.

stick out. **1.** v.tr. Faire dépasser ; sortir. **2.** v.i. Faire saillie ; ressortir.

stick up. **1.** v.tr. Afficher. **2.** v.i. (a) Se dresser ; se tenir debout. (b) **To s. up for,** prendre la défense de.

stickiness, s. Viscosité f.

sticking-plaster, s. Taffetas gommé.

sticky, a. Collant, gluant, visqueux, adhésif.

stiff, a. **1.** (a) Raide, rigide. **S. shirt-front,** plastron empesé. (b) Raide guindé ; contraint. (c) Inflexible, obstiné. **2.** (a) Dur. (b) Ferme. **3.** Difficile ; rude, pénible.

stiffen. **I.** v.tr. Raidir.
II. **stiffen,** v.i. (Se) raidir ; devenir raide.

stiffly, adv. **1.** Raidement ; avec raideur. **2.** D'un air guindé.

stiffness, *s.* **1.** Raideur *f*, rigidité *f*. **2.** Fermeté *f*, consistance *f*. **3.** Difficulté *f*.

stifle. 1. *v.tr.* (*a*) Étouffer, suffoquer. (*b*) Réprimer. **2.** *v.i.* Suffoquer, étouffer.

stifling, *a.* Étouffant, suffocant

stigma, *s.* Stigmate *m*, tache *f*.

stigmatize, *v.tr.* Stigmatiser.

stile, *s.* Échalier *m*.

stiletto, *s.* Stylet *m*.

still¹, *a.* Tranquille. (*a*) Immobile. **To keep s.,** ne pas bouger. (*b*) Silencieux. (*c*) **S. life,** nature morte.

still², *v.tr.* Tranquilliser, calmer.

still³. 1. *adv.* Encore; toujours. **2.** *conj.* Cependant, pourtant, toutefois.

still⁴, *s.* Alambic *m*, cornue *f*.

stillness, *s.* Tranquillité *f*, calme *m*

stilt, *s.* Échasse *f*.

stilted, *a.* Guindé, tendu.

stimulant, *s.* **1.** Stimulant *m*; remontant *m*. **2.** Excitant *m*.

stimulate, *v.tr.* Stimuler; activer, exciter.

stimulation, *s.* Stimulation *f*.

stimulus, *s.* Stimulant *m*; impulsion *f*.

sting¹, *s.* **1.** Dard *m*, aiguillon *m*. **2.** (*a*) Piqûre *f*. (*b*) Douleur cuisante.

sting², *v.tr.* Piquer.

stinginess, *s.* Mesquinerie *f*, ladrerie *f*.

stinging, *a.* Piquant, cuisant brûlant.

stingy, *a.* Mesquin, chiche, ladre.

stink¹, *s.* Puanteur *f*.

stink², *v.i.* Puer; sentir mauvais; empester.

stinking, *a.* Puant, empesté.

stint¹, *s.* Restriction *f*.

stint², *v.tr.* Priver.

stipend, *s.* Traitement *m*.

stipple, *s.* Pointillé *m*.

stipulate. 1. *v.i.* **To s.** for. stipuler. **2.** *v.tr.* Stipuler.

stipulation, *s.* Stipulation *f*.

stir¹, *s.* **1.** Mouvement *m*. **2.** Agitation *f*, émoi *m*. **To make a s.,** faire du bruit.

stir². 1. *v.tr.* (*a*) Remuer, mouvoir; bouger. (*b*) Activer; agiter. (*c*) Émouvoir, troubler. **2.** *v.i.* Bouger remuer. **stir up,** *v.tr.* **1.** Remuer, agiter; activer. **2.** Fomenter.

stirring, *a.* **1.** Actif, remuant. **2.** Émouvant.

stirrup, *s.* Étrier *m*.

stitch¹, *s.* (*a*) Point *m*, piqûre *f*. (*b*) Maille *f*. **To put stitches in a wound,** suturer une plaie.

stitch², *v.tr.* **1.** Coudre. **2.** Suturer.

stoat, *s.* Hermine *f*.

stock¹, *s.* **1.** Race *f*, famille *f*, lignée *f*. **2.** Fût *m*. **3.** (*a*) Provision *f*, approvisionnement *m*. (*b*) Marchandises *fpl*; stock *m*. **In s.,** en magasin. **To take s.,** faire l'inventaire. **4.** Fonds *mpl*, valeurs *fpl*. **5.** Giroflée *f*. **6.** *Attrib.* **S. size,** taille courante.

stock², *v.tr.* **1.** Garnir, stocker (*with*, de). **2.** Tenir, garder, en magasin.

stockade, *s.* Palissade *f*.

stock-broker, *s.* Agent *m* de change.

stock exchange, *s.* Bourse *f* (des valeurs).

stocking, *s.* Bas *m*.

stock-pot, *s.* Pot-au-feu *m inv*.

stock still, *a.* Immobile.

stock-taking, *s.* Inventaire *m*.

stocky, *a.* Trapu.

stodgy, *a.* Lourd.

stoic, *s.* Stoïque *mf*.

stoical, *a.* Stoïque.

stoically, *adv.* Stoïquement.

stoicism, *s.* Stoïcisme *m*

stoke, *v.tr.* Charger.

stoker, *s.* Chauffeur *m*.

stole, *s.* **1.** Étole *f*. **2.** Écharpe *f*.

stolid, *a.* Lourd, lent, impassible

stolidity, *s.* Flegme *m*.

stolidly, *adv.* Avec flegme

stomach, *s.* Estomac *m*.

stone, *s.* **1.** Pierre *f*. **2.** Precious stones, pierres précieuses; pierreries *f*. **3.** Noyau *m*; pépin *m*. **4.** *Attrib.* De, en, pierre.

stone-blind, *a.* Complètement aveugle.

stone-dead, *a.* Raide mort.

stone-deaf, *a.* Complètement sourd.

stone-fruit, *s.* Fruit *m* à noyau.

stoneware, *s.* Poterie *f* de grès.

stony, *a.* **1.** Pierreux; couvert de pierres. **2.** Dur comme la pierre.

stool, *s.* (*a*) Tabouret *m*. **Folding s.,** pliant *m*. (*b*) Escabeau *m*.

stoop, *v.i.* (*a*) Se pencher, se baisser. (*b*) S'abaisser, descendre. (*c*) Être voûté.

stooping, *a.* Penché, courbé; voûté.

stop¹, *s.* **1.** (*a*) Arrêt *m*, interruption *f*. **To put a s. to,** faire cesser. (*b*) Arrêt, halte f. **2.** Point m. **3.** Jeu m, registre m.

stop². I. v.tr. **1.** Boucher; plomber, obturer. **2.** (a) Arrêter. **To s. a blow**, parer un coup. (b) Mettre fin à. **3.** Cesser.

II. **stop**, v.i. **1.** (a) S'arrêter, stopper. **'Cars s. by request,'** "arrêt facultatif." **'All cars s. here,'** "arrêt fixe." (b) Cesser. **2.** Rester; demeurer.

stop-gap, s. Bouche-trou m, pl. bouche-trous.

stoppage, s. **1.** Arrêt m; suspension f. **2.** Obstruction f. **3.** Arrêt, pause f, halte f.

stopper, s. (a) Bouchon m. **Screw s.**, fermeture f à vis. (b) Obturateur m.

stopping, s. **1.** (a) Arrêt m. (b) Suspension f; cessation f. (c) Obturation f. **2.** (a) Tampon m. (b) Plombage m.

stopping-place, s. Arrêt m; halte f.

stop-watch, s. Montre f à arrêt.

storage, s. Emmagasinage m.

store¹, s. **1.** (a) Provision f, approvisionnement m. (b) Abondance f. **To set great s. by**, faire grand cas de. **2.** pl. Provisions. **3.** Entrepôt m, magasin m.

store², v.tr. **1.** Pourvoir, approvisionner (with, de). **2.** Amasser. **3.** (a) Emmagasiner. (b) Prendre en dépôt.

storehouse, s. Magasin m, entrepôt m.

stork, s. Cigogne f.

storm¹, s. **1.** Orage m; tempête f. **2. To take by s.**, prendre d'assaut.

storm². I. v.i. Tempêter. **2.** v.tr. Prendre d'assaut.

stormy, a. Tempétueux; orageux. **S. sea**, mer démontée.

story¹, s. **1.** Histoire f, récit m, conte m. **2. Short s.**, nouvelle f, conte. **3.** Intrigue f.

story², s. Étage m.

story-book, s. Livre m de contes; livre d'histoires.

stout¹, a. **1.** (a) Fort, vigoureux. (b) Vaillant. (c) Résolu. **2.** Fort, solide. **3.** Gros, f. grosse; corpulent.

stout², s. Stout m; bière noire forte.

stoutly, adv. **1.** Fortement, vigoureusement; vaillamment. **2.** Solidement.

stoutness, s. Embonpoint m, corpulence f.

stove, s. (a) Poêle m, fourneau m. **Slow-combustion s.**, calorifère m. (b) Cuisinière f.

stow, v.tr. **To s. (away)**, mettre en place, ranger, serrer.

straddle, v.tr. Enfourcher.

straggle, v.i. Marcher sans ordre.

straggler, s. Traînard m.

straggling, a. Disséminé.

straight. I. a. **1.** (a) Droit. (b) En ligne droite. **2.** Juste, honnête; loyal, -aux. **3.** Net, f. nette. **4.** (a) Droit; d'aplomb. **To put sth. s.**, redresser, ajuster, qch. (b) En ordre.

II. **straight**, s. **To be out of the s.**, être de travers.

III. **straight**, adv. **1.** Droit. **To shoot s.**, tirer juste. **Keep s. on**, continuez tout droit. **2.** Directement. **S. off**, sur-le-champ; tout de suite. **3. S. in the face**, bien en face. **S. out**, franchement; sans détours.

straighten. **1.** v.tr. (a) Rendre droit; (re)dresser. (b) Arranger. **2.** v.i. Se redresser; devenir droit.

straightforward, a. Loyal, -aux; franc, f. franche.

straightforwardly, adv. Loyalement; franchement.

straightforwardness, s. Droiture f, franchise f.

straightness, s. Droiture f.

straightway, adv. Immédiatement, tout de suite, aussitôt.

strain¹, s. **1.** Tension f. **2.** Entorse f, foulure f. **3.** pl. Accords m. **4.** Ton m, sens m.

strain², v.tr. **1.** Tendre. **2. To s. oneself**, se surmener. **3.** (a) Filtrer; tamiser. (b) Faire égoutter.

strain³, s. **1.** Héritage m; fond m. **2.** Race f, lignée f.

strained, a. (a) Tendu. (b) Foulé.

strainer, s. Filtre m; tamis m; passoire f.

strait, s. (a) Détroit m. **The Straits of Dover**, le Pas de Calais. (b) **To be in (great) straits**, être dans l'embarras.

straitened, a. **In s. circumstances**, dans la gêne.

strait-laced, a. Prude; collet monté.

strand¹, s. Rive f, grève f.

strand², s. **1.** Brin m. **2.** Fil m; tresse f.

16

stranded, *a.* **1.** Échoué. **2. To leave s.,** laisser en plan.

strange, *a.* **1.** Inconnu. **2.** Singulier, étrange. **3.** Dépaysé.

strangely, *adv.* Étrangement, singulièrement.

strangeness, *s.* **1.** Étrangeté *f,* singularité *f.* **2.** Nouveauté *f.*

stranger, *s.* Étranger. -ère; inconnu, -ue.

strangle, *v.tr.* Étrangler.

strap, *s.* **1.** Courroie *f.* **2.** Bande *f,* sangle *f.*

stratagem, *s.* Ruse *f;* stratagème *m.*

strategic, *a.* Stratégique.

strategy, *s.* Stratégie *f.*

stratum, *s.* Strate *f,* couche *f,* gisement *m.*

straw, *s.* **1.** Paille *f.* **2.** Chalumeau *m.*

strawberry, *s.* Fraise *f;* fraisier *m.* Wild s., fraise des bois. **S. ice,** glace à la fraise.

straw hat, *s.* Chapeau *m* de paille.

stray¹, *a.* **1.** Égaré, errant. **2. S. bullets,** balles perdues.

stray², *v.i.* S'égarer, errer.

streak¹, *s.* **1.** Raie *f,* bande *f;* trait *m.* **S. of lightning,** éclair *m.* **2.** Trace *f.*

streak², *v.tr.* Rayer, strier.

streaky, *a.* Entrelardé.

stream¹, *s.* **1.** *(a)* Cours *m* d'eau; fleuve *m,* rivière *f.* *(b)* Ruisseau *m.* *(c)* Flot *m.* **2.** Filet *m;* jet *m.* **3.** Courant *m.* **With the s.,** au fil de l'eau. **Against the s.,** à contre courant.

stream², *v.i.* *(a)* Couler; ruisseler. *(b)* Flotter.

streamer, *s.* Banderole *f.* **(Paper) streamers,** serpentins *m.*

streaming, *a.* Ruisselant; inondé.

stream-lined, *a.* Caréné, fuselé.

street, *s.* Rue *f.* **The man in the s.,** l'homme moyen **S. level,** rez-de-chaussée *m inv.*

street-door, *s.* Porte *f* sur la rue; porte d'entrée.

strength, *s.* *(a)* Force(s) *f(pl).* **S. of mind,** fermeté *f* d'esprit. **S. of will,** résolution *f.* **On the s. of,** sur la foi de. *(b)* Solidité *f.*

strengthen, *v.tr.* Consolider; renforcer; affermir.

strengthening, *s.* Renforcement *m;* consolidation *f.*

strenuous, *a.* **1.** Actif, énergique. **2.** Ardu.

strenuously, *adv.* Vigoureusement; énergiquement.

stress¹, *s.* **1.** Force *f,* contrainte *f.* **2.** Tension *f.* **3.** Insistance *f.* **To lay s. on,** insister sur.

stress², *v.tr.* Appuyer, insister, sur; accentuer.

stretch¹, *s.* *(a)* Allongement *m,* extension *f.* *(b)* Tension *f;* effort *m.* *(c)* Étendue *f.* **S. of wing,** envergure *f.* *(d)* Élasticité *f.*

stretch², **1.** *v.tr.* *(a)* Tendre. *(b)* S'étirer. **Stretched out,** étendu. *(c)* Forcer. **2.** *v.i.* *(a)* S'étirer. *(b)* S'étendre. **stretch out.** **1.** *v.tr.* *(a)* Allonger. *(b)* Tendre, avancer. **2.** *v.i.* S'étirer.

stretcher, *s.* Brancard *m,* civière *f.*

strew, *v.tr.* **1.** Répandre. **2.** Joncher.

stricken, *a* Accablé, frappé *(with,* de).

strict, *a.* **1.** Exact; strict. *(a)* Précis. *(b)* Rigoureux. **2. S. orders,** ordres formels. **3.** Sévère.

strictly, *adv.* **1.** Exactement, rigoureusement. **S. speaking,** à proprement parler. **2.** Étroitement; strictement. **3.** Sévèrement.

strictness, *s.* **1.** Exactitude *f,* précision *f.* **2.** Rigueur *f;* sévérité *f.*

stride¹, *s.* Enjambée *f.* **To make great strides,** faire de grands progrès.

stride², *v.i.* *(a)* **To s. along,** avancer à grands pas. *(b)* **To s. over,** enjamber.

stridency, *s.* Stridence *f.*

strident, *a.* Strident.

strife, *s.* Lutte *f.*

strike¹, *s.* **1.** Coup *m.* **2.** Grève *f.*

strike², **I.** *v.tr.* & *ind.tr.* **1.** *(a)* Frapper. **To s. at,** porter un coup à. *(b)* **To s. a bargain,** faire un marché. **2. To s. a match,** frotter une allumette. **3.** *(a)* *Abs.* Foncer. *(b)* Ferrer, piquer. **4.** Struck with terror, saisi d'effroi. **5. To s. into,** pénétrer. **6.** *(a)* Heurter; donner contre. *(b)* **It strikes me,** il me semble. *(c)* Faire impression à; frapper. **7.** Tomber sur, découvrir. **8.** Abattre. **To s. camp,** lever le camp. **9.** *Abs.* Se mettre en grève. **10. To s. an attitude,** poser.

II. strike, *v.i.* Sonner. **strike off,** *v.tr.* **1.** Trancher, abattre. **2.** Rayer. **strike out,** *v.tr.* Rayer, biffer. **strike through,** *v.tr.* *(a)*

Rayer, biffer. (*b*) Percer. **strike up**, *v.tr.* **1.** Entonner ; commencer de jouer. **2. To s. up an acquaintance**, lier connaissance.

striker, *s.* Gréviste *mf.*

striking, *a.* **1. S. clock**, pendule à sonnerie. **2.** Remarquable, frappant.

string[1], *s.* **1.** Ficelle *f* ; corde *f* ; cordon *m.* **To pull the strings**, tirer les ficelles. **2. S. of beads**, collier *m.*

string[2], *v.tr.* **1.** Bander. **2.** Enfiler.

string bag, *s.* Filet *m* à provisions.

stringed, *a.* A cordes.

stringency, *s.* Rigueur *f*, sévérité *f.*

stringent, *a.* Rigoureux, strict.

stringy, *a.* Fibreux, filandreux.

strip[1], *s.* Bande *f.*

strip[2], **I.** *v.tr.* **1.** Mettre tout nu. **2.** (*a*) Dépouiller. (*b*) Dégarnir. **3. To s. off**, ôter, enlever. **II. strip**, *v.i.* **1.** Se dévêtir. **To s. to the skin**, se mettre à poil. **2. To s. off**, se détacher.

stripe[1], *s.* (*a*) Raie *f*, barre *f.* (*b*) Bande *f.* (*c*) Galon *m* ; chevron *m.*

stripe[2], *v.tr.* Rayer, barrer.

striped, *a.* A raies, à barres ; zébré.

stripling, *s.* Tout jeune homme *m.*

strive, *v.i.* **1.** Tâcher, s'efforcer. **To s. after**, rechercher. **2.** Lutter. **se débattre.**

stroke[1], *s.* Coup *m.* **1. Finishing s.**, coup de grâce. **2.** (*a*) Brassée *f.* (*b*) Course *f.* (*c*) **S. of genius**, trait *m* de génie. **A good s. of business**, une bonne affaire. **3.** Attaque *f* d'apoplexie. **4.** Trait (de plume).

stroke[2], *s.* Caresse *f* de la main.

stroke[3], *v.tr.* Caresser de la main.

stroll[1], *s.* **To go for a s.**, faire un tour.

stroll[2], *v.i.* Errer à l'aventure ; flâner.

stroller, *s.* Promeneur, -euse.

strolling, *a.* Vagabond, errant.

strong, *a.* Fort. **1.** Solide ; robuste. **2.** (*a*) Fort, puissant. **S. measures**, mesures énergiques. (*b*) **S. drink**, liqueurs fortes.

stronghold, *s.* Forteresse *f* ; place forte.

strongly, *adv.* Fortement. **1.** Solidement, fermement. **2.** Vigoureusement, énergiquement.

strong-minded, *a.* A l'esprit décidé. **S.-m. person**, forte tête.

strong room, *s.* Chambre blindée ; cave *f* des coffres-forts.

strop[1], *s.* Cuir *m.*

strop[2], *v.tr.* Repasser sur le cuir.

structure, *s.* (*a*) Édifice *m*, structure *f.* (*b*) Ouvrage *m* d'art.

struggle[1], *s.* Lutte *f.*

struggle[2], *v.i.* Lutter ; se débattre.

struggler, *s.* Lutteur *m.*

strut[1], *s.* Démarche fière.

strut[2], *v.i.* Se pavaner, se rengorger.

strut[3], *s.* Support *m*, étai *m.*

strychnine, *s.* Strychnine *f.*

stub, *s.* **1.** Bout *m.* **2.** Souche *f*, talon *m.*

stubble, *s.* Chaume *m.*

stubborn, *a.* Obstiné, opiniâtre, entêté.

stubbornly, *adv.* Obstinément, opiniâtrement.

stubbornness, *s.* Entêtement *m*, obstination *f*, opiniâtreté *f.*

stucco, *s.* Stuc *m.*

stuck-up, *a.* Prétentieux.

stud, *s.* **1.** Clou *m* à grosse tête. **2.** Bouton *m.*

studded, *a.* **1.** Garni de clous ; clouté. **2.** Parsemé (**with**, de).

student, *s.* Étudiant, -ante.

studied, *a.* Étudié ; calculé.

studio, *s.* Atelier *m* ; studio *m.*

studious, *a.* Studieux, appliqué.

studiously, *adv.* **1.** Studieusement. **2.** Avec empressement.

study[1], *s.* **1.** Soin(s) *m*(*pl*), attention *f.* **2. Brown s.**, rêverie *f.* **3.** Étude *f.* **4.** Cabinet *m* de travail.

study[2], *v.tr.* **1.** Étudier ; observer. **2.** S'occuper de, se préoccuper de. **3.** S'étudier, chercher.

stuff[1], *s.* **1.** Matière *f*, substance *f*, étoffe *f.* **2.** Étoffe, tissu *m.*

stuff[2], *v.tr.* **1.** (*a*) Bourrer (**with**, de) ; rembourrer. (*b*) Farcir. (*c*) Empailler. **2. To s. up**, boucher. **3.** Fourrer.

stuffiness, *s.* Odeur *f* de renfermé.

stuffing, *s.* **1.** (*a*) Rembourrage *m.* (*b*) Empaillage *m.* **2.** (*a*) Bourre *f.* (*b*) Farce *f.*

stuffy, *a.* Mal ventilé ; mal aéré.

stumble[1], *s* Trébuchement *m* ; faux pas.

stumble[2], *v.i.* Trébucher ; faire un faux pas. **To s. over**, buter contre.

stumbling-block, *s.* Pierre *f* d'achoppement.

stump, *s.* **1.** Tronçon *m*, souche *f* ; chicot *m* ; moignon *m* ; bout *m.* **2.** Piquet *m.*

stumpy, a. Trapu, ramassé.

stun, v.tr. Étourdir, assommer.

stunning, a. (a) Étourdissant. (b) Accablant.

stunted, a. Rabougri, chétif.

stupefaction, s. Stupéfaction f.

stupefy, v.tr. **1.** Hébéter, abrutir. **2.** Abasourdir. stupéfier.

stupendous, a. Prodigieux.

stupid, a. Stupide ; sot, f. sotte ; bête.

stupidity, s. Stupidité f.

stupidly, adv. Stupidement, sottement ; bêtement.

stupor, s. Stupeur f.

sturdily, adv. **1.** Fortement. **2.** Hardiment, vigoureusement.

sturdiness, s. Vigueur f.

sturdy, a. (a) Vigoureux. robuste. (b) Hardi, résolu, ferme.

stutter[1], s. Bégaiement m.

stutter[2], v.i. & tr. Bégayer, bredouiller.

sty, s. Porcherie f ; étable f.

style[1], s. **1.** (a) Style m, manière f, façon f. **To live in s.,** mener grand train. (b) Style, genre m. (c) Mode f. **2.** Ton m, cachet m. **3.** Titre m, nom m.

style[2], v.tr. Dénommer ; appeler

stylish, a. Élégant, chic m & f.

stylishly, adv. Élégamment ; avec chic.

stylishness, s. Élégance f, chic m.

stylograph, s. Stylographe m.

suave, a. Suave ; doux, f. douce

suavely, adv. Suavement f.

suavity, s. Affabilité f.

subaltern. 1. a. Subalterne, subordonné. **2.** s. Subalterne mf.

subconscious, a. Subconscient.

subconsciously, adv. Inconsciemment.

subdivide, v.tr. Subdiviser.

subdue, v.tr. Subjuguer, maîtriser ; dompter.

subdued, a. **1.** Vaincu, subjugué. **2.** Déprimé **3. In a s. voice,** à mi-voix.

subject[1], s. **1.** Sujet, -ette. **2.** Sujet ; objet m. **To change the s.,** changer de sujet.

subject[2], a. **1.** Assujetti, soumis. **2.** Sujet, -ette, exposé. **3. S. to,** sous réserve de.

subject[3], v.tr. **1.** Assujettir, subjuguer. **2.** Soumettre.

subjection, s. Sujétion f, soumission f. **To bring into s.,** assujettir.

subjugate, v.tr. Subjuguer.

subjugation, s. Subjugation f.

sub-let, v.tr. Sous-louer.

sub-lieutenant, s. Enseigne m.

sublime. 1. a. (a) Sublime. (b) Suprême. **2.** s. Sublime m.

sublimely, adv. Sublimement.

submarine, a. & s. Sous-marin m.

submerge. 1. v.tr. (a) Submerger, immerger. (b) Inonder, noyer. **2.** v.i. Plonger.

submerged, a. Submergé.

submersion, s. Submersion f ; plongée f.

submission, s. (a) Soumission f. (b) Docilité f ; humilité f.

submissive, a. Soumis, résigné.

submissively, adv. Avec docilité.

submissiveness, s. Soumission f, docilité f.

submit. 1. v.i. & pr. Se soumettre. **2.** v.tr. (a) Soumettre. (b) Représenter.

subordinate[1]. **1.** a. (a) Inférieur, -e ; secondaire. (b) Subordonné **2.** s. Subordonné, -ée.

subordinate[2], v.tr. Subordonner.

subordination, s. **1.** Subordination f. **2.** Soumission f.

subpoena[1], s. Assignation f.

subpoena[2], v.tr. Assigner.

subscribe, v.tr. & i. **1.** Souscrire. **2.** S'abonner.

subscriber, s. **1.** Signataire mf souscripteur m. **2.** Abonné, -ée.

subscription, s. **1.** (a) Souscription f ; signature f. (b) Adhésion f. **2.** Cotisation f. **3.** Abonnement m.

subsequent, a. Subséquent, qui suit. **S. to,** postérieur, -e, consécutif, à.

subsequently, adv. Plus tard ; dans la suite.

subservience, s. Soumission f, servilité f.

subservient, a. Obséquieux, servile.

subside, v.i. **1.** S'affaisser, s'enfoncer. **2.** Baisser. **3.** S'apaiser, tomber.

subsidence, s. (a) Affaissement m. (b) Décrue f, baisse f.

subsidiary, a. Subsidiaire.

subsidize, v.tr. Subventionner.

subsidy, s. Subvention f.

subsist, v.i. Subsister. (a) Continuer d'être. (b) S'entretenir, vivre (on. de).

subsistence, s. 1. Existence f. 2. Subsistance f.

substance, s. 1. Substance f, matière f. 2. Substance, fond m. 3. Solidité f.

substantial, a. 1. Substantiel, réel. 2. Important. 3. Solide.

substantially, adv. 1. Substantiellement. 2. Solidement.

substantiate, v.tr. Établir.

substitute¹, s. 1. Suppléant, -ante. 2. (a) Succédané m (for, de). (b) Imitation f.

substitute², v.tr. Substituer.

substitution, s. Substitution f, remplacement m.

subterfuge, s. Subterfuge m.

subterranean, a. Souterrain.

subtle, a. Subtil. 1. (a) Pénétrant. (b) S. distinction, distinction subtile. 2. (a) Fin, raffiné ; (b) Astucieux.

subtlety, s. 1. Subtilité f. 2. Astuce f.

subtly, adv. Subtilement ; avec finesse.

subtract, v.tr. Soustraire.

subtraction, s. Soustraction f.

suburb, s. Faubourg m. **In the** suburbs, dans la banlieue.

suburban, a. Suburbain.

subversive, a. Subversif (of, de).

subvert, v.tr. Renverser, subvertir.

subway, s. Passage souterrain.

succeed, v.tr. & i. 1. Succéder (à) ; hériter (to, de). 2. v.i. Réussir.

succeeding, a. 1. Suivant, subséquent. 2. Futur. 3. Successif.

success, s. Succès m ; réussite f. **To make a s. of,** réussir.

successful, a. Réussi. **S. play,** pièce qui a du succès. **To be s. in,** réussir à. **S. candidate,** candidat élu.

successfully, adv. Avec succès.

succession, s. Succession f. 1. (a) Suite f. **In s.,** successivement. (b) Série f, suite. 2. (a) Héritage m. (b) Descendants mpl.

successive, a. Successif, consécutif.

successively, adv. Successivement.

successor, s. Successeur m.

succinct, a. Succinct, concis.

succour¹, s. Secours m ; aide f.

succour², v.tr. Secourir.

succulent, a. Succulent.

succumb, v.i. Succomber.

such. I. a. Tel, pareil, semblable. 1. **S. men as he,** des gens comme lui. **S. a man,** un tel homme. **I said no**

s. thing, je n'ai rien dit de la sorte. 2. **S. a one,** un tel, une telle. 3. **In s. a way,** de telle sorte. 4. **S. large houses,** de si grandes maisons. II. **such,** pron. 1. Ceux, celles, qui. 2. Ce qui, ce que. 3. **As s., en tant que** tel(le).

suck, v.tr. & i. Sucer. **suck down,** v.tr. Engloutir. **suck in,** v.tr. (a) Sucer, absorber. (b) Engloutir. **suck up,** v.tr. Sucer aspirer ; absorber.

sucking-pig, s. Cochon m de lait.

suckle, v.tr. Allaiter.

suction, s. Succion f ; aspiration f.

sudden, a. (a) Soudain, subit. (b) **S. turning,** tournant brusque. Adv.phr. **All of a s.,** subitement ; tout à coup.

suddenly, adv. Soudain, soudainement ; tout à coup.

suddenness, s. (a) Soudaineté f. (b) Brusquerie f.

sue. 1. v.tr. Poursuivre. 2. v.i. **To sue for,** solliciter.

suède, s. (i) Daim m ; (ii) suède m.

suet, s. Graisse f de rognon.

suffer. I. v.tr. 1. Éprouver, souffrir ; subir. 2. Permettre, tolérer. II. **suffer,** v.i. Souffrir.

sufferance, s. Tolérance f.

sufferer, s. (a) Victime f. (b) Malade mf.

suffering¹, a. Souffrant ; qui souffre.

suffering², s. Souffrance f.

suffice. 1. v.i. Suffire. 2. v.tr. Suffire à.

sufficiency, s. Suffisance f.

sufficient, a. & s. Assez ; suffisant.

sufficiently, adv. Suffisamment ; assez.

suffocate, v.tr. & i. Étouffer, suffoquer.

suffocating, a. Suffocant, étouffant.

suffocation, s. Suffocation f ; étouffement m.

suffrage, s. Suffrage m. (a) Vote m, voix f. (b) Droit m de vote.

suffuse, v.tr. Se répandre sur. **Suffused with tears,** baigné de larmes.

sugar¹, s. Sucre m. **Granulated s.,** sucre cristallisé. **Lump s.,** sucre en morceaux. **Castor s.,** sucre en poudre. **Brown s.,** cassonade f.

sugar², v.tr. Sucrer ; saupoudrer de sucre.

sugar-basin, s. Sucrier m.

sugar-candy, *s.* Sucre candi.

sugar-cane, *s.* Canne *f* à sucre.

sugar-loaf, *s.* Pain *m* de sucre.

sugar-tongs, *s.pl.* Pince *f* à sucre.

sugary, *a.* 1. Sucré. 2. Mielleux.

suggest, *v.tr.* 1. Suggérer, proposer. 2. Inspirer. 3. Insinuer. 4. Évoquer.

suggestion, *s.* Suggestion *f.*

suggestive, *a.* Suggestif ; évocateur, -trice.

suicide¹, *s.* Suicidé, -ée.

suicide², *s.* Suicide *m.* **To commit s.,** se suicider.

suit¹, *s.* 1. Procès *m.* 2. Prière *f,* demande *f,* requête *f.* 3. Cour *f ;* demande en mariage. 4. (a) Complet *m.* (b) Ensemble *m.* 5. Couleur *f.* **To follow s.,** faire de même.

suit², *v.tr.* 1. Accommoder, adapter, approprier. 2. Convenir à, aller à. **This hat suits you,** ce chapeau vous va.

suitability, *s.* Convenance *f ;* à-propos *m ;* aptitude *f.*

suitable, *a.* 1. Convenable, qui convient ; approprié. 2. **S. for,** bon, *f.* bonne, à ; approprié à.

suitably, *adv.* Convenablement ; à propos.

suit-case, *s.* Mallette *f ;* valise *f.*

suite, *s.* 1. Suite *f.* 2. **S. of furniture,** ameublement *m.*

suitor, *s.* Prétendant *m,* soupirant *m.*

sulk, *v.i.* Bouder ; faire la mine.

sulkily, *adv.* En boudant.

sulkiness, *s.* Bouderie *f.*

sulky, *a.* Boudeur, -euse, maussade **To be s.,** bouder.

sullen, *a.* Maussade, morose ; sombre.

sullenly, *adv.* D'un air maussade.

sullenness, *s.* Maussaderie *f.*

sully, *v.tr.* Souiller, ternir.

sulphate, *s.* Sulfate *m.*

sulphide, *s.* Sulfure *m.*

sulphur, *s.* Soufre *m.*

sulphureous, *a.* Sulfureux.

sulphuric, *a.* Sulfurique.

sultan, *s.* Sultan *m.*

sultana, *s.* 1. Sultane *f.* 2. Raisin sec de Smyrne.

sultriness, *s.* Chaleur étouffante.

sultry, *a.* Étouffant, suffocant.

sum¹, *s.* 1. Somme *f,* total *m ;* montant *m.* 2. Problème *m.*

sum², *v.tr.* **To sum up.** (a) Résumer, récapituler. (b) Juger, classer.

summarily, *adv.* Sommairement.

summarize, *v.tr.* Résumer sommairement.

summary. 1. *a.* Sommaire. 2. *s.* Sommaire *m,* résumé *m.*

summer, *s.* Été *m.* **The s. holidays,** les grandes vacances.

summer-house, *s.* Pavillon *m,* kiosque *m.*

summer-time, *s.* 1. L'été *m.* 2. L'heure *f* d'été.

summing-up, *s.* (a) Résumé *m.* (b) Évaluation *f.*

summit, *s.* Sommet *m,* cime *f,* faîte *m.*

summon, *v.tr.* 1. Appeler ; mander ; convoquer. 2. Sommer, requérir. 3. **To s. up,** faire appel à ; rassembler.

summons¹, *s.* 1. Appel ; convocation *f.* 2. Citation *f.*

summons², *v.tr.* Citer ; assigner ; appeler en justice.

sumptuous, *a.* Somptueux, fastueux.

sumptuously, *adv.* Somptueusement.

sum-total, *s.* Somme totale, globale.

sun¹, *s.* Soleil *m.*

sun², *v.tr.* Exposer au soleil.

sunbeam, *s.* Rayon *m* de soleil.

sunburn, *s.* Hâle *m.*

sunburned, *a.* Hâlé.

Sunday, *s.* Dimanche *m.*

sunder, *v.tr.* (a) Séparer, disjoindre. (b) Couper, fendre, en deux.

sun-dial, *s.* Cadran *m* solaire.

sundry. 1. *a.* Divers. 2. *s. pl.* Articles divers.

sunflower, *s.* Tournesol *m.*

sunk, *a.* Submergé ; plongé ; noyé.

sunken, *a.* (a) Noyé, submergé. (b) Affaissé, enfoncé ; creux.

sunlight, *s.* Lumière *f* du soleil. **In the s.,** au soleil.

sunny, *a.* 1. Ensoleillé. 2. Radieux, rayonnant.

sunrise, *s.* Lever *m* du soleil.

sunset, *s.* Coucher *m* du soleil.

sunshade, *s.* 1. Ombrelle *f.* 2. Pare-soleil *m inv.*

sunshine, *s.* Clarté *f* du soleil.

sunstroke, *s.* Insolation *f ;* coup *m* de soleil.

sup, *v.tr.* Prendre à petites gorgées.

superabundance, *s.* Surabondance *f.*

superabundant, *a.* Surabondant.

superannuate, v.tr. Retraiter.
superannuated, a. Retraité.
superannuation, s. Retraite f.
superb, a. Superbe, magnifique.
superbly, adv. Superbement, magnifiquement.
supercilious, a. Sourcilleux, hautain ; dédaigneux.
superciliously, adv. Avec une nuance de dédain.
superficial, a. Superficiel.
superfine, a. Superfin ; surfin.
superfluity, s. 1. Superfluité f. 2. Superflu m.
superfluous, a. Superflu.
superhuman, a. Surhumain.
superintend, v.tr. Diriger, surveiller.
superintendence, s. Direction f, surveillance f, contrôle m.
superintendent, s. Directeur, -trice ; surveillant, -ante.
superior. 1. a. (a) Supérieur, -eure. (b) Sourcilleux, superbe. 2. s. Supérieur, -eure.
superiority, s. Supériorité f.
superlative. 1. a. Suprême. 2. a. & s. Superlatif (m).
superman, s. Surhomme m.
supernatural, a. Surnaturel.
superscription, s. Inscription f ; légende f ; adresse f.
supersede, v.tr. (a) Remplacer. (b) Prendre la place de ; supplanter.
superstition, s. Superstition f.
superstitious, a. Superstitieux.
supervene, v.i. Survenir.
supervise, v.tr. 1. Surveiller. 2. Diriger, conduire.
supervision, s. 1. Surveillance f. 2. Direction f.
supervisor, s. Surveillant, -ante.
supine, a. 1. Couché, étendu. 2. Mou, f. molle ; inerte.
supper, s. Souper m.
supplant, v.tr. Supplanter.
supple, a. Souple.
supplement[1], s. Supplément m.
supplement[2], v.tr. Ajouter à ; augmenter.
supplementary, a. Supplémentaire.
suppliant, a. Suppliant.
supplicant, s. Suppliant, -ante.
supplicate, v.i. & tr. Supplier.
supplication, s. Supplication f.
supply[1], s. 1. Approvisionnement m. 2. (a) Provision f. S. and demand,

l'offre f et la demande. (b) pl. Fournitures f.
supply[2], v.tr. 1. Fournir pourvoir. 2. Réparer ; remplir.
support[1], s. Appui m, soutien m.
support[2], v.tr. 1. Supporter, scutenir, appuyer, maintenir. 2. Entretenir. 3. Supporter, tolérer.
supporter, s. 1. Soutien m. 2. Défenseur m ; partisan, -ane.
suppose, v.tr. (a) Supposer. (b) S'imaginer ; croire, penser.
supposed, a. Supposé, prétendu ; soi-disant.
supposition, s. Supposition f.
suppress, v.tr. 1. (a) Réprimer. (b) Supprimer. 2. Étouffer. 3. Cacher, dissimuler.
suppressed, a. Réprimé ; contenu.
suppression, s. 1. Répression f ; suppression f. 2. Étouffement m. 3. Dissimulation f.
supremacy, s. Suprématie f.
supreme, a. Suprême ; souverain.
supremely, adv. Suprêmement ; au suprême degré.
sure. 1. a. Sûr, certain. (a) To make s., s'assurer. (b) Infaillible ; assuré. (c) Indubitable. (d) He is s. to come, il viendra sûrement. 2. adv. As s. as, aussi sûr que.
sure-footed, a. Au pied sûr.
surely, adv. 1. Sûrement. 2. Assurément.
sureness, s. 1. Sûreté f. 2. Certitude f.
surety, s. Caution f ; garant, -ante.
surf, s. Ressac m ; brisants mpl sur la plage.
surface, s. 1. (a) Surface f. (b) Extérieur m, dehors m. On the s., en apparence. 2. Superficie f.
surf-board, s. Aquaplane m.
surfeit[1], s. 1. Surabondance f. 2. Réplétion f.
surfeit[2], v.tr. Gorger (with, de).
surf-riding, s. Sport m de l'aquaplane.
surge[1], s. Houle f ; vague f.
surge[2], v.i. Refluer.
surgeon, s. 1. Chirurgien, -ienne. 2. Médecin.
surgery, s. 1. Chirurgie f. 2. Cabinet m de consultation ; dispensaire m.
surgical, a. Chirurgical, -aux.
surly, a. (a) Bourru. (b) Hargneux, maussade.

surmise[1], *s.* Conjecture *f*, supposition *f*.

surmise[2], *v.tr.* Conjecturer, deviner.

surmount, *v.tr.* Surmonter.

surname, *s.* Nom *m* de famille.

surpass, *v.tr.* **1.** Surpasser. **2.** Dépasser.

surpassing, *a.* Sans pareil.

surplice, *s.* Surplis *m*.

surplus, *s.* **1.** Surplus *m*, excédent *m*. **2.** *Attrib.* S. stock, soldes *m*.

surprise[1], *s.* Surprise *f*. **1.** To take by s., prendre à l'improviste. **2.** Étonnement *m*.

surprise[2], *v.tr.* Surprendre; étonner. **I am surprised at you!** vous m'étonnez !

surprising, *a.* Surprenant, étonnant.

surrender[1], *s.* **1.** (*a*) Reddition *f*. (*b*) **No s.!** on ne se rend pas ! **2.** Abandon *m*, cession *f*.

surrender[2]. **1.** *v.tr.* (*a*) Rendre, livrer. (*b*) Abandonner, céder. **2.** *v.pr. & i.* Se rendre; se livrer.

surreptitious, *a.* Subreptice, clandestin.

surreptitiously, *adv.* Subrepticement, clandestinement.

surround, *v.tr.* Entourer.

surrounding, *a.* Entourant, environnant.

surroundings, *s.pl.* **1.** Entourage *m*, milieu *m*. **2.** Environs *mpl*, alentours *mpl*.

surveillance, *s.* Surveillance *f*, contrôle *m*.

survey[1], *s.* **1.** (*a*) Aperçu *m* ; vue générale. (*b*) Examen attentif ; étude *f*. **2.** Inspection *f*, visite *f*.

survey[2], *v.tr.* **1.** (*a*) Regarder, contempler. (*b*) Passer en revue. **2.** Relever. **3.** Inspecter ; visiter.

surveyor, *s.* **1.** Arpenteur *m*. **2.** Surveillant *m*, inspecteur *m*.

survival, *s.* Survivance *f*.

survive, **1.** *v.i.* Survivre ; subsister. **2.** *v.tr.* Survivre à.

survivor, *s.* Survivant, -ante.

susceptibility, *s.* **1.** Prédisposition *f*. **2.** Sensibilité *f*, susceptibilité.

susceptible, *a.* **1.** Prédisposé. **2.** (*a*) Sensible, impressionnable. (*b*) Susceptible.

suspect[1], *a. & s.* Suspect, -e.

suspect[2], *v.tr.* Soupçonner. **I suspected as much**, je m'en doutais.

suspend, *v.tr.* Suspendre.

suspended, *a.* Suspendu. **1.** En suspension. **2.** Interrompu.

suspender, *s.* (*a*) Jarretelle *f*. (*b*) *pl.* Bretelles *f*.

suspense, *s.* Suspens *m*.

suspension, *s.* Suspension *f*.

suspicion, *s.* **1.** Soupçon *m*. **With s.**, avec défiance *f*. **To have suspicions about**, avoir des doutes sur ; soupçonner. **2.** Très petite quantité, soupçon.

suspicious, *a.* **1.** Suspect ; louche, équivoque. **2.** Méfiant, soupçonneux.

suspiciously, *adv.* **1.** D'une manière suspecte, équivoque, louche. **2.** Soupçonneusement.

sustain, *v.tr.* **1.** Soutenir, supporter. **2.** Éprouver, subir.

sustained, *a.* Soutenu.

sustaining, *a.* Fortifiant.

sustenance, *s.* Nourriture *f*.

swab, *v.tr.* Nettoyer, essuyer.

swaddle, *v.tr.* Emmailloter.

swaddling-clothes, *s.pl.* Maillot *m*.

swagger[1], *s.* **1.** (*a*) Air important. (*b*) Air cavalier. **2.** Rodomontades *fpl*.

swagger[2], *v.i.* (*a*) Crâner, se pavaner. (*b*) Fanfaronner.

swallow[1], *v.tr.* Avaler ; gober. **swallow up**, *v.tr.* Dévorer, avaler ; engloutir.

swallow[2], *s.* Hirondelle *f*.

swamp[1], *s.* Marais *m*, marécage *m*.

swamp[2], *v.tr.* **1.** Inonder, submerger. **2.** Remplir d'eau.

swampy, *a.* Marécageux.

swan, *s.* Cygne *m*.

sward, *s.* Gazon *m* ; pelouse *f*.

swarm[1], *s.* Essaim *m*, jetée *f*.

swarm[2], *v.i.* (*a*) Essaimer. (*b*) Pulluler, grouiller (*with*, de).

swarthy, *a.* Basané, bistré.

swash, *s.* Clapotement *m*, clapotis *m*.

swastika, *s.* Svastika *m* ; croix gammée.

swathe, *v.tr.* Emmailloter ; envelopper (*in*, de).

sway[1], *s.* **1.** Balancement *m*, oscillation *f*. **2.** Empire *m*, domination *f*.

sway[2]. **1.** *v.i.* (*a*) Se balancer ; osciller. (*b*) Rester indécis ; balancer. (*c*) Pencher. **2.** *v.tr.* (*a*) Balancer. (*b*) Gouverner, influencer.

swear. **1.** *v.tr.* (*a*) Jurer. (*b*) **To s. to secrecy**, faire jurer le secret à.

(*c*) Déclarer sous la foi du serment.
2. *v.i.* Jurer ; proférer un juron.
swear at, *v.ind.tr.* Maudire. **swear to,** *v.ind.tr.* Attester, certifier, sous serment. **I would s. to it,** j'en jurerais.

swearing, *s.* **1.** Attestation *f* sous serment. **2.** Jurons *mpl* ; gros mots.

sweat¹, *s.* Sueur *f*, transpiration *f*.

sweat². **I.** *v.i.* **1.** (*a*) Suer, transpirer. (*b*) Peiner. **2.** Suer, suinter.
II. sweat, *v.tr.* (*a*) Suer. (*b*) Faire suer. (*c*) Exploiter.

sweated, *a.* Mal rétribué.

sweater, *s.* Chandail *m*.

sweating, *s.* **1.** Transpiration *f*.
2. Exploitation *f*.

Swede, *s.* **1.** Suédois, -oise. **2.** Rutabaga *m* ; navet *m* de Suède.

Sweden. *Pr.n.* La Suède.

Swedish. **1.** *a.* Suédois. **2.** *s.* Le suédois.

sweep¹, *s.* **1.** (*a*) At one s., d'un seul coup. (*b*) **To make a clean s.,** faire table rase. **2.** Mouvement *m* circulaire. **3.** Course *f* rapide. **4.** (*a*) Courbe *f* ; boucle *f*. (*b*) Étendue *f*. (*c*) Envergure *f*. **5.** Aviron *m* de queue. **6.** Drague *f*. **7.** Ramoneur *m*. **8.** Sweepstake *m*.

sweep². **I.** *v.tr.* **1.** (*a*) Balayer ; ramoner ; parcourir. (*b*) Draguer. **2.** Emporter, entraîner.
II. sweep, *v.i.* S'étendre. **sweep along,** *v.tr.* Entraîner, emporter. **sweep aside,** *v.tr.* Écarter d'un geste large. **sweep away,** *v.tr.* Balayer ; supprimer, détruire. **sweep down, I.** *v.tr.* Entraîner. **2.** *v.i.* (*a*) S'abattre. (*b*) Dévaler. **sweep off,** *v.tr.* Enlever, emporter ; entraîner. **sweep on,** *v.i.* Continuer d'avancer. **sweep out,** *v.tr.* Balayer. **sweep up,** *v.tr.* Balayer, ramasser.

sweeper, *s.* **1.** Balayeur. -euse. **2.** Balayeuse *f*.

sweeping¹, *a.* **1.** S. gesture, geste large. **2.** S. statement, déclaration par trop générale. S. changes, changement de fond en comble.

sweeping², *s.* **1.** Balayage *m* ; ramonage *m*. **2.** *pl.* Balayures *f*.

sweepstake, *s.* Sweepstake *m*.

sweet. **I.** *a.* Doux, *f.* douce. **1.** Sucré. **2. To smell s.,** sentir bon. **3.** Doux, mélodieux. **4.** Charmant ; gentil, -ille.

II. sweet, *s.* (*a*) Bonbon *m*. (*b*) Entremets sucré.

sweetbread, *s.* Ris *m* de veau, d'agneau.

sweeten, *v.tr.* (*a*) Sucrer. (*b*) Purifier. (*c*) Adoucir.

sweetheart, *s.* Amoureux, -euse.

sweetly, *adv.* (*a*) Doucement ; avec douceur. (*b*) Mélodieusement.

sweetmeat, *s.* Bonbon *m*.

sweetness, *s.* **1.** Douceur *f*. **2.** Gentillesse *f*, charme *m*.

swell¹, *s.* Houle *f*.

swell². **1.** *v.tr.* (R)enfler, gonfler ; augmenter. **2.** *v.i.* (S')enfler, se gonfler ; augmenter, grossir.

swelling, *s.* **1.** Enflement *m*, gonflement *m*. **2.** Tuméfaction *f*. **3.** Bosse *f*, enflure *f* ; fluxion *f*.

sweltering, *a.* **1.** En nage. **2.** Étouffant, accablant.

swerve¹, *s.* Écart *m*, déviation *f*.

swerve², *v.i.* Faire un écart. un crochet ; se dérober.

swift. **I.** *a.* (*a*) Rapide ; vite. (*b*) Prompt.
II. swift, *adv.* Vite, rapidement.
III. swift, *s.* Martinet *m*.

swift-footed, *a.* Au pied léger.

swiftly, *adv.* Vite, rapidement.

swiftness, *s.* **1.** Rapidité *f*. vitesse *f*. **2.** Promptitude *f*.

swill, *v.tr.* Laver à grande eau.

swim¹, *s.* **1.** To go for a s., nager un peu. **2.** In the s., dans le mouvement.

swim². **I.** *v.i.* **1.** (*a*) Nager. To s. across, traverser à la nage. (*b*) Surnager, flotter. **2.** Swimming with tears, inondé de larmes. **3.** My head is swimming, la tête me tourne.
II. swim, *v.tr.* Traverser à la nage.

swimmer, *s.* Nageur, -euse.

swimming, *s.* Nage *f*, natation *f*.

swimming-bath, *s.* Piscine *f*.

swimming-pool, *s.* Piscine *f*.

swindle¹, *s.* **1.** Escroquerie *f*. **2.** Duperie *f*. **3.** Déception *f*.

swindle², *v.tr.* Escroquer.

swindler, *s.* Filou *m*, escroc *m*.

swine, *s.* Cochon *m*, porc *m*.

swing¹, *s.* **1.** Balancement *m*. **2.** (*a*) Oscillation *f*. To be in full s., battre son plein. (*b*) To give a s., balancer. **3.** Escarpolette *f*, balançoire *f*.

swing². **I.** *v.i.* **1.** (*a*) Se balancer ;

branler; osciller. (*b*) Tourner, pivoter; basculer. **2.** Changer de direction. **To s. round,** faire volte-face.

II. **swing,** *v.tr.* **1.** (Faire) balancer; faire osciller. **2.** Faire tourner; lancer, brasser. **3.** Pendre, (ac)crocher (un hamac).

swing-bridge, *s.* Pont tournant.

swing-door, *s.* Porte battante.

swinging[1], *a.* Balançant, oscillant.

swinging[2], *s.* **1.** Balancement *m*, oscillation *f*. **2.** Lancement *m*.

swirl[1], *s.* Remous *m*; tourbillon *m*.

swirl[2], *v.i.* Tournoyer, tourbillonner.

swish[1], *s.* **1.** Bruissement *m*; frou-frou *m*; sifflement *m*. **2.** Coup *m* de fouet.

swish[2]. **1.** *v.i.* Bruire. **2.** *v.tr.* Fouetter.

Swiss. 1. *a.* Suisse. **2.** *s.* Suisse, -esse.

switch[1], *s.* **1.** (*a*) Badine *f*; houssine *f*. (*b*) Coup *m* de baguette. **2.** Interrupteur *m*; commutateur *m*.

switch[2], *v.tr.* **1.** (*a*) Fouetter, cingler. (*b*) Agiter. **2.** Aiguiller, dériver. **switch off,** *v.tr.* Interrompre, couper. **switch on,** *v.tr.* Donner du courant; allumer; tourner le bouton.

switchboard, *s.* Tableau *m* de distribution.

Switzerland. *Pr.n.* La Suisse.

swivel[1], *s.* (*a*) Émerillon *m*. (*b*) Pivot *m*; tourillon *m*.

swivel[2], *v.i.* Pivoter, tourner.

swollen, *a.* Enflé, gonflé; en crue.

swoon[1], *s.* Évanouissement *m*, défaillance *f*.

swoon[2], *v.i.* S'évanouir, défaillir.

swooning, *a.* (*a*) Défaillant. (*b*) Évanoui.

swoop, *v.i.* **To s. down,** s'abattre, foncer.

sword, *s.* (*a*) Épée *f*. (*b*) Sabre *m*.

sword-cut, *s.* Coup *m* de sabre; balafre *f*.

sword-fish, *s.* Espadon *m*.

sword-thrust, *s.* Coup *m* de pointe; coup d'épée.

sworn, *a.* **1.** Assermenté; juré. **2.** Sous serment.

sybarite, *a. & s.* Sybarite (*mf*).

sycamore, *s.* Sycomore *m*.

sycophant, *s.* Flagorneur, -euse.

syllable, *s.* Syllabe *f*.

syllabus, *s.* Programme *m*.

sylph, *s.* Sylphide *f*.

sylvan, *a.* Sylvestre.

symbol, *s.* Symbole *m*.

symbolic(al), *a.* Symbolique.

symbolically, *adv.* Symboliquement.

symmetrical, *a.* Symétrique.

symmetrically, *adv.* Symétriquement.

symmetry, *s.* Symétrie *f*.

sympathetic, *a.* (*a*) De sympathie. (*b*) **S. audience,** auditoire bien disposé. (*c*) Compatissant.

sympathetically, *adv.* **1.** Sympathiquement. **2.** D'une manière compatissante.

sympathize, *v.i.* **1.** Avoir de la compassion (*with,* pour). **2.** **To s. with,** comprendre; partager.

sympathizer, *s.* **1.** **To be a s. in,** compatir à. **2.** Partisan, -ane.

sympathy, *s.* **1.** Compassion *f*. **2.** Sympathie *f*.

symphonic, *a.* Symphonique.

symphony, *s.* Symphonie *f*. **S. concert,** concert *m* symphonique.

symptom, *s.* Symptôme *m*; indice *m*.

synagogue, *s.* Synagogue *f*.

synchronize. 1. *v.tr.* Synchroniser. **2.** *v.i.* Arriver simultanément.

syncope, *s.* Syncope *f*.

syndicate, *s.* Syndicat *m*.

synonym, *s.* Synonyme *m*.

synonymous, *a.* Synonyme (*with,* de).

synopsis, *s.* Résumé *m*, sommaire *m*.

syntax, *s.* Syntaxe *f*.

synthesis, *s.* Synthèse *f*.

synthetic, *a.* Synthétique.

synthetically, *adv.* Synthétiquement.

syringe[1], *s.* Seringue *f*.

syringe[2], *v.tr.* Seringuer.

syrup, *s.* **1.** Sirop *m*. **2.** **Golden s.** mélasse raffinée.

syrupy, *a.* Sirupeux.

system, *s.* **1.** (*a*) Système *m*; organisme *m*. (*b*) Réseau. **2.** Méthode *f*.

systematic, *a.* Systématique, méthodique.

systematically, *adv.* Systématiquement; avec méthode.

T

T, t, *s.* (La lettre) T, t *m.*

tab, *s.* **1.** (*a*) Patte *f.* (*b*) Ferret *m.* (*c*) Attache *f.* **2.** Étiquette *f.*

table, *s.* Table *f.* **1.** (*a*) Occasional t., guéridon *m.* (*b*) To lay the t., mettre la table. To clear the t., desservir. **2.** *pl.* To turn the tables, renverser les rôles. **3.** Table, tableau *m.*

table-cover, *s.* Tapis *m* de table.

table-fork, *s.* Fourchette *f.*

table-knife, *s.* Couteau *m* de table.

table-linen, *s.* Linge *m* de table.

table-spoon, *s.* Cuiller *f* à soupe, à bouche.

tablespoonful, *s.* Cuillerée *f* à bouche.

tablet, *s.* **1.** Plaque commémorative. **2.** (*a*) Comprimé *m.* (*b*) Pain *m.*

table-tennis, *s.* Tennis *m* de salon.

taboo[1]. **1.** *s.* Tabou *m,* -ous. **2.** *Pred. a.* Interdit, proscrit.

taboo[2], *v.tr.* Proscrire, interdire.

tabular, *a.* Tabulaire.

tabulate, *v.tr.* Classifier ; cataloguer.

tacit, *a.* Tacite, implicite.

tacitly, *adv.* Tacitement.

taciturn, *a.* Taciturne.

taciturnity, *s.* Taciturnité *f.*

tack[1], *s.* **1.** Petit clou ; *pl.* semence *f.* **2.** Long point. **3.** Bord *m,* bordée *f.* On the right t., sur la bonne voie.

tack[2], *v.i.* Virer ; louvoyer.

tackle[1], *s.* Attirail *m,* appareil *m,* engins *mpl.*

tackle[2], *v.tr.* Empoigner ; saisir à bras-le-corps ; s'attaquer à.

tact, *s.* Tact *m,* savoir-faire *m.*

tactful, *a.* De tact ; délicat. To be t., avoir du tact.

tactfully, *adv.* Avec tact.

tactical, *a.* Tactique.

tactics, *s.pl.* Tactique *f.*

tactless, *a.* (*a*) Dépourvu de tact. (*b*) Indiscret.

tactlessly, *adv.* Sans tact.

tactlessness, *s.* Manque *m* de tact.

tadpole, *s.* Têtard *m.*

tag, *s.* **1.** (*a*) Morceau *m* (d'étoffe) qui pend. (*b*) Attache *f.* (*c*) Ferret *m.* **2.** Citation banale ; cliché *m.*

tail, *s.* **1.** (*a*) Queue *f.* To turn t., s'enfuir. (*b*) Empennage *m* ; pan *m.* **2.** Pile *f,* revers *m.*

tail-coat, *s.* Habit *m* à queue.

tail-end, *s.* Extrémité *f* arrière ; fin *f.*

tailor[1], *s.* Tailleur *m.*

tailor[2], *v.tr.* Faire, façonner. Tailored dress, robe tailleur.

taint[1], *s.* **1.** (*a*) Corruption *f,* infection *f.* (*b*) Tache *f.* **2.** Tare *f* héréditaire. **3.** Trace *f.*

taint[2], *v.tr.* Infecter, gâter.

tainted, *a.* Infecté, corrompu.

take, *v.* Prendre. I. *v.tr.* **1.** (*a*) To t. sth. from s.o., prendre qch. à qn. To t. sth. from the table, prendre qch. sur la table. (*b*) To t. hold of, saisir, empoigner. She took my arm, elle me prit le bras To t. an opportunity, saisir une occasion. (*c*) To t. prisoner, faire prisonnier. To be taken ill, tomber malade. **2.** (*a*) Louer, prendre. (*b*) 'Taken,' "occupé." (*c*) T. your seats! en voiture ! (*d*) To t. the wrong road, se tromper de chemin. **3.** (*a*) Gagner, remporter. To t. a trick, faire une levée. (*b*) To t. an examination, se présenter à un examen. **4.** (*a*) To t. breath, reprendre haleine. (*b*) To t. a photograph, faire une photographie. (*c*) To t. to pieces, démonter. **5.** (*a*) What will you t. for it? combien en voulez-vous ? (*b*) Tenir. **6.** Prendre ; attraper. **7.** I t. it, je suppose. **8.** (*a*) To t. long, ce sera tôt fait. (*b*) I t. sixes, j'ai six de pointure. **9.** (*a*) Mener, conduire. (*b*) Porter ; transporter.

II. **take,** *v.i.* Avoir du succès ; réussir ; prendre. **take after,** *v.i.* Tenir de. **take away,** *v.tr.* **1.** Enlever, emporter ; emmener. **2.** (*a*) Oter. (*b*) Retirer. **take back,** *v.tr.* **1.** (*a*) Reconduire. (*b*) Reporter. **2.** (*a*) Reprendre. (*b*) Retirer. **take down,** *v.tr.* **1.** Descendre. **2.** To t. down in shorthand, sténographier. **take in,** *v.tr.* **1.** (*a*) Faire entrer. (*b*) Rentrer. To t. in water, faire eau. (*c*) Recevoir. **2.** Inclure. **3.** (*a*) Comprendre ; se rendre compte de. (*b*) To be taken in, se laisser attraper. **take into,** *v.tr.* **1.** To t. i. one's confidence, se confier à. **2.** To t. it i. one's head, s'aviser (*to*, de). **take off.** I. *v.tr.* **1.** Distraire. **2.** (*a*) Enlever. ôter; quitter. (*b*) Emmener. (*c*) Rabattre sur. II. **take off**, *v.i.* Prendre son élan; décoller, s'envoler. **take on.** **1.** *v.tr.* (*a*) Se charger de, entreprendre. (*b*) Accepter. (*c*) Engager. (*d*) Prendre. (*e*) Mener plus loin. **2.** *v.i.* Devenir populaire; réussir. **take out,** *v.tr.* **1.** Sortir; enlever, ôter. **2.** Emmener. **3.** Prendre, obtenir. **take over,** *v.tr.* Prendre (en, à sa, charge). **take to,** *v.i.* **1.** Prendre. **2.** S'adonner à. **3.** (*a*) Prendre en amitié. (*b*) Se faire à. **take up,** *v.tr.* **1.** (*a*) Enlever. (*b*) Embarquer. **2.** Absorber. **3.** (*a*) Relever. (*b*) Adopter. **4.** S'adonner à; épouser. **5.** Arrêter. **6.** Occuper. **take-off,** *s.* (*a*) Élan *m.* (*b*) Décollage *m*; envolée *f.*

taking[1], *a.* Attrayant; séduisant; engageant.

taking[2], *s.* **1.** Prise *f.* **2.** *pl.* Recette *f.*

talcum, *s.* **T. powder.** (poudre *f* de) talc *m.*

tale, *s.* **1.** Conte *m.* (*a*) Récit *m*, histoire *f.* (*b*) Nouvelle *f.* **2.** Rapport *m.*

talent, *s.* Talent *m*; aptitude *f.*

talented, *a.* Qui a du talent; doué.

talk[1], *s.* **1.** (*a*) Paroles *fpl.* (*b*) Bruit *m*, dires *mpl.* (*c*) Propos *mpl*; bavardage *m.* Idle t., paroles en l'air. Small t., menus propos. **2.** Entretien *m*; causerie *f.*

talk[2]. I. *v.i.* **1.** Parler. Talking of, à propos de. **2.** Causer, s'entretenir (*to*, avec). **3.** Jaser, bavarder. II. **talk,** *v.tr.* Parler. **talk over,** *v.tr.* Discuter, débattre.

talkative, *a.* Causeur, -euse.

talkativeness, *s.* Loquacité *f.*

talker, *s.* Causeur, -euse.

talkie, *s.* Film parlant, film parlé.

talking, *s.* **1.** Discours *mpl*, propos *mpl.* **2.** (*a*) Conversation *f.* (*b*) Bavardage *m.*

tall, *a.* **1.** Grand; de haute taille. **2.** Haut, élevé.

tallow, *s.* Suif *m.*

tally[1], *s.* Compte *m.*

tally[2], *v.i.* Correspondre; s'accorder.

talon, *s.* Serre *f*; griffe *f.*

tambourine, *s.* Tambour *m* de basque.

tame[1], *a.* **1.** Apprivoisé, domestiqué. **2.** (*a*) Soumis, dompté. (*b*) Monotone, terne.

tame[2], *v.tr.* (*a*) Apprivoiser. (*b*) Domestiquer

tamely, *adv.* **1.** Sans résistance, lâchement. **2.** Platement.

tameness, *s.* **1.** (*a*) Nature douce. (*b*) Caractère soumis. **2.** Monotonie *f*, fadeur *f.*

tamer, *s.* Dompteur, -euse.

taming, *s.* **1.** (*a*) Apprivoisement *m.* (*b*) Domestication *f.* **2.** Domptement *m.*

tamper, *v.i.* Toucher (*with*, à). To t. with, falsifier.

tan[1], *s.* Hâle *m.*

tan[2]. **1.** *v.tr.* (*a*) Tanner. (*b*) Hâler, bronzer. **2.** *v.i.* Se hâler, se basaner.

tandem. **1.** *s.* Tandem *m.* **2.** *adv.* En flèche.

tang, *s.* Goût vif; saveur *f.*

tangent, *s.* Tangente *f.*

tangerine, *s.* Mandarine *f.*

tangible, *a.* **1.** Tangible. **2.** Réel.

tangle[1], *s.* Embrouillement *m*; emmêlement *m.*

tangle[2], *v.tr.* Embrouiller, (em)mêler

tango[1], *s.* Tango *m.*

tango[2], *v.i.* Danser le tango.

tank, *s.* **1.** Réservoir *m.* **2.** Tank *m.*

tankard, *s.* Pot *m*, chope *f.*

tanker, *s.* Bateau-citerne *m*, *pl.* bateaux-citernes.

tanner, *s.* Tanneur *m.*

tantalize, *v.tr.* Tantaliser, taquiner.

tantalizing, *a.* Provocant.

tap[1], *s.* (*a*) Fausset *m.* (*b*) Robinet *m.*

tap[2], *v.tr.* (*a*) Percer. (*b*) Saigner.

tap[3], *s.* Tape *f*; petit coup.

tap[4]. **1.** *v.tr.* Frapper légèrement; taper. **2.** *v.ind.tr.* Frapper doucement.

tape, *s.* (*a*) Ruban *m* de fil, de coton; ganse *f.* (*b*) Bande *f* d'arrivée.

tape-measure, *s.* Mètre *m* en ruban.

taper[1], *s.* Bougie filée.

taper[2]. **1.** *v.tr.* Effiler. **2.** *v.i.* S'effiler; aller en diminuant.

tapering, *a.* En pointe; effilé, fuselé.

tapestry, *s.* Tapisserie *f.*

tapioca, *s.* Tapioca *m.*

tar[1], *s.* Goudron *m.*

tar[2], *v.tr.* Goudronner.

tardily, *adv.* **1.** Lentement. **2.** Tardivement.

tardiness, s. Lenteur f.

tardy, a. 1. Lent. 2. Tardif.

target, s. Cible f; but m, objectif m.

tariff, s. 1. Tarif m. 2. Tableau m, liste f, des prix.

tarmac, s. 1. Tarmac m. 2. Piste f d'envol.

tarnish. 1. v.tr. Ternir. 2. v.i. Se ternir.

tarpaulin, s. Bâche f.

tart¹, s. (a) Tarte f. (b) Tourte f.

tart², a. (a) Au goût âpre, aigrelet. (b) Aigre; mordant.

tartaric, a. Tartrique.

tartness, s. Acerbité f; acidité f.

task, s. 1. Tâche f; ouvrage m, besogne f. 2. To take to t., prendre à partie.

tassel, s. Gland m; houppe f.

taste¹, s. Goût m. 1. (a) Saveur f, goût. (b) A t., un petit peu. 2. Goût, prédilection f. 3. People of t., les gens de goût.

taste². I. v.tr. 1. Percevoir la saveur de ; sentir. 2. (a) Goûter de à; tâter de. (b) Goûter.

II. **taste,** v.i. Avoir un goût. To t. like, avoir un goût de.

tasteful, a. De bon goût.

tastefully, adv. Avec goût.

tasteless, a. 1. Sans saveur; fade, insipide. 2. Qui manque de goût.

tastelessness, s. 1. Insipidité f, fadeur f. 2. Manque m de goût.

tasty, a. Savoureux; succulent.

tatter, s. Lambeau m.

tattered, a. Dépenaillé, en loques; déguenillé.

tattoo, v.tr. Tatouer.

tattooing, s. Tatouage m.

taunt¹, s. Reproche m; sarcasme m.

taunt², v.tr. (a) Accabler de sarcasmes. (b) To t. s.o. with sth., reprocher qch. à qn.

taunting, a. Sarcastique.

taut, a. Tendu, raidi.

tauten, v.tr. Raidir.

tavern, s. Taverne f, cabaret m.

tawdry, a. D'un mauvais goût criard.

tawny, a. Tanné, basané; fauve.

tax¹, s. 1. Impôt m, contribution f, taxe f. 2. Charge f.

tax², v.tr. 1.(a) Taxer; frapper d'un impôt. (b) Imposer. (c) Mettre à l'épreuve. 2. Taxer, accuser.

taxable, a. Imposable.

taxation, s. (a) Imposition f. (b) Charges fiscales.

tax-collector, s. Percepteur m des contributions.

taxi¹, s. Taxi m.

taxi², v.i. Rouler sur le sol.

taxi-cab, s. Taxi m.

taxi-driver, s. Chauffeur m de taxi.

taximetre, s. Taximètre m.

taxi-rank, s. Station f de taxis.

tax-payer, s. Contribuable mf.

tea, s. 1. Thé m. Afternoon tea, five o'clock m. 2. Tisane f, infusion f.

tea-basket, s. Mallette f de camping.

tea-caddy, s. Boîte f à thé.

teach, v.tr. Enseigner; instruire. To t. s.o. sth. enseigner, apprendre, qch. à qn.

teacher, s. Instituteur, -trice; maître, f. maîtresse; professeur m.

teaching, s. 1. Enseignement m, instruction f. 2. pl. Leçons f. 3. Doctrine f

tea-cloth, s. 1. Nappe f à thé; napperon m. 2. Torchon m.

tea-cosy, s. Couvre-théière m.

tea-cup, s. Tasse f à thé.

tea-kettle, s. Bouilloire f.

team, s. 1. Attelage m. 2. Équipe f.

tea-party, s. Thé m.

tea-plant, s. Arbre m à thé.

tea-pot, s. Théière f.

tear¹, s. Larme f.

tear², s. 1. Déchirement m. 2. Déchirure f, accroc m.

tear³, v.tr. (a) Déchirer. To t. a hole in, faire un trou à. (b) Arracher. **tear away,** v.tr. Arracher. **tear down,** v.tr. Arracher. **tear off,** v.tr. Arracher. **tear out,** v.tr. Arracher. **tear up,** v.tr. Déchirer; mettre en pièces.

tear-drop, s. Larme f.

tearful, a. Éploré; larmoyant.

tearfully, adv. En pleurant; les larmes aux yeux.

tea-room, s. Salon m de thé.

tease¹, s. Taquin, -ine.

tease², v.tr. Taquiner, tourmenter.

teasing¹, a. Taquin; railleur, -euse.

teasing². Taquinerie f, taquinage m.

tea-spoon, s. Cuiller f à thé.

teaspoonful, s. Cuillerée f à thé.

tea-table, s. Table f à thé.

tea-things, s.pl. Service m à thé.

tea-time, s. L'heure f du thé.

technical, *a.* Technique.

technicality, *s.* Détail *m* technique.

technically, *adv.* Techniquement.

technique, *s.* Technique *f.*

tedious, *a.* Fatigant ; ennuyeux.

tedium, *s.* Ennui *m.*

tee, *s.* Tee *m.*

teem, *v.i.* Abonder (*with*, en) ; foisonner, fourmiller (*with*, de).

teetotal, *a.* Antialcoolique.

teetotaller, *s.* Abstinent, -ente.

teetotum, *s.* Toton *m.*

telegram, *s.* Télégramme *m* ; dépêche *f.*

telegraph[1], *s.* Télégraphe *m.* **T. office**, bureau télégraphique.

telegraph[2], *v.i. & tr.* Télégraphier.

telegraphic, *a.* Télégraphique.

telegraphist, *s.* Télégraphiste *mf.*

telegraph-operator, *s.* Télégraphiste *mf.*

telegraph-pole, *s.* Poteau *m* télégraphique.

telegraphy, *s.* Télégraphie *f.*

telepathic, *a.* Télépathique.

telepathy, *s.* Télépathie *f.*

telephone[1], *s.* Téléphone *m.* **Are you on the t.?** avez-vous le téléphone ?

telephone[2]. **1.** *v.i.* Téléphoner. **2.** *v.tr.* (*a*) Téléphoner. (*b*) Téléphoner à.

telephonic, *a.* Téléphonique.

telephone-operator, *s.* Téléphoniste *mf.*

telephonist, *s.* Téléphoniste *mf.*

telephony, *s.* Téléphonie *f.*

telescope[1], *s.* (*a*) Lunette *f* ; longue-vue *f*, *pl.* longues-vues. (*b*) Télescope *m.*

telescope[2]. **1.** *v.tr.* Télescoper **2.** *v.i.* (Se) télescoper.

telescopic, *a.* Télescopique.

television, *s.* Télévision *f.*

tell. I. *v.tr.* **1.** (*a*) Dire. (*b*) To t. s.o. sth., dire, apprendre, qch. à qn. I told you so ! je vous l'avais bien dit ! (*c*) Raconter, conter. (*d*) Annoncer, proclamer ; révéler. **2.** To t. s.o., about s.o., parler de qn à qn. **3.** Ordonner, dire, à. I told him not to, je le lui ai défendu. **4.** (*a*) Discerner, distinguer, reconnaître. (*b*) Savoir. Who can t.? qui sait ? You never can t., on ne sait jamais. **5.** *Abs.* To t. of, annoncer, révéler. **6.** Compter. All told, tout compris. **II. tell**, *v.i.* (*a*) Produire son

effet ; porter. (*b*) Témoigner ; militer.

teller, *s.* **1.** (Ra)conteur, -euse ; narrateur, -trice. **2.** Caissier *m.*

telling[1], *a.* Efficace. **T. blow**, coup *m* qui porte.

telling[2], *s.* **1.** Récit *m* ; narration *f.* **2.** Divulgation *f.* **3. There is no t.**, on ne sait pas.

tell-tale, *s.* **1.** (*a*) Rapporteur, -euse. (*b*) Révélateur, -trice. **2.** Témoin *m.*

temerity, *s.* Témérité *f*, audace *f.*

temper[1], *s.* **1.** Trempe *f.* **2.** Sang-froid *m.* **To be out of t.**, être de mauvaise humeur. **3.** Humeur *f.* (*a*) Caractère *m*, tempérament *m.* (*b*) Mauvaise humeur. **To be in a t.**, être en colère.

temper[2], *v.tr.* **1.** Tremper. **2.** Tempérer ; modérer.

temperament, *s.* Tempérament *m*

temperamental, *a.* Capricieux.

temperance, *s.* Tempérance *f.*

temperate, *a.* **1.** (*a*) Tempérant. sobre. (*b*) Modéré. **2.** Tempéré.

temperately, *adv.* Avec modération

temperature, *s.* Température *f.*

tempest, *s.* Tempête *f.*

tempestuous, *a.* **1.** Tempétueux. **2.** Orageux.

temple[1], *s.* Temple *m.*

temple[2], *s.* Tempe *f.*

tempo, *s.* Tempo *m.*

temporal, *a.* Temporel.

temporarily, *adv.* (*a*) Temporairement, provisoirement. (*b*) Pour le moment.

temporary, *a.* (*a*) Temporaire, provisoire. (*b*) Momentané.

temporize, *v.i.* Temporiser.

tempt, *v.tr.* Tenter.

temptation, *s.* Tentation *f.*

tempter, *s.* Tentateur, -trice.

tempting, *a.* Tentant, alléchant ; séduisant, attrayant.

ten, *num. a. & s.* Dix (*m*).

tenable, *a.* Tenable ; soutenable.

tenacious, *a.* Tenace.

tenaciously, *adv.* Obstinément ; avec ténacité.

tenacity, *s.* Ténacité *f.*

tenancy, *s.* Location *f.*

tenant, *s.* Locataire *mf.*

tend[1], *v.tr.* Soigner.

tend[2], *v.i.* **1.** Tendre, se diriger. **2.** Être sujet(te).

tendency, s. Tendance f.

tender¹, s. Tender m.

tender², a. Tendre. Of t. years, en bas âge.

tender³, s. 1. Soumission f, offre f. 2. To be legal t., avoir cours.

tender⁴. 1. v.tr. Offrir. 2. v.i. Soumissionner.

tender-hearted, a. Compatissant; au cœur tendre.

tenderly, adv. 1. Doucement. 2. Tendrement; avec tendresse.

tenderness, s. 1. Sensibilité f. 2. Délicatesse f. 3. Tendresse f.

tendon, s. Tendon m.

tendril, s. Vrille f.

tenet, s. Doctrine f, dogme m.

tenfold. 1. a. Décuple. 2. adv. To increase t., décupler.

tennis, s. Tennis m.

tennis-ball, s. Balle f de tennis.

tennis-court, s. Tennis m.

tenor, s. 1. Teneur f; sens général. 2. Ténor m.

tense¹, s. Temps m.

tense², a. Tendu.

tenseness, s. 1. Rigidité f. 2. Tension f.

tension, s. Tension f.

tent, s. Tente f.

tentacle, s. Tentacule m.

tentative. 1. a. Expérimental, -aux; d'essai. 2. s. Tentative f, essai m.

tentatively, adv. En guise d'essai.

tenth, num. a. & s. Dixième (m). (On the t. of March, le dix mars.

tent-peg, s. Piquet m de tente

tenure, s. Occupation f.

tepid, a. Tiède.

term¹, s. 1. Terme m, borne f, limite f. 2. (a) Terme, période f. (b) Trimestre m. 3. pl. Conditions f; termes. 4. pl. Relations f. On the best of terms, au mieux. 5. (a) Terme, mot m. (b) pl. Langage m, termes.

term², v.tr. Appeler, nommer.

termagant, s. Mégère f, virago f.

terminable, a. Terminable.

terminal, s. Borne f; borne d'attache.

terminate. 1. v.tr. Terminer. 1. Délimiter. 2. Mettre fin à.
II. **terminate,** v.i. 1. Se terminer, finir. 2. Aboutir.

termination, s. Terminaison f, fin f; cessation f.

terminus, s. (Gare f) terminus m.

terrace, s. 1. Terrasse f; terre-plein m, pl. terre-pleins. 2. Rangée f de maisons formant terrasse.

terra-cotta, s. Terre cuite.

terrestrial, a. Terrestre.

terrible, a. Terrible; affreux.

terribly, adv. Terriblement, affreusement.

terrier, s. Terrier m.

terrific, a. 1. Terrifiant, épouvantable. 2. Terrible; énorme.

terrify, v.tr. Terrifier, effrayer, épouvanter.

terrifying, a. Terrifiant, terrible, épouvantable.

territorial. 1. a. Territorial. -aux. 2. s. Territorial m.

territory, s. Territoire m.

terror, s. Terreur f, effroi m, épouvante f.

terrorism, s. Terrorisme m.

terrorize, v.tr. Terroriser.

terror-struck, a. Saisi de terreur; épouvanté.

terse, a. Concis, net, f. nette.

tersely, adv. Avec concision.

terseness, s. Concision f; netteté f.

test¹, s. 1. (a) Épreuve f. (b) Essai m. 2. Examen.

test², v.tr. (a) Éprouver; mettre à l'épreuve. (b) Essayer; vérifier; examiner.

testament, s. Testament m.

testamentary, a. Testamentaire.

testator, s. Testateur m.

testatrix, s. Testatrice f.

testify. 1. v.tr. Témoigner. 2. (a) Abs. Déposer. (b) v.ind.tr. To t. to, attester.

testimonial, s. 1. Certificat m; recommandation f. 2. Témoignage m d'estime.

testimony, s. Témoignage m.

test-match, s. Rencontre internationale.

test-tube, s. Éprouvette f.

testy, a. Irritable, irascible.

tether¹, s. Longe f; attache f.

tether², v.tr. Attacher.

text, s. Texte m.

text-book, s. Manuel m.

textile, a. & s. Textile (m).

texture, s. Texture f.

Thames (the). Pr.n. La Tamise.

than, conj. Que; de. More t, once, plus d'une fois.

thank, *v.tr.* 1. (a) Remercier (*for*, de); dire merci à. T. goodness! Grâce au ciel! (b) T. you, merci. No, t. you, merci! 2. To have s.o. to t. for sth., devoir qch. à qn.

thankful, *a.* Reconnaissant.

thankfully, *adv.* Avec reconnaissance.

thankfulness, *s.* Reconnaissance *f.*

thankless, *a.* Ingrat.

thanklessness, *s.* Ingratitude *f.*

thanks, *s.pl.* Remerciements. T. to, grâce à.

thanksgiving, *s.* Action *f* de grâce.

that[1]. I. *Dem. pron.* 1. Cela, ça; ce. (a) T. is my opinion, voilà mon avis. What do you mean by t.? qu'entendez-vous par là? T. is, c'est-à-dire. (b) That's right! that's it! c'est cela! That's all, voilà tout. That's curious! voilà qui est curieux! And that's t., et voilà! 2. Celui-là, *f.* celle-là; *pl.* ceux-là, *f.* celles-là. 3. Celui, *f.* celle; *pl.* ceux, *f.* celles. Those of whom I speak, ceux dont je parle.
II. **that,** *dem.a.* (a) Ce, cet; *f.* cette; *pl.* ces. T. book, ce livre(-là). T. one, celui-là, celle-là. (b) Those people who, les gens, ceux, qui.
III. **that,** *dem. adv.* T high, aussi haut que ça.

that[2], *rel. pron. sg. & pl.* 1. Qui; que. 2. Lequel, *f.* laquelle; *pl.* lesquels, *f.* lesquelles. 3. Où; que.

that[3], *conj.* 1. Que; afin que, pour que. 2. O t. it were possible! oh, si c'était possible!

thatch, *s.* Chaume *m.*

thatched, *a.* De chaume. T. cottage, chaumière *f.*

thaw[1], *s.* Dégel *m.*

thaw[2]. 1. *v.tr.* Dégeler. 2. *v.i.* (a) Fondre. (b) *Impers.* It is thawing, il dégèle.

the[1], *def. art.* 1. Le, *f.* la; l'; *pl.* les. (a) I spoke to the coachman, j'ai parlé au cocher. Give that to the woman, donnez cela à la femme. He has gone to the fields, il est allé aux champs. The voice of the people, la voix du peuple. The roof of the house, le toit de la maison. The arrival of the guests, l'arrivée des invités. Edward the Seventh, Edouard Sept. (b) He has the

toothache, il a mal aux dents. (c) By the day, à la journée. 2. Ce, cet, *f.* cette, *pl.* ces At the time, à cette époque.

the[2], *adv.* The sooner the better, le plus tôt sera le mieux.

theatre, *s.* Théâtre *m.*

theatrical, *a.* Théâtral, -aux.

theatricals, *s.pl.* Amateur t., spectacle *m* d'amateurs.

thee, *pers. pron.* 1. Te; t'. 2. Toi.

theft, *s.* (a) Vol *m.* (b) Petty t., larcin *m.*

their, *poss.a.* Leur, *pl.* leurs.

theirs, *poss.pron.* Le leur, la leur, les leurs. He is a friend of t., c'est un de leurs amis.

them, *pers. pron. pl.* 1. Les *mf*; leur *mf.* Speak to t., parlez-leur. 2. Eux, *f.* elles. 3. Many of t., plusieurs d'entre eux. Give me half of t., donnez-m'en la moitié. Every one of t., was killed, ils furent tous tués. Neither of t., ni l'un ni l'autre.

theme, *s.* 1. Sujet *m,* thème *m.* 2. Thème, motif *m.*

themselves, *pers.pron.* (a) Eux-mêmes *m,* elles-mêmes *f.* (b) Se.

then. I. *adv.* 1. Alors; en ce temps-là. T. and there, séance tenante. 2. Puis, ensuite, alors. 3. D'ailleurs; aussi (bien); et puis.
II. **then,** *conj.* En ce cas, donc, alors. But t., mais c'est que.
III. **then,** *quasi-s.* Ce temps-là. Before t., avant cela. By t., déjà. Till t., jusqu'alors; jusque-là. Between now and t., d'ici là.

thence, *adv.* 1. De là. 2. Pour cette raison; par conséquent.

thenceforth, *adv.* Dès lors; désormais.

theological, *a.* Théologique.

theology, *s.* Théologie *f.*

theorem, *s.* Théorème *m.*

theoretical, *a.* Théorique.

theoretically, *adv.* Théoriquement.

theory, *s.* Théorie *f.*

theosophy, *s.* Théosophie *f.*

there. I. *adv.* 1. (a) Là, y. (b) Hurry up t.! dépêchez-vous là-bas! (c) T. is, are, voilà. 2. (a) T. is, are, il est, il y a. (b) T. comes a time, il arrive un moment. 3. Quant à cela; en cela.

II. **there**, *int.* Voilà !

III. **there**, *quasi-s.* In t., là-dedans ; là.

thereabouts, *adv.* **1.** Près de là ; dans le voisinage. **2.** Environ.

thereafter, *adv.* Après (cela) ; par la suite.

thereat, *adv.* Là-dessus.

thereby, *adv.* Par ce moyen ; de cette façon.

therefore, *adv.* Donc ; par conséquent.

therein, *adv.* **1.** En cela ; à cet égard. **2.** (Là-)dedans.

thereof, *adv.* De cela ; en.

thereon, *adv.* (Là-)dessus.

thereupon, *adv.* **1.** Sur ce. **2.** Là-dessus, à ce sujet.

therewith, *adv.* **1.** Avec cela. **2.** Sur ce. **3.** En outre.

thermometer, *s.* Thermomètre *m.*

thesis, *s.* Thèse *f.*

they. **1.** *Pers.pron. pl.* (a) Ils, *f.* elles. Here it **come**, les voici (qui viennent). T. **are rich people**, ce sont des gens riches. (b) Eux, *f.* elles. It is t., ce sont eux. (c) Ceux, celles. **2.** *Indef. pron.* On. T. **say**, on dit.

thick. I. *a.* **1.** Épais, *f.* épaisse ; gros, *f.* grosse. **2.** Épais, serré. **3.** Épais, consistant. T. **soup**, potage *m* crème.

II. **thick**, *s.* Through t. **and thin**, à travers toutes les épreuves.

III. **thick**, *adv.* **1.** En couche épaisse. **2.** Dru.

thicken. **1.** *v.tr.* Épaissir. **2.** *v.i.* (S')épaissir.

thicket, *s.* Hallier *m*, fourré *m.*

thickly, *adv.* **1.** En couche épaisse. **2.** Dru.

thickness, *s.* **1.** (a) Épaisseur *f.* (b) Consistance *f.* **2.** Couche *f.*

thick-set, *a.* Trapu.

thick-skinned, *a.* **1.** A la peau épaisse. **2.** Peu sensible.

thief, *s.* Voleur, -euse.

thieve, *v.tr.* Voler.

thieving[1], *a.* Voleur, -euse.

thieving[2], *s.* Vol *m*, volerie *f.*

thievish, *a.* Voleur, -euse.

thievishness, *s.* Penchant *m* au vol

thigh, *s.* Cuisse *f.*

thimble, *s.* Dé *m.*

thin[1], *a.* **1.** (a) Mince ; ténu ; léger. (b) Maigre, mince. **2.** Clairsemé, rare.

thin[2]. **1.** *v.tr.* (a) Amincir. (b)

Éclaircir. **2.** *v.i.* (a) Maigrir. (b) S'amincir, s'effiler. (c) S'éclaircir.

thine, *poss.pron.* (a) Le tien, la tienne, les tiens, les tiennes. (b) A toi.

thing, *s.* **1.** Chose *f.* (a) Objet *m*, article *m.* (b) *pl.* Vêtements *m*, effets *m.* (c) *pl.* Affaires *f*, effets. **2.** Être *m*, créature *f.* **3.** (a) That's the very t., c'est juste ce qu'il faut. For one t., en premier lieu. (b) *pl.* Things are going badly, les affaires vont mal. **4.** It's not the t., cela ne se fait pas. It's quite the t., c'est tout à fait correct.

think, *v.tr.* & *i.* **1.** Penser, réfléchir. **2.** Songer, s'imaginer. One would have thought, c'était à croire. Anyone would t., on dirait. **3.** Thinking to, dans l'intention de. **4.** (a) I t. so, je pense que oui. (b) *Pred.* Juger, trouver, penser. **5.** I thought so, je m'y attendais. **think about, of**, *v.ind.tr.* **1.** Penser à ; songer à. **2.** S'imaginer, se figurer, songer. **3.** Considérer. To t. of the expense, regarder à la dépense. **4.** (a) *v.tr.* What do you t. of it? qu'en pensez-vous ? To t. too much of, attacher trop d'importance à. (b) To t. well of, estimer. **think out**, *v.tr.* **1.** Imaginer, méditer. **2.** Juger. **think over**, *v.tr.* Réfléchir sur, aviser à.

thinker, *s.* Penseur, -euse.

thinking[1], *a.* Pensant ; qui pense.

thinking[2], *s.* Pensée *f*, réflexion *f.* To my t., à mon avis.

thinly, *adv.* **1.** A peine ; légèrement. **2.** Clair ; peu.

thinness, *s.* **1.** (a) Minceur *f* ; légèreté *f.* (b) Maigreur *f.* **2.** Rareté *f.*

thin-skinned, *a.* Susceptible.

third. **1.** *num.a.* Troisième. T. person, tierce personne, tiers *m.* (On) the t. of March, le trois mars. To travel t., voyager en troisième. **2.** *s.* Tiers *m.*

third-class. **1.** *a.* De troisième. **2.** *adv.* En troisième.

thirdly, *adv.* Troisièmement ; en troisième lieu.

third-rate, *a.* Très inférieur, -eure.

thirst, *s.* Soif *f.*

thirstily, *adv.* Avidement.

thirsting, *a.* Altéré, assoiffé (for, de).

thirsty, *a.* Altéré. To be t., avoir soif. T. for, assoiffé de.

thirteen, *num. a. & s.* Treize (*m*).

thirteenth, *num. a. & s.* Treizième (*m*). (On) **the t. of May,** le treize mai.

thirtieth, *num. a. & s.* Trentième (*m*). (On) **the t. of June,** le trente juin.

thirty, *num. a. & s.* Trente (*m*). **Thirty-first,** trente et unième. **About t.,** une trentaine de.

this. I. *Dem. pron.* **1.** Ceci ; ce. **Who is t.?** quelle est cette personne ? **Before t.,** déjà. **T. is curious,** voici qui est curieux. **T. is where he lives,** c'est ici qu'il demeure. **2.** Celui-ci, *f.* celle-ci, *pl* ceux-ci. *f.* celles-ci.

II. **this,** *dem.a.* Ce, cet, *f.* cette, *pl.* ces. **T. book,** ce livre(-ci). **In these days,** de nos jours. **T. way and that,** de-ci, de-là.

III. **this,** *dem.adv.* **T. high,** aussi haut que ceci.

thistle, *s.* Chardon *m*.

thither, *adv.* Là ; y.

thong, *s.* Lanière *f* de cuir.

thorn, *s.* Épine *f*.

thorny, *a.* Épineux.

thorough, *a.* (a) Minutieux ; complet, -ète ; profond ; consciencieux. (b) Vrai ; achevé.

thoroughbred. **1.** *a.* Pur sang *inv* ; de race. **2.** *s.* (a) Cheval *m* pur sang. (b) Animal, -aux *m*, de race.

thoroughfare, *s.* Voie *f* de communication. **Public t.,** voie publique. 'No t.,' "interdiction de passage."

thoroughly, *adv.* Tout à fait ; parfaitement ; complètement ; à fond.

thou, *pers. pron.* (a) Tu. (b) Toi.

though. I. *conj.* **1.** Quoique, bien que, encore que. **2.** (a) **Strange t.** it may **appear,** si étrange que cela paraisse. (b) **What t.,** qu'importe que. **3.** **As t.,** comme si.

II. **though,** *adv.* Cependant, pourtant.

thought, *s.* (La) pensée. **1.** **Capable of t.,** capable de penser. **2.** (a) Idée *f*. (b) *pl.* Esprit *m*, pensée. **3.** (a) Réflexion *f*, considération *f*. (b) Pensées, rêverie *f*, méditation *f*. **4.** Intention *f*, dessein *m*.

thoughtful, *a.* **1.** (a) Pensif, méditatif ; rêveur, -euse. (b) Réfléchi, prudent. **2.** Prévenant (*of,* pour).

thoughtfully, *adv.* **1.** Pensivement.

2. D'une manière réfléchie. **3.** Avec prévenance.

thoughtfulness, *s.* **1.** Méditation *f*. **2.** Prudence *f*. **3.** Prévenance *f*.

thoughtless, *a.* **1.** Irréfléchi ; étourdi **2.** Peu soucieux.

thoughtlessly, *adv.* Étourdiment.

thoughtlessness, *s.* **1.** Étourderie *f*. **2.** Manque *m* d'égards.

thousand, *num. a. & s.* Mille (*m*) *inv* ; *s.* millier *m*.

thraldom, *s.* Esclavage *m*.

thrash, *v.tr.* (a) Battre ; rosser. (b) Battre à plates coutures. **thrash out,** *v.tr.* Débattre.

thrashing, *s.* Rossée *f*, correction *f*.

thread[1], *s.* **1.** Fil *m*. **2.** (a) **Sewing t.,** fil à coudre. **Lisle t.,** fil d'Écosse. **3.** Filet *m* ; pas *m*.

thread[2], *v.tr.* (a) Enfiler. (b) **To t. one's way,** se faufiler.

threadbare, *a.* Râpé.

threat, *s.* Menace *f*.

threaten, *v.tr.* **1.** Menacer. **2.** *Abs.* **A storm is threatening,** la tempête menace.

threatening, *a.* Menaçant.

three, *num. a. & s.* Trois (*m*).

three-cornered, *a.* Triangulaire.

threefold, *a.* Triple.

thresh, *v.tr.* Battre.

threshing, *s.* Battage *m*.

threshing-machine, *s.* Batteuse *f*.

threshold, *s.* Seuil *m*, pas *m*.

thrice, *adv.* Trois fois.

thrift, *s.* Économie *f*, épargne *f*.

thriftily, *adv.* Avec économie ; frugalement.

thriftiness, *s.* Économie *f*.

thriftless, *a.* Dépensier, prodigue.

thriftlessness, *s.* Prodigalité *f*.

thrifty, *a.* Économe, ménager.

thrill[1], *s.* (a) Frisson *m*, tressaillement *m*. (b) (Vive) émotion.

thrill[2]. **1.** *v.tr.* (a) Faire frémir. (b) Émouvoir. **2.** *v.i.* Tressaillir, frémir.

thriller, *s.* Roman sensationnel.

thrilling, *a.* Empoignant, émouvant.

thrive, *v.i.* (a) Se (bien) développer. (b) Prospérer.

thriving, *a.* Vigoureux ; prospère.

throat, *s.* Gorge *f*.

throb[1], *s.* Pulsation *f*, battement *m*.

throb[2], *v.i.* Battre fort ; palpiter.

throbbing, *s.* Battement *m*, pulsation *f*.

throes, *s.pl.* Douleurs *fpl*, angoisse *f*. **The t. of death,** l'agonie *f*.

throne, *s.* Trône *m*.

throng[1], *s.* (*a*) Foule *f*. (*b*) Cohue *f*.

throng[2]. **1.** *v.i.* Affluer ; se presser. **2.** *v.tr.* Encombrer.

thronged, *a.* Plein de gens ; comble, bondé.

throttle[1], *s.* Étrangleur *m*. **To open out the t.,** mettre les gaz.

throttle[2], *v.tr.* Étrangler.

through. I. *prep.* **1.** (*a*) A travers ; par ; au travers de. **To speak t. one's nose,** parler du nez. (*b*) Pendant, durant. **2.** Par ; par l'entremise de. **3.** En conséquence de. à cause de.

II. through, *adv.* **1.** (*a*) A travers. **To let t.,** laisser passer. (*b*) Right **t.,** de part en part. **To run t.,** transpercer. (*c*) D'un bout à l'autre ; jusqu'au bout. **2.** (*a*) Directement ; (*b*) **To get t. to,** obtenir la communication avec.

III. through, *attrib.a.* Direct.

throughout. 1. *prep.* D'un bout à l'autre de. **2.** *adv.* (*a*) Partout. (*b*) Tout le temps.

throw[1], *s.* Jet *m*, lancement *m*.

throw[2], *v.tr.* **1.** Jeter, lancer ; rejeter. **2.** Projeter. **3.** (*a*) Terrasser. (*b*) Démonter. **throw away,** *v.tr.* **1.** Jeter ; rejeter ; mettre au rebut. **2.** Donner inutilement ; laisser passer. **throw down,** *v.tr.* (*a*) Jeter de haut en bas. (*b*) Jeter à terre. **throw off,** *v.tr.* **1.** (*a*) Jeter, rendre. (*b*) Se débarrasser de ; abandonner. **2. To t. off the scent,** dépister. **throw out,** *v.tr.* **1.** Jeter dehors ; expulser. **2.** Répandre, émettre. **3.** Rejeter. **throw up,** *v.tr.* **1.** Jeter en l'air. **2.** Renoncer à, abandonner.

thrush, *s.* Grive *f*.

thrust[1], *s.* (*a*) Poussée *f*. (*b*) Coup *m* de pointe.

thrust[2], *v.tr.* (*a*) Pousser ; fourrer ; enfoncer. (*b*) **To t. oneself upon,** s'imposer à.

thud[1], *s.* Bruit sourd ; son mat.

thud[2], *v.i.* Tomber avec un bruit sourd ; émettre un bruit mat.

thumb, *s.* Pouce *m*. **Under s.o.'s t.,** sous la domination de qn.

thumb-nail, *s.* Ongle *m* du pouce.

thump[1], *s.* **1.** Coup sourd. **2.** Coup de poing.

thump[2], *v.tr. & i.* Bourrer de coups ; cogner.

thunder[1], *s.* Tonnerre *m*.

thunder[2], *v.i. & tr.* Tonner.

thunderbolt, *s.* Foudre *f*.

thundering, *a.* Tonnant ; fulminant.

thunderous, *a.* **1.** Orageux. **2.** Tonnant ; à tout rompre.

thunder-storm, *s.* Orage *m*.

thunderstruck, *a.* Confondu abasourdi.

Thursday, *s.* Jeudi *m*.

thus, *adv.* **1.** Ainsi ; de cette façon. **2.** Ainsi, donc. **3. T. far,** jusqu'ici ; jusque-là.

thwart[1], *s.* Banc *m* de nage.

thwart[2], *v.tr.* Contrecarrer ; déjouer les menées de.

thy, *poss.a.* Ton, *f.* ta, *pl.* tes.

thyme, *s.* Thym *m*. **Wild t.,** serpolet *m*.

thyroid, *a.* Thyroïde.

thyself, *pron.* (*a*) Toi-même. (*b*) Te.

tiara, *s.* Tiare *f*.

tick[1], *s.* **1.** (*a*) Tic-tac *m*. (*b*) Moment *m*, instant *m*. **2.** Marque *f*, pointage *m*.

tick[2]. **1.** *v.i.* Faire tic-tac. **2.** *v.tr.* Pointer. **tick off,** *v.tr.* Pointer ; faire une marque à.

ticket[1], *s.* **1.** Billet *m* ; ticket *m*. **Platform t.,** billet de quai. **2.** Étiquette *f* ; fiche *f*.

ticket[2], *v.tr.* Étiqueter, marquer.

ticket-collector, *s.* Contrôleur *m*.

ticket-inspector, *s.* Contrôleur *m*.

ticking, *s.* Tic-tac *m*.

tickle[1], *s.* Chatouillement *m*.

tickle[2]. **1.** *v.tr.* (*a*) Chatouiller. (*b*) Amuser. **2.** *v.i.* Chatouiller.

tickling, *s.* Chatouillement *m*.

ticklish, *a.* **1.** Chatouilleux, -euse. **2.** Délicat.

tidal, *a.* **1. T. wave,** vague *f* de fond. **2.** A marée.

tide, *s.* (*a*) Marée *f*. (*b*) Courant *m*.

tidily, *adv.* Proprement ; avec ordre.

tidiness, *s.* Bon ordre ; bonne tenue.

tidings, *s.pl.* Nouvelles *fpl*.

tidy[1], *a.* (*a*) Bien rangé, en bon ordre ; bien tenu. (*b*) Ordonné ; qui a de l'ordre.

tidy[2], *v.tr.* Ranger ; arranger. **To t. oneself,** faire un brin de toilette. *Abs.* **To t. up,** tout remettre en place.

tie¹, s. **1.** (a) Lien m; attache f. (b) Entrave. **2.** (a) Lacet m, cordon m. (b) Nœud m, cravate f. **3.** Match m ou course f à égalité.

tie². I. v.tr. (a) Attacher; lier. (b) Lier, nouer.

II. **tie**, v.i. Être, arriver, à égalité. **tie down**, v.tr. Assujettir. **tie up**, v.tr. Attacher, ficeler; bander, panser.

tie-pin, s. Épingle f de cravate.

tier, s. Rangée f; étage m.

tiger, s. Tigre m.

tiger-cat, s. Chat-tigre m, pl. chats-tigres.

tiger-lily, s. Lis tigré.

tight. I. a. (a) Raide, tendu. To draw t., serrer. (b) Trop juste.

II. **tight**, adv. (a) Fortement, fermement; serré. (b) Étroitement.

tighten. **1.** v.tr. Serrer, resserrer. (b) Renforcer. **2.** v.i. (a) Se (res-)serrer. (b) Se tendre; raidir.

tightly, adv. (a) Fortement. (b) Étroitement; serré.

tightness, s. (a) Tension f, raideur f. (b) Étroitesse f.

tights, s.pl. Collant m, maillot m.

tigress, s. Tigresse f.

tile¹, s. **1.** Tuile f. **2.** Carreau m.

tile², v.tr. Carreler.

tiled, a. **1.** De, en, tuiles. **2.** Carrelé, en carreaux.

till¹, v.tr. Labourer, cultiver.

till², s. Tiroir-caisse m, pl. tiroirs-caisses.

till³. **1.** prep. (a) Jusqu'à. T. now, jusqu'ici. From morning t. night, du matin au soir. (b) Not t., pas avant. **2.** conj. (a) Jusqu'à ce que. To laugh t. one cries, rire aux larmes. (b) Not t., pas avant que.

tilt¹, s. **1.** Inclinaison f, pente f. **2.** Full t., à toute vitesse.

tilt². I. v.i. S'incliner; pencher. To t. up, basculer.

II. **tilt**, v.tr. (a) Pencher, incliner. (b) Faire basculer.

timber, s. **1.** (a) Bois m d'œuvre. (b) Arbres mpl de haute futaie. **2.** Poutre f, madrier m.

timber-yard, s. Chantier m.

time¹, s. **1.** Temps m. In (the course of) t., avec le temps. **2.** Within the required t., dans le délai prescrit. For a long t. to come, d'ici à long-temps. **3.** (a) To take one's t. over sth., mettre le temps à faire qch. (b) To serve one's t., faire son apprentissage. **4.** pl. Époque f. (a) In times past, autrefois, jadis. In times to come, à l'avenir. (b) Behind the times, arriéré. **5.** Moment m. At that t., en ce temps-là. At the present t., à l'heure qu'il est; actuellement. At one t., autrefois, dans le temps. At no t., jamais; à aucun moment. At times, parfois. From that t., dès lors; depuis lors. **6.** Heure f. (a) What is the t.? quelle heure est-il? (b) To be before t., être en avance. To arrive on t., arriver à l'heure. In t., à temps. In good t., de bonne heure. (c) T. of the year, époque de l'année; saison f. **7.** We had a good t., on s'est bien amusé. **8.** Fois f. T. after t., à maintes reprises. **9.** adv.phr. At the same t. (a) En même temps. (b) D'autre part. **10.** (a) Durée f. (b) Mesure f. (c) To keep t., suivre la mesure.

time², v.tr. **1.** (a) Fixer l'heure de. (b) Mesurer. (c) Régler. **2.** Calculer la durée de. **3.** Chronométrer.

timely, a. Opportun, à propos.

timepiece, s. Pendule f; montre f.

time-table, s. Horaire m; indicateur m.

timid, a. Timide, peureux.

timidity, s. Timidité f.

timidly, adv. Timidement.

timorous, a. Peureux, craintif.

tin, s. **1.** Étain m. **2.** Boîte f.

tincture, s. Teinture f.

tinder, s. Amadou m.

tinfoil, s. **1.** Feuille f d'étain. **2.** Papier m simili-étain.

tinge¹, s. Teinte f, nuance f.

tinge², v.tr. Teinter, nuancer.

tingle, v.i. **1.** Tinter. **2.** Picoter.

tinkle¹, s. Tintement m.

tinkle². **1.** v.i. Tinter. **2.** v.tr. Faire tinter.

tinkling, s. Tintement m.

tinned, a. Conservé. T. foods, conserves f alimentaires.

tin-opener, s. Ouvre-boîte m inv.

tinsel, s. **1.** Lamé m, paillettes fpl. (b) Clinquant m.

tint¹, s. Teinte f, nuance f.

tint², v.tr. Teinter, colorer.

tin-tack, s. Broquette f. **Tin-tacks,** semence f.

tiny, a. Minuscule.

tip¹, s. **1.** Bout m, extrémité f, pointe f. **2.** Bout ferré, embout m.

tip², s. **1.** Pourboire m, gratification f. **2.** Tuyau m.

tip³. I. v.tr. **1.** (a) To tip (over), renverser. (b) **To tip** (up), faire basculer. (c) **To tip** (out), déverser. (d) Faire pencher. **2.** Donner un pourboire, une gratification, à. **3.** Tuyauter. **II. tip,** v.i. (a) **To tip** (over), se renverser. (b) **To tip** (up), se soulever, basculer.

tipping, s. Distribution f de pourboires.

tipsiness, s. Ivresse f.

tipsy, a. **1.** Gris, ivre. **To get t.,** se griser. **2.** D'ivrogne.

tiptoe, s. & adv. Sur la pointe des pieds.

tirade, s. Tirade f.

tire. I. v.tr. (a) Fatiguer, lasser. (b) **To t.** out, excéder **2.** v.i. Se lasser, se fatiguer.

tired, a. Fatigué ; las, f. lasse. **T. out,** rompu de fatigue.

tiredness, s. Lassitude f, fatigue f.

tireless, a. Inlassable, infatigable.

tirelessly, adv. Infatigablement.

tiresome, a. **1.** Fatigant ; ennuyeux. **2.** Exaspérant ; assommant.

tissue, s. Tissu m ; étoffe f.

tissue-paper, s. (a) Papier m de soie. (b) Papier pelure.

titanic, a. Titanique, titanesque.

tit-bit, s. Morceau friand ; friandise f.

tithe, s. **1.** Dîme f. **2.** Dixième m.

titillate, v.tr. Titiller, chatouiller.

title, s. (a) Titre m. (b) **Persons of t.,** les nobles m ; la noblesse.

title-page, s. Page f de titre ; titre m.

titter¹, s. Rire étouffé.

titter², v.i. Avoir un petit rire étouffé.

tittering, s. Petits rires.

to. I. prep. A, à. **1.** (a) **He went to France, to Japan, to India,** il est allé en France, au Japon, aux Indes. **I am going to the grocer's,** je vais chez l'épicier. (b) **The road to ruin,** le chemin de la ruine. **2.** Vers, à. **3. Ten minutes to six,** six heures moins dix. **4.** (a) **To this day,** jusqu'à ce jour. (b) **Accurate to a millimetre,** exact à un millimètre près. **5. To this end,** à cet effet. **6. En. To put to flight,** mettre en fuite. **7.** (a) Auprès de, à côté de. (b) **Six votes to four,** six voix contre quatre. **8. To all appearances,** selon les apparences. **9. To drink to s.o.,** boire à la santé de qn. **10.** (a) **What is that to you?** qu'est-ce que cela vous fait ? (b) Envers, pour.

II. to. 1. (a) Pour. **So to speak,** pour ainsi dire. (b) **Happy to do it,** heureux de le faire. **Good to eat,** bon à manger. (c) **To look at her,** à la voir. **2. To lie is shameful,** il est honteux de mentir. **3. I wish him to do it,** je veux qu'il le fasse. **4. You ought to,** vous le devriez.

III. to, adv. **To come to.** reprendre connaissance.

toad, s. Crapaud m.

toadstool, s. Champignon vénéneux.

toast¹, s. **1.** Pain grillé. **Piece of t.,** rôtie f. **Anchovies on t.,** anchois sur canapé. **2.** Toast m.

toast². I. v.tr. (a) Rôtir, griller. (b) Porter un toast à. **2.** v.i. Rôtir, griller.

toasting-fork, s. Fourchette f à rôtir le pain.

toast-rack, s. Porte-rôties m inv.

tobacco, s. Tabac m.

tobacconist, s. Marchand m de tabac. **Tobacconist's,** débit m de tabac.

tobacco-pouch, s. Blague f à tabac.

toboggan¹, s. Toboggan m.

toboggan², v.i. Faire du toboggan.

to-day, adv. & s. Aujourd'hui (m).

toddle, v.i. Marcher à petits pas ; trottiner.

toe, s. **1.** Orteil m ; doigt m de pied. **2.** Bout m, pointe f.

toe-cap, s. Bout rapporté.

toe-clip, s. Cale-pieds m inv.

toe-nail, s. Ongle m d'orteil.

toffee, s. Caramel m au beurre.

together, adv. Ensemble. (a) **T. with,** avec. (b) **To bring t.,** rassembler, réunir. (c) **To act t.,** agir de concert. **All t.,** tous à la fois.

toil¹, s. Labeur m, peine f.

toil², v.i. Travailler, peiner. **To t. up,** gravir péniblement.

toiler, s. Travailleur, -euse.

toilet, s. **1.** Toilette f. **2.** Les toilettes, les cabinets m.

toilet-paper, s. Papier m hygiénique.
toilet-roll, s. Rouleau m de papier hygiénique.
toilet-set, s. Garniture f de toilette.
toilet-soap, s. Savon m de toilette.
toilsome, a. Pénible, fatigant.
token, s. **1.** Signe m, marque f. **2.** Jeton m.
tolerable, a. (a) Tolérable, supportable. (b) Passable.
tolerably, adv. **1.** Tolérablement. **2.** Passablement.
tolerance, s. Tolérance f.
tolerant, a. Tolérant.
tolerate, v.tr. Tolérer, supporter.
toleration, s. Tolérance f.
toll¹, s. Droit m de passage.
toll², v.tr. & i. Tinter, sonner.
toll-call, s. Conversation interurbaine.
tolling, s. (a) Tintement m. (b) Glas m.
tomato, s. Tomate f.
tomb, s. Tombe f; tombeau m
tombstone, s. Pierre tombale.
tome, s. Tome m; gros volume.
tomfoolery, s. Niagauderies fpl.
tommy-gun, s. Mitraillette f.
to-morrow, adv. & s. Demain (m). **To-m. week,** de demain en huit. **The day after to-m.,** après-demain.
ton, s. **1.** Tonne f. **2.** Tonneau m.
tone, s. **1.** Son m, accent m; timbre m. **2.** Ton m.
toneless, a. Atone.
tongs, s.pl. **1.** Pincettes f. **2.** Pince(s) f, tenailles fpl.
tongue, s. **1.** Langue f. **To find one's t.,** retrouver la parole. **To give t.,** donner de la voix. **2.** Langue, idiome m. **3.** Languette f.
tongue-tied, a. Muet, -ette; interdit.
tonic. 1. a. Tonique. **2.** s. (a) Tonique m, fortifiant m. (b) Tonique f.
to-night, adv. & s. Cette nuit; ce soir.
toning, s. Virage m.
tonnage, s. Tonnage m, jauge f.
tonsil, s. Amygdale f.
tonsure¹, s. Tonsure f.
tonsure², v.tr. Tonsurer.
too, adv. **1.** Trop, par trop. **Too much,** (de) trop. **2.** Aussi; également. **3.** D'ailleurs; de plus; en outre.

tool¹, s. **1.** Outil m; instrument m. **2.** Instrument, créature f.
tool², v.tr. Ciseler.
tooling, s. Ciselage m.
toot¹, s. **1.** Son m, appel m. **2.** Cornement m.
toot², v.i. Corner.
tooth, s. Dent f. **Set of teeth,** denture f. **Set of (false) teeth,** dentier m. **T. and nail,** avec acharnement.
toothache, s. Mal m de dents.
tooth-brush, s. Brosse f à dents.
toothless, a. Édenté.
tooth-paste, s. Pâte f dentifrice.
tooth-pick, s. Cure-dents m inv.
tooth-powder, s. Poudre f dentifrice.
toothsome, a. Savoureux.
top¹. I. s. **1.** Haut m, sommet m, cime f, faîte m. **On top of it all,** en sus de tout cela. **2.** Surface f; dessus m. **3.** Tête f. **Gilt top,** tête dorée. **4.** Haut bout. **5. At the top of one's voice,** à tue-tête, à pleine gorge.
II. top, attrib.a. **1.** Supérieur; de dessus, du haut. **The top floor,** le dernier étage. **2.** Premier : principal, -aux.
top², v.tr. **1.** Surmonter, couronner (with, de). **2.** Dépasser. **3.** Calotter. **top up,** v.tr. Reniveler.
top³, s. Toupie f.
topaz, s. Topaze f.
top-coat, s. Pardessus m.
top-heavy, a. Trop lourd du haut.
topic, s. Sujet m, thème m.
topical, a. D'actualités.
topmost, a. Le plus haut.
topography, s. Topographie f.
topple. 1. v.i. (a) **To t.** (over), tomber. (b) Chanceler, branler. **2.** v.tr. **To t. over,** faire tomber.
topsy-turvy, adv. & adj Sens dessus dessous.
torch, s. Torche f, flambeau m.
torment¹, s. Tourment m, torture f.
torment², v.tr. Tourmenter.
tormentor, s. Tourmenteur, -euse.
torpedo¹, s. Torpille f.
torpedo², v.tr. Torpiller.
torpedo-boat, s. Torpilleur m.
torpid, a. Engourdi, inerte.
torrent, s. Torrent m.
torrential, a. Torrentiel.
torrid, a. Torride.
tortoise, s. Tortue f.

tortoise-shell, s. Écaille f.

tortuous, a. Tortueux.

torture[1], s. Torture f, supplice m.

torture[2], v.tr. Torturer ; mettre au supplice.

toss[1], s. **I.** Action f de jeter. (a) Lancement m. (b) Coup m de pile ou face. **2.** T. of the head, mouvement de tête dédaigneux. **3.** Chute f de cheval.

toss[2]. **I.** v.tr. (a) Lancer, jeter ; démonter. (b) Abs. To t. for, jouer à pile ou face. (c) To t. one's head, relever la tête d'un air dédaigneux. (d) Secouer, ballotter. **2.** v.i. S'agiter. (b) To pitch and t., tanguer.

tossing, s. **I.** Lancement m. **2.** Agitation f, ballottement m.

toss-up, s. **I.** Coup m de pile ou face. **2.** Affaire f à issue douteuse.

tot, v.tr. To tot up, additionner.

total. I. a. Total, -aux ; complet, -ète ; global, -aux. **2.** s. Total m ; montant m. **Grand t.,** total global.

totalizator, s. Totalisateur m.

totally, adv. Totalement, complètement.

totter, v.i. Chanceler.

tottering, a. Chancelant.

touch[1], s. **I.** Attouchement m. **2.** Toucher m. **3.** (a) Léger coup. (b) Touche f. To give the finishing touches, mettre la dernière main. **4.** Pointe f ; soupçon m. **5.** Contact m.

touch[2]. **I.** v.tr. **I.** (a) Toucher. (b) Effleurer. To t. a spring, faire jouer un ressort. (c) v.ind.tr. To t. on, toucher, effleurer. (d) Toucher, atteindre. (e) I never t. wine, jamais je ne bois de vin. **2.** Toucher, émouvoir.
 II. touch, v.i. **I.** Se toucher. (a) Être en contact. (b) Venir en contact. **2.** To t. at, faire escale à.

touching. I. a. Touchant, émouvant. **2.** prep. Touchant, concernant.

touchy, a. Susceptible, ombrageux.

tough, a. Dur, résistant ; coriace.

toughen, v.tr. & i. Durcir.

toughness, s. **I.** Dureté f ; résistance f. **2.** Force f, solidité f.

tour, s. **I.** Tour m ; excursion f. **Walking t.,** excursion à pied. **2.** Tournée f.

tourist, s. Touriste mf.

tourist agency, s. Bureau m de tourisme.

tourist ticket, s. Billet m d'excursion.

tournament, s. Tournoi m (de tennis) ; concours m (d'échecs).

tow[1], s. Remorque f.

tow[2], v.tr. Remorquer ; touer ; haler.

tow[3], s. Étoupe f ; filasse f.

towards, prep. **I.** Vers ; du côté de. **2.** Envers ; pour, à l'égard de.

towel, s. Serviette f ; essuie-main(s) m inv.

tower[1], s. (a) Tour f. (b) Church t., clocher m.

tower[2], v.i. **I.** To t. over, dominer. **2.** Monter très haut.

towering, a. **I.** Très haut. **2.** Violent.

towing, s. Remorque f ; touage m, halage m.

tow-line, s. Remorque f ; corde f de halage.

town, s. **I.** Ville f ; cité f. **2.** (a) A man about t., un mondain. (b) He is out of t., il est à la campagne.

town-clerk, s. Greffier municipal.

town-council, s. Conseil municipal.

town-hall, s. Hôtel m de ville.

town-house, s. Hôtel m.

town-planning, s. Urbanisme m ; aménagement m des villes.

township, s. Commune f.

townsman, s. Bourgeois m, citadin m. Fellow t., concitoyen m.

townspeople, s.pl. **I.** Bourgeois m. **2.** Concitoyens m.

tow-path, s. Chemin m de halage.

toy, s. Jouet m ; joujou m, -oux.

toy-shop, s. Magasin m de jouets.

trace[1], s. Trace f, vestige m.

trace[2], v.tr. **I.** Tracer. **2.** Calquer. **3.** Trouver trace de.

tracery, s. **I.** Réseau m ; découpures fpl. **2.** Réseau, nervures fpl.

tracing, s. **I.** (a) Tracé m. (b) Calquage m. **2.** Dessin calqué ; calque m.

tracing-paper, s. Papier m à calquer.

track[1], s. **I.** Erre f, trace f, piste f. To keep t. of, ne pas perdre de vue. To throw off the t., dépister. **2.** Route f, chemin m. **3.** Voie (ferrée).

track[2], v.tr. Suivre à la piste ; traquer. To t. down, dépister.

trackless, a. Sans chemins.

tract[1], s. Étendue f ; région f.

tract[2], s. Brochure f ; tract m.

tractable, *a.* Docile ; traitable.

traction, *s.* Traction *f.*

tractor, *s.* Tracteur *m.*

trade[1], *s.* **1.** État *m*, emploi *m* ; commerce *m* ; métier *m.* **2.** Commerce, négoce *m*, affaires *fpl.* **3.** Commerçants *mpl.* **4.** *Attrib.* **T. price,** prix marchand.

trade[2]. **1.** *v.i.* Faire le commerce, le négoce (*in*, de) ; trafiquer. **2.** *v.tr.* Troquer.

trade-mark, *s.* Marque *f* de fabrique.

trader, *s.* Négociant, -ante ; commerçant, -ante ; marchand, -ande.

tradesman, *s.* Marchand *m*, boutiquier *m*, fournisseur *m.*

tradespeople, *s.pl.* Commerçants *m.*

trade-union, *s.* Syndicat ouvrier.

trade-unionist, *s.* Syndiqué, -ée.

trading, *s.* Commerce *m*, négoce *m.*

tradition, *s.* Tradition *f.*

traditional, *a.* Traditionnel.

traduce, *v.tr.* Calomnier, diffamer.

traffic[1], *s.* **1.** Trafic *m* (*in*, de). **2.** Mouvement *m*, circulation *f.*

traffic[2], *v.i.* Trafiquer ; faire le commerce (*in*, de).

tragedy, *s.* Tragédie *f.*

tragic, *a.* Tragique.

tragically, *adv.* Tragiquement.

trail[1], *s.* **1.** Traînée *f.* **2.** (*a*) Piste *f*, trace *f.* (*b*) Sentier *m* ; piste.

trail[2]. **I.** *v.tr.* **1.** Traîner (après soi). **2.** Traquer.
  II. trail, *v.i.* **1.** Traîner. **2. To t. along,** se traîner. **3.** Ramper.

trailer, *s.* Baladeuse *f.*

trailing, *a.* Grimpant ; rampant.

train[1], *s.* **1.** Traîne *f*, queue *f.* **2.** Suite *f*, équipage *m.* **3.** (*a*) Train, convoi *m* ; succession *f.* **T. of thought,** chaîne *f* d'idées. (*b*) Traînée *f.* **4.** (*a*) Train. **To get into the t.,** monter en wagon. (*b*) Rame *f* (du Métro).

train[2]. **I.** *v.tr.* **1.** (*a*) Former, instruire ; dresser ; exercer. (*b*) Entraîner. **2.** Diriger. **2.** Pointer ; braquer.
  II. train, *v.i.* (*a*) S'exercer. (*b*) S'entraîner.

trainer, *s.* **1.** Dresseur *m.* **2.** Entraîneur *m.*

training, *s.* (*a*) Éducation *f*, instruction *f.* (*b*) Entraînement *m.* **To go into t.,** s'entraîner. (*c*) Dressage.

trait, *s.* Trait *m.*

traitor, *s.* Traître *m.*

traitorous, *a.* Traître, *f.* traîtresse ; perfide.

traitress, *s.* Traîtresse *f.*

tram, *s.* Tramway *m.* **T. driver,** conducteur *m* de tramway ; wattman *m.* **T. conductor,** receveur, -euse.

tram-car, *s.* (Voiture *f* de) tramway *m.*

tramp[1], *s.* **1.** Bruit *m* de pas marqués. **2.** Marche *f* ; promenade *f* à pied. **3.** Chemineau *m.*

tramp[2], *v.i.* **1.** Marcher lourdement. **2.** (*a*) Marcher ; voyager à pied. (*b*) Vagabonder. *v.tr.* **To t. the streets,** battre le pavé.

trample. **I.** *v.i.* **To t. on,** piétiner, écraser. **2.** *v.tr.* **To t. under foot,** fouler aux pieds.

trampling, *s.* Piétinement *m* ; bruit *m* de pas.

tramway, *s.* Voie *f* de tramway.

trance, *s.* (*a*) Extase *f.* (*b*) Transe *f.*

tranquil, *a.* Tranquille ; calme.

tranquillity, *s.* Tranquillité *f.*

tranquilly, *adv.* Tranquillement, paisiblement.

transact, *v.tr.* **To t. business,** faire des affaires.

transaction, *s.* **1.** Conduite *f.* **2. Cash t.,** opération au comptant. **3.** *pl.* Transactions *f.*

transcend, *v.tr.* Surpasser.

transcribe, *v.tr.* Transcrire.

transcription, *s.* Transcription *f.*

transept, *s.* Transept *m.*

transfer[1], *s.* **1.** (*a*) Translation *f*, transport *m* ; déplacement *m.* **T. ticket,** billet de correspondance. (*b*) Transfert *m.* **2.** Acte *m* de cession.

transfer[2], *v.tr.* Transférer. (*a*) Déplacer. (*b*) Transmettre, céder.

transferable, *a.* Transmissible. 'Not t.,' strictement personnel.

transferee, *s.* Cessionnaire *mf.*

transferor, *s.* Cédant, -ante.

transfigure, *v.tr.* Transfigurer.

transfix, *v.tr.* Transpercer.

transform, *v.tr.* Transformer ; métamorphoser.

transformation, *s.* **1.** (*a*) Transformation *f* ; métamorphose *f.* (*b*) Conversion *f.* **2.** Faux toupet ; transformation.

transformer, *s.* Transformateur *m.*

transfuse, *v.tr.* Transfuser.

transfusion, *s.* Transfusion *f.*

transgress, *v.tr.* Transgresser. *Abs.* Pécher. **To t. a rule,** violer une règle.

transgression, *s.* (a) Transgression *f,* violation *f.* (b) Péché *m,* faute *f.*

transgressor, *s.* Transgresseur *m.*

transient, *a.* Transitoire ; passager.

transit, *s.* Passage *m.*

transition, *s.* Transition *f* ; passage *m.*

transitory, *a.* Transitoire ; fugitif

translate, *v.tr.* Traduire.

translation, *s.* Traduction *f*

translator, *s.* Traducteur *m.*

translucent, *a.* Translucide.

transmission, *s.* Transmission *f.*

transmit, *v.tr.* Transmettre.

transmitter, *s.* (a) Transmetteur *m.* (b) Émetteur *m.*

transmitting, *a.* (a) Transmetteur *m.* (b) **T. station,** poste émetteur

transmutation, *s.* Transmutation *f.*

transmute, *v.tr.* Transformer.

transparency, *s.* (a) Transparence *f.* (b) Limpidité *f.*

transparent, *a.* **1.** Transparent ; limpide. **2.** Évident, clair.

transpierce, *v.tr.* Transpercer.

transpire. (a) Transpirer. (b) Se passer.

transport¹, *s.* Transport *m.*

transport², *v.tr.* Transporter.

transpose, *v.tr.* Transposer.

transposition, *s.* Transposition *f.*

transverse, *a.* Transversal, -aux.

trap¹, *s.* **1.** Piège *m.* **2.** Cabriolet *m.*

trap², *v.tr.* Prendre au piège ; cerner.

trap-door, *s.* Trappe *f.*

trapeze, *s.* Trapèze *m.*

trash, *s.* Chose(s) *f(pl)* sans valeur ; camelote *f.*

trashy, *a.* Sans valeur.

travel¹, *s.* Voyages *mpl.*

travel², *v.i.* **1.** (a) Voyager ; faire des voyages. **He is travelling,** il est en voyage. (b) Aller ; circuler. **2.** Être voyageur de commerce.

traveller, *s.* **1.** Voyageur, -euse. **Traveller's cheque,** chèque de voyage. **2.** Commis voyageur.

travelling, *s.* Voyages *mpl* **T. bag,** sac de voyage.

traverse, *v.tr.* Traverser.

travesty¹, *s.* Parodie *f* ; travestissement *m.*

travesty², *v.tr.* Parodier, travestir.

trawler, *s.* Chalutier *m*

tray, *s.* Plateau *m.*

tray-cloth, *s.* Dessus *m.* napperon *m,* de plateau.

treacherous, *a.* Traître : perfide ; infidèle.

treacherously, *adv.* En traître, perfidement.

treachery, *s.* Trahison *f,* perfidie *f*

treacle, *s.* Mélasse *f.*

tread¹, *s.* (a) Pas *m.* (b) Bruit *m* de pas.

tread². **I.** *v.i.* Marcher ; poser les pieds. **To t. on,** mettre le pied sur. **2.** *v.tr.* **To t. under foot,** fouler aux pieds.

treadle, *s.* Pédale *f.*

treason, *s.* Trahison *f.*

treasonable, *a.* **1.** De trahison. **2.** Traître, perfide.

treasure¹, *s.* Trésor *m.*

treasure², *v.tr.* Priser.

treasurer, *s.* Trésorier, -ière.

treasury, *s.* Trésor ; trésorerie *f.*

treat¹, *s.* **1.** Régal *m,* -als ; festin *m* ; fête *f.* **2.** Plaisir *m.*

treat². **I.** *v.i.* Traiter. **II. treat,** *v.tr.* **1.** Traiter. **2.** Régaler ; payer à boire à. **To t. oneself to,** s'offrir, se payer.

treatise, *s.* Traité *m* (on, de).

treatment, *s.* Traitement *m.*

treaty, *s.* **1.** Traité *m* ; convention *f.* **2.** Accord *m,* contrat *m*

treble¹. **I.** *a.* Triple. **II. treble,** *adv.* Trois fois autant. **III. treble,** *s.* **1.** Triple *m.* **2.** Soprano *m.*

treble², *v.tr.* Tripler.

trebly, *adv.* Triplement

tree, *s.* Arbre *m.*

tree-trunk, *s.* Tronc *m* d'arbre.

trefoil, *s.* Trèfle *m.*

trellis, *s.* Treillis *m,* treillage *m.*

trellis-work, *s.* Treillis *m,* treillage *m.*

tremble¹, *s.* Frisson *m* ; tremblotement *m.*

tremble², *v.i.* **1.** Trembler, vibrer. **2.** Trembler, frissonner.

trembling¹, *a.* Tremblant, remblotant

trembling², *s.* Tremblement *m* ; tremblotement *m.*

tremendous, *a.* **1.** Terrible. **2.** Immense.

tremor, *s.* Tremblement *m* ; frémissement *m.*

17.

tremulous, *a* Tremblant, frémissant ; timide. **T. voice,** voix chevrotante.

tremulously, *adv* En tremblant.

trench, *s.* Tranchée *f.*

trenchant, *a.* Tranchant, incisif.

trend, *s.* Direction *f* ; tendance *f.*

trepidation, *s.* Trépidation *f.*

trespass, *v.i.* **1.** Pécher. **2.** (*a*) Empiéter. (*b*) To t. upon, abuser de.

trespasser, *s.* Auteur *m* d'une violation de propriété.

tress, *s.* Tresse *f,* boucle *f.*

trestle, *s.* Tréteau *m,* chevalet *m.*

trial, *s.* **1.** (*a*) Jugement *m.* (*b*) Procès *m.* **Famous trials,** causes *f* célèbres. **2.** Essai *m.* (*a*) Épreuve *f.* (*b*) On t., à l'essai. (**3**) Épreuve douloureuse.

triangle, *s.* Triangle *m.*

triangular, *a.* Triangulaire

tribe, *s.* Tribu *f.*

tribulation, *s.* Tribulation *f.* affliction *f.*

tribunal, *s.* Tribunal *m,* -aux.

tributary. **1.** *a.* Tributaire. **2.** *s.* (*a*) Tributaire *m.* (*b*) Affluent *m.*

tribute, *s.* Tribut *m.*

trick¹, *s.* **1.** (*a*) Tour *m,* ruse *f* ; supercherie *f.* (*b*) Truc *m.* **2.** Farce *f,* tour. **3.** Tour d'adresse. **4.** Manie *f,* habitude *f.* **5.** Levée *f.*

trick², *v.tr.* Attraper, duper.

trickery, *s.* Fourberie *f,* tricherie *f.*

trickle¹, *s.* Filet *m.*

trickle², *v.i.* Couler (goutte à goutte).

trickling, *s.* Écoulement *m* goutte à goutte.

tricky, *a.* Rusé, astucieux, fin.

tricycle, *s.* Tricycle *m.*

tried, *a.* Éprouvé.

trifle¹, *s.* **1.** (*a*) Bagatelle *f,* vétille *f.* (*b*) *Adv.phr.* A t., un tout petit peu ; un soupçon. **2.** Charlotte *f* russe sur biscuit de Savoie.

trifle², **1.** *v.i.* (*a*) Jouer, badiner. **To t. with,** se jouer de. (*b*) S'occuper à des riens. **2.** *v.tr.* **To t. one's time away,** gâcher son temps.

trifler, *s.* Personne *f* frivole.

trifling¹, *a.* Insignifiant ; peu important.

trifling², *s.* **1.** Manque *m* de sérieux. **2.** Futilités *fpl.*

trigger, *s.* Détente *f* ; gâchette *f.*

trim¹, *s.* **1.** Bon ordre. **In good t.,** en forme. **2.** Coupe *f.*

trim², *a.* Soigné ; en bon état.

trim³, *v.tr.* **1.** Tailler. **2.** Orner, parer (*with,* de).

trimming, *s.* **1.** Taille *f.* **2.** (*a*) Garnissage *m.* (*b*) Garniture *f,* ornement *m.*

Trinity, *s.* Trinité *f.*

trinket, *s.* (*a*) Petit objet de parure ; breloque *f.* (*b*) Bibelot *m.*

trio, *s.* Trio *m.*

trip¹, *s.* Excursion *f* ; voyage *m* d'agrément. **Round t.,** croisière *f.*

trip², **1.** *v.i.* Trébucher ; faire un faux pas. **2.** *v.tr.* Donner un croc-en-jambe à ; faire trébucher.

tripe, *s.* Tripes *fpl.*

triple¹, *a.* Triple.

triplicate, *s* In t., en triple exemplaire.

triply, *adv.* Triplement.

tripod, *s.* Trépied *m.*

tripper, *s.* Excursionniste *mf.*

trite, *a.* Banal, -aux.

triumph¹, *s.* Triomphe *m,* succès *m.*

triumph², *v.i.* Triompher (*over,* de).

triumphal, *a.* Triomphal, -aux ; de triomphe.

triumphant, *a.* Triomphant.

triumphantly, *adv.* Triomphalement.

trivial, *a.* **1.** Insignifiant ; sans importance. **2.** Banal, -aux ; trivial, -aux.

trolley, *s.* (*a*) Fardier *m,* chariot *m.* (*b*) Dinner t., serveuse *f.*

trombone, *s.* Trombone *m.*

troop¹, *s.* Troupe *f* ; bande *f.*

troop², *v.i.* **To t. together,** s'attrouper, s'assembler.

trooper, *s.* Cavalier *m*

trophy, *s.* Trophée *m.*

tropic. **1.** *s.* Tropique *m.* **In the tropics,** sous les tropiques. **2.** *a.* Tropical, -aux.

tropical, *a.* Tropical. -aux ; des tropiques.

trot¹, *s.* Trot *m.*

trot², *v.i.* Trotter ; aller au trot.

trouble¹, *s.* **1.** Peine *f,* chagrin *m* ; affliction *f.* **2.** Ennui *m,* difficulté *f.* (*a*) To get into t., s'attirer des ennuis. (*b*) To make t., semer la discorde. **3.** Dérangement *m,* peine. **To put to t.,** déranger. **To have all one's t. for nothing,** en être pour sa peine. **4.** (*a*) Dérangement. **To have heart t., être malade du cœur   (b) **Engine t.,** panne f du moteur.

trouble². **1.** v.tr. (a) Affliger, tourmenter; inquiéter. (b) Affliger, faire souffrir. (c) Déranger, incommoder, gêner. **To t. oneself to,** se donner la peine de. **2.** v.i. (a) S'inquiéter. (b) Se déranger: se mettre en peine.

troubled, a. **1.** Trouble. **2.** Inquiet, -ète; agité.

troublesome, a. **1.** Ennuyeux, gênant. **How t.!** quel ennui! **2.** Difficile, pénible.

trough, s. **1.** Auge f; abreuvoir m. **2.** T. of the sea, creux m de la lame.

trounce, v.tr. Rosser, étriller.

trouncing, s. Raclée f; étrillage m.

troupe, s. Troupe f.

trouser, s. (Pair of) trousers, pantalon m.

trouser-clip, s. Pince f à pantalon.

trouser-press, s. Presse f pour pantalons.

trousseau, s.inv. Trousseau m.

trout, s.inv. Truite f.

trowel, s. **1.** Truelle f. **2.** Déplantoir m.

truant, s. Élève absent(e) (de l'école) sans permission. **To play t.,** faire l'école buissonnière.

truce, s. Trêve f.

truck, s. **1.** (a) Fardier m, camion m, chariot m. (b) Chariot à bagages. **2.** Wagon m (à marchandises).

truculence, s. Truculence f.

truculent, a. Truculent.

trudge, v.i. Marcher lourdement, péniblement.

true. **I.** a. **1.** Vrai; exact. **To come t.,** se réaliser. **2.** Véritable; vrai, réel. **3.** Juste, droit. **4.** Fidèle, loyal, -aux.
     II. true, adv **1.** Vraiment; vrai. **2.** Juste.

truffle, s. Truffe f.

truism, s. Truisme m, axiome m.

truly, adv. **1.** Vraiment, véritablement. **2.** En vérité. **3.** Fidèlement. **4.** Avec vérité; justement.

trump¹, s. Atout m.

trump², v.tr. **1.** Couper. **2.** To t. up, forger.

trumpet¹, s. Trompette f.

trumpet², v.i. Sonner de la trompette.

trumpeter, s. Trompette m.

trumpeting, s. Sonnerie f de trompette.

truncheon, s. Bâton m

trunk, s. **1.** Tronc m. **2.** Malle f, coffre m. **3.** Trompe f.

trunk-call, s. Appel m à longue distance.

truss, v.tr. **1.** Renforcer. **2.** Trousser.

trust¹, s. **1.** Confiance f. **2.** Espérance f, espoir m. **3.** (a) Responsabilité f. (b) Garde f. **4.** Trust m, syndicat m.

trust². **1.** v.tr. (a) Se fier à; mettre sa confiance en. **To t. s.o. with sth.,** confier qch. à qn. (b) Faire crédit à. (c) Espérer. **2.** v.i. (a) Se confier; se fier. (b) Mettre ses espérances (to, en).

trusted, a. De confiance.

trustee, s. **1.** (a) Curateur, -trice. (b) Dépositaire mf **2.** Administrateur, -trice.

trustful, a Plein de confiance; confiant.

trustfully, adv. Avec confiance.

trustfulness, s. Confiance f.

trustiness, s. Fidélité f, loyauté f.

trusting, a. Plein de confiance.

trustworthiness, s. **1.** Loyauté f, fidélité f. **2.** Crédibilité f, exactitude f.

trustworthy, a. **1.** Digne de confiance; honnête. **2.** Croyable, exact.

truth, s. Vérité f.

truthful, a. **1.** Véridique **2.** Vrai; fidèle.

truthfully, adv **1.** Véridiquement. **2.** Fidèlement.

truthfulness, s. Véracité f.

try¹, s. Essai m, tentative f. **At the first try,** du premier coup.

try². **I.** v.tr. **1.** (a) Éprouver; mettre à l'épreuve. (b) Éprouver; affliger. **2.** Essayer; faire l'essai de. **3.** Juger **4.** Essayer; tâcher.
     II. try, v.i. **To try for,** tâcher d'obtenir. **try on,** v.tr. Essayer. **try out,** v.tr. Essayer à fond.

trying, a. **1.** Difficile, pénible. **2.** Vexant; contrariant

tub, s. **1.** Baquet m, bac m **2.** (Bath-)tub, tub m

tube, s. **1.** Tube m; tuyau m. **Inner t.,** chambre f à air. **2.** Voie souterraine.

tuberculosis, s. Tuberculose f.

tubing, s. Tuyautage m, tubes mpl

tubular, a. Tubulaire.

tuck[1], *s* (Petit) pli ; rempli *m*

tuck[2], *v.tr.* Replier, mettre. **tuck in**, *v.tr.* Serrer ; replier. **To t. in the bed-clothes**, border le lit.

Tuesday, *s* Mardi *m* **Shrove T.**, (le) mardi gras.

tuft, *s.* 1. Touffe *f.* 2. Toupet *m.*

tug[1], *s.* 1. Traction *f* ; saccade *f.* 2. Remorqueur *m.*

tug[2], *v.tr. & i.* Tirer avec effort. **To tug at**, tirer sur.

tug-boat, *s.* Remorqueur *m*

tuition, *s.* Instruction *f*

tulip, *s.* Tulipe *f.*

tulle, *s.* Tulle *m.*

tumble[1], *s.* Culbute *f*, chute *f.*

tumble[2]. 1. *v.i.* Tomber ; faire une chute. 2. *v.tr.* Bouleverser, déranger.

tumble-down. *attrib.a.* Croulant, délabré.

tumbler, *s.* Verre *m* sans pied

tumult, *s.* Tumulte *m.*

tumultuous, *a.* Tumultueux.

tune[1], *s.* 1. Air *m.* 2. Accord *m.* **To sing out of t.**, chanter faux.

tune[2], *v.tr.* 1. Accorder, mettre d'accord. 2. **To t. in (to)**, capter. *Abs.* **To t. in**, accorder le récepteur.

tuneful, *a.* Mélodieux, harmonieux.

tunic, *s.* Tunique *f.*

tuning, *s.* Accordage *m*, accord *m.*

tuning-fork, *s* Diapason *m.*

tunnel, *s.* Tunnel *m*

tunny, *s.* Thon *m.*

turban, *s.* Turban *m*

turbid, *a.* Trouble.

turbidity, *s.* Turbidité *f.*

turbine, *s.* Turbine *f.*

turbot, *s.* Turbot *m.*

turbulence, *s.* Turbulence *f.*

turbulent, *a.* Turbulent

tureen, *s.* Soupière *f*

turf, *s.* Gazon *m.*

Turk, *s.* Turc, *f.* Turque.

Turkey[1]. *Pr.n.* La Turquie.

turkey[2], *s.* 1. Dindon *m.* **Young t.**, dindonneau *m* 2. Dinde *f.* dindonneau.

turkey-cock, *s.* Dindon *m.*

turkey-hen, *s.* Dinde *f.*

Turkish. 1. *a.* Turc, *f.* turque ; de Turquie. 2. *s.* Le turc **T. delight**, rahat, loukoum *m.*

turmoil, *s.* Trouble *m* ; agitation *f.*

turn[1], *s.* 1. Tour *m*, révolution *f.* 2. (*a*) Changement *m* de direction ;

virage *m.* (*b*) Tournure *f.* (*c*) **T. of the tide**, changement de la marée. 3. (*a*) Tour **It is your t. (to play)**, c'est à vous de jouer. **In t.**, tour à tour ; à tour de rôle. (*b*) Numéro *m.* 4. **To do a good t.**, rendre service à. 5. **To have a t. for**, avoir des dispositions pour. 6. Tournant *m*, coude *m.* **Sharp t.**, crochet *m*, virage *m.*

turn[2]. I. *v.tr.* 1. Tourner, faire tourner. 2. Donner un autre tour à. 3. Tourner, retourner. 4. Changer, transformer

II. **turn**, *v.i.* 1. Tourner. 2. Se tourner, se retourner. 3. Tourner, se diriger. **To t. to s.o.**, avoir recours à qn. 4. (*a*) **The tide is turning**, la marée change. (*b*) **To t. against**, se retourner contre. 5. (*a*) Se changer, se convertir. (*b*) Devenir **turn aside.** 1. *v.tr.* Détourner. 2. *v.i.* Se détourner, s'écarter. **turn away.** 1. *v.tr.* (*a*) Détourner. (*b*) Renvoyer, congédier. 2. *v.i.* Se détourner. **turn back.** 1. *v.tr.* (*a*) Faire retourner. (*b*) Retrousser. 2. *v.i.* S'en retourner ; rebrousser chemin. **turn down**, *v.tr.* 1. (*a*) Rabattre. (*b*) Faire un pli à. 2. Baisser. **turn off**, *v.tr.* 1. Fermer, couper. 2. Renvoyer, congédier. **turn on**, *v.tr.* Ouvrir. **turn out.** I. *v.tr.* 1. Mettre dehors ; évincer. 2. Vider. 3. Produire. 4. Couper, éteindre. II. **turn out**, *v.i.* 1. (*a*) **As it turned out**, comme il arriva. (*b*) Apparaître ; se trouver. **turn over.** I. *v.tr.* Retourner ; tourner. 2. *v.i.* Se tourner, se retourner ; verser. **turn round.** 1. *v.tr.* Retourner. 2. *v.i.* (*a*) Tourner. (*b*) Se retourner. **turn up.** I. *v.tr.* 1. (*a*) Relever ; retrousser. (*b*) Trouver, se reporter à. 2. Remonter. II. **turn up**, *v.i.* Se relever, se retrousser.

turncoat, *s.* Renégat, -ate.

turning[1], *a.* Tournant ; qui tourne.

turning[2], *s.* 1. (*a*) Rotation *f.* (*b*) Virage *m* ; changement *m* de direction. (*c*) Changement. 2. Tournant *m* ; coude *m* ; virage. **The first t. to the right**, la première à droite.

turning-point, *s.* Point décisif

turnip, *s.* Navet *m.*

turn-over, *s.* 1. (*a*) Chiffre *m*

d'affaires. (b) Écoulement m. **2.
Apple t.-o.,** chausson m aux pommes.
turnstile, s. Tourniquet m.
turpentine, s. Térébenthine f
turquoise, s. Turquoise f
turret, s. Tourelle f.
turtle, s. Tortue f de mer. **To turn
t.,** chavirer.
turtle-dove, s. Tourterelle f.
turtle-soup, s. Potage m à la tortue.
tusk, s. Défense f.
tussle¹, s. Lutte f, mêlée f
tussle², v.i. Lutter.
tutor, s. **1.** Directeur m des études.
2. Private t., précepteur m
twaddle, s. Fadaises fpl.
twang¹, s. **1.** Son aigu. **2.** Nasal t.,
ton nasillard. **To speak with a t.,**
nasiller.
twang², v.i Résonner
tweak, v.tr. Pincer.
tweed, s Cheviote écossaise.
tweezers, s.pl. Petite pince.
twelfth, num. a. & s. Douzième.
(On) the t. of May, le douze mai.
Twelfth-night, s. Veille f des Rois.
twelve, num. a. & s Douze (m).
T. o'clock, midi m; minuit m.
Half past t., midi, minuit, et demi.
twelvemonth, s Année f.
twentieth, num. a. & s. Vingtième
(m). **(On) the t. of June,** le vingt
juin.
twenty, num. a. & s Vingt (m).
T.-first, vingt et unième. **The t.-first
of May,** le vingt et un mai **About
t.,** une vingtaine de.
twice, adv. Deux fois **T. as big,**
deux fois aussi grand. **T. over,** à
deux reprises.
twig, s. Brindille f; ramille f.
twilight, s. **1.** Crépuscule m. **2.**
Attrib. Crépusculaire.
twill, s. Croisé m; twill m.
twin, a. & s. **1.** Jumeau -elle **2.** a
T. beds, lits jumeaux.
twine¹, s. Ficelle f.
twine², **1.** v.tr. Tordre, tortiller;
enrouler. **2.** v.i. (a) Se tordre, se
tortiller. (b) Serpenter.
twinge, s. Élancement m.
twinkle¹, s. **1.** Scintillement m, clignotement m. **2.** Pétillement m.
twinkle², v.i. **1.** Scintiller, clignoter.
2. His eyes twinkled, ses yeux
pétillaient.

twinkling, s. **1.** Scintillement m.
2. Pétillement m.
twirl¹, s. Tournoiement m.
twirl². **1.** v.tr. (a) Faire tournoyer. (b)
Tortiller, friser. **2.** v.i. Tournoyer
twist¹, s. **1.** Fil m retors; cordon m;
cordonnet m. **2. To give sth. a t.,**
exercer une torsion sur qch. **3.**
Twists and turns, tours et retours.
4. Perversion f.
twist². **1.** v.tr. (a) Tordre, tortiller.
(b) **To t.** one's ankle, se fouler la
cheville. **2.** v.i. (a) Se tordre; se
tortiller. (b) Tourner; faire des
détours. **To t. and turn,** serpenter.
twisted, a. Tordu, tors.
twit, v.tr. Taquiner; railler.
twitch¹, s. **1.** Saccade f; petit coup
sec. **2.** Mouvement convulsif.
twitch². **1.** v.tr. Tirer vivement;
donner une saccade à. **2.** v.i. Se
contracter nerveusement; se crisper
nerveusement.
twitter¹, s. Gazouillement m.
twitter², v.i. Gazouiller.
twittering, s. Gazouillement m.
two, num. a. & s. Deux (m).
twofold. **1.** a. Double. **2.** adv.
Doublement.
two-seater, s. Avion m ou voiture f
à deux places.
two-step, s. Pas m de deux.
type¹, s. **1.** Type m; genre m. **2.** (a)
Caractère m, type. (b) Coll. Caractères.
type², v.tr. Écrire à la machine;
dactylographier.
type-script, s. Manuscrit dactylo-
graphié.
typewriter, s. Machine f à écrire.
typewriting, s. Dactylographie f.
typhoid, a. Typhoïde.
typical, a. Typique.
typically, adv. D'une manière
typique.
typist, s. Dactylo(graphe) mf.
tyrannical, a. Tyrannique.
tyrannically, adv. Tyranniquement;
en tyran.
tyrannize, v.i. Faire le tyran **To
t.** over, tyranniser.
tyranny, s. Tyrannie f.
tyrant, s. Tyran m.
tyre, s. (a) Bandage m, cercle m.
(b) **Pneumatic t.,** pneu(matique) m.
tyro, s. Novice mf.

U

U, u, s. (La lettre) U, u m.

ubiquitous, a. Qui se trouve partout.

udder, s. Mamelle f, pis m.

ugliness, s. Laideur f.

ugly, a. Laid ; disgracieux. **To grow u.,** enlaidir.

ulcer, s. Ulcère m.

ulterior, a. **1.** Ultérieur, -eure. **2. U. motive,** motif secret, caché

ultimate, a. Final, -als.

ultimately, adv. A la fin ; en fin de compte.

ultimatum, s. Ultimatum m.

ultimo, adv. Du mois dernier.

ultra, a. Extrême.

ultramarine, a. & s. Outremer m inv.

umber, s. Terre f d'ombre.

umbrage, s. Ombrage m.

umbrella, s. Parapluie m.

umbrella-stand, s. Porte-parapluies m inv.

umpire[1], s. Arbitre m, juge m.

umpire[2], v.tr. Arbitrer.

unabated, a. Non diminué.

unable, a. Incapable. **We are u.,** nous ne pouvons pas.

unacceptable, a. Inacceptable.

unaccompanied, a. Inaccompagné. seul.

unaccountable, a. Inexplicable.

unaccountably, adv. Inexplicablement.

unaccustomed, a. Peu habitué.

unacquainted, a. **To be u. with,** ignorer.

unadorned, a. Sans ornement.

unadulterated, a. Pur.

unaffected, a. Sans affectation. (a) Sincère. (b) Sans pose.

unaided, a. Sans aide ; tout seul.

unalterable, a. Immuable, invariable.

unaltered, a. Toujours le même ; sans changement ; tel quel.

unanimity, s. Unanimité f

unanimous, a. Unanime.

unanimously, adv. A l'unanimité

unanswerable, a. Sans réplique.

unappeased, a. Inapaisé.

unappetizing, a. Peu appétissant.

unappreciated, a. Inapprécié.

unapproachable, a. **1.** Inabordable. **2.** Incomparable.

unarmed, a. Sans armes.

unascertained, a. Non vérifié.

unashamed, a. Sans honte.

unasked, a. Spontanément.

unassuming, a. Modeste.

unattainable, a. Inaccessible (by, à) ; hors de la portée (by, de).

unattended, a. Seul ; sans escorte.

unattractive, a. Peu attrayant ; peu sympathique.

unauthorized, a. Inautorisé ; sans autorisation.

unavailing, a. Inutile ; vain.

unavoidable, a. (a) Inévitable. (b) Qu'on ne peut prévenir.

unavoidably, adv. **1.** Inévitablement. **2. U. absent,** absent pour raison majeure.

unavowed, a. Inavoué.

unaware, a. Ignorant. **To be u. of,** ignorer.

unawares, adv. A l'improviste.

unbearable, a. Insupportable.

unbearably, adv. Insupportablement.

unbeaten, a. Non battu.

unbecoming, a. **1.** Peu convenable ; déplacé. **2.** Peu seyant.

unbelievable, a. Incroyable.

unbeliever, s. Incrédule mf.

unbelieving, a. Incrédule.

unbend, v.i. Se détendre.

unbending, a. Inflexible, raide.

unbiassed, a. Impartial, -aux.

unbidden, a. **1.** Non invité ; intrus. **2.** Spontané.

unbind, v.tr. Délier.

unbleached, a. Écru.

unblemished, a. Sans tache.

unbounded, a. Sans bornes ; illimité ; démesuré.

unbreakable, a. Incassable.

unbridled, a. Débridé, effréné.

unbroken, a. (a) Non brisé, non cassé. (b) Intact. (c) Ininterrompu.

unburden, v.tr. Soulager ; alléger. **To u. oneself,** se délester le cœur.

unbusinesslike, a. Peu pratique.

unbutton, v.tr. Déboutonner.

uncanny, a. Mystérieux.

unceasing, a. Incessant, continu.

unceasingly, adv. Sans cesse.

unceremonious, a. Sans façon, sans gêne.

unceremoniously, *adv.* **1.** Sans cérémonie. **2.** Sans façons.

uncertain, *a.* Incertain. **1.** (*a*) Indéterminé. (*b*) Douteux. **2.** Mal assuré.

uncertainty, *s.* Incertitude *f.*

unchallenged, *a.* Indisputé.

unchanged, *a.* Inchangé ; toujours le même.

unchanging, *a.* Invariable immuable.

uncharitable, *a.* Peu charitable

unchecked, *a.* Sans frein.

uncivil, *a.* Incivil, impoli.

uncivilized, *a.* Incivilisé, barbare

uncivilly, *adv.* Impoliment.

unclaimed, *a.* Non réclamé.

uncle, *s.* Oncle *m.*

unclean, *a.* Impur, immonde.

unclothed, *a.* **1.** Déshabillé. **2.** Nu ; sans vêtements.

unclouded, *a.* Sans nuage ; limpide.

uncoil. 1. *v.tr.* Dérouler. **2.** *v.i.* Se dérouler.

uncomfortable, *a.* **1.** Peu confortable ; incommode. **2.** Désagréable. **3.** To feel u., être mal à l'aise.

uncomfortably, *adv.* **1.** Peu confortablement ; incommodément. **2.** Désagréablement.

uncommon, *a.* Peu commun ; rare ; singulier.

uncomplainingly, *adv.* Sans se plaindre.

uncomplimentary, *a.* Peu flatteur -euse.

uncompromising, *a.* Intransigeant ; intraitable.

unconcerned, *a.* Insouciant.

unconcernedly, *adv.* D'un air indifférent ; avec insouciance.

unconditional, *a.* (*a*) Absolu. (*b*) Sans conditions.

unconditionally, *adv.* Sans réserve.

unconfirmed, *a.* Qui n'est pas confirmé ; sujet, -ette, à caution.

uncongenial, *a.* **1.** Peu sympathique. **2.** (*a*) Peu favorable. (*b*) Ingrat.

unconnected, *a.* (*a*) Sans rapport, sans lien. (*b*) Décousu, sans suite.

unconquerable, *a.* Invincible.

unconscious, *a.* **1.** Inconscient. **2.** Sans connaissance ; évanoui. To become u., perdre connaissance.

unconsciously, *adv.* Inconsciemment.

unconsciousness, *s.* **1.** Inconscience *f.* **2.** Évanouissement *m.*

unconsidered, *a* Inconsidéré, irréfléchi.

unconstrainedly, *adv.* Sans contrainte ; sans aucune gêne ; librement.

uncontrollable, *a* Ingouvernable ; irrésistible.

uncontrollably, *adv* Irrésistiblement.

uncontrolled, *a.* **1.** Indépendant **2.** Absolu ; effréné.

unconventional, *a.* Original, -aux

unconvinced, *a.* Sceptique.

unconvincing, *a.* Peu convaincant.

uncooked, *a.* Non cuit, cru

uncork, *v.tr.* Déboucher.

uncouth, *a.* **1.** Grossier, rude. **2.** Malappris, gauche.

uncover, *v.tr.* Découvrir : mettre à découvert.

unctuous, *a.* Onctueux, graisseux.

uncultivated, *a.* Inculte ; sans culture

uncurbed, *a.* (*a*) Libre ; sans restriction. (*b*) Débridé.

undamaged, *a* Non endommagé ; indemne.

undaunted, *a.* (*a*) Intrépide (*b*) Aucunement intimidé.

undeceive, *v.tr.* Désabuser.

undecided, *a.* (*a*) Indécis (*b*) Irrésolu, hésitant.

undecipherable, *a.* Indéchiffrable.

undefeated, *a.* Invaincu.

undefiled, *a.* Pur ; sans souillure.

undefined, *a* **1.** Non défini. **2.** Indéterminé ; vague.

undemonstrative, *a.* Réservé.

undeniable, *a.* Indéniable, incontestable.

undeniably, *adv.* Incontestablement.

under. I. *prep.* **1.** Sous ; au-dessous de. (*a*) Put it u. that, mettez-le là-dessous. (*b*) U. one's breath, à demi-voix. He is u. thirty, il a moins de trente ans. **2.** (*a*) U. lock and key, sous clef. U. the necessity of, dans la nécessité de. (*b*) To be u. the doctor, être traité par le médecin. **3.** U. repair, en réparation.

II. under, *adv.* **1.** (Au-)dessous. As u., comme ci-dessous. **2.** To keep u., tenir dans la soumission.

under-carriage, *s.* Train *m* d'atterrissage.

underclothes, *s.pl.* Vêtements *mpl* de dessous ; linge *m* de corps ; lingerie *f*.

undercut, *s.* Filet *m* (de bœuf).

underdone, *a.* **1.** Pas assez cuit. **2.** Pas trop cuit ; saignant.

under-exposure, *s.* Sous-exposition *f*.

underfed, *a.* Mal nourri.

underfoot, *adv.* Sous les pieds.

under-garment, *s.* Sous-vêtement *m*.

undergo, *v.tr.* **1.** Subir. **2.** Supporter ; essuyer.

underground. 1. *adv.* (*a*) Sous terre. (*b*) Secrètement ; sous main. **2.** *a.* Souterrain.

undergrowth, *s.* Broussailles *fpl.*

underhand. 1. *adv.* Sous main, sournoisement. **2.** *a.* Secret. -ète ; sournois.

underline, *v.tr.* Souligner.

underlinen, *s.* Linge *m* de corps.

underling, *s.* Subordonné, -ée.

underlying, *a.* **1.** Au-dessous. **2.** Fondamental, -aux. **3.** Caché.

undermentioned, *a.* Sous-mentionné.

undermine, *v.tr.* Miner, saper.

undermost, *a.* Le plus bas, *f.* la plus basse.

underneath. 1. *prep.* Au-dessous de ; sous. From u., de dessous. **2.** *adv.* Au-dessous ; dessous ; par-dessous. **3.** *a.* De dessous ; inférieur, -e.

under-nourished, *a.* Mal nourri.

underpaid, *a.* Mal rétribué.

underrate, *v.tr.* Sous-estimer.

undersigned, *a. & s.* Soussigné. -ée.

under-skirt, *s.* Jupon *m*.

understand, *v.tr.* **1.** Comprendre. (*a*) Se connaître en ; se rendre compte de. (*b*) **To give s.o. to u.,** donner à entendre à qn. **2.** Sous-entendre. **3.** *v.i.* Comprendre.

understandable, *a.* Compréhensible.

understanding, *s.* **1.** Entendement *m*, compréhension *f*. **2.** (*a*) Accord *m*, entente *f*. (*b*) Arrangement *m*. **To come to an u.,** s'entendre. (*c*) **On the u.,** à condition.

understood, *a.* **1.** Compris. **2.** Convenu. **That is u.,** cela va sans dire. **3.** Sous-entendu.

understudy[1], *s.* Doublure *f*.

understudy[2], *v.tr.* Doubler.

undertake, *v.tr.* **1.** Entreprendre. **2.** Se charger de, s'imposer.

undertaker, *s.* Entrepreneur *m* de pompes funèbres.

undertaking, *s.* **1.** Entreprise *f*. **2.** Engagement *m*, promesse *f*.

underwear, *s.* Vêtements *mpl* de dessous ; linge *m* de corps ; lingerie *f*.

undeserved, *a.* Immérité.

undeservedly, *adv.* Injustement.

undeserving, *a.* (*a*) Peu méritant ; sans mérite. (*b*) Indigne.

undesirable, *a. & s.* Indésirable (*mf*)

undeterred, *a.* Non découragé.

undeveloped, *a.* Non développé ; inexploité.

undeviating, *a.* **1.** Droit. direct. **2.** Constant.

undignified, *a.* (*a*) Peu digne. (*b*) **To be u.,** manquer de dignité.

undiluted, *a.* Non dilué.

undiplomatic, *a.* Peu politique.

undiscerning, *a.* Sans discernement.

undisciplined, *a.* Indiscipliné.

undiscovered, *a.* Non découvert ; caché.

undiscriminating, *a.* Sans discernement.

undisguised, *a.* Non déguisé ; non dissimulé.

undismayed, *a.* Sans peur.

undisputed, *a.* Incontesté.

undistinguishable, *a.* **1.** Indistinguible. **2.** Imperceptible.

undistinguished, *a.* Médiocre.

undisturbed, *a.* **1.** Tranquille ; paisible. **2.** Non dérangé.

undivided, *a.* **1.** Indivisé ; entier. **2.** Non partagé.

undo, *v.tr.* **1.** Détruire. **2.** Défaire. dénouer.

undoing, *s.* Ruine *f*, perte *f*.

undone, *a.* **1.** Défait. **To come u.,** se défaire. **2.** Inaccompli.

undoubted, *a.* Indiscutable, incontestable.

undoubtedly, *adv.* Indubitablement, assurément.

undress. 1. *v.i. & pr.* Se déshabiller. **2.** *v.tr.* Déshabiller, dévêtir.

undressed, *a.* Déshabillé, dévêtu.

undue, *a.* (*a*) Illégitime. (*b*) Exagéré, indu.

undulate, *v.i.* Onduler, ondoyer.

undulating, *a.* Ondulé.

undulation, *s.* Ondulation *f* ; accident *m* de terrain.

unduly, adv. **1.** (a) Indûment. (b) Sans raison. **2.** A l'excès.

undying, a. Immortel, impérissable.

unearth, v.tr. Déterrer.

unearthly, a. (a) Surnaturel (b) Sinistre.

uneasily, adv. (a) D'un air gêné. (b) Avec inquiétude.

uneasiness, s. **1.** Gêne f, malaise m **2.** Inquiétude f.

uneasy, a. (a) Mal à l'aise ; gêné. (b) Inquiet, -ète ; anxieux.

uneatable, a. Immangeable.

uneducated, a. Sans instruction ; ignorant.

unemployed, a. Sans emploi. **The u.,** les sans-travail m.

unending, a. **1.** Interminable. **2.** Éternel.

unendurable, a. Insupportable.

unenviable, a. Peu enviable.

unequal, a. **1.** Inégal. -aux. **2.** Inégal, irrégulier.

unequalled, a. Inégalé ; sans égal.

unequally, adv. Inégalement.

unequivocal, a. Clair, net, f. nette.

unerring, a. Infaillible, sûr.

uneven, a. Inégal, -aux. (a) Rugueux. (b) Accidenté. (c) Irrégulier.

unevenly, adv. **1.** Inégalement. **2.** Irrégulièrement.

uneventful, a. Sans incidents.

unexampled, a. Sans exemple, sans égal, sans pareil ; unique.

unexceptionable, a. Irréprochable.

unexpected, a. Inattendu ; imprévu.

unexpectedly, adv. De manière inattendue ; à l'improviste.

unexplained, a. Inexpliqué.

unexplored, a. Inexploré.

unexpurgated, a. Non expurgé.

unfailing, a. Infaillible, sûr. **2.** Intarissable.

unfair, a. **1.** Injuste. **2.** Inéquitable.

unfairly, adv. Injustement.

unfairness, s. Injustice f ; partialité f.

unfaithful, a. Infidèle.

unfamiliar, a. Étranger ; inconnu.

unfashionable, a. Démodé, qui n'est pas de mode.

unfasten, v.tr. **1.** Détacher **2.** Défaire ; ouvrir.

unfathomable, o. Insondable ; impénétrable.

unfathomed, a. Insondé.

unfavourable, a. Défavorable ; désavantageux.

unfeeling, a. Insensible.

unfeigned, a. Sincère ; non simulé.

unfeignedly, adv. Sincèrement.

unfinished, a. Inachevé.

unfit, a. (a) Impropre, peu propre (for, à). (b) Inapte (for, à).

unfitness, s. Inaptitude f (for, à).

unfitted, a. Impropre (for, à) ; inapte.

unflattering, a. Peu flatteur, -euse.

unflinchingly, adv. **1.** Sans broncher. **2.** Stoïquement.

unfold. **1.** v.tr (a) Déplier. (b) Dérouler, déployer. **2.** v.i. & pr. Se déployer, se dérouler.

unforeseen, a. Imprévu, inattendu ; inopiné.

unforgettable, a. Inoubliable.

unforgivable, a. Impardonnable.

unforgiving, a. Implacable.

unforgotten, a. Inoublié.

unfortunate, a. (a) Malheureux, infortuné. (b) Regrettable. **How u.!** quel dommage !

unfortunately, adv. Malheureusement ; par malheur.

unfounded, a. Sans fondement.

unfrequented, a. Peu fréquenté.

unfriendliness, s. Hostilité f.

unfriendly, a. Peu amical. -aux ; mal disposé.

unfruitful, a. Stérile, infécond.

unfurnished, a. Non meublé.

ungainly, a. Gauche, lourd.

ungenerous, a. Peu généreux.

ungovernable, a. Effréné.

ungraceful, a. Disgracieux ; gauche.

ungracious, a. Malgracieux.

ungraciously, adv. Malgracieusement.

ungraciousness, s. Mauvaise grâce.

ungrateful, a. Ingrat.

ungratefully, adv. Avec ingratitude.

ungratefulness, s. Ingratitude f.

ungrudging, a. Généreux.

unguarded, a. **1.** Non gardé. **2.** Indiscret, -ète. **In an u. moment,** dans un moment d'inattention.

unhampered, a. Libre.

unhappily, adv. (a) Malheureusement. (b) Tristement.

unhappiness, s. Chagrin m.

unhappy, a. Malheureux, triste.

unharmed, a. Sain et sauf.

unhealthy, *a.* **1.** Malsain, insalubre. **2.** Maladif.

unheard, *a.* U. of, inouï.

unheeded, *a.* Négligé ; inaperçu.

unheeding, *a.* **1.** Insouciant. **2.** Inattentif.

unhesitating, *a.* Ferme, résolu.

unhesitatingly, *adv.* Sans hésiter.

unhurt, *a.* Sans mal ; indemne ; sain et sauf.

unidentified, *a.* Non identifié.

uniform. 1. *a.* Uniforme. **2.** *s.* Uniforme *m.*

uniformity, *s.* Uniformité *f.*

uniformly, *adv.* Uniformément.

unimpaired, *a.* Non affaibli ; intact.

unimportant, *a.* Sans importance.

uninhabitable, *a.* Inhabitable.

uninhabited, *a.* Inhabité.

uninjured, *a.* **1.** Sain et sauf ; indemne. **2.** Sans dommage.

unintelligent, *a.* Inintelligent.

unintelligible, *a.* Inintelligible.

unintentional, *a.* Involontaire.

unintentionally, *adv.* Involontairement.

uninterested, *a.* Non intéressé ; indifférent.

uninteresting, *a.* Peu intéressant ; sans intérêt.

uninterrupted, *a.* **1.** Ininterrompu. **2.** Continu.

uninviting, *a.* Peu attrayant ; peu appétissant.

union, *s.* **1.** Union *f.* **2.** Concorde *f,* harmonie *f.*

unique, *a.* Unique.

unison, *s.* Unisson *m.*

unit, *s.* Unité *f.*

unite. 1. *v.tr.* (*a*) Unir. (*b*) Mettre d'accord ; unifier. **2.** *v.i.* S'unir, se joindre (*with,* à).

united, *a.* Uni, réuni. **The U. States,** les États-Unis.

unity, *s.* Unité *f* ; concorde *f*

universal, *a.* Universel.

universally, *adv.* Universellement.

universe, *s.* Univers *m.*

university, *s.* Université *f.*

unjust, *a.* Injuste.

unjustifiable, *a.* Injustifiable.

unjustified, *a.* Non justifié.

unjustly, *adv.* Injustement.

unkempt, *a.* Peu soigné ; mal tenu.

unkind, *a.* Dur ; cruel ; peu aimable.

unkindly, *adv.* Méchamment durement ; sans bienveillance.

unkindness, *s.* **1.** Méchanceté *f.* **2.** Manque *m* de bienveillance.

unknown. 1. *a.* Inconnu ; ignoré (*to,* de). **2.** *s.* Inconnu, -ue.

unlace, *v.tr.* Délacer, défaire.

unlawful, *a.* (*a*) Illégal, -aux. (*b*) Illicite.

unless. 1. *conj.* A moins que . . . (ne). U. I hear to the contrary, à moins d'avis contraire. **2.** *prep.* Sauf, excepté.

unlike, *a.* Différent, dissemblable.

unlikely, *a.* Invraisemblable ; peu probable.

unlimited, *a.* Illimité ; sans bornes.

unload, *v.tr.* Décharger.

unlooked, *a.* U. for, inattendu, imprévu.

unlucky, *a.* **1.** (*a*) Malheureux, infortuné. (*b*) Malheureux, malencontreux. **2.** It is u., cela porte malheur.

unmanageable, *a.* **1.** Intraitable. **2.** Difficile à manier.

unmanly, *a.* Indigne d'un homme ; peu viril.

unmannerly, *a.* Malappris ; grossier.

unmarried, *a.* Célibataire.

unmatched, *a.* **1.** Incomparable. **2.** Désassorti, dépareillé.

unmeant, *a.* Involontaire ; fait sans intention.

unmentionable, *a.* Dont il ne faut pas parler.

unmerciful, *a.* Impitoyable.

unmercifully, *adv.* Impitoyablement.

unmerited, *a.* Immérité.

unmistakable, *a.* (*a*) Clair ; évident. (*b*) Facilement reconnaissable.

unmistakably, *adv.* Nettement, évidemment ; à ne pas s'y méprendre.

unmitigated, *a.* Véritable.

unmixed, *a.* Sans mélange ; pur.

unmolested, *a.* Sans être molesté.

unmounted, *a.* Non monté. **1.** (*a*) Non serti. (*b*) Non collé. **2.** A pied.

unnatural, *a.* Non naturel. (*a*) Anormal, -aux. (*b*) Contre nature ; monstrueux.

unnecessarily, *adv.* **1.** Sans nécessité ; inutilement. **2.** Plus que de raison.

unnecessary, *a.* Peu nécessaire ; inutile, superflu.

unnoticed, *a.* Inaperçu, inobservé.

unobjectionable, *a.* Irréprochable

unobservant, *a* Peu observateur -trice.

unobstructed, *a* Inobstrué; non encombré; libre.

unobtainable, *a.* Impossible à obtenir.

unoccupied, *a* **1.** Inoccupé **2.** Inhabité. **3.** Libre, disponible.

unoffending, *a.* Innocent.

unopposed, *a.* Sans opposition

unorthodox, *a.* Peu orthodoxe.

unpack, *v.tr.* **1.** Déballer, dépaqueter. **2.** Défaire. *Abs.* Défaire sa malle.

unpalatable, *a.* Désagréable.

unparalleled, *a.* Incomparable; sans égal, sans pareil.

unpardonable, *a.* Impardonable.

unpatriotic, *a.* Peu patriote; peu patriotique.

unperceived, *a.* Inaperçu.

unperturbed, *a.* **1.** Impassible **2.** Peu ému.

unpleasant, *a.* Désagréable, déplaisant.

unpleasantly, *adv.* Désagréablement.

unpleasantness, *s.* Désagrémen *m*, ennui *m*.

unpolished, *a.* **1.** Non poli; mat. **2.** Rude, grossier.

unpopular, *a.* Impopulaire.

unpopularity, *s.* Impopularité *f.*

unprecedented, *a.* Sans précédent; inouï.

unprejudiced, *a.* Sans préjugés, impartial, -aux; désintéressé.

unprepared, *a.* Au dépourvu

unprepossessing, *a.* Peu engageant.

unpretentious, *a.* Sans prétentions; modeste.

unprincipled, *a.* Sans principes.

unproductive, *a.* Improductif.

unprofitable, *a.* Improfitable; sans profit.

unpropitious, *a.* Impropice.

unprotected, *a.* Inabrité; sans protection, sans défense.

unprovoked, *a.* Fait sans provocation.

unpublished, *a.* Inédit.

unpunctual, *a.* (*a*) Inexact. (*b*) En retard; pas à l'heure.

unpunctuality, *s.* Inexactitude *f*; manque *m* de ponctualité.

unpunished, *a.* Impuni.

unqualified, *a.* **1.** Incompétent. **2.** Catégorique; sans réserve.

unquestionable. *a.* Indiscutable, indubitable.

unquestionably, *adv* Indubitablement.

unquestioned, *a.* Indisputé, incontesté.

unquestioning, *a* Aveugle. sans question.

unquiet, *a.* Inquiet, -ète; agité

unravel, *v.tr.* Débrouiller.

unreadable, *a.* Illisible.

unreal, *a.* Irréel; sans réalité.

unreasonable, *a.* Déraisonnable.

unreasonably, *adv.* Déraisonnablement.

unreasoning, *a.* Aveugle.

unrecognizable, *a.* Méconnaissable.

unregenerate, *a.* Non régénéré.

unrelated, *a.* Sans rapport.

unrelaxing, *a.* Soutenu.

unrelenting, *a.* (*a*) Implacable. impitoyable. (*b*) Acharné.

unreliability, *s.* **1.** Inexactitude ׳. **2.** Instabilité *f.*

unreliable, *a.* Sur lequel on ne peut pas compter; incertain.

unremitting, *a.* **1.** Ininterrompu; sans intermission. **2.** Infatigable.

unrepentant, *a.* Impénitent.

unreserved, *a.* (*a*) Franc, *f.* franche; expansif. (*b*) Complet, -ète; entier.

unreservedly, *adv.* Sans réserve.

unresisting, *a.* Soumis, docile.

unresponsive, *a* Difficile à émouvoir; froid.

unrest, *a.* **1.** Inquiétude *f*. **2.** Agitation *f.*

unrestrained, *a.* Non restreint; libre; immodéré.

unrestrainedly, *adv* Librement; sans contrainte.

unrestricted, *a.* Sans restriction; absolu.

unrewarded, *a.* Sans récompense

unrighteous, *a* **1.** Impie. **2.** Inique, injuste.

unripe, *a.* Vert; qui n'est pas mûr.

unrivalled, *a.* Sans rival; sans pareil.

unroll. 1. *v.tr.* Dérouler. **2.** *v.i. & pr.* Se dérouler.

unruffled, *a.* Calme, placide.

unruly, *a.* Indiscipliné, insoum

unsafe, a. **1.** Dangereux ; peu sûr **2.** Exposé au danger

unsaleable, a. Invendable.

unsanitary, a. Non hygiénique.

unsatisfactory, a Peu satisfaisant ; peu convaincant.

unsatisfied, a. **1.** Mécontent (*with*, de). **2.** Inconvaincu. **3.** Inassouvi.

unscrew, v.tr Dévisser.

unscrupulous, a Peu scrupuleux ; sans scrupules.

unseasonable, a **1.** Hors de saison. **2.** Inopportun ; déplacé.

unseemly, a. Inconvenant.

unseen, a Inaperçu, invisible.

unselfish, a Généreux ; désintéressé.

unselfishly, adv. Généreusement.

unselfishness, s. Générosité *f* ; désintéressement *m*.

unsettle, v.tr. Ébranler ; troubler le repos de.

unsettled, a. **1.** Troublé ; variable. **2.** (a) Indécis. (b) Non réglé.

unsettling, a. Troublant.

unshakeable, a. Inébranlable.

unshaken, a. Inébranlé, ferme.

unshrinkable, a. Irrétrécissable.

unsightly, a. Laid, vilain.

unskilled. a. Inexpérimenté ; inexpert.

unsociable, a. Insociable ; farouche.

unsoiled, a. Propre ; sans tache.

unsold, a. Invendu.

unsolicited, a. Non sollicité ; volontaire, spontané.

unsolved, a Non résolu ; impénétré.

unsophisticated, a. Ingénu, naïf.

unsound, a. **1.** Non sain. **2.** (a) Peu solide. (b) Erroné.

unsparing, a. Prodigue ; infatigable.

unspeakable, a. **1.** Inexprimable. **2.** Détestable, inqualifiable.

unspeakably, adv. Ineffablement, indiciblement.

unspoken, a. Tacite.

unstable, a. **1.** Instable **2.** Peu consistant ; inconstant.

unstained, a. Propre ; sans tache.

unsteadiness, s. Instabilité *f* ; manque *m* de sûreté.

unsteady, a. Peu stable, peu solide ; chancelant ; mal assuré.

unstinted, a. Abondant.

unstudied, a. Naturel ; inétudié.

unsubdued, a. Non subjugué.

unsuccessful, a. **1.** Non réussi ; vain. **2.** Qui n'a pas réussi : refusé ; non élu.

unsuccessfully, adv. Sans succès ; vainement.

unsuitable, a. Impropre mal adapté.

unsullied, a. Immaculé.

unsuspected, a. Insoupçonné.

unswerving, a. Constant, ferme.

unsymmetrical, a. Asymétrique.

unsympathetic, a. Peu compatissant ; froid ; indifférent.

unsympathetically, adv. D'un ai peu compatissant ; froidement.

untamed, a. Inapprivoisé, sauvage ; indompté.

untarnished, a **1.** Non terni. **2.** Sans tache.

untenable, a. **1.** Intenable. **2.** Insoutenable.

untenanted, a. Inoccupé ; inhabité.

unthinkable, a Inimaginable ; inconcevable.

unthinking, a. Irréfléchi, étourdi.

unthinkingly, adv. Sans réflexion ; étourdiment.

untidily, adv. Sans ordre.

untidiness, s. Désordre *m* ; manque *m* d'ordre.

untidy, a. (a) En désordre ; mal tenu ; ébouriffé. (b) Qui manque d'ordre.

untie, v.tr. Dénouer ; défaire.

until. **1.** prep. Jusqu'à. **2.** conj. Jusqu'à ce que.

untimely, a. **1.** Prématuré. **2.** Inopportun, mal à propos.

untiring, a. Inlassable, infatigable.

untold, a. Non compté ; immense.

untrained, a. Inexpert, inexercé.

untried, a. **1.** Inessayé ; non essayé. **2.** Qui n'a pas été mis à l'épreuve.

untroubled, a. Calme, tranquille.

untrue, a. **1.** Faux, *f.* fausse. **2.** Infidèle, déloyal -aux.

untrustworthy, a. **1.** Indigne de confiance. **2.** Douteux, peu sûr.

untruth, s. Mensonge *m*.

untruthful, a. **1.** Menteur, -euse. **2.** Mensonger ; faux, *f.* fausse.

unused, a. **1.** (a) Inutilisé ; non employé. (b) Qui n'a pas encore servi ; neuf. **2.** Peu habitué.

unusual, a. Peu commun ; exceptionnel ; insolite.

unvarying, *a.* Invariable ; constant.

unveil, *v.tr.* Dévoiler. **To u. a statue**, inaugurer une statue.

unveiling, *s.* Inauguration *f.*

unwanted, *a.* **1.** Non désiré, non voulu. **2.** Superflu.

unwarrantable, *a.* Injustifiable.

unwarranted, *a.* Injustifié.

unwary, *a.* Imprudent.

unwavering, *a.* Constant, ferme.

unwearied, *a.* (*a*) Non fatigue (*b*) Infatigable.

unwearying, *a.* Inlassable.

unwelcome, *a.* (*a*) Mal venu, importun. (*b*) Désagréable.

unwell, *a.* Indisposé ; souffrant.

unwholesome, *a.* Malsain ; insalubre.

unwieldy, *a.* **1.** Lourd, gauche. **2.** Peu maniable.

unwilling, *a.* **1.** Peu disposé. **2.** Donné à contre-cœur.

unwillingly, *adv.* A contre-cœur ; de mauvaise grâce ; à regret.

unwillingness, *s.* **1.** Mauvaise volonté ; manque *m* de bonne volonté. **2.** Répugnance *f.*

unwise, *a.* **1.** Imprudent ; peu prudent. **2.** Peu sage ; malavisé.

unwisely, *adv.* Imprudemment.

unwonted, *a.* Inaccoutumé, inhabituel ; peu commun, insolite.

unworthy, *a.* **1.** Indigne. **2.** Méprisable. **3.** Peu méritoire.

unwounded, *a.* Non blessé ; sans blessure.

unwrap, *v.tr.* Défaire, désenvelopper.

unyielding, *a.* Inébranlable ; inflexible.

up. I. *adv.* **1.** (*a*) En montant ; vers le haut. (*b*) **Up and down**, de long en large. **2.** (*a*) Haut ; en haut **Up above**, en haut. **Up above sth.**, au-dessus de qch. **The moon is up**, la lune est levée. (*b*) En dessus. **3.** (*a*) **His blood was up**, il était monté. (*b*) **To be well up in**, connaître à fond. (*c*) **To praise up**, vanter. **4.** (*a*) Debout, levé. (*b*) **To be up all night**, ne pas se coucher de la nuit. (*c*) **To be up against**, se heurter à. **5. What's up?** que se passe-t-il ? qu'y a-t-il ? **6. Time is up**, il est l'heure. **7. Up to.** (*a*) Jusqu'à. (*b*) **Up to now**, jusqu'ici. (*c*) **To be up to**, être à la hauteur de.

II. **up**, *prep.* **1.** En haut de. **2. Up the river**, en amont. **To walk up and down**, se promener de long en large.

III. **up**, *attrib.a.* **Up train**, train montant.

upbraid, *v.tr.* Reprocher.

upbringing, *s.* Éducation *f.*

upheaval, *s.* **1.** Soulèvement *m.* **2.** Bouleversement *m.*

uphold, *v.tr.* Supporter, soutenir

upkeep, *s.* Entretien *m.*

upon, *prep.* Sur.

upper. *a.* **1.** Supérieur, -eure ; (plus) haut, de dessus ; d'au-dessus. **U. part**, dessus *m.* **2. The u. classes**, les hautes classes. **To have the u. hand**, avoir le dessus.

uppermost. **1.** *a.* Le plus haut, le plus élevé. **2.** *adv.* **Face u.**, face en dessus.

upright. I. *a.* **1.** Vertical, -aux ; droit. **To set u.**, mettre debout. **2.** Droit, honnête.

II. **upright**, *s.* Montant *m.*

uprising, *s.* Soulèvement *m* ; insurrection *f.*

uproar, *s.* Vacarme *m*, tapage *m.* **In an u.**, en tumulte.

uproarious, *a.* Tumultueux, tapageur, -euse.

uproot, *v.tr.* Déraciner, extirper.

upset[1]. **1.** *v.tr.* (*a*) Renverser. (*b*) Désorganiser, déranger. (*c*) Troubler. (*d*) Indisposer ; déranger. **2.** *v.i.* Se renverser ; verser ; chavirer.

upset[2], *a.* Bouleversé, ému.

upshot, *s.* Résultat *m*, issue *f.*

upside down, *adv.phr.* (*a*) Sens dessus dessous ; la tête en bas. (*b*) En désordre ; bouleversé.

upstairs. **1.** *adv.* En haut. **To go u.**, monter ; aller en haut. **2.** *a* D'en haut.

upstart, *s.* Parvenu, -ue.

up-stream, *adv.* En amont.

up-to-date, *attrib.a.* **1.** A la page. **2.** Au goût du jour.

upward. **1.** *a.* Ascendant ; à la hausse. **2.** *adv.* = UPWARDS.

upwards, *adv.* **1.** De bas en haut ; vers le haut. **2.** En dessus ; en haut. **3.** Au-dessus ; **U. of**, plus de.

uranium, *s.* Uranium *m.*

urban, *a.* Urbain.

urbane, *a.* Courtois, poli, civil

urge[1], *s.* Incitation *f* ; poussée *f.*

urge[2], *v.tr.* 1. Encourager, exciter ; pousser. 2. Recommander ; insister.

urgency, *s.* Urgence *f.*

urgent, *a.* Urgent, pressant.

urgently, *adv.* Avec instance ; instamment.

urn, *s.* Fontaine *f.*

us, *pers.pron.* Nous.

usage, *s.* 1. Traitement *m.* 2. Usage *m*, coutume *f.*

use[1], *s.* 1. Emploi *m*, usage *m.* To make use of, se servir de. Ready for use, prêt à servir. 2. Jouissance *f*, usage. 3. Utilité *f.* It is of no use, cela ne sert à rien. To have no use for sth., n'avoir que faire de qch. What's the use? à quoi bon. 4. Usage, coutume *f.*

use[2], *v.tr.* 1. (*a*) Employer, se servir de ; utiliser. (*b*) To use force, user de force. 2. To use s.o. well, en user bien avec qn. 3. To use (up), (*a*) User, épuiser. (*b*) Tirer parti de. 4. I used to do it, j'avais l'habitude de le faire.

used, *a.* 1. Usagé ; oblitéré. Hardly u., à l'état de neuf. 2. U. to, habitué, accoutumé, à. To get u. to, s'habituer, s'accoutumer, à.

useful, *a.* Utile.

usefully, *adv.* Utilement.

usefulness, *s.* Utilité *f.*

useless, *a.* Inutile ; bon à rien ; vain. To be u., ne servir à rien.

uselessness, *s.* Inutilité *f.*

usher[1], *s.* Huissier *m.*

usher[2], *v.tr.* Introduire (*in*, dans). To u. out, reconduire.

usherette, *s.* Ouvreuse *f.*

usual, *a.* Usuel, habituel, ordinaire. It is u., il est d'usage. Earlier than u., plus tôt que de coutume. As u., comme à l'ordinaire.

usually, *adv.* Ordinairement ; d'ordinaire.

usurp, *v.tr.* Usurper.

usurper, *s.* Usurpateur, -trice.

utensil, *s.* Ustensile *m.*

utility, *s.* Utilité *f.*

utilize, *v.tr.* Utiliser, se servir de.

utmost, 1. *a.* Extrême ; dernier. With the u. ease, avec la plus grande facilité. 2. *s.* To the u., le plus possible ; au suprême degré. To do one's u., faire tout son possible.

utter[1], *a.* Complet, -ète ; absolu.

utter[2], *v.tr.* (*a*) Pousser, faire entendre ; prononcer. (*b*) Dire ; exprimer.

utterance, *s.* 1. Expression *f.* To give u. to, exprimer. 2. Articulation *f*, prononciation *f.* 3. *pl.* Propos *m.*

utterly, *adv.* Complètement, absolument, tout à fait.

V

V, v, *s.* (La lettre) V, v *m.*

vacancy, *s.* 1. Vide *m.* 2. Vacance *f* ; poste vacant.

vacant, *a.* 1. Vacant, vide, libre. 2. Vague.

vacate, *v.tr.* Quitter.

vacation, *s.* Vacances *fpl.*

vaccinate, *v.tr.* Vacciner.

vaccination, *s.* Vaccination *f.*

vacillate, *v.i.* Vaciller ; hésiter.

vacuum, *s.* Vide *m.*

vacuum-cleaner, *s.* Aspirateur *m.*

vacuum-flask, *s.* Bouteille isolante.

vagabond, *s.* (*a*) Vagabond, -onde. (*b*) Vaurien *m.*

vagrant, 1. *a.* Vagabond, errant. 2. *s.* Vagabond, -onde.

vague, *a.* Vague ; imprécis.

vaguely, *adv.* Vaguement.

vagueness, *s.* Vague *m*, imprécision *f.*

vain, *a.* 1. Vain. 2. Inutile. 3. Vaniteux. 4. In v., en vain ; vainement.

vainly, *adv.* Vainement, en vain.

vale, *s.* Vallon *m.*

valet, *s.* Valet *m* de chambre.

valiant, *a.* Vaillant.

valid, *a.* Valide, valable ; bon.

validity, *s.* Validité *f.*

valise, *s.* Valise *f.*

valley, *s.* Vallée *f.*

valour, *s.* Valeur *f*, vaillance *f.*

valuable. 1. *a.* Précieux ; de valeur, de prix. 2. *s.pl.* Objets *m* de valeur.

valuation, *s.* 1. Évaluation *f*, estimation *f.* 2. Valeur estimée.

value[1], *s.* Valeur *f.*

value[2], *v.tr.* 1. Évaluer, estimer. 2. Estimer ; tenir à.

valued, *a.* Estimé, précieux.

valueless, *a.* Sans valeur.

valuer, s. Estimateur m, expert m.

valve, s. **1.** Soupape f; valve f. **2.** Lampe f. **V. set,** appareil m, poste m, à lampes.

valve-cap, s. Capuchon m (d'une valve de pneu).

vampire, s. Vampire m.

van, s. **1.** (a) Fourgon m. (b) Roulotte f. **2. Recording van,** camion m d'enregistrement. **3.** Wagon m. fourgon.

vandalism, s. Vandalisme m.

vanilla, s. Vanille f. **V. ice,** glace à la vanille.

vanish, v.i. Disparaître.

vanishing, s. Disparition f. **V. cream,** crème f de jour.

vanity, s. Vanité f.

vanquish, v.tr. Vaincre.

vaporize. 1. v.tr. Vaporiser. **2.** v.i. Se vaporiser.

vaporizer, s. Pulvérisateur m; atomiseur m.

vapour, s. Vapeur f.

variable, a. Variable; changeant.

variance, s. Désaccord m. **At v.,** en désaccord.

variation, s Variation f, changement m.

varied, a. Varié; divers.

variegated, a. **1.** Varié; divers **2.** Bigarré, bariolé.

variegation, s. Diversité ' de couleurs; bigarrure f.

variety, s. (a) Variété f, diversité f. (b) Assortiment m.

various, a. **1.** Varié, divers. **2.** (a) Différent, divers. (b) Plusieurs.

varnish[1], s. Vernis m.

varnish[2], v.tr. Vernir.

vary. 1. v.tr. Varier, diversifier; faire varier. **2.** v.i. (a) Varier changer. (b) Différer.

varying, a. Variable changeant; divers.

vase, s. Vase m.

vaseline, s. Vaseline f.

vast, a. Vaste, immense.

vat, s. Cuve f; bac m; bain m.

vault[1], s. **1.** Voûte f. **2.** Souterrain m.

vault[2], v.i. & tr. Sauter.

vaulted, a. Voûté; en voûte.

vaunt, v.tr. Vanter.

veal, s. Veau m.

veer, v.i. Tourner.

vegetable. 1. a. Végétal, -aux. **2.** s. Légume m. **Early vegetables,** primeurs f. **V. garden,** potager m.

vegetable-dish, s. Légumier m.

vegetarian, a. & s Végétarien, -ienne.

vegetarianism, s. Végétarisme m.

vegetation, s. Végétation f.

vehemence, s. Véhémence f.

vehement, a. Véhément.

vehemently, adv. Véhémentement.

vehicle, s. Véhicule m.

veil[1], s. (a) Voile m. (b) Voilette f.

veil[2], v.tr. Voiler.

veiled, a. Voilé.

vein, s. **1.** Veine f. **2.** Nervure f.

vellum, s. Vélin m.

velocity, s. Vitesse f.

velours, s. **1.** Velouté m; velours m de laine. **2. V. hat,** chapeau taupé.

velvet, s. **1.** Velours m. **2.** Attrib. **V. coat,** habit de velours.

velveteen, s. Velours m lisse de coton.

velvety, a. Velouté.

vendor, s. Vendeur, -euse.

veneer, s. **1.** Placage m, revêtement m. **2.** Masque m.

venerable, a. Vénérable.

venerate, v.tr. Vénérer.

veneration, s. Vénération f.

vengeance, s. Vengeance f. **To take v.,** se venger.

Venice. Pr.n. Venise f.

venison, s. Venaison f. **Haunch of v.,** quartier m de chevreuil.

venom, s. Venin m.

venomous, a. Venimeux.

vent[1], s. **1.** Trou m, orifice m. **2. To give v.,** donner libre cours.

vent[2], v.tr. Décharger.

ventilate, v.tr. Aérer; ventiler.

ventilation, s. Aération f, aérage m, ventilation f.

ventilator, s. Ventilateur m; soupirail m, -aux.

ventriloquism, s. Ventriloquie f.

ventriloquist, s. Ventriloque mf.

venture[1], s. **1.** Entreprise f. **2. At a v.,** à l'aventure, au hasard.

venture[2]. **1.** v.tr. (a) Oser. (b) Hasarder. **2.** v.i. (a) To v. upon sth., se risquer à faire qch. (b) S'aventurer. **To v. out of doors,** se risquer à sortir.

venturesome, a. **1.** Aventureux, osé. **2.** Aventuré, risqué.

Venus. Pr.n. Vénus f.

veracious, *a.* Véridique.
veracity, *s.* Véracité *f.*
veranda, *s.* Véranda *f.*
verb, *s.* Verbe *m.*
verbal, *a.* Verbal, -aux ; oral, -aux.
verbally, *adv.* Verbalement ; de vive voix.
verbatim, *adv.* Mot pour mot.
verbena, *s.* Verveine *f.*
verbose, *a.* Verbeux, diffus.
verdant, *a.* Vert, verdoyant.
verdict, *s.* **1.** Verdict *m.* **2.** Jugement *m*, décision *f.*
verdure, *s.* Verdure *f.*
verge[1], *s.* (*a*) Bord *m* ; orée *f.* (*b*) On the v. of, au bord, à deux doigts, de.
verge[2], *v.i.* To v. on, toucher à ; friser.
verger, *s.* Bedeau *m.*
verification, *s.* Vérification *f*, contrôle *m.*
verify, *v.tr.* **1.** Confirmer. **2.** Vérifier, contrôler.
veritable, *a.* Véritable.
vermicelli, *s.* Vermicelle *m.*
vermilion. **1.** *s.* Vermillon *m*, cinabre *m.* **2.** *a.* (De) vermillon ; vermeil.
vermin, *s.* Vermine *f.*
vermouth, *s.* Vermout *m.*
vernacular, *a. & s.* Vernaculaire.
versatile, *a.* (*a*) Aux talents variés. (*b*) Souple.
verse, *s.* **1.** Vers *m.* **2.** Couplet *m.* **3.** *Coll.* Vers *pl.* Light v., poésie légère.
versed, *a.* Versé.
version, *s.* Version *f.* According to his v., d'après lui.
versus, *Lt.prep.* Contre.
vertebrate, *a. & s.* Vertébré (*m*).
vertical, *a.* Vertical, -aux ; à pic.
vertically, *adv.* Verticalement ; d'aplomb.
vertigo, *s.* Vertige *m.*
verve, *s.* Verve *f.*
very. **I.** *a.* **1.** Vrai, véritable. **2.** (*a*) Même. At that v. moment, à cet instant même. To the v. day, jour pour jour. (*b*) At the v. beginning, tout au commencement.
 II. **very**, *adv.* **1.** Très ; fort, bien. It isn't so v. difficult, ce n'est pas tellement difficile. V. much, beaucoup. **2.** The v. first, le tout premier. The v. best, le meilleur de tous.
vespers, *s.pl.* Vêpres *f.*

vessel, *s.* Vaisseau *m*
vest[1], *s.* Gilet *m.*
vest[2]. **1.** *v.tr.* (*a*) Investir. (*b*) Vêtir, revêtir. **2.** *v.i.* To v. in, échoir à.
vesta, *s.* Allumette-bougie *f pl.* allumettes-bougies.
vested, *a.* Dévolu. V. interests, droits acquis.
vestibule, *s.* Vestibule *m.*
vestige, *s.* Vestige *m*, trace *f.*
vestment, *s.* Vêtement *m.*
vestry, *s.* Sacristie *f.*
veteran. **1.** *s.* Vétéran *m.* **2.** *a.* Vieux, *f.* vieille ; aguerri ; expérimenté.
veterinary, *a.* V. surgeon, vétérinaire *m.*
veto[1], *s.* Veto *m.*
veto[2], *v.tr.* Interdire.
vex, *v.tr.* **1.** Vexer, fâcher, chagriner. **2.** Troubler, agiter.
vexation, *s.* **1.** Vexation *f.* **2.** (*a*) Contrariété *f.* (*b*) Chagrin *m*, dépit *m.*
vexatious, *a.* Fâcheux. ennuyeux, contrariant.
vexed, *a.* **1.** Vexé, contrarié, chagrin. **2.** V. question, question non résolue.
vexing, *a.* Vexant, chagrinant.
via, *prep.* Via ; par la voie de ; par.
viaduct, *s.* Viaduc *m.*
vial, *s.* Fiole *f.*
viands, *s. pl.* Aliments *m.*
vibrant, *a.* Vibrant.
vibrate. **1.** *v.i.* Vibrer ; trépider **2.** *v.tr.* Faire vibrer.
vibrating, *a.* Vibrant.
vibration, *s.* Vibration *f.*
vicar, *s.* Curé *m.*
vicarage, *s.* Presbytère *m* ; cure *f.*
vice[1], *s.* **1.** Vice *m.* **2.** Défaut *m.*
vice[2], *s.* Étau *m.*
viceroy, *s.* Vice-roi *m.*
vice versa, *Lt.phr.* Vice versa.
vicinity, *s.* **1.** Voisinage *m*, proximité *f.* **2.** Abords *mpl*; alentours *mpl.*
vicious, *a.* Vicieux ; méchant.
viciously, *adv.* **1.** Vicieusement. **2.** Méchamment.
viciousness, *s.* **1.** Nature vicieuse ; vice *m.* **2.** Méchanceté *f*
victim, *s.* Victime *f.*
victimize, *v.tr.* **1.** Exercer des représailles contre. **2.** Tromper, escroquer.
victor. *s.* Vainqueur *m.*

victorious, *a* Victorieux; vainqueur *m.*

victoriously, *adv.* Victorieusement; en vainqueur.

victory, *s.* Victoire *f.* **To gain the v.,** remporter la victoire.

victuals, *s.pl.* Vivres *m,* provisions *f.*

vie, *v.i.* Le disputer (*with,* à); rivaliser.

view[1], *s.* Vue *f.* **1.** Regard *m;* coup *m* d'œil. **On v.,** exposé; ouvert au public. **2.** (*a*) Vue, perspective *f.* (*b*) **To keep in v.,** ne pas perdre de vue. **3.** Manière *f* de voir; opinion *f.* **In my v.,** à mon avis *m.* **4. In v. of,** en considération de; eu égard à; vu. **5.** Vue, intention *f.*

view[2], *v.tr.* **1.** Regarder; examiner. **2.** Envisager. **3.** Voir, apercevoir.

view-finder, *s.* Viseur *m;* iconoscope *m.*

view-point, *s.* Point *m* de vue; belvédère *m.*

vigil, *s.* Veille *f.*

vigilance, *s.* Vigilance *f.*

vigilant, *a.* Vigilant, éveillé, alerte

vigilantly, *adv.* Avec vigilance.

vignette, *s.* Vignette *f.*

vigorous, *a.* Vigoureux, robuste.

vigorously, *adv.* Vigoureusement.

vigour, *s.* Vigueur *f,* énergie *f;* brio *m.*

vile, *a.* **1.** Vil; bas. *f.* basse, infâme. **2.** Abominable.

vileness, *s.* Bassesse *f.*

vilify, *v.tr.* Vilipender. diffamer.

villa, *s.* Villa *f.*

village, *s.* Village *m.*

villager, *s.* Villageois, -oise.

villain, *s.* Scélérat *m;* gredin *m.*

villainous, *a.* **1.** Vil, infâme. **V. face,** vilain visage. **2.** Abominable.

villainously, *adv.* D'une manière infâme.

villainy, *s.* Scélératesse *f,* infamie *f.*

vindicate, *v.tr.* Défendre; justifier.

vindication, *s.* Défense *f,* apologie *f.* **In v. of,** pour justifier.

vindictive, *a.* Vindicatif; rancunier.

vine, *s.* Vigne *f.*

vinegar, *s.* Vinaigre *m.*

vinegar-cruet, *s.* Burette *f* à vinaigre.

vine-grower, *s.* Viticulteur *m;* vigneron *m.*

vine-growing, *s.* Viticulture *f.*

vine-plant, *s.* Cep *m* de vigne.

vineyard, *s.* Clos *m* de vigne; vigne *f,* vignoble *m.*

vintage, *s.* **1.** Récolte *f* du raisin; vendanges *fpl.* **2.** Année *f* (de belle récolte). **V. wine,** grand vin.

viola[1], *s.* Alto *m.*

viola[2], *s.* Pensée *f.*

violate, *v.tr.* Violer; manquer à.

violation, *s.* Violation *f.*

violence, *s.* **1.** (*a*) Violence *f;* intensité *f.* (*b*) **To do v. to one's feelings,** se faire violence. **2. Robbery with v.,** vol *m* à main armée.

violent, *a.* Violent.

violently, *adv.* Violemment; avec violence.

violet. **1.** *s.* Violette *f.* **2.** (*a*) *s.* Violet *m.* (*b*) *a.* Violet, -ette.

violin, *s.* Violon *m.*

violinist, *s.* Violoniste *mf.*

violoncello, *s.* Violoncelle *m.*

viper, *s.* Vipère *f.*

virago, *s.* Mégère *f.*

virgin, *s. & a.* Vierge (*f*).

virile, *a.* Viril, mâle.

virility, *s.* Virilité *f.*

virtual, *a.* De fait; en fait.

virtually, *adv.* Virtuellement; de fait; en pratique.

virtue, *s.* **1.** Vertu *f.* **2.** Qualité *f;* avantage *m.* **3.** *Prep.phr* **By v. of,** en vertu de, à titre de.

virtuoso, *s.* Virtuose *mf*

virtuous, *a.* Vertueux.

virtuously, *adv.* Vertueusement.

virulence, *s.* Virulence *f.*

virulent, *a.* Virulent.

virulently, *adv.* Avec virulence

visa[1], *a.* Visa *m.*

visa[2], *v.tr.* Viser; apposer un visa à.

visage, *s.* Visage *m,* figure *f.*

viscount, *s.* Vicomte *m.*

viscountess, *s.* Vicomtesse *f.*

viscous, *a.* Visqueux; gluant.

visibility, *s.* Visibilité *f.*

visible, *a.* Visible. **To become v.,** apparaître.

visibly, *adv.* Visiblement, manifestement; à vue d'œil.

vision, *s.* **1.** Vision *f,* vue *f.* **2.** (*a*) Imagination *f,* vision. (*b*) Apparition *f.*

visionary. **1.** *a.* (*a*) Visionnaire. (*b*) Chimérique. **2.** *s.* Visionnaire *mf.*

visit[1], *s.* **1.** Visite *f.* **2.** Séjour *m.*

visit[2], *v.tr.* Rendre visite à ; aller voir.
visitation, *s.* **1.** Calamité *f.* **2.** Apparition *f.*
visiting[1], *a.* En visite.
visiting[2], *s.* Visites *fpl.* **V. hours,** heures de visite.
visiting-card, *s.* Carte *f* de visite.
visitor, *s.* (*a*) Visiteur, -euse. **She has visitors,** elle a du monde. (*b*) Visitors' book, livre *m* des voyageurs.
vista, *s.* **1.** Échappée *f* de vue ; éclaircie *f.* **2.** Perspective *f.*
visual, *a.* Visuel.
visualize, *v.tr.* Se représenter.
vital, *a.* **1.** Vital, -aux. **2.** Essentiel ; capital, -aux.
vitality, *s.* **1.** Vitalité *f.* **2.** Vie *f*, animation *f.*
vitally, *adv.* D'une manière vitale.
vitamin, *s.* Vitamine *f.*
vitiate, *v.tr.* Vicier, corrompre.
vitiation, *s.* Viciation *f.*
vituperation, *s.* Injures *fpl.*
vituperative, *a.* Injurieux.
vivacious, *a.* Vif, animé, enjoué.
vivaciously, *adv.* Avec enjouement ; avec verve.
vivacity, *s.* Vivacité *f* ; animation *f.*
vivid, *a.* Vif, éclatant.
vividly, *adv.* Vivement ; avec éclat.
vividness, *s.* Vivacité *f*, éclat *m.*
vivisection, *s.* Vivisection *f.*
vixen, *s.* **1.** Renarde *f.* **2.** Mégère *f.*
viz., *adv.* A savoir ; c'est-à-dire.
vocabulary, *s.* Vocabulaire *m.*
vocal, *a.* Vocal, -aux.
vocalist, *s.* Chanteur *m*, cantatrice *f.*
vocally, *adv.* Vocalement, oralement.
vocation, *s.* Vocation *f.*
vociferate, *v.i. & tr.* Vociférer.
vociferous, *a.* Vociférant, bruyant.
vogue, *s.* Vogue *f*, mode *f.*
voice[1], *s.* Voix *f.*
voice[2], *v.tr.* Exprimer, énoncer.
voiceless, *a.* Sans voix ; muet, -ette
void. I. *a.* **1.** Vide. **2.** Vacant. **3.** Nul *f.* nulle. **4.** Dépourvu, dénué.
II. **void**, *s.* Vide *m.*
voile, *s.* Voile *m.*
volatile, *a.* **1.** Volatil. **2.** (*a*) Vif, gai. (*b*) Volage, inconstant.

volatilize, *v.i.* Se volatiliser.
volcanic, *a.* Volcanique.
volcano, *s.* Volcan *m.*
volition, *s.* Volition *f.*
volley, *s.* Volée *f* ; salve *f.*
volplane, *v.i.* **1.** Planer. **2.** Descendre en vol plané.
volt, *s.* Volt *m.*
voltage, *s.* Voltage *m.*
volubility, *s.* Volubilité *f.*
voluble, *a.* Facile, aisé ; grand parleur.
volubly, *adv.* Avec volubilité.
volume, *s.* **1.** Volume *m*, livre *m.* **2.** Volume ; grosseur *f.* **3.** Volume ; ampleur *f.*
voluminous, *a.* Volumineux.
voluntarily, *adv.* Volontairement, spontanément.
voluntary, *a.* Volontaire, spontané.
volunteer[1], *s.* Volontaire *m.*
volunteer[2], *v.tr.* Offrir volontairement, spontanément. *Abs.* S'offrir.
voluptuous, *a.* Voluptueux.
vomit, *v.tr. & i.* Vomir.
voracious, *a.* Vorace, dévorant.
voracity, *s.* Voracité *f.*
votary, *s.* Adorateur, -trice.
vote[1], *s.* **1.** (*a*) Vote *m*, scrutin *m.* **To put to the v.,** mettre aux voix. (*b*) Voix *f*, suffrage *m.* **To have a v.,** avoir le droit de vote. **2.** Motion *f*, résolution *f.*
vote[2], *v.i.* Voter.
voting, *s.* Vote *m* ; scrutin *m.*
votive, *a.* Votif.
vouch. **1.** *v.tr.* (*a*) Garantir. (*b*) Prouver. **2.** *v.i.* **To v. for,** répondre de.
voucher, *s.* Fiche *f* ; reçu *m*, bon *m.*
vouchsafe, *v.tr.* Daigner.
vow[1], *s.* Vœu *m*, serment *m.*
vow[2], *v.tr.* Vouer, jurer.
vowel, *s.* Voyelle *f.*
voyage, *s.* Voyage *m* sur mer.
voyager, *s.* Voyageur -euse. par mer ; passager, -ère.
vulgar, *a.* Vulgaire ; commun.
vulgarity, *s.* Vulgarité *f*, trivialité *f.*
vulgarly, *adv.* Vulgairement.
vulnerable, *a.* Vulnérable.
vulture, *s.* Vautour *m.*

W

W, w, s. (La lettre) W, w m.

wad¹, s. (a) Tampon m. (b) Liasse f.

wad², v.tr. Ouater.

wadding, s. 1. Ouatage m, rembourrage m. 2. (a) Ouate f. (b) Tampon m d'ouate.

waddle, v.i. Se dandiner.

wade. 1. v.i. Marcher dans l'eau. 2. v.tr. Passer à gué.

wafer, s. 1. Gaufrette f. 2. Hostie f. 3. Cachet m en papier.

waft, s. Bouffée f, souffle m.

wag¹, s. Farceur m, blagueur m.

wag², s. Agitation f, mouvement m; hochement m.

wag³. 1. v.tr. Agiter, remuer. 2. v.i. S'agiter, se remuer.

wage¹, s. Gages mpl; salaire m, paye f.

wage², v.tr. To w. war, faire la guerre.

wage-earner, s. Salarié, -ée.

wager¹, s. Pari m; gageure f.

wager², v.tr. Parier, gager.

waggon, s. 1. Charrette f; chariot m. 2. Mil: Fourgon m. 3. Wagon m.

wag(g)onette, s. Wagonnette f.

wail¹, s. (a) Cri plaintif; plainte f, gémissement m. (b) Vagissement m.

wail², v.i. Gémir.

wainscot, s. Lambris m.

waist, s. Taille f, ceinture f. W. measurement, tour m de taille.

waistband, s. Ceinture f.

waistcoat, s. Gilet m.

wait¹, s. 1. (a) Attente f; arrêt m. (b) To lie in w., être à l'affût.

wait². 1. v.i. (a) Attendre. To keep waiting, faire attendre. To w. for, attendre. (b) To w. at table, servir. 2. v.tr. Attendre, guetter. **wait on, upon,** v.ind.tr. Servir.

waiter, s. Garçon m. Head w., maître m d'hôtel.

waiting, s. 1. Attente f. 2. Service m.

waiting-maid, s. femme f de chambre.

waiting-room, s. Salle f d'attente; antichambre f.

waitress, s. Fille f de salle; serveuse f. W.! mademoiselle!

waive, v.tr. Renoncer à, abandonner; ne pas insister sur.

wake¹, s. Sillage m.

wake². 1. v.i. (a) **Waking or sleeping,** éveillé ou endormi. (b) Se réveiller. 2. v.tr. Réveiller.

wakeful, a. 1. Éveillé; peu disposé à dormir. 2. Vigilant.

wakefulness, s. 1. (a) Insomnie f. (b) État m de veille. 2. Vigilance f.

waken. 1. v.tr. Éveiller. 2. v.i. Se réveiller.

waking, s. Réveil m. On w. au réveil.

Wales. Pr.n. Le pays de Galles.

walk¹, s. 1. Marche f. 2. Promenade f. To go for a w., aller se promener. 3. Allée f; avenue f, promenade.

walk², v.i. 1. Marcher, cheminer. 2. (a) Aller à pied. (b) Se promener. **walk about,** v.i. Se promener; circuler. **walk along,** v.i. Marcher; s'avancer. **walk away,** v.i. S'en aller; partir. **walk in,** v.i. Entrer. **walk off,** v.i. S'en aller; partir. **walk out,** v.i. Sortir. **walk round,** v.i. 1. Faire le tour de. 2. Faire un détour. **walk up,** v.i. To w. up to, s'approcher de.

walker, s. Marcheur, -euse; promeneur, -euse; piéton m.

walking, s. Marche f; promenades fpl à pied.

walking-stick, s. Canne f.

wall, s. 1. (a) Mur m. (b) Muraille f. 2. Paroi f.

wallet, s. 1. Sacoche f. 2. Portefeuille m.

wallflower, s. Giroflée f des murailles.

wallow, v.i. Se vautrer; croupir.

wall-paper, s. Papier peint.

walnut, s. 1. Noix f. 2. Noyer m.

walnut-shell, s. Coquille f de noix.

walnut-tree, s. Noyer m.

walrus, s. Morse m.

waltz¹, s. Valse f.

waltz², v.i. Valser. To w. with, faire valser.

wan, a. Blême; blafard; pâle.

wand, s. 1. Baguette f. 2. Bâton m; verge f.

wander, v.i. (a) Errer; se promener au hasard. (b) To w. from, s'écarter de. (c) Divaguer; avoir le délire.

wanderer, s. Vagabond, -e; voyageur, -euse.

wandering[1], *a.* (*a*) Errant, vagabond. (*b*) Distrait.

wandering[2], *s.* 1. Vagabondage *m.* 2. Déviation *f.*

wane[1], *s.* Déclin *m.*

wane[2], *v.i.* Décroître, décliner.

want[1], *s.* 1. Manque *m*, défaut *m.* For w. of something better, faute de mieux. For w. of something to do, par désœuvrement. 2. Indigence *f.* 3. Besoin *m.*

want[2]. 1. *v.i.* (*a*) Manquer (*for*, de); être dépourvu (de). (*b*) Être dans le besoin. 2. *v.tr.* (*a*) Manquer de, ne pas avoir. (*b*) Avoir besoin de. Have you all you w.? avez-vous tout ce qu'il vous faut? (*c*) Désirer, vouloir. You are wanted, on vous demande.

wanted, *a.* Désiré, voulu, demandé.

wanting, *pred.a.* Manquant, qui manque. To be w., faire défaut.

wanton, *a.* (*a*) Licencieux, impudique. (*b*) Gratuit; sans motif.

wantonly, *adv.* 1. Impudiquement. 2. De gaieté de cœur. 3. Gratuitement.

war[1], *s.* Guerre *f.*

war[2], *v.i.* To war against, faire la guerre à.

warble, *v.i.* (*a*) Gazouiller (*b*) Chanter.

warbler, *s.* Oiseau chanteur.

warbling, *s.* Gazouillement *m.*

ward[1], *s.* 1. Pupille *mf.* 2. (*a*) Hospital w., salle *f* d'hôpital. (*b*) Quartier *m.* 3. Arrondissement *m.*

ward[2], *v.tr.* To w. off, parer; écarter.

warder, *s.* Gardien *m* (de prison).

wardress, *s.* Gardienne *f* de prison.

wardrobe, *s.* Garde-robe *f* *pl.* garde-robes.

ware, *s.* 1. *Coll:* (*a*) Toilet w., ustensiles *mpl* de toilette. (*b*) China w., porcelaine *f.* 2. *pl.* Marchandise *f.*

warehouse[1], *s.* Entrepôt *m.*

warehouse[2], *v.tr.* Emmagasiner.

warehousing, *s.* Emmagasinage *m*

warfare, *s.* La guerre.

warily, *adv.* Avec circonspection; prudemment.

wariness, *s.* Circonspection *f.*

warlike, *a.* Guerrier; belliqueux.

warm[1], *a.* 1. (*a*) Chaud. To be w., avoir chaud. (*b*) It is w., il fait chaud. 2. Chaleureux.

warm[2]. 1. *v.tr.* Chauffer. 2. *v.i.* (Se)

chauffer; se réchauffer. **warm up**. 1. *v.tr.* Chauffer; réchauffer. 2. *v.i.* S'échauffer.

warm-hearted, *a.* Au cœur chaud, généreux.

warmly, *adv.* 1. Chaudement. 2. (*a*) Chaleureusement. (*b*) Vivement, avec chaleur.

warmth, *s.* 1. Chaleur *f.* 2. (*a*) Ardeur *f*; chaleur. (*b*) Cordialité *f* chaleur. (*c*) Emportement *m.*

warn, *v.tr.* Avertir; prévenir.

warning[1], *s.* Avertisseur, d'avertissement.

warning[2], *s.* Avertissement *m.*

warp. 1. *v.tr.* Haler, touer. II. **warp**, *v.i.* Se déformer; gauchir.

warped, *a.* (*a*) Gauchi. (*b*) Perverti, faussé.

warrant[1], *s.* 1. Garantie *f.* 2. Autorisation *f*; justification *f.* 3. (*a*) Mandat *m.* (*b*) Autorité *f.* (*c*) Certificat *m.*

warrant[2], *v.tr.* 1. Garantir, certifier. 2. Justifier.

warranted, *a.* 1. Garanti. 2. Autorisé.

warren, *s.* Garenne *f.*

warrior, *s.* Guerrier *m*, soldat *m.*

Warsaw, *Pr.n.* Varsovie *f.*

warship, *s.* Vaisseau *m* de guerre.

wart, *s.* Verrue *f.*

war-time, *s.* Temps *m* de guerre.

wary, *a.* (*a*) Avisé, prudent. (*b*) To be w., se méfier.

wash[1], *s.* 1. (*a*) To have a w., se laver. (*b*) Ablutions *fpl.* (*c*) Lessive *f*; blanchissage *m.* 2. Sillage *m.* remous *m.*

wash[2], *v.tr.* 1. (*a*) Laver. To w. one's hands, se laver les mains. (*b*) *v.pr. & i.* Se laver. 2. (*a*) Blanchir, lessiver, laver. (*b*) Material that washes well, étoffe très lavable. 3. Baigner, arroser. 4. To w. ashore, rejeter sur le rivage. **wash away**, *v.tr.* 1. Enlever par le lavage. 2. Emporter, entraîner. **wash off**, *v.tr.* Enlever, effacer, par le lavage. **wash out**, *v.tr.* (*a*) Enlever. (*b*) Laver, rincer. **wash up**, *v.tr.* (*a*) Laver (la vaisselle). (*b*) Rejeter sur le rivage.

wash-basin, *s.* Cuvette *f.*

washer, *s.* Rondelle *f.*

washerwoman, *s.* Blanchisseuse *f*

washing, s. **1.** (a) Lavage m. (b) Ablutions fpl. **2.** Blanchissage m, lessive f.

washing-soda, s. Cristaux mpl (de soude).

washstand, s. Lavabo m

wasp, s. Guêpe f.

wastage, s. Déperdition f; perte f.

waste[1], a. **1.** To lay w., ravager. **2.** De rebut. W. paper, vieux papiers. W.-paper basket, corbeille f à papier(s).

waste[2], s. **1.** Région f inculte. **2.** Gaspillage m. W. of time, perte f de temps. **3.** Déchets mpl, rebut m.

waste[3]. I. v.tr. **1.** Consumer, user. **2.** Gaspiller. To w. one's time, perdre son temps.
    II. **waste,** v.i To w. (away), dépérir.

wasted, a. **1.** Dévasté, ravagé **2.** Amaigri. **3.** Gaspillé.

wasteful, a. Gaspilleur. -euse; prodigue.

watch[1], s. **1.** Garde f; surveillance f. To be on the w. for, guetter. **2.** Quart m. **3.** Montre f.

watch[2]. I. v.i. (a) Veiller. (b) To w. over, garder. (c) To w. for, attendre; guetter. **2.** v.tr. (a) Garder, veiller sur. (b) Observer. (c) Regarder; voir; assister à (d) Guetter.

watch-dog, s. Chien m de garde.

watcher, s. Veilleur, -euse.

watchful, a. Vigilant; alerte; attentif.

watchfulness, s. Vigilance f.

watch-glass, s. Verre m de montre.

watch-maker, s. Horloger m.

watchman, s. Gardien m, garde m.

watchword, s. Mot m d'ordre.

water[1], s. Eau f. **1.** (a) Cold w., eau fraîche. (b) To turn on the w., ouvrir l'eau. **2.** pl. To take the waters, prendre les eaux. **3.** (a) To swim under w., nager entre deux eaux. (b) High w., marée haute.

water[2]. I. v.tr. Arroser. **2.** v.i. Larmoyer.

water bottle, s. **1.** Carafe f. **2.** Gourde f; bidon m.

water-can, s. Broc m.

water-closet, s. Cabinet m; les cabinets; water-closet m, pl. water-closets.

water-colour, s. Aquarelle f.

watercourse, s. Cours m d'eau.

water-cress, s. Cresson m de fontaine.

watered, a. W. silk, soie moirée

waterfall, s. Chute f d'eau.

waterfowl, s. Gibier m d'eau.

water-ice, s. Sorbet m.

watering-can, s. Arrosoir m

watering-place, s. Station f balnéaire.

water-lily, s. Nénuphar m.

water-mark, s. Filigrane m.

water-melon, s. Melon m d'eau; pastèque f.

water-pipe, s. Tuyau m d'eau, conduite f d'eau.

water-polo, s. Polo m nautique.

waterproof, a. & s. Imperméable (m).

watertight, a. Étanche (à l'eau).

wave[1], s. **1.** Vague f; lame f. **2.** Onde f. **3.** Ondulation f **4.** Geste m, signe m.

wave[2]. I. v.i. **1.** S'agiter; flotter; onduler. **2.** Faire signe. **3.** Onduler.
    II. **wave,** v.tr. **1.** Agiter. To w. one's hand, faire signe de la main. **2.** Onduler. To have one's hair waved, se faire onduler.

waved, a. Ondé, ondulé.

waving, s. **1.** (a) Agitation f (b) Ondoiement m. **2.** Ondulation f.

wave-length, s. Longueur f d'onde.

waver, v.i. Vaciller. **1.** Trembloter. **2.** Hésiter; défaillir.

wavering[1], a. **1.** Vacillant, tremblotant. **2.** Hésitant; défaillant.

wavering[2], s. Vacillation f.

wax[1], s. Cire f.

wax[2], v.tr. Cirer.

waxed, a. **1.** Ciré. **2.** W. thread, fil poissé.

waxwork, s. Figure f de cire.

waxy, a. Cireux.

way, s. **1.** Chemin m, route f, voie f. Over the way, de l'autre côté de la rue. **2.** (a) To show the way, montrer la route. To lose one's way, s'égarer. To go the wrong way, faire fausse route. On the way, chemin faisant; en chemin. (b) Way in, entrée f. Way out, sortie f. (c) To make one's way, se diriger. (d) To be in s.o.'s way, gêner qn. To get out of the way, se ranger. To keep out of the way, se tenir à l'écart. To make way for, faire place à. **3. All the way,** jusqu'au bout. **It's a long way from here,** c'est loin d'ici. **4.** (*a*) Côté *m*, direction *f*. **This way,** par ici. (*b*) Sens *m*. **The wrong way,** à contre-sens. **5.** Moyen *m*. **6.** (*a*) Façon *f*, manière *f*. **That's the way!** à la bonne heure! **In one's own way,** à sa guise. (*b*) **To have one's (own) way,** agir à sa guise. **7. In many ways,** à bien des égards. **In some ways,** à certains points de vue. **8.** Cours *m*, course *f*. **9.** (*a*) **By the way,** incidemment; en passant. **By the way!** ah, j'y pense! (*b*) **By way of,** à titre de.

waylay, *v.tr.* Arrêter au passage.

wayside, *s.* Bord *m* de la route.

we, *pers. pron.* (*a*) Nous. (*b*) On.

weak, *a.* **1.** Faible; infirme. **To grow w.,** s'affaiblir. **2.** Dilué. **W tea,** thé léger.

weaken. 1. *v.tr.* Affaiblir; amollir. **2.** *v.i.* S'affaiblir, faiblir.

weakening[1], *a.* Affaiblissant.

weakening[2], *s.* Affaiblissement *m*.

weakly[1], *adv.* (*a*) Faiblement; sans force. (*b*) Sans résolution.

weakly[2], *a.* Débile, faible.

weakness, *s.* Faiblesse *f*.

wealth, *s.* **1.** Richesse *f*; opulence *f*. **2.** Abondance *f*, profusion *f*.

wealthy, *a.* Riche, opulent.

wean, *v.tr* Sevrer.

weapon, *s.* Arme *f*.

wear[1], *s.* **1.** (*a*) Usage *m*. **For evening w.,** pour le soir. **Ladies' w.,** articles *m* pour dames. (*b*) **To be the worse for w.,** être usé. **2.** Usure *f*.

wear[2]. **1.** *v.tr.* Porter. **What shall I w.?** qu'est-ce que je vais mettre? **2.** *v.tr.* User. **To w. holes in,** faire des trous à. **3. To w. well,** être de bon usage. **wear away. 1.** *v.tr.* (*a*) User, ronger. (*b*) Effacer, détruire. **2.** *v.i.* (*a*) S'user. (*b*) S'effacer. **wear off. 1.** *v.tr.* Faire disparaître. **2.** *v.i.* S'effacer, disparaître. **wear out. 1.** *v.tr.* (*a*) User. (*b*) Épuiser, lasser. **2.** *v.i.* S'user.

wearer, *s.* Personne *f* qui porte qch.

wearily, *adv.* **1.** D'un air las, fatigué **2.** Avec fatigue; péniblement.

weariness, *s.* Lassitude *f*, fatigue *f*.

wearing[1], *a.* Fatigant, lassant.

wearing[2], *s.* **W. apparel,** vêtements *mpl*, habits *mpl*.

wearisome, *a.* Ennuyeux.

weary[1], *a.* **1.** Fatigué; las, *f.* lasse. **2.** Las, dégoûté. **3.** Fatigant, obsédant.

weary[2]. **1.** *v.i.* Se lasser, se fatiguer. **2.** *v.tr.* Lasser, fatiguer.

wearying, *a.* Ennuyeux.

weasel, *s.* Belette *f*.

weather, *s.* Temps *m*. **In all weathers,** par tous les temps.

weather-beaten, *a.* Bronzé, hâlé.

weathercock, *s.* Girouette *f*.

weather-forecast, *s.* Bulletin *m* météorologique; prévisions *fpl* du temps.

weave, *v.tr.* (*a*) Tisser. (*b*) Tramer. (*c*) Tresser.

weaver, *s.* Tisserand *m*.

weaving, *s.* **1.** Tissage *m*. **2.** Entrelacement *m*.

web, *s.* **1.** Tissu *m*. **2. Spider's web,** toile *f* d'araignée.

webbed, *a.* Palmé, membrané.

wed. 1. *v.tr.* (*a*) Épouser; se marier avec. (*b*) Unir. **2.** *v.i.* Se marier.

wedded, *a.* Marié.

wedding, *s.* **1.** Noce(s) *f*(*pl*); mariage *m*. **2.** *Attrib.* Nuptial, -aux; de noce(s).

wedding-cake, *s.* Gâteau *m* de noce(s).

wedding-day, *s.* Jour *m* des noces.

wedding-march, *s.* Marche nuptiale.

wedding-present, *s.* Cadeau *m* de noces.

wedding-ring, *s.* Alliance *f*.

wedge[1], *s.* Coin *m*.

wedge[2], *v.tr.* Coincer, assujettir.

Wednesday, *s.* Mercredi *m*.

wee, *a.* Petit; minuscule.

weed[1], *s.* Mauvaise herbe.

weed[2], *v.tr.* Sarcler. **weed out,** *v.tr.* Éliminer; extirper.

weeding, *s.* Sarclage *m*.

weeds, *s.pl.* Vêtements *m* de deuil.

week, *s.* Semaine *f*; huit jours. **To-day w.,** d'aujourd'hui en huit.

weekday, *s.* Jour *m* ouvrable. **On weekdays,** en semaine.

week-end, *s.* Fin *f* de semaine; week-end *m*, *pl.* week-ends.

weekly. 1. *a.* (*a*) De la semaine; hebdomadaire. (*b*) A la semaine. **2.** *s.* Journal *m* hebdomadaire. **3.** *adv.* Par semaine; tout les huit jours.

weep, v.i. Pleurer.
weigh. 1. v.tr. (a) Peser; soupeser. (b) **To w. anchor,** lever l'ancre. **2.** v.i. Peser; avoir du poids. **weigh down,** v.tr. Surcharger; accabler.
weighing-machine, s. Appareil m de pesage.
weight, s. **1.** (a) Poids m; pesant m. (b) Poids, pesanteur f. **To feel the w. of,** soupeser **2. Set of weights,** série f de poids. **3.** Charge f. **4.** Force f. **5.** Importance f.
weightiness, s. **1.** Pesanteur f, lourdeur f. **2.** Importance f, force f.
weighty, a. **1.** Pesant, lourd. **2.** Important, sérieux.
weir, s. Barrage m.
weird, a. (a) Surnaturel; mystérieux. (b) Étrange, singulier.
welcome¹, a. **1.** (a) Bienvenu. **To make w.,** faire bon accueil à. (b) As int. **W.!** soyez le bienvenu! **2.** Agréable; acceptable. **3. You are w. to it,** c'est à votre service.
welcome², s. (a) Bienvenue f. (b) Accueil m.
welcome³, v.tr. **1.** Souhaiter la bienvenue à. **2.** Recevoir avec plaisir.
weld, v.tr. Souder.
welfare, s. Bien-être m.
well¹, s. **1.** Puits m; source f. **2.** Puits, cage f.
well², v.i. **To w.** (up), jaillir; sourdre.
well³. I. adv. Bien. **1. This lad will do w.,** ce garçon ira loin. **To do as w. as one can,** faire de son mieux. **W. done!** très bien! **One might as w. say,** autant dire. **2.** (a) As w., aussi. (b) As w. as, de même que; comme; non moins que. **3.** (a) Eh bien. (b) Well then, eh bien, alors. **II. well,** pred.a. **1.** En bonne santé, bien portant. **2.** (a) **It would be w. to,** il serait bon de. (b) **That's all very w.,** tout cela est bel et bon. **W. and good!** bon! **III. well,** s. Bien m.
well-advised, pred.a. Sage, prudent.
well-being, s. Bien-être m.
well-bred, a. Bien élevé, bien appris.
well-educated, a. Instruit.
well known, a. (Bien) connu; célèbre. **As is w. k.,** comme tout le monde le sait.
well-mannered, a. Bien élevé.

well-meaning, a. Bien intentionné.
well-meant, a. Fait avec une bonne intention.
well-nigh, adv. Presque.
well-off, adj.phr. **1.** Dans l'aisance, à l'aise; riche. **2. W. off for,** bien pourvu, bien fourni, de.
well read, a. Instruit.
well spent, a. Bien utilisé; bien employé.
well-to-do, a. Dans l'aisance; à son aise.
Welsh. 1. a. Gallois; du pays de Galles. **2.** s. (a) pl. Gallois m. (b) Le gallois.
Welshman, s. Gallois m.
Welshwoman, s. Galloise f.
west. 1. s. Ouest m, occident m. **2.** adv. A l'ouest, à l'occident; vers l'ouest. **3.** a. Ouest inv; d'ouest; occidental, -aux.
westerly. 1. a. D'ouest. **2.** adv. Vers l'ouest.
western, a. Ouest inv. de l'ouest; occidental, -aux.
westwards, adv. Vers, à, l'ouest.
wet¹, a. (a) Mouillé, humide. **Wet through,** trempé (jusqu'aux os). (b) Humide, pluvieux.
wet², v.tr. Mouiller. **To wet the tea,** infuser le thé.
wetness, s. Humidité f.
wet-nurse, s. Nourrice f.
wetting, s. **To get a w.,** se faire tremper.
whale, s. Baleine f.
whalebone, s. Baleine f.
whaler, s. Baleinier m.
whaling, s. Pêche f à la baleine. **W. ship,** baleinier m.
wharf, s. Débarcadère m, embarcadère m; quai m.
what. I. a. **1.** (Ce) que, qui. **2.** Quel f. quelle. **W. good is this?** à quoi cela est-il bon? **3. W. an idea!** quelle idée! **W. a lot of people!** que de gens!
II. what, pron. **1.** Ce qui, ce que. **Come w. may,** advienne que pourra. **Say w. he will,** quoi qu'il dise. **2.** (a) Qu'est-ce qui? qu'est-ce que? que? quoi? **W. is that to you?** qu'est-ce que cela vous fait? **What's the use?** à quoi bon? **W. is to be done?** que faire? **W. is he like?** comment est-il? **W. then?** et après? W.

(did you say)? plaît-il? pardon?
(b) Ce qui, ce que. **I don't know
w. to do,** je ne sais que faire.
3. W.? you can't come! comment!
vous ne pouvez pas venir!

whatever. I. *pron.* (a) Tout ce que;
n'importe quoi. (b) Quoi qui, quoi
que. **2.** *a.* (a) Quelque . . . qui, que.
(b) Aucun. **None w.,** pas un seul.
Nothing w., absolument rien.

wheat, *s.* Blé *m,* froment *m.*

wheedle, *v.tr.* Enjôler, cajoler

wheel[1]**,** *s.* **I.** Roue *f;* roulette *f.*
2. *pl.* Rouages *m.* **3.** Volant *m.* **To
take the w.,** prendre la barre.

wheel[2]**. I.** *v.tr.* (a) Tourner. (b)
Rouler. **2.** *v.i.* Tourner en rond;
tournoyer.

wheelbarrow, *s.* Brouette *f.*

wheelwright, *s.* Charron *m.*

wheeze, *v.i.* Respirer péniblement.

whelk, *s.* Buccin *m.*

when. I. *adv.* Quand? pour quand?
II. when, *conj.* **I.** Quand, lorsque
2. Où, que.

whence, *adv.* D'où.

whenever, *adv.* (a) Toutes les fois
que; chaque fois que. (b) A
n'importe quel moment.

where, *adv.* **I.** Où? **2.** (Là) où.

whereabouts, *s.* **No one knows his
w.,** personne ne sait où il est.

whereas, *conj.* **I.** Attendu que, vu
que. **2.** Alors que, tandis que

whereby, *adv.* Par lequel.

wherein, *adv.* **I.** En quoi? **2.** Dans
lequel; où.

whereof, *adv.* De quoi; dont.

whereon, *adv.* Sur quoi, sur lequel.

whereupon, *adv.* Sur quoi, sur lequel.

wherever, *adv.* Partout où; n'importe où.

whet, *v.tr.* **I.** Aiguiser, repasser.
2. Stimuler, exciter.

whether, *conj.* **I.** Si. **2. W. it rains
or blows,** soit qu'il vente, soit qu'il
pleuve. **W. or not,** qu'il en soit
ainsi ou non.

which. I. *a.* **I.** Quel. **W. way do we
go?** par où allons-nous? **W. one?**
lequel? laquelle? **2.** Lequel, *f.*
laquelle; *pl.* lesquels, lesquelles.
II. which, *pron.* **I.** Lequel, etc.
I don't mind w., cela m'est égal.
2. (a) Qui; que; lequel. (b) Ce qui,
ce que. **3.** (a) To w., at w., auquel,

f. à laquelle. *pl.* auxquels, auxquelles;
où. **Of w., from w.,** duquel, *f.* de
laquelle; *pl.* desquels, desquelles;
dont. (b) Quoi.

whichever, *rel. pron. & a.* **I.** (a)
pron. Celui, *f.* celle, *pl.* ceux, celles,
qui, celui, etc., que; n'importe
lequel, etc. (b) *a.* Le . . . que;
n'importe quel. **2.** *a.* N'importe
quel; quelque . . . que.

whiff, *s.* Bouffée *f.*

while[1]**,** *s.* **I.** After a w., après quelque
temps. **In a little w.,** sous peu;
avant peu. **A little w. ago,** il y a
peu de temps. **A long w.,** longtemps.
2. To be worth w., valoir la peine.

while[2]**,** *v.tr.* To w. away, faire passer.

while[3]**,** *conj.* **I.** (a) Pendant que;
tandis que; tout en. (b) Tant que.
2. Quoique, bien que, tout en.

whilst, *conj.* = WHILE[3].

whim, *s.* Caprice *m;* fantaisie *f*

whimper[1]**,** *s.* Geignement *m.*

whimper[2]**,** *v.i.* Pleurnicher, geindre.

whimsical, *a.* Capricieux, fantasque.

whine[1]**,** *s.* Plainte *f;* geignement *m.*

whine[2]**,** *v.i.* Se plaindre; pleurnicher; geindre.

whining[1]**,** *a.* Geignant; pleurnicheur, -euse; plaintif.

whining[2]**,** *s.* (a) Geignement *m*
(b) Plaintes *fpl.*

whip[1]**,** *s.* Fouet *m.*

whip[2]**. I.** *v.tr.* **I.** Fouetter. **2.**
Mouvoir, sortir, vivement.
II. whip, *v.i.* Fouetter.

whipping, *s.* Fouettée *f.*

whirl[1]**,** *s.* Tourbillon *m.*

whirl[2]**. I.** *v.i.* Tourbillonner. tournoyer. **2.** *v.tr.* (a) Faire tourbillonner. (b) **To w. along,** emporter à
toute vitesse.

whirlpool, *s.* Tourbillon *m* (d'eau).

whirlwind, *s.* Tourbillon *m.*

whirr[1]**,** *s.* Bruissement *m.*

whirr[2]**,** *v.i.* Ronronner.

whiskers, *s.pl.* Favoris *m;* moustache *f.*

whisky, *s.* Whisky *m.*

whisper[1]**,** *s.* **I.** Chuchotement *m.*
2. Rumeur *f,* bruit *m.*

whisper[2]**. I.** *v.i.* Chuchoter; parler
bas; murmurer. **2.** *v.tr.* Chuchoter,
souffler à l'oreille.

whispering, *s.* **I.** Chuchotement *m.*
2. Bruissement *m;* murmure *m.*

whistle[1], s. **I.** Sifflement m; coup m de sifflet. **2.** Sifflet m.

whistle[2]. **I.** v.i. (a) Siffler. (b) Donner un coup de sifflet. **2.** v.tr Siffler, siffloter.

Whit, a. **W. Sunday**, (dimanche m de) la Pentecôte.

white. I. a. **I.** Blanc, f. blanche. **As w. as a sheet**, pâle comme la mort. II. **white**, s. **I.** Blanc m; couleur blanche. **2.** Blanc, f. blanche; homme, femme, de la race blanche.

whitebait, s. Blanchaille f.

white-haired, a Aux cheveux blancs.

whiten, v.tr. Blanchir.

whiteness, s. (a) Blancheur f. (b) Pâleur f.

whitethorn, s. Aubépine f.

whitewash[1], s. Blanc m de chaux.

whitewash[2], v.tr. Blanchir à la chaux.

whither, adv. **I.** Où? vers quel lieu? **2.** (Là) où.

whiting, s. Merlan m.

whitish, a. Blanchâtre.

Whitsun(tide), s. La Pentecôte.

whizz[1], s. Sifflement m.

whizz[2], v.i. Siffler. **To w. past**, passer à toute vitesse.

who, pron. **I.** Qui? qui est-ce qui? **2.** (a) Qui. (b) Lequel, f. laquelle; pl. lesquel(le)s.

whoever, pron. nom. **I.** Celui qui; quiconque. **2.** Qui que.

whole. I. a. **I.** Intact. **2.** Intégral -aux; entier; complet, -ète. II. **whole**, s. Tout m, totalité f; ensemble m. **(Up)on the w.**, à tout prendre; somme toute.

wholesale. I. s. **W. and retail**, gros et détail. **2.** a. (a) En gros. (b) En masse. **3.** adv. En gros.

wholesome, a. Sain; salubre.

wholly, adv. **I.** Tout à fait; complètement, entièrement. **2.** Intégralement.

whom, pron. **I.** Qui? **2.** (a) Que; lequel, f. laquelle; pl. lesquels, f. lesquelles. (b) Qui. **Of w.**, dont. **3.** Celui, f. celle, que; qui.

whooping-cough, s. Coqueluche f.

whortleberry, s. Airelle f.

whose, poss.pron. **I.** De qui? à qui? **2.** (a) Dont. (b) De qui; duquel, f. de laquelle; pl. desquel(le)s.

why. **I.** adv. Pourquoi? pour quelle raison? **2.** s. Pourquoi m. **3.** int. Why, what's the matter? mais qu'avez-vous donc?

wick, s. Mèche f.

wicked, a. Mauvais, méchant.

wickedly, adv. Méchamment.

wickedness, s. Méchanceté f.

wicket, s. **I.** Guichet m. **2.** Barrière f.

wide. I. a. **I.** Large. **How w. is the room?** quelle est la largeur de la pièce? **2.** Étendu, ample. **3.** Ample, large. **4.** Éloigné, loin. II. **wide**, adv. **I.** Loin. **W. apart**, espacé. **2.** Largement.

widely, adv. Largement. **W. known**, très connu.

widen. **I.** v.tr. (a) Élargir. (b) Étendre. **2.** v.i. S'élargir.

wide open, a. (Tout) grand ouvert.

wide-spread, a. **I.** Étendu. **2.** Répandu.

widow, s. Veuve f.

widowed, a. Veuve.

widower, s. Veuf m.

widowhood, s. Veuvage m.

width, s. Largeur f; ampleur f.

wield, v.tr. Manier; exercer.

wife, s. Femme f; épouse f.

wig, s. Perruque f.

wild, a. **I.** Sauvage. **2.** (a) **A w. night**, une nuit de tempête. (b) Farouche, inapprivoisé. (c) Dissipé, dissolu. **3.** (a) Affolé. **W. with joy**, fou, f. folle, de joie. (b) Fantasque; insensé; au hasard. **W. talk**, propos en l'air. **4.** s.pl. Région f sauvage.

wilderness, s. Désert m; lieu m sauvage.

wild-fowl, s. Coll: Gibier m à plume.

wiles, s.pl. Ruses f, artifices m.

wilful, a. **I.** Entêté, volontaire. **2.** Fait exprès.

wilfully, adv. **I.** Exprès, à dessein. **2.** Volontairement.

wiliness, s. Astuce f.

will[1], s. **I.** (a) Volonté f. (b) **With a w.**, de bon cœur. **2.** (a) Décision f; volonté. (b) Bon plaisir; gré m. **3.** Testament m.

will[2], v. def. I. Vouloir. **I.** (a) **Do as you w.**, faites comme vous voudrez. **Say what you w.**, quoi que vous disiez. (b) **Would to heaven**, plût au

ciel (que). **2. W. you?** voulez-vous
bien ? **Won't you sit down?** veuillez
(donc) vous asseoir. **3. Accidents
w. happen,** on ne peut pas éviter les
accidents.

    II. **will.** **1.** (*a*) **Will he be there?**
y sera-t-il ? **No, you won't,** pas du
tout. **You won't forget, w. you?**
vous n'oublierez pas, hein ? **You
w. write to me, won't you?** vous
m'écrirez, n'est-ce pas ? (*b*) **He w.
dictate and you w. write,** il va dicter
et vous allez écrire. **2. He would
come if,** il viendrait si.

William. *Pr.n.* Guillaume *m.*

willing, *a.* **1.** (*a*) De bonne volonté ;
bien disposé. **W. hands,** mains empressées. (*b*) Consentant. **2. To be
w.,** vouloir bien. **W. or not,** bon
gré mal gré.

willingly, *adv.* **1.** De plein gré.
2. De bon cœur ; volontiers.

willingness, *s.* **1.** Bonne volonté
2. Consentement *m.*

willow, *s.* Saule *m.*

will-power, *s.* Volonté *f.*

wilt, *v.i.* Se flétrir, se faner.

wily, *a.* Rusé, astucieux.

win[1], *s.* Victoire *f.*

win[2], *v.tr. & i.* **1.** Gagner ; remporter. **2.** Acquérir ; captiver. **3.**
Conquérir. **win over,** *v.tr.* Gagner.

wince, *v.i.* Tressaillir de douleur ;
sourciller ; broncher.

wind[1], *s.* **1.** Vent *m.* (*a*) High w.,
vent fort. **To get the w. up,** avoir
le trac. (*b*) **Head w.,** vent debout.
In the teeth of the w., contre le vent
2. To get w. of, avoir vent de.
3. Souffle *m,* respiration *f,* haleine *f.*

wind[2], *v.tr.* (*a*) Éventer. flairer
(*b*) Essouffler.

wind[3]. I. *v.i.* Tourner ; faire des
détours ; serpenter.

    II. **wind,** *v.tr.* **1.** Enrouler,
dévider. **2. To w. the clock,** remonter l'horloge. **wind up. 1.** *v.tr.*
(*a*) Enrouler. (*b*) Remonter. (*c*) Terminer. **2.** *v.i.* Finir ; terminer.

winded, *a.* Hors d'haleine ; essoufflé.

windfall, *s.* **1.** Fruit tombé. **2.**
Aubaine *f.*

winding[1], *a.* Sinueux, plein de
détours, qui serpente.

winding[2], *s.* **1.** Remontage *m.* **2.** *pl.*
Sinuosités *f,* replis *m,* méandres *m.*

wind-instrument, *s.* Instrument *m*
à vent.

windlass, *s.* Treuil *m.*

windmill, *s.* Moulin *m* à vent.

window, *s.* **1.** (*a*) Fenêtre *f.* **To look
out of the w.,** regarder par la fenêtre.
To break a w., casser une vitre,
un carreau. (*b*) **Stained-glass w.,**
verrière *f* ; vitrail, -aux *m.* (*c*)
Guichet *m.* (*d*) Vitrine *f,* devanture *f,*
montre *f.* **2.** Glace *f.*

window-ledge, *s.* Rebord *m,* appui
m, de fenêtre.

window-pane, *s.* Vitre *f,* carreau *m.*

window-sill, *s.* Appui *m,* rebord *m,*
tablette *f,* de fenêtre.

windscreen, *s.* Pare-brise *m inv*

wind-sleeve, *s.* Sac *m* à vent.

windward. **1.** *a. & adv.* Au vent.
2. *s.* Côté *m* au vent.

windy, *a.* Venteux. **W. day,** journée
de grand vent.

wine, *s.* Vin *m.*

wine-cellar, *s.* Cave *f* au vin.

wine-glass, *s.* Verre *m* à vin.

wine-list, *s.* Carte *f* des vins.

wine-waiter, *s.* Sommelier *m.*

wing, *s.* **1.** Aile *f.* **2.** Vol *m,* essor *m.*
To take w., s'envoler. **3.** Battant *m.*

winged, *a.* Ailé.

wink[1], *s.* Clignement *m* d'œil ; clin
m d'œil.

wink[2], *v.i.* (*a*) Cligner les yeux. (*b*)
To w. at, cligner de l'œil à.

winkle, *s.* Bigorneau *m.*

winner, *s.* Gagnant, -ante.

winning[1], *a.* **1. W. number,** numéro
gagnant. **2.** Attrayant, séduisant.

winning[2], *s.* **1.** Victoire *f.* **2.** *pl.*
Gains *m.*

winning-post, *s.* Poteau *m* d'arrivée.

winnow, *v.tr.* Vanner.

winsome, *a.* Captivant, séduisant.

winter[1], *s.* Hiver *m.* **W. resort,** station
hivernale. **W. sports,** sports d'hiver.

winter[2], *v.i.* Hiverner.

winter-time, *s.* Saison *f* d'hiver.

wipe, *v.tr.* Essuyer. **wipe away,**
v.tr. Essuyer.

wire[1], *s.* **1.** Fil *m* métallique. (*a*)
Copper w., fil de laiton. **W. mattress,** sommier métallique. (*b*) **Telegraph wires,** fils télégraphiques.
2. Télégramme *m,* dépêche *f.*

wire[2], *v.tr.* **1.** Canaliser. **2.** Télégraphier.

wireless¹, *a.* Sans fil. **W. telegraphy,** télégraphie *f* sans fil, T.S.F. **W. telegram,** radiotélégramme *m.* **W. message,** radio *m.*

wireless², *v.tr.* Envoyer par la radio.

wiriness, *s.* Vigueur *f.*

wiring, *s.* Pose *f* de fils électriques ; canalisation *f.*

wiry, *a.* (*a*) Raide, rude (*b*) Sec *f.* sèche, et nerveux.

wisdom, *s.* Sagesse *f.*

wise, *a.* **1.** Sage ; prudent. **2.** He is **none the wiser,** il n'en est pas plus avancé. **No one will be any the wiser,** ni vu ni connu.

wisely, *adv.* Sagement, prudemment.

wish¹, *s.* (*a*) Désir *m* ; vœu *m.* (*b*) Souhait *m*, vœu.

wish². **1.** *v.ind.tr.* To w. for, désirer, souhaiter. **2.** *v.tr.* Vouloir. (*a*) Désirer, vouloir. (*b*) **I w. I were in your place,** je voudrais bien être à votre place. (*c*) **To w. s.o.** good night, souhaiter une bonne nuit à qn ; dire bonsoir à qn.

wishful, *a.* Désireux.

wishing, *s.* Désirs *mpl*, souhaits *mpl*

wisp, *s.* (*a*) Bouchon *m*, poignée *f.* (*b*) **W. of hair,** mèche folle.

wistful, *a.* Désenchanté. **W. smile,** sourire pensif.

wistfully, *adv.* D'un air songeur et triste.

wit, *s.* Esprit *m*, entendement *m* ; intelligence *f.* **To be at one's wit's end,** ne plus savoir de quel côté se tourner.

witch, *s.* (*a*) Sorcière *f.* (*b*) Charmeuse *f.*

witchcraft, *s.* Sorcellerie *f* ; magie noire.

witchery, *s.* (*a*) Ensorcellement *m*, enchantement *m.* (*b*) Fascination *f.*

with, *prep.* Avec. **1.** (*a*) **I shall be w. you in a moment,** je serai à vous dans un moment. (*b*) **Girl w. blue eyes,** jeune fille aux yeux bleus. (*c*) **This decision rests w. you,** c'est à vous de décider. (*d*) **W. all his faults,** malgré tous ses défauts. **2.** (*a*) **I can do nothing w. him,** je ne peux rien en faire. **It is a habit w. me,** c'est une habitude chez moi. (*b*) **W. these words,** ce disant. (*c*) **To fight w.,** se battre contre. **3.** **To part w.,** se défaire de. **4.** (*a*) **To take sth. w.**

both hands, prendre qch. à deux mains. (*b*) **To tremble w. rage,** trembler de rage. **5.** **W. all due respect,** sauf votre respect. **I say so w. regret,** je le dis à regret.

withdraw. **1.** *v.tr.* (*a*) Retirer. (*b*) Soustraire (*from*, à). **2.** *v.i.* Se retirer ; s'éloigner. **To w. into one-self,** se renfermer en soi-même.

withdrawal, *s.* (*a*) Retrait *m.* (*b*) Rappel *m* ; rétractation *f.*

wither. **1.** *v.i.* Se dessécher, dépérir. **2.** *v.tr.* Dessécher, flétrir.

withering, *a.* Foudroyant, écrasant.

withhold, *v.tr.* (*a*) Refuser (*from*, à). (*b*) Cacher (*from*, à). (*c*) Retenir.

within. **1.** *adv.* A l'intérieur ; au dedans. **2.** *prep.* (*a*) A l'intérieur de, en dedans de. (*b*) **To be w. the truth,** être au-dessous de la vérité. **W. a pound,** à une livre près. (*c*) **W. sight,** en vue. **W. call,** à portée de la voix. **W. two miles,** à moins de deux milles. (*d*) **W. an hour,** dans une heure.

without. **1.** *adv.* A l'extérieur, au dehors. **2.** *prep.* (*a*) En dehors de. (*b*) Sans. **To go w.,** se passer de

withstand, *v.tr.* Résister à.

witness¹, *s.* **1.** Témoignage *m.* To bear w. to, témoigner de. **2.** Témoin *m.*

witness². **1.** *v.tr.* (*a*) Être témoin de ; assister à. (*b*) Certifier. **2.** *v.i.* To w. to, témoigner de.

witness-box, *s.* = Barre *f* des témoins.

witticism, *s.* Trait *m* d'esprit : bon mot.

wittily, *adv.* Spirituellement

wittiness, *s.* Esprit *m*

witty, *a.* Spirituel.

wizard, *s.* Sorcier *m*, magicien *m*

wizardry, *s.* Sorcellerie *f*, magie *f*

wizened, *a.* Desséché, ratatiné.

wobble, *v.i.* Ballotter ; branler

woe, *s.* Malheur *m*, chagrin *m.*

woe-begone, *a.* Triste, désolé

woeful, *a.* Triste, affligé.

woefully, *adv.* Tristement.

wolf, *s.* Loup *m.* **She-w.,** louve *f*

wolfish, *a.* Vorace ; cruel.

woman, *s.* **1.** Femme *f.* **An old w.,** une vieille. **2.** *Attrib.* **W. doctor,** femme médecin.

womanlike. **1.** *a.* De femme. **2.** *adv.* En femme ; comme une femme.

womanliness, s. (a) Féminité f. (b) Charme féminin.

womanly, a. De femme; féminin.

wonder[1], s. 1. Merveille f, prodige m For a w., chose remarquable. No w., rien d'étonnant. 2. Étonnement m, surprise f. To fill with w. émerveiller.

wonder[2]. 1. v.i. S'étonner, s'émerveiller (at, de). 2. v.tr. (a) S'étonner. (b) Se demander.

wonderful, a. Merveilleux prodigieux.

wonderfully adv. Merveilleusement.

wondering, a. Étonné, émerveillé

wonderment, s. Étonnement m.

wonder-struck, a. Émerveillé.

wont, s. Coutume f, habitude f.

wonted, a. Habituel, accoutumé.

woo, v.tr. Faire la cour à, courtiser

wood, s. Bois m.

wood-carving, s. Sculpture sur bois.

woodcock, s. Bécasse f.

woodcut, s. Gravure f sur bois

wood-cutter, s. Bûcheron m

wooded, a. Boisé.

wooden, a. 1. De bois en bois. 2. Raide, gauche.

wood-engraving, s. Gravure sur bois.

woodland, s. 1. Pays boisé. 2. Attrib. Des bois; sylvestre.

woodpecker, s. Pic m.

wood-pigeon, s. Ramier m.

woodwork, s. 1. Travail m du bois. 2. (a) Boiserie f. (b) Menuiserie f.

wooer, s. Amoureux m; prétendant m

wooing, s. Cour f.

wool, s. Laine f Steel w. aine d'acier

woollen, a. De laine W. goods, lainages m.

woolly. 1. a. Laineux; de laine 2. s. (Vêtement m en) tricot m.

word, s. 1. Mot m. (a) In other words, en d'autres termes. In so many words, en termes propres. (b) Parole f. Without a w., sans mot dire. With these words, ce disant. (c) To say a good w. for, dire un mot en faveur de. (d) To have words, avoir une altercation. 2. By w. of mouth, de vive voix; verbalement. 3. To send s.o. w. of sth., faire savoir qch à qn; prévenir qn de qch. 4. To keep one's w., tenir parole. To take s.o. at his w., prendre qn au mot. 5. W. of command, ordre m. commandement m

wordy, a. 1. Verbeux, prolixe. 2. W. warfare, lutte f oratoire.

work[1], s. 1. Travail m, -aux The forces at w., les forces en jeu. 2. Travail, ouvrage m, besogne f, tâche f. 3. (a) Good works, (les) bonnes œuvres. (b) Ouvrage, œuvre f. 4. To be out of w., être sans travail; chômer. 5. pl. Constructive works, ouvrages d'art. 6. pl. Rouages mpl, mécanisme m, mouvement m 7. pl. Usine f, atelier m.

work[2]. 1. v.i. 1. Travailler. 2. (a) Fonctionner, aller: marcher (b) Agir; opérer.
II. **work,** v.tr. 1. Faire travailler. 2. Faire fonctionner, faire marcher; faire jouer. 3. Faire; opérer. 4. Broder. 5. Travailler, façonner. 6. Exploiter. **work out,** v.tr. (a) Mener à bien. (b) Développer; élaborer. (c) Supputer; résoudre.

work-basket. s. Corbeille f à ouvrage.

work-box, s. Boîte f à ouvrage.

worker, s. (a) Travailleur -euse. (b) Ouvrier, -ère.

workhouse, s. Asile m des pauvres; hospice m.

working[1], a. The w. classes, la classe ouvrière. W. man, ouvrier m.

working[2], s. 1. Travail m. 2. (a) Manœuvre f. (b) Exploitation f. 3. Marche f, fonctionnement m. In w. order, en état de service

workman, s. Ouvrier m, artisan m.

workmanship, s Exécution f; façon f.

workshop, s. Atelier m.

world, s. Monde m. 1. Map of the w., mappemonde f. All the w. over, dans le monde entier. 2. Man of the w., homme m qui connaît la vie. 3. The theatrical w., le milieu du théâtre.

worldliness, s. Mondanité f.

worldly, a. Mondain.

world-wide, a. Universel; mondial, -aux.

worm, s. Ver m.

wormwood, s. Absinthe f.

worn out, a. **1.** Usé. **2.** Épuisé; exténué.

worried, a. Harassé; soucieux.

worry[1], s. Ennui m; souci m.

worry[2]. **1.** v.tr. Tourmenter, harceler. **2.** v.i. Se tourmenter, s'inquiéter. Don't w.! soyez tranquille!

worse. 1. a. & s. Pire; plus mauvais. To make matters w., par surcroît de malheur. So much the w., tant pis. **2.** s. To change for the w., s'altérer. **3.** adv. Pis; plus mal.

worship[1], s. Culte m, adoration f.

worship[2], v.tr. Adorer.

worshipper, s. Adorateur, -trice.

worst[1]. **1.** a. (Le) pire, (le) plus mauvais. **2.** s. To get the w. of it, avoir le dessous. If the w. comes to the w., en mettant les choses au pis. Do your w.! faites du pis que vous pourrez! **3.** adv. (Le) pis, (le) plus mal.

worst[2], v.tr. Battre, vaincre. To be worsted, avoir le dessous.

worsted, s. Laine f à tricoter.

worth. 1. pred. a. Valant. (a) To be w., valoir. W. the money, avantageux. (b) Book w. reading, livre qui mérite d'être lu. It's w. knowing, c'est bon à savoir. **2.** s. Valeur f.

worthily, adv. Dignement.

worthiness, s. Mérite m.

worthless, a. Sans valeur.

worthy, a. Digne; brave.

wound[1], s. (a) Blessure f. (b) Plaie f.

wound[2], v.tr. Blesser.

woven, a. Tissé.

wraith, s. Apparition spectrale.

wrangle[1], s. Dispute f, querelle f.

wrangle[2], v.i. Se disputer, se quereller.

wrangling, s. Disputes fpl, querelles fpl.

wrap, v.tr. **1.** Envelopper. **2.** Enrouler.

wrapped, a. **1.** (a) Roulé. (b) W. up, emmitouflé. (c) Enveloppé. **2.** W. in meditation, plongé dans ses pensées.

wrapper, s. **1.** (a) Chemise f. (b) Couverture f. **2.** Bande f. **3.** Robe f de chambre.

wrapping, s. (a) Enveloppe f, couverture f. (b) Papier m, toile f, d'emballage.

wrapping-paper, s. Papier m d'emballage.

wrath, s. Colère f.

wrathful, a. Courroucé.

wreak, v.tr. To w. vengeance on, se venger de.

wreath, s. **1.** Couronne f, guirlande f. **2.** Volute f, panache m.

wreathe, v.tr. (a) Enguirlander; couronner. (b) Tresser.

wreck[1], s. **1.** Épave f. **2.** Naufrage m.

wreck[2], v.tr. (a) To be wrecked, faire naufrage. (b) Démolir. (c) Saboter; ruiner.

wreckage, s. Épaves éparses; débris mpl. Piece of w., épave.

wren, s. Roitelet m.

wrench[1], s. **1.** Effort violent. **2.** Clef f; tourne-à-gauche m inv.

wrench[2], v.tr. (a) Tordre; tourner violemment. (b) Arracher (from, à).

wrest, v.tr. Arracher (from, à).

wrestle, **1.** v.i. Lutter. **2.** v.tr Lutter avec, contre.

wrestler, s. Lutteur m.

wrestling, s. Sport m de la lutte; lutte (corps à corps).

wretch, s. **1.** Malheureux, -euse; infortuné, -ée. **2.** Scélérat, -ate. You w.! misérable!

wretched, a. **1.** Misérable, malheureux, infortuné. **2.** Pitoyable.

wretchedly, adv. **1.** Misérablement. **2.** De façon pitoyable, lamentable.

wretchedness, s. Misère f, malheur m.

wriggle[1], s. Tortillement m.

wriggle[2]. **1.** v.i. (a) Se tortiller; s'agiter. (b) To w. out of, se tirer de. **2.** v.tr. Remuer, tortiller.

wring, v.tr. Tordre.

wringing, a. W. wet, mouillé à tordre; trempé jusqu'aux os.

wrinkle[1], s. (a) Ride f. (b) Rugosité f. (c) Faux pli.

wrinkle[2]. **1.** v.tr. Rider, plisser; froncer. **2.** v.i. Se rider; se plisser.

wrist, s. Poignet m.

wristband, s. Poignet m, manchette f.

wrist-watch, s. Montre-bracelet f, pl. montres-bracelets.

writ, s. Acte m judiciaire; mandat m.

write, v.tr. Écrire; rédiger. Abs. Écrire. **write down,** v.tr. Coucher par écrit; inscrire; marquer, noter.

writer, s. Auteur m; écrivain m.

writhe, *v.i.* Se tordre ; se tortiller.

writhing, *s.* Contorsions *fpl.*

writing, *s.* **1.** Écriture *f.* In w., par écrit. **2.** Ouvrage *m* littéraire. *pl.* Écrits *m.*

writing-pad, *s.* Sous-main *m* *pl.* sous-mains.

writing-paper, *s.* Papier *m* à écrire.

written, *a.* Écrit ; par écrit.

wrong¹. I. *a.* **1.** Mauvais ; mal *inv.* **2.** (*a*) Incorrect, inexact ; faux, *f.* fausse. (*b*) To be w., avoir tort ; se tromper. **3.** (*a*) To drive on the w. side of the road, circuler à contre-voie. W. side up, sens dessus dessous. (*b*) To be on the w. track, suivre une mauvaise piste. To say the w. thing, commettre une gaffe.

W. number, erreur *f* de numéro.
W. note, fausse note. **4.** What's w. with you? qu'avez-vous ?
II. **wrong,** *s.* **1.** Mal *m.* **2.** Tort *m,* injustice *f.* **3.** To be in the w., être dans son tort ; avoir tort.
III. **wrong,** *adv.* Mal. (*a*) In-exactement, incorrectement. (*b*) A tort.

wrong², *v.tr.* (*a*) Faire tort à (*b*) Être injuste pour, envers.

wrongful, *a.* Injuste.

wrongfully, *adv.* Injustement ; à tort.

wrongly, *adv.* **1.** A tort **2.** Mal.

wrought, *a.* Ouvré.

wry, *a.* Tordu, tors ; de travers. To pull a wry face, faire la grimace.

X

X, x, *s.* **1.** (La lettre) X, x *m.* **2.** X rays, rayons *m* X.

X-ray¹, *attrib.a.* Radiologique. X-ray

examination, examen radiographique.
X-ray photograph, radiogramme *m.*

X-ray², *v.tr.* Radiographier.

Y

Y, y, *s.* (La lettre) Y, y *m* ; i grec.

yacht, *s.* Yacht *m.*

yacht-club, *s.* Yacht-club *m.* *pl.* yacht-clubs.

yachting, *s.* Yachting *m.*

yachtsman, *s.* Yachtman *m.* *pl.* yachtmen.

yap¹, *s.* Jappement *m.*

yap², *v.i.* Japper.

yard, *s.* **1.** Cour *f.* **2.** (*a*) Chantier *m.* (*b*) Dépôt *m.*

yarn, *s.* **1.** Fil *m* ; filé *m.* **2.** Histoire *f,* conte *m.*

yaw, *v.i.* Faire des embardées.

yawl, *s.* Yole *f.*

yawn¹, *s.* Bâillement *m.* To give a y., bâiller.

yawn², *v.i.* Bâiller.

yawning¹, *a.* Béant.

yawning², *s.* Bâillement *m.*

year, *s.* An *m,* année *f.* (*a*) An. Last y., l'an dernier ; l'année dernière. To be ten years old, avoir dix ans. (*b*) Année. Financial y., année d'exercice. By the y., à l'année. Years ago, il y a bien des années. In after years, dans la suite. To be getting on in years, prendre de l'âge.

year-book, *s.* Annuaire *m.*

yearly. 1. *a.* Annuel. **2.** *adv.* An-nuellement.

yearn, *v.i.* Languir ; avoir bien envie (de).

yearning¹, *a.* Vif, ardent ; plein d'envie.

yearning², *s.* Désir ardent ; envie *f* (*for,* de).

yeast, *s.* Levure *f.*

yell¹, *s.* Hurlement *m* ; cri aigu.

yell². 1. *v.i.* Hurler ; crier à tue-tête. **2.** *v.tr.* To y. out, vociférer, hurler.

yelling, *s.* Hurlements *mpl.*

yellow. 1. *a.* Jaune. **2.** *s.* Jaune *m.*

yellowish, *a.* Jaunâtre.

yelp¹, *s.* Jappement *m.*

yelp², *v.i.* Japper, glapir.

yelping, *s.* Jappement *m.*

yes, *adv.* Oui ; parfaitement ; si ; si fait. Yes, certainly, mais oui.

yesterday, *adv. & s.* Hier (*m*). The day before y., avant-hier (*m*).

yet. I. *adv.* **1.** (*a*) Encore. (*b*) Yet again, encore une fois. **2.** Déjà ; jusqu'ici. As yet, jusqu'à présent. **3.** Malgré tout.
II. **yet,** *conj.* Néanmoins. cepen-dant ; tout de même.

yew, *s.* If *m.*

yield¹, *s.* Production *f* ; rapport *m.*

yield². **1.** *v.tr.* (*a*) Rendre, donner. (*b*) Rapporter, produire. (*c*) Céder. **2.** *v.i.* (*a*) Se rendre ; céder ; succomber. (*b*) S'affaisser, fléchir, plier.

yielding, *a.* **1.** Facile, complaisant. **2.** (*a*) Mou, *f.* molle. (*b*) Souple élastique.

yoke¹, *s.* **1.** Joug *m.* **2.** Palanche *f.* **3.** Empiècement *m* ; tour *m* de gorge.

yoke², *v.tr.* Accoupler ; atteler.

yolk, *s.* Jaune *m* d'œuf.

yonder. 1. *adv.* Over y., là-bas. **2.** *a.* Ce, *f.* cette, *pl.* ces. . . . -là.

you, *pers.pron.* Vous ; tu, te, toi. **1.** Between you and me, entre nous soit dit. **2.** (*a*) If I were you, à votre place. (*b*) You Englishmen, vous autres Anglais. **3.** On. You never can tell, on ne sait jamais.

young. 1. *a.* Jeune. Younger son, fils cadet. **2.** *s.pl.inv.* (*a*) Les jeunes gens ; la jeunesse. (*b*) Animal and its y., animal et ses petits.

youngish, *a.* Assez jeune.

youngster, *s.* Jeune personne *f.*

your, *poss.a.* **1.** Votre, *pl.* vos ; ton, *f.* ta, *pl.* tes. Have you hurt y. hand? vous vous êtes fait mal à la main? **Y. turn!** à vous! **2.** Son, *f.* sa *pl.* ses.

yours, *poss.pron.* Le vôtre, la vôtre, les vôtres ; le tien, la tienne, les tien(ne)s. This is y., ceci est à vous, à toi. He is a friend of yours, c'est un de vos amis.

yourself, *pers.pron.* Vous-même ; toi-même ; vous ; te.

yourselves, *pers.pron.* Vous-mêmes ; vous.

youth, *s.* **1.** Jeunesse *f* **2.** Jeune homme *m.*

youthful, *a* **1.** Jeune **2.** De jeunesse.

youthfulness, *s.* Jeunesse *f.*

Z

Z, z, *s.* (La lettre) Z, z *m.*

zeal, *s.* Zèle *m,* ardeur *f.*

zealous, *a.* Zélé ; empressé.

zealously, *adv.* Avec zèle.

zebra, *s.* Zèbre *m.*

zenith, *s.* Zénith *m.*

zephyr, *s.* Zéphire *m,* zéphyr(e) *m*

zero, *s.* Zéro *m.*

zest, *s.* (*a*) Enthousiasme *m,* entrain *m.* (*b*) Piquant *m.*

zigzag¹, *s.* Zigzag *m.*

zigzag², *v.i.* Zigzaguer.

zinc, *s.* Zinc *m.*

zip, *s.* **Zip fastener,** fermeture *f* éclair *inv.*

zodiac, *s.* Zodiaque *m*

zone, *s.* Zone *f.*

zoological, *a.* Zoologique.

zoologist, *s.* Zoologiste *m.*

zoology, *s.* Zoologie *f.*